MEDAL OF HONOR RECIPIENTS 1863–1994

Volume II
World War II to Somalia

MEDAL OF HONOR RECIPIENTS 1863–1994

Volume II
World War II to Somalia

Compiled by George Lang, M.H.,
Raymond L. Collins and
Gerard F. White

Withdrawn

Facts On File, Inc.

AN INFOBASE HOLDINGS COMPANY

Medal of Honor Recipients 1863–1994

Facts On File, Inc.
460 Park Avenue South
New York, NY 10016

Library of Congress Cataloging-in-Publication Data

Lang, George.
   Medal of Honor recipients, 1863–1994 / compiled by George Lang,
Raymond L. Collins, and Gerard F. White
      p. cm.
   Includes bibliographical references and index.
   ISBN 0-8160-3259-9 (set)
   ISBN 0-8160-3260-2 (vol. 1)
   ISBN 0-8160-3261-0 (vol. 2)
   1. Medal of Honor. 2. United States—Armed Forces—Biography.
I. Collins, Raymond L. (Raymond Luther) II. White, Gerard F.
III. Title.
UB433.L36 1995
355.1'342—dc20   95-12529

Facts On File books are available at special discounts when purchased in bulk quantities
for businesses, associations, institutions or sales promotions. Please call our Special Sales
Department in New York at 212/683-2244 or 800/322-8755.

This book is printed on acid-free paper.

Printed in the United States of America

VB CC 10 9 8 7 6 5 4 3 2 1

TABLE OF CONTENTS

MEDAL OF HONOR RECIPIENTS 1863–1994

Volume II
World War II to Somalia

WORLD WAR II

2595 ◆ ADAMS, LUCIAN

Rank: Staff Sergeant
Service: U.S. Army
Birthday: 26 October 1922
Place of Birth: Port Arthur, Jefferson County, Texas
Entered Service at: Port Arthur, Jefferson County, Texas
Unit: Company I, 3d Battalion, 30th Infantry, 3d Infantry Division
Served as: Squad Leader
Battle or Place of Action: near St. Die, France
Date of Action: 28 October 1944
G.O. Number, Date: 20, 29 March 1945
Date of Presentation: 23 April 1945
Place of Presentation: Zepman Stadium, Nuremberg, Germany, presented by Lt. Gen. Alexander M. Patch III
Citation: For conspicuous gallantry and intrepidity at risk of his life above and beyond the call of duty on 28 October 1944, near St. Die, France. When his company was stopped in its effort to drive through the Mortagne Forest to reopen the supply line to the isolated third battalion, S/Sgt. Adams braved the concentrated fire of machine guns in a lone assault on a force of German troops. Although his company had progressed less than 10 yards and had lost three killed and six wounded, S/Sgt. Adams charged forward dodging from tree to tree firing a borrowed BAR from the hip. Despite intense machine-gun fire which the enemy directed at him and rifle grenades which struck the trees over his head, showering him with broken twigs and branches, S/Sgt. Adams made his way to within 10 yards of the closest machine gun and killed the gunner with a hand grenade. An enemy soldier threw hand grenades at him from a position only 10 yards distant; however, S/Sgt. Adams dispatched him with a single burst of BAR fire. Charging into the vortex of the enemy fire, he killed another machine gunner at 15 yards' range with a hand grenade and forced the surrender of two supporting infantrymen. Although the remainder of the German group concentrated the full force of its automatic-weapon fire in a desperate effort to knock him out, he proceeded through the woods to find and exterminate five more of the enemy. Finally, when the third German machine gun opened up on him at a range of 20 yards, S/Sgt. Adams killed the gunner with BAR fire. In the course of the action, he personally killed nine Germans, eliminated three enemy machine guns, vanquished a specialized force which was armed with automatic weapons, and grenade launchers, cleared the woods of hostile elements and reopened the severed supply lines to the assault companies of his battalion.

2596 ◆ *AGERHOLM, HAROLD CHRIST

Rank: Private First Class
Service: U.S. Marine Corps Reserve
Birthday: 29 January 1925
Place of Birth: Racine, Wisconsin
Date of Death: 7 July 1944
Place of Death: Saipan, Marianas Islands
Cemetery: Mound Cemetery—Racine, Wisconsin
Entered Service at: Wisconsin
Unit: 4th Battalion, 10th Marines, 2d Marine Division
Battle or Place of Action: Saipan, Marianas Islands
Date of Action: 7 July 1944
Citation: For conspicuous gallantry and intrepidity at the risk of his life above and beyond the call of duty while serving with the 4th Battalion, 10th Marines, 2d Marine Division, in action against enemy Japanese forces on Saipan, Marianas Islands, 7 July 1944. When the enemy launched a fierce, determined counterattack against our positions and overran a neighboring artillery battalion, Pfc. Agerholm immediately volunteered to assist in the efforts to check the hostile attack and evacuate our wounded. Locating and appropriating an abandoned ambulance jeep, he repeatedly made extremely perilous trips under heavy rifle and mortar fire and single-handedly loaded and evacuated approximately 45 casualties, working tirelessly and with utter disregard for his own safety during a grueling period of more than three hours. Despite intense, persistent enemy fire, he ran out to aid two men whom he believed to be wounded marines, but was himself mortally wounded by a Japanese sniper while carrying out his hazardous mission. Pfc. Agerholm's brillant initiative, great personal valor, and self-sacrificing efforts in the face of almost certain death reflect the highest credit upon himself and the U.S. Naval Service. He gallantly gave his life for his country.

2597 ◆ ANDERSON, BEAUFORD THEODORE

Rank: Technical Sergeant (highest rank: First Lieutenant)
Service: U.S. Army
Birthday: 6 July 1922
Place of Birth: Eagle, Waukesha County, Wisconsin
Entered Service at: Soldiers Grove, Crawford County, Wisconsin
Unit: Weapons Platoon, Company A, 1st Battalion, 381st Infantry, 96th Infantry Division

Served as: Mortar Section Sergeant
Battle or Place of Action: Okinawa, Ryukyu Islands
Date of Action: 13 April 1945
G.O. Number, Date: 63, 27 June 1946
Date of Presentation: 14 June 1946
Place of Presentation: The White House, Presented by Pres. Harry S. Truman
Citation: He displayed conspicuous gallantry and intrepidity above and beyond the call of duty. When a powerfully conducted predawn Japanese counterattack struck his unit's flank, he ordered his men to take cover in an old tomb, and then, armed only with a carbine, faced the onslaught alone. After emptying one magazine at point-blank range into the screaming attackers, he seized an enemy mortar dud and threw it back among the charging Japs, killing several as it burst. Securing a box of mortar shells, he extracted the safety pins, banged the bases upon a rock to arm them and proceeded alternately to hurl shells and fire his piece among the fanatical foe, finally forcing them to withdraw. Despite the protests of his comrades, and bleeding profusely from a severe shrapnel wound, he made his way to his company commander to report the action. T/Sgt. Anderson's intrepid conduct in the face of overwhelming odds accounted for 25 enemy killed and several machine guns and knee mortars destroyed, thus singlehandedly removing a serious threat to the company's flank.

2598 ◆ *ANDERSON, RICHARD BEATTY

Rank: Private First Class
Service: U.S. Marine Corps
Birthday: 26 June 1921
Place of Birth: Tacoma, Pierce County, Washington
Date of Death: 1 February 1944
Place of Death: Roi Island, Marshall Islands
Cemetery: New Tacoma Cemetery—Tacoma, Washington
Entered Service at: Washington
Unit: Company E, 2d Battalion, 23d Marines, 4th Marine Division
Battle or Place of Action: Roi Island, Kwajalein Atoll, Marshall Islands
Date of Action: 1 February 1944
Place of Presentation: Seattle, WA, presented by Rear Adm. J.A. Taffinder, Commandant, 13th Naval District to his parents
Citation: For conspicuous gallantry and intrepidity at the risk of his life above and beyond the call of duty while serving with the 4th Marine Division during action against enemy Japanese forces on Roi Island, Kwajalein Atoll, Marshall Islands, 1 February 1944. Entering a shell crater occupied by three other marines, Pfc. Anderson was preparing to throw a grenade at an enemy position when it slipped from his hands and rolled toward the men at the bottom of the hole. With insufficient time to retrieve the armed weapon and throw it, Pfc. Anderson fearlessly chose to sacrifice himself and save his companions by hurling his body upon the grenade and taking the full impact of the explosion. His personal valor and exceptional spirit of loyalty in the face of almost certain death were in keeping with the highest traditions of the U.S. Naval Service. He gallantly gave his life for his country.

2599 ◆ *ANTOLAK, SYLVESTER

Rank: Sergeant
Service: U.S. Army
Place of Birth: Clairsville, Ohio
Date of Death: 24 May 1944
Place of Death: Near Cisterna di Littoria, Italy
Cemetery: A.B.M.C. Sicily-Rome Cemetery (C-12-13)—Nettuno, Italy
Entered Service at: Clairsville, Ohio
Unit: Company B, 15th Infantry, 3d Infantry Division
Battle or Place of Action: near Cisterna di Littoria, Italy
Date of Action: 24 May 1944
G.O. Number, Date: 89, 19 October 1945
Citation: Near Cisterna di Littoria, Italy, he charged 200 yards over flat, coverless terrain to destroy an enemy machine-gun nest during the second day of the offensive which broke through the German cordon of steel around the Anzio beachhead. Fully 30 yards in advance of his squad, he ran into withering enemy machine-gun, machine-pistol and rifle fire. Three times he was struck by bullets and knocked to the ground, but each time he struggled to his feet to continue his relentless advance. With one shoulder deeply gashed and his right arm shattered, he continued to rush directly into the enemy fire concentration with his submachine gun wedged under his uninjured arm until within 15 yards of the enemy strongpoint, where he opened fire at deadly close range, killing two Germans and forcing the remaining 10 to surrender. He reorganized his men and, refusing to seek medical attention so badly needed, chose to lead the way toward another strongpoint 100 yards distant. Utterly disregarding the hail of bullets concentrated upon him, he had stormed ahead nearly three-fourths of the space between strongpoints when he was instantly killed by hostile enemy fire. Inspired by his example, his squad went on to overwhelm the enemy troops. By his supreme sacrifice, superb fighting courage, and heroic devotion to the attack, Sgt. Antolak was directly responsible for eliminating 20 Germans, capturing an enemy machine gun, and clearing the path for his company to advance.

2600 ◆ ANTRIM, RICHARD NOTT

Rank: Commander (rank at time of action: Lieutenant) (highest rank: Rear Admiral)
Service: U.S. Navy
Birthday: 17 December 1907
Place of Birth: Peru, Miami County, Indiana
Date of Death: 8 March 1969
Place of Death: Mountain Home, Arkansas
Cemetery: Arlington National Cemetery (35-2613) (MH)—Arlington, Virginia
Entered Service at: Indiana
Unit: U.S.S. *Pope*
Served as: Executive Officer
Battle or Place of Action: Macassar, Celebes, Netherlands East Indies
Date of Action: April 1942
Date of Presentation: 30 January 1947

Place of Presentation: The White House, presented by Pres. Harry S. Truman

Citation: For conspicuous gallantry and intrepidity at the risk of his life above and beyond the call of duty while interned as a prisoner of war of the enemy Japanese in the city of Macassar, Celebes, Netherlands East Indies, in April 1942. Acting instantly on behalf of a naval officer who was subjected to a vicious clubbing by a frenzied Japanese guard venting his insane wrath upon the helpless prisoner, Comdr. (then Lt.) Antrim boldly intervened, attempting to quiet the guard and finally persuading him to discuss the charges against the officer. With the entire Japanese force assembled and making extraordinary preparations for the threatened beating, and with the tension heightened by 2,700 Allied prisoners rapidly closing in, Comdr. Antrim courageously appealed to the fanatic enemy, risking his own life in a desperate effort to mitigate the punishment. When the other had been beaten unconscious by 15 blows of a hawser and was repeatedly kicked by three soldiers to a point beyond which he could not survive, Comdr. Antrim gallantly stepped forward and indicated to the perplexed guards that he would take the remainder of the punishment, throwing the Japanese completely off balance in their amazement and eliciting a roar of acclaim from the suddenly inspired Allied prisoners. By his fearless leadership and valiant concern for the welfare of another, he not only saved the life of a fellow officer and stunned the Japanese into sparing his own life but also brought about a new respect for American officers and men and a great improvement in camp living conditions. His heroic conduct throughout reflects the highest credit upon Comdr. Antrim and the U.S. Naval Service.

2601 ◆ ATKINS, THOMAS E.

Rank: Private First Class
Service: U.S. Army
Birthday: 5 February 1921
Place of Birth: Campobello, Spartanburg County, South Carolina
Entered Service at: Campobello, Spartanburg County, South Carolina
Unit: Company A, 127th Infantry, 32d Infantry Division
Battle or Place of Action: Villa Verde Trail, Luzon, Philippine Islands
Date of Action: 10 March 1945
G.O. Number, Date: 95, 30 October 1945
Date of Presentation: 12 October 1945
Place of Presentation: The White House, presented by Pres. Harry S. Truman
Citation: He fought gallantly on the Villa Verde Trail, Luzon, Philippine Islands. With two companions he occupied a position on a ridge outside the perimeter defense established by the 1st Platoon on a high hill. At about 0300 hours, two companies of Japanese attacked with rifle and machine-gun fire, grenades, TNT charges and land mines, severely wounding Pfc. Atkins and killing his two companions. Despite the intense hostile fire and pain from his deep wound, he held his ground and returned heavy fire. After the attack was repulsed, he remained in his precarious position to

repel any subsequent assaults instead of returning to the American lines for medical treatment. An enemy machine gun, set up within 20 yards of his foxhole, vainly attempted to drive him off or silence his gun. The Japanese repeatedly made fierce attacks, but for four hours Pfc. Atkins determinedly remained in his foxhole, bearing the brunt of each assault and maintaining steady and accurate fire until each charge was repulsed. At 7:00 A.M., 13 enemy dead lay in front of his position; he had fired 400 rounds, all he and his two dead companions possessed, and had used three rifles until each had jammed too badly for further operation. He withdrew during a lull to secure a rifle and more ammunition, and was persuaded to remain for medical treatment. While waiting, he saw a Japanese within the perimeter and, seizing a nearby rifle, killed him. A few minutes later, while lying on a litter, he discovered an enemy group moving up behind the platoon's lines. Despite his severe wounds he sat up, delivered heavy rifle fire against the group, and forced them to withdraw. Pfc. Atkins' superb bravery and his fearless determination to hold his post against the main force of repeated enemy attacks, even though painfully wounded, were major factors in enabling his comrades to maintain their lines against a numerically superior enemy force.

2602 ◆ *BAILEY, KENNETH DILLON

Rank: Major
Service: U.S. Marine Corps
Birthday: 21 October 1910
Place of Birth: Pawnee, Pawnee County, Oklahoma
Date of Death: 27 September 1942
Cemetery: Spring Hill Cemetery (MH)—Danville, Illinois
Entered Service at: Illinois
Unit: Company C, 1st Marine Raider Battalion
Served as: Commanding Officer
Battle or Place of Action: Henderson Field, Guadalcanal, Solomon Islands
Date of Action: 12-13 September 1942
Citation: For extraordinary courage and heroic conduct above and beyond the call of duty as commanding officer of Company C, 1st Marine Raider Battalion, during the enemy Japanese attack on Henderson Field, Guadalcanal, Solomon Islands, 12–13 September 1942. Completely reorganized following the severe engagement of the night before, Maj. Bailey's company, within an hour after taking its assigned position as reserve battalion between the main line and the coveted airport, was threatened on the right flank by the penetration of the enemy into a gap in the main line. In addition to repulsing this threat, while steadily improving his own desperately held position, he used every weapon at his command to cover the forced withdrawal of the main line before a hammering assault by superior enemy forces. After rendering invaluable service to the battalion commander in stemming the retreat, reorganizing the troops, and extending the reverse position to the left, Maj. Bailey, despite a severe head wound, repeatedly led his troops in fierce hand-to-hand combat for a period of 10 hours. His great personal valor while exposed to constant and merciless enemy fire and his indomitable fighting spirit inspired his troops to heights of heroic endeavor

which enabled them to repulse the enemy and hold Henderson Field. He gallantly gave his life in the service of his country.

2603 ◆ *BAKER, ADDISON EARL

Rank: Lieutenant Colonel
Service: U.S. Army Air Corps
Birthday: 1 January 1907
Place of Birth: Chicago, Cook County, Illinois
Date of Death: 1 August 1943
Place of Death: Ploesti, Rumania
Cemetery: A.B.M.C. Florence Cemetery (Wall of the Missing)—Florence, Italy
Entered Service at: Akron, Summit County, Ohio
Unit: 328th Bombardment Squadron, 93d Heavy Bombardment Group, 8th Air Force
Served as: Pilot of a B-24, Squadron Commander
Battle or Place of Action: Ploesti, Rumania
Date of Action: 1 August 1943
G.O. Number, Date: 20, 11 March 1944
Date of Presentation: 1944
Place of Presentation: Akron, Ohio
Citation: For conspicuous gallantry and intrepidity above and beyond the call of duty in action with the enemy on 1 August 1943. On this date he led his command, the 93d Heavy Bombardment Group, on a daring low-level attack against enemy oil refineries and installations at Ploesti, Rumania. Approching the target, his aircraft was hit by a large-caliber antiaircraft shell, seriously damaged, and set on fire. Ignoring the fact he was flying over terrain suitable for safe landing, he refused to jeopardize the mission by breaking up the lead formation and continued unswervingly to lead his group to the target upon which he dropped his bombs with devastating effect. Only then did he leave formation, but his valiant attempts to gain sufficient altitude for the crew to escape by parachute were unavailing and his aircraft crashed in flames after his successful efforts to avoid other planes in formation. By extraordinary flying skill, gallant leadership, and intrepidity, Lt. Col. Baker rendered outstanding, distinguished, and valorous service to our nation.

2604 ◆ *BAKER JR., THOMAS ALEXANDER

Rank: Sergeant (rank at time of action: Private)
Service: U.S. Army
Birthday: 25 June 1916
Place of Birth: Troy, Rensselaer County, New York
Date of Death: 12 July 1944
Cemetery: National Memorial Cemetery of the Pacific (F-162) (MH)—Honolulu, Hawaii
Entered Service at: Troy, Rensselaer County, New York
Unit: Company A, 105th Infantry, 27th Infantry Division
Battle or Place of Action: Saipan, Mariana Islands
Date of Action: 19 June-7 July 1944
G.O. Number, Date: 35, 9 May 1945
Citation: For conspicuous gallantry and intrepidity at the risk of his life above and beyond the call of duty at Saipan, Mariana Islands, 19 June to 7 July 1944. When his entire

company was held up by fire from automatic-weapon and small-arms fire from strongly fortified enemy positions that commanded the view of the company, Sgt. (then Pvt.) Baker voluntarily took a bazooka and dashed alone to within 100 yards of the enemy. Through heavy rifle and machine-gun fire that was directed at him by the enemy, he knocked out the strongpoint, enabling his company to assault the ridge. Some days later while his company advanced across the open field flanked with obstructions and places of concealment for the enemy, Sgt. Baker again voluntarily took up a position in the rear to protect the company against surprise attack and came upon two heavily fortified enemy pockets manned by two officers and 10 enlisted men which had been bypassed. Without regard for such superior numbers, he unhesitatingly attacked and killed all of them. Five hundred yards farther, he discovered six men of the enemy who had concealed themselves behind our lines and destroyed all of them. On 7 July 1944, the perimeter of which Sgt. Baker was a part was attacked from three sides by from 3,000 to 5,000 Japanese. During the early stages of this attack, Sgt. Baker was seriously wounded, but he insisted on remaining in the line and fired at the enemy at ranges sometimes as close as five yards until his ammunition ran out. Without ammunition and with his own weapon battered to uselessness from hand-to-hand combat, he was carried about 50 yards to the rear by a comrade, who was then himself wounded. At this point Sgt. Baker refused to be moved any farther, stating that he preferred to be left to die rather than risk the lives of any more of his friends. A short time later, at his request, he was placed in a sitting position against a small tree. Another comrade, withdrawing, offered assistance. Sgt. Baker refused, insisting that he be left alone and given a soldier's pistol with its remaining eight rounds of ammunition. When last seen alive, Sgt. Baker was propped against a tree, pistol in hand, calmly facing the foe. Later Sgt. Baker's body was found in the same position, gun empty, with eight Japanese lying dead before him. His deeds were in keeping with the highest traditions of the U.S. Army.

2605 ◆ BARFOOT, VAN THOMAS

Rank: Second Lieutenant (rank at time of action: Technical Sergeant) (highest rank: Colonel)
Service: U.S. Army
Birthday: 15 June 1919
Place of Birth: Edinburg, Leake County, Mississippi
Entered Service at: Carthage, Leake County, Mississippi
Unit: 3d Platoon, Company L 3d Battalion, 157th Infantry, 45th Infantry Division
Served as: Platoon Sergeant
Battle or Place of Action: near Carano, Italy
Date of Action: 23 May 1944
G.O. Number, Date: 79, 4 October 1944
Date of Presentation: 28 September 1944
Place of Presentation: Epinal, France, presented by Lt. Gen. Alexander M. Patch III
Citation: For conspicuous gallantry and intrepidity at the risk of life above and beyond the call of duty on 23 May 1944, near Carano, Italy. With his platoon heavily engaged

during an assault against forces well-entrenched on commanding ground, 2d Lt. Barfoot (then T/Sgt.) moved off alone upon the enemy left flank. He crawled to the proximity of one machine-gun nest and made a direct hit on it with a hand grenade, killing two and wounding three Germans. He continued along the German defense line to another machine-gun emplacement, and with his tommy gun killed two and captured three soldiers. Members of another enemy machine-gun crew then abandoned their position and gave themselves up to Sgt. Barfoot. Leaving the prisoners for his support squad to pick up, he proceeded to mop up positions in the immediate area, capturing more prisoners, and bringing his total count to 17. Later that day, after he had reorganized his men and consolidated the newly captured ground, the enemy launched a fierce armored counterattack directly at his platoon positions. Securing a bazooka, Sgt. Barfoot took up an exposed position directly in front of three advancing Mark VI tanks. From a distance of 75 yards his first shot destroyed the track of the leading tank, effectively disabling it, while the other two changed direction toward the flank. As the crew of the disabled tank dismounted, Sgt. Barfoot killed three of them with his tommy gun. He continued onward into enemy terrain and destroyed a recently abandoned German fieldpiece with a demolition charge placed in the breech. While returning to his platoon position, Sgt. Barfoot, though greatly fatigued by his herculean efforts, assisted two of his seriously wounded men 1,700 yards to a position of safety. Sgt. Barfoot's extraordinary heroism, demonstration of magnificent valor, and aggressive determination in the face of point-blank fire are a perpetual inspiration to his fellow soldiers.

2606 ◆ BARRETT, CARLTON WILLIAM

Rank: Private (highest rank: Technical Sergeant)
Service: U.S. Army
Birthday: 24 November 1919
Place of Birth: Fulton, Oswego County, New York
Date of Death: 3 March 1986
Place of Death: Yountville, California
Cemetery: Napa Valley Memorial Gardens (MH)—Napa, California
Entered Service at: Albany, Albany County, New York
Unit: 18th Infantry, 1st Infantry Division
Battle or Place of Action: in the vicinity of St. Laurent-sur-Mer, France
Date of Action: 6 June 1944
G.O. Number, Date: 78, 2 October 1944
Citation: For gallantry and intrepidity at the risk of his life above and beyond the call of duty on 6 June 1944, in the vicinity of St. Laurent-sur-Mer, France. On the morning of D-day, Pvt. Barrett, landing in the face of extremely heavy enemy fire, was forced to wade ashore through neck-deep water. Disregarding the personal danger, he returned to the surf again and again to assist his floundering comrades and save them from drowning. Refusing to remain pinned down by the intense barrage of small-arms and mortar fire poured at the landing points, Pvt. Barrett, working with fierce determination, saved many lives by carrying casualties to an evacuation boat lying offshore. In addition to his assigned mission as

guide, he carried dispatches the length of the fire-swept beach; he assisted the wounded; he calmed the shocked; he arose as a leader in the stress of the occasion. His coolness and his dauntless daring courage while constantly risking his life during a period of many hours had an inestimable effect on his comrades and is in keeping with the highest traditions of the U.S. Army.

2607 ◆ BASILONE, JOHN "MANILA JONN"

Rank: Sergeant (highest rank: Gunnery Sergeant)
Service: U.S. Marine Corps
Birthday: 4 November 1916
Place of Birth: Buffalo, Erie County, New York
Date of Death: 19 February 1945
Place of Death: Iwo Jima, Volcano Islands
Cemetery: Arlington National Cemetery (12-384) (MH)—Arlington, Virginia
Entered Service at: New Jersey
Unit: 1st Battalion, 7th Marines, 1st Marine Division
Battle or Place of Action: Lunga Area, Guadalcanal, Solomon Islands
Date of Action: 24-25 October 1942
Date of Presentation: 21 May 1943
Place of Presentation: Balcombe, Australia, presented by Maj. Gen. Alexander A. Vandegrift, Commanding Gen. 1st Marine Division
Citation: For extraordinary heroism and conspicuous gallantry in action against enemy Japanese forces, above and beyond the call of duty, while serving with the 1st Battalion, 7th Marines, 1st Marine Division in the Lunga area, Guadalcanal, Solomon Islands, on 24 and 25 October 1942. While the enemy was hammering at the Marines' defensive positions, Sgt. Basilone, in charge of two sections of heavy machine guns, fought valiantly to check the savage and determined assault. In a fierce frontal attack with the Japanese blasting his guns with grenades and mortar fire, one of Sgt. Basilone's sections, with its guncrews, was put out of action, leaving only two men able to carry on. Moving an extra gun into position, he placed it in action, then, under continual fire, repaired another and personally manned it, gallantly holding his line until replacements arrived. A little later, with ammunition critically low and the supply lines cut off, Sgt. Basilone, at great risk of his life and in the face of continued enemy attack, battled his way through hostile lines with urgently needed shells for his gunners, thereby contributing in large measure to the virtual annihilation of a Japanese regiment. His great personal valor and courageous initiative were in keeping with the highest traditions of the U.S. Naval Service.

2608 ◆ *BAUER, HAROLD WILLIAM "INDIAN JOE"

Rank: Lieutenant Colonel
Service: U.S. Marine Corps
Birthday: 20 November 1908
Place of Birth: Woodruff, Kansas
Date of Death: 16 November 1942

Place of Death: 15 miles north of Russell Island, Solomon Islands
Cemetery: A.B.M.C. Manila Cemetery (Wall of the Missing)—Manila, Plilippine Islands
Entered Service at: Nebraska
Unit: Marine Fighting Squadron 212
Served as: Squadron Commander/Pilot of F4F Grumman Wildcat
Battle or Place of Action: Guadalcanal, Solomon Islands
Date of Action: 10 May-14 November 1942
Date of Issue: 11 May 1946
Citation: For extraordinary heroism and conspicuous courage as Squadron Commander of Marine Fighting Squadron 212 in the South Pacific area during the period from 10 May to 14 November 1942. Volunteering to pilot a fighter plane in defense of our positions on Guadalcanal, Lt. Col. Bauer participated in two air battles against enemy bombers and fighters outnumbering our force more than two to one, boldly engaged the enemy, and destroyed one Japanese bomber in the engagement of 28 September, and shot down four enemy fighter planes in flames on 3 October, leaving a fifth smoking badly. After successfully leading 26 planes on an over-water ferry flight of more than 600 miles on 16 October, Lt. Col. Bauer, while circling to land, sighted a squadron of enemy planes attacking the U.S.S. *McFarland*. Undaunted by the formidable opposition and with valor above and beyond the call of duty, he engaged the entire squadron and, although alone and his fuel supply nearly exhausted, fought his plane so brillantly that four of the Japanese planes were destroyed before he was forced down by lack of fuel. His intrepid fighting spirit and distinctive ability as a leader and an airman, exemplified in his splendid record of combat achievement, were vital factors in the successful operations in the South Pacific area.
Notes: MIA

2609 ◆ *BAUSELL, LEWIS KENNETH

Rank: Corporal
Service: U.S. Marine Corps
Birthday: 17 April 1924
Place of Birth: Pulaski, Montgomery County, Virginia
Date of Death: 18 September 1944
Cemetery: A.B.M.C. Manila Cemetery (Wall of the Missing)—Manila, Philippine Islands
Entered Service at: Washington, D.C.
Unit: 1st Battalion, 5th Marines, 1st Marine Division
Battle or Place of Action: Peleliu Island, Palau Group
Date of Action: 15 September 1944
Citation: For conspicuous gallantry and intrepidity at the risk of his life above and beyond the call of duty while serving with the 1st Battalion, 5th Marines, 1st Marine Division, during action against enemy Japanese forces on Peleliu Island, Palau Group, 15 September 1944. Valiantly placing himself at the head of his squad, Cpl. Bausell led the charge forward against a hostile pillbox which was covering a vital sector of the beach and, as the first to reach the emplacement, immedi ately started firing his automatic into the aperture while the remainder of his men closed in on the enemy. Swift to act, as

a Japanese grenade was hurled into their midst, Cpl. Bausell threw himself on the deadly weapon, taking the full blast of the explosion and sacrificing his own life to save his men. His unwavering loyalty and inspiring courage reflect the highest credit upon Cpl. Bausell and the U.S. Naval Service. He gallantly gave his life for his country.

2610 ◆ *BEAUDOIN, RAYMOND OVILA

Rank: First Lieutenant
Service: U.S. Army
Birthday: 15 July 1918
Place of Birth: Holyoke, Hampden County, Massachusetts
Date of Death: 6 April 1945
Cemetery: Notre Dame Cemetery (MH)—South Hadley, Massachusetts
Entered Service at: Holyoke, Hampden County, Massachusetts
Unit: Company F, 119th Infantry, 30th Infantry Division
Served as: Platoon Leader
Battle or Place of Action: Hamelin, Germany
Date of Action: 6 April 1945
G.O. Number, Date: 9, 25 January 1946
Citation: He was leading the 2d Platoon of Company F over flat, open terrain to Hamelin, Germany, when the enemy went into action with machine guns and automatic weapons, laying down a devastating curtain of fire which pinned his unit to the ground. By rotating men in firing positions he made it possible for his entire platoon to dig in, defying all the while the murderous enemy fire to encourage his men and to distribute ammunition. He then dug in himself at the most advanced position, where he kept up a steady fire, killing six hostile soldiers and directing his men in inflicting heavy casualties on the numerically superior opposing force. Despite these defensive measures, however, the position of the platoon became more precarious, for the enemy had brought up strong reinforcements and was preparing a coun-terattack. Three men, sent back at intervals to obtain ammu-nition and reinforcements, were killed by sniper fire. To relieve his command from the desperate situation, 1st Lt. Beaudoin decided to make a one-man attack on the most damaging enemy sniper nest 90 yards to the right flank, and thereby divert attention from the runner who would attempt to pierce the enemy's barrier of bullets and secure help. Crawling over completely exposed ground, he relentlessly advanced, undeterred by eight rounds of bazooka fire which threw mud and stones over him or by rifle fire which ripped his uniform. Ten yards from the enemy position he stood up and charged. At point-blank range he shot and killed two occupants of the nest; a third, who tried to bayonet him, he overpowered and killed with the butt of his carbine; and the fourth adversary was cut down by the platoon's rifle fire as he attempted to flee. He continued his attack by running toward a dugout, but there he was struck and killed by a burst from a machine gun. By his intrepidity, great fighting skill, and supreme devotion to his responsibility for the well-being of his platoon, 1st Lt. Beaudoin singlehandedly accomplished a mission that enabled a messenger to secure help which saved

the stricken unit and made possible the decisive defeat of the German forces.

2611 ◆ BELL, BERNARD PIOUS

Rank: Technical Sergeant
Service: U.S. Army
Birthday: 29 December 1911
Place of Birth: Grantsville, Calhoun County, West Virginia
Date of Death: 11 January 1971
Place of Death: Delano, Florida
Cemetery: Arlington National Cemetery (25-3840) (MH)—Arlington, Virginia
Entered Service at: New York, New York
Unit: Company I, 142d Infantry, 36th Infantry Division
Battle or Place of Action: Mittelwihr, France
Date of Action: 18 December 1944
G.O. Number, Date: 73, 30 August 1945
Date of Presentation: 23 August 1945
Place of Presentation: The White House, presented by Pres. Harry S. Truman
Citation: For fighting gallantly at Mittelwihr, France. On the morning of 18 December 1944, he led a squad against a schoolhouse held by enemy troops. While his men covered him, he dashed toward the building, surprised two guards at the door, and took them prisoner without firing a shot. He found that other Germans were in the cellar. These he threatened with hand grenades, forcing 26 in all to emerge and surrender. His squad then occupied the building and prepared to defend it against powerful enemy action. The next day, the enemy poured artillery and mortar barrages into the position, disrupting communications which T/Sgt. Bell repeatedly repaired under heavy small-arms fire as he crossed dangerous terrain to keep his company commander informed of his squad's situation. During the day, several prisoners were taken and other Germans killed when hostile forces were attracted to the schoolhouse by the sound of captured German weapons fired by the Americans. At dawn the next day the enemy prepared to assault the building. A German tank fired round after round into the structure, partially demolishing the upper stories. Despite this heavy fire, T/Sgt. Bell climbed to the second floor and directed artillery fire which forced the hostile tank to withdraw. He then adjusted mortar fire on large forces of enemy foot soldiers attempting to reach the American position and, when this force broke and attempted to retire, he directed deadly machine-gun and rifle fire into their disorganized ranks. Calling for armored support to blast out the German troops hidden behind a wall, he unhesitatingly exposed himself to heavy small-arms fire to stand beside a friendly tank and tell its occupants where to rip holes in walls protecting approaches to the school building. He then trained machine guns on the gaps and mowed down all hostile troops attempting to cross the openings to get closer to the school building. By his intrepidity and bold, aggressive leadership, T/Sgt. Bell enabled his eight-man squad to drive back approximately 150 of the enemy, killing at least 87 and capturing 42. Personally, he killed more than 20 and captured 33 prisoners.

2612 ◆ BENDER, STANLEY

Rank: Staff Sergeant (highest rank: Technical Sergeant)
Service: U.S. Army
Birthday: 31 October 1909
Place of Birth: Carlisle, West Virginia
Date of Death: 22 June 1994
Place of Death: Thacker, West Virginia
Cemetery: High Lawn Memorial Park (MH)—Oak Hill, West Virginia
Entered Service at: Chicago, Cook County, Illinois
Unit: Company E, 7th Infantry, 3d Infantry Division
Battle or Place of Action: La Lande, France
Date of Action: 17 August 1944
G.O. Number, Date: 7, 1 February 1945
Date of Presentation: 21 January 1945
Place of Presentation: France, presented by Lt. Gen. Alexander M. Patch III
Citation: For conspicuous gallantry and intrepidity at risk of life above and beyond the call of duty. On 17 August 1944, near La Lande, France, he climbed on top of a knocked-out tank, in the face of withering machine-gun fire which halted the advance of his company, in an effort to locate the source of this fire. Although bullets ricocheted off the turret at his feet, he nevertheless remained standing upright in full view of the enemy for over two minutes. Locating the enemy machine guns on a knoll 200 yards away, he ordered two squads to cover him and led his men down an irrigation ditch, running a gauntlet of intense machine-gun fire, which completely blanketed 50 yards of his advance and wounded four of his men. While the Germans hurled hand grenades at the ditch, he stood his ground until his squad caught up with him, then advanced alone, in a wide flanking approach, to the rear of the knoll. He walked deliberately a distance of 40 yards, without cover, in full view of the Germans and under a hail of both enemy and friendly fire, to the first machine gun and knocked it out with a single short burst. Then he made his way through the strongpoint, despite bursting hand grenades, toward the second machine gun, 25 yards distant, whose two-man crew swung the machine gun around and fired two bursts at him, but he walked clamly through the fire and, reaching the edge of the emplacement, dispatched the crew. Signaling his men to rush the rifle pits, he then walked 35 yards further to kill an enemy rifleman and returned to lead his squad in the destruction of the eight remaining Germans in the strongpoint. His audacity so inspired the remainder of the assault company that the men charged out of their positions, shouting and yelling, to overpower the enemy roadblock and sweep into town, knocking out two antitank guns, killing 37 Germans, and capturing 26 others. He had sparked and led the assault company in an attack which overwhelmed the enemy, destroying a road block, taking a town, seizing intact three bridges over the Maravenne River, and capturing commanding terrain which dominated the area.

2613 ◆ *BENJAMIN JR., GEORGE

Rank: Private First Class
Service: U.S. Army

Birthday: 24 April 1919
Place of Birth: Philadelphia, Philadelphia County, Pennsylvania
Date of Death: 21 December 1944
Cemetery: A.B.M.C. Manila Cemetery (B-7-156)—Manila, Plilippine Islands
Entered Service at: Carney's Point, Salem County, New Jersey
Unit: Company A, 306th Infantry, 77th Infantry Division
Served as: Radio Operator
Battle or Place of Action: Leyte, Philippine Islands
Date of Action: 21 December 1944
G.O. Number, Date: 49, 28 June 1945
Place of Presentation: Presented by Brig. Gen. Ralph K. Robertson to his Widow
Citation: He was a radio operator, advancing in the rear of his company as it engaged a well-defended Japanese strongpoint holding up the progress of the entire battalion. When a rifle platoon supporting a light tank hesitated in its advance, he voluntarily and with utter disregard for personal safety left his comparatively secure position and ran across bullet-whipped terrain to the tank, waving and shouting to the men of the platoon to follow. Carrying his bulky radio and armed only with a pistol, he fearlessly penetrated intense machine-gun and rifle fire to the enemy position, where he killed one of the enemy in a foxhole and moved to annihilate the crew of a light machine gun. Heedless of the terrific fire now concentrated on him, he continued to spearhead the assault, killing two more of the enemy and exhorting the other men to advance, until he fell mortally wounded. After being evacuated to an aid station, his first thought was still of the American advance. Overcoming great pain he called for the battalion operations officer to report the location of enemy weapons and valuable tactical information he had secured in his heroic charge. The unwavering courage, the unswerving devotion to the task at hand, the aggressive leadership of Pfc. Benjamin were a source of great and lasting inspiration to his comrades and were to a great extent responsible for the success of the battalion's mission.

2614 ◆ BENNETT, EDWARD ANDREW

Rank: Corporal (highest rank: Major)
Service: U.S. Army
Birthday: 11 February 1920
Place of Birth: Middleport, Meigs County, Ohio
Date of Death: 2 May 1983
Place of Death: Campbell, California
Cemetery: Golden Gate National Cemetery (2-B-10714) (MH)—San Bruno, California
Entered Service at: Middleport, Meigs County, Ohio
Unit: Company B, 1st Battalion, 358th Infantry, 90th Infantry Division
Battle or Place of Action: Heckhuscheid, Germany
Date of Action: 1 February 1945
G.O. Number, Date: 95, 30 October 1945
Date of Presentation: 12 October 1945
Place of Presentation: The White House (Rose Garden), presented by Pres. Harry S. Truman

Citation: He was advancing with Company B across open ground to assault Heckhuscheid, Germany, just after dark when vicious enemy machine-gun fire from a house on the outskirts of the town pinned down the group and caused several casualties. He began crawling to the edge of the field in an effort to flank the house, persisting in this maneuver even when the hostile machine gunners located him by the light of burning buildings and attempted to cut him down as he made for the protection of some trees. Reaching safety, he stealthily made his way by a circuitous route to the rear of the buildings occupied by the German gunners. With his trench knife he killed a sentry on guard there and then charged into the darkened house. In a furious hand-to-hand struggle he stormed about a single room which harbored seven Germans. Three he killed with rifle fire, another he clubbed to death with the butt of his gun, and the three others he dispatched with his .45-caliber pistol. The fearless initiative, stalwart combat ability, and outstanding gallantry of Cpl. Bennett eliminated the enemy fire which was decimating his company's ranks and made it possible for the Americans to sweep all resistance from the town.

2615 ◆ *BENNION, MERVYN SHARP

Rank: Captain
Service: U.S. Navy
Birthday: 5 May 1887
Place of Birth: Vernon, Tooele County, Utah
Date of Death: 7 December 1941
Place of Death: Ohau, Territory of Hawaii
Cemetery: City Cemetery (MH)—Salt Lake City, Utah
Entered Service at: Utah
Unit: U.S.S. *West Virginia*
Served as: Commanding Officer
Battle or Place of Action: Pearl Harbor, Ohau, Territory of Hawaii
Date of Action: 7 December 1941
Citation: For conspicuous devotion to duty, extraordinary courage, and complete disregard of his own life, above and beyond the call of duty, during the attack on the Fleet in Pearl Harbor, by Japanese forces on 7 December 1941. As commanding officer of the U.S.S. *West Virginia*, after being mortally wounded, Capt. Bennion evidenced apparent concern only in fighting and saving his ship, and strongly protested against being carried from the bridge.

2616 ◆ *BERRY, CHARLES JOSEPH

Rank: Corporal
Service: U.S. Marine Corps
Birthday: 10 July 1923
Place of Birth: Lorain, Lorain County, Ohio
Date of Death: 3 March 1945
Place of Death: Iwo Jima, Volcano islands
Cemetery: Elmwood Cemetery (MH)—Lorain, Ohio
Entered Service at: Ohio
Unit: 1st Battalion, 26th Marines, 5th Marine Division
Served as: Machine Gunner
Battle or Place of Action: Iwo Jima, Volcano Islands

Date of Action: 3 March 1945
Citation: For conspicuous gallantry and intrepidity at the risk of his life above and beyond the call of duty as a member of a machine-gun crew, serving with the 1st Battalion, 26th Marines, 5th Marine Division, in action against enemy Japanese forces during the seizure of Iwo Jima in the Volcano Islands, on 3 March 1945. Stationed in the front lines, Cpl. Berry manned his weapon with alert readiness as he maintained a constant vigil with other members of his guncrew during the hazardous night hours. When infiltrating Japanese soldiers launched a surprise attack shortly after midnight in an attempt to overrun his position, he engaged in a pitched hand-grenade duel, returning the dangerous weapons with prompt and deadly accuracy until an enemy grenade landed in the fox-hole. Determined to save his comrades, he unhesitatingly chose to sacrifice himself and immediately dived on the deadly missile, absorbing the shattering violence of the exploding charge in his own body and protecting the others from serious injury. Stouthearted and indomitable, Cpl. Berry fearlessly yielded his own life that his fellow marines might carry on the relentless battle against a ruthless enemy, and his superb valor and unfaltering devotion to duty in the face of certain death reflect the highest credit upon himself and upon the U.S. Naval Service. He gallantly gave his life for his country.

2617 ◆ BERTOLDO, VITO R.

Rank: Master Sergeant
Service: U.S. Army
Birthday: 1 December 1916
Place of Birth: Decatur, Macon County, Illinois
Date of Death: 23 July 1966
Cemetery: Golden Gate National Cemetery (C-52-A) (MH)—San Bruno, California
Entered Service at: Decatur, Macon County, Illinois
Unit: Company A, 242d Infantry, 42d Infantry Division
Battle or Place of Action: Hatten, France
Date of Action: 9-10 January 1945
G.O. Number, Date: 5, 10 January 1946
Citation: He fought with extreme gallantry while guarding two command posts against the assault of powerful infantry and armored forces which had overrun the battalion's main line of resistance. On the close approach of enemy soldiers, he left the protection of the building he defended and set up his gun in the street, there to remain for almost 12 hours driving back attacks while in full view of his adversaries and completely exposed to 88-mm, machine-gun, and small-arms fire. He moved back inside the command post, strapped his machine gun to a table, and covered the main approach to the building by firing through a window, remaining steadfast even in the face of 88-mm fire from tanks only 75 yards away. One shell blasted him across the room, but he returned to his weapon. When two enemy personnel carriers led by a tank moved toward his position, he calmly waited for the troops to dismount and then, with the tank firing directly at him, leaned out of the window and mowed down the entire group of more than 20 Germans. Some time later, removal of the command post to another building was ordered. M/Sgt. Bertoldo voluntarily remained behind, covering the withdraw-

al of his comrades and maintaining his stand all night. In the morning he carried his machine gun to an adjacent building used as the command post of another battalion and began a day-long defense of that position. He broke up a heavy attack, launched by a self-propelled 88-mm gun covered by a tank and about 15 infantrymen. Soon afterward another 88-mm weapon moved up to within a few feet of his position, and, placing the muzzle of its gun almost inside the building, fired into the room, knocking him down and seriously wounding others. An American bazooka team set the German weapon afire, and M/Sgt. Bertoldo went back to his machine gun dazed as he was and killed several of the hostile troops as they attempted to withdraw. It was decided to evacuate the command post under the cover of darkness, but before the plan could be put into operation the enemy began an intensive assault supported by fire from their tanks and heavy guns. Disregarding the devastating barrage, he remained at his post and hurled white phosphorous grenades into the advancing enemy troops until they broke and retreated. A tank less than 50 yards away fired at his stronghold, destroyed the machine gun, and blew him across the room again, but he once more returned to the bitter fight and, with a rifle, singlehandedly covered the withdrawal of his fellow soldiers when the post was finally abandoned. With inspiring bravery and intrepidity M/Sgt. Bertoldo withstood the attack of vastly superior forces for more than 48 hours without rest or relief, time after time escaping death only by the slightest margin while killing at least 40 hostile soldiers and wounding many more during his grim battle against the enemy hordes.

2618 ◆ BEYER, ARTHUR O.

Rank: Corporal
Service: U.S. Army
Birthday: 20 May 1909
Place of Birth: Rock Township, Mitchell County, Iowa
Date of Death: 17 February 1965
Place of Death: Near Buffalo, North Dakota
Cemetery: Immanuel Lutheran Church Cemetery—St. Ansgar, Iowa
Entered Service at: St. Ansgar, Mitchell County, Iowa
Unit: Company C, 603d Tank Destroyer Battalion
Battle or Place of Action: near Arloncourt, Belgium
Date of Action: 15 January 1945
G.O. Number, Date: 73, 30 August 1945
Date of Presentation: 23 August 1945
Place of Presentation: The White House, presented by Pres. Harry S. Truman
Citation: He displayed conspicuous gallantry in action. His platoon, in which he was a tank-destroyer gunner, was held up by antitank, machine-gun, and rifle fire from enemy troops dug in along a ridge about 200 yards to the front. Noting a machine-gun position in this defense line, he fired upon it with his 76-mm gun killing one man and silencing the weapon. He dismounted from his vehicle and, under direct enemy observation, crossed open ground to capture the two remaining members of the crew. Another machine gun, about 250 yards to the left, continued to fire on him. Through withering fire, he advanced on the position. Throwing a

grenade into the emplacement, he killed one crew member and again captured the two survivors. He was subjected to concentrated small-arms fire but, with great bravery, he worked his way a quarter mile along the ridge, attacking hostile soldiers in their foxholes with his carbine and grenades. When he had completed his self-imposed mission against powerful German forces, he had destroyed two machine-gun positions, killed eight of the enemy, and captured 18 prisoners, including two bazooka teams. Cpl. Beyer's intrepid action and unflinching determination to close with and destroy the enemy eliminated the German defense line and enabled his task force to gain its objective.

2619 ◆ *BIANCHI, WILLIBALD CHARLES

Rank: First Lieutenant (highest rank: Captain)
Service: U.S. Army
Birthday: 12 March 1915
Place of Birth: New Ulm, Brown County, Minnesota
Date of Death: 9 January 1945
Place of Death: At Sea POW ship sunk by A.A.C. Attack.
Cemetery: National Memorial Cemetery of the Pacific (MA-39) (MH)—Honolulu, Hawaii (marker only)
Entered Service at: New Ulm, Brown County, Minnesota
Unit: Philippine Scouts, 45th Infantry
Served as: Platoon Leader
Battle or Place of Action: near Bagac, Bataan Province, Philippine Islands
Date of Action: 3 February 1942
G.O. Number, Date: 11, 5 March 1942
Place of Presentation: Presented by Gen. Douglas MacArthur
Citation: For conspicuous gallantry and intrepidity above and beyond the call of duty in action with the enemy on 3 February 1942, near Bagac, Province of Bataan, Philippine Islands. When the rifle platoon of another company was ordered to wipe out two strong enemy machine-gun nests, 1st Lt. Bianchi, voluntarily and of his own initiative, advanced with the platoon leading part of the men. When wounded early in the action by two bullets through the left hand, he did not stop for first aid but discarded his rifle and began firing a pistol. He located a machine-gun nest and personally silenced it with grenades. When wounded the second time by two machine-gun bullets through the chest muscles, 1st Lt. Bianchi climbed to the top of an American tank, manned its antiaircraft machine gun, and fired into strongly held enemy position until knocked completely off the tank by a third severe wound.

2620 ◆ BIDDLE, MELVIN EARL

Rank: Private First Class
Service: U.S. Army
Birthday: 28 November 1923
Place of Birth: Daleville, Delaware County, Indiana
Entered Service at: Anderson, Madison County, Indiana
Unit: 1st Squad, 2d Platoon, Company B, 1st Battalion, 517th Parachute Infantry Regiment
Served as: Lead Scout/Rifleman

Battle or Place of Action: between Soy and Hotton, Belgium
Date of Action: 23-24 December 1944
G.O. Number, Date: 95, 30 October 1945
Date of Presentation: 12 October 1945
Place of Presentation: The White House, presented by Pres. Harry S. Truman
Citation: He displayed conspicuous gallantry and intrepidity in action against the enemy near Soy, Belgium, on 23 and 24 December 1944. Serving as lead scout during an attack to relieve the enemy-encircled town of Hotton, he aggressively penetrated a densely wooded area, advanced 400 yards until he came within range of intense enemy rifle fire, and within 20 yards of enemy positions killed three snipers with unerring marksmanship. Courageously continuing his advance an additional 200 yards, he discovered a hostile machine-gun position and dispatched its two occupants. He then located the approximate position of a well-concealed enemy machine-gun nest, and crawling forward threw hand grenades which killed two Germans and fatally wounded a third. After signaling his company to advance, he entered a determined line of enemy defense, cooly and deliberately shifted his position, and shot three more enemy soldiers. Undaunted by enemy fire, he crawled within 20 yards of a machine-gun nest, tossed his last hand grenade into the position, and after the explosion charged the emplacement firing his rifle. When night fell, he scouted enemy positions alone for several hours and returned with valuable information which enabled our attacking infantry and armor to knock out two enemy tanks. At daybreak he again led the advance and, when flanking elements were pinned down by enemy fire, without hesitation made his way toward a hostile machine-gun position and from a distance of 50 yards killed the crew and two supporting riflemen. The remainder of the enemy, finding themselves without automatic-weapon support, fled panic-stricken. Pfc. Biddle's intrepid courage and superb daring during his 20-hour action enabled his battalion to break the enemy grasp on Hotton with a minimum of casualties.

2621 ◆ *BIGELOW, ELMER CHARLES

Rank: Watertender First Class
Service: U.S. Naval Reserve
Birthday: 12 July 1920
Place of Birth: Hebron, McHenry County, Illinois
Date of Death: 15 February 1945
Cemetery: Linn-Hebron Cemetery—Hebron, Illinois
Entered Service at: Illinois
Unit: U.S.S. *Fletcher*
Served as: Watertender
Battle or Place of Action: off Corregidor Island, Philippine Islands
Date of Action: 14 February 1945
Place of Presentation: Great Lakes Naval Base, Illinois, presented by Vice Adm. A. S. Carpender, Commandant, Ninth Naval District to his mother, Mrs. Verna Perry
Citation: For conspicuous gallantry and intrepidity at the risk of his life above and beyond the call of duty while serving on board the U.S.S. *Fletcher* during action against enemy

Japanese forces off Corregidor Island in the Philippines, 14 February 1945. Standing topside when an enemy shell struck the *Fletcher*, Bigelow, acting instantly as the deadly projectile exploded into fragments which penetrated the No. 1 gun magazine and set fire to several powder cases, picked up a pair of fire extinguishers and rushed below in a resolute attempt to quell the raging flames. Refusing to waste the precious time required to don rescue-breathing apparatus, he plunged through the blinding smoke billowing out of the magazine hatch and dropped into the blazing compartment. Despite the acrid, burning powder smoke which seared his lungs with every agonizing breath, he worked rapidly and with instinctive sureness and succeeded in quickly extinguishing the fires and in cooling the cases and bulkheads, thereby preventing further damage to the stricken ship. Although he succumbed to his injuries on the following day, Bigelow, by his dauntless valor, unfaltering skill and prompt action in the critical emergency, had averted a magazine explosion which undoubtedly would have left the ship wallowing at the mercy of the furiously pounding Japanese guns on Corregidor, and his heroic spirit of self-sacrifice in the face of almost certain death enhanced and sustained the highest traditions of the U.S. Naval Service. He gallantly gave his life in the service of his country.

2622 ◆ BJORKLUND, ARNOLD L.

Rank: First Lieutenant
Service: U.S. Army
Birthday: 14 April 1918
Place of Birth: Clinton, Island County, Washington
Date of Death: 28 November 1979
Cemetery: Williamette National Cemetery (0-3446) (MH)—Portland, Oregon
Entered Service at: Seattle, King County, Washington
Unit: 142d Infantry Regiment, 36th Infantry Division
Served as: Platoon Leader
Battle or Place of Action: Altavilla, Italy
Date of Action: 13 September 1943
G.O. Number, Date: 73, 6 September 1944
Date of Presentation: 31 August 1944
Place of Presentation: The White House (Oval Office), presented by Pres. Franklin D. Roosevelt
Citation: For conspicuous gallantry and intrepidity at the risk of his life above and beyond the call of duty in action with the enemy near Altavilla, Italy, 13 September 1943. When his company attacked a German position on Hill 424, the first platoon led by 1st Lt. Bjorklund, moved forward on the right flank to the slope of the hill where it was pinned down by a heavy concentration of machine-gun and rifle fire. Ordering his men to give covering fire, with only three hand grenades, he crept and crawled forward to a German machine-gun position located on a terrace along the forward slope. Approaching within a few yards of the position, and while continuously exposed to enemy fire, he hurled one grenade into the nest, destroyed the gun, and killed three Germans. Discovering a second machine gun 20 yards to the right on a higher terrace, he moved under intense enemy fire to a point within a few yards and threw a second grenade into this position, destroying it and killing two more Germans.

The first platoon was then able to advance 150 yards further up the slope to the crest of the hill, but was again stopped by the fire from a heavy enemy mortar on the reverse slope. First Lt. Bjorklund located the mortar and worked his way under little cover to within ten yards of its position and threw his third grenade, destroying the mortar, killing two of the Germans, and forcing the remaining three to flee. His actions permitted the platoon to take its objective.

2623 ◆ BLOCH, ORVILLE EMIL

Rank: First Lieutenant (highest rank: Colonel)
Service: U.S. Army
Birthday: 10 February 1915
Place of Birth: Big Falls, Waupaca County, Wisconsin
Date of Death: 28 May 1983
Place of Death: Manson, Washington
Cemetery: Evergreen Washelli Memorial Park (MH)—Seattle, Washington
Entered Service at: Streeter, Stutsman County, North Dakota
Unit: Company E, 338th Infantry, 85th Infantry Division
Served as: Platoon Leader
Battle or Place of Action: near Firenzuola, Italy
Date of Action: 22 September 1944
G.O. Number, Date: 9, 10 February 1945
Date of Presentation: 6 February 1945
Place of Presentation: Firenzuloa, Italy, presented by Gen. Mark Clark
Citation: For conspicuous gallantry and intrepidity at the risk of life above and beyond the call of duty. First Lt. Bloch undertook the task of wiping out five enemy machine-gun nests that had held up the advance in that particular sector for one day. Gathering three volunteers from his platoon, the patrol snaked their way to a big rock, behind which a group of three buildings and five machine-gun nests were located. Leaving the three men behind the rock, he attacked the first machine-gun nest alone charging into furious automatic fire, kicking over the machine gun and capturing the machine-gun crew of five. Pulling the pin from a grenade, he held it ready in his hand and dashed into the face of withering automatic fire toward this second machine-gun nest located at the corner of an adjacent building 15 yards distant. When within 20 feet of the machine gun he hurled the grenade, wounding the machine gunner, the other two members of the crew fleeing into a door of the house. Calling one of his volunteer group to accompany him, they advanced to the opposite end of the house, there contacting a machine-gun crew of five running toward this house. First Lt. Bloch and his men opened fire on the enemy crew, forcing them to abandon this machine gun and ammunition and flee into the same house. Without a moment's hesitation, 1st Lt. Bloch, unassisted, rushed through the door into a hail of small-arms fire, firing his carbine from the hip, and captured the seven occupants, wounding three of them. First Lt. Bloch with his men then proceeded to a third house where they discovered an abandoned enemy machine gun and detected another enemy machine-gun nest at the next corner of the building. The crew of six

2624 ◆ BOLDEN, PAUL LUTHER

spotted 1st Lt. Bloch the instant he saw them. Without a moment's hesitation he dashed toward them. The enemy fired pistols wildly in his direction and vanished through a door of the house, 1st Lt. Bloch following them through the door, firing his carbine from the hip, wounding two of the enemy and capturing six. Altogether 1st Lt. Bloch had single-handedly captured 19 prisoners, wounding six of them and eliminating a total of five enemy machine-gun nests. His gallant and heroic actions saved his company many casualties and permitted them to continue the attack with new inspiration and vigor.

2624 ◆ BOLDEN, PAUL LUTHER

Rank: Staff Sergeant (highest rank: Master Sergeant)
Service: U.S. Army
Birthday: 15 June 1922
Place of Birth: Hobbes Island, Alabama
Date of Death: 21 May 1979
Cemetery: Moons Cemetery (MH)—Owens Crossroads, Alabama
Entered Service at: Madison, Madison County, Alabama
Unit: Company I, 120th Infantry, 30th Infantry Division
Battle or Place of Action: Petit-Coo, Belgium
Date of Action: 23 December 1944
G.O. Number, Date: 73, 30 August 1945
Place of Presentation: The White House, presented by Pres. Harry S. Truman
Citation: He voluntarily attacked a formidable enemy strongpoint in Petit-Coo, Belgium, on 23 December 1944, when his company was pinned down by extremely heavy automatic and small-arms fire coming from a house 200 yards to the front. Mortar and tank artillery shells pounded the unit, when S/Sgt. Bolden and a comrade, on their own initiative, moved forward in a hail of bullets to eliminate the ever-increasing fire from the German position. Crawling ahead to close with what they knew was a powerfully armed, vastly superior force, the pair reached the house and took up assault positions, S/Sgt. Bolden under a window, his comrade across the street where he could deliver covering fire. In rapid succession, S/Sgt. Bolden hurled a fragmentation grenade and a white phosphorous grenade into the building; and then, fully realizing that he faced tremendous odds, rushed to the door, threw it open, and fired into 35 SS troopers who were trying to reorganize themselves after the havoc wrought by the grenades. Twenty Germans died under fire of his submachine gun before he was struck in the shoulder, chest, and stomach by part of a burst which killed his comrade across the street. He withdrew from the house, waiting for the surviving Germans to come out and surrender. When none appeared in the doorway, he summoned his ebbing strength, overcame the extreme pain he suffered, and boldly walked back into the house, firing as he went. He had killed the remaining 15 enemy soldiers when his ammunition ran out. S/Sgt. Bolden's heroic advance against great odds, his fearless assault, and his magnificent display of courage in reentering the building where he had been severely wounded cleared the path for his company and insured the success of its mission.

2625 ◆ BOLTON, CECIL HAMILTON

Rank: First Lieutenant
Service: U.S. Army
Birthday: 7 October 1908
Place of Birth: Crawfordville, Wakulla County, Florida
Date of Death: 22 January 1965
Cemetery: Fort Sam Houston National Cemetery (P-C-22-J) (MH)—San Antonio, Texas
Entered Service at: Huntsville, Madison County, Alabama
Unit: Company E, 413th Infantry, 104th Infantry Division
Battle or Place of Action: Mark River, Holland
Date of Action: 2 November 1944
G.O. Number, Date: 74, 1 September 1945
Date of Presentation: 23 August 1945
Place of Presentation: The White House, presented by Pres. Harry S. Truman
Citation: As leader of the weapons platoon of Company E, 413th Infantry, on the night of 2 November 1944, he fought gallantly in a pitched battle which followed the crossing of the Mark River in Holland. When two machine guns pinned down his company, he tried to eliminate, with mortar fire, their grazing fire which was inflicting serious casualties and preventing the company's advance from an area rocked by artillery shelling. In the moonlight it was impossible for him to locate accurately the enemy's camouflaged positions; but he continued to direct fire until wounded severely in the legs and rendered unconscious by a German shell. When he recovered consciousness he instructed his unit and then crawled to the forward rifle platoon positions. Taking a two-man bazooka team on his voluntary mission, he advanced chest-deep in chilling water along a canal toward one enemy machine gun. While the bazooka team covered him, he approached alone to within 15 yards of the hostile emplacement in a house. He charged the remaining distance and killed the two gunners with hand grenades. Returning to his men he led them through intense fire over open ground to assault the second German machine gun. An enemy sniper who tried to block the way was dispatched, and the trio pressed on. When discovered by the machine-gun crew and subjected to direct fire, 1st Lt. Bolton killed one of the three gunners with carbine fire, and his two comrades shot the others. Continuing to disregard his wounds, he led the bazooka team toward an 88-mm artillery piece which was having telling effect on the American ranks, and approached once more through icy canal water until he could dimly make out the gun's silhouette. Under his fire direction, the two soldiers knocked out the enemy weapon with rockets. On the way back to his own lines he was again wounded. To prevent his men being longer subjected to deadly fire, he refused aid and ordered them back to safety, painfully crawling after them until he reached his lines, where he collapsed. First Lt. Bolton's heroic assaults in the face of vicious fire, his inspiring leadership, and continued aggressiveness even through suffering from serious wounds contributed in large measure to overcoming strong enemy resistance and made it possible for his battalion to reach its objective.

2626 ◆ BONG, RICHARD IRA

Rank: Major
Service: U.S. Army Air Corps
Birthday: 24 September 1920
Place of Birth: Superior, Douglas County, Wisconsin
Date of Death: 6 August 1945
Place of Death: Burbank, California
Cemetery: Poplar Cemetery (MH)—Poplar, Wisconsin
Entered Service at: Poplar, Douglas County, Wisconsin
Unit: 49th Fighter Group, 5th Fighter Command, 5th Air Force
Served as: Fighter Pilot of a P-38
Battle or Place of Action: over Borneo and Leyte, Philippine Islands
Date of Action: 10 October-15 November 1944
G.O. Number, Date: 90, 8 December 1944
Date of Presentation: 12 December 1944
Place of Presentation: Tacloban air strip, Leyte, Philippine Islands, presented by Gen. Douglas MacArthur
Citation: For conspicuous gallantry and intrepidity in action above and beyond the call of duty in the southwest Pacific area from 10 October to 15 November 1944. Though assigned to duty as gunnery instructor and neither required nor expected to perform combat duty, Maj. Bong voluntarily and at his own urgent request engaged in repeated combat missions, including unusually hazardous sorties over Balikpapan, Borneo, and in the Leyte area of the Philippines. His aggressiveness and daring resulted in his shooting down eight enemy airplanes during this period.

2627 ◆ *BONNYMAN JR., ALEXANDER "SANDY"

Rank: First Lieutenant
Service: U.S. Marine Corps Reserve
Birthday: 2 May 1910
Place of Birth: Atlanta, Fulton County, Georgia
Date of Death: 22 November 1943
Cemetery: Santa Fe National Cemetery (MA-84) (MH) ('In Memory' marker)—Santa Fe, New Mexico; National Memorial Cemetery of the Pacific (Wall of the Missing)—Honolulu, Hawaii
Entered Service at: New Mexico
Unit: 2d Battalion Shore Party, 8th Marines, 2d Marine Division
Served as: Executive Officer
Battle or Place of Action: Betio Island, Tarawa Atoll, Gilbert Islands
Date of Action: 20-22 November 1943
Citation: For conspicuous gallantry and intrepidity at the risk of his life above and beyond the call of duty as executive officer of the 2d Battalion Shore Party, 8th Marines, 2d Marine Division, during the assault against enemy Japanese-held Tarawa in the Gilbert Islands, 20–22 November 1943. Acting on his own initiative when assault troops were pinned down at the far end of Betio Pier by the overwhelming fire of Japanese shore batteries, 1st Lt. Bonnyman repeatedly defied the blasting fury of the enemy bombardment to organize and lead the besieged men over the long, open pier to the beach and then, voluntarily obtaining flamethrowers and demolitions, organized his pioneer shore party into assault demolitionists and directed the blowing of several hostile installations before the close of D-day. Determined to effect an opening in the enemy's strongly organized defense line the following day, he voluntarily crawled approximately 40 yards forward of our lines and placed demolitions in the entrance of a large Japanese emplacement as the initial move in his planned attack against the heavily garrisoned, bombproof installation which was stubbornly resisting despite the destruction early in the action of a large number of Japanese who had been inflicting heavy casualties on our forces and holding up our advance. Withdrawing only to replenish his ammunition, he led his men in a renewed assault, fearlessly exposing himself to the merciless slash of hostile fire as he stormed the formidable bastion, directed the placement of demolition charges in both entrances, and seized the top of the bombproof position, flushing more than 100 of the enemy who were instantly cut down and effecting the annihilation of approximately 150 troops inside the emplacement. Assailed by additional Japanese after he had gained his objective, he made a heroic stand on the edge of the structure, defending his strategic position with indomitable determination in the face of the desperate charge and killing three of the enemy before he fell, mortally wounded. By his dauntless fighting spirit, unrelenting aggressiveness and forceful leadership throughout three days of unremitting, violent battle, 1st Lt. Bonnyman had inspired his men to heroic effort, enabling them to beat off the counterattack and break the back of hostile resistance in that sector for an immediate gain of 400 yards with no further casualties to our forces in this zone. He gallantly gave his life for his country.

2628 ◆ *BOOKER, ROBERT D.

Rank: Private
Service: U.S. Army
Birthday: 11 July 1920
Place of Birth: Callaway, Custer County, Nebraska
Date of Death: 9 April 1943
Cemetery: Rose Hill Cemetery—Callaway, Nebraska
Entered Service at: Callaway, Custer County, Nebraska
Unit: Company B, 133d Infantry, 34th Infantry Division
Battle or Place of Action: near Fondouk, Tunisia
Date of Action: 9 April 1943
G.O. Number, Date: 34, 25 April 1944
Citation: For conspicuous gallantry and intrepidity at the risk of life above and beyond the call of duty in action. On 9 April 1943 in the vicinity of Fondouk, Tunisia, Pvt. Booker, while engaged in action against the enemy, carried a light machine gun and a box of ammunition over 200 yards of open ground. He continued to advance despite the fact that two enemy machine guns and several mortars were using him as an individual target. Although enemy artillery also began to register on him, upon reaching his objective he immediately commenced firing. After being wounded he silenced one enemy machine gun and was begining to fire at the other when he received a second mortal wound. With his last

remaining strength he encouraged the members of his squad and directed their fire. Pvt. Booker acted without regard for his own safety. His initiative and courage against insurmountable odds are an example of the highest standard of self-sacrifice and fidelity to duty.

2629 ◆ *BORDELON, WILLIAM JAMES

Rank: Staff Sergeant
Service: U.S. Marine Corps
Birthday: 25 December 1920
Place of Birth: San Antonio, Bexar County, Texas
Date of Death: 20 November 1943
Cemetery: National Memorial Cemetery of the Pacific (A-481) (MH)—Honolulu, Hawaii
Entered Service at: Texas
Unit: 1st Battalion, 18th Marines, tactically attached to the 2d Marine Division
Battle or Place of Action: Tarawa, Gilbert Islands
Date of Action: 20 November 1943
Date of Presentation: June 1944
Place of Presentation: Alamo Stadium, Texas, presented by Pres. Franklin D. Roosevelt to his parents
Citation: For valorous and gallant conduct above and beyond the call of duty as a member of an assault engineer platoon of the 1st Battalion, 18th Marines, tactically attached to the 2d Marine Division, in action against the Japanese-held atoll of Tarawa in the Gilbert Islands, 20 November 1943. Landing in the assault waves under withering enemy fire which killed all but four of the men in his tractor, S/Sgt. Bordelon Hurriedly made demolition charges and personally put two pillboxes out of action. Hit by enemy machine-gun fire just as a charge exploded in his hand while assaulting a third position, he courageously remained in action and, although out of demolition, provided himself with a rifle and furnished fire coverage for a group of men scaling the seawall. Disregarding his own serious condition, he unhesitatingly went to the aid of one of his demolition men, wounded and calling for help in the water, rescuing this man and another who had been hit by enemy fire while attempting to make the rescue. Still refusing first aid for himself, he again made up demolition charges and singlehandedly assaulted a fourth Japanese machine-gun position, but was instantly killed when caught in a final burst of fire from the enemy. S/Sgt. Bordelon's great personal valor during a critical phase of securing the limited beachhead was a contributing factor in the ultimate occupation of the island, and his heroic determination throughout three days of violent battle reflects the highest credit upon the U.S. Naval Service. He gallantly gave his life for his country.

2630 ◆ *BOYCE JR., GEORGE W. G.

Rank: Second Lieutenant
Service: U.S. Army
Place of Birth: New York, New York
Date of Death: 23 July 1944
Cemetery: A.B.M.C. Manila Cemetery (A-4-189)—Manila, Philippine Islands

Entered Service at: Cornwall, Orange County, New York
Unit: Troop A, 112th Cavalry Regimental Combat Team
Battle or Place of Action: near Afua, New Guinea
Date of Action: 23 July 1944
G.O. Number, Date: 25, 7 April 1945
Date of Issue: 12 February 1945
Citation: For conspicuous gallantry and intrepidity at the risk of his life above and beyond the call of duty near Afua, New Guinea, on 23 July 1944. 2d Lt. Boyce's troop, having been ordered to the relief of another unit surrounded by superior enemy forces, moved out, and upon gaining contact with the enemy, the two leading platoons deployed and built up a firing line. 2d Lt. Boyce was ordered to attack with his platoon and make the main effort on the right of his troop. He launched his attack but after a short advance encountered such intense rifle, machine-gun, and mortar fire that the forward movement of his platoon was temporarily halted. A shallow depression offered a route of advance, and he worked his squad up this avenue of approach in order to close with the enemy. He was promptly met by a volley of hand grenades, one falling between himself and the men immediately following. Realizing at once that the explosion would kill or wound several of his men, he promptly threw himself upon the grenade and smothered the blast with his own body. By thus deliberately sacrificing his life to save those of his men, this officer exemplified the highest traditions of the U.S. Armed Forces.

2631 ◆ BOYINGTON, GREGORY "PAPPY"

Rank: Major (highest rank: Colonel Ret.)
Service: U.S. Marine Corps Reserve
Birthday: 4 December 1912
Place of Birth: Coeur D'Alene, Kootenai County, Idaho
Date of Death: 11 January 1988
Place of Death: Fresno, California
Cemetery: Arlington National Cemetery (7A-150) (MH)—Arlington, Virginia
Entered Service at: Washington
Unit: Marine Squadron 214, Marine Air Group 11, 1st Marine Air Wing
Served as: Commanding Officer
Battle or Place of Action: Central Solomons area
Date of Action: 12 September 1943—3 January 1944
Date of Presentation: March 1944 (received 5 October 1945)
Place of Presentation: The White House, by Pres. Franklin D. Roosevelt to his Mother; presented by Pres. Harry S. Truman in 1945 to him
Citation: For extraordinary heroism and valiant devotion to duty as commanding officer of Marine Fighting Squadron 214 in action against enemy Japanese forces in the central Solomons area from 12 September 1943 to 3 January 1944. Consistently outnumbered throughout successive hazardous flights over heavily defended hostile territory, Maj. Boyington struck at the enemy with daring and courageous persistence, leading his squadron into combat with devastating results to Japanese shipping, shore installations, and aerial forces. Resolute in his efforts to inflict crippling damage on the

enemy, Maj. Boyington led a formation of 24 fighters over Kahili on 17 October and, persistently circling the airdrome where 60 hostile aircraft were grounded, boldly challenged the Japanese to send up planes. Under his brilliant command, our fighters shot down 20 enemy craft in the ensuing action without the loss of a single ship. A superb airman and determined fighter against overwhelming odds, Maj. Boyington personally destroyed 26 of the many Japanese planes shot down by his squadron and, by his forceful leadership, developed the combat readiness in his command, which was a distinctive factor in the Allied aerial achievements in this vitally strategic area.
Notes: POW

2632 ◆ BRILES, HERSCHEL FLOYD "PETE"

Rank: Staff Sergeant (highest rank: First Sergeant)
Service: U.S. Army
Birthday: 7 February 1914
Place of Birth: Colfax, Jasper County, Iowa
Date of Death: 17 July 1994
Place of Death: Mitchellville, Iowa
Cemetery: Waveland Cemetery (MH)—Prairie City, Iowa
Entered Service at: Fort Des Moines, Polk County, Iowa
Unit: Company C, 899th Tank Destroyer Battalion, attached to the 9th Infantry Division
Served as: Squad Leader
Battle or Place of Action: Scherpenseel, Germany
Date of Action: 20 November 1944
G.O. Number, Date: 77, 10 September 1945
Date of Presentation: 23 August 1945
Place of Presentation: The White House, presented by Pres. Harry S. Truman
Citation: He was leading a platoon of destroyers across an exposed slope near Scherpenseel, Germany, on 20 November 1944, when they came under heavy enemy artillery fire. A direct hit was scored on one of the vehicles, killing one man, seriously wounding two others, and setting the destroyer afire. With a comrade, S/Sgt. Briles left the cover of his own armor and raced across ground raked by artillery and small-arms fire to the rescue of the men in the shattered destroyer. Without hesitation, he lowered himself into the burning turret, removed the wounded, and then extinguished the fire. From a position he assumed the next morning, he observed hostile infantrymen advancing. With his machine gun, he poured such deadly fire into the enemy ranks that an entire pocket of 55 Germans surrendered, clearing the way for a junction between American units which had been held up for two days. Later that day, when another of his destroyers was hit by a concealed enemy tank, he again left protection to give assistance. With the help of another soldier, he evacuated two wounded under heavy fire and, returning to the burning vehicle, braved death from exploding ammunition to put out the flames. By his heroic initiative and complete disregard for personal safety, S/Sgt. Briles was largely responsible for causing heavy enemy casualties, forcing the surrender of 55 Germans, making possible the salvage of our vehicles, and saving the lives of wounded comrades.

2633 ◆ BRITT, MAURICE LEE (FOOTSIE)

Rank: Captain (rank at time of action: Lieutenant) (highest rank: Captain)
Service: U.S. Army
Birthday: 29 June 1919
Place of Birth: Carlisle, Lonoke County, Arkansas
Entered Service at: Lonoke, Lonoke County, Arkansas
Unit: Company L, 3d Battalion, 30th Infantry, 3d Infantry Division
Served as: Company Commander
Battle or Place of Action: North of Mignano, Italy
Date of Action: 10 November 1943
G.O. Number, Date: 23, 24 March 1944
Date of Presentation: 7 June 1944
Place of Presentation: University of Arkansas, Little Rock, Arkansas, presented by Gen. Harry Collins
Citation: For conspicuous gallantry and intrepidity at the risk of his life above and beyond the call of duty. Disdaining enemy hand grenades and close-range machine pistols, machine guns, and rifles, Lt. Britt inspired and led a handful of his men in repelling a bitter counterattack by approximately 100 Germans against his company positions north of Mignano, Italy, on the morning of 10 November 1943. During the intense firefight, Lt. Britt's canteen and field glasses were shattered; a bullet pierced his side; his chest, face, and hands were covered with grenade wounds. Despite his wounds, for which he refused to accept medical attention until ordered to do so by his battalion commander following the battle, he personally killed five and wounded an unknown number of Germans, wiped out one enemy machine-gun crew, fired five clips of carbine and an undetermined amount of M-1 rifle ammunition, and threw 32 fragmentation grenades. His bold, aggressive actions, utterly disregarding superior enemy numbers, resulted in capture of four Germans, two of them wounded, and enabled several captured Americans to escape. Lt. Britt's undaunted courage and prowess in arms were largely responsible for repulsing a German counterattack which, if successful, would have isolated his battalion and destroyed his company.

2634 ◆ *BROSTROM, LEONARD C.

Rank: Private First Class
Service: U.S. Army
Birthday: 23 November 1919
Place of Birth: Preston, Franklin County, Idaho
Date of Death: 28 October 1944
Cemetery: Preston Cemetery District (MH)—Preston, Idaho
Entered Service at: Preston, Franklin County, Idaho
Unit: Company F, 17th Infantry Regiment, 7th Infantry Division
Served as: Rifleman
Battle or Place of Action: near Dagami, Leyte, Philippine Islands
Date of Action: 28 October 1944
G.O. Number, Date: 104, 15 November 1945
Date of Presentation: 29 November 1945

Place of Presentation: Preston, Idaho, presented by Brig. Gen. Robert M. Hardaway to his Father
Citation: He was a rifleman with an assault platoon which ran into powerful resistance near Dagami, Leyte, Philippine Islands, on 28 October 1944. From pillboxes, trenches, and spider holes so well-camouflaged that they could be detected at no more than 20 yards, the enemy poured machine-gun and rifle fire, causing severe casualties in the platoon. Realizing that a key pillbox in the center of the strongpoint would have to be knocked out if the company were to advance, Pfc. Brostrom, without orders and completely ignoring his own safety, ran forward to attack the pillbox with grenades. He immediately became the prime target for all the riflemen in the area, as he rushed to the rear of the pillbox and tossed grenades through the entrance. Six enemy soldiers left a trench in a bayonet charge against the heroic American, but he killed one and drove the others off with rifle fire. As he threw more grenades from his completely exposed position he was wounded several times in the abdomen and knocked to the ground. Although suffering intense pain and rapidly weakening from loss of blood, he slowly rose to his feet and once more hurled his deadly missiles at the pillbox. As he collapsed, the enemy began fleeing from the fortification and were killed by riflemen of his platoon. Pfc. Brostrom died while being carried from the battlefield, but his intrepidity and unhesitating willingness to sacrifice himself in a one-man attack against overwhelming odds enabled his company to reorganize against attack and annihilate the entire enemy position.

2635 ◆ BROWN JR., BOBBIE EVAN

Rank: Captain
Service: U.S. Army
Birthday: 2 September 1903
Place of Birth: Dublin, Laurens County, Georgia
Date of Death: 8 November 1971
Place of Death: Highland Falls, New York
Cemetery: Arlington National Cemetery (46-1021-17) (MH)—Arlington, Virginia
Entered Service at: Atlanta, Fulton County, Georgia
Unit: Company C, 18th Infantry, 1st Infantry Division
Served as: Company Commander
Battle or Place of Action: Crucifix Hill, Aachen, Germany
Date of Action: 8 October 1944
G.O. Number, Date: 74, 1 September 1945
Date of Presentation: 23 August 1945
Place of Presentation: The White House, presented by Pres. Harry S. Truman
Citation: He commanded Company C, 18th Infantry Regiment, on 8 October 1944, when it, with the Ranger Platoon of the 1st Battalion, attacked Crucifix Hill, a key point in the enemy's defense of Aachen, Germany. As the leading rifle platoon assaulted the first of many pillboxes studding the rising ground, heavy fire from a flanking emplacement raked it. An intense artillery barrage fell on the American troops which had been pinned down in an exposed position. Seeing that the pillboxes must be neutralized to prevent the slaughter of his men, Capt. Brown obtained a pole

charge and started forward alone toward the first pillbox, about 100 yards away. Hugging the ground while enemy bullets whipped around him, he crawled and then ran toward the aperture of the fortification, rammed his explosive inside and jumped back as the pillbox and its occupants were blown up. He rejoined the assault platoon, secured another pole charge, and led the way toward the next pillbox under continuous artillery mortar, automatic and small-arms fire. He again ran forward and placed his charge in the enemy fortification, knocking it out. He then found that fire from a third pillbox was pinning down his company; so he returned to his men, secured another charge, and began to creep and crawl toward the hostile emplacement. With heroic bravery he disregarded opposing fire and worked ahead in the face of bullets streaming from the pillbox. Finally reaching his objective, he stood up and inserted his explosive, silencing the enemy. He was wounded by a mortar shell but refused medical attention and, despite heavy hostile fire, moved swiftly among his troops exhorting and instructing them in subduing powerful opposition. Later, realizing the need for information of enemy activity beyond the hill, Capt. Brown went out alone to reconnoiter. He observed possible routes of enemy approach and several times deliberately drew enemy fire to locate gun emplacements. Twice more, on this self-imposed mission, he was wounded; but he succeeded in securing information which led to the destruction of several enemy guns and enabled his company to throw back two powerful counterattacks with heavy losses. Only when Company C's position was completely secure did he permit treatment of his three wounds. By his indomitable courage, fearless leadership, and outstanding skill as a soldier, Capt. Brown contributed in great measure to the taking of Crucifix Hill, a vital link in the American line encircling Aachen.

2636 ◆ BULKELEY, JOHN DUNCAN

Rank: Lieutenant Commander (highest rank: Vice Admiral)
Service: U.S. Navy
Birthday: 19 August 1911
Place of Birth: San Antonio, Bexar County, Texas
Entered Service at: Texas
Unit: Motor Torpedo Boat Squadron 3
Served as: Commanding Officer
Battle or Place of Action: Philippine Waters
Date of Action: 7 December 1941—10 April 1942
Date of Presentation: 4 August 1942
Place of Presentation: The White House, presented by Pres. Franklin D. Roosevelt
Citation: For extraordinary heroism, distinguished service, and conspicuous gallantry above and beyond the call of duty as commander of Motor Torpedo Boat Squadron 3, in Philippine waters during the period from 7 December 1941 to 10 April 1942. The remarkable achievement of Lt. Comdr. Bulkeley's command in damaging or destroying a notable number of Japanese enemy planes, surface combatant and merchant ships, and in dispersing landing parties and land-based enemy forces during the four months and eight days of operation without benefit of repairs, overhaul, or maintenance

facilities for his squadron, is believed to be without precedence in this type of warfare. His dynamic forcefulness and daring in offensive action, his brilliantly planned and skillfully executed attacks, supplemented by a unique resourcefullness and ingenuity, characterize him as an outstanding leader of men and a gallant and intrepid seaman. These qualities coupled with a complete disregard for his own personal safety reflect great credit upon him and the Naval Service.

2637 ◆ BURKE, FRANCIS XAVIER

Rank: First Lieutenant
Service: U.S. Army
Birthday: 29 September 1918
Place of Birth: New York, New York
Date of Death: 6 September 1988
Cemetery: Veterans Memorial Cemetery (KN-1894) (MH)—Arneytown, New Jersey
Entered Service at: Jersey City, Hudson County, New Jersey
Unit: Company D, 1st Battalion, 15th Infantry, 3d Infantry Division
Served as: Battalion Transportation Officer
Battle or Place of Action: Nuremberg, Germany
Date of Action: 17 April 1945
G.O. Number, Date: 4, 9 January 1946
Date of Presentation: 18 December 1945
Place of Presentation: The White House, presented by Pres. Harry S. Truman
Citation: He fought with extreme gallantry in the streets of war-torn Nuremberg, Germany, where the 1st Battalion, 15th Infantry, was engaged in rooting out fanatical defenders of the citadel of Nazism. As battalion transportation officer he had gone forward to select a motor-pool site, when, in a desire to perform more than his assigned duties and participate in the fight, he advanced beyond the lines of the forward riflemen. Detecting a group of about 10 Germans making preparations for a local counterattack, he rushed back to a nearby American company, secured a light machine gun with ammunition, and daringly opened fire on this superior force, which deployed and returned his fire with machine pistols, rifles, and rocket launchers. From another angle a German machine gun tried to blast him from his emplacement, but 1st Lt. Burke killed this guncrew and drove off the survivors of the unit he had originally attacked. Giving his next attention to enemy infantrymen in ruined buildings, he picked up a rifle and dashed more than 100 yards through intense fire and engaged the Germans from behind an abandoned tank. A sniper nearly hit him from a cellar only 20 yards away, but he dispatched this adversary by running directly to the basement window, firing a full clip into it and then plunging through the darkened aperture to complete the job. He withdrew from the fight only long enough to replace his jammed rifle and secure grenades, then reengaged the Germans. Finding his shots ineffective, he pulled the pins from two grenades, and, holding one in each hand, rushed the enemy-held building, hurling his missiles just as the enemy threw a potato-masher grenade at him. In the triple explosion the Germans were wiped out and 1st Lt. Burke was dazed; but he emerged from the shower of debris that engulfed him, recovered his rifle, and went on to kill three more Germans and meet the charge of a machine pistolman, whom he cut down with three calmly delivered shots. He then retired toward the American lines and there assisted a platoon in a raging, 30-minute fight against formidable armed hostile forces. This enemy group was repulsed, and the intrepid fighter moved to another friendly group which broke the power of a German unit armed with a 20-mm gun in a fierce firefight. In four hours of heroic action, 1st Lt. Burke singlehandedly killed 11 and wounded three enemy soldiers and took a leading role in engagements in which an additional 29 enemy were killed or wounded. His extraordinary bravery and superb fighting skill were an inspiration to his comrades, and his entirely voluntary mission into exremely dangerous territory hastened the fall of Nuremberg, in his battalion's sector.

2638 ◆ *BURR, ELMER J.

Rank: First Sergeant
Service: U.S. Army
Birthday: 11 May 1908
Place of Birth: Neenah, Winnebago County, Wisconsin
Date of Death: 24 December 1942
Cemetery: Oak Hill Cemetery—Neenah, Wisconsin
Entered Service at: Menasha, Winnebago County, Wisconsin
Unit: Company I, 127th Infantry, 32d Infantry Division
Battle or Place of Action: Buna, New Guinea
Date of Action: 24 December 1942
G.O. Number, Date: 66, 11 October 1943
Citation: For conspicuous gallantry and intrepidity in action above and beyond the call of duty. During an attack near Buna, New Guinea, on 24 December 1942, 1st Sgt. Burr saw an enemy grenade strike near his company commander. Instantly and with heroic self-sacrifice he threw himself upon it, smothering the explosion with his body. 1st Sgt. Burr thus gave his life in saving that of his commander.

2639 ◆ BURR, HERBERT HOOVER

Rank: Staff Sergeant (rank at time of action: Private First Class)
Service: U.S. Army
Birthday: 13 September 1920
Place of Birth: St. Joseph, Buchanan County, Missouri
Date of Death: 8 February 1990
Cemetery: Mount Washington Cemetery (MH)—Independence, Missouri
Entered Service at: Kansas City, Clay County, Missouri
Unit: Company C, 41st Tank Battalion, 11th Armored Division
Served as: Bow Gunner
Battle or Place of Action: Dorrmoschel, Germany
Date of Action: 19 March 1945
G.O. Number, Date: 73, 30 August 1945
Date of Presentation: 23 August 1945
Place of Presentation: The White House, presented by Pres. Harry S. Truman

Citation: He displayed conspicuous gallantry during action when the tank in which he was bow gunner was hit by an enemy rocket, which severely wounded the platoon sergeant and forced the remainder of the crew to abandon the vehicle. Deafened, but otherwise unhurt, S/Sgt. Burr immediately climbed into the driver's seat and continued on the mission of entering the town to reconnoiter road conditions. As he rounded a turn he encountered an 88-mm antitank gun at point-blank range. Realizing that he had no crew, no one to man the tank's guns, he heroically chose to disregard his personal safety in a direct charge on the German weapon. At considerable speed he headed straight for the loaded gun, which was fully manned by enemy troops who had only to pull the lanyard to send a shell into his vehicle. So unexpected and daring was his assault that he was able to drive his tank completely over the gun, demolishing it and causing its crew to flee in confusion. He then skillfully sideswiped a large truck, overturned it, and wheeling his lumbering vehicle, returned to his company. When medical personnel who had been summoned to treat the wounded sergeant could not locate him, the valiant soldier ran through a hail of sniper fire to direct them to his stricken comrade. The bold, fearless determination of S/Sgt. Burr, his skill and courageous devotion to duty, resulted in the completion of his mission in the face of seemingly impossible odds.

2640 ◆ BURT, JAMES MONTROSS

Rank: Captain
Service: U.S. Army
Birthday: 18 July 1917
Place of Birth: Hinsdale, Berkshire County, Massachusetts
Entered Service at: Lee, Berkshire County, Massachusetts
Unit: Company B, 3d Battalion (Burt's Knights), 66th Armored Regiment, 2d Armored Division
Served as: Company Commander
Battle or Place of Action: Wurselen, Germany
Date of Action: 13 October 1944
G.O. Number, Date: 95, 30 October 1945
Date of Presentation: 12 October 1945
Place of Presentation: The White House, presented by Pres. Harry S. Truman
Citation: Capt. James M. Burt was in command of Company B, 66th Armored Regiment on the western outskirts of Wurselen, Germany on 13 October 1944, when his organization participated in a coordinated infantry-tank attack destined to isolate the large German garrison which was tenaciously defending the city of Aachen. In the first day's action, when infantrymen ran into murderous small-arms and mortar fire, Capt. Burt dismounted from his tank about 200 yards to the rear and moved forward on foot beyond the infantry positions, where, as the enemy concentrated a tremendous volume of fire upon him, he calmly motioned his tanks into good firing positions. As our attack gained momentum, he climbed aboard his tank and directed the action from the rear deck, exposed to hostile volleys which finally wounded him painfully in the face and neck. He maintained his dangerous post despite point-blank self-propelled gunfire until friendly artillery knocked out these enemy

weapons, and then proceeded to the advanced infantry scout's positions to deploy his tanks for the defense of the gains which had been made. The next day, when the enemy counterattacked, he left cover and went 75 yards through heavy fire to assist the infantry battalion commander who was seriously wounded. For the next eight days, through rainy, miserable weather and under constant, heavy shelling, Capt. Burt held the combined forces together, dominating and controlling the critical situation through the sheer force of his heroic example. To direct artillery fire, on 15 October, he took his tank 300 yards into the enemy lines, where he dismounted and remained for one hour giving accurate data to friendly gunners. Twice more on that day he went into enemy territory under deadly fire on reconnaissance. In succeeding days he never faltered in his determination to defeat the strong German forces opposing him. Twice the tank in which he was riding was knocked out by enemy action, and each time he climbed aboard another vehicle and continued the fight. He took great risks to rescue wounded comrades and inflicted prodigious destruction on enemy personnel and material even though suffering from the wounds he received in the battle's opening phase. Capt. Burt's intrepidity and disregard for personal safety were so complete that his own men and the infantry who attached themselves to him were inspired to overcome the wretched and extremely hazardous conditions which accompanied one of the most bitter local actions of the war. The victory achieved closed the Aachen gap.

2641 ◆ BUSH, RICHARD EARL

Rank: Corporal (highest rank: Gunnery Sergeant)
Service: U.S. Marine Corps Reserve
Birthday: 23 December 1923
Place of Birth: Glasgow, Barren County, Kentucky
Entered Service at: Kentucky
Unit: 3d Squad, 3d Platoon, Company C, 1st Battalion, 4th Marines, 6th Marine Division
Served as: Squad Leader
Battle or Place of Action: Mount Yaetake, Okinawa, Ryukyu Islands
Date of Action: 16 April 1945
Date of Presentation: 5 October 1945
Place of Presentation: The White House, presented by Pres. Harry S. Truman
Citation: For conspicuous gallantry and intrepidity at the risk of his life above and beyond the call of duty as a squad leader serving with the 1st Battalion, 4th Marines, 6th Marine Division, in action against enemy Japanese forces, during the final assault against Mount Yaetake on Okinawa, Ryukyu Islands, 16 April 1945. Rallying his men forward with indomitable determination, Cpl. Bush boldly defied the slashing fury of concentrated Japanese artillery fire pouring down from the gun-studded mountain fortress to lead his squad up the face of the rocky precipice, sweep over the ridge, and drive the defending troops from their deeply entrenched position. With his unit, the first to break through the inner defense of Mount Yaetake, he fought relentlessly in the forefront of the action until seriously wounded and evacuated with others under protecting rocks. Although prostrate under

medical treatment when a Japanese hand grenade landed in the midst of the group, Cpl. Bush, alert and courageous in extremity as in battle, unhesitatingly pulled the deadly missile to himself and absorbed the shattering violence of the exploding charge in his body, thereby saving his fellow marines from severe injury or death despite the certain peril to his own life. By his valiant leadership and aggressive tactics in the face of savage opposition, Cpl. Bush contributed materially to the success of the sustained drive toward the conquest of this fiercely defended outpost of the Japanese Empire. His constant concern for the welfare of his men, his resolute spirit of self-sacrifice, and his unwavering devotion to duty throughout the bitter conflict enhance and sustain the highest traditions of the U.S. Naval Service.

2642 ◆ BUSH, ROBERT EUGENE

Rank: Hospital Apprentice First Class
Service: U.S. Navy Reserve
Birthday: 4 October 1926
Place of Birth: Tacoma, Pierce County, Washington
Entered Service at: Washington
Unit: 3d Platoon, Company G, 2d Battalion, 5th Marines, 1st Marine Division
Served as: Medical Corpsman
Battle or Place of Action: Okinawa Jima, Ryukyu Islands
Date of Action: 2 May 1945
Date of Presentation: 5 October 1945
Place of Presentation: The White House, presented by Pres. Harry S. Truman
Citation: For conspicuous gallantry and intrepidity at the risk of life above and beyond the call of duty while serving as medical corpsman with a rifle company, in action against enemy Japanese forces on Okinawa Jima, Ryukyu Islands, 2 May 1945. Fearlessly braving the fury of artillery, mortar, and machine-gun fire from strongly entrenched hostile positions, Bush constantly and unhesitatingly moved from one casualty to another to attend the wounded falling under the enemy's murderous barrages. As the attack passed over a ridge top, Bush was advancing to administer blood plasma to a marine officer lying wounded on the skyline when the Japanese launched a savage counterattack. In this perilously exposed position, he resolutely maintained the flow of lifegiving plasma. With the bottle held high in one hand, Bush drew his pistol with the other and fired into the enemy ranks until his ammunition was expended. Quickly seizing a discarded carbine, he trained his fire on the Japanese charging point-blank over the hill, accounting for six of the enemy despite his own serious wounds and the loss of one eye suffered during his desperate battle in defense of the helpless man. With the hostile force finally routed, he calmly disregarded his own critical condition to complete his mission, valiantly refusing medical treatment for himself until his officer patient had been evacuated, and collapsing only after attempting to walk to the battle aid station. His daring initiative, great personal valor, and heroic spirit of self-sacrifice in service of others reflect great credit upon Bush and enhance the finest traditions of the U.S. Naval Service.

2643 ◆ *BUTTS, JOHN EDWARD

Rank: Second Lieutenant
Service: U.S. Army
Birthday: 8 August 1922
Place of Birth: Medina, Orleans County, New York
Date of Death: 23 June 1944
Cemetery: St. Mary's Cemetery (MH)—Medina, New York
Entered Service at: Buffalo, Erie County, New York
Unit: Company E, 60th Infantry, 9th Infantry Division
Battle or Place of Action: Normandy, France
Date of Action: 14, 16, 23 June 1944
G.O. Number, Date: 58, 19 July 1945
Citation: Heroically led his platoon against an enemy in Normandy, France, on 14, 16, and 23 June 1944. Although painfully wounded on the 14th near Orglandes and again on the 16th while spearheading an attack to establish a bridgehead across the Douve River, he refused medical aid and remained with his platoon. A week later, near Flottemanville Hague, he led an assault on a tactically important and stubbornly defended hill studded with tanks, antitank guns, pillboxes, and machine-gun emplacements and protected by concentrated artillery and mortar fire. As the attack was launched, 2d Lt. Butts, at the head of his platoon, was critically wounded by German machine-gun fire. Although weakened by his injuries, he rallied his men and directed one squad to make a flanking movement while he alone made a frontal assault to draw the hostile fire upon himself. Once more he was struck, but by grim determination and sheer courage continued to crawl ahead. When within 10 yards of his objective, he was killed by direct fire. By his superb courage, unflinching valor, and inspiring actions, 2d Lt. Butts enabled his platoon to take a formidable strongpoint and contributed greatly to the success of his battalion's mission.

2644 ◆ *CADDY, WILLIAM ROBERT

Rank: Private First Class
Service: U.S. Marine Corps Reserve
Birthday: 8 August 1925
Place of Birth: Quincy, Norfolk County, Massachusetts
Date of Death: 3 March 1945
Cemetery: National Memorial Cemetery of the Pacific (C-81) (MH)—Honolulu, Hawaii
Entered Service at: Massachusetts
Unit: Company I, 3d Battalion, 26th Marines, 5th Marine Division
Served as: Rifleman
Battle or Place of Action: Iwo Jima, Volcano Islands
Date of Action: 3 March 1945
Date of Presentation: 8 September 1946
Citation: For conspicuous gallantry and intrepidity at the risk of his life above and beyond the call of duty while serving as a rifleman with Company I, 3d Battalion, 26th Marines, 5th Marine Division, in action against enemy Japanese forces during the seizure of Iwo Jima in the Volcano Islands, 3 March 1945. Consistently aggressive, Pfc. Caddy boldly defied shattering Japanese machine-gun and small-arms fire to move forward with his platoon leader and another marine

during the determined advance of his company through an isolated sector and, gaining the comparative safety of a shell hole, took temporary cover with his comrades. Immediately pinned down by deadly sniper fire from a well-concealed position, he made several unsuccessful attempts to again move forward and then, joined by his platoon leader, engaged the enemy in a fierce exchange of hand grenades until a Japanese grenade fell beyond reach in the shell hole. Fearlessly disregarding all personal danger, Pfc. Caddy instantly dived on the deadly missile, absorbing the exploding charge in his own body and protecting the others from serious injury. Stouthearted and indomitable, he unhesitatingly yielded his own life that his fellow marines might carry on the relentless battle against a fanatic enemy. His dauntless courage and valiant spirit of self-sacrifice in the face of certain death reflect the highest credit upon Pfc. Caddy and upon the U.S. Naval Service. He gallantly gave his life for his comrades.

2645 ◆ *CALLAGHAN, DANIEL JUDSON

Rank: Rear Admiral
Service: U.S. Navy
Birthday: 26 July 1890
Place of Birth: San Francisco, San Francisco County, California
Date of Death: 13 November 1942
Place of Death: Buried at Sea
Cemetery: A.B.M.C. Manila Cemetery (Wall of the Missing)—Manila, Philippine Islands
Entered Service at: Oakland, Alameda County, California
Unit: U.S.S. *San Francisco* (flagship)
Served as: Fleet Commander
Battle or Place of Action: Iron Bottom Sound off Savo Island, Solomon Islands
Date of Action: 12-13 November 1942
Date of Presentation: 9 December 1942
Place of Presentation: The White House, presented by Pres. Franklin D. Roosevelt to his Son
Citation: For extraordinary heroism and conspicuous intrepidity above and beyond the call of duty during action against enemy Japanese forces off Savo Island on the night of 12 to 13 November 1942. Although outbalanced in strength and numbers by a desperate and determined enemy, Rear Adm. Callaghan, with ingenious tactical skill and superb coordination of the units under his command, led his forces into battle against tremendous odds, thereby contributing decisively to the rout of a powerful invasion fleet, and to the consequent frustration of a formidable Japanese offensive. While faithfully directing close-range operations in the face of furious bombardment by superior enemy firepower, he was killed on the bridge of his flagship. His courageous initiative, inspiring leadership, and judicious foresight in a crisis of grave responsibility were in keeping with the finest traditions of the U.S. Naval Service. He gallantly gave his life in the defense of his country.

2646 ◆ CALUGAS, JOSE

Rank: Sergeant (highest rank: Captain)
Service: U.S. Army
Birthday: 29 December 1907
Place of Birth: Barrio Tagsing, Leon, Iloilo, Philippine Islands
Entered Service at: Fort Stotsenburg, Philippine Islands
Unit: Philippine Scouts, Battery B, 1st Battalion, 88th Field Artillery, 23d Division
Served as: Mess Sergeant
Battle or Place of Action: Culis, Bataan Province, Philippine Islands
Date of Action: 16 January 1942
G.O. Number, Date: 10, 24 February 1942
Date of Presentation: 30 April 1945
Place of Presentation: Pampanga, Camp Olivas, Philippine Islands, presented by Gen. George C. Marshall
Citation: The action for which the award was made took place near Culis, Bataan Province, Philippine Islands, on 16 January 1942. A battery gun position was bombed and shelled by the enemy until one gun was put out of commission and all the cannoneers were killed or wounded. Sgt. Calugas, a mess sergeant of another battery, voluntarily and without orders ran 1,000 yards across the shell-swept area to the gun position. There he organized a volunteer squad which placed the gun back in commission and fired effectively against the enemy, although the position remained under constant and heavy Japanese artillery fire.
Notes: POW

2647 ◆ *CANNON, GEORGE HAM

Rank: First Lieutenant
Service: U.S. Marine Corps
Birthday: 5 November 1915
Place of Birth: Webster Groves, St. Louis County, Missouri
Date of Death: 7 December 1941
Place of Death: Sand Island, Midway Islands
Cemetery: National Memorial Cemetery of the Pacific (C-1644) (MH)—Honolulu, Hawaii
Entered Service at: Michigan
Unit: Battery H, 6th Defense Battalion, Fleet Marine Force
Served as: Battery Commander
Battle or Place of Action: Sand Island, Midway Islands
Date of Action: 7 December 1941
Citation: For distinguished conduct in the line of his profession, extraordinary courage, and disregard for his own condition during the bombardment of Sand Island, Midway Islands, by Japanese forces on 7 December 1941. 1st Lt. Cannon, Battery Commander of Battery H, 6th Defense Battalion, Fleet Marine Force, U.S. Marine Corps, was at his command post when he was mortally wounded by enemy shellfire. He refused to be evacuated from his post until after his men who had been wounded by the same shell were evacuated and directed the reorganization of his command post until forcibly removed. As a result of his utter disregard of his own condition he died from loss of blood.

2648 ◆ *CAREY, ALVIN P.

Rank: Staff Sergeant
Service: U.S. Army

Birthday: 16 August 1916
Place of Birth: Lycippus, Pennsylvania
Date of Death: 23 August 1944
Cemetery: Ligonier Valley Cemetery—Ligonier, Pennsylvania
Entered Service at: Laughlintown, Westmoreland County, Pennsylvania
Unit: 38th Infantry, 2d Infantry Division
Served as: Section Leader
Battle or Place of Action: near Plougastel, Brittany, France
Date of Action: 23 August 1944
G.O. Number, Date: 37, 11 May 1945
Citation: For conspicuous gallantry and intrepidity at the risk of his life, above and beyond the call of duty, 23 August 1944. S/Sgt. Carey, leader of a machine-gun section, was advancing with his company in the attack on the strongly held enemy hill 154, near Plougastel, Brittany, France. The advance was held up when the attacking units were pinned down by intense enemy machine-gun fire from a pillbox 200 yards up the hill. From his position covering the right flank, S/Sgt. Carey displaced his guns to an advanced position and then, upon his own initiative, armed himself with as many hand grenades as he could carry and without regard for his personal safety started alone up the hill toward the pillbox. Crawling forward under its withering fire, he proceeded 150 yards when he met a German rifleman whom he killed with his carbine. Continuing his steady forward movement until he reached grenade-throwing distance, he hurled his grenades at the pillbox-opening in the face of intense enemy fire which wounded him mortally. Undaunted, he gathered his strength and continued his grenade attack until one entered and exploded within the pillbox, killing the occupants and putting their guns out of action. Inspired by S/Sgt. Carey's heroic act, the riflemen quickly occupied the position and overpowered the remaining enemy resistance in the vicinity.

2649 ◆ *CAREY JR., CHARLES F.

Rank: Technical Sergeant
Service: U.S. Army
Place of Birth: Canadian, Pittsburg County, Oklahoma
Cemetery: A.B.M.C. Ardennes Cemetery (C-29-12)—Neville-En-Condroz, Belgium
Entered Service at: Cheyenne, Laramie County, Wyoming
Unit: 397th Infantry, 100th Infantry Division
Served as: Platoon Commander
Battle or Place of Action: Rimling, France
Date of Action: 8-9 January 1945
G.O. Number, Date: 53, July 1945
Citation: He was in command of a antitank platoon when about 200 enemy infantrymen and 12 tanks attacked his battalion, overrunning part of its position. After losing his guns, T/Sgt. Carey, acting entirely on his own initiative, organized a patrol and rescued two of his squads from a threatened sector, evacuating those who had been wounded. He organized a second patrol and advanced against an enemy-held house from which vicious fire issued, preventing the free movement of our troops. Covered by fire from his patrol, he approached the house, killed two snipers with his rifle, and threw a

grenade in the door. He entered alone and a few minutes later emerged with 16 prisoners. Acting on information he furnished, the American forces were able to capture an additional 41 Germans in adjacent houses. He assembled another patrol, and, under covering fire, moved to within a few yards of an enemy tank and damaged it with a rocket. As the crew attempted to leave their burning vehicle, he calmly shot them with his rifle, killing three and wounding a fourth. Early in the morning of 9 January, German infantry moved into the western part of the town and encircled a house in which T/Sgt. Carey had previously posted a squad. Four of the group escaped to the attic. By maneuvering an old staircase against the building, T/Sgt. Carey was able to rescue these men. Later that day, when attempting to reach an outpost, he was struck down by sniper fire. The fearless and aggressive leadership of T/Sgt. Carey, his courage in the face of heavy fire from superior enemy forces, provided an inspiring example for his comrades and materially helped his battalion to withstand the German onslaught.

2650 ◆ CARR, CHRIS

True Name: Legally changed from Christos H. Karaberis, under which name the medal was awarded
Rank: Sergeant (highest rank: Sergeant First Class)
Service: U.S. Army
Birthday: 6 April 1914
Place of Birth: Manchester, Hillsborough County, New Hampshire
Date of Death: 16 September 1970
Cemetery: Los Angeles National Cemetery (275-G-15) (MH)—Los Angeles, California
Entered Service at: Manchester, Hillsborough County, New Hampshire
Unit: Company L, 337th Infantry, 85th Infantry Division
Served as: Squad Leader
Battle or Place of Action: near Guignola, Italy
Date of Action: 1-2 October 1944
G.O. Number, Date: 97, 1 November 1945
Date of Presentation: 12 October 1945
Place of Presentation: The White House, presented by Pres. Harry S. Truman
Citation: Leading a squad of Company L, he gallantly cleared the way for his company's approach along a ridge toward its objective, the Casoni di Remagna. When his platoon was pinned down by heavy fire from enemy mortars, machine gun, machine pistols, and rifles, he climbed in advance of his squad on a maneuver around the left flank to locate and eliminate the enemy gun positions. Undeterred by deadly fire that ricocheted off the barren rocky hillside, he crept to the rear of the first machine gun and charged, firing his submachine gun. In this surprise attack he captured eight prisoners and turned them over to his squad before striking out alone for a second machine gun. Discovered in his advance and subjected to direct fire from hostile weapons, he leaped to his feet and ran forward, weaving and crouching, pouring automatic fire into the emplacement that killed four of its defenders and forced the surrender of a lone survivor. He again moved forward through heavy fire to attack a third

machine gun. When close to the emplacement, he closed with a nerve-shattering shout and burst of fire. Paralyzed by his whirlwind attack, all four gunners immediately surrendered. Once more advancing aggressively in the face of a thoroughly alerted enemy, he approached a point of high ground occupied by two machine guns which were firing on his company on the slope below. Charging the first of these weapons, he killed four of the crew and captured three more. The six defenders of the adjacent position, cowed by the savagery of his assault, immediately gave up. By his one-man attack, heroically and voluntarily undertaken in the face of tremendous risks, Sgt. Carr captured five enemy machine-gun positions, killed eight Germans, took 22 prisoners, cleared the ridge leading to his company's objective, and drove a deep wedge into the enemy line, making it possible for his battalion to occupy important, commanding ground.

2651 ◆ *CARSWELL JR., HORACE SEAVER

Rank: Major
Service: U.S. Army Air Corps
Birthday: 16 July 1916
Place of Birth: Fort Worth, Tarrant County, Texas
Date of Death: 26 October 1944
Place of Death: Asiatic Area
Cemetery: Oakwood Cemetery—Fort Worth, Texas
Entered Service at: San Angelo, Tom Green County, Texas
Unit: 374th Bombardment Squadron, 308th Bombardment Group, 14th Air Force
Served as: Pilot of a B-24 Bomber
Battle or Place of Action: Over the South China Sea, near Tungchen, China
Date of Action: 26 October 1944
G.O. Number, Date: 14, 4 February 1946
Citation: He piloted a B-24 bomber in a one-plane strike against a Japanese convoy in the South China Sea on the night of 26 October 1944. Taking the enemy force of 12 ships escorted by at least two destroyers by surprise, he made one bombing run at 600 feet, scoring a near miss on one warship and escaping without drawing fire. He circled and, fully realizing that the convoy was thoroughly alerted and would meet his next attack with a barrage of anitaircraft fire, began a second low-level run which culminated in two direct hits on a large tanker. A hail of steel from Japanese guns riddled the bomber, knocking out two engines, damaging a third, crippling the hydraulic system, puncturing one gasoline tank, ripping uncounted holes in the aircraft, and wounding the copilot; but by a magnificent display of flying skill, Maj. Carswell controlled the plane's plunge toward the sea and carefully forced it into a halting climb in the direction of the China shore. On reaching land, where it would have been possible to abandon the staggering bomber, one of the crew discovered that his parachute had been ripped by flak and rendered useless; the pilot, hoping to cross mountainous terrain and reach a base, continued onward until the third engine failed. He ordered the crew to bail out while he struggled to maintain altitude, and, refusing to save himself, chose to remain with his comrade and attempt a crash landing. He died when the plane struck a mountainside and burned. With consum-

mate gallantry and intrepidity, Maj. Carswell gave his life in a supreme effort to save all members of his crew. His sacrifice, far beyond that required of him, was in keeping with the traditional bravery of America's war heroes.

2652 ◆ CASAMENTO, ANTHONY

Rank: Corporal
Service: U.S. Marine Corps
Birthday: 16 November 1920
Place of Birth: New York, New York
Date of Death: 18 July 1987
Place of Death: Northport, N.Y.
Cemetery: Long Island National Cemetery (DSS-79-A) (MH)—Farmingdale, New York
Entered Service at: New York, New York
Unit: Company D, 1st Battalion, 5th Marines, 1st Marine Division
Served as: Section Leader
Battle or Place of Action: Guadalcanal, Solomon Islands
Date of Action: 1 November 1942
of Presentation: 12 September 1980
Place of Presentation: The White House, presented by Pres. Jimmy Carter
Citation: For conspicuous gallantry and intrepidity at the risk of his life above and beyond the call of duty while serving with Company D, First Battalion, Fifth Marines, First Marine Division on Guadalcanal, British Solomon Islands, in action against the enemy Japanese forces on 1 November 1942. Serving as a leader of a machine gun section, Cpl. Casamento directed his unit to advance along a ridge near the Matanikau River where they engaged the enemy. He positioned his section to provide covering fire for two flanking units and to provide direct support for the main force of his company which was behind him. During the course of this engagement, all members of his section were either killed or severely wounded and he himself suffered multiple, grievous wounds. Nonetheless, Cpl. Casamento continued to provide critical supporting fire for the attack and in defense of his position. Following the loss of all effective personnel, he set up, loaded, and manned his unit's machine gun, tenaciously holding the enemy forces at bay. Cpl. Casamento singlehandedly engaged and destroyed one machine gun emplacement to his front and took under fire the other emplacement on the flank. Despite the heat and ferocity of the engagement, he continued to man his weapon and repeatedly repulsed multiple assaults by the enemy forces, thereby protecting the flanks of the adjoining companies and holding his position until the arrival of his main attacking force. Cpl. Casamento's courageous fighting spirit, heroic conduct, and unwavering dedication to duty reflected great credit upon himself and were in keeping with the highest traditions of the Marine Corps and the U.S. Naval Service.

2653 ◆ *CASTLE, FREDERICK WALKER

Rank: Brigadier General
Service: U.S. Army Air Corps
Birthday: 14 October 1908

2655 ◆ *CHELI, RALPH

Place of Birth: Manila, Philippine Island
Date of Death: 24 December 1944
Place of Death: Over Liege, Belgium
Cemetery: A.B.M.C. Henri-Chapelle Cemetery (D-13-53)—Henri-Chapelle, Belgium
Entered Service at: Mountain Lakes, Morris County, New Jersey
Unit: 4th Bombardment Wing, 8th Air Force
Served as: Wing Commander/Pilot of a B-17
Battle or Place of Action: Germany
Date of Action: 24 December 1944
G.O. Number, Date: 22, 28 February 1946
Place of Presentation: Mountain Lakes, New Jersey, pressented by Gen. Ira Eaker to his Mother
Citation: He was air commander and leader of more than 2,000 heavy bombers in a strike against German airfields on 24 December 1944. En route to the target, the failure of one engine forced him to relinquish his place at the head of the formation. In order not to endanger friendly troops on the ground below, he refused to jettison his bombs to gain speed maneuverability. His lagging, unescorted aircraft became the target of numerous enemy fighters which ripped the left wing with cannon shells, set the oxygen system afire, and wounded two members of the crew. Repeated attacks started fires in two engines, leaving the Flying Fortress in imminent danger of exploding. Realizing the hopelessness of the situation, the bail-out order was given. Without regard for his personal safety he gallantly remained alone at the controls to afford all other crewmembers an opportunity to escape. Still another attack exploded gasoline tanks in the right wing, and the bomber plunged earthward, carrying Gen. Castle to his death. His intrepidity and willing sacrifice of his life to save the members of his crew were in keeping with the highest traditions of the military service.

2654 ◆ CHAMBERS, JUSTICE MARION

Rank: Colonel (rank at time of action: Lieutenant Colonel)
Service: U.S. Marine Corps Reserve
Birthday: 2 February 1908
Place of Birth: Huntington, Cabell County, West Virginia
Date of Death: 29 July 1982
Cemetery: Arlington National Cemetery (6-5813-A-9) (MH)—Arlington, Virginia
Entered Service at: Washington, D.C.
Unit: 3d Assault Battalion Landing Team, 25th Marines, 4th Marine Division
Served as: Commanding Officer
Battle or Place of Action: Iwo Jima, Volcano Islands
Date of Action: 19-22 February 1945
Date of Presentation: 1 November 1950
Place of Presentation: The White House, presented by Pres. Harry S. Truman
Citation: For conspicuous gallantry and intrepidity at the risk of his life above and beyond the call of duty as commanding officer of the 3d Assault Battalion Landing Team, 25th Marines, 4th Marine Division, in action against enemy Japanese forces on Iwo Jima, Volcano Islands, from 19-22 February 1945. Under a furious barrage of enemy machine-

gun and small-arms fire from the commanding cliffs on the right, Col. Chambers (then Lt. Col.) landed immediately after the initial assault waves of his battalion on D-day to find the momentum of the assault threatened by heavy casualties from withering Japanese artillery, mortar rockets, machine-gun, and rifle fire. Exposed to relentless hostile fire, he coolly reorganized his battle-weary men, inspiring them to heroic efforts by his own valor and leading them in an attack on the critical, impregnable high ground from which the enemy was pouring an increasing volume of fire directly onto troops ashore as well as amphibious craft in succeeding waves. Constantly in the front lines encouraging his men to push forward against the enemy's savage resistance, Col. Chambers led an eight-hour battle to carry the flanking ridge top and reduce the enemy's fields of aimed fire, thus protecting the vital foothold gained. In constant defiance of hostile fire while reconnoitering the entire regimental combat team zone of action, he maintained contact with adjacent units and forwarded vital information to the regimental commander. His zealous fighting spirit undiminished despite terrific casualties and the loss of most of his key officers, he again reorganized troops for renewed attack against the enemy's main line of resistance and was directing the fire of the rocket platoon when he fell, critically wounded. Evacuated under heavy Japanese fire, Col. Chambers, by forceful leadership, courage, and fortitude in the face of staggering odds, was directly instrumental in insuring the success of subsequent operations of the 5th Amphibious Corps on Iwo Jima, thereby sustaining and enhancing the finest traditions of the U.S. Naval Service.

2655 ◆ *CHELI, RALPH

Rank: Major
Service: U.S. Army Air Corps
Birthday: 29 October 1919
Place of Birth: San Francisco, San Francisco County, California
Date of Death: 6 March 1944
Cemetery: Jefferson Barracks National Cemetery (Group burial with 20 others) (78-930-934)—St. Louis, Missouri
Entered Service at: Brooklyn, Kings County, New York
Unit: 405th Bombardment Squadron, 38th Bombardment Group, 5th Air Force
Served as: Squadron Leader/Pilot of a B-25
Battle or Place of Action: near Wewak, New Guinea
Date of Action: 18 August 1943
G.O. Number, Date: 72, 28 October 1943
Citation: For conspicuous gallantry and intrepidity above and beyond the call of duty in action with the enemy. While Maj. Cheli was leading his squadron in a dive to attack the heavily defended Dagua airdrome, intercepting enemy aircraft centered their fire on his plane, causing it to burst into flames while still two miles from the objective. His speed would have enabled him to gain necessary altitude to parachute to safety, but this action would have resulted in his formation becoming disorganized and exposed to the enemy. Although a crash was inevitable, he courageously elected to continue leading the attack in his blazing plane. From a minimum altitude, the squadron made a devastating bombing and strafing attack on

the target. The mission completed, Maj. Cheli instructed his wingman to lead the formation and crashed into the sea.

2656 ◆ CHILDERS, ERNEST "CHIEF"

Rank: Second Lieutenant (highest rank: Colonel)
Service: U.S. Army
Birthday: 1 February 1918
Place of Birth: Broken Arrow, Tulsa County, Oklahoma
Entered Service at: Tulsa, Tulsa County, Oklahoma
Unit: Company C, 180th Infantry, 45th Infantry Division
Served as: Platoon Leader
Battle or Place of Action: Oliveto, Italy
Date of Action: 22 September 1943
G.O. Number, Date: 30, 8 April 1944
Date of Presentation: 22 April 1944
Place of Presentation: Naples, Italy, presented by Lt. Gen. Jacob L. Devers on battlefield
Citation: For conspicuous gallantry and intrepidity at risk of life above and beyond the call of duty in action on 22 September 1943, at Oliveto, Italy. Although 2d Lt. Childers previously had just suffered a fractured instep, he, with eight enlisted men, advanced up a hill toward enemy machine-gun nests. The group advanced to a rock wall overlooking a cornfield and 2d Lt. Childers ordered a base of fire laid across the field so that he could advance. When he was fired upon by two enemy snipers from a nearby house he killed both of them. He moved behind the machine-gun nests and killed all occupants of the nearer one. He continued toward the second one and threw rocks into it. When the two occupants of the nest raised up, he shot one. The other was killed by one of the eight enlisted men. 2d Lt. Childers continued his advance toward a house farther up the hill, and singlehandedly, captured an enemy mortar observer. The exceptional leadership, initiative, calmness under fire, and conspicuous gallantry displayed by 2d Lt. Childers were an inspiration to his men.

2657 ◆ CHOATE, CLYDE LEE

Rank: Staff Sergeant
Service: U.S. Army
Birthday: 28 June 1920
Place of Birth: West Frankfort, Franklin County, Illinois
Entered Service at: Anna, Union County, Illinois
Unit: 2d Platoon, Company C, 601st Tank Destroyer Battalion, 3d Infantry Division
Served as: Platoon Sergeant
Battle or Place of Action: Bruyeres, France
Date of Action: 25 October 1944
G.O. Number, Date: 75, 5 September 1945
Date of Presentation: 23 August 1945
Place of Presentation: The White House, presented by Pres. Harry S. Truman
Citation: He commanded a tank destroyer near Bruyeres, France, on 25 October 1944. Our infantry occupied a position on a wooded hill when, at dusk, an enemy Mark IV tank and a company of infantry attacked, threatening to overrun the American position and capture a command post 400 yards to the rear. S/Sgt. Choate's tank destroyer, the only weapon available to oppose the German armor, was set afire by two hits. Ordering his men to abandon the destroyer, S/Sgt. Choate reached comparative safety. He returned to the burning destroyer to search for comrades possibly trapped in the vehicle, risking instant death in an explosion which was imminent and braving enemy fire which ripped his jacket and tore the helmet from his head. Completing the search and seeing the tank and its supporting infantry overrunning our infantry in their shallow foxholes, he secured a bazooka and ran after the tank dodging from tree to tree and passing through the enemy's loose skirmish line. He fired a rocket from a distance of 20 yards, immobilizing the tank but leaving it able to spray the area with cannon and machine-gun fire. Running back to our infantry through vicious fire, he secured another rocket, and, advancing against a hail of machine-gun and small-arms fire reached a position 10 yards from the tank. His second shot shattered the turret. With his pistol he killed two of the crew as they emerged from the tank; and then running to the crippled Mark IV while enemy infantry sniped at him, he dropped a grenade inside the tank and completed its destruction. With their armor gone, the enemy infantry became disorganized and was driven back. S/Sgt. Choate's great daring in assaulting an enemy tank singlehandedly, his determination to follow the vehicle after it had passed his position, and his skill and crushing thoroughness in the attack prevented the enemy from capturing a battalion command post and turned a probable defeat into tactical success.

2658 ◆ *CHRISTENSEN, DALE ELDON

Rank: Second Lieutenant
Service: U.S. Army
Birthday: 31 May 1920
Place of Birth: Cameron Township, Audubon County, Iowa
Date of Death: 4 August 1944
Place of Death: near Afua, Dutch New Guinea
Cemetery: A.B.M.C. Manila Cemetery (A-12-200)— Manila, Philippine Islands
Entered Service at: Gray, Audubon County, Iowa
Unit: Troop E, 112th Cavalry Regiment
Served as: Platoon Leader
Battle or Place of Action: Driniumor River, New Guinea
Date of Action: 16-19 July 1944
G.O. Number, Date: 36, 10 May 1945
Citation: For conspicuous gallantry and intrepidity at the risk of his life above and beyond the call of duty along the Driniumor River, New Guinea, from 16-19 July 1944. 2d Lt. Christensen repeatedly distinguished himself by conspicuous gallantry above and beyond the call of duty in the continuous heavy fighting which occurred in this area from 16-19 July. On 16 July, his platoon engaged in a savage fire fight in which much damage was caused by one enemy machine gun effectively placed. 2d Lt. Christensen ordered his men to remain under cover, crept forward under fire, and at a range of 15 yards put the gun out of action with hand grenades. Again, on 19 July, while attacking an enemy position strong in mortars and machine guns, his platoon was pinned to the ground by intense fire. Ordering his men to remain under

cover, he crept forward alone to locate definitely the enemy automatic weapons and the best direction from which to attack. Although his rifle was struck by enemy fire and knocked from his hands he continued his reconnaissance, locating five enemy machine guns, destroyed one with hand grenades, and rejoined his platoon. He then led his men to the point selected for launching the attack and, calling encouragement, led the charge. This assault was successful and the enemy was driven from the positions with a loss of four mortars and 10 machine guns and leaving many dead on the field. On 4 August 1944, near Afua, Duch New Guinea, 2d Lt. Christensen was killed in action about two yards from his objective while leading his platoon in an attack on an enemy machine-gun position. 2d Lt. Christenson's leadership, intrepidity, and repeatedly demonstrated gallantry in action at the risk of his life, above and beyond the call of duty, exemplify the highest traditions of the U.S. Armed Forces.

2659 ◆ *CHRISTIAN, HERBERT F.

Rank: Private
Service: U.S. Army
Birthday: 18 June 1912
Place of Birth: Byesville, Guernsey County, Ohio
Date of Death: 3 June 1944
Cemetery: Greenwood Cemetery—Byesville, Ohio
Entered Service at: Steubenville, Jefferson County, Ohio
Unit: Battle Patrol, Company E, 15th Infantry, 3d Infantry Division
Battle or Place of Action: near Valmontone, Italy
Date of Action: 2-3 June 1944
G.O. Number, Date: 43, 30 May 1945
Citation: For conspicuous gallantry and intrepidity at the risk of life above and beyond the call of duty. On 2–3 June 1944, at 1:00 A.M., Pvt. Christian elected to sacrifice his life in order that his comrades might extricate themselves from an ambush. Braving massed fire of about 60 riflemen, three machine guns, and three tanks from positions only 30 yards distant, he stood erect and signaled to the patrol to withdraw. The whole area was brightly illuminated by enemy flares. Although his right leg was severed above the knee by cannon fire, Pvt. Christian advanced on his left knee and the bloody stump of his right thigh, firing his submachine gun. Despite excruciating pain, Pvt. Christian continued on his self-assigned mission. He succeeded in distracting the enemy and enabled his 12 comrades to escape. He killed three enemy soldiers almost at once. Leaving a trail of blood behind him, he made his way forward 20 yards, halted at a point within 10 yards of the enemy, and despite intense fire killed a machine-pistol man. Reloading his weapon, he fired directly into the enemy position. The enemy appeared enraged at the success of his ruse, concentrated 20-mm machine-gun, machine-pistol and rifle fire on him, yet he refused to seek cover. Maintaining his erect position, Pvt. Christian fired his weapon to the very last. Just as he emptied his submachine gun, the enemy bullets found their mark and Pvt. Christian slumped forward dead. The courage and spirit of self-sacrifice displayed by this soldier were an inspiration to his comrades and are keeping with the highest traditions of the Armed Forces.

2660 ◆ *CICCHETTI, JOSEPH J.

Rank: Private First Class
Service: U.S. Army
Birthday: 8 June 1923
Place of Birth: Waynesburg, Stark County, Ohio
Date of Death: 9 February 1945
Cemetery: Sandy Valley Cemetery (MH)—Waynesburg, Ohio
Entered Service at: Waynesburg, Stark County, Ohio
Unit: Company A, 148th Infantry, 37th Infantry Division
Battle or Place of Action: South Manila, Luzon, Philippine Islands
Date of Action: 9 February 1945
G.O. Number, Date: 115, 8 December 1945
Citation: He was with troops assaulting the first important line of enemy defenses. The Japanese had converted the partially destroyed Manila Gas Works and adjacent building into a formidable system of mutually supporting strongpoints from which they were concentrating machine-gun, mortar, and heavy artillery fire on the American forces. Casualties rapidly mounted, and the medical aidmen, finding it increasingly difficult to evacuate the wounded, called for volunteer litter bearers. Pfc. Cicchetti immediately responded, organized a litter team, and skillfully led it for more than four hours in rescuing 14 wounded men, constantly passing back and forth over a 400-yard route which was the impact area for a tremendous volume of the most intense enemy fire. On one return trip the path was blocked by machine-gun fire, but Pfc. Cicchetti deliberately exposed himself to draw the automatic fire which he neutralized with his own rifle while ordering the rest of the team to rush past to safety with the wounded. While gallantly continuing his work, he noticed a group of wounded and helpless soldiers some distance away and ran to their rescue although the enemy fire had increased to new fury. As he approached the casualties, he was struck in the head by a shell fragment, but with complete disregard for his gaping wound he continued to his comrades, lifted one and carried him on his shoulders 50 yards to safety. He then collapsed and died. By his skilled leadership, indomitable will, and dauntless courage, Pfc. Cicchetti saved the lives of many of his fellow soldiers at the cost of his own.

2661 ◆ CLARK, FRANCIS J.

Rank: Technical Sergeant
Service: U.S. Army
Birthday: 22 April 1912
Place of Birth: Whitehall, Washington County, New York
Date of Death: 20 October 1981
Cemetery: Evergreen Cemetery—Salem Township, New York
Entered Service at: Salem, New York
Unit: 3d Platoon, Company K, 109th Infantry, 28th Infantry Division
Served as: Squad Leader
Battle or Place of Action: near Kalborn, Luxembourg; near Sevenig, Germany
Date of Action: 12, 17 September 1944

G.O. Number, Date: 77, 10 September 1945
Date of Presentation: 23 August 1945
Place of Presentation: The White House, presented by Pres. Harry S. Truman
Citation: He fought gallantly in Luxembourg and Germany. On 12 September 1944, Company K began fording the Our River near Kalborn, Luxembourg, to take high ground on the opposite bank. Covered by early morning fog, the 3d Platoon, in which T/Sgt. Clark was squad leader, successfully negotiated the crossing; but when the 2d Platoon reached the shore, withering automatic and small-arms fire ripped into it, eliminating the platoon leader and platoon sergeant and pinning down the troops in the open. From his comparatively safe position, T/Sgt. Clark crawled alone across a field through a hail of bullets to the stricken troops. He led the platoon to safety and then unhesitatingly returned to the fire-swept area to rescue a wounded soldier, carrying him to the American line while hostile gunners tried to cut him down. Later, he led his squad and men of the 2d Platoon in dangerous sorties against strong enemy positions to weaken them by lightning-like jabs. He assaulted an enemy machine gun with hand grenades, killing two Germans. He roamed the front and flanks, dashing toward hostile weapons, killing and wounding an undetermined number of the enemy, scattering German patrols and, eventually, forcing the withdrawal of a full company of Germans heavily armed with automatic weapons. On 17 September, near Sevenig, Germany, he advanced alone against an enemy machine gun, killed the gunner and forced the assistant to flee. The Germans counterattacked, and heavy casualties were suffered by Company K. Seeing that two platoons lacked leadership, T/Sgt. Clark took over their command and moved among the men to give encouragement. Although wounded on the morning of 18 September, he refused to be evacuated and took up a position in a pillbox when night came. Emerging at daybreak, he killed a German soldier setting up a machine gun not more than five yards away. When he located another enemy gun, he moved up unobserved and killed two Germans with rifle fire. Later that day he voluntarily braved small-arms fire to take food and water to members of an isolated platoon. T/Sgt. Clark's actions in assuming command when leadership was desperately needed, in launching attacks and beating off counterattacks, in aiding his stranded comrades, and in fearlessly facing powerful enemy fire, were strikingly heroic examples and put fighting heart into the hard-pressed men of Company K.

2662 ◆ COLALILLO, MICHAEL "MIKE"

Rank: Private First Class (highest rank: Staff Sergeant)
Service: U.S. Army
Birthday: 11 December 1925
Place of Birth: Hibbing, St. Louis County, Minnesota
Entered Service at: Duluth, St. Louis County, Minnesota
Unit: 2d Squad, 2d Platoon, Company C, 1st Battalion, 398th Infantry, 100th Infantry Division
Served as: Rifleman
Battle or Place of Action: near Untergriesheim, Germany
Date of Action: 7 April 1945

G.O. Number, Date: 4, 9 January 1945
Date of Presentation: 18 December 1945
Place of Presentation: The White House, presented by Pres. Harry S. Truman
Citation: He was pinned down with other members of his company during an attack against strong enemy positions in the vicinity of Untergriesheim, Germany. Heavy artillery, mortar, and machine-gun fire made any move hazardous, when he stood up, shouted to the company to follow, and ran forward in the wake of a supporting tank, firing his machine pistol. Inspired by his example, his comrades advanced in the face of savage enemy fire. When his weapon was struck by shrapnel and rendered useless, he climbed the deck of the friendly tank, manned an exposed machine gun on the turret of the vehicle, and, while bullets rattled about him, fired at an enemy emplacement with such devastating accuracy that he killed or wounded at least 10 hostile soldiers and destroyed their machine gun. Maintaining his extremely dangerous post as the tank forged ahead, he blasted three more positions, destroyed another machine-gun emplacement, and silenced all resistance in his area, killing at least three and wounding an undetermined number of riflemen as they fled. His machine gun eventually jammed; so he secured a submachine gun from the tank crew to continue his attack on foot. When our armored forces exhausted their ammunition and the order to withdraw was given, he remained behind to help a seriously wounded comrade over several hundred yards of open terrain rocked by an intense enemy artillery and mortar barrage. By his intrepidity and inspiring courage Pfc. Colalillo gave tremendous impetus to his company's attack, killed or wounded 25 of the enemy in bitter fighting, and assisted a wounded soldier in reaching the American lines at great risk to his own life.

2663 ◆ *COLE, DARIL SAMUEL

Rank: Sergeant
Service: U.S. Marine Corps Reserve
Birthday: 20 July 1920
Place of Birth: Flat River, San Francois County, Missouri
Date of Death: 19 February 1945
Cemetery: Park View Cemetery (MH)—Farmington, Missouri
Entered Service at: Esther, San Francois County, Missouri
Unit: Company B, 1st Battalion, 23d Marines, 4th Marine Division
Served as: Section Leader
Battle or Place of Action: Iwo Jima, Volcano Islands
Date of Action: 19 February 1945
Citation: For conspicuous gallantry and intrepidity at the risk of his life above and beyond the call of duty while serving as leader of a machine-gun section of Company B, 1st Battalion, 23d Marines, 4th Marine Division, in action against enemy Japanese forces during the assault on Iwo Jima in the Volcano Islands, 19 February 1945. Assailed by a tremendous volume of small-arms, mortar, and artillery fire as he advanced with one squad of his section in the initial assault wave, Sgt. Cole boldly led his men up the sloping beach toward Airfield No. 1 despite the blanketing curtain of flying shrapnel and,

personally destroying with hand grenades two hostile emplacements which menaced the progress of his unit, continued to move forward until a merciless barrage of fire emanating from three Japanese pillboxes halted the advance. Instantly placing his one remaining machine gun in action, he delivered a shattering fusillade and succeeded in silencing the nearest and most threatening emplacement before his weapon jammed and the enemy, reopening fire with knee mortars and grenades, pinned down his unit for a second time. Shrewdly gauging the tactical situation and evolving a daring plan of counterattack, Sgt. Cole, armed solely with a pistol and one grenade, coolly advanced alone to the hostile pillboxes. Hurling his one grenade at the enemy in sudden, swift attack, he quickly withdrew, returned to his own lines for additional grenades and again advanced, attacked, and withdrew. With enemy guns still active, he ran the gauntlet of slashing fire a third time to complete the total destruction of the Japanese strongpoint and the annihilation of the defending garrison in this final assault. Although instantly killed by an enemy grenade as he returned to his squad, Sgt. Cole had eliminated a formidable Japanese position, thereby enabling his company to storm the remaining fortifications, continue the advance, and seize the objective. By his dauntless initiative, unfaltering courage, and indomitable determination during a critical period of action, Sgt. Cole served as an inspiration to his comrades, and his stouthearted leadership in the face of almost certain death sustained and enhanced the highest tradition of the U.S. Naval Service. He gallantly gave his life for his country.

2664 ◆ *COLE, ROBERT GEORGE

Rank: Lieutenant Colonel
Service: U.S. Army
Birthday: 19 March 1915
Place of Birth: Fort Sam Houston, Bexar County, Texas
Date of Death: 18 September 1944
Cemetery: A.B.M.C. Netherlands Cemetery (B-15-27)—Margraten, Holland
Entered Service at: San Antonio, Bexar County, Texas
Unit: 3d Battalion, 502d Parachute Infantry Regiment, 101st Airborne Division
Served as: Battalion Commander
Battle or Place of Action: near Carentan, France
Date of Action: 11 June 1944
G.O. Number, Date: 79, 4 October 1944
Date of Presentation: 30 October 1944
Place of Presentation: Fort Sam Houston, Texas, presented by Major Gen. Jonathan W. Anderson to his mother, Mrs. Clara Hoff Cole
Citation: For gallantry and intrepidity at the risk of his own life above and beyond the call of duty on 11 June 1944, in France. Lt. Col. Cole was personally leading his battalion in forcing the last four bridges on the road to Carentan when his entire unit was suddenly pinned down to the ground by intense and withering enemy rifle, machine-gun, mortar, and artillery fire placed upon them from well-prepared and heavily fortified positions within 150 yards of the foremost elements. After the devastating and unceasing enemy fire had for over one hour prevented any move and inflicted numerous casual-

ties, Lt. Col. Cole, observing this almost hopeless situation, courageously issued orders to assault the enemy positions with fixed bayonets. With utter disregard for his own safety and completely ignoring the enemy fire, he rose to his feet in front of his battalion and with drawn pistol shouted to his men to follow him in the assault. Catching up a fallen man's rifle and bayonet, he charged on and led the remnants of his battalion across the bullet-swept open ground and into the enemy position. His heroic and valiant action in so inspiring his men resulted in the complete establishment of our bridgehead across the Douve River. The cool fearlessness, personal bravery, and outstanding leadership displayed by Lt. Col. Cole reflect great credit upon himself and are worthy of the highest praise in the military service.

2665 ◆ CONNOR, JAMES PHILLIP

Rank: Sergeant
Service: U.S. Army
Birthday: 12 January 1919
Place of Birth: Wilmington, New Castle County, Delaware
Date of Death: 27 July 1994
Cemetery: Delaware Memorial Veteran Cemetery—Bear, Delaware
Entered Service at: Wilmington, New Castle County, Delaware
Unit: Battle Patrol, 7th Infantry, 3d Infantry Division
Served as: Squad Leader
Battle or Place of Action: Cape Cavalaire, Southern France
Date of Action: 15 August 1944
G.O. Number, Date: 18, 15 March 1945
Date of Presentation: 7 May 1945
Place of Presentation: France, presented by Lt. Gen. Alexander M. Patch III
Citation: For conspicuous gallantry and intrepidity at risk of life above and beyond the call of duty. On 15 August 1944 Sgt. Connor, through sheer grit and determination, led his platoon in clearing an enemy vastly superior in numbers and firepower from strongly entrenched positions on Cape Cavalaire, removing a grave enemy threat to his division during the amphibious landing in southern France, and thereby insured safe and uninterrupted landings for the huge volume of men and material which followed. His battle patrol landed on "Red Beach" with the mission of destroying the strongly fortified enemy positions on Cape Cavalaire with utmost speed. From the penninsula the enemy had commanding observation and seriously menaced the vast landing operations taking place. Though knocked down and seriously wounded in the neck by a hanging mine which killed his platoon lieutenant, Sgt. Connor refused medical aid and with his driving spirit practically carried the platoon across several thousand yards of mine-saturated beach through intense fire from mortars, 20-mm flak guns, machine guns, and snipers. En route to the cape he personally shot and killed two snipers. The platoon sergeant was killed and Sgt. Connor became platoon leader. Receiving a second wound, which lacerated his shoulder and back, he again refused evacuation, expressing determination to carry on until physically unable to continue. He

2666 ◆ COOLEY, RAYMOND HENRY

reassured and prodded the hesitating men of his decimated platoon forward through almost impregnable mortar concentrations. Again emphasizing the prevalent urgency of the mission, he impelled his men toward a group of buildings honeycombed with enenmy snipers and machine guns. Here he received his third grave wound, this time in the leg, felling him in his tracks. Still resolved to carry on, he relinquished command only after his attempts proved that it was physically impossible to stand. Nevertheless, from his prone position, he gave the orders and directed his men in assualting the enemy. Infused with Sgt. Connor's dogged determination, the platoon, though reduced to less than one-third of its original 36 men, outflanked and rushed the enemy with such furiousness that they killed seven, captured 40, seized three machine guns and considerable other material, and took all their assigned objectives, successfully completing their mission. By his repeated examples of tenaciousess and indomitable spirit Sgt. Connor transmitted his heroism to his men until they became a fighting team which could not be stopped.

2666 ◆ COOLEY, RAYMOND HENRY

Rank: Staff Sergeant
Service: U.S. Army
Birthday: 7 May 1914
Place of Birth: Dunlap, Sequatchie County, Tennessee
Date of Death: 12 March 1947
Cemetery: Cumberland View Cemetery (MH)—Jasper, Tennessee
Entered Service at: Richard City, Tennessee
Unit: Company B, 27th Infantry, 25th Infantry Division
Served as: Platoon Guide
Battle or Place of Action: near Lumboy, Luzon, Philippine Islands
Date of Action: 24 February 1945
G.O. Number, Date: 77, 10 September 1945
Date of Presentation: 23 August 1945
Place of Presentation: The White House, presented by Pres. Harry S. Truman
Citation: He was a platoon guide in an assault on a camouflaged entrenchment defended by machine guns, rifles, and mortars. When his men were pinned down by two enemy machine guns, he voluntarily advanced under heavy fire to within 20 yards of one of the guns and attacked it with a hand grenade. The enemy, however, threw the grenade back at him before it could explode. Arming a second grenade, he held it for several seconds of the safe period and then hurled it into the enemy position, where it exploded instantaneously, destroying the gun and crew. He then moved toward the remaining gun, throwing grenades into enemy foxholes as he advanced. Inspired by his actions, one squad of his platoon joined him. After he had armed another grenade and was preparing to throw it into the second machine-gun position, six enemy soldiers rushed at him. Knowing he could not dispose of the armed grenade without injuring his comrades, because of the intermingling in close combat of the men of his platoon and the enemy in the melee which ensued, he deliberately covered the grenade with his body and was severely wounded as it exploded. By his heroic actions, S/Sgt.

Cooley not only silenced a machine gun and so inspired his fellow soldiers that they pressed the attack and destroyed the remaining enemy emplacements, but also, in complete disregard of his own safety, accepted certain injury and possible loss of life to avoid wounding his comrades.

2667 ◆ COOLIDGE, CHARLES HENRY

Rank: Technical Sergeant
Service: U.S. Army
Birthday: 4 August 1921
Place of Birth: Signal Mountain, Hamilton County, Tennessee
Entered Service at: Signal Mountain, Hamilton County, Tennessee
Unit: 2d Platoon, Company M, 3d Battalion, 141st Infantry, 36th Infantry Division
Served as: Machine Gunner
Battle or Place of Action: east of Belmont sur Buttant, France
Date of Action: 24-27 October 1944
G.O. Number, Date: 53, July 1945
Date of Presentation: 18 June 1945
Place of Presentation: near Ulm, Germany, presented by Maj. Gen. Frederick Haislip
Citation: Leading a section of heavy machine guns supported by one platoon of Company K, he took a position near Hill 623, east of Belmont-sur-Buttant, France, 24 October 1944, with the mission of covering the right flank of the 3d Battalion and supporting its action. T/Sgt. Coolidge went forward with a sergeant of Company K to reconnoiter positions for coordinating the fires of the light and heavy machine guns. They ran into an enemy force in the woods estimated to be an infantry company. T/Sgt. Coolidge, attempting to bluff the Germans by a show of assurnace and boldness, called upon them to surrender, whereupon the enemy opened fire. With his carbine, T/Sgt. Coolidge wounded two of them. There being no officer present with the force, T/Sgt. Coolidge at once assumed command. Many of the men were replacements recently arrived; this was their first experience under fire. T/Sgt. Coolidge, unmindful of the enemy fire delivered at close range, walked along the position, calming and encouraging his men and directing their fire. The attack was thrown back. Through 24 and 26 October the enemy launched repeated attacks against the position of this combat group but each was repulsed due to T/Sgt. Coolidge's able leadership. On 27 October, German infantry, supported by two tanks, made a determined attack on the position. The area was swept by enemy small-arms, machine-gun, and tank fire. T/Sgt. Coolidge armed himself with a bazooka and advanced within 25 yards of the tanks. His bazooka failed to function and he threw it aside. Securing all the hand grenades he could carry, he crawled forward and inflicted heavy casualties on the advancing enemy. Finally it became apparent that the enemy, in greatly superior force, supported by tanks, would overrun the position. T/Sgt. Coolidge, displaying great coolness and courage, directed and conducted an orderly withdrawal, being himself the last to leave the position. As a result of T/Sgt. Coolidge's heroic and superior leadership,

the mission of his combat group was accomplished throughout four days of continuous fighting against numerically superior enemy troops in rain and cold and amid dense woods.

2668 ◆ *COURTNEY JR., HENRY ALEXIUS

Rank: Major
Service: U.S. Marine Corps Reserve
Birthday: 6 January 1916
Place of Birth: Duluth, St. Louis County, Minnesota
Date of Death: 15 May 1945
Cemetery: Calvary Cemetery (MH)—Duluth, Minnesota
Entered Service at: Minnesota
Unit: 2d Battalion, 22d Marines, 6th Marine Division
Served as: Executive Officer
Battle or Place of Action: Sugar Loaf Hill, Okinawa Shima, Ryukyu Islands
Date of Action: 14-15 May 1945
Citation: For conspicuous gallantry and intrepidity at the risk of his life above and beyond the call of duty as executive officer of the 2d Battalion, 22d Marines, 6th Marine Division, in action against enemy Japanese forces on Okinawa Shima, in the Ryukyu Islands, 14 and 15 May 1945. Ordered to hold for the night in static defense behind Sugar Loaf Hill after leading the forward elements of his command in a prolonged firefight, Maj. Courtney weighed the effect of a hostile night counterattack against the tactical value of an immediate marine assault, resolved to initiate the assault, and promptly obtained permission to advance and seize the forward slope of the hill. Quickly explaining the situation to his small remaining force, he declared his personal intention of moving forward and then proceeded on his way, boldly blasting nearby cave positions and neutralizing enemy guns as he went. Inspired by his courage, every man followed him without hesitation, and together the intrepid marines braved a terrific concentration of Japanese gunfire to skirt the hill on the right and reach the reverse slope. Temporarily halting, Maj. Courtney sent guides to the rear for more ammunition and possible replacements. Subsequently reinforced by 26 men and an LVT load of grenades, he determined to storm the crest of the hill and crush any planned counterattack before it could gain sufficient momentum to effect a breakthrough. Leading his men by example rather than by command, he pushed ahead with unrelenting aggressiveness, hurling grenades into cave openings on the slope with devastating effect. Upon reaching the crest and observing large numbers of Japanese forming for action less than 100 yards away, he instantly attacked, waged a furious battle, and succeeded in killing many of the enemy and in forcing the remainder to take cover in the caves. Determined to hold, he ordered his men to dig in and, coolly disregarding the continuous hail of flying enemy shrapnel, to rally his weary troops, tirelessly aided casualties and assigned his men to more advantageous positions. Although instantly killed by a hostile mortar burst while moving among his men, Maj. Courtney, by his astute military acumen, indomitable leadership, and decisive action in the face of overwhelming odds, had contributed essentially to the success of the Okinawa campaign. His great personal valor throughout sustained and enhanced the highest tradi-

tions of the U.S. Naval Service. He gallantly gave his life for his country.

2669 ◆ *COWAN, RICHARD ELLER

Rank: Private First Class
Service: U.S. Army
Birthday: 5 December 1922
Place of Birth: Lincoln, Lancaster County, Nebraska
Date of Death: 18 December 1944
Cemetery: Wichita Park Cemetery—Wichita, Kansas
Entered Service at: Wichita, Sedgwick County, Kansas
Unit: Company M, 23d Infantry, 2d Infantry Division
Served as: Heavy Machine Gunner
Battle or Place of Action: near Krinkelter Wald, Belgium
Date of Action: 17 December 1944
G.O. Number, Date: 48, 23 June 1945
Citation: He was a heavy machine gunner in a section attached to Company I in the vicinity of Krinkelter Wald, Belgium, 17 December 1944, when that company was attacked by a numerically superior force of German infantry and tanks. The first six waves of hostile infantrymen were repulsed with heavy casualties, but a seventh drive with tanks killed or wounded all but three of his section, leaving Pvt. Cowan to man his gun, supported by only 15 to 20 riflemen of Company I. He maintained his position, holding off the Germans until the rest of the shattered force had set up a new line along a firebreak. Then, unaided, he moved his machine gun and ammunition to the second position. At the approach of a Royal Tiger tank, he held his fire until about 80 enemy infantrymen supporting the tank appeared at a distance of about 150 yards. His first burst killed or wounded about half of these infantrymen. His position was rocked by an 88-mm shell when the tank opened fire, but he continued to man his gun, pouring deadly fire into the Germans when they again advanced. He was barely missed by another shell. Fire from three machine guns and innumerable small arms struck all about him; an enemy rocket shook him badly, but did not drive him from his gun. Infiltration by the enemy had by this time made the position untenable, and the order was given to withdraw. Pvt. Cowan was the last man to leave, voluntarily covering the withdrawal of his remaining comrades. His heroic actions were entirely responsible for allowing the remaining men to retire successfully from the scene of their last-ditch stand.

2670 ◆ CRAFT, CLARENCE BYRLE

Rank: Private First Class (highest rank: Corporal)
Service: U.S. Army
Birthday: 23 September 1921
Place of Birth: San Bernardino, San Bernardino County, California
Entered Service at: Santa Ana, Orange County, California
Unit: Company G, 2d Battalion, 382d Infantry, 96th Infantry Division
Served as: Rifleman

Battle or Place of Action: Hen Hill, Okinawa, Ryukyu Islands
Date of Action: 31 May 1945
G.O. Number, Date: 97, 1 November 1945
Date of Presentation: 12 October 1945
Place of Presentation: The White House, presented by Pres. Harry S. Truman
Citation: He was a rifleman when his platoon spearheaded an attack on Hen Hill, the tactical position on which the entire Naha-Shuri-Yonaburu line of Japanese defense on Okinawa, Ryukyu Islands, was hinged. For 12 days our forces had been stalled, and repeated, heavy assaults by one battalion and then another had been thrown back by the enemy with serious casualties. With five comrades, Pfc. Craft was dispatched in advance of Company G to feel out the enemy resistance. The group had proceeded only a short distance up the slope when rifle and machine-gun fire, coupled with a terrific barrage of grenades, wounded three and pinned down the others. Against odds that appeared suicidal, Pfc. Craft launched a remarkable one-man attack. He stood up in full view of the enemy and began shooting with deadly marksmanship wherever he saw a hostile movement. He steadily advanced up the hill, killing Japanese soldiers with rapid fire, driving others to cover in their strongly disposed trenches, unhesitatingly facing alone the strength that had previously beaten back attacks in battalion strength. He reached the crest of the hill, where he stood silhouetted against the sky while quickly throwing grenades at extremely short range into the enemy positions. His extraordinary assault lifted the pressure from his company for the moment, allowing members of his platoon to comply with his motions to advance and pass him more grenades. With a chain of his comrades supplying him while he stood atop the hill, he furiously hurled a total of two cases of grenades into a main trench and other positions on the reverse slope of Hen Hill, meanwhile directing the aim of his fellow soldiers who threw grenades from the slope below him. He left his position, where grenades from both sides were passing over his head and bursting on either slope, to attack the main enemy trench as confusion and panic seized the defenders. Straddling the excavation, he pumped rifle fire into the Japanese at point-blank range, killing many and causing the others to flee down the trench. Pursuing them, he came upon a heavy machine gun which was still creating havoc in the American ranks. With rifle fire and a grenade he wiped out this position. By this time the Japanese were in complete rout and American forces were swarming over the hill. Pfc. Craft continued down the central trench to the mouth of a cave where many of the enemy had taken cover. A satchel charge was brought to him, and he tossed it into the cave. It failed to explode. With great daring, the intrepid fighter retrieved the charge from the cave, relighted the fuse, and threw it back, sealing up the Japs in a tomb. In the local action, against tremendously superior forces heavily armed with rifles, machine guns, mortars, and grenades, Pfc. Craft killed at least 25 of the enemy; but his contribution to the campaign on Okinawa was of much more far-reaching consequence, for Hen Hill was the key to the entire defense line, which rapidly crumbled after his utterly fearless and heroic attack.

2671 ◆ *CRAIG, ROBERT

Rank: Second Lieutenant
Service: U.S. Army
Birthday: 1919
Place of Birth: Scotland
Date of Death: 11 July 1943
Cemetery: Toledo Memorial Park—Sylvania, Ohio
Entered Service at: Toledo, Lucas County, Ohio
Unit: Company L, 15th Infantry, 3d Infantry Division
Served as: Platoon Leader
Battle or Place of Action: near Favoratta, Sicily
Date of Action: 11 July 1943
G.O. Number, Date: 41, 26 May 1944
Citation: For conspicuous gallantry and intrepidity at the risk of his life above and beyond the call of duty, on 11 July 1943, at Favoratta, Sicily. Second Lt. Craig voluntarily undertook the perilous task of locating and destroying a hidden enemy machine gun which had halted the advance of his company. Attempts by three other officers to locate the weapon had resulted in failure, with each officer receiving wounds. Second Lt. Craig located the gun and snaked his way to a point within 35 yards of the hostile position before being discovered. Charging headlong into the furious automatic fire, he reached the gun, stood over it, and killed the three crew members with his carbine. With this obstacle removed, his company continued its advance. Shortly thereafter, while advancing down the forward slope of a ridge, 2d Lt. Craig and his platoon, in a position devoid of cover and concealment, encountered the fire of approximately 100 enemy soldiers. Electing to sacrifice himself so that his platoon might carry on the battle, he ordered his men to withdraw to the cover of the crest while he drew the enemy fire to himself. With no hope of survival, he charged toward the enemy unitl he was within 25 yards of them. Assuming a kneeling position, he killed five and wounded three enemy soldiers. While the hostile force concentrated fire on him, his platoon reached the cover of the crest. Second Lt. Craig was killed by enemy fire, but his intrepid action so inspired his men that they drove the enemy from the area, inflicting heavy casualties on the hostile force.

2672 ◆ *CRAIN, MORRIS E.

Rank: Technical Sergeant
Service: U.S. Army
Birthday: 7 October 1924
Place of Birth: Bandana, Ballard County, Kentucky
Date of Death: 13 March 1945
Cemetery: Mount Pleasant Cemetery (MH)—LaCenter, Kentucky
Entered Service at: Paducah, McCracken County, Kentucky
Unit: Company E, 141st Infantry, 36th Infantry Division
Battle or Place of Action: Haguenau, France
Date of Action: 13 March 1945
G.O. Number, Date: 18, 13 February 1946
Citation: He led his platoon against powerful German forces during the struggle to enlarge the bridgehead across the Moder River. With great daring and aggressiveness he spear-

headed the platoon in killing 10 enemy soldiers, capturing 12 more and securing its objective near an important road junction. Although heavy concentrations of artillery, mortar, and self-propelled gunfire raked the area, he moved about among his men during the day, exhorting them to great efforts and encouraging them to stand firm. He carried ammunition and maintained contact with the company command post, exposing himself to deadly enemy fire. At nightfall the enemy barrage became more intense and tanks entered the fray to cover foot troops while they bombarded our positions with grenades and rockets. As buildings were blasted by the Germans, the Americans fell back from house to house. T/Sgt. Crain deployed another platoon which had been sent to his support and then rushed through murderous tank and small-arms fire to the foremost house, which was being defended by five of his men. With the enemy attacking from an adjoining room and a tank firing point-blank at the house, he ordered the men to withdraw while he remained in the face of almost certain death to hold the position. Although shells were crashing through the walls and bullets were hitting all around him, he held his ground and with accurate fire from his submachine gun killed three Germans. He was killed when the building was destroyed by the enemy. T/Sgt. Crain's outstanding valor and intrepid leadership enabled his platoon to organize a new defense, repel the attack, and preserve the hard-won bridgehead.

2673 ◆ *CRAW, DEMAS THURLOW

Rank: Colonel
Service: U.S. Army Air Corps
Birthday: 9 April 1900
Place of Birth: Traverse City, Grand Traverse County, Michigan
Date of Death: 8 November 1942
Place of Death: Near Port Lyautey, French Morocco
Cemetery: Cremated—ashes scattered over Weisbaden, Germany, 24 June 1949
Entered Service at: Michigan
Unit: XII Ground Air Support Command, U.S.A.A.C.
Battle or Place of Action: near Port Lyautey, French Morocco
Date of Action: 8 November 1942
G.O. Number, Date: 11, 4 March 1943
Citation: For conspicuous gallantry and intrepidity in action above and beyond the call of duty. On 8 November 1942, near Port Lyautey, French Morocco, Col. Craw volunteered to accompany the leading wave of assault boats to the shore and pass through the enemy lines to locate the French commander with a view of suspending hostilities. This request was first refused as being too dangerous, but upon the officer's insistence that he was qualified to undertake and accomplish the mission he was allowed to go. Encountering heavy fire while in the landing boat and unable to dock in the river because of shellfire from shore batteries, Col. Craw, accompanied by one officer and one soldier, succeeded in landing on the beach at Mehdia Plage under constant low-level strafing from three enemy planes. Riding in a bantam truck toward French headquarters, progress of the party was hindered by fire from our own naval guns. Nearing Port Lyautey, Col. Craw was instantly killed by a sustained burst of machine-gun fire at point-blank range from a concealed position near the road.

2674 ◆ CRAWFORD, WILLIAM JOHN

Rank: Private (highest rank: Master Sergeant)
Service: U.S. Army
Birthday: 19 May 1918
Place of Birth: Pueblo, Pueblo County, Colorado
Entered Service at: Pueblo, Pueblo County, Colorado
Unit: 3d Platoon, Company I, 3d Battalion, 142d Infantry, 36th Infantry Division
Served as: Squad Scout/Rifleman
Battle or Place of Action: near Altavilla, Italy
Date of Action: 13 September 1943
G.O. Number, Date: 57, 20 July 1944
Date of Presentation: 11 May 1944 & 30 May 1984
Place of Presentation: Camp Carson, Colorado, presented posthumously by Maj. Gen. Terry Allen to his Father 1944. U.S. Air Force Academy, Colorado Springs Colorado; medal presented by Pres. Ronald Reagan to William J. Crawford 30 May 1984
Citation: For conspicuous gallantry and intrepidity at risk of life above and beyond the call of duty in action with the enemy near Altavilla, Italy, 13 September 1943. When Company I attacked an enemy-held position on Hill 424, the 3d Platoon, in which Pvt. Crawford was a squad scout, attacked as base platoon for the company. After reaching the crest of a hill, the platoon was pinned down by intense enemy machine-gun and small-arms fire. Locating one of these guns, which was dug in on a terrace on his immediate front, Pvt. Crawford, without orders and on his own initiative moved over the hill under enemy fire to a point within a few yards of the gun emplacement and singlehandedly destroyed the machine gun and killed three of the crew with a hand grenade, thus enabling his platoon to continue its advance. When the platoon, after reaching the crest, was once more delayed by enemy fire, Pvt. Crawford again, in the face of intense fire, advanced directly to the front midway between two hostile machine-gun nests located on a higher terrace and emplaced in a small ravine. Moving first to the left, with a grenade he destroyed one gun emplacement and killed the crew; he then worked his way, under continuous fire, to the other and with one grenade and the use of his rifle, killed one enemy and forced the remainder to flee. Seizing the enemy machine gun, he fired on the withdrawing Germans and facilitated his company's advance.
Notes: POW

2675 ◆ CREWS, JOHN R.

Rank: Staff Sergeant
Service: U.S. Army
Birthday: 8 March 1923
Place of Birth: Golden, McCurtain County, Oklahoma
Entered Service at: Bowlegs, Seminole County, Oklahoma
Unit: 2d Platoon, Company F, 2d Battalion, 253d Infantry, 63d Infantry Division

Served as: Squad Leader
Battle or Place of Action: Lobenbacherhof, Germany
Date of Action: 8 April 1945
Date of Presentation: 25 June 1948
Place of Presentation: The White House (Rose Garden), presented by Pres. Harry S. Truman
Citation: He displayed conspicous gallantry and intrepidity at the risk of life above and beyond the call of duty on 8 April 1945 near Lobenbacherhof, Germany. As his company was advancing toward the village under heavy fire, an enemy machine gun and automatic rifle with rifle support opened up on it from a hill on the right flank. Seeing that his platoon leader had been wounded by their fire, S/Sgt. Crews, acting upon his own initiative, rushed the strongpoint with two men of his platoon. Despite the fact that one of these men was killed and the other was badly wounded, he continued his advance up the hill in the face of terrific enemy fire. Storming the well dug-in position singlehandedly, he killed two of the crew of the machine gun at point-blank range with his M1 rifle and wrested the gun from the hands of a German whom he had already wounded. He then with his rifle charged the strongly emplaced automatic rifle. Although badly wounded in the thigh by crossfire from the remaining enemy, he kept on and silenced the entire position with his accurate and deadly rifle fire. His actions so unnerved the remaining enemy soldiers that seven of them surrendered and the others fled. His heroism caused the enemy to concentrate on him and permitted the company to move forward into the village.

2676 ◆ *CROMWELL, JOHN PHILIP

Rank: Captain
Service: U.S. Navy
Birthday: 11 September 1901
Place of Birth: Henry, Marshall County, Illinois
Date of Death: 19 November 1943
Cemetery: National Memorial Cemetery of the Pacific (Wall of the Missing)—Honolulu, Hawaii
Entered Service at: Illinois
Unit: U.S.S. Sculpin
Served as: Group Commander
Battle or Place of Action: off Truk Island
Date of Action: 19 November 1943
Date of Presentation: 24 April 1946
Place of Presentation: San Francisco, California, presented to his Widow and Son
Citation: For conspicuous gallantry and intrepidity at the risk of his life above and beyond the call of duty as commander of a submarine coordinated attack group with flag in the U.S.S. Sculpin, during the 9th war patrol of that vessel in enemy-controlled waters off Truk Island, 19 November 1943. Undertaking this patrol prior to the launching of our first large-scale offensive in the Pacific, Capt. Cromwell, alone of the entire Task Group, possessed secret intelligence information of our submarine strategy and tactics, scheduled Fleet movements, and specific attack plans. Constantly vigilant and precise in carrying out his secret orders, he moved his undersea flotilla inexorably forward despite savage opposition and established a line of submarines to southeastward of the main

Japanese stronghold at Truk. Cool and undaunted as the submarine, rocked and battered by Japanese depth charges, sustained terrific battle damage and sank to an excessive depth, he authorized the Sculpin to surface and engage the enemy in a gunfight, thereby providing an opportunity for the crew to abandon ship. Determined to sacrifice himself rather than risk capture and subsequent danger of revealing plans under Japanese torture or use of drugs, he stoically remained aboard the mortally wounded vessel as she plunged to her death. Preserving the security of his mission, at the cost of his own life, he had served his country as he had served the Navy, with deep integrity and an uncompromising devotion to duty. His great moral courage in the face of certain death adds new luster to the traditions of the U.S. Naval Service. He gallantly gave his life for his country.

2677 ◆ CURREY, FRANCIS SHERMAN "FRANK"

Rank: Private First Class (highest rank: Technical Sergeant)
Service: U.S. Army
Birthday: 29 June 1925
Place of Birth: Loch Sheldrake, Sullivan County, New York
Entered Service at: Hurleyville, Sullivan County, New York
Unit: 3d Platoon, Company K, 3d Battalion, 120th Infantry, 30th Infantry Division
Served as: Automatic Rifleman
Battle or Place of Action: Malmedy, Belgium
Date of Action: 21 December 1944
G.O. Number, Date: 69, 17 August 1945
Date of Presentation: 27 July 1945
Place of Presentation: Reims France, presented by Maj. Gen. Leland S. Hobbs
Citation: He was an automatic rifleman with the 3d Platoon defending a strongpoint near Malmedy, Belgium, on 21 December 1944, when the enemy launched a powerful attack. Overrunning tank destroyers and antitank guns located near the strongpoint, German tanks advanced to the 3d Platoon's position, and, after prolonged fighting, forced the withdrawal of this group to a nearby factory. Sgt. Currey found a bazooka in the building and crossed the street to secure rockets, meanwhile enduring intense fire from enemy tanks and hostile infantrymen who had taken up a position at a house a short distance away. In the face of small-arms, machine-gun, and artillery fire, he, with a companion, knocked out a tank with one shot. Moving to another position, he observed three Germans in the doorway of an enemy-held house. He killed or wounded all three with his automatic rifle. He emerged from cover and advanced alone to within 50 yards of the house, intent on wrecking it with rockets. Covered by friendly fire, he stood erect and fired a shot which knocked down half of one wall. While in this forward position, he observed five Americans who had been pinned down for hours by fire from the house and three tanks. Realizing that they could not escape until the enemy tank and infantry guns had been silenced, Sgt. Currey crossed the street to a vehicle, where he procured an armful of antitank grenades. These he launched while under heavy enemy fire, driving tankmen from the vehicles into the house. He then climbed onto a half-track in full

view of the Germans and fired a machine gun at the house. Once again changing his position, he manned another machine gun whose crew had been killed; under covering fire the five soldiers were able to retire to safety. Deprived of tanks and with heavy infantry casualties, the enemy was forced to withdraw. Through his extensive knowledge of weapons and by his heroic and repeated braving of murderous heavy fire, Sgt. Currey was greatly responsible for inflicting heavy losses in men and material on the enemy, for rescuing five comrades, two of whom were wounded, and for stemming an attack which threatened to flank his battalion's position.

2678 ◆ DAHLGREN, EDWARD CARL

Rank: Second Lieutenant (rank at time of action: Sergeant)
Service: U.S. Army
Birthday: 14 March 1916
Place of Birth: Perham, Aroostook County, Maine
Entered Service at: Caribou, Aroostook County, Maine
Unit: 3d Platoon, Company E, 2d Battalion, 142d Infantry, 36th Infantry Division
Served as: Platoon Sergeant
Battle or Place of Action: Oberhoffen, France
Date of Action: 11 February 1945
G.O. Number, Date: 77, 10 September 1945
Date of Presentation: 23 August 1945
Place of Presentation: The White House, presented by Pres. Harry S. Truman
Citation: He led the 3d Platoon to the rescue of a similar unit which had been surrounded in an enemy counterattack at Oberhoffen, France. As he advanced along a street, he observed several Germans crossing a field about 100 yards away. Running into a barn, he took up a position in a window and swept the hostile troops with submachine-gun fire, killing six, wounding others, and completely disorganizing the group. His platoon then moved forward through intermittent sniper fire and made contact with the besieged Americans. When the two platoons had been reorganized, Sgt. Dahlgren continued to advance along the street until he drew fire from an enemy-held house. In the face of machine-pistol and rifle fire, he ran toward the building, hurled a grenade through the door, and blasted his way inside with his gun. This aggressive attack so rattled the Germans that all eight men who had held the strongpoint immediately surrendered. As Sgt. Dahlgren started toward the next house, hostile machine-gun fire drove him to cover. He secured rifle grenades, stepped to an exposed position, and calmly launched his missles from a difficult angle until he had destroyed the machine gun and killed its two operators. He moved to the rear of the house and suddenly came under the fire of a machine gun emplaced in a barn. Throwing a grenade into the structure, he rushed the position, firing his weapon as he ran; within, he overwhelmed five Germans. After reorganizing his unit he advanced to clear hostile riflemen from the building where he had destroyed the machine gun. He entered the house by a window and trapped the Germans in the cellar, where he tossed grenades into their midst, wounding several and forcing 10 more to surrender.

While reconnoitering another street with a comrade, he heard German voices in a house. An attack with rifle grenades drove the hostile troops to the cellar. Sgt. Dahlgren entered the building, kicked open the cellar door, and, firing several bursts down the stairway, called for the trapped enemy to surrender. Sixteen soldiers filed out with their hands in the air. The bold leadership and magnificent courage displayed by Sgt. Dahlgren in his heroic attacks were in a large measure responsible for repulsing an enemy counterattack and saving an American platoon from great danger.

2679 ◆ DALESSONDRO, PETER JOSEPH

Rank: Technical Sergeant
Service: U.S. Army
Birthday: 19 May 1921
Place of Birth: Watervliet, Albany County, New York
Entered Service at: Watervliet, Albany County, New York
Unit: 1st Platoon, Company E, 1st Battalion, 39th Infantry, 9th Infantry Division
Served as: Platoon Sergeant
Battle or Place of Action: Kalterherberg, Germany
Date of Action: 22 December 1944
G.O. Number, Date: 73, 30 August 1945
Date of Presentation: 23 August 1945
Place of Presentation: The White House, presented by Pres. Harry S. Truman
Citation: He was with the 1st Platoon holding an important road junction on high ground near Kalterherberg, Germany, 22 December 1944. In the early morning hours, the enemy, after laying down an intense artillery and mortar barrage, followed through with an all-out attack that threatened to overwhelm the position. T/Sgt. Dalessondro, seeing that his men were becoming disorganized, braved the intense fire to move among them with words of encouragement. Advancing to a fully exposed observation post, he adjusted mortar fire upon the attackers, meanwhile firing upon them with his rifle and encouraging his men in halting and repulsing the attack. Later in the day the enemy launched a second determined attack. Once again, T/Sgt. Dalessondro, in the face of imminent death, rushed to his forward position and immediately called for mortar fire. After exhausting his rifle ammunition, he crawled 30 yards over exposed ground to secure a light machine gun, returned to his position, and fired upon the enemy at almost point-blank range until the gun jammed. He managed to get the gun to fire one more burst, which used up his last round, but with these bullets he killed four German soldiers who were on the verge of murdering an aidman and two wounded soldiers in a nearby foxhole. When the enemy had almost surrounded him, he remained alone, steadfastly facing almost certain death or capture, hurling grenades and calling for mortar fire closer and closer to his outpost as he covered the withdrawal of his platoon to a second line of defense. As the German hordes swarmed about him, he was last heard calling for a barrage, saying, "OK, mortars, let me have it—right in this position!" The gallantry and intrepidity shown by T/Sgt. Dalessondro against an overwhelming enemy attack saved his company from complete rout.

2680 ◆ DALY, MICHAEL JOSEPH

Rank: Captain (rank at time of action: Lieutenant)
Service: U.S. Army
Birthday: 15 September 1924
Place of Birth: New York, New York
Entered Service at: Southport, Fairfield County, Connecticut
Unit: Company A, 1st Battalion, 15th Infantry, 3d Infantry Division
Served as: Company Commander
Battle or Place of Action: Nuremberg, Germany
Date of Action: 18 April 1945
G.O. Number, Date: 77, 10 September 1945
Date of Presentation: 23 August 1945
Place of Presentation: The White House, presented by Pres. Harry S. Truman
Citation: Early in the morning of 18 April 1945, he led his company through the shell-battered, sniper-infested wreckage of Nuremberg, Germany. When blistering machine-gun fire caught his unit in an exposed position, he ordered his men to take cover, dashed forward alone, and, as bullets whined about him, shot the three-man gun-crew with his carbine. Continuing the advance at the head of his company, he located an enemy patrol armed with rocket launchers which threatened friendly armor. He again went forward alone, secured a vantage point, and opened fire on the Germans. Immediately he became the target for concentrated machine-pistol and rocket fire, which blasted the rubble about him. Calmly, he continued to shoot at the patrol until he had killed all six enemy infantrymen. Continuing boldly far in front of his company, he entered a park, where as his men advanced, a German machine gun opened up on them without warning. With his carbine, he killed the gunner; and then, from a completely exposed position, he directed machine-gun fire on the remainder of the crew until all were dead. In a final duel, he wiped out a third machine-gun emplacement with rifle fire at a range of 10 yards. By fearlessly engaging in four singlehanded firefights with a desperate, powerfully armed enemy, Lt. Daly, voluntarily taking all major risks himself and protecting his men at every opportunity, killed 15 Germans, silenced three enemy machine guns, and wiped out an entire enemy patrol. His heroism during the lone bitter struggle with fanatical enemy forces was an inspiration to the valiant Americans who took Nuremberg.

2681 ◆ *DAMATO, ANTHONY PETER

Rank: Corporal
Service: U.S. Marine Corps
Birthday: 28 March 1922
Place of Birth: Shenandoah, Schuylkill County, Pennsylvania
Date of Death: 20 February 1944
Cemetery: National Memorial Cemetery of the Pacific (A-334) (MH)—Honolulu, Hawaii
Entered Service at: Pennsylvania
Battle or Place of Action: Engebi Island, Eniwetok Atoll, Marshall Islands

Date of Action: 19-20 February 1944
Date of Presentation: 9 April 1945
Place of Presentation: Lincoln School, Shenandoah, Pennsylvania, presented to his Mother
Citation: For conspicuous gallantry and intrepidity at the risk of his life above and beyond the call of duty while serving with an assault company in action against enemy Japanese forces on Engebi Island, Eniwetok Atoll, Marshall Islands, on the night of 19–20 February 1944. Highly vulnerable to sudden attack by small, fanatical groups of Japanese still at large despite the efficient and determined efforts of our forces to clear the area, Cpl. Damato lay with two comrades in a large foxhole in his company's defense perimeter which had been dangerously thinned by the forced withdrawal of nearly half of the available men. When one of the enemy approached the foxhole undetected and threw in a hand grenade, Cpl. Damato desperately groped for it in the darkness. Realizing the imminent peril to all three and fully aware of the consequences of his act, he unhesitatingly flung himself on the grenade and, although instantly killed as his body absorbed the explosion, saved the lives of his two companions. Cpl. Damato's splendid initiative, fearless conduct, and valiant sacrifice reflect great credit upon himself and the U.S. Naval Service. He gallantly gave his life for his comrades.

2682 ◆ *DAVID, ALBERT LEROY

Rank: Lieutenant [rank at time of action: Lieutenant (j.g.)]
Service: U.S. Navy
Birthday: 18 July 1902
Place of Birth: Maryville, Nodaway County, Missouri
Date of Death: 17 September 1945
Place of Death: San Diego, California
Cemetery: Fort Rosecrans National Cemetery (OS-125A) (MH)—San Diego, California
Entered Service at: Missouri
Unit: U.S.S. *Pillsbury* DE 133
Served as: Engineering Officer
Battle or Place of Action: off the coast of French West Africa
Date of Action: 4 June 1944
Date of Presentation: 5 October 1945
Place of Presentation: The White House, presented by Pres. Harry S. Truman to his Widow
Citation: For conspicuous gallantry and intrepidity at the risk of his life above and beyond the call of duty while attached to the U.S.S. *Pillsbury* during the capture of an enemy German submarine off French West Africa, 4 June 1944. Taking a vigorous part in the skillfully coordinated attack on the German U-505 which climaxed a prolonged search by the Task Group, Lt. (then Lt. [jg]) David boldly led a party from the *Pillsbury* in boarding the hostile submarine as it circled erratically at five or six knots on the surface. Fully aware that the U-boat might momentarily sink or be blown up by exploding demolition and scuttling charges, he braved the added danger of enemy gunfire to plunge through the conning tower hatch and, with his small party, exerted every effort to keep the ship afloat and to assist the succeeding and more fully equipped salvage parties in making the U-

505 seaworthy for the long tow across the Atlantic to a U.S. port. By his valiant service during the first successful boarding and capture of an enemy man-o-war on the high seas by the U.S. Navy since 1815, Lt. David contributed materially to the effectiveness of our Battle of the Atlantic and upheld the highest traditions of the U.S. Naval Service.

2683 ◆ DAVIS, CHARLES WILLIS

Rank: Major (rank at time of action: Captain) (highest rank: Colonel)
Service: U.S. Army
Birthday: 21 February 1917
Place of Birth: Gordo, Pickens County, Alabama
Date of Death: 18 January 1991
Place of Death: San Francisco, California
Cemetery: Arlington National Cemetery (7-A-170) (MH)—Arlington, Virginia
Entered Service at: Montgomery, Montgomery County, Alabama
Unit: 2d Battalion, 27th Infantry Regiment, 25th Infantry Division
Served as: Battalion Executive Officer
Battle or Place of Action: Guadalcanal, Solomon Islands
Date of Action: 12 January 1943
G.O. Number, Date: 40, 17 July 1943
Date of Presentation: 30 July 1943
Place of Presentation: Guadalcanal, Solomon Islands, presented by Lt. Gen. Millard F. Harmon
Citation: For distinguishing himself conspicuously by gallantry and intrepidity at the risk of his life above and beyond the call of duty in action with the enemy on Guadalcanal Island. On 12 January 1943, Maj. Davis (then Capt.), executive officer of an infantry battalion, volunteered to carry instructions to the leading companies of his battalion which had been caught in crossfire from Japanese machine guns. With complete disregard for his own safety, he made his way to the trapped units, delivered the instructions, supervised their execution, and remained overnight in this exposed position. On the following day, Maj. Davis again volunteered to lead an assault on the Japanese position which was holding up the advance. When his rifle jammed at its first shot, he drew his pistol and, waving his men on, led the assault over the top of the hill. Electrified by this action, another body of soldiers followed and seized the hill. The capture of this position broke Japanese resistance and the battalion was then able to proceed and secure the corps' objective. The courage and leadership displayed by Maj. Davis inspired the entire battalion and unquestionably led to the success of its attack.

2684 ◆ *DAVIS, GEORGE FLEMING

Rank: Commander
Service: U.S. Navy
Birthday: 23 March 1911
Place of Birth: Manila, Philippine Islands
Date of Death: 6 January 1945
Cemetery: A.B.M.C. Manila Cemetery (Wall of the Missing)—Manila, Philippine Islands

Entered Service at: Philippine Islands
Unit: U.S.S. *Walke*
Served as: Commanding Officer
Battle or Place of Action: Lingayen Gulf, Luzon, Philippine Islands
Date of Action: 6 January 1945
Date of Presentation: 15 November 1945
Place of Presentation: Washington, D.C., presented by Sec. of the Navy James Forrestal to his Widow
Citation: For conspicuous gallantry and intrepidity at the risk of his life above and beyond the call of duty as commanding officer of the U.S.S. *Walke* engaged in a detached mission in support of minesweeping operations to clear the waters for entry of our heavy surface and amphibious forces preparatory to the invasion of Lingayen Gulf, Luzon, Philippine Islands, 6 January 1945. Operating without gun support of other surface ships when four Japanese suicide planes were detected flying low overland to attack simultaneously, Comdr. Davis boldly took his position in the exposed wings of the bridge and directed control to pick up the leading plane and open fire. Alert and fearless as the *Walke*'s deadly fire sent the first target crashing into the water and caught the second as it passed close over the bridge to plunge into the sea of portside, he remained steadfast in the path of the third plane plunging swiftly to crash the after end of the bridge structure. Seriously wounded when the craft struck, drenched with gasoline and immediately enveloped in flames, he conned the *Walke* in the midst of the wreckage; he rallied his command to heroic efforts; he exhorted his officers and men to save the ship and, still on his feet, saw the barrage from his guns destroy the fourth suicide bomber. With the fires under control and the safety of the ship assured, he consented to be carried below. Succumbing several hours later, Comdr. Davis by his example of valor and his unhesitating self-sacrifice, steeled the fighting spirit of his command into unyielding purpose in completing a vital mission. He gallantly gave his life in the service of his country.

2685 ◆ *DEALEY, SAMUEL DAVID

Rank: Commander
Service: U.S. Navy
Birthday: 13 September 1906
Place of Birth: Dallas, Collin County, Texas
Date of Death: 24 August 1944 (6th war patrol)
Cemetery: A.B.M.C. Manila Cemetery (Wall of the Missing)—Manila, Philippine Islands
Entered Service at: Texas
Unit: U.S.S. *Harder*
Served as: Commanding Officer
Battle or Place of Action: off Tawi Tawi, Sulu Archipelago
Date of Action: 26 May-3 July 1944 (5th war patrol)
Date of Presentation: 15 November 1945
Place of Presentation: The White House, presented by Pres. Harry S. Truman to his Widow
Citation: For conspicuous gallantry and intrepidity at the risk of his life above and beyond the call of duty as commanding officer of the U.S.S. *Harder* during her 5th war patrol in Japanese-controlled waters. Floodlighted by a bright moon

and disclosed to an enemy destroyer escort which bore down with intent to attack. Comdr. Dealey quickly dived to periscope depth and waited for the pursuer to close range, then opened fire, sending the target and all aboard down in flames with his third torpedo. Plunging deep to avoid fierce depth charges, he again surfaced and, within nine minutes after sighting another destroyer, had sent the enemy down tail first with a hit directly amidship. Evading detection, he penetrated the confined waters off Tawi Tawi with the Japanese Fleet base six miles away and scored death blows on two patrolling destroyers in quick succession. With his ship heeled over by concussion from the first exploding target and the second vessel nose-diving in a blinding detonation, he cleared the area at high speed. Sighted by a large hostile fleet force on the following day, he swung his bow toward the lead destroyer for another "down-the-throat" shot, fired three bow tubes, and promptly crash-dived to be terrifically rocked seconds later by the exploding ship as the *Harder* passed beneath. This remarkable record of five vital Japanese destroyers sunk in five short-range torpedo attacks attests the valiant fighting spirit of Comdr. Dealey and his indomitable command.

2686 ◆ DEBLANC, JEFFERSON JOSEPH

Rank: Captain (highest rank: Colonel)
Service: U.S. Marine Corps Reserve
Birthday: 15 February 1921
Place of Birth: Lockport, Lafourche County, Louisiana
Entered Service at: Lockport, Lafourche County, Louisiana
Unit: Marine Fighting Squadron 112, Marine Air Group 11, 1st Marine Air Wing
Served as: Fighter Pilot of a Grumman Wildcat
Battle or Place of Action: Kolombangara Island, Solomon Islands
Date of Action: 31 January 1943
Date of Presentation: 6 December 1946
Place of Presentation: The White House, presented by Pres. Harry S. Truman
Citation: For conspicuous gallantry and intrepidity at the risk of his life above and beyond the call of duty as leader of a section of six fighter planes in Marine Fighting Squadron 112, during aerial operations against enemy Japanese forces off Kolombangara Island in the Solomon group, 31 January 1943. Taking off with his section as escort for a strike force of dive bombers ordered to attack Japanese surface vessels, 1st Lt. DeBlanc led his flight directly to the target area where, at 14,000 feet, our strike force encountered a large number of Japanese Zeros protecting the enemy's surface craft. In company with the other fighters, 1st Lt. DeBlanc instantly engaged the hostile planes and aggressively countered their repeated attempts to drive off our bombers, persevering in his efforts to protect the diving planes and waging fierce combat until, picking up a call for assistance from the dive bombers, under attack by enemy float planes at 1,000 feet, he broke off his engagement with the Zeros, plunged into the formation of float planes and disrupted the savage attack, enabling our dive bombers to complete their runs on the Japanese surface disposition and withdraw without further incident. Although

his escort mission was fulfilled upon the safe retirement of the bombers, 1st Lt. DeBlanc courageously remained on the scene despite a rapidly diminishing fuel supply and, boldly challenging the enemy's superior number of float planes, fought a valiant battle against terrific odds, seizing the tactical advantage and striking repeatedly to destroy three of the hostile aircraft (two float planes and one Zero) and to disperse the remainder. Prepared to maneuver his damaged plane back to base, he had climbed aloft and set his course when he discovered two Zeros closing in behind. Undaunted, he opened fire and blasted both Zeros from the sky in a short, bitterly fought action which resulted in such hopeless damage to his own plane that other Zeros entering the fight set his aircraft on fire forcing him to bail out over enemy waters between Vella Lavella and enemy-held Kolombangara. A gallant officer, a superb airman, and an indomitable fighter, 1st Lt. DeBlanc had rendered decisive assistance during a critical stage of operations, and his unwavering fortitude in the face of overwhelming opposition reflects the highest credit upon himself and adds new luster to the traditions of the U.S. Naval Service.

2687 ◆ *DEFRANZO, ARTHUR FREDERICK

Rank: Staff Sergeant
Service: U.S. Army
Birthday: 20 March 1919
Place of Birth: Saugus, Essex County, Massachusetts
Date of Death: 10 June 1944
Cemetery: Riverside Cemetery (MH)—Saugus, Massachusetts
Entered Service at: Saugus, Essex County, Massachusetts
Unit: 18th Infantry, 1st Infantry Division
Battle or Place of Action: near Vaubadon, France
Date of Action: 10 June 1944
G.O. Number, Date: 1, 4 January 1945
Citation: For conspicuous gallantry and intrepidity at the risk of his life above and beyond the call of duty on 10 June 1944, near Vaubadon, France. As scouts were advancing across an open field, the enemy suddenly opened fire with several machine guns and hit one of the men. S/Sgt. DeFranzo courageously moved out in the open to the aid of the wounded scout and was himself wounded but brought the man to safety. Refusing aid, S/Sgt. DeFranzo reentered the open field and led the advance upon the enemy. There were always at least two machine-guns bringing unrelenting fire upon him, but S/Sgt. DeFranzo kept going forward, firing into the enemy and one by one the enemy emplacements became silent. While advancing he was again wounded, but continued on until he was within 100 yards of the enemy position and even as he fell, he kept firing his rifle and waving his men forward. When his company came up behind him, S/Sgt. DeFranzo, despite his many severe wounds, suddenly raised himself and once more moved forward in the lead of his men until he was again hit by enemy fire. In a final gesture of indomitable courage, he threw several grenades at the enemy machine-gun position and completely destroyed the gun. In this action S/Sgt. DeFranzo lost his life, but by bearing the brunt of the enemy fire in leading the attack, he pre-

vented a delay in the assault which would have been of considerable benefit to the foe, and he made possible his company's advance with a minimum of casualties. The extraordinary heroism and magnificent devotion to duty displayed by S/Sgt. DeFranzo was a great inspiration to all about him and is in keeping with the highest traditions of the Armed Forces.

2688 ◆ *DEGLOPPER, CHARLES N.

Rank: Private First Class
Service: U.S. Army
Birthday: 30 November 1921
Place of Birth: Grand Island, Erie County, New York
Date of Death: 9 June 1944
Cemetery: Maple Grove Cemetery—Grand Island, New York
Entered Service at: Grand Island, Erie County, New York
Unit: Company C, 325th Glider Infantry, 82d Airborne Division
Served as: Automatic Rifleman
Battle or Place of Action: Merderet River at La Fiere, France
Date of Action: 9 June 1944
G.O. Number, Date: 22, 28 February 1946
Citation: He was a member of Company C, 325th Glider Infantry, on 9 June 1944 advancing with the forward platoon to secure a bridgehead across the Merderet River at La Fiere, France. At dawn the platoon had penetrated an outer line of machine guns and riflemen, but in so doing had become cut off from the rest of the company. Vastly superior forces began a decimation of the stricken unit and put in motion a flanking maneuver which would have completely exposed the American platoon in a shallow roadside ditch where it had taken cover. Detecting this danger, Pfc. DeGlopper volunteered to support his comrades by fire from his automatic rifle while they attempted a withdrawal through a break in a hedgerow 40 yards to the rear. Scorning a concentration of enemy automatic-weapons and rifle fire, he walked from the ditch onto the road in full view of the Germans and sprayed the hostile positions with assault fire. He was wounded, but he continued firing. Struck again, he started to fall; and yet his grim determination and valiant fighting spirit could not be broken. Kneeling in the roadway, weakened by his grievous wounds, he leveled his heavy weapon against the enemy and fired burst after burst until killed outright. He was successful in drawing the enemy action away from his fellow soldiers, who continued the fight from a more advantageous position and established the first bridgehead over the Merderet. In the area where he made his intrepid stand his comrades later found the ground strewn with dead Germans and many machine guns and automatic weapons which he had knocked out of action. Pfc. DeGlopper's gallant sacrifice and unflinching heroism while facing unsurmountable odds were in great measure responsible for a highly important tactical victory in the Normandy Campaign.

2689 ◆ *DELEAU JR., EMILE

Rank: Sergeant
Service: U.S. Army
Birthday: 28 June 1923
Place of Birth: Lansing, Belmont County, Ohio
Date of Death: 2 February 1945
Cemetery: Linwood Cemetery—Blaine, Ohio
Entered Service at: Blaine, Belmont County, Ohio
Unit: Company A, 142d Infantry, 36th Infantry Division
Served as: Squad Leader
Battle or Place of Action: Oberhoffen, France
Date of Action: 1-2 February 1945
G.O. Number, Date: 60, 25 July 1945
Citation: He led a squad in the night attack on Oberhoffen, France, where fierce house-to-house fighting took place. After clearing one building of opposition, he moved his men toward a second house from which heavy machine-gun fire came. He courageously exposed himself to hostile bullets and, firing his submachine gun as he went, advanced steadily toward the enemy position until close enough to hurl grenades through a window, killing three Germans and wrecking their gun. His progress was stopped by heavy rifle and machine-gun fire from another house. Sgt. Deleau dashed through the door with his gun blazing. Within, he captured 10 Germans. The squad then took up a position for the night and awaited daylight to resume the attack. At dawn of 2 February, Sgt. Deleau pressed forward with his unit, killing two snipers as he advanced to a point where machine-gun fire from a house barred the way. Despite vicious small-arms fire, Sgt. Deleau ran across an open area to reach the rear of the building, where he destroyed one machine gun and killed its two operators with a grenade. He worked to the front of the structure and located a second machine gun. Finding it impossible to toss a grenade into the house from his protected position, he fearlessly moved away from the building and was about to hurl his explosive when he was instantly killed by a burst from the gun he sought to knock out. With magnificent courage and daring aggressiveness, Sgt. Deleau cleared four well-defended houses of Germans, inflicted severe losses on the enemy, and at the sacrifice of his own life aided his battalion to reach its objective with a minimum of casualties.

2690 ◆ DERVISHIAN, ERNEST HERBERT

Rank: Second Lieutenant (rank at time of action: Technical Sergeant) (highest rank: Colonel)
Service: U.S. Army
Birthday: 10 August 1916
Place of Birth: Richmond, Richmond County, Virginia
Date of Death: 20 May 1984
Place of Death: Richmond, Virginia
Cemetery: West Hampton Memorial Park—Richmond, Virginia
Entered Service at: Richmond, Richmond County, Virginia
Unit: Company B, 133d Infantry, 34th Infantry Division
Battle or Place of Action: near Cisterna, Italy
Date of Action: 23 May 1944
G.O. Number, Date: 3, 8 January 1945
Date of Presentation: 12 January 1945
Place of Presentation: Piamaggio, Italy, presented by Gen. Mark Clark

Citation: For conspicuous gallantry and intrepidity at the risk of life above and beyond the call of duty on 23 May 1944, in the vicinity of Cisterna, Italy. Second Lt. Dervishian (then T/Sgt.) and four members of his platoon found themselves far ahead of their company after an aggressive advance in the face of enemy artillery and sniper fire. Approaching a railroad embankment, they observed a force of German soldiers hiding in dugouts. Second Lt. Dervishian, directing his men to cover him, boldly moved forward and, firing his carbine, forced 10 Germans to surrender. His men then advanced and captured 15 more Germans occupying adjacent dugouts. The prisoners were returned to the rear to be picked up by advancing units. From the railroad embankment, 2d Lt. Dervishian and his men then observed nine Germans who were fleeing across a ridge. He and his men opened fire and three of the enemy were wounded. As his men were firing, 2d Lt. Dervishian, unnoticed, fearlessly dashed forward alone and captured all of the fleeing enemy before his companions joined him on the ridge. At this point four other men joined 2d Lt. Dervishian's group. An attempt was made to send the four newly arrived men along the left flank of a large, dense vineyard that lay ahead, but murderous machine-gun fire forced them back. Deploying his men, 2d Lt. Dervishian moved to the front of his group and led the advance into the vineyard. He and his men suddenly became pinned down by a machine gun firing at them at a distance of 15 yards. Feigning death while the hostile weapon blazed away at him, 2d Lt. Dervishian assaulted the position during a halt in the firing, using a hand-grenade and carbine fire, and forced the four German crewmembers to surrender. The four men on the left flank were now ordered to enter the vineyard but encountered machine-gun fire which killed one soldier and wounded another. At this moment the enemy intensified the fight by throwing potato-masher grenades at the valiant band of American soldiers within the vineyard. Second Lt. Dervishian ordered his men to withdraw; but instead of following, jumped into the machine-gun position he had just captured and opened fire with the enemy weapon in the direction of the second hostile machine-gun nest. Observing movement in a dugout two or three yards to the rear, 2d Lt. Dervishian seized a machine-pistol. Simultaneously blazing away at the entrance to the dugout to prevent its occupants from firing and firing his machine gun at the other German nest, he forced five Germans in each position to surrender. Determined to rid the area of all Germans, 2d Lt. Dervishian continued his advance alone. Noticing another machine-gun position beside a house, he picked up an abandoned machine-pistol and forced six more Germans to surrender by spraying their position with fire. Unable to locate additional targets in the vicinity, 2d Lt. Dervishian conducted these prisoners to the rear. The prodigous courage and combat skill exhibited by 2d Lt. Dervishian are exemplary of the finest traditions of the U.S. Armed Forces.

2691 ◆ *DIAMOND, JAMES H.

Rank: Private First Class
Service: U.S. Army
Birthday: 22 April 1925

Place of Birth: New Orleans, Orleans County, Louisiana
Date of Death: 14 May 1945
Cemetery: Evergreen Cemetery (MH)—Gulfport, Mississippi
Entered Service at: Gulfport, Harrison County, Mississippi
Unit: Company D, 21st Infantry, 24th Infantry Division
Battle or Place of Action: Mintal, Mindanao, Philippine Islands
Date of Action: 8 to 14 May 1945
G.O. Number, Date: 23, 6 March 1946
Citation: As a member of the machine-gun section, he displayed extreme gallantry and intrepidity above and beyond the call of duty. When a Japanese sniper rose from his foxhole to throw a grenade into their midst, this valiant soldier charged and killed the enemy with a burst from his submachine-gun; then, by delivering sustained fire from his personal arm and simultaneously directing the fire of 105-mm and .50-caliber weapons upon the enemy pillboxes, immobilizing this and another machine-gun section, he enabled them to put their guns into action. When two infantry companies established a bridgehead, he voluntarily assisted in evacuating the wounded under heavy fire; and then, securing an abandoned vehicle, transported casualties to the rear through mortar and artillery fire so intense as to render the vehicle inoperative and despite the fact he was suffering from a painful wound. The following day he again volunteered, this time for the hazardous job of repairing a bridge under heavy enemy fire. On 14 May 1945, when leading a patrol to evacuate casualties from his battalion, which was cut off, he ran through a virtual hail of Japanese fire to secure an abandoned machine gun. Though mortally wounded as he reached the gun, he succeeded in drawing sufficient fire upon himself so that the remaining members of the patrol could reach safety. Pfc. Diamond's indomitable spirit, constant disregard of danger, and eagerness to assist his comrades, will ever remain a symbol of selflessness and heroic sacrifice to those for whom he gave his life.

2692 ◆ *DIETZ, ROBERT H.

Rank: Staff Sergeant
Service: U.S. Army
Place of Birth: Kingston, Ulster County, New York
Date of Death: 29 March 1945
Cemetery: Wiltwych Rural Cemetery—Kingston, New York
Entered Service at: Kingston, Ulster County, New York
Unit: Company A, 38th Armored Infantry Battalion, 7th Armored Division
Served as: Squad Leader
Battle or Place of Action: Kirchain, Germany
Date of Action: 29 March 1945
G.O. Number, Date: 119, 17 December 1945
Citation: He was a squad leader when the task force to which his unit was attached encountered resistance in its advancing on Kirchain, Germany. Between the town's outlying buildings 300 yards distant and the stalled armored column were a minefield and two bridges defended by German rocket-launching teams and riflemen. From the town itself came heavy small-arms fire. Moving forward with his men to

protect engineers while they removed the minefield and the demolition charges attached to the bridges, S/Sgt. Dietz came under intense fire. On his own initiative he advanced alone, scorning the bullets which struck all around him, until he was able to kill the bazooka team defending the first bridge. He continued ahead and had killed another bazooka team, bayoneted an enemy soldier armed with a panzerfaust, and shot two Germans when he was knocked to the ground by another blast of another panzerfaust. He quickly recovered, killed the man who had fired at him, and then jumped into waist-deep water under the second bridge to disconnect the demolition charges. His work was completed; but as he stood up to signal that the route was clear he was killed by another enemy volley from the left flank. S/Sgt. Dietz by his intrepidity and valiant effort on his self-imposed mission, singlehandedly opened the road for the capture of Kirchain and left with his comrades an inspiring example of gallantry in the face of formidable odds.

2693 ◆ DOOLITTLE, JAMES HAROLD

Rank: Brigadier General (highest rank: General)
Service: U.S. Army Air Corps/U.S. Air Force
Birthday: 14 December 1896
Place of Birth: Alameda, Alameda County, California
Date of Death: 27 September 1993
Place of Death: Pebble Beach, California
Cemetery: Arlington National Cemetery (7A-110)—Arlington, Virginia
Entered Service at: Berkeley, Alameda County, California
Unit: Army Air Force Headquarters, Washington, D.C.
Served as: Commanding Officer/Pilot of a B-25
Battle or Place of Action: over Tokyo, Japan
Date of Action: 18 April 1942
G.O. Number, Date: 29, 9 June 1942
Date of Presentation: 20 May 1942
Place of Presentation: The White House, presented by Pres. Franklin D. Roosevelt
Citation: For conspicuous leadership above the call of duty, involving personal valor and intrepidity at an extreme hazard to life. With the apparent certainty of being forced to land in enemy territory or to perish at sea, Gen. Doolittle personally led a squadron of Army bombers, manned by volunteer crews, in a highly destructive raid on the Japanese mainland.

2694 ◆ DOSS, DESMOND THOMAS

Rank: Private First Class (highest rank: Corporal)
Service: U.S. Army
Birthday: 7 February 1919
Place of Birth: Lynchburg, Lynchburg County, Virginia
Entered Service at: Lynchburg, Lynchburg County, Virginia
Unit: 307th Infantry, Medical Detachment, 77th Infantry Division
Served as: Medical Aidman
Battle or Place of Action: Urasoe-Mura, Okinawa, Ryukyu Islands
Date of Action: 29 April-21 May 1945
G.O. Number, Date: 97, 1 November 1945

Date of Presentation: 12 October 1945
Place of Presentation: The White House, presented by Pres. Harry S. Truman
Citation: He was a company aidman when the 1st Battalion assaulted a jagged escarpment 400 feet high. As our troops gained the summit, a heavy concentration of artillery, mortar, and machine-gun fire crashed into them, inflicting approximately 75 casualties and driving the others back. Pfc. Doss refused to seek cover and remained in the fire-swept area with the many stricken, carrying them one by one to the edge of the escarpment and there lowering them on a rope-supported litter down the face of a cliff to friendly hands. On 2 May, he exposed himself to heavy rifle and mortar fire in rescuing a wounded man 200 yards forward of the lines on the same escarpment; and two days later he treated four men who had been cut down while assaulting a strongly defended cave, advancing through a shower of grenades to within eight yards of enemy forces in a cave's mouth, where he dressed his comrades' wounds before making four separate trips under fire to evacuate them to safety. On 5 May, he unhesitatingly braved enemy shelling and small-arms fire to assist an artillery officer. He applied bandages, moved his patient to a spot that offered protection from small-arms fire, and, while artillery and mortar shells fell close by, painstakingly administered plasma. Later that day, when an American was severely wounded by fire from a cave, Pfc. Doss crawled to him where he had fallen 25 feet from the enemy position, rendered aid, and carried him 100 yards to safety while continually exposed to enemy fire. On 21 May, in a night attack on high ground near Shuri, he remained in exposed territory while the rest of his company took cover, fearlessly risking the chance that he would be mistaken for an infiltrating Japanese and giving aid to the injured until he was himself seriously wounded in the legs by the explosion of a grenade. Rather than call another aidman from cover, he cared for his own injuries and waited five hours before litter bearers reached him and started carrying him to cover. The trio was caught in an enemy tank attack and Pfc. Doss, seeing a more critically wounded man nearby, crawled off the litter and directed the bearers to give their first attention to the other man. Awaiting the litter bearers' return, he was again struck, this time suffering a compound fracture of one arm. With magnificent fortitude he bound a rifle stock to his shattered arm as a splint and then crawled 300 yards over rough terrain to the aid station. Through his outstanding bravery and unflinching determination in the face of desperately dangerous conditions Pfc. Doss saved the lives of many soldiers. His name became a symbol throughout the 77th Infantry Division for outstanding gallantry far above and beyond the call of duty.

2695 ◆ DROWLEY, JESSE RAY

Rank: Staff Sergeant
Service: U.S. Army
Birthday: 13 September 1919
Place of Birth: St. Charles, Saginaw County, Michigan
Entered Service at: Wayne County, Michigan
Unit: Weapons Platoon, Company B, 1st Battalion, 132d Infantry, Americal Division

Served as: Squad Leader
Battle or Place of Action: Bougainville, Solomon Islands
Date of Action: 30 January 1944
G.O. Number, Date: 73, 6 September 1944
Date of Presentation: 30 August 1944
Place of Presentation: The White House, presented by Pres. Franklin D. Roosevelt
Citation: For gallantry and intrepidity at the risk of his life above and beyond the call of duty in action with the enemy at Bougainville Island, Solomon Islands, 30 January 1944. S/Sgt. Drowley, a squad leader in a platoon whose mission during an attack was to remain under cover while holding the perimeter defense and acting as a reserve for assaulting echelon, saw three members of the assault company fall badly wounded. When intense hostile fire prevented aid from reaching the casualties, he fearlessly rushed forward to carry the wounded to cover. After rescuing two men, S/Sgt. Drowley discovered an enemy pillbox undetected by assaulting tanks that was inflicting heavy casualties upon the attacking force and was a chief obstacle to the success of the advance. Delegating the rescue of the third man to an assistant, he ran across open terrain to one of the tanks. Signaling to the crew, he climbed to the turret, exchanged his weapon for a submachine gun and voluntarily rode the deck of the tank directing it toward the pillbox by tracer fire. The tank, under constant heavy enemy fire, continued to within 20 feet of the pillbox where S/Sgt. Drowley received a severe bullet wound in the chest. Refusing to return for medical treatment, he remained on the tank and continued to direct its progress until the enemy box was definitely located by the crew. At this point he again was wounded by small-arms fire, losing his left eye and falling to the ground. He remained alongside the tank until the pillbox had been completely demolished and another directly behind the first destroyed. S/Sgt. Drowley, his voluntary mission successfully accomplished, returned alone for medical treatment.

2696 ◆ DUNHAM, RUSSELL

Rank: Technical Sergeant
Service: U.S. Army
Birthday: 23 February 1920
Place of Birth: East Carondelet, St. Clair County, Illinois
Entered Service at: Brighton, Jersey County, Illinois
Unit: 2d Platoon, Company I, 3d Battalion, 30th Infantry, 3d Infantry Division
Served as: Platoon Sergeant
Battle or Place of Action: Kaysersberg, France
Date of Action: 8 January 1945
G.O. Number, Date: 37, 11 May 1945
Date of Presentation: 23 April 1945
Place of Presentation: Zepman Stadium, Nuremberg, Germany, presented by Lt. Gen. Alexander M. Patch III
Citation: For conspicuous gallantry and intrepidity at risk of life above and beyond the call of duty. At about 1430 hours on 8 January 1945, during an attack on Hill 616, near Kaysersberg, France, T/Sgt. Dunham singlehandedly assaulted three enemy machine guns. Wearing a white robe made of a mattress cover, carrying 12 carbine magazines and with a dozen hand grenades snagged in his belt, suspenders, and buttonholes, T/Sgt. Dunham advanced in the attack up a snow-covered hill under fire from two machine guns and supporting riflemen. His platoon 35 yards behind him, T/Sgt. Dunham crawled 75 yards under heavy direct fire toward the timbered emplacement shielding the left machine gun. As he jumped to his feet 10 yards from the gun and charged forward, machine-gun fire tore through his camouflage robe and a rifle bullet seared a 10-inch gash across his back sending him spinning 15 yards downhill into the snow. When the indomitable sergeant sprang to his feet to renew his one-man assault, a German egg grenade landed beside him. He kicked it aside, and as it exploded five yards away, shot and killed the German machine gunner and assistant gunner. His carbine empty, he jumped into the emplacement and hauled out the third member of the gun crew by the collar. Although his back wound was causing him excruciating pain and blood was seeping through his white coat, T/Sgt. Dunham proceeded 50 yards through a storm of automatic and rifle fire to attack the second machine gun. Twenty-five yards from the emplacement he hurled two grenades, destroying the gun and its crew; then fired down into the supporting foxholes with his carbine, dispatching and dispersing the enemy riflemen. Although his coat was so thoroughly blood-soaked that he was a conspicuous target against the white landscape, T/Sgt. Dunham again advanced ahead of his platoon in an assault on enemy positions farther up the hill. Coming under machine-gun fire from 65 yards to his front, while rifle grenades exploded 10 yards from his position, he hit the ground and crawled forward. At 15 yards' range, he jumped to his feet, staggered a few paces toward the timbered machine-gun emplacement, and killed the crew with hand grenades. An enemy rifleman fired at point-blank range, but missed him. After killing the rifleman, T/Sgt. Dunham drove others from their foxholes with grenades and carbine fire. Killing nine Germans—wounding seven and capturing two—firing about 175 rounds of carbine ammunition, and expending 11 grenades, T/Sgt. Dunham, despite a painful wound, spearheaded a spectacular and successful diversionary attack.

2697 ◆ DUNLAP, ROBERT HUGO

Rank: Captain (highest rank: Major)
Service: U.S. Marine Corps Reserve
Birthday: 19 October 1920
Place of Birth: Abingdon, Knox County, Illinois
Entered Service at: Monmouth, Warren County, Illinois
Unit: Company C, 1st Battalion, 26th Marines, 5th Marine Division
Served as: Commanding Officer
Battle or Place of Action: Iwo Jima, Volcano Islands
Date of Action: 20-21 February 1945
Date of Presentation: 18 December 1945
Place of Presentation: The White House, presented by Pres. Harry S. Truman
Citation: For conspicuous gallantry and intrepidity at the risk of his life above and beyond the call of duty as commanding officer of Company C, 1st Battalion, 26th Marines, 5th Marine division, in action against enemy Japanese forces dur-

ing the seizure of Iwo Jima in the Volcano Islands on 20 and 21 February, 1945. Defying uninterrupted blasts of Japanese artillery, mortar, rifle, and machine-gun fire, Capt. Dunlap led his troops in a determined advance from low ground uphill toward the steep cliffs from which the enemy poured a devastating rain of shrapnel and bullets, steadily inching forward until the tremendous volume of enemy fire from the caves located high to his front temporarily halted his progress. Determined not to yield, he crawled alone approximately 200 yards forward of his front lines, took observation at the base of the cliff 50 yards from Japanese lines, located the enemy gun positions, and returned to his own lines where he relayed the vital information to supporting artillery and naval gunfire units. Persistently disregarding his own personal safety, he then placed himself in an exposed vantage point to direct more accurately the supporting fire and, working without respite for two days and two nights under constant enemy fire, skillfully directed a smashing bombardment against the almost impregnable Japanese positions despite numerous obstacles and heavy marine casualties. A brilliant leader, Capt. Dunlap inspired his men to heroic efforts during this critical phase of the battle and by his cool decision, indomitable fighting spirit, and daring tactics in the face of fanatic opposition greatly accelerated the final decisive defeat of Japanese countermeasures in his sector and materially furthered the continued advance of his company. His great personal valor and gallant spirit of self-sacrifice throughout the bitter hostilities reflect the highest credit upon Capt. Dunlap and the U.S. Naval Service.

2698 ◆ *DUTKO, JOHN W.

Rank: Private First Class
Service: U.S. Army
Birthday: 24 October 1916
Place of Birth: Dilltown, Indiana County, Pennsylvania
Date of Death: 23 May 1944
Cemetery: Beverley National Cemetery (DS-1) (MH)—Beverley, New Jersey
Entered Service at: Riverside, Burlington County, New Jersey
Unit: Company A, 30th Infantry, 3d Infantry Division
Battle or Place of Action: near Ponte Rotto, Italy
Date of Action: 23 May 1944
G.O. Number, Date: 80, 5 October 1944
Citation: For conspicuous gallantry and intrepidity at risk of life above and beyond the call of duty, 23 May 1944, near Ponte Rotto, Italy. Pfc. Dutko left the cover of an abandoned enemy trench at the height of an artillery concentration in a singlehanded attack upon three enemy machine-guns and an 88-mm mobile gun. Despite the intense fire of these four weapons which were aimed directly at him, Pfc. Dutko ran 100 yards through the impact area, paused momentarily in a shell crater, and then continued his one-man assault. Although machine-gun bullets kicked up the dirt at his heels, and 88-mm shells exploded within 30 yards of him, Pfc. Dutko nevertheless made his way to a point within 30 yards of the first enemy machine gun and killed both gunners with a hand grenade. Although the second machine gun wounded

him, knocking him to the ground, Pfc. Dutko regained his feet and advanced on the 88-mm gun, firing his Browning automatic rifle from the hip. When he came within 10 yards of this weapon he killed its five-man crew with one long burst of fire. Wheeling on the machine gun which had wounded him, Pfc. Dutko killed the gunner and his assistant. The third German machine gun fired on Pfc. Dutko from a position 20 yards distant wounding him a second time as he proceeded toward the enemy weapon in a half run. He killed both members of its crew with a single burst from his Browning automatic rifle, continued toward the gun and died, his body falling across the dead German crew.

2699 ◆ *DYESS, AQUILLA JAMES

Rank: Lieutenant Colonel
Service: U.S. Marine Corps Reserve
Birthday: 11 January 1909
Place of Birth: Augusta, Richmond County, Georgia
Date of Death: 2 February 1944
Place of Death: Namur Island, Marshall Islands
Cemetery: Westover Memorial Park—Augusta, Georgia
Entered Service at: Georgia
Unit: 1st Battalion, 24th Marines, 4th Marine Division (Rein)
Served as: Commanding Officer
Battle or Place of Action: Namur Island, Kwajalein Atoll, Marshall Islands
Date of Action: 1-2 February 1944
Citation: For conspicuous gallantry and intrepidity at the risk of his life above and beyond the call of duty as commanding officer of the 1st Battalion, 24th Marines (Rein), 4th Marine Division, in action against enemy Japanese forces during the assault on Namur Island, Kwajalein Atoll, Marshall Islands, 1 and 2 February 1944. Undaunted by severe fire from automatic Japanese weapons, Lt. Col. Dyess launched a powerful final attack on the second day of the assault, unhesitatingly posting himself between the opposing lines to point out objectives and avenues of approach and personally leading the advancing troops. Alert and determined to quicken the pace of the offensive against increased enemy fire, he was constantly at the head of advance units, inspiring his men to push forward until the Japanese had been driven back to a small center of resistance and victory assured. While standing on the parapet of the antitank trench directing a group of infantry in a flanking attack against the last enemy position, Lt. Col. Dyess was killed by a burst of enemy machine-gun fire. His daring and forceful leadership and his valiant fighting spirit in the face of terrific opposition were in keeping with the highest traditions of the U.S. Naval Service. He gallantly gave his life for his country.

2700 ◆ EDSON, MERRITT AUSTIN

Rank: Colonel (highest rank: Major General)
Service: U.S. Marine Corps
Birthday: 25 April 1897
Place of Birth: Rutland, Rutland County, Vermont
Date of Death: 14 August 1955

Place of Death: Washington, D.C.
Cemetery: Arlington National Cemetery (2-4960-2)—
Arlington, Virginia
Entered Service at: Vermont
Unit: 1st Marine Raider Battalion
Served as: Commanding Officer
Battle or Place of Action: Guadalcanal, Solomon Islands
Date of Action: 13-14 September 1942
Date of Presentation: 21 May 1943
Place of Presentation: Balcombe, Australia, presented by
Maj. Gen. Alexander A. Vandegrift
Citation: For extraordinary heroism and conspicuous intrepidity above and beyond the call of duty as commanding officer of the 1st Marine Raider Battalion, with Parachute Battalion attached, during action against enemy Japanese forces in the Solomon Islands on the night of 13–14 September 1942. After the airfield on Guadalcanal had been seized from the enemy on 8 August, Col. Edson, with a force of 800 men, was assigned to the occupation and defense of a ridge dominating the jungle on either side of the airport. Facing a formidable Japanese attack which, augmented by infiltration, had crashed through our front lines, he, by skillful handling of his troops, successfully withdrew his forward units to a reserve line with minimum casualties. When the enemy, in a subsequent series of violent assaults, engaged our force in desperate hand-to-hand combat with bayonets, rifles, pistols, grenades, and knives, Col. Edson, although continuously exposed to hostile fire throughout the night, personally directed defense of the reserve position against a fanatical foe of greatly superior numbers. By his astute leadership and gallant devotion to duty, he enabled his men, despite severe losses, to cling tenaciously to their position on the vital ridge, thereby retaining command not only of the Guadalcanal airfield, but also of the 1st Division's entire offensive installations in the surrounding area.

2701 ◆ EHLERS, WALTER DAVID

Rank: Staff Sergeant (highest rank: Second Lieutenant)
Service: U.S. Army
Birthday: 7 May 1921
Place of Birth: Junction City, Geary County, Kansas
Entered Service at: Manhattan, Riley County, Kansas
Unit: 3d Squad, 3d Platoon, Company L, 3d Battalion, 18th Infantry, 1st Infantry Division
Served as: Squad Leader
Battle or Place of Action: near Goville, France
Date of Action: 9-10 June 1944
G.O. Number, Date: 91, 19 December 1944
Date of Presentation: 19 December 1944
Place of Presentation: Paris, France, presented by Lt. Gen. John C.H. Lee
Citation: For conspicuous gallantry and intrepidity at the risk of his life above and beyond the call of duty on 9–10 June 1944 near Goville, France. S/Sgt. Ehlers, always acting as the spearhead of the attack, repeatedly led his men against heavily defended enemy strongpoints, exposing himself to deadly hostile fire whenever the situation required heroic and courageous leadership. Without waiting for an order, S/Sgt.

Ehlers, far ahead of his men, led his squad against a strongly defended enemy strongpoint, personally killing four of an enemy patrol who attacked him en route. Then crawling forward under withering machine-gun fire, he pounced upon the gun-crew and put it out of action. Turning his attention to two mortars protected by the crossfire of two machine guns, S/Sgt. Ehlers led his men through this hail of bullets to kill or put to flight the enemy of the mortar section, killing three men himself. After mopping up the mortar positions, he again advanced on a machine gun, his progress effectively covered by his squad. When he was almost on top of the gun he leaped to his feet and, although greatly outnumbered, he knocked out the position singlehandedly. The next day, having advanced deep into enemy territory, the platoon of which S/Sgt. Ehlers was a member finding itself in an untenable position as the enemy brought increased mortar, machine-gun, and small-arms fire to bear on it, was ordered to withdraw. S/Sgt. Ehlers, after his squad had covered the withdrawal of the remainder of the platoon, stood up and by continuous fire at the semicircle of enemy placements, diverted the bulk of the heavy hostile fire on himself, thus permitting the members of his own squad to withdraw. At this point, though wounded himself, he carried his wounded automatic rifleman to safety and then returned fearlessly over the shell-swept field to retrieve the automatic rifle which he was unable to carry previously. After having his wound treated, he refused to be evacuated, and returned to lead his squad. The intrepid leadership, indomitable courage, and fearless aggressiveness displayed by S/Sgt. Ehlers in the face of overwhelming enemy forces serve as an inspiration to others.

2702 ◆ *ELROD, HENRY TALMAGE

Rank: Captain (highest rank: Major)
Service: U.S. Marine Corps
Birthday: 27 September 1905
Place of Birth: Rebecca, Turner County, Georgia
Date of Death: 23 December 1941
Cemetery: Arlington National Cemetery (12-3246) (MH)—Arlington, Virginia
Entered Service at: Ashburn, Turner County, Georgia
Unit: Marine Fighting Squadron 211
Served as: Pilot of an F4F-3 Grumman Wildcat
Battle or Place of Action: Wake Island
Date of Action: 8-23 December 1941
Citation: For conspicuous gallantry and intrepidity at the risk of his life above and beyond the call of duty while attached to Marine Fighting Squadron 211, during action against enemy Japanese land, surface and aerial units at Wake Island, 8-23 December 1941. Engaging vastly superior forces of enemy bombers and warships on 9 and 12 December, Capt. Elrod shot down two of a flight of 22 hostile planes and, executing repeated bombing and strafing runs at extremely low altitude and close range, succeeded in inflicting deadly damage upon a large Japanese vessel, thereby sinking the first major warship to be destroyed by small-caliber bombs delivered from a fighter-type aircraft. When his plane was disabled by hostile fire and no other ships were operative, Capt. Elrod assumed command of one flank of the line set up

2705 ◆ ERWIN, HENRY EUGENE "RED"

in defiance of the enemy landing and, conducting a brilliant defense, enabled his men to hold their positions and repulse intense hostile fusillades to provide covering fire for unarmed ammunition carriers. Capturing an automatic weapon during one enemy rush in force, he gave his own firearm to one of his men and fought on vigorously against the Japanese. Responsible in a large measure for the strength of his sector's gallant resistance, on 23 December, Capt. Elrod led his men with bold aggressiveness until he fell, mortally wounded. His superb skill as a pilot, daring leadership, and unswerving devotion to duty distinguished him among the defenders of Wake Island, and his valiant conduct reflects the highest credit upon himself and the U.S. Naval Service. He gallantly gave his life for his country.

2703 ◆ *ENDL, GERALD LEON

Rank: Staff Sergeant
Service: U.S. Army
Birthday: 20 August 1915
Place of Birth: Fort Atkinson, Jefferson County, Wisconsin
Date of Death: 11 July 1944
Cemetery: St. Joseph's Cemetery—Fort Atkinson, Wisconsin
Entered Service at: Janesville, Rock County, Wisconsin
Unit: 32d Infantry Division
Battle or Place of Action: near Anamo, New Guinea
Date of Action: 11 July 1944
G.O. Number, Date: 17, 13 March 1945
Citation: For conspicuous gallantry and intrepidity at the risk of his life above and beyond the call of duty near Anamo, New Guinea, 11 July 1944. S/Sgt. Endl was at the head of the leading platoon of his company advancing along a jungle trail when enemy troops were encountered and a firefight developed. The enemy attacked in force under heavy rifle, machine-gun, and grenade fire. His platoon leader wounded, S/Sgt. Endl immediately assumed command and deployed his platoon on a firing line at the fork in the trail toward which the enemy attack was directed. The dense jungle terrain greatly restricted vision and movement, and he endeavored to penetrate down the trail toward an open clearing of kunai grass. As he advanced, he detected the enemy, supported by at least six light and two heavy machine guns, attempting an enveloping movement around both flanks. His commanding officer sent a second platoon to move up on the left flank of the position, but the enemy closed in rapidly, placing our force in imminent danger of being isolated and annihilated. Twelve members of his platoon were wounded, seven being cut off by the enemy. Realizing that if his platoon were forced farther back, these seven men would be hopelessly trapped and at the mercy of a vicious enemy, he resolved to advance at all cost, knowing it meant almost certain death, in an effort to rescue his comrades. In the face of extremely heavy fire he went forward alone and for a period of approximately 10 minutes engaged the enemy in a heroic close-range fight, holding them off while his men crawled forward under cover to evacuate the wounded and to withdraw. Courageously refusing to abandon four more wounded men who were lying along the trail, one by one he brought them back to safety. As he was

carrying the last man in his arms he was struck by a heavy burst of automatic-weapon fire and was killed. By his persistent and daring self-sacrifice and on behalf of his comrades, S/Sgt. Endl made possible the successful evacuation of all but one man, and enabled the two platoons to withdraw with their wounded and to reorganize with the rest of the company.

2704 ◆ *EPPERSON, HAROLD GLENN

Rank: Private First Class
Service: U.S. Marine Corps Reserve
Birthday: 14 July 1923
Place of Birth: Akron, Summit County, Ohio
Date of Death: 25 June 1944
Cemetery: Town Cemetery (MH)—Winchester, Kentucky
Entered Service at: Ohio
Unit: 1st Battalion, 6th Marines, 2d Marine Division
Served as: Machine Gunner
Battle or Place of Action: Saipan Island, Mariana Islands
Date of Action: 25 June 1944
Citation: For conspicuous gallantry and intrepidity at the risk of his life above and beyond the call of duty while serving with the 1st Battalion, 6th Marines, 2d Marine Division, in action against enemy Japanese forces on the island of Saipan in the Marianas, 25 June 1944. With his machine-gun emplacement bearing the full brunt of a fanatic assault initiated by the Japanese under cover of predawn darkness, Pfc. Epperson manned his weapon with determined aggressiveness, fighting furiously in the defense of his battalion's position and maintaining a steady stream of devastating fire against rapidly infiltrating hostile troops to aid materially in annihilating several of the enemy and in breaking the abortive attack. Suddenly a Japanese soldier, assumed to be dead, sprang up and hurled a powerful hand grenade into the emplacement. Determined to save his comrades, Pfc. Epperson unhesitatingly chose to sacrifice himself and, diving upon the deadly missile, absorbed the shattering violence of the exploding charge in his own body. Stouthearted and indomitable in the face of certain death, Pfc. Epperson fearlessly yielded his own life that his able comrades might carry on the relentless battle against a ruthless enemy. His superb valor and unfaltering devotion to duty throughout reflect the highest credit upon himself and upon the U.S. Naval Service. He gallantly gave his life for his country.

2705 ◆ ERWIN, HENRY EUGENE "RED"

Rank: Staff Sergeant (highest rank: Master Sergeant)
Service: U.S. Army Air Corps
Birthday: 8 May 1921
Place of Birth: Adamsville, Jefferson County, Alabama
Entered Service at: Bessemer, Jefferson County, Alabama
Unit: 52d Bombardment Squadron, 29th Bombardment Group, 314th Bombardment Wing, 20th Air Force
Served as: Radio Operator on a B-29
Battle or Place of Action: Koriyama, Japan
Date of Action: 12 April 1945
G.O. Number, Date: 44, 6 June 1945
Date of Presentation: 19 April 1945

Place of Presentation: Fleet Hospital 103, Guam, presented by Gen. Curtis LeMay

Citation: He was the radio operator of a B-29 airplane leading a group formation to attack Koriyama, Japan. He was charged with the additional duty of dropping phosphorus smoke bombs to aid in assembling the group when the launching point was reached. Upon entering the assembly area, aircraft fire and enemy fighter opposition was encountered. Among the phosphorus bombs launched by S/Sgt. Erwin, one proved faulty, exploding in the launching chute, and shot back into the interior of the aircraft, striking him in the face. The burning phosphorus obliterated his nose and completely blinded him. Smoke filled the plane, obscuring the vision of the pilot. S/Sgt. Erwin realized that the aircraft and crew would be lost if the burning bomb remained in the plane. Without regard for his own safety, he picked it up and feeling his way, instictively, crawled around the gun turret and headed for the copilot's window. He found the navigator's table obstructing his passage. Grasping the burning bomb between his forearm and body, he unleashed the spring lock and raised the table. Struggling through the narrow passage he stumbled forward into the smoke-filled pilot's compartment. Groping with his burning hands, he located the window and threw the bomb out. Completely aflame, he fell back upon the floor. The smoke cleared, the pilot, at 300 feet, pulled the plane out of its dive. S/Sgt. Erwin's gallantry and heroism above and beyond the call of duty saved the lives of his comrades.

2706 ◆ *EUBANKS, RAY E.

Rank: Sergeant
Service: U.S. Army
Birthday: 6 February 1922
Place of Birth: Snow Hill, Greene County, North Carolina
Date of Death: 23 July 1944
Cemetery: West View Cemetery (MH)—Kinston, North Carolina
Entered Service at: LaGrange, Lenoir County, North Carolina
Unit: Company D, 503d Parachute Infantry
Battle or Place of Action: Noemfoor Island, Dutch New Guinea
Date of Action: 23 July 1944
G.O. Number, Date: 20, 29 March 1945

Citation: For conspicuous gallantry and intrepidity at the risk of his life above and beyond the call of duty at Noemfoor Island, Dutch New Guinea, 23 July 1944. While moving to the relief of a platoon isolated by the enemy, his company encountered a strong enemy position supported by machine-gun, rifle, and mortar fire. Sgt. Eubanks was ordered to make an attack with one squad to neutralize the enemy by fire in order to assist the advance of his company. He maneuvered his squad to within 30 yards of the enemy where heavy fire checked his advance. Directing his men to maintain their fire, he and two scouts worked their way forward up a shallow depression to within 25 yards of the enemy. Directing the scouts to remain in place, Sgt. Eubanks armed himself with an automatic rifle and worked himself forward over terrain swept by intense fire to within 15 yards of the enemy position when he opened fire with telling effect. The enemy, having located his position, concentrated their fire, with the result that he was wounded and a bullet rendered his rifle useless. In spite of his painful wounds he immediately charged the enemy and using his weapon as a club killed four of the enemy before he was himself again hit and killed. Sgt. Eubanks' heroic action, courage, and example in leadership so inspired his men that their advance was successful. They killed 45 of the enemy and drove the remainder from the position, thus effecting the relief of our beleaguered troops.

2707 ◆ *EVANS, ERNEST EDWIN "CHIEF"

Rank: Commander
Service: U.S. Navy
Birthday: 13 August 1908
Place of Birth: Pawnee, Pawnee County, Oklahoma
Date of Death: 25 October 1944
Cemetery: A.B.M.C. Manila Cemetery (Wall of the Missing)—Manila, Philippine Islands
Entered Service at: Oklahoma
Unit: U.S.S. *Johnston*
Served as: Commanding Officer
Battle or Place of Action: off Samar, Philippine Islands
Date of Action: 25 October 1944
Date of Issue: 28 September 1945

Citation: For conspicuous gallantry and intrepidity at the risk of his life above and beyond the call of duty as commanding officer of the U.S.S. *Johnston* in action against major units of the Japanese fleet during the battle off Samar on 25 October 1944. The first to lay a smoke screen and to open fire as an enemy task force, vastly superior in number, firepower, and armor, rapidly approached, Comdr. Evans gallantly diverted the powerful blasts of hostile guns from the lightly armed and armored carriers under his protection, launching the first torpedo attack when the *Johnston* came under straddling Japanese shellfire. Undaunted by damage sustained under the terrific volume of fire, he unhesitatingly joined others of his group to provide fire support during subsequent torpedo attacks against the Japanese and, outshooting and outmaneuvering the enemy as he consistently interposed his vessel between the hostile fleet units and our carriers despite the crippling loss of engine power and communications with steering aft, shifted command to the fantail, shouted steering orders through an open hatch to men turning the rudder by hand, and battled furiously until the *Johnston*, burning and shuddering from a mortal blow, lay dead in the water after three hours of fierce combat. Seriously wounded early in the engagement, Comdr. Evans, by his indomitable courage and brilliant professional skill, aided materially in turning back the enemy during a critical phase of the action. His valiant fighting spirit throughout this historic battle will venture as an inspiration to all who served with him.

2708 ◆ EVERHART SR., FORREST EUGENE

Rank: Technical Sergeant
Service: U.S. Army

Birthday: 28 August 1921
Place of Birth: Bainbridge, Ross County, Ohio
Date of Death: 30 August 1986
Place of Death: Philadelphia, Pennsylvania
Cemetery: Arlington National Cemetery (60-7516) (MH)—Arlington, Virginia
Entered Service at: Texas City, Galveston County, Texas
Unit: Company H, 359th Infantry, 90th Infantry Division
Battle or Place of Action: near Kerling, France
Date of Action: 12 November 1944
G.O. Number, Date: 77, 10 September 1945
Date of Presentation: 23 August 1945
Place of Presentation: The White House, presented by Pres. Harry S. Truman
Citation: He commanded a platoon that bore the brunt of a desperate enemy counterattack near Korling, France, before dawn on 12 November 1944. When German tanks and self-propelled guns penetrated his left flank and overwhelming infantry forces threatened to overrun the one remaining machine-gun in that section, he ran 400 yards through woods churned by artillery and mortar concentrations to strengthen the defense. With the one remaining gunner, he directed furious fire into the advancing hordes until they swarmed close to the position. He left the gun, boldly charged the attackers, and, after a 15-minute exchange of hand grenades, forced them to withdraw leaving 30 dead behind. He recrossed the fire-swept terrain to his then threatened right flank, exhorted his men and directed murderous fire from the single machine-gun at that position. There, in the light of bursting mortar shells, he again closed with the enemy in a hand-grenade duel and, after a fierce 30-minute battle, forced the Germans to withdraw leaving another 20 dead. The gallantry and intrepidity of T/Sgt. Everhart in rallying his men and refusing to fall back in the face of terrible odds were highly instrumental in repelling the fanatical enemy counterattack directed at the American bridgehead across the Moselle River.

2709 ◆ *FARDY, JOHN PETER

Rank: Corporal
Service: U.S. Marine Corps
Birthday: 15 August 1922
Place of Birth: Chicago, Cook County, Illinois
Date of Death: 7 May 1945
Cemetery: Holy Sepulchre Cemetery—Worth, Illinois
Entered Service at: Illinois
Unit: Company C, 1st Battalion, 1st Marines, 1st Marine Division
Served as: Squad Leader
Battle or Place of Action: Okinawa Shima, Ryukyu Islands
Date of Action: 7 May 1945
Citation: For conspicuous gallantry and intrepidity at the risk of his life above and beyond the call of duty as a squad leader, serving with Company C, 1st Battalion, 1st Marines, 1st Marine Division, in action against enemy Japanese forces on Okinawa Shima in the Ryukyu Islands, 7 May 1945. When his squad was suddenly assailed by extremely heavy small-arms fire from the front during a determined advance against strongly fortified, fiercely defended Japanese positions,

Cpl. Fardy temporarily deployed his men along a nearby drainage ditch. Shortly thereafter, an enemy grenade fell among the marines in the ditch. Instantly throwing himself upon the deadly missile, Cpl. Fardy absorbed the exploding blast in his own body, thereby protecting his comrades from certain and perhaps fatal injuries. Concerned solely for the welfare of his men, he willingly relinquished his own hope of survival that his fellow marines might live to carry on the fight against a fanatic enemy. A stouthearted leader and indomitable fighter, Cpl. Fardy, by his prompt decision and resolute spirit of self-sacrifice in the face of certain death, had rendered valiant service, and his conduct throughout reflects the highest credit upon himself and the U.S. Naval Service. He gallantly gave his life for his country.

2710 ◆ *FEMOYER, ROBERT EDWARD

Rank: Second Lieutenant
Service: U.S. Army Air Corps
Birthday: 31 October 1921
Place of Birth: Huntington, Cabell County, West Virginia
Date of Death: 2 November 1944
Cemetery: Greenlawn Cemetery (MH)—Jacksonville, Florida
Entered Service at: Jacksonville, Duval County, Florida
Unit: 711th Bombardment Squadron, 447th Bombardment Group, 8th Air Force
Served as: Navigator of a B-17
Battle or Place of Action: over Merseburg, Germany
Date of Action: 2 November 1944
G.O. Number, Date: 35, 9 May 1945
Citation: For conspicuous gallantry and intrepidity at the risk of his life above and beyond the call of duty near Merseburg, Germany on 2 November 1944. While on a mission, the bomber, of which 2d Lt. Femoyer was a navigator, was struck by three enemy antiaircraft shells. The plane suffered serious damage and 2d Lt. Femoyer was severely wounded in the side and back by shell fragments which penetrated his body. In spite of extreme pain and great loss of blood he refused an offered injection of morphine. He was determined to keep his mental faculties clear in order that he might direct his plane out of danger and so save his comrades. Not being able to arise from the floor, he asked to be propped up in order to enable him to see his charts and instruments. He successfully directed the navigation of his lone bomber for 21/2 hours so well it avoided enemy flak and returned to the field without further damage. Only when the plane had arrived in the safe area over the English Channel did he feel that he had accomplished his objective; then, and only then, he permitted an injection of a sedative. He died shortly after being moved from the plane. The heroism and self-sacrifice of 2d Lt. Femoyer are in keeping with the highest traditions of the U.S. Army.

2711 ◆ FIELDS, JAMES H.

Rank: First Lieutenant
Service: U.S. Army
Birthday: 26 June 1920

Place of Birth: Caddo, Stephens County, Texas
Date of Death: 17 June 1970
Cemetery: Houston National Cemetery (HB-6) (MH)—Houston, Texas
Entered Service at: Houston, Harris County, Texas
Unit: 10th Armored Infantry, 4th Armored Division
Served as: Platoon Leader
Battle or Place of Action: Rechicourt, France
Date of Action: 27 September 1944
G.O. Number, Date: 13, 27 February 1945
Date of Presentation: 22 February 1945
Place of Presentation: Luxembourg, Belgium, presented by Gen. George S. Patton
Citation: For conspicuous gallantry and intrepidity at the risk of life above and beyond the call of duty, at Rechicourt, France. On 27 September 1944, during a sharp action with the enemy infantry and tank forces, 1st Lt. Fields personally led his platoon in a counterattack on the enemy position. Although his platoon had been seriously depleted, the zeal and fervor of his leadership was such as to inspire his small force to accomplish their mission in the face of overwhelming enemy opposition. Seeing that one of the men had been wounded, he left his slit trench and with complete disregard for his personal safety attended the wounded man and administered first aid. While returning to his slit trench he was seriously wounded by a shell burst, the fragments of which cut through his face and head, tearing his teeth, gums, and nasal passage. Although rendered speechless by his wounds, 1st Lt. Fields refused to be evacuated and continued to lead his platoon by the use of hand signals. On one occasion, when two enemy machine guns had a portion of his unit under deadly crossfire, he left his hole, wounded as he was, ran to a light machine gun, whose crew had been knocked out, picked up the gun, and fired it from the hip with such deadly accuracy that both the enemy gun positions were silenced. His action so impressed his men that they found new courage to take up the firefight, increasing their firepower and exposing themselves more than ever to harass the enemy with additional bazooka and machine-gun fire. Only when his objective had been taken and the enemy scattered did 1st Lt. Fields consent to be evacuated to the battalion command post. At this point he refused to move further back until he had explained to his battalion commander by drawing on paper the position of his men and the disposition of the enemy forces. The dauntless and gallant heroism displayed by 1st Lt. Fields were largely responsible for the repulse of the enemy forces and contributed in a large measure to the successful capture of his battalion objective during this action. His eagerness and determination to close with the enemy and to destroy him were an inspiration to the entire command, and are in the highest traditions of the U.S. Armed Forces.

2712 ◆ FINN, JOHN WILLIAM

Rank: Lieutenant (rank at time of action: Aviation Chief Ordnance Man)
Service: U.S. Navy
Birthday: 24 July 1909
Place of Birth: Los Angeles, Los Angeles County, California
Entered Service at: Belle Vernon Acres, California
Unit: VP-14 Squadron (Patrol Planes Squadron)
Served as: Senior Chief Ordnance Man
Battle or Place of Action: Kaneohe Bay, Territory of Hawaii
Date of Action: 7 December 1941
Date of Presentation: 15 September 1942
Place of Presentation: on board the U.S.S. *Enterprise*, Pearl Harbor, Territory of Hawaii, presented by Adm. Chester W. Nimitz
Citation: For extraordinary heroism distinguished service, and devotion above and beyond the call of duty. During the first attack by Japanese airplanes on the Naval Air Station, Kaneohe Bay, on 7 December 1941, Lt. (then A.C.O.M.) Finn promptly secured and manned a .50-caliber machine gun mounted on an instruction stand in a completely exposed section of the parking ramp, which was under heavy enemy machine-gun strafing fire. Although painfully wounded many times, he continued to man this gun and to return the enemy's fire vigorously and with telling effect throughout the enemy strafing and bombing attacks and with complete disregard for his own personal safety. It was only by specific orders that he was persuaded to leave his post to seek medical attention. Following first-aid treatment, although obviously suffering much pain and moving with great difficulty, he returned to the squadron area and actively supervised the rearming of returning planes. His extraordinary heroism and conduct in this action were in keeping with the highest traditions of the U.S. Naval Service.

2713 ◆ FISHER, ALMOND EDWARD

Rank: Second Lieutenant (highest rank: Lieutenant Colonel)
Service: U.S. Army
Birthday: 28 January 1913
Place of Birth: Hume, Allegany County, New York
Date of Death: 7 January 1982
Place of Death: Concord Township, Ohio
Cemetery: Arlington National Cemetery (6-8751-2)—Arlington, Virginia
Entered Service at: Brooklyn, Kings County, New York
Unit: Company E, 157th Infantry, 45th Infantry Division
Served as: Platoon Leader
Battle or Place of Action: near Grammont, France
Date of Action: 12-13 September 1944
G.O. Number, Date: 32, 23 April 1945
Date of Issue: 23 May 1945
Citation: For conspicuous gallantry and intrepidity at the risk of his life above and beyond the call of duty on the night of 12–13 September 1944, near Grammont, France. In the darkness of the early morning 2d Lt. Fisher was leading a platoon of Company E, 157th Infantry, in single column to the attack of a strongly defended hill position. At 2:30 A.M., the forward elememts were brought under enemy machine-gun fire from a distance of not more than 20 yards. Working his way alone to within 20 feet of the gun emplacement, he opened fire with his carbine and killed the entire guncrew. A few minutes after the advance was resumed, heavy machine-gun fire was encountered from the left flank. Again crawling

forward alone under withering fire, he blasted the gun and crew from their positions with hand grenades. After a halt to replenish ammunition, the advance was again resumed and continued for one hour before being stopped by intense machine-gun and rifle fire. Through the courageous and skillful leadership of 2d Lt. Fisher, the pocket of determined enemy resistance was rapidly obliterated. Spotting an emplaced machine pistol a short time later, with one of his men he moved forward and destroyed the position. As the advance continued the firefight became more intense. When a bypassed German climbed from his foxhole and attempted to tear an M-1 rifle from the hands of one of his men, 2d Lt. Fisher whirled and killed the enemy with a burst from his carbine. About 30 minutes later the platoon came under heavy fire from machine guns from across an open field. Second Lt. Fisher, disregarding the terrific fire, moved across the field with no cover or concealment to within range, knocked the gun from the position, and killed or wounded the crew. Still under heavy fire he returned to his platoon and continued the advance. Once again heavy fire was encountered from a machine gun directly in front. Calling for hand grenades, he found only two remaining in the entire platoon. Pulling the pins and carrying a grenade in each hand, he crawled toward the gun emplacement, moving across areas devoid of cover and under intense fire to within 15 yards when he threw the grenades, demolished the gun, and killed the guncrew. With ammunition low and daybreak near, he ordered his men to dig in and hold the ground already won. Under constant fire from the front and from both flanks, he moved among them directing the preparations for the defense. Shortly after the ammunition supply was replenished, the Germans launched a last determined effort against the depleted group. Attacked by superior numbers from the front, right, and left flank, and even from the rear, the platoon, in bitter hand-to-hand engagements, drove back the enemy at every point. Wounded in both feet by close-range machine pistol fire early in the battle, 2d Lt. Fisher refused medical attention. Unable to walk, he crawled from man to man encouraging them and checking each position. Only after the fighting had subsided did 2d Lt. Fisher crawl 300 yards to the aid station from which he was evacuated. His extraordinary heroism, magnificent valor, and aggressive determination in the face of point-blank enemy fire is an inspiration to his organization and reflects the finest traditions of the U.S. Armed Forces.

2714 ◆ *FLAHERTY, FRANCIS CHARLES

Rank: Ensign
Service: U.S. Naval Reserve
Birthday: 15 March 1919
Place of Birth: Charlotte, Eaton County, Michigan
Date of Death: 7 December 1941
Place of Death: Pearl Harbor, Territory of Hawaii
Cemetery: National Memorial Cemetery of the Pacific (Wall of the Missing)—Honolulu, Hawaii; Maple Hill Cemetery ('In Memory' marker)—Charlotte, Michigan
Entered Service at: Michigan
Unit: U.S.S. *Oklahoma*
Battle or Place of Action: Pearl Harbor, Territory of Hawaii

Date of Action: 7 December 1941
Date of Presentation: 6 March 1946
Place of Presentation: Presented to his Brother
Citation: For conspicuous devotion to duty and extraordinary courage and complete disregard of his own life, above and beyond the call of duty, during the attack on the Fleet in Pearl Harbor, by Japanese forces on 7 December 1941. When it was seen that the U.S.S. *Oklahoma* was going to capsize and the order was given to abandon ship, Ens. Flaherty remained in a turret, holding a flashlight so the remainder of the turret crew could see to escape, thereby sacrificing his own life.

2715 ◆ *FLEMING, RICHARD EUGENE

Rank: Captain
Service: U.S. Marine Corps Reserve
Birthday: 2 November 1917
Place of Birth: St. Paul, Ramsey County, Minnesota
Date of Death: 5 June 1942
Cemetery: National Memorial Cemetery of the Pacific (Wall of the Missing)—Honolulu, Hawaii
Entered Service at: Minnesota
Unit: Marine Scout-Bombing Squadron 241
Served as: Flight Officer
Battle or Place of Action: Midway Island
Date of Action: 4-5 June 1942
Citation: For extraordinary heroism and conspicuous intrepidity above and beyond the call of duty as flight officer, Marine Scout-Bombing Squadron 241, during action against enemy Japanese forces in the battle of Midway on 4 and 5 June 1942. When his squadron commander was shot down during the initial attack upon an enemy aircraft carrier, Capt. Fleming led the remainder of the division with such fearless determination that he dived his own plane to the perilously low altitude of 400 feet before releasing his bomb. Although his craft was riddled by 179 hits in the blistering hail of fire that burst upon him from Japanese fighter guns and antiaircraft batteries, he pulled out with only two minor wounds inflicted upon himself. On the night of 4 June, when the squadron commander lost his way and became separated from the others, Capt. Fleming brought his own plane in for a safe landing at its base despite hazardous weather conditions and total darkness. The following day, after less than four hours' sleep, he led the second division of his squadron in a coordinated glide-bombing and dive-bombing assault upon a Japanese battleship. Undeterred by a fateful approach glide, during which his ship was struck and set afire, he grimly pressed home his attack to an altitude of 500 feet, released his bomb to score a near miss on the stern of his target, then crashed to the sea in flames. His dauntless perseverance and unyielding devotion to duty were in keeping with the highest traditions of the U.S. Naval Service.

2716 ◆ FLUCKEY, EUGENE BENNETT

Rank: Commander (highest rank: Rear Admiral)
Service: U.S. Navy
Birthday: 5 October 1913

Place of Birth: Washington, D.C.
Entered Service at: Neoga, Cumberland County, Illinois
Unit: U.S.S. *Barb*–SS220
Served as: Commanding Officer
Battle or Place of Action: Namkwan Harbor, along coast of China
Date of Action: 19 December 1944—15 February 1945
Date of Presentation: 23 March 1945
Place of Presentation: Washington, D.C., presented by the Sec. of the Navy James V. Forrestal
Citation: For conspicuous gallantry and intrepidity at the risk of his life above and beyond the call of duty as commanding officer of the U.S.S. *Barb* during her 11th war patrol along the east coast of China from 19 December 1944 to 15 February 1945. After sinking a large enemy ammunition ship and damaging additional tonnage during a running two-hour night battle on 8 January, Comdr. Fluckey, in an exceptional feat of brilliant deduction and bold tracking on 25 January, located a concentration of more than 30 enemy ships in the lower reaches of Nankuan Chiang (Mamkwan Harbor). Fully aware that a safe retirement would necessitate an hour's run at full speed through the uncharted, mined, and rock-obstructed waters, he bravely ordered, "Battle station—torpedoes!" In a daring penetration of the heavy enemy screen, and riding in five fathoms of water, he launched the *Barb's* last forward torpedoes at 3,000-yard range. Quickly bringing the ship's stern tubes to bear, he turned loose four more torpedoes into the enemy, obtaining eight direct hits on six of the main targets to explode a large ammunition ship and cause inestimable damage by the resultant flying shells and other pyrotechnics. Clearing the treacherous area at high speed, he brought the *Barb* through to safety, and four days later sank a large Japanese freighter to complete a record of heroic combat achievement, reflecting the highest credit upon Comdr. Fluckey, his gallant officers and men, and the U.S. Naval Service.

2717 ◆ FOSS, JOSEPH JACOB

Rank: Captain (highest rank: Brigadier General)
Service: U.S. Marine Corps Reserve
Birthday: 17 April 1915
Place of Birth: Sioux Falls, Minnehaha County, South Dakota
Entered Service at: Sioux Falls, Minnehaha County, South Dakota
Unit: Marine Fighting Squadron 121, Marine Air Group 11, 1st Marine Aircraft Wing
Served as: Squadron Executive Officer/Pilot of a Grumman F-4F Wildcat
Battle or Place of Action: over Guadalcanal, Solomon Islands
Date of Action: 9 October-19 November 1942; 15, 23 January 1943
Date of Presentation: 18 May 1943
Place of Presentation: The White House (Oval Office), presented by Pres. Franklin D. Roosevelt
Citation: For outstanding heroism and courage above and beyond the call of duty as executive officer of Marine Fighting Squadron 121, 1st Marine Aircraft Wing, at Guadalcanal. Engaging in almost daily combat with the enemy from 9 October to 19 November 1942, Capt. Foss personally shot down 23 Japanese planes and damaged others so severely that their destruction was extremely probable. In addition, during this period, he successfully led a large number of escort missions, skillfully covering reconnaissance, bombing, and photographic planes as well as surface craft. On 15 January 1943, he added three more enemy planes to his already brilliant successes for a record of aerial combat achievement unsurpassed in this war. Boldly searching out an approaching enemy force on 25 January, Capt. Foss led his eight F4F Marine planes and four Army P-38s into action and, undaunted by tremendously superior numbers, intercepted and struck with such force that four Japanese fighters were shot down and the bombers were turned back without releasing a single bomb. His remarkable flying skill, inspiring leadership, and indomitable fighting spirit were distinctive factors in the defense of strategic American positions on Guadalcanal.

2718 ◆ *FOSTER, WILLIAM ADELBERT

Rank: Private First Class
Service: U.S. Marine Corps Reserve
Birthday: 17 February 1915
Place of Birth: Cleveland, Cuyahoga County, Ohio
Date of Death: 2 May 1945
Place of Death: Okinawa Shima, Ryukyu Islands
Cemetery: Calvary Cemetery (MH)—Cleveland, Ohio
Entered Service at: Ohio
Unit: Company K, 3d Battalion, 1st Marines, 1st Marine Division
Served as: Rifleman
Battle or Place of Action: Okinawa Shima, Ryukyu Islands
Date of Action: 2 May 1945
Date of Presentation: 19 August 1945
Place of Presentation: Mayor's office, Cleveland, Ohio, presented by Gen. Alexander A. Vandergrift to his parents
Citation: For conspicuous gallantry and intrepidity at the risk of his life above and beyond the call of duty while serving as a rifleman with the 3d Battalion, 1st Marines, 1st Marine Division, in action against enemy Japanese forces on Okinawa Shima in the Ryukyu Chain, 2 May 1945. Dug in with another marine on the point of the perimeter defense after waging a furious assault against a strongly fortified Japanese position, Pfc. Foster and his comrade engaged in a fierce hand-grenade duel with infiltrating enemy soldiers. Suddenly an enemy grenade landed beyond reach of the foxhole. Instantly diving on the deadly missile, Pfc. Foster absorbed the exploding charge in his own body, thereby protecting the other marine from serious injury. Although mortally wounded as a result of his heroic action, he quickly rallied, handed his own two remaining grenades to his comrade and said, "Make them count." Stouthearted and indomitable, he had unhesitatingly relinquished his own chance of survival that his fellow marine might carry on the relentless fight against a fanatic enemy, and his dauntless determination, cool decision, and valiant spirit of self-sacrifice in the face of certain death reflect the

highest credit upon Pfc. Foster and upon the U.S. Naval Service. He gallantly gave his life in the service of his country.

2719 ◆ *FOURNIER, WILLIAM GRANT

Rank: Sergeant
Service: U.S. Army
Birthday: 21 June 1913
Place of Birth: Norwich, New London County, Connecticut
Date of Death: 10 January 1943
Cemetery: National Memorial Cemetery of the Pacific (L-462) (MH)—Honolulu, Hawaii
Entered Service at: Winterport, Waldo County, Maine
Unit: Company M, 35th Infantry, 25th Infantry Division
Served as: Section Leader
Battle or Place of Action: Mount Austen, Guadalcanal, Solomon Islands
Date of Action: 10 January 1943
G.O. Number, Date: 28, 5 June 1943
Citation: For gallantry and intrepidity above and beyond the call of duty. As leader of a machine-gun section charged with the protection of other battalion units, his group was attacked by a superior number of Japanese, his gunner killed, his assistant gunner wounded, and an adjoining guncrew put out of action. Ordered to withdraw from this hazardous position, Sgt. Fournier refused to retire but rushed forward to the idle gun and, with the aid of another soldier who joined him, held up the machine gun by the tripod to increase its field of action. They opened fire and inflicted heavy casualties upon the enemy. While so engaged both these gallant soldiers were killed, but their sturdy defensive action was a decisive factor in the following success of the attacking battalion.

2720 ◆ *FOWLER, THOMAS WELDON

Rank: Second Lieutenant
Service: U.S. Army
Birthday: 31 October 1921
Place of Birth: Wichita Falls, Wichita County, Texas
Date of Death: 3 June 1944
Cemetery: Crestview Memorial Park (MH)—Wichita Falls, Texas
Entered Service at: Wichita Falls, Wichita County, Texas
Unit: 1st Armored Division
Battle or Place of Action: near Carano, Italy
Date of Action: 23 May 1944
G.O. Number, Date: 84, 28 October 1944
Place of Presentation: Fort Sill, Oklahoma, presented by Maj. Gen. Ralph McT. Pennel to his family
Citation: For conspicuous gallantry and intrepidity at the risk of his life above and beyond the call of duty on 23 May 1944, in the vicinity of Carano, Italy. In the midst of a full-scale armored-infantry attack, 2d Lt. Fowler, while on foot, came upon two completely disorganized infantry platoons held up in their advance by an enemy minefield. Although a tank officer, he immediately reorganized the infantry. He then made a personal reconnaissance through the minefield, clearing a path as he went, by lifting the antipersonnel mines

out of the ground with his hands. After he had gone through the 75-yard belt of deadly explosives, he returned to the infantry and led them through the minefield, a squad at a time. As they deployed, 2d Lt. Fowler, despite small-arms fire and the constant danger of antipersonnel mines, made a reconnaissance into enemy territory in search of a route to continue the advance. He then returned through the minefield and, on foot, he led the tanks through the mines into a position from which they could best support the infantry. Acting as scout 300 yards in front of the infantry, he led the two platoons forward until he had gained his objective, where he came upon several dug-in enemy infantrymen. Having taken them by surprise, 2d Lt. Fowler dragged them out of their foxholes and sent them to the rear; twice, when they resisted, he threw hand grenades into their dugouts. Realizing that a dangerous gap existed between his company and the unit on his right, 2d Lt. Fowler decided to continue his advance until the gap was filled. He reconnoitered to his front, brought the infantry into position where they dug in, and, under heavy mortar and small-arms fire, brought his tanks forward. A few minutes later, the enemy began an armored counterattack. Several Mark VI tanks fired their cannons directly on 2d Lt. Fowler's position. One of his tanks was set afire. With utter disregard for his own life, with shells bursting near him, he ran directly into the enemy tank fire to reach the burning vehicle. For a half-hour, under intense strafing from the advancing tanks, although all other elements had withdrawn, he remained in his forward position, attempting to save the lives of the wounded tank crew. Only when the enemy tanks had almost overrun him, did he withdraw a short distance where he personally rendered first aid to nine wounded infantrymen in the midst of the relentless incoming fire. Second Lt. Fowler's courage, his ability to estimate the situation and to recognize his full responsibility as an officer in the Army of the United States, exemplify the high traditions of the military service for which he later gave his life.

2721 ◆ *FRYAR, ELMER E.

Rank: Private
Service: U.S. Army
Place of Birth: Denver, Denver County, Colorado
Date of Death: 8 December 1944
Cemetery: A.B.M.C. Manila Cemetery (Wall of the Missing)—Manila, Philippine Islands
Entered Service at: Denver, Denver County, Colorado
Unit: Company E, 511th Parachute Infantry, 11th Airborne Division
Battle or Place of Action: Leyte, Philippine Islands
Date of Action: 8 December 1944
G.O. Number, Date: 35, 9 May 1945
Citation: For conspicuous gallantry and intrepidity at the risk of his life above and beyond the call of duty. Pvt. Fryar's battalion encountered the enemy strongly entrenched in a position supported by mortars and automatic weapons. The battalion attacked, but in spite of repeated efforts was unable to take the position. Pvt. Fryar's company was ordered to cover the battalion's withdrawal to a more suitable point from which to attack, but the enemy launched a strong counterat-

tack which threatened to cut off the company. Seeing an enemy platoon moving to outflank his company, he moved to higher ground and opened heavy and accurate fire. He was hit, and wounded, but continuing his attack he drove the enemy back with a loss of 27 killed. While withdrawing to overtake his squad, he found a seriously wounded comrade, helped him to the rear, and soon overtook his platoon leader, who was assisting another wounded. While these four were moving to rejoin their platoon, an enemy sniper appeared and aimed his weapon at the platoon leader. Pvt. Fryar instantly sprang forward, received the full burst of automatic fire in his own body and fell mortally wounded. With his remaining strength he threw a hand grenade and killed the sniper. Pvt. Fryar's indomitable fighting spirit and extraordinary gallantry above and beyond the call of duty contributed outstandingly to the success of the battalion's withdrawal and its subsequent attack and defeat of the enemy. His heroic action in unhesitatingly giving his own life for his comrade in arms exemplifies the highest tradition of the U.S. Armed Forces.

2722 ◆ FUNK JR., LEONARD ALFRED

Rank: First Sergeant
Service: U.S. Army
Birthday: 27 August 1916
Place of Birth: Braddock Township, Allegheny County, Pennsylvania
Date of Death: 20 November 1992
Place of Death: McKeesport, Pennsylvania
Cemetery: Arlington National Cemetery (35-2373-4)— Arlington, Virginia
Entered Service at: Wilkinsburg, Allegheny County, Pennsylvania
Unit: Company C, 1st Battalion, 508th Parachute Infantry, 82d Airborne Division
Served as: Company First Sergeant
Battle or Place of Action: Holzheim, Belgium
Date of Action: 29 January 1945
G.O. Number, Date: 75, 5 September 1945
Date of Presentation: 23 August 1945
Place of Presentation: The White House, presented by Pres. Harry S. Truman
Citation: He distinguished himself by gallant, intrepid actions against the enemy. After advancing 15 miles in a driving snowstorm, the American force prepared to attack through waist-deep drifts. The company executive officer became a casualty, and 1st Sgt. Funk immediately assumed his duties, forming headquarters soldiers into a combat unit for an assault in the face of direct artillery shelling and harassing fire from the right flank. Under his skillful and courageous leadership, this miscellaneous group and the 3d Platoon attacked 15 houses, cleared them, and took 30 prisoners without suffering a casualty. The fierce drive of Company C quickly overran Holzheim, netting some 80 prisoners, who were placed under a four-man guard, all that could be spared, while the rest of the understrength unit went about mopping up isolated points of resistance. An enemy patrol, by means of a ruse, succeeded in capturing the guards and freeing the prisoners, and had begun preparations to attack Company C

from the rear when 1st Sgt. Funk walked around the building and into their midst. He was ordered to surrender by a German officer who pushed a machine pistol into his stomach. Although overwhelmingly outnumbered and facing almost certain death, 1st Sgt. Funk, pretending to comply with the order, began slowly to unsling his submachine-gun from his shoulder and then, with lightning motion, brought the muzzle into line and riddled the German officer. He turned upon the other Germans, firing and shouting to the other Americans to seize the enemy's weapons. In the ensuing fight 21 Germans were killed, many wounded, and the remainder captured. First Sgt. Funk's bold action and heroic disregard for his own safety were directly responsible for the recapture of a vastly superior enemy force, which, if allowed to remain free, could have taken the widespread units of Company C by surprise and endangered the entire attack plan.

2723 ◆ FUQUA, SAMUEL GLENN

Rank: Captain (rank at time of action: Lieutenant Commander) (highest rank: Rear Admiral)
Service: U.S. Navy
Birthday: 15 October 1899
Place of Birth: Laddonia, Audrain County, Missouri
Date of Death: 27 January 1987
Cemetery: Arlington National Cemetery (59-485) (MH)— Arlington, Virginia
Entered Service at: Laddonia, Audrain County, Missouri
Unit: U.S.S. *Arizona*
Battle or Place of Action: Pearl Harbor, Territory Of Hawaii
Date of Action: 7 December 1941
Date of Presentation: 19 March 1942
Citation: For distinguished conduct in action, outstanding heroism, and utter disregard of his own safety above and beyond the call of duty during the attack on the Fleet in Pearl Harbor, by Japanese forces on 7 December 1941. Upon the commencement of the attack, Lt. Comdr. Fuqua rushed to the quarterdeck of the U.S.S. *Arizona*, to which he was attached, where he was stunned and knocked down by the explosion of a large bomb which hit the quarterdeck, penetrated several decks, and started a severe fire. Upon regaining consciousness, he began to direct the fighting of the fire and the rescue of the wounded and injured personnel. Almost immediately there was a tremendous explosion forward, which made the ship appear to rise out of the water, shudder, and settle down by the bow rapidly. The whole forward part of the ship was enveloped in flames which were spreading rapidly, and wounded and burned men were pouring out of the ship to the quarterdeck. Despite these conditions, his harrowing experience, and severe enemy bombing and strafing at the time, Lt. Comdr. Fuqua continued to direct the fighting of the fires in order to check them while the wounded and burned could be taken from the ship, and supervised the rescue of these men in such an amazingly calm and cool manner and with such excellent judgment that it inspired everyone who saw him and undoubtedly resulted in the saving of many lives. After realizing the ship could not be saved and that he

was the senior surviving officer aboard, he directed it to be abandoned, but continued to remain on the quarterdeck and directed abandoning ship and rescue of personnel until satisfied that all personnel that could be had been saved, after which he left his ship with the boatload. The conduct of Lt. Comdr. Fuqua was not only in keeping with the highest traditions of the Naval Service but characterizes him as an outstanding leader of men.

2724 ◆ GALER, ROBERT EDWARD

Rank: Major (highest rank: Brigadier General)
Service: U.S. Marine Corps
Birthday: 23 October 1913
Place of Birth: Seattle, King County, Washington
Entered Service at: Seattle, King County, Washington
Unit: Marine Fighter Squadron 224, Marine Aviation Group 21
Served as: Squadron Commander
Battle or Place of Action: Guadalcanal, Solomon Islands
Date of Action: 1 October 1942
Date of Presentation: 24 March 1943
Place of Presentation: The White House, presented by Pres. Franklin D. Roosevelt
Citation: For conspicuous heroism and courage above and beyond the call of duty as leader of a marine fighter squadron in aerial combat with enemy Japanese forces in the Solomon Islands area. Leading his squadron repeatedly in daring and aggressive raids against Japanese aerial forces, vastly superior in numbers, Maj. Galer availed himself of every favorable attack opportunity, individually shooting down 11 enemy bomber and fighter aircraft over a period of 29 days. Though suffering the extreme physical strain attendant upon protracted fighter operations at an altitude above 25,000 feet, the squadron under his zealous and inspiring leadership shot down a total of 27 Japanese planes. His superb airmanship, his outstanding skill, and personal valor reflect great credit upon Maj. Galer's gallant fighting spirit and upon the U.S. Naval Service.

2725 ◆ *GALT, WILLIAM WYLIE

Rank: Captain
Service: U.S. Army
Birthday: 19 December 1919
Place of Birth: Geyser, Judith Basin County, Montana
Date of Death: 29 May 1944
Cemetery: Mount Olivet Cemetery—Great Falls, Montana
Entered Service at: Stanford, Judith Basin County, Montana
Unit: 1st Battalion, 168th Infantry, 34th Infantry Division
Served as: S-3 Officer
Battle or Place of Action: at Villa Crocetta, Italy
Date of Action: 29 May 1944
G.O. Number, Date: 7, 1 February 1945
Citation: For conspicuous gallantry and intrepidity above and beyond the call of duty. Capt. Galt, Battalion S-3, at a particularly critical period following two unsuccessful attacks by his battalion, of his own volition went forward and ascer-

tained just how critical the situation was. He volunteered, at the risk of his life, personally to lead the battalion against the objective. When the lone remaining tank destroyer refused to go forward, Capt. Galt jumped on the tank destroyer and ordered it to precede the attack. As the tank destroyer moved forward, followed by a company of riflemen, Capt. Galt manned the .30-caliber machine gun in the turret of the tank destroyer, located and directed fire on an enemy 77-mm antitank gun, and destroyed it. Nearing the enemy positions, Capt. Galt stood fully exposed in the turret, ceaselessly firing his machine gun and tossing hand grenades into the enemy zigzag series of trenches despite the hail of sniper and machine-gun bullets ricocheting off the tank destroyer. As the tank destroyer moved, Capt. Galt so maneuvered it that 40 of the enemy were trapped in one trench. When they refused to surrender, Capt. Galt pressed the trigger of the machine gun and dispatched every one of them. A few minutes later an 88-mm shell struck the tank destroyer and Capt. Galt fell mortally wounded across his machine gun. He had personally killed 40 Germans and wounded many more. Capt. Galt pitted his judgment and superb courage against overwhelming odds, exemplifying the highest measure of devotion to his country and the finest traditions of the U.S. Army.

2726 ◆ *GAMMON, ARCHER T.

Rank: Staff Sergeant
Service: U.S. Army
Birthday: 11 September 1918
Place of Birth: Chatham, Pittsylvania County, Virginia
Date of Death: 11 January 1945
Cemetery: Mountain View Cemetery—Danville, Virginia
Entered Service at: Roanoke, Roanoke County, Virginia
Unit: Company A, 9th Armored Infantry Battalion, 6th Armored Division
Served as: Squad Leader
Battle or Place of Action: near Bastogne, Belgium
Date of Action: 11 January 1945
G.O. Number, Date: 18, 13 February 1946
Citation: He charged 30 yards through hip-deep snow to knock out a machine gun and its three-man crew with grenades, saving his platoon from being decimated and allowing it to continue its advance from an open field into some nearby woods. The platoon's advance through the woods had only begun when a machine gun supported by riflemen opened fire and a Tiger Royal tank sent 88-mm shells screaming at the unit from the left flank. S/Sgt. Gammon, disregarding all thoughts of personal safety, rushed forward, then cut to the left, crossing the width of a platoon's skirmish line in an attempt to get within grenade range of the tank and its protecting foot troops. Intense fire was concentrated on him by riflemen and the machine gun emplaced near the tank. He charged the automatic weapon, wiped out its crew of four with grenades, and, with supreme daring, advanced to within 25 yards of the armored vehicle, killing two hostile infantrymen with rifle fire as he moved forward. The tank had started to withdraw, backing a short distance, then firing, backing some more, and then stopping to blast out another round, when the man whose singlehanded relentless attack had put

the ponderous machine on the defensive was struck and instantly killed by a direct hit from the Tiger Royal's heavy gun. By his intrepidity and extreme devotion to the task of driving the enemy back no matter what the odds, S/Sgt. Gammon cleared the woods of German forces, for the tank continued to withdraw, leaving open the path for the gallant squad leader's platoon.

2727 ◆ GARCIA, MARCARIO

Rank: Staff Sergeant (rank at time of action: Private)
Service: U.S. Army
Birthday: 2 January 1920
Place of Birth: Villa de Castano, Mexico
Date of Death: 24 December 1972
Cemetery: Houston National Cemetery (HA-1) (MH)—Houston, Texas
Entered Service at: Sugar Land, Fort Bend County, Texas
Unit: Company B, 22d Infantry, 4th Infantry Division
Served as: Squad Leader
Battle or Place of Action: near Grosshau, Germany
Date of Action: 27 November 1944
G.O. Number, Date: 74, 1 September 1945
Date of Presentation: 23 August 1945
Place of Presentation: The White House, presented by Pres. Harry S. Truman
Citation: While an acting squad leader of Company B, 22d Infantry, on 27 November 1944, near Grosshau, Germany, he singlehandedly assaulted two enemy machine-gun emplacements. Attacking prepared positions on a wooded hill, which could be approached only through meager cover, his company was pinned down by intense machine-gun fire and subjected to a concentrated artillery and mortar barrage. Although painfully wounded, he refused to be evacuated and on his own initiative crawled forward alone until he reached a position near an enemy emplacement. Hurling grenades, he boldly assaulted the position, destroyed the gun, and with his rifle killed three of the enemy who attempted to escape. When he rejoined his company, a second machine gun opened fire and again the intrepid soldier went forward, utterly disregarding his own safety. He stormed the position and destroyed the gun, killed three more Germans, and captured four prisoners. He fought on with his unit until the objective was taken and only then did he permit himself to be removed for medical care. S/Sgt. (then Pvt.) Garcia's conspicuous heroism, his inspiring, courageous conduct, and his complete disregard for his personal safety wiped out two enemy emplacements and enabled his company to advance and secure its objective.

2728 ◆ GARMAN, HAROLD ALVA

Rank: Private (highest rank: Technician Fifth Grade)
Service: U.S. Army
Birthday: 26 February 1918
Place of Birth: Fairfield, Wayne County, Illinois
Date of Death: 13 August 1992
Place of Death: Albion, Illinois
Cemetery: Samaria Baptist Church Cemetery—Albion, Illinois
Entered Service at: Albion, Edwards County, Illinois
Unit: Company B, 5th Medical Battalion, 10th Infantry, 5th Infantry Division
Served as: Litter Bearer
Battle or Place of Action: near Montereau, France
Date of Action: 25 August 1944
G.O. Number, Date: 20, 29 March 1945
Date of Presentation: 6 April 1945
Place of Presentation: Munetx, Germany, presented by Gen. George S. Patton
Citation: For conspicuous gallantry and intrepidity at the risk of his life above and beyond the call of duty. On 25 August 1944, in the vicinity of Montereau, France, the enemy was sharply contesting any enlargement of the bridgehead which our forces had established on the northern bank of the Seine River in this sector. Casualties were being evacuated to the southern shore in assault boats paddled by litter bearers from a medical battalion. Pvt. Garman, also a litter bearer in this battalion, was working on the friendly shore carrying the wounded from the boats to waiting ambulances. As one boatload of wounded reached midstream, a German machine gun suddenly opened fire upon it from a commanding position on the northern bank 100 yards away. All of the men in the boat immediately took to the water except one man who was so badly wounded he could not rise from his litter. Two other patients who were unable to swim because of their wounds clung to the sides of the boat. Seeing the extreme danger of these patients, Pvt. Garman without a moment's hesitation plunged into the Seine. Swimming directly into a hail of machine-gun bullets, he rapidly reached the assault boat and then while still under accurately aimed fire towed the boat with great effort to the southern shore. This soldier's moving heroism not only saved the lives of the three patients but so inspired his comrades that additional assault boats were immediately procured and the evacuation of the wounded resumed. Pvt. Garman's great courage and his heroic devotion to the highest tenets of the Medical Corps may be written with great pride in the annals of the corps.

2729 ◆ GARY, DONALD ARTHUR

Rank: Lieutenant (j.g.) (highest rank: Commander)
Service: U.S. Navy
Birthday: 23 July 1903
Place of Birth: Findlay, Hancock County, Ohio
Date of Death: 9 April 1977
Place of Death: Long Beach, California
Cemetery: Fort Rosecrans National Cemetery (A-13-B) (MH)—San Diego, California
Entered Service at: Ohio
Unit: U.S.S. *Franklin*
Served as: Engineering Officer
Battle or Place of Action: near Kobe, Japan
Date of Action: 19 March 1945
Date of Presentation: 23 January 1946
Place of Presentation: The White House, presented By Pres. Harry S. Truman

Citation: For conspicuous gallantry and intrepidity at the risk of life above and beyond the call of duty as an engineering officer attached to the U.S.S. Franklin when that vessel was fiercely attacked by enemy aircraft during operations against the Japanese Home Islands near Kobe, Japan, 19 March 1945. Stationed on the third deck when the ship was rocked by a series of violent explosions set off in her own ready bombs, rockets and ammunition by the hostile attack, Lt. Gary unhesitantingly risked his life to assist several hundred men trapped in a messing compartment filled with smoke, and with no apparent egress. As the imperiled men below decks became increasingly panic stricken under the raging fury of incessant explosions, he confidently assured them he would find a means of effecting their release and groping through the dark, debris-filled corridors, ultimately discovered an escapeway. Staunchly determined, he struggled back to the messing compartment three despite menacing flames, flooding water, and the ominous threat of sudden additional explosions, on each occasion calmly leading his men through the blanketing pall of smoke until the lst one had been saved. Selfless in his concern for his ship and his fellows, he constantly rallied others about him, repeatedly organized and led firefighting parties into the blazing inferno on the flight deck, and, when firerooms 1 and 2 were found to be inoperable, entered No. 3 fireroom and directed the raising of steam in one boiler in the face of extreme difficulty and hazard. An inspiring and courageous leader, Lt. Gary rendered self-sacrificing service under the most perilous conditions and, by his heroic initiative, fortitude, and valor, was responsible for the saving of several hundred lives. His conduct throughout reflects the highest credit upon himself and upon the U.S. Naval Service.

2730 ✳ GERSTUNG, ROBERT E.

Rank: Technical Sergeant
Service: U.S. Army
Birthday: 6 August 1915
Place of Birth: Chicago, Cook County, Illinois
Date of Death: 17 June 1979
Cemetery: Arlington National Cemetery (66-6152) (MH)—Arlington, Virginia
Entered Service at: Chicago, Cook County, Illinois
Unit: Company H, 313th Infantry, 79th Infantry Division
Served as: Squad Leader
Battle or Place of Action: Siegfried Line, near Berg, Germany
Date of Action: 19 December 1944
G.O. Number, Date: 75, 5 September 1945
Date of Presentation: 23 August 1945
Place of Presentation: The White House, presented by Pres. Harry S. Truman
Citation: On 19 December 1944 he was ordered with his heavy machine-gun squad to the support of an infantry company attacking the outer defenses of the Siegfried line near Berg, Germany. For eight hours he maintained a position made almost untenable by the density of artillery and mortar fire concentrated upon it and the proximity of enemy troops who threw hand grenades into the emplacement. While all

other members of his squad became casualties, he remained at his gun. When he ran out of ammunition, he fearlessly dashed across bullet-swept, open terrain to secure a new supply from a disabled friendly tank. A fierce barrage pierced the water jacket of his gun, but he continued to fire until the weapon overheated and jammed. Instead of withdrawing, he crawled 50 yards across coverless ground to another of his company's machine guns which had been silenced when its entire crew was killed. He continued to man this gun, giving support vitally needed by the infantry. At one time he came under direct fire from a hostile tank, which shot the glove from his hand with an armor-piercing shell but could not drive him from his position or stop his shooting. When the American forces were ordered to retire to their original positions, he remained at his gun, giving the only covering fire. Finally withdrawing, he cradled the heavy weapon in his left arm, slung a belt of ammunition over his shoulder, and walked to the rear, loosing small bursts at the enemy as he went. One hundred yards from safety, he was struck in the leg by a mortar shell; but, with a supreme effort, he crawled the remaining distance, dragging along the gun which had served him and his comrades so well. By his remarkable perseverance, indomitable courage, and heroic devotion to his task in the face of devastating fire, T/Sgt. Gerstung gave his fellow soldiers powerful support in their encounter with formidable enemy forces.

2731 ◆ *GIBSON, ERIC GUNNAR

Rank: Technician Fifth Grade
Service: U.S. Army
Birthday: 3 October 1919
Place of Birth: Nysund, Sweden
Date of Death: 28 January 1944
Cemetery: Nora Cemetery—Rice Lake, Wisconsin
Entered Service at: Chicago, Cook County, Illinois
Unit: Company I, 30th Infantry, 3d Infantry Division
Served as: Company Cook
Battle or Place of Action: near Isola Bella, Italy
Date of Action: 28 January 1944
G.O. Number, Date: 74, 11 September 1944
Date of Presentation: 15 September 1944
Place of Presentation: Camp McCoy, Wisconsin, presented to his parents
Citation: For conspicuous gallantry and intrepidity at the risk of life above and beyond the call of duty. On 28 January 1944, near Isola Bella, Italy, Tech. 5th Grade Gibson, company cook, led a squad of replacements through their initial baptism of fire, destroyed four enemy positions, killed five, and captured two German soldiers, and secured the left flank of his company during an attack on a strongpoint. Placing himself 50 yards in front of his new men, Gibson advanced down the wide stream ditch known as the Fossa Femminamorta, keeping pace with the advance of his company. An enemy soldier allowed Tech. 5th Grade Gibson to come within 20 yards of his concealed position and then opened fire on him with a machine pistol. Despite the stream of automatic fire which barely missed him, Gibson charged the position, firing his submachine gun every few steps.

Reaching the position, Gibson fired point-blank at his opponent, killing him. An artillery concentration fell in and around the ditch; the concussion from one shell knocked him flat. As he got to his feet Gibson was fired on by two soldiers armed with a machine pistol and a rifle from a position only 75 yards distant. Gibson immediately raced toward the foe. Halfway to the position a machine gun opened fire on him. Bullets came within inches of his body, yet Gibson never paused in his forward movement. He killed one and captured the other soldier. Shortly after, when he was fired upon by a heavy machine gun 200 yards down the ditch, Gibson crawled back to his squad and ordered it to lay down a base of fire while he flanked the emplacement. Despite all warnings, Gibson crawled 125 yards through an artillery concentration and the crossfire of two machine guns which showered dirt over his body, threw two hand grenades into the emplacement, and charged it with his submachine gun, killing two of the enemy and capturing a third. Before leading his men around a bend in the stream ditch, Gibson went forward alone to reconnoiter. Hearing an exchange of machine pistol and submachine-gun fire, Gibson's squad went forward to find that its leader had run 35 yards toward an outpost, killed the machine pistol man, and had himself been killed while firing at the Germans.

2732 ◆ *GILMORE, HOWARD WALTER

Rank: Commander
Service: U.S. Navy
Birthday: 29 September 1902
Place of Birth: Selma, Dallas County, Alabama
Date of Death: 7 February 1943
Cemetery: A.B.M.C. Manila Cemetery (Wall of the Missing)—Manila, Philippine Islands
Entered Service at: Louisiana
Unit: U.S.S. *Growler*
Served as: Commanding Officer
Battle or Place of Action: Southwest Pacific
Date of Action: 10 January-7 February 1943
Date of Presentation: 13 July 1943
Place of Presentation: New Orleans, Louisiana, presented by Rear Adm. A.C. Bennett to his Widow
Citation: For distinguished gallantry and valor above and beyond the call of duty as commanding officer of the U.S.S. *Growler* during her fourth war patrol in the southwest Pacific from 10 January to 7 February 1943. Boldly striking at the enemy in spite of continuous hostile air and anti-submarine patrols, Comdr. Gilmore sank one Japanese freighter and damaged another by torpedo fire, successfully evading severe depth charges following each attack. In the darkness of night on 7 February, an enemy gunboat closed range and prepared to ram the *Growler*. Comdr. Gilmore daringly maneuvered to avoid the crash and rammed the attacker instead, ripping into her port side at 17 knots and bursting wide her plates. In the terrific fire of the sinking gunboat's heavy machine guns, Comdr. Gilmore calmly gave the order to clear the bridge, and refusing safety for himself, remained on deck while his men preceded him below. Struck down by the fusillade of bullets and having done his utmost against the enemy, in his final living moments, Comdr. Gilmore gave his last order to

the officer of the deck, "Take her down." The *Growler* dived; seriously damaged but under control, she was brought safely to port by her well-trained crew inspired by the courageous fighting spirit of their dead captain.

2733 ◆ *GONSALVES, HAROLD

Rank: Private First Class
Service: U.S. Marine Corps Reserve
Birthday: 28 January 1926
Place of Birth: Alameda, Alameda County, California
Date of Death: 15 April 1945
Place of Death: Okinawa Shima, Ryukyu Islands
Cemetery: Golden Gate National Cemetery (B-61) (MH)—San Bruno, California
Entered Service at: California
Unit: Battery L, 4th Battalion, 15th Marines, 6th Marine Division
Served as: Acting Scout Sergeant
Battle or Place of Action: Okinawa Shima, Ryukyu Islands
Date of Action: 15 April 1945
Citation: For conspicuous gallantry and intrepidity at the risk of his life above and beyond the call of duty while serving as acting scout sergeant with the 4th Battalion, 15th Marines, 6th Marine Division, during action against enemy Japanese forces on Okinawa Shima in the Ryukyu Chain, 15 April 1945. Undaunted by the powerfully organized opposition encountered on Motobu Peninsula during the fierce assault waged by his battalion against the Japanese stronghold at Mount Yaetake, Pfc. Gonsalves repeatedly braved the terrific enemy bombardment to aid his forward observation team in directing well-placed artillery fire. When his commanding officer determined to move into the front lines in order to register a more effective bombardment in the enemy's defensive position, he unhesitatingly advanced uphill with the officer and another marine despite a slashing barrage of enemy mortar and rifle fire. As they reached the front and a Japanese grenade fell close within the group, instantly Pfc. Gonsalves dived on the deadly missile, absorbing the exploding charge in his own body and thereby protecting the others from serious and perhaps fatal wounds. Stouthearted and indomitable, Pfc. Gonsalves readily yielded his own chances of survival that his fellow marines might carry on the relentless battle against a fanatic enemy, and his cool decision, prompt action, and valiant spirit of self-sacrifice in the face of certain death reflect the highest credit upon himself and upon the U.S. Naval Service.

2734 ◆ *GONZALES, DAVID M.

Rank: Private First Class
Service: U.S. Army
Birthday: 9 June 1923
Place of Birth: Pacoima, Los Angeles County, California
Date of Death: 25 April 1945
Cemetery: Calvary Cemetery—Los Angeles, California
Entered Service at: Pacoima, Los Angeles County, California
Unit: Company A, 127th Infantry, 32d Infantry Division

Battle or Place of Action: Hill 507, Villa Verde Trail, Luzon, Philippine Islands
Date of Action: 25 April 1945
G.O. Number, Date: 115, 8 December 1945
Citation: He was pinned down with his company. As enemy fire swept the area, making any movement extremely hazardous, a 500-pound bomb smashed into the company's perimeter, burying five men with its explosion. Pfc. Gonzales, without hesitation, seized an entrenching tool and under a hail of fire crawled 15 yards to his entombed comrades, where his commanding officer, who had also rushed forward, was beginning to dig the men out. Nearing his goal, he saw the officer struck and instantly killed by machine-gun fire. Undismayed, he set to work swiftly and surely with his hands and entrenching tool while enemy sniper and machine-gun bullets struck all about him. He succeeded in digging one of the men out of the pile of rock and sand. To dig faster he stood up regardless of the greater danger from so exposing himself. He extricated a second man, and then another. As he completed the liberation of the third, he was hit and mortally wounded, but the comrades for whom he so gallantly gave his life were safely evacuated. Pfc. Gonzales' valiant and intrepid conduct exemplifies the highest traditions of the military service.

2735 ◆ GORDON, NATHAN GREEN

Rank: Lieutenant (highest rank: Lieutenant Commander)
Service: U.S. Navy
Birthday: 4 September 1916
Place of Birth: Morrilton, Conway County, Arkansas
Entered Service at: Morrilton, Conway County, Arkansas
Unit: Patrol Squadron 34 (VPB-34), Naval Air Base, Samari Island, New Guinea
Served as: Commander/Pilot of a Catalina Patrol Plane
Battle or Place of Action: Kavieng Harbor, New Ireland, Bismark Sea, southwestern Pacific
Date of Action: 15 February 1944
Date of Presentation: 13 July 1944
Place of Presentation: Brisbane, Australia, presented by Vice Adm. Thomas C. Kincaid
Citation: For extraordinary heroism above and beyond the call of duty as commander of a Catalina patrol plane in rescuing personnel of the U.S. Army 5th Air Force shot down in combat over Kavieng Harbor in the Bismarck Sea, 15 February 1944. On air alert in the vicinity of Vitu Islands, Lt. (then Lt. [jg]) Gordon unhesitatingly responded to a report of the crash and flew boldly into the harbor, defying close-range fire from enemy shore guns to make three separate landings in full view of the Japanese and pick up nine men, several of them injured. With his cumbersome flying boat dangerously overloaded, he made a brilliant takeoff despite heavy swells and almost total absence of wind and set a course for base, only to receive the report of another group stranded in a rubber liferaft 600 yards from the enemy shore. Promptly turning back, he again risked his life to set his plane down under direct fire of the heaviest defenses of Kavieng and take aboard six more survivors, cooly making his fourth dexterous takeoff with 15 rescued officers and men. By his exceptional daring, personal valor, and incomparable airmanship under

most perilous conditions, Lt. Gordon prevented certain death or capture of our airmen by the Japanese.

2736 ◆ *GOTT, DONALD JOSEPH

Rank: First Lieutenant
Service: U.S. Army Air Corps
Birthday: 3 June 1923
Place of Birth: Arnett, Ellis County, Oklahoma
Date of Death: 9 November 1944
Place of Death: Near Saarbrucken, Germany
Cemetery: Harmon Cemetery—Harmon, Oklahoma
Entered Service at: Arnett, Ellis County, Oklahoma
Unit: 729th Bombardment Squadron, 452d Bombardment Group, 8th Air Force
Served as: Pilot of a B-17
Battle or Place of Action: Saarbrucken, Germany
Date of Action: 9 November 1944
G.O. Number, Date: 38, 16 May 1945
Citation: On a bombing run upon the marshaling yards at Saarbrucken, a B-17 aircraft piloted by 1st Lt. Gott was seriously damaged by antiaircraft fire. Three of the aircraft's engines were damaged beyond control and on fire; dangerous flames from the No. 4 engine were leaping back as far as the tail assembly. Flares in the cockpit were ignited and a fire raged therein, which was further increased by free-flowing fluid from two damaged hydraulic lines. The interphone system was rendered useless. In addition to these serious mechanical difficulties the engineer was wounded in the leg and the radio operator's arm was severed below the elbow. Suffering from intense pain, despite the application of a tourniquet, the radio operator fell unconscious. Faced with the imminent explosion of his aircraft and death to his entire crew, mere seconds before bombs away on the target, 1st Lt. Gott and his copilot conferred. Something had to be done immediately to save the life of the wounded radio operator. The lack of a static line and the thought that his unconscious body striking the ground in unknown territory would not bring immediate medical attention forced a quick decision. First Lt. Gott and his copilot decided to fly the flaming aircraft to friendly territory and then attempt to crash land. Bombs were released on the target and the crippled aircraft proceeded alone to Allied-controlled territory. When that had been reached, 1st Lt. Gott had the copilot personally inform all crewmembers to bail out. The copilot chose to remain with 1st Lt. Gott in order to assist in landing the bomber. With only one normally functioning engine, and with the danger of explosion much greater, the aircraft banked into an open field, and when it was at an altitude of 100 feet it exploded, crashed, exploded again, and then disintegrated. All three crew members were instantly killed. First Lt. Gott's loyalty to his crew, his determination to accomplish the task set forth to him, and his deed of knowingly performing what may have been his last service to his country was an example of valor at its highest.

2737 ◆ *GRABIARZ, WILLIAM J.

Rank: Private First Class
Service: U.S. Army

Birthday: 1925
Place of Birth: Buffalo, Erie County, New York
Date of Death: 23 February 1945
Place of Death: Manila, Philippine Islands
Cemetery: St. Stanislaws Cemetery—Cheektowaga, New York
Entered Service at: Buffalo, Erie County, New York
Unit: Troop E, 5th Cavalry, 1st Cavalry Division
Served as: Scout
Battle or Place of Action: Manila, Luzon, Philippine Islands
Date of Action: 23 February 1945
G.O. Number, Date: 115, 8 December 1945
Citation: He was a scout when the unit advanced with tanks along a street in Manila, Luzon, Philippine Islands. Without warning, enemy machine guns and rifle fire from concealed positions in the Customs building swept the street, striking down the troop commander and driving his men to cover. As the officer lay in the open road, unable to move and completely exposed to the point-blank enemy fire, Pfc. Grabiarz voluntarily ran from behind a tank to carry him to safety, but was himself wounded in the shoulder. Ignoring both the pain in his injured, useless arm and his comrades' shouts to seek the cover which was only a few yards distant, the valiant rescuer continued his efforts to drag his commander out of range. Finding this impossible, he rejected the opportunity to save himself and deliberately covered the officer with his own body to form a human shield, calling as he did so for a tank to maneuver into position between him and the hostile emplacement. The enemy riddled him with concentrated fire before the tank could interpose itself. Our troops found that he had been successful in preventing bullets from striking his leader, who survived. Through his magnificent sacrifice in gallantly giving his life to save that of his commander, Pfc. Grabiarz provided an outstanding and lasting inspiration to his fellow soldiers.

2738 ◆ *GRAY, ROSS FRANKLIN

Rank: Sergeant
Service: U.S. Marine Corps Reserve
Birthday: 1 August 1920
Place of Birth: Marvel Valley, Alabama
Date of Death: 27 February 1945
Cemetery: Ada Chapel Cemetery (MH)—West Blocton, Alabama
Entered Service at: Alabama
Unit: Company A, 1st Battalion, 25th Marines, 4th Marine Division
Served as: Platoon Sergeant
Battle or Place of Action: Iwo Jima, Volcano Islands
Date of Action: 21 February 1945
Citation: For conspicuous gallantry and intrepidity at the risk of his life above and beyond the call of duty as a platoon sergeant attached to Company A, 1st Battalion, 25th Marines, 4th Marine Division, in action against enemy Japanese forces on Iwo Jima, Volcano Islands, 21 February 1945. Shrewdly gaging the tactical situation when his platoon was held up by a sudden barrage of hostile grenades while advancing toward the high ground northeast of Airfield No. 1, Sgt. Gray promptly organized the withdrawal of his men from enemy grenade range, quickly moved forward alone to reconnoiter, and discovered a heavily mined area extending along the front of a strong network of emplacements joined by covered trenches. Although assailed by furious gunfire, he cleared a path leading through the minefield to one of the fortifications, then returned to the platoon position and, informing his leader of the serious situation, volunteered to initiate an attack under cover of three fellow marines. Alone and unarmed but carrying a huge satchel charge, he crept up on the Japanese emplacement, boldly hurled the short-fused explosive, and sealed the entrance. Instantly taken under machine-gun fire from a second entrance to the same position, he unhesitatingly braved the increasingly vicious fusillades to crawl back for another charge, returned to his objective, and blasted the second opening, thereby demolishing the position. Repeatedly covering the ground between the savagely defended enemy fortifications and his platoon area, he systematically approached, attacked, and withdrew under blanketing fire to destroy a total of six Japanese positions, more than 25 troops, and a quantity of vital ordnance gear and ammunition. Stouthearted and indomitable, Sgt. Gray had singlehandedly overcome a strong enemy garrison and had completely disarmed a large minefield before finally rejoining his unit. By his great personal valor, daring tactics, and tenacious perseverance in the face of extreme peril, he had contributed materially to the fulfillment of his company's mission. His gallant conduct throughout enhanced and sustained the highest traditions of the U.S. Naval Service.

2739 ◆ GREGG, STEPHEN RAYMOND

Rank: Second Lieutenant (rank at time of action: Technical Sergeant)
Service: U.S. Army
Birthday: 1 September 1914
Place of Birth: New York, New York
Entered Service at: Bayonne, Hudson County, New Jersey
Unit: Weapons Platoon, Company L, 143d Infantry, 36th Infantry Division
Served as: Platoon Sergeant
Battle or Place of Action: near Montelimar, France
Date of Action: 27 August 1944
G.O. Number, Date: 31, 17 April 1945
Date of Presentation: 14 March 1945
Place of Presentation: Berholsheim, France, presented by Lt. Gen. Alexander M. Patch III
Citation: For conspicuous gallantry and intrepidity at risk of life above and beyond the call of duty on 27 August 1944, in the vicinity of Montelimar, France. As his platoon advanced upon the enemy positions, the leading scout was fired upon and 2d Lt. Gregg (then a T/Sgt.) immediately put his machine guns into action to cover the advance of the riflemen. The Germans, who were at close range, threw hand grenades at the riflemen, killing some and wounding seven. Each time a medical aidman attempted to reach the wounded, the Germans fired at him. Realizing the seriousness of the situation, 2d Lt. Gregg took one of the light .30-caliber machine guns and, firing from the hip, started boldly up the

hill with the medical aidman following him. Although the enemy was throwing hand grenades at him, 2d Lt. Gregg remained and fired into the enemy positions while the medical aidman removed the seven wounded men to safety. When 2d Lt. Gregg had expended all his ammunition, he was covered by four Germans who ordered him to surrender. Since the attention of most of the Germans had been diverted by watching this action, friendly riflemen were able to maneuver into firing positions. One, seeing 2d Lt. Gregg's situation, opened fire on his captors. The four Germans hit the ground and thereupon 2d Lt. Gregg recovered a machine pistol from one of the Germans and managed to escape to his other machine-gun positions. He manned a gun, firing at his captors, killed one of them and wounded the other. This action so discouraged the Germans that the platoon was able to continue its advance up the hill to achieve its objective. The following morning, just prior to daybreak, the Germans launched a strong attack, supported by tanks, in an attempt to drive Company L from the hill. As these tanks moved along the valley and their foot troops advanced up the hill, 2d Lt. Gregg immediately ordered his mortars into action. During the day, by careful observation, he was able to direct effective fire on the enemy, inflicting heavy casualties. By late afternoon he had directed 600 rounds when his communication to the mortars was knocked out. Without hesitation he started checking his wires, although the area was under heavy enemy small-arms and artillery fire. When he was within 100 yards of his mortar position, one of his men informed him that the section had been captured and the Germans were using the mortars to fire on the company. Second Lt. Gregg with this man and another nearby rifleman started for the gun position where he could see five Germans firing his mortars. He ordered the two men to cover him, crawled up, threw a hand grenade into the position, and then charged it. The hand grenade killed one, injured two; 2d Lt. Gregg took the other two prisoners, and put his mortars back into action.

2740 ◆ *GRUENNERT, KENNETH E.

Rank: Sergeant
Service: U.S. Army
Birthday: 19 November 1922
Place of Birth: Helenville, Jefferson County, Wisconsin
Date of Death: 24 December 1942
Place of Death: near Buna, New Guinea
Cemetery: Evergreen Lutheran Cemetery—Helenville, Wisconsin
Entered Service at: Helenville, Jefferson County, Wisconsin
Unit: Company L, 127th Infantry, 32d Infantry Division
Battle or Place of Action: near Buna, New Guinea
Date of Action: 24 December 1942
G.O. Number, Date: 66, 11 October 1943
Place of Presentation: The Medal was sent to the parents at their request in the mail
Citation: For conspicuous gallantry and intrepidity in action above and beyond the call of duty. On 24 December 1942, near Buna, New Guinea, Sgt. Gruennert was second in command of a platoon with a misssion to drive through the enemy lines to the beach 600 yards ahead. Within 150 yards

of the objective, the platoon encountered two hostile pillboxes. Sgt. Gruennert advanced alone on the first and put it out of action with hand grenades and rifle fire, killing three of the enemy. Seriously wounded in the shoulder, he bandaged his wound under cover of the pillbox, refusing to withdraw to the aid station and leave his men. He then, with undiminished daring, and under extremely heavy fire, attacked the second pillbox. As he neared it he threw grenades which forced the enemy out where they were easy targets for his platoon. Before the leading elements of his platoon could reach him he was shot by enemy snipers. His inspiring valor cleared the way for his platoon which was the first to attain the beach in this successful effort to split the enemy position.

2741 ◆ *GURKE, HENRY

Rank: Private First Class
Service: U.S. Marine Corps
Birthday: 6 November 1922
Place of Birth: Neche, Pembina County, North Dakota
Date of Death: 9 November 1943
Cemetery: Neche Union Cemetery (MH)—Neche, North Dakota
Entered Service at: North Dakota
Unit: 3d Marine Raider Battalion
Battle or Place of Action: near Empress Augusta Bay, Bougainville, Solomon Islands
Date of Action: 9 November 1943
Citation: For extraordinary heroism and courage above and beyond the call of duty while attached to the 3d Marine Raider Battalion during action against enemy Japanese forces in the Solomon Islands area on 9 November 1943. While his platoon was engaged in the defense of a vital road block near Empress Augusta Bay on Bougainville Island, Pfc. Gurke, in company with another marine, was delivering a fierce stream of fire against the main vanguard of the Japanese. Concluding from the increasing ferocity of grenade barrages that the enemy was determined to annihilate their small, two-man foxhole, he resorted to a bold and desperate measure for holding out despite the torrential hail of shells. When a Japanese grenade dropped squarely into the foxhole, Pfc. Gurke, mindful that his companion manned an automatic weapon of superior firepower and therefore could provide more effective resistance, thrust him roughly aside and flung his own body over the missile to smother the explosion. With unswerving devotion to duty and superb valor, Pfc. Gurke sacrificed himself in order that his comrade might live to carry on the fight. He gallantly gave his life in the service of his country.

2742 ◆ HALL, GEORGE JOHN

Rank: Staff Sergeant
Service: U.S. Army
Birthday: 9 January 1920
Place of Birth: Stoneham, Middlesex County, Massachusetts
Date of Death: 16 February 1946
Place of Death: West Roxbury, Massachusetts
Cemetery: St. Patrick's Cemetery (MH)—Stoneham, Massachusetts

Entered Service at: Boston, Suffolk County, Massachusetts
Unit: Company B, 135th Infantry, 34th Infantry Division
Battle or Place of Action: near Anzio, Italy
Date of Action: 23 May 1944
G.O. Number, Date: 24, 6 April 1945
Date of Presentation: 13 April 1945
Place of Presentation: Boston Common, Massachusetts, presented by Maj. Gen. Sherman Miles
Citation: For conspicuous gallantry and intrepidity at risk of life above and beyond the call of duty. Attacking across flat, open terrain under direct enemy observation, S/Sgt. Hall's company was pinned down by grazing fire from three enemy machine guns and harassing sniper fire. S/Sgt. Hall volunteered to eliminate these obstacles in the path of advance. Crawling along a plowed furrow through furious machine-gun fire, he made his way to a point within hand-grenade range of one of the enemy positions. He pounded the enemy with four hand grenades, and when the smoke had died away, S/Sgt. Hall and two dead Germans occupied the position, while four of the enemy were crawling back to our lines as prisoners. Discovering a quantity of German potato-masher grenades in the position, S/Sgt. Hall engaged the second enemy nest in a deadly exchange of grenades. Each time he exposed himself to throw a grenade the Germans fired machine-gun bursts at him. The vicious duel finally ended in S/Sgt. Hall's favor with five of the enemy surrendered and five others lay dead. Turning his attention to the third machine gun, S/Sgt. Hall left his position and crawled along a furrow, the enemy firing frantically in a effort to halt him. As he neared his final objective, an enemy artillery concentration fell on the area, and S/Sgt. Hall's right leg was severed by a shell burst. With two enemy machine guns eliminated, his company was able to flank the third and continue its advance without incurring excessive casualties. S/Sgt. Hall's fearlessness, his determined fighting spirit, and his prodigious combat skill exemplify the heroic tradition of the American infantryman.

2743 ◆ *HALL, LEWIS R.

Rank: Technician Fifth Grade
Service: U.S. Army
Birthday: 2 March 1895
Place of Birth: Bloom, Ohio
Date of Death: 10 January 1943
Place of Death: Guadalcanal, Mount Austen, Solomon Islands
Cemetery: Glenrest Memorial Estate (MH)—Reynoldsburg, Ohio
Entered Service at: Columbus, Franklin County, Ohio
Unit: Company M, 35th Infantry, 25th Infantry Division
Served as: Squad Leader
Battle or Place of Action: Mount Austen, Guadalcanal, Solomon Islands
Date of Action: 10 January 1943
G.O. Number, Date: 28, 5 June 1943
Citation: For gallantry and intrepidity above and beyond the call of duty. As leader of a machine-gun squad charged with the protection of other battalion units, his group was attacked by a superior number of Japanese, his gunner killed, his assistant gunner wounded, and an adjoining guncrew put out of action. Ordered to withdraw from his hazardous position, he refused to retire but rushed forward to the idle gun and with the aid of another soldier who joined him and held up the machine gun by the tripod to increase its field of action he opened fire and inflicted heavy casualties upon the enemy. While so engaged both these gallant soldiers were killed, but their sturdy defense was a decisive factor in the following success of the attacking battalion.

2744 ◆ HALL, WILLIAM EDWARD

Rank: Lieutenant (j.g.) (highest rank: Lieutenant Commander)
Service: U.S. Navy
Birthday: 31 October 1913
Place of Birth: Storrs, Carbon County, Utah
Entered Service at: Mohrland, Emery County, Utah
Unit: Scouting Squadron 2, Air Group 2, U.S.S. *Lexington*
Served as: Pilot of a Douglas Dauntless
Battle or Place of Action: Coral Sea
Date of Action: 7-8 May 1942
Date of Presentation: 22 November 1942
Place of Presentation: San Diego, California, presented by Vice Adm. Ephraim P. Holmes
Citation: For extreme courage and conspicuous heroism in combat above and beyond the call of duty as pilot of a scouting plane in action against enemy Japanese forces in the Coral Sea on 7 and 8 May 1942. In a resolute and determined attack on 7 May, Lt. (j.g.) Hall dived his plane at an enemy Japanese aircraft carrier, contributing materially to the destruction of that vessel. On 8 May, facing heavy and fierce fighter opposition, he again displayed extraordinary skill as an airman and the aggressive spirit of a fighter in repeated and effectively executed counterattacks against a superior number of enemy planes in which three enemy aircraft were destroyed. Though seriously wounded in this engagement, Lt. (j.g.) Hall, maintaining the fearless and indomitable tactics pursued throughout these actions, succeeded in landing his plane safely.

2745 ◆ *HALLMAN, SHERWOOD H.

Rank: Staff Sergeant
Service: U.S. Army
Birthday: 29 October 1913
Place of Birth: Spring City, Chester County, Pennsylvania
Date of Death: 14 September 1944
Cemetery: A.B.M.C. Brittany Cemetery (M-5-11)—St. James, France
Entered Service at: Spring City, Chester County, Pennsylvania
Unit: Company F, 2d Battalion, 175th Infantry, 29th Infantry Division
Served as: Squad Leader
Battle or Place of Action: Brest, Brittany, France
Date of Action: 13 September 1944
G.O. Number, Date: 31, 17 April 1945

Citation: For conspicuous gallantry and intrepidity at risk of his life above and beyond the call of duty. On 13 September 1944, in Brittany, France, the 2d Battalion in its attack on the fortified city of Brest was held up by a strongly defended enemy position which had prevented its advance despite repeated attacks extending over a three-day period. Finally, Company F advanced to within several hundred yards of the enemy position but was again halted by intense fire. Realizing that the position must be neutralized without delay, S/Sgt. Hallman ordered his squad to cover his movements with fire while he advanced alone to a point from which he could make the assault. Without hesitating, S/Sgt. Hallman leaped over a hedgerow into a sunken road, the central point of the German defenses which was known to contain an enemy machine-gun position and at least 30 enemy riflemen. Firing his carbine and hurling grenades, S/Sgt. Hallman, unassisted, killed or wounded four of the enemy, then ordered the remainder to surrender. Immediately, 12 of the enemy surrendered and the position was shortly secured by the remainder of his company. Seeing the surrender of this position, about 75 of the enemy in the vicinity surrendered, yielding a defensive organization which the battalion with heavy supporting fires had been unable to take. This single heroic act on the part of S/Sgt. Hallman resulted in the immediate advance of the entire battalion for a distance of 2,000 yards to a position from which Fort Keranroux was captured later the same day. S/Sgt. Hallman's fighting determination and intrepidity in battle exemplify the highest tradition of the U.S. Armed Forces.

2746 ◆ *HALYBURTON JR., WILLIAM DAVID

Rank: Pharmacist's Mate Second Class
Service: U.S. Naval Reserve
Birthday: 2 August 1924
Place of Birth: Canton, Haywood County, North Carolina
Date of Death: 10 May 1945
Place of Death: Okinawa Shima, Ryukyu Islands
Cemetery: National Memorial Cemetery of the Pacific (0-274) (MH)—Honolulu, Hawaii
Entered Service at: North Carolina
Unit: 2d Battalion, 5th Marines, 1st Marine Division
Served as: Medical Corpsman
Battle or Place of Action: Okinawa Shima, Ryukyu Islands
Date of Action: 10 May 1945
Citation: For conspicuous gallantry and intrepidity at risk of his life above and beyond the call of duty while serving with a Marine Rifle Company in the 2d Battalion, 5th Marines, 1st Marine Division, during action against enemy Japanese forces on Okinawa Shima in the Ryukyu Chain, 10 May 1945. Undaunted by the deadly accuracy of Japanese counterfire as his unit pushed the attack through a strategically important draw, Halyburton unhesitatingly dashed across the draw and up the hill into an open fire-swept field where the company advance squad was suddenly pinned down under a terrific concentration of mortar, machine-gun, and sniper fire with resultant severe casualties. Moving steadily forward despite the enemy's merciless barrage, he reached the wounded marine who lay farthest away and was rendering first aid when

his patient was struck for a second time by a Japanese bullet. Instantly placing himself in the direct line of fire, he shielded the fallen fighter with his own body and staunchly continued his ministrations although constantly menaced by the slashing fury of shrapnel and bullets falling on all sides. Alert, determined, and completely unselfish in his concern for the helpless marine, he persevered in his efforts until he himself sustained mortal wounds and collapsed, heroically sacrificing himself that his comrade might live. By his outstanding valor and unwavering devotion to duty in the face of tremendous odds, Halyburton sustained and enhanced the highest traditions of the U.S. Naval Service. He gallantly gave his life in the service of his country.

2747 ◆ HAMILTON, PIERPONT MORGAN

Rank: Major (highest rank: Major General)
Service: U.S. Army Air Corps
Birthday: 3 August 1898
Place of Birth: Tuxedo Park, Orange County, New York
Date of Death: 4 March 1982
Place of Death: Los Angeles, California
Cemetery: Santa Barbara Cemetery—Santa Barbara, California
Entered Service at: New York, New York
Unit: Western Task Force
Served as: Assistant Chief of Staff for Intelligence
Battle or Place of Action: near Port Lyautey, French Morocco
Date of Action: 8 November 1942
G.O. Number, Date: 4, 23 January 1943
Citation: For conspicuous gallantry and intrepidity in action above and beyond the call of duty. On 8 November 1942, near Port Lyautey, French Morocco, Lt. Col. Hamilton volunteered to accompany Col. Demas Craw on a dangerous mission to the French commander, designed to bring about a cessation of hostilities. Driven away from the mouth of the Sebou River by heavy shelling from all sides, the landing boat was finally beached at Mehdia Plage despite continuous machine-gun fire from three low-flying hostile planes. Driven in a light truck toward French headquarters, this courageous mission encountered intermittent firing, and as it neared Port Lyautey a heavy burst of machine-gun fire was delivered upon the truck from point-blank range, killing Col. Craw instantly. Although captured immediately after this incident, Lt. Col. Hamilton completed the mission.

2748 ◆ *HAMMERBERG, OWEN FRANCIS PATRICK

Rank: Boatswain's Mate Second Class
Service: U.S. Navy
Birthday: 31 May 1920
Place of Birth: Daggett, Menominee County, Michigan
Date of Death: 17 February 1945
Place of Death: Pearl Harbor, Territory of Hawaii
Cemetery: Holy Sepulchre Cemetery (MH)—Southfield, Michigan
Entered Service at: Michigan

Served as: Diver
Battle or Place of Action: Pearl Harbor, Territory of Hawaii
Date of Action: 17 February 1945
Citation: For conspicuous gallantry and intrepidity at risk of his life above and beyond the call of duty as a diver engaged in rescue operations at West Loch, Pearl Harbor, 17 February 1945. Aware of the danger when two fellow divers were hopelessly trapped in a cave-in of steel wreckage while tunneling with jet nozzles under an LST sunk in 40 feet of water and 20 feet of mud, Hammerberg unhesitatingly went overboard in a valiant attempt to effect their rescue despite the certain hazard of additional cave-ins and the risk of fouling his lifeline on jagged pieces of steel imbedded in the shifting mud. Washing a passage through the original excavation, he reached the first of the trapped men, freed him from the wreckage, and, working desperately in pitch-black darkness, finally effected his release from fouled lines, thereby enabling him to reach the surface. Wearied but undaunted after several hours of arduous labor, Hammerberg resolved to continue his struggle to wash through the oozing submarine, subterranean mud in a determined effort to save the second diver. Venturing still farther under the buried hulk, he held tenaciously to his purpose, reaching a place immediately above the other man just as another cave-in occurred and a heavy piece of steel pinned him crosswise over his shipmate in a position which protected the man beneath from further injury while placing the full brunt of terrific presure on himself. Although he succumbed in agony 18 hours after he had gone to the aid of his fellow divers, Hammerberg, by his cool judgment, unfaltering professional skill, and consistent disregard of all personal danger in the face of tremendous odds, had contributed effectively to the saving of his two comrades. His heroic spirit of self-sacrifice throughout enhanced and sustained the highest traditions of the U.S. Naval Service. He gallantly gave his life in the service of his country.

2749 ◆ *HANSEN, DALE MERLIN

Rank: Private
Service: U.S. Marine Corps
Birthday: 13 December 1922
Place of Birth: Wisner, Cuming County, Nebraska
Date of Death: 11 May 1945
Cemetery: Wisner Cemetery (MH)—Wisner, Nebraska
Entered Service at: Nebraska
Unit: Company E, 2d Battalion, 1st Marines, 1st Marine Division
Battle or Place of Action: Okinawa Shima, Ryukyu Islands
Date of Action: 7 May 1945
Citation: For conspicuous gallantry and intrepidity at risk of his life above and beyond the call of duty while serving with Company E, 2d Battalion, 1st Marines, 1st Marine Division, in action against enemy Japanese forces on Okinawa Shima in the Ryukyu Chain, 7 May 1945. Cool and courageous in combat, Pvt. Hansen unhesitatingly took the initiative during a critical stage of the action and, armed with a rocket launcher, crawled to an exposed position where he attacked and destroyed a strategically located hostile pillbox. With his weapon subsequently destroyed by enemy fire, he seized a rifle and continued his one-man assault. Reaching the crest of a ridge, he leaped across, opened fire on six Japanese, and killed four before his rifle jammed. Attacked by the remaining two Japanese, he beat them off with the butt of his rifle and then climbed back to cover. Promptly returning with another weapon and supply of grenades, he fearlessly advanced, destroyed a strong mortar position, and annihilated eight more of the enemy. In the forefront of battle throughout this bitterly waged engagement, Pvt. Hansen, by his indomitable determination, bold tactics, and complete disregard of all personal danger, contributed essentially to the success of his company's mission and to the ultimate capture of this fiercely defended outpost of the Japanese Empire. His great personal valor in the face of extreme peril reflects the highest credit upon himself and the U.S. Naval Service.

2750 ◆ *HANSON, ROBERT MURRAY

Rank: First Lieutenant (highest rank: Captain)
Service: U.S. Marine Corps Reserve
Birthday: 4 February 1920
Place of Birth: Lucknow, India
Date of Death: 3 February 1944
Cemetery: Newton Cemetery (MH) (Marker Only)—Newton Center, Massachusetts; A.B.M.C. Manila Cemetery (Wall of the Missing)—Manila, Philippine Islands
Entered Service at: Massachusetts
Unit: Marine Fighting Squadron 215
Served as: Fighter Pilot
Battle or Place of Action: Bougainville Island, Soloman Islands & New Britain Island, Bismarck Archipelago
Date of Action: 1 November 1943—24 January 1944
Date of Presentation: 19 August 1944
Place of Presentation: Boston, Massachusetts by Maj. Gen. Lewis G. Merrit to his Mother
Citation: For conspicuous gallantry and intrepidity at risk of his life above and beyond the call of duty as fighter pilot attached to Marine Fighting Squadron 215 in action against enemy Japanese forces at Bougainville Island, 1 November 1943; and New Britain Island, 24 January 1944. Undeterred by fierce opposition, and fearless in the face of overwhelming odds, 1st Lt. Hanson fought the Japanese boldly and with daring aggressiveness. On 1 November, while flying cover for our landing operations at Empress Augusta Bay, he dauntlessly attacked six enemy torpedo bombers, forcing them to jettison their bombs and destroying one Japanese plane during the action. Cut off from his division while deep in enemy territory during a high cover flight over Simpson Harbor on 24 January, 1st Lt. Hanson waged a lone and gallant battle against hostile interceptors as they were orbiting to attack our bombers and, striking with devastating fury, brought down four Zeros and probably a fifth. Handling his plane superbly in both pursuit and attack measures, he was a master of individual air combat, accounting for a total of 25 Japanese aircraft in this theater of war. His great personal valor and invincible fighting spirit were in keeping with the highest traditions of the U.S. Naval Service.

2751 ◆ *HARMON, ROY W.

Rank: Sergeant
Service: U.S. Army
Place of Birth: Talala, Rogers County, Oklahoma
Date of Death: 12 July 1944
Place of Death: Near Casaglia, Italy
Cemetery: A.B.M.C. Florence Cemetery (A-4-37)—Florence, Italy
Entered Service at: Pixley, Tulare County, California
Unit: Company C, 362d Infantry, 91st Infantry Division
Served as: Squad Leader
Battle or Place of Action: near Casaglia, Italy
Date of Action: 12 July 1944
G.O. Number, Date: 83, 2 October 1945
Citation: He was an acting squad leader when heavy machine-gun fire from enemy positions, well dug-in on commanding ground and camouflaged by haystacks, stopped his company's advance and pinned down one platoon where it was exposed to almost certain annihilation. Ordered to rescue the beleaguered platoon by neutralizing the German automatic fire, he led his squad forward along a draw to the right of the trapped unit against three key positions which poured murderous fire into his helpless comrades. When within range, his squad fired tracer bullets in an attempt to set fire to the three haystacks which were strung out in a loose line directly to the front, 75, 150, and 250 yards away. Realizing that this attack was ineffective, Sgt. Harmon ordered his squad to hold their position and voluntarily began a one-man assault. Carrying white phosphorus grenades and a submachine gun, he skillfully took advantage of what little cover the terrain afforded and crept to within 25 yards of the first position. He set the haystack afire with a grenade, and when two of the enemy attempted to flee from the inferno, he killed them with his submachine gun. Crawling toward the second machine-gun emplacement, he attracted fire and was wounded; but he continued to advance and destroyed the position with hand grenades, killing the occupants. He then attacked the third machine gun, running to a small knoll, then crawling over ground which offered no concealment or cover. About halfway to his objective, he was again wounded. But he struggled ahead until within 20 yards of the machine-gun nest, where he raised himself to his knees to throw a grenade. He was knocked down by direct enemy fire. With a final, magnificent effort, he again arose, hurled the grenade and fell dead, riddled by bullets. His missile fired the third position, destroying it. Sgt. Harmon's extraordinary heroism, gallantry, and self-sacrifice saved a platoon from being wiped out, and made it possible for his company to advance against powerful enemy resistance.

2752 ◆ *HARR, HARRY R.

Rank: Corporal
Service: U.S. Army
Birthday: 22 February 1921
Place of Birth: Pine Croft, Pennsylvania
Date of Death: 5 June 1945
Place of Death: Near Maglamin, Philippine Islands
Cemetery: Alto-Reste Park Cemetery (MH)—Altoona, Pennsylvania
Entered Service at: East Freedom, Blair County, Pennsylvania
Unit: Company D, 124th Infantry, 31st Infantry Division
Battle or Place of Action: near Maglamin, Mindanao, Philippine Islands
Date of Action: 5 June 1945
G.O. Number, Date: 28, 28 March 1946
Citation: He displayed conspicuous gallantry and intrepidity. In a fierce counterattack, the Japanese closed in on his machine-gun emplacement, hurling grenades, one of which exploded under the gun, putting it out of action and wounding two of the crew. While the remaining gunners were desperately attempting to repair their weapon, another grenade landed squarely in the emplacement. Quickly realizing he could not safely throw the unexploded missile from the crowded position, Cpl. Harr unhesitatingly covered it with his body to smother the blast. His supremely courageous act, which cost him his life, saved four of his comrades and enabled them to continue their mission.

2753 ◆ HARRELL, WILLIAM GEORGE

Rank: Sergeant
Service: U.S. Marine Corps
Birthday: 26 June 1922
Place of Birth: Rio Grande City, Starr County, Texas
Date of Death: 9 August 1964
Place of Death: San Antonio, Texas
Cemetery: Fort Sam Houston National Cemetery (W-3247) (MH)—San Antonio, Texas
Entered Service at: Mercedes, Hidalgo County, Texas
Unit: Company A, 1st Battalion, 28th Marines, 5th Marine Division
Battle or Place of Action: Iwo Jima, Volcano Islands
Date of Action: 3 March 1945
Date of Presentation: 5 October 1945
Place of Presentation: The White House, presented by Pres. Harry S. Truman
Citation: For conspicuous gallantry and intrepidity at risk of his life above and beyond the call of duty as leader of an assault group attached to the 1st Battalion, 28th Marines, 5th Marine Division during hand-to-hand combat with enemy Japanese at Iwo Jima, Volcano Islands on 3 March 1945. Standing watch alternately with another marine in a terrain studded with caves and ravines, Sgt. Harrell was holding a position in a perimeter defense around the company command post when Japanese troops infiltrated our lines in the early hours of dawn. Awakened by a sudden attack, he quickly opened fire with his carbine and killed two of the enemy as they emerged from a ravine in the light of a star shell burst. Unmindful of his danger as hostile grenades fell closer, he waged a fierce lone battle until an exploding missile tore off his left hand and fractured his thigh. He was vainly attempting to reload the carbine when his companion returned from the command post with another weapon. Wounded again by a Japanese who rushed the foxhole wielding a saber in the

darkness, Sgt. Harrell succeeded in drawing his pistol and killing his opponent and then ordered his wounded companion to a place of safety. Exhausted by profuse bleeding but still unbeaten, he fearlessly met the challenge of two more enemy troops who charged his position and placed a grenade near his head. Killing one man with his pistol, he grasped the sputtering grenade with his good right hand, and, pushing it painfully toward the crouching soldier, saw his remaining assailant destroyed but his own hand severed in the explosion. At dawn Sgt. Harrell was evacuated from a position hedged by the bodies of 12 dead Japanese, at least five of whom he had personally destroyed in his self-sacrificing defense of the command post. His grim fortitude, exceptional valor, and indomitable fighting spirit against almost insurmountable odds reflect the highest credit upon himself and enhance the finest traditions of the U.S. Naval Servic e.

2754 ◆ *HARRIS, JAMES LINDELL

Rank: Second Lieutenant
Service: U.S. Army
Birthday: 27 June 1916
Place of Birth: Hillsboro, Hill County, Texas
Date of Death: 7 October 1944
Place of Death: At Vagney, France
Cemetery: Ridge Park Cemetery—Hillsboro, Texas
Entered Service at: Hillsboro, Hill County, Texas
Unit: Company A, 756th Tank Battalion, 3d Infantry Division
Served as: Tank Commander
Battle or Place of Action: at Vagney, France
Date of Action: 7 October 1944
G.O. Number, Date: 32, 23 April 1945
Citation: For conspicuous gallantry and intrepidity at risk of life above and beyond the call of duty on 7 October 1944, in Vagney, France. At 9 P.M. an enemy raiding party, comprising a tank and two platoons of infantry, infiltrated through the lines under cover of mist and darkness and attacked an infantry battalion command post with hand grenades, retiring a short distance to an ambush position on hearing the approach of the M-4 tank commanded by 2d Lt. Harris. Realizing the need for bold aggressive action, 2d Lt. Harris ordered his tank to halt while he proceeded on foot, fully 10 yards ahead of his six-man patrol and armed only with a service pistol, to probe the darkness for the enemy. Although struck down and mortally wounded by machine-gun bullets which penetrated his solar plexus, he crawled back to his tank, leaving a trail of blood behind him, and, too weak to climb inside it, issued fire orders while lying on the road between the two contending armored vehicles. Although the tank which he commanded was destroyed in the course of the firefight, he stood the enemy off until friendly tanks, preparing to come to his aid, caused the enemy to withdraw and thereby lose an opportunity to kill or capture the entire battalion command personnel. Suffering a second wound, which severed his leg at the hip, in the course of this tank duel, 2d Lt. Harris refused aid until after a wounded member of his crew had been carried to safety. He died before he could be given medical attention.

2755 ◆ *HASTINGS, JOE R.

Rank: Private First Class
Service: U.S. Army
Birthday: 8 April 1925
Place of Birth: Malvern, Carroll County, Ohio
Date of Death: 16 April 1945
Cemetery: Magnolia Cemetery—Magnolia, Ohio
Entered Service at: Magnolia, Stark County, Ohio
Unit: Company C, 386th Infantry, 97th Infantry Division
Served as: Squad Leader
Battle or Place of Action: Drabenderhohe, Germany
Date of Action: 12 April 1945
G.O. Number, Date: 101, 8 November 1945
Citation: He fought gallantly during an attack against strong enemy forces defending Drabenderhohe, Germany, from the dug-in position on commanding ground. As squad leader of a light machine-gun section supporting the advance of the 1st and 3d Platoons, he braved direct rifle, machine-gun, 20-mm, and mortar fire, some of which repeatedly missed him only by inches, and rushed forward over 350 yards of open, rolling fields to reach a position from which he could fire on the enemy troops. From this vantage point he killed the crew of the 20-mm gun and a machine gun, drove several enemy riflemen from their positions, and so successfully shielded the 1st Platoon that it had time to reorganize and remove its wounded to safety. Observing that the 3d Platoon to his right was being met by very heavy 40-mm and machine-gun fire, he ran 150 yards with his gun to the leading elements of that unit, where he killed the crew of the 40-mm gun. As spearhead of the 3d Platoon's attack, he advanced, firing his gun held at hip height, disregarding the bullets that whipped past him, until the assault had carried 175 yards to the objective. In this charge he and the riflemen he led killed or wounded many of the fanatical enemy and put two machine guns out of action. Pfc. Hastings, by his intrepidity, outstanding leadership, and unrelenting determination to wipe out the formidable German opposition, cleared the path for his company's advance into Drabenderhohe. He was killed four days later while again supporting the 3d Platoon.

2756 ◆ *HAUGE JR., LOUIS JAMES

Rank: Corporal
Service: U.S. Marine Corps Reserve
Birthday: 12 December 1924
Place of Birth: Ada, Norman County, Minnesota
Date of Death: 14 May 1945
Place of Death: Okinawa Shima, Ryukyu Islands
Cemetery: National Memorial Cemetery of the Pacific (Wall of the Missing)—Honolulu, Hawaii; Ada Cemetery (marker only)—Ada, Minnesota
Entered Service at: Minnesota
Unit: Company C, 1st Battalion, 1st Marines, 1st Marine Division
Served as: Squad Leader
Battle or Place of Action: Okinawa Shima, Ryukyu Islands
Date of Action: 14 May 1945
Date of Presentation: 14 June 1946

2758 ◆ *HAWKINS, WILLIAM DEANE

Place of Presentation: Presented by Col. Norman E. True to his Father

Citation: For conspicuous gallantry and intrepidity at risk of his life above and beyond the call of duty as leader of a machine-gun squad serving with Company C, 1st Battalion, 1st Marines, 1st Marine Division, in action against enemy Japanese forces on Okinawa Shima in the Ryukyu Chain on 14 May 1945. Alert and aggressive during a determined assault against a strongly fortified Japanese hill position, Cpl. Hauge boldly took the initiative when his company's left flank was pinned down under a heavy machine-gun and mortar barrage with resultant severe casualties and, quickly locating the two machine guns which were delivering the uninterrupted stream of enfilade fire, ordered his squad to maintain a covering barrage as he rushed across an exposed area toward the furiously blazing enemy weapons. Although painfully wounded as he charged the first machine gun, he launched a vigorous singlehanded grenade attack, destroyed the entire hostile gun position, and moved relentlessly forward toward the other emplacement despite his wounds and the increasingly heavy Japanese fire. Undaunted by the savage opposition, he again hurled his deadly grenades with unerring aim and succeeded in demolishing the second enemy gun before he fell under the slashing fury of Japanese sniper fire. By his ready grasp of the critical situation and his heroic one-man assault tactics, Cpl. Hauge had eliminated two strategically placed enemy weapons, thereby releasing the besieged troops from an overwhelming volume of hostile fire and enabling his company to advance. His indomitable fighting spirit and decisive valor in the face of almost certain death reflect the highest credit upon Cpl. Hauge and the U.S. Naval Service. He gallantly gave his life in the service of his country.

2757 ◆ HAWK, JOHN DRUSE "BUD"

Rank: Sergeant
Service: U.S. Army
Birthday: 30 May 1924
Place of Birth: San Francisco, San Francisco County, California
Entered Service at: Bremerton, Kitsap County, Washington
Unit: Weapons Platoon, Company E, 2d Battalion, 359th Infantry, 90th Infantry Division
Served as: Machine Gunner
Battle or Place of Action: near Chambois, France
Date of Action: 20 August 1944
G.O. Number, Date: 55, 13 July 1945
Date of Presentation: 21 June 1945
Place of Presentation: Olympia, Washington, presented by Pres. Harry S. Truman
Citation: He manned a light machine gun on 20 August 1944, near Chambois, France, a key point in the encirclement which created the Falaise pocket. During an enemy counterattack, his position was menaced by a strong force of tanks and infantry. His fire forced the infantry to withdraw, but an artillery shell knocked out his gun and wounded him in the right thigh. Securing a bazooka, he and another man stalked the tanks and forced them to retire to a wooded section. In the lull which followed, Sgt. Hawk reorganized two machine-

gun squads and, in the face of intense enemy fire, directed the assembly of one workable weapon from two damaged guns. When another enemy assault developed, he was forced to pull back from the pressure of spearheading armor. Two of our tank destroyers were brought up. Their shots were ineffective because of the terrain until Sgt. Hawk, despite his wound, boldly climbed to an exposed position on a knoll where, unmoved by fusillades from the enemy, he became a human aiming-stake for the destroyers. Realizing that his shouted fire directions could not be heard above the noise of battle, he ran back to the destroyers through a concentration of bullets and shrapnel to correct the range. He returned to his exposed position, repeating this performance until two of the tanks were knocked out and a third driven off. Still at great risk, he continued to direct the destroyers' fire into the Germans' wooded position until the enemy came out and surrendered. Sgt. Hawk's fearless initiative and heroic conduct, even while suffering from a painful wound, was in large measure responsible for crushing two desperate attempts of the enemy to escape from the Falaise pocket and for taking more that 500 prisoners.

2758 ◆ *HAWKINS, WILLIAM DEANE

Rank: First Lieutenant
Service: U.S. Marine Corps
Birthday: 19 April 1914
Place of Birth: Fort Scott, Bourbon County, Kansas
Date of Death: 21 November 1943
Place of Death: Tarawa, Gilbert Islands
Cemetery: National Memorial Cemetery of the Pacific (B-646) (MH)—Honolulu, Hawaii
Entered Service at: El Paso, El Paso County, Texas
Unit: Scout Sniper Platoon, 2d Marines, 2d Marine Division
Served as: Commanding Officer
Battle or Place of Action: Tarawa, Gilbert Islands
Date of Action: 20-21 November 1943
Citation: For valorous and gallant conduct above and beyond the call of duty as commanding officer of a Scout Sniper Platoon attached to the Assault Regiment in action against Japanese-held Tarawa in the Gilbert Islands, 20 and 21 November 1943. The first to disembark from the jeep lighter, 1st Lt. Hawkins unhesitatingly moved forward under heavy enemy fire at the end of the Betio Pier, neutralizing emplacements in coverage of troops assaulting the main beach positions. Fearlessly leading his men on to join the forces fighting desperately to gain a beachhead, he repeatedly risked his life throughout the day and night to direct and lead attacks on pillboxes and installations with grenades and demolitions. At dawn on the following day, 1st Lt. Hawkins resumed the dangerous mission of clearing the limited beachhead of Japanese resistance, personally initiating an assault on a hostile position fortified by five enemy machine guns, and, crawling forward in the face of withering fire, boldly fired point-blank into the loopholes and completed the destruction with grenades. Refusing to withdraw after being seriously wounded in the chest during this skirmish, 1st Lt. Hawkins steadfastly carried the fight to the enemy, destroying three more pillboxes before he was caught in a burst of Japanese

shellfire and mortally wounded. His relentless fighting spirit in the face of formidable opposition and his exceptionally daring tactics served as an inspiration to his comrades during the most crucial phase of the battle and reflect the highest credit upon the U.S. Naval Service. He gallantly gave his life for his country.

2759 ◆ HAWKS, LLOYD C.

Rank: Private First Class
Service: U.S. Army
Birthday: 13 January 1911
Place of Birth: Becker, Sherburne County, Minnesota
Date of Death: 26 October 1953
Cemetery: Greenwood Cemetery—Park Rapids, Minnesota
Entered Service at: Park Rapids, Hubbard County, Minnesota
Unit: Medical Detachment, Company G, 30th Infantry, 3d Infantry Division
Served as: Medical Aidman
Battle or Place of Action: near Carano, Italy
Date of Action: 30 January 1944
G.O. Number, Date: 5, 15 January 1945
Citation: For conspicuous gallantry and intrepidity at risk of life above and beyond the call of duty. On 30 January 1944, at 3 P.M., near Carano, Italy, Pfc. Hawks braved an enemy counterattack in order to rescue two wounded men who, unable to move, were lying in an exposed position within 30 yards of the enemy. Two riflemen, attempting the rescue, had been forced to return to their fighting holes by extremely severe enemy machine-gun fire, after crawling only 10 yards toward the casualties. An aidman, whom the enemy could plainly identify as such, had been critically wounded in a similar attempt. Pfc. Hawks, nevertheless, crawled 50 yards through a veritable hail of machine-gun bullets and flying mortar fragments to a small ditch, administered first aid to his fellow aidman who had sought cover therein, and continued toward the two wounded men 50 yards distant. An enemy machine-gun bullet penetrated his helmet, knocking it from his head, momentarily stunning him. Thirteen bullets passed through his helmet as it lay on the ground within six inches of his body. Pfc. Hawks crawled to the casualties, administered first aid to the more seriously wounded man, and dragged him to a covered position 25 yards distant. Despite continuous automatic fire from positions only 30 yards away and shells which exploded within 25 yards, Pfc. Hawks returned to the second man and administered first aid to him. As he raised himself to obtain bandages from his medical kit his right hip was shattered by a burst of machine-gun fire and a second burst splintered his left forearm. Displaying dogged determination and extreme self-control, Pfc. Hawks, despite severe pain and his dangling left arm, completed the task of bandaging the remaining casualty and with superhuman effort dragged him to the same depression to which he had brought the first man. Finding insufficient cover for three men at this point, Pfc. Hawks crawled 75 yards in an effort to regain his company, reaching the ditch in which his fellow aidman was lying.

2760 ◆ *HEDRICK, CLINTON M.

Rank: Technical Sergeant
Service: U.S. Army
Birthday: 1 May 1918
Place of Birth: Cherry Grove, West Virginia
Date of Death: 28 March 1945
Place of Death: Near Lembeck, Germany
Cemetery: North Fork Cemetery—Riverton, West Virginia
Entered Service at: Riverton, Pendleton County, West Virginia
Unit: Company I, 194th Glider Infantry, 17th Airborne Division
Battle or Place of Action: near Lembeck, Germany
Date of Action: 27-28 March 1945
G.O. Number, Date: 89, 19 October 1945
Citation: He displayed extraordinary heroism and gallantry in action on 27–28 March 1945, in Germany. Following an airborne landing near Wesel, his unit was assigned as the assault platoon for the assault on Lembeck. Three times the landing elements were pinned down by intense automatic-weapon fire from strongly defended positions. Each time, T/Sgt. Hedrick fearlessly charged through heavy fire, shooting his automatic rifle from his hip. His courageous action so inspired his men that they reduced the enemy positions in rapid succession. When six of the enemy attempted a surprise, flanking movement, he quickly turned and killed the entire party with a burst of fire. Later, the enemy withdrew across a moat into Lembeck Castle. T/Sgt. Hedrick, with utter disregard for his own safety, plunged across the drawbridge alone in pursuit. When a German soldier, with hands upraised, declared the garrison wished to surrender, he entered the castle yard with four of his men to accept the capitulation. The group moved through a sally port, and was met by fire from a German self-propelled gun. Although mortally wounded, T/Sgt. Hedrick fired at the enemy gun and covered the withdrawal of his comrades. He died while being evacuated after the castle was taken. His great personal courage and heroic leadership contributed in large measure to the speedy capture of Lembeck and provided an inspiring example to his comrades.

2761 ◆ HENDRIX, JAMES RICHARD

Rank: Private (highest rank: Master Sergeant)
Service: U.S. Army
Birthday: 20 August 1925
Place of Birth: Lepanto, Poinsett County, Arkansas
Entered Service at: Lepanto, Poinsett County, Arkansas
Unit: 3d Platoon, Company C, 53d Armored Infantry Battalion, 4th Armored Division
Served as: Bazookaman
Battle or Place of Action: near Assenois, Belgium
Date of Action: 26 December 1944
G.O. Number, Date: 74, 1 September 1945
Date of Presentation: 23 August 1945
Place of Presentation: The White House, presented by Pres. Harry S. Truman
Citation: On the night of 26 December 1944, near

Assenois, Belgium, he was with the leading element engaged in the final thrust to break through to the besieged garrison at Bastogne when halted by a fierce combination of artillery and small-arms fire. He dismounted from his half-track and advanced against two 88-mm guns, and, by the ferocity of his rifle fire, compelled the guncrews to take cover and then to surrender. Later in the attack he again left his vehicle, voluntarily, to aid two wounded soldiers, helpless and exposed to intense machine-gun fire. Effectively silencing two hostile machine guns, he held off the enemy by his own fire until the wounded men were evacuated. Pvt. Hendrix again distinguished himself when he hastened to the aid of still another soldier who was trapped in a burning half-track. Braving enemy sniper fire and exploding mines and ammunition in the vehicle, he extricated the wounded man and extinguished his flaming clothing, thereby saving the life of his fellow soldier. Pvt. Hendrix, by his superb courage and heroism, exemplified the highest traditions of the military service.

2762 ◆ *HENRY, ROBERT T.

Rank: Private
Service: U.S. Army
Birthday: 27 November 1923
Place of Birth: Greenville, Washington County, Mississippi
Date of Death: 3 December 1944
Place of Death: Luchem, Germany
Cemetery: Greenville Cemetery—Greenville, Mississippi
Entered Service at: Greenville, Washington County, Mississippi
Unit: 16th Infantry, 1st Infantry Division
Battle or Place of Action: Luchem, Germany
Date of Action: 3 December 1944
G.O. Number, Date: 45, 12 June 1945
Citation: Near Luchem, Germany, he volunteered to attempt the destruction of a nest of five enemy machine guns located in a bunker 150 yards to the flank which had stopped the advance of his platoon. Stripping off his pack, overshoes, helmet, and overcoat, he sprinted alone with his rifle and hand grenades across the open terrain toward the enemy emplacement. Before he had gone half the distance he was hit by a burst of machine-gun fire. Dropping his rifle, he continued to stagger forward until he fell mortally wounded only 10 yards from the enemy emplacement. His singlehanded attack forced the enemy to leave the machine guns. During this break in hostile fire the platoon moved forward and overran the position. Pvt. Henry, by his gallantry and intrepidity and utter disregard for his own life, enabled his company to reach its objective, capturing this key defense and 70 German prisoners.

2763 ◆ HERRERA, SILVESTRE SANTANA

Rank: Private First Class (highest rank: Sergeant)
Service: U.S. Army
Birthday: 17 July 1917
Place of Birth: El Paso, El Paso County, Texas
Entered Service at: Phoenix, Maricopa County, Arizona
Unit: 1st Squad, 1st Platoon, Company E, 2d Battalion, 142d Infantry, 36th Infantry Division

Served as: Acting Squad Leader/Automatic Rifleman
Battle or Place of Action: near Merzwiller, France
Date of Action: 15 March 1945
G.O. Number, Date: 75, 5 September 1945
Date of Presentation: 23 August 1945
Place of Presentation: The White House, presented by Pres. Harry S. Truman
Citation: He advanced with a platoon along a wooded road until stopped by heavy enemy machine-gun fire. As the rest of the unit took cover, he made a one-man frontal assault on a strongpoint and captured eight enemy soldiers. When the platoon resumed its advance and was subjected to fire from a second emplacement beyond an extensive minefield, Pvt. Herrera again moved forward, disregarding the danger of exploding mines, to attack the position. He stepped on a mine and had both feet severed; but, despite intense pain and unchecked loss of blood, he pinned down the enemy with accurate rifle fire while a friendly squad captured the enemy gun by skirting the minefield and rushing in from the flank. The magnificent courage, extraordinary heroism, and willing self-sacrifice displayed by Pvt. Herrera resulted in the capture of two enemy strongpoints and the taking of eight prisoners.

2764 ◆ HERRING, RUFUS GEDDIE

Rank: Lieutenant [rank at time of action: Lieutenant (j.g.)] (highest rank: Lieutenant Commander)
Service: U.S. Navy
Birthday: 11 June 1921
Place of Birth: Roseboro, Sampson County, North Carolina
Entered Service at: Roseboro, Sampson County, North Carolina
Unit: Landing Craft Infantry Gunboat LCI(G)-449, LCI(G) Group 8
Served as: Commanding Officer
Battle or Place of Action: Iwo Jima, Volcano Islands
Date of Action: 17 February 1945
Date of Presentation: 17 September 1945
Place of Presentation: Washington, D.C., presented by Sec. of the Navy James V. Forrestal
Citation: For conspicuous gallantry and intrepidity at the risk of his life above and beyond the call of duty as commanding officer of LCI (G) 449 operating as a unit of LCI (G) Group 8, during the pre-invasion attack on Iwo Jima on 17 February 1945. Boldly closing the strongly fortified shores under the devastating fire of Japanese coastal defense guns, Lt. (then Lt. [jg]) Herring directed shattering barrages of 40-mm and 20-mm gunfire against hostile beaches until struck down by the enemy's savage counterfire which blasted the 449's heavy guns and whipped her decks into sheets of flame. Regaining consciousness despite profuse bleeding he was again critically wounded when a Japanese mortar crashed the conning station, instantly killing or fatally wounding most of the officers and leaving the ship wallowing without navigational control. Upon recovering the second time, Lt. Herring resolutely climbed down to the pilothouse and, fighting against his rapidly waning strength, took over the helm, established communication with the engineroom, and carried on valiantly until relief could be obtained. When no longer

able to stand, he propped himself against empty shell cases and rallied his men to the aid of the wounded; he maintained position in the firing line with his 20-mm guns in action in the face of sustained enemy fire, and conned his crippled ship to safety. His unwavering fortitude, aggressive perseverance, and indomitable spirit against terrific odds reflect the highest credit upon Lt. Herring and uphold the highest traditions of the U.S. Naval Service.

2765 ◆ *HILL, EDWIN JOSEPH

Rank: Chief Boatswain
Service: U.S. Navy
Birthday: 4 October 1895
Place of Birth: Philadelphia, Philadelphia County, Pennsylvania
Date of Death: 7 December 1941
Place of Death: Pearl Harbor, Territory of Hawaii
Cemetery: National Memorial Cemetery of the Pacific (A-895) (MH)—Honolulu, Hawaii
Entered Service at: Pennsylvania
Unit: U.S.S. *Nevada*
Battle or Place of Action: Pearl Harbor, Territory of Hawaii
Date of Action: 7 December 1941
Citation: For distinguished conduct in the line of his profession, extraordinary courage, and disregard of his own safety during the attack on the Fleet in Pearl Harbor, by Japanese forces on 7 December 1941. During the height of the strafing and bombing, Chief Boatswain Hill led his men of the line-handling details of the U.S.S. *Nevada* to the quays, cast off the lines and swam back to his ship. Later, while on the forecastle, attempting to let go the anchors, he was blown overboard and killed by the explosion of several bombs.

2766 ◆ HORNER, FREEMAN VICTOR

Rank: Staff Sergeant (highest rank: Major)
Service: U.S. Army
Birthday: 7 June 1922
Place of Birth: Mount Carmel, Northumberland County, Pennsylvania
Entered Service at: Shamokin, Northumberland County, Pennsylvania
Unit: 2d Platoon, Company K, 2d Battalion, 119th Infantry, 30th Infantry Division
Served as: Acting Platoon Leader
Battle or Place of Action: Wurselen, Germany
Date of Action: 16 November 1944
G.O. Number, Date: 95, 30 October 1945
Date of Presentation: 12 October 1945
Place of Presentation: The White House (Lawn), presented by Pres. Harry S. Truman
Citation: S/Sgt. Horner and other members of his company were attacking Wurselen, Germany, against stubborn resistance on 16 November 1944, when machine-gun fire from houses on the edge of the town pinned the attackers in flat, open terrain 100 yards from their objective. As they lay in the field, enemy artillery observers directed fire upon them, causing serious casualties. Realizing that the machine guns must

be eliminated in order to permit the company to advance from its precarious position, S/Sgt. Horner voluntarily stood up with his submachine gun and rushed into the teeth of concentrated fire, burdened by a heavy load of ammunition and hand grenades. Just as he reached a position of seeming safety, he was fired on by a machine gun which had remained silent up until that time. He coolly wheeled in his fully exposed position while bullets barely missed him and killed two hostile gunners with a single, devastating burst. He turned to face the fire of the other two machine guns and, dodging fire as he ran, charged the two positions 50 yards away. Demoralized by their inability to hit the intrepid infantryman, the enemy abandoned their guns and took cover in the cellar of the house they occupied. S/Sgt. Horner burst into the building, hurled two grenades down the cellar stairs, and called for the Germans to surrender. Four men gave up to him. By his extraordinary courage, S/Sgt. Horner destroyed three enemy machine-gun positions, killed or captured seven enemy, and cleared the path for his company's successful assault on Wurselen.

2767 ◆ HOWARD, JAMES HOWELL

Rank: Lieutenant Colonel (rank at time of action: Major) (highest rank: Brigadier General)
Service: U.S. Army Air Corps/U.S. Air Force
thday: 8 April 1913
Place of Birth: Canton, China
Date of Death: 18 march 1995
Place of Death: Belleair Bluffs, Florida
Cemetery: Arlington national Cemetery (34-2571) (MH)—Arlington, Virginia
Entered Service at: St. Louis, St. Louis County, Missouri
Unit: 356th Fighter Squadron, 354th Fighter Group, 9th Air Force
Served as: Group Commander of P-51s
Battle or Place of Action: over Oschersleben, Germany
Date of Action: 11 January 1944
G.O. Number, Date: 45, 5 June 1944
Date of Presentation: 27 June 1944
Place of Presentation: London, England, presented by Lt. Gen. Carl A. Spaatz, Commander of the Air Forces in Europe
Citation: For conspicuous gallantry and intrepidity above and beyond the call of duty in action with the enemy near Oschersleben, Germany on 11 January 1944. On that day Col. Howard was the leader of a group of P-51 aircraft providing support for a heavy bomber formation on a long-range mission deep in enemy territory. As Col. Howard's group met the bombers in the target area the bomber force was attacked by numerous enemy fighters. Col. Howard, with his group, at once engaged the enemy and himself destroyed a German ME. 110. As a result of this attack Col. Howard lost contact with his group, and at once returned to the level of the bomber formation. He then saw that the bombers were being heavily attacked by enemy airplanes and that no other friendly fighters were at hand. While Col. Howard could have waited to attempt to assemble his group before engaging the enemy, he chose instead to attack singlehandedly a formation of more than 30 German airplanes. With utter disregard for his own

safety he immediately pressed home determined attacks for some 30 minutes, during which time he destroyed three enemy airplanes and probably destroyed and damaged others. Toward the end of this engagement three of his guns went out of action and his fuel supply was becoming dangerously low. Despite these handicaps and the almost insuperable odds against him, Col. Howard continued his aggressive action in an attempt to protect the bombers from the numerous fighters. His skill, courage, and intrepidity on this occasion set an example of heroism which will be an inspiration to the U.S. Armed Forces.

2768 ◆ HUFF, PAUL BERT

Rank: Corporal (highest rank: Command Sergeant Major)
Service: U.S. Army
Birthday: 23 June 1918
Place of Birth: Cleveland, Bradley County, Tennessee
Date of Death: 21 September 1994
Place of Death: Clarksville, Tennessee
Cemetery: Hillcrest Cemetery—Cleveland, Tennessee
Entered Service at: Cleveland, Bradley County, Tennessee
Unit: 1st Squad, 1st Platoon, Company A, 509th Parachute Infantry Battalion, 5th Army
Served as: Acting Platoon Sergeant
Battle or Place of Action: near Carano, Italy
Date of Action: 8 February 1944
G.O. Number, Date: 41, 26 May 1944
Date of Presentation: 8 June 1944
Place of Presentation: Rome, Italy, presented by Lt. Gen. Mark W. Clark
Citation: For conspicuous gallantry and intrepidiity at risk of life above and beyond the call of duty, in action on 8 February 1944, near Carano, Italy. Cpl. Huff volunteered to lead a six-man patrol with the mission of determining the location and strength of an enemy unit which was delivering fire on the exposed right flank of his company. The terrain over which he had to travel consisted of exposed, rolling ground, affording the enemy excellent visibility. As the patrol advanced, its members were subjected to small-arms and machine-gun fire and a concentration of mortar fire, shells bursting within 5 to 10 yards of them and bullets striking the ground at their feet. Moving ahead of his patrol, Cpl. Huff drew fire from three enemy machine guns and a 20-mm weapon. Realizing the danger confronting his patrol, he advanced alone under deadly fire through a minefield and arrived at a point within 75 yards of the nearest machine-gun position. Under direct fire from the rear machine gun, he crawled the remaining 75 yards to the closest emplacement, killed the crew with his submachine gun, and destroyed the gun. During this act he fired from a kneeling position which drew fire from other positions, enabling him to estimate correctly the strength and location of the enemy. Still under concentrated fire, he returned to his patrol and led his men to safety. As a result of the information he gained, a patrol in strength sent out that afternoon, one group under the leadership of Cpl. Huff, succeeded in routing an enemy company of 125 men, killing 27 Germans, and capturing 21 others, with a loss of only three patrol members. Cpl. Huff's intrepid leadership and daring combat skill reflect the finest traditions of the American infantryman.

2769 ◆ *HUGHES, LLOYD HERBERT

Rank: Second Lieutenant
Service: U.S. Army Air Corps
Birthday: 12 July 1921
Place of Birth: Alexandria, Rapides County, Louisiana
Date of Death: 1 August 1943
Cemetery: Fort Sam Houston National Cemetery (U-53) (MH)—San Antonio, Texas
Entered Service at: San Antonio, Bexar County, Texas
Unit: 564th Bombardment Squadron, 389th Bombardment Group, 9th Air Force
Served as: Pilot of a B-24
Battle or Place of Action: Ploesti, Rumania
Date of Action: 1 August 1943
G.O. Number, Date: 17, 26 February 1944
Citation: For conspicuous gallantry in action and intrepidity at risk of his life above and beyond the call of duty. On 1 August 1943, 2d Lt. Hughes served in the capacity of pilot of a heavy bombardment aircraft participating in a long and hazardous minimum-altitude attack against the Axis oil refineries of Ploesti, Rumania, launched from the northern shores of Africa. Flying in the last formation to attack the target, he arrived in the target area after previous flights had thoroughly alerted the enemy defenses. Approaching the target through intense and accurate antiaircraft fire and dense balloon barrages at dangerously low altitude, his plane received several direct hits from both large and small caliber antiaircraft guns which seriously damaged his aircraft, causing sheets of escaping gasoline to stream from the bomb bay and from the left wing. This damage was inflicted at a time prior to reaching the target when 2d Lt. Hughes could have made a forced landing in any of the grain fields readily available at the time. The target area was blazing with burning oil tanks and damaged refinery installations from which flames leaped high above the bombing level of the formation. With full knowledge of the consequences of entering this blazing inferno when his airplane was profusely leaking gasoline in two separate locations, 2d Lt. Hughes, motivated only by his high conception of duty which called for the destruction of his assigned target at any cost, did not elect to make a forced landing or turn back from the attack. Instead, rather than jeopardize the formation and the success of the attack, he unhesitatingly entered the blazing area and dropped his bomb load with great precision. After successfully bombing the objective, his aircraft emerged from the conflagration with the left wing aflame. Only then did he attempt a forced landing, but because of the advanced stage of the fire enveloping his aircraft the plane crashed and was consumed. By 2d Lt. Hughes' heroic decisi on to complete his mission regardless of the consequences, in utter disregard of his own life, and by his gallant and valorous execution of this decision, he has rendered a service to our country in the defeat of our enemies which will everlastingly be outstanding in the annals of our nation's history.

2770 ◆ *HUTCHINS, JOHNNIE DAVID

Rank: Seaman First Class
Service: U.S. Naval Reserve
Birthday: 4 August 1922
Place of Birth: Weimer, Colorado County, Texas
Date of Death: 4 September 1943
Place of Death: Lae, New Guinea
Cemetery: Lakeside Cemetery (MH)—Eagle Lake, Texas
Entered Service at: Texas
Unit: U.S.S. Landing Ship Tank LST-473
Battle or Place of Action: Lae, New Guinea
Date of Action: 4 September 1943
Date of Presentation: September 1944
Place of Presentation: Sam Houston Coliseum, Houston, Texas, presented by Rear Adm. A.C. Bennett to his Mother
Citation: For extraordinary heroism and conspicuous valor above and beyond the call of duty while serving on board a landing ship tank, during the assault on Lae, New Guinea, 4 September 1943. As the ship on which Hutchins was stationed approached the enemy-occupied beach under a veritable hail of fire from Japanese shore batteries and aerial bombardment, a hostile torpedo pierced the surf and bore down upon the vessel with deadly accuracy. In the tense split seconds before the helmsman could steer clear of the threatening missile, a bomb struck the pilothouse, dislodged him from his station, and left the stricken ship helplessly exposed. Fully aware of the dire peril of the situation, Hutchins, although mortally wounded by the shattering explosion, quickly grasped the wheel and exhausted the last of his strength in maneuvering the vessel clear of the advancing torpedo. Still clinging to the helm, he eventually succumbed to his injuries, his final thoughts concerned only with the safety of his ship, his final efforts expended toward the security of his mission. He gallantly gave his life in the service of his country.

2771 ◆ *JACHMAN, ISADORE SEIGFREID

Rank: Staff Sergeant
Service: U.S. Army
Birthday: 14 December 1922
Place of Birth: Berlin, Germany
Date of Death: 4 January 1945
Place of Death: Flamierge, Belgium
Cemetery: Adath Israel Anshe Sfard Cemetery—Baltimore, Maryland
Entered Service at: Baltimore, Baltimore County, Maryland
Unit: Company B, 513th Parachute Infantry Regiment, 17th Airborne Division
Battle or Place of Action: Flamierge, Belgium
Date of Action: 4 January 1945
G.O. Number, Date: 25, 9 June 1950
Place of Presentation: Ft. George Meade, Md., presented by Lt. Gen. Leonard Derow to his parents
Citation: For conspicuous gallantry and intrepidity above and beyond the call of duty at Flamierge, Belgium on 4 January 1945, when his company was pinned down by enemy artillery, mortar, and small-arms fire, two hostile tanks attacked the unit, inflicting heavy casualties. S/Sgt. Jachman, seeing the desperate plight of his comrades, left his place of cover and with total disregard for his own safety dashed across open ground through a hail of fire and, seizing a bazooka from a fallen comrade, advanced on the tanks, which concentrated their fire on him. Firing the weapon alone, he damaged one and forced both to retire. S/Sgt. Jachman's heroic action, in which he suffered fatal wounds, disrupted the entire enemy attack, reflecting the highest credit upon himself and the parachute infantry.

2772 ◆ JACKSON, ARTHUR JUNIOR

Rank: Private First Class (highest rank: Captain)
Service: U.S. Marine Corps
Birthday: 18 October 1924
Place of Birth: Cleveland, Cuyahoga County, Ohio
Entered Service at: Portland, Multnomah County, Oregon
Unit: 3d Squad, 2d Platoon, Company I, 3d Battalion, 7th Marines, 1st Marine Division
Served as: Automatic Rifleman
Battle or Place of Action: Peleliu Island, Palau Islands
Date of Action: 18 September 1944
Date of Presentation: 5 October 1945
Place of Presentation: The White House, presented by Pres. Harry S. Truman
Citation: For conspicuous gallantry and intrepidity at the risk of his life above and beyond the call of duty while serving with the 3d Battalion, 7th Marines, 1st Marine Division, in action against enemy Japanese forces on the island of Peleliu in the Palau group, 18 September 1944. Boldly taking the initiative when his platoon's left flank advance was held up by the fire of Japanese troops concealed in strongly fortified positions, Pfc. Jackson unhesitatingly proceeded forward of our lines and, courageously defying the heavy barrages, charged a large pillbox housing approximately 35 enemy soldiers. Pouring his automatic fire into the opening of the fixed installation to trap the occupying troops, he hurled white phosphorus grenades and explosive charges brought up by a fellow marine, demolishing the pillbox and killing all of the enemy. Advancing alone under the continuous fire from other hostile emplacements, he employed similar means to smash two smaller positions in the immediate vicinity. Determined to crush the entire pocket of resistance although harassed on all sides by the shattering blasts of Japanese weapons and covered only by small rifle parties, he stormed one gun position after another, dealing death and destruction to the savagely fighting enemy in his inexorable drive against the remaining defenses, and succeeded in wiping out a total of 12 pillboxes and 50 Japanese soldiers. Stouthearted and indomitable despite the terrific odds, Pfc. Jackson resolutely maintained control of the platoon's left flank movement throughout his valiant one-man assault and, by his cool decision and relentless fighting spirit during a critical situation, contributed essentially to the complete annihilation of the enemy in the southern sector of the island. His gallant initiative and heroic conduct in the face of extreme peril reflect the highest credit upon Pfc. Jackson and the U.S. Naval Service.

2773 ◆ JACOBSON, DOUGLAS THOMAS

Rank: Private First Class (highest rank: Major)
Service: U.S. Marine Corps Reserve

Birthday: 25 November 1925
Place of Birth: Rochester, Monroe County, New York
Entered Service at: New York
Unit: Company L, 3d Battalion, 24th Marines, 4th Marine Division
Served as: Demolition Specialist/Bazooka/Flamethrower
Battle or Place of Action: Hill 382, Iwo Jima, Volcano Islands
Date of Action: 26 February 1945
Date of Presentation: 5 October 1945
Place of Presentation: The White House, presented by Pres. Harry S. Truman
Citation: For conspicuous gallantry and intrepidity at the risk of his life above and beyond the call of duty while serving with the 3d Battalion, 23d Marines, 4th Marine Division, in combat against enemy Japanese forces during the seizure of Iwo Jima in the Volcano Islands, 26 February 1945. Promptly destroying a stubborn 20-mm antiaircraft gun and its crew after assuming the duties of a bazooka man who had been killed, Pfc. Jacobson waged a relentless battle as his unit fought desperately toward the summit of Hill 382 in an effort to penetrate the heart of Japanese cross-island defense. Employing his weapon with ready accuracy when his platoon was halted by overwhelming enemy fire on 26 February, he first destroyed two hostile machine-gun positions, then attacked a large blockhouse, completely neutralizing the fortification before dispatching the five-man crew of a second pillbox and exploding the installation with a terrific demolitions blast. Moving steadily forward, he wiped out an earth-covered rifle emplacement and, confronted by a cluster of similar emplacements which constituted the perimeter of enemy defenses in his assigned sector, fearlessly advanced, quickly reduced all six positions to a shambles, killed 10 of the enemy, and enabled our forces to occupy the strongpoint. Determined to widen the breach thus forced, he volunteered his services to an adjacent assault company, neutralized a pillbox holding up its advance, opened fire on a Japanese tank pouring a steady stream of bullets on one of our supporting tanks, and smashed the enemy tank's gun turret in a brief but furious action culminating in a singlehanded assault against still another blockhouse and the subsequent neutralization of its firepower. By his dauntless skill and valor, Pfc. Jacobson destroyed a total of 16 enemy positions and annihilated approximately 75 Japanese, thereby contributing essentially to the success of his division's operations against this fanatically defended outpost of the Japanese Empire. His gallant conduct in the face of tremendous odds enhanced and sustained the highest traditions of the U.S. Naval Service.

2774 ◆ *JERSTAD, JOHN LOUIS

Rank: Major
Service: U.S. Army Air Corps
Birthday: 12 February 1918
Place of Birth: Racine, Racine County, Wisconsin
Date of Death: 1 August 1943
Place of Death: near Ploesti, Rumania
Cemetery: A.B.M.C. Ardennes Cemetery (C-24-10)—Neuvile-En-Condroz, Belgium
Entered Service at: Racine, Racine County, Wisconsin

Unit: 201st Provisional Combat Wing, 9th Air Force
Served as: Pilot of a B-24
Battle or Place of Action: Ploesti, Rumania
Date of Action: 1 August 1943
G.O. Number, Date: 72, 28 October 1943
Citation: For conspicuous gallantry and intrepidity above and beyond the call of duty. On 1 August 1943, he served as pilot of the lead aircraft in his group in a daring low-level attack against enemy oil refineries and installations at Ploesti, Rumania. Although he had completed more than his share of missions and was no longer connected with this group, so high was his conception of duty that he volunteered to lead the formation in the correct belief that his participation would contribute materially to the success of this attack. Maj. Jerstad led the formation into attack with full realization of the extreme hazards involved and despite withering fire from heavy and light anitaircraft guns. Three miles from the target his airplane was hit, badly damaged, and set on fire. Ignoring the fact that he was flying over a field suitable for a forced landing, he kept on the course. After the bombs of his aircraft were released on the target, the fire in his ship became so intense as to make further progress impossible and he crashed into the target area. By his voluntary acceptance of a mission he knew was extremely hazardous and his assumption of an intrepid course of action at the risk of life over and above the call of duty, Maj. Jerstad set an example of heroism which will be an inspiration to the U.S. Armed Forces.

2775 ◆ *JOHNSON, ELDEN HARVEY

Rank: Private
Service: U.S. Army
Birthday: 13 February 1921
Place of Birth: Bivale, Cumberland County, New Jersey
Date of Death: 3 June 1944
Cemetery: Union Cemetery (MH)—Scituate, Massachusetts
Entered Service at: East Weymouth, Norfolk County, Massachusetts
Unit: Company H, 15th Infantry, 3d Infantry Division
Battle or Place of Action: near Valmontone, Italy
Date of Action: 3 June 1944
G.O. Number, Date: 38, 16 May 1945
Date of Presentation: 30 May 1945
Place of Presentation: Boston Commons, Boston, Massachusetts, presented by Gen. Sherman Miles to his Mother
Citation: For conspicuous gallantry and intrepidity at the risk of life above and beyond the call of duty. Pvt. Johnson elected to sacrifice his life in order that his comrades might extricate themselves from an ambush. Braving the massed fire of about 60 riflemen, three machine guns, and three tanks from positions only 25 yards distant, he stood erect and signaled his patrol leader to withdraw. The whole area was brightly illuminated by enemy flares. Then, despite 20-mm machine-gun, machine-pistol, and rifle fire directed at him, Pvt. Johnson advanced beyond the enemy in a slow deliberate walk. Firing his automatic rifle from the hip, he succeeded in distracting the enemy and enabled his 12 comrades to escape. Advancing to within five yards of a machine gun, emptying his weapon, Pvt. Johnson killed its crew. Standing in full view

of the enemy, he reloaded and turned on the riflemen to the left, firing directly into their positions. He either killed or wounded four of them. A burst of machine-gun fire tore into Pfc. Johnson and he dropped to his knees. Fighting to the very last, he steadied himself on his knees and sent a final burst of fire crashing into another German. With that he slumped forward dead. Pvt. Johnson had willingly given his life in order that his comrades might live. These acts on the part of Pvt. Johnson were an inspiration to the entire command and are in keeping with the highest traditions of the Armed Forces.

2776 ◆ JOHNSON, LEON WILLIAM

Rank: Colonel (highest rank: General)
Service: U.S. Army Air Corps/U.S. Air Force
Birthday: 13 September 1904
Place of Birth: Columbia, Boone County, Missouri
Entered Service at: Moline, Elk County, Kansas
Unit: 44th Bombardment Group, 2d Bomb Division, 9th Air Force
Served as: Commanding Officer/Pilot of a B-24
Battle or Place of Action: Ploesti, Rumania
Date of Action: 1 August 1943
G.O. Number, Date: 54, 7 September 1943
Date of Presentation: 22 November 1943
Place of Presentation: England, presented by Lt. Gen. Jacob L. Devers
Citation: For conspicuous gallantry in action and intrepidity at the risk of his life above and beyond the call of duty on 1 August 1943. Col. Johnson, as commanding officer of a heavy bombardment group, led the formation of the aircraft of his organization constituting the fourth element of the mass low-level bombing attack of the 9th U.S. Air Force against the vitally important enemy target of the Ploesti oil refineries. While proceeding to the target on this 2,400-mile flight, his element became separated from the leading elements of the mass formation in maintaining the formation of the unit while avoiding dangerous cumulus cloud conditions encountered over mountainous territory. Though temporarily lost, he reestablished contact with the third element and continued on the mission with this reduced force to the prearranged point of attack, where it was discovered that the target assigned to Col. Johnson's group had been attacked and damaged by a preceding element. Though having lost the element of surprise upon which the safety and success of such a daring form of mission in heavy bombardment aircraft so strongly depended, Col. Johnson elected to carry out his planned low-level attack despite the thoroughly alerted defenses, the destructive antiaircraft fire, enemy fighter planes, the imminent danger of exploding delayed-action bombs from the previous element, of oil fires and explosions, and of intense smoke obscuring the target. By his gallant courage, brilliant leadership, and superior flying skill, Col. Johnson so led his formation as to destroy totally the important refining plants and installations which were the object of his mission. Col. Johnson's personal contribution to the success of this historic raid, and the conspicuous gallantry in action and intrepidity at the risk of his life above and beyond the call of duty demonstrated by him on this occasion constitute such deeds of valor and distinguished service as have during our nation's history formed the finest traditions of our Armed Forces.

2777 ◆ *JOHNSON, LEROY

Rank: Sergeant
Service: U.S. Army
Place of Birth: Caney Creek, Louisiana
Date of Death: 15 December 1944
Cemetery: A.B.M.C. Mamila Cemetery (C-10-79)—Manila, Philippine Islands
Entered Service at: Oakdale, Allen County, Louisiana
Unit: Company K, 126th Infantry, 32d Infantry Division
Served as: Squad Leader
Battle or Place of Action: near Limon, Leyte, Philippine Islands
Date of Action: 15 December 1944
G.O. Number, Date: 83, 2 October 1945
Citation: He was a squad leader of a nine-man patrol sent to reconnoiter a ridge held by a well-entrenched enemy force. Seeing an enemy machine-gun position, he ordered his men to remain behind while he crawled to within six yards of the gun. One of the enemy crew jumped up and prepared to man the weapon. Quickly withdrawing, Sgt. Johnson rejoined his patrol and reported the situation to his commanding officer. Ordered to destroy the gun, which covered the approaches to several other enemy positions, he chose three other men, armed them with hand grenades, and led them to a point near the objective. After taking partial cover behind a log, the men had knocked out the gun and begun an assault when hostile troops on the flank hurled several grenades. As he started for cover, Sgt. Johnson saw two unexploded grenades which had fallen near his men. Knowing that his comrades would be wounded or killed by the explosion, he deliberately threw himself on the grenades and received their full charge in his body. Fatally wounded by the blast, he died soon afterward. Through his outstanding gallantry in sacrificing his life for his comrades, Sgt. Johnson provided a shining example of the highest traditions of the U.S. Army.

2778 ◆ JOHNSON JR., OSCAR GODFREY

Rank: Sergeant (rank at time of action: Private First Class) (highest rank: Chief Warrant Officer 4)
Service: U.S. Army
Birthday: 25 March 1921
Place of Birth: Foster City, Dickinson County, Michigan
Entered Service at: Foster City, Dickinson County, Michigan
Unit: Weapons Platoon, Company B, 1st Battalion, 363d Infantry, 91st Infantry Division
Served as: Mortar Gunner
Battle or Place of Action: near Scarperia, Italy
Date of Action: 16-18 September 1944
G.O. Number, Date: 58, 19 July 1945
Date of Presentation: 25 June 1945
Place of Presentation: Northern Italy, presented by Gen. Mark W. Clark

Citation: He practically singlehandedly protected the left flank of his company's position in the offensive to break the Germans's Gothic line. Company B was the extreme left assault unit of the corps. The advance was stopped by heavy fire from Monticelli Ridge, and the company took cover behind an embankment. Sgt. Johnson, a mortar gunner, having expended his ammunition, assumed the duties of a rifleman. As leader of a squad of seven men he was ordered to establish a combat post 50 yards to the left of the company to cover its exposed flank. Repeated enemy counterattacks, supported by artillery, mortar, and machine-gun fire from the high ground to his front, had by the afternoon of 16 September killed or wounded all his men. Collecting weapons and ammunition from his fallen comrades, in the face of hostile fire, he held his exposed position and inflicted heavy casualties upon the enemy, who several times came close enough to throw hand grenades. On the night of 16–17 September, the enemy launched his heaviest attack on Company B, putting his greatest pressure against the lone defender of the left flank. In spite of mortar fire which crashed about him and machine-gun bullets which whipped the crest of his shallow trench, Sgt. Johnson stood erect and repulsed the attack with grenades and small-arms fire. He remained awake and on the alert throughout the night, frustrating all attempts at infiltration. On 17 September, 25 German soldiers surrendered to him. Two men, sent to reinforce him that afternoon, were caught in a devastating mortar and artillery barrage. With no thought of his own safety, Sgt. Johnson rushed to the shell hole where they lay half buried and seriously wounded, covered their position by his fire, and assisted a medical corpsman in rendering aid. That night he secured their removal to the rear and remained on watch until his company was relieved. Five companies of a German parachute regiment had been repeatedly committed to the attack on Company B without success. Twenty dead Germans were found in front of his position. By his heroic stand and utter disregard for personal safety, Sgt. Johnson was in a large measure responsible for defeating the enemy's attempts to turn the exposed left flank.

2779 ◆ JOHNSTON SR., WILLIAM JAMES

Rank: Private First Class
Service: U.S. Army
Birthday: 15 August 1918
Place of Birth: Trenton, Mercer County, New Jersey
Date of Death: 29 May 1990
Place of Death: Newington, Connecticut
Cemetery: Connecticut State Veterans Cemetery (MH)—Middletown, Connecticut
Entered Service at: Colchester, New London County, Connecticut
Unit: Company G, 180th Infantry, 45th Infantry Division
Served as: Machine Gunner
Battle or Place of Action: near Padiglione, Italy
Date of Action: 17-19 February 1944
G.O. Number, Date: 73, 6 September 1944
Place of Presentation: The White House, presented by Pres. Franklin D. Roosevelt
Citation: For conspicuous gallantry and intrepidity at the risk of life above and beyond the call of duty in action against the enemy. On 17 February 1944, near Padiglione, Italy, he observed and fired upon an attacking force of approximately 80 Germans, causing at least 25 casualties and forcing withdrawal of the remainder. All that day he manned his gun without relief, subject to mortar, artillery, and sniper fire. Two Germans individually worked so close to his position that his machine gun was ineffective, whereupon he killed one with his pistol, the second with a rifle taken from another soldier. When a rifleman protecting his gun position was killed by a sniper, he immediately moved the body and relocated the machine gun in that spot in order to obtain a better field of fire. He volunteered to cover the platoon's withdrawal and was the last man to leave that night. In his new position he maintained an all-night vigil, the next day causing seven German casualties. On the afternoon of the 18th, the organization on the left flank having been forced to withdraw, he again covered the withdrawal of his own organization. Shortly thereafter, he was seriously wounded over the heart, and a passing soldier saw him trying to crawl up the embankment. The soldier aided him in resuming his position behind the machine gun which was soon heard in action for about 10 minutes. Though reported killed, Pfc. Johnston was seen returning to the American lines on the morning of 19 February slowly and painfully working his way back from his overrun position through enemy lines. He gave valuable information of new enemy dispositions. His heroic determination to destroy the enemy and his disregard of his own safety aided immeasurably in halting a strong enemy attack, caused an enormous amount of enemy casualties, and so inspired his fellow soldiers that they fought for and held a vitally important position against greatly superior forces.

2780 ◆ *JONES, HERBERT CHARPOIT

Rank: Ensign
Service: U.S. Naval Reserve
Birthday: 1 December 1918
Place of Birth: Los Angeles, Los Angeles County, California
Date of Death: 7 December 1941
Place of Death: Pearl Harbor, Territory of Hawaii
Cemetery: Fort Rosecrans National Cemetery (G-7G) (MH)—San Diego, California
Entered Service at: California
Unit: U.S.S. *California*
Battle or Place of Action: Pearl Harbor, Territory of Hawaii
Date of Action: 7 December 1941
Citation: For conspicuous devotion to duty, extraordinary courage, and complete disregard of his own life, above and beyond the call of duty, during the attack on the Fleet in Pearl Harbor, by Japanese forces on 7 December 1941. Ens. Jones organized and led a party which was supplying ammunition to the antiaircraft battery of the U.S.S. *California* after the mechanical hoists were put out of action, when he was fatally wounded by a bomb explosion. When two men attempted to take him from the area which was on fire, he refused to let them do so, saying in words to the effect, "Leave me alone! I am done for. Get out of here before the magazines go off."

2781 ◆ *JULIAN, JOSEPH RODOLPH

Rank: Platoon Sergeant
Service: U.S. Marine Corps Reserve
Birthday: 3 April 1918
Place of Birth: Sturbridge, Worcester County, Massachusetts
Date of Death: 9 March 1945
Cemetery: Long Island National Cemetery (DSS-12) (MH)—Farmingdale, New York
Entered Service at: Massachusetts
Unit: 1st Battalion, 27th Marines, 5th Marine Division
Served as: Platoon Sergeant
Battle or Place of Action: Iwo Jima, Volcano Islands
Date of Action: 9 March 1945
Citation: For conspicuous gallantry and intrepidity at the risk of his life above and beyond the call of duty as a P/Sgt. Serving with the 1st Battalion, 27th Marines, 5th Marine Division, in action against enemy Japanese forces during the seizure of Iwo Jima in the Volcano Islands, 9 March 1945. Determined to force a breakthrough when Japanese troops occupying trenches and fortified positions on the left front laid down a terrific machine-gun and mortar barrage in a desperate effort to halt his company's advance, P/Sgt. Julian quickly established his platoon's guns in strategic supporting positions, and then, acting on his own initiative, fearlessly moved forward to execute a one-man assault on the nearest pillbox. Advancing alone, he hurled deadly demolitions and white phosphorus grenades into the emplacement, killing two of the enemy and driving the remaining five out into the adjoining trench system. Seizing a discarded rifle, he jumped into the trench and dispatched the five before they could make an escape. Intent on wiping out all resistance, he obtained more explosives and, accompanied by another marine, again charged the hostile fortifications and knocked out two more cave positions. Immediately thereafter, he launched a bazooka attack unassisted, firing four rounds into the one remaining pillbox and completely destroying it before he fell, mortally wounded by a vicious burst of enemy fire. Stouthearted and indomitable, P/Sgt. Julian consistently disregarded all personal danger and, by his bold decision, daring tactics, and relentless fighting spirit during a critical phase of the battle, contributed materially to the continued advance of his company and to the success of his division's operations in the sustained drive toward the conquest of this fiercely defended outpost of the Japanese Empire. His outstanding valor and unfaltering spirit of self-sacrifice throughout the bitter conflict sustained and enhanced the highest traditions of the U.S. Naval Service. He gallantly gave his life for his country.

2782 ◆ *KANDLE, VICTOR LEONARD

Rank: First Lieutenant
Service: U.S. Army
Birthday: 13 June 1921
Place of Birth: Roy, Pierce County, Washington
Date of Death: 31 December 1944
Cemetery: A.B.M.C. Epinal Cemetery (B-14-55)—Epinal, France

Entered Service at: Redwood City, San Mateo County, California
Unit: Company I, 15th Infantry, 3d Infantry Division
Battle or Place of Action: near La Forge, France
Date of Action: 9 October 1944
G.O. Number, Date: 37, 11 May 1945
Place of Presentation: Presidio, San Francisco, CA; presented by Maj. Gen. H.C. Pratt to his Widow and Son
Citation: For conspicuous gallantry and intrepidity at the risk of his life above and beyond the call of duty. On 9 October 1944, at about noon, near La Forge, France, 1st Lt. Kandle, while leading a reconnaissance patrol into enemy territory, engaged in a duel at point-blank range with a German field officer and killed him. Having already taken five enemy prisoners that morning, he led a skeleton platoon of 16 men, reinforced with a light machine-gun squad, through fog and over precipitious mountain terrain to fall on the rear of a German quarry stronghold which had checked the advance of an infantry battalion for two days. Rushing forward, several yards ahead of his assault elements, 1st Lt. Kandle fought his way into the heart of the enemy strongpoint, and by his boldness and audacity, forced the Germans to surrender. Harassed by machine-gun fire from a position which he had bypassed in the dense fog, he moved to within 15 yards of the enemy, killed a German machine gunner with accurate rifle fire and led his men in the destruction of another machine-gun crew and its rifle security elements. Finally, he led his small force against a fortified house held by two German officers and 30 enlisted men. After establishing a base of fire, he rushed forward alone through an open clearing in full view of the enemy, smashed through a barricaded door, and forced all 32 Germans to surrender. His intrepidity and bold leadership resulted in the capture or killing of three enemy officers and 54 enlisted men, the destruction of three enemy strongpoints, and the seizure of enemy positions which had halted a battalion attack.

2783 ◆ KANE, JOHN RILEY

Rank: Colonel
Service: U.S. Army Air Corps/U.S. Air Force
Birthday: 5 January 1907
Place of Birth: McGregor, McLennan County, Texas
Entered Service at: Shreveport, Caddo County, Louisiana
Unit: 98th Bombardment Group, 9th Air Force
Served as: Pilot of a B-24
Battle or Place of Action: Ploesti, Rumania
Date of Action: 1 August 1943
G.O. Number, Date: 54, 9 August 1943
Date of Presentation: 7 September 1943
Place of Presentation: Gezira Sporting Club (Cricket Pitch), Cairo, Egypt, presented by Major Gen. Lewis H. Brereton
Citation: For conspicuous gallantry in action and intrepidity at the risk of his life above and beyond the call of duty, 1 August 1943. On this date he led the third element of heavy bombardment aircraft in a mass low-level bombing attack against the vitally important enemy target of the Ploesti oil refineries. En route to the target, which necessitated a round-trip flight of over 2,400 miles, Col. Kane's element became

separated from the leading portion of the massed formation in avoiding dense and dangerous cumulus cloud conditions over mountainous terrain. Rather than turn back from such a vital mission he elected to proceed to his target. Upon arrival at the target area it was discovered that another group had apparently missed its target and had previously attacked and damaged the target assigned to Col. Kane's element. Despite the thoroughly warned defenses, the intensive antiaircraft fire, enemy fighter airplanes, extreme hazards on a low-level attack of exploding delayed-action bombs from the previous element, of oil fire and explosions and dense smoke over the target area, Col. Kane elected to lead his formation into the attack. By his gallant courage, brilliant leadership, and superior flying skill, he and the formation under his command successfully attacked this vast refinery so essential to our enemies' war effort. Through his conspicuous gallantry in this most hazardous action against the enemy, and by his intrepidity at the risk of his life above and beyond the call of duty, Col. Kane personally contributed vitally to the success of this daring mission and thereby rendered most distinguished service in the furtherance of the defeat of our enemies.

2784 ◆ KEARBY, NEEL ERNEST

Rank: Colonel
Service: U.S. Army Air Corps
Birthday: 5 June 1911
Place of Birth: Wichita Falls, Wichita County, Texas
Date of Death: 5 March 1944
Place of Death: near Wewak, New Guinea
Cemetery: Hillcrest Memorial Park (MH)—Dallas, Texas
Entered Service at: Dallas, Collin County, Texas
Unit: 309th Bombardment Wing, 5th Air Force
Served as: Commanding Officer/Pilot of a P-47
Battle or Place of Action: near Wewak, New Guinea
Date of Action: 11 October 1943
G.O. Number, Date: 3, 6 January 1944
Date of Presentation: 23 January 1944
Place of Presentation: Brisbane, Australia, presented by Gen. Douglas MacArthur
Citation: For conspicuous gallantry and intrepidity above and beyond the call of duty in action with the enemy, Col. Kearby volunteered to lead a flight of four fighters to reconnoiter the strongly defended enemy base at Wewak. Having observed enemy installations and reinforcements at four airfields, and secured important tactical information, he saw an enemy fighter below him, made a diving attack, and shot it down in flames. The small formation then sighted approximately 12 enemy bombers accompanied by 36 fighters. Although his mission had been completed, his fuel was running low, and the numerical odds were 12 to 1, he gave the signal to attack. Diving into the midst of the enemy airplanes he shot down three in quick succession. Observing one of his comrades with two enemy fighters in pursuit, he destroyed both enemy aircraft. The enemy broke off in large numbers to make a multiple attack on his airplane, but despite his peril he made one more pass before seeking cloud protection. Coming into the clear, he called his flight together and led

them to a friendly base. Col. Kearby brought down six enemy aircraft in this action, undertaken with superb daring after his mission was completed.

2785 ◆ *KEATHLEY, GEORGE D.

Rank: Staff Sergeant
Service: U.S. Army
Place of Birth: Olney, Young County, Texas
Date of Death: 14 September 1944
Cemetery: A.B.M.C. Florence Cemetery (D-11-26)—Florence, Italy
Entered Service at: Lamesa, Dawson County, Texas
Unit: 1st Platoon, Company B, 85th Infantry Division
Served as: Platoon Guide
Battle or Place of Action: Mount Altuzzo, Italy
Date of Action: 14 September 1944
G.O. Number, Date: 20, 29 March 1945
Date of Presentation: 11 April 1945
Place of Presentation: Camp Walters, Texas, presented by Major Gen. Bruce Magruder to his Widow Geneva
Citation: For conspicuous gallantry and intrepidity at the risk of his life above and beyond the call of duty, in action on the western ridge of Mount Altuzzo, Italy. After bitter fighting his company had advanced to within 50 yards of the objective, where it was held up due to intense enemy sniper, automatic, small-arms, and mortar fire. The enemy launched three desperate counterattacks in an effort to regain their former positions, but all three were repulsed with heavy casualties on both sides. All officers and noncommissioned officers of the 2d and 3d platoons of Company B had become casualties, and S/Sgt. Keathley, guide of the 1st platoon, moved up and assumed command of both the 2d and 3d platoons, reduced to 20 men. The remnants of the two platoons were dangerously low on ammunition, so S/Sgt. Keathley, under deadly small-arms and mortar fire, crawled from one casualty to another, collecting their ammunition and administering first aid. He then visited each man of his two platoons, issuing the precious ammunition he had collected from the dead and wounded, and giving them words of encouragement. The enemy now delivered their fourth counterattack, which was approximately two companies in strength. In a furious charge they attacked from the front and both flanks, throwing hand grenades, firing automatic weapons, and assisted by a terrific mortar barrage. So strong was the enemy counterattack that the company was given up for lost. The remnants of the 2d and 3d platoons of Company B were now looking to S/Sgt. Keathley for leadership. He shouted his orders precisely and with determination and the men responded with all that was in them. Time after time the enemy tried to drive a wedge into S/Sgt. Keathley's position and each time they were driven back, suffering huge casualties. Suddenly an enemy hand grenade hit and exploded near S/Sgt. Keathley, inflicting a mortal wound in his left side. However, hurling defiance at the enemy, he rose to his feet. Taking his left hand away from his wound and using it to steady his rifle, he fired and killed an attacking enemy soldier, and continued shouting orders to his men. His heroic and intrepid action so inspired his men that they fought with incomparable determination

and viciousness. For 15 minutes S/Sgt. Keathley continued leading his men and effectively firing his rifle. He could have sought a sheltered spot and perhaps saved his life, but instead he elected to set an example for his men and make every possible effort to hold his position. Finally, friendly artillery fire helped to force the enemy to withdraw, leaving behind many of their number either dead or seriously wounded. S/Sgt. Keathley died a few moments later. Had it not been for his indomitable courage and incomparable heroism, the remnants of three rifle platoons of Company B might well have been annihilated by the overwhelming enemy attacking force. His actions were in keeping with the highest traditions of the military service.

2786 ◆ *KEFURT, GUS

Rank: Staff Sergeant
Service: U.S. Army
Place of Birth: Greenville, Mercer County, Pennsylvania
Date of Death: 24 December 1944
Cemetery: A.B.M.C. Epinal Cemetery (A-29-37)—Epinal, France
Entered Service at: Youngstown, Mahoning County, Ohio
Unit: Company K, 15th Infantry, 3d Infantry Division
Battle or Place of Action: near Bennwihr, France
Date of Action: 23, 24 December 1944
Citation: He distinguished himself by conspicuous gallantry and intrepidity above and beyond the call of duty on 23 and 24 December 1944, near Bennwihr, France. Early in the attack S/Sgt. Kefurt jumped through an opening in a wall to be confronted by about 15 Germans. Although outnumbered he opened fire, killing 10 and capturing the others. During a seesaw battle which developed he effectively adjusted artillery fire on an enemy tank close to his position although exposed to small-arms fire. When night fell he maintained a three-man outpost in the center of the town in the middle of the German positions and successfully fought off several hostile patrols attempting to penetrate our lines. Assuming command of his platoon the following morning he led it in hand-to-hand fighting through the town until blocked by a tank. Using rifle grenades he forced surrender of its crew and some supporting infantry. He then continued his attack from house to house against heavy machine-gun and rifle fire. Advancing against a strongpoint that was holding up the company, his platoon was subjected to a strong counterattack and infiltration to its rear. Suffering heavy casualties in their exposed position the men remained there due to S/Sgt. Kefurt's personal example of bravery, determination, and leadership. He constantly exposed himself to fire by going from man to man to direct fire. During this time he killed approximately 15 of the enemy at close range. Although severely wounded in the leg he refused first aid and immediately resumed fighting. When the forces to his rear were pushed back three hours later, he refused to be evacuated, but, during several more counterattacks moved painfully about under intense small-arms and mortar fire, stiffening the resistance of his platoon by encouraging individual men and by his own fire until he was killed. As a result of S/Sgt. Kefurt's gallantry the position was maintained.

2787 ◆ *KELLEY, JONAH EDWARD HIGH

Rank: Staff Sergeant
Service: U.S. Army
Birthday: 13 April 1923
Place of Birth: Roda, West Virginia
Date of Death: 31 January 1945
Cemetery: Queens Point Cemetery (MH)—Keyser, West Virginia
Entered Service at: Keyser, Mineral County, West Virginia
Unit: Company E, 311th Infantry, 78th Infantry Division
Served as: Squad Leader
Battle or Place of Action: Kesternich, Germany
Date of Action: 30-31 January 1945
G.O. Number, Date: 77, 10 September 1945
Date of Presentation: 5 September 1945
Place of Presentation: Fort Hayes, Ohio, presented to his Father
Citation: In charge of the leading squad of Company E, he heroically spearheaded the attack in furious house-to-house fighting. Early on 30 January, he led his men through intense mortar and small-arms fire in repeated assaults on barricaded houses. Although twice wounded, once when struck in the back, the second time when a mortar shell fragment passed through his left hand and rendered it practically useless, he refused to withdraw and continued to lead his squad after hasty dressings had been applied. His serious wounds forced him to fire his rifle with one hand, resting it on rubble or over his left forearm. To blast his way forward with hand grenades, he set aside his rifle to pull the pins with his teeth while grasping the missles with his good hand. Despite these handicaps, he created tremendous havoc in the enemy ranks. He rushed one house, killing three of the enemy and clearing the way for his squad to advance. On approaching the next house, he was fired upon from an upstairs window. He killed the sniper with a single shot and similarly accounted for another enemy soldier who ran from the cellar of the house. As darkness came, he assigned his men to defensive positions, never leaving them to seek medical attention. At dawn the next day, the squad resumed the attack, advancing to a point where heavy automatic and small-arms fire stalled them. Despite his wounds, S/Sgt. Kelley moved out alone, located an enemy gunner dug in under a haystack, and killed him with rifle fire. He returned to his men and found that a German machine gun, from a well-protected position in a neighboring house, still held up the advance. Ordering the squad to remain in comparatively safe positions, he valiantly dashed into the open and attacked the positions singlehandedly through a hail of bullets. He was hit several times and fell to his knees when within 25 yards of his objective; but he summoned his waning strength and emptied his rifle into the machine-gun nest, silencing the weapon before he died. The superb courage, aggressiveness, and utter disregard for his own safety displayed by S/Sgt. Kelley inspired the men he led and enabled them to penetrate the last line of defense held by the enemy in the village of Kesternich.

2788 ◆ *KELLEY, OVA ART

Rank: Private
Service: U.S. Army

Birthday: 27 March 1914
Place of Birth: Norwood, Wright County, Missouri
Date of Death: 10 December 1944
Cemetery: Oak Grove Cemetery (MH)—Norwood, Missouri
Entered Service at: Norwood, Wright County, Missouri
Unit: Company A, 382d Infantry, 96th Infantry Division
Battle or Place of Action: Leyte, Philippine Islands
Date of Action: 8 December 1944
G.O. Number, Date: 89, 19 October 1945
Citation: For conspicuous gallantry and intrepidity at the risk of his life above and beyond the call of duty. Before dawn, near the edge of enemy-held Buri airstrip, the company was immobilized by heavy, accurate rifle and machine-gun fire from hostile troops entrenched in bomb craters and a ditch less than 100 yards distant. The company commander ordered a mortar concentration which destroyed one machine gun but failed to dislodge the main body of the enemy. At this critical moment Pvt. Kelley, on his own initiative, left his shallow foxhole with an armload of hand grenades and began a one-man assault on the foe. Throwing his missles with great accuracy, he moved forward, killing or wounding five men, and forced the remainder to flee in a disorganized route. He picked up an M1 rifle and emptied its clip at the running Japanese, killing three. Discarding this weapon, he took a carbine and killed three more of the enemy. Inspired by his example, his comrades followed him in a charge which destroyed the entire enemy force of 34 enlisted men and two officers and captured two heavy and one light machine guns. Pvt. Kelley continued to press the attack onto an airstrip, where sniper fire wounded him so grievously that he died two days later. His outstanding courage, aggressiveness, and initiative in the face of grave danger was an inspiration to his entire company and led to the success of the attack.

2789   ◆   KELLY, CHARLES E.

Rank: Corporal
Service: U.S. Army
Birthday: 23 September 1920
Place of Birth: Pittsburgh, Allegheny County, Pennsylvania
Date of Death: 11 January 1985
Cemetery: Highwood Cemetery (MH)—Pittsburgh, Pennsylvania
Entered Service at: Pittsburgh, Allegheny County, Pennsylvania
Unit: Company L, 3d Battalion, 143d Infantry, 36th Infantry Division
Battle or Place of Action: near Altavilla, Italy
Date of Action: 13 September 1943
G.O. Number, Date: 13, 18 February 1944
Place of Presentation: Presented by Lt. Gen. Mark W. Clark
Citation: For conspicuous gallantry and intrepidity at the risk of life above and beyond the call of duty. On 13 September 1943, near Altavilla, Italy, Cpl. Kelly voluntarily joined a patrol which located and neutralized enemy machine-gun positions. After this hazardous duty he volunteered to establish contact with a battalion of the U.S. infantry which was beleived to be located on Hill 315, a mile distant. He

travelled over a route commanded by enemy observation and under sniper, mortar, and artillery fire; and later he returned with the correct information that the enemy occupied Hill 315 in organized positions. Immediately thereafter Cpl. Kelly, again a volunteer patrol member, assisted materially in the destruction of two enemy machine-gun nests under conditions requiring great skill and courage. Having effectively fired his weapon until all the ammunition was exhausted, he secured permission to obtain more at an ammunition dump. Arriving at the dump, which was located near a storehouse on the extreme flank of his regiment's position, Cpl. Kelly found that the Germans were attacking ferociously at this point. He obtained his ammunition and was given the mission of protecting the rear of the storehouse. He held his position throughout the night. The following morning the enemy attack was resumed. Cpl. Kelly took a position at an open window of the storehouse. One machine gunner had been killed at this position and several other soldiers wounded. Cpl. Kelly delivered continuous aimed and effective fire upon the enemy with his automatic rifle until the weapon locked from overheating. Finding another automatic rifle, he again directed effective fire upon the enemy until this weapon also locked. At this critical point, with the enemy threatening to overrun the position, Cpl. Kelly picked up 60-mm mortar shells, pulled the safety pins, and used the shells as grenades, killing at least five of the enemy. When it became imperative that the house be evacuated, Cpl. Kelly, de spite his sergeant's injunctions, volunteered to hold the position until the remainder of the detachment could withdraw. As the detachment moved out, Cpl. Kelly was observed deliberately loading and firing a rocket launcher from the window. He was successful in covering the withdrawl of his unit, and later in joining his own organization. Cpl. Kelly's fighting determination and intrepidity in battle exemplify the highest traditions of the U.S. Armed Forces.

2790   ◆   *KELLY, JOHN D.

Rank: Technical Sergeant (rank at time of action: Corporal)
Service: U.S. Army
Birthday: 8 July 1923
Place of Birth: Venango Township, Crawford County, Pennsylvania
Date of Death: 23 November 1944
Cemetery: A.B.M.C. Epinal Cemetery (A-44-7)—Epinal, France
Entered Service at: Cambridge Springs, Crawford County, Pennsylvania
Unit: Company E, 314th Infantry, 79th Infantry Division
Battle or Place of Action: Fort du Roule, Cherbourg, France
Date of Action: 25 June 1944
G.O. Number, Date: 6, 24 January 1945
Date of Presentation: 9 September 1953
Place of Presentation: Presented by Vice Pres. Richard M. Nixon to his Mother
Citation: For conspicuous gallantry and intrepidity at the risk of his life above and beyond the call of duty. On 25 June 1944, in the vicinity of Fort du Roule, Cherbourg, France, when Cpl. Kelly's unit was pinned down by heavy enemy

machine-gun fire emanating from a deeply entrenched strong-point on the slope leading up to the fort, Cpl. Kelly volun-teered to attempt to neutralize the strongpoint. Armed himself with a pole charge about 10 feet long and with 15 pounds of explosive affixed, he climbed the slope under a withering blast of machine-gun fire and placed the charge at the strongpoint's base. The subsequent blast was ineffective, and again, alone and unhesitatingly, he braved the slope to repeat the opera-tion. This second blast blew off the ends of the enemy guns. Cpl. Kelly then climbed the slope a third time to place a pole charge at the strongpoint's rear entrance. When this had been blown open he hurled grenades inside the position, forcing survivors of the enemy guncrews to come out and surrender. The gallantry, tenacity of purpose, and utter disregard for per-sonal safety displayed by Cpl. Kelly were an incentive to his comrades and worthy of emulation by all.

2791 ◆ KELLY, THOMAS JOSEPH

Rank: Corporal
Service: U.S. Army
Birthday: 9 September 1923
Place of Birth: Brooklyn, Kings County, New York
Date of Death: 2 October 1988
Place of Death: Somers Point, New Jersey
Cemetery: Arlington National Cemetery (7-A-125) (MH)—Arlington, Virginia
Entered Service at: Brooklyn, Kings County, New York
Unit: Medical Detachment, 48th Armored Infantry Battalion, 7th Armored Division
Served as: Medical Aidman
Battle or Place of Action: Alemert, Germany
Date of Action: 5 April 1945
G.O. Number, Date: 97, 1 November 1945
Date of Presentation: 12 October 1945
Place of Presentation: The White House, by Pres. Harry S. Truman
Citation: He was an aidman with the 1st Platoon of Company C during an attack on the town of Alemert, Germany. The platoon, committed in a flanking maneuver, had advanced down a small, open valley overlooked by wood-ed slopes hiding enemy machine guns and tanks, when the attack was stopped by murderous fire that inflicted heavy casu-alties in the American ranks. Ordered to withdraw, Cpl. Kelly reached safety with uninjured remnants of his unit, but, on realizing the extent of casualties suffered by the platoon, vol-untarily retraced his steps and began evacuating his comrades under direct machine-gun fire. He was foreced to crawl, drag-ging the injured behind him for most of the 300 yards sepa-rating the exposed area from a place of comparative safety. Two other volunteers who attempted to negotiate the haz-ardous route with him were mortally wounded, but he kept on with his herculean task after dressing their wounds and carry-ing them to friendly hands. In all, he made 10 separate trips throughout the brutal fire, each time bringing out a man from the death trap. Seven more casualties who were able to crawl by themselves he guided and encouraged in escaping from the hail of fire. After he had completed his heroic, self-imposed task and was near collapse from fatigue, he refused to leave his platoon until the attack had been resumed and the objective

taken. Cpl. Kelly's gallantry and intrepidity in face of seeming-ly certain death saved the lives of many of his fellow soldiers and was an example of bravery under fire.

2792 ◆ *KEPPLER, REINHARDT JOHN

Rank: Boatswain's Mate First Class
Service: U.S. Navy
Birthday: 22 January 1918
Place of Birth: Ralston, Washington
Date of Death: 15 November 1942
Place of Death: Naval Hospital, New Hebrides
Cemetery: Golden Gate National Cemetery (C-379) (MH)—San Bruno, California
Entered Service at: Washington
Unit: U.S.S. *San Francisco*
Battle or Place of Action: Iron Bottom Sound, near Savo Island, Solomon Islands
Date of Action: 12-13 November 1942
Date of Presentation: 17 September 1943
Place of Presentation: Naval District Headquarters, San Francisco, California, presented by Vice Adm. John W. Greensale to his Widow
Citation: For extraordinary heroism and distinguished courage above and beyond the call of duty while serving aboard the U.S.S. *San Francisco* during action against enemy Japanese forces in the Solomon Islands, 12–13 November 1942. When a hostile torpedo plane, during a daylight air raid, crashed on the after machine-gun platform, Keppler promptly assisted in removal of the dead and, by his capable supervision of the wounded, undoubtedly helped save the lives of several shipmates who otherwise might have perished. That night, when the ship's hangar was set afire during the great battle off Savo Island, he bravely led a hose into the starboard side of the stricken area and there, without assis-tance and despite frequent hits from terrific enemy bombard-ment, eventually brought the fire under control. Later, although mortally wounded, he labored valiantly in the midst of bursting shells, persistently directing firefighting operations and administering to wounded personnel until he finally col-lapsed from loss of blood. His great personal valor, main-tained with utter disregard of personal safety, was in keeping with the highest traditions of the U.S. Naval Service. He gal-lantly gave his life for his country.

2793 ◆ KERSTETTER, DEXTER JAMES

Rank: Private First Class
Service: U.S. Army
Birthday: 21 December 1907
Place of Birth: Centralia, Lewis County, Washington
Date of Death: 9 July 1972
Cemetery: Drowned in Hood Canal, Puget Sound, Seabeck, Washington. Body not found
Entered Service at: Centralia, Lewis County, Washington
Unit: Company C, 130th Infantry, 33d Infantry Division
Battle or Place of Action: near Galiano, Luzon, Philippine Islands
Date of Action: 13 April 1945
G.O. Number, Date: 97, 1 November 1945

Date of Presentation: 12 October 1945
Place of Presentation: The White House, by Pres. Harry S. Truman
Citation: He was with his unit in a dawn attack against hill positions appoachable only along a narrow ridge paralleled on each side by steep cliffs which were heavily defended by enemy mortars, machine guns, and rifles in well-camouflaged spider holes and tunnels leading to caves. When the leading element was halted by intense fire that inflicted five casualties, Pfc. Kerstetter passed through the American line with his squad. Placing himself well in advance of his men, he grimly worked his way up the narrow steep hogback, meeting the brunt of enemy action. With well-aimed shots and rifle-grenade fire, he forced the Japs to take cover. He left the trail and, moving down a cliff that offered only precarious footholds, dropped among four Japs at the entrance to a cave, fired his rifle from his hip, and killed them all. Climbing back to the trail, he advanced against heavy enemy machine-gun, rifle, and mortar fire to silence a heavy machine gun by killing its crew of four with rifle fire and grenades. He expended his remaining ammunition and grenades on a group of approximately 20 Japs, scattering them, and returned to his squad for more ammunition and first aid for his left hand, which had been blistered by the heat from his rifle. Resupplied, he guided a fresh platoon into a position from which a concerted attack could be launched, killing three hostile soldiers on the way. In all, he dispatched 16 Japs that day. The hill was taken and held against the enemy's counterattacks, which continued for three days. Pfc. Kerstetter's dauntless and gallant heroism was largely responsible for the capture of this key enemy position, and his fearless attack in the face of great odds was an inspiration to his comrades in their dangerous task.

2794 ◆ *KESSLER, PATRICK L.

Rank: Private First Class
Service: U.S. Army
Birthday: 17 March 1922
Place of Birth: Middletown, Butler County, Ohio
Date of Death: 25 May 1944
Cemetery: Woodside Cemetery—Middletown, Ohio
Entered Service at: Middletown, Butler County, Ohio
Unit: Company K, 30th Infantry, 3d Infantry Division
Battle or Place of Action: near Ponte Rotto, Italy
Date of Action: 23 May 1944
G.O. Number, Date: 1, 4 January 1945
Citation: For conspicuous gallantry and intrepidity at the risk of life above and beyond the call of duty. Pfc. Kessler, acting without orders, raced 50 yards through a hail of machine-gun fire, which had killed five of his comrades and halted the advance of his company, in order to form an assault group to destroy the machine gun. Ordering three men to act as a base of fire, he left the cover of a ditch and snaked his way to a point within 50 yards of the enemy machine gun before he was discovered, whereupon he plunged headlong into the furious chain of automatic fire. Reaching a spot within six feet of the emplacement he stood over it and killed both the gunner and his assistant, jumped into the gun position, overpowered and captured a third German after a short struggle. The remaining member of the

crew escaped, but Pfc. Kessler wounded him as he ran. While taking his prisoner to the rear, this soldier saw two of his comrades killed as they assaulted an enemy strongpoint, fire from which had already killed 10 men in the company. Turning his prisoner over to another man, Pfc. Kessler crawled 35 yards to the side of one of the casualties, relieved him of his BAR and ammunition, and continued on toward the strongpoint, 125 yards distant. Although two machine guns concentrated their fire directly on him and shells exploded within 10 yards, bowling him over, Pfc. Kessler crawled 75 yards, passing through an antipersonnel minefield to a point within 50 yards of the enemy and engaged the machine guns in a duel. When an artillery shell burst within a few feet of him, he left the cover of the ditch and advanced upon the position in a slow walk, firing his BAR from the hip. Although the enemy poured heavy machine-gun and small-arms fire at him, Pfc. Kessler succeeded in reaching the edge of their position, killed the gunners, and captured 13 Germans. Then, despite continuous shelling, he started to the rear. After going 25 yards, Pfc. Kessler was fired upon by two snipers only 100 yards away. Several of his prisoners took advantage of this opportunity and attempted to escape; however, Pfc. Kessler hit the ground, fired on either flank of his prisoners, forcing them to cover, and then engaged the two snipers in a firefight and captured them. With this last threat removed, Company K continued its advance, capturing its objective without further opposition. Pfc. Kessler was killed in a subsequent action.

2795 ◆ *KIDD, ISAAC CAMPBELL

Rank: Rear Admiral
Service: U.S. Navy
Birthday: 26 March 1884
Place of Birth: Cleveland, Cuyahoga County, Ohio
Date of Death: 7 December 1941
Place of Death: Pearl Harbor, Territory of Hawaii
Cemetery: U.S.S. *Arizona* (Missing in Action)—Pearl Harbor, Hawaii; National Memorial Cemetery of the Pacific (Wall of the Missing)—Honolulu, Hawaii
Entered Service at: Ohio
Unit: U.S.S. *Arizona*, Battleship Division One
Served as: Commanding Officer
Battle or Place of Action: Pearl Harbor, Territory of Hawaii
Date of Action: 7 December 1941
Citation: For conspicuous devotion to duty, extraordinary courage and complete disregard of his own life, during the attack on the Fleet in Pearl Harbor, by Japanese forces on 7 December 1941. Rear Adm. Kidd immediately went to the bridge and, as Commander Battleship Division One, courageously discharged his duties as senior officer present afloat until the U.S.S. *Arizona*, his flagship, blew up from magazine explosions and a direct bomb hit on the bridge which resulted in the loss of his life.

2796 ◆ *KIMBRO, TRUMAN

Rank: Technician Fourth Grade
Service: U.S. Army
Place of Birth: Madisonville, Madison County, Texas

Date of Death: 19 December 1944
Cemetery: A.B.M.C. Henri-Chapelle Cemetery (F-6-28)—Henri-Chapelle, Belgium
Entered Service at: Houston, Harris County, Texas
Unit: Company C, 2d Engineer Combat Battalion, 2d Infantry Division
Served as: Scout
Battle or Place of Action: near Rocherath, Belgium
Date of Action: 19 December 1944
G.O. Number, Date: 42, 24 May 1945
Citation: On 19 December 1944, as scout, he led a squad assigned to the mission of mining a vital crossroads near Rocherath, Belgium. At the first attempt to reach the objective, he discovered it was occupied by an enemy tank and at least 20 infantrymen. Driven back by the withering fire, Technician Fourth Grade Kimbro made two more attempts to lead his squad to the crossroads, but all approaches were covered by intense enemy fire. Although warned by our own infantrymen of the great danger involved, he left his squad in a protected place and, laden with mines, crawled alone toward the crossroads. When nearing his objective he was severely wounded, but he continued to drag himself forward and laid his mines across the road. As he tried to crawl from the objective his body was riddled with rifle and machine-gun fire. The mines laid by his act of indomitable courage delayed the advance of enemy armor and prevented the rear of our withdrawing columns from being attacked by the enemy.

2797 ◆ *KINER, HAROLD G.

Rank: Private
Service: U.S. Army
Birthday: 14 April 1924
Place of Birth: Aline, Alfalfa County, Oklahoma
Date of Death: 2 October 1944
Cemetery: Eastern Star Cemetery—Aline, Oklahoma
Entered Service at: Enid, Garfield County, Oklahoma
Unit: Company F, 117th Infantry, 30th Infantry Division
Battle or Place of Action: near Palenberg, Germany
Date of Action: 2 October 1944
G.O. Number, Date: 48, 23 June 1945
Citation: With four other men, he was leading in a frontal assault 2 October 1944, on a Siegfried line pillbox near Palenberg, Germany. Machine-gun fire from the strongly defended enemy position 25 yards away pinned down the attackers. The Germans threw hand grenades, one of which dropped between Pvt. Kiner and two other men. With no hesitation, Pvt. Kiner hurled himself upon the grenade, smothering the explosion. By his gallant action and voluntary sacrifice of his own life, he saved his two comrades from serious injury or death.

2798 ◆ *KINGSLEY, DAVID RICHARD

Rank: Second Lieutenant
Service: U.S. Army Air Corps
Birthday: 27 June 1918
Place of Birth: Portland, Multnomah County, Oregon
Date of Death: 23 June 1944

Place of Death: near Polesti, Rumania
Cemetery: Arlington National Cemetery (34-4786) (MH)—Arlington, Virginia
Entered Service at: Portland, Multnomah County, Oregon
Unit: 341st Bombardment Squadron, 97th Bombardment Group, 15th Air Force
Served as: Bombardier of a B-17
Battle or Place of Action: Ploesti, Rumania
Date of Action: 23 June 1944
G.O. Number, Date: 26, 9 April 1945
Place of Presentation: Portland, Oregon presented by Major Gen. Ralph P. Cousins to his Brother, Thomas E. Kingsley
Citation: For conspicuous gallantry and intrepidity in action at the risk of life above and beyond the call of duty, 23 June 1944 near Ploesti, Rumania, while flying as bombardier of a B-17 type aircraft. On the bomb run 2d Lt. Kingsley's aircraft was severely damaged by intense flak and forced to drop out of formation, but the pilot proceeded over the target and 2d Lt. Kingsley successfully dropped his bombs, causing severe damage to vital installations. The damaged aircraft, forced to lose altitude and to lag behind the formation, was aggressively attacked by three ME-109 aircraft, causing more damage to the aircraft and severely wounding the tail gunner in the upper arm. The radio operator and engineer notified 2d Lt. Kingsley that the tail gunner had been wounded and that assistance was needed to check the bleeding. Second Lt. Kingsley made his way back to the radio room, skillfully applied first aid to the wound, and succeeded in checking the bleeding. The tail gunner's parachute harness and heavy clothes were removed and he was covered with blankets, making him as comfortable as possible. Eight ME-109 aircraft again aggressively attacked 2d Lt. Kingsley's aircraft and the ball turret gunner was wounded by 20-mm shell fragments. He went forward to the radio room to have 2d Lt. Kingsley administer first aid. A few minutes later when the pilot gave the order to prepare to bail out, 2d Lt. Kingsley immediately began to assist the wounded gunners in putting on their parachute harness. In the confusion, the tail gunner's harness, believed to have been damaged, could not be located in the bundle of blankets and flying clothes which had been removed from the wounded men. With utter disregard for his own means of escape, 2d Lt. Kingsley unhesitatingly removed his parachute harness and adjusted it to the wounded tail gunner. Due to the extensive damage caused by the accurate and concentrated 20-mm fire by the enemy aircraft the pilot gave the order to bail out, as it appeare d that the aircraft would disintegrate at any moment. Second Lt. Kingsley aided the wounded men in bailing out and when last seen by the crewmembers he was standing on the bomb bay catwalk. The aircraft continued to fly on automatic pilot for a short distance, then crashed and burned. His body was later found in the wreckage. Second Lt. Kingsley by his gallant and heroic action was directly responsible for saving the life of the wounded gunner.

2799 ◆ *KINSER, ELBERT LUTHER

Rank: Sergeant
Service: U.S. Marine Corps Reserve

Birthday: 21 October 1922
Place of Birth: Greeneville, Greene County, Tennessee
Date of Death: 4 May 1945
Cemetery: Solomon Lutheran Church Cemetery—Greeneville, Tennessee
Entered Service at: Tennessee
Unit: Company I, 3d Battalion, 1st Marines, 1st Marine Division
Served as: Acting Platoon Leader
Battle or Place of Action: Okinawa Shima, Ryukyu Islands
Date of Action: 4 May 1945
Citation: For conspicuous gallantry and intrepidity at the risk of his life above and beyond the call of duty while acting as leader of a rifle platoon, serving with Company I, 3d Battalion, 1st Marines, 1st Marine Division, in action against Japanese forces on Okinawa Shima in the Ryukyu Chain, 4 May 1945. Taken under sudden, close attack by hostile troops entrenched on the reverse slope while moving up a strategic ridge along which his platoon was holding newly won positions, Sgt. Kinser engaged the enemy in a fierce hand-grenade battle. Quick to act when a Japanese grenade landed in the immediate vicinity, Sgt. Kinser unhesitatingly threw himself on the deadly missile, absorbing the full charge of the shattering explosion in his own body and thereby protecting his men from serious injury and possible death. Stouthearted and indomitable, he had yielded his own chance of survival that his comrades might live to carry on the relentless battle against the fanatic enemy. His courage, cool decision, and valiant spirit of self-sacrifice in the face of certain death sustained and enhanced the highest traditions of the U.S. Naval Service. He gallantly gave his life for his country.

2800 ◆ KISTERS, GERRY HERMAN

Rank: Second Lieutenant (rank at time of action: Sergeant) (highest rank: First Lieutenant)
Service: U.S. Army
Birthday: 3 March 1919
Place of Birth: Salt Lake City, Salt Lake County, Utah
Date of Death: 11 May 1986
Place of Death: Bloomington, Indiana
Cemetery: Rose Hill Cemetery (MH)—Bloomington, Indiana
Entered Service at: Bloomington, Monroe County, Indiana
Unit: Company B, 91st Reconnaisance Squadron (attached to the 1st Infantry Division), 2d Armored Division
Battle or Place of Action: near Gagliano, Sicily
Date of Action: 31 July 1943
G.O. Number, Date: 13, 18 February 1944
Date of Presentation: 8 February 1944
Place of Presentation: The White House, presented by Pres. Franklin D. Roosevelt
Citation: On 31 July 1943, near Gagliano, Sicily, a detachment of one officer and nine enlisted men, including Sgt. Kisters, advancing ahead of the leading elements of U.S. troops to fill a large crater in the only available vehicle route through Gagliano, was taken under fire by two enemy machine guns. Sgt. Kisters and the officer, unaided and in the face of intense small-arms fire, advanced on the nearest machine-gun emplacement and succeeded in capturing the gun and its crew of four. Although the greater part of the remaining small-arms fire was now directed on the captured machine-gun position, Sgt. Kisters voluntarily advanced alone toward the second gun emplacement. While creeping forward, he was struck five times by enemy bullets, receiving wounds in both legs and his right arm. Despite the wounds, he continued to advance on the enemy, and captured the second machine gun after killing three of its crew and forcing the fourth member to flee. The courage of this soldier and his unhesitating willingness to sacrifice his life, if necessary, served as an inspiration to the command.

2801 ◆ KNAPPENBERGER, ALTON W.

Rank: Private First Class (highest rank: Staff Sergeant)
Service: U.S. Army
Birthday: 31 December 1924
Place of Birth: Coopersburg, Lehigh County, Pennsylvania
Entered Service at: Almount, Bucks County, Pennsylvania
Unit: 1st Platoon, Company C, 15th Battalion, 30th Infantry, 3d Infantry Division
Served as: Automatic Rifleman
Battle or Place of Action: near Cisterna di Littoria, Italy
Date of Action: 1 February 1944
G.O. Number, Date: 41, 26 May 1944
Date of Presentation: August 1944
Place of Presentation: Rome, Italy, presented by Lt. Gen. Mark W. Clark
Citation: For conspicuous gallantry and intrepidity at the risk of his life above and beyond the call of duty in action involving actual conflict with the enemy, on 1 February 1944 near Cisterna di Littoria, Italy. When a heavy German counterattack was launched against his battalion, Pfc. Knappenberger crawled to an exposed knoll and went into position with his automatic rifle. An enemy machine gun 85 yards away opened fire, and bullets struck within six inches of him. Raising to a kneeling position, Pfc. Knappenberger opened fire on the hostile crew, knocked out the gun, killed two members of the crew, and wounded the third. While he fired at this hostile position, two Germans crawled to a point within 20 yards of the knoll and threw potato-masher grenades at him, but Pfc. Knappenberger killed them both with one burst from his automatic rifle. Later, a second machine gun opened fire upon his exposed position from a distance of 100 yards, and this weapon was also silenced by his well-aimed shots. Shortly thereafter, an enemy 20-mm antiaircraft gun directed fire at him, and again Pfc. Knappenberger returned fire to wound one member of the hostile crew. Under tank and artillery shellfire, with shells bursting within 15 yards of him, he held his precarious position and fired at all enemy infantrymen armed with machine pistols and machine guns which he could locate. When his ammunition supply became exhausted, he crawled 15 yards forward through steady machine-gun fire, removed rifle clips from the belt of a casualty, returned to his position, and resumed firing to repel an assaulting German platoon armed with automatic weapons. Finally, his ammunition supply being completely exhausted, he rejoined his company. Pfc.

Knappenberger's intrepid action disrupted the enemy attack for over two hours.

2802 ◆ *KNIGHT, JACK LLEWELLYN

Rank: First Lieutenant
Service: U.S. Army
Birthday: 29 May 1917
Place of Birth: Garner, Texas
Date of Death: 2 February 1945
Cemetery: Holders Chapel Cemetery (MH)—Millsap, Texas
Entered Service at: Weatherford, Parker County, Texas
Unit: 124th Cavalry Regiment, Mars Task Force
Battle or Place of Action: near Loi-Kang, Burma
Date of Action: 2 February 1945
G.O. Number, Date: 44, 6 June 1945
Citation: He led his cavalry troop against heavy concentrations of enemy mortar, artillery, and small-arms fire. After taking the troop's objective and while making preparations for a defense, he discovered a nest of Japanese pillboxes and foxholes to the right front. Preceding his men by at least 10 feet, he immediately led an attack. Singlehandedly he knocked out two enemy pillboxes and killed the occupants of several foxholes. While attempting to knock out a third pillbox, he was struck and blinded by an enemy grenade. Although unable to see, he rallied his platoon and continued forward in the assault on the remaining pillboxes. Before the task was completed he fell mortally wounded. First Lt. Knight's gallantry and intrepidity were responsible for the successful elimination of most of the Japs' positions and served as an inspiration to officers and men of his troop.

2803 ◆ *KNIGHT, RAYMOND LARRY

Rank: First Lieutenant
Service: U.S. Army Air Corps
Birthday: 15 June 1922
Place of Birth: Houston, Harris County, Texas
Date of Death: 25 April 1945
Place of Death: Appenine Mountains, Italy
Cemetery: Houston National Cemetery (H-B-11) (MH)—Houston, Texas
Entered Service at: Houston, Harris County, Texas
Unit: 346th Fighter Squadron, 350th Fighter Group, 12th Air Force
Served as: Pilot of a P-47
Battle or Place of Action: Northern Po Valley, Italy
Date of Action: 24-25 April 1945
G.O. Number, Date: 81, 24 September 1945
Citation: He piloted a fighter-bomber aircraft in a series of low-level strafing missions, destroying 14 grounded enemy aircraft and leading attacks which wrecked 10 others during a critical period of the Allied drive in northern Italy. On the morning of 24 April, he volunteered to lead two other aircraft against the strongly defended enemy airdrome at Ghedi. Ordering his fellow pilots to remain aloft, he skimmed the ground through a deadly curtain of anti-aircraft fire to reconnoiter the field, locating eight German aircraft hidden beneath heavy camouflage. He rejoined his flight, briefed them by radio, and then led them with consummate skill through the hail of enemy fire in a low-level attack, destroying five aircraft, while his flight accounted for two others. Returning to his base, he volunteered to lead three other aircraft in reconnaissance of Bergamo airfield, an enemy base near Ghedi, and one known to be equally well-defended. Again ordering his flight to remain out of range of antiaircraft fire, 1st Lt. Knight flew through an exceptionally intense barrage, which heavily damaged his Thunderbolt, to observe the field at minimum altitude. He discovered a squadron of enemy aircraft under heavy camouflage and led his flight to the assault. Returning alone after the strafing, he made 10 deliberate passes against the field despite being hit by antiaircraft fire twice more, destroying six fully loaded enemy twin-engine aircraft and two fighters. His skillfully led attack enabled his flight to destroy four other twin-engine aircraft and a fighter plane. He then returned to his base in his seriously damaged plane. Early the next morning, when he again attacked Bergamo, he sighted an enemy plane on the runway. Again he led three other American pilots in a blistering low-level sweep through vicious antiaircraft fire that damaged his plane so severely that it was virtually nonflyable. Three of the few remaining twin-engine aircraft at that base were destroyed. Realizing the critical need for aircraft in his unit, he declined to parachute to safety over friendly territory and unhesitatingly attempted to return his shattered plane to his home field. With great skill and strength, he flew homeward until caught by treacherous air conditions in the Apennines Mountains, where he crashed and was killed. The gallant action of 1st Lt. Knight eliminated the German aircraft which were poised to wreak havoc on Allied forces pressing to establish the first firm bridgehead across the Po River; his fearless daring and voluntary self-sacrifice averted possible heavy casualties among ground forces, and the resultant slowing on the German drive culminated in the collapse of enemy resistance in Italy.

2804 ◆ *KRAUS, RICHARD EDWARD

Rank: Private First Class
Service: U.S. Marine Corps Reserve
Birthday: 24 November 1925
Place of Birth: Chicago, Cook County, Illinois
Date of Death: 5 October 1944
Cemetery: Fort Snelling National Cemetery (DS-61A) (MH)—St. Paul, Minnesota
Entered Service at: Minnesota
Unit: 8th Amphibious Tractor Battalion, Fleet Marine Force
Served as: Amphibious Tractor Driver
Battle or Place of Action: Peleliu Island, Palau Islands
Date of Action: 5 October 1944
Citation: For conspicuous gallantry and intrepidity at the risk of his life above and beyond the call of duty while serving with the 8th Amphibious Tractor Battalion, Fleet Marine Force, in action against enemy Japanese forces on Peleliu, Palau Islands on 5 October 1944. Unhesitatingly volunteering for the extremely hazardous mission of evacuating a wounded comrade from the front lines, Pfc. Kraus and three companions courageously made their way forward and suc-

cessfully penetrated the lines for some distance before the enemy opened with an intense, devastating barrage of hand grenades which forced the stretcher party to take cover and subsequently abandon the mission. While returning to the rear, they observed two men approaching who appeared to be marines and immediately demanded the password. When, instead of answering, one of the two Japanese threw a hand grenade into the midst of the group, Pfc. Kraus heroically flung himself upon the grenade and, covering it with his body, absorbed the full impact of the explosion and was instantly killed. By his prompt action and great personal valor in the face of almost certain death, he saved the lives of his three companions, and his loyal spirit of self-sacrifice reflects the highest credit upon himself and the U.S. Naval Service. He gallantly gave his life for his comrades.

2805 ◆ *KROTIAK, ANTON L.

Rank: Private First Class
Service: U.S. Army
Birthday: 15 August 1915
Place of Birth: Chicago, Cook County, Illinois
Date of Death: 8 May 1945
Cemetery: Holy Sepulchre Cemetery (MH)—Worth, Illinois
Entered Service at: Chicago, Cook County, Illinois
Unit: Company I, 148th Infantry, 37th Infantry Division
Served as: Acting Squad Leader
Battle or Place of Action: Balete Pass, Luzon, Philippine Islands
Date of Action: 8 May 1945
G.O. Number, Date: 18, 13 February 1946
Citation: He was an acting squad leader, directing his men in consolidating a newly won position on Hill B when the enemy concentrated small-arms fire and grenades upon him and four others, driving them to cover in an abandoned Japanese trench. A grenade thrown from above landed in the center of the group. Instantly pushing his comrades aside and jamming the grenade into the earth with his rifle butt, he threw himself over it, making a shield of his body to protect the other men. The grenade exploded under him, and he died a few minutes later. By his extraordinary heroism and deliberately giving his life to save those of his comrades, Pfc. Krotiak set an inspiring example of utter devotion and self-sacrifice which reflects the highest traditions of the military service.

2806 ◆ *LA BELLE, JAMES DENNIS

Rank: Private First Class
Service: U.S. Marine Corps Reserve
Birthday: 22 November 1925
Place of Birth: Columbia Heights, Hennepin County, Minnesota
Date of Death: 8 March 1945
Cemetery: Fort Snelling National Cemetery (B-1-422-S) (MH)—St. Paul, Minnesota
Entered Service at: Minnesota
Unit: 27th Marines, 5th Marine Division

Battle or Place of Action: Iwo Jima, Volcano Islands
Date of Action: 8 March 1945
Citation: For conspicuous gallantry and intrepidity at the risk of his life above and beyond the call of duty while attached to the 27th Marines, 5th Marine Division, in action against enemy Japanese forces during the seizure of Iwo Jima in the Volcano Islands, 8 March 1945. Filling a gap in the front lines during a critical phase in the battle, Pfc. La Belle had dug into a foxhole with two other marines and, grimly aware of the enemy's persistent attempts to blast a way through our lines with hand grenades, applied himself with steady concentration to maintaining a sharply vigilant watch during the hazardous night hours. Suddenly a hostile grenade landed beyond reach of his foxhole. Quickly estimating the situation, he determined to save the others if possible, shouted a warning, and instantly dived on the deadly missile, absorbing the exploding charge in his own body and thereby protecting his comrades from serious injury. Stouthearted and indomitable, he had unhesitatingly relinquished his own chance of survival that his fellow marines might carry on the relentless fight against a fanatic enemy. His dauntless courage, cool decision, and valiant spirit of self-sacrifice in the face of certain death reflect the highest credit upon Pfc. La Belle and upon the U.S. Naval Service. He gallantly gave his life in the service of his country.

2807 ◆ LAWLEY JR., WILLIAM ROBERT

Rank: First Lieutenant (highest rank: Colonel)
Service: U.S. Army Air Corps/U.S. Air Force
Birthday: 23 August 1920
Place of Birth: Leeds, Jefferson County, Alabama
Entered Service at: Birmingham, Jefferson County, Alabama
Unit: 364th Bombardment Squadron, 305th Bombardment Group, 40th Combat Wing, 1st Air Division, 8th Air Force
Served as: Pilot of a B-17
Battle or Place of Action: over Liepzig, Germany
Date of Action: 20 February 1944
G.O. Number, Date: 64, 8 August 1944
Date of Presentation: 8 August 1944
Place of Presentation: Headquarters U.S. Army Air Forces Europe, High Wycomb, England, presented by Lt. Gen. Carl A. Spaatz
Citation: For conspicuous gallantry and intrepidity in action above and beyond the call of duty, 20 February 1944, while serving as pilot of a B-17 aircraft on a heavy bombardment mission over enemy-occupied continental Europe. Coming off the target he was attacked by approximately 20 enemy fighters, shot out of formation, and his plane severely crippled. Eight crewmembers were wounded; the copilot was killed by a 20-mm shell. One engine was on fire, the controls shot away, and 1st Lt. Lawley seriously and painfully wounded about the face. Forcing the copilot's body off the controls, he brought the plane out of a steep dive, flying with his left hand only. Blood covered the instruments and windshield and visibility was impossible. With a full bomb load the plane was difficult to maneuver and the bombs could not be released because the racks were frozen. After the order to bail out had been given, one of the waist gunners informed the pilot that

two crewmembers were so severely wounded that it would be impossible for them to bail out. With the fire in the engine spreading, the danger of an explosion was imminent. Because of the helpless condition of his wounded crewmembers 1st Lt. Lawley elected to remain with the ship and bring them to safety if it was humanly possible, giving the other crewmembers the option of bailing out. Enemy fighters again attacked but by using masterful evasive action he managed to lose them. One engine again caught on fire and was extinguished by skillful flying. First Lt. Lawley remained at his post, refusing first aid until he collapsed from sheer exhaustion caused by loss of blood, shock, and the energy he had expended in keeping control of his plane. He was revived by the bombardier and again took over the controls. Coming over the English coast one engine ran out of gasoline and had to be feathered. Another engine started to burn and continued to do so until a successful crash landing was made on a small fighter base. Through his heroism and exceptional flying skill 1st Lt. Lawley rendered outstanding distinguished and valorous service to our nation.

2808 ◆ LAWS, ROBERT EARL

Rank: Staff Sergeant
Service: U.S. Army
Birthday: 18 January 1921
Place of Birth: Altoona, Blair County, Pennsylvania
Date of Death: 1 January 1990
Cemetery: Blair Memorial Park (MH)—Bellwood, Pennsylvania
Entered Service at: Altoona, Blair County, Pennsylvania
Unit: Company G, 169th Infantry, 43d Infantry Division
Served as: Squad Leader
Battle or Place of Action: Pangasinan Province, Luzon, Philippine Islands
Date of Action: 12 January 1945
G.O. Number, Date: 77, 10 September 1945
Date of Presentation: 23 August 1945
Place of Presentation: The White House, presented by Pres. Harry S. Truman
Citation: He led the assault squad when Company G attacked enemy hill positions. The enemy force, estimated to be a reinforced infantry company, was well-supplied with machine guns, ammunition, grenades, and blocks of TNT, and could be attacked only across a narrow ridge 70 yards long. At the end of this ridge an enemy pillbox and rifle positions were set in rising ground. Covered by his squad, S/Sgt. Laws traversed the hogback through vicious enemy fire until close to the pillbox, where he hurled grenades at the fortification. Enemy grenades wounded him, but he persisted in his assault until one of his missiles found its mark and knocked out the pillbox. With more grenades, passed to him by members of his squad who had joined him, he led the attack on the entrenched riflemen. In the advance up the hill, he suffered additional wounds in both arms and legs, about the body and in the head, as grenades and TNT charges exploded near him. Three Japs rushed him with fixed bayonets, and he emptied the magazine of his machine pistol at them, killing two. He closed in hand-to-hand combat with the third, seiz-

ing the Jap's rifle as he met the onslaught. The two fell to the ground and rolled some 50 or 60 feet down a bank. When the dust cleared the Jap lay dead and the valiant American was climbing up the hill with a large gash across the head. He was given first aid and evacuated from the area his courageous determination in the face of formidable odds and while his squad completed the destruction of the enemy position. S/Sgt. Laws' heroic actions provided great inspiration to his comrades, and his courageous determination, in the face of formidable odds and while suffering from multiple wounds, enabled them to secure an important objective with minimum casualties.

2809 ◆ LEE SR., DANIEL WARNEL

Rank: First Lieutenant (rank at time of action: Second Lieutenant)
Service: U.S. Army
Birthday: 23 June 1919
Place of Birth: Alma, Bacon County, Georgia
Date of Death: 22 January 1985
Cemetery: Rose Hill Cemetery (MH)—Alma, Georgia
Entered Service at: Alma, Bacon County, Georgia
Unit: Troop A, 117th Cavalry Reconnaissance Squadron, 7th Army
Served as: Platoon Leader
Battle or Place of Action: Montreval, France
Date of Action: 2 September 1944
G.O. Number, Date: 14, 4 February 1946
Date of Presentation: 23 January 1946
Place of Presentation: Washington, D.C., presented by Pres. Harry S. Truman
Citation: First Lt. (then 2d Lt.) Daniel W. Lee was leader of Headquarters Platoon, Troop A, 117th Cavalry Reconnaissance Squadron, Mechanized, at Montreval, France, on 2 September 1944, when the Germans mounted a strong counterattack, isolating the town and engaging its outnumbered defenders in a pitched battle. After the fight had raged for hours and our forces had withstood heavy shelling and armor-supported infantry attacks, 2d Lt. Lee organized a patrol to knock out mortars which were inflicting heavy casualties on the beleaguered reconnaissance troops. He led the small group to the edge of the town, sweeping enemy riflemen out of position on a ridge from which he observed seven Germans manning two large mortars near an armored half-track about 100 yards down the reverse slope. Armed with a rifle and grenades, he left his men on the high ground and crawled to within 30 yards of the mortars, where the enemy discovered him and unleashed machine-pistol fire which shattered his right thigh. Scorning retreat, bleeding, and suffering intense pain, he dragged himself relentlessly forward. He killed five of the enemy with rifle fire, and the others fled before he reached their position. Fired on by an armored car, he took cover behind the German half-track and there found a panzerfaust with which to neutralize this threat. Despite his wounds, he inched his way toward the car through withering machine-gun fire, maneuvered into range, and blasted the vehicle with a round from the rocket launcher, forcing it to withdraw. Having cleared the slope of hostile troops, he

struggled back to his men, where he collapsed from pain and loss of blood. Second Lt. Lee's outstanding gallantry, willing risk of life, and extreme tenacity of purpose in coming to grips with the enemy, although suffering from grievous wounds, set an example of bravery and devotion to duty in keeping with the highest traditions of the military service.

2810 ◆ LEIMS, JOHN HAROLD

Rank: Second Lieutenant
Service: U.S. Marine Corps Reserve
Birthday: 8 June 1921
Place of Birth: Chicago, Cook County, Illinois
Date of Death: 28 June 1985
Place of Death: Conroe, Texas
Cemetery: Arlington National Cemetery (2-1132-2) (MH)—Arlington, Virginia
Entered Service at: Chicago, Cook County, Illinois
Unit: Company B, 1st Battalion, 9th Marines, 3d Marine Division
Served as: Commanding Officer
Battle or Place of Action: Iwo Jima, Volcano Islands
Date of Action: 7 March 1945
Date of Presentation: 14 June 1946
Place of Presentation: The White House, presented by Pres. Harry S. Truman
Citation: For conspicuous gallantry and intrepidity at the risk of his life above and beyond the call of duty as commanding officer of Company B, 1st Battalion, 9th Marines, 3d Marine Division, in action against enemy Japanese forces on Iwo Jima in the Volcano Islands, 7 March 1945. Launching a surprise attack against the rock-imbedded fortifications of a dominating Japanese hill position, 2d Lt. Leims spurred his company forward with indomitable determination and, skillfully directing his assault platoons against the cave-emplaced enemy troops and heavily fortified pillboxes, succeeded in capturing the objective in the late afternoon. When it became apparent that his assault platoon were cut off in this newly won position, approximately 400 yards forward of adjacent units, and lacked all communication with the command post, he personally advanced and laid telephone lines across the isolating expanse of open, fire-swept terrain. Ordered to withdraw his command after he had joined his forward platoons he immediately complied, adroitly effecting the withdrawal of his troops without incident. Upon arriving at the rear, he was informed that several casualties had been left at the abandoned ridge position beyond the front lines. Although suffering acutely from the strain and exhaustion of battle, he instantly went forward despite darkness and the slashing fury of hostile machine-gun fire, located and carried to safety one seriously wounded marine, and then, running the gauntlet of enemy fire for the third time that night, again made his tortuous way into the bullet-riddled death trap and rescued another of his wounded men. A dauntless leader, concerned at all times for the welfare of his men, 2d Lt. Leims soundly maintained the coordinated strength of his battle-wearied company under extremely difficult conditions and, by his bold tactics, sustained aggressiveness, and heroic disregard of all personal danger, contributed essentially to the success of his division's

operations against this vital Japanese base. His valiant conduct in the face of fanatic opposition sustains and enhances the highest traditions of the U.S. Naval Service.

2811 ◆ *LEONARD, TURNEY WHITE

Rank: First Lieutenant
Service: U.S. Army
Birthday: 18 June 1921
Place of Birth: Dallas, Collin County, Texas
Date of Death: 7 November 1944
Cemetery: Grove Hill Memorial Park (MH)—Dallas, Texas
Entered Service at: Dallas, Collin County, Texas
Unit: Company C, 893d Tank Destroyer Battalion
Served as: Platoon Leader
Battle or Place of Action: Kommerscheidt, Germany
Date of Action: 4-6 November 1944
G.O. Number, Date: 74, 1 September 1945
Citation: He displayed extraordinary heroism while commanding a platoon of mobile weapons at Kommerscheidt, Germany, on 4, 5, and 6 November 1944. During the fierce three-day engagement, he repeatedly braved overwhelming enemy fire in advance of his platoon to direct the fire of his tank destroyer from exposed, dismounted positions. He went on lone reconnaissance missions to discover what opposition his men faced, and on one occasion, when fired upon by a hostile machine gun, advanced alone and eliminated the enemy emplacement with a hand grenade. When a strong German attack threatened to overrun friendly positions, he moved through withering artillery, mortar, and small-arms fire, reorganized confused infantry units whose leaders had become casualties, and exhorted them to hold firm. Although wounded early in battle, he continued to direct fire from his advanced position until he was disabled by a high-explosive shell which shattered his arm, forcing him to withdraw. He was last seen at a medical aid station which was subsequently captured by the enemy. By his superb courage, inspiring leadership, and indomitable fighting spirit, 1st Lt. Leonard enabled our forces to hold off the enemy attack and was personally responsible for the direction of fire which destroyed six German tanks.

2812 ◆ *LESTER, FRED FAULKNER

Rank: Hospital Apprentice First Class
Service: U.S. Navy
Birthday: 29 April 1926
Place of Birth: Downers Grove, Du Page County, Illinois
Date of Death: 8 June 1945
Cemetery: Clarendon Hills Cemetery—Westmont, Illinois
Entered Service at: Illinois
Unit: Assault Rifle Platoon, 1st Battalion, 22d Marines, 6th Marine Division
Served as: Medical Corpsman
Battle or Place of Action: Okinawa Shima, Ryukyu Islands
Date of Action: 8 June 1945
Citation: For conspicuous gallantry and intrepidity at the risk of his life above and beyond the call of duty while serving as a medical corpsman with an assault rifle platoon, attached

to the 1st Battalion, 22d Marines, 6th Marine Division, during action against enemy Japanese forces on Okinawa Shima in the Ryukyu Chain, 8 June 1945. Quick to spot a wounded marine lying in an open field beyond the front lines following the relentless assault against a strategic Japanese hill position, Lester unhesitatingly crawled toward the casualty under a concentrated barrage from hostile machine guns, rifles, and grenades. Torn by enemy rifle bullets as he inched forward, he stoically disregarded the mounting fury of Japanese fire and his own pain to pull the wounded man toward a covered position. Struck by enemy fire a second time before he reached cover, he exerted tremendous effort and succeeded in pulling his comrade to safety where, too seriously wounded himself to administer aid, he instructed two of his squad in proper medical treatment of the rescued marine. Realizing that his own wounds were fatal, he staunchly refused medical attention for himself and, gathering his fast-waning strength with calm determination, coolly and expertly directed his men in the treatment of two other wounded marines, succumbing shortly thereafter. Completely selfless in his concern for the welfare of his fighting comrades, Lester, by his indomitable spirit, outstanding valor, and competent direction of others, had saved the life of one who otherwise must have perished, and had contributed to the safety of countless others. Lester's fortitude in the face of certain death sustains and enhances the highest traditions of the U.S. Naval Service. He gallantly gave his life for his country.

2813 ◆ *LINDSEY, DARRELL ROBINS

Rank: Captain
Service: U.S. Army Air Corps
Birthday: 30 December 1919
Place of Birth: Jefferson, Greene County, Iowa
Date of Death: 9 August 1944
Place of Death: L'Isle Adam railroad bridge over the Seine, France
Cemetery: A.B.M.C. Ardennes Cemetery (Wall of the Missing)—Neuvile-En-Condroz, Belgium
Entered Service at: Storm Lake, Buena Vista County, Iowa
Unit: 585th Bombardment Squadron, 394th Bombardment Group, 9th Air Force
Served as: Pilot of a B-26 Medium Bomber
Battle or Place of Action: L'Isle Adam railroad bridge over the Seine River, France
Date of Action: 9 August 1944
G.O. Number, Date: 43, 30 May 1945
Citation: On 9 August 1944, Capt. Lindsey led a formation of 30 B-26 medium bombers in a hazardous mission to destroy the strategic enemy-held L'Isle Adam railroad bridge over the Seine in occupied France. With most of the bridges over the Seine destroyed, the heavily fortified L'Isle Adam bridge was of inestimable value to the enemy in moving troops, supplies, and equipment to Paris. Capt. Lindsey was fully aware of the fierce resistance that would be encountered. Shortly after reaching enemy territory the formation was buffeted with heavy and accurate antiaircraft fire. By skillful evasive action, Capt. Lindsey was able to elude much of the enemy flak, but just before entering the bombing run his B-

26 was peppered with holes. During the bombing run the enemy fire was even more intense, and Capt. Lindsey's right engine received a direct hit and burst into flames. Despite the fact that his ship was hurled out of formation by the violence of the concussion, Capt. Lindsey brilliantly maneuvered back into the lead position without disrupting the flight. Fully aware that the gasoline tanks might explode at any moment, Capt. Lindsey gallantly elected to continue the perilous bombing run. With fire streaming from his right engine and his right wing half enveloped in flames, he led his formation over the target upon which the bombs were dropped with telling effect. Immediately after the objective was attacked, Capt. Lindsey gave the order for the crew to parachute from the doomed aircraft. With magnificent coolness and superb pilotage, and without regard for his own life, he held the swiftly descending airplane in a steady glide until the members of the crew could jump to safety. With the right wing completely enveloped in flames and an explosion of the gasoline tank imminent, Capt. Lindsey still remained unperturbed. The last man to leave the stricken plane was the bombardier, who offered to lower the wheels so that Capt. Lindsey might escape from the nose. Realizing that this might throw the aircraft into an uncontrollable spin and jeopardize the bombardier's chances to escape, Capt. Lindsey refused the offer. Immediately after the bombardier had bailed out, and before Capt. Lindsey was able to follow, the right gasoline tank exploded. The aircraft sheathed in fire, went into a steep dive and was seen to explode as it crashed. All who are living today from this plane owe their lives to the fact that Capt. Lindsey remained cool and showed supreme courage in this emergency.

2814 ◆ LINDSEY SR., JAKE WILLIAM

Rank: Technical Sergeant (highest rank: Second Lieutenant)
Service: U.S. Army
Birthday: 1 May 1921
Place of Birth: Isney, Alabama
Date of Death: 18 July 1988
Cemetery: White House Cemetery (MH)—Waynesboro, Mississippi
Entered Service at: Lucedale, George County, Mississippi
Unit: Company C, 16th Infantry, 1st Infantry Division
Battle or Place of Action: near Hamich, Germany
Date of Action: 16 November 1944
G.O. Number, Date: 43, 30 May 1945
Date of Presentation: 21 May 1945
Place of Presentation: At a joint session of Congress, Washington, D.C., presented by Pres. Harry S. Truman
Citation: For gallantry and intrepidity in action at the risk of his life above and beyond the call of duty. Technical Sergeant Jake W. Lindsey led a platoon, reduced to six of its original strength of forty, in the attack on an enemy position near Hamich, Germany, 16 November 1944. His men had captured their objective and were digging in when counterattacked by a German infantry company and five tanks. Armed with a rifle and grenades, T/Sgt. Lindsey took position on the left and in advance of the remnant of his platoon, and though exposed to heavy rifle, machine-gun and tank fire,

beat off repeated enemy attacks. Tanks moved to within 50 yards of him but were forced to withdraw because of his accurate rifle and grenade fire. After driving off the tanks, he knocked out two machine guns to his front. Though painfully wounded, T/Sgt. Lindsey continued firing and throwing grenades until his ammunition was expended. An enemy squad attempted to set up a machine gun 50 yards from him. Unmindful of his wounds and enemy fire, he rushed these eight German soldiers, singlehandedly closed with them, killed three with his bayonet, and captured three, the two others escaping. In his fearlessness, inspiring courage and superb leadership, T/Sgt. Lindsey carried on a brilliant defense of his platoon's hard-won ground, securing the position and inflicting heavy casualties on the numerically superior enemy.

2815 ◆ *LINDSTROM, FLOYD K.

Rank: Private First Class
Service: U.S. Army
Birthday: 21 June 1912
Place of Birth: Holdrege, Phelps County, Nebraska
Date of Death: 3 February 1944
Cemetery: Evergreen Cemetery (MH)—Colorado Springs, Colorado
Entered Service at: Colorado Springs, El Paso County, Colorado
Unit: Company H, 7th Infantry Regiment, 3d Infantry Division
Battle or Place of Action: near Mignano, Italy
Date of Action: 11 November 1943
G.O. Number, Date: 32, 20 April 1944
Place of Presentation: Camp Carson, Colorado, presented by Major Gen. Terry Allen, Commanding Gen. 104th Division, to his family
Citation: For conspicuous gallantry and intrepidity at the risk of life above and beyond the call of duty. On 11 November 1943, this soldier's platoon was furnishing machine-gun support for a rifle company attacking a hill near Mignano, Italy, when the enemy counterattacked, forcing the riflemen and half the machine-gun platoon to retire to a defensive position. Pfc. Lindstrom saw that his small section was alone and outnumbered five to one, yet he immediately deployed the few remaining men into position and opened fire with his single gun. The enemy centered fire on him with machine gun, machine pistols, and grenades. Unable to knock out the enemy nest from his original position, Pfc. Lindstrom picked up his own heavy machine gun and staggered 15 yards up the barren, rocky hillside to a new position, completely ignoring enemy small-arms fire which was striking all around him. From this new site, only 10 yards from the enemy machine gun, he engaged it in an intense duel. Realizing that he could not hit the hostile gunners because they were behind a large rock, he charged uphill under a steady stream of fire, killed both gunners with his pistol, and dragged their gun down to his own men, directing them to employ it against the enemy. Disregarding heavy rifle fire, he returned to the enemy machine-gun nest for two boxes of ammunition, came back, and resumed withering fire from his own gun. His spectacular performance completely broke up the German counterattack. Pfc. Lindstrom demonstrated aggressive spirit and complete fearlessness in the face of almost certain death.

2816 ◆ *LLOYD, EDGAR HAROLD

Rank: First Lieutenant
Service: U.S. Army
Birthday: 28 February 1922
Place of Birth: Blytheville, Mississippi County, Arkansas
Date of Death: 16 November 1944
Cemetery: Courthouse Lawn—Blytheville, Arkansas
Entered Service at: Blytheville, Mississippi County, Arkansas
Unit: Company E, 319th Infantry, 80th Infantry Division
Served as: Rifle Platoon Leader
Battle or Place of Action: near Pompey, France
Date of Action: 14 September 1944
G.O. Number, Date: 25, 7 April 1945
Citation: For conspicuous gallantry and intrepidity at the risk of his life above and beyond the call of duty. On 14 September 1944, Company E, 319th Infantry, with which 1st Lt. Lloyd was serving as a rifle platoon leader, was assigned the mission of expelling an estimated enemy force of 200 men from a heavily fortified position near Pompey, France. As the attack progressed, 1st Lt. Lloyd's platoon advanced to within 50 yards of the enemy position where they were caught in a withering machine-gun and rifle crossfire which inflicted heavy casualties and momentarily disorganized the platoon. With complete disregard for his own safety, 1st Lt. Lloyd leaped to his feet and led his men on a run into the raking fire, shouting encouragement to them. He jumped into the first enemy machine-gun position, knocked out the gunner with his fist, dropped a grenade, and jumped out before it exploded. Still shouting encouragement he went from one machine-gun nest to another, pinning the enemy down with submachine-gun fire until he was within throwing distance, and then destroyed them with hand grenades. He personally destroyed five machine guns and many of the enemy, and by his daring leadership and conspicuous bravery inspired his men to overrun the enemy positions and accomplish the objective in the face of seemingly insurmountable odds. His audacious determination and courageous devotion to duty exemplify the highest traditions of the military forces of the United States.

2817 ◆ *LOBAUGH, DONALD RONALD

Rank: Private
Service: U.S. Army
Birthday: 7 February 1925
Place of Birth: Freeport, Armstrong County, Pennsylvania
Date of Death: 22 July 1944
Cemetery: Rimbersburg Cemetery (MH)—Rimbersburg, Pennsylvania
Entered Service at: Freeport, Armstrong County, Pennsylvania
Unit: 127th Infantry, 32d Infantry Division
Battle or Place of Action: near Afua, New Guinea
Date of Action: 22 July 1944

G.O. Number, Date: 31, 17 April 1945
Citation: For conspicuous gallantry and intrepidity at the risk of his life above and beyond the call of duty near Afua, New Guinea, 22 July 1944. While Pvt. Lobaugh's company was withdrawing from its position on 21 July, the enemy attacked and cut off approximately one platoon of our troops. The platoon immediately occupied, organized, and defended a position, which it held throughout the night. Early on 22 July, an attempt was made to effect its withdrawal, but during the preparation therefor, the enemy emplaced a machine gun, protected by the fire of rifles and automatic weapons, which blocked the only route over which the platoon could move. Knowing that it was the key to the enemy position, Pfc. Lobaugh volunteered to attempt to destroy this weapon, even though in order to reach it he would be forced to work his way about 30 yards over ground devoid of cover. When part way across this open space he threw a hand grenade, but exposed himself in the act and was wounded. Heedless of his wound, he boldly rushed the emplacement, firing as he advanced. The enemy concentrated their fire on him, and he was struck repeatedly, but he continued his attack and killed two more before he was himself slain. Pfc. Lobaugh's heroic actions inspired his comrades to press the attack, and to drive the enemy from the position with heavy losses. His fighting determination and intrepidity in battle exemplify the highest traditions of the U.S. Armed Forces.

2818 ◆ LOGAN, JAMES MARION

Rank: Sergeant (highest rank: Technical Sergeant)
Service: U.S. Army
Birthday: 19 December 1920
Place of Birth: McNeil, Travis County, Texas
Entered Service at: Luling, Caldwell County, Texas
Unit: 1st Platoon, Company I, 3d Battalion, 141st Infantry, 36th Infantry Division
Served as: Rifleman
Battle or Place of Action: near Salerno, Italy
Date of Action: 9 September 1943
G.O. Number, Date: 54, 5 July 1944
Date of Presentation: 6 June 1944
Place of Presentation: near Naples, Italy, presented by Lt. Gen. Alexander M. Patch III
Citation: For conspicuous gallantry and intrepidity at the risk of life above and beyond the call of duty in action involving actual conflict on 9 September 1943 in the vicinity of Salerno, Italy. As a rifleman of an infantry company, Sgt. Logan landed with the first wave of the assault echelon on the beaches of the Gulf of Salerno, and after his company had advanced 800 yards inland and taken positions along the forward bank of an irrigation canal, the enemy began a serious counterattack from positions along a rock wall which ran parallel with the canal about 200 yards further inland. Voluntarily exposing himself to the fire of a machine gun located along the rock wall, which sprayed the ground so close to him that he was splattered with dirt and rocks and splinters from the impact of the bullets, Sgt. Logan killed the first three Germans as they came through a gap in the wall. He then attacked the machine gun. As he dashed across the

200 yards of exposed terrain a withering stream of fire followed his advance. Reaching the wall, he crawled along the base, within easy reach of the enemy crouched along the opposite side, until he reached the gun. Jumping up, he shot the two gunners down, hurdled the wall, and seized the gun. Swinging it around, he immediately opened fire on the enemy with the remaining ammunition, raking their flight and inflicting further casualties on them as they fled. After smashing the machine gun over the rocks, Sgt. Logan captured an enemy officer and private who were attempting to sneak away. Later in the morning, Sgt. Logan went after a sniper hidden in a house about 150 yards from the company. Again the intrepid Sergeant ran a gauntlet of fire to reach his objective. Shooting the lock off the door, Sgt. Logan kicked it in and shot the sniper who had just reached the bottom of the stairs. The conspicuous gallantry and intrepidity which characterized Sgt. Logan's exploits proved a constant inspiration to all the men of his company, and aided mate rially in insuring the success of the beachhead at Salerno.

2819 ◆ LOPEZ, JOSE MENDOZA

Rank: Sergeant (highest rank: Sergeant First Class)
Service: U.S. Army
Birthday: 1 June 1912
Place of Birth: Mission, Hidalgo County, Texas
Entered Service at: Brownsville, Cameron County, Texas
Unit: Weapons Platoon, Company M, 3d Battalion, 23d Infantry, 2d Infantry Division
Served as: Machine Gunner
Battle or Place of Action: near Krinkelt, Belgium
Date of Action: 17 December 1944
G.O. Number, Date: 47, 18 June 1945
Date of Presentation: 18 June 1945
Place of Presentation: Zepman Stadium, Nuremberg, Germany, presented by Major Gen. James Van Fleet III
Citation: On his own initiative, he carried his heavy machine gun from Company K's right flank to its left, in order to protect that flank, which was in danger of being overrun by advancing enemy infantry supported by tanks. Occupying a shallow hole offering no protection above the waist, he cut down a group of 10 Germans. Ignoring enemy fire from an advancing tank, he held his position and cut down 25 more enemy infantry attempting to turn his flank. Glancing to his right, he saw a large number of infantry swarming in from the front. Although dazed and shaken from enemy artillery fire which had crashed into the ground only a few yards away, he realized that his position soon would be outflanked. Again, alone, he carried his machine gun to a position to the right rear of the sector; enemy tanks and infantry were forcing a withdrawal. Blown over backwards by the concussion of enemy fire, he immediately reset his gun and continued his fire. Singlehanded he held off the German horde until he was satisfied his company had effected its retirement. Again he loaded his gun on his back and in a hail of small-arms fire he ran to a point where a few of his comrades were attempting to set up another defense against the onrushing enemy. He fired from this position until his ammunition was exhausted. Still carrying his gun, he fell back with his small group to

Krinkelt. Sgt. Lopez's gallantry and intrepidity, on seemingly suicidal missions in which he killed at least 100 of the enemy, were almost solely responsible for allowing Company K to avoid being enveloped, to withdraw successfully, and to give other forces coming up in support time to build a line which repelled the enemy drive.

2820 ◆ LUCAS, JACKLYN HAROLD

Rank: Private First Class
Service: U.S. Marine Corps Reserve
Birthday: 14 February 1928
Place of Birth: Plymouth, Washington County, North Carolina
Entered Service at: Norfolk, Norfolk County, Virginia
Unit: Company C, 1st Battalion, 26th Marines, 5th Marine Division
Served as: Rifleman
Battle or Place of Action: Iwo Jima, Volcano Islands
Date of Action: 20 February 1945
Date of Presentation: 5 October 1945
Place of Presentation: The White House, presented by Pres. Harry S. Truman
Citation: For conspicuous gallantry and intrepidity at the risk of his life above and beyond the call of duty while serving with the 1st Battalion, 26th Marines, 5th Marine Division, during action against enemy Japanese forces on Iwo Jima, Volcano Islands, 20 February 1945. While creeping through a treacherous, twisting ravine which ran in close proximity to a fluid and uncertain front line on D-day plus one, Pfc. Lucas and three other men were suddenly ambushed by a hostile patrol which savagely attacked with rifle fire and grenades. Quick to act when the lives of the small group were endangered by two grenades which landed directly in front of them, Pfc. Lucas unhesitatingly hurled himself over his comrades upon one grenade and pulled the other under him, absorbing the whole blasting forces of the explosions in his own body in order to shield his companions from the concussion and murderous flying fragments. By his inspiring action and valiant spirit of self-sacrifice, he not only protected his comrades from certain injury or possible death but also enabled them to rout the Japanese patrol and continue the advance. His exceptionally courageous initiative and loyalty reflect the highest credit upon Pfc. Lucas and the U.S. Naval Service.

2821 ◆ *LUMMUS, JACK

Rank: First Lieutenant
Service: U.S. Marine Corps Reserve
Birthday: 22 October 1915
Place of Birth: Ennis, Ellis County, Texas
Date of Death: 8 March 1945
Cemetery: Myrtle Cemetery (MH)—Ennis, Texas
Entered Service at: Texas
Unit: Company E, 2d Battalion, 27th Marines, 5th Marine Division
Served as: Rifle Platoon Leader
Battle or Place of Action: Iwo Jima, Volcano Islands
Date of Action: 8 March 1945

Citation: For conspicuous gallantry and intrepidity at the risk of his life above and beyond the call of duty as leader of a rifle platoon attached to the 2d Battalion, 27th Marines, 5th Marine Division, in action against enemy Japanese forces on Iwo Jima in the Volcano Islands, 8 March 1945. Resuming his assault tactics with bold decision after fighting without respite for two days and nights, 1st Lt. Lummus slowly advanced his platoon against an enemy deeply entrenched in a network of mutually supporting positions. Suddenly halted by a terrific concentration of hostile fire, he unhesitatingly moved forward of his front lines in an effort to neutralize the Japanese position. Although knocked to the ground when an enemy grenade exploded close by, he immediately recovered himself and, again moving forward despite the intensified barrage, quickly located, attacked, and destroyed the occupied emplacement. Instantly taken under fire by the garrison of a supporting pillbox and further assailed by the slashing fury of hostile rifle fire, he fell under the impact of a second enemy grenade but, courageously disregarding painful shoulder wounds, staunchly continued his heroic one-man assault and charged the second pillbox, annihilating all the occupants. Subsequently returning to his platoon position, he fearlessly traversed his lines under fire, encouraging his men to advance and directing the fire of supporting tanks against other stubbornly holding Japanese emplacements. Held up again by a devastating barrage, he again moved into the open, rushed a third heavily fortified installation and killed the defending troops. Determined to crush all resistance, he led his men indomitably, personally attacking foxholes and spider traps with his carbine and systematically reducing the fanatic opposition, until, stepping on a land mine, he sustained fatal wounds. By his outstanding valor, skilled tactics, and tenacious perseverance in the face of overwhelming odds, 1st Lt. Lummus had insp ired his stouthearted marines to continue the relentless drive northward, thereby contributing materially to the success of his regimental mission. His dauntless leadership and unwavering devotion to duty throughout sustain and enhance the highest traditions of the U.S. Naval Service. He gallantly gave his life in the service of his country.

2822 ◆ MABRY JR., GEORGE LAFAYETTE

Rank: Lieutenant Colonel (highest rank: Major General)
Service: U.S. Army
Birthday: 14 September 1917
Place of Birth: Sumter, Sumter County, South Carolina
Date of Death: 13 July 1990
Cemetery: Holy Cross Episcopal Church Cemetery (MH)—Stateboro, South Carolina
Entered Service at: Sumter, Sumter County, South Carolina
Unit: 2d Battalion, 8th Infantry, 4th Infantry Division
Served as: Battalion Commander
Battle or Place of Action: Hurtgen Forest near Schevenhutte, Germany
Date of Action: 20 November 1944
G.O. Number, Date: 77, September 1945
Date of Presentation: 23 August 1945
Place of Presentation: The White House, presented by Pres. Harry S. Truman

Citation: He was commanding the 2d Battalion, 8th Infantry, in an attack through the Hurtgen Forest near Schevenhutte, Germany, on 20 November 1944. During the early phases of the assault, the leading elements of his battalion were halted by a minefield and immobilized by heavy hostile fire. Advancing alone into the mined area, Col. Mabry established a safe route of passage. He then moved ahead of the foremost scouts, personally leading the attack, until confronted by a booby-trapped double concertina obstacle. With the assistance of the scouts, he disconnected the explosives and cut a path through the wire. Upon moving through the opening, he observed three enemy in foxholes whom he captured at bayonet point. Driving steadily forward he paced the assault against three log bunkers which housed mutually supported automatic weapons. Racing up a slope ahead of his men, he found the initial bunker deserted, then pushed on to a second where he was suddenly confronted by nine onrushing enemy. Using the butt of his rifle, he felled one adversary and bayoneted a second, before his scouts came to his aid and assisted him in overcoming the others in hand-to-hand combat. Accompanied by the riflemen, he charged the third bunker under point-blank small-arms fire and led the way into the fortification from which he prodded six enemy at bayonet point. Following the consolidation of this area, he led his battalion across 300 yards of fire-swept terrain to seize elevated ground upon which he established a defensive position which menaced the enemy on both flanks, and provided his regiment a firm foothold on the approach to the Cologne Plain. Col. Mabry's superlative courage, daring, and leadership in an operation of major importance exemplify the finest characteristics of the military service.

2823 ◆ MacARTHUR, DOUGLAS

Rank: General of the Armies
Service: U.S. Army
Birthday: 26 January 1880
Place of Birth: Little Rock, Pulaski County, Arkansas
Date of Death: 5 April 1964
Cemetery: Old Norfolk City Hall Memorial (PM)— Norfolk, Virginia
Entered Service at: Ashland, Ashland County, Wisconsin
Unit: U.S. Army Forces in the Far East
Served as: Commanding General
Battle or Place of Action: Bataan Peninsula, Philippine Islands
G.O. Number, Date: 16, 1 April 1942
Date of Presentation: 30 June 1942
Place of Presentation: Melborne, Australia, presented by Nelson Trussler Johnson, Minister of Australia
Citation: For conspicuous leadership in preparing the Philippine Islands to resist conquest, for gallantry and intrepidity above and beyond the call of duty in action against invading Japanese forces, and for the heroic conduct of defensive and offensive operations on the Bataan Peninsula. He mobilized, trained, and led an army which has received world acclaim for its gallant defense against a tremendous superiority of enemy forces in men and arms. His utter disregard of personal danger under heavy fire and aerial bombardment, his

calm judgement in each crisis, inspired his troops, galvanized the spirit of resistance of the Filipino people, and confirmed the faith of the American people in their Armed Forces.

2824 ◆ MacGILLIVARY, CHARLES ANDREW

Rank: Sergeant (highest rank: Technical Sergeant)
Service: U.S. Army
Birthday: 17 January 1917
Place of Birth: Charlottetown, Prince Edward Island, Canada
Entered Service at: Boston, Suffolk County, Massachusetts
Unit: Company I, 463d Battalion, 71st Infantry, 44th Infantry Division
Served as: Platoon Leader
Battle or Place of Action: near Woelfling, France
Date of Action: 1 January 1945
G.O. Number, Date: 77, 10 September 1945
Date of Presentation: 23 August 1945
Place of Presentation: The White House, presented by Pres. Harry S. Truman
Citation: He led a squad when his unit moved forward in darkness to meet the threat of a breakthrough by elements of the 17th German Panzer Grenadier Division. Assigned to protect the left flank, he discovered hostile troops digging in. As he reported this information, several German machine guns opened fire, stopping the American advance. Knowing the position of the enemy, Sgt. MacGillivary volunteered to knock out one of the guns while another company closed in from the right to assault the remaining strongpoints. He circled from the left through woods and snow, carefully worked his way to the emplacement, and shot the two camouflaged gunners at a range of three feet as other enemy forces withdrew. Early in the afternoon of the same day, Sgt. MacGillivary was dispatched on reconnaissance and found that Company I was being opposed by about six machine guns reinforcing a company of fanatically fighting Germans. His unit began to attack but was pinned down by furious automatic and small-arms fire. With a clear idea of where the enemy guns were placed, he voluntarily embarked on a lone combat patrol. Skillfully taking advantage of all available cover, he stalked the enemy, reached a hostile machine gun, and blasted its crew with a grenade. He picked up a submachine gun from the battlefield and pressed on to within 10 yards of another machine gun, where the enemy crew discovered him and feverishly tried to swing their weapon into line to cut him down. He charged ahead, jumped into the midst of the Germans, and killed them with several bursts. Without hesitation, he moved on to still another machine gun, creeping, crawling, and rushing from tree to tree, until close enough to toss a grenade into the emplacement and close with its defenders. He dispatched this crew also, but was himself seriously wounded. Through his indomitable fighting spirit, great initiative, and utter disregard for personal safety in the face of powerful enemy resistance, Sgt. MacGillivary destroyed four hostile machine guns and immeasurably helped his company to continue on its mission with minimum casualties.

2825 ◆ *MAGRATH, JOHN D.

Rank: Private First Class
Service: U.S. Army
Birthday: 4 July 1924
Place of Birth: East Norwalk, Fairfield County, Connecticut
Date of Death: 14 April 1945
Cemetery: Riverside Cemetery (MH)—Norwalk, Connecticut
Entered Service at: East Norwalk, Fairfield County, Connecticut
Unit: Company G, 85th Infantry, 10th Mountain Division
Served as: Scout
Battle or Place of Action: near Castel d'Aiano, Italy
Date of Action: 14 April 1945
G.O. Number, Date: 71, 17 July 1946
Citation: He displayed conspicuous gallantry and intrepidity above and beyond the call of duty when his company was pinned down by heavy artillery, mortar, and small-arms fire, near Castel d'Aiano, Italy. Volunteering to act as scout, armed with only a rifle, he charged headlong into withering fire, killing two Germans and wounding three in order to capture a machine gun. Carrying this weapon across an open field through heavy fire, he neutralized two more machine-gun nests; he then circled behind four other Germans, killing them with a burst as they were firing on his company. Spotting another dangerous enemy position to his right, he knelt with the machine gun in his arms and exchanged fire with the Germans until he had killed two and wounded three. The enemy now poured increased mortar and artillery fire on the company's newly won position. Pfc. Magrath fearlessly volunteered again to brave the shelling in order to collect a report of casualties. Heroically carrying out this task, he made the supreme sacrifice—a climax to the valor and courage that are in keeping with the highest traditions of the military service.

2826 ◆ *MANN, JOE EUGENE

Rank: Private First Class
Service: U.S. Army
Birthday: 12 July 1922
Place of Birth: Reardan, Lincoln County, Washington
Date of Death: 19 September 1944
Cemetery: Greenwood Cemetery—Spokane, Washington
Entered Service at: Seattle, King County, Washington
Unit: Company H, 502d Parachute Infantry, 101st Airborne Division
Served as: Lead Scout
Battle or Place of Action: Best, Holland
Date of Action: 18 September 1944
G.O. Number, Date: 73, 30 August 1945
Date of Presentation: Spring, 1945
Place of Presentation: Baxter Veterans Hospital, Spokane, WA, presented by the hospital commanding officer to his Father
Citation: He distinguished himself by conspicuous gallantry above and beyond the call of duty. On 18 September 1944, in the vicinity of Best, Holland, his platoon, attempting to seize the bridge across the Wilhelmina Canal, was surrounded

and isolated by an enemy force greatly superior in personnel and firepower. Acting as lead scout, Pfc. Mann boldly crept to within rocket-launcher range of an enemy artillery position and, in the face of heavy enemy fire, destroyed an 88-mm gun and an ammunition dump. Completely disregarding the great danger involved, he remained in his exposed position, and, with his M1 rifle, killed the enemy one by one until he was wounded four times. Taken to a covered position, he insisted on returning to a forward position to stand guard during the night. On the following morning the enemy launched a concerted attack and advanced to within a few yards of the position, throwing hand grenades as they approached. One of these landed within a few feet of Pfc. Mann. Unable to raise his arms, which were bandaged to his body, he yelled "Grenade" and threw his body over the grenade, and as it exploded, died. His outstanding gallantry above and beyond the call of duty and his magnificent conduct were an everlasting inspiration to his comrades for whom he gave his life.

2827 ◆ *MARTIN, HARRY LINN

Rank: First Lieutenant
Service: U.S. Marine Corps Reserve
Birthday: 4 January 1911
Place of Birth: Bucyrus, Crawford County, Ohio
Date of Death: 26 March 1945
Cemetery: Oakwood Cemetery (MH)—Bucyrus, Ohio
Entered Service at: Ohio
Unit: Company C, 5th Pioneer Battalion, 5th Marine Division
Served as: Platoon Leader
Battle or Place of Action: Iwo Jima, Volcano Islands
Date of Action: 26 March 1945
Citation: For conspicuous gallantry and intrepidity at the risk of his life above and beyond the call of duty as platoon leader attached to Company C, 5th Pioneer Battalion, 5th Marine Division, in action against enemy Japanese forces on Iwo Jima, Volcano Islands, 26 March 1945. With his sector of the 5th Pioneer Battalion bivouac area penetrated by a concentrated enemy attack launched a few minutes before dawn, 1st Lt. Martin instantly organized a firing line with the marines nearest his foxhole and succeeded in checking momentarily the headlong rush of the Japanese. Determined to rescue several of his men trapped in positions overrun by the enemy, he defied intense hostile fire to work his way through the Japanese to the surrounded marines. Although sustaining two severe wounds, he blasted the Japanese who attempted to intercept him, located his beleaguered men, and directed them to their own lines. When four of the infiltrating enemy took possession of an abandoned machine-gun pit and subjected his sector to a barrage of hand grenades, 1st Lt. Martin, alone and armed only with a pistol, boldly charged the hostile position and killed all its occupants. Realizing that his few remaining comrades could not repulse another organized attack, he called to his men to follow and then charged into the midst of the strong enemy force, firing his weapon and scattering them until he fell, mortally wounded by a grenade. By his outstanding valor, indomitable fighting spirit, and tenacious determination in the face of overwhelming

odds, 1st Lt. Martin permanently disrupted a coordinated Japanese attack and prevented a greater loss of life in his own and adjacent platoons. His inspiring leadership and unswerving devotion to duty reflect the highest credit upon himself and the U.S. Naval Service. He gallantly gave his life in the service of his country.

2828 ◆ *MARTINEZ, JOE P.

Rank: Private
Service: U.S. Army
Birthday: 27 July 1920
Place of Birth: Taos, Taos County, New Mexico
Date of Death: 26 May 1943
Cemetery: Ault Cemetery (MH)—Ault, Colorado
Entered Service at: Ault, Weld County, Colorado
Unit: Company K, 32d Infantry, 7th Infantry Division
Served as: Automatic Rifleman
Battle or Place of Action: on Attu Island, Aleutian Islands
Date of Action: 26 May 1943
G.O. Number, Date: 71, 27 October 1943
Date of Presentation: 11 November 1943
Place of Presentation: Ault, Colorado, presented by Brigadier Gen. Frank L. Culin Jr. to his family
Citation: For conspicuous gallantry and intrepidity above and beyond the call of duty in action with the enemy. Over a period of several days, repeated efforts to drive the enemy from a key defensive position high in the snow-covered precipitous mountains between east arm of Holtz Bay and Chichogof Harbor had failed. On 26 May 1943, troop dispositions were readjusted and a trial coordinated attack on this position by a reinforced battalion was launched. Initially successful, the attack hesitated. In the face of severe hostile machine-gun, rifle, and mortar fire, Pvt. Martinez, an automatic rifleman, rose to his feet and resumed his advance. Occasionally he stopped to urge his comrades on. His example inspired others to follow. After a most difficult climb, Pvt. Martinez eliminated resistance from part of the enemy position by BAR fire and hand grenades, thus assisting the advance of other attacking elements. This success only partially completed the action. The main Holtz-Chichogof Pass rose about 150 feet higher, flanked by steep rocky ridges and reached a snow-filled defile. Passage was barred by enemy fire from either flank and from tiers of snow trenches in front. Despite these obstacles, and knowing of their existence, Pvt. Martinez again led the troops on and up, personally silencing several trenches with BAR fire and ultimately reaching the pass itself. Here, just below the knifelike rim of the pass, Pvt. Martinez encountered a final enemy-occupied trench and as he was engaged in firing into it he was mortally wounded. The pass, however, was taken and its capture was an important preliminary to the end of organized hostile resistance on the island.

2829 ◆ *MASON, LEONARD FOSTER

Rank: Private First Class
Service: U.S. Marine Corps
Birthday: 2 February 1920

Place of Birth: Middlesboro, Bell County, Kentucky
Date of Death: 22 July 1944
Cemetery: National Memorial Cemetery of the Pacific (Wall of the Missing)—Honolulu, Hawaii
Entered Service at: Ohio
Unit: 2d Battalion, 3d Marines, 3d Marine Division
Served as: Automatic Rifleman
Battle or Place of Action: Asan-Adelup Beachhead, Guam, Marianas Islands
Date of Action: 22 July 1944
Citation: For conspicuous gallantry and intrepidity at the risk of his life above and beyond the call of duty as an automatic rifleman serving with the 2d Battalion, 3d Marines, 3d Marine Division, in action against enemy Japanese forces on the Asan-Adelup Beachhead, Guam, Marianas Islands on 22 July 1944. Suddenly taken under fire by two enemy machine guns not more than 15 yards away while clearing out hostile positions holding up the advance of his platoon through a narrow gully, Pfc. Mason, alone and entirely on his own initiative, climbed out of the gully and moved parallel to it toward the rear of the enemy position. Although fired upon immediately by hostile riflemen from a higher position and wounded repeatedly in the arm and shoulder, Pfc. Mason grimly pressed forward and had just reached his objective when hit again by a burst of enemy machine-gun fire, causing a critical wound to which he later succumbed. With valiant disregard for his own peril, he persevered, clearing out the hostile position, killing five Japanese, wounding another, and then rejoining his platoon to report the results of his action before consenting to be evacuated. His exceptionally heroic act in the face of almost certain death enabled his platoon to accomplish its mission and reflects the highest credit upon Pfc. Mason and the U.S. Naval Service. He gallantly gave his life for his country.

2830 ◆ *MATHIES, ARCHIBALD

Rank: Sergeant
Service: U.S. Army Air Corps
Birthday: 3 June 1918
Place of Birth: Scotland
Date of Death: 20 February 1944
Cemetery: Finleyville Cemetery (MH)—Finleyville, Pennsylvania
Entered Service at: Pittsburgh, Allegheny County, Pennsylvania
Unit: 510th Bombardment Squadron, 351st Bombardment Group, 8th Air Force
Served as: Engineer & Ball Turret Gunner on a B-17
Battle or Place of Action: over Europe
Date of Action: 20 February 1944
G.O. Number, Date: 52, 22 June 1944
Place of Presentation: Presented to his Mother
Citation: For conspicuous gallantry and intrepidity at the risk of life above and beyond the call of duty in action against the enemy in connection with a bombing mission over enemy-occupied Europe on 20 February 1944. The aircraft on which Sgt. Mathies was serving as engineer and ball turret gunner was attacked by a squadron of enemy fighters with the

result that the copilot was killed outright, the pilot wounded and rendered unconscious, the radio operator wounded, and the plane severely damaged. Nevertheless, Sgt. Mathies and other members of the crew managed to right the plane and fly it back to their home station, where they contacted the control tower and reported the situation. Sgt. Mathies and the navigator volunteered to attempt to land the plane. Other members of the crew were ordered to jump, leaving Sgt. Mathies and the navigator aboard. After observing the distressed aircraft from another plane, Sgt. Mathies' commanding officer decided the damaged plane could not be landed by the inexperienced crew and ordered them to abandon it and parachute to safety. Demonstrating unsurpassed courage and heroism, Sgt. Mathies and the navigator replied that the pilot was still alive but could not be moved and they would not desert him. They were then told to attempt a landing. After two unsuccessful efforts, the plane crashed into an open field in a third attempt to land. Sgt. Mathies, the navigator, and the wounded pilot were killed.

2831 ◆ *MATHIS, JACK WARREN

Rank: First Lieutenant
Service: U.S. Army Air Corps
Birthday: 25 September 1921
Place of Birth: San Angelo, Tom Green County, Texas
Date of Death: 18 March 1943
Place of Death: over Vegesack, Germany
Cemetery: Fairmount Cemetery—San Angelo, Texas
Entered Service at: San Angelo, Tom Green County, Texas
Unit: 359th Bombardment Squadron, 303d Bombardment Group, 8th Air Force
Served as: Lead Bombardier of a B-17
Battle or Place of Action: over Vegesack, Germany
Date of Action: 18 March 1943
G.O. Number, Date: 38, 12 July 1943
Date of Presentation: 21 September 1943
Place of Presentation: Goodfellow Field, San Angelo, Texas, presented by Maj. Gen. Barton K. Yount to his Mother
Citation: For conspicuous gallantry and intrepidity above and beyond the call of duty in action with the enemy over Vegesack, Germany on 18 March 1943. First Lt. Mathis, as leading bombardier of his squadron, flying through intense and accurate antiaircraft fire, was just starting his bomb run, upon which the entire squadron depended upon for accurate bombing, when he was hit by the enemy antiaircraft fire. His right arm was shattered above the elbow, a large wound was torn in his side and abdomen, and he was knocked from his bombsight to the rear of the bombardier's compartment. Realizing that the success of the mission depended upon him, 1st Lt. Mathis, by sheer determination and willpower, though mortally wounded, dragged himself back to his sights, released his bombs, then died at his post of duty. As the result of this action the airplanes of his bombardment squadron placed their bombs directly upon the assigned target for a perfect attack against the enemy. First Lt. Mathis' undaunted bravery has been a great inspiration to the officers and men of his unit.

2832 ◆ MAXWELL, ROBERT DALE

Rank: Technician Fifth Grade
Service: U.S. Army
Birthday: 26 October 1920
Place of Birth: Boise, Ada County, Idaho
Entered Service at: Creswell, Larimer County, Colorado
Unit: Wire Section, Communications Platoon, Headquarters Company, 3d Battalion, 7th Infantry Regiment, 3d Infantry Division
Served as: Wireman/Switchboard Operator
Battle or Place of Action: near Besancon, France
Date of Action: 7 September 1944
G.O. Number, Date: 24, 6 April 1945
Date of Presentation: 12 May 1945
Place of Presentation: Denver, Colorado, presented by Gen. Danielson
Citation: For conspicuous gallantry and intrepidity at the risk of life above and beyond the call of duty on 7 September 1944, near Besancon, France. Technician 5th Grade Maxwell and three other soldiers, armed only with .45-caliber automatic pistols, defended the battalion observation post against an overwhelming onslaught by enemy infantrymen in approximately platoon strength, supported by 20-mm flak and machine-gun fire, who had infiltrated through the battalion's forward companies and were attacking the observation post with machine-gun, machine pistol, and grenade fire at ranges as close as 10 yards. Despite a hail of fire from automatic weapons and grenade launchers, Technician 5th Grade Maxwell aggressively fought off advancing enemy elements and, by his calmness, tenacity, and fortitude, inspired his fellows to continue the unequal struggle. When an enemy hand grenade was thrown in the midst of his squad, Technician 5th Grade Maxwell unhesitatingly hurled himself squarely upon it, using his blanket and his unprotected body to absorb the full force of the explosion. This act of instantaneous heroism permanently maimed Technican 5th Grade Maxwell, but saved the lives of his comrades in arms and facilitated maintenance of vital military communications during the temporary withdrawal of the battalion's forward headquarters.

2833 ◆ *MAY, MARTIN O.

Rank: Private First Class
Service: U.S. Army
Birthday: 18 April 1922
Place of Birth: Phillipsburg, Warren County, New Jersey
Date of Death: 21 April 1945
Cemetery: National Memorial Cemetery of the Pacific (N-1242) (MH)—Honolulu, Hawaii
Entered Service at: Phillipsburg, Warren County, New Jersey
Unit: 307th Infantry, 77th Infantry Division
Served as: Heavy Machine Gunner
Battle or Place of Action: Iegusuku-Yama, Ie-shima, Ryukyu Islands
Date of Action: 19-20 April 1945
G.O. Number, Date: 9, 25 January 1946
Citation: He gallantly maintained a three-day stand in the

face of terrible odds when American troops fought for possession of the rugged slopes of Iegusuku-Yama on Ie-shima, Ryukyu Islands. After placing his heavy machine gun in an advantageous yet vulnerable position on a ridge to support riflemen, he became the target of fierce mortar and small-arms fire from the counterattacking Japanese. He repulsed this assault by sweeping the enemy with accurate bursts while explosions and ricocheting bullets threw blinding dust and dirt about him. He broke up a second counterattack by hurling grenades into the midst of the enemy forces, and then refused to withdraw, volunteering to maintain his post and cover the movement of American riflemen as they reorganized to meet any further hostile action. The major effort of the enemy did not develop until the morning of 21 April. It found Pfc. May still supporting the rifle company in the face of devastating rifle, machine-gun, and mortar fire. While many of the friendly troops about him became casualties, he continued to fire his machine gun until he was severely wounded and his gun rendered useless by the burst of a mortar shell. Refusing to withdraw from the violent action, he blasted fanatical Japanese troops with hand grenades until wounded again, this time mortally. By his intrepidity and the extreme tenacity with which he held firm until death against overwhelming forces, Pfc. May killed at least 16 Japanese, was largely responsible for maintaining the American lines, and inspired his comrades to efforts which later resulted in complete victory and seizure of the mountain stronghold.

2834 ◆ MAYFIELD, MELVIN

Rank: Corporal
Service: U.S. Army
Birthday: 12 March 1919
Place of Birth: Salem, Harrison County, West Virginia
Date of Death: 19 June 1990
Cemetery: Frazeysburg Cemetery (MH)—Frazeysburg, Ohio
Entered Service at: Nashport, Muskingum County, Ohio
Unit: Company D, 1st Battalion, 20th Infantry, 6th Infantry Division
Served as: Lineman
Battle or Place of Action: Cordillera Mountains, Luzon, Philippine Islands
Date of Action: 29 July 1945
G.O. Number, Date: 49, 31 May 1946
Citation: He displayed conspicuous gallantry and intrepidity above and beyond the call of duty while fighting in the Cordillera Mountains of Luzon, Philippine Islands. When two Filipino companies were pinned down under a torrent of enemy fire that converged on them from a circular ridge commanding their position, Cpl. Mayfield, in a gallant single-handed effort to aid them, rushed from shell hole to shell hole until he reached four enemy caves atop the barren fire-swept hill. With grenades and his carbine, he assaulted each of the caves while enemy fire pounded about him. However, before he annihilated the last hostile redoubt, a machine-gun bullet destroyed his weapon and slashed his left hand. Disregarding his wound, he secured more grenades and dauntlessly charged again into the face of point-blank fire to help destroy a hostile observation post. By his gallant determination and heroic leadership, Cpl. Mayfield inspired the men to eliminate all remaining pockets of resistance in the area and to press the advance against the enemy.

2835 ◆ McCALL, THOMAS EDWARD

Rank: Staff Sergeant
Service: U.S. Army
Birthday: 9 May 1916
Place of Birth: Burrton, Harvey County, Kansas
Date of Death: 19 September 1965
Place of Death: Darlington, Maryland
Cemetery: Spring Vale Cemetery—Lafayette, Indiana
Entered Service at: Veedersburg, Fountain County, Indiana
Unit: Company F, 143d Infantry, 36th Infantry Division
Served as: Commander of a Machine Gun Section
Battle or Place of Action: near San Angelo, Italy
Date of Action: 22 January 1944
G.O. Number, Date: 31, 17 April 1945
Citation: For conspicuous gallantry and intrepidity at risk of life above and beyond the call of duty. On 22 January 1944, Company F had the mission of crossing the Rapido River in the vicinity of San Angelo, Italy, and attacking the well-prepared German positions to the west. For the defense of these positions the enemy had prepared a network of machine-gun positions covering the terrain to the front with a pattern of withering machine-gun fire, and mortar and artillery positions zeroed in on the defilade areas. S/Sgt. McCall commanded a machine-gun section that was to provide added fire support for the riflemen. Under cover of darkness, Company F advanced to the river-crossing site and under intense enemy mortar, artillery, and machine-gun fire crossed an ice-covered bridge which was continually the target for enemy fire. Many casualties occurred on reaching the west side of the river and reorganization was imperative. Exposing himself to the deadly enemy machine-gun and small-arms fire that swept over the flat terrain, S/Sgt. McCall, with unusual calmness, encouraged and welded his men into an effective fighting unit. He then led them forward across the muddy, exposed terrain. Skillfully he guided his men through a barbed-wire entanglement to reach a road where he personally placed the weapons of his two squads into positions of vantage, covering the battalion's front. A shell landed near one of the positions, wounding the gunner, killing the assistant gunner, and destroying the weapon. Even though enemy shells were falling dangerously near, S/Sgt. McCall crawled across the treacherous terrain and rendered first aid to the wounded man, dragging him into a position of cover with the help of another man. The gunners of the second machine gun had been wounded from the fragments of an enemy shell, leaving S/Sgt. McCall the only remaining member of his machine-gun section. Displaying outstanding aggressiveness, he ran forward with the weapon on his hip, reaching a point 30 yards from the enemy, where he fired two bursts of fire into the nest, killing or wounding all of the crew and putting the gun out of action. A second machine gun now opened fire upon him and he rushed its position, firing his weapon from the hip, killing four of the guncrew. A third machine gun, 50 yards in the rear of the first two, was delivering a tremendous

volume of fire upon our troops. S/Sgt. McCall spotted its position and valiantly went toward it in the face of overwhelming enemy fire. He was last seen courageously moving forward on the enemy position, firing his machine gun from the hip. S/Sgt. McCall's intrepidity and unhesitating willingness to sacrifice his life exemplify the highest traditions of the Armed Forces.

2836 ◆ McCAMPBELL, DAVID

Rank: Commander (highest rank: Captain)
Service: U.S. Navy
Birthday: 16 January 1910
Place of Birth: Bessemer, Jefferson County, Alabama
Entered Service at: West Palm Beach, Palm Beach County, Florida
Unit: Air Group 15, U.S.S. *Essex*
Served as: Air Group Commander/Pilot of a Grumman Hellcat
Battle or Place of Action: Battle of the Philippine Sea & Battle of Leyte Gulf
Date of Action: 19 June & 24-25 October 1944
Date of Presentation: 10 January 1945
Place of Presentation: The White House, presented by Pres. Franklin D. Roosevelt
Citation: For conspicuous gallantry and intrepidity at the risk of his life above and beyond the call of duty as commander, Air Group 15, during combat against enemy Japanese aerial forces in the first and second battles of the Philippine Sea. An inspiring leader, fighting boldly in the face of terrific odds, Comdr. McCampbell led his fighter planes against a force of 80 Japanese carrier-based aircraft bearing down on our fleet on 19 June 1944. Striking fiercely in valiant defense of our surface force, he personally destroyed seven hostile planes during this single engagement in which the outnumbering attack force was utterly routed and vitually annihilated. During a major fleet engagement with the enemy on 24 October, Comdr. McCampbell, assisted by but one plane, intercepted and daringly attacked a formation of 60 hostile land-based craft approaching our forces. Fighting desperately but with superb skill against such overwhelming airpower, he shot down nine Japanese planes and, completely disorganizing the enemy group, forced the remainder to abandon the attack before a single aircraft could reach the fleet. His great personal valor and indomitable spirit of aggression under extremely perilous combat conditions reflect the highest credit upon Comdr. McCampbell and the U.S. Naval Service.

2837 ◆ McCANDLESS, BRUCE

Rank: Commander (highest rank: Rear Admiral)
Service: U.S. Navy
Birthday: 12 August 1911
Place of Birth: Washington, D.C.
Date of Death: 24 January 1968
Cemetery: U.S. Naval Academy Cemetery (Lot 1021)—Annapolis, Maryland
Entered Service at: Colorado
Unit: U.S.S. *San Francisco*

Served as: Commanding Officer
Battle or Place of Action: Iron Bottom Sound, off Savo Island, Solomon Islands
Date of Action: 12-13 November 1942
Date of Presentation: 12 December 1942
Place of Presentation: Onboard the U.S.S. *San Francisco*, San Francisco, California, presented by Adm. Ernest J. King
Citation: For conspicuous gallantry and exceptionally distinguished service above and beyond the call of duty as communication officer of the U.S.S. *San Francisco* in combat with enemy Japanese forces in the battle off Savo Island, 12–13 November 1942. In the midst of a violent night engagement, the fire of a determined and desperate enemy seriously wounded Lt. Comdr. McCandless and rendered him unconscious, killed or wounded the admiral in command, his staff, the captain of the ship, the navigator, and all other personnel on the navigating and signal bridges. Faced with the lack of superior command upon his recovery, and displaying superb initiative, he promptly assumed command of the ship and ordered her course and gunfire against an overwhelmingly powerful force. With his superiors in other vessels unaware of the loss of their admiral, and challenged by his great responsibility, Lt. Comdr. McCandless boldly continued to engage the enemy and to lead our column of following vessels to a great victory. Largely through his brilliant seamanship and great courage, the U.S.S. *San Francisco* was brought back to port, saved to fight again in the service of her country.

2838 ◆ *McCARD, ROBERT HOWARD

Rank: Gunnery Sergeant
Service: U.S. Marine Corps
Birthday: 25 November 1918
Place of Birth: Syracuse, Onondaga County, New York
Date of Death: 16 June 1944
Cemetery: National Memorial Cemetery of the Pacific (B-1024) (MH)—Honolulu, Hawaii
Entered Service at: New York
Unit: Company A, 4th Tank Battalion, 4th Marine Division
Served as: Platoon Sergeant
Battle or Place of Action: Saipan, Marianas Islands
Date of Action: 16 June 1944
Date of Presentation: 10 April 1945
Place of Presentation: Centralia, IL, presented by Rear Adm. Arthur C. Carpender, Commandant, 9th Naval District, tohis widow, Lizette McCard
Citation: For conspicuous gallantry and intrepidity at the risk of his life above and beyond the call of duty while serving as platoon sergeant of Company A, 4th Tank Battalion, 4th Marine Division, during the battle for enemy Japanese-held Saipan, Marianas Islands on 16 June 1944. Cut off from the other units of his platoon when his tank was put out of action by a battery of enemy 77-mm guns, G/Sgt. McCard carried on resolutely, bringing all the tank's weapons to bear on the enemy, until the severity of the hostile fire caused him to order his crew out of the escape hatch while he courageously exposed himself to enemy guns by hurling hand grenades in order to cover the evacuation of his men. Seriously wounded during this action and with his supply of grenades exhausted,

G/Sgt. McCard then dismantled one of the tank's machine guns and faced the Japanese for the second time to deliver vigorous fire into their positions, destroying 16 of the enemy but sacrificing himself to insure the safety of his crew. His valiant fighting spirit and supreme loyalty in the face of almost certain death reflect the highest credit upon G/Sgt. McCard and the U.S. Naval Service. He gallantly gave his life for his country.

2839 ◆ McCARTER, LLOYD G.

Rank: Private
Service: U.S. Army
Birthday: 11 May 1917
Place of Birth: St. Maries, Benewah County, Idaho
Date of Death: 2 February 1956
Cemetery: Woodlawn Cemetery (MH)—St. Maries, Idaho
Entered Service at: Tacoma, Pierce County, Washington
Unit: 503d Parachute Infantry
Served as: Scout
Battle or Place of Action: Corregidor, Philippine Islands
Date of Action: 16-19 February 1945
G.O. Number, Date: 77, 10 September 1945
Date of Presentation: 23 August 1945
Place of Presentation: The White House, presented by Pres. Harry S. Truman
Citation: He was a scout with the regiment which seized the fortress of Corregidor, Philippine Islands. Shortly after the initial parachute assault on 16 February 1945, he crossed 30 yards of open ground under intense enemy fire, and at point-blank range silenced a machine gun with hand grenades. On the afternoon of 18 February he killed six snipers. That evening, when a large force attempted to bypass his company, he voluntarily moved to an exposed area and opened fire. The enemy attacked his position repeatedly throughout the night and was each time repulsed. By two o'clock in the morning, all the men about him had been wounded; but shouting encouragement to his comrades and defiance at the enemy, he continued to bear the brunt of the attack, fearlessly exposing himself to locate enemy soldiers and then pouring heavy fire on them. He repeatedly crawled back to the American line to secure more ammunition. When his submachine gun would no longer operate, he seized an automatic rifle and continued to inflict heavy casualties. This weapon, in turn, became too hot to use and, discarding it, he continued with an M1 rifle. At dawn the enemy attacked with renewed intensity. Completely exposing himself to hostile fire, he stood erect to locate the most dangerous enemy positions. He was seriously wounded; but, though he had already killed more than 30 of the enemy, he refused to evacuate until he had pointed out immediate objectives for attack. Through his sustained and outstanding heroism in the face of grave and obvious danger, Pvt. McCarter made outstanding contributions to the success of his company and the recapture of Corregidor.

2840 ◆ McCARTHY, JOSEPH JEREMIAH

Rank: Captain [highest rank: Brigadier General (hon.)]
Service: U.S. Marine Corps Reserve
Birthday: 10 August 1911
Place of Birth: Chicago, Cook County, Illinois
Entered Service at: Chicago, Cook County, Illinois
Unit: Company G, 2d Battalion, 24th Marines, 4th Marine Division
Served as: Company Commander
Battle or Place of Action: Iwo Jima, Volcano Islands
Date of Action: 21 February 1945
Date of Presentation: 5 October 1945
Place of Presentation: The White House, presented by Pres. Harry S. Truman
Citation: For conspicuous gallantry and intrepidity at the risk of his life above and beyond the call of duty as commanding officer of a rifle company attached to the 2d Battalion, 24th Marines, 4th Marine Division, in action against enemy Japanese forces during the seizure of Iwo Jima, Volcano Islands on 21 February 1945. Determined to break through the enemy's cross-island defenses, Capt. McCarthy acted on his own initiative when his company advance was held up by uninterrupted Japanese rifle, machine-gun, and high-velocity 47-mm fire during the approach to Motoyama Airfield No. 2. Quickly organizing a demolition and flamethrower team to accompany his picked rifle squad, he fearlessly led the way across 75 yards of fire-swept ground, charged a heavily fortified pillbox on the ridge of the front, and, personally hurling hand grenades into the emplacement as he directed the combined operations of his small assault group, completely destroyed the hostile installation. Spotting two Japanese soldiers attempting an escape from the shattered pillbox, he boldly stood upright in full view of the enemy and dispatched both troops before advancing to a second emplacement under greatly intensified fire and then blasted the strong fortifications with a well-planted demolitions attack. Subsequently entering the ruins, he found a Japanese taking aim at one of our men and, with alert presence of mind, jumped the enemy, disarmed, and shot him with his own weapon. Then, intent on smashing through the narrow breach, he rallied the remainder of his company and pressed a full attack with furious aggressiveness until he had neutralized all resistance and captured the ridge. An inspiring leader and indomitable fighter, Capt. McCarthy consistently disregarded all personal danger during the fierce conflict and, by his brilliant professional skill, daring tactics, and tenacious perseverance in the face of overwhelming odds, contributed materially to the success of his division's operations again st the savagely defended outpost of the Japanese Empire. His cool decision and outstanding valor reflect the highest credit upon Capt. McCarthy and enhance the finest traditions of the U.S. Naval Service.

2841 ◆ McCOOL JR., RICHARD MILES

Rank: Lieutenant (highest rank: Captain)
Service: U.S. Navy
Birthday: 4 January 1922
Place of Birth: Tishomingo, Johnston County, Oklahoma
Entered Service at: Oklahoma
Unit: U.S.S. LCS (L) (3) 122
Served as: Commanding Officer
Battle or Place of Action: North of Okinawa

Date of Action: 10-11 June 1945
Date of Presentation: 18 December 1945
Place of Presentation: The White House (Oval Office), presented by Pres. Harry S. Truman
Citation: For conspicuous gallantry and intrepidity at the risk of his life above and beyond the call of duty as commanding officer of the U.S.S. LCS (L) (3) 122 during operations against enemy Japanese forces in the Ryukyu Chain, 10 and 11 June 1945. Sharply vigilant during hostile air raids against Allied ships on radar picket duty off Okinawa on 10 June, Lt. McCool aided materially in evacuating all survivors from a sinking destroyer which had sustained mortal damage under the devastating attacks. When his own craft was attacked simultaneously by two of the enemy's suicide squadron early in the evening of 11 June, he instantly hurled the full power of his gun batteries against the plunging aircraft, shooting down the first and damaging the second before it crashed his station in the conning tower and engulfed the immediate area in a mass of flames. Although suffering from shrapnel wounds and painful burns, he rallied his concussion-shocked crew and initiated vigorous firefighting measures and then proceeded to the rescue of several trapped in a blazing compartment, subsequently carrying one man to safety despite the excruciating pain of additional severe burns. Unmindful of all personal danger, he continued his efforts without respite until aid arrived from other ships and he was evacuated. By his staunch leadership, capable direction, and indomitable determination throughout the crisis, Lt. McCool saved the lives of many who otherwise might have perished and contributed materially to the saving of his ship for further combat service. His valiant spirit of self-sacrifice in the face of extreme peril sustains and enhances the highest traditions of the U.S. Naval Service.

2842 ◆ McGAHA, CHARLES L.

Rank: Master Sergeant (highest rank: Major)
Service: U.S. Army
Birthday: 26 February 1914
Place of Birth: Crosby, Tennessee
Date of Death: 8 August 1984
Place of Death: Columbus, Georgia
Cemetery: Union Cemetery—New Port, Tennessee
Entered Service at: Crosby, Tennessee
Unit: Company G, 35th Infantry, 25th Infantry Division
Battle or Place of Action: near Lupao, Luzon, Philippine Islands
Date of Action: 7 February 1945
G.O. Number, Date: 30, 2 April 1946
Citation: He displayed conspicuous gallantry and intrepidity. His platoon and one other from Company G were pinned down in a roadside ditch by heavy fire from five Japanese tanks supported by 10 machine guns and a platoon of riflemen. When one of his men fell wounded 40 yards away, he unhesitatingly crossed the road under a hail of bullets and moved the man 75 yards to safety. Although he had suffered a deep arm wound, he returned to his post. Finding the platoon leader seriously wounded, he assumed command and rallied his men. Once more he braved the enemy fire to go to

the aid of a litter party removing another wounded soldier. A shell exploded in their midst, wounding him in the shoulder and killing two of the party. He picked up the remaining man, carried him to cover, and then moved out in front deliberately to draw the enemy fire while the American forces, thus protected, withdrew to safety. When the last man had gained the new position, he rejoined his command and there collapsed from loss of blood and exhaustion. M/Sgt. McGaha set an example of courage and leadership in keeping with the highest traditions of the service.

2843 ◆ McGARITY, VERNON

Rank: Technical Sergeant
Service: U.S. Army
Birthday: 1 December 1921
Place of Birth: Right, Tennessee
Entered Service at: Model, Tennessee
Unit: 3d Squad, 3d Platoon, Company L, 3d Battalion, 393d Infantry, 99th Infantry Division
Served as: Squad Leader
Battle or Place of Action: near Krinkelt, Belgium
Date of Action: 16 December 1944
G.O. Number, Date: 6, 11 January 1946
Date of Presentation: 12 October 1945
Place of Presentation: The White House, presented by Pres. Harry S. Truman
Citation: He was painfully wounded in an artillery barrage that preceded the powerful counteroffensive launched by the Germans near Krinkelt, Belgium, on the morning of 16 December 1944. He made his way to an aid station, received treatment, and then refused to be evacuated, choosing to return to his hard-pressed men instead. The fury of the enemy's great Western Front offensive swirled about the position held by T/Sgt. McGarity's small force, but so tenaciously did these men fight on orders to stand firm at all costs that they could not be dislodged despite murderous enemy fire and the breakdown of their communications. During the day the heroic squad leader rescued one of his friends who had been wounded in a forward position, and throughout the night he exhorted his comrades to repulse the enemy's attempts of infiltration. When morning came and the Germans attacked with tanks and infantry, he braved heavy fire to run to an advantageous position where he immobilized the enemy's lead tank with a round from a rocket launcher. Fire from his squad drove the attacking infantrymen back, and three supporting tanks withdrew. He rescued, under heavy fire, another wounded American, and then directed devastating fire on a light cannon which had been brought up by the hostile troops to clear resistance from the area. When ammunition began to run low, T/Sgt. McGarity, remembering an old ammunition hole about 100 yards distant in the general direction of the enemy, braved a concentration of hostile fire to replenish his unit's supply. By circuitous route the enemy managed to emplace a machine gun to the rear and flank of the squad's position, cutting off the only escape route. Unhesitatingly, the gallant soldier took it upon himself to destroy this menace singlehandedly. He left cover, and while under steady fire from the enemy, killed or wounded all

the hostile gunners with deadly accurate rifle fire, and prevented all attempts to re-man the gun. Only when his squad's last round had been fired was the enemy able to advance and capture the intrepid leader and his men. The extraordinary bravery and extreme devotion to duty of T/Sgt. McGarity supported a remarkable delaying action which provided the time necessary for assembling reserves and forming a line against which the German striking power was shattered.

Notes: POW

2844 ◆ *McGEE, WILLIAM D.

Rank: Private
Service: U.S. Army
Place of Birth: Indianapolis, Marion County, Indiana
Date of Death: 18 March 1945
Cemetery: A.B.M.C. Luxembourg Cemetery—Luxembourg, France
Entered Service at: Indianapolis, Marion County, Indiana
Unit: Medical Detachment, 304th Infantry, 76th Infantry Division
Served as: Medical Aidman
Battle or Place of Action: near Mulheim, Germany
Date of Action: 18 March 1945
G.O. Number, Date: 21, 26 February 1946
Citation: A medical aidman, he made a night crossing of the Moselle River with troops endeavoring to capture the town of Mulheim. The enemy had retreated in the sector where the assault boats landed, but had left the shore heavily strewn with antipersonnel mines. Two men of the first wave attempting to work their way forward detonated mines which wounded them seriously, leaving them bleeding and in great pain beyond the reach of their comrades. Entirely on his own initiative, Pvt. McGee entered the minefield, brought out one of the injured to comparative safety, and had returned to rescue the second victim when he stepped on a mine and was severely wounded in the resulting explosion. Although suffering intensely and bleeding profusely, he shouted orders that none of his comrades was to risk his life by entering the death-sown field to render first aid that might have saved his life. In making the supreme sacrifice, Pvt. McGee demonstrated a concern for the well-being of his fellow soldiers that transcended all considerations for his own safety and a gallantry in keeping with the highest traditions of the military service.

2845 ◆ *McGILL, TROY A.

Rank: Sergeant
Service: U.S. Army
Birthday: 15 July 1914
Place of Birth: Knoxville, Knox County, Tennessee
Date of Death: 4 March 1944
Cemetery: Knoxville National Cemetery (B-6294) (MH)—Knoxville, Tennessee
Entered Service at: Ada, Pontotoc County, Oklahoma
Unit: Troop G, 5th Cavalry, 1st Cavalry Division
Battle or Place of Action: Admiralty Group, Los Negros Islands

Date of Action: 4 March 1944
G.O. Number, Date: 74, 11 September 1944
Citation: For conspicuous gallantry and intrepidity above and beyond the call of duty in action with the enemy at Los Negros Island, Admiralty Group, on 4 March 1944. In the early morning hours Sgt. McGill, with a squad of eight men, occupied a revetment which bore the brunt of a furious attack by approximately 200 drink-crazed enemy troops. Although covered by crossfire from machine guns on the right and left flank he could receive no support from the remainder of our troops stationed at his rear. All members of the squad were killed or wounded except Sgt. McGill and another man, whom he ordered to return to the next revetment. Courageously resolved to hold his position at all costs, he fired his weapon until it ceased to function. Then, with the enemy only five yards away, he charged from his foxhole in the face of certain death and clubbed the enemy with his rifle in hand-to-hand combat until he was killed. At dawn 105 enemy dead were found around his position. Sgt. McGill's intrepid stand was an inspiration to his comrades and a decisive factor in the defeat of a fanatical enemy.

2846 ◆ *McGRAW, FRANCIS XAVIER

Rank: Private First Class
Service: U.S. Army
Place of Birth: Philadelphia, Philadelphia County, Pennsylvania
Date of Death: 19 November 1944
Cemetery: A.B.M.C. Henri-Chapelle Cemetery—Henri-Chapelle, Belgium
Entered Service at: Camden, Camden County, New Jersey
Unit: Company H, 26th Infantry, 1st Infantry Division
Served as: Heavy Machine Gunner
Battle or Place of Action: near Schevenhutte, Germany
Date of Action: 19 November 1944
G.O. Number, Date: 92, 25 October 1945
Citation: He manned a heavy machine gun emplaced in a foxhole near Schevenhutte, Germany, on 19 November 1944, when the enemy launched a fierce counterattack. Braving an intense hour-long preparatory barrage, he maintained his stand and poured deadly accurate fire into the advancing foot troops until they faltered and came to a halt. The hostile forces brought up a machine gun in an effort to dislodge him but were frustrated when he lifted his gun to an exposed but advantageous position atop a log, courageously stood up in his foxhole, and knocked out the enemy weapon. A rocket blasted his gun from position, but he retrieved it and continued firing. He silenced a second machine gun and then made repeated trips over fire-swept terrain to replenish his ammunition supply. Wounded painfully in this dangerous task, he disregarded his injury and hurried back to his post, where his weapon was showered with mud when another rocket barely missed him. In the midst of the battle, with enemy troops taking advantage of his predicament to press forward, he calmly cleaned his gun, put it back into action and drove off the attackers. He continued to fire until his ammunition was expended, when, with a fierce desire to close with the enemy, he picked up a carbine, killed one enemy soldier, wounded

another, and engaged in a desperate fire-fight with a third until he was mortally wounded by a burst from a machine pistol. The extraordinary heroism and intrepidity displayed by Pvt. McGraw inspired his comrades to great efforts and was a major factor in repulsing the enemy attack.

2847 ◆ *McGUIRE JR., THOMAS BUCHANAN

Rank: Major
Service: U.S. Army Air Corps
Birthday: 1 August 1920
Place of Birth: Ridgewood, Bergen County, New Jersey
Date of Death: 7 January 1945
Place of Death: over Los Negros Island
Cemetery: Arlington National Cemetery (11-426-SH) (MH)—Arlington, Virginia
Entered Service at: Sebring, Highlands County, Florida
Unit: 475th Fighter Group, 5th Air Force
Served as: Pilot/Group Operations Officer
Battle or Place of Action: over Luzon, Philippine Islands
Date of Action: 25-26 December 1944
G.O. Number, Date: 24, 7 March 1946
Date of Presentation: 8 May 1946
Place of Presentation: Patterson, New Jersey, presented by Gen. George C. Kenney to his family
Citation: He fought with conspicuous gallantry and intrepidity over Luzon, Philippine Islands. Voluntarily, he led a squadron of 15 P-38s as top cover for heavy bombers striking Mabalacat Airdrome, where his formation was attacked by 20 aggressive Japanese fighters. In the ensuing action he repeatedly flew to the aid of embattled comrades, driving off enemy assaults while himself under attack and at times outnumbered three to one, and even after his guns jammed, continued the fight by forcing a hostile plane into his wingman's line of fire. Before he started back to his base he had shot down three Zeros. The next day he again volunteered to lead escort fighters on a mission to strongly defended Clark Field. During the resultant engagement he again exposed himself to attacks so that he might rescue a crippled bomber. In rapid succession he shot down one aircraft, parried the attack of four enemy fighters, one of which he shot down, singlehandedly engaged three more Japanese, destroying one, and then shot down still another, his 38th victory in aerial combat. On 7 January 1945, while leading a voluntary fighter sweep over Los Negros Island, he risked an extremely hazardous maneuver at low altitude in an attempt to save a fellow flyer from attack, crashed, and was reported missing in action. With gallant initiative, deep and unselfish concern for the safety of others, and heroic determination to destroy the enemy at all costs, Maj. McGuire set an inspiring example in keeping with the highest traditions of the military service.

2848 ◆ McKINNEY, JOHN R.

Rank: Sergeant (rank at time of action: Private)
Service: U.S. Army
Birthday: 26 February 1921
Place of Birth: Woodcliff, Georgia

Entered Service at: Woodcliff, Georgia
Unit: Company A, 123d Infantry Regiment, 33d Infantry Division
Battle or Place of Action: Tayabas Province, Luzon, Philippine Islands
Date of Action: 11 May 1945
G.O. Number, Date: 14, 4 February 1946
Date of Presentation: 23 January 1946
Place of Presentation: The White House, presented by Pres. Harry S. Truman
Citation: He fought with extreme gallantry to defend the outpost which had been established near Dingalan Bay. Just before daybreak approximately 100 Japanese stealthily attacked the perimeter defense, concentrating on a light machine-gun position manned by three Americans. Having completed a long tour of duty at this gun, Pvt. McKinney was resting a few paces away when an enemy soldier dealt him a glancing blow on the head with a saber. Although dazed by the stroke, he seized his rifle, bludgeoned his attacker, and then shot another assailant who was charging him. Meanwhile, one of his comrades at the machine gun had been wounded and his other companion withdrew carrying the injured man to safety. Alone, Pvt. McKinney was confronted by 10 infantrymen who had captured the machine gun with the evident intent of reversing it to fire into the perimeter. Leaping into the emplacement, he shot seven of them at point-blank range and killed three more with his rifle butt. In the melee the machine gun was rendered inoperative, leaving him only his rifle with which to meet the advancing Japanese, who hurled grenades and directed knee mortar shells into the perimeter. He warily changed position, secured more ammunition, and reloading repeatedly, cut down waves of the fanatical enemy with devastating fire or clubbed them to death in hand-to-hand combat. When assistance arrived, he had thwarted the assault and was in complete control of the area. Thirty-eight dead Japanese around the machine gun and two more at the side of a mortar 45 yards distant was the amazing toll he had exacted singlehandedly. By his indomitable spirit, extraordinary fighting ability, and unwavering courage in the face of tremendous odds, Pvt. McKinney saved his company from possible annihilation and set an example of unsurpassed intrepidity.

2849 ◆ *McTUREOUS JR., ROBERT MILLER

Rank: Private
Service: U.S. Marine Corps
Birthday: 26 March 1924
Place of Birth: Altoona, Lake County, Florida
Date of Death: 11 June 1945
Place of Death: Aboard the Hospital Ship U.S.S. *Relief*
Cemetery: Glendale Cemetery (MH)—Umatilla, Florida
Entered Service at: Florida
Unit: Company H, 3d Battalion, 29th Marines, 6th Marine Division
Battle or Place of Action: Okinawa, Ryukyu Islands
Date of Action: 7 June 1945
Citation: For conspicuous gallantry and intrepidity at the risk of his life above and beyond the call of duty, while serv-

ing with the 3d Battalion, 29th Marines, 6th Marine Division, during action against enemy Japanese forces on Okinawa in the Ryukyu Chain, 7 June 1945. Alert and ready for any hostile counteraction following his company's seizure of an important hill objective, Pvt. McTureous was quick to observe the plight of company stretcher bearers who were suddenly assailed by slashing machine-gun fire as they attempted to evacuate wounded at the rear of the newly won position. Determined to prevent further casualties, he quickly filled his jacket with hand grenades and charged the enemy-occupied caves from which the concentrated barrage was emanating. Coolly disregarding all personal danger as he waged his furious one-man assault, he smashed grenades into the cave entrances, thereby diverting the heaviest fire from the stretcher bearers to his own person and, resolutely returning to his own lines under a blanketing hail of rifle and machine-gun fire to replenish his supply of grenades, dauntlessly continued his systematic reduction of Japanese strength until he himself sustained serious wounds after silencing a large number of the hostile guns. Aware of his own critical condition and unwilling to further endanger the lives of his comrades, he stoically crawled a distance of 200 yards to a sheltered position within friendly lines before calling for aid. By his fearless initiative and bold tactics, Pvt. McTureous had succeeded in neutralizing the enemy fire, killing six Japanese troops, and effectively disorganizing the remainder of the savagely defended garrison. His outstanding valor and heroic spirit of self-sacrifice during a critical stage of operations reflect the highest credit upon himself and the U.S. Naval Service.

2850 ◆ *McVEIGH, JOHN J.

Rank: Sergeant
Service: U.S. Army
Place of Birth: Philadelphia, Philadelphia County, Pennsylvania
Date of Death: 29 August 1944
Cemetery: Holy Sepulchre Cemetery—Philadelphia, Pennsylvania
Entered Service at: Philadelphia, Philadelphia County, Pennsylvania
Unit: Company H, 23d Infantry, 2d Infantry Division
Battle or Place of Action: near Brest, France
Date of Action: 29 August 1944
G.O. Number, Date: 24, 6 April 1945
Citation: For conspicuous gallantry and intrepidity at the risk of his life above and beyond the call of duty near Brest, France, on 29 August 1944. Shortly after dusk an enemy counterattack of platoon strength was launched against one platoon of Company G, 23d Infantry. Since the Company G platoon was not dug in and had just begun to assume defensive positions along a hedge, part of the line sagged momentarily under heavy fire from small-arms and two flak guns, leaving a section of heavy machine guns holding a wide frontage without rifle protection. The enemy drive moved so swiftly that German riflemen were soon almost on top of one machine-gun position. Sgt. McVeigh, heedless of a tremendous amount of small-arms and flak fire directed toward him,

stood up in full view of the enemy and directed the fire of his squad on the attacking Germans until his position was almost overrun. He then drew his trench knife, and singlehandedly charged several of the enemy. In a savage hand-to-hand struggle, Sgt. McVeigh killed one German with the knife, his only weapon, and was advancing on three more of the enemy when he was shot down and killed with small-arms fire at point-blank range. Sgt. McVeigh's heroic act allowed the two remaining men in his squad to concentrate their machine-gun fire on the attacking enemy and then turn their weapons on the three Germans in the road, killing all three. Fire from this machine gun and the other gun of the section was almost entirely responsible for stopping the enemy assault, and allowing the rifle platoon to which it was attached time to reorganize, assume positions on and hold the high ground gained during the day.

2851 ◆ *McWHORTER, WILLIAM A.

Rank: Private First Class (highest rank: Sergeant)
Service: U.S. Army
Birthday: 7 December 1918
Place of Birth: Liberty, Pickins County, South Carolina
Date of Death: 5 December 1944
Cemetery: West View Cemetery (MH)—Liberty, South Carolina
Entered Service at: Liberty, Pickins County, South Carolina
Unit: Company M, 126th Infantry, 32d Infantry Division
Served as: Machine Gunner
Battle or Place of Action: Leyte, Philippine Islands
Date of Action: 5 December 1944
G.O. Number, Date: 82, 27 September 1945
Citation: He displayed gallantry and intrepidity at the risk of his life above and beyond the call of duty while engaged in operations against the enemy. Pfc. McWhorter, a machine gunner, was emplaced in a defensive position with one assistant when the enemy launched a heavy attack. Manning the gun and opening fire, he killed several members of an advancing demolition squad, when one of the enemy succeeded in throwing a fused demolition charge in the entrenchment. Without hesitation and with complete disregard for his own safety, Pfc. McWhorter picked up the improvised grenade and deliberately held it close to his body, bending over and turning away from his companion. The charge exploded, killing him instantly, but leaving his assistant unharmed. Pfc. McWhorter's outstanding heroism and supreme sacrifice in shielding a comrade reflect the highest traditions of the military service.

2852 ◆ MEAGHER, JOHN WILLIAM

Rank: Technical Sergeant
Service: U.S. Army
Birthday: 5 December 1917
Place of Birth: Jersey City, Hudson County, New Jersey
Entered Service at: Jersey City, Hudson County, New Jersey
Unit: 2d Platoon, Company E, 2d Battalion, 305th Infantry, 77th Infantry Division

Served as: Acting Platoon Leader
Battle or Place of Action: near Ozato, Okinawa, Ryukyu Islands
Date of Action: 19 June 1945
G.O. Number, Date: 60, 26 June 1946
Date of Presentation: 14 June 1946
Place of Presentation: The White House (lawn), presented by Pres. Harry S. Truman
Citation: He displayed conspicuous gallantry and intrepidity above and beyond the call of duty. In the heat of the fight, he mounted an assault tank, and, with bullets splattering about him, designated targets to the gunner. Seeing an enemy soldier carrying an explosive charge dash for the tank treads, he shouted fire orders to the gunner, leaped from the tank, and bayonetted the charging soldier. Knocked unconscious and his rifle destroyed, he regained consciousness, secured a machine gun from the tank, and began a furious one-man assault on the enemy. Firing from his hip, moving through vicious crossfire that ripped through his clothing, he charged the nearest pillbox, killing six. Going on amid the hail of bullets and grenades, he dashed for a second enemy gun, running out of ammunition just as he reached the position. He grasped his empty gun by the barrel and in a violent onslaught killed the crew. By his fearless assault T/Sgt. Meagher singlehandedly broke the enemy resistance, enabling his platoon to take its objective and continue the advance.

2853 ◆ MERLI, GINO JOSEPH

Rank: Private First Class (highest rank: Sergeant)
Service: U.S. Army
Birthday: 13 May 1924
Place of Birth: Scranton, Lackawanna County, Pennsylvania
Entered Service at: Peckville, Lackawanna County, Pennsylvania
Unit: Weapons Platoon, Company H, 2d Battalion, 18th Infantry, 1st Infantry Division
Served as: Machine Gunner
Battle or Place of Action: near Sars la Bruyere, Belgium
Date of Action: 4-5 September 1944
G.O. Number, Date: 64, 4 August 1945
Date of Presentation: 15 June 1945
Place of Presentation: The White House, presented by Pres. Harry S. Truman
Citation: He was serving as a machine gunner in the vicinity of Sars-la-Bruyere, Belgium, on the night of 4–5 September 1944, when his company was attacked by a superior German force. Its position was overrun and he was surrounded when our troops were driven back by overwhelming numbers and firepower. Disregarding the fury of the enemy fire concentrated on him he maintained his position, covering the withdrawal of our riflemen and breaking the force of the enemy pressure. His assistant machine gunner was killed and the position captured; the other eight members of the section were forced to surrender. Pfc. Merli slumped down beside the dead assistant gunner and feigned death. No sooner had the enemy group withdrawn than he was up and firing in all directions. Once more his position was taken and the captors found two apparently lifeless bodies. Throughout the night Pfc. Merli stayed at his weapon.

By daybreak the enemy had suffered heavy losses, and as our troops launched an assault, asked for a truce. Our negotiating party, who accepted the German surrender, found Pfc. Merli still at his gun. On the battlefield lay 52 enemy dead, 19 of whom were directly in front of the gun. Pfc. Merli's gallantry and courage, and the losses and confusion that he caused the enemy, contributed materially to our victory.

2854 ◆ *MERRELL, JOSEPH FREDERICK

Rank: Private
Service: U.S. Army
Birthday: 21 August 1926
Place of Birth: Staten Island, Richmond County, New York
Date of Death: 18 April 1945
Cemetery: St. Peter's Cemetery (MH)—Staten Island, New York
Entered Service at: Staten Island, Richmond County, New York
Unit: Company I, 3d Battalion, 15th Infantry, 3d Infantry Division
Battle or Place of Action: near Lohe, Germany
Date of Action: 18 April 1945
G.O. Number, Date: 21, 26 February 1946
Citation: He made a gallant, one-man attack against vastly superior enemy forces near Lohe, Germany. His unit, attempting a quick conquest of hostile hill positions that would open the route to Nuremberg before the enemy could organize his defense of that city, was pinned down by brutal fire from rifles, machine pistols, and two heavy machine guns. Entirely on his own initiative, Pvt. Merrell began a single-handed assault. He ran 100 yards through concentrated fire, barely escaping death at each stride, and at point-blank range engaged four German machine pistolmen with his rifle, killing all of them while their bullets ripped his uniform. As he started forward again, his rifle was smashed by a sniper's bullet, leaving him armed only with three grenades. But he did not hesitate. He zigzagged 200 yards through a hail of bullets to within 10 yards of the first machine gun, where he hurled two grenades and then rushed the position ready to fight with his bare hands if necessary. In the emplacement he seized a Luger pistol and killed what Germans had survived the grenade blast. Rearmed, he crawled toward the second machine gun located 30 yards away, killing four Germans in camouflaged foxholes on the way, but himself receiving a critical wound in the abdomen. And yet he went on, staggering, bleeding, disregarding bullets which tore through the folds of his clothing and glanced off his helmet. He threw his last grenade into the machine-gun nest and stumbled on to wipe out the crew. He had completed this self-appointed task when a machine pistol burst killed him instantly. In his spectacular one-man attack Pvt. Merrell killed six Germans in the first machine-gun emplacement, seven in the next, and an additional 10 infantrymen who were astride his path to the weapons which would have decimated his unit had he not assumed the burden of the assault and stormed the enemy positions with utter fearlessness, intrepidity of the highest order, and a willingness to sacrifice his own life so that his comrades could go on to victory.

2855 ◆ *MESSERSCHMIDT, HAROLD O.

Rank: Sergeant
Service: U.S. Army
Birthday: 1924
Place of Birth: Grier City, Pennsylvania
Date of Death: 17 September 1944
Cemetery: Christ White Church Cemetery—Rush Township, Pennsylvania
Entered Service at: Chester, Delaware County, Pennsylvania
Unit: Company L, 30th Infantry, 3d Infantry Division
Battle or Place of Action: near Radden, France
Date of Action: 17 September 1944
G.O. Number, Date: 71, 17 July 1946
Citation: He displayed conspicuous gallantry and intrepidity above and beyond the call of duty. Braving machine-gun, machine pistol, and rifle fire, he moved fearlessly and calmly from man to man along his 40-yard squad front, encouraging each to hold against the overwhelming assault of a fanatical foe surging up the hillside. Knocked to the ground by a burst from an enemy automatic weapon, he immediately jumped to his feet, and ignoring his grave wounds, fired his submachine gun at the enemy that was now upon them, killing five and wounding many others before his ammunition was spent. Virtually surrounded by a frenzied foe and all of his squad now casualties, he elected to fight alone, using his empty sub-machine gun as a bludgeon against his assailants. Spotting one of the enemy about to kill a wounded comrade, he felled the German with a blow of his weapon. Seeing friendly reinforcements running up the hill, he continued furiously to wield his empty gun against the foe in a new attack, and it was thus that he made the supreme sacrifice. Sgt. Messerschmidt's sustained heroism in hand-to-hand combat with superior enemy forces was in keeping with the highest traditions of the military service.

2856 ◆ *METZGER JR., WILLIAM EDWARD

Rank: Second Lieutenant
Service: U.S. Army Air Corps
Birthday: 9 February 1922
Place of Birth: Lima, Allen County, Ohio
Date of Death: 9 November 1944
Cemetery: Woodlawn Cemetery—Lima, Ohio
Entered Service at: Lima, Allen County, Ohio
Unit: 729th Bombardment Squadron, 452d Bombardment Group, 8th Air Force
Served as: Copilot of a B-17
Battle or Place of Action: Saarbrucken, Germany
Date of Action: 9 November 1944
G.O. Number, Date: 38, 16 May 1945
Citation: On a bombing run upon the marshaling yards at Saarbrucken, Germany, on 9 November 1944, a B-17 aircraft on which 2d Lt. Metzger was serving as copilot was seriously damaged by antiaircraft fire. Three of the aircraft's engines were damaged beyond control and on fire; dangerous flames from the No. 4 engine were leaping back as far as the tail assembly. Flares in the cockpit were ingited and a fire roared therein which was further increased by free-flowing fluid from damaged hydraulic lines. The interphone system was rendered useless. In addition to these serious mechanical diffculties the engineer was wounded in the leg and the radio operator's arm was severed below the elbow. Suffering from intense pain, despite the application of a tourniquet, the radio operator fell unconscious. Faced with the imminent explosion of his aircraft and death to his entire crew, mere seconds before bombs away on the target, 2d Lt. Metzger and his pilot conferred. Something had to be done immediately to save the life of the wounded radio operator. The lack of a static line and the thought that his unconscious body striking the ground in unknown territory would not bring immediate medical attention forced a quick decision. Second Lt. Metzger and his pilot decided to fly the flaming aircraft to friendly territory and then attempt to crash land. Bombs were released on the target and the crippled aircraft proceeded along to Allied-controlled territory. When that had been reached 2d Lt. Metzger personally informed all crewmembers to bail out upon the suggestion of the pilot, 2d Lt. Metzger chose to remain with the pilot for the crash landing in order to assist him in this emergency. With only one normally functioning engine and with the danger of explosion much greater, the aircraft banked into an open field, and when it was at an altitude of 100 feet it exploded, crashed, exploded again, and then disintegrated. All three crewmembers were instantly killed. Second Lt. Metzger's loyalty t o his crew, his determination to accomplish the task set forth to him, and his deed of knowingly performing what may have been his last service to his country was an example of valor at its highest.

2857 ◆ MICHAEL, EDWARD STANLEY

Rank: First Lieutenant (highest rank: Lieutenant Colonel)
Service: U.S. Army Air Corps/U.S. Air Force
Birthday: 2 May 1918
Place of Birth: Chicago, Cook County, Illinois
Date of Death: 10 May 1994
Place of Death: Fairfield, California
Cemetery: Springfield, Utah
Entered Service at: Chicago, Cook County, Illinois
Unit: 364th Bombardment Squadron, 305th Bombardment Group, 40th Combat Wing, 2d Air Division, 8th Air Force
Served as: Aircraft Commander/Pilot of a B-17
Battle or Place of Action: over Stettin, Germany
Date of Action: 11 April 1944
G.O. Number, Date: 5, 15 January 1945
Date of Presentation: 10 January 1945
Place of Presentation: The White House, presented by Pres. Franklin D. Roosevelt
Citation: For conspicuous gallantry and intrepidity above and beyond the call of duty while serving as pilot of a B-17 aircraft on a heavy-bombardment mission to Germany, 11 April 1944. The group in which 1st Lt. Michael was flying was attacked by a swarm of fighters. His plane was singled out and the fighters pressed their attacks home recklessly, completely disregarding the Allied fighter escort and their own intensive flak. His plane was riddled from nose to tail with exploding cannon shells and knocked out of formation, with a large number of fighters following it down, blasting it with

cannon fire as it descended. A cannon shell exploded in the cockpit, wounded the copilot, wrecked the instruments, and blew out the side window. First Lt. Michael was seriously and painfully wounded in the right thigh. Hydraulic fluid filmed over the windshield making visibility impossible, and smoke filled the cockpit. The controls failed to respond and 3,000 feet were lost before he succeeded in leveling off. The radio operator informed him that the whole bomb bay was in flames as a result of the explosion of three cannon shells, which had ignited the incendiaries. With a full load of incendiaries in the bomb bay and a considerable gas load in the tanks, the danger of fire enveloping the plane and the tanks exploding seemed imminent. When the emergency release lever failed to function, 1st Lt. Michael at once gave the order to bail out and seven of the crew left the plane. Seeing the bombardier firing the navigator's gun at the enemy planes, 1st Lt. Michael ordered him to bail out as the plane was liable to explode any minute. When the bombardier looked for his parachute he found that it had been riddled with 20-mm fragments and was useless. First Lt. Michael, seeing the ruined parachute, realized that if the plane was abandoned the bombardier would perish and decided that the only chance would be a crash landing. Completely disregarding his own painful and profusely bleeding wounds , but thinking only of the safety of the remaining crewmembers, he gallantly evaded the enemy using violent evasive action despite the battered condition of his plane. After the plane had been under sustained enemy attack for fully 45 minutes, 1st Lt. Michael finally lost the persistent fighters in a cloud bank. Upon emerging, an accurate barrage of flak caused him to come down to treetop level where flak towers poured a continuous rain of fire on the plane. He continued into France, realizing that at any moment a crash landing might have to be attempted, but trying to get as far as possible to increase the escape possibilities if a safe landing could be achieved. First Lt. Michael flew the plane until he became exhausted from loss of blood, which had formed on the floor in pools, and he lost consciousness. The copilot succeeded in reaching England and sighted an RAF field near the coast. First Lt. Michael finally regained consciousness and insisted upon taking over the controls to land the plane. The undercarriage was useless; the bomb bay doors were jammed open; the hydraulic system and altimeter were shot out. In addition, there was no airspeed indicator, the ball turret was jammed with the guns pointing downward, and the flaps would not respond. Despite these apparently insurmountable obstacles, he landed the plane without mishap.

2858 ◆ *MICHAEL, HARRY J.

Rank: Second Lieutenant
Service: U.S. Army
Birthday: 13 March 1922
Place of Birth: Benton, Indiana
Date of Death: 14 March 1945
Cemetery: Violett Cemetery (MH)—Goshen, Indiana
Entered Service at: Milford, Kosciusko County, Indiana
Unit: Company L, 318th Infantry, 80th Infantry Division
Served as: Platoon Leader

Battle or Place of Action: near Neiderzerf, Germany
Date of Action: 14 March 1945
G.O. Number, Date: 18, 13 February 1946
Citation: He was serving as a rifle platoon leader when his company began an assault on a wooded ridge northeast of the village of Neiderzerf, Germany, early on 13 March 1945. A short distance up the side of the hill, 2d Lt. Michael, at the head of his platoon, heard the click of an enemy machine-gun bolt. Quietly halting the company, he silently moved off into the woods and discovered two enemy machine guns and crews. Executing a sudden charge, he completely surprised the enemy and captured the guns and crews. At daybreak, enemy voices were heard in the thick woods ahead. Leading his platoon in a flanking movement, they charged the enemy with hand grenades and, after a bitter fight, captured 25 members of an SS mountain division, three artillery pieces, and 20 horses. While his company was establishing its position, 2d Lt. Michael made two personal reconnaissance missions of the wood on his left flank. On his first mission he killed two, wounded four, and captured six enemy soldiers singlehandedly. On the second mission he captured seven prisoners. During the afternoon he led his platoon on a frontal assault of a line of enemy pillboxes, successfully capturing the objective, killing 10, and capturing 30 prisoners. The following morning the company was subjected to sniper fire and 2d Lt. Michael, in an attempt to find the hidden sniper, was shot and killed. The inspiring leadership and heroic agressiveness displayed by 2d Lt. Michael upheld the highest traditions of the military service.

2859 ◆ *MILLER, ANDREW

Rank: Staff Sergeant
Service: U.S. Army
Birthday: 11 August 1916
Place of Birth: Manitowoc, Manitowoc County, Wisconsin
Date of Death: 29 November 1944
Cemetery: A.B.M.C. Lorraine Cemetery (A-26-1)—St. Avold, France
Entered Service at: Two Rivers, Manitowoc County, Wisconsin
Unit: Company G, 377th Infantry, 95th Infantry Division
Served as: Squad Leader
Battle or Place of Action: Woippy, France, through Metz to Kerprich Hemmersdorf, Germany
Date of Action: 16-29 November 1944
G.O. Number, Date: 74, 1 September 1945
Citation: For performing a series of heroic deeds from 16 to 29 November 1944, during his company's relentless drive from Woippy, France, through Metz to Kerprich Hemmersdorf, Germany. As he led a rifle squad on 16 November at Woippy, a crossfire from enemy machine guns pinned down his unit. Ordering his men to remain under cover, he went forward alone, entered a building housing one of the guns, and forced five Germans to surrender at bayonet point. He then took the second gun singlehandedly by hurling grenades into the enemy position, killing two, wounding three more, and taking two additional prisoners. At the outskirts of Metz the next day, when his platoon, confused by

heavy explosions and the withdrawal of friendly tanks, retired, he fearlessly remained behind armed with an automatic rifle and exchanged bursts with a German machine gun until he silenced the enemy weapon. His quick action in covering his comrades gave the platoon time to regroup and carry on the fight. On 19 November S/Sgt. Miller led an attack on large enemy barracks. Covered by his squad, he crawled to a barracks window, climbed in, and captured six riflemen occupying the room. His men, and then the entire company, followed through the window, scoured the building, and took 75 prisoners. S/Sgt. Miller volunteered, with three comrades, to capture Gestapo officers who were preventing the surrender of German troops in another building. He ran a gauntlet of machine-gun fire and was lifted through a window. Inside, he found himself covered by a machine pistol, but he persuaded the four Gestapo agents confronting him to surrender. Early the next morning, when strong hostile forces punished his company with heavy fire, S/Sgt. Miller assumed the task of destroying a well-placed machine gun. He was knocked down by a rifle grenade as he climbed an open stairway in a house, but pressed on with a bazooka to find an advantageous spot from which to launch his rocket. He discovered that he could fire only from t he roof, a position where he would draw tremendous enemy fire. Facing the risk, he moved into the open, coolly took aim, and scored a direct hit on the hostile emplacement, wreaking such havoc that the enemy troops became completely demoralized and began surrendering by the score. The following day, in Metz, he captured 12 more prisoners and silenced an enemy machine gun after volunteering for a hazardous mission in advance of his company's position. On 29 November, as Company G climbed a hill overlooking Kerprich Hemmersdorf, enemy fire pinned the unit to the ground. S/Sgt. Miller, on his own initiative, pressed ahead with his squad past the company's leading element to meet the surprise resistance. His men stood up and advanced deliberately, firing as they went. Inspired by S/Sgt. Miller's leadership, the platoon followed, and then another platoon arose and grimly closed with the Germans. The enemy action was smothered, but at the cost of S/Sgt. Miller's life. His tenacious devotion to the attack, his gallant choice to expose himself to enemy action rather than endanger his men, his limitless bravery, assured the success of Company G.

2860 ◆ MILLS, JAMES HENRY

Rank: Private
Service: U.S. Army
Birthday: 2 May 1923
Place of Birth: Fort Meade, Polk County, Florida
Date of Death: 11 November 1973
Cemetery: Oak Hill Burial Park—South Lakeland, Florida
Entered Service at: Fort Meade, Polk County, Florida
Unit: Company F, 15th Infantry, 3d Infantry Division
Battle or Place of Action: near Cisterna di Littoria, Italy
Date of Action: 24 May 1944
G.O. Number, Date: 87, 14 November 1944
Citation: For conspicuous gallantry and intrepidity at the risk of life above and beyond the call of duty. Pvt. Mills, undergoing his baptism of fire, preceded his platoon down a

draw to reach a position from which an attack could be launched against a heavily fortified strongpoint. After advancing about 300 yards, Pvt. Mills was fired on by a machine gun only five yards distant. He killed the gunner with one shot and forced the surrender of the assistant gunner. Continuing his advance, he saw a German soldier in a camouflaged position behind a large bush pulling the pin of a potato-masher grenade. Covering the German with his rifle, Pvt. Mills forced him to drop the grenade and captured him. When another enemy soldier attempted to throw a hand grenade into the draw, Pvt. Mills killed him with one shot. Brought under fire by a machine gun, two machine pistols, and three rifles at a range of only 50 feet, he charged headlong into the furious chain of automatic fire, shooting his M1 from the hip. The enemy was completely demoralized by Pvt. Mills' daring charge, and when he reached a point within 10 feet of their position, all six surrendered. As he neared the end of the draw, Pvt. Mills was brought under fire by a machine gunner 20 yards distant. Despite the fact that he had absolutely no cover, Pvt. Mills killed the gunner with one shot. Two enemy soldiers near the machine gunner fired wildly at Pvt. Mills and then fled. Pvt. Mills fired twice, killing one of the enemy. Continuing on to the position, he captured a fourth soldier. When it became apparent that an assault on the strongpoint would in all probability cause heavy casualties on the platoon, Pvt. Mills volunteered to cover the advance down a shallow ditch to a point within 50 yards of the objective. Standing on the bank in full view of the enemy less than 100 yards away, he shouted and fired his rifle directly into the position. His ruse worked exactly as planned. The enemy centered his fire on Pvt. Mills. Trace rs passed within inches of his body, rifle and machine-pistol bullets ricocheted off the rocks at his feet. Yet he stood there firing until his rifle was empty. Intent on covering the movement of his platoon, Pvt. Mills jumped into the draw, reloaded his weapon, climbed out again, and continued to lay down a base of fire. Repeating this action four times, he enabled his platoon to reach the designated spot undiscovered, from which position it assaulted and overwhelmed the enemy, capturing 22 Germans and taking the objective without casualties.

2861 ◆ *MINICK, JOHN W.

Rank: Staff Sergeant
Service: U.S. Army
Birthday: 14 June 1908
Place of Birth: Wall, Allegheny County, Pennsylvania
Date of Death: 21 November 1944
Cemetery: Westminster Cemetery—Carlisle, Pennsylvania
Entered Service at: Carlisle, Cumberland County, Pennsylvania
Unit: Company I, 3d Battalion, 121st Infantry, 8th Infantry Division
Served as: Squad Leader
Battle or Place of Action: near Hurtgen, Germany
Date of Action: 21 November 1944
Citation: He displayed conspicuous gallantry and intrepidity at the risk of his own life, above and beyond the call of duty, in action involving actual conflict with the enemy on 21 November 1944, near Hurtgen, Germany. S/Sgt. Minick's

battalion was halted in its advance by extensive minefields, exposing troops to heavy concentrations of enemy artillery and mortar fire. Further delay in the advance would result in numerous casualties, and a movement through the minefield was essential. Voluntarily, S/Sgt. Minick led four men through hazardous barbed wire and debris, finally making his way through the minefield for a distance of 300 yards. When an enemy machine gun opened fire, he signaled his men to take covered positions, edged his way alone toward the flank of the weapon, and opened fire, killing two members of the guncrew and capturing three others. Moving forward again, he encountered and engaged singlehandedly an entire company killing 20 Germans and capturing 20, and enabling his platoon to capture the remainder of the hostile group. Again moving ahead and spearheading his battalion's advance, he again encountered machine-gun fire. Crawling forward toward the weapon, he reached a point from which he knocked the weapon out of action. Still another minefield had to be crossed. Undeterred, S/Sgt. Minick advanced forward alone through constant enemy fire and while thus moving, detonated a mine and was instantly killed.

2862 ◆ *MINUE, NICHOLAS

Rank: Private
Service: U.S. Army
Birthday: 1899
Place of Birth: Sedden, Poland
Date of Death: 28 April 1943
Cemetery: A.B.M.C. North Africa Cemetery (E-8-4)—Carthage, Tunisia
Entered Service at: Carteret, Middlesex County, New Jersey
Unit: Company A, 6th Armored Infantry, 1st Armored Division
Battle or Place of Action: near Medjez-el-Bab, Tunisia
Date of Action: 28 April 1943
G.O. Number, Date: 24, 25 March 1944
Citation: For distinguishing himself conspicuously by gallantry and intrepidity at the loss of life above and beyond the call of duty in action with the enemy on 28 April 1943, in the vicinity of Medjez-el-Bab, Tunisia. When the advance of the assault elements of Company A was held up by flanking fire from an enemy machine-gun nest, Pvt. Minue voluntarily, alone, and unhesitatingly, with complete disregard of his own welfare, charged the enemy entrenched position with fixed bayonet. Pvt. Minue assaulted the enemy under a withering machine-gun and rifle fire, killing approximately 10 enemy machine gunners and riflemen. After completely destroying this position, Pvt. Minue continued forward, routing enemy riflemen from dugout positions until he was fatally wounded. The courage, fearlessness, and aggressiveness displayed by Pvt. Minue in the face of inevitable death was unquestionably the factor that gave his company the offensive spirit that was necessary for advancing and driving the enemy from the entire sector.

2863 ◆ *MONTEITH JR., JIMMIE W.

Rank: First Lieutenant
Service: U.S. Army

Birthday: 1 July 1917
Place of Birth: Low Moor, Alleghany County, Virginia
Date of Death: 6 June 1944
Cemetery: A.B.M.C. Normandy Cemetery (I-20-12)—St Laurent-sur-Mer, France
Entered Service at: Richmond, Richmond County, Virginia
Unit: 16th Infantry, 1st Infantry Division
Battle or Place of Action: near Colleville-sur-Mer, France
Date of Action: 6 June 1944
G.O. Number, Date: 20, 29 March 1945
Place of Presentation: Richmond, Virginia, presented by Brig. Gen. Frank Dorn to his family
Citation: For conspicuous gallantry and intrepidity above and beyond the call of duty on 6 June 1944, near Colleville-sur-Mer, France. First Lt. Monteith landed with the initial assault waves on the coast of France under heavy enemy fire. Without regard to his own personal safety he continually moved up and down the beach reorganizing men for further assault. He then led the assault over a narrow protective ledge and across the flat, exposed terrain to the comparative safety of a cliff. Retracing his steps across the field to the beach, he moved over to where two tanks were buttoned up and blind under violent enemy artillery and machine-gun fire. Completely exposed to the intense fire, 1st Lt. Monteith led the tanks on foot through a minefield and into firing positions. Under his direction several enemy positions were destroyed. He then rejoined his company and under his leadership his men captured an advantageous position on the hill. Supervising the defense of his newly won position against repeated vicious counterattacks, he continued to ignore his own personal safety, repeatedly crossing the 200 or 300 yards of open terrain under heavy fire to strengthen links in his defensive chain. When the enemy succeeded in completely surrounding 1st Lt. Monteith and his unit and while leading the fight out of the situation, 1st Lt. Monteith was killed by enemy fire. The courage, gallantry, and intrepid leadership displayed by 1st Lt. Monteith is worthy of emulation.

2864 ◆ MONTGOMERY, JACK CLEVELAND

Rank: First Lieutenant
Service: U.S. Army
Birthday: 23 July 1917
Place of Birth: Long, Oklahoma
Entered Service at: Sallisaw, Sequoyah County, Oklahoma
Unit: 1st Platoon, Company I, 3d Battalion, 180th Infantry, 45th Infantry Division
Served as: Platoon Leader
Battle or Place of Action: near Padiglione, Italy
Date of Action: 22 February 1944
G.O. Number, Date: 5, 15 January 1945
Date of Presentation: 10 January 1945
Place of Presentation: The White House (Oval Office), presented by Pres. Franklin D. Roosevelt
Citation: For conspicuous gallantry and intrepidity at the risk of life above and beyond the call of duty on 22 February 1944, near Padiglione, Italy. Two hours before daybreak a strong force of enemy infantry established themselves in three echelons at 50 yards, 100 yards, and 300 yards, respectively, in front of the rifle platoons commanded by 1st Lt.

Montgomery. The closest position, consisting of four machine guns and one mortar, threatened the immediate security of the platoon position. Seizing an M1 rifle and several hand grenades, 1st Lt. Montgomery crawled up a ditch to within hand-grenade range of the enemy. Then climbing boldly onto a little mound, he fired his rifle and threw his grenades so accurately that he killed eight of the enemy and captured the remaining four. Returning to his platoon, he called for artillery fire on a house, in and around which he suspected that the majority of the enemy had entrenched themselves. Arming himself with a carbine, he proceeded along the shallow ditch, as withering fire from the riflemen and machine gunners in the second position was concentrated on him. He attacked this position with such fury that seven of the enemy surrendered to him, and both machine guns were silenced. Three German dead were found in the vicinity later that morning. First Lt. Montgomery continued boldly toward the house, 300 yards from his platoon position. It was now daylight, and the enemy observation was excellent across the flat open terrain which led to 1st Lt. Montgomery's objective. When the artillery barrage had lifted, 1st Lt. Montgomery ran fearlessly toward the strongly defended position. As the enemy started streaming out of the house, 1st Lt. Montgomery, unafraid of treacherous snipers, exposed himself daringly to assemble the surrendering enemy and send them to the rear. His fearless, aggressive, and intrepid actions that morning accounted for a total of 11 enemy dead, 32 prisoners, and an unknown number of wounded. That night, while aiding an adjacent unit to repulse a counterattack, he was struck by mortar fragments and seriously wounded. The selflessness and courage exhibited by 1st Lt. Montgomery in alone attacking three strong enemy positions inspired his men to a degree beyond estimation.

2865 ◆ *MOON JR., HAROLD HERMAN

Rank: Private
Service: U.S. Army
Birthday: 15 March 1921
Place of Birth: Albuquerque, Bernalillo County, New Mexico
Date of Death: 21 October 1944
Cemetery: Sunset Memorial Park (MH)—Albuquerque, New Mexico
Entered Service at: Gardena, Los Angeles County, California
Unit: Company G, 34th Infantry, 24th Infantry Division
Battle or Place of Action: Pawig, Leyte, Philippine Islands
Date of Action: 21 October 1944
G.O. Number, Date: 104, 15 November 1945
Citation: He fought with conspicuous gallantry and intrepidity when powerful Japanese counterblows were being struck in a desperate effort to annihilate a newly won beachhead. In a forward position, armed with a submachine gun, he met the brunt of a strong, well-supported night attack which quickly enveloped his platoon's flanks. Many men in nearby positions were killed or injured, and Pvt. Moon was wounded as his foxhole became the immediate object of a concentration of mortar and machine-gun fire. Nevertheless, he maintained his stand, poured deadly fire into the enemy,

daringly exposed himself to hostile fire time after time to exhort and inspire what American troops were left in the immediate area. A Japanese officer, covered by machine-gun fire and hidden by an embankment, attempted to knock out his position with grenades, but Pvt. Moon, after protracted and skillful maneuvering, killed him. When the enemy advanced a light machine gun to within 20 yards of the shattered perimeter and fired with telling effects on the remnants of the platoon, he stood up to locate the gun and remained exposed, while calling back range corrections to friendly mortars which knocked out the weapon. A little later he killed two Japanese as they charged an aidman. By dawn his position, the focal point of the attack for more than four hours, was virtually surrounded. In a fanatical effort to reduce it and kill its defender, an entire platoon charged with fixed bayonets. Firing from a sitting position, Pvt. Moon calmly emptied his magazine into the advancing horde, killing 18 and repulsing the attack. In a final display of bravery, he stood up to throw a grenade at a machine gun which had opened fire on the right flank. He was hit and instantly killed, falling in the position from which he had not been driven by the fiercest enemy action. Nearly 200 dead Japanese were found within 100 yards of his foxhole. The continued tenacity, combat sagacity, and magnificent heroism with which Pvt. Moon fought on against overwhelming odds contributed in a large measure to breaking up a powerful enemy threat and did much to insure our initial successes during a most important operation.

2866 ◆ MORGAN, JOHN CARY "RED"

Rank: Second Lieutenant (rank at time of action: Flight Officer) (highest rank: Lieutenant Colonel)
Service: U.S. Army Air Corps/U.S. Air Force
Birthday: 24 August 1914
Place of Birth: Vernon, Wilbarger County, Texas
Date of Death: 17 January 1991
Place of Death: Papillton, Nebraska
Cemetery: Arlington National Cemetery (59-351) (MH)—Arlington, Virginia
Entered Service at: London, England
Unit: 326th Bombardment Squadron, 92d Bombardment Group, 8th Air Force
Served as: Copilot of a B-17
Battle or Place of Action: over Kiel, Germany
Date of Action: 28 July 1943
G.O. Number, Date: 85, 17 December 1943
Date of Presentation: 18 December 1943
Place of Presentation: Widewing, England
Citation: For conspicuous gallantry and intrepidity above and beyond the call of duty, while participating on a bombing mission over enemy-occupied continental Europe, 28 July 1943. Prior to reaching the German coast on the way to the target, the B-17 airplane in which 2d Lt. Morgan was serving as copilot was attacked by a large force of enemy fighters, during which the oxygen system to the tail, waist, and radio gun positions was knocked out. A frontal attack placed a cannon shell through the windshield, totally shattering it, and the pilot's skull was split open by a .303-caliber shell, leaving

him in a crazed condition. The pilot fell over the steering wheel, tightly clamping his arms around it. Second Lt. Morgan at once grasped the controls from his side and, by sheer strength, pulled the airplane back into formation despite the frantic struggles of the semiconscious pilot. The interphone had been destroyed, rendering it impossible to call for help. At this time the top turret gunner fell to the floor and down through the hatch with his arms shot off at the shoulder and a gaping wound in his side. The waist, tail, and radio gunners had lost consciousness from lack of oxygen and, hearing no fire from their guns, the copilot believed they had bailed out. The wounded pilot still offered desperate resistance in his crazed attempts to fly the airplane. There remained the prospect of flying to and over the target and back to a friendly base wholly unassisted. In the face of this desperate situation, 2d Lt. Morgan made his decision to continue the flight and protect any members of the crew who might still be in the ship and for two hours he flew in formation with one hand at the controls and the other holding off the struggling pilot before the navigator entered the steering compartment and relieved the situation. The miraculous and heroic performance of 2d Lt. Morgan on this occasion resulted in the successful completion of a vital bombing mission and the safe return of hi s airplane and crew.
Notes: POW

2867 ◆ *MOSKALA, EDWARD J.

Rank: Private First Class
Service: U.S. Army
Birthday: 6 November 1921
Place of Birth: Chicago, Cook County, Illinois
Date of Death: 9 April 1945
Cemetery: Rock Island National Cemetery (E-293) (MH)—Rock Island, Illinois
Entered Service at: Chicago, Cook County, Illinois
Unit: Company C, 383d Infantry, 96th Infantry Division
Battle or Place of Action: Kakazu Ridge, Okinawa, Ryukyu Islands
Date of Action: 9 April 1945
G.O. Number, Date: 21, 26 February 1946
Citation: He was the leading element when grenade explosions and concentrated machine-gun and mortar fire halted the unit's attack on Kakazu Ridge, Okinawa, Ryukyu Islands. With utter disregard for his personal safety, he charged 40 yards through withering, grazing fire and wiped out two machine-gun nests with well-aimed grenades and deadly accurate fire from his automatic rifle. When strong counterattacks and fierce enemy resistance from other positions forced his company to withdraw, he voluntarily remained behind with eight others to cover the maneuver. Fighting from a critically dangerous position for three hours, he killed more than 25 Japanese before following his surviving companions through screening smoke down the face of the ridge to a gorge where it was discovered that one of the group had been left behind, wounded. Unhesitatingly, Pvt. Moskala climbed the bullet-swept slope to assist in the rescue, and, returning to lower ground, volunteered to protect other wounded while the bulk of the troops quickly took up more favorable positions. He

had saved another casualty and killed four enemy infiltrators when he was struck and mortally wounded himself while aiding still another disabled soldier. With gallant initiative, unfaltering courage, and heroic determination to destroy the enemy, Pvt. Moskala gave his life in his complete devotion to his company's mission and his comrades' well-being. His intrepid conduct provided a lasting inspiration for those with whom he served.

2868 ◆ *MOWER, CHARLES E.

Rank: Sergeant
Service: U.S. Army
Birthday: 29 November 1924
Place of Birth: Chippewa Falls, Chippewa County, Wisconsin
Date of Death: 3 November 1944
Cemetery: A.B.M.C. Manila Cemetery (L-2-110)—Manila, Philippine Islands
Entered Service at: Chippewa Falls, Chippewa County, Wisconsin
Unit: Company A, 34th Infantry, 24th Infantry Division
Served as: Assistant Squad Leader
Battle or Place of Action: near Capoocan, Leyte, Philippine Islands
Date of Action: 3 November 1944
G.O. Number, Date: 17, 11 February 1946
Citation: He was assistant squad leader in an attack against strongly defended enemy positions on both sides of a stream running through a wooded gulch. As the squad advanced through concentrated fire, the leader was killed and Sgt. Mower assumed command. In order to bring direct fire upon the enemy, he had started to lead his men across the stream, which by this time was churned by machine-gun and rifle fire, but he was severely wounded before reaching the opposite bank. After signaling his unit to halt, he realized his own exposed position was the most advantageous point from which to direct the attack, and stood fast. Half submerged, gravely wounded, but refusing to seek shelter or accept aid of any kind, he continued to shout and signal to his squad as he directed it in the destruction of two enemy machine guns and numerous riflemen. Discovering that the intrepid man in the stream was largely responsible for the successful action being taken against them, the remaining Japanese concentrated the full force of their firepower upon him, and he was killed while still urging his men on. Sgt. Mower's gallant initiative and heroic determination aided materially in the successful completion of his squad's mission. His magnificent leadership was an inspiration to those with whom he served.

2869 ◆ *MULLER, JOSEPH E.

Rank: Sergeant
Service: U.S. Army
Birthday: 23 June 1908
Place of Birth: Holyoke, Hampden County, Massachusetts
Date of Death: 16 May 1945
Cemetery: National Memorial Cemetery of the Pacific (M-1259) (MH)—Honolulu, Hawaii

Entered Service at: New York, New York
Unit: Company B, 305th Infantry, 77th Infantry Division
Battle or Place of Action: near Ishimmi, Okinawa, Ryukyu Islands
Date of Action: 15-16 May 1945
G.O. Number, Date: 71, 17 July 1946
Citation: He displayed conspicuous gallantry and intrepidity above and beyond the call of duty. When his platoon was stopped by deadly fire from a strongly defended ridge, he directed men to points where they could cover his attack. Then through the vicious machine-gun and automatic fire, crawling forward alone, he suddenly jumped up, hurled his grenades, charged the enemy, and drove them into the open where his squad shot them down. Seeing enemy survivors about to man a machine gun, he fired his rifle at point-blank range, hurled himself upon them, and killed the remaining four. Before dawn the next day, the enemy counterattacked fiercely to retake the position. Sgt. Muller crawled forward through the flying bullets and explosives, then leaping to his feet, hurling grenades, and firing his rifle, he charged the Japs and routed them. As he moved into his foxhole shared with two other men, a lone enemy, who had been feigning death, threw a grenade. Quickly seeing the danger to his companions, Sgt. Muller threw himself over it and smothered the blast with his body. Heroically sacrificing his life to save his comrades, he upheld the highest traditions of the military service.

2870 ◆ *MUNEMORI, SADAO S.

Rank: Private First Class
Service: U.S. Army
Birthday: 17 August 1922
Place of Birth: Los Angeles, Los Angeles County, California
Date of Death: 5 April 1945
Cemetery: Evergreen Cemetery (MH)—Los Angeles, California
Entered Service at: Los Angeles, Los Angeles County, California
Unit: 442d Combat Team, Company A, 100th Infantry Battalion, 34th Infantry Division
Battle or Place of Action: near Seravezza, Italy
Date of Action: 5 April 1945
G.O. Number, Date: 24, 7 March 1946
Date of Issue: 13 March 1946
Citation: He fought with great gallantry and intrepidity near Seravezza, Italy. When his unit was pinned down by grazing fire from the enemy's strong mountain defense and command of the squad devolved on him with the wounding of its regular leader, he made frontal, one-man attacks through direct fire and knocked out two machine guns with grenades. Withdrawing under murderous fire and showers of grenades from other enemy emplacements, he had nearly reached a shell crater occupied by two of his men when an unexploded grenade bounced on his helmet and rolled toward his helpless comrades. He arose into the withering fire, dived for the missile, and smothered its blast with his body. By his swift, supremely heroic action Pfc. Munemori saved two of his men at the cost of his own life and did much to clear the path for his company's victorious advance.

2871 ◆ *MUNRO, DOUGLAS ALBERT

Rank: Signalman First Class
Service: U.S. Coast Guard
Birthday: 11 October 1919
Place of Birth: Vancouver, British Columbia, Canada
Date of Death: 27 September 1942
Cemetery: Laurel Hill Memorial Park (MH)—Cle Elum, Washington
Entered Service at: Washington
Served as: Petty Officer
Battle or Place of Action: Point Cruz, Guadalcanal, Solomon Islands
Date of Action: 27 September 1942
Date of Presentation: 24 May 1943
Place of Presentation: The White House (Oval Office), presented by Pres. Franklin D. Roosevelt to his mother, Edith Munro
Citation: For extraordinary heroism and conspicuous gallantry in action above and beyond the call of duty as petty officer in charge of a group of 24 Higgins boats, engaged in the evacuation of a battalion of marines trapped by enemy Japanese forces at Point Cruz, Guadalcanal on 27 September 1942. After making preliminary plans for the evacuation of nearly 500 beleaguered marines, Munro, under constant strafing by enemy machine guns on the island, and at great risk of his life, daringly led five of his small craft toward the shore. As he closed the beach, he signaled the others to land, and then in order to draw the enemy's fire and protect the heavily loaded boats, he valiantly placed his craft with its two small guns as a shield between the beachhead and the Japanese. When the perilous task of evacuation was nearly completed, Munro was instantly killed by enemy fire, but his crew, two of whom were wounded, carried on until the last boat had loaded and cleared the beach. By his outstanding leadership, expert planning, and dauntless devotion to duty, he and his courageous comrades undoubtedly saved the lives of many who otherwise would have perished. He gallantly gave his life for his country.

2872 ◆ MURPHY, AUDIE LEON

Rank: Second Lieutenant (highest rank: Major)
Service: U.S. Army
Birthday: 20 June 1924
Place of Birth: near Kingston, Hunt County, Texas
Date of Death: 28 May 1971
Place of Death: near Roanoke, Virginia
Cemetery: Arlington National Cemetery (46-366-11)—Arlington, Virginia
Entered Service at: Dallas, Collin County, Texas
Unit: Company B, 1st Battalion, 15th Infantry, 3d Infantry Division
Served as: Company Commander
Battle or Place of Action: near Holtzwihr, France
Date of Action: 26 January 1945
G.O. Number, Date: 65, 9 August 1945
Date of Presentation: 2 June 1945
Place of Presentation: Airfield near Werfen, Austria, presented by Lt. Gen. Alexander M. Patch III

Citation: Second Lt. Murphy commanded Company B, which was attacked by six tanks and waves of infantry. Second Lt. Murphy ordered his men to withdraw to prepared positions in a woods, while he remained forward at his command post and continued to give fire directions to the artillery by telephone. Behind him, to his right, one of our tank destroyers received a direct hit and began to burn. Its crew withdrew to the woods. Second Lt. Murphy continued to direct artillery fire which killed large numbers of the advancing enemy infantry. With the enemy tanks abreast of his position, 2d Lt. Murphy climbed on the burning tank destroyer, which was in danger of blowing up at any moment, and employed its .50-caliber machine gun against the enemy. He was alone and exposed to German fire from three sides, but his deadly fire killed dozens of Germans and caused their infantry attack to waver. The enemy tanks, losing infantry support, began to fall back. For an hour the Germans tried every available weapon to eliminate 2d Lt. Murphy, but he continued to hold his position and wiped out a squad which was trying to creep up unnoticed on his right flank. Germans reached as close as 10 yards, only to be mowed down by his fire. He received a leg wound, but ignored it and continued the singlehanded fight until his ammunition was exhausted. He then made his way to his company, refused medical attention, and organized the company in a counterattack which forced the Germans to withdraw. His directing of artillery fire wiped out many of the enemy; he killed or wounded about 50. Second Lt. Murphy's indomitable courage and his refusal to give an inch of ground saved his company from possible encirclement and destruction, and enabled it to hold the woods which had been the enemy's objective.

2873 ◆ *MURPHY, FREDERICK C.

Rank: Private First Class
Service: U.S. Army
Birthday: 1918
Place of Birth: Boston, Suffolk County, Massachusetts
Date of Death: 18 March 1945
Cemetery: A.B.M.C. Lorraine Cemetery—St. Avold, France
Entered Service at: Weymouth, Norfolk County, Massachusetts
Unit: Medical Detachment, 259th Infantry, 65th Infantry Division
Served as: Medical Aidman
Battle or Place of Action: Siegfried Line at Saarlautern, Germany
Date of Action: 18 March 1945
G.O. Number, Date: 21, 26 February 1946
Date of Presentation: February 1946
Place of Presentation: City Hall, Quincy, Massachusetts, presented by Lt. Gen. O.W. Griswold to his Widow and Daughter
Citation: An aidman, he was wounded in the right shoulder soon after his comrades had jumped off in a dawn attack, 18 March 1945, against the Siegfried Line at Saarlautern, Germany. He refused to withdraw for treatment and continued forward, administering first aid under heavy machine-gun, mortar, and artillery fire. When the company ran into a

thickly sown antipersonnel minefield and began to suffer more and more casualties, he continued to disregard his own wound and unhesitatingly braved the danger of exploding mines, moving about through heavy fire and helping the injured until he stepped on a mine which severed one of his feet. In spite of his grievous wounds, he struggled on with his work, refusing to be evacuated and crawling from man to man administering to them while in great pain and bleeding profusely. He was killed by the blast of another mine which he had dragged himself across in an effort to reach still another casualty. With indomitable courage, and unquenchable spirit of self-sacrifice and supreme devotion to duty which made it possible for him to continue performing his tasks while barely able to move, Pfc. Murphy saved many of his fellow soldiers at the cost of his own life.

2874 ◆ MURRAY JR., CHARLES PATRICK "CHUCK"

Rank: First Lieutenant (highest rank: Colonel)
Service: U.S. Army
Birthday: 26 September 1921
Place of Birth: Baltimore, Baltimore County, Maryland
Entered Service at: Wilmington, New Hanover County, North Carolina
Unit: Company C, 1st Battalion, 30th Infantry, 3d Infantry Division
Served as: Company Commander
Battle or Place of Action: near Kaysersberg, France
Date of Action: 16 December 1944
G.O. Number, Date: 63, 1 August 1945
Date of Presentation: 5 July 1945
Place of Presentation: Salzburg, Austria, presented by Lt. Gen. Geoffrey Keyes, Commanding Gen. U.S. II Corps
Citation: For commanding Company C, 30th Infantry, displaying supreme courage and heroic initiative near Kaysersberg, France on 16 December 1944, while leading a reinforced platoon into enemy territory. Descending into a valley beneath hilltop positions held by our troops, he observed a force of 200 Germans pouring deadly mortar, bazooka, machine-gun, and small-arms fire into an American battalion occupying the crest of the ridge. The enemy's position in a sunken road, though hidden from the ridge, was open to a flank attack by 1st Lt. Murray's patrol but he hesitated to commit so small a force to battle with the superior and strongly disposed enemy. Crawling out ahead of his troops to a vantage point, he called by radio for artillery fire. His shells bracketed the German force, but when he was about to correct the range his radio went dead. He returned to his patrol, secured grenades and a rifle to launch them, and went back to his self-appointed outpost. His first shots disclosed his position; the enemy directed heavy fire against him as he methodically fired his missiles into the narrow defile. Again he returned to his patrol. With an automatic rifle and ammunition, he once more moved to his exposed position. Burst after burst he fired into the enemy, killing 20, wounding many others, and completely disorganizing its ranks, which began to withdraw. He prevented the removal of three German mortars by knocking out a truck. By that time a mor-

tar had been brought to his support. First Lt. Murray directed the fire of this weapon, causing further casualties and confusion in the German ranks. Calling on his patrol to follow, he then moved out toward his original objective, possession of a bridge and construction of a roadblock. He captured 10 Germans in foxholes. An eleventh, while pretending to surrender, threw a grenade which knocked him to the ground, inflicting eight wounds. Though suffering and bleeding profusely, he refused to return to the rear until he had chosen the spot for the block and had seen his men correctly deployed. By his singlehanded attack on an overwhelming force and by his intrepid and heroic fighting, 1st Lt. Murray stopped a counterattack, established an advance position against formidable odds, and provided an inspiring example for the men of his command.

2875 ◆ *NELSON, WILLIAM LANCASTER

Rank: Sergeant
Service: U.S. Army
Place of Birth: Dover, Kent County, Delaware
Date of Death: 24 April 1943
Cemetery: Silver Brook Cemetery—Wilmington, Delaware
Entered Service at: Middletown, New Castle County, Delaware
Unit: 60th Infantry, 9th Infantry Division
Served as: Mortar Section Leader
Battle or Place of Action: Djebel Dardys, northwest of Sedjenane, Tunisia
Date of Action: 24 April 1943
G.O. Number, Date: 85, 17 December 1943
Date of Presentation: December 1943
Place of Presentation: Fort Dupont, Delaware, presented to his wife Rebecca by Maj. Gen. Lunsford E. Oliver, CG 5th Armored Division
Citation: For conspicuous gallantry and intrepidity at risk of life, above and beyond the call of duty in action involving actual conflict. On the morning of 24 April 1943, Sgt. Nelson led his section of heavy mortars to a forward position where he placed his guns and men. Under intense enemy artillery, mortar, and small-arms fire, he advanced alone to a chosen observation position from which he directed the laying of a concentrated mortar barrage which successfully halted an initial enemy counterattack. Although mortally wounded in the accomplishment of his mission, and with his duty clearly completed, Sgt. Nelson crawled to a still more advanced observation point and continued to direct the fire of his section. Dying of hand-grenade wounds and only 50 yards from the enemy, Sgt. Nelson encouraged his section to continue their fire and by doing so they took a heavy toll of enemy lives. The skill which Sgt. Nelson displayed in this engagement, his courage, and self-sacrificing devotion to duty and heroism resulting in the loss of his life, was a priceless inspiration to our Armed Forces and were in keeping with the highest traditions of the U.S. Army.

2876 ◆ NEPPEL, RALPH GEORGE

Rank: Sergeant
Service: U.S. Army
Birthday: 31 October 1923
Place of Birth: Willey, Carroll County, Iowa
Date of Death: 27 January 1987
Cemetery: Holy Family Cemetery (MH)—Lidderdale, Iowa
Entered Service at: Glidden, Carroll County, Iowa
Unit: Company M, 329th Infantry, 83d Infantry Division
Served as: Squad Leader
Battle or Place of Action: Birgel, Germany
Date of Action: 14 December 1944
G.O. Number, Date: 77, 10 September 1945
Date of Presentation: 23 August 1945
Place of Presentation: The White House, presented by Pres. Harry S. Truman
Citation: He was a leader of a machine-gun squad defending an approach to the village of Birgel, Germany, on 14 December 1944, when an enemy tank, supported by 20 infantrymen, counterattacked. He held his fire until the Germans were within 100 yards and then raked the foot soldiers beside the tank, killing several of them. The enemy armor continued to press forward, and, at the point-blank range of 30 yards, fired a high-velocity shell into the American emplacement, wounding the entire squad. Sgt. Neppel, blown 10 yards from his gun, had one leg severed below the knee and suffered other wounds. Despite his injuries and the danger from the onrushing tank and infantry, he dragged himself back to his position on his elbows, remounted his gun, and killed the remaining enemy riflemen. Stripped of its infantry protection, the tank was forced to withdraw. By his superb courage and indomitable fighting spirit, Sgt. Neppel inflicted heavy casualties on the enemy and broke a determined counterattack.

2877 ◆ NETT, ROBERT BURTON

Rank: Captain (rank at time of action: First Lieutenant) (highest rank: Colonel)
Service: U.S. Army
Birthday: 13 June 1922
Place of Birth: New Haven, New Haven County, Connecticut
Entered Service at: New Haven, New Haven County, Connecticut
Unit: Company E, 2d Battalion, 305th Infantry, 77th Infantry Division
Served as: Company Commander
Battle or Place of Action: near Cognon, Leyte, Philippine Islands
Date of Action: 14 December 1944
G.O. Number, Date: 16, 8 February 1946
Date of Presentation: 8 February 1946
Place of Presentation: New Haven, Connecticut, presented by Lt. Gen. Oscar W. Griswold
Citation: He commanded Company E in an attack against a reinforced enemy battalion which had held up the American advance for two days from its entrenched positions around a three-story concrete building. With another infantry company and armored vehicles, Company E advanced against heavy machine-gun and other automatic-weapon fire with Lt. Nett spearheading the assault against the strongpoint. During the fierce hand-to-hand encounter which ensued, he killed seven

deeply entrenched Japanese with his rifle and bayonet and, although seriously wounded, gallantly continued to lead his men forward, refusing to relinquish his command. Again he was severely wounded, but, still unwilling to retire, pressed ahead with his troops to assure the capture of the objective. Wounded once more in the final assault, he calmly made all arrangements for the resumption of the advance, turned over his command to another officer, and then walked unaided to the rear for medical treatment. By his remarkable courage in continuing forward through sheer determination despite successive wounds, Lt. Nett provided an inspiring example for his men and was instrumental in the capture of a vital strongpoint.

2878 ◆ *NEW, JOHN DURY

Rank: Private First Class
Service: U.S. Marine Corps
Birthday: 12 August 1924
Place of Birth: Mobile, Mobile County, Alabama
Date of Death: 25 September 1944
Cemetery: Mobile National Cemetery (7-2147) (MH)—Mobile, Alabama
Entered Service at: Alabama
Unit: 2d Battalion, 7th Marines, 1st Marine Division
Battle or Place of Action: Peleliu Island, Palau Islands
Date of Action: 25 September 1944
Citation: For conspicuous gallantry and intrepidity at the risk of his life above and beyond the call of duty while serving with the 2d Battalion, 7th Marines, 1st Marine Division, in action against enemy Japanese forces on Peleliu Island, Palau Group, 25 September 1944. When a Japanese soldier emerged from a cave in a cliff directly below an observation post and suddenly hurled a grenade into the position from which two of our men were directing mortar fire against enemy emplacements, Pfc. New instantly perceived the dire peril to the other marines and, with utter disregard for his own safety, unhesitatingly flung himself upon the grenade and absorbed the full impact of the explosion, thus saving the lives of the two observers. Pfc. New's great personal valor and selfless conduct in the face of almost certain death reflect the highest credit upon himself and the U.S. Naval Service. He gallantly gave his life for his country.

2879 ◆ NEWMAN, BERYL RICHARD

Rank: First Lieutenant (highest rank: Captain)
Service: U.S. Army
Birthday: 2 November 1911
Place of Birth: Baraboo, Sauk County, Wisconsin
Entered Service at: Baraboo, Sauk County, Wisconsin
Unit: 1st Platoon, Company F, 2d Battalion, 133d Infantry, 34th Infantry Division
Served as: Platoon Leader
Battle or Place of Action: near Cisterna, Italy
Date of Action: 26 May 1944
G.O. Number, Date: 5, 15 January 1945
Date of Presentation: 10 January 1945
Place of Presentation: The White House, presented by Pres. Franklin D. Roosevelt
Citation: For conspicuous gallantry and intrepidity above

and beyond the call of duty on 26 May 1944. Attacking the strongly held German Anzio-Nettuno defense line near Cisterna, Italy, 1st Lt. Newman, in the lead of his platoon, was suddenly fired upon by two enemy machine guns located on the crest of a hill about 100 yards to his front. The four scouts with him immediately hit the ground, but 1st Lt. Newman remained standing in order to see the enemy positions and his platoon then about 100 yards behind. Locating the enemy nests, 1st Lt. Newman called back to his platoon and ordered one squad to advance to him and the other to flank the enemy to the right. Then, still standing upright in the face of enemy machine-gun fire, 1st Lt. Newman opened up with his tommy gun on the enemy nests. From this range, his fire was not effective in covering the advance of his squads, and one squad was pinned down by the enemy fire. Seeing that his squad was unable to advance, 1st Lt. Newman, in full view of the enemy gunners and in the face of their continuous fire, advanced alone on the enemy nests. He returned their fire with his tommy gun and succeeded in wounding a German in each of the nests. The remaining two Germans fled from the position into a nearby house. Three more enemy soldiers then came out of the house and ran toward a third machine gun. First Lt. Newman, still relentlessly advancing toward them, killed one before he reached the gun, the second before he could fire it. The third fled for his life back into the house. Covering his assault by firing into the doors and windows of the house, 1st Lt. Newman, boldly attacking by himself, called for the occupants to surrender to him. Gaining the house, he kicked in the door and went inside. Although armed with rifles and machine pistols, the 11 Germans there, apparently intimidated, surrendered to the lieutenant without further resistance. 1st Lt. Newman, single-handedly, had silenced three enemy machine guns, wounded two Germa ns, killed two more, and taken 11 prisoners. This demonstration of sheer courage, bravery, and willingness to close with the enemy even in the face of such heavy odds, instilled into these green troops the confidence of veterans and reflect the highest traditions of the U.S. Armed Forces.

2880 ◆ *NININGER JR., ALEXANDER RAMSEY

Rank: Second Lieutenant
Service: U.S. Army
Birthday: 20 October 1918
Place of Birth: Gainesville, Hall County, Georgia
Date of Death: 12 January 1942
Cemetery: Abucay Church Cemetery (grave 9)—Manila, Philippine Islands
Entered Service at: Fort Lauderdale, Broward County, Florida
Unit: Philippine Scouts, Company A, 1st Battalion, 57th Infantry, U.S. Army
Served as: Platoon Leader
Battle or Place of Action: near Abucay, Bataan, Philippine Islands
Date of Action: 12 January 1942
G.O. Number, Date: 9, 5 February 1942
Date of Presentation: 10 February 1942
Place of Presentation: Third Air Force Headquarters, Tampa, Florida, presented by Maj. Gen. Walter H. Frank

Citation: For conspicuous gallantry and intrepidity above and beyond the call of duty in action with the enemy near Abucay, Bataan, Philippine Islands on 12 January 1942. This officer, though assigned to another company not then engaged in combat, voluntarily attached himself to Company K, same regiment, while that unit was being attacked by enemy forces superior in firepower. Enemy snipers in trees and foxholes had stopped a counterattack to regain part of the position. In the hand-to-hand fighting which followed, 2d Lt. Nininger repeatedly forced his way to and into the hostile position. Though exposed to heavy enemy fire, he continued to attack with rifle and hand grenades and succeeded in destroying several enemy groups in foxholes, and enemy snipers. Although wounded three times, he continued his attacks until he was killed after pushing alone far within the enemy position. When his body was found after recapture of the position, one enemy officer and two enemy soldiers lay dead around him.

2881 ◆ *O'BRIEN, WILLIAM JOSEPH

Rank: Lieutenant Colonel
Service: U.S. Army
Birthday: 1899
Place of Birth: Troy, Rensselaer County, New York
Date of Death: 7 July 1944
Cemetery: St. Peter's Cemetery (MH)—Troy, New York
Entered Service at: Troy, Rensselaer County, New York
it: 1st Battalion, 105th Infantry, 27th Infantry Division
Battle or Place of Action: Saipan, Marianas Islands
Date of Action: 20 June-7 July 1944
G.O. Number, Date: 35, 9 May 1945
Citation: For conspicuous gallantry and intrepidity at the risk of his life above and beyond the call of duty at Saipan, Marianas Islands, from 20 June through 7 July 1944. When assault elements of his platoon were held up by intense enemy fire, Lt. Col. O'Brien ordered three tanks to precede the assault companies in an attempt to knock out the strongpoint. Due to direct enemy fire the tanks' turrets were closed, causing the tanks to lose direction and to fire into our own troops. Lt. Col. O'Brien, with complete disregard for his own safety, dashed into full view of the enemy and ran to the leader's tank and pounded on the tank with his pistol butt to attract two of the tank's crew and, mounting the tank fully exposed to the enemy fire, Lt. Col. O'Brien personally directed the assault until the enemy strongpoint had been liquidated. On 28 June 1944, while his platoon was attempting to take a bitterly defended high ridge in the vicinity of Donnay, Lt. Col. O'Brien arranged to capture the ridge by a double envelopment movement of two large combat battalions. He personally took control of the maneuver. Lt. Col. O'Brien crossed 1,200 yards of sniper-infested underbrush alone to arrive at a point where one of his platoons was being held up by the enemy. Leaving some men to contain the enemy, he personally led four men into a narrow ravine behind, and killed or drove off all the Japanese manning that strongpoint. In this action he captured five machine guns and one 77-mm fieldpiece. Lt. Col. O'Brien then organized the two platoons for night defense and against repeated counterattacks directed

them. Meanwhile he managed to hold ground. On 7 July 1944 his battalion and another battalion were attacked by an overwhelming enemy force estimated at between 3,000 and 5,000 Japanese. With bloody hand-to-hand fighting in progress everywhere, their forward positions were finally overrun by the sheer weight of the enemy numbers. With many casualties and ammunition running low, Lt. Col. O' Brien refused to leave the front lines. Striding up and down the lines, he fired at the enemy with a pistol in each hand and his presence there bolstered the spirits of the men, encouraged them in their fight, and sustained them in their heroic stand. Even after he was seriously wounded, Lt. Col. O'Brien refused to be evacuated and after his pistol ammunition was exhausted, he manned a .50-caliber machine gun, mounted on a jeep, and continued firing. When last seen alive he was standing upright firing into the Jap hordes that were enveloping him. Some time later his body was found surrounded by enemy he had killed. His valor was consistent with the highest traditions of the service.

2882 ◆ O'CALLAHAN, JOSEPH TIMOTHY

Rank: Commander (Chaplain Corps)
Service: U.S. Naval Reserve
Birthday: 14 May 1904
Place of Birth: Boston, Suffolk County, Massachusetts
Date of Death: 18 March 1964
Cemetery: Holy Cross College Cemetery—Worcester, Massachusetts
Entered Service at: Massachusetts
Unit: U.S.S. *Franklin*
Served as: Chaplain
Battle or Place of Action: near Kobe, Japan
Date of Action: 19 March 1945
Date of Presentation: 23 January 1946
Place of Presentation: The White House, presented by Pres. Harry S. Truman
Citation: For conspicuous gallantry and intrepidity at the risk of his life above and beyond the call of duty while serving as chaplain on board the U.S.S. *Franklin* when that vessel was fiercely attacked by enemy Japanese aircraft during offensive operations near Kobe, Japan, on 19 March 1945. A valiant and forceful leader, calmly braving the perilous barriers of flame and twisted metal to aid his men and his ship, Lt. Comdr. O'Callahan groped his way through smoke-filled corridors to the open flight deck and into the midst of violently exploding bombs, shells, rockets, and other armament. With the ship rocked by incessant explosions, with debris and fragments raining down and fires raging in ever-increasing fury, he ministered to the wounded and dying, comforting and encouraging men of all faiths; he organized and led firefighting crews into the blazing inferno on the flight deck; he directed the jettisoning of live ammunition and the flooding of the magazine; he manned a hose to cool hot, armed bombs rolling dangerously on the listing deck, continuing his efforts, despite searing, suffocating smoke which forced men to fall back gasping and imperiled others who replaced them. Serving with courage, fortitude, and deep spiritual strength, Lt. Comdr. O'Callahan inspired the gallant officers and men

of the *Franklin* to fight heroically and with profound faith in the face of almost certain death and to return their stricken ship to port.

2883 ◆ OGDEN SR., CARLOS CARNES

Rank: First Lieutenant (highest rank: Major)
Service: U.S. Army
Birthday: 9 May 1917
Place of Birth: Borton, Edgar County, Illinois
Entered Service at: Fairmount, Vermillion County, Illinois
Unit: Company K, 3d Battalion, 314th Infantry, 79th Infantry Division
Served as: Company Commander
Battle or Place of Action: near Fort du Roule, Cherbourg, France
Date of Action: 25 June 1944
G.O. Number, Date: 49, 28 June 1945
Date of Presentation: 30 May 1945
Place of Presentation: Augsburg, Germany, presented by Lt. Gen. Alexander M. Patch III
Citation: On the morning of 25 June 1944, near Fort du Roule, guarding the approaches to Cherbourg, France, 1st Lt. Ogden's company was pinned down by fire from a German 88-mm gun and two machine guns. Arming himself with an M1 rifle, a grenade launcher, and a number of rifle and hand grenades, he left his company in position and advanced alone, under fire, up the slope toward the enemy emplacements. Struck on the head and knocked down by a glancing machine-gun bullet, 1st Lt. Ogden, in spite of his painful wound and enemy fire from close range, continued up the hill. Reaching a vantage point, he silenced the 88-mm gun with a well-placed rifle grenade and then, with hand grenades, knocked out the two machine guns, again being painfully wounded. First Lt. Ogden's heroic leadership and indomitable courage in alone silencing these enemy weapons inspired his men to greater effort and cleared the way for the company to continue the advance and reach its objectives.

2884 ◆ O'HARE, EDWARD HENRY "BUTCH"

Rank: Lieutenant (highest rank: Lieutenant Commander)
Service: U.S. Navy
Birthday: 13 March 1914
Place of Birth: St. Louis, St. Louis County, Missouri
Date of Death: 23 November 1943
Place of Death: South Pacific Area
Cemetery: National Memorial Cemetery of the Pacific (Wall of the Missing)—Honolulu, Hawaii
Entered Service at: St. Louis, St. Louis County, Missouri
Unit: Fighting Squadron 3, U.S.S. *Lexington*
Served as: Section Leader & Pilot
Battle or Place of Action: South Pacific
Date of Action: 20 February 1942
Date of Presentation: 21 April 1942
Place of Presentation: The White House, presented by Pres. Franklin D. Roosevelt
Citation: For conspicuous gallantry and intrepidity in aerial combat, at grave risk of his life above and beyond the call of

duty, as section leader and pilot of Fighting Squadron 3 on 20 February 1942. Having lost the assistance of his teammates, Lt. O'Hare interposed his plane between his ship and an advancing enemy formation of nine attacking twin-engined heavy bombers. Without hesitation, alone and unaided, he repeatedly attacked this enemy formation, at close range in the face of intense combined machine-gun and cannon fire. Despite his concentrated opposition, Lt. O'Hare, by his gallant and courageous action, his extremely skillful marksmanship in making the most of every shot of his limited amount of ammunition, shot down five enemy bombers and severely damaged a sixth before they reached the bomb release point. As a result of his gallant action—one of the most daring, if not the most daring, single action in the history of combat aviation—he undoubtedly saved his carrier from serious damage.

2885 ◆ O'KANE, RICHARD HETHERINGTON

Rank: Commander (highest rank: Rear Admiral)
Service: U.S. Navy
Birthday: 2 February 1911
Place of Birth: Dover, Strafford County, New Hampshire
Date of Death: 16 February 1994
Place of Death: Petaluma, California
Cemetery: Arlington National Cemetery—Arlington, Virginia
Entered Service at: Durham, Strafford County, New Hampshire
Unit: U.S.S. *Tang* SS-306
Served as: Commanding Officer
Battle or Place of Action: Vicinity of Formosa Straits, Philippine Islands
Date of Action: 23-24 October 1944
Date of Presentation: 27 March 1946
Place of Presentation: The White House, presented by Pres. Harry S. Truman
Citation: For conspicuous gallantry and intrepidity at the risk of his life above and beyond the call of duty as commanding officer of the U.S.S. *Tang* operating against two enemy Japanese convoys on 23 and 24 October 1944, during her fifth and last war patrol. Boldly maneuvering on the surface into the midst of a heavily escorted convoy, Comdr. O'Kane stood in the fusillade of bullets and shells from all directions to launch smashing hits on three tankers, coolly swung his ship to fire at a freighter and, in a split-second decision, shot out of the path of an onrushing transport, missing it by inches. Boxed in by blazing tankers, a freighter, transport, and several destroyers, he blasted two of the targets with his remaining torpedoes and, with pyrotechnics bursting on all sides, cleared the area. Twenty-four hours later, he again made contact with a heavily escorted convoy steaming to support the Leyte campaign with reinforcements and supplies and with crated planes piled high on each unit. In defiance of the enemy's relentless fire, he closed the concentration of ships and in quick succession sent two torpedoes each into the first and second transports and an adjacent tanker, finding his mark with each torpedo in a series of violent explosions at less than 1,000-yard range. With ships bearing down from all

sides, he charged the enemy at high speed, exploding the tanker in a burst of flame, smashing the transport dead in the water, and blasting the destroyer with a mighty roar which rocked the *Tang* from stem to stern. Expending his last two torpedoes into the remnants of a once powerful convoy before his own ship went down, Comdr. O'Kane, aided by his gallant command, achieved an illustrious record of heroism in combat, enhancing the finest traditions of the U.S. Naval Service.

2886 ◆ *OLSON, ARLO L.

Rank: Captain
Service: U.S. Army
Birthday: 20 April 1918
Place of Birth: Greenville, Clay County, Iowa
Date of Death: 13 October 1943
Cemetery: Toronto Cemetery—Toronto, South Dakota
Entered Service at: Toronto, Deuel County, South Dakota
Unit: 15th Infantry, 3d Infantry Division
Battle or Place of Action: crossing of the Volturno River, Italy
Date of Action: 13 October 1943
G.O. Number, Date: 71, 31 August 1944
Citation: For conspicuous gallantry and intrepidity at the risk of his life above and beyond the call of duty. On 13 October 1943, when the drive across the Volturno River began, Capt. Olson and his company spearheaded the advance of the regiment through 30 miles of mountainous enemy territory in 13 days. Placing himself at the head of his men, Capt. Olson waded into the chest-deep water of the raging Volturno River and despite point-blank machine-gun fire aimed directly at him made his way to the opposite bank and threw two hand grenades into the gun position, killing the crew. When an enemy machine gun 150 yards distant opened fire on his company, Capt. Olson advanced upon the position in a slow, deliberate walk. Although five German soldiers threw hand grenades at him from a range of five yards, Capt. Olson dispatched them all, picked up a machine pistol, and continued toward the enemy. Advancing to within 15 yards of the position he shot it out with the foe, killing nine and seizing the post. Throughout the next 13 days Capt. Olson led combat patrols, acted as company No. 1 scout, and maintained unbroken contact with the enemy. On 27 October 1943, Capt. Olson conducted a platoon in attack on a strongpoint, crawling to within 25 yards of the enemy and then charging the position. Despite continuous machine-gun fire which barely missed him, Capt. Olson made his way to the gun and killed the crew with his pistol. When the men saw their leader make this desperate attack they followed him and overran the position. Continuing the advance, Capt. Olson led his company to the next objective at the summit of Monte San Nicola. Although the company to his right was forced to take cover from the furious automatic and small-arms fire, which was directed upon him and his men with equal intensity, Capt. Olson waved his company into a skirmish line and despite the fire of a machine gun which singled him out as its sole target led the assault which drove the enemy away. While making a reconnaissance for defensive

positions, Capt. Olson was fatally wounded. Ignoring his severe pain, this intrepid officer completed his reconnaissance, supervised the location of his men in the best defense positions, refused medical aid until all of his men had been cared for, and died as he was being carried down the mountain.

2887 ◆ *OLSON, TRUMAN O.

Rank: Sergeant
Service: U.S. Army
Birthday: 13 October 1917
Place of Birth: Christiana, Wisconsin
Date of Death: 31 January 1944
Cemetery: West Koshkonong Lutheran Cemetery (MH)—Stoughton, Wisconsin
Entered Service at: Cambridge, Dane County, Wisconsin
Unit: Company B, 7th Infantry, 3d Infantry Division
Served as: Light Machine Gunner
Battle or Place of Action: near Cisterna di Littoria, Italy
Date of Action: 30-31 January 1944
G.O. Number, Date: 6, 24 January 1945
Citation: For conspicuous gallantry and intrepidity above and beyond the call of duty. Sgt. Olson, a light machinegunner, elected to sacrifice his life to save his company from annihilation. On the night of 30 January 1944, after a 16-hour assault on entrenched enemy positions in the course of which over one-third of Company B became casualties, the survivors dug in behind a horseshoe elevation, placing Sgt. Olson and his crew, with the one available machine gun, forward of their lines and in an exposed position to bear the brunt of the expected German counterattack. Although he had been fighting without respite, Sgt. Olson stuck grimly to his post all night while his guncrew was cut down, one by one, by accurate and overwhelming enemy fire. Weary from over 24 hours of continuous battle and suffering from an arm wound, received during the night engagement, Sgt. Olson manned his gun alone, meeting the full force of an all-out enemy assault by approximately 200 men supported by mortar and machine-gun fire which the Germans launched at daybreak on the morning of 31 January. After 30 minutes of fighting, Sgt. Olson was mortally wounded, yet, knowing that only his weapons stood between his company and complete destruction, he refused evacuation. For an hour and a half after receiving his second and fatal wound he continued to fire his machine gun, killing at least 20 of the enemy, wounding many more, and forcing the assaulting German elements to withdraw.

2888 ◆ ORESKO, NICHOLAS

Rank: Master Sergeant
Service: U.S. Army
Birthday: 18 January 1917
Place of Birth: Bayonne, Hudson County, New Jersey
Entered Service at: Bayonne, Hudson County, New Jersey
Unit: 1st Platoon, Company C, 1st Battalion, 302d Infantry, 94th Infantry Division
Served as: Platoon Leader
Battle or Place of Action: near Tettington, Germany

Date of Action: 23 January 1945
G.O. Number, Date: 95, 30 October 1945
Date of Presentation: 12 October 1945
Place of Presentation: The White House, presented by Pres. Harry S. Truman
Citation: M/Sgt. Oresko was a platoon leader with Company C, in an attack against strong enemy positions. Deadly automatic fire from the flanks pinned down his unit. Realizing that a machine gun in a nearby bunker must be eliminated, he swiftly worked ahead alone, braving bullets which struck about him, until close enough to throw a grenade into the German position. He rushed the bunker and, with point-blank rifle fire, killed all the hostile occupants who survived the grenade blast. Another machine gun opened up on him, knocking him down and seriously wounding him in the hip. Refusing to withdraw from the battle, he placed himself at the head of his platoon to continue the assault. As withering machine-gun and rifle fire swept the area, he struck out alone in advance of his men to a second bunker. With a grenade, he crippled the dug-in machine gun defending this position and then wiped out the troops manning it with his rifle, completing his second self-imposed, one-man attack. Although weak from loss of blood, he refused to be evacuated until assured the mission was successfully accomplished. Through quick thinking, indomitable courage, and unswerving devotion to the attack in the face of bitter resistance and while wounded, M/Sgt. Oresko killed 12 Germans, prevented a delay in the assault, and made it possible for Company C to obtain its objective with minimum casualties.

2889 ◆ *OWENS, ROBERT ALLEN

Rank: Sergeant
Service: U.S. Marine Corps
Birthday: 13 September 1920
Place of Birth: Greenville, Greenville County, South Carolina
Date of Death: 1 November 1943
Cemetery: A.B.M.C. Manila Cemetery (N-12-200)—Manila, Philippine Islands
Entered Service at: South Carolina
Battle or Place of Action: Cape Torokina, Bougainville, Solomon Islands
Date of Action: 1 November 1943
Citation: For conspicuous gallantry and intrepidity at the risk of his life above and beyond the call of duty while serving with a marine division, in action against enemy Japanese forces during extremely hazardous landing operations at Cape Torokina, Bougainville Island, Solomon Islands, on 1 November 1943. Forced to pass within disastrous range of a strongly protected, well-camouflaged Japanese 75-mm regimental gun strategically located on the beach, our landing units were suffering heavy losses in casualties and boats while attempting to approach the beach, and the success of the operations was seriously threatened. Observing the ineffectiveness of marine rifle and grenade attacks against the incessant, devastating fire of the enemy weapon and aware of the urgent need for prompt action, Sgt. Owens unhesitatingly determined to charge the gun bunker from the front and,

calling on four of his comrades to assist him, carefully placed them to cover the fire of the two adjacent hostile bunkers. Choosing a moment that provided a fair opportunity for passing these bunkers, he immediately charged into the mouth of the steadily firing cannon and entered the emplacement through the fire port, driving the guncrew out of the rear door and insuring their destruction before he himself was wounded. Indomitable and aggressive in the face of almost certain death, Sgt. Owens silenced a powerful gun which was of inestimable value to the Japanese defense and, by his brilliant initiative and heroic spirit of self-sacrifice, contributed immeasurably to the success of the vital landing operations. His valiant conduct throughout reflects the highest credit upon himself and the U.S. Naval Service.

2890 ◆ *OZBOURN, JOSEPH WILLIAM

Rank: Private
Service: U.S. Marine Corps
Birthday: 24 October 1919
Place of Birth: Herrin, Williamson County, Illinois
Date of Death: 28 July 1944
Cemetery: National Memorial Cemetery of the Pacific (F-77) (MH)—Honolulu, Hawaii
Entered Service at: Illinois
Unit: 1st Battalion, 23d Marines, 4th Marine Division
Served as: Browning Automatic Rifleman
Battle or Place of Action: Tinian Island, Marianas Islands
Date of Action: 28 July 1944
Citation: For conspicuous gallantry and intrepidity at the risk of his life above and beyond the call of duty as a Browning automatic rifleman serving with the 1st Battalion, 23d Marines, 4th Marine Division, during the battle for enemy Japanese-held Tinian Island, Marianas Islands, 30 July 1944. As a member of a platoon assigned the mission of clearing the remaining Japanese troops from dugouts and pillboxes along a treeline, Pvt. Ozbourn, flanked by two men on either side, was moving forward to throw an armed hand grenade into a dugout when a terrific blast from the entrance severely wounded the four men and himself. Unable to throw the grenade into the dugout and with no place to hurl it without endangering the other men, Pvt. Ozbourn unhesitatingly grasped it close to his body and fell upon it, sacrificing his own life to absorb the full impact of the explosion, but saving his comrades. His great personal valor and unwavering loyalty reflect the highest credit upon Pvt. Ozbourn and the U.S. Naval Service. He gallantly gave his life for his country.

2891 ◆ PAIGE, MITCHELL

Rank: Platoon Sergeant (highest rank: Colonel)
Service: U.S. Marine Corps
Birthday: 31 August 1918
Place of Birth: Charleroi, Washington County, Pennsylvania
Entered Service at: Pennsylvania
Unit: Company H, 2d Battalion, 7th Marine Regiment, 1st Marine Division
Served as: Platoon Sergeant
Battle or Place of Action: Guadalcanal, Solomon Islands

Date of Action: 26 October 1942
Date of Presentation: 21 May 1943
Place of Presentation: Balcombe, Australia, presented by Major Gen. Alexander A. Vandegrift, Commanding Gen. 1st Marine Division
Citation: For extraordinary heroism and conspicuous gallantry in action above and beyond the call of duty while serving with a company of marines in combat against enemy Japanese forces in the Solomon Islands on 26 October 1942. When the enemy broke through the line directly in front of his position, P/Sgt. Paige, commanding a machine-gun section with fearless determination, continued to direct the fire of his gunners until all his men were either killed or wounded. Alone, against the deadly hail of Japanese shells, he fought with his gun and when it was destroyed, took over another, moving from gun to gun, never ceasing his withering fire against the advancing hordes until reinforcements finally arrived. Then, forming a new line, he dauntlessly and aggressively led a bayonet charge, driving the enemy back and preventing a breakthrough in our lines. His great personal valor and unyielding devotion to duty were in keeping with the highest traditions of the U.S. Naval Service.

2892 ◆ *PARLE, JOHN JOSEPH

Rank: Ensign
Service: U.S. Naval Reserve
Birthday: 26 May 1920
Place of Birth: Omaha, Douglas County, Nebraska
Date of Death: 17 July 1943
Cemetery: Holy Sepulchre Cemetery—Omaha, Nebraska
Entered Service at: Nebraska
Unit: U.S.S. *LST 375*
Battle or Place of Action: Sicily
Date of Action: 9-10 July 1943
Citation: For valor and courage above and beyond the call of duty as officer-in-charge of small boats in the U.S.S. LST 375 during the amphibious assault on the island of Sicily, 9–10 July 1943. Realizing that a detonation of explosives would prematurely disclose to the enemy the assault about to be carried out, and with full knowledge of the peril involved, Ens. Parle unhesitatingly risked his life to extinguish a smoke pot accidentally ignited in a boat carrying charges of high explosives, detonating fuses and ammunition. Undaunted by fire and blinding smoke, he entered the craft, quickly snuffed out a burning fuse, and after failing in his desperate efforts to extinguish the fire pot, finally seized it with both hands and threw it over the side. Although he succumbed a week later from smoke and fumes inhaled, Ens. Parle's heroic self-sacrifice prevented grave damage to the ship and personnel and insured the security of a vital mission. He gallantly gave his life in the service of his country.

2893 ◆ *PARRISH, LAVERNE

Rank: Technician Fourth Grade
Service: U.S. Army
Birthday: 16 July 1918
Place of Birth: Knox City, Montana

Date of Death: 24 January 1945
Cemetery: Mountain View Cemetery—Ronon, Montana
Entered Service at: Ronan, Lake County, Montana
Unit: Medical Detachment, 161st Infantry, 25th Infantry Division
Served as: Medical Aidman
Battle or Place of Action: Binalonan, Luzon, Philippine Islands
Date of Action: 18-24 January 1945
G.O. Number, Date: 55, 13 July 1945
Citation: He was medical aidman with Company C during the fighting in Binalonan, Luzon, Philippine Islands. On the 18th, he observed two wounded men under enemy fire and immediately went to their rescue. After moving one to cover, he crossed 25 yards of open ground to administer aid to the second. In the early hours of the 24th, his company, crossing an open field near San Manuel, encountered intense enemy fire and was ordered to withdraw to the cover of a ditch. While treating casualties, Technician Parrish observed two wounded still in the field. Without hesitation he left the ditch, crawled forward under enemy fire, and in two successive trips brought both men to safety. He next administered aid to 12 casualties in the same field, crossing and recrossing the open area raked by hostile fire. Making successive trips, he then brought three wounded to cover. After treating nearly all of the 37 casualties suffered by his company, he was mortally wounded by mortar fire, and shortly after was killed. The indomitable spirit, intrepidity, and gallantry of Technician Parrish saved many lives at the cost of his own.

2894 ◆ *PEASE JR., HARL

Rank: Captain
Service: U.S. Army Air Corps
Birthday: 10 April 1917
Place of Birth: Plymouth, Grafton County, New Hampshire
Date of Death: 8 October 1942
Place of Death: New Guinea
Cemetery: A.B.M.C. Manila Cemetery (Wall of the Missing)—Manila, Philippine Islands
Entered Service at: Boston, Suffolk County, Massachusetts
Unit: Heavy Bombardment Squadron, 19th Bombardment Group, 509th Bombardment Wing, 5th Air Force
Served as: Pilot of a B-17
Battle or Place of Action: near Rabaul, New Britain, Bismarck Archipelago
Date of Action: 6-7 August 1942
G.O. Number, Date: 59, 4 November 1942
Date of Presentation: 2 December 1942
Place of Presentation: The White House, presented by Pres. Franklin D. Roosevelt to his parents Mr. & Mrs. Harl Pease Sr
Citation: For conspicuous gallantry and intrepidity above and beyond the call of duty in action with the enemy on 6–7 August 1942. When one engine of the bombardment airplane of which he was a pilot failed during a bombing mission over New Guinea, Capt. Pease was forced to return to base in Australia. Knowing that all available airplanes of his group were to participate the next day in an attack on an enemy-held airdrome near Rabaul, New Britain, although he was not

scheduled to take part in this mission, Capt. Pease selected the most serviceable airplane at this base and prepared it for combat, knowing that it had been found and declared unserviceable for combat missions. With the members of his combat crew, who volunteered to accompany him, he rejoined his squadron at Port Moresby, New Guinea, at 1 A.M. on 7 August, after having flown almost continuously since early in the preceding morning. With only three hours' rest, he took off with his squadron for the attack. Throughout the long flight to Rabaul, New Britain, he managed by skillful flying of his unserviceable airplane to maintain his position in the group. When the formation was intercepted by about 30 enemy fighter airplanes before reaching the target, Capt. Pease, on the wing which bore the brunt of the hostile attack, by gallant action and the accurate shooting by his crew, succeeded in destroying several Zeros before dropping his bombs on the hostile base as planned, this in spite of continuous enemy attacks. The fight with the enemy pursuit lasted 25 minutes until the group dived into cloud cover. After leaving the target, Capt. Pease's aircraft fell behind the balance of the group due to unknown difficulties as a result of the combat and was unable to reach this cover before the enemy pursuit succeeded in igniting one of his bomb bay tanks. He was seen to drop the flaming tank. It is believed that Capt. Pease's airplane and crew were subsequently shot down in flames, as they did not return to th eir base. In voluntarily performing this mission Capt. Pease contributed materially to the success of the group and displayed high devotion to duty, valor, and complete contempt for personal danger. His undaunted bravery has been a great inspiration to the officers and men of his unit.

2895 ◆ *PEDEN, FORREST E.

Rank: Technician Fifth Grade
Service: U.S. Army
Birthday: 3 October 1913
Place of Birth: St. Joseph, Buchanan County, Missouri
Date of Death: 3 February 1945
Cemetery: Mount Olive Cemetery—Troy, Kansas
Entered Service at: Wathena, Doniphan County, Kansas
Unit: Battery C, 10th Field Artillery Battalion, 3d Infantry Division
Served as: Forward Artillery Observer
Battle or Place of Action: near Biesheim, France
Date of Action: 3 February 1945
G.O. Number, Date: 18, 13 February 1946
Citation: He was a forward artillery observer when the group of about 45 infantrymen with whom he was advancing was ambushed in the uncertain light of a waning moon. Enemy forces outnumbering the Americans by four to one poured withering artillery, mortar, machine-gun, and small-arms fire into the stricken unit from the flanks, forcing our men to seek the cover of a ditch which they found already occupied by enemy foot troops. As the opposing infantrymen struggled in hand-to-hand combat, Technician Peden courageously went to the assistance of two wounded soldiers and rendered first aid under heavy fire. With radio cummunications inoperative, he realized that the unit would be wiped

out unless help could be secured from the rear. On his own initiative, he ran 800 yards to the battalion command post through a hail of bullets which pierced his jacket, and there secured two light tanks to go to the relief of his hard-pressed comrades. Knowing the terrible risk involved, he climbed upon the hull of the lead tank and guided it into battle. Through a murderous concentration of fire the tank lumbered onward, bullets and shell fragments ricocheting from its steel armor within inches of the completely exposed rider, until it reached the ditch. As it was about to go into action it was turned into a flaming pyre by a direct hit which killed Technican Peden. However, his intrepidity and gallant sacrifice was not in vain. Attracted by the light from the burning tank, reinforcements found the beleaguered Americans and drove off the enemy.

2896 ◆ *PENDLETON, JACK JAMES

Rank: Staff Sergeant
Service: U.S. Army
Birthday: 31 March 1918
Place of Birth: Sentinel Butte, Golden Valley County, North Dakota
Date of Death: 12 October 1944
Cemetery: Tahoma Cemetery—Yakima, Washington
Entered Service at: Yakima, Yakima County, Washington
Unit: Company I, 120th Infantry, 30th Infantry Division
Served as: Squad Leader
Battle or Place of Action: Bardenberg, Germany
Date of Action: 12 October 1944
G.O. Number, Date: 24, 6 April 1945
Citation: For conspicuous gallantry and intrepidity at the risk of his life above and beyond the call of duty on 12 October 1944. When Company I was advancing on the town of Bardenberg, Germany, they reached a point approximately two-thirds of the distance through the town when they were pinned down by fire from a nest of enemy machine guns. This enemy strongpoint was protected by a lone machine gun strategically placed at an intersection and firing down a street which offered little or no cover or concealment for the advancing troops. The elimination of this protecting machine gun was imperative in order that the stronger position it protected could be neutralized. After repeated and unsuccessful attempts had been made to knock out this position, S/Sgt. Pendleton volunteered to lead his squad in an attempt to neutralize this strongpoint. S/Sgt. Pendleton started his squad slowly forward, crawling about 10 yards in front of his men in the advance toward the enemy gun. After advancing approximately 130 yards under the withering fire, S/Sgt. Pendleton was seriously wounded in the leg by a burst from the gun he was assaulting. Disregarding his grievous wound, he ordered his men to remain where they were, and with a supply of hand grenades he slowly and painfully worked his way forward alone. With no hope of surviving the veritable hail of machine-gun fire which he deliberately drew onto himself, he succeeded in advancing within 10 yards of the enemy position when he was instantly killed by a burst from the enemy gun. By deliberately diverting the attention of the enemy machine-gunners upon himself, a second squad was

able to advance, undetected, and with the help of S/Sgt. Pendleton's squad, neutralized the lone machine gun, while another platoon of his company advanced up the intersecting street and knocked out the machine-gun nest which the first gun had been covering. S/Sgt. Pendleton's sacrifice enabled the entire company to continue the advance and complete their missi on at a critical phase of the action.

2897 ◆ *PEREGORY, FRANK D.

Rank: Technical Sergeant
Service: U.S. Army
Birthday: 10 April 1915
Place of Birth: Esmont, Albemarle County, Virginia
Date of Death: 14 June 1944
Cemetery: A.B.M.C. Normandy Cemetery (G-21-7)—St. Laurent-Sur-Mer, France
Entered Service at: Charlottesville, Charlottesville County, Virginia
Unit: Company K, 3d Battalion, 116th Infantry, 29th Infantry Division
Battle or Place of Action: Grandcampe, France
Date of Action: 8 June 1944
G.O. Number, Date: 43, 30 May 1945
Citation: On 8 June 1944, the 3d Battalion of the 116th Infantry was advancing on the strongly held German defenses at Grandcampe, France, when the leading elements were suddenly halted by decimating machine-gun fire from a firmly entrenched enemy force on the high ground overlooking the town. After numerous attempts to neutralize the enemy position by supporting artillery and tank fire had proved ineffective, T/Sgt. Peregory, on his own initiative, advanced up the hill under withering fire and worked his way to the crest, where he discovered an entrenchment leading to the main fortifications 200 yards away. Without hesitating, he leaped into the trench and moved toward the emplacement. Encountering a squad of enemy riflemen, he fearlessly attacked them with hand grenades and bayonet, killed eight, and forced three to surrender. Continuing along the trench, he singlehandedly forced the surrender of 32 more riflemen, captured the machine gunners, and opened the way for the leading elements of the battalion to advance and secure its objective. The extraordinary gallantry and aggressiveness displayed by T/Sgt. Peregory are exemplary of the highest traditions of the Armed Forces.

2898 ◆ *PEREZ JR., MANUEL

Rank: Private First Class
Service: U.S. Army
Birthday: 3 March 1923
Place of Birth: Oklahoma City, Oklahoma County, Oklahoma
Date of Death: 14 March 1945
Cemetery: Fairlawn Cemetery (MH)—Oklahoma City, Oklahoma
Entered Service at: Chicago, Cook County, Illinois
Unit: Company A, 511th Parachute Infantry, 11th Airborne Division
Served as: Scout

Battle or Place of Action: Fort William McKinley, Luzon, Philippine Islands
Date of Action: 13 February 1945
G.O. Number, Date: 124, 27 December 1945
Citation: He was lead scout for Company A, which had destroyed 11 of 12 pillboxes in a strongly fortified sector defending the approach to enemy-held Fort William McKinley on Luzon, Philippine Islands. In the reduction of these pillboxes, he killed five Japanese in the open and blasted others in pillboxes with grenades. Realizing the urgent need for taking the last emplacement, which contained two twin-mount .50-caliber dual-purpose machine guns, he took a circuitous route to within 20 yards of the position, killing four of the enemy in his advance. He threw a grenade into the pillbox, and, as the crew started withdrawing through a tunnel just to the rear of the emplacement, shot and killed four before exhausting his clip. He had reloaded and killed four more when an escaping Jap threw his rifle with fixed bayonet at him. In warding off this thrust, his own rifle was knocked to the ground. Seizing the Jap rifle, he continued firing, killing two more of the enemy. He rushed the remaining Japanese, killed three of them with the butt of the rifle, and entered the pillbox, where he bayoneted the one surviving hostile soldier. Singlehandedly, he killed 18 of the enemy in neutralizing the position that had held up the advance of his entire company. Through his courageous determination and heroic disregard of grave danger, Pfc. Perez made possible the successful advance of his unit toward a valuable objective and provided a lasting inspiration for his comrades.

2899 ◆ *PETERS, GEORGE J.

Rank: Private
Service: U.S. Army
Place of Birth: Cranston, Providence County, Rhode Island
Date of Death: 24 March 1945
Cemetery: A.B.M.C. Netherlands Cemetery (6-17-8)—Margraten, Holland
Entered Service at: Cranston, Providence County, Rhode Island
Unit: Company G, 507th Parachute Infantry, 17th Airborne Division
Served as: Platoon Radio Operator
Battle or Place of Action: near Fluren, Germany
Date of Action: 24 March 1945
G.O. Number, Date: 16, 8 February 1946
Citation: Pvt. Peters, a platoon radio operator with Company G, made a descent into Germany near Fluren, east of the Rhine. With 10 others, he landed in a field about 75 yards from a German machine gun supported by riflemen and was immediately pinned down by heavy, direct fire. The position of the small unit seemed hopeless, with the men struggling to free themselves of their parachutes in a hail of bullets that cut them off from their nearby equipment bundles, when Pvt. Peters stood up without orders and began a one-man charge against the hostile emplacement armed only with a rifle and grenades. His singlehanded assault immediately drew the enemy fire away from his comrades. He had run halfway to his objective, pitting rifle fire against that of the machine gun, when he was struck and knocked to the ground by a

burst. Heroically, he regained his feet and struggled onward. Once more he was torn by bullets, and this time he was unable to rise. With gallant devotion to his self-imposed mission, he crawled directly into the fire that had mortally wounded him until close enough to hurl grenades which knocked out the machine gun, killed two of its operators, and drove protecting riflemen from their positions into the safety of a woods. By his intrepidity and supreme sacrifice, Pvt. Peters saved the lives of many of his fellow soldiers and made it possible for them to reach their equipment, organize, and seize their first objective.

2900 ◆ *PETERSON, GEORGE

Rank: Staff Sergeant
Service: U.S. Army
Place of Birth: Brooklyn, Kings County, New York
Date of Death: 30 March 1945
Cemetery: A.B.M.C. Netherlands Cemetery (D-21-10)—Margraten, Holland
Entered Service at: Brooklyn, Kings County, New York
Unit: Company K, 18th Infantry, 1st Infantry Division
Served as: Acting Platoon Sergeant
Battle or Place of Action: near Eisern, Germany
Date of Action: 30 March 1945
G.O. Number, Date: 88, 17 October 1945
Citation: He was an acting platoon sergeant with Company K, near Eisern, Germany. When his company encountered an enemy battalion and came under heavy small-arms, machine-gun, and mortar fire, the 2d Platoon was given the mission of flanking the enemy positions while the remaining units attacked frontally. S/Sgt. Peterson crept and crawled to a position in the lead and motioned for the 2d Platoon to follow. A mortar shell fell close by and severely wounded him in the legs, but, although bleeding and suffering intense pain, he refused to withdraw and continued forward. Two hostile machine guns went into action at close range. Braving this grazing fire, he crawled steadily toward the guns and worked his way alone to a shallow draw, where, despite the hail of bullets, he raised himself to his knees and threw a grenade into the nearest machine-gun nest, silencing the weapon and killing or wounding all its crew. The second gun was immediately turned on him, but he calmly and deliberately threw a second grenade which rocked the position and killed all four Germans who occupied it. As he continued forward he was spotted by an enemy rifleman, who shot him in the arm. Undeterred, he crawled some 20 yards until a third machine gun opened fire on him. By almost superhuman effort, weak from loss of blood and suffering great pain, he again raised himself to his knees and fired a grenade from his rifle, killing three of the enemy guncrew and causing the remaining one to flee. With the first objective seized, he was being treated by the company aidman when he observed one of his outpost men seriously wounded by a mortar burst. He wrenched himself from the hands of the aidman and began to crawl forward to assist his comrade, whom he had almost reached when he was struck and fatally wounded by an enemy bullet. S/Sgt. Peterson, by his gallant, intrepid actions, unrelenting fighting spirit, and outstanding initiative, silenced three enemy machine guns against great odds and while suffering from

severe wounds, enabling his company to advance with minimum casualties.

2901 ◆ *PETERSON, OSCAR VERNER

Rank: Chief Watertender
Service: U.S. Navy
Birthday: 27 August 1899
Place of Birth: Prentice, Price County, Wisconsin
Date of Death: 7 May 1942
Cemetery: A.B.M.C. Manila Cemetery (Wall of the Missing)—Manila, Philippine Islands
Entered Service at: Wisconsin
Unit: U.S.S. *Neosho*
Date of Action: 7 May 1942
Citation: For extraordinary courage and conspicuous heroism above and beyond the call of duty while in charge of a repair party during an attack on the U.S.S. *Neosho* by enemy Japanese aerial forces on 7 May 1942. Lacking assistance because of injuries to the other members of his repair party and severely wounded himself, Peterson, with no concern for his own life, closed the bulkhead stop valves and in so doing received additional burns which resulted in his death. His spirit of self-sacrifice and loyalty, characteristic of a fine seaman, was in keeping with the highest traditions of the U.S. Naval Service. He gallantly gave his life in the service of his country.

2902 ◆ *PETRARCA, FRANK JOSEPH

Rank: Private First Class
Service: U.S. Army
Birthday: 31 July 1918
Place of Birth: Cleveland, Cuyahoga County, Ohio
Date of Death: 31 July 1943
Cemetery: Calvary Cemetery (MH)—Cleveland, Ohio
Entered Service at: Cleveland, Cuyahoga County, Ohio
Unit: Medical Detachment, 145th Infantry, 37th Infantry Division
Served as: Medical Aidman
Battle or Place of Action: Horseshoe Hill, New Georgia, Solomon Islands
Date of Action: 27 July 1943
G.O. Number, Date: 86, 23 December 1943
Citation: For conspicuous gallantry and intrepidity in action above and beyond the call of duty. Pfc. Petrarca advanced with the leading troop element to within 100 yards of the enemy fortifications where mortar and small-arms fire caused a number of casualties. Singling out the most seriously wounded, he worked his way to the aid of Pfc. Scott, lying within 75 yards of the enemy, whose wounds were so serious that he could not even be moved out of the direct line of fire. Pfc. Petrarca fearlessly administered first aid to Pfc. Scott and two other soldiers and shielded the former until his death. On 29 July 1943, Pfc. Petrarca, during an intense mortar barrage, went to the aid of his sergeant who had been partly buried in a foxhole under the debris of a shell explosion, dug him out, restored him to consciousness, and caused his evacuation. On 31 July 1943 and against the warning of a fellow soldier, he went to the aid of a mortar fragment casualty where his path

over the crest of a hill exposed him to enemy observation from only 20 yards distance. A target for intense knee mortar and automatic fire, he resolutely worked his way to within two yards of his objective where he was mortally wounded by hostile mortar fire. Even on the threshold of death he continued to display valor and contempt for the foe; raising himself to his knees, this intrepid soldier shouted defiance at the enemy, made a last attempt to reach his wounded comrade and fell in glorious death.

2903 ◆ PHARRIS, JACKSON CHARLES

Rank: Lieutenant (rank at time of action: Gunner) (highest rank: Lieutenant Commander)
Service: U.S. Navy
Birthday: 26 June 1912
Place of Birth: Columbus, Muscogee County, Georgia
Date of Death: 17 October 1966
Cemetery: Arlington National Cemetery (13-16281) (MH)—Arlington, Virginia
Entered Service at: California
Unit: U.S.S. *California*
Battle or Place of Action: Pearl Harbor, Territory of Hawaii
Date of Action: 7 December 1941
Citation: For conspicuous gallantry and intrepidity at the risk of his life above and beyond the call of duty while attached to the U.S.S. *California* during the surprise enemy Japanese aerial attack on Pearl Harbor, Territory of Hawaii, 7 December 1941. In charge of the ordnance repair party on the third deck when the first Japanese torpedo struck almost directly under his station, Lt. (then Gunner) Pharris was stunned and severely injuried by the concussion which hurled him to the overhead and back to the deck. Quickly recovering, he acted on his own initiative to set up a hand-supply ammunition train for the antiaircraft guns. With water and oil rushing in where the port bulkhead had been torn up from the deck, with many of the remaining crewmembers overcome by oil fumes, and the ship without power and listing heavily to port as a result of a second torpedo hit, Lt. Pharris ordered the shipfitters to counterflood. Twice rendered unconscious by the nauseous fumes and handicapped by his painful injuries, he persisted in his desperate efforts to speed up the supply of ammunition and at the same time repeatedly risked his life to enter the flooding compartments and drag to safety unconscious shipmates who were gradually being submerged in oil. By his inspiring leadership, his valiant efforts, and extreme loyalty to his ship and her crew, he saved many of his shipmates from death and was largely responsible for keeping the *California* in action during the attack. His heroic conduct throughout this first eventful engagement of World War II reflects the highest credit upon Lt. Pharris and enhances the finest traditions of the U.S. Naval Service.

2904 ◆ *PHELPS, WESLEY

Rank: Private
Service: U.S. Marine Corps Reserve
Birthday: 12 June 1923
Place of Birth: Neafus, Grayson County, Kentucky

Date of Death: 4 October 1944
Cemetery: Rosine Cemetery (MH)—Rosine, Kentucky
Entered Service at: Kentucky
Unit: 3d Battalion, 7th Marines, 1st Marine Division
Battle or Place of Action: Peleliu Island, Palau Islands
Date of Action: 4 October 1944
Citation: For conspicuous gallantry and intrepidity at the risk of his life above and beyond the call of duty while serving with the 3d Battalion, 7th Marines, 1st Marine Division, in action against enemy Japanese forces on Peleliu Island, Palau Group, during a savage hostile counterattack on the night of 4 October 1944. Stationed with another marine in an advanced position when a Japanese hand grenade landed in his foxhole, Pfc. Phelps instantly shouted a warning to his comrade and rolled over on the deadly bomb, absorbing with his own body the full, shattering impact of the exploding charge. Courageous and indomitable, Pfc. Phelps fearlessly gave his life that another might be spared serious injury, and his great valor and heroic devotion to duty in the face of certain death reflect the highest credit upon himself and the U.S. Naval Service. He gallantly gave his life for his country.

2905 ◆ *PHILLIPS, GEORGE

Rank: Private
Service: U.S. Marine Corps Reserve
Birthday: 14 July 1926
Place of Birth: Rich Hill, Vernon County, Missouri
Date of Death: 14 March 1945
Cemetery: Bethel Cemetery (MH)—Labadie, Missouri
Entered Service at: Labadie, Franklin County, Missouri
Unit: 2d Battalion, 28th Marines, 5th Marine Division
Battle or Place of Action: Iwo Jima, Volcano Islands
Date of Action: 14 March 1945
Citation: For conspicuous gallantry and intrepidity at the risk of his life above and beyond the call of duty while serving with the 2d Battalion, 28th Marines, 5th Marine Division, in action against enemy Japanese forces during the seizure of Iwo Jima in the Volcano Islands on 14 March 1945. Standing the foxhole watch while other members of his squad rested after a night of bitter hand-grenade fighting against infiltrating Japanese troops, Pvt. Phillips was the only member of his unit alerted when an enemy hand grenade was tossed into their midst. Instantly shouting a warning, he unhesitatingly threw himself on the deadly missile, absorbing the shattering violence of the exploding charge in his own body and protecting his comrades from serious injury. Stouthearted and indomitable, Pvt. Phillips willingly yielded his own life that his fellow marines might carry on the relentless battle against a fanatic enemy. His superb valor and unfaltering spirit of self-sacrifice in the face of certain death reflect the highest credit upon himself and upon the U.S. Naval Service. He gallantly gave his life for his country.

2906 ◆ PIERCE, FRANCIS JUNIOR

Rank: Pharmacist's Mate First Class
Service: U.S. Navy
Birthday: 7 December 1924

Place of Birth: Earlville, Delaware County, Iowa
Date of Death: 21 December 1986
Cemetery: Holy Cross Cemetery—Grand Rapids, Michigan
Entered Service at: Iowa
Unit: 2d Battalion, 24th Marines, 4th Marine Division
Served as: Medical Corpsman
Battle or Place of Action: Iwo Jima, Volcano Islands
Date of Action: 15-16 March 1945
Date of Issue: 1948
Citation: For conspicuous gallantry and intrepidity at the risk of his life above and beyond the call of duty while attached to the 2d Battalion, 24th Marines, 4th Marine Division, during the Iwo Jima campaign, 15 and 16 March 1945. Almost continuously under fire while carrying out the most dangerous volunteer assignments, Pierce gained valuable knowledge of the terrain and disposition of troops. Caught in heavy enemy rifle and machine-gun fire which wounded a corpsman and two of the eight stretcher bearers who were carrying two wounded marines to a forward aid station on 15 March, Pierce quickly took charge of the party, carried the newly wounded men to a sheltered position, and rendered first aid. After directing the evacuation of three of the casualties, he stood in the open to draw the enemy's fire and, with his weapon blasting, enabled the litter bearers to reach cover. Turning his attention to the other two casualties, he was attempting to stop the profuse bleeding of one man when a Japanese fired from a cave less than 20 yards away and wounded his patient again. Risking his own life to save his patient, Pierce deliberately exposed himself to draw the attacker from the cave and destroyed him with the last of his ammunition. Then lifting the wounded man to his back, he advanced unarmed through deadly rifle fire across 200 feet of open terrain. Despite exhaustion and in the face of warnings against such a suicidal mission, he again traversed the same fire-swept path to rescue the remaining marine. On the following morning, he led a combat patrol to the sniper nest and, while aiding a stricken marine, was seriously wounded. Refusing aid for himself, he directed treatment for the casualty, at the same time maintaining protective fire for his comrades. Completely fearless, completely devoted to the care of his patients, Pierce inspired the entire battalion. His valor in the face of extreme peril sustains and enhances the finest traditions of the U.S. Naval Service.

2907 ◆ *PINDER JR., JOHN J.

Rank: Technician Fifth Grade
Service: U.S. Army
Birthday: 7 June 1912
Place of Birth: McKees Rocks, Allegheny County, Pennsylvania
Date of Death: 6 June 1944
Cemetery: Grand View Cemetery—Hanover Township, Pennsylvania
Entered Service at: Burgettstown, Washington County, Pennsylvania
Unit: 16th Infantry, 1st Infantry Division
Battle or Place of Action: near Colleville-sur-Mer, France
Date of Action: 6 June 1944

G.O. Number, Date: 1, 4 January 1945
Citation: For conspicuous gallantry and intrepidity above and beyond the call of duty on 6 June 1944, near Colleville-sur-Mer, France. On D-day, Technician Fifth Grade Pinder landed on the coast 100 yards offshore under devastating enemy machine-gun and artillery fire which caused severe casualties among the boatload. Carrying a vitally important radio, he struggled towards shore in waist-deep water. Only a few yards from his craft he was hit by enemy fire and was gravely wounded. Technician Fifth Grade Pinder never stopped. He made shore and delivered the radio. Refusing to take cover afforded, or to accept medical attention for his wounds, Technician Fifth Grade Pinder, though terribly weakened by loss of blood and in fierce pain, on three occasions went into the fire-swept surf to salvage communication equipment. He recovered many vital parts and equipment, including another workable radio. On the third trip he was again hit, suffering machine-gun bullet wounds in the legs. Still this valiant soldier would not stop for rest or medical attention. Remaining exposed to heavy enemy fire, growing steadily weaker, he aided in establishing the vital radio communications on the beach. While so engaged this dauntless soldier was hit for the third time and killed. The indomitable courage and personal bravery of Technician Fifth Grade Pinder was a magnificent inspiration to the men with whom he served.

2908 ◆ POPE, EVERETT PARKER

Rank: Captain (highest rank: Major)
Service: U.S. Marine Corps
Birthday: 16 July 1919
Place of Birth: Milton, Norfolk County, Massachusetts
Entered Service at: Quincy, Norfolk County, Massachusetts
Unit: Company C, 1st Battalion, 1st Marines, 1st Marine Division
Served as: Commanding Officer
Battle or Place of Action: Peleliu Island, Palau Islands
Date of Action: 19 September 1944
Date of Presentation: 15 June 1945
Place of Presentation: The White House, presented by Pres. Harry S. Truman
Citation: For conspicuous gallantry and intrepidity at the risk of his life above and beyond the call of duty while serving as commanding officer of Company C, 1st Battalion, 1st Marines, 1st Marine Division, during action against enemy Japanese forces on Peleliu Island, Palau Group on 19–20 September 1944. Subjected to point-blank cannon fire which caused heavy casualties and badly disorganized his company while assaulting a steep coral hill, Capt. Pope rallied his men and gallantly led them to the summit in the face of machine-gun, mortar, and sniper fire. Forced by widespread hostile attack to deploy the remnants of his company thinly in order to hold the ground won, and with his machine guns out of order and insufficient water and ammunition, he remained on the exposed hill with 12 men and one wounded officer, determined to hold through the night. Attacked continuously with grenades, machine guns, and rifles from three sides, he and his valiant men fiercely beat back or destroyed the enemy,

resorting to hand-to-hand combat as the supply of ammunition dwindled, and still maintaining his lines with his eight remaining riflemen when daylight brought more deadly fire and he was ordered to withdraw. His valiant leadership against devastating odds while protecting the units below from heavy Japanese attack reflects the highest credit upon Capt. Pope and the U.S. Naval Service.

2909 ◆ *POWER, JOHN VINCENT

Rank: First Lieutenant
Service: U.S. Marine Corps
Birthday: 20 November 1918
Place of Birth: Worcester, Worcester County, Massachusetts
Date of Death: 1 February 1944
Cemetery: St. John's Cemetery—Worcester, Massachusetts
Entered Service at: Massachusetts
Unit: 4th Marine Division
Served as: Platoon Leader
Battle or Place of Action: Namur Island, Kwajalein Atoll, Marshall Islands
Date of Action: 1 February 1944
Citation: For conspicuous gallantry and intrepidity at the risk of his life above and beyond the call of duty as platoon leader, attached to the 4th Marine Division, during the landing and battle of Namur Island, Kwajalein Atoll, Marshall Islands, 1 February 1944. Severely wounded in the stomach while setting a demolition charge on a Japanese pillbox, 1st Lt. Power was steadfast in his determination to remain in action. Protecting his wound with his left hand and firing with his right, he courageously advanced as another hostile position was taken under attack, fiercely charging the opening made by the explosion and emptying his carbine into the pillbox. While attempting to reload and continue the attack, 1st Lt. Power was shot again in the stomach and head and collapsed in the doorway. His exceptional valor, fortitude and indomitable fighting spirit in the face of withering enemy fire were in keeping with the highest traditions of the U.S. Naval Service. He gallantly gave his life for his country.

2910 ◆ *POWERS, JOHN JAMES

Rank: Lieutenant
Service: U.S. Navy
Birthday: 13 July 1912
Place of Birth: New York, New York
Date of Death: 8 May 1942
Cemetery: A.B.M.C. Manila Cemetery (Wall of the Missing)—Manila, Philippine Islands
Entered Service at: New York
Unit: Bombing Squadron 5, U.S.S. *Yorktown*
Served as: Pilot
Battle or Place of Action: Coral Sea
Date of Action: 4-8 April 1942
Date of Presentation: 7 September 1942
Place of Presentation: Washington, D.C., presented by Adm. Royal E. Ingersoll to his Mother
Citation: For distinguished and conspicuous gallantry and intrepidity at the risk of his life above and beyond the call of duty, while pilot of a airplane of Bombing Squadron 5, Lt. Powers participated, with his squadron, in five engagements with Japanese forces in the Coral Sea area and adjacent waters during the period from 4 to 8 May 1942. Three attacks were made on enemy objectives at or near Tulagi on 4 May. In these attacks he scored a direct hit which instantly demolished a large enemy gunboat or destroyer and is credited with two close misses, one of which severely damaged a large aircraft tender, the other damaging a 20,000-ton transport. He fearlessly strafed a gunboat, firing all his ammunition into it amid intense antiaircraft fire. This gunboat was then observed to be leaving a heavy oil slick in its wake and later was seen beached on a nearby island. On 7 May, an attack was launched against an enemy airplane carrier and other units of the enemy's invasion force. He fearlessly led his attack section of three Douglas Dauntless dive bombers, to attack the carrier. On this occasion he dived in the face of heavy antiaircraft fire, to an altitude well below the safety altitude, at the risk of his life and almost certain damage to his own plane, in order that he might positively obtain a hit in a vital part of the ship, which would insure her complete destruction. This bomb hit was noted by many pilots and observers to cause a tremendous explosion engulfing the ship in a mass of flame, smoke, and debris. The ship sank soon after. That evening, in his capacity as squadron gunnery officer, Lt. Powers gave a lecture to the squadron on point-of-aim and diving technique. During this discourse he advocated low release point in order to insure greater accuracy; yet he stressed the danger not only from enemy fire and the resultant low pull-out, but from own bomb blast and bomb fragments. Thus his low dive bombing attacks were deliberate and premeditated, since he well knew and realized the dangers of such tactics, but went far beyond the call of duty in order to further the cause which he knew to be right. The next morning, 8 May, as the pilots of the attack group left the ready room to man planes, his indomitable spirit and leadership were well-expressed in his own words, "Remember the folks back home are counting on us. I am going to get a hit if I have to lay it on their flight deck." He led his section of dive bombers down to the target from an altitude of 18,000 feet, through a wall of bursting antiaircraft shells and into the face of enemy fighter planes. Again, completely disregarding the safety altitude and without fear or concern for his safety, Lt. Powers courageously pressed home his attack, almost to the very deck of an enemy carrier and did not release his bomb until he was sure of a direct hit. He was last seen attempting recovery from his dive at the extremely low altitude of 200 feet, and amid a terrific barrage of shell and bomb fragments, smoke, flame, and debris from the stricken vessel.

2911 ◆ POWERS, LEO J.

Rank: Private First Class (highest rank: Sergeant)
Service: U.S. Army
Birthday: 5 April 1909
Place of Birth: Anselmo, Custer County, Nebraska
Date of Death: 16 July 1967
Cemetery: Holy Cross Cemetery (MH)—Butte, Montana
Entered Service at: Alder Gulch, Madison County, Montana

Unit: Company L, 133d Infantry, 34th Infantry Division
Served as: Rifleman
Battle or Place of Action: Hill 175, northwest of Casino, Italy
Date of Action: 3 February 1944
G.O. Number, Date: 5, 15 January 1945
Date of Presentation: 10 January 1945
Place of Presentation: Washington, D.C., presented by Pres. Franklin D. Roosevelt
Citation: For conspicuous gallantry and intrepidity at the risk of his life above and beyond the call of duty. On 3 February 1944, this soldier's company was assigned the mission of capturing Hill 175, the key enemy strongpoint northwest of Cassino, Italy. The enemy, estimated to be at least 50 in strength, supported by machine guns emplaced in three pillboxes and mortar fire from behind the hill, was able to pin the attackers down and inflict eight casualties. The company was unable to advance, but Pfc. Powers, a rifleman in one of the assault platoons, on his own initiative and in the face of terrific fire, crawled forward to assault one of the enemy pillboxes which he had spotted. Armed with two hand grenades and well aware that if the enemy should see him it would mean almost certain death, Pfc. Powers crawled up the hill to within 15 yards of the enemy pillbox. Then standing upright in full view of the enemy gunners in order to throw his grenade into the small opening in the roof, he tossed a grenade into the pillbox. At this close, the grenade entered the pillbox, killed two of the occupants and three or four more fled the position, probably wounded. This enemy gun silenced, the center of the line was able to move forward again, but almost immediately came under machine-gun fire from a second pillbox on the left flank. Pfc. Powers, however, had located this pillbox, and crawled toward it, with absolutely no cover if the enemy should see him. Raising himself in full view of the enemy gunners about 15 feet from the pillbox, Pfc. Powers threw his grenade into the pillbox, silencing the gun, killing another German, and probably wounding three or four more who fled. Pfc. Powers, still acting on his own initiative, commenced crawling toward the third enemy pillbox in the face of heavy machine-pistol and machine-gun fire. Skillfully availing himself of meager cover and concealment, Pfc. Powers crawled up to within 10 yards of this pillbox, fully exposed himself to the enemy gunners, stood upright, and tossed the two grenades into the small opening in the roof of the pillbox. His grenades killed two of the enemy and four more, all wounded, came out and surrendered to Pfc. Powers, who was now unarmed. Pfc. Powers had worked his way over the entire company front, and against tremendous odds had singlehandedly broken the backbone of this heavily defended and strategic enemy position, and enabled his regiment to advance into the city of Cassino. Pfc. Powers' fighting determination and intrepidity in battle exemplify the highest traditions of the U.S. Armed Forces.

2912 ◆ PRESTON, ARTHUR MURRAY

Rank: Lieutenant Commander (rank at time of action: Lieutenant) (highest rank: Commander)
Service: U.S. Naval Reserve

Birthday: 1 November 1913
Place of Birth: Washington, D.C.
Date of Death: 7 January 1968
Cemetery: Arlington National Cemetery (3-1847-A-1)—Arlington, Virginia
Entered Service at: Maryland
Unit: Torpedo Boat Squadron 33
Served as: Commanding Officer
Battle or Place of Action: Wasile Bay, Halmahera Island, Moluccas, Netherlands Indies
Date of Action: 16 September 1944
Date of Presentation: 19 December 1947
Place of Presentation: The White House, presented by Pres. Harry S. Truman
Citation: For conspicuous gallantry and intrepidity at the risk of his life above and beyond the call of duty as commander, Motor Torpedo Boat Squadron 33, while effecting the rescue of a Navy pilot shot down in Wasile Bay, Halmahera Island, less than 200 yards from a strongly defended Japanese dock and supply area, 16 September 1944. Volunteering for a perilous mission unsuccessfully attempted by the pilot's squadron mates and a PBY plane, Lt. Comdr. (then Lt.) Preston led PT-489 and PT-363 through 60 miles of restricted, heavily mined waters. Twice turned back while running the gauntlet of fire from powerful coastal defense guns guarding the 11-mile strait at the entrance to the bay, he was again turned back by furious fire in the immediate area of the downed airman. Aided by an aircraft smoke screen, he finally succeeded in reaching his objective and, under vicious fire delivered at 150-yard range, took the pilot aboard and cleared the area, sinking a small hostile cargo vessel with 40-mm fire during retirement. Increasingly vulnerable when covering aircraft were forced to leave because of insufficient fuel, Lt. Comdr. Preston raced PT boats 489 and 363 at high speed for 20 minutes through shell-splashed water and across minefields to safety. Under continuous fire for 2 1/2 hours, Lt. Comdr. Preston successfully achieved a mission considered suicidal in its tremendous hazards and brought his boats through without personnel casualties and with but superficial damage from shrapnel. His exceptional daring and great personal valor enhance the finest traditions of the U.S. Naval Service.

2913 ◆ *PRUSSMAN, ERNEST W.

Rank: Private First Class
Service: U.S. Army
Place of Birth: Baltimore, Baltimore County, Maryland
Date of Death: 8 September 1944
Cemetery: A.B.M.C. Brittany Cemetery (A-12-14)—St. James, France
Entered Service at: Brighton, Suffolk County, Massachusetts
Unit: 13th Infantry, 8th Infantry Division
Battle or Place of Action: near Les Coates, Brittany, France
Date of Action: 8 September 1944
G.O. Number, Date: 31, 17 April 1945
Citation: For conspicuous gallantry and intrepidity at the risk of life above and beyond the call of duty on 8 September

1944, near Les Coates, Brittany, France. When the advance of flank companies of two battalions was halted by intense enemy mortar, machine-gun, and sniper fire from a fortified position on his left, Pfc. Prussman maneuvered his squad to assault the enemy fortifications. Hurdling a hedgerow, he came upon two enemy riflemen whom he disarmed. After leading his squad across an open field to the next hedgerow, he advanced to a machine-gun position, destroyed the gun, captured its crew and two riflemen. Again advancing ahead of his squad in the assault, he was mortally wounded by an enemy rifleman, but as he fell to the ground he threw a hand grenade, killing his opponent. His superb leadership and heroic action at the cost of his life so demoralized the enemy that resistance at this point collapsed, permitting the two battalions to continue their advance.

2914 ◆ *PUCKET, DONALD DALE

Rank: First Lieutenant
Service: U.S. Army Air Corps
Birthday: 19 December 1915
Place of Birth: Longmont, Boulder County, Colorado
Date of Death: 9 July 1944
Cemetery: Jefferson Barracks National Cemetery (One of six in group burial) (84-270-271-272)—St. Louis, Missouri
Entered Service at: Boulder, Boulder County, Colorado
Unit: 343d Bombardment Squadron, 98th Bombardment Group, 8th Air Force
Served as: Pilot of a B-24
Battle or Place of Action: Ploesti, Rumania
Date of Action: 9 July 1944
G.O. Number, Date: 48, 23 June 1945
Citation: He took part in a highly effective attack against vital oil installations in Ploesti on 9 July 1944. Just after "bombs away," the plane received heavy and direct hits from antiaircraft fire. One crewmember was instantly killed and six others severely wounded. The airplane was badly damaged, two were knocked out, the controls cables cut, the oxygen system on fire, and the bomb bay flooded with gas and hydraulic fluid. Regaining control of his crippled plane, 1st Lt. Pucket turned its direction over to the copilot. He calmed the crew, administered first aid, and surveyed the damage. Finding the bomb bay doors jammed, he used the hand crank to open them to allow the gas to escape. He jettisoned all guns and equipment but the plane continued to lose altitude rapidly. Realizing that it would be impossible to reach friendly territory he ordered the crew to abandon ship. Three of the crew, uncontrollable from fright or shock, would not leave. First Lt. Pucket urged the others to jump. Ignoring their entreaties to follow, he refused to abandon the three hysterical men and was last seen fighting to regain control of the plane. A few moments later the flaming bomber crashed on a mountainside. First Lt. Pucket, unhesitatingly and with supreme sacrifice, gave his life in his courageous attempt to save the lives of three others.

2915 ◆ RAMAGE, LAWSON PATERSON "RED"

Rank: Commander (highest rank: Vice Admiral)
Service: U.S. Navy
Birthday: 19 January 1909
Place of Birth: Monroe Bridge, Franklin County, Massachusetts
Date of Death: 15 April 1990
Place of Death: Bethesda, Maryland
Cemetery: Arlington National Cemetery (7-A-184)—Arlington, Virginia
Entered Service at: Vermont
Unit: U.S.S. Parche
Served as: Commanding Officer
Battle or Place of Action: off Taiwan, South China Sea
Date of Action: 31 July 1944
Date of Presentation: 10 January 1945
Place of Presentation: The White House, presented by Pres. Franklin D. Roosevelt
Citation: For conspicuous gallantry and intrepidity at the risk of his life above and beyond the call of duty as commanding officer of the U.S.S. Parche in a predawn attack on a Japanese convoy, 31 July 1944. Boldly penetrating the screen of a heavily escorted convoy, Comdr. Ramage launched a perilous surface attack by delivering a crippling stern shot into a freighter and quickly following up with a series of bow and stern torpedoes to sink the leading tanker and damage the second one. Exposed by the light of bursting flares and bravely defiant of terrific shellfire passing close overhead, he struck again, sinking a transport by two forward reloads. In the mounting fury of fire from the damaged and sinking tanker, he calmly ordered his men below, remaining on the bridge to fight it out with an enemy now disorganized and confused. Swift to act as a fast transport closed in to ram, Comdr. Ramage daringly swung the stern of the speeding Parche as she crossed the bow of the onrushing ship, clearing by less than 50 feet but placing his submarine in a deadly crossfire from escorts on all sides and with the transport dead ahead. Undaunted, he sent three smashing "down the throat" bow shots to stop the target, then scored a killing hit as a climax to 46 minutes of violent action with the Parche and her valiant fighting company retiring victorious and unscathed.

2916 ◆ *RAY, BERNARD JAMES

Rank: First Lieutenant
Service: U.S. Army
Birthday: 9 June 1921
Place of Birth: Brooklyn, Kings County, New York
Date of Death: 17 November 1944
Cemetery: Long Island National Cemetery (DSS-6) (MH)—Farmingdale, New York
Entered Service at: Baldwin, Nassau County, New York
Unit: Company F, 8th Infantry, 4th Infantry Division
Served as: Platoon Leader
Battle or Place of Action: Hurtgen Forest, near Schevenhutte, Germany
Date of Action: 17 November 1944
G.O. Number, Date: 115, 8 December 1945
Citation: He was platoon leader with Company F, 8th Infantry, on 17 November 1944, during the drive through the Hurtgen Forest near Schevenhutte, Germany. The American forces attacked in wet, bitterly cold weather over rough, wooded terrain, meeting brutal resistance from posi-

tions spaced throughout the forest behind minefields and wire obstacles. Small arms, machine-gun, mortar, and artillery fire caused heavy casualties in the ranks when Company F was halted by a concertina-type wire barrier. Under heavy fire, 1st Lt. Ray reorganized his men and prepared to blow a path through the entanglement, a task which appeared impossible of accomplishment and from which others tried to dissuade him. With impacable determination to clear the way, he placed explosive caps in his pockets, obtained several banga-lore torpedoes, and then wrapped a length of highly explosive primer cord about his body. He dashed forward under direct fire, reached the barbed wire and prepared his demolition charge as mortar shells, which were being aimed at him alone, came steadily nearer his completely exposed position. He had placed a torpedo under the wire and was connecting it to a charge he carried when he was severely wounded by a burst-ing mortar shell. Apparently realizing that he would fail in his self-imposed mission unless he completed it in a few moments, he made a supremely gallant decision. With the primer cord still wound around his body and the explosive caps in his pocket, he completed a hasty wiring system and unhesitatingly thrust down on the handle of the charger, destroying himself with the wire barricade in the resulting blast. By the deliberate sacrifice of his life, 1st Lt. Ray enabled his company to continue its attack, the resumption of which was of positive significance in gaining the approaches to the Cologne Plain.

2917 ◆ *REESE, JAMES W.

Rank: Private
Service: U.S. Army
Birthday: 1920
Place of Birth: Chester, Delaware County, Pennsylvania
Date of Death: 5 August 1943
Cemetery: Chester Rural Cemetery—Chester, Pennsylvania
Entered Service at: Chester, Delaware County, Pennsylvania
Unit: 26th Infantry, 1st Infantry Division
Served as: Acting Squad Leader
Battle or Place of Action: at Mount Vassillio, Sicily
Date of Action: 5 August 1943
G.O. Number, Date: 85, 17 December 1943
Date of Presentation: December 1943
Place of Presentation: Fort Dupont, Delaware, presented by Maj. Gen. Lunsford Oliver to his family
Citation: For conspicuous gallantry and intrepidity at the risk of life, above and beyond the call of duty in action involv-ing actual conflict with the enemy. When the enemy launched a counterattack which threatened the position of his compa-ny, Pvt. Reese, as the acting squad leader of a 60-mm mortar squad, displayed superior leadership on his own initiative, maneuvered his squad forward to a favorable position from which, by skillfully directing the fire of his weapon, he caused many casualties in the enemy ranks, and aided materially in repulsing the counterattack. When the enemy fire became so severe as to make his position untenable, he ordered the other members of his squad to withdraw to a safer position, but declined to seek safety for himself. So as to bring more effec-tive fire upon the enemy, Pvt. Reese, without assistance, moved his mortar to a new position and attacked an enemy

machine-gun nest. He had only three rounds of ammunition but secured a direct hit with his last round, completely destroying the nest and killing the occupants. Ammunition being exhausted, he abandoned the mortar, seized a rifle, and continued to advance, moving into an exposed position over-looking the enemy. Despite a heavy concentration of machine-gun, mortar, and artillery fire, the heaviest experi-enced by his unit throughout the entire Sicilian campaign, he remained at this position and continued to inflict casualties upon the enemy until he was killed. His bravery, coupled with his gallant and unswerving determination to close with the enemy, regardless of consequences and obstacles which he faced, are a priceless inspiration to our Armed Forces.

2918 ◆ *REESE JR., JOHN N.

Rank: Private First Class
Service: U.S. Army
Birthday: 13 June 1923
Place of Birth: Muskogee, Muskogee County, Oklahoma
Date of Death: 9 February 1945
Cemetery: Fort Gibson National Cemetery (2-1259-E) (MH)—Fort Gibson, Oklahoma
Entered Service at: Pryor, Mayes County, Oklahoma
Unit: Company B, 148th Infantry, 37th Infantry Division
Battle or Place of Action: Paco Railroad Station, Manila, Philippine Islands
Date of Action: 9 February 1945
G.O. Number, Date: 89, 19 October 1945
Citation: He was engaged in the attack on the Paco Railroad Station, which was strongly defended by 300 deter-mined enemy soldiers with machine guns and rifles, support-ed by several pillboxes, three 20-mm guns, one 37-mm gun, and heavy mortars. While making a frontal assault across an open field, his platoon was halted 100 yards from the station by intense enemy fire. On his own initiative he left the pla-toon, accompanied by a comrade, and continued forward to a house 60 yards from the objective. Although under constant enemy observation, the two men remained in this position for an hour, firing at targets of opportunity, killing more than 35 Japanese and wounding many more. Moving closer to the sta-tion and discovering a group of Japanese replacements attempting to reach pillboxes, they opened heavy fire, killed more than 40 and stopped all subsequent attempts to man the emplacements. Enemy fire became more intense as they advanced to within 20 yards of the station. From that point Pfc. Reese provided effective covering fire and courageously drew enemy fire to himself while his companion killed seven Japanese and destroyed a 20-mm gun and heavy machine gun with hand grenades. With their ammunition running low, the two men started to return to the American lines, alternately providing covering fire for each other as they withdrew. During this movement, Pfc. Reese was killed by enemy fire as he reloaded his rifle. The intrepid team, in 21/2 hours of fierce fighting, killed more than 82 Japanese, completely dis-organized their defense, and paved the way for subsequent complete defeat of the enemy at this strongpoint. By his gal-lant determination in the face of tremendous odds, aggressive fighting spirit, and extreme heroism at the cost of his life, Pfc. Reese materially aided the advance of our troops in Manila

and provided a lasting inspiration to all those with whom he served.

2919 ◆ *REEVES, THOMAS JAMES

Rank: Radio Electrician (highest rank: Warrant Officer)
Service: U.S. Navy
Birthday: 9 December 1895
Place of Birth: Thomaston, Litchfield County, Connecticut
Date of Death: 7 December 1941
Cemetery: National Memorial Cemetery of the Pacific (A-884) (MH)—Honolulu, Hawaii
Entered Service at: Connecticut
Unit: U.S.S. *California*
Battle or Place of Action: Pearl Harbor, Territory of Hawaii
Date of Action: 7 December 1941
Citation: For distinguished conduct in the line of his profession, extraordinary courage, and disregard of his own safety during the attack on the Fleet in Pearl Harbor, by Japanese forces on 7 December 1941. After the mechanized ammunition hoists were put out of action on the U.S.S. *California*, Reeves, on his own initiative, in a burning passageway, assisted in the maintenance of an ammunition supply by hand to the antiaircraft guns until he was overcome by smoke and fire, which resulted in his death.

2920 ◆ *RICKETTS, MILTON ERNEST

Rank: Lieutenant
Service: U.S. Navy
Birthday: 5 August 1913
Place of Birth: Baltimore, Baltimore County, Maryland
Date of Death: 8 May 1942
Place of Death: Coral Sea
Cemetery: A.B.M.C. Manila Cemetery (Wall of the Missing)—Manila, Philippine Islands
Entered Service at: Maryland
Unit: U.S.S. *Yorktown*
Served as: Officer-in-Charge of the Engineering Repair Party
Battle or Place of Action: Coral Sea
Date of Action: 8 May 1942
Citation: For extraordinary and distinguished gallantry above and beyond the call of duty as officer-in-charge of the Engineering Repair Party of the U.S.S. *Yorktown* in action against enemy Japanese forces in the Battle of the Coral Sea on 8 May 1942. During the severe bombing of the *Yorktown* by enemy Japanese forces, an aerial bomb passed through and exploded directly beneath the compartment in which Lt. Ricketts' battle station was located, killing, wounding, or stunning all of his men and mortally wounding him. Despite his ebbing strength, Lt. Ricketts promptly opened the valve of a near-by fireplug, partially led out the firehose, and directed a heavy stream of water into the fire before dropping dead beside the hose. His courageous action, which undoubtedly prevented the rapid spread of fire to serious proportions, and his unflinching devotion to duty were in keeping with the highest traditions of the U.S. Naval Service. He gallantly gave his life for his country.

2921 ◆ *RIORDAN, PAUL F.

Rank: Second Lieutenant
Service: U.S. Army
Birthday: 8 November 1920
Place of Birth: Charles City, Floyd County, Iowa
Date of Death: 8 February 1944
Place of Death: Cassino, Italy
Cemetery: Mount Olivet Cemetery (MH)—Kansas City, Missouri
Entered Service at: Kansas City, Clay County, Missouri
Unit: Company L, 133d Infantry, 34th Infantry Division
Served as: Platoon Leader
Battle or Place of Action: near Cassino, Italy
Date of Action: 3-8 February 1944
G.O. Number, Date: 74, 11 September 1944
Date of Presentation: 11 September 1944
Place of Presentation: Kansas City, Missouri, presented to his parents at their home
Citation: For conspicuous gallantry and intrepidity above and beyond the call of duty. In the attack on the approaches to the city of Cassino on 3 February 1944, 2d Lt. Riordan led one of the assault platoons. Attacking Hill 175, his command was pinned down by enemy machine-gun fire from the hill and from a pillbox about 45 yards to the right of the hill. In the face of intense fire, 2d Lt. Riordan moved out in full view of the enemy gunners to reach a position from where he could throw a hand grenade into the pillbox. Then, getting to his knees, he hurled the grenade approximately 45 yards, scoring a direct hit. The grenade killed one and wounded the other two Germans in the nest and silenced the gun. Another soldier then cleaned out the enemy pillboxes on the hill itself, and the company took its objective. Continuing the assault into Cassino itself on 8 February 1944, 2d Lt. Riordan and his platoon were given the mission of taking the city jailhouse, one of the enemy's several strongpoints. Again 2d Lt. Riordan took the lead and managed to get through the ring of enemy fire covering the approaches and reached the building. His platoon, however, could not get through the intense fire and was cut off. Second Lt. Riordan, aware that his men were unable to follow, determined to carry on singlehandedly, but the numerically superior enemy force was too much for him to overcome, and he was killed by enemy small-arms fire after disposing of at least two of the defenders. Second Lt. Riordan's bravery and extraordinary heroism in the face of almost certain death were an inspiration to his men and exemplify the highest traditions of the U.S. Armed Forces.

2922 ◆ *ROAN, CHARLES HOWARD

Rank: Private First Class
Service: U.S. Marine Corps Reserve
Birthday: 16 August 1923
Place of Birth: Claude, Armstrong County, Texas
Date of Death: 18 September 1944
Cemetery: A.B.M.C. Manila Cemetery (Wall of the Missing)—Manila, Philippine Islands; Claude Cemetery ('In Memory' marker)—Claude, Texas
Entered Service at: Texas

Unit: 2d Battalion, 7th Marines, 1st Marine Division
Battle or Place of Action: Peleliu Island, Palau Islands
Date of Action: 18 September 1944
Citation: For conspicuous gallantry and intrepidity at the risk of his life above and beyond the call of duty while serving with the 2d Battalion, 7th Marines, 1st Marine Division, in action against enemy Japanese forces on Peleliu, Palau Islands, 18 September 1944. Shortly after his leader ordered a withdrawal upon discovering that his squad was partly cut off from their company as a result of the rapid advance along an exposed ridge during an aggressive attack on the strongly entrenched enemy, Pfc. Roan and his companions were suddenly engaged in a furious exchange of hand grenades by Japanese forces emplaced in a cave on higher ground and to the rear of the squad. Seeking protection with four other marines in a depression in the rocky, broken terrain, Pfc. Roan was wounded by an enemy grenade which fell close to their position and, immediately realizing the imminent peril to his comrades when another grenade landed in the midst of the group, unhesitatingly flung himself upon it, covering it with his body and absorbing the full impact of the explosion. By his prompt action and selfless conduct in the face of almost certain death, he saved the lives of four men. His great personal valor reflects the highest credit upon himself and the U.S. Naval Service. He gallantly gave his life for his comrades.

2923 ◆ *ROBINSON JR., JAMES E.

Rank: First Lieutenant
Service: U.S. Army
Birthday: 10 July 1918
Place of Birth: Toledo, Lucas County, Ohio
Date of Death: 6 April 1945
Cemetery: Fort Sam Houston National Cemetery (T-98) (MH)—San Antonio, Texas
Entered Service at: Waco, McLennan County, Texas
Unit: Battery A, 861st Field Artillery Battalion, 63d Infantry Division
Served as: Forward Observer
Battle or Place of Action: near Untergriesheim, Germany
Date of Action: 6 April 1945
G.O. Number, Date: 117, 11 December 1945
Citation: He was a field artillery observer attached to Company A, 253d Infantry, near Untergriesheim, Germany, on 6 April 1945. Eight hours of desperate fighting over open terrain swept by German machine-gun, mortar, and small-arms fire had decimated Company A, robbing it of its commanding officer and most of its key enlisted personnel, when 1st Lt. Robinson rallied the 23 remaining uninjured riflemen and a few walking wounded, and, while carrying his heavy radio for communications with American batteries, led them through intense fire in a charge against the objective. Ten German infantrymen in foxholes threatened to stop the assault, but the gallant leader killed them all at point-blank range with rifle and pistol fire and then pressed on with his men to sweep the area of all resistance. Soon afterward he was ordered to seize the defended town of Kressbach. He went to each of the 19 exhausted survivors with cheering words, instilling in them courage and fortitude, before leading the

little band forward once more. In the advance he was seriously wounded in the throat by a shell fragment, but, despite great pain and loss of blood, he refused medical attention and continued the attack, directing supporting artillery fire even though he was mortally wounded. Only after the town had been taken and he could no longer speak did he leave the command he had inspired in victory and walk nearly two miles to an aid station where he died from his wounds. By his intrepid leadership 1st Lt. Robinson was directly responsible for Company A's accomplishing its mission against tremendous odds.

2924 ◆ RODRIGUEZ, CLETO L.

Rank: Technical Sergeant (rank at time of action: Private) (highest rank: Master Sergeant)
Service: U.S. Army
Birthday: 26 April 1923
Place of Birth: San Marcos, Hays County, Texas
Date of Death: 7 December 1990
Place of Death: San Antonio, Texas
Cemetery: Fort Sam Houston National Cemetery (MH)—San Antonio, Texas
Entered Service at: San Antonio, Bexar County, Texas
Unit: Company B, 148th Infantry, 37th Infantry Division
Served as: Automatic Rifleman
Battle or Place of Action: Paco Railroad Station, Manila, Philippine Islands
Date of Action: 9 February 1945
G.O. Number, Date: 97, 1 November 1945
Date of Presentation: 12 October 1945
Place of Presentation: The White House, presented by Pres. Harry S. Truman
Citation: He was an automatic rifleman when his unit attacked the strongly defended Paco Railroad Station during the battle for Manila, Philippine Islands. While making a frontal assault across an open field, his platoon was halted 100 yards from the station by intense enemy fire. On his own initiative, he left the platoon, accompanied by a comrade, and continued forward to a house 60 yards from the objective. Although under constant enemy observation, the two men remained in this position for an hour, firing at targets of opportunity, killing more than 35 hostile soldiers, and wounding many more. Moving closer to the station and discovering a group of Japanese replacements attempting to reach pillboxes, they opened heavy fire, killed more than 40, and stopped all subsequent attempts to man the emplacements. Enemy fire became more intense as they advanced to within 20 yards of the station. Then, covered by his companion, Pvt. Rodriguez boldly moved up to the building and threw five grenades through a doorway, killing seven Japanese, destroying a 20-mm gun, and wrecking a heavy machine gun. With their ammunition running low, the two men started to return to the American lines, alternately providing covering fire for each other's withdrawal. During this movement, Pvt. Rodriguez' companion was killed. In 2 1/2 hours of fierce fighting the intrepid team killed more than 82 Japanese, completely disorganized their defense, and paved the way for the subsequent overwhelming defeat of the

enemy at this strongpoint. Two days later, Pvt. Rodriguez again enabled his comrades to advance when he singlehandedly killed six Japanese and destroyed a well-placed 20-mm gun. By his outstanding skill with his weapon, gallant determination to destroy the enemy, and heroic courage in the face of tremendous odds, Pvt. Rodriguez, on two occasions, materially aided the advance of our troops in Manila.

2925 ◆ *ROEDER, ROBERT E.

Rank: Captain
Service: U.S. Army
Birthday: 25 July 1917
Place of Birth: Summit Station, Schuylkill County, Pennsylvania
Date of Death: 28 September 1944
Cemetery: Arlington National Cemetery (12-6116) (MH)—Arlington, Virginia
Entered Service at: Summit Station, Schuylkill County, Pennsylvania
Unit: Company G, 350th Infantry, 88th Infantry Division
Served as: Company Commander
Battle or Place of Action: Mount Battaglia, Italy
Date of Action: 27-28 September 1944
G.O. Number, Date: 31, 17 April 1945
Citation: For conspicuous gallantry and intrepidity at the risk of life above and beyond the call of duty. Capt. Roeder commanded his company in defense of the strategic Mount Battaglia. Shortly after the company had occupied the hill, the Germans launched the first of a series of determined counterattacks to regain this dominating height. Completely exposed to ceaseless enemy artillery and small-arms fire, Capt. Roeder constantly circulated among his men, encouraging them and directing their defense against the persistent enemy. During the sixth counterattack, the enemy, by using flamethrowers and taking advantage of the fog, succeeded in overrunning the position. Capt. Roeder led his men in a fierce battle at close quarters to repulse the attack with heavy losses to the Germans. The following morning, while the company was engaged in repulsing an enemy counterattack in force, Capt. Roeder was seriously wounded and rendered unconscious by shell fragments. He was carried to the company command post, where he regained consciousness. Refusing medical treatment, he insisted on rejoining his men. Although in a weakened condition, Capt. Roeder dragged himself to the door of the command post and, picking up a rifle, braced himself in a sitting position. He began firing his weapon, shouted words of encouragement, and issued orders to his men. He personally killed two Germans before he himself was killed instantly by an exploding shell. Through Capt. Roeder's able and intrepid leadership his men held Mount Battaglia against the aggressive and fanatical enemy attempts to retake this important and strategic height. His valorous performance is exemplary of the fighting spirit of the U.S. Army.

2926 ◆ *ROOKS, ALBERT HAROLD

Rank: Captain
Service: U.S. Navy
Birthday: 29 December 1891
Place of Birth: Colton, Whitman County, Washington
Date of Death: 1 March 1942
Cemetery: A.B.M.C. Manila Cemetery (Wall of the Missing)—Manila, Philippine Islands
Entered Service at: Washington
Unit: U.S.S. Houston
Served as: Commanding Officer
Battle or Place of Action: from Darwin to Koepang, Timor, Netherlands East Indies
Date of Action: 4-27 February 1942
Date of Presentation: 24 June 1943
Place of Presentation: The White House (Oval Office), presented by Pres. Franklin D. Roosevelt to his Widow and Son
Citation: For extraordinary heroism, outstanding courage, gallantry in action, and distinguished service in the line of his profession, as commanding officer of the U.S.S. Houston during the period from 4 to 27 February 1942, while in action with superior Japanese enemy aerial and surface forces. While proceeding to attack an enemy amphibious expedition, as a unit in a mixed force, Houston was heavily attacked by bombers; after evading four attacks, she was heavily hit in a fifth attack, lost 60 killed and had one turret wholly disabled. Capt. Rooks made his ship again seaworthy and sailed within three days to escort an important reinforcing convoy from Darwin to Koepang, Timor, Netherlands East Indies. While so engaged, another powerful air attack developed which by Houston's marked efficiency was fought off without much damage to the convoy. The commanding general of all forces in the area thereupon canceled the movement and Capt. Rooks escorted the convoy back to Darwin. Later, while in a considerable American-British-Dutch force engaged with an overwhelming force of Japanese surface ships, Houston with H.M.S. Exeter carried the brunt of the battle, and her fire alone heavily damaged one and possibly two heavy cruisers. Although heavily damaged in the actions, Capt. Rooks succeeded in disengaging his ship when the flag officer commanding broke off the action and got her safely away from the vicinity, whereas one-half of the cruisers were lost.

2927 ◆ *ROOSEVELT JR., THEODORE

Rank: Brigadier General
Service: U.S. Army
Birthday: 13 September 1887
Place of Birth: Oyster Bay, Nassau County, New York
Date of Death: 12 July 1944
Place of Death: Normandy, France
Cemetery: A.B.M.C. Normandy Cemetery (D-28-45)—St. Laurent-sur-Mer, France
Entered Service at: Oyster Bay, Nassau County, New York
Unit: 4th Infantry Division
Served as: Assistant Division Commander
Battle or Place of Action: Normandy Invasion, France
Date of Action: 6 June 1944
G.O. Number, Date: 77, 28 September 1944
Date of Presentation: 21 September 1944
Place of Presentation: The Pentagon, presented by Sec. of War Henry L. Stimson to his Widow

Citation: For gallantry and intrepidity at the risk of his life above and beyond the call of duty on 6 June 1944, in France. After two verbal requests to accompany the leading assault elements in the Normandy invasion had been denied, Brig. Gen. Roosevelt's written request for this mission was approved and he landed with the first wave of the forces assaulting the enemy-held beaches. He repeatedly led groups from the beach, over the seawall, and established them inland. His valor, courage, and presence in the very front of the attack and his complete unconcern at being under heavy fire inspired the troops to heights of enthusiasm and self-sacrifice. Although the enemy had the beach under constant direct fire, Brig. Gen. Roosevelt moved from one locality to another, rallying men around him, directed, and personally led them against the enemy. Under his seasoned, precise, calm, and unfaltering leadership, assault troops reduced beach strongpoints and rapidly moved inland with minimum casualties. He thus contributed substantially to the successful establishment of the beachhead in France.

2928 ◆ ROSS, DONALD KIRBY

Rank: Warrant Machinist (highest rank: Captain)
Service: U.S. Navy
Birthday: 8 December 1910
Place of Birth: Beverly, Lincoln County, Kansas
Date of Death: 27 May 1992
Place of Death: Port Orchard, Washington
Cemetery: At sea, over U.S.S. *Nevada* (Pacific Ocean)
Entered Service at: Denver, Denver County, Colorado
Unit: U.S.S. *Nevada*
Battle or Place of Action: Pearl Harbor, Territory of Hawaii
Date of Action: 7 December 1941
Date of Presentation: 18 April 1942
Place of Presentation: Pearl Harbor, Territory of Hawaii, presented by Adm. Chester W. Nimitz
Citation: For distinguished conduct in the line of his profession, extraordinary courage, and disregard for his own life during the attack on the Fleet at Pearl Harbor, Territory of Hawaii, by Japanese forces on 7 December 1941. When his station in the forward dynamo room of the U.S.S. *Nevada* became almost untenable due to smoke, steam, and heat, Machinist Ross forced his men to leave that station and performed all the duties himself until blinded and unconscious. Upon being rescued and resuscitated, he returned and secured the forward dynamo room and proceeded to the after dynamo room where he was later again rendered unconscious by exhaustion. Again recovering consciousness he returned to his station where he remained until directed to abandon it.

2929 ◆ ROSS, WILBURN KIRBY

Rank: Private (highest rank: Master Sergeant)
Service: U.S. Army
Birthday: 12 May 1922
Place of Birth: Strunk, McCreary County, Kentucky
Entered Service at: Strunk, McCreary County, Kentucky
Unit: Weapons Platoon, Company G, 2d Battalion, 30th Infantry, 3d Infantry Division

Served as: Light Machine Gunner
Battle or Place of Action: near St. Jacques, France
Date of Action: 30 October 1944
G.O. Number, Date: 30, 14 April 1945
Date of Presentation: 23 April 1945
Place of Presentation: Zepman Stadium, Nuremberg, Germany, presented by Lt. Gen. Alexander M. Patch III
Citation: For conspicuous gallantry and intrepidity at the risk of life above and beyond the call of duty near St. Jacques, France. At 11:30 A.M. on 30 October 1944, after his company had lost 55 out of 88 men in an attack on an entrenched, full-strength German company of elite mountain troops, Pvt. Ross placed his light machine gun 10 yards in advance of the foremost supporting riflemen in order to absorb the initial impact of an enemy counterattack. With machine-gun and small-arms fire striking the earth near him, he fired with deadly effect on the assaulting force and repelled it. Despite the hail of automatic fire and the explosion of rifle grenades within a stone's throw of his position, he continued to man his machine gun alone, holding off six more German attacks. When the eighth assault was launched, most of his supporting riflemen were out of ammunition. They took positions in echelon behind Pvt. Ross and crawled up, during the attack, to extract a few rounds of ammunition from his machine-gun ammunition belt. Pvt. Ross fought on virtually without assistance and, despite the fact that enemy grenadiers crawled to within four yards of his position in an effort to kill him with hand grenades, he again directed accurate and deadly fire on the hostile force and hurled it back. After expending his last rounds, Pvt. Ross was advised to withdraw to the company command post, together with eight surviving riflemen, but, as more ammunition was expected, he declined to do so. The Germans launched their last all-out attack, converging their fire on Pvt. Ross in a desperate attempt to destroy the machine gun which stood between them and a decisive breakthrough. As his supporting riflemen fixed bayonets for a last-ditch stand, fresh ammunition arrived and was brought to Pvt. Ross just as the advance assault elements were about to swarm over his position. He opened murderous fire on the oncoming enemy, killed 40 and wounded 10 of the attacking force, broke the assault sin glehandedly, and forced the Germans to withdraw. Having killed or wounded at least 58 Germans in more than five hours of continuous combat and saved the remnants of his company from destruction, Pvt. Ross remained at his post that night and the following day for a total of 36 hours. His actions throughout this engagement were an inspiration to his comrades and maintained the high traditions of the military service.

2930 ◆ ROUH, CARLTON ROBERT

Rank: First Lieutenant (highest rank: Captain)
Service: U.S. Marine Corps Reserve
Birthday: 11 May 1919
Place of Birth: Lindenwold, Camden County, New Jersey
Date of Death: 8 December 1977
Cemetery: Berlin Cemetery (MH)—Berlin, New Jersey
Entered Service at: New Jersey
Unit: 1st Battalion, 5th Marines, 1st Marine Division

Battle or Place of Action: Peleliu Island, Palau Islands
Date of Action: 15 September 1944
Date of Presentation: 15 June 1945
Place of Presentation: The White House, presented by Pres. Harry S. Truman
Citation: For conspicuous gallantry and intrepidity at the risk of his life above and beyond the call of duty while attached to the 1st Battalion, 5th Marines, 1st Marine Division, during action against enemy Japanese forces on Peleliu Island, Palau Group, 15 September 1944. Before permitting his men to use an enemy dugout as a position for an 81-mm mortar observation post, 1st Lt. Rouh made a personal reconnaissance of the pillbox and, upon entering, was severely wounded by Japanese rifle fire from within. Emerging from the dugout, he was immediately assisted by two marines to a less exposed area but, while receiving first aid, was further endangered by an enemy grenade which was thrown into their midst. Quick to act in spite of his weakened condition, he lurched to a crouching position and thrust both men aside, placing his own body between them and the grenade and taking the full blast of the explosion himself. His exceptional spirit of loyalty and self-sacrifice in the face of almost certain death reflects the highest credit upon 1st Lt. Rouh and the U.S. Naval Service.

2931 ◆ RUDOLPH, DONALD EUGENE

Rank: Second Lieutenant (rank at time of action: Technical Sergeant)
Service: U.S. Army
Birthday: 21 February 1921
Place of Birth: South Haven, Wright County, Minnesota
Entered Service at: Minneapolis, Hennepin County, Minnesota
Unit: Weapons Platoon, Company E, 2d Battalion, 20th Infantry, 6th Infantry Division
Served as: Acting Platoon Leader
Battle or Place of Action: Munoz, Luzon, Philippine Islands
Date of Action: 5 February 1945
G.O. Number, Date: 77, 10 September 1945
Date of Presentation: 23 August 1945
Place of Presentation: The White House (Gold Room), presented by Pres. Harry S. Truman
Citation: Second Lt. Rudolph (then T/Sgt.) was acting as platoon leader at Munoz, Luzon, Philippine Islands. While administering first aid on the battlefield, he observed enemy fire issuing from a nearby culvert. Crawling to the culvert with rifle and grenades, he killed three of the enemy concealed there. He then worked his way across open terrain toward a line of enemy pillboxes which had immobilized his company. Nearing the first pillbox, he hurled a grenade through its embrasure and charged the position. With his bare hands he tore away the wood and tin covering, then dropped a grenade through the opening, killing the enemy gunners and destroying their machine gun. Ordering several riflemen to cover his further advance, 2d Lt. Rudolph seized a pick mattock and made his way to a second pillbox. Piercing its top with the mattock, he dropped a grenade through the

hole, firing several rounds from his rifle into it, and smothered any surviving enemy by sealing the hole and the embrasure with earth. In quick succession he attacked and neutralized six more pillboxes. Later, when his platoon was attacked by an enemy tank, he advanced under covering fire, climbed to the top of the tank, and dropped a white phosphorus grenade through the turret, destroying the crew. Through his outstanding heroism, superb courage, and leadership, and complete disregard for his own safety, 2d Lt. Rudolph cleared a path for an advance which culminated in one of the most decisive victories of the Philippine campaign.

2932 ◆ *RUHL, DONALD JACK

Rank: Private First Class
Service: U.S. Marine Corps Reserve
Birthday: 2 July 1923
Place of Birth: Columbus, Stillwater County, Montana
Date of Death: 21 February 1945
Cemetery: Hillside Cemetery (MH)—Greybull, Wyoming
Entered Service at: Montana
Unit: Company E, 2d Battalion, 28th Marines, 5th Marine Division
Served as: Rifleman
Battle or Place of Action: Iwo Jima, Volcano Islands
Date of Action: 19-21 February 1945
Citation: For conspicuous gallantry and intrepidity at the risk of his life above and beyond the call of duty while serving as a rifleman in an assault platoon of Company E, 28th Marines, 5th Marine Division, in action against enemy Japanese forces on Iwo Jima, Volcano Islands from 19–21 February 1945. Quick to press the advantage after eight Japanese had been driven from a blockhouse on D-day, Pfc. Ruhl singlehandedly attacked the group, killing one of the enemy with his bayonet and another by rifle fire in his determined attempt to annihilate the escaping troops. Cool and undaunted as the fury of hostile resistance steadily increased throughout the night, he voluntarily left the shelter of his tank trap early in the morning of D-day plus one and moved out under a tremendous volume of mortar and machine-gun fire to rescue a wounded marine lying in an exposed position approximately 40 yards forward of the line. Half pulling and half carrying the wounded man, he removed him to a defiladed position, called for an assistant and a stretcher and, again running the gauntlet of hostile fire, carried the casualty to an aid station some 300 yards distant on the beach. Returning to his platoon, he continued his valiant efforts, volunteering to investigate an apparently abandoned Japanese gun emplacement 75 yards forward of the right flank during consolidation of the front lines, and subsequently occupying the position through the night to prevent the enemy from repossessing the valuable weapon. Pushing forward in the assault against the vast network of fortifications surrounding Mt. Suribachi the following morning, he crawled with his platoon guide to the top of a Japanese bunker to bring fire to bear on enemy troops located on the far side of the bunker. Suddenly a hostile grenade landed between the two marines. Instantly Pfc. Ruhl called a warning to his fellow marine and dived on the deadly missile, absorbing the full impact of the shattering

explosion in his own body and protecting all within range from the danger of flying fragments although he might easily have dropped from his position on the edge of the bunker to the ground below. An indomitable fighter, Pfc. Ruhl rendered heroic service toward the defeat of a ruthless enemy, and his valor, initiative, and unfaltering spirit of self-sacrifice in the face of almost certain death sustain and enhance the highest traditions of the U.S. Naval Service. He gallantly gave his life for his country.

2933 ◆ RUIZ, ALEJANDRO RENTERIA

Rank: Private First Class (highest rank: Sergeant)
Service: U.S. Army
Birthday: 26 June 1924
Place of Birth: Loving, Eddy County, New Mexico
Entered Service at: Carlsbad, Eddy County, New Mexico
Unit: 1st Platoon, Company A, 1st Battalion, 165th Infantry, 27th Infantry Division
Served as: Rifleman
Battle or Place of Action: Okinawa, Ryukyu Islands
Date of Action: 28 April 1945
G.O. Number, Date: 60, 26 June 1946
Date of Presentation: 14 June 1946
Place of Presentation: The White House, presented by Pres. Harry S. Truman
Citation: When his unit was stopped by a skillfully camouflaged enemy pillbox, he displayed conspicuous gallantry and intrepidity above and beyond the call of duty. His squad, suddenly brought under a hail of machine-gun fire and a vicious grenade attack, was pinned down. Jumping to his feet, Pfc. Ruiz seized an automatic rifle and lunged through the flying grenades and rifle and automatic fire for the top of the emplacement. When an enemy soldier charged him, his rifle jammed. Undaunted, Pfc. Ruiz whirled on his assailant and clubbed him down. Then he ran back through bullets and grenades, seized more ammunition and another automatic rifle, and again made for the pillbox. Enemy fire now was concentrated on him, but he charged on, miraculously reaching the position, and in plain view he climbed to the top. Leaping from one opening to another, he sent burst after burst into the pillbox, killing 12 of the enemy and completely destroying the position. Pfc. Ruiz's heroic conduct, in the face of overwhelming odds, saved the lives of many comrades and eliminated an obstacle that long would have checked his unit's advance.

2934 ◆ *SADOWSKI, JOSEPH JOHN

Rank: Sergeant
Service: U.S. Army
Birthday: 7 December 1916
Place of Birth: Perth Amboy, Middlesex County, New Jersey
Date of Death: 14 September 1944
Place of Death: Valhey, France
Cemetery: St. Stephen's Cemetery—Keasby, New Jersey
Entered Service at: Perth Amboy, Middlesex County, New Jersey

Unit: Company A, 37th Tank Battalion, 4th Armored Division
Served as: Tank Commander
Battle or Place of Action: Valhey, France
Date of Action: 14 September 1944
G.O. Number, Date: 32, 23 April 1945
Place of Presentation: Fort George Meade, Maryland, presented by Maj. Gen. Francis B. Melon to his family
Citation: For conspicuous gallantry and intrepidity at the risk of his life above and beyond the call of duty at Valhey, France. On the afternoon of 14 September 1944, Sgt. Sadowski as a tank commander was advancing with the lead elements of Combat Command A, 4th Armored Division, through an intensely severe barrage of enemy fire from the streets and buildings of the town of Valhey. As Sgt. Sadowski's tank advanced through the hail of fire, it was struck by a shell from an 88-mm gun fired at a range of 20 yards. The tank was disabled and burst into flames. The suddenness of the enemy attack caused confusion and hesitation among the crews of the remaining tanks of our forces. Sgt. Sadowski immediately ordered his crew to dismount and take cover in the adjoining buildings. After his crew had dismounted, Sgt. Sadowski discovered that one member of the crew, the bow gunner, had been unable to leave the tank. Although the tank was being subjected to a withering hail of enemy small-arms, bazooka, grenade, and mortar fire from the streets and from the windows of adjacent buildings, Sgt. Sadowski unhesitatingly returned to his tank and endeavored to pry up the bow gunner's hatch. While engaged in this attempt to rescue his comrade from the burning tank, he was cut down by a stream of machine-gun fire which resulted in his death. The gallant and noble sacrifice of his life in the aid of his comrade, undertaken in the face of almost certain death, so inspired the remainder of the tank crews that they pressed forward with greater ferocity and completely destroyed the enemy forces in this town without further loss to themselves. The heroism and selfless devotion to duty displayed by Sgt. Sadowski, which resulted in his death, inspired the remainder of his forces to press forward to victory and reflect the highest traditions of the Armed Forces.

2935 ◆ *SARNOSKI, JOSEPH RAYMOND

Rank: Second Lieutenant
Service: U.S. Army Air Corps
Birthday: 30 January 1915
Place of Birth: Simpson, Lackawanna County, Pennsylvania
Date of Death: 16 June 1943
Place of Death: Over Buka Area, Solomon Islands
Cemetery: National Memorial Cemetery of the Pacific (A-582) (MH)—Honolulu, Hawaii
Entered Service at: Simpson, Lackawanna County, Pennsylvania
Unit: 65th Bombardment Squadron, 43d Bombardment Group, 5th Air Force
Served as: Bombardier of a B-17
Battle or Place of Action: over Buka area, Solomon Islands
Date of Action: 16 June 1943

G.O. Number, Date: 85, 17 December 1943
Place of Presentation: Presented to his Widow
Citation: For conspicuous gallantry and intrepidity in action above and beyond the call of duty. On 16 June 1943, 2d Lt. Sarnoski volunteered as bombardier of a crew on an important photographic mapping mission covering the heavily defended Buka area, Solomon Islands. When the mission was nearly completed, about 20 enemy fighters intercepted. At the nose guns, 2d Lt. Sarnoski fought off the first attackers, making it possible for the pilot to finish the plotted course. When a coordinated frontal attack by the enemy extensively damaged his bomber and seriously injured five of the crew, 2d Lt. Sarnoski though wounded, continued firing and shot down two enemy planes. A 20-millimeter shell which burst in the nose of the bomber knocked him into the catwalk under the cockpit. With indomitable fighting spirit, he crawled back to his post and kept on firing until he collapsed on his guns. Second Lt. Sarnoski, by resolute defense of his aircraft at the price of his life, made possible the completion of a vitally important mission.

2936 ◆ *SAYERS, FOSTER JOSEPH

Rank: Private First Class
Service: U.S. Army
Birthday: 27 April 1924
Place of Birth: Marshalls Creek, Monroe County, Pennsylvania
Date of Death: 12 November 1944
Place of Death: near Thionville, France
Cemetery: Schenck Cemetery (MH)—Howard Township, Pennsylvania
Entered Service at: Howard, Centre County, Pennsylvania
Unit: Company L, 357th Infantry, 90th Infantry Division
Served as: Machine Gunner
Battle or Place of Action: near Thionville, France
Date of Action: 12 November 1944
G.O. Number, Date: 89, 19 October 1945
Citation: He displayed conspicuous gallantry above and beyond the call of duty in combat on 12 November 1944, near Thionville, France. During an attack on strong hostile forces entrenched on a hill he fearlessly ran up the steep approach toward his objective and set up his machine gun 20 yards from the enemy. Realizing it would be necessary to attract full attention of the dug-in Germans while his company crossed an open area and flanked the enemy, he picked up his gun, charged through withering machine-gun and rifle fire to the very edge of the emplacement, and there killed 12 German soldiers with devastating close-range fire. He took up a position behind a log and engaged the hostile infantry from the flank in an heroic attempt to distract their attention while his comrades attained their objective at the crest of the hill. He was killed by the very heavy concentration of return fire; but his fearless assault enabled his company to sweep the hill with a minimum of casualties, killing or capturing every enemy soldier on it. Pfc. Sayers' indomitable fighting spirit, aggressiveness, and supreme devotion to duty live on as an example of the highest traditions of the military service.

2937 ◆ SCHAEFER, JOSEPH EDWARD

Rank: Staff Sergeant
Service: U.S. Army
Birthday: 27 December 1918
Place of Birth: New York, New York
Date of Death: 16 March 1987
Place of Death: Staten Island, New York
Cemetery: Long Island National Cemetery (DSS-80) (MH)—Farmingdale, New York
Entered Service at: Long Island, New York
Unit: 2d Platoon, Company I, 18th Infantry, 1st Infantry Division
Served as: Squad Leader
Battle or Place of Action: near Stolberg, Germany
Date of Action: 24 September 1944
G.O. Number, Date: 71, 22 August 1945
Citation: He was in charge of a squad of the 2d Platoon in the vicinity of Stolberg, Germany, early in the morning of 24 September 1944, when two enemy companies supported by machine guns launched an attack to seize control of an important crossroads which was defended by his platoon. One American squad was forced back, another captured, leaving only S/Sgt. Schaefer's men to defend the position. To shift his squad into a house which would afford better protection, he crawled about under heavy small-arms and machine-gun fire, instructed each individual, and moved to the building. A heavy concentration of enemy artillery fire scored hits on his strongpoint. S/Sgt. Schaefer assigned his men to positions and selected for himself the most dangerous one at the door. With his M1 rifle, he broke the first wave of infantry thrown toward the house. The Germans attacked again with grenades and flamethrowers but were thrown back a second time, S/Sgt. Schaefer killing and wounding several. Regrouped for a final assault, the Germans approached from two directions. One force drove at the house from the front, while a second group advanced stealthily along a hedgerow. Recognizing the threat, S/Sgt. Schaefer fired rapidly at the enemy before him, killing or wounding all six; then, with no cover whatever, dashed to the hedgerow and poured deadly accurate shots into the second group, killing five, wounding two others, and forcing the enemy to withdraw. He scoured the area near his battered stronghold and captured 10 prisoners. By this time the rest of his company had begun a counterattack; he moved forward to assist another platoon to regain its position. Remaining in the lead, crawling and running in the face of heavy fire, he overtook the enemy, and liberated the American squad captured earlier in the battle. In all, single-handed and armed only with his rifle, he killed between 15 and 20 Germans, wounded at least as many more, and took 10 prisoners. S/Sgt. Schaefer's indomitable courage and his determination to hold his position at all costs were responsible for stopping an enemy breakthrough.

2938 ◆ SCHAUER, HENRY

Rank: Private First Class (highest rank: Technical Sergeant)
Service: U.S. Army
Birthday: 9 October 1918

Place of Birth: Clinton, Custer County, Oklahoma
Entered Service at: Scobey, Daniels County, Montana
Unit: Battle Patrol, Company F, 2d Battalion, 15th Infantry Regiment, 3d Infantry Division
Served as: Automatic Rifleman
Battle or Place of Action: near Cisterna di Littoria, Italy
Date of Action: 23-24 May 1944
G.O. Number, Date: 83, 27 October 1944
Date of Presentation: 4 October 1944
Place of Presentation: France, presented by Lt. Gen. Alexander M. Patch III
Citation: For conspicuous gallantry and intrepidity at risk of life above and beyond the call of duty. On 23 May 1944, at 12 noon, Pfc. (now T/Sgt.) Schauer left the cover of a ditch to engage four German snipers who opened fire on the patrol from its rear. Standing erect he walked deliberately 30 yards toward the enemy, stopped amid the fire of four rifles centered on him, and with four bursts from his BAR, each at a different range, killed all of the snipers. Catching sight of a fifth sniper waiting for the patrol behind a house chimney, Pfc. Schauer brought him down with another burst. Shortly after, when a heavy enemy artillery concentration and two machine guns temporarily halted the patrol, Pfc. Schauer again left cover to engage the enemy weapons singlehandedly. While shells exploded within 15 yards, showering dirt over him, and strings of grazing German tracer bullets whipped past him at chest level, Pfc. Schauer knelt, killed the two gunners of the machine gun only 60 yards from him with a single burst from his BAR, and crumpled two other enemy soldiers who ran to man the gun. Inserting a fresh magazine in his BAR, Pfc. Schauer shifted his body to fire at the other weapon 500 yards distant and emptied his weapon into the enemy crew, killing all four Germans. Next morning, when shells from a German Mark VI tank and a machine gun only 100 yards distant again forced the patrol to seek cover, Pfc. Schauer crawled toward the enemy machine gun, stood upright only 80 yards from the weapon as its bullets cut the surrounding ground, and four tank shells fired directly at him burst within 20 yards. Raising his BAR to his shoulder, Pfc. Schauer killed the four members of the German machine-gun crew with one burst of fire.

2939 ◆ SCHONLAND, HERBERT EMERY

Rank: Commander (highest rank: Rear Admiral)
Service: U.S. Navy
Birthday: 7 September 1900
Place of Birth: Portland, Cumberland County, Maine
Date of Death: 13 November 1984
Place of Death: New London, Connecticut
Cemetery: Arlington National Cemetery (7-A-168) (MH)—Arlington, Virginia
Entered Service at: Portland, Cumberland County, Maine
Unit: U.S.S. *San Francisco*
Served as: Damage Control Officer
Battle or Place of Action: Iron Bottom Sound, off Savo Island, Solomon Islands
Date of Action: 12-13 November 1943
Date of Presentation: 5 January 1943

Place of Presentation: The White House (Oval Office), presented by Pres. Franklin D. Roosevelt
Citation: For extreme heroism and courage above and beyond the call of duty as damage control officer of the U.S.S. *San Francisco* in action against greatly superior enemy forces in the battle off Savo Island, 12–13 November 1942. In the same violent night engagement in which all of his superior officers were killed or wounded, Lt. Comdr. Schonland was fighting valiantly to free the *San Francisco* of large quantities of water flooding the second deck compartments through numerous shell holes caused by enemy fire. Upon being informed that he was commanding officer, he ascertained that the conning of the ship was being efficiently handled, then directed the officer who had taken over that task to continue while he himself resumed the vitally important work of maintaining the stability of the ship. In water waist deep, he carried on his efforts in darkness illuminated only by hand lanterns until water in flooded compartments had been drained or pumped off and watertight integrity had again been restored to the *San Francisco*. His great personal valor and gallant devotion to duty at great peril to his own life were instrumental in bringing his ship back to port under her own power, saved to fight again in the service of her country.

2940 ◆ *SCHWAB, ALBERT ERNEST

Rank: Private First Class
Service: U.S. Marine Corps Reserve
Birthday: 17 July 1920
Place of Birth: Washington, D.C.
Date of Death: 7 May 1945
Cemetery: Memorial Park Cemetery (MH)—Tulsa, Oklahoma
Entered Service at: Tulsa, Tulsa County, Oklahoma
: Headquarters Company, 1st Battalion, 5th Marines, 1st Marine Division
Served as: Flamethrower Operator
Battle or Place of Action: Okinawa Shima, Ryukyu Islands
Date of Action: 7 May 1945
Date of Presentation: 31 May 1946
Place of Presentation: Presented by Rear Adm. Joseph J. Clark to his Son
Citation: For conspicuous gallantry and intrepidity at the risk of his life above and beyond the call of duty as a flamethrower operator in action against enemy Japanese forces on Okinawa Shima in the Ryukyu Islands, 7 May 1945. Quick to take action when his company was pinned down in a valley and suffered resultant heavy casualties under blanketing machine-gun fire emanating from a high ridge to the front, Pfc. Schwab, unable to flank the enemy emplacement because of steep cliffs on either side, advanced up the face of the ridge in bold defiance of the intense barrage and, skillfully directing the fire of his flamethrower, quickly demolished the hostile gun position, thereby enabling his company to occupy the ridge. Suddenly a second enemy machine gun opened fire, killing and wounding several marines with its initial bursts. Estimating with split-second decision the tactical difficulties

confronting his comrades, Pfc. Schwab elected to continue his one-man assault despite a diminished supply of fuel for his flamethrower. Cool and indomitable, he moved forward in the face of a direct concentration of hostile fire, relentlessly closed with the enemy position, and attacked. Although severely wounded by a final vicious blast from the enemy weapon, Pfc. Schwab had succeeded in destroying two highly strategic Japanese gun positions during a critical stage of the operation and, by his dauntless, singlehanded efforts, had materially furthered the advance of his company. His aggressive initiative, outstanding valor, and professional skill throughout the bitter conflict sustain and enhance the highest traditions of the U.S. Naval Service.

2941 ◆ *SCOTT, NORMAN

Rank: Rear Admiral
Service: U.S. Navy
Birthday: 10 August 1889
Place of Birth: Indianapolis, Marion County, Indiana
Date of Death: 13 November 1942
Cemetery: A.B.M.C. Manila Cemetery (Wall of the Missing)—Manila, Philippine Islands
Entered Service at: Indiana
Unit: U.S.S. *Atlanta* (flagship)
Served as: Fleet Commander
Battle or Place of Action: Iron Bottom Sound, off Savo Island, Solomon Islands
Date of Action: 12-13 November 1942
Date of Presentation: 9 December 1942
Place of Presentation: The White House, presented by Pres. Franklin D. Roosevelt to his Son
Citation: For extraordinary heroism and conspicuous intrepidity above and beyond the call of duty during action against enemy Japanese forces off Savo Island on the night of 11–12 October and again on the night of 12–13 November 1942. In the earlier action, intercepting a Japanese task force intent upon storming our island positions and landing reinforcements at Guadalcanal, Rear Adm. Scott, with courageous skill and superb coordination of the units under his command, destroyed eight hostile vessels and put the others to flight. Again challenged, a month later, by the return of a stubborn and persistent foe, he led his force into a desperate battle against tremendous odds, directing close-range operations against the invading enemy until he himself was killed in the furious bombardment by their superior firepower. On each of these occasions his dauntless initiative, inspiring leadership, and judicious foresight in a crisis of grave responsibility contributed decisively to the rout of a powerful invasion fleet and to the consequent frustration of a formidable Japanese offensive. He gallantly gave his life in the service of his country.

2942 ◆ *SCOTT, ROBERT RAYMOND

Rank: Machinist's Mate First Class
Service: U.S. Navy
Birthday: 13 July 1915
Place of Birth: Massillon, Stark County, Ohio
Date of Death: 7 December 1941
Cemetery: Arlington National Cemetery (34-3939) (MH)—Arlington, Virginia
Entered Service at: Ohio
Unit: U.S.S. *California*
Battle or Place of Action: Pearl Harbor, Territory of Hawaii
Date of Action: 7 December 1941
Citation: For conspicuous devotion to duty, extraordinary courage, and complete disregard for his own life, above and beyond the call of duty, during the attack on the Fleet in Pearl Harbor by Japanese forces on 7 December 1941. The compartment in the U.S.S. *California* in which the air compressor to which Scott was assigned as his battle station was flooded as the result of a torpedo hit. The remainder of the personnel evacuated that compartment but Scott refused to leave, saying words to the effect "This is my station and I will stay and give them air as long as the guns are going."

2943 ◆ SCOTT, ROBERT SHELDON

Rank: Captain (rank at time of action: 2d Lieutenant) (highest rank: Colonel)
Service: U.S. Army
Birthday: 30 November 1913
Place of Birth: Washington, D.C.
Entered Service at: Santa Fe, Santa Fe County, New Mexico
Unit: 1st Platoon, Company C, 1st Battalion, 17th Infantry, 43d Infantry Division
Served as: Platoon Leader
Battle or Place of Action: near Munda Air Strip, New Georgia, Solomon Islands
Date of Action: 29 July 1943
G.O. Number, Date: 81, 14 October 1944
Date of Presentation: 14 October 1944
Place of Presentation: Aitape, New Guinea, presented by Maj. Gen. Leonard F. (Red) Wing
Citation: For conspicuous gallantry and intrepidity at the risk of his life above and beyond the call of duty near Munda Airstrip, New Georgia, Solomon Islands on 29 July 1943. After 27 days of bitter fighting, the enemy held a hilltop salient which commanded the approach to Munda Airstrip. Our troops were exhausted from prolonged battle and heavy casualties, but Lt. Scott advanced with the leading platoon of his company to attack the enemy position, urging his men forward in the face of enemy rifle and enemy machine-gun fire. He had pushed forward alone to a point midway across the barren hilltop within 75 yards of the enemy when the enemy launched a desperate counterattack, which if successful would have gained undisputed possession of the hill. Enemy riflemen charged out on the plateau, firing and throwing grenades as they moved to engage our troops. The company withdrew, but Lt. Scott, with only a blasted tree stump for cover, stood his ground against the wild enemy assault. By firing his carbine and throwing the grenades in his possession he momentarily stopped the enemy advance, using the brief respite to obtain more grenades. Disregarding small-arms fire and exploding grenades aimed at him, suffering a bullet wound in the left hand and a painful shrapnel wound in the head after his carbine had been shot from his hand, he threw

grenade after grenade with devastating accuracy until the beaten enemy withdrew. Our troops, inspired to renewed effort by Lt. Scott's intrepid stand and incomparable courage, swept across the plateau to capture the hill, and from this strategic position four days later captured Munda Airstrip.

2944 ◆ SHEA, CHARLES WILLIAM

Rank: Second Lieutenant (rank at time of action: Staff Sergeant) (highest rank: Colonel)
Service: U.S. Army
Birthday: 24 August 1921
Place of Birth: Bronx County, New York
Date of Death: 7 April 1994
Place of Death: Plainview, New York
Cemetery: Long Island National Cemetery (DSS 71-A)—Farmingdale, New York
Entered Service at: New York, New York
Unit: 2d Squad, 2d Platoon, Company F, 2d Battalion, 350th Infantry, 88th Infantry Division
Served as: Squad Leader
Battle or Place of Action: near Mount Damiano, Italy
Date of Action: 12 May 1944
G.O. Number, Date: 4, 12 January 1945
Date of Presentation: 1 December 1944
Place of Presentation: Montecatini, Italy, presented by Lt. Gen. Mark Clark
Citation: For conspicuous gallantry and intrepidity at the risk of life above and beyond the call of duty, on 12 May 1944, near Mount Damiano, Italy. As 2d Lt. Shea and his company were advancing toward a hill occupied by the enemy, three enemy machine guns suddenly opened fire, inflicting heavy casualties upon the company and halting its advance. Second Lt. Shea immediately moved forward to eliminate these machine-gun nests in order to enable his company to continue its attack. The deadly hail of machine-gun fire at first pinned him down, but boldly continuing his advance, 2d Lt. Shea crept up to the first nest. Throwing several hand grenades, he forced the four enemy soldiers manning this position to surrender, and disarming them, he sent them to the rear. He then crawled to the second machine-gun position and after a short firefight forced two more German soldiers to surrender. At this time, the third machine gun fired at him, and while deadly small-arms fire pitted the earth around him, 2d Lt. Shea crawled toward the nest. Suddenly he stood up and rushed the emplacement and with well-directed fire from his rifle, he killed all three of the enemy machine gunners. Second Lt. Shea's display of personal valor was an inspiration to the officers and men of his company.

2945 ◆ *SHERIDAN, CARL VERNON

Rank: Private First Class
Service: U.S. Army
Birthday: 5 January 1925
Place of Birth: Baltimore, Baltimore County, Maryland
Date of Death: 26 November 1944
Cemetery: Druid Ridge Cemetery (MH)—Pikesville, Maryland

Entered Service at: Baltimore, Baltimore County, Maryland
Unit: Company K, 2d Battalion, 47th Infantry, 9th Infantry Division
Served as: Bazooka Gunner
Battle or Place of Action: Frenzenberg Castle, Weisweiler, Germany
Date of Action: 26 November 1944
G.O. Number, Date: 43, 30 May 1945
Date of Presentation: June 1945
Place of Presentation: To his parents
Citation: Attached to the 2d Battalion of the 47th Infantry on 26 November 1944, for the attack on Frenzenberg Castle, in the vicinity of Weisweiler, Germany, Company K, after an advance of 1,000 yards through a shattering barrage of enemy artillery and mortar fire, had captured two buildings in the courtyard of the castle but was left with an effective fighting strength of only 35 men. During the advance, Pfc. Sheridan, acting as a bazooka gunner, had braved the enemy fire to stop and procure the additional rockets carried by his ammunition bearer who was wounded. Upon rejoining his company in the captured buildings, he found it in a furious fight with approximately 70 enemy paratroopers occupying the castle gatehouse. This was a solidly built stone structure surrounded by a deep water-filled moat 20 feet wide. The only approach to the heavily defended position was across the courtyard and over a drawbridge leading to a barricaded oaken door. Pfc. Sheridan, realizing that his bazooka was the only available weapon with sufficient power to penetrate the heavy oak planking, with complete disregard for his own safety left the protection of the buildings and in the face of heavy and intense small-arms and grenade fire, crossed the courtyard to the drawbridge entrance where he could bring direct fire to bear against the door. Although handicapped by the lack of an assistant, and a constant target for the enemy fire that burst around him, he skillfully and effectively handled his awkward weapon to place two well-aimed rockets into the structure. Observing that the door was only weakened, and realizing that a gap must be made for a successful assault, he loaded his last rocket, took careful aim, and blasted a hole through the heavy planks. Turning to his company he shouted, "Come on, let's get them!" With his .45 pistol blazing, he charged into the gaping entrance and was killed by the withering fire that met him. The final assault on Frenzenberg Castle was made through the gap which Pfc. Sheridan gave his life to create.

2946 ◆ *SHOCKLEY, WILLIAM RALPH

Rank: Private First Class
Service: U.S. Army
Birthday: 4 December 1918
Place of Birth: Bokoshe, LeFlore County, Oklahoma
Date of Death: 31 March 1945
Place of Death: Villa Verde Trail, Luzon, Philippine Islands
Cemetery: Floral Memorial Park—Selma, California
Entered Service at: Selma, Fresno County, California
Unit: Company L, 128th Infantry, 32d Infantry Division
Battle or Place of Action: Villa Verde Trail, Luzon, Philippine Islands

Date of Action: 31 March 1945
G.O. Number, Date: 89, 19 October 1945
Citation: He was in position with his unit on a hill when the enemy, after a concentration of artillery fire, launched a counterattack. He maintained his position under intense enemy fire and urged his comrades to withdraw, saying that he would "remain to the end" to provide cover. Although he had to clear two stoppages which impeded the reloading of his weapon, he halted one enemy charge. Hostile troops then began moving in on his left flank, and he quickly shifted his gun to fire on them. Knowing that the only route of escape was being cut off by the enemy, he ordered the remainder of his squad to withdraw to safety and deliberately remained at his post. He continued to fire until he was killed during the ensuing enemy charge. Later, four Japanese were found dead in front of his position. Pfc. Shockley, facing certain death, sacrificed himself to save his fellow soldiers, but the heroism and gallantry displayed by him enabled his squad to reorganize and continue its attack.

2947 ◆ SHOMO, WILLIAM ARTHUR

Rank: Major (highest rank: Colonel)
Service: U.S. Army Air Corps/U.S. Air Force
Birthday: 30 May 1918
Place of Birth: Jeannette, Westmoreland County, Pennsylvania
Date of Death: 25 June 1990
Place of Death: Warren, Pennsylvania
Cemetery: St. Clair Cemetery—Greenburg, Pennsylvania
Entered Service at: Westmoreland County, Pennsylvania
Unit: 82d Tactical Reconnaissance Squadron, 71st Reconnaissance Gp., 308th Bombardment Wing, 5th Air Force
Served as: Pilot of a P-51
Battle or Place of Action: over Luzon, Philippine Islands
Date of Action: 11 January 1945
G.O. Number, Date: 25, 7 April 1945
Date of Presentation: 3 April 1945
Place of Presentation: Luzon, Philippine Islands, presented by Maj. Gen. Ennis C. Whitehead
Citation: For conspicuous gallantry and intrepidity at the risk of his life above and beyond the call of duty. Maj. Shomo was lead pilot of a flight of two fighter planes charged with an armed photographic and strafing mission against the Aparri and Laoag airdromes. While en route to the objective, he observed an enemy twin engine bomber, protected by 12 fighters, flying about 2,500 feet above him and in the opposite direction. Although the odds were 13 to 2, Maj. Shomo immediately ordered an attack. Accompanied by his wingman he closed on the enemy formation in a climbing turn and scored hits on the leading plane of the third element, which exploded in midair. Maj. Shomo then attacked the second element from the left side of the formation and shot another fighter down in flames. When the enemy formed for counterattack, Maj. Shomo moved to the other side of the formation and hit a third fighter which exploded and fell. Diving below the bomber, he put a burst into its underside and it crashed and burned. Pulling up from this pass he encountered a fifth plane firing head on and destroyed it. He next dived upon the first element and shot down the lead plane; then diving to 300 feet in pursuit of another fighter he caught it with his initial burst and it crashed in flames. During this action his wingman had shot down three planes, while the three remaining enemy fighters had fled into a cloud bank and escaped. Maj. Shomo's extraordinary gallantry and intrepidity in attacking such a far superior force and destroying seven enemy aircraft in one action is unparalleled in the southwest Pacific area.

2948 ◆ *SHOUP, CURTIS F.

Rank: Staff Sergeant
Service: U.S. Army
Birthday: 11 January 1921
Place of Birth: Napanoch, Ulster County, New York
Date of Death: 7 January 1945
Cemetery: North Scriba Church Cemetery (MH)—Scriba, New York
Entered Service at: Buffalo, Erie County, New York
Unit: Company I, 346th Infantry, 87th Infantry Division
Battle or Place of Action: near Tillet, Belgium
Date of Action: 7 January 1945
G.O. Number, Date: 60, 25 July 1945
Citation: On 7 January 1945, near Tillet, Belgium, his company attacked German troops on rising ground. Intense hostile machine-gun fire pinned down and threatened to annihilate the American unit in an exposed position where frozen ground made it impossible to dig in for protection. Heavy mortar and artillery fire from enemy batteries was added to the storm of destruction falling on the Americans. Realizing that the machine gun must be silenced at all costs, S/Sgt. Shoup, armed with an automatic rifle, crawled to within 75 yards of the enemy emplacement. He found that his fire was ineffective from this position, and completely disregarding his own safety, stood up and grimly strode ahead into the murderous stream of bullets, firing his low-held weapon as he went. He was hit several times and finally was knocked to the ground. But he struggled to his feet and staggered forward until close enough to hurl a grenade, wiping out the enemy machine-gun nest with his dying action. By his heroism, fearless determination, and supreme sacrifice, S/Sgt. Shoup eliminated a hostile weapon which threatened to destroy his company and turned a desperate situation into victory.

2949 ◆ SHOUP, DAVID MONROE

Rank: Colonel (highest rank: General)
Service: U.S. Marine Corps
Birthday: 30 December 1904
Place of Birth: Battle Ground, Tippecanoe County, Indiana
Date of Death: 13 January 1983
Place of Death: Alexandria, Virginia
Cemetery: Arlington National Cemetery (7-A-189) (MH)—Arlington, Virginia
Entered Service at: Indiana
Unit: 2d Marines, 2d Marine Division
Served as: Commanding Officer of all Marines on Betio Island

Battle or Place of Action: Betio Island, Tarawa Atoll, Gilbert Islands
Date of Action: 20-22 November 1943
Date of Presentation: 22 January 1945
Place of Presentation: Presented by Sec. of the Navy James V. Forrestal
Citation: For conspicuous gallantry and intrepidity at the risk of his life above and beyond the call of duty as commanding officer of all Marine Corps troops in action against enemy Japanese forces on Betio Island, Tarawa Atoll, Gilbert Islands from 20–22 November 1943. Although severely shocked by an exploding enemy shell soon after landing at the pier and suffering from a serious, painful leg wound which had become infected, Col. Shoup fearlessly exposed himself to the terrific and relentless artillery, machine-gun, and rifle fire from hostile shore emplacements. Rallying his hesitant troops by his own inspiring heroism, he gallantly led them across the fringing reefs to charge the heavily fortified island and reinforce our hard-pressed, thinly held lines. Upon arrival onshore, he assumed command of all landed troops and, working without rest under constant, withering enemy fire during the next two days, conducted smashing attacks against unbelievably strong and fanatically defended Japanese positions despite innumerable obstacles and heavy casualties. By his brilliant leadership, daring tactics, and selfless devotion to duty, Col. Shoup was largely responsible for the final decisive defeat of the enemy, and his indomitable fighting spirit reflects great credit upon the U.S. Naval Service.

2950 ◆ SIGLER, FRANKLIN EARL

Rank: Private (highest rank: Private First Class)
Service: U.S. Marine Corps Reserve
Birthday: 6 November 1924
Place of Birth: Glen Ridge, Essex County, New Jersey
Date of Death: 20 January 1995
Cemetery: Arlington National Cemetery (12-2799)—Arlington, Virginia
Entered Service at: Little Falls, Passaic County, New Jersey
Unit: 2d Squad, 3d Platoon, Company F, 2d Battalion, 26th Marines, 5th Marine Division
Served as: Squad Leader
Battle or Place of Action: Iwo Jima, Volcano Islands
Date of Action: 14 March 1945
Date of Presentation: 5 October 1945
Place of Presentation: The White House, presented by Pres. Harry S. Truman
Citation: For conspicuous gallantry and intrepidity at the risk of his life above and beyond the call of duty while serving with the 2d Battalion, 26th Marines, 5th Marine Division, in action against enemy Japanese forces during the seizure of Iwo Jima in the Volcano Islands on 14 March 1945. Voluntarily taking command of his rifle squad when the leader became a casualty, Pvt. Sigler fearlessly led a bold charge against an enemy gun installation which had held up the advance of his company for several days and, reaching the position in advance of the others, assailed the emplacement with hand grenades and personally annihilated the entire crew. As additional Japanese troops opened fire from con-

cealed tunnels and caves above, he quickly scaled the rocks leading to the attacking guns, surprised the enemy with a furious one-man assault and, although severely wounded in the encounter, deliberately crawled back to his squad position where he steadfastly refused evacuation, persistently directing heavy machine-gun and rocket barrages on the Japanese cave entrances. Undaunted by the merciless rain of hostile fire during the intensified action, he gallantly disregarded his own painful wounds to aid casualties, carrying three wounded squad members to safety behind the lines and returning to continue the battle with renewed determination until ordered to retire for medical treatment. Stouthearted and indomitable in the face of extreme peril, Pvt. Sigler, by his alert initiative, unfaltering leadership, and daring tactics in a critical situation, effected the release of his besieged company from enemy fire and contributed essentially to its further advance against a savagely fighting enemy. His superb valor, resolute fortitude, and heroic spirit of self-sacrifice throughout reflect the highest credit upon Pvt. Sigler and the U.S. Naval Service.

2951 ◆ SILK, EDWARD A.

Rank: First Lieutenant
Service: U.S. Army
Birthday: 8 June 1916
Place of Birth: Johnstown, Cambria County, Pennsylvania
Date of Death: 19 November 1955
Cemetery: Arlington National Cemetery (30-1045-C) (MH)—Arlington, Virginia
Entered Service at: Johnstown, Cambria County, Pennsylvania
Unit: Company E, 398th Infantry, 100th Infantry Division
Served as: Weapons Platoon Leader
Battle or Place of Action: near St. Pravel, France
Date of Action: 23 November 1944
G.O. Number, Date: 97, 1 November 1945
Date of Presentation: 12 October 1945
Place of Presentation: The White House, presented by Pres. Harry S. Truman
Citation: First Lt. Edward A. Silk commanded the weapons platoon of Company E, 398th Infantry, on 23 November 1944, when the end battalion was assigned the mission of seizing high ground overlooking Moyenmoutier, France, prior to an attack on the city itself. His company jumped off in the lead at dawn and by noon had reached the edge of the woods in the vicinity of St. Pravel where scouts saw an enemy sentry standing guard before a farmhouse in a valley below. One squad, engaged in reconnoitering the area, was immediately pinned down by intense machine-gun and automatic-weapon fire from within the house. Skillfully deploying his light machine-gun section, 1st Lt. Silk answered enemy fire, but when 15 minutes had elapsed with no slackening of resistance, he decided to eliminate the strongpoint by a one-man attack. Running 100 yards across an open field to the shelter of a low stone wall directly in front of the farmhouse, he fired into the door and windows with his carbine; then, in full view of the enemy, vaulted the wall and dashed 50 yards through a hail of bullets to the left side of the house, where he hurled a grenade through a window, silencing a machine gun and

2952 ◆ SJOGREN, JOHN CARLETON

killing two gunners. In attempting to move to the right side of the house he drew fire from a second machine gun emplaced in the woodshed. With magnificent courage he rushed this position in the face of direct fire and succeeded in neutralizing the weapon and killing the two gunners by throwing grenades into the structure. His supply of grenades was by now exhausted, but undaunted, he dashed back to the side of the farmhouse and began to throw rocks through a window, demanding the surrender of the remaining enemy. Twelve Germans, overcome by his relentless assault and confused by his unorthodox methods, gave up to the lone American. By his gallant willingness to assume the full burden of the attack and the intrepidity with which he carried out his extremely hazardous mission, 1st Lt. Silk enabled his battalion to continue its advance and seize its objective.

2952 ◆ SJOGREN, JOHN CARLETON

Rank: Staff Sergeant (highest rank: Major)
Service: U.S. Army
Birthday: 19 August 1916
Place of Birth: Rockford, Kent County, Michigan
Date of Death: 30 August 1987
Cemetery: Rockford Cemetery (MH)—Rockford, Michigan
Entered Service at: Rockford, Kent County, Michigan
Unit: Company I, 160th Infantry, 40th Infantry Division
Battle or Place of Action: near San Jose Hacienda, Negros, Philippine Islands
Date of Action: 23 May 1945
G.O. Number, Date: 97, 1 November 1945
Date of Presentation: 12 October 1945
Place of Presentation: The White House, presented by Pres. Harry S. Truman
Citation: He led an attack against a high precipitous ridge defended by a company of enemy riflemen, who were entrenched in spider holes and supported by well-sealed pillboxes housing automatic weapons with interlocking bands of fire. The terrain was such that only one squad could advance at a time; and from a knoll atop a ridge a pillbox covered the only approach with automatic fire. Against this enemy stronghold, S/Sgt. Sjogren led the first squad to open the assault. Deploying his men, he moved forward and was hurling grenades when he saw that his next in command, at the opposite flank, was gravely wounded. Without hesitation he crossed 20 yards of exposed terrain in the face of enemy fire and exploding dynamite charges, moved the man to cover, and administered first aid. He then worked his way forward and, advancing directly into the enemy fire, killed eight Japanese in spider holes guarding the approach to the pillbox. Crawling to within a few feet of the pillbox while his men concentrated their bullets on the fire port, he began dropping grenades through the narrow firing slit. The enemy immediately threw two or three of these unexploded grenades out, and fragments from one wounded him in the hand and back. However, by hurling grenades through the embrasure faster than the enemy could return them, he succeeded in destroying the occupants. Despite his wounds, he directed his squad to follow him in a systematic attack on the remaining positions, which he eliminated in like manner, taking tremendous

risks, overcoming bitter resistance, and never hesitating in his relentless advance. To silence one of the pillboxes, he wrenched a light machine gun out through the embrasure as it was firing before blowing up the occupants with hand grenades. During this action, S/Sgt. Sjogren, by his heroic bravery, aggressiveness, and skill as a soldier, singlehandedly killed 43 enemy soldiers and destroyed nine pillboxes, thereby paving the way for his company's successful advance.

2953 ◆ SKAGGS JR., LUTHER

Rank: Private First Class (highest rank: Corporal)
Service: U.S. Marine Corps Reserve
Birthday: 3 March 1923
Place of Birth: Henderson, Henderson County, Kentucky
Date of Death: 6 April 1976
Place of Death: Sarasota, Florida
Cemetery: Arlington National Cemetery (46-1066-8) (MH)—Arlington, Virginia
Entered Service at: Kentucky
Unit: 3d Battalion, 3d Marines, 3d Marine Division
Served as: Squad Leader
Battle or Place of Action: Asan-Adelup Beachhead, Guam, Mariana Islands
Date of Action: 21-22 July 1944
Date of Presentation: 15 June 1945
Place of Presentation: The White House, presented by Pres. Harry S. Truman
Citation: For conspicuous gallantry and intrepidity at the risk of his life above and beyond the call of duty while serving as a squad leader with a mortar section of a rifle company in the 3d Battalion, 3d Marines, 3d Marine Division, during action against enemy Japanese forces on the Asan-Adelup beachhead, Guam, Mariana Islands, 21–22 July 1944. When the section leader became a casualty under a heavy mortar barrage shortly after landing, Pfc. Skaggs promptly assumed command and led the section through intense fire for a distance of 200 yards to a position from which to deliver effective coverage of the assault on a strategic cliff. Valiantly defending this vital position against strong enemy counterattacks during the night, Pfc. Skaggs was critically wounded when a Japanese grenade lodged in his foxhole and exploded, shattering the lower part of one leg. Quick to act, he applied an improvised tourniquet and, while propped up in his foxhole, gallantly returned the enemy's fire with his rifle and hand grenades for a period of eight hours, later crawling unassisted to the rear to continue the fight until the Japanese had been annihilated. Uncomplaining and calm throughout this critical period, Pfc. Skaggs served as a heroic example of courage and fortitude to other wounded men and, by his courageous leadership and inspiring devotion to duty, upheld the high traditions of the U.S. Naval Service.

2954 ◆ SLATON, JAMES DANIEL

Rank: Corporal
Service: U.S. Army
Birthday: 2 April 1912
Place of Birth: Laurel, Jones County, Mississippi

MEDAL OF HONOR RECIPIENTS

Date of Death: 25 February 1961
Place of Death: Laurel, Mississippi
Cemetery: Harmony Cemetery—Laurel, Mississippi
Entered Service at: Gulfport, Harrison County, Mississippi
Unit: Company K, 157th Infantry, 45th Infantry Division
Served as: Lead Scout
Battle or Place of Action: near Oliveto, Italy
Date of Action: 23 September 1943
G.O. Number, Date: 44, 30 May 1944
Date of Presentation: 7 June 1944
Place of Presentation: Algiers, presented by Lt. Gen. Jacob S. Devers
Citation: For conspicuous gallantry and intrepidity at the risk of life above and beyond the call of duty in action with the enemy in the vicinity of Oliveto, Italy, on 23 September 1943. Cpl. Slaton was lead scout of an infantry squad which had been committed to a flank to knock out enemy resistance which had succeeded in pinning two attacking platoons to the ground. Working ahead of his squad, Cpl. Slaton crept upon an enemy machine-gun nest and, assaulting it with his bayonet, succeeded in killing the gunner. When his bayonet stuck, he detached it from the rifle and killed another gunner with rifle fire. At that time he was fired upon by a machine gun to his immediate left. Cpl. Slaton then moved over open ground under constant fire to within throwing distance, and on his second try scored a direct hit on the second enemy machine-gun nest, killing two enemy gunners. At that time a third machine gun fired on him 100 yards to his front, and Cpl. Slaton killed both of these enemy gunners with rifle fire. As a result of Cpl. Slaton's heroic action in immobilizing three enemy machine-gun nests with bayonet, grenade, and rifle fire, the two rifle platoons which were receiving heavy casualties from enemy fire were able to withdraw to covered positions and again take the initiative. Cpl. Slaton withdrew under mortar fire on order of his platoon leader at dusk that evening. The heroic actions of Cpl. Slaton were far above and beyond the call of duty and are worthy of emulation.

2955 ◆ *SMITH, FURMAN L.

Rank: Private
Service: U.S. Army
Birthday: 11 May 1925
Place of Birth: Six Mile, Pickins County, South Carolina
Date of Death: 31 May 1944
Cemetery: Pleasant Hill Church Cemetery—Central, South Carolina
Entered Service at: Central, Pickins County, South Carolina
Unit: Company L, 135th Infantry, 34th Infantry Division
Served as: Rifleman
Battle or Place of Action: near Lanuvio, Italy
Date of Action: 31 May 1944
G.O. Number, Date: 6, 24 January 1945
Citation: For conspicuous gallantry and intrepidity at the risk of his life above and beyond the call of duty. In its attack on a strongpoint, an infantry company was held up by intense enemy fire. The group to which Pvt. Smith belonged was far in the lead when attacked by a force of 80 Germans. The squad leader and one other man were seriously wounded and

other members of the group withdrew to the company position, but Pvt. Smith refused to leave his wounded comrades. He placed them in the shelter of shell craters and then alone faced a strong enemy counterattack, temporarily checking it by his accurate rifle fire at close range, killing and wounding many of the foe. Against overwhelming odds, he stood his ground until shot down and killed, rifle in hand.

2956 ◆ SMITH, JOHN LUCIAN

Rank: Major (highest rank: Colonel)
Service: U.S. Marine Corps
Birthday: 26 December 1914
Place of Birth: Lexington, Cleveland County, Oklahoma
Date of Death: 9 June 1972
Cemetery: Arlington National Cemetery (3-2503-H-2)—Arlington, Virginia
Entered Service at: Oklahoma
Unit: Marine Fighting Squadron 223
Served as: Commanding Officer
Battle or Place of Action: Guadalcanal, Solomon Islands
Date of Action: August-September 1942
Date of Presentation: 24 February 1943
Place of Presentation: The White House, presented by Pres. Franklin D. Roosevelt
Citation: For conspicuous gallantry and heroic achievement in aerial combat above and beyond the call of duty as commanding officer of Marine Fighting Squadron 233 during operations against enemy Japanese forces in the Solomon Islands area, August–September 1942. Repeatedly risking his life in aggressive and daring attacks, Maj. Smith led his squadron against a determined force, greatly superior in numbers, personally shooting down 16 Japanese planes between 21 August and 15 September 1942. In spite of the limited combat experience of many of the pilots of this squadron, they achieved the notable record of a total of 83 enemy aircraft destroyed in this period, mainly attributable to the thorough training under Maj. Smith and to his intrepid and inspiring leadership. His bold tactics and indomitable fighting spirit, and the valiant and zealous fortitude of the men of his command not only rendered the enemy's attacks ineffective and costly to Japan, but contributed to the security of our advance base. His loyal and courageous devotion to duty sustains and enhances the finest traditions of the U.S. Naval Service.

2957 ◆ SMITH SR., MAYNARD HARRISON

Rank: Sergeant (highest rank: Staff Sergeant)
Service: U.S. Army Air Corps
Birthday: 19 May 1911
Place of Birth: Cairo, Michigan
Date of Death: 11 May 1984
Place of Death: Bay Pines, Florida
Cemetery: Arlington National Cemetery (66-7375) (MH)—Arlington, Virginia
Entered Service at: Cairo, Michigan
Unit: 423d Bombardment Squadron, 306th Bombardment Group, 8th Air Force
Served as: Gunner on a B-17

Battle or Place of Action: Brest, France
Date of Action: 1 May 1943
G.O. Number, Date: 38, 12 July 1943
Place of Presentation: Eighth Army Airfield, England, presented by Sec. of War Henry L. Stimson
Citation: For conspicuous gallantry and intrepidity in action above and beyond the call of duty. The aircraft of which Sgt. Smith was a gunner was subjected to intense enemy antiaircraft fire and determined fighter airplane attacks while returning from a mission over enemy-occupied continental Europe on 1 May 1943. The airplane was hit several times by antiaircraft fire and cannon shells of the fighter airplanes, two of the crew were seriously wounded, the aircraft's oxygen system shot out, and several vital control cables severed when intense fires were ignited simultaneously in the radio compartment and waist sections. The situation became so acute that three of the crew bailed out into the comparative safety of the sea. Sgt. Smith, then on his first combat mission, elected to fight the fire by himself, administered first aid to the wounded tail gunner, manned the waist guns, and fought the intense flames alternately. The escaping oxygen fanned the fire to such intense heat that the ammunition in the radio compartment began to explode, the radio, gun mount, and camera were melted, and the compartment completely gutted. Sgt. Smith threw the exploding ammunition overboard, fought the fire until all the firefighting aids were exhausted, manned the workable guns until the enemy fighter were driven away, further administered first aid to his wounded comrade, and then by wrapping himself in protecting cloth, completely extinguished the fire by hand. This soldier's gallantry in action, undaunted bravery, and loyalty to his aircraft and fellow crewmembers, without regard for his own personal safety, is an inspiration to the U.S Armed Forces.

2958 ◆ SODERMAN, WILLIAM ADOLPH

Rank: Private First Class
Service: U.S. Army
Birthday: 20 March 1912
Place of Birth: West Haven, New Haven County, Connecticut
Date of Death: 20 October 1980
Cemetery: Oak Grove Cemetery (MH)—West Haven, Connecticut
Entered Service at: West Haven, New Haven County, Connecticut
Unit: Company K, 9th Infantry, 2d Infantry Division
Served as: Bazooka Gunner
Battle or Place of Action: near Rocherath, Belgium
Date of Action: 17 December 1944
G.O. Number, Date: 97, 1 November 1945
Date of Presentation: 12 October 1945
Place of Presentation: The White House, presented by Pres. Harry S. Truman
Citation: Armed with a bazooka, he defended a key road junction near Rocherath, Belgium, on 17 December 1944, during the German Ardennes counteroffensive. After a heavy artillery barrage had wounded and forced the withdrawal of his assistant, he heard enemy tanks approaching the position

where he calmly waited in the gathering darkness of early evening until the five Mark V tanks which made up the hostile force were within point-blank range. He then stood up, completely disregarding the firepower that could be brought to bear upon him, and launched a rocket into the lead tank, setting it afire and forcing its crew to abandon it as the other tanks pressed on before Pfc. Soderman could reload. The daring bazookaman remained at his post all night under severe artillery, mortar, and machine-gun fire, awaiting the next onslaught, which was made shortly after dawn by five more tanks. Running along a ditch to meet them, he reached an advantageous point and there leaped to the road in full view of the tank gunners, deliberately aimed his weapon and disabled the lead tank. The other vehicles, thwarted by a deep ditch in their attempt to go around the crippled machine, withdrew. While returning to his post Pfc. Soderman, braving heavy fire to attack an enemy infantry platoon from close range, killed at least three Germans and wounded several others with a round from his bazooka. By this time, enemy pressure had made Company K's position untenable. Orders were issued for withdrawal to an assembly area, where Pfc. Soderman was located when he once more heard enemy tanks approaching. Knowing that elements of the company had not completed their disengaging maneuver and were consequently extremely vulnerable to an armored attack, he hurried from his comparatively safe position to meet the tanks. Once more he disabled the lead tank with a single rocket, his last; but before he could reach cover, machine-gun bullets from the tank ripped into his right shoulder. Unarmed and seriously wounded he dragged himself along a ditch to the American lines and was evacuated. Through his unfaltering courage against overwhelming odds, Pfc. Soderman contributed in great measure to the defense of Rocherath, exhibiting to a superlative degree the intrepidity and heroism with which American soldiers met and smashed the savage power of the last great German offensive.

2959 ◆ SORENSON, RICHARD KEITH

Rank: Private (highest rank: First Lieutenant)
Service: U.S. Marine Corps Reserve
Birthday: 28 August 1924
Place of Birth: Anoka, Anoka County, Minnesota
Entered Service at: Anoka, Anoka County, Minnesota
Unit: 1st Squad, 1st Platoon, Company M, 3d Battalion, 24th Marine Regiment, 4th Marine Division
Served as: Machinegun Crewman
Battle or Place of Action: Namur Island, Kwajalein Atoll, Marshall Islands
Date of Action: 1-2 February 1944
Date of Presentation: 19 July 1944
Place of Presentation: Seattle Naval Hospital, Seattle, Washington, presented by Maj. Gen. Joseph C. Fegan
Citation: For conspicuous gallantry and intrepidity at the risk of his life above and beyond the call of duty while serving with an assault battalion attached to the 4th Marine Division during the battle of Namur Island, Kwajalein Atoll, Marshall Islands on 1–2 February 1944. Putting up a brave defense against a particularly violent counterattack by the enemy dur-

ing invasion operations, Pvt. Sorenson and five other marines occupying a shell hole were endangered by a Japanese grenade thrown into their midst. Unhesitatingly, and with complete disregard for his own safety, Pvt. Sorenson hurled himself upon the deadly weapon, heroically taking the full impact of the explosion. As a result of his gallant action, he was severely wounded, but the lives of his comrades were saved. His great personal valor and exceptional spirit of self-sacrifice in the face of almost certain death were in keeping with the highest traditions of the U.S. Naval Service.

2960 ◆ *SPECKER, JOE C.

Rank: Sergeant
Service: U.S. Army
Birthday: 10 January 1921
Place of Birth: Odessa, Lafayette County, Missouri
Date of Death: 7 January 1944
Cemetery: Odessa Cemetery—Odessa, Missouri
Entered Service at: Odessa, Lafayette County, Missouri
Unit: 48th Combat Engineer Battalion
Battle or Place of Action: at Mount Porchia, Italy
Date of Action: 7 January 1944
G.O. Number, Date: 56, 12 July 1944
Citation: For conspicuous gallantry and intrepidity at the risk of life above and beyond the call of duty, in action involving actual conflict. On the night of 7 January 1944, Sgt. Specker, with his company, was advancing up the slope of Mount Porchia, Italy. He was sent forward on reconnaissance and on his return he reported to his company commander the fact that there was an enemy machine-gun nest and several well-placed snipers directly in the path and awaiting the company. Sgt. Specker requested and was granted permission to place one of his machine guns in a position near the enemy machine gun. Voluntarily and alone he made his way up the mountain with a machine gun and a box of ammunition. He was observed by the enemy as he walked along and was severely wounded by the deadly fire directed at him. Though so seriously wounded that he was unable to walk, he continued to drag himself over the jagged edges of rock and rough terrain until he reached the position at which he desired to set up his machine gun. He set up the gun so well and fired so accurately that the enemy machine-gun nest was silenced and the remainder of the snipers forced to retire, enabling his platoon to obtain their objective. Sgt. Specker was found dead at his gun. His personal bravery, self-sacrifice, and determination were an inspiration to his officers and fellow soldiers.

2961 ◆ SPURRIER, JUNIOR JAMES

Rank: Staff Sergeant
Service: U.S. Army
Birthday: 14 December 1922
Place of Birth: Russell County, Kentucky
Date of Death: 25 February 1984
Place of Death: Limestone, Tennessee
Cemetery: Mountain Home National Cemetery (HH-15-8) (MH)—Johnson, Tennessee
Entered Service at: Riggs, Kentucky

Unit: Company G, 134th Infantry, 35th Infantry Division
Served as: Automatic Rifleman
Battle or Place of Action: Achain, France
Date of Action: 13 November 1944
G.O. Number, Date: 18, 15 March 1945
Citation: For conspicuous gallantry and intrepidity at the risk of his life above and beyond the call of duty in action against the enemy at Achain, France, on 13 November 1944. At 2:00 P.M., Company G attacked the village of Achain from the east. S/Sgt. Spurrier armed with a BAR passed around the village and advanced alone. Attacking from the west, he immediately killed three Germans. From this time until dark, S/Sgt. Spurrier, using at different times his BAR and M1 rifle, American and German rocket launchers, a German automatic pistol, and hand grenades, continued his solitary attack against the enemy regardless of all types of small-arms and automatic-weapon fire. As a result of his heroic actions he killed an officer and 24 enlisted men and captured two officers and two enlisted men. His valor has shed fresh honor on the U.S. Armed Forces.

2962 ◆ *SQUIRES, JOHN C.

Rank: Sergeant (rank at time of action: Private First Class)
Service: U.S. Army
Birthday: 19 May 1925
Place of Birth: Louisville, Jefferson County, Kentucky
Date of Death: 23 May 1944
Cemetery: Zachary Taylor National Cemetery (A-1359) (MH)—Louisville, Kentucky
Entered Service at: Louisville, Jefferson County, Kentucky
Unit: Company A, 30th Infantry, 3d Infantry Division
Served as: Platoon Messenger
Battle or Place of Action: near Padiglione, Italy
Date of Action: 23-24 April 1944
G.O. Number, Date: 78, 2 October 1944
Citation: For conspicuous gallantry and intrepidity at the risk of his life above and beyond the call of duty. At the start of his company's attack on strongly held enemy positions in and around Spaccasassi Creek, near Padiglione, Italy, on the night of 23–24 April 1944, Pfc. Squires, platoon messenger, participating in his first offensive action, braved intense artillery, mortar, and antitank gun fire in order to investigate the effect of an antitank mine explosion on the leading platoon. Despite shells which burst close to him, Pfc. Squires made his way 50 yards forward to the advance element, noted the situation, reconnoitered a new route of advance, and informed his platoon leader of the casualties sustained and the alternate route. Acting without orders, he rounded up stragglers, organized a group of lost men into a squad and led them forward. When the platoon reached Spaccasassi Creek and established an outpost, Pfc. Squires, knowing that almost all of the noncommissioned officers were casualties, placed eight men in position of his own volition, disregarding enemy machine-gun, machine-pistol, and grenade fire which covered the creek draw. When his platoon had been reduced to 14 men, he brought up reinforcements twice. On each trip he went through barbed wire and across an enemy minefield, under intense artillery and mortar fire. Three times in the early morning the outpost was

counterattacked. Each time Pfc. Squires ignored withering enemy automatic fire and grenades which struck all around him, and fired hundreds of rounds of rifle, Browning automatic rifle, and captured German Spandau machine-gun ammunition at the enemy, inflicting numerous casualties and materially aiding in repulsing the attacks. Following these fights, he moved 50 yards to the south end of the outpost and engaged 21 German soldiers in individual machine-gun duels at point-blank range, forcing all 21 enemy to surrender and capturing 13 more Spandau guns. Learning the function of this weapon by questioning a German officer prisoner, he placed the captured guns in position and instructed other members of his platoon in their operation. The next night when the Germans attacked the outpost again he killed three and wounded more Germans with captured potato-masher grenades and fire from his Spandau gun. Pfc. Squires was killed in a subsequent action.

2963 ◆ *STEIN, TONY

Rank: Corporal
Service: U.S. Marine Corps Reserve
Birthday: 30 September 1921
Place of Birth: Dayton, Montgomery County, Ohio
Date of Death: 1 March 1945
Cemetery: Calvary Cemetery (MH)—Dayton, Ohio
Entered Service at: Ohio
Unit: Company A, 1st Battalion, 28th Marines, 5th Marine Division
Battle or Place of Action: Iwo Jima, Volcano Islands
Date of Action: 19 February 1945
Citation: For conspicuous gallantry and intrepidity at the risk of his life above and beyond the call of duty while serving with Company A, 1st Battalion, 28th Marines, 5th Marine Division, in action against enemy Japanese forces on Iwo Jima, in the Volcano Islands, 19 February 1945. The first man of his unit to be on station after hitting the beach in the initial assault, Cpl. Stein, armed with a personally improvised aircraft-type weapon, provided rapid covering fire as the remainder of his platoon attempted to move into position. When his comrades were stalled by a concentrated machine-gun and mortar barrage, he gallantly stood upright and exposed himself to the enemy's view, thereby drawing the hostile fire to his own person and enabling him to observe the location of the furiously blazing hostile guns. Determined to neutralize the strategically placed weapons, he boldly charged the enemy pillboxes one by one and succeeded in killing 20 of the enemy during the furious singlehanded assault. Cool and courageous under the merciless hail of exploding shells and bullets which fell on all sides, he continued to deliver the fire of his skillfully improvised weapon at a tremendous rate of speed which rapidly exhausted his ammunition. Undaunted, he removed his helmet and shoes to expedite his movements and ran back to the beach for additional ammunition, making a total of eight trips under intense fire and carrying or assisting a wounded man back each time. Despite the unrelenting savagery and confusion of battle, he rendered prompt assistance to his platoon whenever the unit was in position, directing the fire of a half-track against a stubborn pillbox until he

had effected the ultimate destruction of the Japanese fortification. Later in the day, although his weapon was twice shot from his hands, he personally covered the withdrawal of his platoon to the company position. Stouthearted and indomitable, Cpl. Stein, by his aggressive initiative, sound judgment, and unwavering d evotion to duty in the face of terrific odds, contributed materially to the fulfillment of his mission, and his outstanding valor throughout the bitter hours of conflict sustains and enhances the highest traditions of the U.S. Naval Service.

2964 ◆ STREET III, GEORGE LEVICK

Rank: Commander (highest rank: Captain)
Service: U.S. Navy
Birthday: 27 July 1913
Place of Birth: Richmond, Richmond County, Virginia
Entered Service at: Richmond, Richmond County, Virginia
Unit: U.S.S. *Tirante* SS 420
Served as: Commanding Officer
Battle or Place of Action: harbor of Quelpart Island off the coast of Korea
Date of Action: 14 April 1945
Date of Presentation: 5 October 1945
Place of Presentation: The White House, presented by Pres. Harry S. Truman
Citation: For conspicuous gallantry and intrepidity at the risk of his life above and beyond the call of duty as commanding officer of the U.S.S. *Tirante* during the first war patrol of that vessel against enemy Japanese surface forces in the harbor of Quelpart Island, off the coast of Korea on 14 April 1945. With the crew at surface battle stations, Comdr. (then Lt. Comdr.) Street approached the hostile anchorage from the south within 1,200 yards of the coast to complete a reconnoitering circuit of the island. Leaving the 10-fathom curve far behind, he penetrated the mined and shoal-obstructed waters of the restricted harbor despite numerous patroling vessels and in defiance of five shore-based radar stations and menacing aircraft. Prepared to fight it out on the surface if attacked, Comdr. Street went into action, sending two torpedoes with deadly accuracy into a large Japanese ammunition ship and exploding the target in a mountainous and blinding glare of white flames. With the *Tirante* instantly spotted by the enemy as she stood out plainly in the flare of light, he ordered the torpedo data computer set up while retiring and fired his last two torpedoes to disintegrate in quick succession the leading frigate and a similar flanking vessel. Clearing the gutted harbor at emergency full speed ahead, he slipped undetected along the shoreline, diving deep as a pursuing patrol dropped a pattern of depth charges at the point of submergence. His illustrious record of combat achievement during the first war patrol of the *Tirante* characterizes Comdr. Street as a daring and skillful leader and reflects the highest credit upon himself, his valiant command, and the U.S. Naval Service.

2965 ◆ *STRYKER, STUART S.

Rank: Private First Class
Service: U.S. Army

2967 ◆ *TERRY, SEYMOUR W.

Birthday: 30 October 1924
Place of Birth: Portland, Multnomah County, Oregon
Date of Death: 24 March 1945
Cemetery: Golden Gate National Cemetery (B-719)
(MH)—San Bruno, California
Entered Service at: Portland, Multnomah County, Oregon
Unit: Company E, 513th Parachute Infantry, 17th Airborne
Division
Served as: Platoon Runner
Battle or Place of Action: near Wesel, Germany
Date of Action: 24 March 1945
G.O. Number, Date: 117, 11 December 1945
Citation: He was a platoon runner, when the unit assembled
near Wesel, Germany, after a descent east of the Rhine.
Attacking along a railroad, Company E reached a point about
250 yards from a large building used as an enemy headquarters and manned by a powerful force of Germans with rifles,
machine guns, and four field pieces. One platoon made a
frontal assault but was pinned down by intense fire from the
house after advancing only 50 yards. So badly stricken that it
could not return the raking fire, the platoon was at the mercy
of the German machine gunners when Pfc. Stryker voluntarily
left a place of comparative safety, and, armed with a carbine,
ran to the head of the unit. In full view of the enemy and
under constant fire, he exhorted the men to get to their feet
and follow him. Inspired by his fearlessness, they rushed after
him in a desperate charge through an increased hail of bullets.
Twenty-five yards from the objective the heroic soldier was
killed by the enemy fusillades. His gallant and wholly voluntary action in the face of overwhelming firepower, however,
so encouraged his comrades and diverted the enemy's attention that other elements of the company were able to surround the house, capturing more than 200 hostile soldiers
and much equipment, besides freeing three members of an
American bomber crew held prisoner there. The intrepidity
and unhesitating self-sacrifice of Pfc. Stryker were in keeping
with the highest traditions of the military service.

2966 ◆ SWETT, JAMES ELMS

Rank: First Lieutenant (highest rank: Colonel)
Service: U.S. Marine Corps Reserve
Birthday: 15 June 1920
Place of Birth: Seattle, King County, Washington
Entered Service at: San Mateo, San Mateo County,
California
Unit: Marine Fighting Squadron 221, Marine Aircraft
Group 12, 1st Marine Air Wing
Served as: Division Leader
Battle or Place of Action: Solomon Islands area
Date of Action: 7 April 1943
Date of Presentation: 12 October 1943
Place of Presentation: Espirito Santo Island, New Hebrides,
presented by Maj. Gen. Ralph Mitchell
Citation: For extraordinary heroism and personal valor
above and beyond the call of duty, as division leader of
Marine Fighting Squadron 221 with Marine Aircraft Group
12, 1st Marine Aircraft Wing, in action against enemy
Japanese aerial forces in the Solomon Islands area, 7 April

1943. In a daring flight to intercept a wave of 150 Japanese
planes, 1st Lt. Swett unhesitatingly hurled his four-plane division into action against a formation of 15 enemy bombers and
personally exploded three hostile planes in midair with accurate and deadly fire during his dive. Although separated from
his division while clearing the heavy concentration of antiaircraft fire, he boldly attacked six enemy bombers, engaged the
first four in turn and, unaided, shot down all in flames.
Exhausting his ammunition as he closed the fifth enemy
Japanese bomber, he relentlessly drove his attack against terrific opposition which partially disabled his engine, shattered the
windscreen, and slashed his face. In spite of this, he brought
his battered plane down with skillful precision in the water off
Tulagi without further injury. The superb airmanship and
tenacious fighting spirit which enabled 1st Lt. Swett to
destroy seven enemy bombers in a single flight were in keeping with the highest traditions of the U.S. Naval Service.

2967 ◆ *TERRY, SEYMOUR W.

Rank: Captain
Service: U.S. Army
Birthday: 11 December 1918
Place of Birth: Little Rock, Pulaski County, Arkansas
Date of Death: 11 May 1945
Cemetery: Roselawn Cemetery—Little Rock, Arkansas
Entered Service at: Little Rock, Pulaski County, Arkansas
Unit: Company B, 382d Infantry, 96th Infantry Division
Served as: Company Commander
Battle or Place of Action: Zebra Hill, Okinawa, Ryukyu
Islands
Date of Action: 11 May 1945
G.O. Number, Date: 23, 6 March 1946
Citation: First Lt. Terry was leading an attack against heavily
defended Zebra Hill when devastating fire from five pillboxes
halted the advance. He braved the hail of bullets to secure
satchel charges and white phosphorus grenades, and then ran
30 yards directly at the enemy with an ignited charge to the
first stronghold, demolished it, and moved on to the other
pillboxes, bombarding them with his grenades and calmly
cutting down their defenders with rifle fire as they attempted
to escape. When he had finished this job by sealing the four
pillboxes with explosives, he had killed 20 Japanese and
destroyed three machine guns. The advance was again held
up by an intense grenade barrage which inflicted several casualties. Locating the source of enemy fire in trenches on the
reverse slope of the hill, 1st Lt. Terry, burdened by six satchel
charges, launched a one-man assault. He wrecked the enemy's
defenses by throwing explosives into their positions and he
himself accounted for 10 of the hostile troops killed when his
men overran the area. Pressing forward again toward a nearby
ridge, his two assault platoons were stopped by slashing
machine-gun and mortar fire. He fearlessly ran across 100
yards of fire-swept terrain to join the support platoon and
urge it on in a flanking maneuver. This thrust, too, was halted
by stubborn resistance. First Lt. Terry began another one-
man drive, hurling grenades upon the strongly entrenched
defenders until they fled in confusion, leaving five dead
behind them. Inspired by this bold action, the support pla-

toon charged the retreating enemy and annihilated them. Soon afterward, while organizing his company to repulse a possible counterattack, the gallant company commander was mortally wounded by the burst of an enemy mortar shell. By his indomitable fighting spirit, brilliant leadership, and unwavering courage in the face of tremendous odds, 1st Lt. Terry made possible the accomplishment of his unit's mission and set an example of heroism in keeping with the highest traditions of the military service.

2968 ◆ *THOMAS, HERBERT JOSEPH

Rank: Sergeant
Service: U.S. Marine Corps Reserve
Birthday: 8 February 1918
Place of Birth: Columbus, Franklin County, Ohio
Date of Death: 7 November 1943
Cemetery: Sunset Memorial Park—South Charleston, West Virginia
Entered Service at: West Virginia
Unit: 3d Marines, 3d Marine Division
Battle or Place of Action: Koromokina River, Bougainville Island, Solomon Islands
Date of Action: 7 November 1943
Citation: For extraordinary heroism and conspicuous gallantry above and beyond the call of duty while serving with the 3d Marines, 3d Marine Division, in action against enemy Japanese forces during the battle at the Koromokina River, Bougainville Island, Solomon Islands, on 7 November 1943. Although several of his men were struck by enemy bullets as he led his squad through dense jungle undergrowth in the face of severe hostile machine-gun fire, Sgt. Thomas and his group fearlessly pressed forward into the center of the Japanese position and destroyed the crews of two machine guns by accurate rifle fire and grenades. Discovering a third gun more difficult to approach, he carefully placed his men closely around him in strategic positions from which they were to charge after he had thrown a grenade into the emplacement. When the grenade struck vines and fell back into the midst of the group, Sgt. Thomas deliberately flung himself upon it to smother the explosion, valiantly sacrificing his life for his comrades. Inspired by his selfless action, his men unhesitatingly charged the enemy machine gun and, with fierce determination, killed the crew and several other nearby-defenders. The splendid initiative and extremely heroic conduct of Sgt. Thomas in carrying out his prompt decision with full knowledge of his fate reflect great credit upon himself and the U.S. Naval Service. He gallantly gave his life for his country.

2969 ◆ *THOMAS, WILLIAM H.

Rank: Private First Class
Service: U.S. Army
Birthday: 13 January 1923
Place of Birth: Wynne, Cross County, Arkansas
Date of Death: 22 April 1945
Cemetery: A.B.M.C. Manila Cemetery (F-16-90)—Manila, Philippine Islands
Entered Service at: Ypsilanti, Washtenaw County, Michigan

Unit: 149th Infantry, 38th Infantry Division
Served as: Automatic Rifleman
Battle or Place of Action: Zambales Mountains, Luzon, Philippine Islands
Date of Action: 22 April 1945
G.O. Number, Date: 81, 24 September 1945
Citation: He was a member of the leading squad of Company B, which was attacking along a narrow, wooded ridge. The enemy, strongly entrenched in camouflaged emplacements on the hill beyond, directed heavy fire and hurled explosive charges on the attacking riflemen. Pfc. Thomas, an automatic rifleman, was struck by one of these charges, which blew off both his legs below the knees. He refused medical aid and evacuation, and continued to fire at the enemy until his weapon was put out of action by an enemy bullet. Still refusing aid, he threw his last two grenades. He destroyed three of the enemy after suffering the wounds from which he died later that day. The effective fire of Pfc. Thomas prevented the repulse of his platoon and assured the capture of the hostile position. His magnificent courage and heroic devotion to duty provided a lasting inspiration for his comrades.

2970 ◆ *THOMASON, CLYDE A.

Rank: Sergeant
Service: U.S. Marine Corps Reserve
Birthday: 23 May 1914
Place of Birth: Atlanta, Fulton County, Georgia
Date of Death: 18 August 1942
Place of Death: Makin Island, Gilbert Islands
Cemetery: National Memorial Cemetery of the Pacific (Wall of the Missing)—Honolulu, Hawaii
Entered Service at: Georgia
Unit: 2d Marine Raider Battalion
Battle or Place of Action: Makin Island, Gilbert Islands
Date of Action: 17-18 August 1942
Date of Presentation: 20 January 1943
Place of Presentation: Presented by Sec. of the Navy James Forrestal to stepmother, Mrs. Amy M. Thomason
Citation: For conspicuous heroism and intrepidity above and beyond the call of duty during the Marine Raider Expedition against the Japanese-held island of Makin on 17–18 August 1942. Leading the advance element of the assault echelon, Sgt. Thomason disposed his men with keen judgment and discrimination and, by his exemplary leadership and great personal valor, exhorted them to like fearless efforts. On one occasion, he dauntlessly walked up to a house which concealed an enemy Japanese sniper, forced in the door, and shot the man before he could resist. Later in the action, while leading an assault on an enemy position, he gallantly gave his life in the service of his country. His courage and loyal devotion to duty in the face of grave peril were in keeping with the finest traditions of the U.S. Naval Service.

2971 ◆ THOMPSON, MAX

Rank: Sergeant (highest rank: Technical Sergeant)
Service: U.S. Army

Birthday: 21 July 1922
Place of Birth: Bethel, Pitt County, North Carolina
Entered Service at: Canton, Haywood County, North Carolina
Unit: 3d Squad, 3d Platoon, Company K, 3d Battalion, 18th Infantry, 1st Infantry Division
Served as: Assistant Squad Leader
Battle or Place of Action: near Haaren, Germany
Date of Action: 18 October 1944
G.O. Number, Date: 47, 18 June 1945
Date of Presentation: 18 June 1945
Place of Presentation: near Cheb, Czechoslovakia, presented by Lt. Gen. Clarence R. Hubner
Citation: On 18 October 1944, Company K, 18th Infantry, occupying a position on a hill near Haaren, Germany, was attacked by an enemy infantry battalion supported by tanks. The assault was preceded by an artillery concentration, lasting an hour, which inflicted heavy casualties on the company. While engaged in moving wounded men to cover, Sgt. Thomason observed that the enemy had overrun the positions of the 3d Platoon. He immediately attempted to stem the enemy's advance singlehandedly. He manned an abandoned machine gun and fired on the enemy until a direct hit from a hostile tank destroyed the gun. Shaken and dazed, Sgt. Thomason picked up an automatic rifle and, although alone against the enemy force which was pouring into the gap in our lines, he fired burst after burst, halting the leading elements of the attack and dispersing those following. Throwing aside his automatic rifle, which had jammed, he took up a rocket gun, and fired on a light tank, setting it on fire. By evening the enemy had been driven from the greater part of the captured position but still held three pillboxes. Sgt. Thomason's squad was assigned the task of dislodging the enemy from these emplacements. Darkness having fallen and finding that fire of his squad was ineffective from a distance, Sgt. Thomason crawled forward alone to within 20 yards of one of the pillboxes and fired grenades into it. The Germans holding the emplacement concentrated their fire upon him. Though wounded, he held his position fearlessly, continued his grenade fire, and finally forced the enemy to abandon the blockhouse. Sgt. Thomason's courageous leadership inspired his men and materially contributed to the clearing of the enemy from his last remaining hold on this important hill position.

2972 ◆ *THORNE, HORACE MARVIN

Rank: Corporal
Service: U.S. Army
Birthday: 29 September 1918
Place of Birth: Keansburg, Monmouth County, New Jersey
Date of Death: 21 December 1944
Cemetery: Fairview Cemetery (MH)—Red Bank, New Jersey
Entered Service at: Keyport, Monmouth County, New Jersey
Unit: Troop D, 89th Cavalry Reconnaissance Squadron, 9th Armored Division
Served as: Light Machine Gunner

Battle or Place of Action: near Grufflingen, Belgium
Date of Action: 21 December 1944
G.O. Number, Date: 80, 19 September 1945
Citation: He was the leader of a combat patrol on 21 December 1944, near Grufflingen, Belgium, with the mission of driving German forces from dug-in positions in a heavily wooded area. As he advanced his light machine gun, a German Mark III tank emerged from the enemy position and was quickly immobilized by fire from American light tanks supporting the patrol. Two of the enemy tankmen attempted to abandon their vehicle but were killed by Cpl. Thorne's shots before they could jump to the ground. To complete the destruction of the tank and its crew, Cpl. Thorne left his covered position and crept forward alone through intense machine-gun fire until close enough to toss two grenades into the tank's open turret, killing two more Germans. He returned across the same fire-beaten zone as heavy mortar fire began falling in the area, seized his machine gun, and, without help, dragged it to the knocked-out tank and set it up on the vehicle's rear deck. He fired short rapid bursts into the enemy positions from his advantageous but exposed location, killing or wounding eight. Two enemy machine-gun crews abandoned their positions and retreated in confusion. His gun jammed; but rather than leave his self-chosen post he attempted to clear the stoppage; enemy small-arms fire, concentrated on the tank, killed him instantly. Cpl. Thorne, displaying heroic initiative and intrepid fighting qualities, inflicted costly casualties on the enemy and insured the success of his patrol's mission by the sacrifice of his life.

2973 ◆ *THORSON, JOHN F.

Rank: Private First Class
Service: U.S. Army
Birthday: 10 May 1920
Place of Birth: Armstrong, Emmet County, Iowa
Date of Death: 29 October 1944
Cemetery: Keokuk National Cemetery (D-71) (MH)—Keokuk, Iowa
Entered Service at: Armstrong, Emmet County, Iowa
Unit: Company G, 17th Infantry, 7th Infantry Division
Served as: Automatic Rifleman
Battle or Place of Action: Dagami, Leyte, Philippine Islands
Date of Action: 28 October 1944
G.O. Number, Date: 58, 19 July 1945
Citation: He was an automatic rifleman on 28 October 1944, in the attack on Dagami, Leyte, Philippine Islands. A heavily fortified enemy position consisting of pillboxes and supporting trenches held up the advance of his company. His platoon was ordered to outflank and neutralize the strongpoint. Voluntarily moving well out in front of his group, Pvt. Thorson came upon an enemy fire trench defended by several hostile riflemen and, disregarding the intense fire directed at him, attacked singlehandedly. He was seriously wounded and fell about six yards from the trench. Just as the remaining 20 members of the platoon reached him, one of the enemy threw a grenade into their midst. Shouting a warning and making a final effort, Pvt. Thorson rolled onto the grenade and smothered the explosion with his body. He was instantly

killed, but his magnificent courage and supreme self-sacrifice prevented the injury and possible death of his comrades and remain with them as a lasting inspiration.

2974 ◆ *TIMMERMAN, GRANT FREDERICK

Rank: Sergeant
Service: U.S. Marine Corps
Birthday: 14 February 1919
Place of Birth: Americus, Lyon County, Kansas
Date of Death: 8 July 1944
Cemetery: National Memorial Cemetery of the Pacific (A-844) (MH)—Honolulu, Hawaii
Entered Service at: Kansas
Unit: 2d Battalion, 6th Marines, 2d Marine Division
Served as: Tank Commander
Battle or Place of Action: Saipan, Mariana Islands
Date of Action: 8 July 1944
Citation: For conspicuous gallantry and intrepidity at the risk of his life above and beyond the call of duty as tank commander serving with the 2d Battalion, 6th Marines, 2d Marine Division, during action against enemy Japanese forces on Saipan, Mariana Islands, on 8 July 1944. Advancing with his tank a few yards ahead of the infantry in support of a vigorous attack on hostile positions, Sgt. Timmerman maintained steady fire from his antiaircraft sky-mount machine gun until progress was impeded by a series of enemy trenches and pillboxes. Observing a target of opportunity, he immediately ordered the tank stopped and, mindful of the danger from the muzzle blast as he prepared to open fire with the 75-mm., fearlessly stood up in the exposed turret and ordered the infantry to hit the deck. Quick to act, as a grenade, hurled by the Japanese, was about to drop into the open turret hatch, Sgt. Timmerman unhesitatingly blocked the opening with his body, holding the grenade against his chest and taking the brunt of the explosion. His exceptional valor and loyalty in saving his men at the cost of his own life reflect the highest credit upon Sgt. Timmerman and the U.S. Naval Service. He gallantly gave his life in the service of his country.

2975 ◆ *TOMICH, PETER

Rank: Chief Watertender
Service: U.S. Navy
Birthday: 3 June 1893
Place of Birth: Prolog, Austria
Date of Death: 7 December 1941
Cemetery: National Memorial Cemetery of the Pacific (Wall of the Missing)—Honolulu, Hawaii
Entered Service at: New Jersey
Unit: U.S.S. Utah
Served as: Chief Watertender
Battle or Place of Action: Pearl Harbor, Territory of Hawaii
Date of Action: 7 December 1941
Date of Presentation: 4 January 1944
Place of Presentation: U.S.S. Tomich, presented to the ship by Rear Adm. Monroe Kelly. When the ship was decommissioned on September 20, 1946, Tomich's Medal of Honor was returned to the Navy Department. (No living relatives could be found.) On May 25, 1947 Uath Gov. Herbert B. Maw formally named Tomich an honorary citizen of Utah, the state in whose honor the battleship on which Tomich gave his life was named. On the occasion Rear Adm. Mahlon S. Tisdale, Commander of the U.S. Navy Base, San Francisco, awarded Tomich's Medal of Honor to the State of Utah as the official guardian of the dead hero. The presentation was made with full military honors in the rotunda of the Utah Capitol
Citation: For distinguished conduct in the line of his profession, and extraordinary courage and disregard of his own safety, during the attack on the Fleet in Pearl Harbor by the Japanese forces on 7 December 1941. Although realizing that the ship was capsizing as a result of enemy bombing and torpedoing, Tomich remained at his post in the engineering plant of the U.S.S. Utah until he saw that all boilers were secured and all fireroom personnel had left their stations, and by so doing lost his own life.

2976 ◆ TOMINAC, JOHN JOSEPH

Rank: First Lieutenant (highest rank: Colonel)
Service: U.S. Army
Birthday: 29 April 1922
Place of Birth: Conemaugh, Cambria County, Pennsylvania
Entered Service at: Conemaugh, Cambria County, Pennsylvania
Unit: 3d Platoon, Company I, 3d Battalion, 15th Infantry, 3d Infantry Division
Served as: Platoon Leader
Battle or Place of Action: Saulx de Vesoul, France
Date of Action: 12 September 1944
G.O. Number, Date: 20, 29 March 1945
Date of Presentation: 23 April 1945
Place of Presentation: Zepman Stadium, Nuremberg, Germany, presented by Lt. Gen. Alexander M. Patch III
Citation: For conspicuous gallantry and intrepidity at the risk of life above and beyond the call of duty on 12 September 1944, in an attack on Saulx de Vesoul, France. First Lt. Tominac charged alone over 50 yards of exposed terrain onto an enemy roadblock to dispatch a three-man crew of German machine gunners with a single burst from his Thompson machine gun. After smashing the enemy outpost, he led one of his squads in the annihilation of a second hostile group defended by mortar, machine-gun, automatic-pistol, rifle, and grenade fire, killing about 30 of the enemy. Reaching the suburbs of the town, he advanced 50 yards ahead of his men to reconnoiter a third enemy position which commanded the road with a 77-mm SP gun supported by infantry elements. The SP gun opened fire on his supporting tank, setting it afire with a direct hit. A fragment from the same shell painfully wounded 1st Lt. Tominac in the shoulder, knocking him to the ground. As the crew abandoned the M-4 tank, which was running downhill toward the enemy, 1st Lt. Tominac picked himself up and jumped onto the hull of the burning vehicle. Despite withering enemy machine-gun, mortar, pistol, and sniper fire, which was ricocheting off the hull and turret of the M-4, 1st Lt. Tominac climbed into the turret and gripped the .50-caliber antiaircraft machine gun.

Plainly silhouetted against the sky, painfully wounded, and with the tank burning beneath his feet, he directed bursts of machine-gun fire on the roadblock, the SP gun, and the supporting German infantrymen, and forced the enemy to withdraw from his prepared position. Jumping off the tank before it exploded, 1st Lt. Tominac refused evacuation despite his painful wound. Calling upon a sergeant to extract the shell fragments from his shoulder with a pocketknife, he continued to direct the assault, led his squad in a hand-grenade attack against a fortified position occupied by 32 of the enemy armed with machine guns, machine pistols, and rifles, and compelle d them to surrender. His outstanding heroism and exemplary leadership resulted in the destruction of four successive enemy defensive positions, surrender of a vital sector of the city Saulx de Vesoul, and the death or capture of at least 60 of the enemy.

2977 ◆ *TOWLE, JOHN RODERICK

Rank: Private
Service: U.S. Army
Birthday: 19 October 1924
Place of Birth: Cleveland, Cuyahoga County, Ohio
Date of Death: 21 September 1944
Cemetery: Calvary Cemetery (MH)—Cleveland, Ohio
Entered Service at: Cleveland, Cuyahoga County, Ohio
Unit: Company C, 504th Parachute Infantry, 82d Airborne Division
Served as: Rocket Launcher Gunner
Battle or Place of Action: near Oosterhout, Holland
Date of Action: 21 September 1944
G.O. Number, Date: 18, 15 March 1945
Date of Presentation: 25 March 1945
Place of Presentation: Fort Knox, Kentucky, presented to his parents by Maj. Gen. C.L. Scott
Citation: For conspicuous gallantry and intrepidity at the risk of life above and beyond the call of duty on 21 September 1944, near Oosterhout, Holland. The rifle company in which Pvt. Towle served as rocket launcher gunner was occupying a defensive position in the west sector of the recently established Nijmegen bridgehead when a strong enemy force of approximately 100 infantry supported by two tanks and a half-track formed a counterattack. With full knowledge of the disastrous consequences resulting not only to his company but to the entire bridgehead by an enemy breakthrough, Pvt. Towle immediately and without orders left his foxhole and moved 200 yards in the face of intense small-arms fire to a position on an exposed dike roadbed. From this precarious position Pvt. Towle fired his rocket launcher at and hit both tanks to his immediate front. Armored skirting on both tanks prevented penetration by the projectiles, but both vehicles withdrew slightly damaged. Still under intense fire and fully exposed to the enemy, Pvt. Towle then engaged a nearby house which nine Germans had entered and were using as a strongpoint, and with one round killed all nine. Hurriedly replenishing his supply of ammunition, Pvt. Towle, motivated only by his high conception of duty which called for the destruction of the enemy at any cost, then rushed approximately 125 yards through grazing

enemy fire to an exposed position from which he could engage the enemy half-track with his rocket launcher. While in a kneeling position preparatory to firing on the enemy vehicle, Pvt. Towle was mortally wounded by a mortar shell. By his heroic tenacity, at the price of his life, Pvt. Towle saved the lives of many of his comrades and was directly instrumental in breaking up the enemy counterattack.

2978 ◆ TREADWELL, JACK LEMASTER

Rank: Captain (rank at time of action: First Lieutenant) (highest rank: Colonel)
Service: U.S. Army
Birthday: 31 March 1919
Place of Birth: Ashland, Clay County, Alabama
Date of Death: 12 December 1977
Cemetery: Fort Sill Post Cemetery (Y-11-8) (MH)—Fort Sill, Oklahoma
Entered Service at: Snyder, Kiowa County, Oklahoma
Unit: Company F, 180th Infantry, 45th Infantry Division
Served as: Commanding Officer
Battle or Place of Action: near Nieder-Wurzbach, Germany
Date of Action: 18 March 1945
G.O. Number, Date: 79, 14 September 1945
Date of Presentation: 23 August 1945
Place of Presentation: The White House, presented by Pres. Harry S. Truman
Citation: Capt. Treadwell (then 1st Lt.), commanding officer of Company F, near Nieder-Wurzbach, Germany, in the Siegfried line, singlehandedly captured six pillboxes and 18 prisoners. Murderous enemy automatic and rifle fire with intermittent artillery bombardments had pinned down his company for hours at the base of a hill defended by concrete fortifications and interlocking trenches. Eight men sent to attack a single point had all become casualties on the bare slope when Capt. Treadwell, armed with a submachine gun and hand grenades, went forward alone to clear the way for his stalled company. Over the terrain devoid of cover and swept by bullets, he fearlessly advanced, firing at the aperture of the nearest pillbox and, when within range, hurling grenades at it. He reached the pillbox, thrust the muzzle of his gun through the port, and drove four Germans out with their hands in the air. A fifth was found dead inside. Waving these prisoners back to the American lines, he continued under terrible, concentrated fire to the next pillbox and took it in the same manner. In this fort he captured the commander of the hill defenses, whom he sent to the rear with the other prisoners. Never slackening his attack, he then ran across the crest of the hill to a third pillbox, traversing this distance in full view of hostile machine gunners and snipers. He was again successful in taking the enemy position. The Germans quickly fell prey to his further rushes on three more pillboxes in the confusion and havoc caused by his whirlwind assaults and capture of their commander. Inspired by the electrifying performance of their leader, the men of Company F stormed after him and overwhelmed resistance on the entire hill, driving a wedge into the Siegfried line and making it possible for their battalion to take its objective. By his courageous willingness to face nearly impossible odds and by his

overwhelming one-man offensive, Capt. Treadwell reduced a heavily fortified, seemingly impregnable enemy sector.

2979 ◆ *TRUEMPER, WALTER EDWARD

Rank: Second Lieutenant
Service: U.S. Army Air Corps
Birthday: 31 October 1918
Place of Birth: Aurora, Du Page County, Illinois
Date of Death: 20 February 1944
Cemetery: St. Paul's Lutheran Cemetery—Aurora, Illinois
Entered Service at: Aurora, Du Page County, Illinois
Unit: 510th Bombardment Squadron, 351st Bombardment Group, 8th Air Force
Served as: Navigator of a B-17
Battle or Place of Action: over Leipzig, Germany
Date of Action: 20 February 1944
G.O. Number, Date: 52, 22 June 1944
Citation: For conspicuous gallantry and intrepidity at the risk of life above and beyond the call of duty in action against the enemy in connection with a bombing mission over enemy-occupied Europe on 20 February 1944. The aircraft on which 2d Lt. Truemper was serving as navigator was attacked by a squadron of enemy fighters with the result that the copilot was killed outright, the pilot wounded and rendered unconscious, the radio operator wounded, and the plane severely damaged. Nevertheless, 2d Lt. Truemper and other members of his crew managed to right the plane and fly it back to their home station, where they contacted the control tower and reported the situation. Second Lt. Truemper and the engineer volunteered to attempt to land the plane. Other members of the crew were ordered to jump, leaving 2d Lt. Truemper and the engineer aboard. After observing the distressed aircraft from another plane, 2d Lt. Truemper's commanding officer decided the damaged plane could not be landed by the inexperienced crew and ordered them to abandon it and parachute to safety. Demonstrating unsurpassed courage and heroism, 2d Lt. Truemper and the engineer replied that the pilot was still alive but could not be moved and that they would not desert him. They were then told to attempt a landing. After two unsuccessful efforts their plane crashed into an open field in a third attempt to land. Second Lt. Truemper, the engineer, and the wounded pilot were killed.

2980 ◆ *TURNER, DAY G.

Rank: Sergeant
Service: U.S. Army
Place of Birth: Berwick, Columbia County, Pennsylvania
Date of Death: 8 February 1945
Cemetery: A.B.M.C. Luxembourg Cemetery (E-10-72)—Luxembourg City, Luxembourg
Entered Service at: Nescopeck, Luzerne County, Pennsylvania
Unit: Company B, 319th Infantry, 80th Infantry Division
Served as: Squad Leader
Battle or Place of Action: at Dahl, Luxembourg
Date of Action: 8 January 1945
G.O. Number, Date: 49, 28 June 1945

Citation: He commanded a nine-man squad with the mission of holding a critical flank position. When overwhelming numbers of the enemy attacked under cover of withering artillery, mortar, and rocket fire, he withdrew his squad into a nearby house, determined to defend it to the last man. The enemy attacked again and again and were repulsed with heavy losses. Supported by direct tank fire, they finally gained entrance, but the intrepid sergeant refused to surrender although five of his men were wounded and one was killed. He boldly flung a can of flaming oil at the first wave of attackers, dispersing them, and fought doggedly from room to room, closing with the enemy in fierce hand-to-hand encounters. He hurled hand grenade for hand grenade, bayoneted two fanatical Germans who rushed a doorway he was defending, and fought on with the enemy's weapons when his own ammunition was expended. The savage fight raged for four hours, and finally, when only three men of the defending squad were left unwounded, the enemy surrendered. Twenty-five prisoners were taken, 11 enemy dead and a great number of wounded were counted. Sgt. Turner's valiant stand will live on as a constant inspiration to his comrades. His heroic, inspiring leadership, his determination, and courageous devotion to duty exemplify the highest traditions of the military service.

2981 ◆ TURNER, GEORGE BENTON

Rank: Private First Class
Service: U.S. Army
Birthday: 27 June 1899
Place of Birth: Longview, Gregg County, Texas
Date of Death: 29 June 1963
Cemetery: Arlington National Cemetery (41-589) (MH)—Arlington, Virginia
Entered Service at: Los Angeles, Los Angeles County, California
Unit: Battery C, 499th Armored Field Artillery Battalion, 14th Armored Division
Battle or Place of Action: Philippsbourg, France
Date of Action: 3 January 1945
G.O. Number, Date: 79, 14 September 1945
Date of Presentation: 23 August 1945
Place of Presentation: The White House, presented by Pres. Harry S. Truman
Citation: At Philippsbourg, France, he was cut off from his artillery unit by an enemy armored infantry attack. Coming upon a friendly infantry company withdrawing under the vicious onslaught, he noticed two German tanks and approximately 75 supporting foot soldiers advancing down the main street of the village. Seizing a rocket launcher, he advanced under intense small-arms and cannon fire to meet the tanks and, standing in the middle of the road, fired at them, destroying one and disabling the second. From a nearby half-track he then dismounted a machine gun, placed it in the open street and fired into the enemy infantrymen, killing or wounding a great number and breaking up the attack. In the American counterattack which followed, two supporting tanks were disabled by an enemy antitank gun. Firing a light machine gun from the hip, Pfc. Turner held off the enemy so

that the crews of the disabled vehicles could extricate themselves. He ran through a hail of fire to one of the tanks which had burst into flames and attempted to rescue a man who had been unable to escape; but an explosion of the tank's ammunition frustrated his effort and wounded him painfully. Refusing to be evacuated, he remained with the infantry until the following day, driving off an enemy patrol with serious casualties, assisting in capturing a hostile strongpoint, and voluntarily and fearlessly driving a truck through heavy enemy fire to deliver wounded men to the rear aid station. The great courage displayed by Pfc. Turner and his magnificently heroic initiative contributed materially to the defense of the French town and inspired the troops about him.

2982 ◆ URBAN, MATT LOUIS

Rank: Lieutenant Colonel (rank at time of action: Captain)
Service: U.S. Army
Birthday: 25 August 1919
Place of Birth: Buffalo, Erie County, New York
Date of Death: 4 March 1995
Place of Death: Holland, Michigan
Cemetery: Arlington National Cemetery (7A-40) (MH)—Arlington, Virginia
Entered Service at: Fort Bragg, Cumberland County, North Carolina
Unit: Company F, 2d Battalion, 60th Infantry Regiment, 9th Infantry Division
Served as: Company Commander/Battalion Commander
Battle or Place of Action: France & Belgium
Date of Action: 14 June-3 September 1944
Date of Presentation: 19 July 1980
Place of Presentation: The White House, presented by Pres. Jimmy Carter
Citation: Lt. Col. (then Capt.) Matt Urban, 112-22-2414, United States Army, who distinguished himself by a series of bold, heroic actions, exemplified by singularly outstanding combat leadership, personal bravery, and tenacious devotion to duty, during the period from 14 June to 3 September 1944 while assigned to the 2d Battalion, 60th Infantry Regiment, 9th Infantry Division. On 14 June, Capt. Urban's company, attacking at Renouf, France, encountered heavy enemy small-arms and tank fire. The enemy tanks were unmercifully raking his unit's positions and inflicting heavy casualties. Capt. Urban, realizing that his company was in imminent danger of being decimated, armed himself with a bazooka. He worked his way with an ammo carrier through hedgerows, under a continuing barrage of fire, to a point near the tanks. He brazenly exposed himself to the enemy fire and, firing the bazooka, destroyed both tanks. Responding to Capt. Urban's action, his company moved forward and routed the enemy. Later that same day, still in the attack near Orglandes, Capt. Urban was wounded in the leg by direct fire from a 37-mm tank gun. He refused evacuation and continued to lead his company until they moved into defensive positions for the night. At 0500 hours the next day, still in the attack near Orglandes, Capt. Urban, though badly wounded, directed his company in another attack. One hour later he was again wounded. Suffering from two wounds, one serious,

he was evacuated to England. In mid-July, while recovering from his wounds, he learned of his unit's severe losses in the hedgerows of Normandy. Realizing his unit's need for battle-tested leaders, he voluntarily left the hospital and hitchhiked his way back to his unit near Saint-Lo, France. Arriving at the 2d Battalion Command Post at 1130 hours on 25 July, he found that his unit had jumped off at 1100 hours in the first attack of "Operation Cobra." Still limping from his leg wound, Capt. Urban made his way forward to retake command of h is company. He found his company held up by strong enemy opposition. Two supporting tanks had been destroyed and another, intact but with no tank commander or gunner, was not moving. He located a lieutenant in charge of the support tanks and directed a plan of attack to eliminate the enemy strongpoint. The lieutenant and a sergeant were immediately killed by the heavy enemy fire when they tried to mount the tank. Capt. Urban, though physically hampered by his leg wound and knowing quick action had to be taken, dashed through the scathing fire and mounted the tank. With enemy bullets ricocheting from the tank, Capt. Urban ordered the tank forward and, completely exposed to the enemy fire, manned the machine gun and placed devastating fire on the enemy. His action, in the face of enemy fire, galvanized the battalion into action and they attacked and destroyed the enemy position. On 2 August, Capt. Urban was wounded in the chest by shell fragments and, disregarding the recommendation of the battalion surgeon, again refused evacuation. On 6 August, Capt. Urban became the commander of the 2d Battalion. On 15 August, he was again wounded but remained with his unit. On 3 September, the 2d Battalion was given the mission of establishing a crossing-point on the Meuse River near Heer, Belgium. The enemy planned to stop the advance of the Allied Army by concentrating heavy forces at the Meuse. The 2d Battalion, attacking toward the crossing-point, encountered fierce enemy artillery, small-arms, and mortar fire which stopped the attack. Capt. Urban quickly moved from his command post to the lead position of the battalion. Reorganizing the attacking elements, he personally led a charge toward the enemy's strongpoint. As the charge moved across the open terrain, Capt. Urban was seriously wounded in the neck. Although unable to talk above a whisper from the paralyzing neck wound, and in danger of losing his life, he refused to be evacuated until the enemy was routed and his battalion had secured the crossing-point on the Meuse River. Capt. Urban's personal leadership, limitless bravery, and repeated extraordinary exposure to enemy fire served as an inspiration to his entire battalion. His valorous and intrepid actions reflect the utmost credit upon him and uphold the noble traditions of the United States Army.

2983 ◆ *VALDEZ, JOSE F.

Rank: Private First Class
Service: U.S. Army
Birthday: 3 January 1925
Place of Birth: Governador, New Mexico
Date of Death: 17 February 1945
Cemetery: Santa Fe National Cemetery (Q-29) (MH)—Santa Fe, New Mexico

Entered Service at: Pleasant Grove, Utah County, Utah
Unit: Company B, 7th Infantry, 3d Infantry Division
Battle or Place of Action: near Rosenkrantz, France
Date of Action: 25 January 1945
G.O. Number, Date: 16, 8 February 1946
Citation: He was on outpost duty with five others when the enemy counterattacked with overwhelming strength. From his position near some woods 500 yards beyond the American lines he observed a hostile tank about 75 yards away, and raked it with automatic rifle fire until it withdrew. Soon afterward he saw three Germans stealthily approaching through the woods. Scorning cover as the enemy soldiers opened up with heavy automatic-weapon fire from a range of 30 yards, he engaged in a firefight with the attackers until he had killed all three. The enemy quickly launched an attack with two full companies of infantrymen, blasting the patrol with murderous concentrations of automatic and rifle fire and beginning an encircling movement which forced the patrol leader to order a withdrawal. Despite the terrible odds, Pfc. Valdez immediately volunteered to cover the maneuver, and as the patrol one by one plunged through a hail of bullets toward the American lines, he fired burst after burst into the swarming enemy. Three of his companions were wounded in their dash for safety and he was struck by a bullet that entered his stomach and, passing through his body, emerged from his back. Overcoming agonizing pain, he regained control of himself and resumed his firing position, delivering a protective screen of bullets until all others of the patrol were safe. By field telephone he called for artillery and mortar fire on the Germans and corrected the range until he had shells falling within 50 yards of his position. For 15 minutes he refused to be dislodged by more than 200 of the enemy; then, seeing that the barrage had broken the counterattack, he dragged himself back to his own lines. He died later as a result of his wounds. Through his valiant, intrepid stand and at the cost of his own life, Pfc. Valdez made it possible for his comrades to escape, and was directly responsible for repulsing an attack by vastly superior enemy forces.

2984 ◆ *VANCE JR., LEON ROBERT

Rank: Lieutenant Colonel
Service: U.S. Army Air Corps
Birthday: 11 August 1916
Place of Birth: Enid, Garfield County, Oklahoma
Date of Death: 26 July 1944
Place of Death: Between Iceland & Newfoundland
Cemetery: A.B.M.C. Cambridge Cemetery (Wall of the Missing)—Cambridge, England
Entered Service at: Garden City, Nassau County, New York
Unit: 489th Bombardment Group, 8th Air Force
Served as: Deputy Group Commander/Pilot of a B-24-H
Battle or Place of Action: over Wimereaux, France
Date of Action: 5 June 1944
G.O. Number, Date: 1, 4 January 1945
Date of Presentation: 11 October 1946
Place of Presentation: Enid Air Force Base, Enid, Oklahoma, presented by Maj. Gen. James P. Hodges to his Widow and Daughter

Citation: For conspicuous gallantry and intrepidity above and beyond the call of duty on 5 June 1944, when he led a Heavy Bombardment Group in an attack against defended enemy coastal positions in the vicinity of Wimereaux, France. Approaching the target, his aircraft was hit repeatedly by anti-aircraft fire which seriously crippled the ship, killed the pilot, and wounded several members of the crew, including Lt. Col. Vance, whose right foot was practically severed. In spite of his injury, and with three engines lost to the flak, he led his formation over the target, bombing it successfully. After applying a tourniquet to his leg with the aid of the radar operator, Lt. Col. Vance, realizing that the ship was approaching a stall altitude with the one remaining engine failing, struggled to a semi-upright position beside the copilot and took over control of the ship. Cutting the power and feathering the last engine he put the aircraft in glide sufficiently steep to maintain his airspeed. Gradually losing altitude, he at last reached the English coast, whereupon he ordered all members of the crew to bail out as he knew they would all safely make land. But he received a message over the interphone system which led him to believe one of the crewmembers was unable to jump due to injuries; so he made the decision to ditch the ship in the channel, thereby giving this man a chance for life. To add further to the danger of ditching the ship in his crippled condition, there was a 500-pound bomb hung up in the bomb bay. Unable to climb into the seat vacated by the copilot, since his foot, hanging on to his leg by a few tendons, had become lodged behind the copilot's seat, he nevertheless made a successful ditching while lying on the floor using only aileron and elevators for control and the side window of the cockpit for visual reference. On coming to rest in the water the aircraft commenced to sink rapidly with Lt. Col. Vance pinned in the cockpit by the upper turret which had crash ed in during the landing. As it was settling beneath the waves an explosion occurred which threw Lt. Col. Vance clear of the wreckage. After clinging to a piece of floating wreckage until he could muster enough strength to inflate his life vest, he began searching for the crewmember whom he believed to be aboard. Failing to find anyone he began swimming and was found approximately 50 minutes later by an air-sea rescue craft. By his extraordinary flying skill and gallant leadership, despite his grave injury, Lt. Col. Vance led his formation to a successful bombing of the assigned target and returned the crew to a point where they could bail out with safety. His gallant and valorous decision to ditch the aircraft in order to give the crewmember he believed to be aboard a chance for life exemplifies the highest traditions of the U.S. Armed Forces.

2985 ◆ VANDEGRIFT, ALEXANDER ARCHER

Rank: Major General (highest rank: General)
Service: U.S. Marine Corps
Birthday: 13 March 1887
Place of Birth: Charlottesville, Charlottesville County, Virginia
Date of Death: 8 May 1973
Place of Death: Bethesda, Maryland
Cemetery: Arlington National Cemetery (2-4965-B-RH)—Arlington, Virginia

Entered Service at: Virginia
Unit: 1st Marine Division
Served as: Commanding Officer
Battle or Place of Action: Solomon Islands
Date of Action: 7 August-9 December 1942
Citation: For outstanding and heroic accomplishment above and beyond the call of duty as commanding officer of the 1st Marine Division in operations against enemy Japanese forces in the Solomon Islands during the period from 7 August to 9 December 1942. With the adverse factors of weather, terrain, and disease making his task a difficult and hazardous undertaking, and with his command eventually including sea, land, and air forces of Army, Navy, and Marine Corps, Maj. Gen. Vandegrift achieved marked success in commanding the initial landings of the U.S. forces in the Solomon Islands and in their subsequent occupation. His tenacity, courage, and resourcefulness prevailed against a strong, determined, and experienced enemy, and the gallant fighting spirit of the men under his inspiring leadership enabled them to withstand aerial, land, and sea bombardment, to surmount all obstacles, and leave a disorganized and ravaged enemy. This dangerous but vital mission, accomplished at the constant risk of his life, resulted in securing a valuable base for further operations of our forces against the enemy, and its successful completion reflects great credit upon Maj. Gen. Vandegrift, his command, and the U.S. Naval Service.

2986 ◆ *VAN NOY JR., NATHAN

Rank: Private
Service: U.S. Army
Birthday: 9 August 1924
Place of Birth: Grace, Caribou County, Idaho
Date of Death: 17 October 1943
Cemetery: Grace Cemetery (MH)—Grace, Idaho
Entered Service at: Preston, Franklin County, Idaho
Unit: Headquarters Company, Shore Battalion, 532d Engineer Boat & Shore Regiment
Served as: Machine Gunner
Battle or Place of Action: near Finschafen, New Guinea
Date of Action: 17 October 1943
G.O. Number, Date: 17, 26 February 1944
Date of Presentation: 17 March 1944
Place of Presentation: Preston, Idaho, presented by Col. A.E. Merrill to his Mother
Citation: For conspicuous gallantry and intrepidity above and beyond the call of duty in action with the enemy near Finschafen, New Guinea, on 17 October 1943. When wounded late in September, Pvt. Van Noy declined evacuation and continued on duty. On 17 October 1943 he was gunner in charge of a machine-gun post only five yards from the water's edge when the alarm was given that three enemy barges loaded with troops were approaching the beach in the early morning darkness. One landing barge was sunk by Allied fire, but the other two beached 10 yards from Pvt. Van Noy's emplacement. Despite his exposed position, he poured a withering hail of fire onto the debarking enemy troops. His loader was wounded by a grenade and evacuated. Pvt. Van Noy, also grievously wounded, remained at his post, ignoring

calls of nearby soldiers urging him to withdraw, and continued to fire with deadly accuracy. He expended every round and was found, covered with wounds, dead beside his gun. In this action Pvt. Van Noy killed at least half of the 39 enemy taking part in the landing. His heroic tenacity at the price of his life not only saved the lives of many of his comrades, but enabled them to annihilate the attacking detachment.

2987 ◆ *VAN VALKENBURGH, FRANKLIN

Rank: Captain
Service: U.S. Navy
Birthday: 5 April 1888
Place of Birth: Minneapolis, Hennepin County, Minnesota
Date of Death: 7 December 1941
Place of Death: Pearl Harbor, Territory of Hawaii
Cemetery: National Memorial Cemetery of the Pacific (Wall of the Missing)—Honolulu, Hawaii
Entered Service at: Wisconsin
Unit: U.S.S. *Arizona*
Served as: Commanding Officer
Battle or Place of Action: Pearl Harbor, Territory of Hawaii
Date of Action: 7 December 1941
Citation: For conspicuous devotion to duty, extraordinary courage and complete disregard of his own life, during the attack on the Fleet in Pearl Harbor, Territory of Hawaii, by Japanese forces on 7 December 1941. As commanding officer of the U.S.S. *Arizona*, Capt. Van Valkenburgh gallantly fought his ship until the U.S.S. *Arizona* blew up from magazine explosions and a direct bomb hit on the bridge which resulted in the loss of his life.

2988 ◆ *VAN VOORHIS, BRUCE AVERY

Rank: Lieutenant Commander (highest rank: Commander)
Service: U.S. Navy
Birthday: 29 January 1908
Place of Birth: Aberdeen, Grays Harbor County, Washington
Date of Death: 6 July 1943
Place of Death: off Greenwich Island, Solomon Islands
Cemetery: Jefferson Barracks National Cemetery (one of six in a group burial) (79-279-280-281)—St. Louis, Missouri; Arlington National Cemetery (MI-86) (MH)—Arlington, Virginia
Entered Service at: Nevada
Unit: Bombing Squadron 102
Served as: Squadron Commander/Pilot of a PB4Y-1
Battle or Place of Action: Greenwich Island, Solomon Islands
Date of Action: 6 July 1943
Citation: For conspicuous gallantry and intrepidity at the risk of his life above and beyond the call of duty as squadron commander of Bombing Squadron 102 and as plane commander of a PB4Y-1 patrol bomber operating against the enemy on Japanese-held Greenwich Island during the battle of the Solomon Islands, 6 July 1943. Fully aware of the limited chance of surviving an urgent mission, voluntarily undertaken to prevent a surprise Japanese attack against our forces,

Lt. Comdr. Van Voorhis took off in total darkness on a perilous 700-mile flight without escort or support. Successful in reaching his objective despite treacherous and varying winds, low visibility, and difficult terrain, he fought a lone but relentless battle under fierce antiaircraft fire and overwhelming aerial opposition. Forced lower and lower by pursuing planes, he coolly persisted in his mission of destruction. Abandoning all chances of a safe return, he executed six bold, ground-level attacks to demolish the enemy's vital radio station, installations, antiaircraft guns and crews with bombs and machine-gun fire, and to destroy one fighter plane in the air and three on the water. Caught in his own bomb blast, Lt. Comdr. Van Voorhis crashed into the lagoon off the beach, sacrificing himself in a singlehanded fight against almost insuperable odds, to make a distinctive contribution to our continued offensive in driving the Japanese from the Solomons and, by his superb daring, courage, and resoluteness of purpose, enhanced the finest traditions of the U.S. Naval Service. He gallantly gave his life for his country.

2989 ◆ *VIALE, ROBERT M.

Rank: Second Lieutenant
Service: U.S. Army
Birthday: 21 April 1916
Place of Birth: Bayside, Humboldt County, California
Date of Death: 5 February 1945
Cemetery: Ocean View Cemetery (MH)—Eureka, California
Entered Service at: Ukiah, Mendocino County, California
Unit: Company K, 148th Infantry, 37th Infantry Division
Served as: Platoon Leader
Battle or Place of Action: Manila, Luzon, Philippine Islands
Date of Action: 5 February 1945
G.O. Number, Date: 92, 25 October 1945
Citation: He displayed conspicuous gallantry and intrepidity above and beyond the call of duty. Forced by the enemy's detonation of prepared demolitions to shift the course of his advance through the city, he led the 1st platoon toward a small bridge, where heavy fire from three enemy pillboxes halted the unit. With two men he crossed the bridge behind screening grenade smoke to attack the pillboxes. The first he knocked out himself while covered by his men's protecting fire; the other two were silenced by one of his companions and a bazooka team which he had called up. He suffered a painful wound in the right arm during the action. After his entire platoon had joined him, he pushed ahead through mortar fire and encircling flames. Blocked from the only escape route by an enemy machine gun placed at a street corner, he entered a nearby building with his men to explore possible means of reducing the emplacement. In one room he found civilians huddled together, in another, a small window placed high in the wall and reached by a ladder. Because of the relative position of the window, ladder, and enemy emplacement, he decided that he, being left-handed, could better hurl a grenade than one of his men who had made an unsuccessful attempt. Grasping an armed grenade, he started up the ladder. His wounded right arm weakened and, as he tried to steady himself, the grenade fell to the floor. In the

five seconds before the grenade would explode, he dropped down, recovered the grenade and looked for a place to dispose of it safely. Finding no way to get rid of the grenade without exposing his own men or the civilians to injury or death, he turned to the wall, held it close to his body and bent over it as it exploded. Second Lt. Viale died in a few minutes, but his heroic act saved the lives of others.

2990 ◆ *VILLEGAS, YSMAEL R.

Rank: Staff Sergeant
Service: U.S. Army
Birthday: 21 March 1924
Place of Birth: Casa Blanca, California
Date of Death: 20 March 1945
Place of Death: Villa Verde Trail, Philippine Islands
Cemetery: Riverside National Cemetery (5-1178) (MH)—Riverside, California
Entered Service at: Casa Blanca, California
Unit: Company F, 127th Infantry, 32d Infantry Division
Served as: Squad Leader
Battle or Place of Action: Villa Verde Trail, Luzon, Philippine Islands
Date of Action: 20 March 1945
G.O. Number, Date: 89, 19 October 1945
Citation: He was a squad leader when his unit, in a forward position, clashed with an enemy strongly entrenched in connected caves and foxholes on commanding ground. He moved boldly from man to man, in the face of bursting grenades and demolition charges, through heavy machine-gun and rifle fire, to bolster the spirit of his comrades. Inspired by his gallantry, his men pressed forward to the crest of the hill. Numerous enemy riflemen, refusing to flee, continued firing from their foxholes. S/Sgt. Villegas, with complete disregard for his own safety and the bullets which kicked up the dirt at his feet, charged an enemy position and, firing at point-blank range, killed the Japanese in a foxhole. He rushed a second foxhole while bullets missed him by inches and killed one more of the enemy. In rapid succession he charged a third, a fourth, a fifth foxhole, each time destroying the enemy within. The fire against him increased in intensity, but he pressed onward to attack a sixth position. As he neared his goal, he was hit and killed by enemy fire. Through his heroism and indomitable fighting spirit, S/Sgt. Villegas, at the cost of his life, inspired his men to a determined attack in which they swept the enemy from the field.

2991 ◆ VLUG, DIRK JOHN

Rank: Private First Class
Service: U.S. Army
Birthday: 20 August 1916
Place of Birth: Maple Lake, Wright County, Minnesota
Entered Service at: Grand Rapids, Kent County, Michigan
Unit: Headquarters Company, 1st Battalion, 126th Infantry, 32d Infantry Division
Served as: Ammunition Bearer
Battle or Place of Action: near Limon, Leyte, Philippine Islands

Date of Action: 15 December 1944
G.O. Number, Date: 60, 26 June 1946
Date of Presentation: 14 June 1946
Place of Presentation: The White House, presented by Pres. Harry S. Truman
Citation: He displayed conspicuous gallantry and intrepidity above and beyond the call of duty when an American road-block on the Ormoc Road was attacked by a group of enemy tanks. He left his covered position and, with a rocket launcher and six rounds of ammunition, advanced alone under intense machine-gun and 37-mm fire. Loading singlehandedly, he destroyed the first tank, killing its occupants with a single round. As the crew of the second tank started to dismount and attack him, he killed one of the foe with his pistol, forcing the survivors to return to their vehicle, which he then destroyed with a second round. Three more hostile tanks moved up the road, so he flanked the first and eliminated it, and then, despite a hail of enemy fire, pressed forward again to destroy another. With his last round of ammunition he struck the remaining vehicle, causing it to crash down a steep embankment. Through his sustained heroism in the face of superior forces, Pfc. Vlug alone destroyed five enemy tanks and greatly facilitated successful accomplishment of his battalion's mission.

2992 ◆ VOSLER, FORREST LEE "WOODY"

Rank: Technical Sergeant
Service: U.S. Army Air Corps
Birthday: 29 July 1923
Place of Birth: Lyndonville, Orleans County, New York
Date of Death: 17 February 1992
Place of Death: Titusville, Florida
Cemetery: Arlington National Cemetery (60-4924) (MH)—Arlington, Virginia
Entered Service at: Rochester, Monroe County, New York
Unit: 358th Bombardment Squadron, 303d Bombardment Group, 8th Air Force
Served as: Radio Operator/Gunner on a B-17
Battle or Place of Action: over Bremen, Germany
Date of Action: 20 December 1943
G.O. Number, Date: 73, 6 September 1944
Date of Presentation: 31 August 1944
Place of Presentation: The White House (Oval Office), presented by Pres. Franklin D. Roosevelt
Citation: For conspicuous gallantry in action against the enemy above and beyond the call of duty while serving as a radio operator-air gunner on a heavy bombardment aircraft in a mission over Bremen, Germany, 20 December 1943. After bombing the target, the aircraft in which T/Sgt. Vosler was serving was severely damaged by antiaircraft fire, forced out of formation, and immediately subjected to repeated vicious attacks by enemy fighters. Early in the engagement a 20-mm cannon shell exploded in the radio compartment, painfully wounding T/Sgt. Vosler in the legs and thighs. At about the same time a direct hit on the tail of the ship seriously wounded the tail gunner and rendered the tail guns inoperative. Realizing the great need for firepower in protecting the vulnerable tail of the ship, T/Sgt. Vosler, with grim determina-

tion, kept up a steady stream of deadly fire. Shortly thereafter another 20-mm enemy shell exploded, wounding T/Sgt. Vosler in the chest and about the face. Pieces of metal lodged in both eyes, impairing his vision to such extent that he could only distinguish blurred shapes. Displaying remarkable tenacity and courage, he kept firing his guns and declined to take first-aid treatment. The radio equipment had been rendered inoperative during the battle, and when the pilot announced that he would have to ditch, although unable to see and working entirely by touch, T/Sgt. Vosler finally got the set operating and sent out distress signals despite several lapses into unconsciousness. When the ship ditched, T/Sgt. Vosler managed to get out on the wing by himself and hold the wounded tail gunner from slipping off until the other crewmembers could help him into the dinghy. T/Sgt. Vosler's actions on this occasion were an inspiration to all serving with him. The extraordinary courage, coolness, and skill he displayed in the face of great odds, when handicapped by injuries that would have incapacitated the average crewmember, were outstanding.

2993 ◆ WAHLEN, GEORGE EDWARD

Rank: Pharmacist's Mate Second Class (highest rank: Major, USA ret.)
Service: U.S. Navy
Birthday: 8 August 1924
Place of Birth: Ogden, Weber County, Utah
Entered Service at: Ogden, Weber County, Utah
Unit: 1st Platoon, Company F, 2d Battalion, 26th Marines, 5th Marine Division
Served as: Medical Corpsman
Battle or Place of Action: Iwo Jima, Volcano Islands
Date of Action: 3 March 1945
Date of Presentation: 5 October 1945
Place of Presentation: The White House, presented by Pres. Harry S. Truman
Citation: For conspicuous gallantry and intrepidity at the risk of his life above and beyond the call of duty while serving with the 2d Battalion, 26th Marines, 5th Marine Division, during action against enemy Japanese forces on Iwo Jima in the Volcano Group on 3 March 1945. Painfully wounded in the bitter action on 26 February, Wahlen remained on the battlefield, advancing well forward of the front lines to aid a wounded marine and carrying him back to safety despite a terrific concentration of fire. Tireless in his ministrations, he consistently disregarded all danger to attend his fighting comrades as they fell under the devastating rain of shrapnel and bullets, and rendered prompt assistance to various elements of his combat group as required. When an adjacent platoon suffered heavy casualties, he defied the continuous pounding of heavy mortars and deadly fire of enemy rifles to care for the wounded, working rapidly in an area swept by constant fire and treating 14 casualties before returning to his own platoon. Wounded again on 2 March, he gallantly refused evacuation, moving out with his company the following day in a furious assault across 600 yards of open terrain and repeatedly rendering medical aid while exposed to the blasting fury of powerful Japanese guns. Stouthearted and indomitable, he

persevered in his determined efforts as his unit waged fierce battle and, unable to walk after sustaining a third agonizing wound, resolutely crawled 50 yards to administer first aid to still another fallen fighter. By his dauntless fortitude and valor, Wahlen served as a constant inspiration and contributed vitally to the high morale of his company during critical phases of this strategically important engagement. His heroic spirit of self-sacrifice in the face of overwhelming enemy fire upheld the highest traditions of the U.S. Naval Service.

2994 ◆ WAINWRIGHT IV, JONATHAN MAYHEW

Rank: General
Service: U.S. Army
Birthday: 23 August 1883
Place of Birth: Fort Walla Walla, Walla Walla County, Washington
Date of Death: 2 September 1953
Place of Death: San Antonio, Texas
Cemetery: Arlington National Cemetery (1-358-B)—Arlington, Virginia
Entered Service at: Skaneateles, Onondaga County, New York
Unit: U.S. Army
Served as: Commanding General of U.S. Armed Forces in the Philippines
Battle or Place of Action: Philippine Islands
Date of Action: 12 March-7 May 1942
G.O. Number, Date: 80, 19 September 1945
Date of Presentation: 10 September 1945
Place of Presentation: The White House (Rose Garden), presented by Pres. Harry S. Truman
Citation: Distinguished himself by intrepid and determined leadership against greatly superior enemy forces. At the repeated risk of life above and beyond the call of duty in his position, he frequented the firing line of his troops where his presence provided the example and incentive that helped make the gallant efforts of these men possible. The final stand on beleaguered Corregidor, for which he was in an important measure personally responsible, commanded the admiration of the nation's allies. It reflected the high morale of American arms in the face of overwhelming odds. His courage and resolution were a vitally needed inspiration to the then sorely pressed freedom-loving peoples of the world.
Notes: POW

2995 ◆ *WALKER, KENNETH NEWTON

Rank: Brigadier General
Service: U.S. Army Air Corps
Birthday: 17 July 1898
Place of Birth: Cerrillos, Santa Fe County, New Mexico
Date of Death: 5 January 1943
Place of Death: Near Rabaul, New Britain
Cemetery: A.B.M.C. Manila Cemetery (Wall of the Missing)—Manila, Philippine Islands
Entered Service at: Denver, Denver County, Colorado
Unit: 5th Bomber Command, 5th Air Force
Served as: Commanding Officer/Pilot of a B-17
Battle or Place of Action: over Rabaul, New Britain, Bismarck Archipelago
Date of Action: 5 January 1943
G.O. Number, Date: 13, 11 March 1943
Date of Presentation: 25 March 1943
Place of Presentation: The White House, presented by Pres. Franklin D. Roosevelt to his family
Citation: For conspicuous leadership above and beyond the call of duty involving personal valor and intrepidity at an extreme hazard to life. As commander of the 5th Bomber Command during the period from 5 September 1942 to 5 January 1943, Brig. Gen. Walker repeatedly accompanied his units on bombing missions deep into enemy-held territory. From the lessons personally gained under combat conditions, he developed a highly efficient technique for bombing when opposed by enemy fighter airplanes and by antiaircraft fire. On 5 January 1943, in the face of extremely heavy antiaircraft fire and determined opposition by enemy fighters, he led an effective daylight bombing attack against shipping in the harbor at Rabaul, New Britain, which resulted in direct hits on nine enemy vessels. During this action his airplane was disabled and forced down by the attack of an overwhelming number of enemy fighters.

2996 ◆ *WALLACE, HERMAN C.

Rank: Private First Class
Service: U.S. Army
Birthday: 1924
Place of Birth: Marlow, Stephens County, Oklahoma
Date of Death: 27 February 1945
Cemetery: City of Lubbock Cemetery (MH)—Lubbock, Texas
Entered Service at: Lubbock, Lubbock County, Texas
Unit: Company B, 301st Combat Engineer Battalion, 76th Infantry Division
Battle or Place of Action: near Prumzurley, Germany
Date of Action: 27 February 1945
G.O. Number, Date: 92, 25 October 1945
Citation: He displayed conspicuous gallantry and intrepidity. While helping clear enemy mines from a road, he stepped on a well-concealed S-type antipersonnel mine. Hearing the characteristic noise indicating that the mine had been activated and, if he stepped aside, would be thrown upward to explode above the ground and spray the area with fragments, surely killing two comrades directly behind him and endangering other members of his squad, he deliberately placed his other foot on the mine even though his best chance for survival was to fall prone. Pvt. Wallace was killed when the charge detonated, but his supreme heroism at the cost of his life confined the blast to the ground and his own body and saved his fellow soldiers from death or injury.

2997 ◆ WALSH, KENNETH AMBROSE

Rank: First Lieutenant (highest rank: Lieutenant Colonel)
Service: U.S. Marine Corps
Birthday: 24 November 1916

Place of Birth: Brooklyn, Kings County, New York
Entered Service at: Brooklyn, Kings County, New York
Unit: Marine Fighting Squadron 124, Marine Air Group 12, 1st Marine Air Wing
Served as: Flight Leader/Pilot of an F4U Corsair
Battle or Place of Action: Vella Lavella & Kahili, Solomon Islands
Date of Action: 15, 30 August 1943
Date of Presentation: 8 February 1944
Place of Presentation: The White House (Oval Office), presented by Pres. Franklin D. Roosevelt
Citation: For extraordinary heroism and intrepidity above and beyond the call of duty as a pilot in Marine Fighting Squadron 124 in aerial combat against enemy Japanese forces in the Solomon Islands area. Determined to thwart the enemy's attempt to bomb Allied ground forces and shipping at Vella Lavella on 15 August 1943, 1st Lt. Walsh repeatedly dived his plane into an enemy formation outnumbering his own division six to one and, although his plane was hit numerous times, shot down two Japanese dive bombers and one fighter. After developing engine trouble on 30 August during a vital escort mission, 1st Lt. Walsh landed his mechanically disabled plane at Munda, quickly replaced it with another, and proceeded to rejoin his flight over Kahili. Separated from his escort group when he encountered approximately 50 Japanese Zeros, he unhesitatingly attacked, striking with relentless fury in his lone battle against a powerful force. He destroyed four hostile fighters before cannon shellfire forced him to make a dead-stick landing off Vella Lavella where he was later picked up. His valiant leadership and his daring skill as a flier served as a source of confidence and inspiration to his fellow pilots and reflect the highest credit upon the U.S. Naval Service.

2998 ◆ *WALSH, WILLIAM GARY

Rank: Gunnery Sergeant
Service: U.S. Marine Corps Reserve
Birthday: 7 April 1922
Place of Birth: Roxbury, Suffolk County, Massachusetts
Date of Death: 27 February 1945
Cemetery: Arlington National Cemetery (12-487) (MH)—Arlington, Virginia
Entered Service at: Massachusetts
Unit: Company G, 3d Battalion, 27th Marines, 5th Marine Division
Served as: Platoon Leader
Battle or Place of Action: Iwo Jima, Volcano Islands
Date of Action: 27 February 1945
Citation: For extraordinary gallantry and intrepidity at the risk of his life above and beyond the call of duty as leader of an assault platoon, attached to Company G, 3d Battalion, 27th Marines, 5th Marine Division, in action against enemy Japanese forces at Iwo Jima, Volcano Islands, on 27 February 1945. With the advance of his company toward Hill 362 disrupted by vicious machine-gun fire from a forward position which guarded the approaches to this key enemy stronghold, G/Sgt. Walsh fearlessly charged at the head of his platoon against the Japanese entrenched on the ridge above him,

utterly oblivious to the unrelenting fury of hostile automatic-weapons fire and hand grenades employed with fanatic desperation to smash his daring assault. Thrown back by the enemy's savage resistance, he once again led his men in a seemingly impossible attack up the steep, rocky slope, boldly defiant of the annihilating streams of bullets which saturated the area. Despite his own casualty losses and the overwhelming advantage held by the Japanese in superior numbers and dominant position, he gained the ridge's top only to be subjected to an intense barrage of hand grenades thrown by the remaining Japanese staging a suicidal last stand on the reverse slope. When one of the grenades fell in the midst of his surviving men, huddled together in a small trench, G/Sgt. Walsh, in a final valiant act of complete self-sacrifice, instantly threw himself upon the deadly bomb, absorbing with his own body the full and terrific force of the explosion. Through his extraordinary initiative and inspiring valor in the face of almost certain death, he saved his comrades from injury and possible loss of life and enabled his company to seize and hold this vital enemy position. He gallantly gave his life for his country.

2999 ◆ *WARD, JAMES RICHARD

Rank: Seaman First Class
Service: U.S. Navy
ay: 10 September 1921
Place of Birth: Springfield, Clark County, Ohio
Date of Death: 7 December 1941
Cemetery: National Memorial Cemetery of the Pacific (Wall of the Missing)—Honolulu, Hawaii; Ferncliff Cemetery ('In Memory' marker)—Springfield, Ohio
Entered Service at: Springfield, Clark County, Ohio
Unit: U.S.S. *Oklahoma*
Battle or Place of Action: Pearl Harbor, Territory of Hawaii
Date of Action: 7 December 1941
Citation: For conspicuous devotion to duty, extraordinary courage, and complete disregard of his life, above and beyond the call of duty, during the attack on the Fleet in Pearl Harbor by Japanese forces on 7 December 1941. When it was seen that the U.S.S. *Oklahoma* was going to capsize and the order was given to abandon ship, Ward remained in a turret holding a flashlight so the remainder of the turret crew could see to escape, thereby sacrificing his own life.

3000 ◆ WARE, KEITH LINCOLN

Rank: Lieutenant Colonel (highest rank: Major General)
Service: U.S. Army
Birthday: 23 November 1915
Place of Birth: Denver, Denver County, Colorado
Date of Death: 13 September 1968
Place of Death: Cambodia
Cemetery: Arlington National Cemetery (30-258-3) (MH)—Arlington, Virginia
Entered Service at: Glendale, Los Angeles County, California
Unit: 1st Battalion, 15th Infantry, 3d Infantry Division
Served as: Battalion Commander

Battle or Place of Action: near Sigolsheim, France
Date of Action: 26 December 1944
G.O. Number, Date: 47, 18 June 1945
Date of Presentation: 23 April 1945
Place of Presentation: Zepman Stadium, Nuremberg, Germany, presented by Lt. Gen. Alexander M. Patch III
Citation: Commanding the 1st Battalion attacking a strongly held enemy position on a hill near Sigolsheim, France, on 26 December 1944, Lt. Col. Ware found that one of his assault companies had been stopped and forced to dig in by a concentration of enemy artillery, mortar, and machine-gun fire. The company had suffered casualties in attempting to take the hill. Realizing that his men must be inspired to new courage, Lt. Col. Ware went forward 150 yards beyond the most forward elements of his command, and for two hours reconnoitered the enemy positions, deliberately drawing fire upon himself which caused the enemy to disclose his dispositions. Returning to his company, he armed himself with an automatic rifle and boldly advanced upon the enemy, followed by two officers, nine enlisted men, and a tank. Approaching an enemy machine gun, Lt. Col. Ware shot two German riflemen and fired tracers into the emplacement, indicating its position to his tank, which promptly knocked the gun out of action. Lt. Col. Ware turned his attention to a second machine gun, killing two of its supporting riflemen and forcing the others to surrender. The tank destroyed the gun. Having expended the ammunition for the automatic rifle, Lt. Col. Ware took up an M1 rifle, killed a German rifleman, and fired upon a third machine gun 50 yards away. His tank silenced the gun. Upon his approach to a fourth machine gun, its supporting riflemen surrendered and his tank disposed of the gun. During this action Lt. Col. Ware's small assault group was fully engaged in attacking enemy positions that were not receiving his direct and personal attention. Five of his party of 11 were casualties and Lt. Col. Ware was wounded, but refused medical attention until this important hill position was cleared of the enemy and securely occupied by his command.

3001 ◆ *WARNER, HENRY F.

Rank: Corporal
Service: U.S. Army
Birthday: 23 August 1923
Place of Birth: Troy, Montgomery County, North Carolina
Date of Death: 21 December 1944
Cemetery: South Side Cemetery (MH)—Troy, North Carolina
Entered Service at: Troy, Montgomery County, North Carolina
Unit: Antitank Company, 2d Battalion, 26th Infantry, 1st Infantry Division
Served as: 57-mm Antitank Gunner
Battle or Place of Action: near Dom Butgenbach, Belgium
Date of Action: 20-21 December 1944
G.O. Number, Date: 48, 23 June 1945
Citation: Serving as 57-mm antitank gunner with the 2d Battalion, he was a major factor in stopping enemy tanks during heavy attacks against the battalion position near Dom Butgenbach, Belgium, on 20–21 December 1944. In the first attack, launched early in the morning on the 20th, enemy tanks succeeded in penetrating parts of the line. Cpl. Warner, disregarding the concentrated cannon and machine-gun fire from two tanks bearing down on him and ignoring the imminent danger of being overrun by the infantry moving under tank cover, destroyed the first tank and scored a direct and deadly hit upon the second. A third tank approached to within five yards of his position while he was attempting to clear a jammed breach lock. Jumping from his gun pit, he engaged in a pistol duel with the tank commander standing in the turret, killing him and forcing the tank to withdraw. Following a day and night during which our forces were subjected to constant shelling, mortar barrages, and numerous unsuccessful infantry attacks, the enemy struck in great force on the early morning of the 21st. Seeing a Mark IV tank looming out of the mist and heading toward his position, Cpl. Warner scored a direct hit. Disregarding his injuries, he endeavored to finish the loading and again fire at the tank, whose motor was now aflame, when a second machine-gun burst killed him. Cpl. Warner's gallantry and intrepidity at the risk of life above and beyond the call of duty contributed materially to the successful defense against the enemy attacks.

3002 ◆ WATSON, WILSON DOUGLAS

Rank: Private (highest rank: Staff Sergeant)
Service: U.S. Marine Corps Reserve
Birthday: 18 February 1922
Place of Birth: Tuscumbia, Colbert County, Alabama
Date of Death: 19 December 1994
Place of Death: Russellville, Arkansas
Cemetery: Russell Cemetery—Ozone, Arkansas
Entered Service at: Earle, Crittenden County, Arkansas
Unit: 2d Squad, 3d Platoon, Company G, 2d Battalion, 9th Marines, 3d Marine Division
Served as: Automatic Rifleman
Battle or Place of Action: Iwo Jima, Volcano Islands
Date of Action: 26-27 February 1945
Date of Presentation: 5 October 1945
Place of Presentation: The White House, presented by Pres. Harry S. Truman
Citation: For conspicuous gallantry and intrepidity at the risk of his life above and beyond the call of duty as automatic rifleman serving with the 2d Battalion, 9th Marines, 3d Marine Division, during action against enemy Japanese forces on Iwo Jima, Volcano Islands, 26 and 27 February 1945. With his squad abruptly halted by intense fire from enemy fortifications in the high rocky ridges and crags commanding the line of advance, Pvt. Watson boldly rushed one pillbox and fired into the embrasure with his weapon, keeping the enemy pinned down singlehandedly until he was in a position to hurl in a grenade and then running to the rear of the emplacement to destroy the retreating Japanese and enable his platoon to take its objective. Again pinned down at the foot of a small hill, he dauntlessly scaled the jagged incline under fierce mortar and machine-gun barrages and, with his assistant BAR man, charged the crest of the hill, firing from

his hip. Fighting furiously against Japanese troops attacking with grenades and knee mortars from the reverse slope, he stood fearlessly erect in his exposed position to cover the hostile entrenchments and held the hill under savage fire for 15 minutes, killing 60 Japanese before his ammunition was exhausted and his platoon was able to join him. His courageous initiative and valiant fighting spirit against devastating odds were directly responsible for the continued advance of his platoon, and his inspiring leadership throughout this bitterly fought action reflects the highest credit upon Pvt. Watson and the U.S. Naval Service.

3003 ◆ *WAUGH, ROBERT T.

Rank: First Lieutenant
Service: U.S. Army
Place of Birth: Ashton, Rhode Island
Date of Death: 19 May 1944
Cemetery: A.B.M.C. Sicily-Rome Cemetery (H-13-37)—Nettuno, Italy
Entered Service at: Augusta, Kennebec County, Maine
Unit: 339th Infantry, 85th Infantry Division
Served as: Platoon Leader
Battle or Place of Action: near Tremensucli, Italy
Date of Action: 11-14 May 1944
G.O. Number, Date: 79, 4 October 1944
Place of Presentation: Fort Dupont, Delaware, presented by Maj. Gen. Henry Terrell Jr. to his family
Citation: For conspicuous gallantry and intrepidity at the risk of life above and beyond the call of duty in action with the enemy. In the course of an attack upon an enemy-held hill on 11 May, 1st Lt. Waugh personally reconnoitered a heavily mined area before entering it with his platoon. Directing his men to deliver fire on six bunkers guarding this hill, 1st Lt. Waugh advanced alone against them, reached the first bunker, threw phosphorus grenades into it, and, as the defenders emerged, killed them with a burst from his tommy gun. He repeated this process on the five remaining bunkers, killing or capturing the occupants. On the morning of 14 May, 1st Lt. Waugh ordered his platoon to lay a base of fire on two enemy pillboxes located on a knoll which commanded the only trail up the hill. He then ran to the first pillbox, threw several grenades into it, drove the defenders into the open, and killed them. The second pillbox was next taken by this intrepid officer by similar methods. The fearless actions of 1st Lt. Waugh broke the Gustav Line at that point, neutralizing six bunkers and two pillboxes, and he was personally responsible for the death of 30 of the enemy and the capture of 25 others. He was later killed in action in Itri, Italy, while leading his platoon in an attack.

3004 ◆ WAYBUR, DAVID CROWDER

Rank: First Lieutenant
Service: U.S. Army
Place of Birth: Oakland, Alameda County, California
Date of Death: 28 March 1945
Cemetery: A.B.M.C. Lorraine Cemetery (E-22-44) (MH)—St. Avold, France

Entered Service at: Piedmont, Alameda County, California
Unit: 3d Reconnaissance Troop, 3d Infantry Division
Battle or Place of Action: near Agrigento, Sicily
Date of Action: 17 July 1943
G.O. Number, Date: 69, 21 October 1943
Citation: For conspicuous gallantry and intrepidity at the risk of life above and beyond the call of duty in action involving actual conflict with the enemy. Commander of a reconnaissance platoon, 1st Lt. Waybur volunteered to lead a three-vehicle patrol into enemy-held territory to locate an isolated Ranger unit. Proceeding under cover of darkness, over roads known to be heavily mined and strongly defended by road blocks and machine-gun positions, the patrol's progress was halted at a bridge which had been destroyed by enemy troops and was suddenly cut off from its supporting vehicles by four enemy tanks. Although hopelessly outnumbered and outgunned, and himself and his men completely exposed, he quickly dispersed his vehicles and ordered his gunners to open fire with their .30 and .50-caliber machine guns. Then, with ammunition exhausted, three of his men hit, and himself seriously wounded, he seized his .45-caliber Thompson submachine gun and, standing in the bright moonlight directly in the line of fire, alone engaged the leading tank at 30 yards and succeeded in killing the crewmembers, causing the tank to run onto the bridge and crash into the stream bed. After dispatching one of the men for aid, he rallied the rest to cover and withstood the continued fire of the tanks until the arrival of aid the following morning.

3005 ◆ *WEICHT, ELLIS R.

Rank: Sergeant
Service: U.S. Army
Place of Birth: Clearville, Bedford County, Pennsylvania
Date of Death: 3 December 1944
Cemetery: A.B.M.C. Epinal Cemetery (B-42-20) (MH)—Epinal, France
Entered Service at: Bedford, Bedford County, Pennsylvania
Unit: Company F, 142d Infantry, 36th Infantry Division
Served as: Squad Leader
Battle or Place of Action: St. Hippolyte, France
Date of Action: 3 December 1944
G.O. Number, Date: 58, 19 July 1945
Citation: For commanding an assault squad in Company F's attack against the strategically important Alsatian town of St. Hippolyte on 3 December 1944. He aggressively led his men down a winding street, clearing the houses of opposition as he advanced. Upon rounding a bend, the group was suddenly brought under the fire of two machine guns emplaced in the door and window of a house 100 yards distant. While his squad members took cover, Sgt. Weicht moved rapidly forward to a high rock wall and, fearlessly exposing himself to the enemy action, fired two clips of ammunition from his rifle. His fire proving ineffective, he entered a house opposite the enemy gun position, and, firing from a window, killed the two hostile gunners. Continuing the attack, the advance was again halted when two 20-mm guns opened fire on the company. An artillery observer ordered friendly troops to evacuate the area and then directed artillery fire upon the gun posi-

tions. Sgt. Weicht remained in the shelled area and continued to fire on the hostile weapons. When the barrage lifted and the enemy soldiers attempted to remove their gun, he killed two crewmembers and forced the others to flee. Sgt. Weicht continued to lead his squad forward until he spotted a road block approximately 125 yards away. Moving to the second floor of a nearby house and firing from a window, he killed three and wounded several of the enemy. Instantly becoming a target for heavy and direct fire, he disregarded personal safety to continue his fire, with unusual effectiveness, until he was killed by a direct hit from an antitank gun.

3006 ◆ *WETZEL, WALTER C.

Rank: Private First Class
Service: U.S. Army
Place of Birth: Huntington, Cabell County, West Virginia
Date of Death: 3 April 1945
Cemetery: A.B.M.C. Netherlands Cemetery (N-18-10) (MH)—Margraten, Holland
Entered Service at: Roseville, Macomb County, Michigan
Unit: Antitank Company, 13th Infantry, 8th Infantry Division
Served as: Acting Squad Leader
Battle or Place of Action: Birken, Germany
Date of Action: 3 April 1945
G.O. Number, Date: 21, 26 February 1946
Citation: Pfc. Wetzel, an acting squad leader with the Antitank Company of the 13th Infantry, was guarding his platoon's command post in a house at Birken, Germany, during the early morning hours of 3 April 1945, when he detected strong enemy forces moving in to attack. He ran into the house, alerted the occupants, and immediately began defending the post against heavy automatic-weapon fire coming from the hostile troops. Under cover of darkness the Germans forced their way close to the building where they hurled grenades, two of which landed in the room where Pfc. Wetzel and the others had taken up firing positions. Shouting a warning to his fellow soldiers, Pfc. Wetzel threw himself on the grenades and, as they exploded, absorbed their entire blast, suffering wounds from which he died. The supreme gallantry of Pfc. Wetzel saved his comrades from death or serious injury and made it possible for them to continue the defense of the command post and break the power of a dangerous local counterthrust by the enemy. His unhesitating sacrifice of his life was in keeping with the U.S. Army's highest traditions of bravery and heroism.

3007 ◆ WHITELEY, ELI LAMAR

Rank: First Lieutenant
Service: U.S. Army
Birthday: 10 December 1913
Place of Birth: Florence, Williamson County, Texas
Date of Death: 2 December 1986
Cemetery: City Cemetery (MH)—College Station, Texas
Entered Service at: Georgetown, Williamson County, Texas
Unit: Company L, 15th Infantry, 3d Infantry Division
Served as: Platoon Leader

Battle or Place of Action: Sigolsheim, France
Date of Action: 27 December 1944
G.O. Number, Date: 79, 14 September 1945
Date of Presentation: 23 August 1945
Place of Presentation: The White House, presented by Pres. Harry S. Truman
Citation: While leading his platoon on 27 December 1944, in savage house-to-house fighting through the fortress town of Sigolsheim, France, he attacked a building through a street swept by withering mortar and automatic-weapon fire. He was hit and severely wounded in the arm and shoulder; but he charged into the house alone and killed its two defenders. Hurling smoke and fragmentation grenades before him, he reached the next house and stormed inside, killing two and capturing 11 of the enemy. He continued leading his platoon in the extremely dangerous task of clearing hostile troops from strongpoints along the street until he reached a building held by fanatical Nazi troops. Although suffering from wounds which had rendered his left arm useless, he advanced on this strongly defended house and, after blasting out a wall with bazooka fire, charged through a hail of bullets. Wedging his submachine gun under his uninjured arm, he rushed into the house through the hole torn by his rockets, killed five of the enemy, and forced the remaining 12 to surrender. As he emerged to continue his fearless attack, he was again hit and critically wounded. In agony and with one eye pierced by a shell fragment, he shouted for his men to follow him to the next house. He was determined to stay in the fighting and remained at the head of his platoon until forcibly evacuated. By his disregard for personal safety, his aggressiveness while suffering from severe wounds, his determined leadership and superb courage, 1st Lt. Whiteley killed nine Germans, captured 23 more, and spearheaded an attack which cracked the core of enemy resistance in a vital area.

3008 ◆ WHITTINGTON, HULON BROOKE

Rank: Sergeant (highest rank: Major)
Service: U.S. Army
Birthday: 9 July 1921
Place of Birth: Bogalusa, Washington County, Louisiana
Date of Death: 17 January 1969
Cemetery: Arlington National Cemetery (13-8-W)—Arlington, Virginia
Entered Service at: Bastrop, Morehouse County, Louisiana
Unit: 41st Armored Infantry, 2d Armored Division
Served as: Squad Leader
Battle or Place of Action: near Grimesnil, France
Date of Action: 29 July 1944
G.O. Number, Date: 32, 23 April 1945
Citation: For conspicuous gallantry and intrepidity at the risk of life above and beyond the call of duty. On the night of 29 July 1944, near Grimesnil, France, during an enemy armored attack, Sgt. Whittington, a squad leader, assumed command of his platoon when the platoon leader and platoon sergeant became missing in action. He reorganized the defense and, under fire, courageously crawled between gun positions to check the actions of his men. When the advancing enemy attempted to penetrate a roadblock, Sgt.

Whittington, completely disregarding intense enemy action, mounted a tank and, by shouting through the turret, directed it into position to fire point-blank at the leading Mark V German tank. The destruction of this vehicle blocked all movement of the remaining enemy column consisting of over 100 vehicles of a Panzer unit. The blocked vehicles were then destroyed by hand grenades, bazooka, tank, and artillery fire, and large numbers of enemy personnel were wiped out by a bold and resolute bayonet charge inspired by Sgt. Whittington. When the medical aidman had become a casualty, Sgt. Whittington personally administered first aid to his wounded men. The dynamic leadership, the inspiring example, and the dauntless courage of Sgt. Whittington, above and beyond the call of duty, are in keeping with the highest traditions of the military service.

3009 ◆ WIEDORFER, PAUL JOSEPH

Rank: Staff Sergeant (rank at time of action: Private) (highest rank: Master Sergeant)
Service: U.S. Army
Birthday: 17 January 1921
Place of Birth: Baltimore, Baltimore County, Maryland
Entered Service at: Baltimore, Baltimore County, Maryland
Unit: 2d Squad, 2d Platoon, Company G, 2d Battalion, 318th Infantry, 80th Infantry Division
Served as: Rifleman
Battle or Place of Action: near Chaumont, Belgium
Date of Action: 25 December 1944
G.O. Number, Date: 45, 12 June 1945
Date of Presentation: 29 May 1945
Place of Presentation: 137th Gen. Hospital, Ellesmere, Shropshire, England, presented by Brigadier Gen. E. F. Koenig, UK Base Commander
Citation: He alone made it possible for his company to advance until its objective was seized. Company G had cleared a wooded area of snipers, and one platoon was advancing across an open clearing toward another wood when it was met by heavy machine-gun fire from two German positions dug in at the edge of the second wood. These positions were flanked by enemy riflemen. The platoon took cover behind a small ridge approximately 40 yards from the enemy position. There was no other available protection and the entire platoon was pinned down by the German fire. It was about noon and the day was clear, but the terrain extremely difficult due to a three-inch snowfall the night before over ice-covered ground. Pvt. Wiedorfer, realizing that the platoon advance could not continue until the two enemy machine-gun nests were destroyed, voluntarily charged alone across the slippery open ground with no protecting cover of any kind. Running in a crouched position, under a hail of enemy fire, he slipped and fell in the snow, but quickly rose and continued forward with the enemy concentrating automatic and small-arms fire on him as he advanced. Miraculously escaping injury, Pvt. Wiedorfer reached a point some 10 yards from the first machine-gun emplacement and hurled a hand grenade into it. With his rifle he killed the remaining Germans, and, without hesitation, wheeled to the right and attacked the second emplacement. One of the enemy was

wounded by his fire and the other six immediately surrendered. This heroic action by one man enabled the platoon to advance from behind its protecting ridge and continue successfully to reach its objective. A few minutes later, when both the platoon leader and the platoon sergeant were wounded, Pvt. Wiedorfer assumed command of the platoon, leading it forward with inspired energy until the mission was accomplished.

3010 ◆ *WIGLE, THOMAS W.

Rank: Second Lieutenant
Service: U.S. Army
Birthday: 18 May 1909
Place of Birth: Indianapolis, Marion County, Indiana
Date of Death: 16 September 1944
Cemetery: Arlington National Cemetery (34-3307) (MH)—Arlington, Virginia
Entered Service at: Detroit, Wayne County, Michigan
Unit: Company K, 135th Infantry, 34th Infantry Division
Served as: Executive Officer
Battle or Place of Action: Monte Frassino, Italy
Date of Action: 14 September 1944
G.O. Number, Date: 8, 7 February 1945
Citation: For conspicuous gallantry and intrepidity at the risk of life above and beyond the call of duty in the vicinity of Monte Frassino, Italy. The 3d Platoon, in attempting to seize a strongly fortified hill position protected by three parallel high terraced stone walls, was twice thrown back by the withering crossfire. Second Lt. Wigle, acting company executive, observing that the platoon was without an officer, volunteered to command it on the next attack. Leading his men up the bare, rocky slopes through intense and concentrated fire, he succeeded in reaching the first of the stone walls. Having himself boosted to the top and perching there in full view of the enemy, he drew and returned their fire while his men helped each other up and over. Following the same method, he successfully negotiated the second. Upon reaching the top of the third wall, he faced three houses which were the key point of the enemy defense. Ordering his men to cover him, he made a dash through a hail of machine-pistol fire to reach the nearest house. Firing his carbine as he entered, he drove the enemy before him out of the back door and into the second house. Following closely on the heels of the foe, he drove them from this house to the third where they took refuge in the cellar. When his men rejoined him, they found him mortally wounded on the cellar stairs which he had started to descend to force the surrender of the enemy. His heroic action resulted in the capture of 36 German soldiers and the seizure of the strongpoint.

3011 ◆ WILBUR, WILLIAM HALE

Rank: Colonel (highest rank: Brigadier General)
Service: U.S. Army
Birthday: 24 September 1888
Place of Birth: Palmer, Hampden County, Massachusetts
Date of Death: 27 December 1979
Place of Death: Sanibel, Florida

Cemetery: U.S. Military Academy Cemetery (7-C-148)—West Point, New York
Entered Service at: Palmer, Hampden County, Massachusetts
Unit: Western Task Force, North Africa
Battle or Place of Action: Fedala, North Africa
Date of Action: 8 November 1942
G.O. Number, Date: 2, 13 January 1943
Date of Presentation: 24 January 1943
Place of Presentation: Casablanca, Algiers, presented by Pres. Franklin D. Roosevelt
Citation: For conspicuous gallantry and intrepidity in action above and beyond the call of duty. Col. Wilbur prepared the plan for making contact with French commanders in Casablanca and obtaining an armistice to prevent unnecessary bloodshed. On 8 November 1942, he landed at Fedala with the leading assault waves where opposition had developed into a firm and continuous defensive line across his route of advance. Commandeering a vehicle, he was driven toward the hostile defenses under incessant fire, finally locating a French officer who accorded him passage through the forward positions. He then proceeded in total darkness through 16 miles of enemy-occupied country intermittently subjected to heavy bursts of fire, and accomplished his mission by delivering his letters to appropriate French officials in Casablanca. Returning toward his command, Col. Wilbur detected a hostile battery firing effectively on our troops. He took charge of a platoon of American tanks and personally led them in an attack and capture of the battery. From the moment of landing until the cessation of hostile resistance, Col. Wilbur's conduct was voluntary and exemplary in its coolness and daring.

3012 ◆ *WILKIN, EDWARD G.

Rank: Corporal
Service: U.S. Army
Birthday: 25 May 1917
Place of Birth: Burlington, Chittenden County, Vermont
Date of Death: 18 April 1945
Cemetery: Longmeadow Cemetery (MH)—Longmeadow, Massachusetts
Entered Service at: Longmeadow, Hampden County, Massachusetts
Unit: Company C, 157th Infantry, 45th Infantry Division
Battle or Place of Action: Siegfried Line, Germany
Date of Action: 18 March 1945
G.O. Number, Date: 119, 17 December 1945
Citation: He spearheaded his unit's assault of the Siegfried line in Germany. Heavy fire from enemy riflemen and camouflaged pillboxes had pinned down his comrades when he moved forward on his own initiative to reconnoiter a route of advance. He cleared the way into an area studded with pillboxes, where he repeatedly stood up and walked into vicious enemy fire, storming one fortification after another with automatic rifle fire and grenades, killing enemy troops, taking prisoners as the enemy defense became confused, and encouraging his comrades by his heroic example. When halted by heavy barbed wire entanglements, he secured bangalore torpedoes and blasted a path toward still more pillboxes, all the

time braving bursting grenades and mortar shells and direct rifle and automatic-weapon fire. He engaged in fierce firefights, standing in the open while his adversaries fought from the protection of concrete emplacements, and on one occasion pursued enemy soldiers across an open field and through interlocking trenches, disregarding the crossfire from two pillboxes until he had penetrated the formidable line 200 yards in advance of any American element. That night, although terribly fatigued, he refused to rest and insisted on distributing rations and supplies to his comrades. Hearing that a nearby company was suffering heavy casualties, he secured permission to guide litter bearers and assist them in evacuating the wounded. All that night he remained in the battle area on his mercy missions, and for the following two days he continued to remove casualties, venturing into enemy-held territory, scorning cover, and braving devastating mortar and artillery bombardments. In three days he neutralized and captured six pillboxes singlehandedly, killed at least nine Germans, wounded 13, took 13 prisoners, aided in the capture of 14 others, and saved many American lives by his fearless performance as a litter bearer. Through his superb fighting skill, dauntless courage, and gallant, in spiring actions, Cpl. Wilkin contributed in large measure to his company's success in cracking the Siegfried line. One month later he was killed in action while fighting deep in Germany.

3013 ◆ *WILKINS, RAYMOND HARRELL

Rank: Major
Service: U.S. Army Air Corps
Birthday: 28 September 1917
Place of Birth: Portsmouth, Portsmouth County, Virginia
Date of Death: 2 November 1943
Place of Death: Rabaul, New Britain
Cemetery: A.B.M.C. Manila Cemetery (Wall of the Missing)—Manila, Philippine Islands; Olive Branch Cemetery ('In Memory' marker) (MH)—Portsmouth, Va.
Entered Service at: Portsmouth, Portsmouth County, Virginia
Unit: 89th Bombardment Squadron, 3d Bombardment Group, 5th Air Force
Served as: Squadron Leader/Pilot of a B-25
Battle or Place of Action: near Rabaul, New Britain, Bismarck Archipelago
Date of Action: 2 November 1943
G.O. Number, Date: 23, 24 March 1944
Date of Presentation: 1 December 1944
Place of Presentation: Vandalia, Ohio, presented to his family
Citation: For conspicuous gallantry and intrepidity above and beyond the call of duty in action with the enemy near Rabaul, New Britain, on 2 November 1943. Leading his squadron in an attack on shipping in Simpson Harbor, during which intense antiaircraft fire was expected, Maj. Wilkins briefed his squadron so that his airplane would be in the position of greatest risk. His squadron was the last of three in the group to enter the target area. Smoke from bombs dropped by preceding aircraft necessitated a last-second revision of tactics on his part, which still enabled his squadron to strike vital

shipping targets, but forced it to approach through concentrated fire and increased the danger of Maj. Wilkins' left flank position. His airplane was hit almost immediately, the right wing damaged, and control rendered extremely difficult. Although he could have withdrawn, he held fast and led his squadron into the attack. He strafed a group of small harbor vessels, and then, at low level, attacked an enemy destroyer. His 1,000 pound bomb struck squarely amidships, causing the vessel to explode. Although antiaircraft fire from this vessel had seriously damaged his left vertical stabilizer, he refused to deviate from the course. From below-masthead height he attacked a transport of some 9,000 tons, scoring a hit which engulfed the ship in flames. Bombs expended, he began to withdraw his squadron. A heavy cruiser barred the path. Unhesitatingly, to neutralize the cruiser's guns and attract its fire, he went in for a strafing run. His damaged stabilizer was completely shot off. To avoid swerving into his wing planes he had to turn so as to expose the belly and full wing surfaces of his plane to the enemy fire; it caught and crumpled his left wing. Now past control, the bomber crashed into the sea. In the fierce engagement Maj. Wilkins destroyed two enemy vessels, and his heroic self-sacrifice made possible the safe withdrawal of the remaining planes of his squadron.

3014 ◆ *WILL, WALTER J.

Rank: First Lieutenant
Service: U.S. Army
Place of Birth: Pittsburgh, Allegheny County, Pennsylvania
Date of Death: 30 March 1945
Cemetery: A.B.M.C. Netherlands Cemetery (D-3-32) (MH)—Margraten, Holland
Entered Service at: West Winfield, Herkimer County, New York
Unit: Company K, 18th Infantry, 1st Infantry Division
Battle or Place of Action: near Eisern, Germany
Date of Action: 30 March 1945
G.O. Number, Date: 88, 17 October 1945
Citation: He displayed conspicuous gallantry during an attack on powerful enemy positions. He courageously exposed himself to withering hostile fire to rescue two wounded men and then, although painfully wounded himself, made a third trip to carry another soldier to safety from an open area. Ignoring the profuse bleeding of his wound, he gallantly led men of his platoon forward until they were pinned down by murderous flanking fire from two enemy machine guns. He fearlessly crawled alone to within 30 feet of the first enemy position, killed the crew of four, and silenced the gun with accurate grenade fire. He continued to crawl through intense enemy fire to within 20 feet of the second position where he leaped to his feet, made a lone, ferocious charge, and captured the gun and its nine-man crew. Observing another platoon pinned down by two more German machine guns, he led a squad on a flanking approach and, rising to his knees in the face of direct fire, coolly and deliberately lobbed three grenades at the Germans, silencing one gun and killing its crew. With tenacious aggressiveness, he ran toward the other gun and knocked it out with grenade fire. He then returned to his platoon and led it in a fierce,

inspired charge, forcing the enemy to fall back in confusion. First Lt. Will was mortally wounded in this last action, but his heroic leadership, indomitable courage, and unflinching devotion to duty live on as a perpetual inspiration to all those who witnessed his deeds.

3015 ◆ WILLIAMS, HERSHEL WOODROW "WOODY"

Rank: Corporal (highest rank: Chief Warrant Officer 4)
Service: U.S. Marine Corps Reserve
Birthday: 2 October 1923
Place of Birth: Quiet Dell, Marion County, West Virginia
Entered Service at: Fairmont, Marion County, West Virginia
Unit: Headquarters Company, 1st Battalion, 21st Marines, 3d Marine Division
Served as: Demolition Sergeant
Battle or Place of Action: Iwo Jima, Volcano Islands
Date of Action: 23 February 1945
Date of Presentation: 5 October 1945
Place of Presentation: The White House, presented by Pres. Harry S. Truman
Citation: For conspicuous gallantry and intrepidity at the risk of his life above and beyond the call of duty as demolition sergeant serving with the 21st Marines, 3d Marine Division, in action against enemy Japanese forces on Iwo Jima, Volcano Islands, 23 February 1945. Quick to volunteer his services when our tanks were maneuvering vainly to open a lane for the infantry through the network of reinforced concrete pillboxes, buried mines, and black volcanic sands, Cpl. Williams daringly went forward alone to attempt the reduction of devastating machine-gun fire from the unyielding positions. Covered only by four riflemen, he fought desperately for four hours under terrific enemy small-arms fire and repeatedly returned to his own lines to prepare demolition charges and obtain serviced flamethrowers, struggling back, frequently to the rear of hostile emplacements, to wipe out one position after another. On one occasion, he daringly mounted a pillbox to insert the nozzle of his flamethrower through the air vent, killing the occupants, and silencing the gun; on another he grimly charged enemy riflemen who attempted to stop him with bayonets and destroyed them with a burst of flame from his weapon. His unyielding determination and extraordinary heroism in the face of ruthless enemy resistance were directly instrumental in neutralizing one of the most fanatically defended Japanese strongpoints encountered by his regiment and aided vitally in enabling his company to reach its objective. Cpl. Williams' aggressive fighting spirit and valiant devotion to duty throughout this fiercely contested action sustain and enhance the highest traditions of the U.S. Naval Service.

3016 ◆ *WILLIAMS, JACK

Rank: Pharmacist's Mate Third Class
Service: U.S. Naval Reserve
Birthday: 18 October 1924
Place of Birth: Harrison, Boone County, Arkansas

Date of Death: 3 March 1945
Cemetery: Springfield National Cemetery (30-2375) (MH)—Springfield, Missouri
Entered Service at: Arkansas
Unit: 3d Battalion, 28th Marines, 5th Marine Division
Served as: Medical Corpsman
Battle or Place of Action: Iwo Jima, Volcano Islands
Date of Action: 3 March 1945
Citation: For conspicuous gallantry and intrepidity at the risk of his life above and beyond the call of duty while serving with the 3d Battalion, 28th Marines, 5th Marine Division, during the occupation of Iwo Jima, Volcano Islands, 3 March 1945. Gallantly going forward on the front lines under intense enemy small-arms fire to assist a marine wounded in a fierce grenade battle, Williams dragged the man to a shallow depression and was kneeling, using his own body as a screen from the sustained fire as he administered first aid, when struck in the abdomen and groin three times by hostile rifle fire. Momentarily stunned, he quickly recovered and completed his ministration before applying battle dressings to his own multiple wounds. Unmindful of his own urgent need for medical attention, he remained in the perilous fire-swept area to care for another marine casualty. Heroically completing his task despite pain and profuse bleeding, he then endeavored to make his way to the rear in search of adequate aid for himself when struck down by a Japanese sniper bullet which caused his collapse. Succumbing later as a result of his self-sacrificing service to others, Williams, by his courageous determination, unwavering fortitude, and valiant performance of duty, served as an inspiring example of heroism, in keeping with the highest traditions of the U.S. Naval Service. He gallantly gave his life for his country.

3017 ◆ *WILLIS, JOHN HARLAN

Rank: Pharmacist's Mate First Class
Service: U.S. Navy
Birthday: 10 June 1921
Place of Birth: Columbia, Maury County, Tennessee
Date of Death: 28 February 1945
Cemetery: Rose Hill Cemetery—Columbia, Tennessee
Entered Service at: Tennessee
Unit: 3d Battalion, 27th Marines, 5th Marine Division
Served as: Platoon Medical Corpsman
Battle or Place of Action: Iwo Jima, Volcano Islands
Date of Action: 28 February 1945
Citation: For conspicuous gallantry and intrepidity at the risk of his life above and beyond the call of duty as platoon corpsman serving with the 3d Battalion, 27th Marines, 5th Marine Division, during operations against enemy Japanese forces on Iwo Jima, Volcano Islands, 28 February 1945. Constantly imperiled by artillery and mortar fire from strong and mutually supporting pillboxes and caves studding Hill 362 in the enemy cross-island defenses, Willis resolutely administered first aid to the many marines wounded during the furious close-in fighting until he himself was struck by shrapnel and was ordered back to the battle-aid station. Without waiting for official medical release, he quickly returned to his company and, during a savage hand-to-hand

enemy counterattack, daringly advanced to the extreme front lines under mortar and sniper fire to aid a marine lying wounded in a shell hole. Completely unmindful of his own danger as the Japanese intensified their attack, Willis calmly continued to administer blood plasma to his patient, promptly returning the first hostile grenade which landed in the shell hole while he was working and hurling back seven more in quick succession before the ninth one exploded in his hand and instantly killed him. By his great personal valor in saving others at the sacrifice of his own life, he inspired his companions, although terrifically outnumbered, to launch a fiercely determined attack and repulse the enemy force. His exceptional fortitude and courage in the performance of duty reflect the highest credit upon Willis and the U.S. Naval Service. He gallantly gave his life for his country.

3018 ◆ *WILSON, ALFRED LEONARD

Rank: Technician Grade Five
Service: U.S. Army
Birthday: 18 September 1918
Place of Birth: Fairchance, Fayette County, Pennsylvania
Date of Death: 8 November 1944
Cemetery: Maple Grove Cemetery (MH)—Fairchance, Pennsylvania
Entered Service at: Fairchance, Fayette County, Pennsylvania
Unit: Medical Detachment, 328th Infantry, 26th Infantry Division
Served as: Medical Aidman
Battle or Place of Action: near Bezange la Petite, France
Date of Action: 8 November 1944
G.O. Number, Date: 47, 18 June 1945
Citation: He volunteered to assist as an aidman a company other than his own, which was suffering casualties from constant artillery fire. He administered to the wounded and returned to his own company when a shell burst injured a number of its men. While treating his comrades he was seriously wounded, but refused to be evacuated by litter bearers sent to relieve him. In spite of great pain and loss of blood, he continued to administer first aid until he was too weak to stand. Crawling from one patient to another, he continued his work until excessive loss of blood prevented him from moving. He then verbally directed unskilled enlisted men in continuing the first aid for the wounded. Still refusing asistance himself, he remained to instruct others in dressing the wounds of his comrades until he was unable to speak above a whisper and finally lapsed into unconsciousness. The effects of his injury later caused his death. By steadfastly remaining at the scene without regard for his own safety, Cpl. Wilson through distinguished devotion to duty and personal sacrifice helped to save the lives of at least 10 wounded men.

3019 ◆ WILSON JR., LOUIS HUGH

Rank: Captain (highest rank: General)
Service: U.S. Marine Corps
Birthday: 11 February 1920
Place of Birth: Brandon, Rankin County, Mississippi

Entered Service at: Mississippi
Unit: Company F, 2d Battalion, 9th Marines, 3d Marine Division
Served as: Commanding Officer
Battle or Place of Action: Fonte Hill, Guam, Mariana Islands
Date of Action: 25-26 July 1944
Date of Presentation: 5 October 1945
Place of Presentation: The White House, presented by Pres. Harry S. Truman
Citation: For conspicuous gallantry and intrepidity at the risk of his life above and beyond the call of duty as commanding officer of a rifle company attached to the 2d Battalion, 9th Marines, 3d Marine Division, in action against enemy Japanese forces at Fonte Hill, Guam, 25–26 July 1944. Ordered to take that portion of the hill within his zone of action, Capt. Wilson initiated his attack in midafternoon, pushed up the rugged, open terrain against terrific machine-gun and rifle fire for 300 yards, and successfully captured the objective. Promptly assuming command of other disorganized units and motorized equipment in addition to his own company and one reinforcing platoon, he organized his night defenses in the face of continuous hostile fire and, although wounded three times during this five-hour period, completed his disposition of men and guns before retiring to the company command post for medical attention. Shortly thereafter, when the enemy launched the first of a series of savage counterattacks lasting all night, he voluntarily rejoined his besieged units and repeatedly exposed himself to the merciless hail of shrapnel and bullets, dashing 50 yards into the open on one occasion to rescue a wounded marine lying helpless beyond the front lines. Fighting fiercely in hand-to-hand encounters, he led his men in furiously waged battle for approximately 10 hours, tenaciously holding his line and repelling the fanatically renewed counterthrusts until he succeeded in crushing the last efforts of the hard-pressed Japanese early the following morning. Then organizing a 17-man patrol, he immediately advanced upon a strategic slope essential to the security of his position and, boldly defying intense mortar, machine-gun, and rifle fire which struck down 13 of his men, drove relentlessly forward with the remnants of his patrol to seize the vital ground. By his indomitable leadership, daring combat tactics, and valor in the face of overwhelming odds, Capt. Wilson succeede d in capturing and holding the strategic high ground in his regimental sector, thereby contributing essentially to the success of his regimental mission and to the annihilation of 350 Japanese troops. His inspiring conduct throughout the critical periods of this decisive action sustains and enhances the highest traditions of the U.S. Naval Service.

3020 ◆ *WILSON, ROBERT LEE

Rank: Private First Class
Service: U.S. Marine Corps
Birthday: 24 May 1921
Place of Birth: Centralia, Marion County, Illinois
Date of Death: 4 August 1944
Cemetery: Hillcrest Memorial Park (MH)—Centralia, Illinois

Entered Service at: Illinois
Unit: 2d Battalion, 6th Marines, 2d Marine Division
Battle or Place of Action: Tinian Island, Mariana Islands
Date of Action: 4 August 1944
Citation: For conspicuous gallantry and intrepidity at the risk of his life above and beyond the call of duty while serving with the 2d Battalion, 6th Marines, 2d Marine Division, during action against enemy Japanese forces at Tinian Island, Marianas Group, on 4 August 1944. As one of a group of marines advancing through heavy underbrush to neutralize isolated points of resistance, Pfc. Wilson daringly preceded his companions toward a pile of rocks where Japanese troops were supposed to be hiding. Fully aware of the danger involved, he was moving forward while the remainder of the squad, armed with automatic rifles, closed together in the rear when an enemy grenade landed in the midst of the group. Quick to act, Pfc. Wilson cried a warning to the men and unhesitatingly threw himself on the grenade, heroically sacrificing his own life that the others might live and fulfill their mission. His exceptional valor, his courageous loyalty and unwavering devotion to duty in the face of grave peril reflect the highest credit upon Pfc. Wilson and the U.S. Naval Service. He gallantly gave his life for his country.

3021 ◆ WISE, HOMER L.

Rank: Staff Sergeant (highest rank: First Sergeant)
Service: U.S. Army
Birthday: 27 February 1917
Place of Birth: Baton Rouge, East Baton Rouge County, Louisiana
Date of Death: 22 April 1974
Place of Death: Springdale, Connecticut
Cemetery: St. John's Cemetery (MH)—Darien, Connecticut
Entered Service at: Baton Rouge, East Baton Rouge County, Louisiana
Unit: Company L, 142d Infantry, 36th Infantry Division
Battle or Place of Action: Magliano, Italy
Date of Action: 14 June 1944
G.O. Number, Date: 90, 8 December 1944
Citation: While his platoon was pinned down by enemy small-arms fire from both flanks, he left his position of comparative safety and assisted in carrying one of his men, who had been seriously wounded and who lay in an exposed position, to a point where he could receive medical attention. The advance of the platoon was resumed, but was again stopped by enemy frontal fire. A German officer and two enlisted men, armed with automatic weapons, threatened the right flank. Fearlessly exposing himself, he moved to a position from which he killed all three with his submachine gun. Returning to his squad, he obtained an M1 rifle and several antitank grenades, then took up a position from which he delivered accurate fire on the enemy holding up the advance. As the battalion moved forward it was again stopped by enemy frontal and flanking fire. He procured an automatic rifle and, advancing ahead of his men, neutralized an enemy machine gun with his fire. When the flanking fire became more intense he ran to a nearby tank and, exposing himself

on the turret, restored a jammed machine gun to operating efficiency and used it so effectively that the enemy fire from the adjacent ridge was materially reduced, thus permitting the battalion to occupy its objective.

3022 ◆ *WITEK, FRANK PETER

Rank: Private First Class
Service: U.S. Marine Corps Reserve
Birthday: 10 December 1921
Place of Birth: Derby, New Haven County, Connecticut
Date of Death: 3 August 1944
Cemetery: Rock Island National Cemetery (E-72) (MH)—Rock Island, Illinois
Entered Service at: Illinois
Unit: 1st Battalion, 9th Marines, 3d Marine Division
Battle or Place of Action: Finegayen, Guam, Mariana Islands
Date of Action: 3 August 1944
Citation: For conspicuous gallantry and intrepidity at the risk of his life above and beyond the call of duty while serving with the 1st Battalion, 9th Marines, 3d Marine Division, during the battle of Finegayen at Guam, Marianas, on 3 August 1944. When his rifle platoon was halted by heavy surprise fire from well-camouflaged enemy positions, Pfc. Witek daringly remained standing to fire a full magazine from his automatic at point-blank range into a depression housing Japanese troops, killing eight of the enemy and enabling the greater part of his platoon to take cover. During his platoon's withdrawal for consolidation of lines, he remained to safeguard a severely wounded comrade, courageously returning the enemy's fire until the arrival of stretcher bearers and then covering the evacuation by sustained fire as he moved backward toward his own lines. With his platoon again pinned down by a hostile machine gun, Pfc. Witek, on his own initiative, moved forward boldly to the reinforcing tanks and infantry, alternately throwing hand grenades and firing as he advanced to within 5 to 10 yards of the enemy position, and destroying the hostile machine-gun emplacement and an additional eight Japanese before he himself was struck down by an enemy rifleman. His valiant and inspiring action effectively reduced the enemy's firepower, thereby enabling his platoon to attain its objective, and reflects the highest credit upon Pfc. Witek and the U.S. Naval Service. He gallantly gave his life for his country.

3023 ◆ *WOODFORD, HOWARD E.

Rank: Staff Sergeant
Service: U.S. Army
Birthday: 21 June 1921
Place of Birth: Barberton, Summit County, Ohio
Date of Death: 6 June 1945
Cemetery: Greenlawn Memorial Park (MH)—Akron, Ohio
Entered Service at: Barberton, Summit County, Ohio
Unit: Company I, 130th Infantry, 33d Infantry Division
Battle or Place of Action: near Tabio, Luzon, Philippine Islands
Date of Action: 6 June 1945
G.O. Number, Date: 14, 4 February 1946
Citation: He volunteered to investigate the delay in a scheduled attack by an attached guerrilla battalion. Reaching the line of departure, he found that the lead company, in combat for the first time, was immobilized by intense enemy mortar, machine-gun, and rifle fire which had caused casualties to key personnel. Knowing that further failure to advance would endanger the flanks of adjacent units as well as delay capture of the objective, he immediately took command of the company, evacuated the wounded, reorganized the unit under fire, and prepared to attack. He repeatedly exposed himself to draw revealing fire from the Japanese strongpoints and then moved forward with a five-man covering force to determine exact enemy positions. Although intense enemy machine-gun fire killed two and wounded his other three men, S/Sgt. Woodford resolutely continued his patrol before returning to the company. Then, against bitter resistance, he guided the guerrillas up a barren hill and captured the objective, personally accounting for two hostile machine gunners and courageously reconnoitering strong defensive positions before directing neutralizing fire. After organizing a perimeter defense for the night, he was given permission by radio to return to his battalion, but, feeling that he was needed to maintain proper control, he chose to remain with the guerrillas. Before dawn the next morning the enemy launched a fierce suicide attack with mortars, grenades, and small-arms fire, and infiltrated through the perimeter. Though wounded by a grenade, S/Sgt. Woodford remained at his post calling for mortar support until bullets knocked out his radio. Then, seizing a rifle he began working his way around the perimeter, encouraging the men until he reached a weak spot where two guerrillas had been killed. Filling the gap himself, he fought off the enemy. At daybreak he was found dead in his foxhole, but 37 enemy dead were lying in and around his position. By his daring, skillful, and inspiring leadership as well as by his gallant determination to search out and kill the enemy, S/Sgt. Woodford led an inexperienced unit in capturing and securing a vital objective and was responsible for the successful continuance of a vitally important general advance.

3024 ◆ YOUNG, CASSIN

Rank: Commander (highest rank: Captain)
Service: U.S. Navy
Birthday: 6 March 1894
Place of Birth: Washington, D.C.
Date of Death: 13 November 1942
Place of Death: At Sea Off Guadalcanal
Cemetery: A.B.M.C. Manila Cemetery (Wall of the Missing)—Manila, Buried at sea; Mt. Pleasant Memorial Park ('In Memory' marker only) (MH)—Mt. Pleasant, South Carolina
Entered Service at: Wisconsin
Unit: U.S.S. *Vestal*
Served as: Commanding Officer
Battle or Place of Action: Pearl Harbor, Territory of Hawaii
Date of Action: 7 December 1941
Date of Presentation: 18 April 1942

Place of Presentation: Pearl Harbor, Territory of Hawaii, presented by Adm. Chester W. Nimitz
Citation: For distinguished conduct in action, outstanding heroism and utter disregard of his own safety, above and beyond the call of duty, as commanding officer of the U.S.S. *Vestal*, during the attack on the Fleet in Pearl Harbor, Territory of Hawaii, by enemy Japanese forces on 7 December 1941. Comdr. Young proceeded to the bridge and later took personal command of the three-inch antiaircraft gun. When blown overboard by the blast of the forward magazine explosion of the U.S.S. *Arizona*, to which the U.S.S. *Vestal* was moored, he swam back to his ship. The entire forward part of the U.S.S. *Arizona* was a blazing inferno with oil afire on the water between the two ships; as a result of several bomb hits, the U.S.S. *Vestal* was afire in several places, was settling and taking on a list. Despite severe enemy bombing and strafing at the time and his shocking experience of having been blown overboard, Comdr. Young, with extreme coolness and calmness, moved his ship to an anchorage distant from the U.S.S. *Arizona*, and subsequently beached the U.S.S. *Vestal* upon determining that such action was required to save his ship.

3025 ◆ *YOUNG, RODGER W.

Rank: Private
Service: U.S. Army
Birthday: 28 April 1918
Place of Birth: Tiffin, Seneca County, Ohio
Date of Death: 31 July 1943
Cemetery: McPherson Cemetery—Clyde, Ohio
Entered Service at: Clyde, Sandusky County, Ohio
Unit: 148th Infantry, 37th Infantry Division
Battle or Place of Action: New Georgia, Solomon Islands
Date of Action: 31 July 1943
G.O. Number, Date: 3, 6 January 1944
Date of Presentation: 17 January 1944
Place of Presentation: Fort Knox, Kentucky, presented by Maj. Gen. Charles Scott to his family
Citation: On 31 July 1943, the infantry company of which Pvt. Young was a member, was ordered to make a limited withdrawal from the battle line in order to adjust the battalion's position for the night. At this time, Pvt. Young's platoon was engaged with the enemy in a dense jungle where observation was very limited. The platoon suddenly was pinned down by intense fire from a Japanese machine gun concealed on higher ground only 75 yards away. The initial burst wounded Pvt. Young. As the platoon started to obey the order to withdraw, Pvt. Young called out that he could see the enemy emplacement, whereupon he started creeping toward it. Another burst from the machine gun wounded him the second time. Despite the wounds, he continued his heroic advance, attracting enemy fire and answering with rifle fire. When he was close enough to his objective, he began throwing hand grenades, and while doing so was hit again and killed. Pvt. Young's bold action in closing with this Japanese pillbox, and thus diverting its fire, permitted his platoon to disengage itself, without loss, and was responsible for several enemy casualties.

3026 ◆ ZEAMER JR., JAY

Rank: Major (rank at time of action: Captain) (highest rank: Lieutenant Colonel)
Service: U.S. Army Air Corps
Birthday: 25 July 1918
Place of Birth: Carlisle, Cumberland County, Pennsylvania
Entered Service at: Machias, Washington County, Maine
Unit: 65th Bombardment Squadron, 43d Bombardment Group, 5th Air Force
Served as: Aircraft Commander/Pilot of a B-17
Battle or Place of Action: over Buka area, Solomon Islands
Date of Action: 16 June 1943
G.O. Number, Date: 14 January 1944
Date of Presentation: 16 January 1944
Place of Presentation: The Pentagon, presented by Gen. Henry H. (Hap) Arnold in his office
Citation: On 16 June 1943, Maj. Zeamer (then Capt.) volunteered as pilot of a bomber on an important photographic mapping mission covering the formidably defended area in the vicinity of Buka, Solomon Islands. While photographing the Buka airdrome, his crew observed about 20 enemy fighters on the field, many of them taking off. Despite the certainty of a dangerous attack by this strong force, Maj. Zeamer proceeded with his mapping run, even after the enemy attack began. In the ensuing engagement, Maj. Zeamer sustained gunshot wounds in both arms and legs, one leg being broken. Despite his injuries, he maneuvered the damaged plane so skillfully that his gunners were able to fight off the enemy during a running flight which lasted 40 minutes. The crew destroyed at least five hostile planes, of which Maj. Zeamer himself shot down one. Although weak from loss of blood, he refused medical aid until the enemy had broken combat. He then turned over the controls, but continued to exercise command despite lapses into unconsciousness, and directed the flight to a base 580 miles away. In this voluntary action, Maj. Zeamer, with superb skill, resolution, and courage, accomplished a mission of great value.

3027 ◆ *ZUSSMAN, RAYMOND

Rank: Second Lieutenant
Service: U.S. Army
Birthday: 23 July 1917
Place of Birth: Hamtramck, Wayne County, Michigan
Date of Death: 21 September 1944
Cemetery: The Machpelah Cemetery—Ferndale, Michigan
Entered Service at: Detroit, Wayne County, Michigan
Unit: Company A, 756th Tank Battalion, 3d Infantry Division
Served as: Tank Commander
Battle or Place of Action: Noroy le Bourg, France
Date of Action: 12 September 1944
G.O. Number, Date: 42, 24 May 1945
Citation: On 12 September 1944, 2d Lt. Zussman was in command of two tanks operating with an infantry company in the attack on enemy forces occupying the town of Noroy-le-bourg, France. At 7:00 P.M., his command tank bogged down. Throughout the ensuing action, armed only with a

carbine, he reconnoitered alone on foot far in advance of his remaining tank and the infantry. Returning only from time to time to designate targets, he directed the action of the tank and turned over to the infantry the numerous German soldiers he had caused to surrender. He located a road block and directed his tanks to destroy it. Fully exposed to fire from enemy positions only 50 yards distant, he stood by his tank directing its fire. Three Germans were killed and eight surrendered. Again he walked before his tank, leading it against an enemy-held group of houses, machine-gun and small-arms fire kicking up dust at his feet. The tank fire broke the resistance and 20 enemy surrendered. Going forward again alone he passed an enemy-occupied house from which Germans fired on him and threw grenades in his path. After a brief firefight, he signaled his tank to come up and fire on the house. Eleven German soldiers were killed and 15 surrendered. Going on alone, he disappeared around a street corner. The fire of his carbine could be heard and in a few minutes he reappeared driving 30 prisoners before him. Under 2d Lt. Zussman's heroic and inspiring leadership, 18 enemy soldiers were killed and 92 captured.

KOREAN WAR

3028 ◆ *ABRELL, CHARLES GENE

Rank: Corporal
Service: U.S. Marine Corps
Birthday: 12 August 1931
Place of Birth: Terre Haute, Vigo County, Indiana
Date of Death: 10 June 1951
Cemetery: Westlawn Cemetery—Farmersburg, Indiana
Entered Service at: Terre Haute, Vigo County, Indiana
Unit: Company E, 2d Battalion, 1st Marines, 1st Marine Division (Rein)
Served as: Fire Team Leader
Battle or Place of Action: Hangnyong, Korea
Date of Action: 10 June 1951
Date of Presentation: 4 September 1952
Place of Presentation: The Pentagon, presented by Sec. of the Navy Dan A. Kimball to his Mother
Citation: For conspicuous gallantry and intrepidity at the risk of his life above and beyond the call of duty while serving as a fire team leader in Company E, in action against enemy aggressor forces. While advancing with his platoon in an attack against well-concealed and heavily fortified enemy hill positions, Cpl. Abrell voluntarily rushed forward through the assaulting squad which was pinned down by a hail of intense and accurate automatic-weapons fire from a hostile bunker situated on commanding ground. Although previously wounded by enemy hand-grenade fragments, he proceeded to carry out a bold, single-handed attack against the bunker, exhorting his comrades to follow him. Sustaining two additional wounds as he stormed toward the emplacement, he resolutely pulled the pin from a grenade clutched in his hand and hurled himself bodily into the bunker with the live missile still in his grasp. Fatally wounded in the resulting explosion which killed the entire enemy gun crew within the stronghold, Cpl. Abrell, by his valiant spirit of self-sacrifice in the face of certain death, served to inspire all his comrades and contributed directly to the success of his platoon in attaining its objective. His superb courage and heroic initiative sustain and enhance the highest traditions of the U.S. Naval Service. He gallantly gave his life for his country.

3029 ◆ ADAMS, STANLEY TAYLOR

Rank: Master Sergeant (rank at time of action: Sergeant First Class) (highest rank: Lieutenant Colonel)
Service: U.S. Army
Birthday: 9 May 1922
Place of Birth: DeSoto, Johnson County, Kansas
Entered Service at: Olathe, Johnson County, Kansas
Unit: 1st Platoon, Company A, 1st Battalion, 19th Infantry Regiment, 24th Infantry Division
Served as: Platoon Sergeant
Battle or Place of Action: Sesim-ni, Korea
Date of Action: 4 February 1951
G.O. Number, Date: 66, 2 August 1951
Date of Presentation: 5 July 1951
Place of Presentation: The White House, presented by Pres. Harry S. Truman
Citation: M/Sgt. Adams, Company A, distinguished himself by conspicuous gallantry and intrepidity above and beyond the call of duty in action against an enemy. At approximately 0100 hours M/Sgt. Adams' platoon, holding an outpost some 200 yards ahead of his company, came under a determined attack by an estimated 250 enemy troops. Intense small-arms, machine-gun, and mortar fire from three sides pressed the platoon back against the main line of resistance. Observing approximately 150 hostile troops silhouetted against the skyline advancing against his platoon, M/Sgt. Adams leaped to his feet, urged his men to fix bayonets, and he, with 13 members of his platoon, charged this hostile force with indomitable courage. Within 50 yards of the enemy M/Sgt. Adams was knocked to the ground when pierced in the leg by an enemy bullet. He jumped to his feet and, ignoring his wound, continued on to close with the enemy when he was knocked down four times from the concussion of grenades which had bounced off his body. Shouting orders he charged the enemy positions and engaged them in hand-to-hand combat where man after man fell before his terrific onslaught with bayonet and rifle butt. After nearly an hour of vicious action M/Sgt. Adams and his comrades routed the fanatical foe, killing over 50 and forcing the remainder to withdraw. Upon receiving orders that his battalion was moving back he provided cover fire while his men withdrew. M/Sgt. Adams' superb leadership, incredible courage, and consummate devotion to duty so inspired his comrades that the enemy attack was completely thwarted, saving his battalion from possible disaster. His sustained personal bravery and indomitable fighting spirit against overwhelming odds reflect the utmost glory upon himself and uphold the finest traditions of the infantry and the military service.

3030 ◆ BARBER, WILLIAM EARL

Rank: Captain (highest rank: Colonel)
Service: U.S. Marine Corps
Birthday: 30 November 1919
Place of Birth: Dehart, Morgan County, Kentucky
Entered Service at: West Liberty, Morgan County, Kentucky

Unit: Company F, 2d Battalion, 7th Marines, 1st Marine Division (Rein)
Served as: Commanding Officer
Battle or Place of Action: Chosin Reservoir, Korea
Date of Action: 2 December 1950
Date of Presentation: 20 August 1952
Place of Presentation: The White House, presented by Pres. Harry S. Truman
Citation: For conspicuous gallantry and intrepidity at the risk of his life above and beyond the call of duty as commanding officer of Company F in action against enemy aggressor forces. Assigned to defend a three-mile mountain pass along the division's main supply line and commanding the only route of approach in the march from Yudam-ni to Hagaru-ri, Capt. Barber took position with his battle-weary troops, and, before nightfall, had dug in and set up a defense along the frozen, snow-covered hillside. When a force of estimated regimental strength savagely attacked during the night, inflicting heavy casualties and finally surrounding his position following a bitterly fought seven-hour conflict, Capt. Barber, after repulsing the enemy, gave assurance that he could hold if supplied by airdrops and requested permission to stand fast when orders were received by radio to fight his way back to a relieving force after two reinforcing units had been driven back under fierce resistance in their attempts to reach the isolated troops. Aware that leaving the position would sever contact with the 8,000 marines trapped at Yudam-ni and jeopardize their chances of joining the 3,000 more awaiting their arrival in Hagaru-ri for the continued drive to the sea, he chose to risk loss of his command rather than sacrifice more men if the enemy seized control and forced a renewed battle to regain the position, or abandon his many wounded who were unable to walk. Although severely wounded in the leg in the early morning of the 29th, Capt. Barber continued to maintain personal control, often moving up and down the lines on a stretcher to direct the defense and consistently encouraging and inspiring his men to supreme efforts despite the staggering opposition. Waging desperate battle throughout five days and six nights of repeated onslaughts launched by the fanatical aggressors, he and his heroic command accounted for approximately 1,000 enemy dead in this epic stand in bitter subzero weather, and when the company was relieved, only 82 of his original 220 men were able to walk away from the position so valiantly defended against insuperable odds. His profound faith and courage, great personal valor, and unwavering fortitude were decisive factors in the successful withdrawal of the division from the deathtrap in the Chosin Reservoir sector and reflect the highest credit upon Capt. Barber, his intrepid officers and men, and the U.S. Naval Service.

3031 ◆ *BARKER, CHALRES H.

Rank: Private First Class
Service: U.S. Army
Birthday: 12 April 1935
Place of Birth: Pickens County, South Carolina
Date of Death: 4 June 1953
Cemetery: National Memorial of the Pacific (Wall of the Missing)—Honolulu, Hawaii
Entered Service at: Pickens County, South Carolina

Unit: Company K, 17th Infantry Regiment, 7th Infantry Division
Served as: Rifleman
Battle or Place of Action: Sokkogae, Korea
Date of Action: 4 June 1953
G.O. Number, Date: 37, 7 June 1955
Citation: Pfc. Barker, a member of Company K, distinguished himself by conspicuous gallantry and indomitable courage above and beyond the call of duty in action against the enemy. While participating in a combat patrol engaged in screening an approach to "Pork-Chop Outpost," Pfc. Barker and his companions surprised and engaged an enemy group digging emplacements on the slope. Totally unprepared, the hostile troops sought cover. After ordering Pfc. Barker and a comrade to lay down a base of fire, the patrol leader maneuvered the remainder of the platoon to a vantage point on higher ground. Pfc. Barker moved to an open area firing his rifle and hurling grenades on the hostile positions. As enemy action increased in volume and intensity, mortar bursts fell on friendly positions, ammunition was in critical supply, and the platoon was ordered to withdraw into a perimeter defense preparatory to moving back to the outpost. Voluntarily electing to cover the retrograde movement, he gallantly maintained a defense and was last seen in close hand-to-hand combat with the enemy. Pfc. Barker's unflinching courage, consummate devotion to duty, and supreme sacrifice enabled the patrol to complete the mission and effect an orderly withdrawal to friendly lines, reflecting lasting glory upon himself and upholding the highest traditions of the military service.
Notes: MIA

3032 ◆ *BAUGH, WILLIAM BERNARD

Rank: Private First Class
Service: U.S. Marine Corps
Birthday: 7 July 1930
Place of Birth: McKinney, Lincoln County, Kentucky
Date of Death: 29 November 1950
Cemetery: Glen Haven Cemetery (MH)—Harrison, Ohio
Entered Service at: Harrison, Hamilton County, Ohio
Unit: Company G, 3d Battalion, 1st Marines, 1st Marine Division (Rein)
Battle or Place of Action: along the road from Koto-ri to Hagaru-ri, Korea
Date of Action: 29 November 1950
Date of Presentation: 27 August 1952
Place of Presentation: Dayton, Ohio, presented to parents
Citation: For conspicuous gallantry and intrepidity at the risk of his life above and beyond the call of duty while serving as a member of an antitank assault squad attached to Company G, during a nighttime enemy attack against a motorized column. Acting instantly when a hostile hand grenade landed in his truck as he and his squad prepared to alight and assist in the repulse of an enemy force delivering intense automatic-weapons and grenade fire from deeply entrenched and well-concealed roadside positions, Pfc. Baugh quickly shouted a warning to the other men in the vehicle and, unmindful of his personal safety, hurled himself upon the deadly missile, thereby saving his comrades from serious injury or possible death. Sustaining severe wounds from

which he died a short time afterward, Pfc. Baugh, by his superb courage and valiant spirit of self-sacrifice, upheld the highest traditions of the U.S. Naval Service. He gallantly gave his life for his country.

3033 ◆ *BENFOLD, EDWARD CLYDE "TED"

Rank: Hospital Corpsman Third Class
Service: U.S. Navy
Birthday: 15 January 1931
Place of Birth: Staten Island, Richmond County, New York
Date of Death: 5 September 1952
Cemetery: Beverly National Cemetery (N-804) (MH)—Beverly, New Jersey
Entered Service at: Philadelphia, Philadelphia County, Pennsylvania
Unit: Attached to a company in the 1st Marine Division
Served as: Medical Corpsman
Battle or Place of Action: Korea
Date of Action: 5 September 1952
Date of Presentation: 16 July 1953
Place of Presentation: Philadelphia Naval Base, Pa., presented by Rear Adm. John H. Brown Jr., Commandant 4th Naval District, to his son Edward Joseph Benfold
Citation: For gallantry and intrepidity at the risk of his life above and beyond the call of duty while serving in operations against enemy aggressor forces. When his company was subjected to heavy artillery and mortar barrages, followed by a determined assault during the hours of darkness by an enemy force estimated at battalion strength, HC3c. Benford resolutely moved from position to position in the face of intense hostile fire, treating the wounded and lending words of encouragement. Leaving the protection of his sheltered position to treat the wounded when the platoon area in which he was working was attacked from both the front and rear, he moved forward to an exposed ridgeline where he observed two marines in a large crater. As he approached the two men to determine their condition, an enemy soldier threw two grenades into the crater while two other enemy charged the position. Picking up a grenade in each hand, HC3c. Benford leaped out of the crater and hurled himself against the onrushing hostile soldiers, pushing the grenades against their chests and killing both the attackers. Mortally wounded while carrying out this heroic act, HC3c. Benford, by his great personal valor and resolute spirit of self-sacrifice in the face of almost certain death, was directly responsible for saving the lives of his two comrades. His exceptional courage reflects the highest credit upon himself and enhances the finest traditions of the U.S. Naval Service. He gallantly gave his life for others.

3034 ◆ *BENNETT, EMORY L.

Rank: Private First Class
Service: U.S. Army
Birthday: 20 December 1929
Place of Birth: New Smyrna Beach, Volusia County, Florida
Date of Death: 24 June 1951
Cemetery: Pine Crest Cemetery—Cocoa, Florida
Entered Service at: Cocoa, Brevard County, Florida

Unit: Company B, 15th Infantry Regiment, 3d Infantry Division
Served as: Automatic Rifleman
Battle or Place of Action: Sobangsan, Korea
Date of Action: 24 June 1951
G.O. Number, Date: 11, 1 February 1952
Date of Presentation: 16 January 1952
Place of Presentation: The Pentagon, presented by the Sec. of Defense Robert Lovett to his Father
Citation: Pfc. Bennett, a member of company B, distinguished himself by conspicuous gallantry and intrepidity at the risk of his life above and beyond the call of duty in action against an armed enemy of the United Nations. At approximately 0200 hours, two enemy battalions swarmed up the ridgeline in a ferocious banzai charge in an attempt to dislodge Pfc. Bennett's company from its defensive positions. Meeting the challenge, the gallant defenders delivered destructive retaliation, but the enemy pressed the assault with fanatical determination and the integrity of the perimeter was imperiled. Fully aware of the odds against him, Pfc. Bennett unhesitatingly left his foxhole, moved through withering fire, stood within full view of the enemy, and, employing his automatic rifle, poured crippling fire into the ranks of the onrushing assailants, inflicting numerous casualties. Although wounded, Pfc. Bennett gallantly maintained his one-man defense and the attack was momentarily halted. During this lull in battle, the company regrouped for counterattack, but the numerically superior foe soon infiltrated into the position. Upon orders to move back, Pfc. Bennett voluntarily remained to provide covering fire for the withdrawing elements, and, defying the enemy, continued to sweep the charging foe with devastating fire until mortally wounded. His willing self-sacrifice and intrepid actions saved the position from being overrun and enabled the company to effect an orderly withdrawal. Pfc. Bennett's unflinching courage and consummate devotion to duty reflect lasting glory on himself and the military service.

3035 ◆ BLEAK, DAVID BRUCE

Rank: Sergeant
Service: U.S. Army
Birthday: 27 February 1932
Place of Birth: Idaho Falls, Bonneville County, Idaho
Entered Service at: Shelley, Bingham County, Idaho
Unit: Medical Company, 2d, Battalion, 223d Infantry Regiment, 40th Infantry Division
Served as: Medical Aidman
Battle or Place of Action: Minari-gol, Korea
Date of Action: 14 June 1952
G.O. Number, Date: 83, 2 November 1953
Date of Presentation: 27 October 1953
Place of Presentation: The White House, presented by Pres. Dwight D. Eisenhower
Citation: Sgt. Bleak, a member of the medical company, distinguished himself by conspicuous gallantry and indomitable courage above and beyond the call of duty in action against the enemy. As a medical aidman, he volunteered to accompany a reconnaissance patrol committed to engage the enemy and capture a prisoner for interrogation. Forging up the

rugged slope of the key terrain, the group was subjected to intense automatic-weapons and small-arms fire and suffered several casualties. After administering to the wounded, he continued to advance with the patrol. Nearing the military crest of the hill, while attempting to cross the fire-swept area to attend the wounded, he came under hostile fire from a small group of the enemy concealed in a trench. Entering the trench he closed with the enemy, killed two with bare hands and a third with his trench knife. Moving from the emplacement, he saw a concussion grenade fall in front of a companion and, quickly shifting his position, shielded the man from the impact of the blast. Later, while ministering to the wounded, he was struck by a hostile bullet but, despite the wound, he undertook to evacuate a wounded comrade. As he moved down the hill with his heavy burden, he was attacked by two enemy soldiers with fixed bayonets. Closing with the aggressors, he grabbed them and smacked their heads together, then carried his helpless comrade down the hill to safety. Sgt. Bleak's dauntless courage and intrepid actions reflect utmost credit upon himself and are in keeping with the honored traditions of the military service.

3036 ◆ *BRITTIN, NELSON VOGEL

Rank: Sergeant First Class
Service: U.S. Army
Birthday: 31 October 1920
Place of Birth: Audubon, Camden County, New Jersey
Date of Death: 7 March 1951
Cemetery: Beverly National Cemetery (OS-2) (MH)—Beverly, New Jersey
Entered Service at: Audubon, Camden County, New Jersey
Unit: Company I, 19th Infantry Regiment
Served as: Squad Leader
Battle or Place of Action: Yonggong-ni, Korea
Date of Action: 7 March 1951
G.O. Number, Date: 12, 1 February 1952
Date of Presentation: 16 January 1952
Place of Presentation: The Pentagon, presented by the Sec. of Defense Robert Lovett to his parents
Citation: Sfc. Brittin, a member of Company I, distinguished himself by conspicuous gallantry and intrepidity above and beyond the call of duty in action. Volunteering to lead his squad up a hill, with meager cover against murderous fire from the enemy, he ordered his squad to give him support and, in the face of withering fire and bursting shells, he tossed a grenade at the nearest enemy position. On returning to his squad, he was knocked down and wounded by an enemy grenade. Refusing medical attention, he replenished his supply of grenades and returned, hurling grenades into hostile positions and shooting the enemy as they fled. When his weapon jammed, he leaped without hesitation into a foxhole and killed the occupants with his bayonet and the butt of his rifle. He continued to wipe out foxholes and, noting that his squad had been pinned down, he rushed to the rear of a machine-gun position, threw a grenade into the nest, and ran around to its front, where he killed all three occupants with his rifle. Less than 100 yards up the hill, his squad again came under vicious fire from another camouflaged, sand-

bagged, machine-gun nest well-flanked by supporting riflemen. Sfc. Brittin again charged this new position in an aggressive endeavor to silence this remaining obstacle and ran directly into a burst of automatic fire which killed him instantly. In his sustained and driving action, he had killed 20 enemy soldiers and destroyed four automatic weapons. The conspicuous courage, consummate valor, and noble self-sacrifice displayed by Sfc. Brittin enabled his inspired company to attain its objective and reflect the highest glory on himself and the heroic traditions of the military service.

3037 ◆ *BROWN, MELVIN L.

Rank: Private First Class
Service: U.S. Army
Birthday: 22 February 1931
Place of Birth: Mahaffey, Clearfield County, Pennsylvania
Date of Death: 5 September 1950
Cemetery: Mahaffey Cemetery—Mahaffey, Pennsylvania
Entered Service at: Erie, Erie County, Pennsylvania
Unit: Company D, 8th Combat Engineer Battalion, 1st Cavalry Div.
Served as: Rifleman
Battle or Place of Action: Kasan, Korea
Date of Action: 4 September 1950
G.O. Number, Date: 11, 16 February 1951
Date of Presentation: 9 January 1951
Place of Presentation: The White House, presented by Pres. Harry S. Truman to his Father
Citation: Pfc. Brown, Company D, distinguished himself by conspicuous gallantry and intrepidity above and beyond the call of duty in action against the enemy. While his platoon was securing Hill 755 (the Walled City), the enemy, using heavy automatic weapons and small arms, counterattacked. Taking a position on a 50-foot-high wall he delivered heavy rifle fire on the enemy. His ammunition was soon expended and although wounded, he remained at his post and threw his few grenades into the attackers, causing many casualties. When his supply of grenades was exhausted his comrades from nearby foxholes tossed others to him and he left his position, braving a hail of fire, to retrieve and throw them at the enemy. The attackers continued to assault his position and Pfc. Brown, weaponless, drew his entrenching tool from his pack and calmly waited until they one by one peered over the wall, delivering each a crushing blow upon the head. Knocking 10 or 12 enemy from the wall, his daring action so inspired his platoon that they repelled the attack and held their position. Pfc. Brown's extraordinary heroism, gallantry, and intrepidity reflect the highest credit upon himself and was in keeping with the honored traditions of the military service. Reportedly missing in action and officially killed in action, September 5, 1950.

3038 ◆ BURKE, LLOYD LESLIE "SCOOTER"

Rank: First Lieutenant (highest rank: Colonel)
Service: U.S. Army
Birthday: 29 September 1924
Place of Birth: Tichnor, Arkansas County, Arkansas

Entered Service at: Stuttgart, Arkansas County, Arkansas
Unit: Company G, 2d Battalion, 5th Cavalry Regiment, 1st Cavalry Division
Served as: Company Commander
Battle or Place of Action: Chong-dong, Korea
Date of Action: 28 October 1951
G.O. Number, Date: 43
Date of Presentation: 12 April 1952
Place of Presentation: The White House, presented by Pres. Harry S. Truman
Citation: First Lt. Burke, distinguished himself by conspicuous gallantry and outstanding courage above and beyond the call of duty in action against the enemy. Intense enemy fire had pinned down leading elements of his company committed to secure commanding ground when 1st Lt. Burke left the command post to rally and urge the men to follow him toward three bunkers impeding the advance. Dashing to an exposed vantage point he threw several grenades at the bunkers, then, returning for an M1 rifle and adapter, he made a lone assault, wiping out the position and killing the crew. Closing on the center bunker he lobbed grenades through the opening and, with his pistol, killed three of its occupants attempting to surround him. Ordering his men forward he charged the third emplacement, catching several grenades in midair and hurling them back at the enemy. Inspired by his display of valor his men stormed forward, overran the hostile position, but were again pinned down by increased fire. Securing a light machine gun and three boxes of ammunition, 1st Lt. Burke dashed through the impact area to an open knoll, set up his gun, and poured a crippling fire into the ranks of the enemy, killing approximately 75. Although wounded, he ordered more ammunition, reloading and destroying two mortar emplacements and a machine-gun position with his accurate fire. Cradling the weapon in his arms he then led his men forward, killing some 25 more of the retreating enemy and securing the objective. First Lt. Burke's heroic action and daring exploits inspired his small force of 35 troops. His unflinching courage and outstanding leadership reflect the highest credit upon himself, the infantry, and the U.S. Army.

3039 ◆ *BURRIS, TONY K.

Rank: Sergeant First Class
Service: U.S. Army
Birthday: 30 May 1929
Place of Birth: Blanchard, McClain County, Oklahoma
Date of Death: 9 October 1951
Cemetery: Blanchard Cemetery (MH)—Blanchard, Oklahoma
Entered Service at: Blanchard, McClain County, Oklahoma
Unit: Company L, 38th Infantry Regiment, 2d Infantry Division
Battle or Place of Action: Mundung-ni, Korea
Date of Action: 8-9 October 1951
G.O. Number, Date: 84, 5 September 1952
Date of Presentation: 14 August 1952
Place of Presentation: The Pentagon, presented by Gen. Omar N. Bradley to his Mother
Citation: Sfc. Burris, a member of Company L, distin-

guished himself by conspicuous gallantry and outstanding courage above and beyond the call of duty. On 8 October, when his company encountered intense fire from an entrenched hostile force, Sfc. Burris charged forward alone, throwing grenades into the position and destroying approximately 15 of the enemy. On the following day, spearheading a renewed assault on enemy positions on the next ridge, he was wounded by machine-gun fire but continued the assault, reaching the crest of the ridge ahead of his unit and sustaining a second wound. Calling for a 57-mm recoilless-rifle team, he deliberately exposed himself to draw hostile fire and reveal the enemy position. The enemy machine-gun emplacement was destroyed. The company then moved forward and prepared to assault other positions on the ridgeline. Sfc. Burris, refusing evacuation and submitting only to emergency treatment, joined the unit in its renewed attack but fire from hostile emplacement halted the advance. Sfc. Burris rose to his feet, charged forward and destroyed the first emplacement with its heavy machine gun and crew of six men. Moving out to the next emplacement, and throwing his last grenade, which destroyed this position, he fell mortally wounded by enemy fire. Inspired by his consummate gallantry, his comrades renewed a spirited assault which overran enemy positions and secured Hill 605, a strategic position in the battle for "Heartbreak Ridge." Sfc. Burris' indomitable fighting spirit, outstanding heroism, and gallant self-sacrifice reflect the highest glory upon himself, the infantry, and the U.S. Army.

3040 ◆ CAFFERATA JR., HECTOR ALBERT

Rank: Private
Service: U.S. Marine Corps Reserve
Birthday: 4 November 1929
Place of Birth: New York, New York
Entered Service at: Dover, Morris County, New Jersey
Unit: Company F, 2d Battalion, 7th Marines, 1st Marine Division (Rein)
Served as: Rifleman
Battle or Place of Action: Toktong Pass, Korea
Date of Action: 28 November 1950
Date of Presentation: 24 November 1952
Place of Presentation: The White House, presented by Pres. Harry S. Truman
Citation: For conspicuous gallantry and intrepidity at the risk of his life above and beyond the call of duty while serving as a rifleman with Company F, in action against enemy aggressor forces. When all the other members of his fire team became casualties, creating a gap in the lines, during the initial phase of a vicious attack launched by a fanatical enemy of regimental strength against his company's hill position, Pvt. Cafferata waged a lone battle with grenades and rifle fire as the attack gained momentum and the enemy threatened penetration through the gap and endangered the integrity of the entire defensive perimeter. Making a target of himself under the devastating fire from automatic weapons, rifles, grenades, and mortars, he maneuvered up and down the line and delivered accurate and effective fire against the onrushing force, killing 15, wounding many more, and forcing the others to withdraw so that reinforcements could move up and consoli-

date the position. Again fighting desperately against a renewed onslaught later that same morning when a hostile grenade landed in a shallow entrenchment occupied by wounded marines, Pvt. Cafferata rushed into the gully under heavy fire, seized the deadly missile in his right hand and hurled it free of his comrades before it detonated, severing part of one finger and seriously wounding him in the right hand and arm. Courageously ignoring the intense pain, he stanchly fought on until he was struck by a sniper's bullet and forced to submit to evacuation for medical treatment. Stouthearted and indomitable, Pvt. Cafferata, by his fortitude, great personal valor, and dauntless perseverance in the face of almost certain death, saved the lives of several of his fellow marines and contributed essentially to the success achieved by his company in maintaining its defensive position against tremendous odds. His extraordinary heroism throughout was in keeping with the highest traditions of the U.S. Naval Service.

3041 ◆ *CHAMPAGNE, DAVID BERNARD

Rank: Corporal
Service: U.S. Marine Corps
Birthday: 13 November 1932
Place of Birth: Waterville, Kennebec County, Maine
Date of Death: 28 May 1952
Cemetery: St. Francis de Sales Cemetery (MH)—Waterville, Maine
Entered Service at: Wakefield, Washington County, Rhode Island
Unit: Company A, 1st Battalion, 7th Marines, 1st Marine Division (Rein)
Served as: Fire Team Leader
Battle or Place of Action: Korea
Date of Action: 28 May 1952
Citation: For conspicuous gallantry and intrepidity at the risk of his life above and beyond the call of duty while serving as a fire team leader of Company A, in action against enemy aggressor forces. Advancing with his platoon in the initial assault of the company against a strongly fortified and heavily defended hill position, Cpl. Champagne skillfully led his fire team through a veritable hail of intense enemy machine-gun, small-arms, and grenade fire, overrunning trenches and a series of almost impregnable bunker positions before reaching the crest of the hill and placing his men in defensive positions. Suffering a painful leg wound while assisting in repelling the ensuing hostile counterattack, which was launched under cover of a murderous hail of mortar and artillery fire, he steadfastly refused evacuation and fearlessly continued to control his fire team. When the enemy counterattack increased in intensity, and a hostile grenade landed in the midst of the fire team, Cpl. Champagne unhesitatingly seized the deadly missile and hurled it in the direction of the approaching enemy. As the grenade left his hand, it exploded, blowing off his hand and throwing him out of the trench. Mortally wounded by enemy mortar fire while in this exposed position, Cpl. Champagne, by his valiant leadership, fortitude, and gallant spirit of self-sacrifice in the face of almost certain death, undoubtedly saved the lives of several of his fellow marines. His heroic actions served to inspire all who observed

him and reflect the highest credit upon himself and the U.S. Naval Service. He gallantly gave his life for his country.

3042 ◆ CHARETTE, WILLIAM RICHARD

Rank: Hospital Corpsman Third Class (highest rank: Master Chief Hospital Corpsman)
Service: U.S. Navy
Birthday: 29 March 1932
Place of Birth: Ludington, Mason County, Michigan
Entered Service at: Ludington, Mason County, Michigan
Unit: Attached to Company F, 2d Battalion, 7th Marines, 1st Marine Division
Served as: Hospital Corpsman
Battle or Place of Action: Panmunjom Corridor (DMZ), Korea
Date of Action: 27 March 1953
Date of Presentation: 12 January 1954
Place of Presentation: The White House, presented by Pres. Dwight D. Eisenhower
Citation: For conspicuous gallantry and intrepidity at the risk of his life above and beyond the call of duty in action against enemy aggressor forces during the early morning hours. Participating in a fierce encounter with a cleverly concealed and well-entrenched enemy force occupying positions on a vital and bitterly contested outpost far in advance of the main line of resistance, HC3c. Charette repeatedly and unhesitatingly moved about through a murderous barrage of hostile small-arms and mortar fire to render assistance to his wounded comrades. When an enemy grenade landed within a few feet of a marine he was attending, he immediately threw himself upon the stricken man and absorbed the entire concussion of the deadly missile with his body. Although sustaining painful facial wounds and undergoing shock from the intensity of the blast which ripped the helmet and medical aid kit from his person, HC3c. Charette resourcefully improvised emergency bandages by tearing off part of his clothing, and gallantly continued to administer medical aid to the wounded in his own unit and to those in adjacent platoon areas as well. Observing a seriously wounded comrade whose armored vest had been torn from his body by the blast from an exploding shell, he selflessly removed his own battle vest and placed it upon the helpless man although fully aware of the added jeopardy to himself. Moving to the side of another casualty who was suffering excruciating pain from a serious leg wound, HC3c. Charette stood upright in the trench line and exposed himself to a deadly hail of enemy fire in order to lend more effective aid to the victim and to alleviate his anguish while being removed to a position of safety. By his indomitable courage and inspiring efforts in behalf of his wounded comrades, HC3c. Charette was directly responsible for saving many lives. His great personal valor reflects the highest credit upon himself and enhances the finest traditions of the U.S. Naval Service.

3043 ◆ *CHARLTON, CORNELIUS H.

Rank: Sergeant
Service: U.S. Army

Birthday: 24 July 1929
Place of Birth: East Gulf, Raleigh County, West Virginia
Date of Death: 2 June 1951
Place of Death: Chipo-ri, Korea
Cemetery: American Legion Cemetery (MH)—Beckley, West Virginia
Entered Service at: Bronx County, New York
Unit: Company C, 24th Infantry Regiment, 25th Infantry Division
Served as: Platoon Sergeant
Battle or Place of Action: Chipo-ri, Korea
Date of Action: 2 June 1951
G.O. Number, Date: 30, 19 March 1952
Date of Presentation: 12 March 1952
Place of Presentation: The Pentagon, presented by Sec. of the Army Frank C. Pace to his parents
Citation: Sgt. Charlton, a member of Company C, distinguished himself by conspicuous gallantry and intrepidity above and beyond the call of duty in action against the enemy. His platoon was attacking heavily defended hostile positions on commanding ground when the leader was wounded and evacuated. Sgt. Charlton assumed command, rallied the men, and spearheaded the assault against the hill. Personally eliminating two hostile positions and killing six of the enemy with his rifle fire and grenades, he continued up the slope until the unit suffered heavy casualties and became pinned down. Regrouping the men, he led them forward only to be again hurled back by a shower of grenades. Despite a severe chest wound, Sgt. Charlton refused medical attention and led a third daring charge which carried to the crest of the ridge. Observing that the remaining emplacement which had retarded the advance was situated on the reverse slope, he charged it alone, was again hit by a grenade but raked the position with a devastating fire which eliminated it and routed the defenders. The wounds received during his daring exploits resulted in his death, but his indomitable courage, superb leadership, and gallant self-sacrifice reflect the highest credit upon himself, the infantry, and the military service.

3044 ◆ *CHRISTIANSON, STANLEY REUBEN

Rank: Private First Class
Service: U.S. Marine Corps
Birthday: 24 January 1925
Place of Birth: Mindoro, La Crosse County, Wisconsin
Date of Death: 29 September 1950
Cemetery: Wet Coulee Cemetery (MH)—Mindoro, Wisconsin
Entered Service at: Mindoro, La Crosse County, Wisconsin
Unit: Company E, 2d Battalion, 1st Marines, 1st Marine Division (Rein)
Battle or Place of Action: Seoul, Korea
Date of Action: 29 September 1950
Date of Presentation: 30 August 1951
Place of Presentation: The Pentagon, presented by Sec. of the Navy Dan A. Kimball to his parents
Citation: For conspicuous gallantry and intrepidity at the risk of his life above and beyond the call of duty while serving with Company E, in action against enemy aggressor forces at

Hill 132, in the early morning hours. Manning one of the several listening posts covering approaches to the platoon area when the enemy commenced the attack, Pfc. Christianson quickly sent another marine to alert the rest of the platoon. Without orders, he remained in his position and, with full knowledge that he would have slight chance of escape, fired relentlessly at oncoming hostile troops attacking furiously with rifles, automatic weapons, and incendiary grenades. Accounting for seven enemy dead in the immediate vicinity before his position was overrun and he himself fatally struck down, Pfc. Christianson, by his superb courage, valiant fighting spirit, and devotion to duty, was responsible for allowing the rest of the platoon time to man positions, build up a stronger defense on that flank, and repel the attack with 41 of the enemy destroyed, many more wounded, and three taken prisoner. His self-sacrificing actions in the face of overwhelming odds sustain and enhance the finest traditions of the U.S. Naval Service. Pfc. Christianson gallantly gave his life for his country.

3045 ◆ *COLLIER, GILBERT GEORGIE

Rank: Sergeant (rank at time of action: Corporal)
Service: U.S. Army
Birthday: 30 December 1930
Place of Birth: Hunter, Woodruff County, Arkansas
Date of Death: 22 July 1953
Cemetery: DeWitt Cemetery—DeWitt, Arkansas
Entered Service at: Tichnor, Arkansas County, Arkansas
Unit: Company F, 223d Infantry Regiment, 40th Infantry Division
Served as: Pointman/Assistant Squad Leader
Battle or Place of Action: Tutayon, Korea
Date of Action: 19-20 July 1953
G.O. Number, Date: 3, 12 January 1955
Citation: Sgt. Collier, a member of Company F, distinguished himself by conspicuous gallantry and indomitable courage above and beyond the call of duty in action against the enemy. Sgt. Collier was point man and assistant leader of a combat patrol committed to make contact with the enemy. As the patrol moved forward through the darkness, he and his commanding officer slipped and fell from a steep, 60-foot cliff and were injured. Incapacitated by a badly sprained ankle which prevented immediate movement, the officer ordered the patrol to return to the safety of friendly lines. Although suffering from a painful back injury, Sgt. Collier elected to remain with his leader, and before daylight they managed to crawl back up and over the mountainous terrain to the opposite valley, where they concealed themselves in the brush until nightfall, then edged toward their company positions. Shortly after leaving the daylight retreat they were ambushed and, in the ensuing firefight, Sgt. Collier killed two hostile soldiers, received painful wounds, and was separated from his companion. Then, ammunition expended, he closed in hand-to-hand combat with four attacking hostile infantrymen, killing, wounding, and routing the foe with his bayonet. He was mortally wounded during this action, but made a valiant attempt to reach and assist his leader in a desperate effort to save his comrade's life without regard for his own personal safety. Sgt.

Collier's unflinching courage, consummate devotion to duty, and gallant self-sacrifice reflect lasting glory upon himself and uphold the noble traditions of the military service.

3046 ◆ *COLLIER, JOHN WALTON

Rank: Corporal
Service: U.S. Army
Birthday: 3 April 1929
Place of Birth: Worthington, Greenup County, Kentucky
Date of Death: 19 September 1950
Cemetery: Arlington National Cemetery (12-4637) (MH)—Arlington, Virginia
Entered Service at: Worthington, Greenup County, Kentucky
Unit: Company C, 27th Infantry Regiment, 25th Infantry Division
Battle or Place of Action: Chindoing-ni, Korea
Date of Action: 19 September 1950
G.O. Number, Date: 86, 2 August 1951
Date of Presentation: 21 June 1951
Place of Presentation: The Pentagon, presented by Gen. Omar N. Bradley to his Father
Citation: Cpl. Collier, Company C, distinguished himself by conspicuous gallantry and intrepidity above and beyond the call of duty in action. While engaged in an assault on a strategic ridge strongly defended by a fanatical enemy, the leading elements of his company encountered intense automatic-weapons and grenade fire. Cpl. Collier and three comrades volunteered and moved forward to neutralize an enemy machine-gun position which was hampering the company's advance, but they were twice repulsed. On the third attempt, Cpl. Collier, despite heavy enemy fire and grenade barrages, moved to an exposed position ahead of his comrades, assaulted and destroyed the machine-gun nest, killing at least four enemy soldiers. As he returned down the rocky, fire-swept hill and joined his squad, an enemy grenade landed in their midst. Shouting a warning to his comrades, he, selflessly and unhesitatingly, threw himself upon the grenade and smothered its explosion with his body. This intrepid action saved his comrades from death or injury. Cpl. Collier's supreme, personal bravery, consummate gallantry, and noble self-sacrifice reflect untold glory upon himself and uphold the honored traditions of the military service.

3047 ◆ COMMISKEY SR., HENRY ALFRED

Rank: First Lieutenant (rank at time of action: Second Lieutenant) (highest rank: Major)
Service: U.S. Marine Corps
Birthday: 10 January 1927
Place of Birth: Hattiesburg, Forrest County, Mississippi
Date of Death: 16 August 1971
Place of Death: Meridian, Mississippi
Cemetery: Cremated, ashes scattered over the Gulf of Mexico
Entered Service at: Hattiesburg, Forrest County, Mississippi
Unit: Company C, 1st Battalion, 1st Marines, 1st Marine Division

Served as: Platoon Leader
Battle or Place of Action: Yongdungp'o, Korea
Date of Action: 20 September 1950
Date of Presentation: 1 August 1951
Place of Presentation: The White House, presented by Pres. Harry S. Truman
Citation: For conspicuous gallantry and intrepidity at the risk of his life above and beyond the call of duty while serving as a platoon leader in Company C, in action against enemy aggressor forces. Directed to attack hostile forces well dug in on Hill 85, 1st Lt. Commiskey spearheaded the assault, charging up the steep slopes on the run. Coolly disregarding the heavy enemy machine-gun and small-arms fire, he plunged on well forward of the rest of his platoon and was the first man to reach the crest of the objective. Armed only with a pistol, he jumped into a hostile machine-gun emplacement occupied by five enemy troops and quickly disposed of four of the soldiers with his automatic pistol. Grappling with the fifth, 1st Lt. Commiskey knocked him to the ground and held him until he could obtain a weapon from another member of his platoon and killed the last of the enemy gun crew. Continuing his bold assault, he moved to the next emplacement, killed two more of the enemy and then led his platoon toward the rear nose of the hill to rout the remainder of the hostile troops and destroy them as they fled from their positions. His valiant leadership and courageous fighting spirit served to inspire the men of his company to heroic endeavor in seizing the objective, and reflect the highest credit upon 1st Lt. Commiskey and the U.S. Naval Service.

3048 ◆ *COURSEN, SAMUEL STREIT

Rank: First Lieutenant
Service: U.S. Army
Birthday: 4 August 1926
Place of Birth: Madison, Morris County, New Jersey
Date of Death: 12 October 1950
Place of Death: Kaesong, Korea
Cemetery: U.S. Military Academy Cemetery (7-230)—West Point, New York
Entered Service at: Madison, Morris County, New Jersey
Unit: Company C, 5th Cavalry Regiment, 1st Cavalry Division
Served as: Platoon Leader
Battle or Place of Action: Kaesong, Korea
Date of Action: 12 October 1950
G.O. Number, Date: 57, 2 August 1951
Date of Presentation: 21 June 1951
Place of Presentation: The Pentagon, presented by Gen. Omar N. Bradley to his Son
Citation: First Lt. Coursen distinguished himself by conspicuous gallantry and intrepidity above and beyond the call of duty in action. While Company C was attacking Hill 174 under heavy enemy small-arms fire, his platoon received enemy fire from close-range. The platoon returned the fire and continued to advance. During this phase, one of his men moved into a well-camouflaged emplacement, which was thought to be unoccupied, and was wounded by the enemy who were hidden within the emplacement. Seeing the soldier

in difficulty, he rushed to the man's aid and, without regard for his personal safety, engaged the enemy in hand-to-hand combat in an effort to protect his wounded comrade until he himself was killed. When his body was recovered after the battle, seven enemy dead were found in the emplacement. As the result of 1st Lt. Coursen's violent struggle several of the enemies' heads had been crushed with his rifle. His aggressive and intrepid actions saved the life of the wounded man, eliminated the main position of the enemy roadblock, and greatly inspired the men in his command. First Lt. Coursen's extraordinary heroism and intrepidity refect the highest credit on himself and are in keeping with the honored traditions of the military service.

3049 ◆ *CRAIG, GORDON MAYNARD

Rank: Corporal
Service: U.S. Army
Birthday: 3 August 1929
Place of Birth: Brockton, Plymouth County, Massachusetts
Date of Death: 10 September 1950
Cemetery: Village Cemetery of Elmwood (MH)—East Bridgewater, Massachusetts
Entered Service at: Brockton, Plymouth County, Massachusetts
Unit: Reconnaissance Company, 1st Cavalry Division
Battle or Place of Action: Kasan, Korea
Date of Action: 10 September 1950
G.O. Number, Date: 23, 25 April 1951
Date of Presentation: 3 April 1951
Place of Presentation: The Pentagon, presented by Gen. Omar N. Bradley to his Mother
Citation: Cpl. Craig, 16th Reconnaissance Company, distinguished himself by conspicuous gallantry and intrepidity above and beyond the call of duty in action against the enemy. During the attack on a strategic enemy-held hill, his company's advance was subjected to intense hostile grenade, mortar, and small-arms fire. Cpl. Craig and four comrades moved forward to eliminate an enemy machine-gun nest that was hampering the company's advance. At that instance an enemy machine gunner hurled a hand grenade at the advancing men. Without hesitating or attempting to seek cover for himself, Cpl. Craig threw himself on the grenade and smothered its burst with his body. His intrepid and selfless act, in which he unhesitantly gave his life for his comrades, inspired them to attack with such ferocity that they annihilated the enemy machine-gun crew, enabling the company to continue its attack. Cpl. Craig's noble self-sacrifice reflects the highest credit upon himself and upholds the esteemed traditions of the military service.

3050 ◆ CRUMP, JERRY KIRT

Rank: Corporal
Service: U.S. Army
Birthday: 18 February 1933
Place of Birth: Charlotte, Mecklenburg County, North Carolina
Date of Death: 10 January 1977

Place of Death: Lincolnton, North Carolina
Cemetery: Mt. Zion Cemetery (MH)—Cornelius, North Carolina
Entered Service at: Forest City, Rutherford County, North Carolina
Unit: Company L, 7th Infantry Regiment, 3d Infantry Division
Battle or Place of Action: Chorwon, Korea
Date of Action: 6-7 September 1951
G.O. Number, Date: 68, 11 July 1952
Date of Presentation: 27 June 1952
Place of Presentation: The White House (Rose Garden), presented by Pres. Harry S. Truman
Citation: Cpl. Crump, a member of Company L, distinguished himself by conspicuous gallantry and outstanding courage above and beyond the call of duty in action against the enemy. During the night a numerically superior hostile force launched an assault against his platoon on Hill 284, overrunning friendly positions and swarming into the sector. Cpl. Crump repeatedly exposed himself to deliver effective fire into the ranks of the assailants, inflicting numerous casualties. Observing two enemy soldiers endeavoring to capture a friendly machine gun, he charged and killed both with his bayonet, regaining control of the weapon. Returning to his position, now occupied by four of his wounded comrades, he continued his accurate fire into enemy troops surrounding his emplacement. When a hostile soldier hurled a grenade into the position, Cpl. Crump immediately flung himself over the missile, absorbing the blast with his body and saving his comrades from death or serious injury. His aggressive actions had so inspired his comrades that a spirited counterattack drove the enemy from the perimeter. Cpl. Crump's heroic devotion to duty, imdomitable fighting spirit, and willingness to sacrifice himself to save his comrades reflect the highest credit upon himself, the infantry and the U.S. Army.

3051 ◆ *DAVENPORT, JACK ARDEN

Rank: Corporal
Service: U.S. Marine Corps
Birthday: 7 September 1931
Place of Birth: Kansas City, Clay County, Missouri
Date of Death: 21 September 1951
Cemetery: Mount Moriah Cemetery (MH)—Kansas City, Missouri
Entered Service at: Mission, Johnson County, Kansas
Unit: Company G, 3d Battalion, 5th Marines, 1st Marine Division (Rein)
Served as: Squad Leader
Battle or Place of Action: Songnae-dong, Korea
Date of Action: 21 September 1951
Date of Presentation: 7 January 1953
Place of Presentation: The Pentagon, presented by Sec. of the Navy Dan A. Kimball to his Father
Citation: For conspicuous gallantry and intrepidity at the risk of his life above and beyond the call of duty while serving as a squad leader in Company G, in action against enemy aggressor forces early in the morning. While expertly directing the defense of his position during a probing attack by hostile

forces attempting to infiltrate the area, Cpl. Davenport, acting quickly when an enemy grenade fell into the foxhole which he was occupying with another marine, skillfully located the deadly projectile in the dark and, undeterred by the personal risk involved, heroically threw himself over the live missile, thereby saving his companion from serious injury or possible death. His cool and resourceful leadership were contributing factors in the successful repulse of the enemy attack and his superb courage and admirable spirit of self-sacrifice in the face of almost certain death enhance and sustain the highest traditions of the U.S. Naval Service. Cpl. Davenport gallantly gave his life for his country.

3052 ◆ *DAVIS JR., GEORGE ANDREW

Rank: Major (highest rank: Lieutenant Colonel)
Service: U.S. Air Force
Birthday: 1 December 1920
Place of Birth: Dublin, Erath County, Texas
Date of Death: 10 February 1952
Place of Death: Sinuiju-Yalu River area, Korea
Cemetery: National Memorial of the Pacific (Wall of the Missing)—Honolulu, Hawaii; City of Lubbock Cemetery (MH)(Headstone Only)—Lubbock, Texas
Entered Service at: Lubbock, Lubbock County, Texas
Unit: 4th Fighter Group, 334th Fighter Squadron,, 5th Air Force
Served as: Flight Commander/Pilot F-86 Saberjet
Battle or Place of Action: Sinuiju-Yalu River area, Korea
Date of Action: 10 February 1952
Date of Presentation: 14 May 1954
Place of Presentation: Reese Air Force Base, Texas, presented by Gen. Nathan F. Twining to his widow
Citation: Maj. Davis distinguished himself by conspicuous gallantry and intrepidity at the risk of his life above and beyond the call of duty. While leading a flight of four F-86 Saberjets on a combat aerial patrol mission near the Manchurian border, Maj. Davis' element leader ran out of oxygen and was forced to retire from the flight with his wingman accompanying him. Maj. Davis and the remaining F-86s continued the mission and sighted a formation of approximately 12 enemy MIG-15 aircraft speeding southward toward an area where friendly fighter-bombers were conducting low-level operations against the Communist lines of communcations. With selfless disregard for the numerical superiority of the enemy, Maj. Davis positioned his two aircraft, then dove at the MIG formation. While speeding through the formation from the rear, he singled out a MIG-15 and destroyed it with a concentrated burst of fire. Although he was now under continuous fire from the enemy fighters to his rear, Maj. Davis sustained his attack. He fired at another MIG-15 which, bursting into smoke and flames, went into a vertical dive. Rather than maintain his superior speed and evade the enemy fire being concentrated on him, he elected to reduce his speed and sought out still a third MIG-15. During this latest attack his aircraft sustained a direct hit, went out of control, then crashed into a mountain 30 miles south of the Yalu River. Maj. Davis' bold attack completely disrupted the enemy formation, permitting the friendly fighter-bombers to

successfully complete their interdiction mission. Maj. Davis, by his indomitable fighting spirit, heroic aggressiveness, and superb courage in engaging the enemy against formidable odds exemplified valor at its highest.
Notes: MIA

3053 ◆ DAVIS, RAYMOND GILBERT

Rank: Lieutenant Colonel (highest rank: General)
Service: U.S. Marine Corps
Birthday: 13 January 1915
Place of Birth: Fitzgerald, Ben Hill County, Georgia
Entered Service at: Atlanta, Fulton County, Georgia
Unit: 1st Battalion, 7th Marines, 1st Marine Division (Rein)
Served as: Battalion Commander
Battle or Place of Action: Hagaru-ri, Korea
Date of Action: 1-4 December 1950
Date of Presentation: 24 November 1952
Place of Presentation: The White House, presented by Pres. Harry S. Truman
Citation: For conspicuous gallantry and intrepidity at the risk of his life above and beyond the call of duty as commanding officer of the 1st Battalion, in action against enemy aggressor forces. Although keenly aware that the operation involved breaking through a surrounding enemy and advancing eight miles along primitive icy trails in the bitter cold with every passage disputed by a savage and determined foe, Lt. Col. Davis boldly led his battalion into the attack in a daring attempt to relieve a beleaguered rifle company and to seize, hold, and defend a vital mountain pass controlling the only route available for two marine regiments in danger of being cut off by numerically superior hostile forces during their redeployment to the port of Hungnam. When the battalion immediately encountered strong opposition from entrenched enemy forces commanding high ground in the path of the advance, he promptly spearheaded his unit in a fierce attack up the steep, ice-covered slopes in the face of withering fire and, personally leading the assault groups in a hand-to-hand encounter, drove the hostile troops from their position, rested his men, and reconnoitered the area under enemy fire to determine the best route for continuing the mission. Always in the thick of the fighting, Lt. Col. Davis led his battalion over three successive ridges in the deep snow in continuous attacks against the enemy and, constantly inspiring and encouraging his men throughout the night, brought his unit to a point within 1,500 yards of the surrounded rifle company by daybreak. Although knocked to the ground when a shell fragment struck his helmet and two bullets pierced his clothing, he arose and fought his way forward at the head of his men until he reached the isolated marines. On the following morning, he bravely led his battalion in securing the vital mountain pass from a strongly entrenched and numerically superior hostile force, carrying all his wounded with him, including 22 litter cases and numerous ambulatory patients. Despite repeated savage and heavy assaults by the enemy, he stubbornly held the vital terrrain until the two regiments of the division had deployed through the pass and, on the morning of 4 December, led his battalion into Hagaru-ri intact. By his superb leadership, outstanding courage, and

brilliant tactical ability, Lt. Col. Davis was directly instrumental in saving the beleagured rifle company from complete annihilation and enabled the two marine regiments to escape possible destruction. His valiant devotion to duty and unyielding fighting spirit in the face of almost insurmountable odds enhance and sustain the highest traditions of the U.S. Naval Service.

3054 ◆ DEAN SR., WILLIAM FRISHE

Rank: Major General
Service: U.S. Army
Birthday: 1 August 1899
Place of Birth: Carlyle, Clinton County, Illinois
Date of Death: 24 August 1981
Cemetery: San Francisco National Cemetery (353-B) (MH)—San Francisco, California
Entered Service at: California
Unit: 24th Infantry Division
Served as: Commanding General
Battle or Place of Action: Taejon, Korea
Date of Action: 20-21 July 1950
G.O. Number, Date: 7, 16 February 1951
Date of Presentation: 9 January 1951
Place of Presentation: White House, presented by Pres. Harry S. Truman to his Wife
Citation: Maj. Gen. Dean distinguished himself by conspicuous gallantry and intrepidity at the repeated risk of his life above and beyond the call of duty. In command of a unit suddenly relieved from occupation duties in Japan and as yet untried in combat, faced with a ruthless and determined enemy, highly trained and overwhelmingly superior in numbers, he felt it his duty to take action which, to a man of his military experience and knowledge, was clearly apt to result in his death. He personally and alone attacked an enemy tank while armed only with a hand grenade. He also directed the fire of his tanks from an exposed position with neither cover nor concealment while under observed artillery and small-arms fire. When the town of Taejon was finally overrun he refused to ensure his own safety by leaving with the leading elements but remained behind organizing his retreating forces, directing stragglers, and was last seen assisting the wounded to a place of safety. These actions indicate that Maj. Gen. Dean felt it necessary to sustain the courage and resolution of his troops by examples of excessive gallantry committed always at the threatened portions of his front lines. The magnificent response of his unit to this willing and cheerful sacrifice, made with full knowledge of its certain cost, is history. The success of this phase of the campaign is in large measure due to Maj. Gen. Dean's heroic leadership, courageous and loyal devotion to his men, and his complete disregard for personal safety.
Notes: POW

3055 ◆ *DESIDERIO, REGINALD BENJAMIN

Rank: Captain
Service: U.S. Army
Birthday: 12 September 1912

Place of Birth: Clairton, Allegheny County, Pennsylvania
Date of Death: 27 November 1950
Cemetery: San Francisco National Cemetery (OS20-128-30) (MH)—San Francisco, California
Entered Service at: Gilroy, Santa Clara County, California
Unit: Company E, 27th Infantry Regiment, 25th Infantry Division
Served as: Company Commander
Battle or Place of Action: Ipsok, Korea
Date of Action: 27 November 1950
G.O. Number, Date: 58, 2 August 1951
Date of Presentation: 21 June 1951
Place of Presentation: The Pentagon, presented by Gen. Omar N. Bradley to his Widow
Citation: Capt. Desiderio distinguished himself by conspicuous gallantry and intrepidity at the repeated risk of his life above and beyond the call of duty. His company was given the mission of defending the command post of a task force against an enemy breakthrough. After personal reconnaissance during darkness and under intense enemy fire, he placed his men in defensive positions to repel an attack. Early in the action he was wounded, but refused evacuation and despite enemy fire continued to move among his men checking their positions and making sure that each element was prepared to receive the next attack. Again wounded, he continued to direct his men. By his inspiring leadership he encouraged them to hold their position. In the subsequent fighting when the fanatical enemy succeeded in penetrating the position, he personally charged them with carbine, rifle, and grenades, inflicting many casualties until he himself was mortally wounded. His men, spurred on by his intrepid example, repelled this final attack. Capt. Desiderio's heroic leadership, courageous and loyal devotion to duty, and his complete disregard for personal safety reflect the highest honor on him and are in keeping with the esteemed traditions of the U.S. Army.

3056 ◆ *DEWERT, RICHARD DAVID

Rank: Hospital Corpsman
Service: U.S. Navy
Birthday: 17 November 1931
Place of Birth: Taunton, Bristol County, Massachusetts
Date of Death: 5 April 1951
Cemetery: Massachusetts National Cemetery (5-167) (MH)—Bourne, Massachusetts
Entered Service at: Taunton, Bristol County, Massachusetts
Unit: Hospital corpsman attached to Marine Infantry Company, 1st Marine Division
Served as: Medical Corpsman
Battle or Place of Action: Korea
Date of Action: 5 April 1951
Date of Presentation: 27 May 1952
Place of Presentation: Presented by Sec. of the Navy Dan A. Kimball to his Mother
Citation: For conspicuous gallantry and intrepidity at the risk of his life above and beyond the call of duty while serving as an HC, in action against enemy aggressor forces. When a fire team from the point platoon of his company was pinned

down by a deadly barrage of hostile automatic-weapons fire and suffered many casualties, HC Dewert rushed to the assistance of one of the more seriously wounded and, despite a painful leg wound sustained while dragging the stricken marine to safety, steadfastly refused medical treatment for himself and immediately dashed back through the fire-swept area to carry a second wounded man out of the line of fire. Undaunted by the mounting hail of devastating enemy fire, he bravely moved forward a third time and received another serious wound in the shoulder after discovering that a wounded marine had already died. Still persistent in his refusal to submit to first aid, he resolutely answered the call of a fourth stricken comrade and, while rendering medical assistance, was himself mortally wounded by a burst of enemy fire. His courageous initiative, great personal valor, and heroic spirit of self-sacrifice in the face of overwhelming odds reflect the highest credit upon HC Dewert and enhance the finest traditions of the U.S. Naval Service. He gallantly gave his life for his country.

3057 ◆ DEWEY, DUANE EDGAR

Rank: Corporal
Service: U.S. Marine Corps Reserve
Birthday: 16 November 1931
ace of Birth: Grand Rapids, Kent County, Michigan
Entered Service at: Muskegon, Muskegon County, Michigan
Unit: 3d Squad, Weapons Platoon, Company E, 2d Battalion, 5th Marines, 1st Marine Division (Rein)
Served as: Squad Leader/Machine Gunner
Battle or Place of Action: near Panmunjom, Korea
Date of Action: 16 April 1952
Date of Presentation: 12 March 1953
Place of Presentation: The White House (Oval Office), presented by Pres. Dwight D. Eisenhower
Citation: For conspicuous gallantry and intrepidity at the risk of his life above and beyond the call of duty while serving as a gunner in a machine-gun platoon of Company E, in action against enemy aggressor forces. When an enemy grenade landed close to his position while he and his assistant gunner were receiving medical attention for their wounds during a fierce night attack by numerically superior hostile forces, Cpl. Dewey, although suffering intense pain, immediately pulled the corpsman to the ground and, shouting a warning to the other marines around him, bravely smothered the deadly missile with his body, personally absorbing the full force of the explosion to save his comrades from possible injury or death. His indomitable courage, outstanding initiative, and valiant efforts in behalf of others in the face of almost certain death reflect the highest credit upon Cpl. Dewey and enhance the finest traditions of the U.S. Naval Service.

3058 ◆ DODD, CARL HENRY

Rank: First Lieutenant (rank at time of action: Second Lieutenant) (highest rank: Major)
Service: U.S. Army
Birthday: 21 April 1925
Place of Birth: Coats, Harlan County, Kentucky

Entered Service at: Kenvir, Harlan County, Kentucky
Unit: 2d Platoon, Company E, 2d Battalion, 5th Infantry Regiment, 24th Infantry Division
Served as: Platoon Leader
Battle or Place of Action: Subuk, Korea
Date of Action: 30-31 January 1951
G.O. Number, Date: 37, 4 June 1951
Date of Presentation: 19 May 1951
Place of Presentation: Blair House, presented by Pres. Harry S. Truman
Citation: First Lt. Dodd, Company E, distinguished himself by conspicuous gallantry and intrepidity above and beyond the call of duty in action against the enemy. First Lt. Dodd, given the responsibility of spearheading an attack to capture Hill 256, a key terrain feature defended by a well-armed, crafty foe who had withstood several previous assaults, led his platoon forward over hazardous terrain under hostile small-arms, mortar, and artillery fire from well-camouflaged enemy emplacements which reached such intensity that his men faltered. With utter disregard for his safety, 1st Lt. Dodd moved among his men, reorganized and encouraged them, and then singlehandedly charged the first hostile machine-gun nest, killing or wounding all its occupants. Inspired by his incredible courage, his platoon responded magnificiently and, fixing bayonets and throwing grenades, closed on the enemy and wiped out every hostile position as it moved relentlessly onward to its initial objective. Securing the first series of enemy positions, 1st Lt. Dodd again reorganized his platoon and led them across a narrow ridge and onto Hill 256. Firing his rifle and throwing grenades, he advanced at the head of his platoon despite the intense concentrated hostile fire which was brought to bear on their narrow avenue of approach. When his platoon was still 200 yards from the objective he moved ahead and with his last grenade destroyed an enemy mortar, killing the crew. Darkness then halted the advance, but at daybreak 1st Lt. Dodd, again boldly advancing ahead of his unit, led the platoon through a dense fog against the remaining hostile positions. With bayonet and grenades he continued to set pace without regard for the danger to his life, until he and his troops had eliminated the last of the defenders and had secured the final objective. First Lt. Dodd's superb leadership and extraordinary heroism inspired his men to overcome this strong enemy defense reflecting the highest credit upon himself and upholding the esteemed traditions of the military service.

3059 ◆ *DUKE, RAY E.

Rank: Sergeant First Class (highest rank: Master Sergeant)
Service: U.S. Army
Birthday: 9 May 1923
Place of Birth: Whitwell, Marion County, Tennessee
Date of Death: 11 November 1951
Cemetery: Chattanooga National Cemetery (Z-373) (MH)—Chattanooga, Tennessee
Entered Service at: Whitwell, Marion County, Tennessee
Unit: Company C, 21st Infantry Regiment, 24th Infantry Division
Battle or Place of Action: Mugok, Korea
Date of Action: 26 April 1951

G.O. Number, Date: 20, 19 March 1954
Citation: Sfc. Duke, a member of Company C, distinguished himself by conspicuous gallantry and outstanding courage above and beyond the call of duty in action against the enemy. Upon learning that several of his men were isolated and heavily engaged in an area yielded by his platoon when ordered to withdraw, he led a small force in a daring assault which recovered the position and the beleaguered men. Another enemy attack in strength resulted in numerous casualties but Sfc. Duke, although wounded by mortar fragments, calmly moved along his platoon line to coordinate fields of fire and urge his men to hold firm in the bitter encounter. Wounded a second time, he received first aid and returned to his position. When the enemy again attacked shortly after dawn, despite his wounds, Sfc. Duke repeatedly braved withering fire to ensure maximum defense of each position. Threatened with annihilation and with mounting casualties, the platoon was again ordered to withdraw when Sfc. Duke was wounded a third time in both legs and was unable to walk. Realizing that he was impeding the progress of two comrades who were carrying him from the hill, he urged them to leave him and seek safety. He was last seen pouring devastating fire into the ranks of the onrushing assailants. The consummate courage, superb leadership, and heroic actions of Sfc. Duke, displayed during intensive action against overwhelming odds, reflect the highest credit upon himself, the infantry, and the U.S. Army.

3060 ◆ *EDWARDS, JUNIOR DEAN

Rank: Sergeant First Class
Service: U.S. Army
Birthday: 7 October 1926
Place of Birth: Indianola, Warren County, Iowa
Date of Death: 2 January 1951
Cemetery: I.O.O.F. Cemetery (MH)—Indianola, Iowa
Entered Service at: Indianola, Warren County, Iowa
Unit: Company E, 23d Infantry Regiment, 2d Infantry Division
Battle or Place of Action: Changbong-ni, Korea
Date of Action: 2 January 1951
G.O. Number, Date: 13, 1 February 1952
Date of Presentation: 16 January 1952
Place of Presentation: The Pentagon, presented by the Sec. of Defense Robert A. Lovett to his Father
Citation: Sfc. Edwards, Company E, distinguished himself by conspicuous gallantry and intrepidity above and beyond the call of duty in action against the enemy. When his platoon, while assisting in the defense of a strategic hill, was forced out of its position and came under vicious raking fire from an enemy machine gun set up on adjacent high ground, Sfc. Edwards individually charged the hostile emplacement, throwing grenades as he advanced. The enemy withdrew, but returned to deliver devastating fire when he had expended his ammunition. Securing a fresh supply of grenades, he again charged the emplacement, neutralized the weapon, and killed the crew, but was forced back by hostile small-arms fire. When the enemy emplaced another machine gun and resumed fire, Sfc. Edwards again renewed his supply of grenades, rushed a third time through a vicious hail of fire,

silenced this second gun, and annihilated its crew. In this third daring assault he was mortally wounded, but his indomitable courage and successful action enabled his platoon to regain and hold the vital strongpoint. Sfc. Edwards' consummate valor and gallant self-sacrifice reflect the utmost glory upon himself and are in keeping with the esteemed traditions of the infantry and military service.

3061 ◆ *ESSEBAGGER JR., JOHN

Rank: Corporal
Service: U.S. Army
Birthday: 29 October 1928
Place of Birth: Holland, Ottawa County, Michigan
Date of Death: 25 April 1951
Cemetery: Pilgrim Home Cemetery—Holland, Michigan
Entered Service at: Holland, Ottawa County, Michigan
Unit: Company A, 7th Infantry Regiment, 3d Infantry Division
Battle or Place of Action: Popsu-dong, Korea
Date of Action: 25 April 1951
G.O. Number, Date: 61, 24 April 1952
Date of Presentation: 26 March 1952
Place of Presentation: The Pentagon, presented by Sec. of the Army Frank C. Pace to his Widow
Citation: Cpl. Essebagger, a member of Company A, distinguished himself by conspicuous gallantry and outstanding courage above and beyond the call of duty in action against the enemy. Committed to effect a delaying action to cover the 3d Battalion's withdrawal through Company A, Cpl. Essebagger, a member of one of two squads maintaining defensive positions in key terrain and defending the company's right flank, had participated in repulsing numerous attacks. In a frenzied banzai charge the numerically superior enemy seriously threatened the security of the planned route of withdrawal and the isolation of the small force. Badly shaken, the grossly outnumbered detachment started to fall back and Cpl. Essebagger, realizing the impending danger, voluntarily remained to provide security for the withdrawal. Gallantly maintaining a one-man stand, Cpl. Essebagger raked the menacing hordes with crippling fire and, with the foe closing on the position, left the comparative safety of his shelter and advanced in the face of overwhelming odds, firing his weapon and hurling grenades to disconcert the enemy and afford time for displacement of friendly elements to more tenable positions. Scorning the withering fire and bursting shells, Cpl. Essebagger continued to move forward, inflicting destruction upon the fanatical foe until he was mortally wounded. Cpl. Essebagger's intrepid action and supreme sacrifice exacted a heavy toll in enemy dead and wounded, stemmed the onslaught, and enabled the retiring squads to reach safety. His valorous conduct and devotion to duty reflected lasting glory upon himself and was in keeping with the noblest traditions of the infantry and the U.S. Army.

3062 ◆ *FAITH JR., DON CARLOS

Rank: Lieutenant Colonel
Service: U.S. Army

Birthday: 26 August 1918
Place of Birth: Washington, Daviess County, Indiana
Date of Death: 1 December 1950
Cemetery: National Memorial of the Pacific (Wall of the Missing)—Honolulu, Hawaii; Arlington National Cemetery (4-3016) ('In Memory' inscription on reverse side of parent's headstone)—Arlington, Virginia
Entered Service at: Washington, Daviess County, Indiana
Unit: 1st Battalion, 32d Infantry Regiment, 7th Infantry Division
Served as: Battalion Commander
Battle or Place of Action: Hagaru-ri, Korea
Date of Action: 27 November-1 December 1950
G.O. Number, Date: 59, 2 August 1951
Date of Presentation: 21 June 1951
Place of Presentation: The Pentagon, presented by Gen. Omar N. Bradley to his Widow
Citation: Lt. Col. Faith, commanding 1st Battalion, distinguished himself conspicuously by gallantry and intrepidity in action above and beyond the call of duty in the area of the Chosin Reservoir. When the enemy launched a fanatical attack against his battalion, Lt. Col. Faith unhesitatingly exposed himself to heavy enemy fire as he moved about directing the action. When the enemy penetrated the positions, Lt. Col. Faith personally led counterattacks to restore the position. During an attack by his battalion to effect a junction with another U.S. unit, Lt. Col. Faith reconnoitered the route for, and personally directed, the first elements of his command across the ice-covered reservoir and then directed the movement of his vehicles, which were loaded with wounded, until all of his command had passed through the enemy fire. Having completed this he crossed the reservoir himself. Assuming command of the force his unit had joined, he was given the mission of attacking to join friendly elements to the south. Lt. Col. Faith, although physically exhausted in the bitter cold, organized and launched an attack which was soon stopped by enemy fire. He ran forward under enemy small-arms and automatic-weapons fire, got his men on their feet, and personally led the fire attack as it blasted its way through the enemy ring. As they came to a hairpin curve, enemy fire from a roadblock again pinned the column down. Lt. Col. Faith organized a group of men and directed their attack on the enemy positions on the right flank. He then placed himself at the head of another group of men and in the face of direct enemy fire led an attack on the enemy roadblock, firing his pistol and throwing grenades. When he had reached a position approximately 30 yards from the roadblock, he was mortally wounded, but continued to direct the attack until the roadblock was overrun. Throughout the five days of action Lt. Col. Faith gave no thought to his safety and did not spare himself. His presence each time in the position of greatest danger was an inspiration to his men. Also, the damage he personally inflicted, firing from his position at the head of his men, was of material assistance on several occasions. Lt. Col. Faith's outstanding gallantry and noble self-sacrifice above and beyond the call of duty reflect the highest honor on him and are in keeping with the highest traditions of the U.S. Army.
Notes: MIA

3063 ◆ *GARCIA, FERNANDO LUIS

Rank: Private First Class
Service: U.S. Marine Corps
Birthday: 14 October 1929
Place of Birth: Utuado, Utuado County, Puerto Rico
Date of Death: 5 September 1952
Cemetery: Puerto Rico National Cemetery ('In Memory' marker only)—Bayamon, Puerto Rico; National Memorial of the Pacific—Honolulu, Hawaii
Entered Service at: San Juan, San Juan County, Puerto Rico
Unit: Company I, 3d Battalion, 5th Marines, 1st Marine Division (Rein)
Battle or Place of Action: Korea
Date of Action: 5 September 1952
Date of Presentation: 25 October 1953
Place of Presentation: City Hall, Utuado, Puerto Rico, presented to parents
Citation: For conspicuous gallantry and intrepidity at the risk of his life above and beyond the call of duty while serving as a member of Company I, in action against enemy aggressor forces. While participating in the defense of a combat outpost located more than one mile forward of the main line of resistance during a savage night attack by a fanatical enemy force employing grenades, mortars, and artillery, Pfc. Garcia, although suffering painful wounds, moved through the intense hail of hostile fire to a supply point to secure more hand grenades. Quick to act when a hostile grenade landed nearby, endangering the life of another marine, as well as his own, he unhesitatingly chose to sacrifice himself and immediately threw his body upon the deadly missile, receiving the full impact of the explosion. His great personal valor and cool decision in the face of almost certain death sustain and enhance the finest traditions of the U.S. Naval Service. He gallantly gave his life for his country.
Notes: MIA

3064 ◆ *GEORGE, CHARLES

Rank: Private First Class
Service: U.S. Army
Birthday: 23 August 1932
Place of Birth: Cherokee, Swain County, North Carolina
Date of Death: 30 November 1952
Cemetery: Yellow Hill Cemetery (MH)—Cherokee, North Carolina
Entered Service at: Whittier, Jackson County, North Carolina
Unit: Company C, 179th Infantry Regiment, 45th Infantry Division
Battle or Place of Action: Songnae-dong, Korea
Date of Action: 30 November 1952
G.O. Number, Date: 19, 18 March 1954
Citation: Pfc. George, a member of Company C, distinguished himself by conspicuous gallantry and outstanding courage above and beyond the call of duty in action against the enemy on the night of 30 November 1952. He was a member of a raiding party committed to engage the enemy and capture a prisoner for interrogation. Forging up the

rugged slope of the key terrain feature, the group was subjected to intense mortar and machine-gun fire and suffered several casualties. Throughout the advance, he fought valiantly and, upon reaching the crest of the hill, leaped into the trenches and closed with the enemy in hand-to-hand combat. When friendly troops were ordered to move back upon completion of the assignment, he and two comrades remained to cover the withdrawal. While in the process of leaving the trenches a hostile soldier hurled a grenade into their midst. Pfc. George shouted a warning to one comrade, pushed the other soldier out of danger, and, with full knowledge of the consequences, unhesitatingly threw himself upon the grenade, absorbing the full blast of the explosion. Although seriously wounded in this display of valor, he refrained from any outcry which would divulge the position of his companions. The two soldiers evacuated him to the forward aid station and shortly thereafter he succumbed to his wound. Pfc. George's indomitable courage, consummate devotion to duty, and willing self-sacrifice reflect the highest credit upon himself and uphold the finest traditions of the military service.

3065 ◆ *GILLILAND, CHARLES L.

Rank: Corporal (rank at time of action: Private First Class)
Service: U.S. Army
Birthday: 24 May 1933
Place of Birth: Mountain Home, Baxter County, Arkansas
Date of Death: 25 April 1951
Cemetery: National Memorial of the Pacific—Honolulu, Hawaii
Entered Service at: Yellville, Marion County, Arkansas
Unit: Company I, 7th Infantry Regiment, 3d Infantry Division
Served as: Automatic Rifleman
Battle or Place of Action: Tongmang-ni, Korea
Date of Action: 25 April 1951
G.O. Number, Date: 2, 11 January 1955
Citation: Cpl. Gilliland, a member of Company I, distinguished himself by conspicuous gallantry and outstanding courage above and beyond the call of duty in action against the enemy. A numerically superior hostile force launched a coordinated assault against his company perimeter, the brunt of which was directed up a defile covered by his automatic rifle. His assistant was killed by enemy fire, but Cpl. Gilliland, facing the full force of the assault, poured a steady fire into the foe, which stemmed the onslaught. When two enemy soldiers escaped his raking fire and infiltrated the sector, he leaped from his foxhole, overtook and killed them both with his pistol. Sustaining a serious head wound in this daring exploit, he refused medical attention and returned to his emplacement to continue his defense of the defile. His unit was ordered back to new defensive positions, but Cpl. Gilliland volunteered to remain to cover the withdrawal and hold the enemy at bay. His heroic actions and indomitable devotion to duty prevented the enemy from completely overrunning his company positions. Cpl. Gilliland's incredible valor and supreme sacrifice reflect lasting glory upon himself and are in keeping with the honored traditions of the military service.
Notes: MIA

3066 ◆ *GOMEZ, EDWARD

Rank: Private First Class
Service: U.S. Marine Corps
Birthday: 10 August 1932
Place of Birth: Omaha, Douglas County, Nebraska
Date of Death: 14 September 1951
Cemetery: St. Mary's Cemetery (MH)—Omaha, Nebraska
Entered Service at: Omaha, Douglas County, Nebraska
Unit: Company E, 2d Battalion, 1st Marines, 1st Marine Division (Rein)
Served as: Ammunition Bearer
Battle or Place of Action: Hill 749, Korea
Date of Action: 14 September 1951
Citation: For conspicuous gallantry and intrepidity at the risk of his life above and beyond the call of duty while serving as an ammunition bearer in Company E, in action against enemy aggressor forces. Boldly advancing with his squad in support of a group of riflemen assaulting a series of strongly fortified and bitterly defended hostile positions on Hill 749, Pfc. Gomez consistently exposed himself to the withering barrage to keep his machine gun supplied with ammunition during the drive forward to seize the objective. As his squad deployed to meet an imminent counterattack, he voluntarily moved down an abandoned trench to search for a new location for the gun and, when a hostile grenade landed between himself and his weapon, shouted a warning to those around him as he grasped the activated charge in his hand. Determined to save his comrades, he unhesitatingly chose to sacrifice himself and, diving into the ditch with the deadly missile, absorbed the shattering violence of the explosion in his body. By his stouthearted courage, incomparable valor, and decisive spirit of self-sacrifice, Pfc. Gomez inspired the others to heroic efforts in subsequently repelling the outnumbering foe, and his valiant conduct throughout sustained and enhanced the finest traditions of the U.S. Naval Service. He gallantly gave his life for his country.

3067 ◆ *GOODBLOOD, CLAIR

Rank: Corporal
Service: U.S. Army
Birthday: 18 September 1929
Place of Birth: Fort Kent, Aroostook County, Maine
Date of Death: 25 April 1951
Cemetery: Chandler Cemetery (MH)—Burham, Maine
Entered Service at: Burnham, Waldo County, Maine
Unit: Company D, 7th Infantry Regiment, 3d Infantry Division
Served as: Machine Gunner
Battle or Place of Action: Popsu-dong, Korea
Date of Action: 24-25 April 1951
G.O. Number, Date: 14, 1 February 1952
Date of Presentation: 16 January 1952
Place of Presentation: The Pentagon, presented by Sec. of Defense Robert A. Lovett to his Mother
Citation: Cpl. Goodblood, a member of Company D, distinguished himself by conspicuous gallantry and intrepidity at the risk of his life above and beyond the call of duty in action

against an armed enemy of the United Nations. Cpl. Goodblood, a machine gunner, was attached to Company B in defensive positions on thickly wooded key terrain under attack by a ruthless foe. In the bitter fighting which ensued, the numerically superior enemy infiltrated the perimeter, rendering the friendly positions untenable. Upon order to move back, Cpl. Goodblood voluntarily remained to cover the withdrawal and, constantly vulnerable to heavy fire, inflicted withering destruction on the assaulting force. Seeing a grenade lobbed at his position, he shoved his assistant to the ground and flinging himself upon the soldier attempted to shield him. Despite his valorous act both men were wounded. Rejecting aid for himself, he ordered the ammunition bearer to evacuate the injured man for medical treatment. He fearlessly maintained his one-man defense, sweeping the onrushing assailants with fire until an enemy banzai charge carried the hill and silenced his gun. When friendly elements regained the commanding ground, Cpl. Goodblood's body was found lying beside his gun and approximately 100 hostile dead lay in the wake of his field of fire. Through his unflinching courage and willing self-sacrifice the onslaught was retarded, enabling his unit to withdraw, regroup, and resecure the strongpoint. Cpl. Goodblood's inspirational conduct and devotion to duty reflect lasting glory on himself and are in keeping with the noble traditions of the military service.

3068 ◆ *GUILLEN, AMBROSIO

Rank: Staff Sergeant
Service: U.S. Marine Corps
Birthday: 7 December 1929
Place of Birth: La Junta, Otero County, Colorado
Date of Death: 25 July 1953
Cemetery: Fort Bliss National Cemetery (E-9171) (MH)—Fort Bliss, Texas
Entered Service at: El Paso, El Paso County, Texas
Unit: Company F, 2d Battalion, 7th Marines, 1st Marine Division (Rein)
Served as: Platoon Sergeant
Battle or Place of Action: Songuch-on, Korea
Date of Action: 25 July 1953
Citation: For conspicuous gallantry and intrepidity at the risk of his life above and beyond the call of duty while serving as a platoon sergeant of Company F in action against enemy aggressor forces. Participating in the defense of an outpost forward of the main line of resistance, S/Sgt. Guillen maneuvered his platoon over unfamiliar terrain in the face of hostile fire and placed his men in fighting positions. With his unit pinned down when the outpost was attacked under cover of darkness by an estimated force of two enemy battalions supported by mortar and artillery fire, he deliberately exposed himself to the heavy barrage and attacks to direct his men in defending their positions and personally supervise the treatment and evacuation of the wounded. Inspired by his leadership, the platoon quickly rallied and engaged the enemy in fierce hand-to-hand combat. Although critically wounded during the course of the battle, S/Sgt. Guillen refused medical aid and continued to direct his men throughout the remainder of the engagement until the enemy was defeated

and thrown into disorderly retreat. Succumbing to his wounds within a few hours, S/Sgt. Guillen, by his outstanding courage and indomitable fighting spirit, was directly responsible for the success of his platoon in repelling a numerically superior enemy force. His personal valor reflects the highest credit upon himself and enhances the finest traditions of the U.S. Naval Service. He gallantly gave his life for his country.

3069 ◆ *HAMMOND, FRANCIS COLTON

Rank: Hospitalman
Service: U.S. Navy
Birthday: 9 November 1931
Place of Birth: Alexandria, Alexandria County, Virginia
Date of Death: 26 March 1953
Cemetery: Arlington National Cemetery (33-9011) (MH)—Arlington, Virginia
Entered Service at: Alexandria, Alexandria County, Virginia
Unit: 1st Battalion, 5th Marines (Attached), 1st Marine Division
Served as: Medical Corpsman
Battle or Place of Action: near Sanae-dong, Korea
Date of Action: 26-27 March 1953
Date of Presentation: 29 December 1953
Place of Presentation: The Pentagon, Presented by Sec. of the Navy Robert B. Anderson to his infant Son
Citation: For conspicuous gallantry and intrepidity at the risk of his life above and beyond the call of duty as an HC serving with the 1st Marine Division in action against enemy aggressor forces on the night of 26-27 March 1953. After reaching an intermediate objective during a counterattack against a heavily entrenched and numerically superior hostile force occupying ground on a bitterly contested outpost far in advance of the main line of resistance, HC Hammond's platoon was subjected to a murderous barrage of hostile mortar and artillery fire, followed by a vicious assault by onrushing enemy troops. Resolutely advancing through the veritable curtain of fire to aid his stricken comrades, HC Hammond moved among the stalwart garrison of marines and, although critically wounded himself, valiantly continued to administer aid to the other wounded throughout an exhausting four-hour period. When the unit was ordered to withdraw, he skillfully directed the evacuation of casualties and remained in the fire-swept area to assist the corpsmen of the relieving unit until he was struck by a round of enemy mortar fire and fell, mortally wounded. By his exceptional fortitude, inspiring initiative, and self-sacrificing efforts, HC Hammond undoubtedly saved the lives of many marines. His great personal valor in the face of overwhelming odds enhances and sustains the finest traditions of the U.S. Naval Service. He gallantly gave his life for his country.

3070 ◆ *HAMMOND JR., LESTER

Rank: Corporal
Service: U.S. Army
Birthday: 25 March 1931
Place of Birth: Wayland, Clark County, Missouri

Date of Death: 14 August 1952
Cemetery: Sunset Cemetery (MH)—Quincy, Illinois
Entered Service at: Quincy, Adams County, Illinois
Unit: Company A, 187th Airborne Regimental Combat Team
Served as: Radio Operator
Battle or Place of Action: Kumwha, Korea
Date of Action: 14 August 1952
G.O. Number, Date: 63, 17 August 1953
Date of Presentation: 5 August 1953
Place of Presentation: The Pentagon auditorium, presented by Under Sec. of the Army Earl D. Johnson to his Father
Citation: Cpl. Hammond, a radio operator with Company A, distinguished himself by conspicuous gallantry and outstanding courage above and beyond the call of duty in action against the enemy. Cpl. Hammond was a member of a six man reconnaissance patrol which had penetrated approximately 3,500 yards into enemy-held territory. Ambushed and partially surrounded by a large hostile force, the small group opened fire, then quickly withdrew up a narrow ravine in search of protective cover. Despite a wound sustained in the initial exchange of fire and imminent danger of being overrun by the numerically superior foe, he refused to seek shelter and, remaining in an exposed place, called for artillery fire to support a defensive action. Constantly vulnerable to enemy observation and action, he coordinated and directed crippling fire on the assailants, inflicting heavy casualties and repulsing several attempts to overrun friendly positions. Although wounded a second time, he remained steadfast and maintained his stand until mortally wounded. His indomitable fighting spirit set an inspiring example of valor to his comrades and, through his actions, the onslaught was stemmed, enabling a friendly platoon to reach the beleaguered patrol, evacuate the wounded, and effect a safe withdrawal to friendly lines. Cpl. Hammond's unflinching courage and consummate devotion to duty reflect lasting glory on himself and uphold the finest traditions of the military service.

3071 ◆ *HANDRICH, MELVIN O.

Rank: Master Sergeant
Service: U.S. Army
Birthday: 26 January 1919
Place of Birth: Manawa, Waupaca County, Wisconsin
Date of Death: 26 August 1950
Cemetery: Little Wolf Cemetery (MH)—Manawo, Wisconsin
Entered Service at: Manawa, Waupaca County, Wisconsin
Unit: Company C, 5th Infantry Regiment
Battle or Place of Action: Sobuk San Mountain, Korea
Date of Action: 25-26 August 1950
G.O. Number, Date: 60, 2 August 1951
Date of Presentation: 21 June 1951
Place of Presentation: The Pentagon, presented by Gen. Omar N. Bradley to his Father
Citation: M/Sgt. Handrich, Company C, distinguished himself by conspicuous gallantry and intrepidity above and beyond the call of duty in action. His company was engaged in repulsing an estimated 150 enemy who were threatening to overrun its position. Near midnight on 25 August, a hostile group over 100 strong attempted to infiltrate the company perimeter. M/Sgt. Handrich, despite the heavy enemy fire, voluntarily left the comparative safety of the defensive area and moved to a forward position where he could direct mortar and artillery fire upon the advancing enemy. He remained at this post for eight hours, directing fire against the enemy who often approached to within 50 feet of his position. Again, on the morning of 26 August, another strong hostile force made an attempt to overrun the company's position. With complete disregard for his safety, M/Sgt. Handrich rose to his feet and from this exposed position fired his rifle and directed mortar and artillery fire on the attackers. At the peak of this action he observed elements of his company preparing to withdraw. He perilously made his way across fire-swept terrain to the defense area where, by example and forceful leadership, he reorganized the men to continue the fight. During the action M/Sgt. Handrich was severely wounded. Refusing to take cover or be evacuated, he returned to his forward position and continued to direct the company's fire. Later a determined enemy attack overran M/Sgt. Handrich's position and he was mortally wounded. When the position was retaken, over 70 enemy dead were counted in the area he had so intrepidly defended. M/Sgt. Handrich's sustained personal bravery, consummate courage, and gallant self-sacrifice reflect untold glory upon himself and the heroic traditions of the military service.

3072 ◆ *HANSON, JACK G.

Rank: Private First Class
Service: U.S. Army
Birthday: 18 September 1930
Place of Birth: Escatawpa, Jackson County, Mississippi
Date of Death: 7 June 1951
Cemetery: Robinson Cemetery—Escatawpa, Mississippi
Entered Service at: Galveston, Galveston County, Texas
Unit: Company F, 31st Infantry Regiment
Served as: Machine Gunner
Battle or Place of Action: Pachi-dong, Korea
Date of Action: 7 June 1951
G.O. Number, Date: 15, 1 February 1952
Date of Presentation: 16 January 1952
Place of Presentation: The Pentagon, presented by the Sec. of Defense Robert A. Lovett to his Father
Citation: Pfc. Hanson, a machine gunner with the 1st Platoon, Company F, distinguished himself by conspicuous gallantry and intrepidity at the risk of his life above and beyond the call of duty in action against an armed enemy of the United Nations. The company, in defensive positions on two strategic hills separated by a wide saddle, was ruthlessly attacked at approximately 0300 hours, the brunt of which centered on the approach to the divide within range of Pfc. Hanson's machine gun. In the initial phase of the action, four riflemen were wounded and evacuated, and the numerically superior enemy, advancing under cover of darkness, infiltrated and posed an imminent threat to the security of the command post and weapons platoon. Upon orders to move to key terrain above and to the right of Pfc. Hanson's position,

he voluntarily remained to provide protective fire for the withdrawal. Subsequent to the retiring elements' fighting a rearguard action to the new location, it was learned that Pfc. Hanson's assistant gunner and three riflemen had been wounded and had crawled to safety, and that he was maintaining a lone-man defense. After the 1st Platoon reorganized, counterattacked, and rescued its original positions at approximately 0530 hours, Pfc. Hanson's body was found lying in front of his emplacement, his machine-gun ammunition expended, his empty pistol in his right hand, and a machete with blood on the blade in his left hand, and approximately 22 enemy dead lay in the wake of his action. Pfc. Hanson's consummate valor, inspirational conduct, and willing self-sacrifice enabled the company to contain the enemy and regain the commanding ground, and reflect lasting glory on himself and the noble traditions of the military service.

3073 ◆ *HARTELL, LEE ROSS

Rank: First Lieutenant
Service: U.S. Army
Birthday: 23 August 1923
Place of Birth: Philadelphia, Philadelphia County, Pennsylvania
Date of Death: 27 August 1951
Place of Death: Hill 700, South Korea
Cemetery: St. Peter's Cemetery (MH)—Danbury, Connecticut
Entered Service at: Danbury, Fairfield County, Connecticut
Unit: Battery A, 15th Field Artillery Battalion, 2d Infantry Division
Served as: Forward Observer
Battle or Place of Action: Kobangsan-ni, Korea
Date of Action: 27 August 1951
G.O. Number, Date: 16, 1 February 1952
Date of Presentation: 16 January 1952
Place of Presentation: The Pentagon, presented by the Sec. of Defense Robert A. Lovett to his Widow
Citation: 1st Lt. Hartell, a member of Battery A, distinguished himself by conspicuous gallantry and intrepidity at the risk of his life above and beyond the call of duty in action against an armed enemy of the United Nations. During the darkness of early morning, the enemy launched a ruthless attack against friendly positions on a rugged mountainous ridge. 1st Lt. Hartell, attached to Company B, 9th Infantry Regiment, as forward observer, quickly moved his radio to an exposed vantage on the ridgeline to adjust defensive fires. Realizing the tactical advantage of illuminating the area of approach, he called for flares and then directed crippling fire into the onrushing assailants. At this juncture a large force of hostile troops swarmed up the slope in banzai charge and came within 10 yards of 1st Lt. Hartell's position. 1st Lt. Hartell sustained a severe hand wound in the ensuing encounter, but grasped the microphone with his other hand and maintained his magnificent stand until the front and left flank of the company were protected by a close-in wall of withering fire, causing the fanatical foe to disperse and fall back momentarily. After the numerically superior enemy overran an outpost and was closing on his position, 1st Lt. Hartell, in a final radio call, urged the friendly elements to

fire both batteries continuously. Although mortally wounded, 1st Lt. Hartell's intrepid actions contributed significantly to stemming the onslaught and enabled his company to maintain the strategic strongpoint. His consummate valor and unwavering devotion to duty reflect lasting glory on himself and uphold the noble traditions of the military service.

3074 ◆ HARVEY, RAYMOND

Rank: Captain (highest rank: Lieutenant Colonel)
Service: U.S. Army
Birthday: 1 March 1920
Place of Birth: Ford City, Armstrong County, Pennsylvania
Entered Service at: Pasadena, Los Angeles County, California
Unit: Company C, 1st Battalion, 17th Infantry Regiment, 7th Infantry Division
Served as: Company Commander
Battle or Place of Action: vicinity of Taemi-Dong, Korea
Date of Action: 9 March 1951
G.O. Number, Date: 67, 2 August 1951
Date of Presentation: 5 July 1951
Place of Presentation: The White House, presented by Pres. Harry S. Truman
Citation: Capt. Harvey, Company C, distinguished himself by conspicuous gallantry and intrepidity above and beyond the call of duty in action. When his company was pinned down by a barrage of automatic-weapons fire from numerous well-entrenched emplacements, imperiling accomplishment of its mission, Capt. Harvey braved a hail of fire and exploding grenades to advance to the first enemy machine-gun nest, killing its crew with grenades. Rushing to the edge of the next emplacement, he killed its crew with carbine fire. He then moved the 1st Platoon forward until it was again halted by a curtain of automatic fire from well-fortified hostile positions. Disregarding the hail of fire, he personally charged and neutralized a third emplacement. Miraculously escaping death from intense crossfire, Capt. Harvey continued to lead the assault. Spotting an enemy pillbox well-camouflaged by logs, he moved close enough to sweep the emplacement with carbine fire and throw grenades through the openings, annihilating its five occupants. Though wounded he then turned to order the company forward, and, suffering agonizing pain, he continued to direct the reduction of the remaining hostile positions, refusing evacuation until assured that the mission would be accomplished. Capt. Harvey's valorous and intrepid actions served as an inspiration to his company, reflecting the utmost glory upon himself and upholding the heroic traditions of the military service.

3075 ◆ *HENRY, FREDERICK F.

Rank: First Lieutenant
Service: U.S. Army
Place of Birth: Vian, Sequoyah County, Oklahoma
Date of Death: 1 September 1950
Cemetery: National Memorial of the Pacific (Wall of the Missing)—Honolulu, Hawaii
Entered Service at: Clinton, Custer County, Oklahoma
Unit: Company F, 28th Infantry Regiment

Served as: Platoon Leader
Battle or Place of Action: Am-Dong, Korea
Date of Action: 1 September 1950
G.O. Number, Date: 8, 16 February 1951
Date of Presentation: 9 January 1951
Place of Presentation: The White House, presented by Pres. Harry S. Truman to his Widow
Citation: 1st Lt. Henry, Company F, distinguished himself by conspicuous gallantry and intrepidity above and beyond the call of duty in action. His platoon was holding a strategic ridge near the town when they were attacked by a superior enemy force, supported by heavy mortar and artillery fire. Seeing his platoon disorganized by this fanatical assault, he left his foxhole and moving along the line ordered his men to stay in place and keep firing. Encouraged by this heroic action, the platoon reformed a defensive line and rained devastating fire on the enemy, checking its advance. Enemy fire had knocked out all communications and 1st Lt. Henry was unable to determine whether or not the main line of resistance was altered to this heavy attack. On his own initiative, although severely wounded, he decided to hold his position as long as possible and ordered the wounded evacuated and their weapons and ammunition brought to him. Establishing a one-man defensive position, he ordered the platoon's withdrawal and despite his wound and with complete disregard for himself remained behind to cover the movement. When last seen he was singlehandedly firing all available weapons so effectively that he caused an estimated 50 enemy casualties. His ammunition was soon expended and his position overrun, but this intrepid action saved the platoon and halted the enemy's advance until the main line of resistance was prepared to throw back the attack. 1st Lt. Henry's outstanding gallantry and noble self-sacrifice above and beyond the call of duty reflect the highest honor on him and are in keeping with the esteemed traditions of the U.S. Army.
Notes: MIA

3076 ◆ HERNANDEZ, RODOLFO PEREZ

Rank: Corporal
Service: U.S. Army
Birthday: 14 April 1931
Place of Birth: Colton, San Bernardino County, California
Entered Service at: Fowler, Fresno County, California
Unit: 3d Squad, 3d Platoon, Company G, 2d Battalion, 187th Airborne Regimental Combat Team
Served as: Squad Leader
Battle or Place of Action: near Wontong-ni, Korea
Date of Action: 31 May 1951
G.O. Number, Date: 40, 21 April 1952
Date of Presentation: 12 April 1952
Place of Presentation: The White House, presented by Pres. Harry S. Truman
Citation: Cpl. Hernandez, a member of Company G, distinguished himself by conspicuous gallantry and intrepidity above and beyond the call of duty in action against the enemy. His platoon, in defensive positions on Hill 420, came under ruthless attack by a numerically superior and fanatical hostile force, accompanied by heavy artillery, mortar, and machine-gun fire which inflicted numerous casualties on the

platoon. His comrades were forced to withdraw due to lack of ammunition, but Cpl. Hernandez, although wounded in an exchange of grenades, continued to deliver deadly fire into the ranks of the onrushing assailants until a ruptured cartridge rendered his rifle inoperative. Immediately leaving his position, Cpl. Hernandez rushed the enemy armed only with rifle and bayonet. Fearlessly engaging the foe, he killed six of the enemy before falling unconscious from grenade, bayonet, and bullet wounds, but his heroic action momentarily halted the enemy advance and enabled his unit to counterattack and retake the lost ground. The indomitable fighting spirit, outstanding courage, and tenacious devotion to duty clearly demonstrated by Cpl. Hernandez reflect the highest credit upon himself, the infantry, and the U.S. Army.

3077 ◆ HUDNER JR., THOMAS JEROME

Rank: Lieutenant (j.g.) (highest rank: Captain)
Service: U.S. Navy
Birthday: 31 August 1924
Place of Birth: Fall River, Bristol County, Massachusetts
Entered Service at: Fall River, Bristol County, Massachusetts
Unit: Fighter Squadron 32, Air Group 3, U.S.S. *Leyte*
Served as: Pilot of a F-4U-4 Corsair
Battle or Place of Action: Chosin Reservoir, Korea
Date of Action: 4 December 1950
Date of Presentation: 13 April 1951
Place of Presentation: The White House, presented by Pres. Harry S. Truman
Citation: For conspicuous gallantry and intrepidity at the risk of his life above and beyond the call of duty as a pilot in Fighter Squadron 32, while attempting to rescue a squadron mate whose plane, struck by antiaircraft fire and trailing smoke, was forced down behind enemy lines. Quickly maneuvering to circle the downed pilot and protect him from enemy troops infesting the area, Lt. (j.g.) Hudner risked his life to save the injured flier who was trapped alive in the burning wreckage. Fully aware of the extreme danger in landing on the rough mountainous terrain, and the scant hope of escape or survival in subzero temperature, he put his plane down skillfully in a deliberate wheels-up landing in the presence of enemy troops. With his bare hands, he packed the fuselage with snow to keep the flames away from the pilot and struggled to pull him free. Unsuccessful in this he returned to his crashed aircraft and radioed other airborne planes, requesting that a helicopter be dispatched with an ax and fire extinguisher. He then remained on the spot despite the continuing danger from enemy action and, with the assistance of the rescue pilot, renewed a desperate but unavailing battle against time, cold, and flames. Lt. (j.g.) Hudner's exceptionally valiant action and selfless devotion to a shipmate sustain and enhance the highest traditions of the U.S. Naval Service.

3078 ◆ INGMAN JR., EINAR HAROLD

Rank: Sergeant (rank at time of action: Corporal) (highest rank: Staff Sergeant)
Service: U.S. Army

Birthday: 6 October 1929
Place of Birth: Milwaukee, Milwaukee County, Wisconsin
Entered Service at: West Bend, Washington County, Wisconsin
Unit: 3d Platoon, Company E, 17th Infantry Regiment, 7th Infantry Division
Served as: Acting Platoon Sergeant
Battle or Place of Action: near Maltari, Korea
Date of Action: 26 February 1951
G.O. Number, Date: 68, 2 August 1951
Date of Presentation: 5 July 1951
Place of Presentation: The White House, presented by Pres. Harry S. Truman
Citation: Sgt. Ingman, a member of Company E, distinguished himself by conspicuous gallantry and intrepidity above and beyond the call of duty in action against the enemy. The two leading squads of the assault platoon of his company, while attacking a strongly fortified ridge held by the enemy, were pinned down by withering fire, and both squad leaders and several men were wounded. Cpl. Ingman assumed command, reorganized, and combined the two squads, then moved from one position to another, designating fields of fire and giving advice and encouragement to the men. Locating an enemy machine-gun position that was raking his men with devastating fire, he charged it alone, threw a grenade into the position, and killed the remaining crew with rifle fire. Another enemy machine gun opened fire approximately 15 yards away and inflicted additional casualties to the group and stopped the attack. When Cpl. Ingman charged the second position he was hit by grenade fragments and a hail of fire which seriously wounded him about the face and neck and knocked him to the ground. With incredible courage and stamina, he arose instantly and, using only his rifle, killed the entire gun crew before falling unconscious from his wounds. As a result of the singular action by Cpl. Ingman, the defense of the enemy was broken, his squad secured its objective, and more than 100 hostile troops abandoned their weapons and fled in disorganized retreat. Cpl. Ingman's indomitable courage, extraordinary heroism, and superb leadership reflect the highest credit on himself and are in keeping with the esteemed traditions of the infantry and the U.S. Army.

3079 ◆ *JECELIN, WILLIAM R.

Rank: Sergeant
Service: U.S. Army
Place of Birth: Baltimore, Baltimore County, Maryland
Date of Death: 19 September 1950
Cemetery: Bohemin National Cemetery—Baltimore, Maryland
Entered Service at: Baltimore, Baltimore County, Maryland
Unit: Company C, 35th Infantry Regiment, 25th Infantry Division
Served as: Platoon Sergeant
Battle or Place of Action: near Saga, Korea
Date of Action: 19 September 1950
G.O. Number, Date: 24, 25 April 1951
Date of Presentation: 3 April 1951

Place of Presentation: The Pentagon, presented by Gen. Omar N. Bradley to his Father
Citation: Sgt. Jecelin, Company C, distinguished himself by conspicuous gallantry and intrepidity above and beyond the call of duty in action against the enemy. His company was ordered to secure a prominent, saw-toothed ridge from a well-entrenched and heavily armed enemy. Unable to capture the objective in the first attempt, a frontal and flanking assault was launched. He led his platoon through heavy enemy fire and bursting shells, across rice fields and rocky terrain, in direct frontal attack on the ridge in order to draw fire away from the flanks. The unit advanced to the base of the cliff, where intense, accurate hostile fire stopped the attack. Realizing that an assault was the only solution, Sgt. Jecelin rose from his position firing his rifle and throwing grenades as he called on his men to follow him. Despite the intense enemy fire this attack carried to the crest of the ridge where the men were forced to take cover. Again he rallied his men and stormed the enemy strongpoint. With fixed bayonets they charged into the face of antitank fire and engaged the enemy in hand-to-hand combat. After clubbing and slashing this force into submission the platoon was forced to take cover from direct frontal fire of a self-propelled gun. Refusing to be stopped he leaped to his feet and through sheer personal courage and fierce determination led his men in a new attack. At this instant a well-camouflaged enemy soldier threw a grenade at the remaining members of the platoon. He immediately lunged and covered the grenade with his body, absorbing the full force of the explosion to save those around him. This incredible courage and willingness to sacrifice himself for his comrades so imbued them with fury that they completely eliminated the enemy force. Sgt. Jecelin's heroic leadership and outstanding gallantry reflect the highest credit upon himself and uphold the esteemed traditions of the military service.

3080 ◆ *JOHNSON, JAMES EDMUND

Rank: Sergeant
Service: U.S. Marine Corps
Birthday: 1 January 1926
Place of Birth: Pocatello, Bannock County, Idaho
Date of Death: 2 November 1953
Cemetery: National Memorial of the Pacific (Wall of the Missing)—Honolulu, Hawaii; Arlington National Cemetery ('In Memory' marker) (451) (MH)—Arlington, Virginia
Entered Service at: Washington, D.C.
Unit: Company J, 3d Battalion, 7th Marines, 1st Marine Division (Rein)
Served as: Squad Leader
Battle or Place of Action: Yudam-ni, Korea
Date of Action: 2 December 1950
Date of Presentation: 29 March 1954
Place of Presentation: Washington, D.C., presented by Sec. of the Navy Robert B. Anderson to his Widow
Citation: For conspicuous gallantry and intrepidity at the risk of his life above and beyond the call of duty while serving as a squad leader in a provisional rifle platoon composed of artillerymen and attached to Company J, in action against

enemy aggressor forces. Vastly outnumbered by a well-entrenched and cleverly concealed enemy force wearing the uniforms of friendly troops and attacking his platoon's open and unconcealed positions, Sgt. Johnson unhesitatingly took charge of his platoon in the absence of the leader and, exhibiting great personal valor in the face of a heavy barrage of hostile fire, coolly proceeded to move about among his men, shouting words of encouragement and inspiration and skillfully directing their fire. Ordered to displace his platoon during the firefight, he immediately placed himself in an extremely hazardous position from which he could provide covering fire for his men. Fully aware that his voluntary action meant either certain death or capture to himself, he courageously continued to provide effective cover for his men and was last observed in a wounded condition single-handedly engaging enemy troops in close hand-grenade and hand-to-hand fighting. By his valiant and inspiring leadership, Sgt. Johnson was directly responsible for the successful completion of the platoon's displacement and the saving of many lives. His dauntless fighting spirit and unfaltering devotion to duty in the face of terrific odds reflect the highest credit upon himself and the U.S. Naval Service.

Notes: MIA

3081 ◆ *JORDON, MACK A.

Rank: Private First Class
Service: U.S. Army
Birthday: 8 December 1928
Place of Birth: Collins, Covington County, Mississippi
Date of Death: 15 November 1951
Cemetery: Station Creek Cemetery—Collins, Mississippi
Entered Service at: Collins, Covington County, Mississippi
Unit: 3d Platoon, Company K, 21st Infantry Regiment, 24th Infantry Division
Served as: Squad Leader
Battle or Place of Action: near Kumsong, Korea
Date of Action: 15 November 1951
G.O. Number, Date: 3, 8 January 1953
Date of Presentation: 7 January 1953
Place of Presentation: The Pentagon, presented by Sec. of the Army Frank C. Pace to his family
Citation: Pfc. Jordan, a member of Company K, distinguished himself by conspicuous gallantry and indomitable courage above and beyond the call of duty in action against the enemy. As a squad leader of the 3d Platoon, he was participating in a night attack on key terrain against a fanatical hostile force when the advance was halted by intense small-arms and automatic-weapons fire and a vicious barrage of hand grenades. Upon orders for the platoon to withdraw and reorganize, Pfc. Jordan voluntarily remained behind to provide covering fire. Crawling toward an enemy machine-gun emplacement, he threw three grenades and neutralized the gun. He then rushed the position delivering a devastating hail of fire, killing several of the enemy and forcing the remainder to fall back to new positions. He courageously attempted to move forward to silence another machine gun but, before he could leave his position, the ruthless foe hurled explosives down the hill and in the ensuing blast both legs were severed.

Despite mortal wounds, he continued to deliver deadly fire and held off the assailants until the platoon returned. Pfc. Jordan's unflinching courage and gallant self-sacrifice reflect lasting glory upon himself and uphold the noble traditions of the infantry and the military service.

3082 ◆ *KANELL, BILLIE GENE

Rank: Private
Service: U.S. Army
Birthday: 26 June 1931
Place of Birth: Poplar Bluff, Butler County, Missouri
Date of Death: 7 September 1951
Cemetery: Fairdealing Cemetery—Fairdealing, Missouri
Entered Service at: Poplar Bluff, Butler County, Missouri
Unit: Company I, 35th Infantry Regiment, 25th Infantry Division
Battle or Place of Action: near Pyongyang, Korea
Date of Action: 7 September 1951
G.O. Number, Date: 57, 13 June 1952
Date of Presentation: 26 March 1952
Place of Presentation: The Pentagon, presented by Sec. of the Army Frank C. Pace to his Father
Citation: Pvt. Kanell, a member of Company I, distinguished himself by conspicuous gallantry and outstanding courage above and beyond the call of duty in action against the enemy. A numerically superior hostile force had launched a fanatical assault against friendly positions, supported by mortar and artillery fire, when Pvt. Kanell stood in his emplacement exposed to enemy observation and action and delivered accurate fire into the ranks of the assailants. An enemy grenade was hurled into his emplacement and Pvt. Kanell threw himself upon the grenade, absorbing the blast with his body to protect two of his comrades from serious injury and possible death. A few seconds later another grenade was thrown into the emplacement and, although seriously wounded by the first missile, he summoned his waning strength to roll toward the second grenade and used his body as a shield to again protect his comrades. He was mortally wounded as a result of his heroic actions. His indomitable courage, sustained fortitude against overwhelming odds, and gallant self-sacrifice reflect the highest credit upon himself, the infantry, and the U.S. Army.

3083 ◆ *KAUFMAN, LOREN R.

Rank: Sergeant First Class
Service: U.S. Army
Birthday: 27 July 1923
Place of Birth: The Dalles, Wasco County, Oregon
Date of Death: 10 February 1951
Cemetery: Willamette National Cemetery (G-2812) (MH)—Portland, Oregon
Entered Service at: The Dalles, Wasco County, Oregon
Unit: Company G, 9th Infantry Regiment, 2d Infantry Division
Battle or Place of Action: near Yongsan, Korea
Date of Action: 4-5 September 1950
G.O. Number, Date: 61, 2 August 1951

Date of Presentation: 21 June 1951
Place of Presentation: The Pentagon, presented by Gen. Omar N. Bradley to his Father
Citation: Sfc. Kaufman distinguished himself by conspicuous gallantry and intrepidity above and beyond the call of duty in action. On the night of 4 September the company was in a defensive position on two adjoining hills. His platoon was occupying a strong point two miles away protecting the battalion flank. Early on 5 September the company was attacked by enemy battalion and his platoon was ordered to reinforce the company. As his unit moved along a ridge it encountered a hostile encircling force. Sfc. Kaufman, running forward, bayoneted the lead scout and engaged the column in a rifle and grenade assault. His quick, vicious attack so surprised the enemy that they retreated in confusion. When his platoon joined the company he discovered that the enemy had taken commanding ground and pinned the company down in a draw. Without hesitation Sfc. Kaufman charged the enemy lines firing his rifle and throwing grenades. During the action, he bayoneted two enemy and, seizing an unmanned machine gun, delivered deadly fire on the defenders. Following this encounter the company regrouped and resumed the attack. Leading the assault, he reached the ridge, destroyed a hostile machine-gun position, and routed the remaining enemy. Pursuing the hostile troops, he bayoneted two more and then rushed a mortar position, shooting the gunners. Remnants of the enemy fled to a village and Sfc. Kaufman led a patrol into the town, dispersed them, and burned the buildings. The dauntless courage and resolute intrepid leadership of Sfc. Kaufman were directly responsible for the success of his company in regaining its positions, reflecting distinct credit upon himself and upholding the esteemed traditions of the military service.

3084 ◆ *KELLY, JOHN DORAN

Rank: Private First Class
Service: U.S. Marine Corps
Birthday: 8 July 1928
Place of Birth: Youngstown, Mahoning County, Ohio
Date of Death: 28 May 1952
Cemetery: Jefferson Memorial Cemetery (MH)—Pittsburgh, Pennsylvania
Entered Service at: Homestead, Allegheny County, Pennsylvania
Unit: Company C, 1st Battalion, 7th Marines, 1st Marine Division (Rein)
Served as: Radio Operator
Battle or Place of Action: Korea
Date of Action: 28 May 1952
Date of Presentation: 9 September 1953
Place of Presentation: Washington, D.C., Marine Corps Barracks, presented by Vice Pres. Richard M. Nixon to his Mother
Citation: For conspicuous gallantry and intrepidity at the risk of his life above and beyond the call of duty while serving as a radio operator of Company C, in action against enemy aggressor forces. With his platoon pinned down by a numerically superior enemy force employing intense mortar, artillery, small-arms, and grenade fire, Pfc. Kelly requested permission to leave his radio in the care of another man and to participate in an assault on enemy key positions. Fearlessly charging forward in the face of a murderous hail of machine-gun fire and hand grenades, he initiated a daring attack against a hostile strongpoint and personally neutralized the position, killing two of the enemy. Unyielding in the face of heavy odds, he continued forward and singlehandedly assaulted a machine-gun bunker. Although painfully wounded, he bravely charged the bunker and destroyed it, killing three of the enemy. Courageously continuing his one-man assault, he again stormed forward in a valiant attempt to wipe out a third bunker and boldly delivered point-blank fire into the aperture of the hostile emplacement. Mortally wounded by enemy fire while carrying out this heroic action, Pfc. Kelly, by his great personal valor and aggressive fighting spirit, inspired his comrades to sweep on, overrun and secure the objective. His extraordinary heroism in the face of almost certain death reflects the highest credit upon himself and enhances the finest traditions of the U.S. Naval Service. He gallantly gave his life for his country.

3085 ◆ *KELSO, JACK WILLIAM

Rank: Private First Class
Service: U.S. Marine Corps
Birthday: 23 January 1934
Place of Birth: Madera, Madera County, California
Date of Death: 2 October 1952
Place of Death: Korea
Cemetery: Washington Colony Cemetery (MH)—Fresno, California
Entered Service at: Caruthers, Fresno County, California
Unit: Company I, 3d Battalion, 7th Marines, 1st Marine Division (Rein)
Served as: Rifleman
Battle or Place of Action: Korea
Date of Action: 2 October 1952
Date of Presentation: 9 September 1953
Place of Presentation: Marine Corps Barracks, Washington, D.C., presented by Vice Pres. Richard M. Nixon to his parents
Citation: For conspicuous gallantry and intrepidity at the risk of his life above and beyond the call of duty while serving as a rifleman of Company I, in action against enemy aggressor forces. When both the platoon commander and the platoon sergeant became casualties during the defense of a vital outpost against a numerically superior enemy force attacking at night under cover of intense small-arms, grenade, and mortar fire, Pfc. Kelso bravely exposed himself to the hail of enemy fire in a determined effort to reorganize the unit and to repel the onrushing attackers. Forced to seek cover, along with four other marines, in a nearby bunker which immediately came under attack, he unhesitatingly picked up an enemy grenade which landed in the shelter, rushed out into the open, and hurled it back at the enemy. Although painfully wounded when the grenade exploded as it left his hand, and again forced to seek the protection of the bunker when the hostile fire became more intensified, Pfc. Kelso refused to remain in

his position of comparative safety and moved out into the fire-swept area to return the enemy fire, thereby permitting the pinned-down marines in the bunker to escape. Mortally wounded while providing covering fire for his comrades, Pfc. Kelso, by his valiant fighting spirit, aggressive determination, and self-sacrificing efforts in behalf of others, served to inspire all who observed him. His heroic actions sustain and enhance the highest traditions of the U.S. Naval Service. He gallantly gave his life for his country.

3086 ◆ KENNEMORE, ROBERT SIDNEY

Rank: Staff Sergeant
Service: U.S. Marine Corps
Birthday: 21 June 1920
Place of Birth: Greenville, Greenville County, South Carolina
Date of Death: 26 April 1989
Cemetery: San Francisco National Cemetery (H-CA-404) (MH)—San Francisco, California
Entered Service at: Greenville, Greenville County, South Carolina
Unit: Company E, 2d Battalion, 7th Marines, 1st Marine Division (Rein)
Served as: Section Leader
Battle or Place of Action: north of Yudam-ni, Korea
Date of Action: 27-28 November 1950
Citation: For conspicuous gallantry and intrepidity at the risk of his life above and beyond the call of duty as leader of a machine-gun section in Company E, in action against enemy aggressor forces. With the company's defensive perimeter overrun by a numerically superior hostile force during a savage night attack north of Yudam-ni and his platoon commander seriously wounded, S/Sgt. Kennemore unhesitatingly assumed command, quickly reorganized the unit and directed the men in consolidating the position. When an enemy grenade landed in the midst of a machine-gun squad, he bravely placed his foot on the missile and, in the face of almost certain death, personally absorbed the full force of the explosion to prevent injury to his fellow marines. By his indomitable courage, outstanding leadership, and selfless efforts in behalf of his comrades, S/Sgt. Kennemore was greatly instrumental in driving the enemy from the area and upheld the highest traditions of the U.S. Naval Service.

3087 ◆ *KILMER, JOHN EDWARD

Rank: Hospital Corpsman
Service: U.S. Navy
Birthday: 15 August 1930
Place of Birth: Highland Park, Lake County, Illinois
Date of Death: 13 August 1952
Cemetery: San Jose Burial Park (MH)—San Antonio, Texas
Entered Service at: Houston, Harris County, Texas
Unit: Attached to duty as a medical corpsman with a Marine rifle company in the 1st Marine Division
Served as: Medical Corpsman
Battle or Place of Action: Korea

Date of Action: 13 August 1952
Citation: For conspicuous gallantry and intrepidity at the risk of his life above and beyond the call of duty in action against enemy aggressor forces. With his company engaged in defending a vitally important hill position well forward of the main line of resistance during an assault by large concentrations of hostile troops, HC Kilmer repeatedly braved intense enemy mortar, artillery, and sniper fire to move from one position to another, administering aid to the wounded and expediting their evacuation. Painfully wounded himself when struck by mortar fragments while moving to the aid of a casualty, he persisted in his efforts and inched his way to the side of the stricken marine through a hail of enemy shells falling around him. Undaunted by the devastating hostile fire, he skillfully administered first aid to his comrade and, as another mounting barrage of enemy fire shattered the immediate area, unhesitatingly shielded the wounded man with his body. Mortally wounded by flying shrapnel while carrying out this heroic action, HC Kilmer, by his great personal valor and gallant spirit of self-sacrifce in saving the life of a comrade, served to inspire all who observed him. His unyielding devotion to duty in the face of heavy odds reflects the highest credit upon himself and enhances the finest traditions of the U.S. Naval Service. He gallantly gave his life for another.

3088 ◆ *KNIGHT, NOAH ODELL

Rank: Private First Class
Service: U.S. Army
Birthday: 29 October 1929
Place of Birth: Chesterfield County, South Carolina
Date of Death: 24 November 1951
Cemetery: Union Hill Baptist Church (MH)—Pageland, South Carolina
Entered Service at: Jefferson, Chesterfield County, South Carolina
Unit: Company F, 7th Infantry Regiment, 3d Infantry Division
Battle or Place of Action: near Kowang-San, Korea
Date of Action: 23-24 November 1951
G.O. Number, Date: 2, 7 January 1953
Date of Presentation: 7 January 1953
Place of Presentation: The Pentagon, presented by Sec. of the Army Frank C. Pace to his family
Citation: Pfc. Knight, a member of Company F, distinguished himself by conspicuous gallantry and indomitable courage above and beyond the call of duty in action against the enemy. He occupied a key position in the defense perimeter when waves of enemy troops passed through their own artillery and mortar concentrations and charged the company position. Two direct hits from an enemy emplacement demolished his bunker and wounded him. Disregarding personal safety, he moved to a shallow depression for a better firing vantage. Unable to deliver effective fire from his defilade position, he left his shelter, moved through heavy fire in full view of the enemy and, firing into the ranks of the relentless assailants, inflicted numerous casualties, momentarily stemming the attack. Later during another vicious onslaught, he observed an enemy squad infiltrating the position and, coun-

terattacking, killed or wounded the entire group. Expending the last of his ammunition, he discovered three enemy soldiers entering the friendly position with demolition charges. Realizing the explosives would enable the enemy to exploit the breach, he fearlessly rushed forward and disabled two assailants with the butt of his rifle when the third exploded a demolition charge killing the three enemy soldiers and mortally wounding Pfc. Knight. Pfc. Knight's supreme sacrifice and consummate devotion to duty reflect lasting glory on himself and uphold the noble traditions of the military service.

3089 ◆ *KOELSCH, JOHN KELVIN

Rank: Lieutenant (j.g.)
Service: U.S. Navy
Birthday: 22 December 1925
Place of Birth: London, England
Date of Death: 16 October 1951
Place of Death: Prison Camp, North Korea
Cemetery: Arlington National Cemetery (30-1123-RH) (MH)—Arlington, Virginia
Entered Service at: Los Angeles, Los Angeles County, California
Unit: Navy Helicopter Rescue Unit, U.S.S. *Princeton*
Served as: Helicopter Pilot
Battle or Place of Action: near Wonsan, North Korea
Date of Action: 3 July 1951
Date of Presentation: August 1955
Place of Presentation: The Pentagon, presented by Secretary of the Navy Charles S. Thomas to his mother
Citation: For conspicuous gallantry and intrepidity at the risk of his life above and beyond the call of duty while serving with a Navy helicopter rescue unit. Although darkness was rapidly approaching when information was received that a marine aviator had been shot down and was trapped by the enemy in mountainous terrain deep in hostile territory, Lt. (j.g.) Koelsch voluntarily flew a helicopter to the reported position of the downed airman in an attempt to effect a rescue. With an almost solid overcast concealing everything below the mountain peaks, he descended in his unarmed and vulnerable aircraft without the accompanying fighter escort to an extremely low altitude beneath the cloud level and began a systematic search. Despite the increasingly intense enemy fire, which struck his helicopter on one occasion, he persisted in his mission until he succeeded in locating the downed pilot, who was suffering from serious burns on the arms and legs. While the victim was being hoisted into the aircraft, it was struck again by an accurate burst of hostile fire and crashed on the side of the mountain. Quickly extricating his crewmen and the aviator from the wreckage, Lt. (j.g.) Koelsch led them from the vicinity in an effort to escape from hostile troops, evading the enemy forces for nine days and rendering such medical attention as possible to his severely burned companion until all were captured. Up to the time of his death while still a captive of the enemy, Lt. (j.g.) Koelsch steadfastly refused to aid his captors in any manner and served to inspire his fellow prisoners by his fortitude and consideration for others. His great personal valor and heroic spirit of self-sacrifice

throughout sustain and enhance the finest traditions of the U.S. Naval Service.
Notes: POW

3090 ◆ KOUMA, ERNEST RICHARD

Rank: Master Sergeant (rank at time of action: Sergeant First Class)
Service: U.S. Army
Birthday: 23 November 1919
Place of Birth: Dwight, Butler County, Nebraska
Date of Death: 19 December 1993
Place of Death: McDaniels, Kentucky
Cemetery: Fort Knox Post Cemetery (MH)—Fort Knox, Kentucky
Entered Service at: Dwight, Butler County, Nebraska
Unit: 4th Platoon, Company A, 72d Tank Battalion, 2d Infantry Division
Served as: Tank Commander
Battle or Place of Action: vicinity of Agok, Korea
Date of Action: 31 August-1 September 1951
G.O. Number, Date: 38, 4 June 1951
Date of Presentation: 19 May 1951
Place of Presentation: Blair House, presented by Pres. Harry S. Truman
Citation: M/Sgt. Kouma, a tank commander in Company A, distinguished himself by conspicuous gallantry and intrepidity at the risk of his life above and beyond the call of duty in action against the enemy. His unit was engaged in supporting infantry elements on the Naktong River front. Near midnight on 31 August, a hostile force estimated at 500 crossed the river and launched a fierce attack against the infantry positions, inflicting heavy casualties. A withdrawal was ordered and his armored unit was given the mission of covering the movement until a secondary position could be established. The enemy assault overran two tanks, destroyed one, and forced another to withdraw. Suddenly M/Sgt. Kouma discovered that his tank was the only obstacle in the path of the hostile onslaught. Holding his ground, he gave fire orders to his crew and remained in position throughout the night, fighting off repeated enemy attacks. During one fierce assault, the enemy surrounded his tank and he leaped from the armored turret, exposing himself to a hail of hostile fire, manned the .50 caliber machine gun mounted on the rear deck, and delivered point-blank fire into the fanatical foe. His machine gun emptied, he fired his pistol and threw grenades to keep the enemy from his tank. After more than nine hours of constant combat and close-in fighting, he withdrew his vehicle to friendly lines. During the withdrawal through eight miles of hostile territory, M/Sgt. Kouma continued to inflict casualties upon the enemy and exhausted his ammunition in destroying three hostile machine-gun positions. During this action, M/Sgt. Kouma killed an estimated 250 enemy soldiers. His magnificent stand allowed the infantry sufficient time to reestablish defensive positions. Rejoining his company, although suffering intensely from his wounds, he attempted to resupply his tank and return to the battle area. While being evacuated for medical treatment, his courage was again displayed when he requested to return to the front. M/Sgt.

Kouma's superb leadership, heroism, and intense devotion to duty reflect the highest credit on himself and uphold the esteemed traditions of the U.S. Army.

3091 ◆ *KRZYZOWSKI, EDWARD C.

Rank: Captain
Service: U.S. Army
Birthday: 16 January 1914
Place of Birth: Chicago, Cook County, Illinois
Date of Death: 3 September 1951
Cemetery: Resurrection Cemetery—Justice, Illinois
Entered Service at: Cicero, Cook County, Illinois
Unit: Company B, 9th Infantry Regiment, 2d Infantry Division
Served as: Company Commander
Battle or Place of Action: near Tondul, Korea
Date of Action: 31 August-3 September 1951
G.O. Number, Date: 56, 12 June 1952
Date of Presentation: 26 March 1952
Place of Presentation: The Pentagon, presented by Sec. of the Army Frank C. Pace to his Widow
Citation: Capt. Krzyzowski, distinguished himself by conspicuous gallantry and indomitable courage above and beyond the call of duty in action against the enemy as commanding officer of Company B. Spearheading an assault against strongly defended Hill 700, his company came under vicious cross-fire and grenade attack from enemy bunkers. Creeping up the fire-swept hill, he personally eliminated one bunker with his grenades and wiped out a second with carbine fire. Forced to retire to more tenable positions for the night, the company, led by Capt. Krzyzowski, resumed the attack the following day, gaining several hundred yards and inflicting numerous casualties. Overwhelmed by the numerically superior hostile force, he ordered his men to evacuate the wounded and move back. Providing protective fire for their safe withdrawal, he was wounded again by grenade fragments, but refused evacuation and continued to direct the defense. On 3 September, he led his valiant unit in another assault which overran several hostile positions, but again the company was pinned down by murderous fire. Courageously advancing alone to an open knoll to plot mortar concentrations against the hill, he was killed instantly by an enemy sniper's fire. Capt. Krzyzowski's consummate fortitude, heroic leadership, and gallant self-sacrifice, so clearly demonstrated throughout three days of bitter combat, reflect the highest credit and lasting glory on himself, the infantry, and the U.S. Army.

3092 ◆ *KYLE, DARWIN K.

Rank: Second Lieutenant
Service: U.S. Army
Birthday: 1 June 1918
Place of Birth: Jenkins, Letcher County, Kentucky
Date of Death: 16 February 1951
Cemetery: Sunset Memorial Park—South Charleston, West Virginia
Entered Service at: Racine, Boone County, West Virginia
Unit: Company K, 7th Infantry Regiment, 3d Infantry Division

Served as: Platoon Leader
Battle or Place of Action: near Kamil-ni, Korea
Date of Action: 16 February 1951
G.O. Number, Date: 17, 1 February 1952
Date of Presentation: 16 January 1952
Place of Presentation: The Pentagon, presented by Sec. of Defense Robert Lovett to his Widow
Citation: 2d Lt. Kyle, distinguished himself by conspicuous gallantry and intrepidity above and beyond the call of duty in action against the enemy. When his platoon had been pinned down by intense fire, he completely exposed himself to move among and encourage his men to continue the advance against enemy forces strongly entrenched on Hill 185. Inspired by his courageous leadership, the platoon resumed the advance but was again pinned down when an enemy machine gun opened fire, wounding six of the men. 2d Lt. Kyle immediately charged the hostile emplacement alone, engaged the crew in hand-to-hand combat, killing all three. Continuing on toward the objective, his platoon suddenly received an intense automatic-weapons fire from a well-concealed hostile position on its right flank. Again leading his men in a daring bayonet charge against this position, firing his carbine and throwing grenades, 2d Lt. Kyle personally destroyed four of the enemy before he was killed by a burst from an enemy submachine gun. The extraordinary heroism and outstanding leadership of 2d Lt. Kyle, and his gallant self-sacrifice, reflect the highest credit upon himself and are in keeping with the esteemed traditions of the military service.

3093 ◆ LEE, HUBERT LOUIS

Rank: Master Sergeant
Service: U.S. Army
Birthday: 2 February 1915
Place of Birth: Arburg, Missouri
Date of Death: 5 November 1982
Place of Death: Jackson, Mississippi
Cemetery: Leland-Stoneville Cemetery (MH)—Stoneville, Mississippi
Entered Service at: Leland, Washington County, Mississippi
Unit: Company I, 23d Infantry Regiment, 2d Infantry Division
Served as: Platoon Sergeant
Battle or Place of Action: near Ip-o-ri, Korea
Date of Action: 1 February 1951
G.O. Number, Date: 21, 5 February 1952
Date of Presentation: 29 January 1952
Place of Presentation: The White House, presented by Pres. Harry S. Truman
Citation: M/Sgt. Lee, a member of Company I, distinguished himself by conspicuous gallantry and intrepidity above and beyond the call of duty in action against the enemy. When his platoon was forced from its position by a numerically superior enemy force, and his platoon leader wounded, M/Sgt. Lee assumed command, regrouped the remnants of his unit, and led them in repeated assaults to regain the position. Within 25 yards of his objective he received a leg wound from grenade fragments, but refused

assistance and continued the attack. Although forced to withdraw five times, each time he regrouped his remaining men and renewed the assault. Moving forward at the head of his small group in the fifth attempt, he was struck by an exploding grenade, knocked to the ground, and seriously wounded in both legs. Still refusing assistance, he advanced by crawling, rising to his knees to fire, and urging his men to follow. While thus directing the final assault, he was wounded a third time, by small-arms fire. Persistently continuing to crawl forward, he directed his men in a final and successful attack which regained the vital objective. His intrepid leadership and determination led to the destruction of 83 of the enemy and withdrawal of the remainder, and was a vital factor in stopping the enemy attack. M/Sgt. Lee's indomitable courage, consummate valor, and outstanding leadership reflect the highest credit upon himself and are in keeping with the finest traditions of the infantry and the U.S. Army.

3094 ◆ *LIBBY, GEORGE DALTON

Rank: Sergeant
Service: U.S. Army
Birthday: 4 December 1919
Place of Birth: Bridgton, Cumberland County, Maine
Date of Death: 20 July 1950
Cemetery: Arlington National Cemetery (34-1317) (MH)—Arlington, Virginia
Entered Service at: Waterbury, New Haven County, Connecticut
Unit: Company C, 3d Combat Engineer Battalion, 24th Infantry Division
Battle or Place of Action: near Taejon, Korea
Date of Action: 20 July 1950
G.O. Number, Date: 62, 2 August 1951
Date of Presentation: 21 June 1951
Place of Presentation: The Pentagon, presented by Gen. Omar N. Bradley to his Sister
Citation: Sgt. Libby distinguished himself by conspicuous gallantry and intrepidity above and beyond the call of duty in action. While breaking through an enemy encirclement, the vehicle in which he was riding approached an enemy roadblock and encountered devastating fire which disabled the truck, killing or wounding all the passengers except Sgt. Libby. Taking cover in a ditch, Sgt. Libby engaged the enemy and despite the heavy fire crossed the road twice to administer aid to his wounded comrades. He then hailed a passing M-5 artillery tractor and helped the wounded aboard. The enemy directed intense small-arms fire at the driver, and Sgt. Libby, realizing that no one else could operate the vehicle, placed himself between the driver and the enemy thereby shielding him while he returned the fire. During this action he received several wounds in the arms and body. Continuing through the town, the tractor made frequent stops and Sgt. Libby helped more wounded aboard. Refusing first aid, he continued to shield the driver and return the fire of the enemy when another roadblock was encountered. Sgt. Libby received additional wounds but held his position until he lost consciousness. Sgt. Libby's sustained, heroic actions enabled his comrades to reach friendly lines. His dauntless courage

and gallant self-sacrifice reflect the highest credit upon himself and uphold the esteemed traditions of the U.S. Army.

3095 ◆ *LITTLETON, HERBERT A.

Rank: Private First Class
Service: U.S. Marine Corps Reserve
Birthday: 1 July 1930
Place of Birth: Mena, Polk County, Arkansas
Date of Death: 22 April 1951
Cemetery: Kohler Lawn Cemetery (MH)—Nampa, Idaho
Entered Service at: Black Hawk, Meade County, South Dakota
Unit: Company C, 1st Battalion, 7th Marines, 1st Marine Division
Served as: Radio Operator
Battle or Place of Action: Chungchon, Korea
Date of Action: 22 April 1951
Citation: For conspicuous gallantry and intrepidity at the risk of his life above and beyond the call of duty while serving as a radio operator with an artillery forward observation team of Company C, in action against enemy aggressor forces. Standing watch when a well-concealed and numerically superior enemy force launched a violent night attack from nearby positions against his company, Pfc. Littleton quickly alerted the forward observation team and immediately moved into an advantageous position to assist in calling down artillery fire on the hostile force. When an enemy hand grenade was thrown into his vantage point shortly after the arrival of the remainder of the team, he unhesitatingly hurled himself on the deadly missle, absorbing its full, shattering impact in his body. By his prompt action and heroic spirit of self-sacrifice, he saved the other members of his team from serious injury or death and enabled them to carry on the vital mission which culminated in the repulse of the hostile attack. His indomitable valor in the face of almost certain death reflects the highest credit upon Pfc. Littleton and the U.S. Naval Service. He gallantly gave his life for his country.

3096 ◆ *LONG, CHARLES RICHARD

Rank: Sergeant
Service: U.S. Army
Birthday: 10 December 1923
Place of Birth: Kansas City, Clay County, Missouri
Date of Death: 12 February 1951
Cemetery: Mount Washington Cemetery (MH)—Independence, Missouri
Entered Service at: Kansas City, Clay County, Missouri
Unit: Company M, 38th Infantry Regiment, 2d Infantry Division
Served as: Forward Observer
Battle or Place of Action: near Hoeng-song, Korea
Date of Action: 12 February 1951
G.O. Number, Date: 18, 1 February 1952
Date of Presentation: 16 January 1952
Place of Presentation: The Pentagon, presented by Sec. of Defense Robert Lovett to his Widow
Citation: Sgt. Long, a member of Company M, distin-

guished himself by conspicuous gallantry and intrepidity above and beyond the call of duty in action against an armed enemy of the United Nations. When Company M, in a defensive perimeter on Hill 300, was viciously attacked by a numerically superior hostile force at approximately 0300 hours and ordered to withdraw, Sgt. Long, a forward observer for the mortar platoon, voluntarily remained at his post to provide cover by directing mortar fire on the enemy. Maintaining radio contact with his platoon, Sgt. Long coolly directed accurate mortar fire on the advancing foe. He continued firing his carbine and throwing hand grenades until his position was surrounded and he was mortally wounded. Sgt. Long's inspirational, valorous action halted the onslaught, exacted a heavy toll of enemy casualties, and enabled his company to withdraw, reorganize, counterattack, and regain the hill strongpoint. His unflinching courage and noble self-sacrifice reflect the highest credit on himself and are in keeping with the honored traditions of the military service.

3097 ◆ *LOPEZ, BALDOMERO

Rank: First Lieutenant
Service: U.S. Marine Corps
Birthday: 23 August 1925
Place of Birth: Tampa, Hillsborough County, Florida
Date of Death: 15 September 1950
Cemetery: Centre Adorim Memorial Park (MH)—Tampa, Florida
Entered Service at: Tampa, Hillsborough County, Florida
Unit: Company A, 1st Battalion, 5th Marines, 1st Marine Division (Rein)
Served as: Rifle Platoon Commander
Battle or Place of Action: Inchon, Korea
Date of Action: 15 September 1950
Date of Presentation: 30 August 1951
Place of Presentation: The Pentagon, presented by Sec. of the Navy Dan A. Kimball to his parents
Citation: For conspicuous gallantry and intrepidity at the risk of his life above and beyond the call of duty as a rifle platoon commander of Company A, in action against enemy aggressor forces. With his platoon 1st Lt. Lopez was engaged in the reduction of immediate enemy beach defenses after landing with the assault waves. Exposing himself to hostile fire, he moved forward alongside a bunker and prepared to throw a hand grenade into the next pillbox whose fire was pinning down that sector of the beach. Taken under fire by an enemy automatic weapon and hit in the right shoulder and chest as he lifted his arm to throw, he fell backward and dropped the deadly missile. After a moment, he turned and dragged his body forward in an effort to retrieve the grenade and throw it. In critical condition from pain and loss of blood, and unable to grasp the hand grenade firmly enough to hurl it, he chose to sacrifice himself rather than endanger the lives of his men and, with a sweeping motion of his wounded right arm, cradled the grenade under him and absorbed the full impact of the explosion. His exceptional courage, fortitude, and devotion to duty reflect the highest credit upon 1st Lt. Lopez and the U.S. Naval Service. He gallantly gave his life for his country.

3098 ◆ *LORING JR., CHARLES JOSEPH

Rank: Major
Service: U.S. Air Force
Birthday: 2 October 1918
Place of Birth: Portland, Cumberland County, Maine
Date of Death: 22 November 1952
Cemetery: National Memorial of the Pacific (Wall of the Missing)—Honolulu, Hawaii
Entered Service at: Portland, Cumberland County, Maine
Unit: 80th Fighter-Bomber Squadron, 8th Fighter-Bomber Wing
Served as: Flight Leader/Pilot of a F-80
Battle or Place of Action: near Sniper Ridge, North Korea
Date of Action: 22 November 1952
Date of Presentation: 5 May 1954
Place of Presentation: The White House, presented by Pres. Dwight D. Eisenhower to his Widow
Citation: Maj. Loring distinguished himself by conspicuous gallantry and intrepidity at the risk of his life above and beyond the call of duty. While leading a flight of four F-80 type aircraft on a close support mission, Maj. Loring was briefed by a controller to dive-bomb enemy gun positions which were harassing friendly ground troops. After verifying the location of the target, Maj. Loring rolled into his dive bomb run. Throughout the run, extremely accurate ground fire was directed on his aircraft. Disregarding the accuracy and intensity of the ground fire, Maj. Loring aggressively continued to press the attack until his aircraft was hit. At approximately 4,000 feet, he deliberately altered his course and aimed his diving aircraft at active gun emplacements concentrated on a ridge northwest of the briefed target, turned his aircraft 45 degrees to the left, pulled up in a deliberate, controlled manuever, and elected to sacrifice his life by diving his aircraft directly into the midst of the enemy emplacements. His selfless and heroic action completely destroyed the enemy gun emplacement and eliminated a dangerous threat to United Nations ground forces. Maj. Loring's noble spirit, superlative courage, and conspicuous self-sacrifice in inflicting maximum damage on the enemy exemplified valor of the highest degree, and his actions were in keeping with the finest traditions of the U.S. Air Force.
Notes: POW WWII—MIA Korea

3099 ◆ *LYELL, WILLIAM FRANKLIN

Rank: Corporal
Service: U.S. Army
Birthday: 14 February 1929
Place of Birth: Hickman County, Tennessee
Date of Death: 31 August 1951
Place of Death: Chup'a-ri, Korea
Cemetery: Nashville National Cemetery (1-151) (MH)—Madison, Tennessee
Entered Service at: Old Hickory, Davidson County, Tennessee
Unit: Company F, 17th Infantry Regiment, 7th Infantry Division
Battle or Place of Action: near Chup'a-ri, Korea

Date of Action: 31 August 1951
G.O. Number, Date: 4, 9 January 1953
Date of Presentation: 7 January 1953
Place of Presentation: The Pentagon, presented by Sec. of the Army Frank C. Pace to his family
Citation: Cpl. Lyell, a member of company F, distinguished himself by conspicuous gallantry and outstanding courage above and beyond the call of duty in action against the enemy. When his platoon leader was killed, Cpl. Lyell assumed command and led his unit in an assault on strongly fortified enemy positions located on commanding terrain. When his platoon came under vicious, raking fire which halted the forward movement, Cpl. Lyell seized a 57-mm recoilless rifle and unhesitatingly moved ahead to a suitable firing position from which he delivered deadly accurate fire completely destroying an enemy bunker, killing its occuppants. He then returned to his platoon and was resuming the assault when the unit was again subjected to intense hostile fire from two other bunkers. Disregarding his personal safety, armed with grenades, he charged forward hurling grenades into one of the enemy emplacements, and although painfully wounded in this action he pressed on, destroying the bunker and killing six of the foe. He then continued his attack against a third enemy position, throwing grenades as he ran forward, annihilating four enemy soldiers. He then led his platoon to the north slope of the hill where positions were occupied from which effective fire was delivered against the enemy in support of friendly troops moving up. Fearlessly exposing himself to enemy fire, he continuously moved about, directing and encouraging his men until he was mortally wounded by enemy mortar fire. Cpl. Lyell's extraordinary heroism, indomitable courage, and aggressive leadership reflect great credit on himself and are in keeping with the highest traditions of the military service.

3100 ◆ *MARTINEZ, BENITO

Rank: Corporal
Service: U.S. Army
Birthday: 21 April 1932
Place of Birth: Fort Hancock, Hudspeth County, Texas
Date of Death: 6 September 1952
Cemetery: Fort Bliss National Cemetery (B-366A) (MH)—Fort Bliss, Texas
Entered Service at: Fort Hancock, Hudspeth County, Texas
Unit: Company A, 1st Battalion, 27th Infantry Regiment, 25th Infantry Division
Served as: Machine Gunner
Battle or Place of Action: near Satae-ri, Korea
Date of Action: 6 September 1952
G.O. Number, Date: 96, 29 December 1953
Date of Presentation: 16 December 1953
Citation: Cpl. Martinez, a machine gunner with Company A, distinguished himself by conspicuous gallantry and outstanding courage above and beyond the call of duty in action against the enemy. While manning a listening post forward of the main line of resistance, his position was attacked by a hostile force of reinforced company strength. In the bitter fighting which ensued, the enemy infiltrated the defense perimeter and, realizing that encirclement was imminent, Cpl. Martinez elected to remain at his post in an attempt to stem the onslaught. In a daring defense, he raked the attacking troops with crippling fire, inflicting numerous casualties. Although contacted by sound power phone several times, he insisted that no attempt be made to rescue him because of the danger involved. Soon thereafter, the hostile forces rushed the emplacement, forcing him to make a limited withdrawal with only an automatic rifle and pistol to defend himself. After a courageous six-hour stand and shortly before dawn, he called in for the last time, stating that the enemy was converging on his position. His magnificent stand enabled friendly elements to reorganize, attack, and regain the key terrain. Cpl. Martinez' incredible valor and supreme sacrifice reflect lasting glory upon himself and are in keeping with the honored traditions of the military service.

3101 ◆ *MATTHEWS, DANIEL PAUL

Rank: Sergeant
Service: U.S. Marine Corps
Birthday: 31 December 1931
Place of Birth: Van Nuys, Los Angeles County, California
Date of Death: 28 March 1953
Place of Death: Vegas Hill, Korea
Cemetery: Glen Haven Memorial Park (MH)—San Fernando, California
Entered Service at: Van Nuys, Los Angeles County, California
Unit: Company F, 2d Battalion, 7th Marines, 1st Marine Division (Rein)
Served as: Squad Leader
Battle or Place of Action: Vegas Hill, Korea
Date of Action: 28 March 1953
Date of Issue: 29 March 1954
Citation: For conspicuous gallantry and intrepidity at the risk of his life above and beyond the call of duty while serving as a squad leader of Company F, in action against enemy aggressor forces. Participating in a counterattack against a firmly entrenched and well-concealed hostile force which had repelled six previous assaults on a vital enemy-held outpost far forward of the main line of resistance, Sgt. Matthews fearlessly advanced in the attack until his squad was pinned down by a murderous sweep of fire from an enemy machine gun located on the peak of the outpost. Observing that the deadly fire prevented a corpsman from removing a wounded man lying in an open area fully exposed to the brunt of the devastating gunfire, he worked his way to the base of the hostile machine-gun emplacement, leaped onto the rock fortification surrounding the gun and, taking the enemy by complete surprise, singlehandedly charged the hostile emplacement with his rifle. Although severely wounded when the enemy brought a withering hail of fire to bear upon him, he gallantly continued his valiant one-man assault and, firing his rifle with deadly effectiveness, succeeded in killing two of the enemy, routing a third, and completely silencing the enemy weapon, thereby enabling his comrades to evacuate the stricken marine to a safe position. Succumbing to his wounds before aid could reach him, Sgt. Matthews, by his indomitable fighting spirit,

courageous initiative, and resolute determination in the face of almost certain death, served to inspire all who observed him and was directly instrumental in saving the life of his wounded comrade. His great personal valor reflects the highest credit upon himself and enhances the finest traditions of the U.S. Naval Service. He gallantly gave his life for his country.

3102 ◆ *MAUSERT III, FREDERICK WILLIAM

Rank: Sergeant
Service: U.S. Marine Corps
Birthday: 2 May 1931
Place of Birth: Cambridge, Washington County, New York
Date of Death: 12 September 1951
Cemetery: Arlington National Cemetery (12-5559) (MH)—Arlington, Virginia
Entered Service at: Dresher, Montgomery County, Pennsylvania
Unit: Company B, 1st Battalion, 7th Marines, 1st Marine Division (Rein)
Served as: Squad Leader
Battle or Place of Action: Songnap-yong, Korea
Date of Action: 12 September 1951
Date of Presentation: 4 September 1952
Place of Presentation: The Pentagon, presented by Sec. of the Navy Dan A. Kimball to his Mother
Citation: For conspicuous gallantry and intrepidity at the risk of his life above and beyond the call of duty while serving as a squad leader in Company B, in action against enemy aggressor forces. With his company pinned down and suffering heavy casualties under murderous machine-gun, rifle, artillery, and mortar fire laid down from heavily fortified, deeply entrenched hostile strongholds on Hill 673, Sgt. Mausert unhesitatingly left his covered position and ran through a heavily mined and fire-swept area to bring back two critically wounded men to the comparative safety of the lines. Staunchly refusing evacuation despite a painful head wound sustained during his voluntary act, he insisted on remaining with his squad and, with his platoon ordered into the assault moments later, took the point position and led his men in a furious bayonet charge against the first of a literally impregnable series of bunkers. Stunned and knocked to the ground when another bullet struck his helmet, he regained his feet and resumed his drive, personally silencing the machine gun and leading his men in eliminating several other emplacements in the area. Promptly reorganizing his unit for a renewed fight to the final objective on top of the ridge, Sgt. Mausert boldly left his position when the enemy's fire gained momentum and, making a target of himself, boldly advanced alone into the face of the machine gun, drawing the fire away from his men and enabling them to move into position to assault. Again severely wounded when the enemy's fire found its mark, he still refused aid and continued spearheading the assault to the topmost machine-gun nest and bunkers, the last bulwark of the fanatic aggressors. Leaping into the wall of fire, he destroyed another machine gun with grenades before he was mortally wounded by bursting grenades and machine-gun fire. Stouthearted and indomitable, Sgt. Mausert, by his fortitude, great personal valor, and extraordinary heroism in

the face of almost certain death, had inspired his men to sweep on, overrun, and finally secure the objective. His unyielding courage throughout reflects the highest credit upon himself and the U.S. Naval Service. He gallantly gave his life for his country.

3103 ◆ *McGOVERN, ROBERT MILTON

Rank: First Lieutenant
Service: U.S. Army
Birthday: 24 January 1928
Place of Birth: Washington, D.C.
Date of Death: 30 January 1951
Cemetery: Arlington National Cemetery (3-1212-C)—Arlington, Virginia
Entered Service at: Washington, D.C.
Unit: Company A, 5th Cavalry Regiment, 1st Cavalry Division
Served as: Platoon Leader
Battle or Place of Action: near Kamyangjan-ni, Korea
Date of Action: 30 January 1951
G.O. Number, Date: 2, 8 January 1952
Citation: 1st Lt. McGovern, a member of Company A, distinguished himself by conspicuous gallantry and intrepidity at the risk of life above and beyond the call of duty in action against an armed enemy of the United Nations. As 1st Lt. McGovern led his platoon up a slope to engage hostile troops emplaced in bunker-type pillbox with connecting trenches, the unit came under heavy machine-gun and rifle fire from the crest of the hill, approximately 75 yards distant. Despite a wound sustained in this initial burst of withering fire, 1st Lt. McGovern, assured the men of his ability to continue on and urged them forward. Forging up the rocky incline, he fearlessly led the platoon to within several yards of its objective when the ruthless foe threw and rolled a vicious barrage of hand grenades on the group and halted the advance. Enemy fire increased in volume and intensity, and 1st Lt. McGovern, realizing that casualties were rapidly increasing and the morale of his men badly shaken, hurled back several grenades before they exploded. Then, disregarding his painful wound and weakened condition, he charged a machine-gun emplacement which was raking his position with flanking fire. When he was within 10 yards of the position a burst of fire ripped the carbine from his hands, but, undaunted, he continued his one-man assault and, firing his pistol and throwing grenades, killed seven hostile soldiers before falling mortally wounded in front of the gun he had silenced. 1st Lt. McGovern's incredible display of valor imbued his men with indomitable resolution to avenge his death. Fixing bayonets and throwing grenades, they charged with such ferocity that hostile positions were overrun and the enemy routed from the hill. The inspirational leadership, unflinching courage, and intrepid actions of 1st Lt. McGovern reflected utmost glory on himself and the honored tradition of the military services.

3104 ◆ McLAUGHLIN, ALFORD LEE

Rank: Private First Class
Service: U.S. Marine Corps

Birthday: 18 March 1928
Place of Birth: Leeds, Jefferson County, Alabama
Date of Death: 15 January 1977
Cemetery: Mount Hebron Cemetery (MH)—Leeds, Alabama
Entered Service at: Leeds, Jefferson County, Alabama
Unit: Company L, 3d Battalion, 5th Marines, 1st Marine Division (Rein)
Served as: Machine Gunner
Battle or Place of Action: Outpost Bruce, Korea
Date of Action: 4-5 September 1952
Date of Presentation: 27 October 1953
Place of Presentation: The White House, presented by Pres. Dwight D. Eisenhower
Citation: For conspicuous gallantry and intrepidity at the risk of his life above and beyond the call of duty while serving as a machine gunner of Company L, in action against enemy aggressor forces on the night of 4-5 September 1952. Volunteering for his second continuous tour of duty on a strategic combat outpost far in advance of the main line of resistance, Pfc. McLaughlin, although operating under a barrage of enemy artillery and mortar fire, set up plans for the defense of his position which proved decisive in the successful defense of the outpost. When hostile forces attacked in battalion strength during the night, he maintained a constant flow of devastating fire upon the enemy, alternately employing two machine guns, a carbine, and hand grenades. Although painfully wounded, he bravely fired the machine guns from the hip until his hands became blistered by the extreme heat of the weapons and, placing the guns on the ground to allow them to cool, continued to defend the position with his carbine and grenades. Standing up in full view, he shouted words of encouragement to his comrades above the din of battle and, throughout a series of fanatical enemy attacks, sprayed the surrounding area with deadly fire, accounting for an estimated 150 enemy dead and 50 wounded. By his indomitable courage, superb leadership, and valiant fighting spirit in the face of overwhelming odds, Pfc. McLaughlin served to inspire his fellow marines in their gallant stand against the enemy and was directly instrumental in preventing the vital outpost from falling into the hands of a determined and numerically superior hostile force. His outstanding heroism and unwavering devotion to duty reflect the highest credit upon himself and enhance the finest traditions of the U.S. Naval Service.

3105 ◆ *MENDONCA, LEROY A.

Rank: Sergeant
Service: U.S. Army
Birthday: 2 August 1932
Place of Birth: Honolulu, Honolulu County, Territory of Hawaii
Date of Death: 4 July 1951
Cemetery: National Memorial Cemetery of the Pacific (Q-1408) (MH)—Honolulu, Hawaii
Entered Service at: Honolulu, Honolulu County, Territory of Hawaii
Unit: Company B, 7th Infantry Regiment, 3d Infantry Division

Battle or Place of Action: near Chich-on, Korea
Date of Action: 4 July 1951
G.O. Number, Date: 83, 3 September 1952
Date of Presentation: 14 August 1952
Place of Presentation: The Pentagon, presented by Gen. Omar N. Bradley to his Mother
Citation: Sgt. LeRoy A. Mendonca, distinguished himself by conspicuous gallantry above and beyond the call of duty in action against the enemy. After his platoon, in an exhaustive fight, had captured Hill 586, the newly won positions were assaulted during the night by a numerically superior enemy force. When the 1st Platoon positions were outflanked and under great pressure and the platoon was ordered to withdraw to a secondary line of defense, Sgt. Mendonca voluntarily remained in an exposed position and covered the platoon's withdrawal. Although under murderous enemy fire, he fired his weapon and hurled grenades at the onrushing enemy until his supply of ammunition was exhausted. He fought on, clubbing with his rifle and using his bayonet until he was mortally wounded. After the action it was estimated that Sgt. Mendonca had accounted for 37 enemy casualties. His daring actions stalled the crushing assault, protecting the platoon's withdrawal to secondary positions, and enabling the entire unit to repel the enemy attack and retain possession of the vital hilltop position. Sgt. Mendonca's extraordinary gallantry and exemplary valor are in keeping with the highest traditions of the U.S. Army.

3106 ◆ MILLETT, LEWIS LEE "RED"

Rank: Captain (highest rank: Colonel)
Service: U.S. Army
Birthday: 15 December 1920
Place of Birth: Mechanic Falls, Androscoggin County, Maine
Entered Service at: Mechanic Falls, Androscoggin County, Maine
Unit: Company E, 2d Battalion, 27th Infantry Regiment, 25th Infantry Division
Served as: Company Commander
Battle or Place of Action: vicinity of Hill 180, Soam-Ni, Korea
Date of Action: 7 February 1951
G.O. Number, Date: 69, 2 August 1951
Date of Presentation: 5 July 1951
Place of Presentation: The White House (Rose Garden), presented by Pres. Harry S. Truman
Citation: Capt. Millett, Company E, distinguished himself by conspicuous gallantry and intrepidity above and beyond the call of duty in action. While personally leading his company in an attack against a strongly held position, he noted that the 1st Platoon was pinned down by small-arms, automatic, and antitank fire. Capt. Millett ordered the 3d Platoon forward, placed himself at the head of the two platoons, and, with fixed bayonet, led the assault up the fire-swept hill. In the fierce charge Capt. Millett bayoneted two enemy soldiers and boldly continued on, throwing grenades, clubbing and bayoneting the enemy, while urging his men forward by shouting encouragement. Despite vicious opposing fire, the

whirlwind hand-to-hand assault carried to the crest of the hill. His dauntless leadership and personal courage so inspired his men that they stormed into the hostile position and used their bayonets with such lethal effect that the enemy fled in wild disorder. During this fierce onslaught Capt. Millett was wounded by grenade fragments but refused evacuation until the objective was taken and firmly secured. The superb leadership, conspicuous courage, and consummate devotion to duty demonstrated by Capt. Millett were directly responsible for the successful accomplishment of a hazardous mission and reflect the highest credit on himself and the heroic traditions of the military service.

3107 ◆ *MITCHELL, FRANK NICIAS

Rank: First Lieutenant
Service: U.S. Marine Corps
Birthday: 18 August 1921
Place of Birth: Indian Gap, Hamilton County, Texas
Date of Death: 26 November 1950
Cemetery: National Memorial of the Pacific (Wall of the Missing)—Honolulu, Hawaii; Roaring Springs Cemetery (MH)('In Memory' marker)—Roaring Springs, Texas
Entered Service at: Roaring Springs, Motley County, Texas
Unit: Company A, 1st Battalion, 7th Marines, 1st Marine Division (Rein)
Served as: Platoon Leader
Battle or Place of Action: near Hansan-ni, Korea
Date of Action: 26 November 1950
Place of Presentation: Atlanta, GA, to his widow, Beverly Banks Mitchell and his daughter, Barbara
Citation: For conspicuous gallantry and intrepidity at the risk of his life above and beyond the call of duty as leader of a rifle platoon of Company A, in action against enemy aggressor forces. Leading his platoon in point position during a patrol by his company through a thickly wooded and snow-covered area in the vicinity of Hansan-ni, 1st Lt. Mitchell acted immediately when the enemy suddenly opened fire at point-blank range, pinning down his forward elements and inflicting numerous casualties in his ranks. Boldly dashing to the front under blistering fire from automatic weapons and small arms, he seized an automatic rifle from one of the wounded men and effectively trained it against the attackers and, when his ammunition was expended, picked up and hurled grenades with deadly accuracy, at the same time directing and encouraging his men in driving the outnumbering enemy from his position. Maneuvering to set up a defense when the enemy furiously counterattacked to the front and left flank, 1st Lt. Mitchell, despite wounds sustained early in the action, reorganized his platoon under the devastating fire and spearheaded a fierce hand-to-hand struggle to repulse the onslaught. Asking for volunteers to assist in searching for and evacuating the wounded, he personally led a party of litter bearers through the hostile lines in growing darkness and, although suffering intense pain from multiple wounds, stormed ahead and waged a singlehanded battle against the enemy, successfully covering the withdrawal of his men before he was fatally struck down by a burst of small-arms fire. Stouthearted and indomitable in the face of tremendous

odds, 1st Lt. Mitchell, by his fortitude, great personal valor, and extraordinary heroism, saved the lives of several marines and inflicted heavy casualties among the aggressors. His unyielding courage throughout reflects the highest credit upon himself and the U.S. Naval Service. He gallantly gave his life for his country.
Notes: MIA

3108 ◆ MIYAMURA, HIROSHI

Rank: Corporal (highest rank: Staff Sergeant)
Service: U.S. Army
Birthday: 6 October 1925
Place of Birth: Gallup, McKinley County, New Mexico
Entered Service at: Gallup, McKinley County, New Mexico
Unit: Company H, 2d Battalion, 7th Infantry Regiment, 3d Infantry Division
Served as: Squad Leader
Battle or Place of Action: near Taejon-ni, Korea
Date of Action: 24-25 April 1951
G.O. Number, Date: 85, 4 November 1953
Date of Presentation: 27 October 1953
Place of Presentation: The White House, presented by Pres. Dwight D. Eisenhower
Citation: Cpl. Miyamura, a member of Company H, distinguished himself by conspicuous gallantry and intrepidity above and beyond the call of duty in action against the enemy. On the night of 24 April, Company H was occupying a defensive position when the enemy fanatically attacked, threatening to overrun the position. Cpl. Miyamura, a machine-gun squad leader, aware of the imminent danger to his men, unhesitatingly jumped from his shelter wielding his bayonet in close hand-to-hand combat, killing approximately 10 of the enemy. Returning to his position, he administered first aid to the wounded and directed their evacuation. As another savage assault hit the line, he manned his machine gun and delivered withering fire until his ammunition was expended. He ordered the squad to withdraw while he stayed behind to render the gun inoperative. He then bayoneted his way through infiltrated enemy soldiers to a second gun emplacement and assisted in its operation. When the intensity of the attack necessitated the withdrawal of the company Cpl. Miyamura ordered his men to fall back while he remained to cover their movement. He killed more than 50 of the enemy before his ammunition was depleted and he was severely wounded. He maintained his magnificent stand despite his painful wounds, continuing to repel the attack until his position was overrun. When last seen he was fighting ferociously against an overwhelming number of enemy soldiers. Cpl. Miyamura's indomitable heroism and consummate devotion to duty reflect the utmost glory on himself and uphold the illustrious traditions on the military service.
Notes: POW

3109 ◆ MIZE, OLA LEE

Rank: Master Sergeant (rank at time of action: Sergeant) (highest rank: Colonel)
Service: U.S. Army

Birthday: 28 August 1931
Place of Birth: Albertville, Marshall County, Alabama
Entered Service at: Gadsden, Etowah County, Alabama
Unit: 2d Platoon, Company K, 15th Infantry Regiment, 3d Infantry Division
Served as: Assistant Platoon Sergeant
Battle or Place of Action: near Surang-ni, Korea
Date of Action: 10-11 June 1953
G.O. Number, Date: 70, 24 September 1954
Date of Presentation: 7 September 1954
Place of Presentation: Denver Colorado, presented by Pres. Dwight D. Eisenhower
Citation: M/Sgt. Mize, a member of Company K, distinguished himself by conspicuous gallantry and outstanding courage above and beyond the call of duty in action against the enemy. Company K was committed to the defense of "Outpost Harry," a strategically valuable position, when the enemy launched a heavy attack. Learning that a comrade on a friendly listening post had been wounded, he moved through the intense barrage, accompanied by a medical aidman, and rescued the wounded soldier. On returning to the main position he established an effective defense system and inflicted heavy casualties against attacks from determined enemy assault forces which had penetrated into trenches within the outpost area. During his fearless actions he was blown down by artillery and grenade blasts three times, but each time he dauntlessly returned to his position, tenaciously fighting and successfully repelling hostile attacks. When enemy onslaughts ceased, he took his few men and moved from bunker to bunker, firing through apertures and throwing grenades at the foe, neutralizing their positions. When an enemy soldier stepped out behind a comrade, prepared to fire, M/Sgt. Mize killed him, saving the life of his fellow soldier. After rejoining the platoon, moving from man to man, distributing ammunition, and shouting words of encouragement he observed a friendly machine-gun position overrun. He immediately fought his way to the position, killing 10 of the enemy and dispersing the remainder. Fighting back to the command post, and finding several friendly wounded there, he took a position to protect them. Later, securing a radio, he directed friendly artillery fire upon the attacking enemy's routes of approach. At dawn he helped regroup for a counterattack which successfully drove the enemy from the outpost. M/Sgt. Mize's valorous conduct and unflinching courage reflect lasting glory upon himself and uphold the noble traditions of the military service.

3110 ◆ *MONEGAN JR., WALTER CARLETON

Rank: Private First Class
Service: U.S. Marine Corps
Birthday: 25 December 1930
Place of Birth: Melrose, Middlesex County, Massachusetts
Date of Death: 20 September 1950
Cemetery: Arlington National Cemetery (34-4513) (MH)—Arlington, Virginia
Entered Service at: Seattle, King County, Washington
Unit: Company F, 2d Battalion, 1st Marines, 1st Marine Division (Rein)

Served as: Rocket Gunner
Battle or Place of Action: near Sosa-ri, Korea
Date of Action: 17-20 September 1950
Date of Presentation: 8 February 1952
Place of Presentation: The Pentagon, presented by Under Sec. of the Navy Francis P. Whitehair to his Widow
Citation: For conspicuous gallantry and intrepidity at the risk of his life above and beyond the call of duty while serving as a rocket gunner attached to Company F, and in action against enemy aggressor forces. Dug in on a hill overlooking the main Seoul highway when six enemy tanks threatened to break through the battalion position during a predawn attack on 17 September, Pfc. Monegan promptly moved forward with his bazooka, under heavy hostile automatic-weapons fire and engaged the lead tank at a range of less than 50 yards. After scoring a direct hit and killing the sole surviving tankman with his carbine as he came through the escape hatch, he boldly fired two more rounds of ammunition at the oncoming tanks, disorganizing the attack and enabling our tank crews to continue blasting with their 90-mm guns. With his own and an adjacent company's position threatened by annihilation when an overwhelming enemy tank-infantry force bypassed the area and proceeded toward the battalion command post during the early morning of September 20, he seized his rocket launcher and, in total darkness, charged down the slope of the hill where the tanks had broken through. Quick to act when an illuminating shell lit the area, he scored a direct hit on one of the tanks as hostile rifle and automatic-weapons fire raked the area at close-range. Again exposing himself, he fired another round to destroy a second tank and, as the rear tank turned to retreat, stood upright to fire and was fatally struck down by hostile machine-gun fire when another illuminating shell silhouetted him against the sky. Pfc. Monegan's daring initiative, gallant fighting spirit, and courageous devotion to duty were contributing factors in the success of his company in repelling the enemy, and his self-sacrificing efforts throughout sustain and enhance the highest traditions of the U.S. Naval Service. He gallantly gave his life for his country.

3111 ◆ *MORELAND, WHITT LLOYD

Rank: Private First Class
Service: U.S. Marine Corps
Birthday: 7 March 1930
Place of Birth: Waco, McLennan County, Texas
Date of Death: 29 May 1951
Cemetery: Whittington Cemetery (MH)—Mount Ida, Arkansas
Entered Service at: Austin, Travis County, Texas
Unit: Company C, 1st Battalion, 5th Marines, 1st Marine Division (Rein)
Served as: Intelligence Scout
Battle or Place of Action: Kwagch'i-Dong, Korea
Date of Action: 29 May 1951
Date of Presentation: 19 July 1951
Place of Presentation: Austin Texas
Citation: For conspicuous gallantry and intrepidity at the risk of his life above and beyond the call of duty while serving

as an intelligence scout attached to Company C, in action against enemy aggressor forces. Voluntarily accompanying a rifle platoon in a daring assault against a strongly defended enemy hill position, Pfc. Moreland delivered accurate rifle fire on the hostile emplacement and thereby aided materially in seizing the objective. After the position had been secured, he unhesitatingly led a party forward to neutralize an enemy bunker which he had observed some 400 meters beyond, and moving boldly through a fire-swept area, almost reached the hostile emplacement when the enemy launched a volley of hand grenades on his group. Quick to act despite the personal danger involved, he kicked several of the grenades off the ridgeline where they exploded harmlessly and, while attempting to kick away another, slipped and fell near the deadly missile. Aware that the sputtering grenade would explode before he could regain his feet and dispose of it, he shouted a warning to his comrades, covered the missile with his body and absorbed the full blast of the explosion, but in saving his companions from possible injury or death, was mortally wounded. His heroic initiative and valiant spirit of self-sacrifice in the face of certain death reflect the highest credit upon Pfc. Moreland and the U.S. Naval Service. He gallantly gave his life for his country.

3112 ◆ *MOYER, DONALD RAYMOND

Rank: Sergeant First Class
Service: U.S. Army
Birthday: 15 April 1930
Place of Birth: Pontiac, Oakland County, Michigan
Date of Death: 20 May 1951
Cemetery: Perry Mount Park Cemetery (MH)—Pontiac, Michigan
Entered Service at: Keego Harbor, Oakland County, Michigan
Unit: Company E, 35th Infantry Regiment, 25th Infantry Division
Served as: Assistant Platoon Leader
Battle or Place of Action: near Seoul, Korea
Date of Action: 20 May 1951
G.O. Number, Date: 19, 1 February 1952
Date of Presentation: 16 January 1952
Place of Presentation: The Pentagon, presented by Sec. of Defense Robert Lovett to his Father
Citation: Sfc. Moyer, assistant platoon leader, Company E, distinguished himself by conspicuous gallantry and intrepidity at the risk of his life above and beyond the call of duty in action against an armed enemy of the United Nations. Sfc. Moyer's platoon was committed to attack and secure commanding terrain stubbornly defended by a numerically superior hostile force emplaced in well-fortified positions. Advancing up the rocky hill, the leading elements came under intense automatic-weapons, small-arms, and grenade fire, wounding the platoon leader and platoon sergeant. Sfc. Moyer, realizing the success of the mission was imperiled, rushed to the head of the faltering column, assumed command, and urged the men forward. Inspired by Sfc. Moyer's unflinching courage, the troops responded magnificently, but as they reached the final approaches to the rugged crest of the hill, enemy fire increased in volume and intensity and the fanatical foe showered the platoon with grenades. Undaunted, the valiant group forged ahead, and as they neared the top of the hill, the enemy hurled a grenade into their midst. Sfc. Moyer, fully aware of the odds against him, unhesitatingly threw himself on the grenade, absorbing the full blast of the explosion with his body. Although mortally wounded in this fearless display of valor, Sfc. Moyer's intrepid act saved several of his comrades from death or serious injury, and his inspirational leadership and consummate devotion to duty contributed significantly to the subsequent seizure of the enemy stronghold and reflect lasting glory on himself and the noble traditions of the military service.

3113 ◆ MURPHY, RAYMOND GERALD

Rank: Second Lieutenant (highest rank: Captain)
Service: U.S. Marine Corps
Birthday: 14 January 1930
Place of Birth: Pueblo, Pueblo County, Colorado
Entered Service at: Pueblo, Pueblo County, Colorado
Unit: 1st Platoon, Company A, 1st Battalion, 5th Marines, 1st Marine Division (Rein)
Served as: Platoon Commander
Battle or Place of Action: Ungok Hill, west of Panmunjan, Korea
Date of Action: 3 February 1953
Date of Presentation: 27 October 1953
Place of Presentation: The White House, presented by Pres. Dwight D. Eisenhower
Citation: For conspicuous gallantry and intrepidity at the risk of his life above and beyond the call of duty as a platoon commander of Company A, in action against enemy aggressor forces. Although painfully wounded by fragments from an enemy mortar shell while leading his evacuation platoon in a support of assault units attacking a cleverly concealed and well-entrenched hostile force occupying commanding ground, 2d Lt. Murphy steadfastly refused medical aid and continued to lead his men up a hill through a withering barrage of hostile mortar and small-arms fire, skillfully maneuvering his force from one position to the next and shouting words of encouragement. Undeterred by the increasing intense enemy fire, he immediately located casualties as they fell and made several trips up and down the fire-swept hill to direct evacuation teams to the wounded, personally carrying many of the stricken marines to safety. When reinforcements were needed by the assaulting elements, 2d Lt. Murphy employed part of his unit as support and, during the ensuing battle, personally killed two of the enemy with his pistol. With all the wounded evacuated and the assaulting units beginning to disengage, he remained behind with a carbine to cover the movement of friendly forces off the hill and, though suffering intense pain from his previous wounds, seized an automatic rifle to provide more firepower when the enemy reappeared in the trenches. After reaching the base of the hill, he organized a search party and again ascended the slope for a final check on missing marines, locating and carrying the bodies of a machine-gun crew back down the hill. Wounded a second time while conducting the entire force to the line of depar-

ture through a continuing barrage of enemy small-arms, artillery, and mortar fire, he again refused medical assistance until assured that every one of his men, including all casualties, had preceded him to the main lines. His resolute and inspiring leadership, exceptional fortitude, and great personal valor reflect the highest credit upon 2d Lt. Murphy and enhance the finest traditions of the U.S. Naval Service.

3114 ◆ MYERS, REGINALD RODNEY

Rank: Major (highest rank: Colonel)
Service: U.S. Marine Corps
Birthday: 26 November 1919
Place of Birth: Boise, Ada County, Idaho
Entered Service at: Boise, Ada County, Idaho
Unit: 3d Battalion, 1st Marines, 1st Marine Division (Rein)
Served as: Battalion Executive Officer
Battle or Place of Action: near Hagaru-ri, Korea
Date of Action: 29 November 1950
Date of Presentation: 29 October 1951
Place of Presentation: The White House, presented by Pres. Harry S. Truman
Citation: For conspicuous gallantry and intrepidity at the risk of his life above and beyond the call of duty as executive officer of the 3d Battalion, in action against enemy aggressor forces. Assuming command of a composite unit of Army and Marine service and headquarters elements totaling approximately 250 men, during a critical stage in the vital defense of the strategically important military base at Hagaru-ri, Maj. Myers immediately initiated a determined and aggressive counterattack against a well-entrenched and cleverly concealed enemy force numbering an estimated 4,000. Severely handicapped by a lack of trained personnel and experienced leaders in his valiant efforts to regain maximum ground prior to daylight, he persisted in constantly exposing himself to intense, accurate, and sustained hostile fire in order to direct and supervise the employment of his men and to encourage and spur them on in pressing the attack. Inexorably moving forward up the steep, snow-covered slope with his depleted group in the face of apparently insurmountable odds, he concurrently directed artillery and mortar fire with superb skill and although losing 170 of his men during 14 hours of raging combat in subzero temperature, continued to reorganize his unit and spearhead the attack which resulted in 600 enemy killed and 500 wounded. By his exceptional and valorous leadership throughout, Maj. Myers contributed directly to the success of his unit in restoring the perimeter. His resolute spirit of self-sacrifice and unfaltering devotion to duty enhance and sustain the highest traditions of the U.S. Naval Service.

3115 ◆ *OBREGON, EUGENE ARNOLD

Rank: Private First Class
Service: U.S. Marine Corps
Birthday: 12 November 1930
Place of Birth: Los Angeles, Los Angeles County, California
Date of Death: 26 September 1950
Place of Death: Seoul, Korea
Cemetery: Calvary Cemetery—East Los Angeles, California

Entered Service at: Los Angeles, Los Angeles County, California
Unit: Company G, 3d Battalion, 5th Marines, 1st Marine Division (Rein)
Served as: Ammunition Carrier
Battle or Place of Action: Seoul, Korea
Date of Action: 26 September 1950
Date of Presentation: 30 August 1951
Place of Presentation: The Pentagon, presented by Sec. of the Navy Dan A. Kimball to his parents
Citation: For conspicuous gallantry and intrepidity at the risk of his life above and beyond the call of duty while serving with Company G, in action against enemy aggressor forces. While serving as an ammunition carrier of a machine-gun squad in a marine rifle company which was temporarily pinned down by hostile fire, Pfc. Obregon observed a fellow marine fall wounded in the line of fire. Armed only with a pistol, he unhesitating dashed from his covered position to the side of the casualty. Firing his pistol with one hand as he ran, he grasped his comrade by the arm with his other hand and, despite the great peril to himself dragged him to the side of the road. Still under enemy fire, he was bandaging the man's wounds when hostile troops of approximately platoon strength began advancing toward his position. Quickly seizing the wounded marine's carbine, he placed his own body as a shield in front of him and lay there firing accurately and effectively into the hostile group until he himself was fatally wounded by enemy machine-gun fire. By his courageous fighting spirit, fortitude, and loyal devotion to duty, Pfc. Obregon enabled his fellow marines to rescue the wounded man and aided essentially in repelling the attack, thereby sustaining and enhancing the highest traditions of the U.S. Naval Service. He gallantly gave his life for his country.

3116 ◆ O'BRIEN JR., GEORGE HERMAN

Rank: Second Lieutenant (highest rank: Major)
Service: U.S. Marine Corps Reserve
Birthday: 10 September 1926
Place of Birth: Fort Worth, Tarrant County, Texas
Entered Service at: Big Spring, Howard County, Texas
Unit: 1st Platoon, Company H, 3d Battalion, 7th Marines, 1st Marine Division (Rein)
Served as: Rifle Platoon Commander
Battle or Place of Action: The Hook, Korea
Date of Action: 27 October 1952
Date of Presentation: 27 October 1953
Place of Presentation: The White House, presented by Pres. Dwight D. Eisenhower
Citation: For conspicuous gallantry and intrepidity at the risk of his life above and beyond the call of duty as a rifle platoon commander of Company H, in action against enemy aggressor forces. With his platoon subjected to an intense mortar and artillery bombardment while preparing to assault a vitally important hill position on the main line of resistance which had been overrun by a numerically superior enemy force on the preceding night, 2d Lt. O'Brien leaped from his trench when the attack signal was given and, shouting for his men to follow, raced across an exposed saddle and up the

enemy-held hill through a virtual hail of deadly small-arms, artillery, and mortar fire. Although shot through the arm and thrown to the ground by hostile automatic-weapons fire as he neared the well-entrenched enemy position, he bravely regained his feet, waved his men onward, and continued to spearhead the assault, pausing only long enough to go to the aid of a wounded marine. Encountering the enemy at close-range, he proceeded to hurl hand grenades into the bunkers and, utilizing his carbine to best advantage in savage hand-to-hand combat, succeeded in killing at least three of the enemy. Struck down by the concussion of grenades on three occasions during the subsequent action, he steadfastly refused to be evacuated for medical treatment and continued to lead his platoon in the assault for a period of nearly four hours, repeatedly encouraging his men and maintaining superb direction of the unit. With the attack halted, he set up a defense with his remaining forces to prepare for a counterattack, personally checking each position, attending to the wounded and expediting their evacuation. When a relief of the position was effected by another unit, he remained to cover the withdrawal and to assure that no wounded were left behind. By his exceptionally daring and forceful leadership in the face of overwhelming odds, 2d Lt. O'Brien served as a constant source of inspiration to all who observed him and was greatly instrumental in the recapture of a strategic position on the main line of resistance. His indomitable determination and valiant fighting spirit reflect the highest credit upon himself and enhance the finest traditions of the U.S. Naval Service.

3117 ◆ *OUELLETTE, JOSEPH R.

Rank: Private First Class
Service: U.S. Army
Birthday: 1930
Place of Birth: Lowell, Middlesex County, Massachusetts
Date of Death: 3 September 1950
Cemetery: St. Joseph's Cemetery (MH)—East Chelmsford, Massachusetts
Entered Service at: Lowell, Middlesex County, Massachusetts
Unit: Company H, 9th Infantry Regiment, 2d Infantry Division
Battle or Place of Action: near Yongsan, Korea
Date of Action: 31 August-3 September 1950
G.O. Number, Date: 25, 25 April 1951
Date of Presentation: 3 April 1951
Place of Presentation: The Pentagon, presented by Gen. Omar N. Bradley to his Mother
Citation: Pfc. Ouellette distinguished himself by conspicuous gallantry and intrepidity in action against the enemy in the Makioug-Chang River salient. When an enemy assault cut off and surrounded his unit, he voluntarily made a reconnaissance of a nearby hill under intense enemy fire to locate friendly troop positions and obtain information of the enemy's strength and location. Finding that friendly troops were not on the hill, he worked his way back to his unit under heavy fire. Later, when an airdrop of water was made outside the perimeter, he again braved enemy fire in an

attempt to retrieve water for his unit. Finding the dropped cans broken and devoid of water, he returned to his unit. His heroic attempt greatly increased his comrades' morale. When ammunition and grenades ran low, Pfc. Ouellette again slipped out of the perimeter to collect these from the enemy dead. After collecting grenades he was attacked by an enemy soldier. He killed this enemy in hand-to-hand combat, gathered up the ammunition, and returned to his unit. When the enemy attacked on 3 September, they assaulted his position with grenades. On six occasions Pfc. Ouellette leaped from his foxhole to escape exploding grenades. In doing so, he had to face enemy small-arms fire. He continued his resistance, despite a severe wound, until he lost his life. The extraordinary heroism and intrepidity displayed by Pfc. Ouellette reflect the highest credit on himself and are in keeping with the esteemed traditions of the military service.

3118 ◆ *PAGE, JOHN UPSHUR DENNIS

Rank: Lieutenant Colonel
Service: U.S. Army
Birthday: 8 February 1904
Place of Birth: Malahi Island, Luzon, Philippine Islands
Date of Death: 10 December 1950
Cemetery: Arlington National Cemetery (4-2743-A-B)—Arlington, Virginia
Entered Service at: St. Paul, Ramsey County, Minnesota
Unit: Attached to the 52d Transportation Truck Battalion, X Corps Artillery
Served as: Artillery Officer
Battle or Place of Action: near Chosin Reservoir, Korea
Date of Action: 29 November-10 December 1950
G.O. Number, Date: 21, 25 April 1957
Date of Issue: 19 December 1956
Citation: Lt. Col. Page, a member of X Corps Artillery, distinguished himself by conspicuous gallantry and intrepidity in action above and beyond the call of duty in a series of exploits. On 29 November, Lt. Col. Page left X Corps Headquarters at Hamhung with the mission of establishing traffic control on the main supply route to 1st Marine Division positions and those of some Army elements on the Chosin Reservoir plateau. Having completed his mission Lt. Col. Page was free to return to the safety of Hamhung but chose to remain on the plateau to aid an isolated signal station, thus being cut off with elements of the marine division. After rescuing his jeep driver by breaking up an ambush near a destroyed bridge, Lt. Col. Page reached the lines of a surrounded marine garrison at Koto-ri. He then voluntarily developed and trained a reserve force of assorted army troops trapped with the marines. By exemplary leadership and tireless devotion he made an effective tactical unit available. In order that casualties might be evacuated, an airstrip was improvised on frozen ground partly outside of the Koto-ri defense perimeter which was continually under enemy attack. During two such attacks, Lt. Col. Page exposed himself on the airstrip to direct fire on the enemy and twice mounted the rear deck of a tank, manning the machine gun on the turret to drive the enemy back into a no man's land. On 3 December while being flown low over enemy lines in a light

observation plane, Lt. Col. Page dropped hand grenades on Chinese positions and sprayed foxholes with automatic fire from his carbine. After 10 days of constant fighting the marine and army units in the vicinity of the Chosin Reservoir had succeeded in gathering at the edge of the plateau and Lt. Col. Page was flown to Hamhung to arrange for artillery support of the beleaguered troops attempting to break out. Again Lt. Col. Page refused an opportunity to remain in safety and returned to give every assistance to his comrades. As the column slowly moved south Lt. Col. Page joined the rear guard. When it neared the entrance to a narrow pass it came under frequent attacks on both flanks. Mounting an abandoned tank Lt. Col. Page manned the machine gun, braved heavy return fire, and covered the passing vehicles until the danger diminished. Later when another attack threatened his section of the convoy, then in the middle of the pass, Lt. Col. Page took a machine gun to the hillside and delivered effective counterfire, remaining exposed while men and vehicles passed through the ambuscade. On the night of 10 December the convoy reached the bottom of the pass but was halted by a strong enemy force at the front and on both flanks. Deadly small-arms fire poured into the column. Realizing the danger to the column as it lay motionless, Lt. Col. Page fought his way to the head of the column and plunged forward into the heart of the hostile position. His intrepid action so surprised the enemy that their ranks became disordered and suffered heavy casualties. Heedless of his safety, as he had been throughout the preceding 10 days, Lt. Col. Page remained forward, fiercely engaging the enemy singlehandedly until mortally wounded. By his valiant and aggressive spirit Lt. Col. Page enabled friendly forces to stand off the enemy. His outstanding courage, unswerving devotion to duty, and supreme self-sacrifice reflect great credit upon Lt. Col. Page and are in the highest tradition of the military service.

3119 ◆ *PENDLETON, CHARLES F.

Rank: Corporal
Service: U.S. Army
Birthday: 26 September 1931
Place of Birth: Camden, Benton County, Tennessee
Date of Death: 17 July 1953
Cemetery: Laurel Land Memorial Cemetery—Fort Worth, Texas
Entered Service at: Fort Worth, Texas
Unit: Company D, 15th Infantry Regiment, 3d Infantry Division
Served as: Machine Gunner
Battle or Place of Action: near Choo Gung-Dong, Korea
Date of Action: 16-17 July 1953
Citation: Cpl. Pendleton, a machine gunner with Company D, distinguished himself by conspicuous gallantry and indomitable courage above and beyond the call of duty in action against the enemy. After consolidating and establishing a defensive perimeter on a key terrain feature, friendly elements were attacked by a large hostile force. Cpl. Pendleton delivered deadly accurate fire into the approaching troops, killing approximately 15 and disorganizing the remainder with grenades. Unable to protect the flanks because of the narrow confines of the trench, he removed the machine gun from the tripod and, exposed to enemy observation, positioned it on his knee to improve his firing vantage. Observing a hostile infantryman jumping into the position, intent on throwing a grenade at his comrades, he whirled about and killed the attacker, then inflicted such heavy casualties on the enemy force that they retreated to regroup. After reorganizing, a second wave of hostile soldiers moved forward in an attempt to overrun the position and, later, when a hostile grenade landed nearby, Cpl. Pendleton quickly retrieved and hurled it back at the foe. Although he was burned by the hot shells ejecting from his weapon, and he was wounded by a grenade, he refused evacuation and continued to fire on the assaulting force. As enemy action increased in tempo, his machine gun was destroyed by a grenade but, undaunted, he grabbed a carbine and continued his heroic defense until mortally wounded by a mortar burst. Cpl. Pendleton's unflinching courage, gallant self-sacrifice, and consummate devotion to duty reflect lasting glory upon himself and uphold the finest traditions of the military service.

3120 ◆ *PHILLIPS, LEE HUGH

Rank: Corporal
Service: U.S. Marine Corps
Birthday: 3 February 1930
Place of Birth: Stockbridge, Henry County, Georgia
Date of Death: 27 November 1950
Cemetery: National Memorial of the Pacific (Wall of the Missing)—Honolulu, Hawaii; Marietta National Cemetery (B8) ('In Memory' marker)—Marietta, Georgia
Entered Service at: Ben Hill, Fulton County, Georgia
Unit: Company E, 2d Battalion, 7th Marines, 1st Marine Division (Rein)
Served as: Squad Leader
Battle or Place of Action: Korea
Date of Action: 4 November 1950
Citation: For conspicuous gallantry and intrepidity at the risk of his life above and beyond the call of duty while serving as a squad leader of Company E, in action against enemy aggressor forces. Assuming the point position in the attack against a strongly defended and well-entrenched numerically superior enemy force occupying a vital hill position which had been unsuccessfully assaulted on five separate occasions by units of the Marine Corps and other friendly forces, Cpl. Phillips fearlessly led his men in a bayonet charge up the precipitous slope under a deadly hail of hostile mortar, small-arms, and machine-gun fire. Quickly rallying his squad when it was pinned down by heavy and accurate mortar barrage, he continued to lead his men through the bombarded area and, although only five members were left in the casualty-ridden unit, gained the military crest of the hill where he was immediately subjected to an enemy counterattack. Although greatly outnumbered by an estimated enemy squad, Cpl. Phillips boldly engaged the hostile force with hand grenades and rifle fire and, exhorting his gallant group of marines to follow him, stormed forward to completely overwhelm the enemy. With only three men now left in his squad, he proceeded to spearhead an assault on the last remaining strongpoint which was

3123 ◆ *POMEROY, RALPH EUGENE

defended by four of the enemy on a rocky and almost inaccessible portion of the hill position. Using one hand to climb up the extremely hazardous precipice, he hurled grenades with the other and, with two remaining comrades, succeeded in annihilating the pocket of resistance and in consolidating the position. Immediately subjected to a sharp counterattack by an estimated enemy squad, he skillfully directed the fire of his men and employed his own weapon with deadly effectiveness to repulse the numerically superior hostile force. By his valiant leadership, indomitable fighting spirit, and resolute determination in the face of heavy odds, Cpl. Phillips served to inspire all who observed him and was directly responsible for the destruction of the enemy stronghold. His great personal valor refects the highest credit upon himself and enhances and sustains the finest traditions of the U.S. Naval Service.
Notes: MIA

3121 ◆ *PILILAAU, HERBERT K.

Rank: Private First Class
Service: U.S. Army
Birthday: 10 October 1928
Place of Birth: Waianae, Oahu, Territory of Hawaii
Date of Death: 17 September 1951
Cemetery: National Memorial Cemetery of the Pacific (P-127)—Honolulu, Hawaii
Entered Service at: Oahu, Territory of Hawaii
Unit: Company C, 23d Infantry Regiment, 2d Infantry Division
Battle or Place of Action: near Pia-ri, Korea
Date of Action: 17 September 1951
G.O. Number, Date: 58, 18 June 1952
Date of Presentation: 26 March 1952
Place of Presentation: The Pentagon, presented by Sec. of the Army Frank C. Pace to his Father
Citation: Pfc. Pililaau, a member of Company C, distinguished himself by conspicuous gallantry and outstanding courage above and beyond the call of duty in action against the enemy. The enemy sent wave after wave of fanatical troops against his platoon which held a key terrain feature on "Heartbreak Ridge." Valiantly defending its position, the unit repulsed each attack until ammunition became practically exhausted and it was ordered to withdraw to a new position. Voluntarily remaining behind to cover the withdrawal, Pfc. Pililaau fired his automatic weapon into the ranks of the assailants, threw all his grenades, and, with ammunition exhausted, closed with the foe in hand-to-hand combat, courageously fighting with his trench knife and bare fists until finally overcome and mortally wounded. When the position was subsequently retaken, more than 40 enemy dead were counted in the area he had so valiantly defended. His heroic devotion to duty, indomitable fighting spirit, and gallant self-sacrifice reflect the highest credit upon himself, the infantry, and the U.S. Army.

3122 ◆ PITTMAN, JOHN ALBERT

Rank: Sergeant
Service: U.S. Army
Birthday: 15 October 1928
Place of Birth: Carrollton, Carroll County, Mississippi
Date of Death: 8 April 1995
Place of Death: Greenwood, Mississippi
Cemetery: New Hope Church Cemetery—Greenwood Mississippi
Entered Service at: Carrollton, Carroll County, Mississippi
Unit: 1st Platoon, Company C, 1st Battalion, 23d Infantry Regiment, 2d Infantry Division
Served as: Squad Leader
Battle or Place of Action: near Kujang-dong, Korea
Date of Action: 26 November 1950
G.O. Number, Date: 39, 4 June 1951
Date of Presentation: 19 May 1951
Place of Presentation: Blair House, presented by Pres. Harry S. Truman
Citation: Sgt. Pittman distinguished himself by conspicuous gallantry and intrepidity above and beyond the call of duty in action against the enemy. He volunteered to lead his squad in a counterattack to regain commanding terrain lost in an earlier engagement. Moving aggressively forward in the face of intense artillery, mortar, and small-arms fire, he was wounded by mortar fragments. Disregarding his wounds, he continued to lead and direct his men in a bold advance against the hostile strongpoint. During this daring action, an enemy grenade was thrown in the midst of his squad, endangering the lives of his comrades. Without hesitation, Sgt. Pittman threw himself on the grenade and absorbed its burst with his body. When a medical aidman reached him, his first request was to be informed as to how many of his men were hurt. This intrepid and selfless act saved several of his men from death or serious injury and was an inspiration to the entire command. Sgt. Pittman's extraordinary heroism reflects the highest credit upon himself and is in keeping with the esteemed traditions of the military service.

3123 ◆ *POMEROY, RALPH EUGENE

Rank: Private First Class
Service: U.S. Army
Birthday: 26 March 1930
Place of Birth: Quinwood, Greenbrier County, West Virginia
Date of Death: 15 October 1952
Cemetery: At The End Of The Trail Cemetery (MH)—Clintonville, West Virginia
Entered Service at: Quinwood, Greenbrier County, West Virginia
Unit: Company E, 31st Infantry Regiment, 7th Infantry Division
Served as: Machine Gunner
Battle or Place of Action: near Kumhwa, Korea
Date of Action: 15 October 1952
G.O. Number, Date: 97, 30 December 1953
Citation: Pfc. Pomeroy, a machine gunner with Company E, distinguished himself by conspicuous gallantry and indomitable courage above and beyond the call of duty in action against the enemy. While his comrades were consolidating on a key terrain feature, he manned a machine gun at

the end of a communication trench on the forward slope to protect the platoon flank and prevent a surprise attack. When the enemy attacked through a ravine leading directly to his firing posiiton, he immediately opened fire on the advancing troops, inflicting a heavy toll in casualties and blunting the assault. At this juncture the enemy directed intense concentrations of artillery and mortar fire on his position in an attempt to neutralize his gun. Despite withering fire and bursting shells, he maintained his heroic stand and poured crippling fire into the ranks of the hostile force until a mortar burst severely wounded him and rendered the gun mount inoperable. Quickly removing the hot, heavy weapon, he cradled it in his arms and, moving forward with grim determination, raked the attacking forces with a hail of fire. Although wounded a second time he pursued his relentless course until his ammunition was expended to within 10 feet of the foe and then, using the machine gun as a club, he courageously closed with the enemy in hand-to-hand combat until mortally wounded. Pfc. Pomeroy's consummate valor, inspirational actions, and supreme sacrifice enabled the platoon to contain the attack and maintain the integrity of the perimeter, reflecting lasting glory upon himself and upholding the noble traditions of the military service.

3124 ◆ *PORTER, DONN F.

Rank: Sergeant
Service: U.S. Army
Birthday: 1 March 1931
Place of Birth: Sewickley, Allegheny County, Pennsylvania
Date of Death: 7 September 1952
Place of Death: Mundung-ni, Korea
Cemetery: Arlington National Cemetery (33-4357) (MH)—Arlington, Virginia
Entered Service at: Baltimore, Baltimore County, Maryland
Unit: Company G, 14th Infantry Regiment, 25th Infantry Division
Battle or Place of Action: near Mundung-ni, Korea
Date of Action: 7 September 1952
G.O. Number, Date: 64, 18 August 1953
Date of Presentation: 5 August 1953
Place of Presentation: The Pentagon (Auditorium), presented by Under Sec. of the Army Earl D. Johnson to his Father
Citation: Sgt. Porter, a member of Company G, distinguished himself by conspicuous gallantry and outstanding courage above and beyond the call of duty in action against the enemy. Advancing under cover of intense mortar and artillery fire, two hostile platoons attacked a combat outpost commanded by Sgt. Porter, destroyed communications, and killed two of his three-man crew. Gallantly maintaining his position, he poured deadly accurate fire into the ranks of the enemy, killing 15 and dispersing the remainder. After falling back under a hail of fire, the determined foe reorganized and stormed forward in an attempt to overrun the outpost. Without hesitation, Sgt. Porter jumped from his position with bayonet fixed and, meeting the onslaught and in close combat, killed six hostile soldiers and routed the attack. While returning to the outpost, he was killed by an artillery burst, but his courageous actions forced

the enemy to break off the engagement and thwarted a surprise attack on the main line of resistance. Sgt. Porter's incredible display of valor, gallant self-sacrifice, and consummate devotion to duty reflect the highest credit upon himself and uphold the noble traditions of the military service.

3125 ◆ *POYNTER, JAMES IRSLEY

Rank: Sergeant
Service: U.S. Marine Corps Reserve
Birthday: 1 December 1916
Place of Birth: Bloomington, McLean County, Illinois
Date of Death: 4 November 1950
Place of Death: Sudong, Korea
Cemetery: Fort Rosecrans National Cemetery (0-729) (MH)—San Diego, California
Entered Service at: Downey, Los Angeles County, California
Unit: Company A, 1st Battalion, 7th Marines, 1st Marine Division (Rein)
Served as: Squad Leader
Battle or Place of Action: near Sudong, Korea
Date of Action: 4 November 1950
Date of Presentation: 4 September 1952
Place of Presentation: The Pentagon, presented by Sec. of the Navy Dan A. Kimball to his Widow
Citation: For conspicuous gallantry and intrepidity at the risk of his life above and beyond the call of duty while serving as a squad leader in a rifle platoon of Company A, in action against enemy aggressor forces during the defense of Hill 532, south of Sudong, Korea. When a vastly outnumbering, well-concealed hostile force launched a sudden, vicious counterattack against his platoon's hasty defensive position, Sgt. Poynter displayed superb skill and courage in leading his squad and directing its fire against the onrushing enemy. With his ranks critically depleted by casualties and he himself critically wounded as the onslaught gained momentum and the hostile force surrounded his position, he seized his bayonet and engaged in bitter hand-to-hand combat as the breakthrough continued. Observing three machine guns closing in at a distance of 25 yards, he dashed from his position and, grasping hand grenades from fallen marines as he ran, charged the emplacements in rapid succession, killing the crews of two and putting the other out of action before he fell, mortally wounded. By his self-sacrificing and valiant conduct, Sgt. Poynter inspired the remaining members of his squad to heroic endeavor in bearing down upon and repelling the disorganized enemy, thereby enabling the platoon to move out of the trap to a more favorable tactical position. His indomitable fighting spirit, fortitude, and great personal valor maintained in the face of overwhelming odds sustain and enhance the finest traditions of the U.S. Naval Service. He gallantly gave his life for his country.

3126 ◆ *RAMER, GEORGE HENRY

Rank: Second Lieutenant
Service: U.S. Marine Corps Reserve
Birthday: 27 March 1927
Place of Birth: Meyersdale, Somerset County, Pennsylvania

Date of Death: 12 September 1951
Place of Death: Korea
Cemetery: Lewisburg Cemetery (MH)—Lewisburg, Pennsylvania
Entered Service at: Lewisburg, Union County, Pennsylvania
Unit: 3d Platoon, Company I, 3d Battalion, 7th Marines, 1st Marine Division (Rein)
Served as: Platoon Leader
Battle or Place of Action: Korea
Date of Action: 12 September 1951
Date of Presentation: 7 January 1953
Place of Presentation: The Pentagon, presented by Sec. of the Navy Dan A. Kimball to his Widow
Citation: For conspicuous gallantry and intrepidity at the risk of his life above and beyond the call of duty as leader of the 3d Platoon in Company I, in action against enemy aggressor forces. Ordered to attack and seize hostile positions atop a hill, vigorously defended by well-entrenched enemy forces delivering massed small-arms mortar, and machine-gun fire, 2d Lt. Ramer fearlessly led his men up the steep slopes and, although he and the majority of his unit were wounded during the ascent, boldly continued to spearhead the assault. With the terrain becoming more precipitous near the summit and the climb more perilous as the hostile forces added grenades to the devastating hail of fire, he staunchly carried the attack to the top, personally annihilated one enemy bunker with grenade and carbine fire and captured the objective with his remaining eight men. Unable to hold the position against an immediate, overwhelming hostile counterattack, he ordered his group to withdraw and singlehandedly fought the enemy to furnish cover for his men and for the evacuation of three fatally wounded marines. Severely wounded a second time, 2d Lt. Ramer refused aid when his men returned to help him and, after ordering them to seek shelter, courageously manned his post until the hostile troops overran his position and he fell mortally wounded. His indomitable fighting spirit, inspiring leadership and unselfish concern for others in the face of death, reflect the highest credit upon 2d Lt. Ramer and the U.S. Naval Service. He gallantly gave his life for his country.

3127 ◆ *RED CLOUD JR., MITCHELL

Rank: Corporal
Service: U.S. Army
Birthday: 2 July 1924
Place of Birth: Hatfield, Wisconsin
Date of Death: 5 November 1950
Place of Death: Chonghyon, Korea
Cemetery: Decorah Cemetery—Komensky, Wisconsin
Entered Service at: Merrillan, Jackson County, Wisconsin
Unit: Company E, 19th Infantry Regiment, 24th Infantry Division
Served as: Automatic Rifleman
Battle or Place of Action: near Chonghyon, Korea
Date of Action: 5 November 1950
G.O. Number, Date: 26, 25 April 1951
Date of Presentation: 3 April 1951
Place of Presentation: The Pentagon, presented by Gen. Omar N. Bradley to his Mother

Citation: Cpl. Red Cloud, Company E, distinguished himself by conspicuous gallantry and intrepidity above and beyond the call of duty in action against the enemy. From his position on the point of a ridge immediately in front of the company command post, he was the first to detect the approach of the Chinese Communist forces and give the alarm as the enemy charged from a brush-covered area less that 100 feet from him. Springing up he delivered devastating point-blank automatic rifle into the advancing enemy. His accurate and intense fire checked this assault and gained time for the company to consolidate its defense. With utter fearlessness he maintained his firing position until severely wounded by enemy fire. Refusing assistance he pulled himself to his feet and wrapping his arm around a tree continued his deadly fire again, until he was fatally wounded. This heroic act stopped the enemy from overrunning his company's position and gained time for reorganization and evacuation of the wounded. Cpl. Red Cloud's dauntless courage and gallant self-sacrifice reflects the highest credit upon himself and upholds the esteemed traditions of the U.S. Army.

3128 ◆ *REEM, ROBERT DALE

Rank: Second Lieutenant
Service: U.S. Marine Corps
Birthday: 20 October 1925
Place of Birth: Lancaster, Lancaster County, Pennsylvania
Date of Death: 6 November 1950
Place of Death: Chinhung-ni, Korea
Cemetery: Arlington National Cemetery (6-9376-B) (MH)—Arlington, Virginia
Entered Service at: Elizabethtown, Lancaster County, Pennsylvania
Unit: Company H, 3d Battalion, 7th Marines, 1st Marine Division (Rein)
Served as: Platoon Commander
Battle or Place of Action: vicinity of Chinhung-ni, Korea
Date of Action: 6 November 1950
Date of Presentation: 8 February 1952
Place of Presentation: The Pentagon, presented by Under Sec. of the Navy Francis P. Whitehair to his Widow
Citation: For conspicuous gallantry and intrepidity at the risk of his life above and beyond the call of duty as a platoon commander in Company H, in action against enemy aggressor forces. Grimly determined to dislodge a group of heavy enemy infantry units occupying well-concealed and strongly fortified positions on commanding ground overlooking unprotected terrain, 2d Lt. Reem moved slowly forward up the side of the ridge with his platoon in the face of a veritable hail of shattering hostile machine-gun, grenade, and rifle fire. Three times repulsed by a resolute enemy force in achieving his objective, and pinned down by the continuing fury of hostile fire, he rallied and regrouped the heroic men in his depleted and disorganized platoon in preparation for a fourth attack. Issuing last-minute orders to his non-commissioned officers when an enemy grenade landed in a depression of the rocky ground in which the group was standing, 2d Lt. Reem unhesitatingly chose to sacrifice himself and, springing upon the deadly missile, absorbed the full impact of the explosion

in his body, thus protecting others from serious injury and possible death. Stouthearted and indomitable, he readily yielded his own chance of survival that his subordinate leaders might live to carry on the fight against a fanatic enemy. His superb courage, cool decisiveness, and valiant spirit of self-sacrifice in the face of certain death reflect the highest credit upon 2d Lt. Reem and the U.S. Naval Service. He gallantly gave his life for his country.

3129 ◆ RODRIGUEZ, JOSEPH CHARLES

Rank: Sergeant (rank at time of action: Private First Class) (highest rank: Colonel)
Service: U.S. Army
Birthday: 14 November 1928
Place of Birth: San Bernardino, San Bernardino County, California
Entered Service at: San Bernardino, San Bernardino County, California
Unit: 2d Squad, 2d Platoon, Company F, 2d Battalion, 17th Infantry Regiment, 7th Infantry Division
Served as: Assistant Squad Leader
Battle or Place of Action: near Munye-ri, Korea
Date of Action: 21 May 1951
G.O. Number, Date: 22, 5 February 1952
Date of Presentation: 29 January 1952
Place of Presentation: The White House, presented by Pres. Harry S. Truman
Citation: Sgt. Rodriguez distinguished himself by conspicuous gallantry and intrepidity at the risk of his life above and beyond the call of duty in action against an armed enemy of the Unites Nations. Sgt. Rodriguez, an assistant squad leader of the 2d Platoon, was participating in an attack against a fanatical hostile force occupying well-fortified positions on rugged command terrain, when his squad's advance was halted within approximately 60 yards by a withering barrage of automatic-weapons and small-arms fire from five emplacements directly to the front and right and left flanks, together with grenades which the enemy rolled down the hill toward the advancing troops. Fully aware of the odds against him, Sgt. Rodriguez leaped to his feet, dashed 60 yards up the fire-swept slope, and, after lobbing grenades into the first foxhole with deadly accuracy, ran around the left flank, silenced an automatic weapon with two grenades and continued his whirlwind assault to the top of the peak, wiping out two more foxholes and then, reaching the right flank, he tossed grenades into the remaining emplacement, destroying the gun and annihilating its crew. Sgt. Rodriguez' intrepid actions exacted a toll of 15 enemy dead and, as a result of his incredible display of valor, the defense of the opposition was broken, and the enemy routed, and the strategic strongpoint secured. His unflinching courage under fire and inspirational devotion to duty reflect highest credit on himself and uphold the honored traditions of the military service.

3130 ◆ ROSSER, RONALD EUGENE

Rank: Corporal (highest rank: Sergeant First Class Ret.)
Service: U.S. Army
Birthday: 24 October 1929
Place of Birth: Columbus, Franklin County, Ohio
Entered Service at: Crooksville, Perry County, Ohio
Unit: Headquarters Company (Heavy Mortar), 38th Infantry Regiment, 2d Infantry Division
Served as: Forward Observer
Battle or Place of Action: near Ponggilli, Korea
Date of Action: 12 January 1952
G.O. Number, Date: 67, 7 July 1952
Date of Presentation: 27 June 1952
Place of Presentation: The White House (Rose Garden), presented by Pres. Harry S. Truman
Citation: Cpl. Rosser distinguished himself by conspicuous gallantry above and beyond the call of duty. While assaulting heavily fortified enemy hill positions, Company L, 38th Infantry Regiment, was stopped by fierce automatic-weapons, small-arms, artillery, and mortar fire. Cpl. Rosser, a forward observer was with the lead platoon of Company L, when it came under fire from two directions. Cpl. Rosser turned his radio over to his assistant and, disregarding the enemy fire, charged the enemy positions armed with only carbine and a grenade. At the first bunker, he silenced its occupants with a burst from his weapon. Gaining the top of the hill, he killed two enemy soldiers, and then went down the trench, killing five more as he advanced. He then hurled his grenade into a bunker and shot two other soldiers as they emerged. Having exhausted his ammunition, he returned through the enemy fire to obtain more ammunition and grenades and charged the enemy bunkers. Although those who attempted to join him became casualties, Cpl. Rosser once again exhausted his ammunition, obtained a new supply, and returning to the hilltop a third time hurled grenades into the enemy positions. During this heroic action Cpl. Rosser singlehandedly killed at least 13 of the enemy. After exhausting his ammunition he accompanied the withdrawing platoon, and though himself wounded, made several trips across open terrain still under enemy fire to help remove other men injured more seriously than himself. This outstanding soldier's courageous and selfless devotion to duty is worthy of emulation by all men. He has contributed magnificently to the high traditions of the military service.

3131 ◆ *SCHOONOVER, DAN D.

Rank: Corporal
Service: U.S. Army
Birthday: 8 October 1933
Place of Birth: Boise, Ada County, Idaho
Date of Death: 10 July 1953
Place of Death: Sokkogae, Korea
Cemetery: National Memorial of the Pacific (Wall of the Missing)—Honolulu, Hawaii
Entered Service at: Boise, Ada County, Idaho
Unit: Company A, 13th Combat Engineer Battalion Attached to Company G, 17th Infantry, 7th Infantry Division
Served as: Squad Leader
Battle or Place of Action: Pork Chop Hill, near Sokkogae, Korea
Date of Action: 8-10 July 1953
G.O. Number, Date: 5, 14 January 1955
Date of Presentation: July 1954

Place of Presentation: Presented to his Mother
Citation: Cpl. Schoonover distinguished himself by conspicuous gallantry and outstanding courage above and beyond the call of duty in action against the enemy. He was in charge of an engineer demolition squad attached to an infantry company which was committed to dislodge the enemy from a vital hill. Realizing that the heavy fighting and intense enemy fire made it impossible to carry out his mission, he voluntarily employed his unit as a rifle squad and, forging up the steep barren slope, participated in the assault on hostile positions. When an artillery round exploded on the roof of an enemy bunker, he courageously ran forward and leaped into the position, killing one hostile infantryman and taking another prisoner. Later in the action, when friendly forces were pinned down by vicious fire from another enemy bunker, he dashed through the hail of fire, hurled grenades in the nearest aperture, then ran to the doorway and emptied his pistol, killing the remainder of the enemy. His brave action neutralized the position and enabled friendly troops to continue their advance to the crest of the hill. When the enemy counterattacked he constantly exposed himself to the heavy bombardment to direct the fire of his men and to call in an effective artillery barrage on hostile forces. Although the company was relieved early the following morning, he voluntarily remained in the area, manned a machine gun for several hours, and subsequently joined another assault on enemy emplacements. When last seen he was operating an automatic rifle with devastating effect until mortally wounded by artillery fire. Cpl. Schoonover's heroic leadership during two days of heavy fighting, superb personal bravery, and willing self-sacrifice inspired his comrades and saved many lives, reflecting lasting glory upon himself and upholding the honored traditions of the military service.
Notes: MIA

3132 ◆ SCHOWALTER JR., EDWARD RIGHTOR

Rank: First Lieutenant (highest rank: Colonel)
Service: U.S. Army
Birthday: 24 December 1927
Place of Birth: New Orleans, Orleans County, Louisiana
Entered Service at: Metairie, Jefferson County, Louisiana
Unit: Company A, 1st Battalion, 31st Infantry Regiment, 7th Infantry Division
Served as: Company Commander
Battle or Place of Action: near Kumhwa, Korea
Date of Action: 14 October 1952
G.O. Number, Date: 6, 28 January 1954
Date of Presentation: 12 October 1953
Place of Presentation: The White House, presented by Pres. Dwight D. Eisenhower
Citation: 1st Lt. Schowalter, commanding officer, Company A, distinguished himself by conspicuous gallantry and indomitable courage above and beyond the call of duty in action against the enemy. Committed to attack and occupy a key approach to the primary objective, the 1st Platoon of his company came under heavy vicious small-arms, grenade, and mortar fire within 50 yards of the enemy-held strong-point, halting the advance and inflicting several casualties. The 2d Platoon moved up in support at this juncture, and although wounded, 1st Lt. Schowalter continued to spearhead the assault. Nearing the objective he was severely wounded by a grenade fragment but, refusing medical aid, he led his men into the trenches and began routing the enemy from the bunkers with grenades. Suddenly from a burst of fire from a hidden cove off the trench he was again wounded. Although suffering from his wounds, he refused to relinquish command and continued issuing orders and encouraging his men until the commanding ground was secured and then he was evacuated. 1st Lt. Schowalter's unflinching courage, extraordinary heroism, and inspirational leadership reflect the highest credit upon himself and are in keeping with the highest traditions of the military service.

3133 ◆ *SEBILLE, LOUIS JOSEPH

Rank: Major
Service: U.S. Air Force
Birthday: 21 November 1915
Place of Birth: Harbor Beach, Huron County, Michigan
Date of Death: 5 August 1950
Place of Death: Near Hanchang, Korea
Cemetery: Forest Home Cemetery—Chicago, Illinois
Entered Service at: Chicago, Cook County, Illinois
Unit: 67th Fighter-Bomber Squadron, 18th Fighter-Bomber Group, 5th Air Force
Served as: Pilot of a F-51
Battle or Place of Action: near Hanchang, Korea
Date of Action: 5 August 1950
Date of Presentation: 24 August 1951
Place of Presentation: March AFB, Riverside, California, presented by Gen. Hoyt Sanford Vandenberg to his Widow
Citation: Maj. Sebille distinguished himself by conspicuous gallantry and intrepidity at the risk of his life above and beyond the call of duty. During an attack on a camouflaged area containing a concentration of enemy troops, artillery, and armored vehicles, Maj. Sebille's F-51 aircraft was severely damaged by antiaircraft fire. Although fully cognizant of the short period he could remain airborne, he deliberately ignored the possibility of survival by abandoning the aircraft or by crash landing, and continued his attack against the enemy forces threatening the security of friendly ground troops. In his determination to inflict maximum damage upon the enemy, Maj. Sebille again exposed himself to the intense fire of enemy gun batteries and dived on the target to his death. The superior leadership, daring, and selfless devotion to duty which he displayed in the execution of an extremely dangerous mission were an inspiration to both his subordinates and superiors and reflect the highest credit upon himself, the U.S. Air Force, and the armed forces of the United Nations.

3134 ◆ *SHEA JR., RICHARD THOMAS

Rank: First Lieutenant
Service: U.S. Army
Birthday: 3 January 1927
Place of Birth: Portsmouth, Portsmouth County, Virginia
Date of Death: 8 July 1953

Place of Death: Sokkogae, Korea
Cemetery: Olive Branch Cemetery (MH)—Portsmouth, Virginia
Entered Service at: Portsmouth, Portsmouth County, Virginia
Unit: Company A, 17th Infantry Regiment, 7th Infantry Division
Served as: Executive Officer
Battle or Place of Action: Pork Chop Hill, near Sokkogae, Korea
Date of Action: 7-8 June 1953
G.O. Number, Date: 38, 8 June 1955
Date of Presentation: 16 May 1955
Place of Presentation: Parade Grounds, Ft. Meyers, Va., by the Secretary of the Army Robert T. Stevens to his widow
Citation: 1st Lt. Shea, executive officer, Company A, distinguished himself by conspicuous gallantry and indomitable courage above and beyond the call of duty in action against the enemy. On the night of 6 July, he was supervising the reinforcement of defensive positions when the enemy attacked with great numerical superiority. Voluntarily proceeding to the area most threatened, he organized and led a counterattack and, in the bitter fighting which ensued, closed with and killed two hostile soldiers with his trench knife. Calmly moving among the men, checking positions, steadying and urging the troops to hold firm, he fought side by side with them throughout the night. Despite heavy losses, the hostile force pressed the assault with determination, and at dawn made an all-out attempt to overrun friendly elements. Charging forward to meet the challenge, 1st Lt. Shea and his gallant men drove back the hostile troops. Elements of Company G joined the defense on the afternoon of 7 July, having lost key personnel through casualties. Immediately integrating these troops into his unit, 1st Lt. Shea rallied a group of 20 men and again charged the enemy. Although wounded in this action, he refused evacuation and continued to lead the counterattack. When the assaulting element was pinned down by heavy machine-gun fire, he personally rushed the emplacement and, firing his carbine and lobbing grenades with deadly accuracy, neutralized the weapon and killed three of the enemy. With forceful leadership and by his heroic example, 1st Lt. Shea coordinated and directed a holding action throughout the night and the following morning. On 8 July, the enemy attacked again. Despite additional wounds, he launched a determined counterattack and was last seen in close hand-to-hand combat with the enemy. 1st Lt. Shea's inspirational leadership and unflinching courage set an illustrious example of valor to the men of his regiment, reflecting lasting glory upon himself and upholding the noble traditions of the military service.

3135 ◆ *SHUCK JR., WILLIAM EDWARD

Rank: Staff Sergeant (highest rank: Master Sergeant)
Service: U.S. Marine Corps
Birthday: 16 August 1926
Place of Birth: Cumberland, Allegany County, Maryland
Date of Death: 3 July 1952
Place of Death: Korea

Cemetery: St. Peter's & Paul Cemetery (MH)—Cumberland, Maryland
Entered Service at: Cumberland, Allegany County, Maryland
Unit: Company G, 3d Battalion, 7th Marines, 1st Marine Division (Rein)
Served as: Squad Leader
Battle or Place of Action: Korea
Date of Action: 3 July 1952
Date of Presentation: 9 September 1953
Place of Presentation: Marine Corps Barracks, Washington, D.C., presented by Vice Pres. Richard M. Nixon to his Widow
Citation: For conspicuous gallantry and intrepidity at the risk of his life above and beyond the call of duty while serving as a squad leader of Company G, in action against enemy aggressor forces. When his platoon was subjected to a devastating barrage of enemy small-arms, grenade, artillery, and mortar fire during an assault against strongly fortified hill positions well forward of the main line of resistance, S/Sgt. Shuck, although painfully wounded, refused medical attention and continued to lead his machine-gun squad in the attack. Unhesitatingly assuming command of a rifle squad when the leader became a casualty, he skillfully organized the two squads into an attacking force and led two more daring assaults upon the hostile positions. Wounded a second time, he steadfastly refused evacuation and remained in the foremost position under heavy fire until assured that all dead and wounded were evacuated. Mortally wounded by an enemy sniper bullet while voluntarily assisting in the removal of the last casualty, S/Sgt. Shuck, by his fortitude and great personal valor in the face of overwhelming odds, served to inspire all who observed him. His unyielding courage throughout reflects the highest credit upon himself and the U.S. Naval Service. He gallantly gave his life for his country.

3136 ◆ SIMANEK, ROBERT ERNEST

Rank: Private First Class
Service: U.S. Marine Corps
Birthday: 26 April 1930
Place of Birth: Detroit, Wayne County, Michigan
Entered Service at: Detroit, Wayne County, Michigan
Unit: 2d Squad, 2d Platoon, Company F, 2d Battalion, 5th Marines, 1st Marine Division (Rein)
Served as: Radio Operator
Battle or Place of Action: Outpost Irene, Korea
Date of Action: 17 August 1952
Date of Presentation: 27 October 1953
Place of Presentation: The White House, presented by Pres. Dwight D. Eisenhower
Citation: For conspicuous gallantry and intrepidity at the risk of his life above and beyond the call of duty while serving with Company F, in action against enemy aggressor forces. While accompanying a patrol en route to occupy a combat outpost forward of friendly lines, Pfc. Simanek exhibited a high degree of courage and a resolute spirit of self-sacrifice in protecting the lives of his fellow marines. With his unit ambushed by an intense concentration of enemy mortar and

small-arms fire, and suffering heavy casualties, he was forced to seek cover with the remaining members of the patrol in a nearby trench line. Determined to save his comrades when a hostile grenade was hurled into their midst, he unhesitatingly threw himself on the deadly missile absorbing the shattering violence of the exploding charge in his body and shielding his fellow marines from serious injury or death. Gravely wounded as a result of his heroic action, Pfc. Simanek, by his daring initiative and great personal valor in the face of almost certain death, served to inspire all who observed him and upheld the highest traditions of the U.S. Naval Service.

3137 ◆ *SITMAN, WILLIAM S.

Rank: Sergeant First Class
Service: U.S. Army
Birthday: 9 August 1923
Place of Birth: Bellwood, Blair County, Pennsylvania
Date of Death: 14 February 1951
Place of Death: Chipyong-ni, Korea
Cemetery: Logan Valley Cemetery (MH)—Bellwood, Pennsylvania
Entered Service at: Bellwood, Blair County, Pennsylvania
Unit: Company A, 23d Infantry Regiment, 2d Infantry Division
Served as: Section Leader
Battle or Place of Action: near Chipyong-ni, Korea
Date of Action: 14 February 1951
G.O. Number, Date: 20, 1 February 1952
Date of Presentation: 16 January 1952
Place of Presentation: The Pentagon, presented by Sec. of Defense Robert Lovett to his Widow
Citation: Sfc. Sitman distinguished himself by conspicuous gallantry and intrepidity above and beyond the call of duty in action against an armed enemy of the United Nations. Sfc. Sitman, a machine-gun section leader of Company M, was attached to Company I, under attack by a numerically superior hostile force. During the encounter when an enemy grenade knocked out his machine gun, a squad from Company I immediately emplaced a light machine gun, and Sfc. Sitman and his men remained to provide security for the crew. In the ensuing action, the enemy lobbed a grenade into the position and Sfc. Sitman, fully aware of the odds against him, selflessly threw himself on it, absorbing the full force of the explosion with his body. Although mortally wounded in this fearless display of valor, his intrepid act saved five men from death or serious injury, and enabled them to continue inflicting withering fire on the ruthless foe throughout the attack. Sfc. Sitman's noble self-sacrifice and consummate devotion to duty reflect lasting glory on himself and uphold the honored traditions of the military service.

3138 ◆ SITTER, CARL LEONARD

Rank: Captain (highest rank: Colonel)
Service: U.S. Marine Corps
Birthday: 2 December 1922
Place of Birth: Syracuse, Morgan County, Missouri
Entered Service at: Pueblo, Pueblo County, Colorado

Unit: Company G, 3d Battalion, 1st Marines, 1st Marine Division (Rein)
Served as: Commanding Officer
Battle or Place of Action: Hagaru-ri, Korea
Date of Action: 29-30 November 1950
Date of Presentation: 29 October 1951
Place of Presentation: The White House, presented by Pres. Harry S. Truman
Citation: For conspicuous gallantry and intrepidity at the risk of his life above and beyond the call of duty as commanding officer of Company G, in action against enemy aggressor forces. Ordered to break through enemy-infested territory to reinforce his battalion the morning of 29 November, Capt. Sitter continuously exposed himself to enemy fire as he led his company forward and, despite 25 percent casualties suffered in the furious action, succeeded in driving through to his objective. Assuming the responsibility of attempting to seize and occupy a strategic area occupied by a hostile force of regiment strength deeply entrenched on a snow-covered hill commanding the entire valley southeast of the town, as well as the line of march of friendly troops withdrawing to the south, he reorganized his depleted units the following morning and boldly led them up the steep, frozen hillside under blistering fire, encouraging and redeploying his troops as casualties occurred and directing forward platoons as they continued the drive to the top of the ridge. During the night when a vastly outnumbering enemy launched a sudden, vicious counterattack, setting the hill ablaze with mortar, machine-gun, and automatic-weapons fire and taking a heavy toll in troops, Capt. Sitter visited each foxhole and gun position, coolly deploying and integrating reinforcing units consisting of service personnel unfamiliar with infantry tactics into a coordinated combat team and instilling in every man the will and determination to hold his position at all costs. With the enemy penetrating his lines in repeated counterattacks which often required hand-to-hand combat, and, on one occasion infiltrating to the command post with hand grenades, he fought gallantly with his men in repulsing and killing the fanatic attackers in each encounter. Painfully wounded in the face, arms, and chest by bursting grenades, he staunchly refused to be evacuated and continued to fight on until a successful defense of the area was assured with a loss to the enemy of more than 50 percent dead, wounded, and captured. His valiant leadership, superb tactics, and great personal valor throughout 36 hours of bitter combat reflect the highest credit upon Capt. Sitter and the U.S. Naval Service.

3139 ◆ *SKINNER JR., SHERROD EMERSON

Rank: Second Lieutenant
Service: U.S. Marine Corps Reserve
Birthday: 29 October 1929
Place of Birth: Hartford, Hartford County, Connecticut
Date of Death: 26 October 1952
Place of Death: Korea
Cemetery: Arlington National Cemetery (3-2032-RH) (MH)—Arlington, Virginia
Entered Service at: East Lansing, Ingham County, Michigan

Unit: Battery F, 2d Battalion, 11th Marines, 1st Marine Division (Rein)
Served as: Forward Observer
Battle or Place of Action: Korea
Date of Action: 26 October 1952
Date of Presentation: 9 September 1953
Place of Presentation: Marine Corps Barracks, Washington, D.C., presented by Vice Pres. Richard M. Nixon to his parents
Citation: For conspicuous gallantry and intrepidity at the risk of his life above and beyond the call of duty as an artillery forward observer of Battery F, in action against enemy aggressor forces on the night of 26 October 1952. When his observation post in an extremely critical and vital sector of the main line of resistance was subjected to a sudden and fanatical attack by hostile forces, supported by a devastating barrage of artillery and mortar fire which completely severed communication lines connecting the outpost with friendly firing batteries, 2d Lt. Skinner, in a determined effort to hold his position, immediately organized and directed the surviving personnel in the defense of the outpost, continuing to call down fire on the enemy by means of radio alone until his equipment became damaged beyond repair. Undaunted by the intense hostile barrage and the rapidly-closing attackers, he twice left the protection of his bunker in order to direct accurate machine-gun fire and to replenish the depleted supply of ammunition and grenades. Although painfully wounded on each occasion, he steadfastly refused medical aid until the rest of the men received treatment. As the ground attack reached its climax, he gallantly directed the final defense until the meager supply of ammunition was exhausted and the position overrun. During the three hours that the outpost was occupied by the enemy, several grenades were thrown into the bunker which served as protection for 2d Lt. Skinner and his remaining comrades. Realizing that there was no chance for other than passive resistance, he directed his men to feign death even though the hostile troops entered the bunker and searched their persons. Later, when an enemy grenade was thrown between him and two other survivors, he immediately threw himself on the deadly missile in an effort to protect the others, absorbing the full force of the explosion and sacrificing his life for his comrades. By his indomitable fighting spirit, superb lea dership, and great personal valor in the face of tremendous odds, 2d Lt. Skinner served to inspire his fellow marines in their heroic stand against the enemy and upheld the highest traditions of the U.S. Naval Service. He gallantly gave his life for his country.

3140 ◆ *SMITH, DAVID MONROE

Rank: Private First Class
Service: U.S. Army
Birthday: 10 November 1926
Place of Birth: Livingston, Rockcastle County, Kentucky
Date of Death: 1 September 1950
Place of Death: Yongsan, Korea
Cemetery: Smith Cemetery on the Hill Ponder (MH)—Livingston, Kentucky
Entered Service at: Livingston, Rockcastle County, Kentucky

Unit: Company E, 9th Infantry Regiment, 2d Infantry Division
Served as: Mortar Gunner
Battle or Place of Action: near Yongsan, Korea
Date of Action: 1 September 1950
G.O. Number, Date: 78, 21 August 1952
Date of Presentation: 14 August 1952
Place of Presentation: The Pentagon, presented by Gen. Omar N. Bradley to his Mother
Citation: Pfc. Smith distinguished himself by conspicuous gallantry and outstanding courage above and beyond the call of duty in action. Pfc. Smith was a gunner in the mortar section of Company E, emplaced in rugged mountainous terrain and under attack by a numerically superior hostile force. Bitter fighting ensued and the enemy overran forward elements, infiltrated the perimeter, and rendered friendly positions untenable. The mortar section was ordered to withdraw, but the enemy had encircled and closed in on the position. Observing a grenade lobbed at his emplacement, Pfc. Smith shouted a warning to his comrades and, fully aware of the odds against him, flung himself upon it and smothered the explosion with his body. Although mortally wounded in this display of valor, his intrepid act saved five men from death or serious injury. Pfc. Smith's inspirational conduct and supreme sacrifice reflect lasting glory on himself and are in keeping with the noble traditions of the infantry of the U.S. Army.

3141 ◆ *SPEICHER, CLIFTON T.

Rank: Corporal
Service: U.S. Army
Birthday: 25 March 1931
Place of Birth: Gray, Somerset County, Pennsylvania
Date of Death: 14 June 1952
Place of Death: Minarigol, Korea
Cemetery: Beam Cemetery—Jenner Township, Pennsylvania
Entered Service at: Gray, Somerset County, Pennsylvania
Unit: Company F, 223d Infantry Regiment, 40th Infantry Division
Battle or Place of Action: near Minarigol, Korea
Date of Action: 14 June 1952
G.O. Number, Date: 65, 19 August 1953
Date of Presentation: 5 August 1953
Place of Presentation: The Pentagon Auditorium, presented by Under Sec. of the Army Earl D. Johnson to his Father
Citation: Cpl. Speicher distinguished himself by conspicuous gallantry and indomitable courage above and beyond the call of duty in action against the enemy. While participating in an assault to secure a key terrain feature, Cpl. Speicher's squad was pinned down by withering small-arms, mortar, and machine-gun fire. Although already wounded he left the comparative safety of his position, and made a daring charge against the machine-gun emplacement. Within 10 yards of the goal, he was again wounded by small-arms fire but continued on, entered the bunker, killed two hostile soldiers with his rifle, a third with his bayonet, and silenced the machine gun. Inspired by this incredible display of valor, the men quickly moved up and completed the mission. Dazed and

3144 ◆ *SUDUT, JEROME A.

shaken, he walked to the foot of the hill where he collapsed and died. Cpl. Speicher's consummate sacrifice and unflinching devotion to duty reflect lasting glory upon himself and uphold the noble traditions of the military service.

3142 ◆ STONE, JAMES LAMAR

Rank: First Lieutenant (highest rank: Colonel)
Service: U.S. Army
Birthday: 27 December 1922
Place of Birth: Pine Bluff, Jefferson County, Arkansas
Entered Service at: Houston, Harris County, Texas
Unit: 3d Platoon, Company F, 2d Battalion, 8th Cavalry Regiment, 1st Cavalry Division
Served as: Platoon Leader
Battle or Place of Action: near Sokkogae, Korea
Date of Action: 21-22 November 1951
G.O. Number, Date: 82, 20 October 1953
Date of Presentation: 27 October 1953
Place of Presentation: The White House, presented by Pres. Dwight D. Eisenhower
Citation: 1st Lt. Stone distinguished himself by conspicuous gallantry and indomitable courage above and beyond the call of duty in action against the enemy. When his platoon, holding a vital outpost position, was attacked by overwhelming Chinese forces, 1st Lt. Stone stood erect and exposed to the terrific enemy fire calmly directed his men in the defense. A defensive flamethrower failing to function, he personally moved to its location, further exposing himself, and personally repaired the weapon. Throughout a second attack, 1st Lt. Stone, though painfully wounded, personally carried the only remaining light machine gun from place to place in the position in order to bring fire upon the Chinese advancing from two directions. Throughout he continued to encourage and direct his depleted platoon in its hopeless defense. Although again wounded, he continued the fight with his carbine, still exposing himself as an example to his men. When this final overwhelming assault swept over the platoon's position his voice could still be heard faintly urging his men to carry on, until he lost consciousness. Only because of this officer's driving spirit and heroic action was the platoon emboldened to make its brave but hopeless last ditch stand.
Notes: POW

3143 ◆ *STORY, LUTHER H.

Rank: Private First Class
Service: U.S. Army
Birthday: 20 July 1931
Place of Birth: Buena Vista, Marion County, Georgia
Date of Death: 1 September 1950
Place of Death: Agok, Korea
Cemetery: National Memorial Cemetery of the Pacific (Wall of the Missing)—Honolulu, Hawaii; Andersonville National Cemetery ('In Memory' marker)—Andersonville, Georgia
Entered Service at: Georgia
Unit: Company A, 9th Infantry Regiment, 2d Infantry Division
Served as: Weapons Squad Leader

Battle or Place of Action: near Agok, Korea
Date of Action: 1 September 1950
G.O. Number, Date: 70, 2 August 1951
Date of Presentation: 21 June 1951
Place of Presentation: The Pentagon, presented by Gen. Omar N. Bradley to his Father
Citation: Pfc. Story distinguished himself by conspicuous gallantry and intrepidity above and beyond the call of duty in action. A savage daylight attack by elements of three enemy divisions penetrated the thinly held lines of the 9th Infantry. Company A beat off several banzai attacks but was bypassed and in danger of being cut off and surrounded. Pfc. Story, a weapons squad leader, was heavily engaged in stopping the early attacks and had just moved his squad to a position overlooking the Naktong River when he observed a large group of the enemy crossing the river to attack Company A. Seizing a machine gun from his wounded gunner he placed deadly fire on the hostile column killing or wounding an estimated 100 enemy soldiers. Facing certain encirclement, the company commander ordered a withdrawal. During the move Pfc. Story noticed the approach of an enemy truck loaded with troops and towing an ammunition trailer. Alerting his comrades to take cover, he fearlessly stood in the middle of the road, throwing grenades into the truck. Out of grenades, he crawled to his squad, gathered up additional grenades, and again attacked the vehicle. During the withdrawal the company was attacked by such superior numbers that it was forced to deploy in a rice field. Pfc. Story was wounded in this action, but, disregarding his wounds, rallied the men about him and repelled the attack. Realizing that his wounds would hamper his comrades, he refused to retire to the next position but remained to cover the company's withdrawal. When last seen he was firing every weapon available and fighting off another hostile assault. Pvt. Story's extraordinary heroism, aggressive leadership, and supreme devotion to duty reflect the highest credit upon himself and were in keeping with the esteemed traditions of the military service.
Notes: MIA

3144 ◆ *SUDUT, JEROME A.

Rank: Second Lieutenant
Service: U.S. Army
Birthday: 20 October 1930
Place of Birth: Wausau, Marathon County, Wisconsin
Date of Death: 12 September 1951
Place of Death: Kumhwa, Korea
Cemetery: Restlawn Memorial Cemetery—Wausau, Wisconsin
Entered Service at: Wisconsin
Unit: Company B, 27th Infantry Regiment, 25th Infantry Division
Served as: Platoon Leader
Battle or Place of Action: near Kumhwa, Korea
Date of Action: 12 September 1951
G.O. Number, Date: 31, 21 March 1952
Date of Presentation: 13 March 1952
Place of Presentation: Presented by Sec. of the Army Frank C. Pace to his parents

Citation: 2d Lt. Sudut distinguished himself by conspicuous gallantry above and beyond the call of duty in action against the enemy. His platoon, attacking heavily fortified and stategically located hostile emplacements, had been stopped by intense fire from a large bunker containing several firing posts. Armed with submachine gun, pistol, and grenades, 2d Lt. Sudut charged the emplacement alone through vicious hostile fire, killing three of the occupants and dispersing the remainder. Painfully wounded, he returned to reorganize his platoon, refused evacuation, and led his men in a renewed attack. The enemy had returned to the bunker by means of connecting trenches from other emplacements and the platoon was again halted by devastating fire. Accompanied by an automatic-rifleman, 2d Lt. Sudut again charged into close-range fire to eliminate the postion. When the rifleman was wounded, 2d Lt. Sudut seized his weapon and continued alone, killing three of the four remaining occupants. Though mortally wounded and his ammunition exhausted, he jumped into the emplacement and killed the remaining enemy soldier with his trench knife. His singlehanded assaults so inspired his comrades that they continued the attack and drove the enemy from the hill, securing the objective. Second Lt. Sudut's consummate fighting spirit, outstanding leadership, and gallant self-sacrifice are in keeping with the finest traditions of the infantry and the U.S. Army.

3145 ◆ *THOMPSON, WILLIAM HENRY

Rank: Private First Class
Service: U.S. Army
Birthday: 16 August 1927
Place of Birth: New York, New York
Date of Death: 6 August 1950
Place of Death: Haman, Korea
Cemetery: Long Island National Cemetery (DSS-19) (MH)—Farmingdale, New York
Entered Service at: Bronx County, New York
Unit: Company M, 24th Infantry Regiment, 25th Infantry Division
Served as: Machine Gunner
Battle or Place of Action: near Haman, Korea
Date of Action: 6 August 1950
G.O. Number, Date: 63, 2 August 1951
Date of Presentation: 21 June 1951
Place of Presentation: The Pentagon, presented by Gen. Omar Bradley to his Mother
Citation: Pfc. Thompson distinguished himself by conspicuous gallantry and intrepidity above and beyond the call of duty in action against the enemy. While his platoon was reorganizing under cover of darkness, fanatical enemy forces in overwhelming strength launched a surprise attack on the unit. Pfc. Thompson set up his machine gun in the path of the onslaught and swept the enemy with withering fire, pinning them down momentarily, thus permitting the remainder of his platoon to withdraw to a more tenable position. Although hit repeatedly by grenade fragments and small-arms fire, he resisted all efforts of his comrades to induce him to withdraw, steadfastly remained at his machine gun and continued to deliver deadly, accurate fire until mortally wounded by an enemy grenade. Pfc. Thompson's dauntless courage and gal-

lant self-sacrifice reflect the highest credit on himself and uphold the esteemed traditions of military service.

3146 ◆ *TURNER, CHARLES WILLIAM

Rank: Sergeant First Class
Service: U.S. Army
Birthday: 28 May 1921
Place of Birth: Boston, Suffolk County, Massachusetts
Date of Death: 1 September 1950
Place of Death: Yongsan, Korea
Cemetery: Arlington National Cemetery (12-7762) (MH)—Arlington, Virginia
Entered Service at: Massachusetts
Unit: 2d Reconnaissance Company, 2d Infantry Division
Served as: Section Leader
Battle or Place of Action: near Yongsan, Korea
Date of Action: 2 September 1950
G.O. Number, Date: 10, 16 February 1951
Date of Presentation: 9 January 1951
Place of Presentation: The White House, presented by Pres. Harry S. Truman to his Mother
Citation: Sfc. Turner distinguished himself by conspicuous gallantry and intrepidity above and beyond the call of duty in action against the enemy. A large enemy force launched a mortar-and automatic-weapon-supported assault against his platoon. Sfc. Turner, a section leader, quickly organized his unit for defense and then observed that the attack was directed at the tank section 100 yards away. Leaving his secured section, he dashed through a hail of fire to the threatened position and, mounting a tank, manned the exposed turret machine gun. Disregarding the intense enemy fire he calmly held this position, delivering deadly accurate fire and pointing out targets for the tank's 75-mm gun. His action resulted in the destruction of seven enemy machine-gun nests. Although severely wounded he remained at the gun shouting encouragement to his comrades. During the action the tank received over 50 direct hits; the periscopes and antenna were shot away and three rounds hit the machine-gun mount. Despite this fire he remained at his post until a burst of enemy fire cost his life. This intrepid and heroic performance enabled the platoon to withdraw and later launch an attack which routed the enemy. Sfc. Turner's valor and example reflect the highest credit upon himself and are in keeping with the esteemed traditions of the U.S. Army.

3147 ◆ VAN WINKLE, ARCHIE

Rank: Staff Sergeant (highest rank: Colonel)
Service: U.S. Marine Corps Reserve
Birthday: 17 March 1925
Place of Birth: Juneau, Juneau County, Alaska
Date of Death: 20 May 1986
Place of Death: Ketchikan, Alaska
Cemetery: Cremated, ashes scattered at sea
Entered Service at: Arlington, Snohomish County, Washington
Unit: 3 Platoon, Company B, 1st Battalion, 7th Marines, 1st Marine Division (Rein)
Served as: Platoon Sergeant

Battle or Place of Action: near Sudong, Korea
Date of Action: 2 November 1950
Date of Presentation: 6 February 1951
Place of Presentation: The White House, presented by Pres. Harry S. Truman
Citation: For conspicuous gallantry and intrepidity at the risk of his life above and beyond the call of duty while serving as a platoon sergeant in company B, in action against enemy aggressor forces. Immediately rallying the men in his area after a fanatical and numerically superior enemy force penetrated the center of the line under cover of darkness and pinned down the platoon with a devastating barrage of deadly automatic-weapons and grenade fire, S/Sgt. Van Winkle boldly spearheaded a determined attack through withering fire against hostile frontal positions and, though he and all the others who charged with him were wounded, succeeded in enabling his platoon to gain the fire superiority and the opportunity to reorganize. Realizing that the left-flank squad was isolated from the rest of the unit, he rushed through 40 yards of fierce enemy fire to reunite his troops despite an elbow wound which rendered one of his arms totally useless. Severely wounded a second time when a direct hit in the chest from a hostile hand grenade caused serious and painful wounds, he staunchly refused evacuation and continued to shout orders and words of encouragement to his depleted and battered platoon. Finally carried from his position unconscious from shock and from loss of blood, S/Sgt. Van Winkle served to inspire all who observed him to heroic efforts in successfully repulsing the enemy attack. His superb leadership, valiant fighting spirit, and unfaltering devotion to duty in the face of heavy odds reflect the highest credit upon himself and the U.S. Naval Service.

3148 ◆ *VITTORI, JOSEPH

Rank: Corporal
Service: U.S. Marine Corps Reserve
Birthday: 1 August 1929
Place of Birth: Beverly, Essex County, Massachusetts
Date of Death: 16 September 1951
Place of Death: Hill 749, Korea
Cemetery: St. Mary's Cemetery (MH)—Beverly, Massachusetts
Entered Service at: Beverly, Essex County, Massachusetts
Unit: Company F, 2d Battalion, 1st Marines, 1st Marine Division (Rein)
Served as: Automatic Rifleman
Battle or Place of Action: Hill 749, Korea
Date of Action: 15-16 September 1951
Place of Presentation: The Pentagon, presented by Sec. of the Navy Dan A. Kimball to his family
Citation: For conspicuous gallantry and intrepidity at the risk of his life above and beyond the call of duty while serving as an automatic-rifleman in Company F, in action against enemy aggressor forces. With a forward platoon suffering heavy casualties and forced to withdraw under a vicious enemy counterattack as his company assaulted strong hostile forces entrenched on Hill 749, Cpl. Vittori boldly rushed through the withdrawing troops with two other volunteers from his reserve platoon and plunged directly into the midst

of the enemy. Overwhelming them in a fierce hand-to-hand struggle, he enabled his company to consolidate its positions to meet further imminent onslaught. Quick to respond to an urgent call for a rifleman to defend a heavy machine gun positioned on the extreme point of the northern flank and virtually isolated from the remainder of the unit when the enemy again struck in force during the night, he assumed position under the devastating barrage and, fighting a singlehanded battle, leaped from one flank to the other, covering each foxhole in turn as casualties continued to mount, manning a machine gun when the gunner was struck down, and making repeated trips through the heaviest shellfire to replenish ammunition. With the situation becoming extremely critical, reinforcing units to the rear pinned down under the blistering attack, and foxholes left practically void by dead and wounded for a distance of 100 yards, Cpl. Vittori continued his valiant stand, refusing to give ground as the enemy penetrated to within feet of his position, simulating strength in the line and denying the foe physical occupation of the ground. Mortally wounded by the enemy machine-gun and rifle bullets while persisting in his magnificent defense of the sector where approximately 200 enemy dead were found the following morning, Cpl. Vittori, by his fortitude, stouthearted courage, and great personal valor, had kept the point position intact despite the tremendous odds and undoubt edly prevented the entire battalion position from collapsing. His extraordinary heroism throughout the furious nightlong battle reflects the highest credit upon himself and the U.S. Naval Service. He gallantly gave his life for his country.

3149 ◆ *WALMSLEY JR., JOHN SPRINGER

Rank: Captain
Service: U.S. Air Force
Birthday: 7 January 1920
Place of Birth: Baltimore, Baltimore County, Maryland
Date of Death: 14 September 1951
Place of Death: Yangdok, Korea
Cemetery: Honolulu, Hawaii
Entered Service at: Baltimore, Baltimore County, Maryland
Unit: 8th Bombardment Squadron, 3d Bombardment Group
Served as: Pilot of a Douglas B-26
Battle or Place of Action: near Yangdok, Korea
Date of Action: 14 September 1951
Date of Presentation: 12 June 1954
Place of Presentation: Bolling AFB, presented by Sec. of the Air Force Talbott to his Widow
Citation: Capt. Walmsley distinguished himself by conspicuous gallantry and intrepidity at the risk of his life above and beyond the call of duty. While flying a B-26 aircraft on a night combat mission with the objective of developing new tactics, Capt. Walmsley sighted an enemy supply train which had been assigned top priority as a target of opportunity. He immediately attacked, producing a strike which disabled the train, and, when his ammunition was expended, radioed for friendly aircraft in the area to complete destruction of the target. Employing the searchlight mounted on his aircraft, he guided another B-26 aircraft to the target area, meanwhile constantly exposing himself to enemy fire. Directing an

incoming B-26 pilot, he twice boldly aligned himself with the target, his searchlight illuminating the area, in a determined effort to give the attacking aircraft full visibility. As the friendly aircraft prepared for the attack, Capt. Walmsley descended into the valley in a low-level run over the target with searchlight blazing, selflessly exposing himself to vicious enemy antiaircraft fire. In his determination to inflict maximum damage on the enemy, he refused to employ evasive tactics and valiantly pressed forward straight through an intense barrage, thus insuring complete destruction of the enemy's vitally needed war cargo. While he courageously pressed his attack Capt. Walmsley's plane was hit and crashed into the surrounding mountains, exploding upon impact. His heroic initiative and daring aggressiveness in completing this important mission in the face of overwhelming opposition and at the risk of his life, refects the highest credit upon himself and the U.S. Air Force.

Notes: MIA

3150 ◆ *WATKINS, LEWIS GEORGE

Rank: Staff Sergeant
Service: U.S. Marine Corps
Birthday: 6 June 1925
Place of Birth: Seneca, Oconee County, South Carolina
Date of Death: 7 October 1952
Place of Death: Korea
Cemetery: Honolulu, Hawaii
Entered Service at: Seneca, Oconee County, South Carolina
Unit: Company I, 3d Battalion, 7th Marines, 1st Marine Division (Rein)
Battle or Place of Action: Korea
Date of Action: 7 October 1952
Date of Presentation: 9 September 1953
Place of Presentation: Marine Corps Barracks, Washington, D.C., presented by Vice Pres. Richard M. Nixon to his parents
Citation: For conspicuous gallantry and intrepidity at the risk of his life above and beyond the call of duty while serving as a guide of a rifle platoon of Company I, in action against enemy aggressor forces during the hours of darkness on the morning of 7 October 1952. With his platoon assigned the mission of retaking an outpost which had been overrun by the enemy earlier in the night, S/Sgt. Watkins skillfully led his unit in the assault up the designated hill. Although painfully wounded when a well-entrenched hostile force at the crest of the hill engaged the platoon with intense small-arms and grenade fire, he gallantly continued to lead his men. Obtaining an automatic rifle from one of the wounded men, he assisted in pinning down an enemy machine gun holding up the assault. When an enemy grenade landed among S/Sgt. Watkins and several other marines while they were moving forward through a trench on the hill crest, he immediately pushed his companions aside, placed himself in a position to shield them, and picked up the deadly missile in an attempt to throw it outside the trench. Mortally wounded when the grenade exploded in his hand, S/Sgt. Watkins, by his great personal valor in the face of almost certain death, saved the lives of several of his comrades and contributed materially to

the success of the mission. His extraordinary heroism, inspiring leadership, and resolute spirit of self-sacrifice reflect the highest credit upon himself and enhance the finest traditions of the U.S. Naval Service. He gallantly gave his life for his country.

Notes: MIA

3151 ◆ *WATKINS, TRAVIS E.

Rank: Master Sergeant
Service: U.S. Army
Birthday: 5 September 1920
Place of Birth: Waldo, Columbia County, Arkansas
Date of Death: 3 September 1950
Place of Death: Yongsan, Korea
Cemetery: Gladewater Memorial Park (PM)—Gladewater, Texas
Entered Service at: Texas
Unit: Company H, 9th Infantry Regiment, 2d Infantry Division
Battle or Place of Action: near Yongsan, Korea
Date of Action: 31 August-3 September 1950
G.O. Number, Date: 9, 16 February 1951
Date of Presentation: 9 January 1951
Place of Presentation: The White House, presented by Pres. Harry S. Truman to his Widow
Citation: M/Sgt. Watkins distinguished himself by conspicuous gallantry and intrepidity above and beyond the call of duty in action against the enemy. When an overwhelming enemy force broke through and isolated 30 men of his unit, he took command, established a perimeter defense and directed action which repelled continuous, fanatical enemy assaults. With his group completely surrounded and cut off, he moved from foxhole to foxhole exposing himself to enemy fire, giving instructions, and offering encouragement to his men. Later when the need for ammunition and grenades became critical he shot two enemy soldiers 50 yards outside the perimeter and went out alone for their ammunition and weapons. As he picked up their weapons he was attacked by three others and wounded. Returning their fire he killed all three and gathering up the weapons of the five enemy dead returned to his amazed comrades. During a later assault, six enemy soldiers gained a defiladed spot and began to throw grenades into the perimeter making it untenable. Realizing the desperate situation and disregarding his wound, he rose from his foxhole to engage them with rifle fire. Although immediately hit by a burst from an enemy machine gun he continued to fire until he had killed the grenade throwers. With this threat eliminated he collapsed and despite being paralyzed from the waist down, encouraged his men to hold on. He refused all food, saving it for his comrades, and when it became apparent that help would not arrive in time to hold the position ordered his men to escape to friendly lines. Refusing evacuation as his hopeless condition would burden his comrades, he remained in his position and cheerfully wished them luck. Through his aggressive leadership and intrepid actions, this small force destroyed nearly 500 of the enemy before abandoning their position. M/Sgt. Watkins' sustained personal bravery and noble self-sacrifice reflect the

highest glory upon himself and is in keeping with the esteemed tradi tions of the U.S. Army.

3152 ◆ WEST, ERNEST EDISON

Rank: Private First Class
Service: U.S. Army
Birthday: 2 September 1931
Place of Birth: Russell, Greenup County, Kentucky
Entered Service at: Wurtland, Greenup County, Kentucky
Unit: 2d Squad, 3d Platoon, Company L, 3d Battalion, 14th Infantry Regiment, 25th Infantry Division
Served as: Acting Sergeant/Squad Leader
Battle or Place of Action: near Sataeri, Korea
Date of Action: 12 October 1952
G.O. Number, Date: 7, 29 January 1954
Date of Presentation: 12 January 1954
Place of Presentation: The White House, presented by Pres. Dwight D. Eisenhower
Citation: Pfc. West distinguished himself by conspicuous gallantry above and beyond the call of duty in action against the enemy. He voluntarily accompanied a contingent to locate and destroy a reported enemy outpost. Nearing the objective, the patrol was ambushed and suffered numerous casualties. Observing his wounded leader lying in an exposed position, Pfc. West ordered the troops to withdraw, then braved intense fire to reach and assist him. While attempting evacuation, he was attacked by three hostile soldiers employing grenades and small-arms fire. Quickly shifting his body to shelter the officer, he killed the assailants with his rifle, then carried the helpless man to safety. He was critically wounded and lost an eye in this action, but courageously returned through withering fire and bursting shells to assist the wounded. While evacuating two comrades, he closed with and killed three more of the foe. Pfc. West's indomitable spirit, consummate valor, and intrepid actions inspired all who observed him, reflect the highest credit on himself, and uphold the honored traditions of the military service.

3153 ◆ WILSON, BENJAMIN F.

Rank: First Lieutenant (rank at time of action: Master Sergeant) (highest rank: Major)
Service: U.S. Army
Birthday: 2 June 1922
Place of Birth: Vashon, King County, Washington
Date of Death: 1 March 1988
Place of Death: Honolulu, Hawaii
Cemetery: National Memorial Cemetery of the Pacific (A-1060-A) (MH)—Honolulu, Hawaii
Entered Service at: Vashon, King County, Washington
Unit: Company I, 31st Infantry Regiment, 7th Infantry Division
Battle or Place of Action: near Hwach'on-Myon, Korea
Date of Action: 5 June 1951
G.O. Number, Date: 69, 23 September 1954
Date of Presentation: 7 September 1954
Place of Presentation: Army Hospital, Denver, CO, presented by Pres. Dwight D. Eisenhower

Citation: 1st Lt. Wilson distinguished himself by conspicuous gallantry and indomitable courage above and beyond the call of duty in action against the enemy. Company I was committed to attack and secure commanding terrain stubbornly defended by a numerically superior hostile force emplaced in well-fortified positions. When the spearheading element was pinned down by withering hostile fire, he dashed forward and, firing his rifle and throwing grenades, neutralized the position denying the advance, and killed four enemy soldiers manning submachine guns. After the assault platoon moved up, occupied the position, and a base of fire was established, he led a bayonet attack which reduced the objective and killed approximately 27 hostile soldiers. While friendly forces were consolidating the newly won gain, the enemy launched a counterattack and 1st Lt. Wilson, realizing the imminent threat of being overrun, made a determined lone-man charge, killing seven and wounding two of the enemy, and routing the remainder in disorder. After the position was organized, he led an assault carrying to approximately 15 yards of the final objective, when enemy fire halted the advance. He ordered the platoon to withdraw and, although painfully wounded in this action, remained to provide covering fire. During an ensuing counterattack, the commanding officer and 1st Platoon leader became casualties. Unhesitatingly, 1st Lt. Wilson charged the enemy ranks and fought valiantly, killing three enemy soldiers with his rifle before it was wrested from his hands, and annihilating four others with his entrenching tool. His courageous delaying action enabled his comrades to reorganize and effect an orderly withdrawal. While directing evacuation of the wounded, he suffered a second wound, but elected to remain on the position until assured that all of the men had reached safety. 1st Lt. Wilson's sustained valor and intrepid actions reflect utmost credit upon himself and uphold the honored traditions of th e military service.

3154 ◆ WILSON, HAROLD EDWARD "SPEEDY"

Rank: Technical Sergeant (highest rank: Chief Warrant Officer 4)
Service: U.S. Marine Corps Reserve
Birthday: 5 December 1921
Place of Birth: Birmingham, Jefferson County, Alabama
Entered Service at: Birmingham, Jefferson County, Alabama
Unit: 3d Platoon, Company G, 3d Battalion, 1st Marines, 1st Marine Division
Served as: Platoon Sergeant
Battle or Place of Action: Korea
Date of Action: 23-24 April 1951
Date of Presentation: 12 April 1952
Place of Presentation: The White House, presented by Pres. Harry S. Truman
Citation: For gallantry and intrepidity at the risk of his life above and beyond the call of duty while serving as platoon sergeant of a rifle platoon attached to Company G, in action against enemy aggressor forces on the night from 23 to 24 April 1951. When the company outpost was overrun by the enemy while his platoon, firing from hastily constructed fox-

holes, was engaged in resisting the brunt of a fierce mortar, machine-gun, grenade, and small-arms attack launched by hostile forces from high ground under cover of darkness, T/Sgt. Wilson braved intense fire to assist the survivors back into the line and to direct the treatment of casualties. Although twice wounded by gunfire, in the right arm and the left leg, he refused medical aid for himself and continued to move about among his men, shouting words of encouragement. After receiving further wounds in the head and shoulder as the attack increased in intensity, he again insisted upon remaining with his unit. Unable to use either arm to fire, and with mounting casualties among our forces, he resupplied his men with rifles and ammunition taken from the wounded. Personally reporting to his company commander on several occasions, he requested and received additional assistance when the enemy attack became even more fierce and, after placing the reinforcements in strategic positions in the line, directed effective fire until blown off his feet by the bursting of a hostile mortar round in his face. Dazed and suffering from concussion, he still refused medical aid and, despite weakness from loss of blood, moved from foxhole to foxhole, directing fire, resupplying ammunition, rendering first aid, and encouraging his men. By his heroic actions in the face of almost certain death, when the unit's ability to hold the disadvantageous position was doubtful, he instilled confidence in his troops, inspiring them to rally repeatedly and turn back the furious assaults. At dawn, after the final attack had been repulsed, he personally accounted for each man in his platoon before walking unassisted one-half mile to the aid station where he submitted to treatment. His outstanding courage, initiative, and skilled leadership in the face of overwhelming odds were contributing factors in the success of his company's mission and reflect the highest credit upon T/Sgt. Wilson and the U.S. Naval Service.

3155 ◆ *WILSON, RICHARD G.

Rank: Private First Class
Service: U.S. Army
Birthday: 19 August 1931
Place of Birth: Marion, Williamson County, Illinois
Date of Death: 21 October 1950
Place of Death: Opari, Korea
Cemetery: Cape County Memorial Park—Cape Girardeau, Missouri
Entered Service at: Cape Girardeau, Cape Girardeau County, Missouri
Unit: Medical Company, Company I, 187th Airborne Infantry Regiment
Served as: Medical Aidman
Battle or Place of Action: near Opari, Korea
Date of Action: 21 October 1950
G.O. Number, Date: 64, 2 August 1951
Date of Presentation: 21 June 1951
Place of Presentation: The Pentagon, presented by Gen. Omar N. Bradley to his Widow
Citation: Pfc. Wilson distinguished himself by conspicuous gallantry and intrepidity above and beyond the call of duty in action. As medical aidman attached to Company I, he accompanied the unit during a reconnaissance-in-force through the hilly country near Opari. The main body of the company was passing through a narrow valley flanked on three sides by high hills when the enemy laid down a barrage of mortar, automatic-weapons, and small-arms fire. The company suffered a large number of casualties from the intense hostile fire while fighting its way out of the ambush. Pfc. Wilson proceeded at once to move among the wounded and administered aid to them oblivious of the danger to himself, constantly exposing himself to hostile fire. The company commander ordered a withdrawal as the enemy threatened to encircle and isolate the company. As his unit withdrew Pvt. Wilson assisted wounded men to safety and assured himself that none were left behind. After the company had pulled back he learned that a comrade previously thought dead had been seen to be moving and attempting to crawl to safety. Despite the protests of his comrades, unarmed and facing a merciless enemy, Pfc. Wilson returned to the dangerous position in search of his comrade. Two days later a patrol found him lying beside the man he returned to aid. He had been shot several times while trying to shield and administer to the wounded man. Pfc. Wilson's superb personal bravery, consummate courage, and willing self-sacrifice for his comrades reflect untold glory upon himself and uphold the esteemed traditions of the military service.

3156 ◆ *WINDRICH, WILLIAM GORDON

Rank: Staff Sergeant
Service: U.S. Marine Corps
Birthday: 14 May 1921
Place of Birth: Chicago, Cook County, Illinois
Date of Death: 2 December 1950
Cemetery: Arlington National Cemetery (31-4856) (MH)—Arlington, Virginia
Entered Service at: Hammond, Lake County, Indiana
Unit: Company I, 3d Battalion, 5th Marines, 1st Marine Division (Rein)
Served as: Platoon Sergeant
Battle or Place of Action: vinicity of Yudam-ni, Korea
Date of Action: 1 December 1950
Date of Presentation: 8 February 1952
Place of Presentation: The Pentagon, presented by Under Sec. of the Navy Francis P. Whitehair to his Widow
Citation: For conspicuous gallantry and intrepidity at the risk of his life above and beyond the call of duty as a platoon sergeant of Company I, in action against enemy aggressor forces the night of 1 December 1950. Promptly organizing a squad of men when the enemy launched a sudden, vicious counterattack against the forward elements of his company's position, rendering it untenable, S/Sgt. Windrich, armed with a carbine, spearheaded the assault to the top of the knoll immediately confronting the overwhelming forces and, under shattering hostile automatic-weapons, mortar, and grenade fire, directed effective fire to hold back the attackers and cover the withdrawal of our troops to commanding ground. With seven of his men struck down during the furious action and himself wounded in the head by a bursting grenade, he made his way to his company's position and, organizing a

small group of volunteers, returned with them to evacuate the wounded and dying from the frozen hillside, staunchly refusing medical attention himself. Immediately redeploying the remainder of his troops, S/Sgt. Windrich placed them on the left flank of the defensive sector before the enemy again attacked in force. Wounded in the leg during the bitter fight that followed, he bravely fought on with his men, shouting words of encouragement and directing their fire until the attack was repelled. Refusing evacuation although unable to stand, he still continued to direct his platoon in setting up defensive positions until weakened by the bitter cold, excessive loss of blood, and severe pain, he lapsed into unconsciousness and died. His valiant leadership, fortitude, and courageous fighting spirit against tremendous odds served to inspire others to heroic endeavor in holding the objective and reflect the highest credit upon S/Sgt. Windrich and the U.S. Naval Service. He gallantly gave his life for his country.

3157 ◆ *WOMACK, BRYANT HOMER

Rank: Private
Service: U.S. Army
Birthday: 12 May 1931
Place of Birth: Mill Spring, Polk County, North Carolina
Date of Death: 12 March 1952
Place of Death: Sokso-ri, Korea
Cemetery: Lebanon Church Cemetery (MH)—Mill Spring, North Carolina
Entered Service at: Mill Spring, Polk County, North Carolina
Unit: Medical Company, 14th Infantry Regiment, 25th Infantry Division
Served as: Medical Aidman
Battle or Place of Action: near Sokso-ri, Korea
Date of Action: 12 March 1952
G.O. Number, Date: 5, 12 January 1953
Date of Presentation: 7 January 1953
Place of Presentation: The Pentagon, presented by Sec. of the Army Frank C. Pace to his family
Citation: Pfc. Womack distinguished himself by conspicuous gallantry above and beyond the call of duty in action against the enemy. Pfc. Womack was the only medical aidman attached to a night combat patrol when sudden contact with a numerically superior enemy produced numerous casualties. Pfc. Womack went immediately to their aid, although this necessitated exposing himself to a devastating hail of enemy fire, during which he was seriously wounded. Refusing medical aid for himself, he continued moving among his comrades to administer aid. While he was aiding one man, he was again struck by enemy mortar fire, this time suffering the loss of his right arm. Although he knew the consequences should immediate aid not be administered, he still refused aid and insisted that all efforts be made for the benefit of others that were wounded. Although unable to perform the task himself, he

remained on the scene and directed others in first-aid techniques. The last man to withdraw, he walked until he collapsed from loss of blood, and died a few minutes later while being carried by his comrades. The extraordinary heroism, outstanding courage, and unswerving devotion to his duties displayed by Pfc. Womack reflect the utmost distinction upon himself and uphold the esteemed traditions of the U.S. Army.

3158 ◆ *YOUNG, ROBERT HARLEY

Rank: Private First Class (highest rank: Corporal)
Service: U.S. Army
Birthday: 4 March 1929
Place of Birth: Oroville, Butte County, California
Date of Death: 5 November 1950
Cemetery: Golden Gate National Cemetery (0-8) (MH)—San Bruno, California
Entered Service at: Vallejo, Solano County, California
Unit: Company E, 8th Cavalry Regiment, 1st Cavalry Division
Battle or Place of Action: north of Kaesong, Korea
Date of Action: 9 October 1950
G.O. Number, Date: 65, 2 August 1951
Date of Presentation: 21 June 1951
Place of Presentation: The Pentagon, presented by Gen. Omar N. Bradley to his Father
Citation: Pfc. Young distinguished himself by conspicuous gallantry and intrepidity above and beyond the call of duty in action. His company, spearheading a battalion drive deep in enemy territory, suddenly came under a devastating barrage of enemy mortar and automatic-weapons crossfire which inflicted heavy casualties among his comrades and wounded him in the face and shoulder. Refusing to be evacuated, Pfc. Young remained in position and continued to fire at the enemy until wounded a second time. As he awaited first aid near the company command post, the enemy attempted an enveloping movement. Disregarding medical treatment he took an exposed position and firing with deadly accuracy killed five of the enemy. During this action he was again hit by hostile fire which knocked him to the ground and destroyed his helmet. Later when supporting tanks moved forward, Pfc. Young, his wounds still unattended, directed tank fire which destroyed three enemy gun positions and enabled the company to advance. Wounded again by an enemy mortar burst, and while aiding several of his injured comrades, he demanded that all others be evacuated first. Throughout the course of this action the leadership and combative instinct displayed by Pfc. Young exerted a profound influence on the conduct of the company. His aggressive example affected the whole course of the action and was responsible for its success. Pfc. Young's dauntless courage and intrepidity reflect the highest credit upon himself and uphold the esteemed traditions of the U.S. Army.

3159 ◆ *ADAMS, WILLIAM EDWARD

Rank: Major
Service: U.S. Army
Birthday: 16 June 1939
Place of Birth: Casper, Natrona County, Wyoming
Date of Death: 25 May 1971
Place of Death: Republic of Vietnam
Cemetery: Fort Logan National Cemetery (P-3831) (MH)—Denver, Colorado
Entered Service at: Kansas City, Clay County, Missouri
Unit: A/227th Assault Helicopter Company, 52d Aviation Battalion, 17th Aviation Group, 1st Aviation Brigade
Served as: Helicopter Pilot
Battle or Place of Action: Kontum Province, Republic of Vietnam
Date of Action: 25 May 1971
G.O. Number, Date: 38, 6 September 1974
Date of Presentation: 8 August 1974
Place of Presentation: Blair House, presented by Vice Pres. Gerald R. Ford to his family
Citation: Maj. Adams distinguished himself on 25 May 1971 while serving as a helicopter pilot in Kontum province in the Republic of Vietnam. On that date, Maj. Adams volunteered to fly a lightly armed helicopter in an attempt to evacuate three seriously wounded soldiers from a small fire base which was under attack by a large enemy force. He made the decision with full knowledge that numerous antiaircraft weapons were positioned around the base and that the clear weather would afford the enemy gunners an unobstructed view of all routes into the base. As he approached the base, the enemy gunners opened fire with heavy machine guns, rocket-propelled grenades, and small arms. Undaunted by the fusillade, he continued his approach determined to accomplish the mission. Displaying tremendous courage under fire, he calmly directed the attacks of supporting gunships while maintaining absolute control of the helicopter he was flying. He landed the aircraft at the fire base despite the ever-increasing enemy fire and calmly waited until the wounded soldiers were placed on board. As his aircraft departed from the fire base, it was struck and seriously damaged by enemy antiaircraft fire and began descending. Flying with exceptional skill, he immediately regained control of the crippled aircraft and attempted a controlled landing. Despite his valiant efforts, the helicopter exploded, overturned, and plummeted to earth amid the hail of enemy fire. Maj. Adams' conspicuous gallantry, intrepidity, and humanitarian regard for his fellow man were in keeping with the most cherished traditions of the military service and reflected utmost credit on him and the U.S. Army.

3160 ◆ *ALBANESE, LEWIS

Rank: Private First Class
Service: U.S. Army
Birthday: 27 April 1946
Place of Birth: Venice, Italy
Date of Death: 1 December 1966
Place of Death: Republic of Vietnam
Cemetery: Evergreen-Washelli Memorial Park—Seattle, Washington
Entered Service at: Seattle, King County, Washington
Unit: Company B, 5th Battalion, 7th Cavalry, 1st Cavalry Division (Airmobile)
Battle or Place of Action: near Phu Muu II, Republic of Vietnam
Date of Action: 1 December 1966
G.O. Number, Date: 12, 3 April 1968
Date of Presentation: 16 February 1968
Place of Presentation: The Pentagon, presented by Sec. of the Army Stanley R. Resor to his family
Citation: For conspicuous gallantry and intrepidity in action at the risk of his life above and beyond the call of duty. Pfc. Albanese's platoon, while advancing through densely covered terrain to establish a blocking position, received intense automatic-weapons fire from close range. As other members maneuvered to assault the enemy position, Pfc. Albanese was ordered to provide security for the left flank of the platoon. Suddenly, the left flank received fire from enemy located in a well-concealed ditch. Realizing the imminent danger to his comrades from this fire, Pfc. Albanese fixed his bayonet and moved aggressively into the ditch. His action silenced the sniper fire, enabling the platoon to resume movement toward the main enemy position. As the platoon continued to advance, the sound of heavy firing emanated from the left flank from a pitched battle that ensued in the ditch which Pfc. Albanese had entered. The ditch was actually a well-organized complex of enemy defenses designed to bring devastating flanking fire on the forces attacking the main position. Pfc. Albanese, disregarding the danger to himself, advanced 100 meters along the trench and killed six of the snipers, who were armed with automatic weapons. Having exhausted his ammunition, Pfc. Albanese was mortally wounded when he engaged and killed two more enemy soldiers in fierce hand-to-hand combat. His unparalleled actions saved the lives of many members of his platoon who otherwise would have fallen to the sniper fire from the ditch, and enabled his platoon to successfully advance against an enemy force of overwhelming numerical superiority. Pfc. Albanese's extraordinary heroism and supreme dedication to his comrades were commensurate with the finest traditions of the military service and remain a tribute to himself, his unit, and the U.S. Army.

3161 ◆ *ANDERSON JR., JAMES

Rank: Private First Class
Service: U.S. Marine Corps
Birthday: 22 January 1947
Place of Birth: Los Angeles, Los Angeles County, California
Date of Death: 28 February 1967
Place of Death: Republic of Vietnam
Cemetery: Lincoln Memorial Park—Compton, California
Entered Service at: Los Angeles, Los Angeles County, California
Unit: 2d Platoon, Company F, 2d Battalion, 3d Marines, 3d Marine Division (Rein) FMF
Served as: Rifleman
Battle or Place of Action: northwest of Cam Lo, Republic of Vietnam
Date of Action: 28 February 1967
Date of Presentation: 21 August 1968
Place of Presentation: Marine Barracks, Washington, D.C., presented by Sec. of the Navy Paul R. Ignatius to his family
Citation: For conspicuous gallantry and intrepidity at the risk of his life above and beyond the call of duty. Company F was advancing in dense jungle northwest of Cam Lo in an effort to extract a heavily besieged reconnaissance patrol. Pfc. Anderson's platoon was the lead element and had advanced only about 200 meters when they were brought under extremely intense enemy small-arms and automatic-weapons fire. The platoon reacted swiftly, getting on line as best they could in the thick terrain, and began returning fire. Pfc. Anderson found himself tightly bunched together with the other members of the platoon only 20 meters from the enemy positions. As the firefight continued several of the men were wounded by the deadly enemy assault. Suddenly, an enemy grenade landed in the midst of the marines and rolled alongside Pfc. Anderson's head. Unhesitatingly and with complete disregard for his personal safety, he reached out, grasped the grenade, pulled it to his chest and curled around it as it went off. Although several marines received shrapnel from the grenade, his body absorbed the major force of the explosion. In this singularly heroic act, Pfc. Anderson saved his comrades from serious injury and possible death. His personal heroism, extraordinary valor, and inspirational supreme self-sacrifice reflected great credit upon himself and the Marine Corps and upheld the highest traditions of the U.S. Naval Service. He gallantly gave his life for his country.

3162 ◆ *ANDERSON, RICHARD ALLEN

Rank: Lance Corporal
Service: U.S. Marine Corps
Birthday: 16 April 1948
Place of Birth: Washington, D.C.
Date of Death: 24 August 1969
Place of Death: Republic of Vietnam
Cemetery: Forest Park Cemetery—Houston, Texas
Entered Service at: Houston, Harris County, Texas
Unit: Company E, 3d Reconnaissance Battalion, 3d Marine Division (Rein) FMF
Served as: Assistant Team Leader
Battle or Place of Action: Quang Tri Province, Republic of Vietnam
Date of Action: 24 August 1969
Date of Presentation: 15 September 1971
Place of Presentation: The White House, presented by Vice Pres. Spiro T. Agnew to his family
Citation: For conspicuous gallantry and intrepidity at the risk of his life above and beyond the call of duty while serving as an assistant team leader with Company E, in connection with combat operations against an armed enemy. While conducting a patrol during the early morning hours L/Cpl. Anderson's reconnaissance team came under a heavy volume of automatic-weapons and machine-gun fire from a numerically superior and well-concealed enemy force. Although painfully wounded in both legs and knocked to the ground during the initial moments of the fierce firefight, L/Cpl. Anderson assumed a prone position and continued to deliver intense suppressive fire in an attempt to repulse the attackers. Moments later he was wounded a second time by an enemy soldier who had approached to within eight feet of the team's position. Undaunted, he continued to pour a relentless stream of fire at the assaulting unit, even while a companion was treating his leg wounds. Observing an enemy grenade land between himself and the other marine, L/Cpl. Anderson immediately rolled over and covered the lethal weapon with his body, absorbing the full effects of the detonation. By his indomitable courage, inspiring initiative, and selfless devotion to duty, L/Cpl. Anderson was instrumental in saving several marines from serious injury or possible death. His actions were in keeping with the highest traditions of the Marine Corps and of the U.S. Naval Service. He gallantly gave his life in the service of his country.

3163 ◆ ANDERSON, WEBSTER

Rank: Sergeant First Class (rank at time of action: Staff Sergeant)
Service: U.S. Army
Birthday: 15 July 1933
Place of Birth: Winnsboro, Fairfield County, South Carolina
Entered Service at: Winnsboro, Fairfield County, South Carolina
Unit: Battery A, 2d Battalion, 320th Artillery, 101st Airborne Division (Airmobile)
Served as: Battery Section Chief
Battle or Place of Action: Tam Ky, Republic of Vietnam
Date of Action: 15 October 1967
G.O. Number, Date: 80, 4 December 1969
Date of Presentation: 24 November 1969
Place of Presentation: The White House, presented by Pres. Richard M. Nixon
Citation: Sfc. Anderson (then S/Sgt.) distinguished himself by conspicuous gallantry and intrepidity in action while serving as chief of section in Battery A, against a hostile force. During the early morning hours Battery A's defensive position was attacked by a determined North Vietnamese Army infantry unit supported by heavy mortar, recoilless-rifle, rocket-propelled-grenade and automatic-weapons fire. The initial enemy onslaught breached the battery defensive perimeter. Sfc. Anderson, with complete disregard for his personal safety,

mounted the exposed parapet of his howitzer position and became the mainstay of the defense of the battery position. Sfc. Anderson directed devastating direct howitzer fire on the assaulting enemy while providing rifle and grenade defensive fire against enemy soldiers attempting to overrun his gun section position. While protecting his crew and directing their fire against the enemy from his exposed position, two enemy grenades exploded at his feet knocking him down and severely wounding him in the legs. Despite the excruciating pain and though not able to stand, Sfc. Anderson valorously propped himself on the parapet and continued to direct howitzer fire upon the closing enemy and to encourage his men to fight on. Seeing an enemy grenade land within the gun pit near a wounded member of his gun crew, Sfc. Anderson heedless of his own safety, seized the grenade and attempted to throw it over the parapet to save his men. As the grenade was thrown from the position it exploded and Sfc. Anderson was again grievously wounded. Although only partially conscious and severely wounded, Sfc. Anderson refused medical evacuation and continued to encourage his men in the defense of the position. Sfc. Anderson, by his inspirational leadership, professionalism, devotion to duty, and complete disregard for his welfare, was able to maintain the defense of his section position and to defeat a determined attack. Sfc. Anderson's gallantry and extraordinary heroism at the risk of his life above and beyond the call of duty are in the highest traditions of the military service and reflect great credit upon himself, his unit, and the U.S. Army.

3164 ◆ *ASHLEY JR., EUGENE

Rank: Sergeant First Class
Service: U.S. Army
Birthday: 12 October 1931
Place of Birth: Wilmington, New Hanover County, North Carolina
Date of Death: 7 February 1968
Place of Death: Republic of Vietnam
Cemetery: Rochfish Memorial Cemetery (MH)—Fayetteville, North Carolina
Entered Service at: New York, New York
Unit: Detachment A-101, Company C, 5th Special Forces Group (Airborne), 1st Special Forces
Served as: Senior Advisor
Battle or Place of Action: near Lang Vei, Republic of Vietnam
Date of Action: 6-7 February 1968
G.O. Number, Date: 84, 12 December 1969
Date of Presentation: 2 December 1969
Place of Presentation: The White House, presented by Vice Pres. Spiro T. Agnew to his family
Citation: Sfc. Ashley distinguished himself by conspicuous gallantry and intrepidity while serving with Detachment A-101, Company C. Sfc. Ashley was the senior Special Forces Advisor of a hastily organized assault force whose mission was to rescue entrapped U.S. Special Forces advisers at Camp Lang Vei. During the initial attack on the Special Forces camp by North Vietnamese Army forces, Sfc. Ashley supported the camp with high-explosive and illumination mortar rounds. When communications were lost with the main camp, he assumed the additional responsibility of directing air strikes and artillery support. Sfc. Ashley organized and equipped a small assault force composed of local friendly personnel. During the ensuing battle, Sfc. Ashley led a total of five vigorous assaults against the enemy, continuously exposing himself to a voluminous hail of enemy grenades, machine gun and automatic-weapons fire. Throughout these assaults, he was plagued by numerous boobytrapped satchel charges in all bunkers on his avenue of approach. During his fifth and final assault, he adjusted air strikes nearly on top of his assault element, forcing the enemy to withdraw and resulting in friendly control of the summit of the hill. While exposing himself to intense enemy fire, he was seriously wounded by machine-gun fire but continued his mission without regard for his personal safety. After the fifth assault he lost consciousness and was carried from the summit by his comrades only to suffer a fatal wound when an enemy artillery round landed in the area. Sfc. Ashley displayed extraordinary heroism in risking his life in an attempt to save the lives of his entrapped comrades and commanding officer. His total disregard for his personal safety while exposed to enemy observation and automatic-weapons fire was an inspiration to all men committed to the assault. The resolute valor with which he led five gallant charges placed critical diversionary pressure on the attacking enemy and his valiant efforts carved a channel in the overpowering enemy forces and weapons positions through which the survivors of Camp Lang Vei eventually escaped to freedom. Sfc. Ashley's bravery at the cost of his life was in the highest traditions of the military service, and reflects great credit upon himself, his unit, and the U.S. Army.

3165 ◆ *AUSTIN, OSCAR PALMER

Rank: Private First Class
Service: U.S. Marine Corps
Birthday: 15 January 1948
Place of Birth: Nacogdoches, Nacogdoches County, Texas
Date of Death: 23 February 1969
Place of Death: Republic of Vietnam
Cemetery: Greenwood Memorial Park—Phoenix, Arizona
Entered Service at: Phoenix, Maricopa County, Arizona
Unit: Company E, 2d Battalion, 7th Marines, 1st Marine Division (Rein) FMF
Served as: Assistant Machine Gunner
Battle or Place of Action: west of Da Nang, Republic of Vietnam
Date of Action: 23 February 1969
Date of Presentation: 20 April 1970
Place of Presentation: The White House, presented by Vice Pres. Spiro T. Agnew to his family
Citation: For conspicuous gallantry and intrepidity at the risk of his life above and beyond the call of duty while serving as an assistant machine gunner with Company E, in connection with operations against enemy forces. During the early morning hours Pfc. Austin's observation post was subjected to a fierce ground attack by a large North Vietnamese Army force supported by a heavy volume of hand grenades, satchel charges, and small-arms fire. Observing that one of his

wounded companions had fallen unconscious in a position dangerously exposed to the hostile fire, Pfc. Austin unhesitatingly left the relative security of his fighting hole and, with complete disregard for his safety, raced across the fire-swept terrain to assist the marine to a covered location. As he neared the casualty, he observed an enemy grenade land nearby and reacting instantly, leaped between the injured marine and the lethal object, absorbing the effects of its detonation. As he ignored his painful injuries and turned to examine the wounded man, he saw a North Vietnamese Army soldier aiming a weapon at his unconscious companion. With full knowledge of the probable consequences and thinking only to protect the marine, Pfc. Austin resolutely threw himself between the casualty and the hostile soldier, and in so doing, was mortally wounded. Pfc. Austin's indomitable courage, inspiring initiative and selfless devotion to duty upheld the highest traditions of the Marine Corps and the U.S. Naval Service. He gallantly gave his life for his country.

3166 ◆ BACA, JOHN PHILIP

Rank: Specialist Fourth Class (highest rank: Sergeant)
Service: U.S. Army
Birthday: 10 January 1949
Place of Birth: Providence, Providence County, Rhode Island
Entered Service at: Fort Ord, Monterey County, California
Unit: 4th Platoon, Company D, 1st Battalion, 12th Cavalry, 1st Cavalry Division
Served as: Recoilless Rifle Team Member
Battle or Place of Action: near Quan Loi, Phuoc Long Province, Republic of Vietnam
Date of Action: 10 February 1970
G.O. Number, Date: 37, 16 July 1971
Date of Presentation: 15 June 1971
Place of Presentation: The White House (East Ballroom), presented by Pres. Richard M. Nixon
Citation: For conspicuous gallantry and intrepidity in action at the risk of his life above and beyond the call of duty. Sp4c. Baca, Company D, distinguished himself while serving on a recoilless-rifle team during a night ambush mission. A platoon from his company was sent to investigate the detonation of an automatic ambush device forward of his unit's main position and soon came under intense enemy fire from concealed positions along the trail. Hearing the heavy firing from the platoon position and realizing that his recoilless-rifle team could assist the members of the besieged patrol, Sp4c. Baca led his team through the hail of enemy fire to a firing position within the patrol's defensive perimeter. As they prepared to engage the enemy, a fragmentation grenade was thrown into the midst of the patrol. Fully aware of the danger to his comrades, Sp4c. Baca unhesitatingly and with complete disregard for his own safety, covered the grenade with his steel helmet and fell on it as the grenade exploded, thereby absorbing the lethal fragments and concussion with his body. His gallant action and total disregard for his personal well-being directly saved eight men from certain serious injury or death. The extraordinary courage and selflessness displayed by Sp4c.

Baca, at the risk of his life, are in the highest traditions of the military service and reflect great credit on him, his unit, and the U.S. Army.

3167 ◆ BACON, NICKY DANIEL

Rank: Staff Sergeant (highest rank: First Sergeant)
Service: U.S. Army
Birthday: 25 November 1945
Place of Birth: Caraway, Craighead County, Arkansas
Entered Service at: Phoenix, Maricopa County, Arizona
Unit: Company B, 4th Battalion, 21st Infantry, 11th Infantry Brigade, Americal Division
Served as: Squad Leader
Battle or Place of Action: west of Tam Ky, Republic of Vietnam
Date of Action: 26 August 1968
G.O. Number, Date: 81, 4 December 1969
Date of Presentation: 24 November 1969
Place of Presentation: The White House, presented by Pres. Richard M. Nixon
Citation: For conspicuous gallantry and intrepidity in action at the risk of his life above and beyond the call of duty. S/Sgt. Bacon distinguished himself while serving as a squad leader with the 1st Platoon, Company B, during an operation west of Tam Ky. When Company B came under fire from an enemy bunker line to the front, S/Sgt. Bacon quickly organized his men and led them forward in an assault. He advanced on a hostile bunker and destroyed it with grenades. As he did so, several fellow soldiers, including the 1st Platoon leader, were struck by machine-gun fire and fell wounded in an exposed position forward of the rest of the platoon. S/Sgt. Bacon immediately assumed command of the platoon and assaulted the hostile gun position, finally killing the enemy gun crew in a singlehanded effort. When the 3d Platoon moved to S/Sgt. Bacon's location, its leader was also wounded. Without hesitation S/Sgt. Bacon took charge of the additional platoon and continued the fight. In the ensuing action he personally killed four more enemy soldiers and silenced an antitank weapon. Under his leadership and example, the members of both platoons accepted his authority without question. Continuing to ignore the intense hostile fire, he climbed up on the exposed deck of a tank and directed fire into the enemy position while several wounded men were evacuated. As a result of S/Sgt. Bacon's extraordinary efforts, his company was able to move forward, eliminate the enemy positions, and rescue the men trapped to the front. S/Sgt. Bacon's bravery at the risk of his life was in the highest traditions of the military service and reflects great credit upon himself, his unit, and the U.S. Army.

3168 ◆ BAKER JR., JOHN FRANKLIN

Rank: Sergeant (rank at time of action: Private First Class) (highest rank: Master Sergeant)
Service: U.S. Army
Birthday: 30 October 1945
Place of Birth: Davenport, Scott County, Iowa
Entered Service at: Moline, Rock Island County, Illinois

Unit: Company A, 2d Battalion, 27th Infantry, 25th Infantry Division
Served as: Machine Gunner
Battle or Place of Action: near Dau Tieng, Republic of Vietnam
Date of Action: 5 November 1966
G.O. Number, Date: 24, 13 June 1968
Date of Presentation: 1 May 1968
Place of Presentation: The White House (East Ballroom), presented by Pres. Lyndon B. Johnson
Citation: For conspicuous gallantry and intrepidity in action at the risk of his life above and beyond the call of duty. En route to assist another unit that was engaged with the enemy, Company A came under intense enemy fire and the lead man was killed instantly. Sgt. Baker immediately moved to the head of the column and together with another soldier knocked out two enemy bunkers. When his comrade was mortally wounded, Sgt. Baker, spotting four Viet Cong snipers, killed all of them, evacuated the fallen soldier, and returned to lead repeated assaults against the enemy positions, killing several more Viet Cong. Moving to attack two additional enemy bunkers, he and another soldier drew intense enemy fire and Sgt. Baker was blown from his feet by an enemy grenade. He quickly recovered and singlehandedly destroyed one bunker before the other soldier was wounded. Seizing his fallen comrade's machine gun, Sgt. Baker charged through the deadly fusillade to silence the other bunker. He evacuated his comrade, replenished his ammunition, and returned to the forefront to brave the enemy fire and continue the fight. When the forward element was ordered to withdraw, he carried one wounded man to the rear. As he returned to evacuate another soldier, he was taken under fire by snipers, but raced beyond the friendly troops to attack and kill the snipers. After evacuating the wounded man, he returned to cover the deployment of the unit. His ammunition now exhausted, he dragged two more of his fallen comrades to the rear. Sgt. Baker's selfless heroism, indomitable fighting spirit, and extraordinary gallantry were directly responsible for saving the lives of several of his comrades, and inflicting serious damage on the enemy. His acts were in keeping with the highest traditions of the U.S. Army and reflect great credit upon himself and the Armed Forces of his country.

3169 ◆ BALLARD, DONALD EVERETT

Rank: Hospital Corpsman Second Class (current rank: Lieutenant Colonel (ARNG)
Service: U.S. Navy
Birthday: 5 December 1945
Place of Birth: Kansas City, Clay County, Missouri
Entered Service at: Kansas City, Clay County, Missouri
Unit: Company M, 3d Battalion, 4th Marines, 3d Marine Division
Served as: Medical Corpsman
Battle or Place of Action: Quang Tri Province, Republic of Vietnam
Date of Action: 16 May 1968
Date of Presentation: 14 May 1970

Place of Presentation: The White House, presented by Pres. Richard M. Nixon
Citation: For conspicuous gallantry and intrepidity at the risk of his life above and beyond the call of duty while serving as a HC2c. with Company M, in connection with operations against enemy aggressor forces. During the afternoon hours, Company M was moving to join the remainder of the 3d Battalion in Quang Tri province. After treating and evacuating two heat casualies, HC2c. Ballard was returning to his platoon from the evacuation landing zone when the company was ambushed by a North Vietnamese Army unit employing automatic weapons and mortars, and sustained numerous casualies. Observing a wounded marine, HC2c. Ballard unhesitatingly moved across the fire-swept terrain to the injured man and swiftly rendered medical assistance to his comrade. HC2c. Ballard then directed four marines to carry the casualty to a position of relative safety. As the four men prepared to move the wounded marine, an enemy soldier suddenly left his concealed position and, after hurling a hand grenade which landed near the casualty, commenced firing upon the small group of men. Instantly shouting a warning to the marines, HC2c. Ballard fearlessly threw himself upon the lethal explosive device to protect his comrades from the deadly blast. When the grenade failed to detonate, he calmly arose from his dangerous position and resolutely continued his determined efforts in treating other marine casualties. HC2c. Ballard's heroic actions and selfless concern for the welfare of his companions served to inspire all who observed him and prevented possible injury or death to his fellow marines. His courage, daring initiative, and unwavering devotion to duty in the face of extreme personal danger, sustain and enhance the finest traditions of the U.S. Naval Service.

3170 ◆ *BARKER, JEDH COLBY

Rank: Lance Corporal
Service: U.S. Marine Corps
Birthday: 20 June 1945
ce of Birth: Franklin, Merrimack County, New Hampshire
Date of Death: 21 September 1967
Place of Death: Republic of Vietnam
Cemetery: George Washington Memorial Cemetery (MH)—Paramus, New Jersey
Entered Service at: Park Ridge, Bergen County, New Jersey
Unit: Company F, 2d Battalion, 4th Marines, 3d Marine Division (Rein) FMF
Served as: Machine Gunner
Battle or Place of Action: near Con Thein, Republic of Vietnam
Date of Action: 21 September 1967
Date of Presentation: 31 October 1969
Place of Presentation: The White House, presented by Vice Pres. Spiro T. Agnew to his family
Citation: For conspicuous gallantry and intrepidity at the risk of his life above and beyond the call of duty while serving as a machine gunner with Company F. During a reconnaissance operation L/Cpl. Barker's squad was suddenly hit by enemy sniper fire. The squad immediately deployed to a combat formation and advanced to a strongly fortified enemy

position, when it was again struck by small-arms and auto-matic-weapons fire, sustaining numerous casualties. Although wounded by the initial burst of fire, L/Cpl. Barker boldly remained in the open, delivering a devastating volume of accurate fire on the numerically superior force. The enemy was intent upon annihilating the small marine force and, real-izing that L/Cpl. Barker was a threat to their position, direct-ed the preponderance of their fire on his position. He was again wounded, this time in the right hand, which prevented him from operating his vitally needed machine gun. Suddenly and without warning, an enemy grenade landed in the midst of the few surviving marines. Unhesitatingly and with com-plete disregard for his personal safety, L/Cpl. Barker threw himself upon the deadly grenade, absorbing with his body the full and tremendous force of the explosion. In a final act of bravery, he crawled to the side of a wounded comrade and administered first aid before succumbing to his grievous wounds. His bold initiative, intrepid fighting spirit and unwa-vering devotion to duty in the face of almost certain death undoubtedly saved his comrades from further injury or possi-ble death and reflect great credit upon himself, the Marine Corps, and the U.S. Naval Service. He gallantly gave his life for his country.

3171 ◆ *BARNES III, JOHN ANDREW

Rank: Private First Class
Service: U.S. Army
Birthday: 16 April 1945
Place of Birth: Boston, Suffolk County, Massachusetts
Date of Death: 12 November 1967
Place of Death: Republic of Vietnam
Cemetery: Brookdale Cemetery (MH)—Dedham, Massachusetts
Entered Service at: Boston, Suffolk County, Massachusetts
Unit: Company C, 1st Battalion, 503d Infantry, 173d Airborne Brigade
Served as: Grenadier
Battle or Place of Action: Dak To, Republic of Vietnam
Date of Action: 12 November 1967
G.O. Number, Date: 73, 20 November 1969
Date of Presentation: 4 November 1969
Place of Presentation: The White House, presented by Vice Pres. Spiro T. Agnew to his family
Citation: For conspicuous gallantry and intrepidity in action at the risk of his life above and beyond the call of duty. Pfc. Barnes distinguished himself by exceptional heroism while engaged in combat against hostile forces. Pfc. Barnes was serving as a grenadier when his unit was attacked by a North Vietnamese force, estimated to be a battalion. Upon seeing the crew of a machine-gun team killed, Pfc. Barnes, without hesitation, dashed through the bullet-swept area, manned the machinegun, and killed nine enemy soldiers as they assaulted his position. While pausing just long enough to retrieve more ammunition, Pfc. Barnes observed an enemy grenade thrown into the midst of some severely wounded personnel close to his position. Realizing that the grenade could further injure or kill the majority of the wounded presonnel, he sacrificed his life by throwing himself directly onto the hand grenade as

it exploded. Through his indomitable courage, complete dis-regard for his own safety, and profound concern for his fellow soldiers, he averted a probable loss of life and injury to the wounded members of his unit. Pfc. Barnes' extraordinary heroism and intrepidity at the cost of his life, above and beyond the call of duty, are in the highest traditions of mili-tary service and reflect great credit upon himself, his unit, and the U.S. Army.

3172 ◆ BARNUM JR., HARVEY CURTISS "BARNEY"

Rank: Captain (rank at time of action: First Lieutenant) (highest rank: Colonel)
Service: U.S. Marine Corps
Birthday: 21 July 1940
Place of Birth: Cheshire, New Haven County, Connecticut
Entered Service at: Cheshire, New Haven County, Connecticut
Unit: Company H, 2d Battalion, 9th Marines, 3d Marine Division (Rein) FMF
Served as: Forward Observer
Battle or Place of Action: outside the village of Ky Phu, Quang Tin Province, Republic of Vietnam
Date of Action: 18 December 1965
Date of Presentation: 27 February 1967
Place of Presentation: Marine Barracks, Washington, D.C., presented by Sec. of the Navy Paul H. Nitze
Citation: For conspicuous gallantry and intrepidity at the risk of his life above and beyond the call of duty. When the company was suddenly pinned down by a hail of extremely accurate enemy fire and was quickly separated from the remainder of the battalion by over 500 meters of open and fire-swept ground and casualties mounted rapidly, Lt. Barnum quickly made a hazardous reconnaissance of the area, seeking targets for his artillery. Finding the rifle company commander mortally wounded and the radio operator killed, he, with complete disregard for his safety, gave aid to the dying com-mander, then removed the radio from the dead operator and strapped it to himself. He immediately assumed command of the rifle company, and moving at once into the midst of the heavy fire, rallying and giving encouragement to all units, reorganizing them to replace the loss of key personnel and lead their attack on enemy positions from which deadly fire continued to come. His sound and swift decisions and his obvious calm served to stabalize the badly decimated units and his gallant example as he stood exposed repeatedly to point out targets served as an inspiration to all. Provided with two armed helicopters, he moved fearlessly through enemy fire to control the air attacks against the firmly entrenched enemy while skillfully directing one platoon in a successful counterattack on the key enemy positions. Having thus cleared a small area, he requested and directed the landing of two transport helicopters for the evacuation of the dead and wounded. He then assisted in the mopping-up and final seizure of the battalion's objective. His gallant initiative and heroic conduct reflected great credit upon himself and were in keeping with the highest traditions of the Marine Corps and the U.S. Naval Service.

3173 ◆ BEIKIRCH, GARY BURNELL

Rank: Sergeant
Service: U.S. Army
Birthday: 29 August 1947
Place of Birth: Rochester, Monroe County, New York
Entered Service at: Buffalo, Erie County, New York
Unit: Detachment 8245, Company B, 5th Special Forces Group (Airborne), 1st Special Forces
Served as: Medical Aidman
Battle or Place of Action: Dak Seang Special Forces A Camp, Kontum Province, Republic of Vietnam
Date of Action: 1 April 1970
G.O. Number, Date: 37, 5 November 1973
Date of Presentation: 15 October 1973
Place of Presentation: The White House, presented by Pres. Richard M. Nixon
Citation: For conspicuous gallantry and intrepidity in action at the risk of his life above and beyond the call of duty. Sgt. Beikirch, medical aidman, Detachment B-24, Company B, distinguished himself during the defense of Camp Dak Seang. The allied defenders suffered a number of casualties as a result of an intense, devastating attack launched by the enemy from well-concealed positions surrounding the camp. Sgt. Beikirch, with complete disregard for his personal safety, moved unhesitatingly through the withering enemy fire to his fallen comrades, applied first aid to their wounds and assisted them to the medical-aid station. When informed that a seriously injured American officer was lying in an exposed position, Sgt. Beikirch ran immediately through the hail of fire. Although he was wounded seriously by fragments from an exploding enemy mortar shell, Sgt. Beikirch carried the officer to a medical aid station. Ignoring his own serious injuries, Sgt. Beikirch left the relative safety of the medical bunker to search for and evacuate other men who had been injured. He was again wounded as he dragged a critically injured Vietnamese soldier to the medical bunker while simultaneously applying mouth-to-mouth resuscitation to sustain his life. Sgt. Beikirch again refused treatment and continued his search for other casualties until he collapsed. Only then did he permit himself to be treated. Sgt. Beikirch's complete devotion to the welfare of his comrades, at the risk of his life, are in keeping with the highest traditions of the military service and reflect great credit on him, his unit, and the U.S. Army.

3174 ◆ *BELCHER, TED

Rank: Sergeant
Service: U.S. Army
Birthday: 21 July 1924
Place of Birth: Accoville, Logan County, West Virginia
Date of Death: 19 November 1966
Place of Death: Republic of Vietnam
Cemetery: Greenwood Cemetery—Zanesville, Ohio
Entered Service at: Huntington, Cabell County, West Virginia
Unit: Company C, 1st Battalion, 14th Infantry, 25th Infantry Division
Served as: Squad Leader
Battle or Place of Action: Plei Djerang, Republic of Vietnam
Date of Action: 19 November 1966
G.O. Number, Date: 82, 20 December 1968
Date of Presentation: 6 December 1968
Place of Presentation: The Pentagon, presented by Sec. of the Army Stanley R. Resor to his family
Citation: Distinguishing himself by conspicuous gallantry and intrepidity at the risk of his life. Sgt. Belcher's unit was engaged in a search-and-destroy mission with Company B, 1st Battalion, 14th Infantry, the Battalion Reconnaissance Platoon, and a Special Forces company of Civilian Irregular Defense Group personnel. As a squad leader of the 2d Platoon of Company C, Sgt. Belcher was leading his men when they encountered a bunker complex. The reconnaissance platoon, located a few hundred meters northwest of Company C, received a heavy volume of fire from well-camouflaged snipers. As the 2d Platoon moved forward to assist the unit under attack, Sgt. Belcher and his squad, advancing only a short distance through the dense jungle terrain, met heavy and accurate automatic-weapons and sniper fire. Sgt. Belcher and his squad were momentarily stopped by the deadly volume of enemy fire. He quickly gave the order to return fire and resume the advance toward the enemy. As he moved up with his men, a hand grenade landed in the midst of the sergeant's squad. Instantly realizing the immediate danger to his men, Sgt. Belcher, unhesitatingly and with complete disregard for his safety, lunged forward, covering the grenade with his body. Absorbing the grenade blast at the cost of his life, he saved his comrades from becoming casualties. Sgt. Belcher's profound concern for his fellow soldiers, at the risk of his life above and beyond the call of duty, are in keeping with the highest tradition of the U.S. Army and reflect credit upon himself and the Armed Forces of his country.

3175 ◆ *BELLRICHARD, LESLIE ALLEN

Rank: Private First Class
Service: U.S. Army
Birthday: 4 December 1941
Place of Birth: Janesville, Rock County, Wisconsin
Date of Death: 20 May 1967
Place of Death: Republic of Vietnam
Cemetery: Oakhill Cemetery (MH)—Janesville, Wisconsin
Entered Service at: Oakland, Alameda County, California
Unit: Company C, 1st Battalion, 8th Infantry, 4th Infantry Division
Served as: Fire Team Leader
Battle or Place of Action: Kontum Province, Republic of Vietnam
Date of Action: 20 May 1967
G.O. Number, Date: 53, 8 August 1969
Date of Presentation: 10 July 1969
Place of Presentation: The White House, presented by Pres. Richard M. Nixon to his family
Citation: For conspicuous gallantry and intrepidity in action at the risk of his life above and beyond the call of duty.

Acting as a fire-team leader with Company C during combat operations Pfc. Bellrichard was with four fellow soldiers in a foxhole on their unit's perimeter when the position came under a massive enemy attack. Following a 30-minute mortar barrage, the enemy launched a strong ground assault. Pfc. Bellrichard rose in face of a group of charging enemy soldiers and threw hand grenades into their midst, eliminating several of the foe and forcing the remainder to withdraw. Failing in their initial attack, the enemy repeated the mortar and rocket bombardment of the friendly perimeter, then once again charged against the defenders in a concerted effort to overrun the position. Pfc. Bellrichard resumed throwing hand grenades at the onrushing attackers. As he was about to hurl a grenade, a mortar round exploded just in front of his position, knocking him into the foxhole and causing him to lose his grip on the already armed grenade. Recovering instantly, Pfc. Bellrichard recognized the threat to the lives of his four comrades and threw himself upon the grenade, shielding his companions from the blast that followed. Although seriously wounded, Pfc. Bellrichard struggled into an upright position in the foxhole and fired his rifle at the enemy until he succumbed to his wounds. His selfless heroism contributed greatly to the successful defense of the position, and he was directly responsible for saving the lives of several of his comrades. His acts are in keeping with the highest traditions of the military service and reflect great credit upon himself and the U.S. Army.

3176 ◆ BENAVIDEZ, ROY PEREZ

Rank: Master Sergeant (rank at time of action: Staff Sergeant)
Service: U.S. Army
Birthday: 5 August 1935
Place of Birth: Cuero, DeWitt County, Texas
Entered Service at: Houston, Harris County, Texas
Unit: 5th Special Forces Group (Airborne), Detachment B-56, 1st Special Forces
Served as: Operation Intelligence Sergeant
Battle or Place of Action: west of Loc Ninh, Cambodia
Date of Action: 2 May 1968
G.O. Number, Date: 8, 16 March 1981
Date of Presentation: 24 February 1981
Place of Presentation: The Pentagon (courtyard), presented by Pres. Ronald Reagan
Citation: M/Sgt. (then S/Sgt.) Roy P. Benavidez, 455-02-5039, United States Army, who distinguished himself by a series of daring and extremely valorous actions on 2 May 1968 while assigned to Detachment B-56, 5th Special Forces Group (Airborne), 1st Special Forces, Republic of Vietnam. On the morning of 2 May 1968, a 12-man Special Forces Reconnaissance Team was inserted by helicopters in a dense jungle area west of Loc Ninh, Vietnam, to gather intelligence information about confirmed large-scale enemy activity. This area was controlled and routinely patrolled by the North Vietnamese Army. After a short period of time on the ground, the team met heavy enemy resistance, and requested emergency extraction. Three helicopters attempted extraction, but were unable to land due to intense enemy small-arms and anti-aircraft fire. Sgt. Benavidez was at the Forward Operating Base in Loc Ninh monitoring the operation by radio when these helicopters returned to off-load wounded crewmembers and to assess aircraft damage. Sgt. Benavidez voluntarily boarded a returning aircraft to assist in another extraction attempt. Realizing that all the team members were either dead or wounded and unable to move to the pickup zone, he directed the aircraft to a nearby clearing while he jumped from the hovering helicopter, and ran approximately 75 meters under withering small-arms fire to the crippled team. Prior to reaching the team's position he was wounded in his right leg, face, and head. Despite these painful injuries, he took charge, repositioning the team members and directing their fire to facilitate the landing of the extraction aircraft and the loading of the wounded and dead team members. He then threw smoke canisters to direct the aircraft to the team's position. Despite his severe wounds and under intense enemy fire, he carried and dragged half of the wounded team members to the awaiting aircraft. He then provided protective fire by running alongside the aircraft as it moved to pick up the remaining team members. As the enemy's fire intensified, he hurried to recover the body and classified documents on the dead team leader. When he reached the leader's body, Sgt. Benavidez was severely wounded by small-arms fire in the abdomen and grenade fragments in his back. At nearly the same moment, the aircraft pilot was mortally wounded, and his helicopter crashed. Although in extremely critical condition due to his multiple wounds, Sgt. Benavidez secured the classified documents and made his way back to the wreckage, where he aided the wounded out of the overturned aircraft, and gathered the stunned survivors into a defensive perimeter. Under increasing enemy automatic-weapons and grenade fire, he moved around the perimeter distributing water and ammunition to his weary men, reinstilling in them a will to live and fight. Facing a buildup of enemy opposition with a beleaguered team, Sgt. Benavidez mustered his strength, began calling in tactical air strikes and directed the fire from supporting gunships to suppress the enemy's fire and so permitted another extraction attempt. He was wounded again in his thigh by small-arms fire while administering first aid to a wounded team member just before another extraction helicopter was able to land. His indomitable spirit kept him going as he began to ferry his comrades to the craft. On his second trip with the wounded, he was clubbed from additional wounds to his head and arms before killing his adversary. He then continued under devastating fire to carry the wounded to the helicopter. Upon reaching the aircraft, he spotted and killed two enemy soldiers who were rushing the craft from an angle that prevented the aircraft door-gunner from firing upon them. With little strength remaining, he made one last trip to the perimeter to ensure that all classified material had been collected or destroyed and to bring in the remaining wounded. Only then, in extremely serious condition from numerous wounds and loss of blood, did he allow himself to be pulled into the extraction aircraft. Sgt. Benavidez' gallant choice to join voluntarily his comrades who were in critical straits, to expose himself constantly to withering enemy fire, and his refusal to be stopped despite numerous severe wounds, saved the lives of at least eight

men. His fearless personal leadership, tenacious devotion to duty, and extremely valorous actions in the face of overwhelming odds were in keeping with the highest traditions of the military service and reflect the utmost credit on him and the United States Army.

3177 ◆ *BENNETT, STEVEN LOGAN

Rank: Captain
Service: U.S. Air Force
Birthday: 22 April 1946
Place of Birth: Palestine, Anderson County, Texas
Date of Death: 29 June 1972
Place of Death: Gulf of Tonkin
Cemetery: Lafayette Memorial Park—Lafayette, Louisiana
Entered Service at: Lafayette, Lafayette County, Louisiana
Unit: 20th Tactical Air Support Squadron, Da Nang Air Base, Pacific Air Forces
Served as: Forward Air Controller; Pilot of a OV-10 Bronco
Battle or Place of Action: Quang Tri Province, Republic of Vietnam
Date of Action: 29 June 1972
G.O. Number, Date: GB-1007, 6 September 1974
Date of Presentation: 8 August 1974
Place of Presentation: Blair House, presented by Vice Pres. Gerald R. Ford to his family
Citation: Capt. Bennett was the pilot of a light aircraft flying an artillery adjustment mission along a heavily defended segment of route structure. A large concentration of enemy troops were massing for an attack on a friendly unit. Capt. Bennett requested tactical air support but was advised that none was available. He also requested artillery support, but this too was denied due to the close proximity of friendly troops to the target. Capt. Bennett was determined to aid the endangered unit and elected to strafe the hostile positions. After four such passes, the enemy forces began to retreat. Capt. Bennett continued the attack, but, as he completed his fifth strafing pass, his aircraft was struck by a surface-to-air missile which severely damaged the left engine and the left main landing gear. As fire spread in the left engine, Capt. Bennett realized that recovery at a friendly airfield was impossible. He instructed his observer to prepare for ejection, but was informed by the observer that his parachute had been shredded by the force of the impacting missile. Although Capt. Bennett had a good parachute, he knew that if he ejected, the observer would have no chance of survival. With complete disregard for his own life, Capt. Bennett elected to ditch the aircraft into the Gulf of Tonkin, even though he realized that a pilot of this type aircraft had never survived a ditching. The ensuing impact upon the water caused the aircraft to cartwheel and severely damage the front cockpit, making escape for Capt. Bennett impossible. The observer successfully made his way out of the aircraft and was rescued. Capt. Bennett's unparalleled concern for his companion, extraordinary heroism, and intrepidity above and beyond the call of duty, at the cost of his life, were in keeping with the highest traditions of the military service and reflect great credit upon himself and the U.S. Air Force.

3178 ◆ *BENNETT, THOMAS WILLIAM

Rank: Corporal
Service: U.S. Army
Birthday: 7 April 1947
Place of Birth: Morgantown, Monongalia County, West Virginia
Date of Death: 11 February 1969
Place of Death: Republic of Vietnam
Cemetery: East Oak Grove Cemetery—Morgantown, West Virginia
Entered Service at: Fairmont, Marion County, West Virginia
Unit: 2d Platoon, Company B, 1st Battalion, 14th Infantry, 4th Infantry Division
Served as: Medical Aidman
Battle or Place of Action: Chu Pa Region, Pleiku Province, Republic of Vietnam
Date of Action: 9-11 February 1969
G.O. Number, Date: 10, 23 April 1970
Date of Presentation: 7 April 1970
Place of Presentation: The White House (Oval Office), presented by Pres. Richard M. Nixon to his family
Citation: For conspicuous gallantry and intrepidity in action at the risk of his life above and beyond the call of duty. Cpl. Bennett distinguished himself while serving as a platoon medical aidman with the 2d Platoon, Company B, during a reconnaissance-in-force mission. On 9 February the platoon was moving to assist the 1st Platoon of Company D, which had run into a North Vietnamese ambush, when it became heavily engaged by the intense small-arms, automatic-weapons, mortar and rocket fire from a well-fortified and numerically superior enemy unit. In the initial barrage of fire, three of the point members of the platoon fell wounded. Cpl. Bennett, with complete disregard for his safety, ran through the heavy fire to his fallen comrades, administered life-saving first aid under fire, and then made repeated trips carrying the wounded men to positions of relative safety from which they would be medically evacuated from the battle position. Cpl. Bennett repeatedly braved the intense enemy fire, moving across open areas to give aid and comfort to his wounded comrades. He valiantly exposed himself to the heavy fire in order to retrieve the bodies of several fallen personnel. Throughout the night and following day, Cpl. Bennett moved from position to position treating and comforting several personnel who had suffered shrapnel and gunshot wounds. On 11 February, Company B again moved in an assault on the well-fortified enemy positions and became heavily engaged with the numerically superior enemy force. Five members of the company fell wounded in the initial assault. Cpl. Bennett ran to their aid without regard to the heavy fire. He treated one wounded comrade and began running toward another seriously wounded man. Although the wounded man was located forward of the company position covered by heavy enemy grazing fire and Cpl. Bennett was warned that it was impossible to reach the position, he leaped forward with complete disregard for his safety to save his comrade's life. In an attempt to save his fellow soldier, he was mortally wounded. Cpl. Bennett's undaunted concern for his comrades at the cost of his life

above and beyond the call of duty are in keeping with the highest traditions of the military service and reflect great credit upon himself, his unit, and the U.S. Army.

3179 ◆ *BLANCHFIELD, MICHAEL REINERT

Rank: Specialist Fourth Class
Service: U.S. Army
Birthday: 4 January 1950
Place of Birth: Minneapolis, Hennepin County, Minnesota
Date of Death: 3 July 1969
Place of Death: Republic of Vietnam
Cemetery: All Saints Cemetery (MH)—Des Plains, Illinois
Entered Service at: Chicago, Cook County, Illinois
Unit: Company A, 4th Battalion, 503d Infantry, 173d Airborne Brigade
Served as: Rifleman
Battle or Place of Action: Binh Dinh Province, Republic of Vietnam
Date of Action: 3 July 1969
G.O. Number, Date: 25, 21 May 1971
Date of Presentation: 22 April 1971
Place of Presentation: The White House, presented by Pres. Richard M. Nixon to his family
Citation: For conspicuous gallantry and intrepidity in action at the risk of his life above and beyond the call of duty. Sp4c. Blanchfield distinguished himself while serving as a rifleman in Company A on a combat patrol. The patrol surrounded a group of houses to search for suspects. During the search of one of the huts, a man suddenly ran out toward a nearby treeline. Sp4c. Blanchfield, who was on guard outside the hut, saw the man, shouted for him to halt, and began firing at him as the man ignored the warning and continued to run. The suspect suddenly threw a grenade toward the hut and its occupants. Although the exploding grenade severely wounded Sp4c. Blanchfield and several others, he regained his feet to continue the pursuit of the enemy. The fleeing enemy threw a second grenade which landed near Sp4c. Blanchfield and several members of his patrol. Instantly realizing the danger, he shouted a warning to his comrades. Sp4c. Blanchfield unhesitatingly and with complete disregard for his safety threw himself on the grenade, absorbing the full and fatal impact of the explosion. By his gallant action and self-sacrifice, he was able to save the lives and prevent injury to four members of the patrol and several Vietnamese civilians in the immediate area. Sp4c. Blanchfield's extraordinary courage and gallantry at the cost of his life above and beyond the call of duty are in keeping with the highest traditions of the military service and reflect great credit upon himself, his unit, and the U.S. Army.

3180 ◆ *BOBO, JOHN PAUL

Rank: Second Lieutenant
Service: U.S. Marine Corps Reserve
Birthday: 14 February 1943
Place of Birth: Niagara Falls, Niagara County, New York
Date of Death: 30 March 1967
Place of Death: Republic of Vietnam

Cemetery: Gate of Heaven Cemetery—Niagara Falls, New York
Entered Service at: Buffalo, Erie County, New York
Unit: Company I, 3d Battalion, 9th Marines, 3d Marine Division (Rein) FMF
Served as: Weapons Platoon Commander
Battle or Place of Action: Quang Tri Province, Republic of Vietnam
Date of Action: 30 March 1967
Date of Presentation: 27 August 1968
Place of Presentation: Marine Barracks, Washington, D.C., presented by Sec. of the Navy Paul R. Ignatius to his family
Citation: For conspicuous gallantry and intrepidity at the risk of his life above and beyond the call of duty. Company I was establishing night ambush sites when the command group was attacked by a reinforced North Vietnamese company supported by heavy automatic-weapons and mortar fire. 2d Lt. Bobo immediately organized a hasty defense and moved from position to position encouraging the outnumbered marines despite the murderous enemy fire. Recovering a rocket launcher from among the friendly casualties, he organized a new launcher team and directed its fire into the enemy machine-gun positions. When an exploding enemy mortar round severed 2d Lt. Bobo's right leg below the knee, he refused to be evacuated and insisted upon being placed in a firing position to cover the movement of the command group to a better location. With a web belt around his leg serving as a tourniquet and with his leg jammed into the dirt to contain the bleeding he remained in this position and delivered devastating fire into the ranks of the enemy attempting to overrun the marines. 2d Lt. Bobo was mortally wounded while firing his weapon into the mainpoint of the enemy attack but his valiant spirit inspired his men to heroic efforts, and his tenacious stand enabled the command group to gain a protective position where it repulsed the enemy onslaught. 2d Lt. Bobo's superb leadership, dauntless courage, and bold initiative reflected great credit upon himself and upheld the highest traditions of the Marine Corps and the U.S. Naval Service. He gallantly gave his life for his country.

3181 ◆ BONDSTEEL, JAMES LEROY

Rank: Staff Sergeant (highest rank: Master Sergeant)
Service: U.S. Army
Birthday: 18 July 1947
Place of Birth: Jackson, Jackson County, Michigan
Date of Death: 9 April 1987
Place of Death: Kinik River Bridge, Anchorage, Alaska
Cemetery: Fort Richardson National Cemetery (H-19) (MH)—Fort Richardson, Alaska
Entered Service at: Detroit, Wayne County, Michigan
Unit: Company A, 2d Battalion, 2d Infantry, 1st Infantry Division
Served as: Platoon Sergeant
Battle or Place of Action: near the village of Lang Sau, An Loc Province, Republic of Vietnam
Date of Action: 24 May 1969
G.O. Number, Date: 38, 5 November 1973
Date of Presentation: 15 October 1973

Place of Presentation: The White House, presented by Pres. Richard M. Nixon

Citation: For conspicuous gallantry and intrepidity in action at the risk of his life above and beyond the call of duty. S/Sgt. Bondsteel distinguished himself while serving as a platoon sergeant with Company A, near the village of Lang Sau. Company A was directed to assist a friendly unit which was endangered by intense fire from a North Vietnamese battalion located in a heavily fortified base camp. S/Sgt. Bondsteel quickly organized the men of his platoon into effective combat teams and spearheaded the attack by destroying four enemy-occupied bunkers. He then raced some 200 meters under heavy enemy fire to reach an adjoining platoon which had begun to falter. After rallying this unit and assisting their wounded, S/Sgt. Bondsteel returned to his own sector with critically needed munitions. Without pausing he moved to the forefront and destroyed four enemy-occupied bunkers and a machine gun which had threatened his advancing platoon. Although painfully wounded by an enemy grenade, S/Sgt. Bondsteel refused medical attention and continued his assault by neutralizing two more enemy bunkers nearby. While searching one of these emplacements, S/Sgt. Bondsteel narrowly escaped death when an enemy soldier detonated a grenade at close range. Shortly thereafter, he ran to the aid of a seriously wounded officer and struck down an enemy soldier who was threatening the officer's life. S/Sgt. Bondsteel then continued to rally his men and lead them through the entrenched enemy until his company was relieved. His exemplary leadership and great personal courage throughout the four-hour battle ensured the success of his own and nearby units, and resulted in the saving of numerous lives of his fellow soldiers. By individual acts of bravery he destroyed 10 enemy bunkers and accounted for a large toll of the enemy, including two key enemy commanders. His extraordinary heroism at the risk of his life was in the highest traditions of the military service and reflect great credit upon him, his unit, and the U.S. Army.

3182 ◆ *BOWEN JR., HAMMETT LEE

Rank: Staff Sergeant
Service: U.S. Army
Birthday: 30 November 1947
Place of Birth: LaGrange, Troup County, Georgia
Date of Death: 27 June 1969
Place of Death: Republic of Vietnam
Cemetery: Restlawn Memory Garden Cemetery (MH)—La Grange, Georgia
Entered Service at: Jacksonville, Duval County, Florida
Unit: Company C, 2d Battalion, 14th Infantry, 25th Infantry Division
Served as: Platoon Sergeant
Battle or Place of Action: Binh Duong Province, Republic of Vietnam
Date of Action: 27 June 1969
G.O. Number, Date: 43, 12 September 1974
Date of Presentation: 17 July 1974
Place of Presentation: Blair House (Courtyard), presented by Vice Pres. Gerald R. Ford to his family

Citation: S/Sgt. Bowen distinguished himself while serving as a platoon sergeant during combat operations in Binh Duong Province, Republic of Vietnam. S/Sgt. Bowen's platoon was advancing on a reconnaissance mission into enemy-controlled terrain when it came under the withering crossfire of small arms and grenades from an enemy ambush force. S/Sgt. Bowen placed heavy suppressive fire on the enemy positions and ordered his men to fall back. As the platoon was moving back, an enemy grenade was thrown amid S/Sgt. Bowen and three of his men. Sensing the danger to his comrades, S/Sgt. Bowen shouted a warning to his men and hurled himself on the grenade, absorbing the explosion with his body while saving the lives of his fellow soldiers. S/Sgt. Bowen's extraordinary courage and concern for his men at the cost of his life served as an inspiration to his comrades and are in the highest traditions of the military service and the U.S. Army.

3183 ◆ BRADY, PATRICK HENRY

Rank: Major (highest rank: Major General)
Service: U.S. Army
Birthday: 1 October 1936
Place of Birth: Philip, Haakon County, South Dakota
Entered Service at: Seattle, King County, Washington
Unit: Medical Service Corps, 54th Medical Detachment, 67th Medical Group, 44th Medical Brigade
Served as: Medivac Helicopter Pilot
Battle or Place of Action: near Chu Lai, Republic of Vietnam
Date of Action: 6 January 1968
G.O. Number, Date: 62, 27 October 1969
Date of Presentation: 9 October 1969
Place of Presentation: The White House, presented by Pres. Richard M. Nixon

Citation: For conspicuous gallantry and intrepidity in action at the risk of his life above and beyond the call of duty, Maj. Brady distinguished himself while serving in the Republic of Vietnam commanding a UH-1H ambulance helicopter, volunteered to rescue wounded men from a site in enemy-held territory which was reported to be heavily defended and to be blanketed by fog. To reach the site, he descended through heavy fog and smoke and hovered slowly along a valley trail, turning his ship sideward to blow away the fog with the backwash from his rotor blades. Despite the unchallenged, close-range enemy fire, he found the dangerously small site, where he successfully landed and evacuated two badly wounded South Vietnamese soldiers. He was then called to another area completely covered by dense fog where American casualties lay only 50 meters from the enemy. Two aircraft had previously been shot down and others had made unsuccessful attempts to reach this site earlier in the day. With unmatched skill and extraordinary courage, Maj. Brady made four flights to this embattled landing zone and successfully rescued all of the wounded. On his third mission of the day, Maj. Brady once again landed at a site surrounded by the enemy. The friendly ground force, pinned down by enemy fire, had been unable to reach and secure the landing zone. Although his aircraft had been badly damaged and his controls partially shot away during his initial entry into this area, he returned minutes later and rescued the remaining injured. Shortly thereafter obtaining a replacement aircraft, Maj. Brady was requested to land in an enemy mine field where a platoon of American soldiers was trapped. A mine detonated near his helicopter, wounding two crewmembers and damaging his ship. In spite of this, he managed to fly six severely injured patients to medical aid. Throughout that day Maj. Brady utilized three helicopters to evacuate a total of 51 seriously wounded men, many of whom would have perished without prompt medical treatment. Maj. Brady's bravery was in the highest traditions of the military service and reflects great credit upon himself and the U.S. Army.

3184 ◆ *BRUCE, DANIEL DEAN

Rank: Private First Class
Service: U.S. Marine Corps
Birthday: 18 May 1950
Place of Birth: Michigan City, La Porte County, Indiana
Date of Death: 1 March 1969
Place of Death: Republic of Vietnam
Cemetery: Greenwood Cemetery—Michigan City, Indiana
Entered Service at: Chicago, Cook County, Illinois
Unit: Headquarters & Service Company, 3d Battalion, 5th Marines, 1st Marine Division (Rein) FMF
Served as: Mortar Man
Battle or Place of Action: Fire Support Base Tomahawk, Quang Nam Province, Republic of Vietnam
Date of Action: 1 March 1969
Date of Presentation: 16 February 1971
Place of Presentation: The White House (East Ballroom), presented by Pres. Richard M. Nixon to his family
Citation: For conspicuous gallantry and intrepidity at the risk of his life above and beyond the call of duty while serving as a mortar man with Headquarters and Service Company 3d Battalion, against the enemy. Early in the morning Pfc. Bruce was on watch in his night defensive position at Fire Support Base Tomahawk when he heard movements ahead of him. An enemy explosive charge was thrown toward his position and he reacted instantly, catching the device and shouting to alert his companions. Realizing the danger to the adjacent position with its two occupants, Pfc. Bruce held the device to his body and attempted to carry it from the vicinity of the entrenched marines. As he moved away, the charge detonated and he absorbed the full force of the explosion. Pfc. Bruce's indomitable courage, inspiring valor and selfless devotion to duty saved the lives of three of his fellow marines and upheld the highest traditions of the Marine Corps and the U.S. Naval Service. He gallantly gave his life for his country.

3185 ◆ *BRYANT, WILLIAM MAUD

Rank: Sergeant First Class
Service: U.S. Army
Birthday: 16 February 1933
Place of Birth: Cochran, Bleckley County, Georgia
Date of Death: 24 March 1969
Place of Death: Republic of Vietnam

Cemetery: Raleigh National Cemetery (15-1227) (MH)—Raleigh, North Carolina
Entered Service at: Detroit, Wayne County, Michigan
Unit: Company A, 5th Special Forces Group, 1st Special Forces
Served as: Commanding Officer of C.I.D.G.Co. 321
Battle or Place of Action: Long Khanh Province, Republic of Vietnam
Date of Action: 24 March 1969
G.O. Number, Date: 8, 9 March 1971
Date of Presentation: 16 February 1971
Place of Presentation: The White House (East Ballroom), presented by Pres. Richard M. Nixon to his family
Citation: For conspicuous gallantry and intrepidity in action at the risk of his life above and beyond the call of duty. Sfc. Bryant, assigned to Company A, distinguished himself while serving as commanding officer of Civilian Irregular Defense Group Company 321, 2d Battalion, 3d Mobile Strike Force Command, during combat operations. The battalion came under heavy fire and became surrounded by the elements of three enemy regiments. Sfc. Bryant displayed extraordinary heroism throughout the succeeding 34 hours of incessant attack as he moved throughout the company position heedless of the intense hostile fire while establishing and improving the defensive perimeter, directing fire during critical phases of the battle, distributing ammunition, assisting the wounded, and providing the leadership and inspirational example of courage to his men. When a helicopter drop of ammunition was made to resupply the beleaguered force, Sfc. Bryant with complete disregard for his safety ran through the heavy enemy fire to retrieve the scattered ammunition boxes and distributed needed ammunition to his men. During a lull in the intense fighting, Sfc. Bryant led a patrol outside the perimeter to obtain information of the enemy. The patrol came under intense automatic-weapons fire and was pinned down. Sfc. Bryant singlehandedly repulsed one enemy attack on his small force and by his heroic action inspired his men to fight off other assaults. Seeing a wounded enemy soldier some distance from the patrol location, Sfc. Bryant crawled forward alone under heavy fire to retrieve the soldier for intelligence purposes. Finding that the enemy soldier had expired, Sfc. Bryant crawled back to his patrol and led his men back to the company position where he again took command of the defense. As the siege continued, Sfc. Bryant organized and led a patrol in a daring attempt to break through the enemy encirclement. The patrol had advanced some 200 meters by heavy fighting when it was pinned down by the intense automatic-weapons fire from heavily fortified bunkers and Sfc. Bryant was severely wounded. Despite his wounds he rallied his men, called for helicopter gunship support, and directed heavy suppressive fire upon the enemy positions. Following the last gunship attack, Sfc. Bryant fearlessly charged an enemy automatic-weapons position, overrunning it and singlehandedly destroying its three defenders. Inspired by his heroic example, his men renewed their attack on the entrenched enemy. While regrouping his small force for the final assault against the enemy, Sfc. Bryant fell mortally wounded by an enemy rocket. Sfc. Bryant's selfless concern for his comrades, at the cost of his life above and beyond the

call of duty, are in keeping with the highest traditions of the military service and reflect great credit upon himself, his unit, and the U.S. Army.

3186 ◆ BUCHA, PAUL WILLIAM

Rank: Captain
Service: U.S. Army
Birthday: 1 August 1943
Place of Birth: Washington, D.C.
Entered Service at: USMA West Point, Orange County, New York
Unit: Company D, 3d Battalion, 187th Infantry, 3d Brigade, 101st Airborne Division
Served as: Company Commander
Battle or Place of Action: near Phuoc Vinh, Binh Duong Province, Republic of Vietnam
Date of Action: 16-19 March 1968
G.O. Number, Date: 30, 5 June 1970
Date of Presentation: 14 May 1970
Place of Presentation: The White House, presented by Pres. Richard M. Nixon
Citation: For conspicuous gallantry and intrepidity in action at the risk of his life above and beyond the call of duty. Capt. Bucha distinguished himself while serving as commanding officer, Company D, on a reconnaissance-in-force mission against enemy forces near Phuoc Vinh. The company was inserted by helicopter into the suspected enemy stronghold to locate and destroy the enemy. During this period Capt. Bucha aggressively and courageously led his men in the destruction of enemy fortifications and base areas and eliminated scattered resistance impeding the advance of the company. On 18 March while advancing to contact, the lead elements of the company became engaged by the heavy automatic-weapon, heavy machine-gun, rocket-propelled-grenade, claymore-mine and small-arms fire of an estimated battalion-size force. Capt. Bucha, with complete disregard for his safety, moved to the threatened area to direct the defense and ordered reinforcements to the aid of the lead element. Seeing that his men were pinned down by heavy machine-gun fire from a concealed bunker located some 40 meters to the front of the positions, Capt. Bucha crawled through the hail of fire to singlehandedly destroy the bunker with grenades. During this heroic action Capt. Bucha received a painful shrapnel wound. Returning to the perimeter, he observed that his unit could not hold its positions and repel the human wave assaults launched by the determined enemy. Capt. Bucha ordered the withdrawal of the unit elements and covered the withdrawal to positions of a company perimeter from which he could direct fire upon the charging enemy. When one friendly element retrieving casualties was ambushed and cut off from the perimeter, Capt. Bucha ordered them to feign death and he directed artillery fire around them. During the night Capt. Bucha moved throughout the position, distributing ammunition, providing encouragement, and insuring the integrity of the defense. He directed artillery, helicopter-gunship and Air Force-gunship fire on the enemy strong points and attacking forces, marking the positions with smoke grenades. Using flashlights in complete view of enemy snipers, he directed the medical evacuation of three air-ambu-

lance loads of seriously wounded personnel and the helicopter supply of his company. At daybreak Capt. Bucha led a rescue party to recover the dead and wounded members of the ambushed element. During the period of intensive combat, Capt. Bucha, by his extraordinary heroism, inspirational example, outstanding leadership, and professional competence, led his company in the decimation of a superior enemy force which left 156 dead on the battlefield. His bravery and gallantry at the risk of his life are in the highest traditions of the military service. Capt. Bucha has reflected great credit on himself, his unit, and the U.S. Army.

3187 ◆ *BUKER, BRIAN LEROY

Rank: Sergeant
Service: U.S. Army
Birthday: 3 November 1949
Place of Birth: Benton, Maine
Date of Death: 5 April 1970
Place of Death: Republic of Vietnam
Cemetery: Brown Cemetery (MH)—Benton, Maine
Entered Service at: Bangor, Penobscot County, Maine
Unit: Detachment B-55, 5th Special Forces Group (Airborne), 1st Special Forces
Served as: Platoon Advisor
Battle or Place of Action: Chau Doc Province, Republic of Vietnam
Date of Action: 5 April 1970
G.O. Number, Date: 6, 25 January 1972
Date of Presentation: 16 December 1971
Place of Presentation: Old Executive Office Building, presented by Vice Pres. Spiro T. Agnew to his family
Citation: For conspicuous gallantry and intrepidity in action at the risk of his life above and beyond the call of duty. Sgt. Buker, Detachment B-55, distinguished himself while serving as a platoon adviser of a Vietnamese mobile strike force company during an offensive mission. Sgt. Buker personally led the platoon, cleared a strategically located well-guarded pass, and established the first foothold at the top of what had been an impenetrable mountain fortress. When the platoon came under intense fire from a determined enemy located in two heavily fortified bunkers, and realizing that withdrawal would result in heavy casualties, Sgt. Buker unhesitatingly, and with complete disregard for his personal safety, charged through the hail of enemy fire and destroyed the first bunker with hand grenades. While reorganizing his men for the attack on the second bunker, Sgt. Buker was seriously wounded. Despite his wounds and the deadly fire, he crawled forward and destroyed the second bunker. Sgt. Buker refused medical attention and was reorganizing his men to continue the attack when he was mortally wounded. As a direct result of his heroic actions, many casualties were averted, and the assault of the enemy position was successful. Sgt. Buker's extraordinary heroism at the cost of his life are in the highest traditions of the military service and reflect great credit on him, his unit, and the U.S. Army.

3188 ◆ *BURKE, ROBERT CHARLES

Rank: Private First Class
Service: U.S. Marine Corps

Birthday: 7 November 1949
Place of Birth: Monticello, Piatt County, Illinois
Date of Death: 17 May 1968
Place of Death: Republic of Vietnam
Cemetery: Monticello Cemetery (MH)—Monticello, Illinois
Entered Service at: Chicago, Cook County, Illinois
Unit: Company I, 3d Battalion, 27th Marines, 1st Marine Division (Rein) FMF
Served as: Machine Gunner
Battle or Place of Action: Le Nam 1, Go Nai Island, southern Quang Nam Province, Republic of Vietnam
Date of Action: 17 May 1968
Date of Presentation: 20 April 1970
Place of Presentation: The White House, presented by Vice Pres. Spiro T. Agnew to his family
Citation: For conspicuous gallantry and intrepidity at the risk of his life above and beyond the call of duty for service as a machine gunner with Company I. While on Operation Allen Brook, Company I was approaching a dry river bed with a heavily wooded treeline that borders the hamlet of Le Nam (1), when they suddenly came under intense mortar, rocket-propelled-grenade, automatic-weapons, and small-arms fire from a large, well-concealed enemy force which halted the company's advance and wounded several marines. Realizing that key points of resistance had to be eliminated to allow the units to advance and casualties to be evacuated, Pfc. Burke, without hesitation, seized his machine gun and launched a series of one-man assaults against the fortified emplacements. As he aggressively maneuvered to the edge of the steep river bank, he delivered accurate suppressive fire upon several enemy bunkers, which enabled his comrades to advance and move the wounded marines to positions of relative safety. As he continued his combative actions, he located an opposing automatic-weapons emplacement and poured intense fire into the position, killing three North Vietnamese soldiers as they attempted to flee. Pfc. Burke then fearlessly moved from one position to another, quelling the hostile fire until his weapon malfunctioned. Obtaining a casualty's rifle and hand grenades, he advanced further into the midst of the enemy fire in an assault against another pocket of resistance, killing two more of the enemy. Observing that a fellow marine had cleared his malfunctioning machine gun, he grasped his weapon and moved into a dangerously exposed area and saturated the hostile treeline until he fell mortally wounded. Pfc. Burke's gallant actions upheld the highest traditions of the Marine Corps and the U.S. Naval Service. He gallantly gave his life for his country.

3189 ◆ *CAPODANNO, VINCENT ROBERT

Rank: Lieutenant
Service: U.S. Navy
Birthday: 13 February 1929
Place of Birth: Staten Island, Richmond County, New York
Date of Death: 4 September 1967
Place of Death: Republic of Vietnam
Cemetery: Saint Peter's Cemetery—Staten Island, New York
Entered Service at: Staten Island, Richmond County, New York

Unit: Chaplain Corps, 3d Battalion, 5th Marines, 1st Marine Division (Rein) FMF
Served as: Chaplain
Battle or Place of Action: Quang Tin Province, Republic of Vietnam
Date of Action: 4 September 1967
Date of Presentation: 7 January 1969
Place of Presentation: The Washington Navy Yard, presented by Sec. of the Navy Paul R. Ignatius to his family
Citation: For conspicuous gallantry and intrepidity at the risk of his life above and beyond the call of duty as Chaplain of the 3d Battalion, in connection with operations against enemy forces. In response to reports that the 2d Platoon of M Company was in danger of being overrun by a massed enemy assaulting force, Lt. Capodanno left the relative safety of the company command post and ran through an open area raked with fire, directly to the beleaguered platoon. Disregarding the intense enemy small-arms, automatic-weapons, and mortar fire, he moved about the battlefield administering last rites to the dying and giving medical aid to the wounded. When an exploding mortar round inflicted painful multiple wounds to his arms and legs, and severed a portion of his right hand, he steadfastly refused all medical aid. Instead, he directed the corpsmen to help their wounded comrades and, with calm vigor, continued to move about the battlefield as he provided encouragement by voice and example to the valiant marines. Upon encountering a wounded corpsman in the direct line of fire of an enemy machine gunner positioned approximately 15 yards away, Lt. Capodanno rushed in a daring attempt to aid and assist the mortally wounded corpsman. At that instant, only inches from his goal, he was struck down by a burst of machine-gun fire. By his heroic conduct on the battlefield, and his inspiring example, Lt. Capodanno upheld the finest traditions of the U.S. Naval Service. He gallantly gave his life in the cause of freedom.

3190 ◆ *CARON, WAYNE MAURICE

Rank: Hospital Corpsman Third Class
Service: U.S. Navy
Birthday: 2 November 1946
Place of Birth: Middleboro, Plymouth County, Massachusetts
Date of Death: 28 July 1968
Place of Death: Republic of Vietnam
Cemetery: Arlington National Cemetery (51-2600) (MH)—Arlington, Virginia
Entered Service at: Boston, Suffolk County, Massachusetts
Unit: Headquarters & Service Company, 3d Battalion, 7th Marines, 1st Marine Division (Rein) FMF
Served as: Medical Corpsman
Battle or Place of Action: Quang Nam Province, Republic of Vietnam
Date of Action: 28 July 1968
Date of Presentation: 20 April 1970
Place of Presentation: The White House, presented by Vice Pres. Spiro T. Agnew to his family
Citation: For conspicuous gallantry and intrepidity at the risk of his life above and beyond the call of duty while serving as platoon corpsman with Company K, during combat opera-

tions against enemy forces. While on a sweep through an open rice field, HC3c. Caron's unit started receiving enemy small-arms fire. Upon seeing two marine casualties fall, he immediately ran forward to render first aid, but found that they were dead. At this time the platoon was taken under intense small-arms and automatic-weapons fire, sustaining additional casualties. As he moved to the aid of his wounded comrades, HC3c. Caron was hit in the arm by enemy fire. Although knocked to the ground, he regained his feet and continued to the injured marines. He rendered medical assistance to the first marine he reached, who was grievously wounded, and undoubtedly was instrumental in saving the man's life. HC3c. Caron then ran toward the second wounded marine, but was again hit by enemy fire, this time in the leg. Nonetheless, he crawled the remaining distance and provided medical aid for this severely wounded man. HC3c. Caron started to make his way to yet another injured comrade, when he was again struck by enemy small-arms fire. Courageously and with unbelievable determination, HC3c. Caron continued his attempt to reach the third marine until he was killed by an enemy rocket round. His inspiring valor, steadfast determination, and selfless dedication in the face of extreme danger, sustain and enhance the finest traditions of the U.S. Naval Service.

3191 ◆ *CARTER, BRUCE WAYNE

Rank: Private First Class
Service: U.S. Marine Corps
Birthday: 7 May 1950
Place of Birth: Schenectady, Schenectady County, New York
Date of Death: 7 August 1969
Place of Death: Republic of Vietnam
Cemetery: Vista Memorial Gardens (MH)—Hialeah, Florida
Entered Service at: Jacksonville, Duval County, Florida
Unit: Company H, 2d Battalion, 3d Marines, 3d Marine Division (Rein) FMF
Served as: Grenadier
Battle or Place of Action: Quang Tri Province, Republic of Vietnam
Date of Action: 7 August 1969
Date of Presentation: 9 September 1971
Place of Presentation: The White House, presented by Vice Pres. Spiro T. Agnew to his family
Citation: For conspicuous gallantry and intrepidity at the risk of his life above and beyond the call of duty while serving as grenadier with Company H in connection with combat operations against the enemy. Pfc. Carter's unit was maneuvering against the enemy during Operation Idaho Canyon and came under a heavy volume of fire from a numerically superior hostile force. The lead element soon became separated from the main body of the squad by a brush fire. Pfc. Carter and his fellow marines were pinned down by vicious crossfire when, with complete disregard for his safety, he stood in full view of the North Vietnamese Army soldiers to deliver a devastating volume of fire at their positions. The accuracy and aggressiveness of his attack caused several enemy casualties and forced the remainder of the soldiers to retreat

from the immediate area. Shouting directions to the marines around him, Pfc. Carter then commenced leading them from the path of the rapidly approaching brush fire when he observed a hostile grenade land between him and his companions. Fully aware of the probable consequences of his action but determined to protect the men following him, he unhesitatingly threw himself over the grenade, absorbing the full effects of its detonation with his body. Pfc. Carter's indomitable courage, inspiring initiative, and selfless devotion to duty upheld the highest traditions of the Marine Corps and the U.S. Naval Service. He gallantly gave his life in the service of his country.

3192 ◆ CAVAIANI, JON ROBERT

Rank: Staff Sergeant (highest rank: Sergeant Major)
Service: U.S. Army
Birthday: 2 August 1943
Place of Birth: Royston, England
Entered Service at: Fresno, Fresno County, California
Unit: Vietnam Training Advisory Group, Republic of Vietnam
Served as: Platoon Leader
Battle or Place of Action: Hill 1050, overlooking Khesahn Airfield, Republic of Vietnam
Date of Action: 4-5 June 1971
G.O. Number, Date: 2, 3 January 1975
Date of Presentation: 12 December 1974
Place of Presentation: The White House, presented by Pres. Gerald R. Ford
Citation: S/Sgt. Cavaiani distinguished himself by conspicuous gallantry and intrepidity at the risk of his life above and beyond the call of duty in action in the Republic of Vietnam on 4 and 5 June 1971 while serving as a platoon leader to a security platoon providing security for an isolated radio relay site located within enemy-held territory. On the morning of 4 June 1971, the entire camp came under an intense barrage of enemy small-arms, automatic-weapons, rocket-propelled-grenade and mortar fire from a superior size enemy force. S/Sgt. Cavaiani acted with complete disregard for his personal safety as he repeatedly exposed himself to heavy enemy fire in order to move about the camp's perimeter directing the platoon's fire and rallying the platoon in a desperate fight for survival. S/Sgt. Cavaiani also returned heavy suppressive fire upon the assaulting enemy force during this period with a variety of weapons. When the entire platoon was to be evacuated, S/Sgt. Cavaiani unhesitatingly volunteered to remain on the ground and direct the helicopters into the landing zone. S/Sgt. Cavaiani was able to direct the first three helicopters in evacuating a major portion of the platoon. Due to intense increase in enemy fire, S/Sgt. Cavaiani was forced to remain at the camp overnight where he calmly directed the remaining platoon members in strengthening their defenses. On the morning of 5 June, a heavy ground fog restricted visibility. The superior size enemy force launched a major ground attack in an attempt to completely annihilate the remaining small force. The enemy force advanced in two ranks, first firing a heavy volume of small-arms, automatic-weapons, and rocket-propelled-grenade fire while the second rank continuously threw a steady barrage of hand grenades at the belea-

guered force. S/Sgt. Cavaiani returned a heavy barrage of small-arms and hand-grenade fire on the assaulting enemy force but was unable to slow them down. He ordered the remaining platoon members to attempt to escape while he provided them with cover fire. With one last courageous exertion, S/Sgt. Cavaiani recovered a machine gun, stood up, completely exposing himself to the heavy enemy fire directed at him, and began firing the machine gun in a sweeping motion along the two ranks of advancing enemy soldiers. Through S/Sgt. Cavaiani's valiant efforts with complete disregard for his safety, the majority of the remaining platoon members were able to escape. While inflicting severe losses on the advancing enemy force, S/Sgt. Cavaiani was wounded numerous times. S/Sgt. Cavaiani's conspicuous gallantry, extraordinary heroism, and intrepidity at the risk of his life, above and beyond the call of duty, were in keeping with the highest traditions of the military service and reflect great credit upon himself and the U.S. Army.

3193 ◆ CLAUSEN JR., RAYMOND MICHAEL "RED"

Rank: Private First Class
Service: U.S. Marine Corps
Birthday: 14 October 1947
Place of Birth: New Orleans, Orleans County, Louisiana
Entered Service at: New Orleans, Orleans County, Louisiana
Unit: Marine Medium Helicopter Squadron 263, Marine Aircraft Group 16, 1st Marine Aircraft Wing
Served as: Crew Chief of a HC-46 Helicopter
Battle or Place of Action: Republic of Vietnam
Date of Action: 31 January 1970
Date of Presentation: 15 June 1971
Place of Presentation: The White House (East Ballroom), presented by Pres. Richard M. Nixon
Citation: For conspicuous gallantry and intrepidity at the risk of his life above and beyond the call of duty while serving with Marine Medium Helicopter Squadron 263 during operations against enemy forces. Participating in a helicopter rescue mission to extract elements of a platoon which had inadvertently entered a minefield while attacking enemy positions, Pfc. Clausen skillfully guided the helicopter pilot to a landing in an area cleared by one of several mine explosions. With 11 marines wounded, and one dead, and the remaining eight marines holding their positions for fear of detonating other mines, Pfc. Clausen quickly leaped from the helicopter and, in the face of enemy fire, moved across the extremely hazardous mineladen area to assist in carrying casualties to the waiting helicopter and in placing them aboard. Despite the ever-present threat of further mine explosions, he continued his valiant efforts, leaving the comparatively safe area of the helicopter on six separate occasions to carry out his rescue efforts. On one occasion while he was carrying one of the wounded, another mine detonated, killing a corpsman and wounding three other men. Only when he was certain that all marines were safely aboard did he signal the pilot to lift the helicopter. By the courageous, determined, and inspiring efforts in the face of the utmost danger, Pfc. Clausen upheld the highest traditions of the Marine Corps and of the U.S. Naval Service.

3194 ◆ *COKER, RONALD LEROY

Rank: Private First Class
Service: U.S. Marine Corps
Birthday: 9 August 1947
Place of Birth: Alliance, Box Butte County, Nebraska
Date of Death: 24 March 1969
Place of Death: Republic of Vietnam
Cemetery: Fairview Cemetery—Alliance, Nebraska
Entered Service at: Denver, Denver County, Colorado
Unit: 2d Platoon, Company M, 3d Battalion, 3d Marines, 3d Marine Division (Rein) FMF
Served as: Rifleman
Battle or Place of Action: northwest Quang Tri Province, Republic of Vietnam
Date of Action: 24 March 1969
Date of Presentation: 20 April 1970
Place of Presentation: The White House, presented by Vice Pres. Spiro T. Agnew to his family
Citation: For conspicuous gallantry and intrepidity at the risk of his life above and beyond the call of duty while serving as a rifleman with Company M in action against enemy forces. While serving as point man for the 2d Platoon, Pfc. Coker was leading his patrol when he encountered five enemy soldiers on a narrow jungle trail. Pfc. Coker's squad aggressively pursued them to a cave. As the squad neared the cave, it came under intense hostile fire, seriously wounding one marine and forcing the others to take cover. Observing the wounded man lying exposed to continuous enemy fire, Pfc. Coker disregarded his safety and moved across the fire-swept terrain toward his companion. Although wounded by enemy small-arms fire, he continued to crawl across the hazardous area and skillfully threw a hand grenade into the enemy positions, suppressing the hostile fire sufficiently to enable him to reach the wounded man. As he began to drag his injured comrade toward safety, a grenade landed on the wounded marine. Unhesitatingly, Pfc. Coker grasped it with both hands and turned away from his wounded companion, but before he could dispose of the grenade it exploded. Severely wounded, but undaunted, he refused to abandon his comrade. As he moved toward friendly lines, two more enemy grenades exploded near him, inflicting still further injuries. Concerned only for the safety of his comrade, Pfc. Coker, with supreme effort, continued to crawl and pull the wounded marine with him. His heroic deeds inspired his fellow marines to such aggressive action that the enemy fire was suppressed sufficiently to enable others to reach him and carry him to a relatively safe area where he succumbed to his extensive wounds. Pfc. Coker's indomitable courage, inspiring initiative, and selfless devotion to duty upheld the highest traditions of the Marine Corps and of the U.S. Naval Service. He gallantly gave his life for his country.

3195 ◆ *CONNOR, PETER SPENCER

Rank: Staff Sergeant
Service: U.S. Marine Corps
Birthday: 4 September 1932
Place of Birth: Orange, Essex County, New Jersey
Date of Death: 8 March 1966

Place of Death: on board Hospital Ship U.S.S. *Repose*
Cemetery: Fort Rosecrans National Cemetery (A-E-1005) (MH)—San Diego, California
Entered Service at: South Orange, Essex County, New Jersey
Unit: Company F, 2d Battalion, 3d Marines, 1st Marine Division (Rein) FMF
Served as: Platoon Sergeant
Battle or Place of Action: Quang Ngai Province, Republic of Vietnam
Date of Action: 25 February 1966
Date of Presentation: 2 May 1967
Place of Presentation: The White House (Rose Garden), presented by Pres. Lyndon B. Johnson to his family
Citation: For conspicuous gallantry and intrepidity in action against enemy Viet Cong forces at the risk of his life above and beyond the call of duty. Leading his platoon on a search-and-destroy operation in an area made particularly hazardous by extensive cave and tunnel complexes, S/Sgt. Connor maneuvered his unit aggressively forward under intermittent enemy small-arms fire. Exhibiting particular alertness and keen observation, he spotted an enemy spider hole emplacement approximately 15 meters to his front. He pulled the pin from a fragmentation grenade intending to charge the hole boldly and drop the missile into its depths. Upon pulling the pin he realized that the firing mechanism was faulty, and that even as he held the safety device firmly in place, the fuse charge was already activated. With only precious seconds to decide, he further realized that he could not cover the distance to the small opening of the spider hole in sufficient time, and that to hurl the deadly bomb in any direction would result in death or injury to some of his comrades tactically deployed near him. Manifesting extraordinary gallantry and with utter disregard for his personal safety, he chose to hold the grenade against his body in order to absorb the terrific explosion and spare his comrades. His act of extreme valor and selflessness in the face of virtually certain death, although leaving him mortally wounded, spared many of his fellow marines from death or injury. His gallant action in giving his life in the cause of freedom reflects the highest credit upon the Marine Corps and the Armed Forces of the United States.

3196 ◆ *COOK, DONALD GILBERT

Rank: Colonel (rank at time of action: Captain)
Service: U.S. Marine Corps
Birthday: 9 August 1934
Place of Birth: Brooklyn, Kings County, New York
Date of Death: 8 December 1967
Place of Death: Republic of Vietnam
Cemetery: Arlington National Cemetery ('In Memory' marker) (M1-110)—Arlington, Virginia
Entered Service at: Brooklyn, Kings County, New York
Unit: Naval Advisor Group, Military Assistance Command
Served as: Battalion Advisor
Battle or Place of Action: in the vicinity of Binh Gia, Phouc Tuy Province, Republic of Vietnam
Date of Action: 31 December 1964—8 December 1967
Date of Presentation: 16 May 1980

Place of Presentation: The Pentagon (Hall of Heroes), presented by Sec. of the Navy Edward Hidalgo to his family
Citation: For conspicuous gallantry and intrepidity at the risk of his life above and beyond the call of duty while interned as a Prisoner of War by the Viet Cong in the Republic of Vietnam during the period from 31 December 1964 to 8 December 1967. Despite the fact that by so doing he would bring about harsher treatment for himself, Col. (then Capt.) Cook established himself as the senior prisoner, even though in actuality he was not. Repeatedly assuming more than his share of the manual labor in order that the other Prisoners of War could improve the state of their health, Col. Cook willingly and unselfishly put the interests of his comrades before that of his own well-being and, eventually, his life. Giving more needy men his medicine and drug allowance while constantly nursing them, he risked infection from contagious diseases while in a rapidly deteriorating state of health. This unselfish and exemplary conduct, coupled with his refusal to stray even the slightest from the Code of Conduct, earned him the deepest respect from not only his fellow prisoners, but his captors as well. Rather than negotiate for his own release or better treatment, he steadfastly frustrated attempts by the Viet Cong to break his indomitable spirit, and passed this same resolve on to the men with whose well-being he so closely associated himself. Knowing his refusals would prevent his release prior to the end of the war, and also knowing his chances for prolonged survival would be small in the event of continued refusal, he chose nevertheless to adhere to a Code of Conduct far above that which could be expected. His personal valor and exceptional spirit of loyalty in the face of almost certain death reflected the highest credit upon Col. Cook, the Marine Corps, and the United States Naval Service.
Notes: POW from 31 December 1964—8 December 1967

3197 ◆ *CREEK, THOMAS ELBERT

Rank: Lance Corporal
Service: U.S. Marine Corps
Birthday: 7 April 1950
Place of Birth: Joplin, Jasper County, Missouri
Date of Death: 13 February 1969
Place of Death: Republic of Vietnam
Cemetery: Lland Cemetery (MH)—Amarillo, Texas
Entered Service at: Amarillo, Potter County, Texas
Unit: Company I, 3d Battalion, 9th Marines, 3d Marine Division (Rein) FMF
Served as: Rifleman
Battle or Place of Action: near Cam Lo, Republic of Vietnam
Date of Action: 13 February 1969
Date of Presentation: 20 April 1970
Place of Presentation: The White House, presented by Vice Pres. Spiro T. Agnew to his family
Citation: For conspicuous gallantry and intrepidity at the risk of his life above and beyond the call of duty while serving as a rifleman with Company I in action against enemy forces. L/Cpl. Creek's squad was providing security for a convoy moving to resupply the Vandergrift Command Base when an

enemy command-detonated mine destroyed one of the vehicles and halted the convoy near the Cam Lo Resettlement Village. Almost immediately, the marines came under a heavy volume of hostile mortar fire followed by intense small-arms fire from a well-concealed enemy force. As his squad deployed to engage the enemy, L/Cpl. Creek quickly moved to a fighting position and aggressively engaged in the firefight. Observing a position from which he could more effectively deliver fire against the hostile forces, he completely disregarded his own safety as he fearlessly dashed across the fire-swept terrain and was seriously wounded by enemy fire. At the same time, an enemy grenade was thrown into the gully where he had fallen, landing between him and several companions. Fully realizing the inevitable results of his action, L/Cpl. Creek rolled on the grenade and absorbed the full force of the explosion with his body, thereby saving the lives of five of his fellow marines. As a result of his heroic action, his men were inspired to such aggressive action that the enemy was defeated and the convoy was able to continue its vital mission. L/Cpl. Creek's indomitable courage inspired the Marine Corps and the U.S. Naval Service. He gallantly gave his life for his country.

3198 ◆ *CRESCENZ, MICHAEL JOSEPH

Rank: Corporal
Service: U.S. Army
Birthday: 14 January 1949
Place of Birth: Philadelphia, Philadelphia County, Pennsylvania
Date of Death: 20 November 1968
Place of Death: Republic of Vietnam
Cemetery: Holy Sepulchre Cemetery—Philadelphia, Pennsylvania
Entered Service at: Philadelphia, Philadelphia County, Pennsylvania
Unit: Company A, 4th Battalion, 31st Infantry, 196th Infantry Brigade, Americal Division
Served as: Rifleman
Battle or Place of Action: Hiep Duc Valley area, Republic of Vietnam
Date of Action: 20 November 1968
G.O. Number, Date: 11, 23 April 1970
Date of Presentation: 7 April 1970
Place of Presentation: The White House, presented by Pres. Richard M. Nixon to his family
Citation: Cpl. Crescenz distinguished himself by conspicuous gallantry and intrepidity in action while serving as a rifleman with Company A. In the morning his unit engaged a large, well-entrenched force of the North Vietnamese Army whose initial burst of fire pinned down the lead squad and killed the two point men, halting the advance of Company A. Immediately, Cpl. Crescenz left the relative safety of his own position, seized a nearby machine gun and, with complete disregard for his safety, charged 100 meters up a slope toward the enemy bunkers which he effectively silenced, killing the two occupants of each. Undaunted by the withering machine-gun fire around him, Cpl. Crescenz courageously moved forward toward a third bunker which he also succeeded in silenc-

ing, killing two more of the enemy and momentarily clearing the route of advance for his comrades. Suddenly, intense machine-gun fire erupted from an unseen, camouflaged bunker. Realizing the danger to his fellow soldiers, Cpl. Crescenz disregarded the barrage of hostile fire directed at him and daringly advanced toward the position. Assaulting with his machine gun, Cpl. Crescenz was within five meters of the bunker when he was mortally wounded by the fire from the enemy machine gun. As a direct result of his heroic actions, his company was able to maneuver freely with minimal danger and to complete its mission, defeating the enemy. Cpl. Crescenz's bravery and extraordinary heroism at the cost of his life are in the highest traditions of the military service and reflect great credit on himself, his unit, and the U.S. Army.

3199 ◆ *CUTINHA, NICHOLAS JOSEPH

Rank: Specialist Fourth Class
Service: U.S. Army
Birthday: 13 January 1945
Place of Birth: Fernandina Beach, Nassau County, Florida
Date of Death: 2 March 1968
Place of Death: Republic of Vietnam
Cemetery: Fort Denaud Cemetery—Fort Denaud, Florida
Entered Service at: Coral Gables, Dade County, Florida
Unit: Company C, 4th Battalion, 9th Infantry Regiment, 25th Infantry Division
Served as: Machine Gunner
Battle or Place of Action: near Gia Dinh, Republic of Vietnam
Date of Action: 2 March 1968
G.O. Number, Date: 26, 23 April 1970
Date of Presentation: 7 April 1970
Place of Presentation: The White House, presented by Pres. Richard M. Nixon to his family
Citation: For conspicuous gallantry and intrepidity in action at the risk of his life above and beyond the call of duty. While serving as a machine gunner with Company C, Sp4c. Cutinha accompanied his unit on a combat mission near Gia Dinh. Suddenly his company came under small-arms, automatic-weapons, mortar, and rocket-propelled grenade fire, from a battalion-size enemy unit. During the initial hostile attack, communications with the battalion was lost and the company commander and numerous members of the company became casualties. When Sp4c. Cutinha observed that his company was pinned down and disorganized, he moved to the front with complete disregard for his safety, firing his machine gun at the charging enemy. As he moved forward he drew fire on his own position and was seriously wounded in the leg. As the hostile fire intensified and half of the company was killed or wounded, Sp4c. Cutinha assumed command of all the survivors in his area and initiated a withdrawal while providing cover fire for the evacuation of the wounded. He killed several enemy soldiers but sustained another leg wound when his machine gun was destroyed by incoming rounds. Undaunted, he crawled through a hail of enemy fire to an operable machine gun in order to continue the defense of his injured comrades who were being administered medical treatment. Sp4c. Cutinha maintained this position, refused assistance,

and provided defensive fire for his comrades until he fell mortally wounded. He was solely responsible for killing 15 enemy soldiers while saving the lives of at least nine members of his own unit. Sp4c. Cutinha's gallantry and extraordinary heroism were in keeping with the highest traditions of the military service and reflect great credit upon himself, his unit, and the U.S. Army.

3200   ◆   *DAHL, LARRY GILBERT

Rank: Specialist Fourth Class
Service: U.S. Army
Birthday: 10 June 1949
Place of Birth: Oregon City, Clackamas County, Oregon
Date of Death: 23 February 1971
Place of Death: Republic of Vietnam
Cemetery: Willamette National Cemetery (S-3512) (MH)—Portland, Oregon
Entered Service at: Portland, Multnomah County, Oregon
Unit: 359th Transportation Company, 27th Transportation Battalion, U.S. Army Support Command
Served as: Machine Gunner
Battle or Place of Action: An Khe, Binh Dinh Province, Republic of Vietnam
Date of Action: 23 February 1971
G.O. Number, Date: 36, 6 September 1974
Date of Presentation: 8 August 1974
Place of Presentation: Blair House, presented by Vice Pres. Gerald R. Ford to his family
Citation: Sp4c. Dahl distinguished himself by conspicuous gallantry and intrepidity while serving as a machine gunner on a gun truck near An Khe, Binh Dinh Province. The gun truck in which Sp4c. Dahl was riding was sent with two other gun trucks to assist in the defense of a convoy that had been ambushed by an enemy force. The gun trucks entered the battle zone and engaged the attacking enemy troops with a heavy volume of machine-gun fire, causing a large number of casualties. After a brief period of intense fighting the attack subsided. As the gun trucks were preparing to return to their normal escort duties, an enemy hand grenade was thrown into the truck in which Sp4c. Dahl was riding. Instantly realizing the great danger, Sp4c. Dahl called a warning to his companions and threw himself directly onto the grenade. Through his indomitable courage, complete disregard for his safety, and profound concern for his fellow soldiers, Sp4c. Dahl saved the lives of the other members of the truck crew while sacrificing his own. Sp4c. Dahl's conspicuous gallantry, extraordinary heroism, and intrepidity at the cost of his life, above and beyond the call of duty, are in keeping with the highest traditions of the military service and reflect great credit on himself, his unit, and the U.S. Army.

3201   ◆   *DAVIS, RODNEY MAXWELL

Rank: Sergeant
Service: U.S. Marine Corps
Birthday: 7 April 1942
Place of Birth: Macon, Bibb County, Georgia
Date of Death: 6 September 1967

Place of Death: Republic of Vietnam
Cemetery: Linwood Cemetery—Macon, Georgia
Entered Service at: Macon, Bibb County, Georgia
Unit: 2d Platoon, Company B, 1st Battalion, 5th Marines, 1st Marine Division
Served as: Right Guide
Battle or Place of Action: Quang Nam Province, Republic of Vietnam
Date of Action: 6 September 1967
Date of Presentation: 26 March 1969
Place of Presentation: The Executive Office Building, presented by Vice Pres. Spiro T. Agnew to his family
Citation: For conspicuous gallantry and intrepidity at the risk of his life above and beyond the call of duty while serving as the right guide of the 2d Platoon, Company B, in action against enemy forces. Elements of the 2d Platoon were pinned down by a numerically superior force of attacking North Vietnamese Army regulars. Remnants of the platoon were located in a trench line where Sgt. Davis was directing the fire of his men in an attempt to repel the enemy attack. Disregarding the enemy hand grenades and high volume of small-arms and mortar fire, Sgt. Davis moved from man to man shouting words of encouragement to each of them while firing and throwing grenades at the onrushing enemy. When an enemy grenade landed in the trench in the midst of his men, Sgt. Davis realizing the gravity of the situation, and in a final valiant act of complete self-sacrifice, instantly threw himself upon the grenade, absorbing with his body the full and terrific force of the explosion. Through his extraordinary initiative and inspiring valor in the face of almost certain death, Sgt. Davis saved his comrades from injury and possible loss of life, enabled his platoon to hold its vital position, and upheld the highest traditions of the Marine Corps and the U.S. Naval Service. He gallantly gave his life for his country.

3202   ◆   DAVIS, SAMMY LEE

Rank: Sergeant (rank at time of action: Private First Class) (highest rank: Sergeant First Class)
Service: U.S. Army
Birthday: 1 November 1946
Place of Birth: Dayton, Montgomery County, Ohio
Entered Service at: Indianapolis, Marion County, Indiana
Unit: Battery C, 2d Battalion, 4th Artillery, 9th Infantry Division
Served as: Cannoneer
Battle or Place of Action: Firebase Cudgil, west of Cai Lay, Republic of Vietnam
Date of Action: 18 November 1967
G.O. Number, Date: 75, 10 December 1968
Date of Presentation: 19 November 1968
Place of Presentation: The White House, presented by Pres. Lyndon B. Johnson
Citation: For conspicuous gallantry and intrepidity in action at the risk of his life above and beyond the call of duty. Sgt. Davis (then Pfc.) distinguished himself during the early morning hours while serving as a cannoneer with Battery C, at a remote fire support base. At approximately 0200 hours the fire support base was under heavy enemy mortar attack.

Simultaneously, an estimated reinforced Viet Cong battalion launched a fierce ground assault upon the fire support base. The attacking enemy drove to within 25 meters of the friendly positions. Only a river separated the Viet Cong from the fire support base. Detecting a nearby enemy position, Sgt. Davis seized a machine gun and provided covering fire for his gun crew, as they attempted to bring direct artillery fire on the enemy. Despite his efforts, an enemy recoilless-rifle round scored a direct hit upon the artillery piece. The resultant blast hurled the gun crew from their weapon and blew Sgt. Davis into a foxhole. He struggled to his feet and returned to the howitzer, which was burning furiously. Ignoring repeated warnings to seek cover, Sgt. Davis rammed a shell into the gun. Disregarding a withering hail of enemy fire directed against his position, he aimed and fired the howitzer which rolled backward, knocking Sgt. Davis violently to the ground. Undaunted, he returned to the weapon to fire again when an enemy mortar round exploded within 20 meters of his position, injuring him painfully. Nevertheless, Sgt. Davis loaded the artillery piece, aimed, and fired. Again he was knocked down by the recoil. In complete disregard for his safety, Sgt. Davis loaded and fired three more shells into the enemy. Disregarding his extensive injuries and his inability to swim, Sgt. Davis picked up an air mattress and struck out across the deep river to rescue three wounded comrades on the far side. Upon reaching the three wounded men, he stood upright and fired into the dense vegetation to prevent the Viet Cong from advancing. While the most seriously wounded soldier was helped across the river, Sgt. Davis protected the two remaining casualties until he could pull them across the river to the fire support base. Though suffering from painful wounds, he refused medical attention, joining another howitzer crew which fired at the large Viet Cong force until it broke contact and fled. Sgt. Davis' extraordinary heroism, at the risk of his life, is in keeping with the highest traditions of the military service and reflect great credit upon himself and the U.S. Army.

3203 ◆ DAY, GEORGE EVERETTE "BUD"

Rank: Colonel (rank at time of action: Major)
Service: U.S. Air Force
Birthday: 24 February 1925
Place of Birth: Sioux City, Woodbury County, Iowa
Entered Service at: Sioux City, Woodbury County, Iowa
Unit: Misty Super FAC's F-100 Squadron, Phu Cat Air Base
Served as: Pilot of an F-100
Battle or Place of Action: over North Vietnam
Date of Action: 26 August 1967
G.O. Number, Date: GB-180, 22 March 1976
Date of Presentation: 6 March 1976
Place of Presentation: The White House, presented by Pres. Gerald R. Ford
Citation: On 26 August 1967, Col. Day was forced to eject from his aircraft over North Vietnam when it was hit by ground fire. His right arm was broken in three places, and his left knee was badly sprained. He was immediately captured by hostile forces and taken to a prison camp where he was interrogated and severely tortured. After causing the guards to

relax their vigilance, Col. Day escaped into the jungle and began the trek toward South Vietnam. Despite injuries inflicted by fragments of a bomb or rocket, he continued southward surviving only on a few berries and uncooked frogs. He successfully evaded enemy patrols and reached the Ben Hai River, where he encountered U.S. artillery barrages. With the aid of a bamboo log float, Col. Day swam across the river and entered the demilitarized zone. Due to delirium, he lost his sense of direction and wandered aimlessly for several days. After several unsuccessful attempts to signal U.S. aircraft, he was ambushed and recaptured by the Viet Cong, sustaining gunshot wounds to his left hand and thigh. He was returned to the prison from which he had escaped and later was moved to Hanoi after giving his captors false information to questions put before him. Physically, Col. Day was totally debilitated and unable to perform even the simplest task for himself. Despite his many injuries, he continued to offer maximum resistance. His personal bravery in the face of deadly enemy pressure was significant in saving the lives of fellow aviators who were still flying against the enemy. Col. Day's conspicuous gallantry and intrepidity at the risk of his life above and beyond the call of duty are in keeping with the highest traditions of the U.S. Air Force and reflect great credit upon himself and the U.S. Armed Forces.
Notes: POW from 26 August 1967—February 1973 Shot down over North Vietnam on 26 August 1967, he spent 67 months as a prisoner of war. Col. Day was the only POW to escape from prison in North Vietnam and then be recaptured by the Viet Cong in the South.

3204 ◆ *DE LA GARZA JR., EMILIO ALBERT

Rank: Lance Corporal
Service: U.S. Marine Corps
Birthday: 23 June 1949
Place of Birth: East Chicago, Lake County, Indiana
Date of Death: 11 April 1970
Place of Death: Republic of Vietnam
Cemetery: Saint John's Cemetery (MH)—Hammond, Indiana
Entered Service at: Chicago, Cook County, Illinois
Unit: Company E, 2d Battalion, 1st Marines, 1st Marine Division (Rein) FMF
Served as: Machine Gunner
Battle or Place of Action: near Da Nang, Republic of Vietnam
Date of Action: 11 April 1970
Date of Presentation: 9 September 1971
Place of Presentation: The White House, presented by Vice Pres. Spiro T. Agnew to his family
Citation: For conspicuous gallantry and intrepidity at the risk of his life above and beyond the call of duty while serving as a machine gunner with Company E. Returning with his squad from a night ambush operation, L/Cpl. De La Garza joined his platoon commander and another marine in searching for two enemy soldiers who had been observed fleeing for cover toward a small pond. Moments later, he located one of the enemy soldiers hiding among the reeds and brush. As the three marines attempted to remove the resisting soldier from

the pond, L/Cpl. De La Garza observed him pull the pin on a grenade. Shouting a warning, L/Cpl. De La Garza placed himself between the other two marines and the ensuing blast from the grenade, thereby saving the lives of his comrades at the sacrifice of his life. By his prompt and decisive action and his great personal valor in the face of almost certain death, L/Cpl. De La Garza upheld and further enhanced the finest traditions of the Marine Corps and the U.S. Naval Service.

3205 ◆ DETHLEFSEN, MERLYN HANS

Rank: Major (rank at time of action: Captain) (highest rank: Colonel)
Service: U.S. Air Force
Birthday: 29 June 1934
Place of Birth: Greenville, Clay County, Iowa
Date of Death: 14 December 1987
Place of Death: Fort Worth, Texas
Cemetery: Arlington National Cemetery (65-1626) (MH)—Arlington, Virginia
Entered Service at: Royal, Clay County, Iowa
Unit: 354th Tactical Fighter Squadron, Takhli Royal Thai AFB, Thailand
Served as: Pilot of an F-105
Battle or Place of Action: Thai Nguyen, North Vietnam
Date of Action: 10 March 1967
G.O. Number, Date: GB-51, 8 February 1968
Date of Presentation: 1 February 1968
Place of Presentation: The White House, presented by Pres. Lyndon B. Johnson
Citation: Maj. Dethlefsen was one of a flight of F-105 aircraft engaged in a fire suppression mission designed to destroy a key antiaircraft defensive complex containing surface-to-air missiles (SAM), an exceptionally heavy concentration of antiaircraft artillery, and other automatic weapons. The defensive network was situated to dominate the approach and provide protection to an important North Vietnam industrial center that was scheduled to be attacked by fighter bombers immediately after the strike by Maj. Dethlefsen's flight. In the initial attack on the defensive complex the lead aircraft was crippled, and Maj. Dethlefsen's aircraft was extensively damaged by the intense enemy fire. Realizing that the success of the impending fighter bomber attack on the center now depended on his ability to effectively suppress the defensive fire, Maj. Dethlefsen ignored the enemy's overwhelming firepower and the damage to his aircraft and pressed his attack. Despite a continuing hail of antiaircraft fire, deadly surface-to-air missiles, and counterattacks by MIG interceptors, Maj. Dethlefsen flew repeated close-range strikes to silence the enemy defensive positions with bombs and cannon fire. His action in rendering ineffective the defensive SAM and antiaircraft artillery sites enabled the ensuing fighter bombers to strike successfully the important industrial target without loss or damage to their aircraft, thereby appreciably reducing the enemy's ability to provide essential war material. Maj. Dethlefsen's consummate skill and selfless dedication to this significant mission were in keeping with the highest traditions of the U.S. Air Force and reflect great credit upon himself and the Armed Forces of his country.

3206 ◆ *DEVORE JR., EDWARD ALLEN

Rank: Specialist Fourth Class
Service: U.S. Army
Birthday: 15 June 1947
Place of Birth: Torrance, Los Angeles County, California
Date of Death: 17 March 1968
Place of Death: Republic of Vietnam
Cemetery: Green Hills Memorial Park—San Pedro, California
Entered Service at: Harbor City, Los Angeles County, California
Unit: Company B, 4th Battalion, 39th Infantry, 9th Infantry Division
Served as: Machine Gunner
Battle or Place of Action: near Saigon, Republic of Vietnam
Date of Action: 17 March 1968
G.O. Number, Date: 16, 23 April 1970
Date of Presentation: 7 April 1970
Place of Presentation: The White House, presented by Pres. Richard M. Nixon to his family
Citation: For conspicuous gallantry and intrepidity in action at the risk of his life above and beyond the call of duty. Sp4c. Devore distinguished himself by exceptionally valorous actions on the afternoon of 17 March 1968, while serving as a machine gunner with Company B, on a reconnaissance-in-force mission approximately five kilometers south of Saigon. Sp4c. Devore's platoon, the company's lead element, abruptly came under intense fire from automatic weapons, claymore mines, rockets, and grenades from well-concealed bunkers in a nipa palm swamp. One man was killed and three wounded about 20 meters from the bunker complex. Sp4c. Devore raced through a hail of fire to provide a base of fire with his machine gun, enabling the point element to move the wounded back to friendly lines. After supporting artillery, gunships, and air strikes had been employed on the enemy positions, a squad was sent forward to retrieve their fallen comrades. Intense enemy frontal and enfilading automatic-weapons fire pinned down this element in the kill zone. With complete disregard for his personal safety, Sp4c. Devore assaulted the enemy positions. Hit in the shoulder and knocked down about 35 meters short of his objectives, Sp4c. Devore, ignoring his pain and the warnings of his fellow soldiers, jumped to his feet and continued his assault under intense hostile fire. Although mortally wounded during this advance, he continued to place highly accurate suppressive fire upon the entrenched insurgents. By drawing the enemy fire upon himself, Sp4c. Devore enabled the trapped squad to rejoin the platoon in safety. Sp4c. Devore's extraordinary heroism and devotion to duty in close combat were in keeping with the highest traditions of the military service and reflect great credit upon himself, the 39th Infantry, and the U.S. Army.

3207 ◆ *DIAS, RALPH ELLIS

Rank: Private First Class
Service: U.S. Marine Corps
Birthday: 15 July 1950

Place of Birth: Shelocta, Armstrong County, Pennsylvania
Date of Death: 12 November 1969
Place of Death: Republic of Vietnam
Cemetery: Oakdale Cemetery (MH)—Leetonia, Ohio
Entered Service at: Pittsburgh, Allegheny County, Pennsylvania
Unit: 3d Platoon, Company D, 1st Battalion, 7th Marines, 1st Marine Division (Rein) FMF
Served as: Rifleman
Battle or Place of Action: Que Son Mountains, Republic of Vietnam
Date of Action: 12 November 1969
Date of Presentation: 17 July 1974
Place of Presentation: Blair House, presented by Vice Pres. Gerald R. Ford to his family
Citation: As a member of a reaction force which was pinned down by enemy fire while assisting a platoon in the same circumstance, Pfc. Dias, observing that both units were sustaining casualties, initiated an aggressive assault against an enemy machine-gun bunker which was the principal source of hostile fire. Severely wounded by enemy snipers while charging across the open area, he pulled himself to the shelter of a nearby rock. Braving enemy fire for a second time, Pfc. Dias was again wounded. Unable to walk, he crawled 15 meters to the protection of a rock located near his objective and, repeatedly exposing himself to intense hostile fire, unsuccessfully threw several hand grenades at the machine-gun emplacement. Still determined to destroy the emplacement, Pfc. Dias again moved into the open and was wounded a third time by sniper fire. As he threw a last grenade, which destroyed the enemy position, he was mortally wounded by another enemy round. Pfc. Dias' indomitable courage, dynamic initiative, and selfless devotion to duty upheld the highest traditions of the Marine Corps and the U.S. Naval Service. He gallantly gave his life in the service of his country.

3208 ◆ *DICKEY, DOUGLAS EUGENE

Rank: Private First Class
Service: U.S. Marine Corps
Birthday: 24 December 1946
Place of Birth: Greenville, Darke County, Ohio
Date of Death: 26 March 1967
Place of Death: Republic of Vietnam
Cemetery: Brock Cemetery (MH)—Rossburg, Ohio
Entered Service at: Cincinnati, Hamilton County, Ohio
Unit: 2d Platoon, Company C, 1st Battalion, 4th Marines, 9th Marine Amphibious Brigade, 3d Marine Division (Rein) FMF
Served as: Rifleman
Battle or Place of Action: near Gio An, Quang Tri Province, Republic of Vietnam
Date of Action: 26 March 1967
Date of Presentation: 16 April 1968
Place of Presentation: Marine Barracks, Washington, D.C., presented by Sec. of the Navy Paul R. Ignatius to his family
Citation: For conspicuous gallantry and intrepidity at the risk of his life above and beyond the call of duty. While participating in Operation Beacon Hill 1, the 2d Platoon was

engaged in a fierce battle with the Viet Cong at close-range in dense jungle foliage. Pfc. Dickey had come forward to replace a radio operator who had been wounded in this intense action and was being treated by a medical corpsman. Suddenly an enemy grenade landed in the midst of a group of marines, which included the wounded radio operator who was immobilized. Fully realizing the inevitable result of his actions, Pfc. Dickey, in a final valiant act, quickly and unhesitatingly threw himself upon the deadly grenade, absorbing with his body the full and complete force of the explosion. Pfc. Dickey's personal heroism, extraordinary valor and selfless courage saved a number of his comrades from certain injury and possible death at the cost of his life. His actions reflected great credit upon himself, the Marine Corps, and the U.S. Naval Service. He gallantly gave his life for his country.

3209 ◆ DIX, DREW DENNIS

Rank: Staff Sergeant (highest rank: Major)
Service: U.S. Army
Birthday: 14 December 1944
Place of Birth: West Point, Orange County, New York
Entered Service at: Denver, Denver County, Colorado
Unit: Senior Advisor Group, IV Corps, Military Assistance Command
Served as: Unit Advisor
Battle or Place of Action: Chau Doc Province, Republic of Vietnam
Date of Action: 31 January-1 February 1968
G.O. Number, Date: 10, 6 February 1969
Date of Presentation: 16 January 1969
Place of Presentation: The White House, presented by Pres. Lyndon B. Johnson
Citation: For conspicuous gallantry and intrepidity in action at the risk of his life above and beyond the call of duty. S/Sgt. Dix distinguished himself by exceptional heroism while serving as a unit adviser. Two heavily armed Viet Cong battalions attacked the province capital city of Chau Phu resulting in the complete breakdown and fragmentation of the defenses of the city. S/Sgt. Dix with a patrol of Vietnamese soldiers, was recalled to assist in defense of Chau Phu. Learning that a nurse was trapped in a house near the center of the city, S/Sgt. Dix organized a relief force, successfully rescued the nurse, and returned her to the safety of the Tactical Operations Center. Being informed of other trapped civilians within the city, S/Sgt. Dix voluntarily led another force to rescue eight civilian employees located in a building which was under heavy mortar and small-arms fire. S/Sgt. Dix then returned to the center of the city. Upon approaching a building, he was subjected to intense automatic rifle and machine-gun fire from an unknown number of Viet Cong. He personally assaulted the building, killing six Viet Cong, and rescuing two Filipinos. The following day S/Sgt. Dix, still on his own volition, assembled a 20-man force and though under intense enemy fire cleared the Viet Cong out of the hotel, theater, and other adjacent buildings within the city. During this portion of the attack, Army of the Republic of Vietnam soldiers inspired by the heroism and success of S/Sgt. Dix, rallied and commenced firing upon the Viet

Cong. S/Sgt. Dix captured 20 prisoners, including a high-ranking Viet Cong official. He then attacked enemy troops who had entered the residence of the Deputy Province Chief and was successful in rescuing the official's wife and children. S/Sgt. Dix's personal heroic actions resulted in 14 confirmed Viet Cong killed in action and possibly 25 more, the capture of 20 prisoners, 15 weapons, and the rescue of the 14 United States and free-world civilians. The heroism of S/Sgt. Dix was in the highest tradition and reflects great credit upon the U.S. Army.

3210 ◆ *DOANE, STEPHEN HOLDEN

Rank: First Lieutenant
Service: U.S. Army
Birthday: 13 October 1947
Place of Birth: Beverly, Essex County, Massachusetts
Date of Death: 25 March 1969
Place of Death: Republic of Vietnam
Cemetery: Arlington National Cemetery (59-1617) (MH)—Arlington, Virginia
Entered Service at: Albany, Albany County, New York
Unit: Company B, 1st Battalion, 5th Infantry, 25th Infantry Division
Served as: Platoon Leader
Battle or Place of Action: Hau Nghia Province, Republic of Vietnam
Date of Action: 25 March 1969
G.O. Number, Date: 7, 9 March 1971
Date of Presentation: 16 February 1971
Place of Presentation: The White House (East Ballroom), presented by Pres. Richard M. Nixon to his family
Citation: For conspicuous gallantry and intrepidity in action at the risk of his life above and beyond the call of duty. 1st Lt. Doane was serving as a platoon leader when his company, engaged in a tactical operation, abruptly contacted an enemy force concealed in protected bunkers and trenches. Three of the leading soldiers were pinned down by enemy crossfire. One was seriously wounded. After efforts of one platoon to rescue these men had failed, it became obvious that only a small group could successfully move close enough to destroy the enemy position and rescue or relieve the trapped soldiers. 1st Lt. Doane, although fully aware of the danger of such an action, crawled to the nearest enemy bunker and silenced it. He was wounded but continued to advance to a second enemy bunker. As he prepared to throw a grenade, he was again wounded. Undaunted, he deliberately pulled the pin on the grenade and lunged with it into the enemy bunker, destroying this final obstacle. 1st Lt. Doane's supreme act enabled his company to rescue the trapped men without further casualties. The extraordinary courage and selflessness displayed by this officer were an inspiration to his men and are in the highest traditions of the U.S. Army.

3211 ◆ DOLBY, DAVID CHARLES

Rank: Sergeant (rank at time of action: Specialist Fourth Class) (highest rank: Staff Sergeant)
Service: U.S. Army
Birthday: 14 May 1946
Place of Birth: Norristown, Montgomery County, Pennsylvania
Entered Service at: Philadelphia, Philadelphia County, Pennsylvania
Unit: Company B, 1st Battalion (Airborne), 8th Cavalry, 1st Cavalry Division
Served as: Machine Gunner
Battle or Place of Action: Republic of Vietnam
Date of Action: 21 May 1966
G.O. Number, Date: 45, 20 October 1967
Date of Presentation: 28 September 1967
Place of Presentation: The White House, presented by Pres. Lyndon B. Johnson
Citation: For conspicuous gallantry and intrepidity at the risk of his life above and beyond the call of duty, when his platoon, while advancing tactically, suddenly came under intense fire from the enemy located on a ridge immediately to the front. Six members of the platoon were killed instantly and a number were wounded, including the platoon leader. Sgt. Dolby's every move brought fire from the enemy. However, aware that the platoon leader was critically wounded, and that the platoon was in a precarious situation, Sgt. Dolby moved the wounded men to safety and deployed the remainder of the platoon to engage the enemy. Subsequently, his dying platoon leader ordered Sgt. Dolby to withdraw the forward elements to rejoin the platoon. Despite the continuing intense enemy fire and with utter disregard for his own safety, Sgt. Dolby positioned abled-bodied men to cover the withdrawal of the forward elements, assisted the wounded to the new position, and he, alone, attacked enemy positions until his ammunition was expended. Replenishing his ammunition, he returned to the area of most intense action, single-handedly killed three enemy machine gunners, and neutralized the enemy fire, thus enabling friendly elements on the flank to advance on the enemy redoubt. He defied the enemy fire to personally carry a seriously wounded soldier to safety where he could be treated and, returning to the forward area, he crawled through withering fire to within 50 meters of the enemy bunkers and threw smoke grenades to mark them for air strikes. Although repeatedly under fire at close range from enemy snipers and automatic weapons, Sgt. Dolby directed artillery fire on the enemy and succeeded in silencing several enemy weapons. He remained in his exposed location until his comrades had displaced to more secure positions. His actions of unsurpassed valor during four hours of intense combat were a source of inspiration to his entire company, contributed significantly to the success of the overall assault on the enemy position, and were directly responsible for saving the lives of a number of his fellow soldiers. Sgt. Dolby's heroism was in the highest traditions of the U.S. Army.

3212 ◆ DONLON, ROGER HUGH CHARLES

Rank: Captain (highest rank: Colonel)
Service: U.S. Army
Birthday: 30 January 1934
Place of Birth: Saugerties, Ulster County, New York
Entered Service at: Saugerties, Ulster County, New York

Unit: Detachment A-726, 7th Special Forces Group (Airborne), 1st Special Forces
Served as: Commanding Officer
Battle or Place of Action: near Nam Dong, Republic of Vietnam
Date of Action: 6 July 1964
G.O. Number, Date: 41, 17 December 1964
Date of Presentation: 5 December 1964
Place of Presentation: The White House (East Ballroom), presented by Pres. Lyndon B. Johnson
Citation: For conspicuous gallantry and intrepidity at the risk of his life above and beyond the call of duty while defending a U.S. military installation against a fierce attack by hostile forces. Capt. Donlon was serving as the commanding officer of the U.S. Army Special Forces Detachment A-726 at Camp Nam Dong when a reinforced Viet Cong battalion suddenly launched a full-scale, predawn attack on the camp. During the violent battle that ensued, lasting five hours and resulting in heavy casualties on both sides, Capt. Donlon directed the defense operations in the midst of an enemy barrage of mortar shells, falling grenades, and extremely heavy gunfire. Upon the initial onslaught, he swiftly marshaled his forces and ordered the removal of the needed ammunition from a blazing building. He then dashed through a hail of small arms and exploding hand grenades to abort a breach of the main gate. En route to this position he detected an enemy demolition team of three in the proximity of the main gate and quickly annihilated them. Although exposed to the intense grenade attack, he then succeeded in reaching a 60-mm mortar position despite sustaining a severe stomach wound as he was within five yards of the gun pit. When he discovered that most of the men in this gun pit were also wounded, he completely disregarded his own injury, directed their withdrawal to a location 30 meters away, and again risked his life by remaining behind and covering the movement with the utmost effectiveness. Noticing that his team sergeant was unable to evacuate the gun pit he crawled toward him and, while dragging the fallen soldier out of the gun pit, an enemy mortar exploded and inflicted a wound in Capt. Donlon's left shoulder. Although suffering from multiple wounds, he carried the abandoned 60-mm mortar weapon to a new location 30 meters away where he found three wounded defenders. After administering first aid and encouragement to these men, he left the weapon with them, headed toward another position, and retrieved a 57-mm recoilless rifle. Then with great courage and coolness under fire, he returned to the abandoned gun pit, evacuated ammunition for the two weapons, and while crawling and dragging the urgently needed ammunition, received a third wound in his leg by an enemy hand grenade. Despite his critical physical condition, he again crawled 175 meters to an 81-mm mortar position and directed firing operations which protected the seriously threatened east sector of the camp. He then moved to an eastern 60-mm mortar position and upon determining that the vicious enemy assault had weakened, crawled back to the gun pit with the 60-mm mortar, set it up for defensive operations, and turned it over to two defenders with minor wounds. Without hesitation, he left this sheltered position, and moved from position to position around the beleaguered perimeter while hurling hand grenades at the enemy and inspiring his men to superhuman effort. As he bravely continued to move around the perimeter, a mortar shell exploded, wounding him in the face and body. As the long awaited daylight brought defeat to the enemy forces and their retreat back to the jungle leaving behind 54 of their dead, many weapons, and grenades, Capt. Donlon immediately reorganized his defenses and administered first aid to the wounded. His dynamic leadership, fortitude, and valiant efforts inspired not only the American personnel but the friendly Vietnamese defenders as well and resulted in the successful defense of the camp. Capt. Donlon's extraordinary heroism, at the risk of his life above and beyond the call of duty, are in the highest traditions of the U.S. Army and reflect great credit upon himself and the Armed Forces of his country.

3213 ◆ DUNAGAN, KERN WAYNE

Rank: Major (rank at time of action: Captain) (highest rank: Colonel)
Service: U.S. Army
Birthday: 20 February 1934
Place of Birth: Superior, Pinal County, Arizona
Date of Death: 27 December 1991
Place of Death: Nevada City, California
Cemetery: Golden Gate National Cemetery (1-3-92) (WS-117-1) (MH)—San Francisco, California
Entered Service at: Los Angeles, Los Angeles County, California
Unit: Company A, 1st Battalion, 46th Infantry, Americal Division
Served as: Commanding Officer
Battle or Place of Action: Quang Tin Province, Republic of Vietnam
Date of Action: 13 May 1969
G.O. Number, Date: 39, 23 July 1971
Date of Presentation: 15 June 1971
Place of Presentation: The White House (East Ballroom), presented by Pres. Richard M. Nixon
Citation: For conspicuous gallantry and intrepidity in action at the risk of his life above and beyond the call of duty. Maj. (then Capt.) Dunagan distinguished himself during the period 13 and 14 May 1969, while serving as commanding officer, Company A. On 13 May 1969, Maj. Dunagan was leading an attack to relieve pressure on the battalion's forward support base when his company came under intense fire from a well-entrenched enemy battalion. Despite continuous hostile fire from a numerically superior force, Maj. Dunagan repeatedly and fearlessly exposed himself in order to locate enemy positions, direct friendly supporting artillery, and position the men of his company. In the early evening, while directing an element of his unit into perimeter guard, he was seriously wounded during an enemy mortar attack, but he refused to leave the battlefield and continued to supervise the evacuation of dead and wounded and to lead his command in the difficult task of disengaging from an aggressive enemy. In spite of painful wounds and extreme fatigue, Maj. Dunagan risked heavy fire on two occasions to rescue critically wounded men. He was again seriously wounded. Undaunted, he

continued to display outstanding courage, professional competence, and leadership and successfully extricated his command from its untenable position on the evening of 14 May. Having maneuvered his command into contact with an adjacent friendly unit, he learned that a six-man party from his company was under fire and had not reached the new perimeter. Maj. Dunagan unhesitatingly went back and searched for his men. Finding one soldier critically wounded, Maj. Dunagan, ignoring his wounds, lifted the man to his shoulders and carried him to the comparative safety of the friendly perimeter. Before permitting himself to be evacuated, he insured all of his wounded received emergency treatment and were removed from the area. Throughout the engagement, Maj. Dunagan's actions gave great inspiration to his men and were directly responsible for saving the lives of many of his fellow soldiers. Maj. Dunagan's extraordinary heroism, above and beyond the call of duty, are in the highest traditions of the U.S. Army and reflect great credit on him, his unit, and the U.S. Army.

3214 ◆ *DURHAM JR., HAROLD BASCOM

Rank: Second Lieutenant
Service: U.S. Army
Birthday: 12 October 1942
Place of Birth: Rocky Mount, Edgecombe County, North Carolina
Date of Death: 17 October 1967
Place of Death: Republic of Vietnam
Cemetery: Oakridge Cemetery—Tifton, Georgia
Entered Service at: Atlanta, Fulton County, Georgia
Unit: Battery C, 6th Battalion, 15th Artillery, 1st Infantry Division
Served as: Forward Observer
Battle or Place of Action: Republic of Vietnam
Date of Action: 17 October 1967
G.O. Number, Date: 74, 20 November 1969
Date of Presentation: 31 October 1969
Place of Presentation: The Executive Office Building, presented by Vice Pres. Spiro T. Agnew to his family
Citation: 2nd Lt. Durham, Artillery, distinguished himself by conspicuous gallantry and intrepidity at the cost of his life above and beyond the call of duty while assigned to Battery C. 2nd Lt. Durham was serving as a forward observer with Company D, 2d Battalion, 28th Infantry during a battalion reconnaissance-in-force mission. At approximately 1015 hours contact was made with an enemy force concealed in well-camouflaged positions and fortified bunkers. 2nd Lt. Durham immediately moved into an exposed position to adjust the supporting artillery fire onto the insurgents. During a brief lull in the battle he administered emergency first aid to the wounded in spite of heavy enemy sniper fire directed toward him. Moments later, as enemy units assaulted friendly positions, he learned that Company A, bearing the brunt of the attack, had lost its forward observer. While he was moving to replace the wounded observer, the enemy detonated a claymore mine, severely wounding him in the head and impairing his vision. In spite of the intense pain, he continued to direct the supporting artillery fire and to employ his individual weapon in support of the hard-pressed infantrymen. As the enemy pressed their attack, 2d Lt. Durham called for supporting fire to be placed almost directly on his position. Twice the insurgents were driven back, leaving many dead and wounded behind. 2nd Lt. Durham was then taken to a secondary defensive position. Even in his extremely weakened condition, he continued to call artillery fire onto the enemy. He refused to seek cover and instead positioned himself in a small clearing which offered a better vantage point from which to adjust the fire. Suddenly, he was severely wounded a second time by enemy machine-gun fire. As he lay on the ground near death, he saw two Viet Cong approaching, shooting the defenseless wounded men. With his last effort, 2d Lt. Durham shouted a warning to a nearby soldier who immediately killed the insurgents. 2nd Lt. Durham died moments later, still grasping the radio handset. 2nd Lt. Durham's gallant actions in close combat with an enemy force are in keeping with the highest traditions of the military service and reflect great credit upon himself, his unit, and the U.S. Army.

3215 ◆ *ENGLISH JR., GLENN HARRY

Rank: Staff Sergeant
Service: U.S. Army
Birthday: 23 April 1940
Place of Birth: Altoona, Blair County, Pennsylvania
Date of Death: 7 September 1970
Place of Death: Republic of Vietnam
Cemetery: Fort Bragg Post Cemetery (I-288-A) (MH)—Fort Bragg, North Carolina
Entered Service at: Philadelphia, Philadelphia County, Pennsylvania
Unit: Company E, 3d Battalion, 503d Infantry, 173d Airborne Brigade
Served as: Squad Leader
Battle or Place of Action: Phu My District, Republic of Vietnam
Date of Action: 7 September 1970
G.O. Number, Date: 39, 6 September 1974
Date of Presentation: 8 August 1974
Place of Presentation: Blair House, presented by Vice Pres. Gerald R. Ford to his family
Citation: S/Sgt. English was riding in the lead armored personnel carrier in a four-vehicle column when an enemy mine exploded in front of his vehicle. As the vehicle swerved from the road, a concealed enemy force waiting in ambush opened fire with automatic weapons and antitank grenades, striking the vehicle several times and setting it on fire. S/Sgt. English escaped from the disabled vehicle and, without pausing to extinguish the flames on his clothing, rallied his stunned unit. He then led it in a vigorous assault, in the face of heavy enemy automatic-weapons fire, on the entrenched enemy position. This prompt and courageous action routed the enemy and saved his unit from destruction. Following the assault, S/Sgt. English heard the cries of three men still trapped inside the vehicle. Paying no heed to warnings that the ammunition and fuel in the burning personnel carrier might explode at any moment, S/Sgt. English raced to the vehicle and climbed inside to rescue his wounded comrades. As he was lifting one of the men to safety, the vehicle exploded, mortally wounding him and the man he was attempting

to save. By his extraordinary devotion to duty, indomitable courage, and utter disregard for his own safety, S/Sgt. English saved his unit from destruction and selflessly sacrificed his life in a brave attempt to save three comrades. S/Sgt. English's conspicuous gallantry and intrepidity in action at the cost of his life were an inspiration to his comrades and are in the highest traditions of the U.S. Army.

3216 ◆ *ESTOCIN, MICHAEL JOHN

Rank: Captain (rank at time of action: Lieutenant Commander)
Service: U.S. Navy
Birthday: 27 April 1931
Place of Birth: Turtle Creek, Allegheny County, Pennsylvania
Date of Death: 26 April 1967
Place of Death: North Vietnam
Cemetery: Fort Rosecrans National Cemetery ('In Memory' marker) (MA-112)—San Diego, California
Entered Service at: Akron, Summit County, Ohio
Unit: Attack Squadron 192, U.S.S. *Ticonderoga* (CVA-14)
Served as: Pilot
Battle or Place of Action: Haiphong, North Vietnam
Date of Action: 20, 26 April 1967
Date of Presentation: 27 February 1978
Place of Presentation: The Pentagon (Hall of Heroes), presented by Sec. of the Navy W. Graham Claytor Jr. to his family
Citation: For conspicuous gallantry and intrepidity at the risk of his life above and beyond the call of duty on 20 and 26 April 1967 as a pilot in Attack Squadron 192, embarked in U.S.S. *Ticonderoga* (CVA-14). Leading a three-plane group of aircraft in support of a coordinated strike against two thermal powerplants in Haiphong, North Vietnam, on 20 April 1967, Capt. Estocin provided continuous warnings to the strike group leaders of the surface-to-air missile (SAM) threats, and personally neutralized three SAM sites. Although his aircraft was severely damaged by an exploding missile, he reentered the target area and relentlessly prosecuted a SHRIKE attack in the face of intense antiaircraft fire. With less than five minutes of fuel remaining he departed the target area and commenced in-flight refueling which continued for over 100 miles. Three miles aft of the *Ticonderoga*, and without enough fuel for a second approach, he disengaged from the tanker and executed a precise approach to a fiery arrested landing. On 26 April 1967, in support of a coordinated strike against the vital fuel facilities in Haiphong, he led an attack on a threatening SAM site, during which his aircraft was seriously damaged by an exploding SAM, nevertheless, he regained control of his burning aircraft and courageously launched his SHRIKE missiles before departing the area. By his inspiring courage and unswerving devotion to duty in the face of grave personal danger, Capt. Estocin upheld the highest traditions of the U.S. Naval Service.

3217 ◆ *EVANS JR., DONALD WARD

Rank: Specialist Fourth Class
Service: U.S. Army
Birthday: 23 July 1943

Place of Birth: Covina, Los Angeles County, California
Date of Death: 27 January 1967
Place of Death: Republic of Vietnam
Cemetery: Oakdale Memorial Park—Glendora, California
Entered Service at: Covina, Los Angeles County, California
Unit: Company A, 2d Battalion, 12th Infantry, 4th Infantry Division
Served as: Medical Aidman
Battle or Place of Action: Tri Tam, Republic of Vietnam
Date of Action: 27 January 1967
G.O. Number, Date: 34, 5 July 1968
Date of Presentation: 4 June 1968
Place of Presentation: The Pentagon, presented by Sec. of the Army Stanley R. Resor to his family
Citation: For conspicuous gallantry and intrepidity in action at the risk of his life above and beyond the call of duty. He left his position of relative safety with his platoon which had not yet been committed to the battle to answer the calls for medical aid from the wounded men of another platoon which was heavily engaged with the enemy force. Dashing across 100 meters of open area through a withering hail of enemy fire and exploding grenades, he administered lifesaving treatment to one individual and continued to expose himself to the deadly enemy fire as he moved to treat each of the other wounded men and to offer them encouragement. Realizing that the wounds of one man required immediate attention, Sp4c. Evans dragged the injured soldier back across the dangerous fire-swept area, to a secure position from which he could be further evacuated. Miraculously escaping the enemy fusillade, Sp4c. Evans returned to the forward location. As he continued the treatment of the wounded, he was struck by fragments from an enemy grenade. Despite his serious and painful injury he succeeded in evacuating another wounded comrade, rejoined his platoon as it was committed to battle and was soon treating other wounded soldiers. As he evacuated another wounded man across the fire-covered field, he was severely wounded. Continuing to refuse medical attention and ignoring advice to remain behind, he managed with his waning strength to move yet another wounded comrade across the dangerous open area to safety. Disregarding his painful wounds and seriously weakened from profuse bleeding, he continued his lifesaving medical aid and was killed while treating another wounded comrade. Sp4c. Evan's extraordinary valor, dedication, and indomitable spirit saved the lives of several of his fellow soldiers, served as an inspiration to the men of his company, were instrumental in the success of their mission, and reflect great credit upon himself and the Armed Forces of his country.

3218 ◆ *EVANS, RODNEY JOHN

Rank: Sergeant
Service: U.S. Army
Birthday: 17 July 1948
Place of Birth: Chelsea, Suffolk County, Massachusetts
Date of Death: 18 July 1969
Place of Death: Republic of Vietnam
Cemetery: Liberty Hill Cemetery—Florala, Alabama
Entered Service at: Montgomery, Montgomery County, Alabama

Unit: Company D, 1st Battalion, 12th Cavalry, 1st Cavalry Division
Served as: Squad Leader
Battle or Place of Action: Tay Ninh Province, Republic of Vietnam
Date of Action: 18 July 1969
G.O. Number, Date: 29, 5 July 1972
Date of Presentation: 22 April 1971
Place of Presentation: The White House, presented by Pres. Richard M. Nixon to his family
Citation: For conspicuous gallantry and intrepidity in action at the risk of his life above and beyond the call of duty. Sgt. Evans distinguished himself by extraordinary heroism while serving as a squad leader in a reconnaissance sweep through heavy vegetation to reconnoiter a strong enemy position. As the force approached a well-defined trail, the platoon scout warned that the trail was booby-trapped. Sgt. Evans led his squad on a route parallel to the trail. The force had started to move forward when a nearby squad was hit by the blast of a concealed mine. Looking to his right Sgt. Evans saw a second enemy device. With complete disregard for his safety he shouted a warning to his men, dived to the ground, and crawled toward the mine. Just as he reached it an enemy soldier detonated the explosive and Sgt. Evans absorbed the full impact with his body. His gallant and selfless action saved his comrades from probable death or injury and served as an inspiration to his entire unit. Sgt. Evans' gallantry in action at the cost of his life was in keeping with the highest traditions of the military service and reflect great credit upon himself, his unit, and the U.S. Army.

3219 ◆ FERGUSON, FREDERICK EDGAR

Rank: Chief Warrant Officer (highest rank: Major)
Service: U.S. Army
Birthday: 18 August 1939
Place of Birth: Pilot Point, Denton County, Texas
Entered Service at: Phoenix, Maricopa County, Arizona
Unit: Company C, 227th Aviation Battalion, 1st Cavalry Division (Airmobile)
Served as: Helicopter Commander
Battle or Place of Action: Hue, Republic of Vietnam
Date of Action: 31 January 1968
G.O. Number, Date: 38, 13 June 1969
Date of Presentation: 17 May 1969
Place of Presentation: The White House, presented by Pres. Richard M. Nixon
Citation: For conspicuous gallantry and intrepidity in action at the risk of his life above and beyond the call of duty. CWO Ferguson, commander of a resupply helicopter monitoring an emergency call from wounded passengers and crewmen of a downed helicopter under heavy attack within the enemy-controlled city of Hue, unhesitatingly volunteered to attempt evacuation. Despite warnings from all aircraft to stay clear of the area due to heavy antiaircraft fire, CWO Ferguson began a low-level flight at maximum airspeed along the Perfume River toward the tiny, isolated South Vietnamese Army compound in which the crash survivors had taken refuge. Coolly and skillfully maintaining his course in the face of intense, short-range fire

from enemy-occupied buildings and boats, he displayed superior flying skill and tenacity of purpose by landing his aircraft in an extremely confined area in a blinding dust cloud under heavy mortar and small-arms fire. Although the helicopter was severely damaged by mortar fragments during the loading of the wounded, CWO Ferguson disregarded the damage and, taking off through the continuing hail of mortar fire, he flew his crippled aircraft on the return route through the rain of fire that he had experienced earlier and safely returned his wounded passengers to friendly control. CWO Ferguson's extraordinary determination saved the lives of five of his comrades. His actions are in the highest traditions of the military service and reflect great credit on himself and the U.S. Army.

3220 ◆ *FERNANDEZ, DANIEL

Rank: Specialist Fourth Class
ice: U.S. Army
Birthday: 30 June 1944
Place of Birth: Albuquerque, Bernalillo County, New Mexico
Date of Death: 18 February 1966
Place of Death: Republic of Vietnam
Cemetery: Santa Fe National Cemetery (S-249) (MH)—Santa Fe, New Mexico
Entered Service at: Albuquerque, Bernalillo County, New Mexico
Unit: Company C, 1st Battalion, 5th Infantry (Mechanized), 25th Infantry Division
Battle or Place of Action: Cu Chi, Hau Nghia Province, Republic of Vietnam
Date of Action: 18 February 1966
G.O. Number, Date: 21, 26 April 1967
Date of Presentation: 6 April 1967
Place of Presentation: The White House (Rose Garden), presented by Pres. Lyndon B. Johnson to his family
Citation: For conspicuous gallantry and intrepidity at the risk of his life above and beyond the call of duty. Sp4c. Fernandez demonstrated indomitable courage when the patrol was ambushed by a Viet Cong rifle company and driven back by the intense enemy automatic-weapons fire before it could evacuate an American soldier who had been wounded in the Viet Cong attack. Sp4c. Fernandez, a sergeant, and two other volunteers immediately fought their way through devastating fire and exploding grenades to reach the fallen soldier. Upon reaching their fallen comrade the sergeant was struck in the knee by machine-gun fire and immobilized. Sp4c. Fernandez took charge, rallied the left flank of his patrol, and began to assist in the recovery of the wounded sergeant. While first aid was being administered to the wounded man, a sudden increase in the accuracy and intensity of the enemy fire forced the volunteer group to take cover. As they did, an enemy grenade landed in the midst of the group, although some men did not see it. Realizing there was no time for the wounded sergeant or the other men to protect themselves from the grenade blast, Sp4c. Fernandez vaulted over the wounded sergeant and threw himself on the grenade as it exploded, saving the lives of his four comrades at the sacrifice of his life. Sp4c. Fernandez' profound concern for his fellow soldiers, at

the risk of his life above and beyond the call of duty, are in the highest traditions of the U.S. Army and reflect great credit upon himself and the Armed Forces of his country.

3221 ◆ FISHER, BERNARD FRANCIS

Rank: Major (highest rank: Colonel)
Service: U.S. Air Force
Birthday: 11 January 1927
Place of Birth: San Bernardino, San Bernardino County, California
Entered Service at: Kuna, Ada County, Idaho
Unit: 1st Air Commandos, United States Air Force
Served as: Pilot of a A-1E Skyraider
Battle or Place of Action: Bien Hoa and Pleiku, Republic of Vietnam
Date of Action: 10 March 1966
G.O. Number, Date: GB-41, 23 January 1967
Date of Presentation: 19 January 1967
Place of Presentation: The White House, presented by Pres. Lyndon B. Johnson
Citation: For conspicuous gallantry and intrepidity at the risk of his life above and beyond the call of duty. On that date, the Special Forces camp at A Shau was under attack by 2,000 North Vietnamese Army regulars. Hostile troops had positioned themselves between the airstrip and the camp. Other hostile troops had surrounded the camp and were continuously raking it with automatic-weapons fire from the surrounding hills. The tops of the 1,500-foot hills were obscured by an 800 foot ceiling, limiting aircraft maneuverability and forcing pilots to operate within range of hostile gun positions, which often were able to fire down on attacking aircraft. During the battle, Maj. Fisher observed a fellow airman crash land on the battle-torn airstrip. In the belief that the downed pilot was seriously injured and in imminent danger of capture, Maj. Fisher announced his intention to land on the airstrip to effect a rescue. Although aware of the extreme danger and likely failure of such an attempt, he elected to continue. Directing his own air cover, he landed his aircraft and taxied almost the full length of the runway, which was littered with battle debris and parts of an exploded aircraft. While effecting a successful rescue of the downed pilot, heavy ground fire was observed, with 19 bullets striking his aircraft. In the face of withering ground fire, he applied power and gained enough speed to lift-off at the overrun of the airstrip. Maj. Fisher's profound concern for his fellow airman, at the risk of his life above and beyond the call of duty, are in the highest traditions of the U.S. Air Force and reflect great credit upon himself and the Armed Forces of his country.

3222 ◆ FITZMAURICE, MICHAEL JOHN

Rank: Specialist Fourth Class
Service: U.S. Army
Birthday: 9 March 1950
Place of Birth: Jamestown, Stutsman County, North Dakota
Entered Service at: Cavour, Beadle County, South Dakota
Unit: 3d Squad, Troop D, 2d Squadron, 17th Cavalry, 101st Airborne Division (Airmobile)

Served as: Rifleman
Battle or Place of Action: Khesanh, Republic of Vietnam
Date of Action: 23 March 1971
G.O. Number, Date: 39, 5 November 1973
Date of Presentation: 15 October 1973
Place of Presentation: The White House, presented by Pres. Richard M. Nixon
Citation: For conspicuous gallantry and intrepidity in action at the risk of his life above and beyond the call of duty. Sp4c. Fitzmaurice, 3d Platoon, Troop D, distinguished himself at Khesanh. Sp4c. Fitzmaurice and three fellow soldiers were occupying a bunker when a company of North Vietnamese sappers infiltrated the area. At the onset of the attack Sp4c. Fitzmaurice observed three explosive charges which had been thrown into the bunker by the enemy. Realizing the imminent danger to his comrades, and with complete disregard for his personal safety, he hurled two of the charges out of the bunker. He then threw his flak vest and himself over the remaining charge. By this courageous act he absorbed the blast and shielded his fellow soldiers. Although suffering from serious multiple wounds and partial loss of sight, he charged out of the bunker and engaged the enemy until his rifle was damaged by the blast of an enemy hand grenade. While in search of another weapon, Sp4c. Fitzmaurice encountered and overcame an enemy sapper in hand-to-hand combat. Having obtained another weapon, he returned to his original fighting position and inflicted additional casualties on the attacking enemy. Although seriously wounded, Sp4c. Fitzmaurice refused to be medically evacuated, preferring to remain at his post. Sp4c. Fitzmaurice's extraordinary heroism in action at the risk of his life contributed significantly to the successful defense of the position and resulted in saving the lives of a number of his fellow soldiers. These acts of heroism go above and beyond the call of duty, are in keeping with the highest traditions of the military service, and reflect great credit on Sp4c. Fitzmaurice and the U.S. Army.

3223 ◆ *FLEEK, CHARLES CLINTON

Rank: Sergeant
Service: U.S. Army
Birthday: 28 August 1947
Place of Birth: Petersburg, Boone County, Kentucky
Date of Death: 27 May 1967
Place of Death: Republic of Vietnam
Cemetery: Petersburg Cemetery (MH)—Petersburg, Kentucky
Entered Service at: Cincinnati, Hamilton County, Ohio
Unit: Company C, 1st Battalion, 27th Infantry, 25th Infantry Division
Served as: Squad Leader
Battle or Place of Action: Binh Duong Province, Republic of Vietnam
Date of Action: 27 May 1967
G.O. Number, Date: 10, 9 March 1971
Date of Presentation: 16 February 1971
Place of Presentation: The White House (East Ballroom), presented by Pres. Richard M. Nixon to his family
Citation: For conspicuous gallantry and intrepidity in action

at the risk of his life above and beyond the call of duty. Sgt. Fleek distinguished himself while serving as a squad leader in Company C, during an ambush operation. Sgt. Fleek's unit was deployed in ambush locations when a large enemy force approached the position. Suddenly, the leading enemy element, sensing the ambush, halted and started to withdraw. Reacting instantly, Sgt. Fleek opened fire and directed the effective fire of his men upon the numerically superior enemy force. During the fierce battle that followed, an enemy soldier threw a grenade into the squad position. Realizing that his men had not seen the grenade, Sgt. Fleek, although in a position to seek cover, shouted a warning to his comrades and threw himself onto the grenade, absorbing its blast. His gallant action undoubtedly saved the lives or prevented the injury of at least eight of his fellow soldiers. Sgt. Fleek's gallantry and willing self-sacrifice were in keeping with the highest traditions of the military service and reflect great credit on himself, his unit, and the U.S. Army.

3224 ◆ FLEMING, JAMES PHILLIP

Rank: Captain (rank at time of action: First Lieutenant) (highest rank: Colonel)
Service: U.S. Air Force
Birthday: 12 March 1943
Place of Birth: Sedalia, Pettis County, Missouri
Entered Service at: Pullman, Whitman County, Washington
Unit: 20th Special Operations Squadron, United States Air Force
Served as: UF-1F Helicopter Commander
Battle or Place of Action: near Duc Co, Republic of Vietnam
Date of Action: 26 November 1968
G.O. Number, Date: GB-477, 23 June 1970
Date of Presentation: 14 May 1970
Place of Presentation: The White House, presented by Pres. Richard M. Nixon
Citation: For conspicuous gallantry and intrepidity in action at the risk of his life above and beyond the call of duty. Capt. Fleming (then 1st Lt.) distinguished himself as the aircraft commander of a UH-1F transport helicopter. Capt. Fleming went to the aid of a six-man Special Forces long-range reconnaissance patrol that was in danger of being overrun by a large, heavily armed hostile force. Despite the knowledge that one helicopter had been downed by intense hostile fire, Capt. Fleming descended, and balanced his helicopter on a river bank with the tail boom hanging over open water. The patrol could not penetrate to the landing site and he was forced to withdraw. Dangerously low on fuel, Capt. Fleming repeated his original landing maneuver. Disregarding his own safety, he remained in this exposed position. Hostile fire crashed through his windscreen as the patrol boarded his helicopter. Capt. Fleming made a successful takeoff through a barrage of hostile fire and recovered safely at a forward base. Capt. Fleming's profound concern for his fellow men, at the risk of his life above and beyond the call of duty, are in keeping with the highest traditions of the U.S. Air Force and reflect great credit upon himself and the Armed Forces of his country.

3225 ◆ FOLEY, ROBERT FRANKLIN

Rank: Captain (highest rank: Major General)
Service: U.S. Army
Birthday: 30 May 1941
Place of Birth: Newton, Middlesex County, Massachusetts
Entered Service at: Newton, Middlesex County, Massachusetts
Unit: Company A, 2d Battalion, 27th Infantry, 25th Infantry Division
Served as: Company Commander
Battle or Place of Action: near Quan Dau Tieng, Republic of Vietnam
Date of Action: 5 November 1966
G.O. Number, Date: 28, 21 June 1968
Date of Presentation: 1 May 1968
Place of Presentation: The White House, presented by Pres. Lyndon B. Johnson
Citation: For conspicuous gallantry and intrepidity in action at the risk of his life above and beyond the call of duty. Capt. Foley's company was ordered to extricate another company of the battalion. Moving through the dense jungle to aid the besieged unit, Company A encountered a strong enemy force occupying well-concealed, defensive positions, and the company's leading element quickly sustained several casualties. Capt. Foley immediately ran forward to the scene of the most intense action to direct the company's efforts. Deploying one platoon on the flank, he led the other two platoons in an attack on the enemy in the face of intense fire. During this action both radio operators accompanying him were wounded. At grave risk to himself, he defied the enemy's murderous fire and helped the wounded operators to a position where they could receive medical care. As he moved forward again one of his machine-gun crews was wounded. Seizing the weapon, he charged forward firing the machine gun, shouting orders, and rallying his men, thus maintaining the momentum of the attack. Under increasingly heavy enemy fire he ordered his assistant to take cover and, alone, Capt. Foley continued to advance firing the machine gun until the wounded had been evacuated and the attack in this area could be resumed. When movement on the other flank was halted by the enemy's fanatical defense, Capt. Foley moved to personally direct this critical phase of the battle. Leading the renewed effort he was blown off his feet and wounded by an enemy grenade. Despite his painful wounds he refused medical aid and persevered in the forefront of the attack on the enemy redoubt. He led the assault on several enemy gun emplacements and, singlehandedly, destroyed three such positions. His outstanding personal leadership under intense enemy fire during the fierce battle which lasted for several hours inspired his men to heroic efforts and was instrumental in the ultimate success of the operation. Capt. Foley's magnificent courage, selfless concern for his men, and professional skill reflect the utmost credit upon himself and the U.S. Army.

3226 ◆ *FOLLAND, MICHAEL FLEMING

Rank: Corporal
Service: U.S. Army

Birthday: 15 April 1949
Place of Birth: Richmond, Richmond County, Virginia
Date of Death: 3 July 1969
Place of Death: Republic of Vietnam
Cemetery: Glendale National Cemetery (H-846) (MH)—Richmond, Virginia
Entered Service at: Richmond, Richmond County, Virginia
Unit: Weapons Platoon, Company D, 2d Battalion, 3d Infantry, 199th Infantry Brigade
Served as: Ammunition Bearer
Battle or Place of Action: Long Khanh Province, Republic of Vietnam
Date of Action: 3 July 1969
G.O. Number, Date: 8, 25 January 1972
Date of Presentation: 16 December 1971
Place of Presentation: The Executive Office Building, presented by Vice Pres. Spiro T. Agnew to his family
Citation: For conspicuous gallantry and intrepidity in action at the risk of his life above and beyond the call of duty. Cpl. Folland distinguished himself while serving as an ammunition bearer with the weapons platoon of Company D, during a reconnaissance patrol mission. As the patrol was moving through a dense jungle area, it was caught in an intense crossfire from heavily fortified and concealed enemy ambush positions. As the patrol reacted to neutralize the ambush, it became evident that the heavy weapons could not be used in the cramped fighting area. Cpl. Folland dropped his recoilless-rifle ammunition and ran forward to join his commander in an assault on the enemy bunkers. The assaulting force moved forward until it was pinned down directly in front of the heavily fortified bunkers by machine-gun fire. Cpl. Folland stood up to draw enemy fire on himself and to place suppressive fire on the enemy positions while his commander attempted to destroy the machine-gun positions with grenades. Before the officer could throw a grenade, an enemy grenade landed in the position. Cpl. Folland alerted his comrades and his commander hurled the grenade from the position. When a second enemy grenade landed in the position, Cpl. Folland again shouted a warning to his fellow soldiers. Seeing that no one could reach the grenade and realizing that it was about to explode, Cpl. Folland, with complete disregard for his safety, threw himself on the grenade. By his dauntless courage, Cpl. Folland saved the lives of his comrades although he was mortally wounded by the explosion. Cpl. Folland's extraordinary heroism, at the cost of his life, was in keeping with the highest traditions of the military service and reflect great credit upon himself, his unit, and the U.S. Army.

3227 ◆ *FOSTER, PAUL HELLSTROM

Rank: Sergeant
Service: U.S. Marine Corps Reserve
Birthday: 17 April 1939
Place of Birth: San Mateo, San Mateo County, California
Date of Death: 14 October 1967
Place of Death: Republic of Vietnam
Cemetery: Golden Gate National Cemetery (V-4764) (MH)—San Bruno, California

Entered Service at: San Francisco, San Francisco County, California
Unit: 2d Battalion, 4th Marines, 3d Marine Division (Rein) FMF
Served as: Artillery Liaison Operations Chief
Battle or Place of Action: near Con Thien, Quang Tri Province, Republic of Vietnam
Date of Action: 14 October 1967
Date of Presentation: 20 June 1969
Place of Presentation: The White House, presented by Pres. Richard M. Nixon to his family
Citation: For conspicuous gallantry and intrepidity at the risk of his life above and beyond the call of duty while serving as an artillery liaison operations chief with the 2d Battalion. In the early morning hours the 2d Battalion was occupying a defensive position which protected a bridge on the road leading from Con Thien to Cam Lo. Suddenly, the marines' position came under a heavy volume of mortar and artillery fire, followed by an aggressive enemy ground assault. In the ensuing engagement, the hostile forces penetrated the perimeter and brought a heavy concentration of small-arms, automatic-weapons, and rocket fire to bear on the battalion command post. Although his position in the fire support coordination center was dangerously exposed to enemy fire and he was wounded when an enemy hand grenade exploded near his position, Sgt. Foster resolutely continued to direct accurate mortar and artillery fire on the advancing North Vietnamese troops. As the attack continued, a hand grenade landed in the midst of Sgt. Foster and his five companions. Realizing the danger, he shouted a warning, threw his armored vest over the grenade, and unhesitatingly placed his body over the armored vest. When the grenade exploded, Sgt. Foster absorbed the entire blast with his body and was mortally wounded. His heroic actions undoubtedly saved his comrades from further injury or possible death. Sgt. Foster's courage, extraordinary heroism, and unfaltering devotion to duty reflected great credit upon himself and the Marine Corps and upheld the highest traditions of the U.S. Naval Service. He gallantly gave his life for his country.

3228 ◆ *FOURNET, DOUGLAS BERNARD

Rank: First Lieutenant
Service: U.S. Army
Birthday: 7 May 1943
Place of Birth: Lake Charles, Calcasieu County, Louisiana
Date of Death: 4 May 1968
Place of Death: Republic of Vietnam
Cemetery: McGrill Cemetery—Kinder, Louisiana
Entered Service at: New Orleans, Orleans County, Louisiana
Unit: 2d Platoon, Company B, 1st Battalion, 7th Cavalry, 1st Cavalry Division (Airmobile)
Served as: Platoon Leader
Battle or Place of Action: A Shau Valley, Republic of Vietnam
Date of Action: 4 May 1968
G.O. Number, Date: 18, 23 April 1970
Date of Presentation: 7 April 1970

Place of Presentation: The White House, presented by Pres. Richard M. Nixon to his family

Citation: For conspicuous gallantry and intrepidity in action at the risk of his life above and beyond the call of duty. 1st Lt. Fournet, Infantry, distinguished himself in action while serving as rifle platoon leader of the 2d Platoon, Company B. While advancing uphill against fortified enemy positions in the A Shau Valley, the platoon encountered intense sniper fire, making movement very difficult. The right flank man suddenly discovered an enemy claymore mine covering the route of advance and shouted a warning to his comrades. Realizing that the enemy would also be alerted, 1st Lt. Fournet ordered his men to take cover and ran uphill toward the mine, drawing a sheath knife as he approached it. With complete disregard for his safety and realizing the imminent danger to members of his command, he used his body as a shield in front of the mine as he attempted to slash the control wires leading from the enemy positions to the mine. As he reached for the wire the mine was detonated, killing him instantly. Five men nearest the mine were slightly wounded, but 1st Lt. Fournet's heroic and unselfish act spared his men of serious injury or death. His gallantry and willing self-sacrifice are in keeping with the highest traditions of the military service and reflect great credit upon himself, his unit, and the U.S. Army.

3229 ◆ *FOUS, JAMES WILLIAM

Rank: Private First Class
Service: U.S. Army
Birthday: 14 October 1946
Place of Birth: Omaha, Douglas County, Nebraska
Date of Death: 14 May 1968
Place of Death: Republic of Vietnam
Cemetery: Fort McPherson National Cemetery (G-685) (MH)—Maxwell, Nebraska
Entered Service at: Omaha, Douglas County, Nebraska
Unit: Company E, 4th Battalion, 47th Infantry, 9th Infantry Division
Served as: Rifleman
Battle or Place of Action: Kien Hoa Province, Republic of Vietnam
Date of Action: 14 May 1968
G.O. Number, Date: 8, 23 April 1970
Date of Presentation: 7 April 1970
Place of Presentation: The White House, presented by Pres. Richard M. Nixon to his family

Citation: For conspicuous gallantry and intrepidity in action at the risk of his life above and beyond the call of duty. Pfc. Fous distinguished himself at the risk of his life while serving as a rifleman with Company E. Pfc. Fous was participating in a reconnaissance-in-force mission when his unit formed its perimeter defense for the night. Pfc. Fous, together with three other American soldiers, occupied a position in a thickly vegetated area facing a woodline. Pfc. Fous detected three Viet Cong maneuvering toward his position and, after alerting the other men, directed accurate fire upon the enemy soldiers, silencing two of them. The third Viet Cong soldier managed to escape in the thick vegetation after throwing a hand grenade into Pfc. Fous' position. Without hesitation, Pfc. Fous shouted a warning to his comrades and leaped upon the lethal explosive, absorbing the blast with his body to save the lives of the three men in the area at the sacrifice of his life. Pfc. Fous' extraordinary heroism at the cost of his life were in keeping with the highest traditions of the military service and reflect great credit upon himself, his unit, and the U.S. Army.

3230 ◆ FOX, WESLEY LEE

Rank: Captain (rank at time of action: First Lieutenant) (highest rank: Colonel)
Service: U.S. Marine Corps
Birthday: 30 September 1931
Place of Birth: Herndon, Fairfax County, Virginia
Entered Service at: Leesburg, Loudoun County, Virginia
Unit: Company A, 1st Battalion, 9th Marines, 3d Marine Division (Rein) FMF
Served as: Commanding Officer
Battle or Place of Action: A Shau Valley, Quang Tri Province, Republic of Vietnam
Date of Action: 22 February 1969
Date of Presentation: 2 March 1971
Place of Presentation: The White House (East Ballroom), presented by Pres. Richard M. Nixon

Citation: For conspicuous gallantry and intrepidity at the risk of his life above and beyond the call of duty while serving as commanding officer of Company A, in action against the enemy in the northern A Shau Valley. Capt. (then 1st Lt.) Fox's company came under intense fire from a large well-concealed enemy force. Capt. Fox maneuvered to a position from which he could assess the situation and confer with his platoon leaders. As they departed to execute the plan he had devised, the enemy attacked and Capt. Fox was wounded along with all of the other members of the command group, except the executive officer. Capt. Fox continued to direct the activity of his company. Advancing through heavy enemy fire, he personally neutralized one enemy position and calmly ordered an assault against the hostile emplacements. He then moved through the hazardous area coordinating aircraft support with the activities of his men. When his executive officer was mortally wounded, Capt. Fox reorganized the company and directed the fire of his men as they hurled grenades against the enemy and drove the hostile forces into retreat. Wounded again in the final assault, Capt. Fox refused medical attention, established a defensive posture, and supervised the preparation of casualties for medical evacuation. His indomitable courage, inspiring initiative, and unwavering devotion to duty in the face of grave personal danger inspired his marines to such aggressive action that they overcame all enemy resistance and destroyed a large bunker complex. Capt. Fox's heroic actions reflect great credit upon himself and the Marine Corps and uphold the highest traditions of the U.S. Naval Service.

3231 ◆ *FRATELLENICO, FRANK ROCCO

Rank: Corporal
Service: U.S. Army

Birthday: 14 July 1951
Place of Birth: Sharon, Litchfield County, Connecticut
Date of Death: 19 August 1970
Place of Death: Republic of Vietnam
Cemetery: Private Cemetery (MH)—Chatham, New York
Entered Service at: Albany, Albany County, New York
Unit: Company B, 2d Battalion, 502d Infantry, 1st Brigade, 101st Airborne Division
Served as: Rifleman
Battle or Place of Action: near Fire Base Barnett, Quang Tri Province, Republic of Vietnam
Date of Action: 19 August 1970
G.O. Number, Date: 37, 6 September 1974
Date of Presentation: 8 August 1974
Place of Presentation: Blair House, presented by Vice Pres. Gerald R. Ford to his family
Citation: Cpl. Fratellenico distinguished himself while serving as a rifleman with Company B. Cpl. Fratellenico's squad was pinned down by intensive fire from two well-fortified enemy bunkers. At great personal risk Cpl. Fratellenico maneuvered forward and, using hand grenades, neutralized the first bunker which was occupied by a number of enemy soldiers. While attacking the second bunker, enemy fire struck Cpl. Fratellenico, causing him to fall to the ground and drop a grenade which he was preparing to throw. Alert to the imminent danger to his comrades, Cpl. Fratellenico retrieved the grenade and fell upon it an instant before it exploded. His heroic actions prevented death or serious injury to four of his comrades nearby and inspired his unit, which subsequently overran the enemy position. Cpl. Fratellenico's conspicuous gallantry, extraordinary heroism, and intrepidity at the cost of his life, above and beyond the call of duty, are in keeping with the highest traditions of the military service and reflect great credit upon him, his unit, and the U.S. Army.

3232 ◆ FRITZ, HAROLD ARTHUR

Rank: Captain (rank at time of action: First Lieutenant) (highest rank: Lieutenant Colonel)
Service: U.S. Army
Birthday: 21 February 1944
Place of Birth: Chicago, Cook County, Illinois
Entered Service at: Milwaukee, Milwaukee County, Wisconsin
Unit: Troop A, 1st Squadron, 11th Armored Cavalry Regiment
Served as: Platoon Leader
Battle or Place of Action: near An Loc, Binh Long Province, Republic of Vietnam
Date of Action: 11 January 1969
G.O. Number, Date: 15, 24 March 1971
Date of Presentation: 2 March 1971
Place of Presentation: The White House (East Ballroom), presented by Pres. Richard M. Nixon
Citation: For conspicuous gallantry and intrepidity in action at the risk of his life above and beyond the call of duty. Capt. (then 1st Lt.) Fritz, Armor, U.S. Army, distinguished himself while serving as a platoon leader with Troop A, near Quan Loi. Capt. Fritz was leading his seven-vehicle armored col-

umn along Highway 13 to meet and escort a truck convoy when the column suddenly came under intense crossfire from a reinforced enemy company deployed in ambush positions. In the initial attack, Capt. Fritz' vehicle was hit and he was seriously wounded. Realizing that his platoon was completely surrounded, vastly outnumbered, and in danger of being overrun, Capt. Fritz leaped to the top of his burning vehicle and directed the positioning of his remaining vehicles and men. With complete disregard for his wounds and safety, he ran from vehicle to vehicle in complete view of the enemy gunners in order to reposition his men, to improve the defenses, to assist the wounded, to distribute ammunition, to direct fire, and to provide encouragement to his men. When a strong enemy force assaulted the position and attempted to overrun the platoon, Capt. Fritz manned a machine gun and through his exemplary action inspired his men to deliver intense and deadly fire which broke the assault and routed the attackers. Moments later a second enemy force advanced to within two meters of the position and threatened to overwhelm the defenders. Capt. Fritz, armed only with a pistol and bayonet, led a small group of his men in a fierce and daring charge which routed the attackers and inflicted heavy casualties. When a relief force arrived, Capt. Fritz saw that it was not deploying effectively against the enemy positions, and he moved through the heavy enemy fire to direct its deployment against the hostile positions. This deployment forced the enemy to abandon the ambush site and withdraw. Despite his wounds, Capt. Fritz returned to his position, assisted his men, and refused medical attention until all of his wounded comrades had been treated and evacuated. The extraordinary courage and selflessness displayed by Capt. Fritz, at the repeated risk of his own life above and beyond the call of duty, were in keeping with the highest traditions of the U.S. Army and reflect greatest credit upon himself, his unit, and the Armed Forces.

3233 ◆ *GARDNER, JAMES ALTON

Rank: First Lieutenant
Service: U.S. Army
Birthday: 7 February 1943
Place of Birth: Dyersburg, Dyer County, Tennessee
Date of Death: 7 February 1966
Place of Death: Republic of Vietnam
Cemetery: Fairview Cemetery—Dyersburg, Tennessee
Entered Service at: Memphis, Shelby County, Tennessee
Unit: Headquarters & Headquarters Company, 1st Battalion (Airborne), 327th Infantry, 1st Brigade, 101st Airborne Division
Served as: Platoon Leader
Battle or Place of Action: My Canh, Republic of Vietnam
Date of Action: 7 February 1966
G.O. Number, Date: 49, 30 November 1967
Date of Presentation: 19 October 1967
Place of Presentation: The Pentagon, presented by Sec. of the Army Stanley R. Resor to his family
Citation: For conspicuous gallantry and intrepidity in action at the risk of his life above and beyond the call of duty. 1st Lt. Gardner's platoon was advancing to relieve a company of

the 1st Battalion that had been pinned down for several hours by a numerically superior enemy force in the village of My Canh, Vietnam. The enemy occupied a series of strongly fortified bunker positions which were mutually supporting and expertly concealed. Approaches to the position were well-covered by an integrated pattern of fire including automatic weapons, machine guns, and mortars. Air strikes and artillery placed on the fortifications had little effect. 1st Lt. Gardner's platoon was to relieve the friendly company by encircling and destroying the enemy force. Even as it moved to begin the attack, the platoon was under heavy enemy fire. During the attack, the enemy fire intensified. Leading the assault and disregarding his own safety, 1st Lt. Gardner charged through a withering hail of fire across an open rice paddy. On reaching the first bunker he destroyed it with a grenade and without hesitation dashed to the second bunker and eliminated it by tossing a grenade inside. Then, crawling swiftly along the dike of a rice paddy, he reached the third bunker. Before he could arm a grenade, the enemy gunner leaped forth, firing at him. 1st Lt. Gardner instantly returned the fire and killed the enemy gunner at a distance of six feet. Following the seizure of the main enemy position, he reorganized the platoon to continue the attack. Advancing to the new assault position, the platoon was pinned down by an enemy machine gun emplaced in a fortified bunker. 1st Lt. Gardner immediately collected several grenades and charged the enemy position, firing his rifle as he advanced to neutralize the defenders. He dropped a grenade into the bunker and vaulted beyond. As the bunker blew up, he came under fire again. Rolling into a ditch to gain cover, he moved toward the new source of fire. Nearing the position, he leaped from the ditch and advanced with a grenade in one hand and firing his rifle with the other. He was gravely wounded just before he reached the bunker, but with a last valiant effort he staggered forward and destroyed the bunker, and its defenders, with a grenade. Although he fell dead on the rim of the bunker, his extraordinary actions so inspired the men of his platoon that they resumed the attack and completely routed the enemy. 1st Lt. Gardner's conspicuous gallantry were in the highest traditions of the U.S. Army.

3234 ◆ *GERTSCH, JOHN GERRY

Rank: Staff Sergeant
Service: U.S. Army
Birthday: 29 September 1944
Place of Birth: Jersey City, Hudson County, New Jersey
Date of Death: 19 July 1969
Place of Death: Republic of Vietnam
Cemetery: Northside Catholic Cemetery (MH)—Pittsburgh, Pennsylvania
Entered Service at: Buffalo, Erie County, New York
Unit: Company E, 1st Battalion, 327th Infantry, 101st Airborne Division
Served as: Platoon Sergeant/Platoon Leader
Battle or Place of Action: A Shau Valley, Republic of Vietnam
Date of Action: 15-19 July 1969
G.O. Number, Date: 34, 6 September 1974

Date of Presentation: 17 July 1974
Place of Presentation: Blair House (Courtyard), presented by Vice Pres. Gerald R. Ford to his family
Citation: S/Sgt. Gertsch distinguished himself while serving as a platoon sergeant and platoon leader during combat operations in the A Shau Valley. During the initial phase of an operation to seize a strongly defended enemy position, S/Sgt. Gertsch's platoon leader was seriously wounded and lay exposed to intense enemy fire. Forsaking his own safety, without hesitation S/Sgt. Gertsch rushed to aid his fallen leader and dragged him to a sheltered position. He then assumed command of the heavily engaged platoon and led his men in a fierce counterattack that forced the enemy to withdraw. Later, a small element of S/Sgt. Gertsch's unit was reconnoitering when attacked again by the enemy. S/Sgt. Gertsch moved forward to his besieged element and immediately charged, firing as he advanced. His determined assault forced the enemy troops to withdraw in confusion and made possible the recovery of two wounded men who had been exposed to heavy enemy fire. Sometime later his platoon came under attack by an enemy force employing automatic-weapons, grenade, and rocket fire. S/Sgt. Gertsch was severely wounded during the onslaught but continued to command his platoon despite his painful wound. While moving under fire and encouraging his men he sighted an aidman treating a wounded officer from an adjacent unit. Realizing that both men were in imminent danger of being killed, he rushed forward and positioned himself between them and the enemy nearby. While the wounded officer was being moved to safety S/Sgt. Gertsch was mortally wounded by enemy fire. Without S/Sgt. Gertsch's courage, ability to inspire others, and profound concern for the welfare of his men, the loss of life among his fellow soldiers would have been significantly greater. His conspicuous gallantry, extraordinary heroism, and intrepidity at the cost of his life, above and beyond the call of duty, are in the highest traditions of the U.S. Army and reflect great credit on him and the Armed Forces of his country.

3235 ◆ *GONZALEZ, ALFREDO (FREDDY)

Rank: Sergeant
Service: U.S. Marine Corps
Birthday: 23 May 1946
Place of Birth: Edinburg, Hidalgo County, Texas
Date of Death: 4 February 1968
Place of Death: Republic of Vietnam
Cemetery: Hillcrest Cemetery (MH)—Edenburg, Texas
Entered Service at: San Antonio, Bexar County, Texas
Unit: 3d Platoon, Company A, 1st Battalion, 1st Marines, 1st Marine Division (Rein) FMF
Served as: Platoon Commander
Battle or Place of Action: near Thua Thien, Republic of Vietnam
Date of Action: 4 February 1968
Date of Presentation: 31 October 1969
Place of Presentation: The White House, presented by Vice Pres. Spiro T. Agnew to his family
Citation: For conspicuous gallantry and intrepidity at the risk of his life above and beyond the call of duty while serving

as platoon commander, 3d Platoon, Company A. On 31 January 1968, during the initial phase of Operation Hue City, Sgt. Gonzalez' unit was formed as a reaction force and deployed to Hue to relieve the pressure on the beleaguered city. While moving by truck convoy along Route No. 1, near the village of Lang Van Lrong, the marines received a heavy volume of enemy fire. Sgt. Gonzalez aggressively maneuvered the marines in his platoon, and directed their fire until the area was cleared of snipers. Immediately after crossing a river south of Hue, the column was again hit by intense enemy fire. One of the marines on top of a tank was wounded and fell to the ground in an exposed position. With complete disregard for his safety, Sgt. Gonzalez ran through the fire-swept area to the assistance of his injured comrade. He lifted him up and though receiving fragmentation wounds during the rescue, he carried the wounded marine to a covered position for treatment. Due to the increased volume and accuracy of enemy fire from a fortified machine-gun bunker on the side of the road, the company was temporarily halted. Realizing the gravity of the situation, Sgt. Gonzalez exposed himself to the enemy fire and moved his platoon along the east side of a bordering rice paddy to a dike directly across from the bunker. Though fully aware of the danger involved, he moved to the fire-swept road and destroyed the hostile position with hand grenades. Although seriously wounded again on 3 February, he steadfastly refused medical treatment and continued to supervise his men and lead the attack. On 4 February, the enemy had again pinned the company down, inflicting heavy casualties with automatic-weapons and rocket fire. Sgt. Gonzalez, utilizing a number of light antitank assault weapons, fearlessly moved from position to position firing numerous rounds at the heavily fortified enemy emplacements. He successfully knocked out a rocket position and suppressed much of the enemy fire before falling mortally wounded. The heroism, courage, and dynamic leadership displayed by Sgt. Gonzalez reflected great credit upon himself and the Marine Corps and were in keeping with the highest traditions of the U.S. Naval Service. He gallantly gave his life for his country.

3236 ◆ *GRAHAM, JAMES ALBERT

Rank: Captain
Service: U.S. Marine Corps
Birthday: 25 August 1940
Place of Birth: Wilkinsburg, Allegheny County, Pennsylvania
Date of Death: 2 June 1967
Place of Death: Republic of Vietnam
Cemetery: Arlington National Cemetery (13-8576-F) (MH)—Arlington, Virginia
Entered Service at: Prince Georges, Prince Georges County, Maryland
Unit: Company F, 2d Battalion, 5th Marines, 1st Marine Division (Rein) FMF
Served as: Company Commander
Battle or Place of Action: Quang Tin Province, Republic of Vietnam
Date of Action: 2 June 1967

Date of Presentation: 29 October 1968
Place of Presentation: Marine Barracks, Washington D.C., presented by Sec. of the Navy Paul R. Ignatius to his family
Citation: For conspicuous gallantry and intrepidity at the risk of his life above and beyond the call of duty. During Operation Union II, the 1st Battalion, 5th Marines, consisting of Companies A and D, with Capt. Graham's company attached, launched an attack against an enemy-occupied position with two companies assaulting and one in reserve. Company F, a leading company, was proceeding across a clear paddy area 1,000 meters wide, attacking toward the assigned objective, when it came under fire from mortars and small arms which immediately inflicted a large number of casualties. Hardest hit by the enemy fire was the 2d platoon of Company F, which was pinned down in the open paddy area by intense fire from two concealed machine guns. Forming an assault unit from members of his small company headquarters, Capt. Graham boldly led a fierce assault through the second platoon's position, forcing the enemy to abandon the first machine-gun position, thereby relieving some of the pressure on his second platoon, and enabling evacuation of the wounded to a more secure area. Resolute to silence the second machine gun, which continued its devastating fire, Capt. Graham's small force stood steadfast in its hard-won enclave. Subsequently, during the afternoon's fierce fighting, he suffered two minor wounds while personally accounting for an estimated 15 enemy killed. With the enemy position remaining invincible upon each attempt to withdraw to friendly lines, and although knowing that he had no chance of survival, he chose to remain with one man who could not be moved due to the seriousness of his wounds. The last radio transmission from Capt. Graham reported that he was being assaulted by a force of 25 enemy soldiers; he died while protecting himself and the wounded man he chose not to abandon. Capt. Graham's actions throughout the day were a series of heroic achievements. His outstanding courage, superb leadership, and indomitable fighting spirit undoubtedly saved the second platoon from annihilation and reflected great credit upon himself, the Marine Corps, and the U.S. Naval Service. He gallantly gave his life for his country.

3237 ◆ *GRANDSTAFF, BRUCE ALAN

Rank: Platoon Sergeant
Service: U.S. Army
Birthday: 2 June 1934
Place of Birth: Spokane, Spokane County, Washington
Date of Death: 18 May 1967
Place of Death: Republic of Vietnam
Cemetery: Greenwood Riverside Memorial Park—Spokane, Washington
Entered Service at: Spokane, Spokane County, Washington
Unit: Weapons Platoon, Company B, 1st Battalion, 8th Infantry, 4th Infantry Division
Served as: Platoon Leader
Battle or Place of Action: Pleiku Province, Republic of Vietnam
Date of Action: 18 May 1967
G.O. Number, Date: 52, 8 August 1967

Date of Presentation: 10 July 1969
Place of Presentation: The White House, presented by Pres. Richard M. Nixon to his family
Citation: For conspicuous gallantry and intrepidity in action at the risk of his life above and beyond the call of duty. P/Sgt. Grandstaff distinguished himself while leading the Weapons Platoon, Company B, on a reconnaissance mission near the Cambodian border. His platoon was advancing through intermittent enemy contact when it was struck by heavy small-arms and automatic-weapons fire from three sides. As he established a defensive perimeter, P/Sgt. Grandstaff noted that several of his men had been struck down. He raced 30 meters through the intense fire to aid them but could only save one. Denied freedom to maneuver his unit by the intensity of the enemy onslaught, he adjusted artillery to within 45 meters of his position. When helicopter gunships arrived, he crawled outside the defensive position to mark the location with smoke grenades. Realizing his first marker was probably ineffective, he crawled to another location and threw his last smoke grenade but the smoke did not penetrate the jungle foliage. Seriously wounded in the leg during this effort he returned to his radio and, refusing medical aid, adjusted the artillery even closer as the enemy advanced on his position. Recognizing the need for additional firepower, he again braved the enemy fusillade, crawled to the edge of his position, and fired several magazines of tracer ammunition through the jungle canopy. He succeeded in designating the location to the gunships but this action again drew the enemy fire and he was wounded in the other leg. Now enduring intense pain and bleeding profusely, he crawled to within 10 meters of an enemy machine gun which had caused many casualties among his men. He destroyed the position with hand grenades but received additional wounds. Rallying his remaining men to withstand the enemy assaults, he realized his position was being overrun and asked for artillery directly on his location. He fought until mortally wounded by an enemy rocket. Although every man in the platoon was a casualty, survivors attest to the indomitable spirit and exceptional courage of this outstanding combat leader who inspired his men to fight courageously against overwhelming odds and cost the enemy heavy casualties. P/Sgt. Grandstaff's selfless gallantry, above and beyond the call of duty, are in the highest traditions of the U.S. Army and reflect great credit upon himself and the Armed Forces of his country.

3238 ◆ *GRANT, JOSEPH XAVIER

Rank: Captain (rank at time of action: First Lieutenant)
Service: U.S. Army
Birthday: 28 March 1940
Place of Birth: Cambridge, Middlesex County, Massachusetts
Date of Death: 13 November 1966
Place of Death: Republic of Vietnam
Cemetery: Arlington National Cemetery (30-1648-2) (MH)—Arlington, Virginia
Entered Service at: Boston, Suffolk County, Massachusetts
Unit: Company A, 1st Battalion, 14th Infantry, 25th Infantry Division

Served as: Platoon Leader
Battle or Place of Action: near Plei Djereng, Republic of Vietnam
Date of Action: 13 November 1966
G.O. Number, Date: 4, 29 January 1968
Date of Presentation: 30 November 1967
Place of Presentation: The Pentagon, presented by Sec. of the Army Stanley R. Resor to his family
Citation: For conspicuous gallantry and intrepidity in action at the risk of his life above and beyond the call of duty. Company A was participating in a search-and-destroy operation when the leading platoon made contact with the enemy and a fierce fire-fight ensued. Capt. Grant was ordered to disengage the two remaining platoons and to maneuver them to envelop and destroy the enemy. After beginning their movement, the platoon encountered intense automatic-weapons and mortar fire from the front and flank. Capt. Grant was ordered to deploy the platoons in a defensive position. As this action was underway, the enemy attacked, using "human wave" assaults, in an attempt to literally overwhelm Capt. Grant's force. In a magnificent display of courage and leadership, Capt. Grant moved under intense fire along the hastily formed defensive line repositioning soldiers to fill gaps created by the mounting casualties and inspiring and directing the efforts of his men to successfully repel the determined enemy onslaught. Seeing a platoon leader wounded, Capt. Grant hastened to his aid, in the face of the mass of fire of the entire enemy force, and moved him to a more secure position. During this action, Capt. Grant was wounded in the shoulder. Refusing medical treatment, he returned to the forward part of the perimeter, where he continued to lead and to inspire his men by his own indomitable example. While attempting to evacuate a wounded soldier, he was pinned down by fire from an enemy machine gun. With a supply of hand grenades, he crawled forward under a withering hail of fire and knocked out the machine gun, killing the crew, after which he moved the wounded man to safety. Learning that several other wounded men were pinned down by enemy fire forward of his position, Capt. Grant disregarded his painful wound and led five men across the fire-swept open ground to effect a rescue. Following the return of the wounded men to the perimeter, a concentration of mortar fire landed in their midst and Capt. Grant was killed instantly. His heroic actions saved the lives of a number of his comrades and enabled the task force to repulse the vicious assaults and defeat the enemy. Capt. Grant's actions reflect great credit upon himself and were in keeping with the finest traditions of the U.S. Army.

3239 ◆ *GRAVES, TERRENCE COLLINSON

Rank: Second Lieutenant
Service: U.S. Marine Corps
Birthday: 6 July 1945
Place of Birth: Corpus Christi, Nueces County, Texas
Date of Death: 17 February 1968
Place of Death: Republic of Vietnam
Cemetery: Woodlawn Cemetery (MH)—Hamilton, New York
Entered Service at: New York

Unit: 3d Force Reconnaissance Company, 3d Reconnaissance Battalion, 3d Marine Division (Rein) FMF
Served as: Platoon Commander
Battle or Place of Action: Quang Tri Province, Republic of Vietnam
Date of Action: 16 February 1968
Date of Presentation: 2 December 1969
Place of Presentation: The White House, presented by Vice Pres. Spiro T. Agnew to his family
Citation: For conspicuous gallantry and intrepidity at the risk of his life above and beyond the call of duty as a platoon commander with the 3d Force Reconnaissance Company. While on a long-range reconnaissance mission, 2d Lt. Graves' eight-man patrol observed seven enemy soldiers approaching their position. Reacting instantly, he deployed his men and directed their fire on the approaching enemy. After the fire had ceased, he and two patrol members commenced a search on the area, and suddenly came under a heavy volume of hostile small-arms and automatic-weapons fire from a numerically superior enemy force. When one of his men was hit by the enemy fire, 2d Lt. Graves moved through the fire-swept area to his radio and, while directing suppressive fire from his men, requested air support and adjusted a heavy volume of artillery and helicopter gunship fire upon the enemy. After attending the wounded, 2d Lt. Graves, accompanied by another marine, moved from his relatively safe position to confirm the results of the earlier engagement. Observing that several of the enemy were still alive, he launched a determined assault, eliminating the remaining enemy troops. He then began moving the patrol to a landing zone for extraction, when the unit again came under intense fire which wounded two more marines and 2d Lt. Graves. Refusing medical attention, he once more adjusted air strikes and artillery fire upon the enemy while directing the fire of his men. He led his men to a new landing site into which he skillfully guided the incoming aircraft and boarded his men while remaining exposed to the hostile fire. Realizing that one of the wounded had not embarked, he directed the aircraft to depart and, along with another marine, moved to the side of the casualty. Confronted with a shortage of ammunition, 2d Lt. Graves utilized supporting arms and directed fire until a second helicopter arrived. At this point, the volume of enemy fire intensified, hitting the helicopter and causing it to crash shortly after liftoff. All aboard were killed. Second Lt. Graves' outstanding courage, superb leadership, and indomitable fighting spirit throughout the day were in keeping with the highest traditions of the Marine Corps and the U.S. Naval Service. He gallantly gave his life for his country.

3240 ◆ *GUENETTE, PETER MATHEW

Rank: Specialist Fourth Class
Service: U.S. Army
Birthday: 4 January 1948
Place of Birth: Troy, Rensselaer County, New York
Date of Death: 18 May 1968
Place of Death: Republic of Vietnam
Cemetery: Saint John's Cemetery—North Troy, New York
Entered Service at: Albany, Albany County, New York

Unit: Company D, 2d Battalion (Airborne), 506th Infantry, 101st Airborne Division
Served as: Machine Gunner
Battle or Place of Action: Quan Tan Uyen Province, Republic of Vietnam
Date of Action: 18 May 1968
G.O. Number, Date: 9, 23 April 1970
Date of Presentation: 7 April 1970
Place of Presentation: The White House, presented by Pres. Richard M. Nixon to his family
Citation: For conspicuous gallantry and intrepidity in action at the risk of his life above and beyond the call of duty. Sp4c. Guenette distinguished himself serving as a machine gunner with Company D, during combat operations. While Sp4c. Guenette's platoon was sweeping a suspected enemy base camp, it came under light harassing fire from a well-equipped and firmly entrenched squad of North Vietnamese Army regulars which was serving as a delaying force at the entrance to their base camp. As the platoon moved within 10 meters of the fortified positions, the enemy fire became intense. Sp4c. Guenette and his assistant gunner immediately began to provide a base of suppressive fire, ceasing momentarily to allow the assistant gunner time to throw a grenade into the bunker. Seconds later, an enemy grenade was thrown to Sp4c. Guenette's right flank. Realizing that the grenade would kill or wound at least four men and destroy the machine gun, he shouted a warning and smothered the grenade with his body, absorbing its blast. Through his actions, he prevented loss of life or injury to at least three men and enabled his comrades to maintain their fire superiority. By his gallantry at the cost of his life in keeping with the highest traditions of the military service, Sp4c. Guenette has reflected great credit upon himself, his unit, and the U.S. Army.

3241 ◆ HAGEMEISTER, CHARLES CRIS

Rank: Specialist Fifth Class (rank at time of action: Specialist Fourth Class) (highest rank: Lieutenant Colonel)
Service: U.S. Army
Birthday: 21 August 1946
Place of Birth: Lincoln, Lancaster County, Nebraska
Entered Service at: Lincoln, Lancaster County, Nebraska
Unit: Headquarters & Headquarters Company, 1st Battalion, 5th Cavalry, 1st Cavalry Division (Airmobile)
Served as: Medical Aidman
Battle or Place of Action: Binh Dinh Province, Republic of Vietnam
Date of Action: 20 March 1967
G.O. Number, Date: 29, 24 June 1968
Date of Presentation: 14 May 1968
Place of Presentation: Pentagon (Inner Courtyard), Hall of Heroes, presented by Pres. Lyndon B. Johnson
Citation: For conspicuous gallantry and intrepidity in action at the risk of his life above and beyond the call of duty. While conducting combat operations against a hostile force, Sp5c. Hagemeister's platoon suddenly came under heavy attack from three sides by an enemy force occupying well-concealed, fortified positions and supported by machine guns and mortars. Seeing two of his comrades seriously wounded in the ini-

tial action, Sp5c. Hagemeister, unhesitatingly and with total disregard for his safety, raced through the deadly hail of enemy fire to provide them medical aid. Upon learning that the platoon leader and several other soldiers had been wounded, Sp5c. Hagemeister continued to brave the withering enemy fire and crawled forward to render lifesaving treatment and to offer words of encouragement. Attempting to evacuate the seriously wounded soldiers, Sp5c. Hagemeister was taken under fire at close range by an enemy sniper. Realizing that the lives of his fellow soldiers depended on his actions, Sp5c. Hagemeister seized a rifle from a fallen comrade, killed the sniper, three other enemy soldiers who were attempting to encircle his position, and silenced an enemy machine gun that covered the area with deadly fire. Unable to remove the wounded to a less exposed location and aware of the enemy efforts to isolate his unit, he dashed through the fusillade of fire to secure help from a nearby platoon. Returning with help, he placed men in positions to cover his advance as he moved to evacuate the wounded forward of his location. These efforts successfully completed, he then moved to the other flank and evacuated additional wounded men despite the fact that his every move drew fire from the enemy. Sp5c. Hagemeister's repeated heroic and selfless actions at the risk of his life saved the lives of many of his comrades and inspired their actions in repelling the enemy assault. Sp5c. Hagemeister's indomitable courage was in the highest traditions of the Armed Forces and reflect great credit upon himself.

3242 ◆ *HAGEN, LOREN DOUGLAS

Rank: First Lieutenant
Service: U.S. Army
Birthday: 25 February 1946
Place of Birth: Fargo, Cass County, North Dakota
Date of Death: 7 August 1971
Place of Death: Republic of Vietnam
Cemetery: Arlington National Cemetery (28-1204) (MH)—Arlington, Virginia
Entered Service at: Fargo, Cass County, North Dakota
Unit: U.S. Army Training Advisory Group
Served as: Team Leader
Battle or Place of Action: Republic of Vietnam
Date of Action: 7 August 1971
G.O. Number, Date: 40, 6 September 1974
Date of Presentation: 8 August 1974
Place of Presentation: Blair House, presented by Vice Pres. Gerald R. Ford to his family
Citation: 1st Lt. Hagen distinguished himself in action while serving as the team leader of a small reconnaissance team operating deep within enemy-held territory. At approximately 0600 hours on the morning of 7 August 1971 the small team came under a fierce assault by a superior-sized enemy force using heavy small-arms, automatic-weapons, mortar, and rocket fire. 1st Lt. Hagen immediately began returning small-arms fire upon the attackers and successfully led his team in repelling the first enemy onslaught. He then quickly deployed his men into more strategic defense locations before the enemy struck again in an attempt to overrun

and annihilate the beleaguered team's members. 1st Lt. Hagen repeatedly exposed himself to the enemy fire directed at him as he constantly moved about the team's perimeter, directing fire, rallying the members, and resupplying the team with ammunition, while courageously returning small-arms and hand-grenade fire in a valorous attempt to repel the advancing enemy force. The courageous actions and expert leadership abilities of 1st Lt. Hagen were a great source of inspiration and instilled confidence in the team members. After observing an enemy rocket make a direct hit on and destroy one of the team's bunkers, 1st Lt. Hagen moved toward the wrecked bunker in search for team members despite the fact that the enemy force now controlled the bunker area. With total disregard for his own personal safety, he crawled through the enemy fire while returning small-arms fire upon the enemy force. Undaunted by the enemy rockets and grenades impacting all around him, 1st Lt. Hagen desperately advanced upon the destroyed bunker until he was fatally wounded by enemy small-arms and automatic-weapons fire. With complete disregard for his personal safety, 1st Lt. Hagen's courageous gallantry, extraordinary heroism, and intrepidity above and beyond the call of duty, at the cost of his own life, were in keeping with the highest traditions of the military service and reflect great credit upon him and the U.S. Army.

3243 ◆ *HARTSOCK, ROBERT WILLARD

Rank: Staff Sergeant
Service: U.S. Army
Birthday: 24 January 1945
Place of Birth: Cumberland, Allegany County, Maryland
Date of Death: 23 February 1969
Place of Death: Republic of Vietnam
Cemetery: Rocky Gap Veterans Cemetery (MH)—Flintstone, Maryland
Entered Service at: Fairmont, Marion County, West Virginia
Unit: 44th Infantry Platoon (Scout Dog), 3d Brigade, 25th Infantry Division
Served as: Section Leader
Battle or Place of Action: Dau Tieng Base Camp, Hau Nghia Province, Republic of Vietnam
Date of Action: 23 February 1969
G.O. Number, Date: 47, 8 September 1970
Date of Presentation: 6 August 1970
Place of Presentation: The White House, presented by Pres. Richard M. Nixon to his family
Citation: For conspicuous gallantry and intrepidity in action at the risk of his life above and beyond the call of duty. S/Sgt. Hartsock distinguished himself in action while serving as section leader with the 44th Infantry Platoon. When the Dau Tieng Base Camp came under a heavy enemy rocket and mortar attack, S/Sgt. Hartsock and his platoon commander spotted an enemy sapper squad which had infiltrated the camp undetected. Realizing the enemy squad was heading for the brigade tactical operations center and nearby prisoner compound, they concealed themselves and, although heavily outnumbered, awaited the approach of the enemy soldiers.

When the enemy was almost upon them, S/Sgt. Hartsock and his platoon commander opened fire on the squad. As a wounded enemy soldier fell, he managed to detonate a satchel charge he was carrying. S/Sgt. Hartsock, with complete disregard for his life, threw himself on the charge and was gravely wounded. In spite of his wounds, S/Sgt. Hartsock crawled about five meters to a ditch and provided heavy suppressive fire, completely pinning down the enemy and allowing his commander to seek shelter. S/Sgt. Hartsock continued his deadly stream of fire until he succumbed to his wounds. S/Sgt. Hartsock's extraordinary heroism and profound concern for the lives of his fellow soldiers were in keeping with the highest traditions of the military service and reflect great credit upon him, his unit, and the U.S. Army.

3244 ◆ *HARVEY JR., CARMEL BERNON

Rank: Specialist Fourth Class
Service: U.S. Army
Birthday: 6 October 1946
Place of Birth: Montgomery, Fayette County, West Virginia
Date of Death: 21 June 1967
Place of Death: Republic of Vietnam
Cemetery: Cedar Park Cemetery—Chicago, Illinois
Entered Service at: Chicago, Cook County, Illinois
Unit: Company B, 1st Battalion, 5th Cavalry, 1st Cavalry Division (Airmobile)
Served as: Fire Team Leader
Battle or Place of Action: Binh Dinh Province, Republic of Vietnam
Date of Action: 21 June 1967
G.O. Number, Date: 67, 27 October 1969
Date of Presentation: 16 October 1969
Place of Presentation: The White House, presented by Pres. Richard M. Nixon to his family
Citation: For conspicuous gallantry and intrepidity in action at the risk of his life above and beyond the call of duty. Sp4c. Harvey distinguished himself as a fire team leader with Company B, during combat operations. Ordered to secure a downed helicopter, his platoon established a defensive perimeter around the aircraft, but shortly thereafter a large enemy force attacked the position from three sides. Sp4c. Harvey and two members of his squad were in a position directly in the path of the enemy onslaught, and their location received the brunt of the fire from an enemy machine gun. In short order, both of his companions were wounded, but Sp4c. Harvey covered this loss by increasing his deliberate rifle fire at the foe. The enemy machine gun seemed to concentrate on him and the bullets struck the ground all around his position. One round hit and armed a grenade attached to his belt. Quickly, he tried to remove the grenade but was unsuccessful. Realizing the danger to his comrades if he remained and despite the hail of enemy fire, he jumped to his feet, shouted a challenge at the enemy, and raced toward the deadly machine gun. He nearly reached the enemy position when the grenade on his belt exploded, mortally wounding Sp4c. Harvey, and stunning the enemy machine-gun crew. His final act caused a pause in the enemy fire, and the wounded men were moved from the danger area. Sp4c.

Harvey's dedication to duty, high sense of responsibility, and heroic actions inspired the others in his platoon to decisively beat back the enemy attack. His acts are in keeping with the highest traditions of the military service and reflect great credit upon himself and the U.S. Army.

3245 ◆ HERDA, FRANK ALOYSIOUS

Rank: Specialist Fourth Class (rank at time of action: Private First Class)
Service: U.S. Army
Birthday: 13 September 1947
Place of Birth: Cleveland, Cuyahoga County, Ohio
Entered Service at: Cleveland, Cuyahoga County, Ohio
Unit: Company A, 1st Battalion (Airborne), 506th Infantry, 101st Airborne Division (Airmobile)
Served as: Grenadier
Battle or Place of Action: near Dak To, Quang Trang Province, Republic of Vietnam
Date of Action: 29 June 1968
G.O. Number, Date: 32, 5 June 1970
Date of Presentation: 14 May 1970
Place of Presentation: The White House, presented by Pres. Richard M. Nixon
Citation: For conspicuous gallantry and intrepidity in action at the risk of his life above and beyond the call of duty. Sp4c. Herda (then Pfc.) distinguished himself while serving as a grenadier with Company A. Company A was part of a battalion-size night defensive perimeter when a large enemy force initiated an attack on the friendly units. While other enemy elements provided diversionary fire and indirect weapons fire to the west, a sapper force of approximately 30 men armed with hand grenades and small charges attacked Company A's perimeter from the east. As the sappers were making a last, violent assault, five of them charged the position defended by Sp4c. Herda and two comrades, one of whom was wounded and lay helpless in the bottom of the foxhole. Sp4c. Herda fired at the aggressors until they were within 10 feet of his position and one of their grenades landed in the foxhole. He fired one last round from his grenade launcher, hitting one of the enemy soldiers in the head, and then, with no concern for his safety, Sp4c. Herda immediately covered the blast of the grenade with his body. The explosion wounded him grievously, but his selfless action prevented his two comrades from being seriously injured or killed and enabled the remaining defender to kill the other sappers. By his gallantry at the risk of his life in the highest traditions of the military service, Sp4c. Herda has reflected great credit on himself, his unit, and the U.S. Army.

3246 ◆ *HIBBS, ROBERT JOHN

Rank: Second Lieutenant
Service: U.S. Army
Birthday: 21 April 1943
Place of Birth: Omaha, Douglas County, Nebraska
Date of Death: 5 March 1966
Place of Death: Republic of Vietnam
Cemetery: Greenwood Cemetery (MH)—Cedar Falls, Iowa

Entered Service at: Des Moines, Polk County, Iowa
Unit: Company B, 2d Battalion, 28th Infantry, 1st Infantry Division
Served as: Patrol Commander
Battle or Place of Action: Don Dien Lo Ke, Republic of Vietnam
Date of Action: 5 March 1966
G.O. Number, Date: 8, 24 February 1967
Date of Presentation: 26 January 1967
Place of Presentation: Fort Myers, Virginia, presented by Sec. of the Army Stanley R. Resor to his family
Citation: For conspicuous gallantry and intrepidity at the risk of his life above and beyond the call of duty. 2d Lt. Hibbs was in command of a 15-man ambush patrol of the 2d Battalion, when his unit observed a company of Viet Cong advancing along the road toward the 2d Battalion's position. Informing his command post by radio of the impending attack, he prepared his men for the oncoming Viet Cong, emplaced two mines in their path, and, when the insurgents were within 20 feet of the patrol's position, he fired the two antipersonnel mines, wounding or killing half of the enemy company. Then, to cover the withdrawl of his patrol, he threw hand grenades, stepped onto the open road, and opened fire on the remainder of the Viet Cong force of approximately 50 men. Having rejoined his men, he was leading them toward the battalion perimeter when the patrol encountered the rear elements of another Viet Cong company deployed to attack the battalion. With the advantage of surprise, he directed a charge against the Viet Cong, which carried the patrol through the insurgent force, completely disrupting its attack. Learning that a wounded patrol member was wandering in the area between the two opposing forces and although moments from safety and wounded in the leg himself, he and a sergeant went back to the battlefield to recover the stricken man. After they maneuvered through the withering fire of two Viet Cong machine guns, the sergeant grabbed the dazed soldier and dragged him back toward the friendly lines while 2d Lt. Hibbs remained behind to provide covering fire. Armed only with a M-16 rifle and a pistol, but determined to destroy the enemy positions, he then charged the two machine-gun emplacements and was struck down. Before succumbing to his mortal wounds, he destroyed the starlight telescopic sight attached to his rifle to prevent its capture and use by the Viet Cong. 2d Lt. Hibbs' profound concern for his fellow soldiers and his intrepidity at the risk of his life above and beyond the call of duty are in the highest traditions of the U.S. Army and reflect great credit upon himself and the Armed Forces of his country.

3247 ◆ *HOLCOMB, JOHN NOBLE

Rank: Sergeant
Service: U.S. Army
Birthday: 11 June 1946
Place of Birth: Baker, Baker County, Oregon
Date of Death: 3 December 1968
Place of Death: Republic of Vietnam
Cemetery: Eagle Valley Cemetery (MH)—Richland, Oregon

Entered Service at: Corvallis, Benton County, Oregon
Unit: Company D, 2d Battalion, 7th Cavalry, 1st Cavalry Division
Served as: Squad Leader
Battle or Place of Action: near Quan Loi, Republic of Vietnam
Date of Action: 3 December 1968
G.O. Number, Date: 9, 9 March 1971
Date of Presentation: 16 February 1971
Place of Presentation: The White House (East Ballroom), presented by Pres. Richard M. Nixon to his family
Citation: For conspicuous gallantry and intrepidity in action at the risk of his life above and beyond the call of duty. Sgt. Holcomb distinguished himself while serving as a squad leader in Company D during a combat assault mission. Sgt. Holcomb's company assault had landed by helicopter and deployed into a hasty defensive position to organize for a reconnaissance-in-force mission when it was attacked from three sides by an estimated battalion-size enemy force. Sgt. Holcomb's squad was directly in the path of the main enemy attack. With complete disregard for the heavy fire, Sgt. Holcomb moved among his men giving encouragement and directing fire on the assaulting enemy. When his machine gunner was knocked out, Sgt. Holcomb seized the weapon, ran to a forward edge of the position, and placed withering fire on the enemy. His gallant actions caused the enemy to withdraw. Sgt. Holcomb treated and carried his wounded to a position of safety and reorganized his defensive sector despite a raging grass fire ignited by the incoming enemy mortar and rocket rounds. When the enemy assaulted the position a second time, Sgt. Holcomb again manned the forward machine gun, devastating the enemy attack and forcing the enemy to again break contact and withdraw. During the enemy withdrawal an enemy rocket hit Sgt. Holcomb's position, destroying his machine gun and severely wounding him. Despite his painful wounds, Sgt. Holcomb crawled through the grass fire and exploding mortar and rocket rounds to move the members of his squad, every one of whom had been wounded, to more secure positions. Although grievously wounded and sustained solely by his indomitable will and courage, Sgt. Holcomb as the last surviving leader of his platoon organized his men to repel the enemy, crawled to the platoon radio, and reported the third enemy assault on his position. His report brought friendly supporting fires on the charging enemy and broke the enemy attack. Sgt. Holcomb's inspiring leadership, fighting spirit, in action at the cost of his life, were in keeping with the highest traditions of the military service and reflect great credit on himself, his unit, and the U.S. Army.

3248 ◆ HOOPER, JOE RONNIE

Rank: Staff Sergeant (rank at time of action: Sergeant) (highest rank: Captain)
Service: U.S. Army
Birthday: 8 August 1938
Place of Birth: Piedmont, Greenville County, South Carolina
Date of Death: 6 May 1979
Place of Death: Louisville, Kentucky

Cemetery: Arlington National Cemetery (46-656-17)
(MH)—Arlington, Virginia
Entered Service at: Los Angeles, Los Angeles County,
California
Unit: Company A, 1st Battalion (Airborne), 506th Infantry,
101st Airborne Division (Airmobile)
Served as: Squad Leader
Battle or Place of Action: near Hue, Republic of Vietnam
Date of Action: 21 February 1968
G.O. Number, Date: 24, 17 April 1969
Date of Presentation: 7 March 1969
Place of Presentation: The White House, presented by Pres.
Richard M. Nixon
Citation: For conspicuous gallantry and intrepidity in action
at the risk of his life above and beyond the call of duty.
S/Sgt. (then Sgt.) Hooper, U.S. Army, distinguished himself
while serving as squad leader with Company D. Company D
was assaulting a heavily defended enemy position along a river
bank when it encountered a withering hail of fire from rockets, machine guns, and automatic weapons. S/Sgt. Hooper
rallied several men and stormed across the river, overrunning
several bunkers on the opposite shore. Thus inspired, the rest
of the company moved to the attack. With utter disregard for
his own safety, he moved out under the intense fire again and
pulled back the wounded, moving them to safety. During this
act S/Sgt. Hooper was seriously wounded, but he refused
medical aid and returned to his men. With the relentless
enemy fire disrupting the attack, he singlehandedly stormed
three enemy bunkers, destroying them with hand grenades
and rifle fire, and shot two enemy soldiers who had attacked
and wounded the chaplain. Leading his men forward in a
sweep of the area, S/Sgt. Hooper destroyed three buildings
housing enemy riflemen. At this point he was attacked by a
North Vietnamese officer whom he fatally wounded with his
bayonet. Finding his men under heavy fire from a house to
the front, he proceeded alone to the building, killing its occupants with rifle fire and grenades. By now his initial body
wound had been compounded by grenade fragments, yet
despite the multiple wounds and loss of blood, he continued
to lead his men against the intense enemy fire. As his squad
reached the final line of enemy resistance, it received devastating fire from four bunkers in line on its left flank. S/Sgt.
Hooper gathered several hand grenades and raced down a
small trench which ran the length of the bunker line, tossing
grenades into each bunker as he passed by, killing all but two
of the occupants. With these positions destroyed, he concentrated on the last bunkers facing his men, destroying the first
with an incendiary grenade and neutralizing two more by rifle
fire. He then raced across an open field, still under enemy
fire, to rescue a wounded man who was trapped in a trench.
Upon reaching the man, he was faced by an armed enemy
soldier whom he killed with a pistol. Moving his comrade to
safety and returning to his men, he neutralized the final pocket of enemy resistance by fatally wounding three North
Vietnamese officers with rifle fire. S/Sgt. Hooper then established a final line and reorganized his men, not accepting
treatment until this was accomplished and not consenting to
evacuation until the following morning. His supreme valor,
inspiring leadership, and heroic self-sacrifice were directly

responsible for the company's success and provided a lasting
example in personal courage for every man on the field.
S/Sgt. Hooper's actions were in keeping with the highest traditions of the military service and reflect great credit upon
himself and the U.S. Army.

3249 ◆ *HOSKING JR., CHARLES ERNEST

Rank: Master Sergeant (rank at time of action: Staff Sergeant)
Service: U.S. Army
Birthday: 12 May 1924
Place of Birth: Ramsey, Bergen County, New Jersey
Date of Death: 21 March 1967
Place of Death: Republic of Vietnam
Cemetery: Valleau Cemetery—Ridgewood, New Jersey
Entered Service at: Fort Dix, Mercer County, New Jersey
Unit: Detachment A-302, Company A, 5th Special Forces
Group (Airborne), 1st Special Forces
Served as: Company Advisor
Battle or Place of Action: Don Luan District, Phuoc Long
Province, Republic of Vietnam
Date of Action: 21 March 1967
G.O. Number, Date: 39, 13 June 1969
Date of Presentation: 23 May 1969
Place of Presentation: The White House, presented by Pres.
Richard M. Nixon to his Widow
Citation: For conspicuous gallantry and intrepidity in action
at the risk of his life above and beyond the call of duty.
M/Sgt. Hosking (then Sfc.), Detachment A-302, Company
A, greatly distinguished himself while serving as company
adviser in the III Corps Civilian Irregular Defense Group
Reaction Battalion during combat operations in Don Luan
District. A Viet Cong suspect was apprehended and subsequently identified as a Viet Cong sniper. While M/Sgt.
Hosking was preparing the enemy for movement back to the
base camp, the prisoner suddenly grabbed a hand grenade
from M/Sgt. Hosking's belt, armed the grenade, and started
running towards the company command group which consisted of two Americans and two Vietnamese who were standing a few feet away. Instantly realizing that the enemy intended to kill the other men, M/Sgt. Hosking immediately leaped
upon the Viet Cong's back. With utter disregard for his personal safety, he grasped the Viet Cong in a "Bear Hug" forcing the grenade against the enemy soldier's chest. He then
wrestled the Viet Cong to the ground and covered the
enemy's body with his body until the grenade detonated. The
blast instantly killed both M/Sgt. Hosking and the Viet Cong.
By absorbing the full force of the exploding grenade with his
body and that of the enemy, he saved the other members of
his command group from death or serious injury. M/Sgt.
Hosking's risk of his life above and beyond the call of duty are
in the highest traditions of the U.S. Army and reflect great
credit upon himself and the Armed Forces of his country.

3250 ◆ HOWARD, JIMMIE EARL

Rank: Gunnery Sergeant (rank at time of action: Staff
Sergeant) (highest rank: First Sergeant)
Service: U.S. Marine Corps

Birthday: 27 July 1929
Place of Birth: Burlington, Des Moines County, Iowa
Date of Death: 12 November 1993
Place of Death: San Diego, California
Cemetery: Fort Rosecrans National Cemetery (O-3759)—San Diego, California
Entered Service at: Burlington, Des Moines County, Iowa
Unit: Company C, 1st Reconnaissance Battalion, 1st Marine Division (Rein) FMF
Served as: Platoon Sergeant
Battle or Place of Action: near Chu Lai, Republic of Vietnam
Date of Action: 16 June 1966
Date of Presentation: 21 August 1967
Place of Presentation: The White House, presented by Pres. Lyndon B. Johnson
Citation: For conspicuous gallantry and intrepidity at the risk of his life above and beyond the call of duty. G/Sgt. Howard and his 18-man platoon were occupying an observation post deep within enemy-controlled territory. Shortly after midnight a Viet Cong force of estimated battalion size approached the marines' position and launched a vicious attack with small-arms, automatic-weapons, and mortar fire. Reacting swiftly and fearlessly in the face of the overwhelming odds, G/Sgt. Howard skillfully organized his small but determined force into a tight perimeter defense and calmly moved from position to position to direct his men's fire. Throughout the night, during assault after assault, his courageous example and firm leadership inspired and motivated his men to withstand the unrelenting fury of the hostile fire in the seemingly hopeless situation. He constantly shouted encouragement to his men and exhibited imagination and resourcefulness in directing their return fire. When fragments of an exploding enemy grenade wounded him severely and prevented him from moving his legs, he distributed his ammunition to the remaining members of his platoon and proceeded to maintain radio communications and direct air strikes on the enemy with uncanny accuracy. At dawn, despite the fact that five men were killed and all but one wounded, his beleaguered platoon was still in command of its position. When evacuation helicopters approached his position, G/Sgt. Howard warned them away and called for additional air strikes and directed devastating small-arms fire and air strikes against enemy automatic-weapons positions in order to make the landing zone as secure as possible. Through his extraordinary courage and resolute fighting spirit, G/Sgt. Howard was largely responsible for preventing the loss of his entire platoon. His valiant leadership and courageous fighting spirit served to inspire the men of his platoon to heroic endeavor in the face of overwhelming odds, and reflect the highest credit upon G/Sgt. Howard, the Marine Corps, and the U.S. Naval Service.

3251 ◆ HOWARD, ROBERT LEWIS

Rank: First Lieutenant (rank at time of action: Sergeant First Class) (highest rank: Colonel)
Service: U.S. Army
Birthday: 11 July 1939
Place of Birth: Opelika, Lee County, Alabama

Entered Service at: Montgomery, Montgomery County, Alabama
Unit: 5th Special Forces Group (Airborne), 1st Special Forces
Served as: Platoon Sergeant
Battle or Place of Action: Republic of Vietnam
Date of Action: 30 December 1968
G.O. Number, Date: 16, 24 March 1971
Date of Presentation: 2 March 1971
Place of Presentation: The White House (East Ballroom), presented by Pres. Richard M. Nixon
Citation: For conspicuous gallantry and intrepidity in action at the risk of his life above and beyond the call of duty. 1st Lt. Howard (then Sfc.) distinguished himself while serving as platoon sergeant of an American-Vietnamese platoon which was on a mission to rescue a missing American soldier in enemy-controlled territory in the Republic of Vietnam. The platoon had left its helicopter landing zone and was moving out on its mission when it was attacked by an estimated two-company force. During the initial engagement, 1st Lt. Howard was wounded and his weapon destroyed by a grenade explosion. 1st Lt. Howard saw his platoon leader had been wounded seriously and was exposed to fire. Although unable to walk, and weaponless, 1st Lt. Howard unhesitatingly crawled through a hail of fire to retrieve his wounded leader. As 1st Lt. Howard was administering first aid and removing the officer's equipment, an enemy bullet struck one of the ammunition pouches on the lieutenant's belt, detonating several magazines of ammunition. 1st Lt. Howard momentarily sought cover and then realizing that he must rejoin the platoon, which had been disorganized by the enemy attack, he again began dragging the seriously wounded officer toward the platoon area. Through his outstanding example of indomitable courage and bravery, 1st Lt. Howard was able to rally the platoon into an organized defense force. With complete disregard for his safely, 1st Lt. Howard crawled from position to position, administering first aid to the wounded, giving encouragement to the defenders and directing their fire on the encircling enemy. For 3 1/2 hours 1st Lt. Howard's small force and supporting aircraft successfully repulsed enemy attacks and finally were in sufficient control to permit the landing of rescue helicopters. 1st Lt. Howard personally supervised the loading of his men and did not leave the bullet-swept landing zone until all were aboard safely. 1st Lt. Howard's gallantry in action, his complete devotion to the welfare of his men at the risk of his life were in keeping with the highest traditions of the military service and reflect great credit on himself, his unit, and the U.S. Army.

3252 ◆ *HOWE, JAMES DONNIE

Rank: Lance Corporal
Service: U.S. Marine Corps
Birthday: 17 December 1948
Place of Birth: Six Mile, Pickens County, South Carolina
Date of Death: 6 May 1970
Place of Death: Republic of Vietnam
Cemetery: Liberty Memorial Gardens Cemetery (MH)—Liberty, South Carolina

Entered Service at: Fort Jackson, Richland County, South Carolina
Unit: Company I, 3d Battalion, 7th Marines, 1st Marine Division (Rein) FMF
Served as: Rifleman
Battle or Place of Action: Republic of Vietnam
Date of Action: 6 May 1970
Date of Presentation: 15 September 1971
Place of Presentation: The White House, presented by Vice Pres. Spiro T. Agnew to his family
Citation: For conspicuous gallantry and intrepidity at the risk of his life above and beyond the call of duty while serving as a rifleman with Company I, during operations against enemy forces. In the early morning hours L/Cpl. Howe and two other marines were occupying a defensive position in a sandy beach area fronted by bamboo thickets. Enemy sappers suddenly launched a grenade attack against the position, utilizing the cover of darkness to carry out their assault. Following the initial explosions of the grenades, L/Cpl. Howe and his two comrades moved to a more advantageous position in order to return suppressive fire. When an enemy grenade landed in their midst, L/Cpl. Howe immediately shouted a warning and then threw himself upon the deadly missile, thereby protecting the lives of the fellow marines. His heroic and selfless action was in keeping with the finest traditions of the Marine Corps and of the U.S. Naval Service. He valiantly gave his life in the service of his country.

3253 ◆ *INGALLS, GEORGE ALAN

Rank: Specialist Fourth Class
Service: U.S. Army
Birthday: 9 March 1946
Place of Birth: Hanford, Kings County, California
Date of Death: 16 April 1967
Place of Death: Republic of Vietnam
Cemetery: Crestlawn Memorial Park (MH)—Riverside, California
Entered Service at: Los Angeles, Los Angeles County, California
Unit: Company A, 2d Battalion, 5th Cavalry, 1st Cavalry Division (Airmobile)
Served as: Rifleman
Battle or Place of Action: near Duc Pho, Republic of Vietnam
Date of Action: 16 April 1967
G.O. Number, Date: 11, 6 February 1969
Date of Presentation: 30 January 1969
Place of Presentation: The Pentagon, presented by Sec. of the Army Stanley R. Resor to his family
Citation: For conspicuous gallantry and intrepidity in action at the risk of his life above and beyond the call of duty. Sp4c. Ingalls, a member of Company A, accompanied his squad on a night ambush mission. Shortly after the ambush was established, an enemy soldier entered the killing zone and was shot when he tried to evade capture. Other enemy soldiers were expected to enter the area, and the ambush was maintained in the same location. Two quiet hours passed without incident, then suddenly a hand grenade was thrown from the nearby dense undergrowth into the center of the squad's position. The grenade did not explode, but shortly thereafter a second grenade landed directly between Sp4c. Ingalls and a nearby comrade. Although he could have jumped to a safe position, Sp4c. Ingalls, in a spontaneous act of great courage, threw himself on the grenade and absorbed its full blast. The explosion mortally wounded Sp4c. Ingalls, but his heroic action saved the lives of the remaining members of his squad. His gallantry and selfless devotion to his comrades are in keeping with the highest traditions of the military service and reflects great credit upon Sp4c. Ingalls, his unit, and the U.S. Army.

3254 ◆ JACKSON, JOE MADISON

Rank: Lieutenant Colonel (highest rank: Colonel)
Service: U.S. Air Force
Birthday: 14 March 1923
Place of Birth: Newnan, Coweta County, Georgia
Entered Service at: Newnan, Coweta County, Georgia
Unit: 311th Air Commando Squadron, Da Nang, Republic of Vietnam
Served as: Pilot of an C-123
Battle or Place of Action: Kham Duc, Republic of Vietnam
Date of Action: 12 May 1968
G.O. Number, Date: GB-40, 27 January 1969
Date of Presentation: 16 January 1969
Place of Presentation: The White house, presented by Pres. Lyndon B. Johnson
Citation: For conspicuous gallantry and intrepidity in action at the risk of his life above and beyond the call of duty. Lt. Col. Jackson distinguished himself as a pilot of a C-123 aircraft. Lt. Col. Jackson volunteered to attempt the rescue of a three-man USAF Combat Control Team from the Special Forces camp at Kham Duc. Hostile forces had overrun the forward outpost and established gun positions on the airstrip. They were raking the camp with small-arms, mortars, light and heavy automatic-weapons, and recoilless-rifle fire. The camp was engulfed in flames and ammunition dumps were continuously exploding and littering the runway with debris. In addition, eight aircraft had been destroyed by the intense enemy fire and one aircraft remained on the runway reducing its usable length to only 2,200 feet. To further complicate the landing, the weather was deteriorating rapidly, thereby permitting only one air strike prior to his landing. Although fully aware of the extreme danger and likely failure of such an attempt, Lt. Col. Jackson elected to land his aircraft and attempt to rescue. Displaying superb airmanship and extraordinary heroism, he landed his aircraft near the point where the combat control team was reported to be hiding. While on the ground, his aircraft was the target of intense hostile fire. A rocket landed in front of the nose of the aircraft but failed to explode. Once the combat control team was aboard, Lt. Col. Jackson succeeded in getting airborne despite the hostile fire directed across the runway in front of his aircraft. Lt. Col. Jackson's profound concern for his fellow men, at the risk of his life above and beyond the call of duty, are in keeping with the highest traditions of the U.S. Air Force and reflect great credit upon himself and the Armed Forces of his country.

3255 ◆ JACOBS, JACK HOWARD

Rank: Captain (rank at time of action: First Lieutenant) (highest rank: Colonel)
Service: U.S. Army
Birthday: 2 August 1945
Place of Birth: Brooklyn, Kings County, New York
Entered Service at: Trenton, Mercer County, New Jersey
Unit: U.S. Military Assistance Command, Army Element
Served as: Assistant Battalion Advisor
Battle or Place of Action: Kien Phong Province, Republic of Vietnam
Date of Action: 9 March 1968
G.O. Number, Date: 63, 27 October 1969
Date of Presentation: 9 October 1969
Place of Presentation: The White House, presented by Pres. Richard M. Nixon
Citation: For conspicuous gallantry and intrepidity in action at the risk of his life above and beyond the call of duty. Capt. Jacobs (then 1st Lt.), Infantry, distinguished himself while serving as assistant battalion adviser, 2d Battalion, 16th Infantry, 9th Infantry Division, Army of the Republic of Vietnam. The 2d Battalion was advancing to contact when it came under intense heavy machine-gun and mortar fire from a Viet Cong battalion positioned in well-fortified bunkers. As the 2d Battalion deployed into attack formation, its advance was halted by devastating fire. Capt. Jacobs, with the command element of the lead company, called for and directed air strikes on the enemy positions to facilitate a renewed attack. Due to the intensity of the enemy fire and heavy casualties to the command group, including the company commander, the attack stopped and the friendly troops became disorganized. Although wounded by mortar fragments, Capt. Jacobs assumed command of the allied company, ordered a withdrawal from the exposed position, and established a defensive perimeter. Despite profuse bleeding from head wounds which impaired his vision, Capt. Jacobs, with complete disregard for his safety, returned under intense fire to evacuate a seriously wounded adviser to the safety of a wooded area where he administered lifesaving first aid. He then returned through heavy automatic-weapons fire to evacuate the wounded company commander. Capt. Jacobs made repeated trips across the fire-swept, open rice paddies, evacuating wounded and their weapons. On three separate occasions, Capt. Jacobs contacted and drove off Viet Cong squads who were searching for allied wounded and weapons, singlehandedly killing three and wounding several others. His gallant actions and extraordinary heroism saved the lives of one U.S. adviser and 13 allied soldiers. Through his effort the allied company was restored to an effective fighting unit and prevented defeat of the friendly forces by a strong and determined enemy. Capt. Jacobs, by his gallantry and bravery in action in the highest traditions of the military service, has reflected great credit upon himself, his unit, and the U.S. Army.

3256 ◆ JENKINS, DON

Rank: Staff Sergeant (rank at time of action: Private First Class)
Service: U.S. Army
Birthday: 18 April 1948
Place of Birth: Quality, Butler County, Kentucky
Entered Service at: Nashville, Davidson County, Tennessee
Unit: Company A, 2d Battalion, 39th Infantry, 9th Infantry Division
Served as: Machine Gunner
Battle or Place of Action: Kien Phong Province, Republic of Vietnam
Date of Action: 6 January 1969
G.O. Number, Date: 17, 24 March 1971
Date of Presentation: 2 March 1971
Place of Presentation: The White House (East Ballroom), presented by Pres. Richard M. Nixon
Citation: For conspicuous gallantry and intrepidity in action at the risk of his life above and beyond the call of duty. S/Sgt. Jenkins (then Pfc.), Company A, distinguished himself while serving as a machine gunner on a reconnaissance mission. When his company came under heavy crossfire from an enemy complex, S/Sgt. Jenkins unhesitatingly maneuvered forward to a perilously exposed position and began placing suppressive fire on the enemy. When his own machine gun jammed, he immediately obtained a rifle and continued to fire into the enemy bunkers until his machine gun was made operative by his assistant. He exposed himself to extremely heavy fire when he repeatedly both ran and crawled across open terrain to obtain resupplies of ammunition until he had exhausted all that was available for his machine gun. Displaying tremendous presence of mind, he then armed himself with two antitank weapons and, by himself, maneuvered through the hostile fusillade to within 20 meters of an enemy bunker to destroy that position. After moving back to the friendly defensive perimeter long enough to secure yet another weapon, a grenade launcher, S/Sgt. Jenkins moved forward to a position providing no protection and resumed placing accurate fire on the enemy until his ammunition was again exhausted. During this time he was seriously wounded by shrapnel. Undaunted and displaying great courage, he moved forward 100 meters to aid a friendly element that was pinned down only a few meters from the enemy. This he did with complete disregard for his own wound and despite having been advised that several previous rescue attempts had failed at the cost of the life of one and wounding of others. Ignoring the continuing intense fire and his painful wounds, and hindered by darkness, he made three trips to the beleaguered unit, each time pulling a wounded comrade back to safety. S/Sgt. Jenkins' extraordinary valor, dedication, and indomitable spirit inspired his fellow soldiers to repulse the determined enemy attack and ultimately to defeat the larger force. S/Sgt. Jenkins' risk of his life reflect great credit upon himself, his unit, and the U.S. Army.

3257 ◆ *JENKINS JR., ROBERT HENRY

Rank: Private First Class
Service: U.S. Marine Corps
Birthday: 1 June 1948
Place of Birth: Interlachen, Putnam County, Florida
Date of Death: 5 March 1969
Place of Death: Republic of Vietnam

Cemetery: Sister Spring Baptist Cemetery (MH)—Interlachen, Florida
Entered Service at: Jacksonville, Duval County, Florida
Unit: 3d Reconnaissance Battalion, 3d Marine Division (Rein) FMF
Served as: Machine Gunner
Battle or Place of Action: Fire Support Base Argonne, DMZ
Date of Action: 5 March 1969
Date of Presentation: 20 April 1970
Place of Presentation: The White House, presented by Vice Pres. Spiro T. Agnew to his family
Citation: For conspicuous gallantry and intrepidity at the risk of his life above and beyond the call of duty while serving as a machine gunner with Company C, 3d Reconnaissance Battalion, in connection with operations against enemy forces. Early in the morning Pfc. Jenkins' 12-man reconnaissance team was occupying a defensive position at Fire Support Base Argonne south of the Demilitarized Zone. Suddenly, the marines were assaulted by a North Vietnamese Army platoon employing mortars, automatic weapons, and hand grenades. Reacting instantly, Pfc. Jenkins and another marine quickly moved into a two-man fighting emplacement, and as they boldly delivered accurate machine-gun fire against the enemy, a North Vietnamese soldier threw a hand grenade into the friendly emplacement. Fully realizing the inevitable results of his actions, Pfc. Jenkins quickly seized his comrade, and pushing the man to the ground, he leaped on top of the marine to shield him from the explosion. Absorbing the full impact of the detonation, Pfc. Jenkins was seriously injured and subsequently succumbed to his wounds. His courage, inspiring valor, and selfless devotion to duty saved a fellow marine from serious injury or possible death and upheld the highest traditions of the Marine Corps and the U.S. Naval Service. He gallantly gave his life for his country.

3258 ◆ JENNINGS, DELBERT OWEN

Rank: Staff Sergeant (highest rank: Command Sergeant Major)
Service: U.S. Army
Birthday: 23 July 1936
Place of Birth: Silver City, Grant County, New Mexico
Entered Service at: San Francisco, San Francisco County, California
Unit: 3d Squad, 4th Platoon, Company C, 1st Battalion (Airborne), 12th Cavalry, 1st Air Cavalry Division
Served as: Squad Leader
Battle or Place of Action: Kim Song Valley, Republic of Vietnam
Date of Action: 27 December 1966
G.O. Number, Date: 60, 22 October 1968
Date of Presentation: 19 September 1968
Place of Presentation: The White House, presented by Pres. Lyndon B. Johnson
Citation: For conspicuous gallantry and intrepidity at the risk of his life above and beyond the call of duty. Part of Company C was defending an artillery position when attacked by a North Vietnamese Army regiment supported by mortar, recoilless-rifle, and machine-gun fire. At the outset, Sgt.

Jennings sprang to his bunker, astride the main attack route, and slowed the on-coming enemy wave with highly effective machine-gun fire. Despite a tenacious defense in which he killed at least 12 of the enemy, his squad was forced to the rear. After covering the withdrawal of the squad, he rejoined his men, destroyed an enemy demolition crew about to blow up a nearby howitzer, and killed three enemy soldiers at his initial bunker position. Ordering his men back into a secondary position, he again covered their withdrawal, killing one enemy with the butt of his weapon. Observing that some of the defenders were unaware of a enemy force in their rear, he raced through a fire-swept area to warn the men, turn their fire on the enemy, and lead them into a secondary perimeter. Assisting in the defense of the new position, he aided the air-landing of reinforcements by throwing white phosphorous grenades on the landing zone despite dangerously silhouetting himself with the light. After helping to repulse the final enemy assaults, he led a group of volunteers well beyond friendly lines to an area where eight seriously wounded men lay. Braving enemy sniper fire and ignoring the presence of booby traps in the area, they recovered the eight men who would have probably perished without early medical treatment. Sgt. Jenning's extraordinary heroism and inspirational leadership saved the lives of many of his comrades and contributed greatly to the defeat of a superior enemy force. His actions stand with the highest traditions of the military profession and reflect great credit upon himself, his unit, and the U.S. Army.

3259 ◆ *JIMENEZ, JOSE FRANCISCO

Rank: Lance Corporal
Service: U.S. Marine Corps
Birthday: 20 March 1946
Place of Birth: Mexico City, Mexico
Date of Death: 28 August 1969
Place of Death: Republic of Vietnam
Cemetery: Panteon Municipal Cemetery (MH)—Morelia, Mexico
Entered Service at: Phoenix, Maricopa County, Arizona
Unit: Company K, 3d Battalion, 7th Marines, 1st Marine Division (Rein) FMF
Served as: Fire Team Leader
Battle or Place of Action: south of Da Nang, Quang Nam Province, Republic of Vietnam
Date of Action: 28 August 1969
Date of Presentation: 6 August 1970
Place of Presentation: The White House, presented by Pres. Richard M. Nixon to his family
Citation: For conspicuous gallantry and intrepidity at the risk of his life above and beyond the call of duty while serving as a fire team leader with Company K, in operations against the enemy. L/Cpl. Jimenez' unit came under heavy attack by North Vietnamese soldiers concealed in well-camouflaged emplacements. L/Cpl. Jimenez reacted by seizing the initiative and plunging forward toward the enemy positions. He personally destroyed several enemy personnel and silenced an antiaircraft weapon. Shouting encouragement to his companions, L/Cpl. Jimenez continued his aggressive forward movement. He slowly maneuvered to within 10 feet of hostile sol-

diers who were firing automatic weapons from a trench and, in the face of vicious enemy fire, destroyed the position. Although he was by now the target of concentrated fire from hostile gunners intent upon halting his assault, L/Cpl. Jimenez continued to press forward. As he moved to attack another enemy soldier, he was mortally wounded. L/Cpl. Jimenez' indomitable courage, aggressive fighting spirit, and unfaltering devotion to duty upheld the highest traditions of the Marine Corps and of the U.S. Naval Service.

3260 ◆ JOEL, LAWRENCE

Rank: Specialist Sixth Class (rank at time of action: Specialist Fifth Class) (highest rank: Sergeant First Class)
Service: U.S. Army
Birthday: 22 February 1928
Place of Birth: Winston-Salem, Forsyth County, North Carolina
Date of Death: 4 February 1984
Place of Death: Winston-Salem, North Carolina
Cemetery: Arlington National Cemetery (46-15-1) (MH)—Arlington, Virginia
Entered Service at: New York, New York
Unit: Headquarters & Headquarters Company, 1st Battalion (Airborne), 503d Infantry, 173d Airborne Brigade
Served as: Medical Aidman
Battle or Place of Action: Republic of Vietnam
Date of Action: 8 November 1965
G.O. Number, Date: 15, 5 April 1967
Date of Presentation: 9 March 1967
Place of Presentation: The White House (Lawn), presented by Pres. Lyndon b. Johnson
Citation: For conspicuous gallantry and intrepidity at the risk of his life above and beyond the call of duty. Sp6c. Joel demonstrated indomitable courage, determination, and professional skill when a numerically superior and well-concealed Viet Cong element launched a vicious attack which wounded or killed nearly every man in the lead squad of the company. After treating the men wounded by the initial burst of gunfire, he bravely moved forward to assist others who were wounded while proceeding to their objective. While moving from man to man, he was struck in the right leg by machine-gun fire. Although painfully wounded his desire to aid his fellow soldiers transcended all personal feeling. He bandaged his own wound and self-administered morphine to deaden the pain enabling him to continue his dangerous undertaking. Through this period of time, he constantly shouted words of encouragement to all around him. Then, completely ignoring the warnings of others and his pain, he continued his search for wounded, exposing himself to hostile fire; and, as the bullets dug up the dirt around him, he held plasma bottles high while kneeling completely engrossed in his lifesaving mission. Then, after being struck a second time and with a bullet lodged in his thigh, he dragged himself over the battlefield and succeeded in treating 13 more men before his medical supplies ran out. Displaying resourcefulness, he saved the life of one man by placing a plastic bag over a severe chest wound to congeal the blood. As one of the platoons pursued the Viet Cong, an insurgent force in concealed positions opened fire

on the platoon and wounded many more soldiers. With a new stock of medical supplies, Sp6c. Joel again shouted words of encouragement as he crawled through an intense hail of gunfire to the wounded men. After the 24-hour battle subsided and the Viet Cong dead numbered 410, snipers continued to harass the company. Throughout the long battle, Sp6c. Joel never lost sight of his mission as a medical aidman and continued to comfort and treat the wounded until his own evacuation was ordered. His meticulous attention to duty saved a large number of lives and his unselfish, daring example under most adverse conditions was an inspiration to all. Sp6c. Joel's profound concern for his fellow soldiers, at the risk of his life above and beyond the call of duty, are in the highest traditions of the U.S. Army and reflect great credit upon himself and the Armed Forces of his country.

3261 ◆ JOHNSON, DWIGHT HAL

Rank: Specialist Fifth Class
Service: U.S. Army
Birthday: 7 May 1947
Place of Birth: Detroit, Wayne County, Michigan
Date of Death: 30 April 1971
Place of Death: Detroit, Michigan
Cemetery: Arlington National Cemetery (31-471) (MH)—Arlington, Virginia
Entered Service at: Detroit, Wayne County, Michigan
Unit: Company B, 1st Battalion, 69th Armor, 4th Infantry Division
Served as: Tank Driver
Battle or Place of Action: near Dak To, Kontum Province, Republic of Vietnam
Date of Action: 15 January 1968
G.O. Number, Date: 76, 10 December 1968
Date of Presentation: 19 November 1968
Place of Presentation: The White House, presented by Pres. Lyndon B. Johnson
Citation: For conspicuous gallantry and intrepidity at the risk of his life above and beyond the call of duty. Sp5c. Johnson, a tank driver with Company B, was a member of a reaction force moving to aid other elements of his platoon, which was in heavy contact with a battalion-size North Vietnamese force. Sp5c. Johnson's tank, upon reaching the point of contact, threw a track and became immobilized. Realizing that he could do no more as a driver, he climbed out of the vehicle, armed only with a .45 caliber pistol. Despite intense hostile fire, Sp5c. Johnson killed several enemy soldiers before he had expended his ammunition. Returning to his tank through a heavy volume of antitank-rocket, small-arms and automatic weapon fire, he obtained a submachine gun with which to continue his fight against the advancing enemy. Armed with this weapon, Sp5c. Johnson again braved deadly enemy fire to return to the center of the ambush site where he courageously eliminated more of the determined foe. Engaged in extremely close combat when the last of his ammunition was expended, he killed an enemy soldier with the stock end of his submachine gun. Now weaponless, Sp5c. Johnson ignored the enemy fire around him, climbed into his platoon sergeant's tank, extricated a wound-

ed crewmember and carried him to an armored personnel carrier. He then returned to the same tank and assisted in firing the main gun until it jammed. In a magnificent display of courage, Sp5c. Johnson exited the tank and again armed only with a .45 caliber pistol, engaged several North Vietnamese troops in close proximity to the vehicle. Fighting his way through devastating fire and remounting his own immobilized tank, he remained fully exposed to the enemy as he bravely and skillfully engaged them with the tank's externally mounted .50 caliber machine gun, where he remained until the situation was brought under control. Sp5c. Johnson's profound concern for his fellow soldiers, at the risk of his life above and beyond the call of duty, are in keeping with the highest traditions of the military service and reflect great credit upon himself and the U.S. Army.

3262 ◆ *JOHNSON, RALPH HENRY

Rank: Private First Class
Service: U.S. Marine Corps
Birthday: 11 January 1949
Place of Birth: Charleston, Charleston County, South Carolina
Date of Death: 5 March 1968
Place of Death: Republic of Vietnam
Cemetery: Beaufort National Cemetery (3-21) (MH)—Beaufort, South Carolina
Entered Service at: Oakland, Alameda County, California
Unit: Company A, 1st Reconnaissance Battalion, 1st Marine Division (Rein) FMF
Served as: Reconnaissance Scout
Battle or Place of Action: Hill-146, near Quan Duc Valley, Republic of Vietnam
Date of Action: 5 March 1968
Date of Presentation: 20 April 1970
Place of Presentation: The White House, presented by Vice Pres. Spiro T. Agnew to his family
Citation: For conspicuous gallantry and intrepidity at the risk of his life above and beyond the call of duty while serving as a reconnaissance scout with Company A, in action against the North Vietnamese Army and Viet Cong forces. In the early morning hours during Operation Rock, Pfc. Johnson was a member of a 15-man reconnaissance patrol manning an observation post on Hill 146 overlooking the Quan Duc Valley deep in enemy-controlled territory. They were attacked by a platoon-size hostile force employing automatic weapons, satchel charges, and hand grenades. Suddenly, a hand grenade landed in the three-man fighting hole occupied by Pfc. Johnson and two fellow marines. Realizing the inherent danger to his two comrades, he shouted a warning and unhesitatingly hurled himself on the explosive device. When the grenade exploded, Pfc. Johnson absorbed the tremendous impact of the blast and was killed instantly. His prompt and heroic act saved the life of one marine at the cost of his life and undoubtedly prevented the enemy from penetrating his sector of the patrol's perimeter. Pfc. Johnson's courage, inspiring valor, and selfless devotion to duty were in keeping with the highest traditions of the Marine Corps and the U.S. Naval Service. He gallantly gave his life for his country.

3263 ◆ *JOHNSTON, DONALD RAY

Rank: Specialist Fourth Class
Service: U.S. Army
Birthday: 19 November 1947
Place of Birth: Columbus, Muscogee County, Georgia
Date of Death: 21 March 1969
Place of Death: Republic of Vietnam
Cemetery: Fort Benning Post Cemetery (E-43-A) (MH)—Fort Benning, Georgia
Entered Service at: Columbus, Muscogee County, Georgia
Unit: Company D, 1st Battalion, 8th Cavalry, 1st Cavalry Division
Served as: Mortarman
Battle or Place of Action: Tay Ninh Province, Republic of Vietnam
Date of Action: 21 March 1969
G.O. Number, Date: 11, 9 March 1971
Date of Presentation: 16 February 1971
Place of Presentation: The White House (East Ballroom), presented by Pres. Richard M. Nixon to his family
Citation: For conspicuous gallantry and intrepidity in action at the risk of his life above and beyond the call of duty. Sp4c. Johnston distinguished himself while serving as a mortarman with Company D, at a fire support base in Tay Ninh Province. Sp4c. Johnston's company was in defense positions when it came under a devastating rocket and mortar attack. Under cover of the bombardment, enemy sappers broke through the defensive perimeter and began hurling explosive charges into the main defensive bunkers. Sp4c. Johnston and six of his comrades had moved from their exposed position to one of the bunkers to continue their fight against the enemy attackers. As they were firing from the bunker, an enemy soldier threw three explosive charges into their position. Sensing the danger to his comrades, Sp4c. Johnston, with complete disregard for his safety, hurled himself onto the explosive charges, smothering the detonations with his body and shielding his fellow soldiers from the blast. His heroic action saved the lives of six of his comrades. Sp4c. Johnston's concern for his fellow men at the cost of his life were in the highest traditions of the military service and reflect great credit upon himself, his unit, and the U.S. Army.

3264 ◆ *JONES III, WILLIAM ATKINSON

Rank: Colonel
Service: U.S. Air Force
Birthday: 31 May 1922
Place of Birth: Norfolk, Norfolk County, Virginia
Date of Death: 15 November 1969
Place of Death: near Woodbridge, Virginia
Cemetery: Saint John's Church Cemetery—Warsaw, Virginia
Entered Service at: Charlottesville, Charlottesville County, Virginia
Unit: 602d Special Operations Squadron, Nakon Phanom Royal Thai AFB Thailand
Served as: Pilot of an A-1H Skyraider
Battle or Place of Action: near Dong Hoi, North Vietnam

Date of Action: 1 September 1968
G.O. Number, Date: GB-826, 23 June 1970
Date of Presentation: 6 August 1970
Place of Presentation: The White House, presented by Pres. Richard M. Nixon to his family
Citation: For conspicuous gallantry and intrepidity in action at the risk of his life above and beyond the call of duty. Col. Jones distinguished himself as the pilot of an A-1H Skyraider aircraft near Dong Hoi, North Vietnam. On that day, as the on-scene commander in the attempted rescue of a downed U.S. pilot, Col. Jones' aircraft was repeatedly hit by heavy and accurate antiaircraft fire. On one of his low passes, Col. Jones felt an explosion beneath his aircraft and his cockpit rapidly filled with smoke. With complete disregard of the possibility that his aircraft might still be burning, he unhesitatingly continued his search for the downed pilot. On this pass, he sighted the survivor and a multiple-barrel gun position firing at him from near the top of a karst formation. He could not attack the gun position on that pass for fear he would endanger the downed pilot. Leaving himself exposed to the gun position, Col. Jones attacked the position with cannon and rocket fire on two successive passes. On his second pass, the aircraft was hit with multiple rounds of automatic-weapons fire. One round impacted the Yankee Extraction System rocket mounted directly behind the headrest, igniting the rocket. His aircraft was observed to burst into flames in the center fuselage section, with flames engulfing the cockpit area. He pulled the extraction handle, jettisoning the canopy. The influx of fresh air made the fire burn with greater intensity for a few moments, but since the rocket motor had already burned, the extraction system did not pull Col. Jones from the aircraft. Despite searing pains from severe burns sustained on his arms, hands, neck, shoulders, and face, Col. Jones pulled his aircraft into a climb and attempted to transmit the location of the downed pilot and the enemy gun position to the other aircraft in the area. His calls were blocked by other aircraft transmissions repeatedly directing him to bail out and within seconds his transmitters were disabled and he could receive only on one channel. Completely disregarding his injuries, he elected to fly his crippled aircraft back to his base and pass on essential information for the rescue rather than bail out. Col. Jones successfully landed his heavily damaged aircraft and passed the information to a debriefing officer while on the operating table. As a result of his heroic actions and complete disregard for his personal safety, the downed pilot was rescued later in the day. Col. Jones' profound concern for his fellow man at the risk of his life, above and beyond the call of duty, are in keeping with the highest traditions of the U.S. Air Force and reflect great credit upon himself and the Armed Forces of his country.

3265 ◆ *KAROPCZYC, STEPHEN EDWARD

Rank: First Lieutenant
Service: U.S. Army
Birthday: 5 March 1944
Place of Birth: New York, New York
Date of Death: 12 March 1967
Place of Death: Republic of Vietnam

Cemetery: Long Island National Cemetery (DSS-5-A) (MH)—Farmingdale, New York
Entered Service at: Bethpage, Nassau County, New York
Unit: 3d Platoon, Company A, 2d Battalion, 35th Infantry, 25th Infantry Division
Served as: Platoon Leader
Battle or Place of Action: Kontum Province, Republic of Vietnam
Date of Action: 12 March 1967
G.O. Number, Date: 4, 24 January 1969
Date of Presentation: 9 January 1969
Place of Presentation: The Pentagon, presented by Sec. of the Army Stanley R. Resor to his family
Citation: For conspicuous gallantry and intrepidity in action at the risk of his life above and beyond the call of duty. While leading the 3d Platoon, Company A, on a flanking maneuver against a superior enemy force, 1st Lt. Karopczyc observed that his lead element was engaged with a small enemy unit along his route. Aware of the importance of quickly pushing through to the main enemy force in order to provide relief for a hard-pressed friendly platoon, he dashed through the intense enemy fire into the open and hurled colored smoke grenades to designate the foe for attack by helicopter gunships. He moved among his men to embolden their advance, and he guided their attack by marking enemy locations with bursts of fire from his own weapon. His forceful leadership quickened the advance, forced the enemy to retreat, and allowed his unit to close with the main hostile force. Continuing the deployment of his platoon, he constantly exposed himself as he ran from man to man to give encouragement and to direct their efforts. A shot from an enemy sniper struck him above the heart but he refused aid for this serious injury, plugging the bleeding wound with his finger until it could be properly dressed. As the enemy strength mounted, he ordered his men to organize a defensive position in and around some abandoned bunkers where he conducted a defense against the increasingly strong enemy attacks. After several hours, a North Vietnamese soldier hurled a hand grenade to within a few feet of 1st Lt. Karopczyc and two other wounded men. Although his position protected him, he leaped up to cover the deadly grenade with a steel helmet. It exploded to drive fragments into 1st Lt. Karopczyc's legs, but his action prevented further injury to the two wounded men. Severely weakened by his multiple wounds, he continued to direct the actions of his men until he succumbed two hours later. 1st Lt. Karopczyc's heroic leadership, unyielding perseverance, and selfless devotion to his men were directly responsible for the successful and spirited action of his platoon throughout the battle and are in keeping with the highest traditions of the U.S. Army.

3266 ◆ *KAWAMURA, TERRY TERUO

Rank: Corporal
Service: U.S. Army
Birthday: 10 December 1949
Place of Birth: Wahiawa, Honolulu County, Oahu, Hawaii
Date of Death: 20 March 1969
Place of Death: Republic of Vietnam

Cemetery: Mililani Memorial Park—Pearl City, Hawaii
Entered Service at: Oahu, Hawaii
Unit: 173d Engineer Company, 173d Airborne Brigade
Battle or Place of Action: Camp Radcliff, Republic of Vietnam
Date of Action: 20 March 1969
G.O. Number, Date: 12, 9 March 1971
Date of Presentation: 16 February 1971
Place of Presentation: The White House (East Ballroom), presented by Pres. Richard M. Nixon to his family
Citation: For conspicuous gallantry and intrepidity in action at the risk of his life above and beyond the call of duty. Cpl. Kawamura distinguished himself by heroic action while serving as a member of the 173d Engineer Company. An enemy demolition team infiltrated the unit quarters area and opened fire with automatic weapons. Disregarding the intense fire, Cpl. Kawamura ran for his weapon. At that moment, a violent explosion tore a hole in the roof and stunned the occupants of the room. Cpl. Kawamura jumped to his feet, secured his weapon and, as he ran toward the door to return the enemy fire, he observed that another explosive charge had been thrown through the hole in the roof to the floor. He immediately realized that two stunned fellow soldiers were in great peril and shouted a warning. Although in a position to escape, Cpl. Kawamura unhesitatingly wheeled around and threw himself on the charge. In completely disregarding his safety, Cpl. Kawamura prevented serious injury or death to several members of his unit. The extraordinary courage and selflessness displayed by Cpl. Kawamura are in the highest traditions of the military service and reflect great credit upon himself, his unit, and the U.S. Army.

3267 ◆ KAYS, KENNETH MICHAEL

Rank: Private First Class (rank at time of action: Private)
Service: U.S. Army
Birthday: 22 September 1949
Place of Birth: Mount Vernon, Jefferson County, Illinois
Date of Death: 25 November 1991
Place of Death: Fairfield, Illinois
Cemetery: Maple Hill Cemetery Veterans Section (MH)—Fairfield, Illinois
Entered Service at: Fairfield, Wayne County, Illinois
Unit: Headquarters & Headquarters Company, 1st Battalion, 506th Infantry, 101st Airborne Division
Served as: Medical Aidman
Battle or Place of Action: Thua Thien Province, Republic of Vietnam
Date of Action: 7 May 1970
G.O. Number, Date: 40, 5 November 1973
Date of Presentation: 15 October 1973
Place of Presentation: The White House, presented by Pres. Richard M. Nixon
Citation: For conspicuous gallantry and intrepidity in action at the risk of his life above and beyond the call of duty. Pfc. (then Pvt.) Kays distinguished himself while serving as a medical aidman with Company D, 1st Battalion, 101st Airborne Division near Fire Support Base Maureen. A heavily armed force of enemy sappers and infantrymen assaulted Company

D's night defensive position, wounding and killing a number of its members. Disregarding the intense enemy fire and ground assault, Pfc. Kays began moving toward the perimeter to assist his fallen comrades. In doing so he became the target of concentrated enemy fire and explosive charges, one of which severed the lower portion of his left leg. After applying a tourniquet to his leg, Pfc. Kays moved to the fire-swept perimeter, administered medical aid to one of the wounded, and helped move him to an area of relative safety. Despite his severe wound and excruciating pain, Pfc. Kays returned to the perimeter in search of other wounded men. He treated another wounded comrade, and, using his own body as a shield against enemy bullets and fragments, moved him to safety. Although weakened from a great loss of blood, Pfc. Kays resumed his heroic lifesaving efforts by moving beyond the company's perimeter into the enemy-held territory to treat a wounded American lying there. Only after his fellow wounded soldiers had been treated and evacuated did Pfc. Kays allow his own wounds to be treated. These courageous acts by Pfc. Kays resulted in the saving of numerous lives and inspired others in his company to repel the enemy. Pfc. Kays' heroism at the risk of his life are in keeping with the highest traditions of the service and reflect great credit upon him, his unit, and the U.S. Army.

3268 ◆ *KEDENBURG, JOHN JAMES

Rank: Specialist Fifth Class
Service: U.S. Army
Birthday: 31 July 1946
Place of Birth: Brooklyn, Kings County, New York
Date of Death: 14 June 1968
Place of Death: Republic of Vietnam
Cemetery: Long Island National Cemetery (2H-3684) (MH)—Farmingdale, New York
Entered Service at: Brooklyn, Kings County, New York
Unit: Command and Control Detachment North, Forward Operating Base 2, 5th Special Forces Group (Airborne), 1st Special Forces
Served as: Advisor
Battle or Place of Action: Republic of Vietnam
Date of Action: 13 June 1968
G.O. Number, Date: 17, 23 April 1970
Date of Presentation: 7 April 1970
Place of Presentation: The White House, presented by Pres. Richard M. Nixon to his family
Citation: For conspicuous gallantry and intrepidity in action at the risk of his life above and beyond the call of duty. Sp5c. Kedenburg, U.S. Army, Command and Control Detachment North, Forward Operating Base 2, 5th Special Forces Group (Airborne), distinguished himself while serving as adviser to a long-range reconnaissance team of South Vietnamese irregular troops. The team's mission was to conduct counterguerrilla operations deep within enemy-held territory. Prior to reaching the day's objective, the team was attacked and encircled by a battalion-size North Vietnamese Army force. Sp5c. Kedenburg assumed immediate command of the team which succeeded, after a fierce fight, in breaking out of the encirclement. As the team moved through thick jungle to a posi-

tion from which it could be extracted by helicopter, Sp5c. Kedenburg conducted a gallant rear guard fight against the pursuing enemy and called for tactical air support and rescue helicopters. His withering fire against the enemy permitted the team to reach a preselected landing zone with the loss of only one man, who was unaccounted for. Once in the landing zone, Sp5c. Kedenburg deployed the team into a perimeter defense against the numerically superior enemy force. When tactical air support arrived, he skillfully directed air strikes against the enemy, suppressing their fire so that helicopters could hover over the area and drop slings to be used in the extraction of the team. After half of the team was extracted by helicopter, Sp5c. Kedenburg and the remaining three members of the team harnessed themselves to the sling on a second hovering helicopter. Just as the helicopter was to lift them out of the area, the South Vietnamese team member who had been unaccounted for after the initial encounter with the enemy appeared in the landing zone. Sp5c. Kedenburg unhesitatingly gave up his place in the sling to the man and directed the helicopter pilot to leave the area. He then continued to engage the enemy who were swarming into the landing zone, killing six enemy soldiers before he was overpowered. Sp5c. Kedenburg's inspiring leadership, consummate courage, and willing self-sacrifice permitted his small team to inflict heavy casualties on the enemy and escape almost certain annihilation. His actions reflect great credit upon himself and the U.S. Army.

3269 ◆ *KEITH, MIGUEL

R Lance Corporal
Service: U.S. Marine Corps
Birthday: 2 June 1951
Place of Birth: San Antonio, Bexar County, Texas
Date of Death: 8 May 1970
Place of Death: Republic of Vietnam
Cemetery: Forest Lawn Cemetery (MH)—Omaha, Nebraska
Entered Service at: Omaha, Douglas County, Nebraska
Unit: Combined Action Platoon 1-3-2, III Marine Amphibious Force
Served as: Machine Gunner
Battle or Place of Action: Quang Ngai Province, Republic of Vietnam
Date of Action: 8 May 1970
Date of Presentation: 15 September 1971
Place of Presentation: The White House, presented by Vice Pres. Spiro T. Agnew to his family
Citation: For conspicuous gallantry and intrepidity at the risk of his life above and beyond the call of duty while serving as a machine gunner with Combined Action Platoon 1-3-2. During the early morning L/Cpl. Keith was seriously wounded when his platoon was subjected to a heavy ground attack by a greatly outnumbering enemy force. Despite his painful wounds, he ran across the fire-swept terrain to check the security of vital defensive positions and then, while completely exposed to view, proceeded to deliver a hail of devastating machine-gun fire against the enemy. Determined to stop five of the enemy soldiers approaching the command post, he

rushed forward, firing as he advanced. He succeeded in disposing of three of the attackers and in dispersing the remaining two. At this point, a grenade detonated near L/Cpl. Keith, knocking him to the ground and inflicting further severe wounds. Fighting pain and weakness from loss of blood, he again braved the concentrated hostile fire to charge an estimated 25 enemy soldiers who were massing to attack. The vigor of his assault and his well-placed fire eliminated four of the enemy soldiers while the remainder fled for cover. During this valiant effort, he was mortally wounded by an enemy soldier. By his courageous and inspiring performance in the face of almost overwhelming odds, L/Cpl. Keith contributed in large measure to the success of his platoon in routing a numerically superior enemy force, and upheld the finest traditions of the Marine Corps and of the U.S. Naval Service.

3270 ◆ KELLER, LEONARD BERT

Rank: Sergeant
Service: U.S. Army
Birthday: 25 February 1947
Place of Birth: Rockford, Winnebago County, Illinois
Entered Service at: Chicago, Cook County, Illinois
Unit: Company A, 3d Battalion, 60th Infantry, 9th Infantry Division
Served as: Machine Gunner
Battle or Place of Action: Ap Bac Zone, Republic of Vietnam
Date of Action: 2 May 1967
G.O. Number, Date: 61, 22 October 1968
Date of Presentation: 19 September 1968
Place of Presentation: The White House, presented by Pres. Lyndon B. Johnson
Citation: For conspicuous gallantry and intrepidity in action at the risk of his life above and beyond the call of duty. Sweeping through an area where an enemy ambush had occurred earlier, Sgt. Keller's unit suddenly came under intense automatic-weapons and small-arms fire from a number of enemy bunkers and numerous snipers in nearby trees. Sgt. Keller quickly moved to a position where he could fire at a bunker from which automatic fire was received, killing one Viet Cong who attempted to escape. Leaping to the top of a dike, he and a comrade charged the enemy bunkers, dangerously exposing themselves to the enemy fire. Armed with a light machine gun, Sgt. Keller and his comrade began a systematic assault on the enemy bunkers. While Sgt. Keller neutralized the fire from the first bunker with his machine gun, the other soldier threw in a hand grenade killing its occupant. Then he and the other soldier charged a second bunker, killing its occupant. A third bunker contained a automatic rifleman who had pinned down much of the friendly platoon. Again, with utter disregard for the fire directed to them, the two-men charged, killing the enemy within. Continuing their attack, Sgt. Keller and his comrade assaulted four more bunkers, killing the enemy within. During their furious assault, Sgt. Keller and his comrade had been almost continuously exposed to intense sniper fire as the enemy desperately sought to stop their attack. The ferocity of their assault had

carried the soldiers beyond the line of bunkers into the tree-line, forcing the snipers to flee. The two men gave immediate chase, driving the enemy away from the friendly unit. When his ammunition was exhausted, Sgt. Keller returned to the platoon to assist in the evacuation of the wounded. The two man assault had driven an enemy platoon from a well-pre-pared position, accounted for numerous enemy dead, and prevented further friendly casualties. Sgt. Keller's selfless hero-ism and indomitable fighting spirit saved the lives of many of his comrades and inflicted serious damage on the enemy. His acts were in keeping with the highest traditions of the military service and reflect great credit upon himself and the U.S. Army.

3271 ◆ KELLEY, THOMAS GUNNING

Rank: Lieutenant Commander (rank at time of action: Lieutenant) (highest rank: Captain)
Service: U.S. Navy
Birthday: 13 May 1939
Place of Birth: Boston, Suffolk County, Massachusetts
Entered Service at: Boston, Suffolk County, Massachusetts
Unit: River Assault Division 152
Served as: Division Commander
Battle or Place of Action: Ong Muong Canal, Kien Hoa Province, Republic of Vietnam
Date of Action: 15 June 1969
Date of Presentation: 14 May 1970
Place of Presentation: The White House, presented by Pres. Richard M. Nixon
Citation: For conspicuous gallantry and intrepidity at the risk of his life above and beyond the call of duty in the after-noon while serving as commander of River Assault Division 152 during combat operations against enemy aggressor forces. Lt. Comdr. (then Lt.) Kelley was in charge of a col-umn of eight river assault craft which were extracting one company of U.S. Army infantry troops on the east bank of the Ong Muong Canal in Kien Hoa Province, when one of the armored troop carriers reported a mechanical failure of a loading ramp. At approximately the same time, Viet Cong forces opened fire from the opposite bank of the canal. After issuing orders for the crippled troop carrier to raise its ramp manually, and for the remaining boats to form a protective cordon around the disabled craft, Lt. Comdr. Kelley, realizing the extreme danger to his column and its inability to clear the ambush site until the crippled unit was repaired, boldly maneuvered the monitor in which he was embarked to the exposed side of the protective cordon in direct line with the enemy's fire, and ordered the monitor to commence firing. Suddenly, an enemy rocket scored a direct hit on the coxswain's flat, the shell penetrating the thick armor plate, and the explosion spraying shrapnel in all directions. Sustaining serious head wounds from the blast, which hurled him to the deck of the monitor, Lt. Comdr. Kelley disregard-ed his severe injuries and attempted to continue directing the other boats. Although unable to move from the deck or to speak clearly into the radio, he succeeded in relaying his com-mands through one of his men until the enemy attack was

silenced and the boats were able to move to an area of safety. Lt. Comdr. Kelley's brilliant leadership, bold initiative, and resolute determination served to inspire his men and provide the impetus needed to carry out the mission after he was medically evacuated by helicopter. His extraordinary courage under fire and his selfless devotion to duty sustain and enhance the finest traditions of the U.S. Naval Service.

3272 ◆ KELLOGG JR., ALLAN JAY

Rank: Gunnery Sergeant (rank at time of action: Staff Sergeant) (highest rank: Sergeant Major)
Service: U.S. Marine Corps
Birthday: 1 October 1943
Place of Birth: Bethel, Fairfield County, Connecticut
Entered Service at: Bridgeport, Fairfield County, Connecticut
Unit: Company G, 2d Battalion, 5th Marines, 1st Marine Division
Served as: Platoon Sergeant
Battle or Place of Action: Quang Nam Province, Republic of Vietnam
Date of Action: 11 March 1970
Date of Presentation: 15 October 1973
Place of Presentation: The White House, presented by Pres. Richard M. Nixon
Citation: For conspicuous gallantry and intrepidity at the risk of his life above and beyond the call of duty while serving as a platoon sergeant with Company G, in connection with combat operations against the enemy on the night of 11 March 1970. Under the leadership of G/Sgt. Kellogg, a small unit from Company G was evacuating a fallen comrade when the unit came under a heavy volume of small-arms and auto-matic-weapons fire from a numerically superior enemy force occupying well-concealed emplacements in the surrounding jungle. During the ensuing fierce engagement, an enemy sol-dier managed to maneuver through the dense foliage to a position near the marines, and hurled a hand grenade into their midst which glanced off the chest of G/Sgt. Kellogg. Quick to act, he forced the grenade into the mud in which he was standing, threw himself over the lethal weapon and absorbed the full effects of its detonation with his body, thereby preventing serious injury or possible death to several of his fellow marines. Although suffering multiple injuries to his chest and his right shoulder and arm, G/Sgt. Kellogg res-olutely continued to direct the efforts of his men until all were able to maneuver to the relative safety of the company perimeter. By his heroic and decisive action in risking his life to save the lives of his comrades, G/Sgt. Kellogg reflected the highest credit upon himself and upheld the finest traditions of the Marine Corps and the U.S. Naval Service.

3273 ◆ KERREY, JOSEPH ROBERT

Rank: Lieutenant (j.g.)
Service: U.S. Naval Reserve
Birthday: 27 August 1943
Place of Birth: Lincoln, Lancaster County, Nebraska
Entered Service at: Omaha, Douglas County, Nebraska

Unit: Sea, Air, and Land Team 1 (SEAL)
Served as: SEAL Team Leader
Battle or Place of Action: near Nha Trang Bay, Republic of Vietnam
Date of Action: 14 March 1969
Date of Presentation: 14 May 1970
Place of Presentation: The White House, presented by Pres. Richard M. Nixon
Citation: For conspicuous gallantry and intrepidity at the risk of his life above and beyond the call of duty while serving as a SEAL team leader during action against enemy aggressor (Viet Cong) forces. Acting in response to reliable intelligence, Lt. (j.g.) Kerrey led his SEAL team on a mission to capture important members of the enemy's area political cadre known to be located on an island in the bay of Nha Trang. In order to surprise the enemy, he and his team scaled a 350-foot sheer cliff to place themselves above the ledge on which the enemy was located. Splitting his team in two elements and coordinating both, Lt. (j.g.) Kerrey led his men in the treacherous downward descent to the enemy's camp. Just as they neared the end of their descent, intense enemy fire was directed at them, and Lt. (j.g.) Kerrey received massive injuries from a grenade which exploded at his feet and threw him backward on the jagged rocks. Although bleeding profusely and suffering great pain, he displayed outstanding courage and presence of mind in immediately directing his element's fire into the heart of the enemy camp. Utilizing his radioman, Lt. (j.g.) Kerrey called in a second element's fire support which caught the confused Viet Cong in a devastating crossfire. After successfully suppressing the enemy's fire, and although immobilized by his multiple wounds, he continued to maintain calm, superlative control as he ordered his team to secure and defend an extraction site. Lt. (j.g.) Kerrey resolutely directed his men, despite his near-unconscious state, until he was eventually evacuated by helicopter. The havoc brought to the enemy by this very successful mission cannot be over-estimated. The enemy soldiers who were captured provided critical intelligence to the allied effort. Lt. (j.g.) Kerrey's courageous and inspiring leadership, valiant fighting spirit, and tenacious devotion to duty in the face of almost overwhelming opposition sustain and enhance the finest traditions of the U.S. Naval Service.

3274 ◆ KINSMAN, THOMAS JAMES

Rank: Specialist Fourth Class (rank at time of action: Private First Class)
Service: U.S. Army
Birthday: 4 March 1945
Place of Birth: Renton, King County, Washington
Entered Service at: Seattle, King County, Washington
Unit: Company B, 3d Battalion, 60th Infantry, 9th Infantry Division
Served as: Rifleman
Battle or Place of Action: near Vinh Long, Republic of Vietnam
Date of Action: 6 February 1968
G.O. Number, Date: 40, 13 June 1969
Date of Presentation: 17 May 1969

Place of Presentation: The White House (Lawn), presented by Pres. Richard M. Nixon
Citation: For conspicuous gallantry and intrepidity in action at the risk of his life above and beyond the call of duty Sp4c. Kinsman (then Pfc.) distinguished himself in action in the afternoon while serving as a rifleman with Company B, on a reconnaissance-in-force mission. As his company was proceeding up a narrow canal in armored troop carriers, it came under sudden and intense rocket, automatic-weapons and small-arms fire from a well-entrenched Viet Cong force. The company immediately beached and began assaulting the enemy bunker complex. Hampered by exceedingly dense undergrowth which limited visibility to 10 meters, a group of eight men became cut off from the main body of the company. As they were moving through heavy enemy fire to effect a link-up, an enemy soldier in a concealed position hurled a grenade into their midst. Sp4c. Kinsman immediately alerted his comrades of the danger, then unhesitatingly threw himself on the grenade and blocked the explosion with his body. As a result of his courageous action, he received severe head and chest wounds. Through his indomitable courage, complete disregard for his personal safety and profound concern for his fellow soldiers, Sp4c. Kinsman averted loss of life and injury to the other seven men in his element. Sp4c. Kinsman's extraordinary heroism at the risk of his life, above and beyond the call of duty, are in keeping with the highest traditions of the military service and reflect great credit upon himself, his unit, and the U.S. Army.

3275 ◆ LAMBERS, PAUL RONALD

Rank: Staff Sergeant
Service: U.S. Army
Birthday: 25 June 1942
Place of Birth: Holland, Ottawa County, Michigan
Date of Death: 1 December 1970
Place of Death: Holland, Michigan
Cemetery: Drowned in Lake Michigan, body not recovered.
Entered Service at: Holland, Ottawa County, Michigan
Unit: 3d Platoon, Company A, 2d Battalion, 27th Infantry, 25th Infantry Division
Battle or Place of Action: Tay Ninh Province, Republic of Vietnam
Date of Action: 20 August 1968
G.O. Number, Date: 79, 4 December 1969
Date of Presentation: 24 November 1969
Place of Presentation: The White House, presented by Pres. Richard M. Nixon
Citation: For conspicuous gallantry and intrepidity in action at the risk of his life above and beyond the call of duty. S/Sgt. (then Sgt.) Lambers distinguished himself in action while serving with the 3d Platoon, Company A. The unit had established a night defensive position astride a suspected enemy infiltration route, when it was attacked by an estimated Viet Cong battalion. During the initial enemy onslaught, the platoon leader fell seriously wounded and S/Sgt. Lambers assumed command of the platoon. Disregarding the intense enemy fire, S/Sgt. Lambers left his covered position, secured the platoon radio, and moved to the command post to direct

3277 ♦ *LANGHORN, GARFIELD McCONNELL

the defense. When his radio became inoperative due to enemy action, S/Sgt. Lambers crossed the fire-swept position to secure the 90-mm recoilless-rifle crew's radio in order to re-establish communications. Upon discovering that the 90-mm recoilless rifle was not functioning, S/Sgt. Lambers assisted in the repair of the weapon and directed cannister fire at point-blank range against the attacking enemy who had breached the defensive wire of the position. When the weapon was knocked out by enemy fire, he singlehandedly repulsed a penetration of the position by detonating claymore mines and throwing grenades into the midst of the attackers, killing four more of the Viet Cong with well-aimed hand grenades. S/Sgt. Lambers maintained command of the platoon elements by moving from position to position under the hail of enemy fire, providing assistance where the assault was the heaviest and by his outstanding example inspiring his men to the utmost efforts of courage. He displayed great skill and valor throughout the five-hour battle by personally directing artillery and helicopter fire, placing them at times within five meters of the defensive position. He repeatedly exposed himself to hostile fire at great risk to his own life in order to redistribute ammunition and to care for seriously wounded comrades and to move them to sheltered positions. S/Sgt. Lambers' superb leadership, professional skill, and magnificent courage saved the lives of his comrades, resulted in the virtual annihilation of a vastly superior enemy force, and were largely instrumental in thwarting an enemy offensive against Tay Ninh City. His gallantry at the risk of his life is in keeping with the highest traditions of the military service and reflects great credit upon himself, his unit, and the U.S. Army.

3276 ♦ LANG, GEORGE CHARLES

Rank: Specialist Fourth Class
Service: U.S. Army
Birthday: 20 April 1947
Place of Birth: Flushing, Queens County, New York
Entered Service at: Brooklyn, Kings County, New York
Unit: 3d Squad, 3d Platoon, Company A, 4th Battalion, 47th Infantry, 9th Infantry Division
Served as: Squad Leader
Battle or Place of Action: near Ben Tre City, Kien Hoa Province, Republic of Vietnam
Date of Action: 22 February 1969
G.O. Number, Date: 18, 24 March 1971
Date of Presentation: 2 March 1971
Place of Presentation: The White House (East Ballroom), presented by Pres. Richard M. Nixon
Citation: For conspicuous gallantry and intrepidity in action at the risk of his life above and beyond the call of duty. Sp4c. Lang, Company A, was serving as a squad leader when his unit, on a reconnaissance-in-force mission, encountered intense fire from a well-fortified enemy bunker complex. Sp4c. Lang observed an emplacement from which heavy fire was coming. Unhesitatingly, he assaulted the position and destroyed it with hand grenades and rifle fire. Observing another emplacement approximately 15 meters to his front, Sp4c. Lang jumped across a canal, moved through heavy

enemy fire to within a few feet of the position, and eliminated it, again using hand grenades and rifle fire. Nearby, he discovered a large cache of enemy ammunition. As he maneuvered his squad forward to secure the cache, they came under fire from yet a third bunker. Sp4c. Lang immediately reacted, assaulted this position, and destroyed it with the remainder of his grenades. After returning to the area of the arms cache, his squad again came under heavy enemy rocket and automatic-weapons fire from three sides and suffered six casualties. Sp4c. Lang was one of those seriously wounded. Although immobilized and in great pain, he continued to direct his men until his evacuation was ordered over his protests. The sustained extraordinary courage and selflessness exhibited by this soldier over an extended period of time were an inspiration to his comrades and are in keeping with the highest traditions of the U.S. Army.

3277 ♦ *LANGHORN, GARFIELD McCONNELL

Rank: Private First Class
Service: U.S. Army
Birthday: 10 September 1948
Place of Birth: Cumberland, Cumberland County, Virginia
Date of Death: 15 January 1969
Place of Death: Republic of Vietnam
Cemetery: Riverhead Cemetery (MH)—Riverhead, New York
Entered Service at: Brooklyn, Kings County, New York
Unit: Troop C, 7th Squadron (Airmobile), 17th Cavalry, 1st Aviation Brigade
Served as: Radio Operator
Battle or Place of Action: near Plei Djereng, Pleiku Province, Republic of Vietnam
Date of Action: 15 January 1969
G.O. Number, Date: 19, 23 April 1970
Date of Presentation: 7 April 1970
Place of Presentation: The White House, presented by Pres. Richard M. Nixon to his family
Citation: For conspicuous gallantry and intrepidity in action at the risk of his life above and beyond the call of duty. Pfc. Langhorn distinguished himself while serving as a radio operator with Troop C, near Plei Djereng in Pleiku Province. Pfc. Langhorn's platoon was inserted into a landing zone to rescue two pilots of a Cobra helicopter shot down by enemy fire on a heavily timbered slope. He provided radio coordination with the command-and-control aircraft overhead while the troops hacked their way through dense undergrowth to the wreckage, where both aviators were found dead. As the men were taking the bodies to a pickup site, they suddenly came under intense fire from North Vietnamese soldiers in camouflaged bunkers to the front and right flank, and within minutes they were surrounded. Pfc. Langhorn immediately radioed for help from the orbiting gunships, which began to place minigun and rocket fire on the aggressors. He then lay between the platoon leader and another man, operating the radio and providing covering fire for the wounded who had been moved to the center of the small perimeter. Darkness

VIETNAM WAR   707 soon fell, making it impossible for the gunships to give accurate support, and the aggressors began to probe the perimeter. An enemy hand grenade landed in front of Pfc. Langhorn and a few feet from personnel who had become casualties. Choosing to protect these wounded, he unhesitatingly threw himself on the grenade, scooped it beneath his body, and absorbed the blast. By sacrificing himself, he saved the lives of his comrades. Pfc. Langhorn's extraordinary heroism at the cost of his life was in keeping with the highest traditions of the military service and reflect great credit on himself, his unit, and the U.S. Army.

3278 ◆ *LAPOINTE JR., JOSEPH GUY

Rank: Specialist Fourth Class
Service: U.S. Army
Birthday: 2 July 1948
Place of Birth: Dayton, Montgomery County, Ohio
Date of Death: 2 June 1969
Place of Death: Republic of Vietnam
Cemetery: Riverside Cemetery—West Milton, Ohio
Entered Service at: Cincinnati, Hamilton County, Ohio
Unit: Headquarters & Headquarters Troop, 2d Squadron, 17th Cavalry, 101st Airborne Division
Served as: Medical Aidman
Battle or Place of Action: Quang Tin Province, Republic of Vietnam
Date of Action: 2 June 1969
G.O. Number, Date: 7, 25 January 1972
Date of Presentation: 16 December 1971
Place of Presentation: Old Executive Office Building, presented by Vice Pres. Spiro T. Agnew to his family
Citation: For conspicuous gallantry and intrepidity in action at the risk of his life above and beyond the call of duty. Sp4c. LaPointe, Headquarters and Headquarters Troop, 2d Squadron, distinguished himself while serving as a medical aidman during a combat helicopter assault mission. Sp4c. LaPointe's patrol was advancing from the landing zone through an adjoining valley when it suddenly encountered heavy automatic-weapons fire from a large enemy force entrenched in well-fortified bunker positions. In the initial hail of fire, two soldiers in the formation vanguard were seriously wounded. Hearing a call for aid from one of the wounded, Sp4c. LaPointe ran forward through heavy fire to assist his fallen comrades. To reach the wounded men, he was forced to crawl directly in view of an enemy bunker. As members of his unit attempted to provide covering fire, he administered first aid to one man, shielding the other with his body. He was hit by a burst of fire from the bunker while attending the wounded soldier. In spite of his painful wounds, Sp4c. LaPointe continued his lifesaving duties until he was again wounded and knocked to the ground. Making strenuous efforts, he moved back again into a shielding position to continue administering first aid. An exploding enemy grenade mortally wounded all three men. Sp4c. LaPointe's courageous actions at the cost of his life were an inspiration to his comrades. His gallantry and selflessness are in the highest traditions of the military service and reflect great credit on him, his unit, and the U.S. Army.

3279 ◆ LASSEN, CLYDE EVERETT

Rank: Lieutenant (highest rank: Commander)
Service: U.S. Navy
Birthday: 14 March 1942
Place of Birth: Fort Myers, Lee County, Florida
Date of Death: 1 April 1994
Place of Death: Pensacola, Florida
Cemetery: Barrancas National Cemetery (MH)(38-113)—Pensacola, Florida
Entered Service at: Jacksonville, Duval County, Florida
Unit: U.S.S. *Preble* (DLG-15), Detachment 104, Helicopter Support Squadron 7
Served as: Search & Rescue Helicopter Pilot
Battle or Place of Action: Republic of Vietnam
Date of Action: 19 June 1968
Date of Presentation: 16 January 1969
Place of Presentation: The White House, presented by Pres. Lyndon B. Johnson
Citation: For conspicuous gallantry and intrepidity at the risk of his life above and beyond the call of duty as pilot and aircraft commander of a search-and-rescue helicopter, attached to Helicopter Support Squadron 7, during operations against enemy forces in North Vietnam. Launched shortly after midnight to attempt the rescue of two downed aviators, Lt. (then Lt. (j.g.) Lassen skillfully piloted his aircraft over unknown and hostile terrain to a steep, tree-covered hill on which the survivors had been located. Although enemy fire was being directed at the helicopter, he initially landed in a clear area near the base of the hill, but, due to the dense undergrowth, the survivors could not reach the helicopter. With the aid of flare illumination, Lt. Lassen successfully accomplished a hover between two trees at the survivors' position. Illumination was abruptly lost as the last of the flares were expended, and the helicopter collided with a tree, commencing a sharp descent. Expertly righting his aircraft and maneuvering clear, Lt. Lassen remained in the area, determined to make another rescue attempt, and encouraged the downed aviators while awaiting resumption of flare illumination. After another unsuccessful, illuminated rescue attempt, and with his fuel dangerously low and his aircraft significantly damaged, he launched again and commenced another approach in the face of the continuing enemy opposition. When flare illumination was again lost, Lt. Lassen, fully aware of the dangers in clearly revealing his position to the enemy, turned on his landing lights and completed the landing. On this attempt, the survivors were able to make their way to the helicopter. En route to the coast he encountered and successfully evaded additional hostile antiaircraft fire and, with fuel for only five minutes of flight remaining, landed safely aboard U.S.S. *Jouett* (DLG-29).

3280 ◆ *LAUFFER, BILLY LANE

Rank: Private First Class
Service: U.S. Army
Birthday: 20 October 1945
Place of Birth: Murray, Calloway County, Kentucky
Date of Death: 21 September 1966

Place of Death: Republic of Vietnam
Cemetery: Murray Memorial Gardens—Murray, Kentucky
Entered Service at: Phoenix, Maricopa County, Arizona
Unit: Company C, 2d Battalion, 5th Cavalry, 1st Air Cavalry Division
Served as: Rifleman
Battle or Place of Action: near Bon Son, Binh Dinh Province, Republic of Vietnam
Date of Action: 21 September 1966
G.O. Number, Date: 49, 14 September 1968
Date of Presentation: 15 August 1968
Place of Presentation: The Pentagon, presented by Sec. of the Army Stanley R. Resor to his family
Citation: For conspicuous gallantry and intrepidity in action at the risk of his life above and beyond the call of duty. Pfc. Lauffer's squad, a part of Company C, was suddenly struck at close range by an intense machine-gun crossfire from two concealed bunkers astride the squad's route. Pfc. Lauffer, the second man in the column, saw the leadman fall and noted that the remainder of the squad was unable to move. Two comrades, previously wounded and being carried on litters, were lying helpless in the beaten zone of the enemy fire. Reacting instinctively, Pfc. Lauffer quickly engaged both bunkers with fire from his rifle, but when the other squad members attempted to maneuver under his cover fire, the enemy fusillade increased in volume and thwarted every attempt to move. Seeing this and his wounded comrades helpless in the open, Pfc. Lauffer rose to his feet and charged the enemy machine-gun positions, firing his weapon and drawing the enemy's attention. Keeping the enemy confused and off balance, his one-man assault provided the crucial moments for the wounded point man to crawl to a covered position, the squad to move the exposed litter patients to safety, and his comrades to gain more advantageous positions. Pfc. Lauffer was fatally wounded during his selfless act of courage and devotion to his fellow soldiers. His gallantry at the cost of his life served as an inspiration to his comrades and saved the lives of an untold number of his companions. His actions are in keeping with the highest traditions of military service and reflect great credit upon himself, his unit, and the U.S. Army.

3281   ◆   *LAW, ROBERT DAVID

Rank: Specialist Fourth Class
Service: U.S. Army
Birthday: 15 September 1944
Place of Birth: Fort Worth, Tarrant County, Texas
Date of Death: 22 February 1969
Place of Death: Republic of Vietnam
Cemetery: Mount Olivet Cemetery—Fort Worth, Texas
Entered Service at: Dallas, Collin County, Texas
Unit: Company I (Ranger), 75th Infantry, 1st Infantry Division
Battle or Place of Action: Tinh Phuoc Thanh Province, Republic of Vietnam
Date of Action: 22 February 1969
G.O. Number, Date: 45, 28 August 1970
Date of Presentation: 6 August 1970

Place of Presentation: The White House, presented by Pres. Richard M. Nixon to his family
Citation: For conspicuous gallantry and intrepidity in action at the risk of his life above and beyond the call of duty. Sp4c. Law distinguished himself while serving with Company I. While on a long-range reconnaissance patrol in Tinh Phuoc Thanh Province, Sp4c. Law and five comrades made contact with a small enemy patrol. As the opposing elements exchanged intense fire, he maneuvered to a perilously exposed position flanking his comrades and began placing suppressive fire on the hostile troops. Although his team was hindered by a low supply of ammunition and suffered from an unidentified irritating gas in the air, Sp4c. Law's spirited defense and challenging counterassault rallied his fellow soldiers against the well-equipped hostile troops. When an enemy grenade landed in his team's position, Sp4c. Law, instead of diving into the safety of a stream behind him, threw himself on the grenade to save the lives of his comrades. Sp4c. Law's extraordinary courage and profound concern for his fellow soldiers were in keeping with the highest traditions of the military service and reflect great credit on himself, his unit, and the U.S. Army.

3282   ◆   LEE, HOWARD VINCENT

Rank: Major (rank at time of action: Captain) (highest rank: Colonel)
Service: U.S. Marine Corps
Birthday: 1 August 1933
Place of Birth: New York, New York
Entered Service at: Dumfries, Prince William County, Virginia
Unit: Company E, 2d Battalion, 4th Marines, 3d Marine Division (Rein) FMF
Served as: Company Commander
Battle or Place of Action: near Cam Lo, Republic of Vietnam
Date of Action: 8-9 August 1966
Date of Presentation: 25 October 1967
Place of Presentation: The White House, presented by Pres. Lyndon B. Johnson
Citation: For conspicuous gallantry and intrepidity at the risk of his life above and beyond the call of duty. A platoon of Maj. (then Capt.) Lee's company, while on an operation deep in enemy territory, was attacked and surrounded by a large Vietnamese force. Realizing that the unit had suffered numerous casualties, depriving it of effective leadership, and fully aware that the platoon was even then under heavy attack by the enemy, Maj. Lee took seven men and proceeded by helicopter to reinforce the beleaguered platoon. Maj. Lee disembarked from the helicopter with two of his men and, braving withering enemy fire, led them into the perimeter, where he fearlessly moved from position to position, directing and encouraging the overtaxed troops. The enemy then launched a massive attack with the full might of their forces. Although painfully wounded by fragments from an enemy grenade in several areas of his body, including his eye, Maj. Lee continued undauntedly throughout the night to direct the valiant defense, coordinate supporting fire, and apprise higher headquarters of the plight of the platoon. The next morning he

collapsed from his wounds and was forced to relinquish command. However the small band of marines had held their position and repeatedly fought off many vicious enemy attacks for a grueling six hours until their evacuation was effected the following morning. Maj. Lee's actions saved his men from capture, minimized the loss of lives, and dealt the enemy a severe defeat. His indomitable fighting spirit, superb leadership, and great personal valor in the face of tremendous odds, reflect great credit upon himself and are in keeping with the highest traditions of the Marine Corps and the U.S. Naval Service.

3283 ◆ *LEE, MILTON ARTHUR

Rank: Private First Class
Service: U.S. Army
Birthday: 28 February 1949
Place of Birth: Shreveport, Caddo County, Louisiana
Date of Death: 26 April 1968
Place of Death: Republic of Vietnam
Cemetery: Fort Sam Houston National Cemetery (X-2475) (MH)—San Antonio, Texas
Entered Service at: San Antonio, Bexar County, Texas
Unit: 3d Platoon, Company B, 2d Battalion, 502d Infantry, 1st Brigade, 101st Airborne Division (Airmobile)
Served as: Radio Operator
Battle or Place of Action: near Phu Bai, Thua Thien Province, Republic of Vietnam
Date of Action: 26 April 1968
G.O. Number, Date: 13, 23 April 1970
Date of Presentation: 7 April 1970
Place of Presentation: The White House, presented by Pres. Richard M. Nixon to his family
Citation: For conspicuous gallantry and intrepidity in action at the risk of his life above and beyond the call of duty. Pfc. Lee distinguished himself near the city of Phu Bai in the province of Thua Thien. Pfc. Lee was serving as the radio telephone operator with the 3d Platoon, Company B. As lead element for the company, the 3d Platoon received intense surprise hostile fire from a force of North Vietnamese Army regulars in well-concealed bunkers. With 50 percent casualties, the platoon maneuvered to a position of cover to treat their wounded and reorganize, while Pfc. Lee moved through the heavy enemy fire giving lifesaving first aid to his wounded comrades. During the subsequent assault on the enemy defensive positions, Pfc. Lee continuously kept close radio contact with the company commander, relaying precise and understandable orders to his platoon leader. While advancing with the front rank toward the objective, Pfc. Lee observed four North Vietnamese soldiers with automatic weapons and a rocket launcher lying in wait for the lead element of the platoon. As the element moved forward, unaware of the concealed danger, Pfc. Lee immediately and with utter disregard for his own personal safety, passed his radio to another soldier and charged through the murderous fire. Without hesitation he continued his assault, overrunning the enemy position, killing all occupants, and capturing four automatic weapons and a rocket launcher. Pfc. Lee continued his one-man assault on the second position through a heavy barrage of enemy automatic-weapons fire. Grievously wounded, he continued to press the attack, crawling forward into a firing position and delivering accurate covering fire to enable his platoon to maneuver and destroy the position. Not until the position was overrun did Pfc. Lee falter in his steady volume of fire and succumb to his wounds. Pfc. Lee's heroic actions saved the lives of the lead element and were instrumental in the destruction of the key position of the enemy defense. Pfc. Lee's gallantry at the risk of life above and beyond the call of duty are in keeping with the highest traditions of the military service and reflect great credit on himself, the 502d Infantry, and the U.S. Army.

3284 ◆ *LEISY, ROBERT RONALD

Rank: Second Lieutenant
Service: U.S. Army
Birthday: 1 March 1945
Place of Birth: Stockton, San Joaquin County, California
Date of Death: 2 December 1969
Place of Death: Republic of Vietnam
Cemetery: Evergreen-Washelli Memorial Park—Seattle, Washington
Entered Service at: Seattle, King County, Washington
Unit: Company B, 1st Battalion, 8th Cavalry, 1st Cavalry Division
Served as: Platoon Leader
Battle or Place of Action: Phuoc Long Province, Republic of Vietnam
Date of Action: 2 December 1969
G.O. Number, Date: 4, 25 January 1972
Date of Presentation: 16 December 1971
Place of Presentation: Old Executive Office Building, presented by Vice Pres. Sprio T. Agnew to his family
Citation: For conspicuous gallantry and intrepidity in action at the risk of his life above and beyond the call of duty. 2d Lt. Leisy, Infantry, Company B, distinguished himself while serving as platoon leader during a reconnaissance mission. One of his patrols became heavily engaged by the fire from a numerically superior enemy force located in a well-entrenched bunker complex. As 2d Lt. Leisy deployed the remainder of his platoon to rescue the beleaguered patrol, the platoon also came under intense enemy fire from the front and both flanks. In complete disregard for his safety, 2d Lt. Leisy moved from position to position deploying his men to effectively engage the enemy. Accompanied by his radio operator he moved to the front and spotted an enemy sniper in a tree in the act of firing a rocket-propelled grenade at them. Realizing there was neither time to escape the grenade nor shout a warning, 2d Lt. Leisy unhesitatingly, and with full knowledge of the consequences, shielded the radio operator with his body and absorbed the full impact of the explosion. This valorous act saved the life of the radio operator and protected other men of his platoon who were nearby from serious injury. Despite his mortal wounds, 2d Lt. Leisy calmly and confidently continued to direct the platoon's fire. When medical aid arrived 2d Lt. Leisy valiantly refused attention until the other seriously wounded were treated. His display of extraordinary courage and exemplary devotion to duty provided the inspiration and leadership that enabled his platoon to successfully withdraw without further casualties. 2d Lt.

Leisy's gallantry at the cost of his life are in keeping with the highest traditions of the military service and reflect great credit on him, his unit, and the U.S. Army

3285 ◆ LEMON, PETER CHARLES

Rank: Sergeant (rank at time of action: Specialist Fourth Class)
Service: U.S. Army
Birthday: 5 June 1950
Place of Birth: Toronto, Canada
Entered Service at: Tawas City, Iosco County, Michigan
Unit: Company E (Recon), 2d Battalion, 8th Cavalry, 1st Cavalry Division
Served as: Assistant Machine Gunner
Battle or Place of Action: Fire Support Base Illingworth, Tay Ninh Province, Republic of Vietnam
Date of Action: 1 April 1970
G.O. Number, Date: 36, 16 July 1971
Date of Presentation: 15 June 1971
Place of Presentation: The White House, presented by Pres. Richard M. Nixon
Citation: For conspicuous gallantry and intrepidity in action at the risk of his life above and beyond the call of duty. Sgt. Lemon (then Sp4c.), Company E, distinguished himself while serving as an assistant machine gunner during the defense of Fire Support Base Illingworth. When the base came under heavy enemy attack, Sgt. Lemon engaged a numerically superior enemy with machine-gun and rifle fire from his defensive position until both weapons malfunctioned. He then used hand grenades to fend off the intensified enemy attack launched in his direction. After eliminating all but one of the enemy soldiers in the immediate vicinity, he pursued and disposed of the remaining soldier in hand-to-hand combat. Despite fragment wounds from an exploding grenade, Sgt. Lemon regained his position, carried a more seriously wounded comrade to an aid station, and, as he returned, was wounded a second time by enemy fire. Disregarding his personal injuries, he moved to his position through a hail of small-arms and grenade fire. Sgt. Lemon immediately realized that the defensive sector was in danger of being overrun by the enemy and unhesitatingly assaulted the enemy soldiers by throwing hand grenades and engaging in hand-to-hand combat. He was wounded yet a third time, but his determined efforts successfully drove the enemy from the position. Securing an operable machine gun, Sgt. Lemon stood atop an embankment fully exposed to enemy fire, and placed effective fire upon the enemy until he collapsed from his multiple wounds and exhaustion. After regaining consciousness at the aid station, he refused medical evacuation until his more seriously wounded comrades had been evacuated. Sgt. Lemon's gallantry and extraordinary heroism are in keeping with the highest traditions of the military service and reflect great credit on him, his unit, and the U.S. Army.

3286 ◆ *LEONARD, MATTHEW

Rank: Sergeant First Class
Service: U.S. Army
Birthday: 26 November 1929

Place of Birth: Eutaw, Greene County, Alabama
Date of Death: 28 February 1967
Place of Death: Republic of Vietnam
Cemetery: Shadow Lawn Cemetery (MH)—Birmingham, Alabama
Entered Service at: Birmingham, Jefferson County, Alabama
Unit: Company B, 1st Battalion, 16th Infantry, 1st Infantry Division
Served as: Platoon Sergeant
Battle or Place of Action: near Suoi Da, Republic of Vietnam
Date of Action: 28 February 1967
G.O. Number, Date: 2, 9 January 1969
Date of Presentation: 19 December 1968
Place of Presentation: The Pentagon, presented by Sec. of the Army Stanley R. Resor to his family
Citation: For conspicuous gallantry and intrepidity in action at the risk of his life above and beyond the call of duty. His platoon was suddenly attacked by a large enemy force employing small-arms, automatic weapons, and hand grenades. Although the platoon leader and several other key leaders were among the first wounded, P/Sgt. Leonard quickly rallied his men to throw back the initial enemy assaults. During the short pause that followed, he organized a defensive perimeter, redistributed ammunition, and inspired his comrades through his forceful leadership and words of encouragement. Noticing a wounded companion outside the perimeter, he dragged the man to safety but was struck by a sniper's bullet which shattered his left hand. Refusing medical attention and continuously exposing himself to the increasing fire as the enemy again assaulted the perimeter, P/Sgt. Leonard moved from position to position to direct the fire of his men against the well-camouflaged foe. Under the cover of the main attack, the enemy moved a machine gun into a location where it could sweep the entire perimeter. This threat was magnified when the platoon machine gun in this area malfunctioned. P/Sgt. Leonard quickly crawled to the gun position and was helping to clear the malfunction when the gunner and other men in the vicinity were wounded by fire from the enemy machine gun. P/Sgt. Leonard rose to his feet, charged the enemy gun, and destroyed the hostile crew despite being hit several times by enemy fire. He moved to a tree, propped himself against it, and continued to engage the enemy until he succumbed to his many wounds. His fighting spirit, heroic leadership, and valiant acts inspired the remaining members of his platoon to hold back the enemy until assistance arrived. P/Sgt. Leonard's profound courage and devotion to his men are in keeping with the highest traditions of the military service, and his gallant actions reflect great credit upon himself and the U.S. Army.

3287 ◆ LEVITOW, JOHN LEE

Rank: Sergeant (rank at time of action: Airman First Class)
Service: U.S. Air Force
Birthday: 1 November 1945
Place of Birth: Hartford, Hartford County, Connecticut
Entered Service at: New Haven, New Haven County, Connecticut
Unit: 3d Special Operations Squadron

Served as: Loadmaster
Battle or Place of Action: over Long Binh Army Post, Republic of Vietnam
Date of Action: 24 February 1969
G.O. Number, Date: GB-476, 23 June 1970
Date of Presentation: 14 May 1970
Place of Presentation: The White House, presented by Pres. Richard M. Nixon
Citation: For conspicuous gallantry and intrepidity in action at the risk of his life above and beyond the call of duty. Sgt. Levitow (then A1c.), U.S. Air Force, distinguished himself by exceptional heroism while assigned as a loadmaster aboard an AC-47 aircraft flying a night mission in support of Long Binh Army Post. Sgt. Levitow's aircraft was struck by a hostile mortar round. The resulting explosion ripped a hole two feet in diameter through the wing and fragments made over 3,500 holes in the fuselage. All occupants of the cargo compartment were wounded and helplessly slammed against the floor and fuselage. The explosion tore an activated flare from the grasp of a crewmember who had been launching flares to provide illumination for Army ground troops engaged in combat. Sgt. Levitow, though stunned by the concussion of the blast and suffering from over 40 fragment wounds in the back and legs, staggered to his feet and turned to assist the man nearest to him who had been knocked down and was bleeding heavily. As he was moving his wounded comrade forward and away from the opened cargo compartment door, he saw the smoking flare ahead of him in the aisle. Realizing the danger involved and completely disregarding his own wounds, Sgt. Levitow started toward the burning flare. The aircraft was partially out of control and the flare was rolling wildly from side to side. Sgt. Levitow struggled forward despite the loss of blood from his many wounds and the partial loss of feeling in his right leg. Unable to grasp the rolling flare with his hands, he threw himself bodily upon the burning flare. Hugging the deadly device to his body, he dragged himself back to the rear of the aircraft and hurled the flare through the open cargo door. At that instant the flare separated and ignited in the air, but clear of the aircraft. Sgt. Levitow, by his selfless and heroic actions, saved the aircraft and its entire crew from certain death and destruction. Sgt. Levitow's gallantry, his profound concern for his fellow men, at the risk of his life above and beyond the call of duty, are in keeping with the highest traditions of the U.S. Air Force and reflect great credit upon himself and the Armed Forces of his country.

3288 ◆ LITEKY, CHARLES JAMES (ANGELO)

Rank: Captain
Service: U.S. Army
Birthday: 14 February 1931
Place of Birth: Washington, D.C.
Entered Service at: Fort Hamilton, Kings County, New York
Unit: Headquarters & Headquarters Company, 199th Infantry Brigade (Separate) (Light)
Served as: Chaplain
Battle or Place of Action: near Phuoc-Lac, Bien Hoa Province, Republic of Vietnam

Date of Action: 6 December 1967
G.O. Number, Date: 77, 10 December 1968
Date of Presentation: 19 November 1968
Place of Presentation: The White House, presented by Pres. Lyndon B. Johnson
Citation: Chaplain Liteky distinguished himself by exceptional heroism while serving with Company A, 4th Battalion, 12th Infantry, 199th Light Infantry Brigade. He was participating in a search-and-destroy operation when Company A came under intense fire from a battalion-size enemy force. Momentarily stunned from the immediate encounter that ensued, the men hugged the ground for cover. Observing two wounded men, Chaplain Liteky moved to within 15 meters of an enemy machine-gun position to reach them, placing himself between the enemy and the wounded men. When there was a brief respite in the fighting, he managed to drag them to the relative safety of the landing zone. Inspired by his courageous actions, the company rallied and began placing a heavy volume of fire upon the enemy positions. In a magnificent display of courage and leadership, Chaplain Liteky began moving upright through the enemy fire, administering last rites to the dying and evacuating the wounded. Noticing another trapped and seriously wounded man, Chaplain Liteky crawled to his aid. Realizing that the wounded man was too heavy to carry, he rolled on his back, placed the man on his chest and through sheer determination and fortitude crawled back to the landing zone using his elbows and heels to push himself along. Pausing for breath momentarily, he returned to the action and came upon a man entangled in the dense, thorny underbrush. Once more intense enemy fire was directed at him, but Chaplain Liteky stood his ground and calmly broke the vines and carried the man to the landing zone for evacuation. On several occasions when the landing zone was under small-arms and rocket fire, Chaplain Liteky stood up in the face of hostile fire and personally directed the medivac helicopters into and out of the area. With the wounded safely evacuated, Chaplain Liteky returned to the perimeter, constantly encouraging and inspiring the men. Upon the unit's relief on the morning of 7 December 1967, it was discovered that despite painful wounds in the neck and foot, Chaplain Liteky had personally carried over 20 men to the landing zone for evacuation during the savage fighting. Through his indomitable inspiration and heroic actions, Chaplain Liteky saved the lives of a number of his comrades and enabled the company to repulse the enemy. Chaplain Liteky's actions reflect great credit upon himself and were in keeping with the highest traditions of the U.S. Army.

3289 ◆ LITTRELL, GARY LEE

Rank: Sergeant First Class (highest rank: Command Sergeant Major)
Service: U.S. Army
Birthday: 26 October 1944
Place of Birth: Henderson, Henderson County, Kentucky
Entered Service at: Los Angeles, Los Angeles County, California
Unit: U.S. Military Assistance Command, II Corps Advisory Group, Advisory Team 21

Served as: Light Weapons Infantry Advisor
Battle or Place of Action: Kontum Province, Republic of Vietnam
Date of Action: 4-8 April 1970
G.O. Number, Date: 41, 5 November 1973
Date of Presentation: 15 October 1973
Place of Presentation: The White House, presented by Pres. Richard M. Nixon
Citation: For conspicuous gallantry and intrepidity in action at the risk of his life above and beyond the call of duty. Sfc. Littrell, U.S. Military Assistance Command, Vietnam, Advisory Team 21, distinguished himself while serving as a Light Weapons Infantry adviser with the 23d Battalion, 2d Ranger Group, Republic of Vietnam Army, near Dak Seang. After establishing a defensive perimeter on a hill on 4 April, the battalion was subjected to an intense enemy mortar attack which killed the Vietnamese commander, one adviser, and seriously wounded all the advisers except Sfc. Littrell. During the ensuing four days, Sfc. Littrell exhibited near superhuman endurance as he singlehandedly bolstered the besieged battalion. Repeatedly abandoning positions of relative safety, he directed artillery and air support by day and marked the unit's location by night, despite the heavy, concentrated enemy fire. His dauntless will instilled in the men of the 23d Battalion a deep desire to resist. Assault after assault was repulsed as the battalion responded to the extraordinary leadership and personal example exhibited by Sfc. Littrell as he continuously moved to those points most seriously threatened by the enemy, redistributed ammunition, strengthened faltering defenses, cared for the wounded, and shouted encouragement to the Vietnamese in their own language. When the beleaguered battalion was finally ordered to withdraw, numerous ambushes were encountered. Sfc. Littrell repeatedly prevented widespread disorder by directing air strikes to within 50 meters of their position. Through his indomitable courage and complete disregard for his safety, he averted excessive loss of life and injury to the members of the battalion. The sustained extraordinary courage and selflessness displayed by Sfc. Littrell over an extended period of time were in keeping with the highest traditions of the military service and reflect great credit on him and the U.S. Army.

3290   ◆   LIVINGSTON, JAMES EVERTTE

Rank: Captain (current rank: Major General)
Service: U.S. Marine Corps
Birthday: 12 January 1940
Place of Birth: Towns, Telfair County, Georgia
Entered Service at: McRae, Telfair County, Georgia
Unit: Company E, 2d Battalion, 4th Marines, 9th Marine Amphibious Brigade
Served as: Commanding Officer
Battle or Place of Action: Dai Do, Quang Tri Province, Republic of Vietnam
Date of Action: 2 May 1968
Date of Presentation: 14 May 1970
Place of Presentation: The White House, presented by Pres. Richard M. Nixon
Citation: For conspicuous gallantry and intrepidity at the

risk of his life above and beyond the call of duty while serving as Commanding Officer, Company E, in action against enemy forces. Company E launched a determined assault on the heavily fortified village of Dai Do, which had been seized by the enemy on the preceding evening isolating a marine company from the remainder of the battalion. Skillfully employing screening agents, Capt. Livingston maneuvered his men to assault positions across 500 meters of dangerous open rice paddy while under intense enemy fire. Ignoring hostile rounds impacting near him, he fearlessly led his men in a savage assault against enemy emplacements within the village. While adjusting supporting arms fire, Capt. Livingston moved to the points of heaviest resistance, shouting words of encouragement to his marines, directing their fire, and spurring the dwindling momentum of the attack on repeated occasions. Although twice painfully wounded by grenade fragments, he refused medical treatment and courageously led his men in the destruction of over 100 mutually supporting bunkers, driving the remaining enemy from their positions and relieving the pressure on the stranded marine company. As the two companies consolidated positions and evacuated casualties, a third company passed through the friendly lines launching an assault on the adjacent village of Dinh To, only to be halted by a furious counterattack of an enemy battalion. Swiftly assessing the situation and disregarding the heavy volume of enemy fire, Capt. Livingston boldly maneuvered the remaining effective men of his company forward, joined forces with the heavily engaged marines, and halted the enemy's counterattack. Wounded a third time and unable to walk, he steadfastly remained in the dangerously exposed area, deploying his men to more tenable positions and supervising the evacuation of casualties. Only when assured of the safety of his men did he allow himself to be evacuated. Capt. Livingston's gallant actions uphold the highest traditions of the Marine Corps and the U.S. Naval Service.

3291   ◆   *LONG, DONALD RUSSELL

Rank: Sergeant
Service: U.S. Army
Birthday: 27 August 1939
Place of Birth: Blackfork, Ohio
Date of Death: 30 June 1966
Place of Death: Republic of Vietnam
Cemetery: Union Baptist Church Cemetery—Blackfork, Ohio
Entered Service at: Ashland, Boyd County, Kentucky
Unit: Troop C, 1st Squadron, 4th Cavalry, 1st Infantry Division
Served as: Assistant Platoon Leader
Battle or Place of Action: Republic of Vietnam
Date of Action: 30 June 1966
G.O. Number, Date: 13, 4 April 1968
Date of Presentation: 8 February 1968
Place of Presentation: The Pentagon, presented by Sec. of the Army Stanley R. Resor to his family
Citation: For conspicuous gallantry and intrepidity in action at the risk of his life above and beyond the call of duty. Troops B and C, while conducting a reconnaissance mission

along a road were suddenly attacked by a Viet Cong regiment, supported by mortars, recoilless rifles, and machine guns from concealed positions astride the road. Sgt. Long abandoned the relative safety of his armored personnel carrier and braved a withering hail of enemy fire to carry wounded men to evacuation helicopters. As the platoon fought its way forward to resupply advanced elements, Sgt. Long repeatedly exposed himself to enemy fire at point-blank range to provide the needed supplies. While assaulting the Viet Cong position, Sgt. Long inspired his comrades by fearlessly standing unprotected to repel the enemy with rifle fire and grenades as they attempted to mount his carrier. When the enemy threatened to overrun a disabled carrier nearby, Sgt. Long again disregarded his own safety to help the severely wounded crew to safety. As he was handing arms to the less seriously wounded and reorganizing them to press the attack, an enemy grenade was hurled onto the carrier deck. Immediately recognizing the imminent danger, he instinctively shouted a warning to the crew and pushed to safety one man who had not heard his warning over the roar of battle. Realizing that these actions would not fully protect the exposed crewmen from the deadly explosion, he threw himself over the grenade to absorb the blast and thereby saved the lives of eight of his comrades at the expense of his life. Throughout the battle, Sgt. Long's extraordinary heroism, courage and supreme devotion to his men were in the finest tradition of the military service, and reflect great credit upon himself and the U.S. Army.

3292 ◆ *LOZADA, CARLOS JAMES

Rank: Private First Class
Service: U.S. Army
Birthday: 6 September 1946
Place of Birth: Caguas, Caguas County, Puerto Rico
Date of Death: 20 November 1967
Place of Death: Republic of Vietnam
Cemetery: Long Island National Cemetery (T-2295) (MH)—Farmingdale, New York
Entered Service at: New York, New York
Unit: 1st Platoon, Company A, 2d Battalion, 503d Infantry, 173d Airborne Brigade
Served as: Machine Gunner
Battle or Place of Action: Hill 875, near Dak To, Kontum Province, Republic of Vietnam
Date of Action: 20 November 1967
G.O. Number, Date: 77, 4 December 1969
Date of Presentation: 18 November 1969
Place of Presentation: The White House, presented by Vice Pres. Spiro T. Agnew to his family
Citation: For conspicuous gallantry and intrepidity in action at the risk of his life above and beyond the call of duty. Pfc. Lozada, U.S. Army, distinguished himself at the risk of his life above and beyond the call of duty in the battle of Dak To. While serving as a machine gunner with 1st Platoon, Company A, Pfc. Lozada was part of a four-man early warning outpost, located 35 meters from his company's lines. At 1400 hours a North Vietnamese Army company rapidly approached the outpost along a well-defended trail. Pfc.

Lozada alerted his comrades and commenced firing at the enemy who were within 10 meters of the outpost. His heavy and accurate machine-gun fire killed at least 20 North Vietnamese soldiers and completely disrupted their initial attack. Pfc. Lozada remained in an exposed position and continued to pour deadly fire upon the enemy despite the urgent pleas of his comrades to withdraw. The enemy continued their assault, attempting to envelop the outpost. At the same time enemy forces launched a heavy attack on the forward west flank of Company A with the intent to cut them off from their battalion. Company A was given the order to withdraw. Pfc. Lozada apparently realized that if he abandoned his position there would be nothing to hold back the surging North Vietnamese soldiers and that the entire company withdrawal would be jeopardized. He called for his comrades to move back and that he would stay and provide cover for them. He made this decision realizing that the enemy was converging on three sides of his position and only meters away, and a delay in withdrawal meant almost certain death. Pfc. Lozada continued to deliver a heavy, accurate volume of suppressive fire against the enemy until he was mortally wounded and had to be carried during the withdrawal. His heroic deed served as an example and an inspiration to his comrades throughout the ensuing four-day battle. Pfc. Lozada's actions are in the highest traditions of the U.S. Army and reflect great credit upon himself, his unit, and the U.S. Army.

3293 ◆ *LUCAS, ANDRE CAVARO

Rank: Lieutenant Colonel
Service: U.S. Army
Birthday: 2 October 1930
Place of Birth: Washington, D.C.
Date of Death: 23 July 1970
Place of Death: Republic of Vietnam
Cemetery: U.S Military Academy Cemetery (7-C-160)—West Point, New York
Entered Service at: West Point, Orange County, New York
Unit: 2d Battalion, 506th Infantry, 101st Airborne Division
Served as: Battalion Commander
Battle or Place of Action: Fire Support Base Ripcord, Republic of Vietnam
Date of Action: 1-23 July 1970
G.O. Number, Date: 33, 6 September 1974
Date of Presentation: 17 July 1974
Place of Presentation: Blair House (Courtyard), presented by Vice Pres. Gerald R. Ford to his family
Citation: Lt. Col. Lucas distinguished himself by extraordinary heroism while serving as the commanding officer of the 2d Battalion. Although the fire base was constantly subjected to heavy attacks by a numerically superior enemy force throughout this period, Lt. Col. Lucas, forsaking his own safety, performed numerous acts of extraordinary valor in directing the defense of the allied position. On one occasion, he flew in a helicopter at treetop level above an entrenched enemy directing the fire of one of his companies for over three hours. Even though his helicopter was heavily damaged by enemy fire, he remained in an exposed position until the

company expended its supply of grenades. He then transferred to another helicopter, dropped critically needed
grenades to the troops, and resumed his perilous mission of
directing fire on the enemy. These courageous actions by Lt.
Col. Lucas prevented the company from being encircled and
destroyed by a larger enemy force. On another occasion, Lt.
Col. Lucas attempted to rescue a crewman trapped in a burning helicopter. As the flames in the aircraft spread, and enemy
fire became intense, Lt. Col. Lucas ordered all members of
the rescue party to safety. Then, at great personal risk, he
continued the rescue effort amid concentrated enemy mortar
fire, intense heat, and exploding ammunition until the aircraft
was completely engulfed in flames. Lt. Col. Lucas was mortally wounded while directing the successful withdrawal of his
battalion from the fire base. His actions throughout this
extended period inspired his men to heroic efforts, and were
instrumental in saving the lives of many of his fellow soldiers
while inflicting heavy casualties on the enemy. Lt. Col. Lucas'
conspicuous gallantry and intrepidity in action, at the cost of
his own life, were in keeping with the highest traditions of
the military service and reflect great credit on him, his unit,
and the U.S. Army.

3294 ◆ LYNCH, ALLAN JAMES

Rank: Sergeant (rank at time of action: Specialist Fourth
Class)
Service: U.S. Army
Birthday: 28 October 1945
Place of Birth: Chicago, Cook County, Illinois
Entered Service at: Chicago, Cook County, Illinois
Unit: Company D, 1st Battalion (Airmobile), 12th Cavalry,
1st Cavalry Division
Served as: Radio Operator
Battle or Place of Action: near My An (2), Binh Dinh
Province, Republic of Vietnam
Date of Action: 15 December 1967
G.O. Number, Date: 33, 5 June 1970
Date of Presentation: 14 May 1970
Place of Presentation: The White House, presented by Pres.
Richard M. Nixon
Citation: For conspicuous gallantry and intrepidity in action
at the risk of his life above and beyond the call of duty. Sgt.
Lynch (then Sp4c.) distinguished himself while serving as a
radio telephone operator with Company D. While serving in
the forward element on an operation near the village of My
An, his unit became heavily engaged with a numerically superior enemy force. Quickly and accurately assessing the situation, Sgt. Lynch provided his commander with information
which subsequently proved essential to the unit's successful
actions. Observing three wounded comrades lying exposed to
enemy fire, Sgt. Lynch dashed across 50 meters of open
ground through a withering hail of enemy fire to administer
aid. Reconnoitering a nearby trench for a covered position to
protect the wounded from intense hostile fire, he killed two
enemy soldiers at point-blank range. With the trench cleared,
he unhesitatingly returned to the fire-swept area three times
to carry the wounded men to safety. When his company was
forced to withdraw by the superior firepower of the enemy,

Sgt. Lynch remained to aid his comrades at the risk of his life
rather than abandon them. Alone, he defended his isolated
position for two hours against the advancing enemy. Using
only his rifle and a grenade, he stopped them just short of his
trench, killing five. Again, disregarding his safety in the face
of withering hostile fire, he crossed 70 meters of exposed terrain five times to carry his wounded comrades to a more
secure area. Once he had assured their comfort and safety,
Sgt. Lynch located the counterattacking friendly company to
assist in directing the attack and evacuating the three casualties. His gallantry at the risk of his life is in the highest traditions of the military service. Sgt. Lynch has reflected great
credit on himself, the 12th Cavalry, and the U.S. Army.

3295 ◆ MARM JR., WALTER JOSEPH

Rank: First Lieutenant (rank at time of action: Second
Lieutenant) (current rank: Colonel)
Service: U.S. Army
Birthday: 20 November 1941
Place of Birth: Washington, Washington County,
Pennsylvania
Entered Service at: Pittsburgh, Allegheny County,
Pennsylvania
Unit: Company A, 1st Battalion, 7th Cavalry, 1st Cavalry
Division (Airmobile)
Served as: Platoon Leader
Battle or Place of Action: vicinity of Ia Drang Valley,
Republic of Vietnam
Date of Action: 14 November 1965
G.O. Number, Date: 7, 15 February 1967
Date of Presentation: 19 December 1966
Place of Presentation: The Pentagon, presented by Sec. of
the Army Stanley R. Resor
Citation: For conspicuous gallantry and intrepidity at the
risk of his life above and beyond the call of duty. As a platoon
leader in the 1st Cavalry Division (Airmobile), 1st Lt. Marm
demonstrated indomitable courage during a combat operation. His company was moving through the valley to relieve a
friendly unit surrounded by an enemy force of estimated regimental size. 1st Lt. Marm led his platoon through withering
fire until they were finally forced to take cover. Realizing that
his platoon could not hold very long, and seeing four enemy
soldiers moving into his position, he moved quickly under
heavy fire and annihilated all four. Then, seeing that his platoon was receiving intense fire from a concealed machine gun,
he deliberately exposed himself to draw its fire. Thus locating
its position, he attempted to destroy it with an antitank
weapon. Although he inflicted casualties, the weapon did not
silence the enemy fire. Quickly, disregarding the intense fire
directed on him and his platoon, he charged 30 meters across
open ground and hurled grenades into the enemy position,
killing some of the eight insurgents manning it. Although
severely wounded, when his grenades were expended, armed
with only a rifle, he continued the momentum of his assault
on the position and killed the remainder of the enemy. 1st Lt.
Marm's selfless actions reduced the fire on his platoon, broke
the enemy assault, and rallied his unit to continue toward the
accomplishment of this mission. 1st Lt. Marm's gallantry on

the battlefield and his extraordinary intrepidity at the risk of his life are in the highest traditions of the U.S. Army and reflect great credit upon himself and the Armed Forces of his country.

3296 ◆ *MARTINI, GARY WAYNE

Rank: Private First Class
Service: U.S. Marine Corps
Birthday: 21 September 1948
Place of Birth: Lexington, Lexington County, Virginia
Date of Death: 21 April 1967
Place of Death: Republic of Vietnam
Cemetery: Rosewood Cemetery—Lewisburg, West Virginia
Entered Service at: Portland, Multnomah County, Oregon
Unit: Company F, 2d Battalion, 1st Marines, 1st Marine Division (Rein) FMF
Served as: Rifleman
Battle or Place of Action: Binh Son, Republic of Vietnam
Date of Action: 21 April 1967
Date of Presentation: 22 October 1968
Place of Presentation: Marine Barracks, Washington D.C., presented by Secretary of the Navy Paul R. Ignatius to his family
Citation: For conspicuous gallantry and intrepidity at the risk of his life above and beyond the call of duty. On 21 April 1967, during Operation Union, elements of Company F, conducting offensive operations at Binh Son, encountered a firmly entrenched enemy force and immediately deployed to engage them. The marines in Pfc. Martini's platoon assaulted across an open rice paddy to within 20 meters of the enemy trench line where they were suddenly struck by hand grenades, intense small-arms, automatic-weapons, and mortar fire. The enemy onslaught killed 14 and wounded 18 marines, pinning the remainder of the platoon down behind a low paddy dike. In the face of imminent danger, Pfc. Martini immediately crawled over the dike to a forward open area within 15 meters of the enemy position where, continuously exposed to the hostile fire, he hurled hand grenades, killing several of the enemy. Crawling back through the intense fire, he rejoined his platoon which had moved to the relative safety of a trench line. From this position he observed several of his wounded comrades lying helpless in the fire-swept paddy. Although he knew that one man had been killed attempting to assist the wounded, Pfc. Martini raced through the open area and dragged a comrade back to a friendly position. In spite of a serious wound received during this first daring rescue, he again braved the unrelenting fury of the enemy fire to aid another companion lying wounded only 20 meters in front of the enemy trench line. As he reached the fallen marine, he received a mortal wound, but disregarding his own condition, he began to drag the marine toward his platoon's position. Observing men from his unit attempting to leave the security of their position to aid him, concerned only for their safety, he called to them to remain under cover, and through a final supreme effort, moved his injured comrade to where he could be pulled to safety, before he fell, succumbing to his wounds. Stouthearted and indomitable, Pfc. Martini unhesitatingly yielded his life to save two of his comrades and

insure the safety of the remainder of his platoon. His outstanding courage, valiant fighting spirit and selfless devotion to duty reflected the highest credit upon himself, the Marine Corps, and the U.S. Naval Service. He gallantly gave his life for his country.

3297 ◆ *MAXAM, LARRY LEONARD

Rank: Corporal
Service: U.S. Marine Corps
Birthday: 9 January 1948
Place of Birth: Glendale, Los Angeles County, California
Date of Death: 2 February 1968
Place of Death: Republic of Vietnam
Cemetery: National Memorial Cemetery of the Pacific (J-388) (MH)—Honolulu, Hawaii
Entered Service at: Los Angeles, Los Angeles County, California
Unit: Company D, 1st Battalion, 4th Marines, 3d Marine Division (Rein) FMF
Served as: Fire Team Leader
Battle or Place of Action: Cam Lo District, Quang Tri Province, Republic of Vietnam
Date of Action: 2 February 1968
Date of Presentation: 20 April 1970
Place of Presentation: The White House, presented by Pres. Richard M. Nixon to his family
Citation: For conspicuous gallantry and intrepidity at the risk of his life above and beyond the call of duty while serving as a fire team leader with Company D. The Cam Lo District Headquarters came under extremely heavy rocket, artillery, mortar, and recoilless-rifle fire from a numerically superior enemy force destroying a portion of the defense perimeter. Cpl. Maxam observing the enemy massing for an assault into the compound across the remaining defensive wire, instructed his assistant fire team leader to take charge of the fire team, and unhesitatingly proceeded to the weakened section of the perimeter. Completely exposed to the concentrated enemy fire, he sustained multiple fragmentation wounds from exploding grenades as he ran to an abandoned machine-gun position. Reaching the emplacement, he grasped the machine gun and commenced to deliver effective fire on the advancing enemy. As the enemy directed maximum firepower against the determined marine, Cpl. Maxam's position received a direct hit from a rocket-propelled grenade, knocking him backwards and inflicting severe fragmentation wounds to his face and right eye. Although momentarily stunned and in intense pain, Cpl. Maxam courageously assumed his firing position and subsequently was struck again by small-arms fire. With resolute determination, he gallantly continued to deliver intense machine-gun fire, causing the enemy to retreat through the defensive wire to positions of cover. In a desperate attempt to silence his weapon, the North Vietnamese threw hand grenades and directed recoilless-rifle fire against him inflicting two additional wounds. Too weak to reload his machine gun, Cpl. Maxam fell to a prone position and valiantly continued to deliver effective fire with his rifle. After 1 1/2 hours, during which he was hit repeatedly by fragments from exploding grenades and concentrated small-arms

fire, he succumbed to his wounds, having successfully defended nearly half of the perimeter singlehandedly. Cpl. Maxam's aggressive fighting spirit, inspiring valor and selfless devotion to duty, reflected great credit upon himself and the Marine Corps and upheld the highest traditions of the U.S. Naval Service. He gallantly gave his life for his country.

3298 ◆ McCLEERY, FINNIS DAWSON

Rank: Sergeant First Class
Service: U.S. Army
Birthday: 25 December 1927
Place of Birth: Stephenville, Erath County, Texas
Entered Service at: San Angelo, Tom Green County, Texas
Unit: 1st Platoon, Company A, 1st Battalion, 6th U.S. Infantry, Americal Division
Served as: Platoon Leader
Battle or Place of Action: Quang Tin Province, Republic of Vietnam
Date of Action: 14 May 1968
G.O. Number, Date: 19, 24 March 1971
Date of Presentation: 2 March 1971
Place of Presentation: The White House (East Ballroom), presented by Pres. Richard M. Nixon
Citation: For conspicuous gallantry and intrepidity in action at the risk of his life above and beyond the call of duty. P/Sgt. McCleery, U.S. Army, distinguished himself while serving as platoon leader of the 1st Platoon of Company A. A combined force was assigned the mission of assaulting a reinforced company of North Vietnamese Army regulars, well-entrenched on Hill 352, 17 miles west of Tam Ky. As P/Sgt. McCleery led his men up the hill and across an open area to close with the enemy, his platoon and other friendly elements were pinned down by tremendously heavy fire coming from the fortified enemy positions. Realizing the severe damage that the enemy could inflict on the combined force in the event that their attack was completely halted, P/Sgt. McCleery rose from his sheltered position and began a one-man assault on the bunker complex. With extraordinary courage, he moved across 60 meters of open ground as bullets struck all around him and rockets and grenades literally exploded at his feet. As he came within 30 meters of the key enemy bunker, P/Sgt. McCleery began firing furiously from the hip and throwing hand grenades. At this point in his assault, he was painfully wounded by shrapnel, but, with complete disregard for his wound, he continued his advance on the key bunker and killed all of its occupants. Having successfully and singlehandedly reached the enemy perimeter, he climbed to the top of the bunker he had just captured and, in full view of the enemy, shouted encouragement to his men to follow his assault. As the friendly forces moved forward, P/Sgt. McCleery began a lateral assault on the enemy bunker line. He continued to expose himself to the intense enemy fire as he moved from bunker to bunker, destroying each in turn. He was wounded a second time by shrapnel as he destroyed and routed the enemy from the hill. P/Sgt. McCleery is personally credited with eliminating several key enemy positions and inspiring the assault that resulted in gaining control of Hill 352. His extraordinary heroism at the risk of his life above and beyond the call of duty was in keeping with the highest standards of the military service, and reflects great credit on him, the Americal Division, and the U.S. Army.

3299 ◆ *McDONALD, PHILL GENE

Rank: Private First Class
Service: U.S. Army
Birthday: 13 September 1941
Place of Birth: Avondale, McDowell County, West Virginia
Date of Death: 7 June 1968
Place of Death: Republic of Vietnam
Cemetery: Guilford Memorial Park (MH)—Greensboro, North Carolina
Entered Service at: Beckley, Raleigh County, West Virginia
Unit: 1st Platoon, Company A, 1st Battalion, 14th Infantry, 4th Infantry Division
Served as: Team Leader
Battle or Place of Action: near Kontum City, Republic of Vietnam
Date of Action: 7 June 1968
G.O. Number, Date: 20, 23 April 1970
Date of Presentation: 7 April 1970
Place of Presentation: The White House, presented by Pres. Richard M. Nixon to his family
Citation: For conspicuous gallantry and intrepidity in action at the risk of his life above and beyond the call of duty. Pfc. McDonald distinguished himself while serving as a team leader with the 1st Platoon of Company A. While on a combat mission his platoon came under heavy barrage of automatic-weapons fire from a well-concealed company-size enemy force. Volunteering to escort two wounded comrades to an evacuation point, Pfc. McDonald crawled through intense fire to destroy with a grenade an enemy automatic weapon threatening the safety of the evacuation. Returning to his platoon, he again volunteered to provide covering fire for the maneuver of the platoon from its exposed position. Realizing the threat he posed, enemy gunners concentrated their fire on Pfc. McDonald's position, seriously wounding him. Despite his painful wounds, Pfc. McDonald recovered the weapon of a wounded machine gunner to provide accurate covering fire for the gunner's evacuation. When other soldiers were pinned down by a heavy volume of fire from a hostile machine gun to his front, Pfc. McDonald crawled toward the enemy position to destroy it with grenades. He was mortally wounded in this intrepid action. Pfc. McDonald's gallantry at the risk of his life, which resulted in the saving of the lives of his comrades, is in keeping with the highest traditions of the military service and reflect great credit upon himself, his unit, and the U.S. Army.

3300 ◆ McGINTY III, JOHN JAMES

Rank: Second Lieutenant (rank at time of action: Staff Sergeant) (highest rank: Captain)
Service: U.S. Marine Corps
Birthday: 21 January 1940
Place of Birth: Boston, Suffolk County, Massachusetts

Entered Service at: Laurel Bay, South Carolina
Unit: Company K, 3d Battalion, 4th Marines, 3d Marine Division (Rein) FMF
Served as: Acting Platoon Leader
Battle or Place of Action: Quang Tri Province, Republic of Vietnam
Date of Action: 18 July 1966
Date of Presentation: 12 March 1968
Place of Presentation: The White House, presented by Pres. Lyndon B. Johnson
Citation: For conspicuous gallantry and intrepidity at the risk of his life above and beyond the call of duty. 2d Lt. McGinty's platoon, which was providing rear security to protect the withdrawal of the battalion from a position which had been under attack for three days, came under heavy small-arms, automatic-weapons, and mortar fire from an estimated enemy regiment. With each successive human wave which assaulted his 32-man platoon during the four-hour battle, 2d Lt. McGinty rallied his men to beat off the enemy. In one bitter assault, two of the squads became separated from the remainder of the platoon. With complete disregard for his safety, 2d Lt. McGinty charged through intense automatic-weapons and mortar fire to their position. Finding 20 men wounded and the medical corpsman killed, he quickly reloaded ammunition magazines and weapons for the wounded men and directed their fire upon the enemy. Although he was painfully wounded as he moved to care for the disabled men, he continued to shout encouragement to his troops and to direct their fire so effectively that the attacking hordes were beaten off. When the enemy tried to out-flank his position, he killed five of them at point-blank range with his pistol. When they again seemed on the verge of overrunning the small force, he skillfully adjusted artillery and air strikes within 50 yards of his position. This destructive firepower routed the enemy, who left an estimated 500 bodies on the battlefield. 2d Lt. McGinty's personal heroism, indomitable leadership, selfless devotion to duty, and bold fighting spirit inspired his men to resist the repeated attacks by a fanatical enemy, reflected great credit upon himself, and upheld the highest traditions of the Marine Corps and the U.S. Naval Service.

3301 ◆ McGONAGLE, WILLIAM LOREN

Rank: Captain (rank at time of action: Commander)
Service: U.S. Navy
Birthday: 19 November 1925
Place of Birth: Wichita, Sedgwick County, Kansas
Entered Service at: Thermal, Riverside County, California
Unit: U.S.S. *Liberty* (AGTR-5)
Served as: Captain
Battle or Place of Action: International waters, Eastern Mediterranean
Date of Action: 8-9 June 1967
Date of Presentation: 6 June 1968
Place of Presentation: Admiral Leutze Park, Washington Navy Yard, presented by Sec. of the Navy Paul R. Ignatius
Citation: For conspicuous gallantry and intrepidity at the risk of his life above and beyond the call of duty. Sailing in international waters, the *Liberty* was attacked without warning by a jet fighter aircraft and motor torpedo boats which inflicted many casualties among the crew and caused extreme damage to the ship. Although severely wounded during the first air attack, Capt. McGonagle remained at his battle station on the badly damaged bridge and, with full knowledge of the seriousness of his wounds, subordinated his own welfare to the safety and survival of his command. Steadfastly refusing any treatment which would take him away from his post, he calmly continued to exercise firm command of his ship. Despite continuous exposure to fire, he maneuvered his ship, directed its defense, supervised the control of flooding and fire, and saw to the care of the casualties. Capt. McGonagle's extraordinary valor under these conditions inspired the surviving members of the *Liberty*'s crew, many of them seriously wounded, to heroic efforts to overcome the battle damage and keep the ship afloat. Subsequent to the attack, although in great pain and weak from loss of blood, Capt. McGonagle remained at his battle station and continued to command his ship for more than 17 hours. It was only after rendezvous with a U.S. destroyer that he relinquished personal control of the *Liberty* and permitted himself to be removed from the bridge. Even then, he refused much needed medical attention until convinced that the seriously wounded among his crew had been treated. Capt. McGonagle's superb professionalism, courageous fighting spirit, and valiant leadership saved his ship and many lives. His actions sustain and enhance the finest traditions of the U.S. Naval Service.

3302 ◆ *McKIBBEN, RAY

Rank: Sergeant
Service: U.S. Army
Birthday: 27 October 1946
Place of Birth: Felton, Haralson County, Georgia
Date of Death: 8 December 1968
Place of Death: Republic of Vietnam
Cemetery: Center Baptist Cemetery (MH)—Felton, Georgia
Entered Service at: Atlanta, Fulton County, Georgia
Unit: Troop B, 7th Squadron (Airmobile), 17th Cavalry, 1st Aviation Brigade
Served as: Team Leader
Battle or Place of Action: near Song Mao, Republic of Vietnam
Date of Action: 8 December 1968
G.O. Number, Date: 21, 23 April 1970
Date of Presentation: 7 April 1970
Place of Presentation: The White House, presented by Pres. Richard M. Nixon to his family
Citation: For conspicuous gallantry and intrepidity in action at the risk of his life above and beyond the call of duty. Sgt. McKibben distinguished himself in action while serving as team leader of the point element of a reconnaissance patrol of Troop B, operating in enemy territory. Sgt. McKibben was leading his point element in a movement to contact along a well-traveled trail when the lead element came under heavy automatic-weapons fire from a fortified bunker position, forcing the patrol to take cover. Sgt. McKibben, appraising the situation and without regard for his own safety, charged

through bamboo and heavy brush to the fortified position, killed the enemy gunner, secured the weapon and directed his patrol element forward. As the patrol moved out, Sgt. McKibben observed enemy movement to the flank of the patrol. Fire support from helicopter gunships was requested and the area was effectively neutralized. The patrol again continued its mission and as the lead element rounded the bend of a river it came under heavy automatic-weapons fire from camouflaged bunkers. As Sgt. McKibben was deploying his men to covered positions, he observed one of his men fall wounded. Although bullets were hitting all around the wounded man, Sgt. McKibben, with complete disregard for his safety, sprang to his comrade's side and under heavy enemy fire pulled him to safety behind the cover of a rock emplacement where he administered hasty first aid. Sgt. McKibben, seeing that his comrades were pinned down and were unable to deliver effective fire against the enemy bunkers, again undertook a singlehanded assault of the enemy defenses. He charged through the brush and hail of automatic-weapons fire closing on the first bunker, killing the enemy with accurate rifle fire and securing the enemy's weapon. He continued his assault against the next bunker, firing his rifle as he charged. As he approached the second bunker his rifle ran out of ammunition, however; he used the captured enemy weapon until it too was empty, at that time he silenced the bunker with well-placed hand grenades. He reloaded his weapon and covered the advance of his men as they moved forward. Observing the fire of another bunker impeding the patrol's advance, Sgt. McKibben again singlehandedly assaulted the new position. As he neared the bunker he was mortally wounded but was able to fire a final burst from his weapon killing the enemy and enabling the patrol to continue the assault. Sgt. McKibben's indomitable courage, extraordinary heroism, profound concern for the welfare of his fellow soldiers, and disregard for his personal safety saved the lives of his comrades and enabled the patrol to accomplish its mission. Sgt. McKibben's gallantry in action at the cost of his life above and beyond the call of duty are in the highest traditions of the military service and reflect great credit upon himself, his unit, and the U.S. Army.

3303 ◆ *McMAHON, THOMAS JOSEPH

Rank: Specialist Fourth Class
Service: U.S. Army
Birthday: 24 June 1948
Place of Birth: Washington, D.C.
Date of Death: 19 March 1969
Place of Death: Republic of Vietnam
Cemetery: Mount Hope Cemetery (MH)—Lewiston, Maine
Entered Service at: Portland, Cumberland County, Maine
Unit: Company A, 2d Battalion, 1st Infantry, 196th Infantry Brigade, Americal Division
Served as: Medical Aidman
Battle or Place of Action: Quang Tin Province, Republic of Vietnam
Date of Action: 19 March 1969
G.O. Number, Date: 46, 28 August 1970

Date of Presentation: 6 August 1970
Place of Presentation: The White House, presented by Pres. Richard M. Nixon to his family
Citation: For conspicuous gallantry and intrepidity in action at the risk of his life above and beyond the call of duty. Sp4c. McMahon distinguished himself while serving as medical aidman with Company A. When the lead elements of his company came under heavy fire from well-fortified enemy positions, three soldiers fell seriously wounded. Sp4c. McMahon, with complete disregard for his safety, left his covered position and ran through intense enemy fire to the side of one of the wounded, administered first aid, and then carried him to safety. He returned through the hail of fire to the side of a second wounded man. Although painfully wounded by an exploding mortar round while returning the wounded man to a secure position, Sp4c. McMahon refused medical attention and heroically ran back through the heavy enemy fire toward his remaining wounded comrade. He fell mortally wounded before he could rescue the last man. Sp4c. McMahon's undaunted concern for the welfare of his comrades at the cost of his life are in keeping with the highest traditions of the military service and reflect great credit on himself, his unit, and the U.S. Army.

3304 ◆ McNERNEY, DAVID HERBERT

Rank: First Sergeant
Service: U.S. Army
Birthday: 2 June 1931
Place of Birth: Lowell, Middlesex County, Massachusetts
Entered Service at: Fort Bliss, El Paso County, Texas
Unit: Company A, 1st Battalion, 8th Infantry, 4th Infantry Division
Served as: Company First Sergeant
Battle or Place of Action: Polei Doc, Republic of Vietnam
Date of Action: 22 March 1967
G.O. Number, Date: 62, 22 October 1968
Date of Presentation: 19 September 1968
Place of Presentation: The White House, presented by Pres. Lyndon B. Johnson
Citation: 1st Sgt. McNerney distinguished himself when his unit was attacked by a North Vietnamese battalion near Polei Doc. Running through the hail of enemy fire to the area of heaviest contact, he was assisting in the development of a defensive perimeter when he encountered several enemy at close range. He killed the enemy but was painfully injured when blown from his feet by a grenade. In spite of this injury, he assaulted and destroyed an enemy machine-gun position that had pinned down five of his comrades beyond the defensive line. Upon learning his commander and artillery forward observer had been killed, he assumed command of the company. He adjusted artillery fire to within 20 meters of the position in a daring measure to repulse enemy assaults. When the smoke grenades used to mark the position were gone, he moved into a nearby clearing to designate the location to friendly aircraft. In spite of enemy fire he remained exposed until he was certain the position was spotted and then climbed into a tree and tied the identification panel to its highest branches. Then he moved among his men readjusting

their position, encouraging the defenders and checking the wounded. As the hostile assaults slackened, he began clearing a helicopter landing site to evacuate the wounded. When explosives were needed to remove large trees, he crawled outside the relative safety of his perimeter to collect demolition material from abandoned rucksacks. Moving through a fusillade of fire he returned with the explosives that were vital to the clearing of the landing zone. Disregarding the pain of his injury and refusing medical evacuation, 1st Sgt. McNerney remained with his unit until the next day when the new commander arrived. 1st Sgt. McNerney's outstanding heroism and leadership were inspirational to his comrades. His actions were in keeping with the highest traditions of the U.S. Army and reflect great credit upon himself and the Armed Forces of his country.

3305 ◆ *McWETHY JR., EDGAR LEE

Rank: Specialist Fifth Class
Service: U.S. Army
Birthday: 22 November 1944
Place of Birth: Leadville, Lake County, Colorado
Date of Death: 21 June 1967
Place of Death: Republic of Vietnam
Cemetery: Pence Cemetery—Baxter Springs, Kansas
Entered Service at: Denver, Denver County, Colorado
Unit: Company B, 1st Battalion, 5th Cavalry, 1st Cavalry Division (Airmobile)
Served as: Medical Aidman
Battle or Place of Action: Binh Dinh Province, Republic of Vietnam
Date of Action: 21 June 1967
G.O. Number, Date: 68, 27 October 1969
Date of Presentation: 16 October 1969
Place of Presentation: The White House, presented by Pres. Richard M. Nixon to his family
Citation: For conspicuous gallantry and intrepidity in action at the risk of his life above and beyond the call of duty. Serving as a medical aidman with Company B, Sp5c. McWethy accompanied his platoon to the site of a downed helicopter. Shortly after the platoon established a defensive perimeter around the aircraft, a large enemy force attacked the position from three sides with a heavy volume of automatic-weapons fire and grenades. The platoon leader and his radio operator were wounded almost immediately, and Sp5c. McWethy rushed across the fire-swept area to their assistance. Although he could not help the mortally wounded radio operator, Sp5c. McWethy's timely first aid enabled the platoon leader to retain command during this critical period. Hearing a call for aid, Sp5c. McWethy started across the open toward the injured men, but was wounded in the head and was knocked to the ground. He regained his feet and continued on but was hit again, this time in the leg. Struggling onward despite his wounds, he gained the side of his comrades and treated their injuries. Observing another fallen rifleman lying in an exposed position raked by enemy fire, Sp5c. McWethy moved toward him without hesitation. Although the enemy fire wounded him a third time, Sp5c. McWethy reached his fallen companion. Though weakened and in

extreme pain, Sp5c. McWethy gave the wounded man artificial respiration but suffered a fourth and fatal wound. Through his indomitable courage, complete disregard for his safety, and demonstrated concern for his fellow soldiers, Sp5c. McWethy inspired the members of his platoon and contributed in great measure to their successful defense of the position and the ultimate rout of the enemy force. Sp5c. McWethy's profound sense of duty, bravery, and his willingness to accept extraordinary risks in order to help the men of his unit are characteristic of the highest traditions of the military service and reflect great credit upon himself and the U.S. Army.

3306 ◆ *MICHAEL, DON LESLIE

Rank: Specialist Fourth Class
Service: U.S. Army
Birthday: 31 July 1947
Place of Birth: Florence, Lauderdale County, Alabama
Date of Death: 8 April 1967
Place of Death: Republic of Vietnam
Cemetery: Mount Pleasant Cemetery (MH)—Lexington, Alabama
Entered Service at: Montgomery, Montgonery County, Alabama
Unit: Company C, 4th Battalion, 503d Infantry, 173d Airborne Brigade
Served as: Rifleman
Battle or Place of Action: Republic of Vietnam
Date of Action: 8 April 1967
G.O. Number, Date: 41, 13 June 1969
Date of Presentation: 23 May 1969
Place of Presentation: The White House, presented by Pres. Richard M. Nixon to his family
Citation: For conspicuous gallantry and intrepidity at the risk of his life above and beyond the call of duty. Sp4c. Michael, U.S. Army, distinguished himself while serving with Company C. Sp4c. Michael was part of a platoon which was moving through an area of suspected enemy activity. While the rest of the platoon stopped to provide security, the squad to which Sp4c. Michael was assigned moved forward to investigate signs of recent enemy activity. After moving approximately 125 meters, the squad encountered a single Viet Cong soldier. When he was fired upon by the squad's machine gunner, other Viet Cong opened fire with automatic weapons from a well-concealed bunker to the squad's right front. The volume of enemy fire was so withering as to pin down the entire squad and halt all forward movement. Realizing the gravity of the situation, Sp4c. Michael exposed himself to throw two grenades, but failed to eliminate the enemy position. From his position on the left flank, Sp4c. Michael maneuvered forward with two more grenades until he was within 20 meters of the enemy bunkers, when he again exposed himself to throw two grenades, which failed to detonate. Undaunted, Sp4c. Michael made his way back to the friendly positions to obtain more grenades. With two grenades in hand, he again started his perilous move towards the enemy bunker, which by this time was under intense artillery fire from friendly positions. As he neared the bunker,

an enemy soldier attacked him from a concealed position. Sp4c. Michael killed him with his rifle and, in spite of the enemy fire and the exploding artillery rounds, was successful in destroying the enemy positions. Sp4c. Michael took up pursuit of the remnants of the retreating enemy. When his comrades reached Sp4c. Michael, he had been mortally wounded. His inspiring display of determination and courage saved the lives of many of his comrades and successfully eliminated a destructive enemy force. Sp4c. Michael's actions were in keeping with the highest traditions of the military service and reflect the utmost credit upon himself and the U.S. Army.

3307 ◆ MILLER, FRANKLIN DOUGLAS

Rank: Staff Sergeant (highest rank: Command Sergeant Major)
Service: U.S. Army
Birthday: 27 January 1945
Place of Birth: Elizabeth City, Pasquotank County, North Carolina
Entered Service at: Albuquerque, Bernalillo County, New Mexico
Unit: 5th Special Forces Group, 1st Special Forces
Served as: Team Leader
Battle or Place of Action: Kontum Province, Republic of Vietnam
Date of Action: 5 January 1970
G.O. Number, Date: 35, 16 July 1971
Date of Presentation: 15 June 1971
Place of Presentation: The White House, presented by Pres. Richard M. Nixon
Citation: For conspicuous gallantry and intrepidity in action at the risk of his life above and beyond the call of duty. S/Sgt. Miller, 5th Special Forces Group, distinguished himself while serving as team leader of an American-Vietnamese long-range reconnaissance patrol operating deep within enemy-controlled territory. Leaving the helicopter insertion point, the patrol moved forward on its mission. Suddenly, one of the team members tripped a hostile booby trap which wounded four soldiers. S/Sgt. Miller, knowing that the explosion would alert the enemy, quickly administered first aid to the wounded and directed the team into positions across a small stream bed at the base of a steep hill. Within a few minutes, S/Sgt. Miller saw the lead element of what he estimated to be a platoon-size enemy force moving toward his location. Concerned for the safety of his men, he directed the small team to move up the hill to a more secure position. He remained alone, separated from the patrol, to meet the attack. S/Sgt. Miller singlehandedly repulsed two determined attacks by the numerically superior enemy force and caused them to withdraw in disorder. He rejoined his team, established contact with a forward air controller, and arranged the evacuation of his patrol. However, the only suitable extraction location in the heavy jungle was a bomb crater some 150 meters from the team location. S/Sgt. Miller reconnoitered the route to the crater and led his men through the enemy-controlled jungle to the extraction site. As the evacuation helicopter hovered over the crater to pick up the patrol, the enemy

launched a savage automatic-weapons and rocket-propelled-grenade attack against the beleaguered team, driving off the rescue helicopter. S/Sgt. Miller led the team in a valiant defense which drove back the enemy in its attempt to overrun the small patrol. Although seriously wounded and with every man in his patrol a casualty, S/Sgt. Miller moved forward to again singlehandedly meet the hostile attackers. From his forward exposed position, S/Sgt. Miller gallantly repelled two attacks by the enemy before a friendly relief force reached the patrol location. S/Sgt. Miller's gallantry, intrepidity in action, and selfless devotion to the welfare of his comrades are in keeping with the highest traditions of the military service and reflect great credit on him, his unit, and the U.S. Army.

3308 ◆ *MILLER, GARY LEE

Rank: First Lieutenant
Service: U.S. Army
Birthday: 19 March 1947
Place of Birth: Covington, Covington County, Virginia
Date of Death: 16 February 1969
Place of Death: Republic of Vietnam
Cemetery: Allegheny Memorial Park—Covington, Virginia
Entered Service at: Roanoke, Roanoke County, Virginia
Unit: Company A, 1st Battalion, 28th Infantry, 1st Infantry Division
Served as: Platoon Leader
Battle or Place of Action: Binh Duong Province, Republic of Vietnam
Date of Action: 16 February 1969
G.O. Number, Date: 44, 28 August 1970
Date of Presentation: 6 August 1970
Place of Presentation: The White House, presented by Pres. Richard M. Nixon to his family
Citation: For conspicuous gallantry and intrepidity in action at the risk of his life above and beyond the call of duty. 1st Lt. Miller, Infantry, Company A, was serving as a platoon leader at night when his company ambushed a hostile force infiltrating from Cambodian sanctuaries. After contact with the enemy was broken, 1st Lt. Miller led a reconnaissance patrol from their prepared positions through the early evening darkness and dense tropical growth to search the area for enemy casualties. As the group advanced they were suddenly attacked. 1st Lt. Miller was seriously wounded. However, the group fought back with telling effect on the hostile force. An enemy grenade was thrown into the midst of the friendly patrol group and all took cover except 1st Lt. Miller, who in the dim light located the grenade and threw himself on it, absorbing the force of the explosion with his body. His action saved nearby members of his patrol from almost certain serious injury. The extraordinary courage and selflessness displayed by this officer were an inspiration to his comrades and are in the highest traditions of the U.S. Army.

3309 ◆ MODRZEJEWSKI, ROBERT JOSEPH

Rank: Major (rank at time of action: Captain) (highest rank: Colonel)
Service: U.S. Marine Corps

Birthday: 3 July 1934
Place of Birth: Milwaukee, Milwaukee County, Wisconsin
Entered Service at: Milwaukee, Milwaukee County, Wisconsin
Unit: Company K, 3d Battalion, 4th Marines, 3d Marine Division (Rein) FMF
Served as: Company Commander
Battle or Place of Action: Republic of Vietnam
Date of Action: 15-18 July 1966
Date of Presentation: 12 March 1968
Place of Presentation: The White House, presented by Pres. Lyndon B. Johnson
Citation: For conspicuous gallantry and intrepidity at the risk of his life above and beyond the call of duty. On 15 July, during Operation Hastings, Company K was landed in an enemy-infested jungle area to establish a blocking position at a major enemy trail network. Shortly after landing, the company encountered a reinforced enemy platoon in a well-organized, defensive position. Maj. Modrzejewski led his men in the successful seizure of the enemy redoubt, which contained large quantities of ammunition and supplies. That evening, a numerically superior enemy force counterattacked in an effort to retake the vital supply area, thus setting the pattern of activity for the next 2 1/2 days. In the first series of attacks, the enemy assaulted repeatedly in overwhelming numbers but each time was repulsed by the gallant marines. The second night, the enemy struck in battalion strength, and Maj. Modrzejewski was wounded in this intensive action which was fought at close quarters. Although exposed to enemy fire, and despite his painful wounds, he crawled 200 meters to provide critically needed ammunition to an exposed element of his command and was constantly present wherever the fighting was the heaviest; despite numerous casualties, a dwindling supply of ammunition, and the knowledge that they were surrounded, he skillfully directed artillery fire to within a few meters of his position and courageously inspired the efforts of his company in repelling the aggressive enemy attack. On 18 July, Company K was attacked by a regimental-size enemy force. Although his unit was vastly outnumbered and weakened by the previous fighting, Maj. Modrzejewski reorganized his men and calmly moved among them to encourage and direct their efforts to heroic limits as they fought to overcome the vicious enemy onslaught. Again he called in air and artillery strikes at close-range with devastating effect on the enemy, which together with the bold and determined fighting of the men of Company K, repulsed the fanatical attack of the larger North Vietnamese force. His unparalleled personal heroism and indomitable leadership inspired his men to a significant victory over the enemy force and reflected great credit upon himself, the Marine Corps, and the U.S. Naval Service.

3310 ◆ *MOLNAR, FRANKIE ZOLY

Rank: Staff Sergeant
Service: U.S. Army
Birthday: 14 February 1943
Place of Birth: Logan, Logan County, West Virginia
Date of Death: 20 May 1967

Place of Death: Republic of Vietnam
Cemetery: Highland Memorial Gardens Cemetery—Logan, West Virginia
Entered Service at: Fresno, Fresno County, California
Unit: Company B, 1st Battalion, 8th Infantry, 4th Infantry Division
Served as: Squad Leader
Battle or Place of Action: Kontum Province, Republic of Vietnam
Date of Action: 20 May 1967
G.O. Number, Date: 51, 8 August 1969
Date of Presentation: 10 July 1969
Place of Presentation: The White House, presented by Pres. Richard M. Nixon to his family
Citation: For conspicuous gallantry and intrepidity in action at the risk of his life above and beyond the call of duty. S/Sgt. Molnar distinguished himself while serving as a squad leader with Company B, during combat operations. Shortly after the battalion's defensive perimeter was established, it was hit by intense mortar fire as the prelude to a massive enemy night attack. S/Sgt. Molnar immediately left his sheltered location to insure the readiness of his squad to meet the attack. As he crawled through the position, he discovered a group of enemy soldiers closing in on his squad area. His accurate rifle fire killed five of the enemy and forced the remainder to flee. When the mortar fire stopped, the enemy attacked in a human wave supported by grenades, rockets, automatic-weapons, and small-arms fire. After assisting to repel the first enemy assault, S/Sgt. Molnar found that his squad's ammunition and grenade supply were nearly expended. Again leaving the relative safety of his position, he crawled through intense enemy fire to secure additional ammunition and distribute it to his squad. He rejoined his men to beat back the renewed enemy onslaught, and he moved about his area providing medical aid and assisting in the evacuation of the wounded. With the help of several men, he was preparing to move a severely wounded soldier when an enemy hand grenade was thrown into the group. The first to see the grenade, S/Sgt. Molnar threw himself on it and absorbed the deadly blast to save his comrades. His demonstrated selflessness and inspirational leadership on the battlefield were a major factor in the successful defense of the American position and are in keeping with the finest traditions of the U.S. Army. S/Sgt. Molnar's actions reflect great credit upon himself, his unit, and the U.S. Army.

3311 ◆ *MONROE, JAMES HOWARD

Rank: Private First Class
Service: U.S. Army
Birthday: 17 October 1944
Place of Birth: Aurora, Du Page County, Illinois
Date of Death: 16 February 1967
Place of Death: Republic of Vietnam
Cemetery: Wheaton Cemetery—Wheaton, Illinois
Entered Service at: Chicago, Cook County, Illinois
Unit: Headquarters & Headquarters Company, 1st Battalion, 8th Cavalry, 1st Cavalry Division (Airmobile)
Served as: Medical Aidman

Battle or Place of Action: Bong Son, Hoai Nhon Province, Republic of Vietnam
Date of Action: 16 February 1967
G.O. Number, Date: 68, 5 November 1968
Date of Presentation: 17 October 1968
Place of Presentation: The Pentagon, presented by Sec. of the Army Stanley R. Resor to his family
Citation: For conspicuous gallantry and intrepidity in action at the risk of his life above and beyond the call of duty. His platoon was deployed in a night ambush when the position was suddenly subjected to an intense and accurate grenade attack, and one foxhole was hit immediately. Responding without hesitation to the calls for help from the wounded men, Pfc. Monroe moved forward through heavy small-arms fire to the foxhole but found that all of the men had expired. He turned immediately and crawled back through the deadly hail of fire toward other calls for aid. He moved to the platoon sergeant's position where he found the radio operator bleeding profusely from fragmentation and bullet wounds. Ignoring the continuing enemy attack, Pfc. Monroe began treating the wounded man when he saw a live grenade fall directly in front of the position. He shouted a warning to all those nearby, pushed the wounded radio operator and the platoon sergeant to one side, and lunged forward to smother the grenade's blast with his body. Through his valorous actions, performed in a flash of inspired selflessness, Pfc. Monroe saved the lives of two of his comrades and prevented the probable injury of several others. His gallantry and intrepidity were in the highest traditions of the U.S. Army, and reflect great credit upon himself and the Armed Forces of his country.

3312 ◆ *MORGAN, WILLIAM DAVID

Rank: Corporal
Service: U.S. Marine Corps
Birthday: 17 September 1947
Place of Birth: Pittsburgh, Allegheny County, Pennsylvania
Date of Death: 25 February 1969
Place of Death: Republic of Vietnam
Cemetery: Mount Lebanon Cemetery (MH)—Pittsburgh, Pennsylvania
Entered Service at: Pittsburgh, Allegheny County, Pennsylvania
Unit: Company H, 2d Battalion, 9th Marines, 3d Marine Division (Rein) FMF
Served as: Squad Leader
Battle or Place of Action: southeast of Vandegrift Combat Base, Quang Tri Province, Republic of Vietnam
Date of Action: 25 February 1969
Date of Presentation: 6 August 1970
Place of Presentation: The White House, presented by Pres. Richard M. Nixon to his family
Citation: For conspicuous gallantry and intrepidity at the risk of his life above and beyond the call of duty while serving as a squad leader with Company H, in operations against the enemy. While participating in Operation Dewey Canyon southeast of Vandegrift Combat Base, one of the squads of Cpl. Morgan's platoon was temporarily pinned down and sus-

tained several casualties while attacking a North Vietnamese Army force occupying a heavily fortified bunker complex. Observing that two of the wounded marines had fallen in a position dangerously exposed to the enemy fire and that all attempts to evacuate them were halted by a heavy volume of automatic-weapons fire and rocket-propelled grenades. Cpl. Morgan unhesitatingly maneuvered through the dense jungle undergrowth to a road that passed in front of a hostile emplacement which was the principal source of enemy fire. Fully aware of the possible consequences of his valiant action, but thinking only of the welfare of his injured companions, Cpl. Morgan shouted words of encouragement to them as he initiated an aggressive assault against the hostile bunker. While charging across the open road, he was clearly visible to the hostile soldiers who turned their fire in his direction and mortally wounded him, but his diversionary tactic enabled the remainder of his squad to retrieve their casualties and overrun the North Vietnamese Army position. His heroic and determined actions saved the lives of two fellow marines and were instrumental in the subsequent defeat of the enemy. Cpl. Morgan's indomitable courage, inspiring initiative, and selfless devotion to duty upheld the highest traditions of the Marine Corps and of the U.S. Naval Service. He gallantly gave his life for his country.

3313 ◆ MORRIS, CHARLES BEDFORD

Rank: Staff Sergeant (rank at time of action: Sergeant) (highest rank: Sergeant Major)
Service: U.S. Army
Birthday: 29 December 1931
Place of Birth: Carroll County, Virginia
Entered Service at: Roanoke, Roanoke County, Virginia
Unit: Company A, 2d Battalion (Airborne), 503d Infantry, 173d Airborne Brigade (Separate)
Served as: Platoon Sergeant
Battle or Place of Action: near Xuan Loc, Republic of Vietnam
Date of Action: 29 June 1966
G.O. Number, Date: 51, 14 December 1967
Date of Presentation: 16 November 1967
Place of Presentation: The White House, presented by Pres. Lyndon B. Johnson
Citation: For conspicuous gallantry and intrepidity at the risk of his life above and beyond the call of duty. Seeing indications of the enemy's presence in the area, S/Sgt. Morris deployed his squad and continued forward alone to make a reconnaissance. He unknowingly crawled within 20 meters of an enemy machine gun, whereupon the gunner fired, wounding him in the chest. S/Sgt. Morris instantly returned the fire and killed the gunner. Continuing to crawl within a few feet of the gun, he hurled a grenade and killed the remainder of the enemy crew. Although in pain and bleeding profusely, S/Sgt. Morris continued his reconnaissance. Returning to the platoon area, he reported the results of his reconnaissance to the platoon leader. As he spoke, the platoon came under heavy fire. Refusing medical attention for himself, he deployed his men in better firing positions confronting the entrenched enemy to his front. Then for eight hours the pla-

toon engaged the numerically superior enemy force. Withdrawal was impossible without abandoning many wounded and dead. Finding the platoon medic dead, S/Sgt. Morris administered first aid to himself and was returning to treat the wounded members of his squad with the medic's first-aid kit when he was again wounded. Knocked down and stunned, he regained consciousness and continued to treat the wounded, reposition his men, and inspire and encourage their efforts. Wounded again when an enemy grenade shattered his left hand, nonetheless he personally took up the fight and armed and threw several grenades which killed a number of enemy soldiers. Seeing that an enemy machine gun had maneuvered behind his platoon and was delivering the fire upon his men, S/Sgt. Morris and another man crawled toward the gun to knock it out. His comrade was killed and S/Sgt. Morris sustained another wound, but, firing his rifle with one hand, he silenced the enemy machine gun. Returning to the platoon, he courageously exposed himself to the devastating enemy fire to drag the wounded to a protected area, and with utter disregard for his personal safety and the pain he suffered, he continued to lead and direct the efforts of his men until relief arrived. Upon termination of the battle, important documents were found among the enemy dead revealing a planned ambush of a Republic of Vietnam battalion. Use of this information prevented the ambush and saved many lives. S/Sgt. Morris' gallantry was instrumental in the successful defeat of the enemy, saved many lives, and was in the highest traditions of the U.S. Army.

3314 ◆ *MURRAY, ROBERT CHARLES

Rank: Staff Sergeant
Service: U.S. Army
Birthday: 10 December 1946
Place of Birth: Bronx County, New York
Date of Death: 7 June 1970
Place of Death: Republic of Vietnam
Cemetery: Gate of Heaven Cemetery—Hawthorne, New York
Entered Service at: New York, New York
Unit: Company B, 4th Battalion, 31st Infantry, 196th Infantry Brigade, Americal Division
Served as: Squad Leader
Battle or Place of Action: near the village of Hiep Duc, Republic of Vietnam
Date of Action: 7 June 1970
G.O. Number, Date: 41, 6 September 1974
Date of Presentation: 8 August 1974
Place of Presentation: Blair House, presented by Vice Pres. Gerald R. Ford to his family
Citation: S/Sgt. Murray distinguished himself while serving as a squad leader with Company B. S/Sgt. Murray's squad was searching for an enemy mortar that had been threatening friendly positions when a member of the squad tripped an enemy grenade rigged as a booby trap. Realizing that he had activated the enemy booby trap, the soldier shouted for everybody to take cover. Instantly assessing the danger to the men of his squad, S/Sgt. Murray unhesitatingly and with complete disregard for his own safety threw himself on the grenade

absorbing the full and fatal impact of the explosion. By his gallant action and self sacrifice, he prevented the death or injury of the other members of his squad. S/Sgt. Murray's extraordinary courage and gallantry, at the cost of his life above and beyond the call to duty, are in keeping with the highest traditions of the military service and reflect great credit on him, his unit, and the U.S. Army.

3315 ◆ *NASH, DAVID PAUL

Rank: Private First Class
Service: U.S. Army
Birthday: 3 November 1947
Place of Birth: Whitesville, Daviess County, Kentucky
Date of Death: 29 December 1968
Place of Death: Republic of Vietnam
Cemetery: Saint Mary's of the Woods Cemetery (MH)—Whitesville, Kentucky
Entered Service at: Louisville, Jefferson County, Kentucky
Unit: Company B, 2d Battalion, 39th Infantry, 9th Infantry Division
Served as: Grenadier
Battle or Place of Action: Giao Duc District, Dinh Tuong Province, Republic of Vietnam
Date of Action: 29 December 1968
G.O. Number, Date: 23, 23 April 1970
Date of Presentation: 7 April 1970
Place of Presentation: The White House, presented by Pres. Richard M. Nixon to his family
Citation: For conspicuous gallantry and intrepidity in action at the risk of his life above and beyond the call of duty. Pfc. Nash distinguished himself while serving as a grenadier with Company B, in Giao Duc district. When an ambush patrol of which he was a member suddenly came under intense attack before reaching its destination, he was the first to return the enemy fire. Taking an exposed location, Pfc. Nash suppressed the hostile fusillade with a rapid series of rounds from his grenade launcher, enabling artillery fire to be adjusted on the enemy. After the foe had been routed, his small element continued to the ambush site where he established a position with three fellow soldiers on a narrow dike. Shortly past midnight, while Pfc. Nash and a comrade kept watch and the two other men took their turn sleeping, an enemy grenade wounded two soldiers in the adjacent position. Seconds later, Pfc. Nash saw another grenade land only a few feet from his own position. Although he could have escaped harm by rolling down the other side of the dike, he shouted a warning to his comrades and leaped upon the lethal explosive. Absorbing the blast with his body, he saved the lives of the three men in the area at the sacrifice of his life. By his gallantry at the cost of his life and in the highest traditions of the military service, Pfc. Nash has reflected great credit on himself, his unit, and the U.S. Army.

3316 ◆ *NEWLIN, MELVIN EARL

Rank: Private First Class
Service: U.S. Marine Corps
Birthday: 27 September 1948

Place of Birth: Wellsville, Columbiana County, Ohio
Date of Death: 4 July 1967
Place of Death: Republic of Vietnam
Cemetery: Spring Hill Cemetery (MH)—Wellsville, Ohio
Entered Service at: Cleveland, Cuyahoga County, Ohio
Unit: Company F, 2d Battalion, 5th Marines, 1st Marine Division (Rein) FMF
Served as: Machine Gunner
Battle or Place of Action: Quang Nam Province, Republic of Vietnam
Date of Action: 3-4 July 1967
Date of Presentation: 18 March 1969
Place of Presentation: The White House, presented by Pres. Richard M. Nixon to his family
Citation: For conspicuous gallantry and intrepidity at the risk of his life above and beyond the call of duty while serving as a machine gunner attached to the 1st Platoon, Company F, 2d Battalion, on 3 and 4 July 1967. Pfc. Newlin, with four other marines, was manning a key position on the perimeter of the Nong Son outpost when the enemy launched a savage and well-coordinated mortar and infantry assault, seriously wounding him and killing his four comrades. Propping himself against his machine gun, he poured a deadly accurate stream of fire into the charging ranks of the Viet Cong. Though repeatedly hit by small-arms fire, he twice repelled enemy attempts to overrun his position. During the third attempt, a grenade explosion wounded him again and knocked him to the ground, unconscious. The Viet Cong guerrillas, believing him dead, bypassed him and continued their assault on the main force. Meanwhile, Pfc. Newlin regained consciousness, crawled back to his weapon, and brought it to bear on the rear of the enemy causing havoc and confusion among them. Spotting the enemy attempting to bring a captured 106 recoilless weapon to bear on other marine positions, he shifted his fire, inflicting heavy casualties on the enemy and preventing them from firing the captured weapon. He then shifted his fire back to the primary enemy force, causing the enemy to stop their assault on the marine bunkers and to once again attack his machine-gun position. Valiantly fighting off two more enemy assaults, he firmly held his ground until mortally wounded. Pfc. Newlin had single-handedly broken up and disorganized the entire enemy assault force, causing them to lose momentum and delaying them long enough for his fellow marines to organize a defense and beat off their secondary attack. His indomitable courage, fortitude, and unwavering devotion to duty in the face of almost certain death reflected great credit upon himself and the Marine Corps and upheld the highest traditions of the U.S. Naval Service.

3317 ◆ *NOONAN JR., THOMAS PATRICK

Rank: Lance Corporal
Service: U.S. Marine Corps
Birthday: 18 November 1943
Place of Birth: Brooklyn, Kings County, New York
Date of Death: 5 February 1969
Place of Death: Republic of Vietnam
Cemetery: First Calvary Cemetery—Woodside, New York

Entered Service at: Brooklyn, Kings County, New York
Unit: Company G, 2d Battalion, 9th Marines, 3d Marine Division (Rein) FMF
Served as: Fire Team Leader
Battle or Place of Action: near Vandergrift Combat Base, A Shau Valley, Republic of Vietnam
Date of Action: 5 February 1969
Date of Presentation: 16 February 1971
Place of Presentation: The White House (East Ballroom), presented by Pres. Richard M. Nixon to his family
Citation: For conspicuous gallantry and intrepidity at the risk of his life above and beyond the call of duty while serving as a fire team leader with Company G, in operations against the enemy in Quang Tri province. Company G was directed to move from a position which they had been holding southeast of the Vandergrift Combat Base to an alternate location. As the marines commenced a slow and difficult descent down the side of the hill made extremely slippery by the heavy rains, the leading element came under a heavy fire from a North Vietnamese Army unit occupying well-concealed positions in the rocky terrain. Four men were wounded, and repeated attempts to recover them failed because of the intense hostile fire. L/Cpl. Noonan moved from his position of relative security and, maneuvering down the treacherous slope to a location near the injured men, took cover behind some rocks. Shouting words of encouragement to the wounded men to restore their confidence, he dashed across the hazardous terrain and commenced dragging the most seriously wounded man away from the fire-swept area. Although wounded and knocked to the ground by an enemy round, L/Cpl. Noonan recovered rapidly and resumed dragging the man toward the marginal security of a rock. He was, however, mortally wounded before he could reach his destination. His heroic actions inspired his fellow marines to such aggressiveness that they initiated a spirited assault which forced the enemy soldiers to withdraw. L/Cpl. Noonan's indomitable courage, inspiring initiative, and selfless devotion to duty upheld the highest traditions of the Marine Corps and the U.S. Naval Service. He gallantly gave his life for his country.

3318 ◆ NORRIS, THOMAS ROLLAND

Rank: Lieutenant
Service: U.S. Navy
Birthday: 14 January 1944
Place of Birth: Jacksonville, Duval County, Florida
Entered Service at: Silver Spring, Montgomery County, Maryland
Unit: United States Military Assistance Command, Headquarters, SEAL Advisor, Strategic Technical Directorate Assistance Team
Served as: SEAL Advisor
Battle or Place of Action: Quang Tri Province, Republic of Vietnam
Date of Action: 10-13 April 1972
Date of Presentation: 6 March 1976
Place of Presentation: The White House, presented by Pres. Gerald R. Ford
Citation: Lt. Norris completed an unprecedented ground

rescue of two downed pilots deep within heavily controlled enemy territory in Quang Tri Province. Lt. Norris, on the night of 10 April, led a five-man patrol through 2,000 meters of heavily controlled territory, located one of the downed pilots at daybreak, and returned to the Forward Operating Base (FOB). On 11 April, after a devastating mortar and rocket attack on the small FOB, Lt. Norris led a three-man team on two unsuccessful rescue attempts for the second pilot. On the afternoon of the 12th, a forward air controller located the pilot and notified Lt. Norris. Dressed in fishermen disguises and using a sampan, Lt. Norris and one Vietnamese traveled throughout the night and found the injured pilot at dawn. Covering the pilot with bamboo and vegetation, they began the return journey, successfully evading a North Vietnamese patrol. Approaching the FOB, they came under heavy machine-gun fire. Lt. Norris called in an air strike which provided suppression fire and a smoke screen, allowing the rescue party to reach the FOB. By his outstanding display of decisive leadership, undaunted courage, and selfless dedication in the face of extreme danger, Lt. Norris enhanced the finest traditions of the U.S. Naval service.

3319 ◆ NOVOSEL, MICHAEL JOSEPH

Rank: Chief Warrant Officer (highest rank: Chief Warrant Officer 4)
Service: U.S. Army
Birthday: 3 September 1922
Place of Birth: Etna, Allegheny County, Pennsylvania
Entered Service at: Kenner, Jefferson County, Louisiana
Unit: 82d Medical Detachment, 45th Medical Company, 68th Medical Group
Served as: Commander of a Medivac Helicopter
Battle or Place of Action: Kien Tuong Province, Republic of Vietnam
Date of Action: 2 October 1969
G.O. Number, Date: 34, 16 July 1971
Date of Presentation: 15 June 1971
Place of Presentation: The White House, presented by Pres. Richard M. Nixon
Citation: For conspicuous gallantry and intrepidity in action at the risk of his life above and beyond the call of duty. CWO Novosel, 82d Medical Detachment, distinguished himself while serving as commander of a medical evacuation helicopter. He unhesitatingly maneuvered his helicopter into a heavily fortified and defended enemy training area where a group of wounded Vietnamese soldiers were pinned down by a large enemy force. Flying without gunship or other cover and exposed to intense machine-gun fire, CWO Novosel was able to locate and rescue a wounded soldier. Since all communications with the beleaguered troops had been lost, he repeatedly circled the battle area, flying at low level under continuous heavy fire, to attract the attention of the scattered friendly troops. This display of courage visibly raised their morale, as they recognized this as a signal to assemble for evacuation. On six occasions he and his crew were forced out of the battle area by the intense enemy fire, only to circle and return from another direction to land and extract additional troops. Near the end of the mission, a wounded soldier was

spotted close to an enemy bunker. Fully realizing that he would attract a hail of enemy fire, CWO Novosel nevertheless attempted the extraction by hovering the helicopter backward. As the man was pulled on board, enemy automatic weapons opened fire at close-range, damaged the aircraft and wounded CWO Novosel. He momentarily lost control of the aircraft, but quickly recovered and departed under the withering enemy fire. In all 15 extremely hazardous extractions were performed in order to remove wounded personnel. As a direct result of his selfless conduct, the lives of 29 soldiers were saved. The extraordinary heroism displayed by CWO Novosel was an inspiration to his comrades in arms and reflect great credit on him, his unit, and the U.S. Army.

3320 ◆ *OLIVE III, MILTON LEE

Rank: Private First Class
Service: U.S. Army
Birthday: 7 November 1946
Place of Birth: Chicago, Cook County, Illinois
Date of Death: 22 October 1965
Place of Death: Republic of Vietnam
Cemetery: West Grove Cemetery—Lexington, Mississippi
Entered Service at: Chicago, Cook County, Illinois
Unit: 3d Platoon, Company B, 2d Battalion [Airborne], 503d Infantry, 173d Airborne Brigade
Battle or Place of Action: Phu Cuong, Republic of Vietnam
Date of Action: 22 October 1965
G.O. Number, Date: 18, 26 April 1966
Date of Presentation: 21 April 1966
Place of Presentation: The White house, presented by Pres. Lyndon B. Johnson to his family
Citation: For conspicuous gallantry and intrepidity at the risk of his life above and beyond the call of duty. Pfc. Olive was a member of the 3d Platoon of Company B, as it moved through the jungle to find the Viet Cong operating in the area. Although the platoon was subjected to a heavy volume of enemy gunfire and pinned down temporarily, it retaliated by assaulting the Viet Cong positions, causing the enemy to flee. As the platoon pursued the insurgents, Pfc. Olive and four other soldiers were moving through the jungle together when a grenade was thrown into their midst. Pfc. Olive saw the grenade, and then saved the lives of his fellow soldiers at the sacrifice of his by grabbing the grenade in his hand and falling on it to absorb the blast with his body. Through his bravery, unhesitating actions, and complete disregard for his safety, he prevented additional loss of life or injury to the members of his platoon. Pfc. Olive's extraordinary heroism, at the risk of his life above and beyond the call of duty, are in the highest traditions of the U.S. Army and reflect great credit upon himself and the Armed Forces of his country.

3321 ◆ *OLSON, KENNETH LEE

Rank: Specialist Fourth Class
Service: U.S. Army
Birthday: 26 May 1945
Place of Birth: Willmar, Kandiyohi County, Minnesota
Date of Death: 13 May 1968

Place of Death: Republic of Vietnam
Cemetery: Paynesville Cemetery (MH)—Paynesville, Minnesota
Entered Service at: Minneapolis, Hennepin County, Minnesota
Unit: Company A, 5th Battalion, 12th Infantry, 199th Infantry Brigade (Separate)
Served as: Team Leader
Battle or Place of Action: Republic of Vietnam
Date of Action: 13 May 1968
G.O. Number, Date: 22, 23 April 1970
Date of Presentation: 7 April 1970
Place of Presentation: The White House, presented by Pres. Richard M. Nixon to his family
Citation: For conspicuous gallantry and intrepidity in action at the risk of his life above and beyond the call of duty. Sp4c. Olson distinguished himself at the cost of his life while serving as a team leader with Company A. Sp4c. Olson was participating in a mission to reinforce a reconnaissance platoon which was heavily engaged with a well-entrenched Viet Cong force. When his platoon moved into the area of contact and had overrun the first line of enemy bunkers, Sp4c. Olson and a fellow soldier moved forward of the platoon to investigate another suspected line of bunkers. As the two men advanced they were pinned down by intense automatic-weapons fire from an enemy position 10 meters to their front. With complete disregard for his safety, Sp4c. Olson exposed himself and hurled a hand grenade into the Viet Cong position. Failing to silence the hostile fire, he again exposed himself to the intense fire in preparation to assault the enemy position. As he prepared to hurl the grenade, he was wounded, causing him to drop the activated device within his own position. Realizing that it would explode immediately, Sp4c. Olson threw himself upon the grenade and pulled it in to his body to take the full force of the explosion. By this unselfish action Sp4c. Olson sacrificed his own life to save the lives of his fellow comrades-in-arms. His extraordinary heroism inspired his fellow soldiers to renew their efforts and totally defeat the enemy force. Sp4c. Olson's profound courage and intrepidity were in keeping with the highest traditions of the military service and reflect great credit upon himself, his unit, and the U.S. Army.

3322 ◆ O'MALLEY, ROBERT EMMETT

Rank: Sergeant (rank at time of action: Corporal)
Service: U.S. Marine Corps
Birthday: 3 June 1943
Place of Birth: Woodside, Queens County, New York
Entered Service at: New York, New York
Unit: Company I, 3d Battalion, 3d Marine Regiment, 3d Marine Division (Rein) FMF
Served as: Squad Leader
Battle or Place of Action: near An Cu'ong 2, Republic of Vietnam
Date of Action: 18 August 1965
Date of Presentation: 6 December 1966
Place of Presentation: The Federal Building, Austin, Texas, presented by Pres. Lyndon B. Johnson

Citation: For conspicuous gallantry and intrepidity in action against the communist (Viet Cong) forces at the risk of his life above and beyond the call of duty. While leading his squad in the assault against a strongly entrenched enemy force, his unit came under intense small-arms fire. With complete disregard for his personal safety, Sgt. O'Malley raced across an open rice paddy to a trench line where the enemy forces were located. Jumping into the trench, he attacked the Viet Cong with his rifle and grenades, singlehandedly killed eight of the enemy. He then led his squad to the assistance of an adjacent marine unit which was suffering heavy casualties. Continuing to press forward, he reloaded his weapon and fired with telling effect into the enemy emplacement. He personally assisted in the evacuation of several wounded marines, and again regrouping the remnants of his squad, he returned to the point of the heaviest fighting. Ordered to an evacuation point by an officer, Sgt. O'Malley gathered his besieged and badly wounded squad, and boldly led them under fire to a helicopter for withdrawal. Although three times wounded in this encounter, and facing imminent death from a fanatic and determined enemy, he steadfastly refused evacuation and continued to cover his squad's boarding of the helicopters while, from an exposed position, he delivered fire against the enemy until his wounded men were evacuated. Only then, with his last mission accomplished, did he permit himself to be removed from the battlefield. By his valor, leadership, and courageous efforts in behalf of his comrades, he served as an inspiration to all who observed him, and reflected the highest credit upon the Marine Corps and the U.S. Naval Service.

3323 ◆ *OUELLET, DAVID GEORGE

Rank: Seaman
Service: U.S. Navy
Birthday: 13 June 1944
Place of Birth: Newton, Middlesex County, Massachusetts
Date of Death: 6 March 1967
Place of Death: Republic of Vietnam
Cemetery: Woodlawn Cemetery (MH)—Wellesley, Massachusetts
Entered Service at: Boston, Suffolk County, Massachusetts
Unit: River Patrol Boat (PBR-124), My Tho Detachment 532, River Squadron 5
Served as: Forward Machine Gunner
Battle or Place of Action: Mekong River, Republic of Vietnam
Date of Action: 6 March 1967
Date of Presentation: 30 January 1968
Place of Presentation: The Pentagon, presented by Sec. of the Navy Paul R. Ignatius to his family
Citation: For conspicuous gallantry and intrepidity at the risk of his life above and beyond the call of duty. As the forward machine gunner on River Patrol Boat (PBR) 124, which was on patrol during the early evening hours, Seaman Ouellet observed suspicious activity near the river bank, alerted his boat captain, and recommended movement of the boat to the area to investigate. While the PBR was making a high-speed

run along the river bank, Seaman Ouellet spotted an incoming enemy grenade falling toward the boat. He immediately left the protected position of his gun mount and ran aft for the full length of the speeding boat, shouting to his fellow crewmembers to take cover. Observing the boat captain standing unprotected on the boat, Seaman Ouellet bounded on to the engine compartment cover, and pushed the boat captain down to safety. In the split second that followed the grenade's landing, and in the face of certain death, Seaman Ouellet fearlessly placed himself between the deadly missile and his shipmates, courageously absorbing most of the blast fragments with his body in order to protect his shipmates from injury and death. His extraordinary heroism and his selfless and courageous actions on behalf of his comrades at the expense of his life were in the finest traditions of the U.S. Naval Service.

3324 ◆ PATTERSON, ROBERT MARTIN

Rank: Sergeant (rank at time of action: Specialist Fourth Class) (highest rank: Command Sergeant Major)
Service: U.S. Army
Birthday: 16 April 1948
Place of Birth: Durham, Durham County, North Carolina
Entered Service at: Raleigh, Wake County, North Carolina
Unit: 3d Platoon, Troop B, 2d Squadron, 17th Cavalry, 101st Airborne Division
Served as: Fire Team Leader
Battle or Place of Action: near La Chu, Republic of Vietnam
Date of Action: 6 May 1968
G.O. Number, Date: 65, 25 October 1969
Date of Presentation: 9 October 1969
Place of Presentation: The White House, presented by Pres. Richard M. Nixon
Citation: For conspicuous gallantry and intrepidity in action at the risk of his life above and beyond the call of duty. Sgt. Patterson (then Sp4c.) distinguished himself while serving as a fire team leader of the 3d Platoon, Troop B, during an assault against a North Vietnamese Army battalion which was entrenched in a heavily fortified position. When the leading squad of the 3d Platoon was pinned down by heavy interlocking automatic-weapons and rocket-propelled-grenade fire from two enemy bunkers, Sgt. Patterson and the two other members of his assault team moved forward under a hail of enemy fire to destroy the bunkers with grenade and machine-gun fire. Observing that his comrades were being fired on from a third enemy bunker covered by enemy gunners in one-man spider holes, Sgt. Patterson, with complete disregard for his safety and ignoring the warnings of his comrades that he was moving into a bunker complex, assaulted and destroyed the position. Although exposed to intensive small-arms and grenade fire from the bunkers and their mutually supporting emplacements, Sgt. Patterson continued his assault upon the bunkers which were impeding the advance of his unit. Sgt. Patterson singlehandedly destroyed by rifle and grenade fire five enemy bunkers, killed eight enemy soldiers,

and captured seven weapons. His dauntless courage and heroism inspired his platoon to resume the attack and to penetrate the enemy defensive position. Sgt. Patterson's action at the risk of his life has reflected great credit upon himself, his unit, and the U.S. Army.

3325 ◆ *PAUL, JOE CALVIN

Rank: Lance Corporal
Service: U.S. Marine Corps
Birthday: 23 April 1946
Place of Birth: Williamsburg, Whitley County, Kentucky
Date of Death: 19 August 1965
Place of Death: Republic of Vietnam
Cemetery: Memorial Park—Dayton, Ohio
Entered Service at: Dayton, Montgomery County, Ohio
Unit: Company H, 2d Battalion, 4th Marines, 3d Marine Division (Rein) FMF
Served as: Fire Team Leader
Battle or Place of Action: near Chu Lai, Republic of Vietnam
Date of Action: 18 August 1965
Date of Presentation: 7 February 1967
Place of Presentation: Marine Barracks, Washington D.C., presented by Under Sec. of the Navy to his family
Citation: For conspicuous gallantry and intrepidity at the risk of his life above and beyond the call of duty. In violent battle, L/Cpl. Paul's platoon sustained five casualties as it was temporarily pinned down, by devastating mortar, recoilless-rifle, automatic-weapons, and rifle fire delivered by insurgent communist (Viet Cong) forces in well-entrenched positions. The wounded marines were unable to move from their perilously exposed positions forward of the remainder of their platoon, and were suddenly subjected to a barrage of white phosphorous rifle grenades. L/Cpl. Paul, fully aware that his tactics would almost certainly result in serious injury or death to himself, chose to disregard his safety and boldly dashed across the fire-swept rice paddies, placed himself between his wounded comrades and the enemy, and delivered effective suppressive fire with his automatic weapon in order to divert the attack long enough to allow the casualties to be evacuated. Although critically wounded during the course of the battle, he resolutely remained in his exposed position and continued to fire his rifle until he collapsed and was evacuated. By his fortitude and gallant spirit of self-sacrifice in the face of almost certain death, he saved the lives of several of his fellow marines. His heroic action served to inspire all who observed him and reflect the highest credit upon himself, the Marine Corps, and the U.S. Naval Service. He gallantly gave his life in the cause of freedom.

3326 ◆ PENRY, RICHARD ALLEN

Rank: Sergeant
Service: U.S. Army
Birthday: 18 November 1948
Place of Birth: Petaluma, Sonoma County, California
Date of Death: 9 May 1994
Place of Death: Petaluma, California

Cemetery: Cypress Hills Memorial Park (MH)—Petaluma, California
Entered Service at: Oakland, Alameda County, California
Unit: Company C, 4th Battalion, 12th Infantry, 199th Infantry Brigade
Served as: Rifleman
Battle or Place of Action: Binh Tuy Province, Republic of Vietnam
Date of Action: 31 January 1970
G.O. Number, Date: 40, 23 July 1971
Date of Presentation: 15 June 1971
Place of Presentation: The White House, presented by Pres. Richard M. Nixon
Citation: For conspicuous gallantry and intrepidity in action at the risk of his life above and beyond the call of duty. Sgt. Penry, Company C, distinguished himself while serving as a rifleman during a night ambush mission. As the platoon was preparing the ambush position, it suddenly came under an intense enemy attack from mortar, rocket, and automatic-weapons fire which seriously wounded the company commander and most of the platoon members, leaving small isolated groups of wounded men throughout the area. Sgt. Penry, seeing the extreme seriousness of the situation, worked his way through the deadly enemy fire to the company command post where he administered first aid to the wounded company commander and other personnel. He then moved the command post to a position which provided greater protection and visual communication and control of other platoon elements. Realizing the company radio was damaged and recognizing the urgent necessity to reestablish communications with the battalion headquarters, he ran outside the defensive perimeter through a fusillade of hostile fire to retrieve a radio. Finding it inoperable, Sgt. Penry returned through heavy fire to retrieve two more radios. Turning his attention to the defense of the area, he crawled to the edge of the perimeter, retrieved needed ammunition and weapons, and resupplied the wounded men. During a determined assault by over 30 enemy soldiers, Sgt. Penry occupied the most vulnerable forward position, placing heavy, accurate fire on the attacking enemy and exposing himself several times to throw hand grenades into the advancing enemy troops. He succeeded virtually singlehandedly in stopping the attack. Learning that none of the radios were operable, Sgt. Penry again crawled outside the defensive perimeter, retrieved a fourth radio, and established communications with higher headquarters. Sgt. Penry then continued to administer first aid to the wounded and repositioned them to better repel further enemy attacks. Despite continuous and deadly sniper fire, he again left the defensive perimeter, moved to within a few feet of enemy positions, located five isolated wounded soldiers, and led them to safety. When evacuation helicopters approached, Sgt. Penry voluntarily left the perimeter, set up a guiding beacon, established the priorities for evacuation, and successively carried 18 wounded men to the extraction site. After all wounded personnel had been evacuated, Sgt. Penry joined another platoon and assisted in the pursuit of the enemy. Sgt. Penry's extraordinary heroism at the risk of his own life are in keeping with the highest traditions of the military service and reflect great credit on him, his unit, and the U.S. Army.

3327   ◆   *PERKINS JR., WILLIAM THOMAS

Rank: Corporal
Service: U.S. Marine Corps
Birthday: 10 August 1947
Place of Birth: Rochester, Monroe County, New York
Date of Death: 12 October 1967
Place of Death: Republic of Vietnam
Cemetery: San Fernando Mission Cemetery—San Fernando, California
Entered Service at: San Francisco, San Francisco County, California
Unit: Company C, 1st Battalion, 1st Marines, 1st Marine Division (Rein) FMF
Served as: Combat Photographer
Battle or Place of Action: Quang Tri Province, Republic of Vietnam
Date of Action: 12 October 1967
Date of Presentation: 20 June 1969
Place of Presentation: The White House, presented by Pres. Richard M. Nixon to his family
Citation: For conspicuous gallantry and intrepidity at the risk of his life above and beyond the call of duty while serving as a combat photographer attached to Company C. During Operation Medina, a major reconnaissance-in-force southwest of Quang Tri, Company C made heavy combat contact with a numerically superior North Vietnamese Army force estimated at from two to three companies. The focal point of the intense fighting was a helicopter landing zone which was also serving as the Command Post of Company C. In the course of a strong hostile attack, an enemy grenade landed in the immediate area occupied by Cpl. Perkins and three other marines. Realizing the inherent danger, he shouted the warning, "Incoming Grenade" to his fellow marines, and in a valiant act of heroism, hurled himself upon the grenade absorbing the impact of the explosion with his body, thereby saving the lives of his comrades at the cost of his life. Through his exceptional courage and inspiring valor in the face of certain death, Cpl. Perkins reflected great credit upon himself and the Marine Corps and upheld the highest traditions of the U.S. Naval Service. He gallantly gave his life for his country.

3328   ◆   *PETERS, LAWRENCE DAVID

Rank: Sergeant
Service: U.S. Marine Corps
Birthday: 16 September 1946
Place of Birth: Johnson City, Broome County, New York
Date of Death: 4 September 1967
Place of Death: Republic of Vietnam
Cemetery: Chenango Valley Cemetery (MH)—Binghamton, New York
Entered Service at: Binghamton, Broome County, New York
Unit: Company M, 3d Battalion, 5th Marines, 1st Marine Division (Rein) FMF
Served as: Squad Leader
Battle or Place of Action: Quang Tin Province, Republic of Vietnam

Date of Action: 4 September 1967
Date of Presentation: 20 April 1970
Place of Presentation: The White House, presented by Vice Pres. Spiro T. Agnew to his family
Citation: For conspicuous gallantry and intrepidity at the risk of his life above and beyond the call of duty while serving as a squad leader with Company M. During Operation Swift, the marines of the 2d Platoon of Company M were struck by intense mortar, machine-gun, and small-arms fire from an entrenched enemy force. As the company rallied its forces, Sgt. Peters maneuvered his squad in an assault on an enemy-defended knoll. Disregarding his safety, as enemy rounds hit all about him, he stood in the open, pointing out enemy positions until he was painfully wounded in the leg. Disregarding his wound, he moved forward and continued to lead his men. As the enemy fire increased in accuracy and volume, his squad lost its momentum and was temporarily pinned down. Exposing himself to devastating enemy fire, he consolidated his position to render more effective fire. While directing the base of fire, he was wounded a second time in the face and neck from an exploding mortar round. As the enemy attempted to infiltrate the position of an adjacent platoon, Sgt. Peters stood erect in the full view of the enemy firing burst after burst forcing them to disclose their camouflaged positions. Sgt. Peters steadfastly continued to direct his squad in spite of two additional wounds and persisted in his efforts to encourage and supervise his men until he lost consciousness and succumbed. Inspired by his selfless actions, the squad regained fire superiority and once again carried the assault to the enemy. By his outstanding valor, indomitable fighting spirit and tenacious determination in the face of overwhelming odds, Sgt. Peters upheld the highest traditions of the Marine Corps and the U.S. Naval Service. He gallantly gave his life for his country.

3329 ◆ *PETERSEN, DANNY JOHN

Rank: Specialist Fourth Class
Service: U.S. Army
Birthday: 11 March 1949
Place of Birth: Horton, Brown County, Kansas
Date of Death: 9 January 1970
Place of Death: Republic of Vietnam
Cemetery: Netawaka Cemetery (MH)—Netawaka, Kansas
Entered Service at: Kansas City, Clay County, Missouri
Unit: Company B, 4th Battalion, 23d Infantry, 25th Infantry Division
Served as: A.P.C. Commander
Battle or Place of Action: Tay Ninh Province, Republic of Vietnam
Date of Action: 9 January 1970
G.O. Number, Date: 44, 12 September 1974
Date of Presentation: 17 July 1974
Place of Presentation: Blair House, presented by Vice Pres. Gerald R. Ford to his family
Citation: Sp4c. Petersen distinguished himself while serving as an armored personnel carrier commander with Company B during a combat operation against a North Vietnamese Army force estimated to be of battalion size. During the initial contact with the enemy, an armored personnel carrier was dis-

abled and the crewmen were pinned down by the heavy onslaught of enemy small-arms, automatic-weapons, and rocket-propelled-grenade fire. Sp4c. Petersen immediately maneuvered his armored personnel carrier to a position between the disabled vehicle and the enemy. He placed suppressive fire on the enemy's well-fortified position, thereby enabling the crewmembers of the disabled personnel carrier to repair their vehicle. He then maneuvered his vehicle, while still under heavy hostile fire, to within 10 feet of the enemy's defensive emplacement. After a period of intense fighting, his vehicle received a direct hit and the driver was wounded. With extraordinary courage and selfless disregard for his own safety, Sp4c. Petersen carried his wounded comrade 45 meters across the bullet-swept field to a secure area. He then voluntarily returned to his disabled armored personnel carrier to provide covering fire for both the other vehicles and the dismounted personnel of his platoon as they withdrew. Despite heavy fire from three sides, he remained with his disabled vehicle, alone and completely exposed. Sp4c. Petersen was standing on top of his vehicle, firing his weapon, when he was mortally wounded. His heroic and selfless actions prevented further loss of life in his platoon. Sp4c. Petersen's conspicuous gallantry and extraordinary heroism are in the highest traditions of the military service and reflect great credit upon him, his unit, and the U.S. Army.

3330 ◆ *PHIPPS, JIMMY WAYNE

Rank: Private First Class
Service: U.S. Marine Corps
Birthday: 1 November 1950
Place of Birth: Santa Monica, Los Angeles County, California
Date of Death: 27 May 1969
Place of Death: Republic of Vietnam
Cemetery: Woodlawn Cemetery—Santa Monica, California
Entered Service at: Culver City, Los Angeles County, California
Unit: Company B, 1st Engineer Battalion, 1st Marine Division (Rein) FMF
Served as: Combat Engineer
Battle or Place of Action: near An Hoa, Republic of Vietnam
Date of Action: 27 May 1969
Date of Presentation: 20 April 1970
Place of Presentation: The White House, presented by Vice Pres. Spiro T. Agnew to his family
Citation: For conspicuous gallantry and intrepidity at the risk of his life above and beyond the call of duty while serving as a combat engineer with Company B in connection with combat operations against the enemy. Pfc. Phipps was a member of a two-man combat engineer demolition team assigned to locate and destroy enemy artillery ordnance and concealed firing devices. After he had expended all of his explosives and blasting caps, Pfc. Phipps discovered a 175-mm high-explosive artillery round in a rice paddy. Suspecting that the enemy had attached the artillery round to a secondary explosive device, he warned other marines in the area to move to covered positions and perpared to destroy the

round with a hand grenade. As he was attaching the hand grenade to a stake beside the artillery round, the fuse of the enemy's secondary explosive device ignited. Realizing that his assistant and the platoon commander were both within a few meters of him and that the imminent explosion could kill all three men, Pfc. Phipps grasped the hand grenade to his chest and dived forward to cover the enemy's explosive and the artillery round with his body, thereby shielding his companions from the detonation while absorbing the full and tremendous impact with his body. Pfc. Phipps' indomitable courage, inspiring initiative, and selfless devotion to duty saved the lives of two marines and upheld the highest traditions of the Marine Corps and the U.S. Naval Service. He gallantly gave his life for his country.

3331 ◆ *PIERCE, LARRY STANLEY

Rank: Sergeant
Service: U.S. Army
Birthday: 6 July 1941
Place of Birth: Wewoka, Seminole County, Oklahoma
Date of Death: 20 September 1965
Place of Death: Republic of Vietnam
Cemetery: Wasco Cemetery—Wasco, California
Entered Service at: Fresno, Fresno County, California
Unit: Headquarters & Headquarters Company, 1st Battalion (Airborne), 503d Infantry, 173d Airborne Brigade
Served as: Squad Leader
Battle or Place of Action: near Ben Cat, Republic of Vietnam
Date of Action: 20 September 1965
G.O. Number, Date: 7, 24 February 1966
Date of Presentation: 24 February 1966
Place of Presentation: The White House, presented by Pres. Lyndon B. Johnson to his family
Citation: For conspicuous gallantry and intrepidity at the risk of his life above and beyond the call of duty. Sgt. Pierce was serving as squad leader in a reconnaissance platoon when his patrol was ambushed by hostile forces. Through his inspiring leadership and personal courage, the squad succeeded in eliminating an enemy machine gun and routing the opposing force. While pursuing the fleeing enemy, the squad came upon a dirt road and, as the main body of his men entered the road, Sgt. Pierce discovered an antipersonnel mine emplaced in the road bed. Realizing that the mine could destroy the majority of his squad, Sgt. Pierce saved the lives of his men at the sacrifice of his life by throwing himself directly onto the mine as it exploded. Through his indomitable courage, complete disregard for his safety, and profound concern for his fellow soldiers, he averted loss of life and injury to the members of his squad. Sgt. Pierce's extraordinary heroism, at the cost of his life, are in the highest traditions of the U.S. Army and reflect great credit upon himself and the Armed Forces of his country.

3332 ◆ PITTMAN, RICHARD ALLAN

Rank: Sergeant (rank at time of action: Lance Corporal) (highest rank: Master Sergeant)
Service: U.S. Marine Corps

Birthday: 26 May 1945
Place of Birth: French Camp, San Joaquin County, California
Entered Service at: Stockton, San Joaquin County, California
Unit: Company I, 3d Battalion, 5th Marines, 1st Marine Division (Rein) FMF
Served as: Rifleman/Squad Leader
Battle or Place of Action: near the Demilitarized Zone, Republic of Vietnam
Date of Action: 24 July 1966
Date of Presentation: 14 May 1968
Place of Presentation: The Pentagon (Inner Courtyard), Hall of Heroes, presented by Pres. Lyndon B. Johnson
Citation: For conspicuous gallantry and intrepidity at the risk of his life above and beyond the call of duty. While Company I was conducting an operation along the axis of a narrow jungle trail, the leading company elements suffered numerous casualties when they suddenly came under heavy fire from a well-concealed and numerically superior force. Hearing the engaged marines' calls for more firepower, Sgt. Pittman quickly exchanged his rifle for a machine gun and several belts of ammunition, left the relative safety of his platoon, and unhesitatingly rushed forward to aid his comrades. Taken under intense enemy small-arms fire at point-blank range during his advance, he returned the fire, silencing the enemy position. As Sgt. Pittman continued to forge forward to aid members of the leading platoon, he again came under heavy fire from two automatic weapons which he promptly destroyed. Learning that there were additional wounded marines 50 yards further along the trail, he braved a withering hail of enemy mortar and small-arms fire to continue onward. As he reached the position where the leading marines had fallen, he was suddenly confronted with a bold frontal attack by 30 to 40 enemy. Totally disregarding his safety, he calmly established a position in the middle of the trail and raked the advancing enemy with devastating machine-gun fire. His weapon rendered ineffective, he picked up an enemy submachine gun and, together with a pistol seized from a fallen comrade, continued his lethal fire until the enemy force had withdrawn. Having exhausted his ammunition except for a grenade which he hurled at the enemy, he then rejoined his platoon. Sgt. Pittman's daring initiative, bold fighting spirit, and selfless devotion to duty inflicted many enemy casualties, disrupted the enemy attack, and saved the lives of many of his wounded comrades. His personal valor at grave risk to himself reflects the highest credit upon himself, the Marine Corps, and the U.S. Naval Service.

3333 ◆ *PITTS, RILEY LEROY

Rank: Captain
Service: U.S. Army
Birthday: 15 October 1937
Place of Birth: Fallis, Oklahoma
Date of Death: 31 October 1967
Place of Death: Republic of Vietnam
Cemetery: Hillcrest Memorial Gardens Cemetery (MH)—Spencer, Oklahoma
Entered Service at: Wichita, Sedgwick County, Kansas

Unit: Company C, 2d Battalion, 27th Infantry, 25th Infantry Division
Served as: Company Commander
Battle or Place of Action: Ap Dong, Republic of Vietnam
Date of Action: 31 October 1967
G.O. Number, Date: 84, 31 December 1968
Date of Presentation: 10 December 1968
Place of Presentation: The White House, presented by Pres. Lyndon B. Johnson to his family
Citation: Distinguishing himself by exceptional heroism while serving as company commander during an airmobile assault. Immediately after his company landed in the area, several Viet Cong opened fire with automatic weapons. Despite the enemy fire, Capt. Pitts forcefully led an assault which overran the enemy positions. Shortly thereafter, Capt. Pitts was ordered to move his unit to the north to reinforce another company heavily engaged against a strong enemy force. As Capt. Pitts' company moved forward to engage the enemy, intense fire was received from three directions, including fire from four enemy bunkers, two of which were within 15 meters of Capt. Pitts' position. The severity of the incoming fire prevented Capt. Pitts from maneuvering his company. His rifle fire proving ineffective against the enemy due to the dense jungle foliage, he picked up an M-79 grenade launcher and began pinpointing the targets. Seizing a Chinese Communist grenade which had been taken from a captured Viet Cong's web gear, Capt. Pitts lobbed the grenade at a bunker to his front, but it hit the dense jungle foliage and rebounded. Without hesitation, Capt. Pitts threw himself on top of the grenade which, fortunately, failed to explode. Capt. Pitts then directed the repositioning of the company to permit friendly artillery to be fired. Upon completion of the artillery fire mission, Capt. Pitts again led his men toward the enemy positions, personally killing at least one more Viet Cong. The jungle growth still prevented effective fire to be placed on the enemy bunkers. Capt. Pitts, displaying complete disregard for his life and personal safety, quickly moved to a position which permitted him to place effective fire on the enemy. He maintained a continuous fire, pinpointing the enemy's fortified positions, while at the same time directing and urging his men forward, until he was mortally wounded. Capt. Pitts' conspicuous gallantry, extraordinary heroism, and intrepidity at the cost of his life, above and beyond the call of duty, are in the highest traditions of the U.S. Army and reflect great credit upon himself, his unit, and the Armed Forces of his country.

3334 ◆ PLESS, STEPHEN WESLEY

Rank: Major (rank at time of action: Captain)
Service: U.S. Marine Corps
Birthday: 6 September 1939
Place of Birth: Newnan, Coweta County, Georgia
Date of Death: 20 July 1969
Place of Death: Pensacola, Florida
Cemetery: Barrancas National Cemetery (21-929A) (MH)—Pensacola, Florida
Entered Service at: Atlanta, Fulton County, Georgia

Unit: Marine Observation Squadron 6, Marine Aircraft Group 36, 1st Marine Aircraft Wing
Served as: Helicopter Gunship Pilot
Battle or Place of Action: near Quang Nai, Republic of Vietnam
Date of Action: 19 August 1967
Date of Presentation: 16 January 1969
Place of Presentation: The White House, presented by Pres. Lyndon B. Johnson
Citation: For conspicuous gallantry and intrepidity at the risk of his life above and beyond the call of duty while serving as a helicopter gunship pilot attached to Marine Observation Squadron 6 in action against enemy forces. During an escort mission Maj. Pless monitored an emergency call that four American soldiers stranded on a nearby beach were being overwhelmed by a large Viet Cong force. Maj. Pless flew to the scene and found 30 to 50 enemy soldiers in the open. Some of the enemy were bayoneting and beating the downed Americans. Maj. Pless displayed exceptional airmanship as he launched a devastating attack against the enemy force, killing or wounding many of the enemy and driving the remainder back into a treeline. His rockets and machine-gun attacks were made at such low levels that the aircraft flew through debris created by explosions from its rockets. Seeing one of the wounded soldiers gesture for assistance, he maneuvered his helicopter into a position between the wounded man and the enemy, providing a shield which permitted his crew to retrieve the wounded. During the rescue the enemy directed intense fire at the helicopter and rushed the aircraft again and again, closing to within a few feet before being beaten back. When the wounded men were aboard, Maj. Pless maneuvered the helicopter out to sea. Before it became safely airborne, the overloaded aircraft settled four times into the water. Displaying superb airmanship, he finally got the helicopter aloft. Maj. Pless' extraordinary heroism coupled with his outstanding flying skill prevented the annihilation of the tiny force. His courageous actions reflect great credit upon himself and uphold the highest traditions of the Marine Corps and the U.S. Naval Service.

3335 ◆ *PORT, WILLIAM DAVID

Rank: Sergeant (rank at time of action: Private First Class)
Service: U.S. Army
Birthday: 31 October 1941
Place of Birth: Petersburg, Huntingdon County, Pennsylvania
Date of Death: 27 November 1968
Place of Death: Republic of Vietnam
Cemetery: Arlington National Cemetery (7-8120-B) (MH)—Arlington, Virginia
Entered Service at: Harrisburg, Dauphin County, Pennsylvania
Unit: Company C, 5th Battalion, 7th Cavalry, 1st Air Cavalry Division
Served as: Rifleman
Battle or Place of Action: Que Son Valley, Heip Duc Province
Date of Action: 12 January 1968

G.O. Number, Date: 48, 8 September 1970
Date of Presentation: 6 August 1970
Place of Presentation: The White House, presented by Pres. Richard M. Nixon to his family
Citation: For conspicuous gallantry and intrepidity at the risk of his life above and beyond the call of duty. Sgt. Port distinguished himself while serving as a rifleman with Company C, which was conducting combat operations against an enemy force in the Que Son Valley. As Sgt. Port's platoon was moving to cut off a reported movement of enemy soldiers, the platoon came under heavy fire from an entrenched enemy force. The platoon was forced to withdraw due to the intensity and ferocity of the fire. Although wounded in the hand as the withdrawal began, Sgt. Port, with complete disregard for his safety, ran through the heavy fire to assist a wounded comrade back to the safety of the platoon perimeter. As the enemy forces assaulted in the perimeter, Sgt. Port and three comrades were in position behind an embankment when an enemy grenade landed in their midst. Sgt. Port, realizing the danger to his fellow soldiers, shouted the warning, "Grenade," and unhesitatingly hurled himself towards the grenade to shield his comrades from the explosion. Through his exemplary courage and devotion he saved the lives of his fellow soldiers and gave the members of his platoon the inspiration needed to hold their position. Sgt. Port's selfless concern for his comrades, at the risk of his life above and beyond the call of duty, are in keeping with the highest traditions of the military service and reflect great credit on himself, his unit, and the U.S. Army.
Notes: POW from 12 January 1968—27 November 1968

3336 ◆ *POXON, ROBERT LESLIE

Rank: First Lieutenant
Service: U.S. Army
Birthday: 3 January 1947
Place of Birth: Detroit, Wayne County, Michigan
Date of Death: 2 June 1969
Place of Death: Republic of Vietnam
Cemetery: Forest Lawn Cemetery—Detroit, Michigan
Entered Service at: Detroit, Wayne County, Michigan
Unit: Troop B, 1st Squadron, 9th Cavalry, 1st Cavalry Division
Served as: Platoon Leader
Battle or Place of Action: Tay Ninh Province, Republic of Vietnam
Date of Action: 2 June 1969
G.O. Number, Date: 6, 9 March 1971
Date of Presentation: 16 February 1971
Place of Presentation: The White House (East Ballroom), presented by Pres. Richard M. Nixon to his family
Citation: For conspicuous gallantry and intrepidity in action at the risk of his life above and beyond the call of duty. 1st Lt. Poxon, Armor, Troop B, distinguished himself while serving as a platoon leader on a reconnaissance mission. Landing by helicopter in a area suspected of being occupied by the enemy, the platoon came under intense fire from enemy soldiers in concealed positions and fortifications around the landing zone. A soldier fell, hit by the first burst of fire. 1st

Lt. Poxon dashed to his aid, drawing the majority of the enemy fire as he crossed 20 meters of open ground. The fallen soldier was beyond help and 1st Lt. Poxon was seriously and painfully wounded. 1st Lt. Poxon, with indomitable courage, refused medical aid and evacuation and turned his attention to seizing the initiative from the enemy. With sure instinct he marked a central enemy bunker as the key to success. Quickly instructing his men to concentrate their fire on the bunker, and in spite of his wound, 1st Lt. Poxon crawled toward the bunker, readied a hand grenade, and charged. He was hit again but continued his assault. After succeeding in silencing the enemy guns in the bunker he was struck once again by enemy fire and fell, mortally wounded. 1st Lt. Poxon's comrades followed their leader, pressed the attack, and drove the enemy from their positions. 1st Lt. Poxon's gallantry, indomitable will, and courage are in keeping with the highest traditions of the military service and reflect great credit on himself, his unit, and the U.S. Army.

3337 ◆ *PROM, WILLIAM RAYMOND

Rank: Lance Corporal
Service: U.S. Marine Corps
Birthday: 17 November 1948
Place of Birth: Pittsburgh, Allegheny County, Pennsylvania
Date of Death: 9 February 1969
Place of Death: Republic of Vietnam
Cemetery: Allegheny County Memorial Park (MH)—Pittsburgh, Pennsylvania
Entered Service at: Pittsburgh, Allegheny County, Pennsylvania
Unit: Company I, 3d Battalion, 3d Marines, 3d Marine Division (Rein) FMF
Served as: Squad Leader/Machine Gunner
Battle or Place of Action: near An Hoa, Republic of Vietnam
Date of Action: 9 February 1969
Date of Presentation: 20 April 1970
Place of Presentation: The White House, presented by Vice Pres. Spiro T. Agnew to his family
Citation: For conspicuous gallantry and intrepidity at the risk of his life above and beyond the call of duty while serving as a machine-gun squad leader with Company I, in action against the enemy. While returning from a reconnaissance operation during Operation Taylor Common, two platoons of Company I came under an intense automatic-weapons fire and grenade attack from a well-concealed North Vietnamese Army force in fortified positions. The leading element of the platoon was isolated and several marines were wounded. L/Cpl. Prom immediately assumed control of one of his machine guns and began to deliver return fire. Disregarding his safety he advanced to a position from which he could more effectively deliver covering fire while first aid was administered to the wounded men. Realizing that the enemy would have to be destroyed before the injured marines could be evacuated, L/Cpl. Prom again moved forward and delivered a heavy volume of fire with such accuracy that he was instrumental in routing the enemy, thus permitting his men to regroup and resume their march. Shortly thereafter, the

platoon again came under heavy fire in which one man was critically wounded. Reacting instantly, L/Cpl. Prom moved forward to protect his injured comrade. Unable to continue his fire because of severe wounds, he continued to advance to within a few yards to the enemy positions. There, standing in full view of the enemy, he accurately directed the fire of his support elements until he was mortally wounded. Inspired by his heroic actions, the marines launched an assault that destroyed the enemy. L/Cpl. Prom's indomitable courage, inspiring initiative and selfless devotion to duty upheld the highest traditions of the Marine Corps and the U.S. Naval Service. He gallantly gave his life for his country.

3338 ◆ *PRUDEN, ROBERT JOSEPH

Rank: Staff Sergeant
Service: U.S. Army
Birthday: 9 September 1949
Place of Birth: St.Paul, Ramsey County, Minnesota
Date of Death: 29 November 1969
Place of Death: Republic of Vietnam
Cemetery: Fort Snelling National Cemetery (M-5710) (MH)—Minneapolis, Minnesota
Entered Service at: Minneapolis, Hennepin County, Minnesota
Unit: Company G, 75th Infantry, Americal Division
Served as: Reconnaissance Team Leader
Battle or Place of Action: Quang Ngai Province, Republic of Vietnam
Date of Action: 29 November 1969
G.O. Number, Date: 26, 26 May 1971
Date of Presentation: 22 April 1971
Place of Presentation: The White House, presented by Pres. Richard M. Nixon to his family
Citation: For conspicuous gallantry and intrepidity in action at the risk of his life above and beyond the call of duty. S/Sgt. Pruden, Company G, distinguished himself while serving as a reconnaissance team leader during an ambush mission. The six-man team was inserted by helicopter into enemy-controlled territory to establish an ambush position and to obtain information concerning enemy movements. As the team moved into the preplanned area, S/Sgt. Pruden deployed his men into two groups on the opposite sides of a well-used trail. As the groups were establishing their defensive positions, one member of the team was trapped in the open by the heavy fire from an enemy squad. Realizing that the ambush position had been compromised, S/Sgt. Pruden directed his team to open fire on the enemy force. Immediately, the team came under heavy fire from a second enemy element. S/Sgt. Pruden, with full knowledge of the extreme danger involved, left his concealed position and, firing as he ran, advanced toward the enemy to draw the hostile fire. He was seriously wounded twice but continued his attack until he fell for a third time, in front of the enemy positions. S/Sgt. Pruden's actions resulted in several enemy casualties and withdrawal of the remaining enemy force. Although grievously wounded, he directed his men into defensive positions and called for evacuation helicopters, which safely withdrew the members of the team. S/Sgt. Pruden's outstanding

courage, selfless concern for the welfare of his men, and intrepidity in action at the cost of his life were in keeping with the highest traditions of the military service and reflect great credit upon himself, his unit, and the U.S. Army.

3339 ◆ *RABEL, LASZLO

Rank: Staff Sergeant
Service: U.S. Army
Birthday: 21 September 1937
Place of Birth: Budapest, Hungary
Date of Death: 13 November 1968
Place of Death: Republic of Vietnam
Cemetery: Arlington National Cemetery (52-1326) (MH)—Arlington, Virginia
Entered Service at: Minneapolis, Hennepin County, Minnesota
Unit: Team Delta, 74th Infantry Detachment (Long Range Patrol), 173d Airborne Brigade
Served as: Team Leader
Battle or Place of Action: Binh Dinh Province, Republic of Vietnam
Date of Action: 13 November 1968
G.O. Number, Date: 6, 23 April 1970
Date of Presentation: 7 April 1970
Place of Presentation: The White House, presented by Pres. Richard M. Nixon to his family
Citation: For conspicuous gallantry and intrepidity in action at the risk of his life above and beyond the call of duty. S/Sgt. Rabel distinguished himself while serving as leader of Team Delta, 74th Infantry Detachment. At 1000 hours on this date, Team Delta was in a defensive perimeter conducting reconnaissance of enemy trail networks when a member of the team detected enemy movement to the front. As S/Sgt. Rabel and a comrade prepared to clear the area, he heard an incoming grenade as it landed in the midst of the team's perimeter. With complete disregard for his life, S/Sgt. Rabel threw himself on the grenade and, covering it with his body, received the complete impact of the immediate explosion. Through his indomitable courage, complete disregard for his safety, and profound concern for his fellow soldiers, S/Sgt. Rabel averted the loss of life and injury to the other members of Team Delta. By his gallantry at the cost of his life in the highest traditions of the military service, S/Sgt. Rabel has reflected great credit upon himself, his unit, and the U.S. Army.

3340 ◆ *RAY, DAVID ROBERT

Rank: Hospital Corpsman Second Class
Service: U.S. Navy
Birthday: 14 February 1945
Place of Birth: McMinnville, Warren County, Tennessee
Date of Death: 19 March 1969
Place of Death: Republic of Vietnam
Cemetery: Mountain View Cemetery—McMinnville, Tennessee
Entered Service at: Nashville, Davidson County, Tennessee
Unit: Battery D, 2d Battalion, 11th Marines, 1st Marine Division

Served as: Medical Corpsman
Battle or Place of Action: Phu Loc 6, near An Hoa, Quang Nam Province, Republic of Vietnam
Date of Action: 19 March 1969
Date of Presentation: 20 April 1970
Place of Presentation: The White House, presented by Vice Pres. Spiro T. Agnew to his family
Citation: For conspicuous gallantry and intrepidity at the risk of his life above and beyond the call of duty while serving as a HC2c. with Battery D, 2d Battalion, at Phu Loc 6, near An Hoa. During the early morning hours, an estimated battalion-size enemy force launched a determined assault against the battery's position, and succeeded in effecting a penetration of the barbed-wire perimeter. The initial burst of enemy fire caused numerous casualties among the marines who had immediately manned their howitzers during the rocket and mortar attack. Undaunted by the intense hostile fire, HC2c. Ray moved from parapet to parapet, rendering emergency medical treatment to the wounded. Although seriously wounded himself while administering first aid to a marine casualty, he refused medical aid and continued his lifesaving efforts. While he was bandaging and attempting to comfort another wounded marine, HC2c. Ray was forced to battle two enemy soldiers who attacked his position, personally killing one and wounding the other. Rapidly losing his strength as a result of his severe wounds, he nonetheless managed to move through the hail of enemy fire to other casualties. Once again, he was faced with the intense fire of oncoming enemy troops and, despite the grave personal danger and insurmountable odds, succeeded in treating the wounded and holding off the enemy until he ran out of ammunition, at which time he sustained fatal wounds. HC2c. Ray's final act of heroism was to protect the patient he was treating. He threw himself upon the wounded marine, thus saving the man's life when an enemy grenade exploded nearby. By his determined and persevering actions, courageous spirit, and selfless devotion to the welfare of his marine comrades, HC2c. Ray served to inspire the men of Battery D to heroic efforts in defeating the enemy. His conduct throughout was in keeping with the finest traditions of the U.S. Naval Service.

3341 ◆ RAY, RONALD ERIC

Rank: Captain (rank at time of action: First Lieutenant) (highest rank: Lieutenant Colonel)
Service: U.S. Army
Birthday: 7 December 1941
Place of Birth: Cordele, Crisp County, Georgia
Entered Service at: Atlanta, Fulton County, Georgia
Unit: Company A, 2d Battalion, 35th Infantry, 25th Infantry Division
Served as: Platoon Leader
Battle or Place of Action: Ia Drang Valley, Republic of Vietnam
Date of Action: 19 June 1966
G.O. Number, Date: 31, 5 June 1970
Date of Presentation: 14 May 1970
Place of Presentation: The White House, presented by Pres. Richard M. Nixon

Citation: For conspicuous gallantry and intrepidity in action at the risk of his life above and beyond the call of duty. Capt. Ray distinguished himself while serving as a platoon leader with Company A. When one of his ambush patrols was attacked by an estimated reinforced Viet Cong company, Capt. Ray organized a reaction force and quickly moved through two kilometers of mountainous jungle terrain to the contact area. After breaking through the hostile lines to reach the beleaguered patrol, Capt. Ray began directing the reinforcement of the site. When an enemy position pinned down three of his men with a heavy volume of automatic-weapons fire, he silenced the emplacement with a grenade and killed four Viet Cong with his rifle fire. As medics were moving a casualty toward a sheltered position, they began receiving intense hostile fire. While directing suppressive fire on the enemy position, Capt. Ray moved close enough to silence the enemy with a grenade. A few moments later Capt. Ray saw an enemy grenade land, unnoticed, near two of his men. Without hesitation or regard for his safety he dove between the grenade and the men, thus shielding them from the explosion while receiving wounds in his exposed feet and legs. He immediately sustained additional wounds in his legs from an enemy machine gun, but nevertheless he silenced the emplacement with another grenade. Although suffering great pain from his wounds, Capt. Ray continued to direct his men, providing the outstanding courage and leadership they vitally needed, and prevented their annihilation by successfully leading them from their surrounded position. Only after assuring that his platoon was no longer in immediate danger did he allow himself to be evacuated for medical treatment. By his gallantry at the risk of his life in the highest traditions of the military service, Capt. Ray has reflected great credit upon himself, his unit, and the U.S. Army.

3342 ◆ *REASONER, FRANK STANLEY

Rank: First Lieutenant
Service: U.S. Marine Corps
Birthday: 16 September 1937
Place of Birth: Spokane, Spokane County, Washington
Date of Death: 12 July 1965
Place of Death: Republic of Vietnam
Cemetery: Greenwood Cemetery (MH)—Kellogg, Idaho
Entered Service at: Kellogg, Shoshone County, Idaho
Unit: Company A, 3d Reconnaissance Battalion, 3d Marine Division (Rein) FMF
Served as: Commanding Officer
Battle or Place of Action: near Da Nang, Republic of Vietnam
Date of Action: 12 July 1965
Date of Presentation: 31 January 1967
Place of Presentation: The Pentagon, presented by the Sec. of the Navy Paul H. Nitze to his family
Citation: For conspicuous gallantry and intrepidity at the risk of his life above and beyond the call of duty. The reconnaissance patrol led by 1st Lt. Reasoner had deeply penetrated heavily controlled enemy territory when it came under extremely heavy fire from an estimated 50 to 100 Viet Cong insurgents. Accompanying the advance party and the point

that consisted of five men, he immediately deployed his men for an assault after the Viet Cong had opened fire from numerous concealed positions. Boldly shouting encouragement, and virtually isolated from the main body, he organized a base of fire for an assault on the enemy positions. The slashing fury of the Viet Cong machine-gun and automatic-weapons fire made it impossible for the main body to move forward. Repeatedly exposing himself to the devastating attack he skillfully provided covering fire, killing at least two Viet Cong and effectively silencing an automatic-weapons position in a valiant attempt to effect evacuation of a wounded man. As casualties began to mount his radio operator was wounded and 1st Lt. Reasoner immediately moved to his side and tended his wounds. When the radio operator was hit a second time while attempting to reach a covered position, 1st Lt. Reasoner courageously running to his aid through the grazing machine-gun fire fell mortally wounded. His indomitable fighting spirit, valiant leadership, and unflinching devotion to duty provided the inspiration that was to enable the patrol to complete its mission without further casualties. In the face of almost certain death he gallantly gave his life in the service of his country. His actions upheld the highest traditions of the Marine Corps and the U.S. Naval Service.

3343 ◆ *ROARK, ANUND CHARLES

Rank: Sergeant
Service: U.S. Army
Birthday: 17 February 1948
Place of Birth: Vallejo, Solano County, California
Date of Death: 16 May 1968
Place of Death: Republic of Vietnam
Cemetery: Fort Rosecrans National Cemetery (0-1855) (MH)—San Diego, California
Entered Service at: Los Angeles, Los Angeles County, California
Unit: Company C, 1st Battalion, 12th Infantry, 4th Infantry Division
Served as: Squad Leader
Battle or Place of Action: Kontum Province, Republic of Vietnam
Date of Action: 16 May 1968
G.O. Number, Date: 25, 23 April 1970
Date of Presentation: 7 April 1970
Place of Presentation: The White House, presented by Pres. Richard M. Nixon to his family
Citation: For conspicuous gallantry and intrepidity in action at the risk of his life above and beyond the call of duty. Sgt. Roark distinguished himself by extraordinary gallantry while serving with Company C. Sgt. Roark was the point squad leader of a small force which had the mission of rescuing 11 men in a hilltop observation post under heavy attack by a company-size force, approximately 1,000 meters from the battalion perimeter. As lead elements of the relief force reached the besieged observation post, intense automatic-weapons fire from enemy-occupied bunkers halted their movement. Without hesitation, Sgt. Roark maneuvered his squad, repeatedly exposing himself to withering enemy fire to hurl grenades and direct the fire of his squad to gain fire

superiority and cover the withdrawal of the outpost and evacuation of its casualties. Frustrated in their effort to overrun the position, the enemy swept the hilltop with small arms and volleys of grenades. Seeing a grenade land in the midst of his men, Sgt. Roark, with complete disregard for his safety, hurled himself upon the grenade, absorbing its blast with his body. Sgt. Roark's magnificent leadership and dauntless courage saved the lives of many of his comrades and were the inspiration for the successful relief of the outpost. His actions which culminated in the supreme sacrifice of his life were in keeping with the highest traditions of the military service, and reflect great credit on himself and the U.S. Army.

3344 ◆ ROBERTS, GORDON RAY

Rank: Sergeant (rank at time of action: Specialist Fourth Class) (highest rank: Master Sergeant)
Service: U.S. Army
Birthday: 14 June 1950
Place of Birth: Middletown, Butler County, Ohio
Entered Service at: Cincinnati, Hamilton County, Ohio
Unit: Company B, 1st Battalion, 506th Infantry, 101st Airborne Division (Airmobile)
Served as: Rifleman
Battle or Place of Action: Thua Thien Province, Republic of Vietnam
Date of Action: 11 July 1969
G.O. Number, Date: 20, 24 March 1971
Date of Presentation: 2 March 1971
Place of Presentation: The White House (East Ballroom), presented by Pres. Richard M. Nixon
Citation: For conspicuous gallantry and intrepidity in action at the risk of his life above and beyond the call of duty. Sgt. Roberts distinguished himself while serving as a rifleman with Company B, during combat operations. Sgt. Roberts' platoon was maneuvering along a ridge to attack heavily fortified enemy bunker positions which had pinned down an adjoining friendly company. As the platoon approached the enemy positions, it was suddenly pinned down by heavy automatic-weapons and grenade fire from camouflaged enemy fortifications atop the overlooking hill. Seeing his platoon immobilized and in danger of failing in its mission, Sgt. Roberts crawled rapidly toward the closest enemy bunker. With complete disregard for his safety, he leaped to his feet and charged the bunker, firing as he ran. Despite the intense enemy fire directed at him, Sgt. Roberts silenced the two-man bunker. Without hesitation, Sgt. Roberts continued his one-man assault on a second bunker. As he neared the second bunker, a burst of enemy fire knocked his rifle from his hands. Sgt. Roberts picked up a rifle dropped by a comrade and continued his assault, silencing the bunker. He continued his charge against a third bunker and destroyed it with well-thrown hand grenades. Although Sgt. Roberts was now cut off from his platoon, he continued his assault against a fourth enemy emplacement. He fought through a heavy hail of fire to join elements of an adjoining company which had been pinned down by the enemy fire. Although continually exposed to hostile fire, he assisted in moving wounded personnel from exposed positions on the hilltop to an evacuation

area before returning to his unit. By his gallant and selfless actions, Sgt. Roberts contributed directly in saving the lives of his comrades and served as an inspiration to his fellow soldiers in the defeat of the enemy force. Sgt. Roberts' extraordinary heroism in action at the risk of his life were in keeping with the highest traditions of the military service and reflect great credit upon himself, his unit, and the U.S. Army.

3345 ◆ *ROBINSON JR., JAMES WILLIAM

Rank: Sergeant
Service: U.S. Army
Birthday: 30 August 1940
Place of Birth: Hinsdale, Du Page County, Illinois
Date of Death: 11 April 1966
Place of Death: Republic of Vietnam
Cemetery: Clarendon Hills Cemetery (MH)—Westmont, Illinois
Entered Service at: Chicago, Cook County, Illinois
Unit: Company D, 2d Battalion, 16th Infantry, 1st Infantry Division
Served as: Fire Team Leader
Battle or Place of Action: Republic of Vietnam
Date of Action: 11 April 1966
G.O. Number, Date: 35, 13 September 1967
Date of Presentation: 16 July 1967
Place of Presentation: The Pentagon, presented by Sec. of the Army Stanley R. Resor to his family
Citation: For conspicuous gallantry and intrepidity in action at the risk of his life above and beyond the call of duty. Company C was engaged in fierce combat with a Viet Cong battalion. Despite the heavy fire, Sgt. Robinson moved among the men of his fire team, instructing and inspiring them, and placing them in advantageous positions. Enemy snipers located in nearby trees were inflicting heavy casualties on forward elements of Sgt. Robinson's unit. Upon locating the enemy sniper whose fire was taking the heaviest toll, he took a grenade launcher and eliminated the sniper. Seeing a medic hit while administering aid to a wounded sergeant in front of his position and aware that now the two wounded men were at the mercy of the enemy, he charged through a withering hail of fire and dragged his comrades to safety, where he rendered first aid and saved their lives. As the battle continued and casualties mounted, Sgt. Robinson moved about under intense fire to collect from the wounded their weapons and ammunition and redistribute them to able-bodied soldiers. Adding his fire to that of his men, he assisted in eliminating a major enemy threat. Seeing another wounded comrade in front of his position, Sgt. Robinson again defied the enemy's fire to effect a rescue. In so doing he was himself wounded in the shoulder and leg. Despite his painful wounds, he dragged the soldier to shelter and saved his life by administering first aid. While patching his own wounds, he spotted an enemy machine gun which had inflicted a number of casualties on the American force. His rifle ammunition expended, he seized two grenades and, in an act of unsurpassed heroism, charged toward the entrenched enemy weapon. Hit again in the leg, this time with a tracer round which set fire to his clothing, Sgt. Robinson ripped the burning clothing from his body and staggered indomitably through the enemy fire, now concentrated solely on him, to within grenade range of the enemy machine-gun position. Sustaining two additional chest wounds, he marshalled his fleeting physical strength and hurled the two grenades, thus destroying the enemy gun position, as he fell dead upon the battlefield. His magnificent display of leadership and bravery saved several lives and inspired his soldiers to defeat the numerically superior enemy force. Sgt. Robinson's conspicuous gallantry and intrepidity, at the cost of his life, are in keeping with the finest traditions of the U.S. Army and reflect great credit upon the 1st Infantry Division and the U.S. Armed Forces.

3346 ◆ ROCCO, LOUIS RICHARD

Rank: Warrant Officer (rank at time of action: Sergeant First Class) (highest rank: Chief Warrant Officer 2)
Service: U.S. Army
Birthday: 19 November 1938
Place of Birth: Albuquerque, Bernalillo County, New Mexico
Entered Service at: Los Angeles, Los Angeles County, California
Unit: U.S. Military Assistance Command, Advisory Team 162
Served as: Medical Advisor
Battle or Place of Action: Northeast of Katum, Republic of Vietnam
Date of Action: 24 May 1970
G.O. Number, Date: 1, 3 January 1975
Date of Presentation: 12 December 1974
Place of Presentation: The White House, presented by Pres. Gerald R. Ford
Citation: WO Rocco distinguished himself when he volunteered to accompany a medical evacuation team on an urgent mission to evacuate eight critically wounded Army of the Republic of Vietnam personnel. As the helicopter approached the landing zone, it became the target for intense enemy automatic-weapons fire. Disregarding his own safety, WO Rocco identified and placed accurate suppressive fire on the enemy positions as the aircraft descended toward the landing zone. Sustaining major damage from the enemy fire, the aircraft was forced to crash land, causing WO Rocco to sustain a fractured wrist and hip and severely bruised back. Ignoring his injuries, he extracted the survivors from the burning wreckage, sustaining burns to his own body. Despite intense enemy fire, WO Rocco carried each unconscious man across approximately 20 meters of exposed terrain to the Army of the Republic of Vietnam perimeter. On each trip, his severely burned hands and broken wrist caused excruciating pain, but the lives of the unconscious crash survivors were more important than his personal discomfort, and he continued his rescue efforts. Once inside the friendly position, WO Rocco helped administer first aid to his wounded comrades until his wounds and burns caused him to collapse and lose consciousness. His bravery under fire and intense devotion to duty were directly responsible for saving three of his fellow soldiers from certain death. His unparalleled bravery in the face of enemy fire, his complete disregard for his own pain and injuries, and his per-

formance were far above and beyond the call of duty and were in keeping with the highest traditions of self-sacrifice and courage of the military service.

3347 ◆ ROGERS, CHARLES CALVIN

Rank: Lieutenant Colonel (highest rank: Major General)
Service: U.S. Army
Birthday: 6 September 1929
Place of Birth: Claremont, West Virginia
Date of Death: 21 September 1990
Place of Death: Munich, Germany
Cemetery: Arlington National Cemetery (7-A-99) (MH)—Arlington, Virginia
Entered Service at: Institute, Kanawha County, West Virginia
Unit: 1st Battalion, 5th Artillery, 1st Infantry Division
Served as: Battalion Commander
Battle or Place of Action: Fishhook near Cambodian border, Republic of Vietnam
Date of Action: 1 November 1968
G.O. Number, Date: 29, 5 June 1970
Date of Presentation: 14 May 1970
Place of Presentation: The White House, presented by Pres. Richard M. Nixon
Citation: For conspicuous gallantry and intrepidity in action at the risk of his life above and beyond the call of duty. Lt. Col. Rogers, Field Artillery, distinguished himself in action while serving as commanding officer, 1st Battalion, during the defense of a forward fire support base. In the early morning hours, the fire support base was subjected to a concentrated bombardment of heavy mortar, rocket, and rocket-propelled grenade fire. Simultaneously the position was struck by a human wave ground assault, led by sappers who breached the defensive barriers with bangalore torpedoes and penetrated the defensive perimeter. Lt. Col. Rogers with complete disregard for his safety moved through the hail of fragments from bursting enemy rounds to the embattled area. He aggressively rallied the dazed artillery crewmen to man their howitzers and he directed their fire on the assaulting enemy. Although knocked to the ground and wounded by an exploding round, Lt. Col. Rogers sprang to his feet and led a small counterattack force against an enemy element that had penetrated the howitzer position. Although painfully wounded a second time during the assault, Lt. Col. Rogers pressed the attack killing several of the enemy and driving the remainder from their positions. Refusing medical treatment, Lt. Col. Rogers reestablished and reinforced the defensive positions. As a second human wave attack was launched against another sector of the perimeter, Lt. Col. Rogers directed artillery fire on the assaulting enemy and led a second counterattack against the charging forces. His valorous example rallied the beleaguered defenders to repulse and defeat the enemy onslaught. Lt. Col. Rogers moved from position to position through the heavy enemy fire, giving encouragement and direction to his men. At dawn the determined enemy launched a third assault against the fire base in an attempt to overrun the position. Lt. Col. Rogers moved to the threatened area and directed lethal fire on the enemy f orces. Seeing a howitzer inoperative due to casualties, Lt. Col. Rogers joined the surviving members of the crew to return the howitzer to action. While directing the position defense, Lt. Col. Rogers was seriously wounded by fragments from a heavy mortar round which exploded on the parapet of the gun position. Although too severely wounded to physically lead the defenders, Lt. Col. Rogers continued to give encouragement and direction to his men in the defeating and repelling of the enemy attack. Lt. Col. Rogers' dauntless courage and heroism inspired the defenders of the fire support base to the heights of valor to defeat a determined and numerically superior enemy force. His relentless spirit of aggressiveness in action are in the highest traditions of the military service and reflect great credit upon himself, his unit, and the U.S. Army.

3348 ◆ *RUBIO, EURIPIDES

Rank: Captain
Service: U.S. Army
Birthday: 1 March 1938
Place of Birth: Ponce, Ponce County, Puerto Rico
Date of Death: 8 November 1966
Place of Death: Republic of Vietnam
Cemetery: Puerto Rico National Cemetery (HSA-5) (MH)—Bayamon, Puerto Rico
Entered Service at: Fort Buchanan, San Juan County, Puerto Rico
Unit: Headquarters & Headquarters Company, 1st Battalion, 28th Infantry, 1st Infantry Division
Served as: Communications Officer
Battle or Place of Action: Tay Ninh Province, Republic of Vietnam
Date of Action: 8 November 1966
G.O. Number, Date: 39, 2 August 1968
Date of Presentation: 11 July 1968
Place of Presentation: The Pentagon, presented by Sec. of the Army Stanley R. Resor to his family
Citation: For conspicuous gallantry and intrepidity in action at the risk of his life above and beyond the call of duty. Capt. Rubio, Infantry, was serving as communications officer, 1st Battalion, when a numerically superior enemy force launched a massive attack against the battalion defense position. Intense enemy machine-gun fire raked the area while mortar rounds and rifle grenades exploded within the perimeter. Leaving the relative safety of his post, Capt. Rubio received two serious wounds as he braved the withering fire to go to the area of most intense action where he distributed ammunition, reestablished positions, and rendered aid to the wounded. Disregarding the painful wounds, he unhesitatingly assumed command when a rifle company commander was medically evacuated. Capt. Rubio was wounded a third time as he selflessly exposed himself to the devastating enemy fire to move among his men to encourage them to fight with renewed effort. While aiding the evacuation of wounded personnel, he noted that a smoke grenade which was intended to mark the Viet Cong position for air strikes had fallen dangerously close to the friendly lines. Capt. Rubio ran to reposition the grenade but was immediately struck to his knees by enemy

fire. Despite his several wounds, Capt. Rubio scooped up the grenade, ran through the deadly hail of fire to within 20 meters of the enemy position and hurled the already smoking grenade into the midst of the enemy before he fell for the final time. Using the reposition grenade as a marker, friendly air strikes were directed to destroy the hostile positions. Capt. Rubio's singularly heroic act turned the tide of battle, and his extraordinary leadership and valor were a magnificent inspiration to his men. His remarkable bravery and selfless concern for his men are in keeping with the highest traditions of the military service and reflect great credit on Capt. Rubio and the U.S. Army.

3349 ◆ *SANTIAGO-COLON, HECTOR

Rank: Specialist Fourth Class
Service: U.S. Army
Birthday: 20 December 1942
Place of Birth: Salinas, Salinas County, Puerto Rico
Date of Death: 28 June 1968
Place of Death: Republic of Vietnam
Cemetery: Salinas Municipal Cemetery (MH)—Salinas, Puerto Rico
Entered Service at: New York, New York
Unit: Company B, 5th Battalion, 7th Cavalry, 1st Cavalry Division (Airmobile)
Served as: Gunner in Mortar Platoon
Battle or Place of Action: Quang Tri Province, Republic of Vietnam
Date of Action: 28 June 1968
G.O. Number, Date: 24, 23 April 1970
Date of Presentation: 7 April 1970
Place of Presentation: The White House, presented by Pres. Richard M. Nixon to his family
Citation: For conspicuous gallantry and intrepidity in action at the risk of his life above and beyond the call of duty. Sp4c. Santiago-Colon distinguished himself at the cost of his life while serving as a gunner in the mortar platoon of Company B. While serving as a perimeter sentry, Sp4c. Santiago-Colon heard distinct movement in the heavily wooded area to his front and flanks. Immediately he alerted his fellow sentries in the area to move to their foxholes and remain alert for any enemy probing forces. From the wooded area around his position heavy enemy automatic-weapons and small-arms fire suddenly broke out, but extreme darkness rendered difficult the precise location and identification of the hostile force. Only the muzzle flashes from the enemy weapons indicated their positions. Sp4c. Santiago-Colon and the other members of his platoon immediately began to repel the attackers, utilizing hand grenades, antipersonnel mines and small-arms fire. Due to the heavy volume of enemy fire and exploding grenades around them, a North Vietnamese soldier was able to crawl, undetected, to their position. Suddenly, the enemy soldier lobbed a hand grenade into Sp4c. Santiago-Colon's foxhole. Realizing that there was no time to throw the grenade out of his position, Sp4c. Santiago-Colon retrieved the grenade, tucked it into his stomach and, turning away from his comrades, absorbed the full impact of the blast. His heroic self-sacrifice saved the lives of those who occupied the foxhole with him, and provided them with the inspiration to continue fighting until they had forced the enemy to retreat from the perimeter. By his gallantry at the cost of his life and in the highest traditions of the military service, Sp4c. Santiago-Colon has reflected great credit upon himself, his unit, and the U.S. Army.

3350 ◆ *SARGENT, RUPPERT LEON

Rank: First Lieutenant
Service: U.S. Army
Birthday: 6 January 1938
Place of Birth: Hampton, Hampton County, Virginia
Date of Death: 15 March 1967
Place of Death: Republic of Vietnam
Cemetery: Hampton National Cemetery (F-17596) (MH)—Hampton Virginia,
Entered Service at: Richmond, Richmond County, Virginia
Unit: Company B, 4th Battalion, 9th Infantry, 25th Infantry Division
Served as: Platoon Leader
Battle or Place of Action: Hau Nghia Province, Republic of Vietnam
Date of Action: 15 March 1967
G.O. Number, Date: 25, 17 April 1969
Date of Presentation: 10 March 1969
Place of Presentation: At Widow's home, Hampton, Va., presented by Gen. Donley P. Bolton
Citation: For conspicuous gallantry and intrepidity in action at the risk of his life above and beyond the call of duty. While leading a platoon of Company B, 1st Lt. Sargent was investigating a reported Viet Cong meetinghouse and weapons cache. A tunnel entrance which 1st Lt. Sargent observed was booby-trapped. He tried to destroy the booby trap and blow the cover from the tunnel using hand grenades, but this attempt was not successful. He and his demolition man moved in to destroy the booby trap and cover which flushed a Viet Cong soldier from the tunnel, who was immediately killed by the nearby platoon sergeant. First Lt. Sargent, the platoon sergeant, and a forward observer moved toward the tunnel entrance. As they approached, another Viet Cong emerged and threw two hand grenades that landed in the midst of the group. First Lt. Sargent fired three shots at the enemy then turned and unhesitatingly threw himself over the two grenades. He was mortally wounded, and his two companions were lightly wounded when the grenades exploded. By his courageous and selfless act of exceptional heroism, he saved the lives of the platoon sergeant and forward observer and prevented the injury or death of several other nearby comrades. First Lt. Sargent's actions were in keeping with the highest traditions of the military service and reflect great credit upon himself and the U.S. Army.

3351 ◆ SASSER, CLARENCE EUGENE

Rank: Specialist Fifth Class (rank at time of action: Private First Class)
Service: U.S. Army
Birthday: 12 September 1947

Place of Birth: Chenango, Texas
Entered Service at: Houston, Harris County, Texas
Unit: Headquarters & Headquarters Company, 3d Battalion, 60th Infantry, 9th Infantry Division
Served as: Medical Aidman
Battle or Place of Action: Ding Tuong Province, Republic of Vietnam
Date of Action: 10 January 1968
G.O. Number, Date: 26, 17 April 1969
Date of Presentation: 7 March 1969
Place of Presentation: The White House, presented by Pres. Richard M. Nixon
Citation: For conspicuous gallantry and intrepidity in action at the risk of his life above and beyond the call of duty. Sp5c. Sasser distinguished himself while assigned to Headquarters and Headquarters Company, 3d Battalion. He was serving as a medical aidman with Company A, 3d Battalion, on a reconnaissance-in-force operation. His company was making an air assault when suddenly it was taken under heavy small-arms, recoilless-rifle, machine-gun, and rocket fire from well-fortified enemy positions on three sides of the landing zone. During the first few minutes, over 30 casualties were sustained. Without hesitation, Sp5c. Sasser ran across an open rice paddy through a hail of fire to assist the wounded. After helping one man to safety, he was painfully wounded in the left shoulder by fragments of an exploding rocket. Refusing medical attention, he ran through a barrage of rocket and automatic-weapons fire to aid casualties of the initial attack and, after giving them urgently needed treatment, continued to search for other wounded. Despite two additional wounds immobilizing his legs, he dragged himself through the mud toward another soldier 100 meters away. Although in agonizing pain and faint from loss of blood, Sp5c. Sasser reached the man, treated him, and proceeded on to encourage another group of soldiers to crawl 200 meters to relative safety. There he attended their wounds for five hours until they were evacuated. Sp5c. Sasser's extraordinary heroism is in keeping with the highest traditions of the military service and reflect great credit upon himself, his unit, and the U.S. Army.

3352 ◆ *SEAY, WILLIAM WAYNE

Rank: Sergeant
Service: U.S. Army
Birthday: 24 October 1948
Place of Birth: Brewton, Escambia County, Alabama
Date of Death: 25 August 1968
Place of Death: Republic of Vietnam
Cemetery: Weaver Cemetery—Brewton, Alabama
Entered Service at: Montgomery, Montgomery County, Alabama
Unit: 62d Transportation Company (Medium Truck), 7th Transportation Battalion, 48th Transportation Group
Served as: Driver
Battle or Place of Action: near Ap Nhi, Republic of Vietnam
Date of Action: 25 August 1968
G.O. Number, Date: 12, 23 April 1970
Date of Presentation: 7 April 1970

Place of Presentation: The White House, presented by Pres. Richard M. Nixon to his family
Citation: For conspicuous gallantry and intrepidity in action at the risk of his life above and beyond the call of duty. Sgt. Seay distinguished himself while serving as a driver with the 62d Transportation Company, on a resupply mission. The convoy with which he was traveling, carrying critically needed ammunition and supplies from Long Binh to Tay Ninh, was ambushed by a reinforced battalion of the North Vietnamese Army. As the main elements of the convoy entered the ambush killing zone, they were struck by intense rocket, machine-gun, and automatic-weapons fire from the well-concealed and entrenched enemy force. When his convoy was forced to stop, Sgt. Seay immediately dismounted and took a defensive position behind the wheels of a vehicle loaded with high-explosive ammunition. As the violent North Vietnamese assault approached to within 10 meters of the road, Sgt. Seay opened fire, killing two of the enemy. He then spotted a sniper in a tree approximately 75 meters to his front and killed him. When an enemy grenade was thrown under an ammunition trailer near his position, without regard for his own safety he left his protective cover, exposing himself to intense enemy fire, picked up the grenade, and threw it back to the North Vietnamese position, killing four more of the enemy and saving the lives of the men around him. Another enemy grenade landed approximately three meters from Sgt. Seay's position. Again Sgt. Seay left his covered position and threw the armed grenade back upon the assaulting enemy. After returning to his position he was painfully wounded in the right wrist, however, Sgt. Seay continued to give encouragement and direction to his fellow soldiers. After moving to the relative cover of a shallow ditch, he detected three enemy soldiers who had penetrated the position and were preparing to fire on his comrades. Although weak from loss of blood and with his right hand immobilized, Sgt. Seay stood up and fired his rifle with his left hand, killing all three and saving the lives of the other men in his location. As a result of his heroic action, Sgt. Seay was mortally wounded by a sniper's bullet. Sgt. Seay, by his gallantry in action at the cost of his life, has reflected great credit upon himself, his unit, and the U.S. Army.

3353 ◆ *SHEA, DANIEL JOHN

Rank: Private First Class
Service: U.S. Army
Birthday: 29 January 1947
Place of Birth: Norwalk, Fairfield County, Connecticut
Date of Death: 14 May 1969
Place of Death: Republic of Vietnam
Cemetery: Saint John's Cemetery (MH)—Norwalk, Connecticut
Entered Service at: New Haven, New Haven County, Connecticut
Unit: Headquarters Company, 3d Battalion, 21st Infantry, 196th Infantry Brigade, Americal Division
Served as: Medical Aidman
Battle or Place of Action: Quang Tri Province, Republic of Vietnam

Date of Action: 14 May 1969
G.O. Number, Date: 13, 9 March 1971
Date of Presentation: 16 February 1971
Place of Presentation: The White House, presented by Pres. Richard M. Nixon presented to his family
Citation: For conspicuous gallantry and intrepidity in action at the risk of his life above and beyond the call of duty. Pfc. Shea, Headquarters and Headquarters Company, 3d Battalion, distinguished himself while serving as a medical aidman with Company C, 3d Battalion, during a combat patrol mission. As the lead platoon of the company was crossing a rice paddy, a large enemy force in ambush positions opened fire with mortars, grenades, and automatic weapons. Under heavy crossfire from three sides, the platoon withdrew to a small island in the paddy to establish a defensive perimeter. Pfc. Shea, seeing that a number of his comrades had fallen in the initial hail of fire, dashed from the defensive position to assist the wounded. With complete disregard for his safety and braving the intense hostile fire sweeping the open rice paddy, Pfc. Shea made four trips to tend wounded soldiers and to carry them to the safety of the platoon position. Seeing a fifth wounded comrade directly in front of one of the enemy strong points, Pfc. Shea ran to his assistance. As he reached the wounded man, Pfc. Shea was grievously wounded. Disregarding his welfare, Pfc. Shea tended his wounded comrade and began to move him back to the safety of the defensive perimeter. As he neared the platoon position, Pfc. Shea was mortally wounded by a burst of enemy fire. By his heroic actions Pfc. Shea saved the lives of several of his fellow soldiers. Pfc. Shea's gallantry in action at the cost of his life were in keeping with the highest traditions of the military service and reflect great credit upon himself, his unit, and the U.S. Army.

3354 ◆ *SHIELDS, MARVIN GLEN

Rank: Construction Mechanic Third Class
Service: U.S. Navy
Birthday: 30 December 1939
Place of Birth: Port Townsend, Jefferson County, Washington
Date of Death: 10 June 1965
Place of Death: Republic of Vietnam
Cemetery: Gardiner Cemetery (MH)—Gardiner, Washington
Entered Service at: Seattle, King County, Washington
Unit: Seabee Team 1104, Mobile Construction Battalion 11
Served as: Seabee
Battle or Place of Action: Dong Xoai, Republic of Vietnam
Date of Action: 10 June 1965
Date of Presentation: 13 September 1966
Place of Presentation: The White House, presented by Pres. Lyndon B. Johnson to his family
Citation: For conspicuous gallantry and intrepidity at the risk of his life above and beyond the call of duty. Although wounded when the compound of Detachment A-342, 5th Special Forces Group (Airborne), 1st Special Forces, came under intense fire from an estimated reinforced Viet Cong regiment employing machine guns, heavy weapons, and small

arms, Shields continued to resupply his fellow Americans who needed ammunition and to return the enemy fire for a period of approximately three hours, at which time the Viet Cong launched a massive attack at close-range with flamethrowers, hand grenades and small-arms fire. Wounded a second time during this attack, Shields nevertheless assisted in carrying a more critically wounded man to safety, and then resumed firing at the enemy for four more hours. When the commander asked for a volunteer to accompany him in an attempt to knock out an enemy machine-gun emplacement which was endangering the lives of all personnel in the compound because of the accuracy of its fire, Shields unhesitatingly volunteered for this extremely hazardous mission. Proceeding toward their objective with a 3.5-inch rocket launcher, they succeeded in destroying the enemy machine-gun emplacement, thus undoubtedly saving the lives of many of their fellow servicemen in the compound. Shields was mortally wounded by hostile fire while returning to his defensive position. His heroic initiative and great personal valor in the face of intense enemy fire sustain and enhance the finest traditions of the U.S. Naval Service.

3355 ◆ *SIJAN, LANCE PETER

Rank: Captain
Service: U.S. Air Force
Birthday: 13 April 1942
Place of Birth: Milwaukee, Milwaukee County, Wisconsin
Date of Death: 22 January 1968
Place of Death: Hoa Lo Prison, Hanoi, North Vietnam
Cemetery: Arlington Park Cemetery (MH)—Milwaukee, Wisconsin
Entered Service at: Milwaukee, Milwaukee County, Wisconsin
Unit: 480th Tactical Fighter Squadron, Da Nang AFB, Republic of Vietnam
Served as: Pilot of an F-4C Aircraft
Battle or Place of Action: Ban Loboy Ford, Laos and Ban Kari Pass & Hoa Lo Prison, North Vietnam
Date of Action: 9 November 1967
G.O. Number, Date: GB-181, 23 March 1976
Date of Presentation: 6 March 1976
Place of Presentation: The White House, presented by Pres. Gerald R. Ford to his family
Citation: While on a flight over North Vietnam, Capt. Sijan ejected from his disabled aircraft and successfully evaded capture for more than six weeks. During this time, he was seriously injured and suffered from shock and extreme weight loss due to lack of food. After being captured by North Vietnamese soldiers, Capt. Sijan was taken to a holding point for subsequent transfer to a prisoner-of-war camp. In his emaciated and crippled condition, he overpowered one of his guards and crawled into the jungle, only to be recaptured after several hours. He was then transferred to another prison camp where he was kept in solitary confinement and interrogated at length. During interrogation, he was severely tortured; however, he did not divulge any information to his captors. Capt. Sijan lapsed into delirium and was placed in the care of another prisoner. During his intermittent periods of

consciousness until his death, he never complained of his physical condition and, on several occasions, spoke of future escape attempts. Capt. Sijan's extraordinary heroism and intrepidity above and beyond the call of duty at the cost of his life are in keeping with the highest traditions of the U.S. Air Force and reflect great credit upon himself and the U.S. Armed Forces.

Notes: POW from 9 November 1967—22 January 1968

3356 ◆ *SIMS, CLIFFORD CHESTER

Rank: Staff Sergeant
Service: U.S. Army
Birthday: 18 June 1942
Place of Birth: Port St. Joe, Gulf County, Florida
Date of Death: 21 February 1968
Place of Death: Republic of Vietnam
Cemetery: Barrancas National Cemetery (29-546) (MH)—Pensacola, Florida
Entered Service at: Jacksonville, Duval County, Florida
Unit: Company D, 2d Battalion (Airborne), 501st Infantry, 101st Airborne Division
Served as: Squad Leader
Battle or Place of Action: near Hue, Republic of Vietnam
Date of Action: 21 February 1968
G.O. Number, Date: 83, 12 December 1969
Date of Presentation: 2 December 1969
Place of Presentation: The White House, presented by Vice Pres. Spiro T. Agnew to his family
Citation: For conspicuous gallantry and intrepidity in action at the risk of his life above and beyond the call of duty. S/Sgt. Sims distinguished himself while serving as a squad leader with Company D. Company D was assaulting a heavily fortified enemy position concealed within a dense wooded area when it encountered strong enemy defensive fire. Once within the woodline, S/Sgt. Sims led his squad in a furious attack against an enemy force which had pinned down the 1st Platoon and threatened to overrun it. His skillful leadership provided the platoon with freedom of movement and enabled it to regain the initiative. S/Sgt. Sims was then ordered to move his squad to a position where he could provide covering fire for the company command group and to link up with the 3d Platoon which was under heavy enemy pressure. After moving no more than 30 meters S/Sgt. Sims noticed that a brick structure in which ammunition was stocked was on fire. Realizing the danger, S/Sgt. Sims took immediate action to move his squad from this position. Though in the process of leaving the area two members of his squad were injured by the subsequent explosion of the ammunition, S/Sgt. Sims' prompt actions undoubtedly prevented more serious casualties from occurring. While continuing through the dense woods amidst heavy enemy fire, S/Sgt. Sims and his squad were approaching a bunker when they heard an unmistakable noise of a concealed booby trap being triggered immediately to their front. S/Sgt. Sims warned his comrades of the danger and unhesitatingly hurled himself upon the device as it exploded, taking the full impact of the blast. In so protecting his fellow soldiers, he willingly sacrificed his life. S/Sgt. Sims' extraordinary heroism at the cost of his life is in keeping with the highest traditions of the military service and reflect great credit upon himself and the U.S. Army.

3357 ◆ *SINGLETON, WALTER KEITH

Rank: Sergeant
Service: U.S. Marine Corps
Birthday: 7 December 1944
Place of Birth: Memphis, Shelby County, Tennessee
Date of Death: 24 March 1967
Place of Death: Republic of Vietnam
Cemetery: Memory Hill Gardens Cemetery—Memphis, Tennessee
Entered Service at: Memphis, Shelby County, Tennessee
Unit: Company A, 1st Battalion, 9th Marines, 3d Marine Division (Rein) FMF
Served as: Supply Sergeant
Battle or Place of Action: Gio Linh District, Quang Tri Province, Republic of Vietnam
Date of Action: 24 March 1967
Date of Presentation: 4 September 1968
Place of Presentation: Marine Barracks, Washington, D.C., presented by Secretary of the Navy Paul R. Ignatius to his family
Citation: For conspicuous gallantry and intrepidity at the risk of his life above and beyond the call of duty. Sgt. Singleton's company was conducting combat operations when the lead platoon received intense small-arms, automatic-weapons, rocket, and mortar fire from a well-entrenched enemy force. As the company fought its way forward, the extremely heavy enemy fire caused numerous friendly casualties. Sensing the need for early treatment of the wounded, Sgt. Singleton quickly moved from his relatively safe position in the rear of the foremost point of the advance and made numerous trips through the enemy killing zone to move the injured men out of the danger area. Noting that a large part of the enemy fire was coming from a hedgerow, he seized a machine gun and assaulted the key enemy location, delivering devastating fire as he advanced. He forced his way through the hedgerow directly into the enemy strong point. Although he was mortally wounded, his fearless attack killed eight of the enemy and drove the remainder from the hedgerow. Sgt. Singleton's bold actions completely disorganized the enemy defense and saved the lives of many of his comrades. His daring initiative, selfless devotion to duty and indomitable fighting spirit reflected great credit upon himself and the Marine Corps, and his performance upheld the highest traditions of the U.S. Naval Service.

3358 ◆ *SISLER, GEORGE KENTON

Rank: First Lieutenant
Service: U.S. Army
Birthday: 19 September 1937
Place of Birth: Dexter, Stoddard County, Missouri
Date of Death: 7 February 1967
Place of Death: Republic of Vietnam
Cemetery: Dexter Cemetery—Dexter, Missouri
Entered Service at: Dexter, Stoddard County, Missouri

Unit: Headquarters & Headquarters Company, 5th Special Forces Group (Airborne), 1st Special Forces
Served as: Platoon Leader/Advisor
Battle or Place of Action: Republic of Vietnam
Date of Action: 7 February 1967
G.O. Number, Date: 35, 16 July 1968
Date of Presentation: 27 June 1968
Place of Presentation: The Pentagon, presented by Sec. of the Army Stanley R. Resor to his family
Citation: For conspicuous gallantry and intrepidity at the risk of his life above and beyond the call of duty. 1st Lt. Sisler was the platoon leader/adviser to a Special United States/Vietnam exploitation force. While on patrol deep within enemy-dominated territory, 1st Lt. Sisler's platoon was attacked from three sides by a company-sized enemy force. 1st Lt. Sisler quickly rallied his men, deployed them to a better defensive position, called for air strikes, and moved among his men to encourage and direct their efforts. Learning that two men had been wounded and were unable to pull back to the perimeter, 1st Lt. Sisler charged from the position through intense enemy fire to assist them. He reached the men and began carrying one of them back to the perimeter, when he was taken under more intensive weapons fire by the enemy. Laying down his wounded comrade, he killed three onrushing enemy soldiers by firing his rifle and silenced the enemy machine gun with a grenade. As he returned the wounded man to the perimeter, the left flank of the position came under extremely heavy attack by the superior enemy force and several additional men of his platoon were quickly wounded. Realizing the need for instant action to prevent his position from being overrun, 1st Lt. Sisler picked up some grenades and charged singlehandedly into the enemy onslaught, firing his weapon and throwing grenades. This singularly heroic action broke up the vicious assault and forced the enemy to begin withdrawing. Despite the continuing enemy fire, 1st Lt. Sisler was moving about the battlefield directing force and several men of his platoon were quickly wounded. His extraordinary leadership, infinite courage, and selfless concern for his men saved the lives of a number of his comrades. His actions reflect great credit upon himself and uphold the highest traditions of the military service.

3359 ◆ *SKIDGEL, DONALD SIDNEY

Rank: Sergeant
Service: U.S. Army
Birthday: 13 October 1948
Place of Birth: Caribou, Aroostook County, Maine
Date of Death: 14 September 1969
Place of Death: Republic of Vietnam
Cemetery: Sawyer Cemetery (MH)—Plymouth, Maine
Entered Service at: Bangor, Penobscot County, Maine
Unit: Troop D, 1st Squadron, 9th Cavalry, 1st Cavalry Division
Served as: Reconnaissance Section Leader
Battle or Place of Action: near Song Be, Republic of Vietnam
Date of Action: 14 September 1969
G.O. Number, Date: 5, 25 January 1972

Date of Presentation: 16 December 1971
Place of Presentation: Old Executive Office Building, presented by Vice Pres. Spiro T. Agnew to his family
Citation: For conspicuous gallantry and intrepidity in action at the risk of his life above and beyond the call of duty. Sgt. Skidgel distinguished himself while serving as a reconnaissance section leader in Troop D. On a road near Song Be in Binh Long Province, Sgt. Skidgel and his section with other elements of his troop were acting as a convoy security-and-screening force when contact occurred with an estimated enemy battalion concealed in tall grass and in bunkers bordering the road. Sgt. Skidgel maneuvered off the road and began placing effective machine-gun fire on the enemy automatic-weapons and rocket-propelled-grenade positions. After silencing at least one position, he ran with his machine gun across 60 meters of bullet-swept ground to another location from which he continued to rake the enemy positions. Running low on ammunition, he returned to his vehicle over the same terrain. Moments later he was alerted that the command element was receiving intense automatic-weapons, rocket-propelled-grenade and mortar fire. Although he knew the road was saturated with enemy fire, Sgt. Skidgel calmly mounted his vehicle and with his driver advanced toward the command group in an effort to draw the enemy fire onto himself. Despite the hostile fire concentrated on him, he succeeded in silencing several enemy positions with his machine gun. Moments later Sgt. Skidgel was knocked down onto the rear fender by the explosion of an enemy rocket-propelled grenade. Ignoring his extremely painful wounds, he staggered back to his feet and placed effective fire on several other enemy positions until he was mortally wounded by hostile small-arms fire. His selfless actions enabled the command group to withdraw to a better position without casualties and inspired the rest of his fellow soldiers to gain fire superiority and defeat the enemy. Sgt. Skidgel's gallantry at the cost of his life were in keeping with the highest traditions of the military service and reflect great credit upon himself, his unit, and the U.S. Army.

3360 ◆ *SMEDLEY, LARRY EUGENE

Rank: Corporal
Service: U.S. Marine Corps
Birthday: 4 March 1949
Place of Birth: Front Royal, Warren County, Virginia
Date of Death: 21 December 1967
Place of Death: Republic of Vietnam
Cemetery: Arlington National Cemetery (31-6486) (MH)—Arlington, Virginia
Entered Service at: Orlando, Orange County, Florida
Unit: Company D, 1st Battalion, 7th Marines, 1st Marine Division (Rein) FMF
Served as: Squad Leader
Battle or Place of Action: at the mouth of Happy Valley, near Phouc Ninh (2), Quang Nam Province, Republic of Vietnam
Date of Action: 20-21 December 1967
Date of Presentation: 20 June 1969
Place of Presentation: The White House, presented by Pres. Richard M. Nixon to his family

Citation: For conspicuous gallantry and intrepidity at the risk of his life above and beyond the call of duty while serving as a squad leader with Company D, in connection with operations against the enemy. On the evenings of 20 and 21 December 1967, Cpl. Smedley led his six-man squad to an ambush site at the mouth of Happy Valley, near Phouc Ninh (2) in Quang Nam Province. Later that night an estimated 100 Viet Cong and North Vietnamese Army regulars, carrying 122-mm rocket launchers and mortars, were observed moving toward Hill 41. Realizing this was a significant enemy move to launch an attack on the vital Da Nang complex, Cpl. Smedley immediately took sound and courageous action to stop the enemy threat. After he radioed for a reaction force, he skillfully maneuvered his men to a more advantageous position and led an attack on the numerically superior enemy force. A heavy volume of fire from an enemy machine-gun positioned on the left flank of the squad inflicted several casualties on Cpl. Smedley's unit. Simultaneously, an enemy rifle grenade exploded nearby, wounding him in the right foot and knocking him to the ground. Cpl. Smedley disregarded this serious injury and valiantly struggled to his feet, shouting words of encouragement to his men. He fearlessly led a charge against the enemy machine-gun emplacement, firing his rifle and throwing grenades, until he was again struck by enemy fire and knocked to the ground. Gravely wounded and weak from loss of blood, he rose and commenced a one-man assault against the enemy position. Although his aggressive and singlehanded attack resulted in the destruction of the machine gun, he was struck in the chest by enemy fire and fell mortally wounded. Cpl. Smedley's inspiring and courageous actions, bold initiative, and selfless devotion to duty in the face of certain death were in keeping with the highest traditions of the Marine Corps and the U.S. Naval Service. He gallantly gave his life for his country.

3361 ◆ *SMITH, ELMELINDO RODRIQUES

Rank: Sergeant First Class (rank at time of action: Staff Sergeant)
Service: U.S. Army
Birthday: 27 July 1935
Place of Birth: Honolulu, Honolulu County, Hawaii
Date of Death: 16 February 1967
Place of Death: Republic of Vietnam
Cemetery: National Memorial Cemetery of the Pacific (W-131) (MH)—Honolulu, Hawaii
Entered Service at: Honolulu, Honolulu County, Hawaii
Unit: 1st Platoon, Company C, 2d Battalion, 8th Infantry, 4th Infantry Division
Served as: Platoon Sergeant
Battle or Place of Action: Republic of Vietnam
Date of Action: 16 February 1967
G.O. Number, Date: 63, 22 October 1968
Date of Presentation: 3 October 1968
Place of Presentation: The Pentagon, presented by Sec. of the Army Stanley R. Resor to his family
Citation: For conspicuous gallantry and intrepidity at the risk of his life above and beyond the call of duty. During a reconnaissance patrol, his platoon was suddenly engaged by intense machine-gun fire hemming in the platoon on three sides. A defensive perimeter was hastily established, but the enemy added mortar and rocket fire to the deadly fusillade and assaulted the position from several directions. With complete disregard for his safety, P/Sgt. Smith moved through the deadly fire along the defensive line, positioning soldiers, distributing ammunition, and encouraging his men to repel the enemy attack. Struck to the ground by enemy fire which caused a severe shoulder wound, he regained his feet, killed the enemy soldier, and continued to move about the perimeter. He was again wounded in the shoulder and stomach but continued moving on his knees to assist in the defense. Noting the enemy massing at a weakened point on the perimeter, he crawled into the open and poured deadly fire into the enemy ranks. As he crawled on, he was struck by a rocket. Moments later, he regained consciousness, and drawing on his fast dwindling strength, continued to crawl from man to man. When he could move no farther, he chose to remain in the open where he could alert the perimeter to the approaching enemy. P/Sgt. Smith perished, never relenting in his determined effort against the enemy. The valorous acts and heroic leadership of this outstanding soldier inspired those remaining members of his platoon to beat back the enemy assaults. P/Sgt. Smith's gallant actions were in keeping with the highest traditions of the U.S. Army and they reflect great credit upon him and the Armed Forces of his country.

3362 ◆ SPRAYBERRY, JAMES MICHAEL

Rank: Captain (rank at time of action: First Lieutenant) (highest rank: Lieutenant Colonel)
Service: U.S. Army
Birthday: 24 April 1947
Place of Birth: LaGrange, Troup County, Georgia
Entered Service at: Montgomery, Montgomery County, Alabama
Unit: Company D, 5th Battalion, 7th Cavalry, 1st Cavalry Division (Airmobile)
Served as: Executive Officer
Battle or Place of Action: Republic of Vietnam
Date of Action: 25 April 1968
G.O. Number, Date: 64, 27 October 1969
Date of Presentation: 9 October 1969
Place of Presentation: The White House (South Lawn), presented by Pres. Richard M. Nixon
Citation: For conspicuous gallantry and intrepidity in action at the risk of his life above and beyond the call of duty. Capt. Sprayberry, Armor, U.S. Army, distinguished himself by exceptional bravery while serving as executive officer of Company D. His company commander and a great number of the men were wounded and separated from the main body of the company. A daylight attempt to rescue them was driven back by the well-entrenched enemy's heavy fire. Capt. Sprayberry then organized and led a volunteer night patrol to eliminate the intervening enemy bunkers and to relieve the surrounded element. The patrol soon began receiving enemy machine-gun fire. Capt. Sprayberry quickly moved the men to protective cover and without regard for his own safety, crawled within close range of the bunker from which the fire

was coming. He silenced the machine gun with a hand grenade. Identifying several one-man enemy positions nearby, Capt. Sprayberry immediately attacked them with the rest of his grenades. He crawled back for more grenades and when two grenades were thrown at his men from a position to the front, Capt. Sprayberry, without hesitation, again exposed himself and charged the enemy-held bunker, killing its occupants with a grenade. Placing two men to cover his advance, he crawled forward and neutralized three more bunkers with grenades. Immediately thereafter, Capt. Sprayberry was surprised by an enemy soldier who charged from a concealed position. He killed the soldier with his pistol and with continuing disregard for the danger neutralized another enemy emplacement. Capt. Sprayberry then established radio contact with the isolated men, directing them toward his position. When the two elements made contact he organized his men into litter parties to evacuate the wounded. As the evacuation was nearing completion, he observed an enemy machine-gun position which he silenced with a grenade. Capt. Sprayberry returned to the rescue party, established security, and moved to friendly lines with the wounded. This rescue operation, which lasted approximately 7 1/2 hours, saved the lives of many of his fellow soldiers. Capt. Sprayberry personally killed 12 enemy soldiers, eliminated two machine guns, and destroyed numerous enemy bunkers. Capt. Sprayberry's indomitable spirit and gallant action at great personal risk to his life are in keeping with the highest traditions of the military service and reflect great credit upon himself, his unit, and the U.S. Army.

3363 ◆ *STEINDAM, RUSSELL ALBERT

Rank: First Lieutenant
Service: U.S. Army
Birthday: 27 August 1946
Place of Birth: Austin, Travis County, Texas
Date of Death: 1 February 1970
Place of Death: Republic of Vietnam
Cemetery: Restland Memorial Park (MH)—Dallas, Texas
Entered Service at: Austin, Travis County, Texas
Unit: Troop B, 3d Squadron, 4th Cavalry, 25th Infantry Division
Served as: Platoon Leader
Battle or Place of Action: Tay Ninh Province, Republic of Vietnam
Date of Action: 1 February 1970
G.O. Number, Date: 3, 25 January 1972
Date of Presentation: 16 December 1971
Place of Presentation: Old Executive Office Building, presented by Vice Pres. Spiro T. Agnew to his family
Citation: For conspicuous gallantry and intrepidity in action at the risk of his life above and beyond the call of duty. First Lt. Steindam, Troop B, while serving as a platoon leader, led members of his platoon on a night ambush operation. On the way to the ambush site, suspected enemy movement was detected on one flank and the platoon's temporary position was subjected to intense small-arms and automatic-weapons fire as well as a fusillade of hand and rocket-propelled grenades. After the initial barrage, 1st Lt. Steindam ordered

fire placed on the enemy position and the wounded men to be moved to a shallow bomb crater. As he directed the return fire against the enemy from his exposed position, a fragmentation grenade was thrown into the site occupied by his command group. Instantly realizing the extreme gravity of the situation, 1st Lt. Steindam shouted a warning to alert his fellow soldiers in the immediate vicinity. Then, unhesitatingly and with complete disregard for his safety, 1st Lt. Steindam deliberately threw himself on the grenade, absorbing the full and fatal force of the explosion as it detonated. By his gallant action and self-sacrifice, he was able to save the lives of the nearby members of his command group. The extraordinary courage and selflessness displayed by 1st Lt. Steindam were an inspiration to his comrades and are in the highest traditions of the U.S. Army.

3364 ◆ *STEWART, JIMMY GOETHEL

Rank: Staff Sergeant
Service: U.S. Army
Birthday: 25 December 1942
Place of Birth: West Columbia, Mason County, West Virginia
Date of Death: 18 May 1966
Place of Death: Republic of Vietnam
Cemetery: Riverview Cemetery—Middleport, Oklahoma
Entered Service at: Ashland, Boyd County, Kentucky
Unit: Company B, 2d Battalion, 12th Cavalry, 1st Cavalry Division (Airmobile)
Battle or Place of Action: Republic of Vietnam
Date of Action: 18 May 1966
G.O. Number, Date: 41, 22 September 1967
Date of Presentation: 24 August 1967
Place of Presentation: The Pentagon, presented by Sec. of the Army Stanley R. Resor to his family
Citation: For conspicuous gallantry and intrepidity in action at the risk of his life above and beyond the call of duty. Early in the morning a reinforced North Vietnamese company attacked Company B, which was manning a defensive perimeter in Vietnam. The surprise onslaught wounded five members of a six-man squad caught in the direct path of the enemy's thrust. S/Sgt. Stewart became a lone defender of vital terrain—virtually one man against a hostile platoon. Refusing to take advantage of a lull in the firing which would have permitted him to withdraw, S/Sgt. Stewart elected to hold his ground to protect his fallen comrades and prevent an enemy penetration of the company perimeter. As the full force of the platoon-sized attack struck his lone position, he fought like a man possessed; emptying magazine after magazine at the determined, oncharging enemy. The enemy drove almost to his position and hurled grenades, but S/Sgt. Stewart decimated them by retrieving and throwing the grenades back. Exhausting his ammunition, he crawled, under intense fire, to his wounded team members and collected ammunition that they were unable to use. Far past the normal point of exhaustion, he held his position for four harrowing hours and through three assaults, annihilating the enemy as they approached and before they could get a foothold. As a result of his defense, the company position held until the

arrival of a reinforcing platoon which counterattacked the enemy, now occupying foxholes to the left of S/Sgt. Stewart's position. After the counterattack, his body was found in a shallow enemy hole where he had advanced in order to add his fire to that of the counterattacking platoon. Eight enemy dead were found around his immediate position, with evidence that 15 others had been dragged away. The wounded whom he gave his life to protect were recovered and evacuated. S/Sgt. Stewart's indomitable courage, in the face of overwhelming odds, stands as a tribute to himself and an inspiration to all men of his unit. His actions were in the highest traditions of the U.S. Army and the Armed Forces of his country.

3365 ◆ STOCKDALE, JAMES BOND

Rank: Rear Admiral (rank at time of action: Captain) (highest rank: Vice Admiral)
Service: U.S. Navy
Birthday: 23 December 1923
Place of Birth: Abingdon, Knox County, Illinois
Entered Service at: Abingdon, Knox County, Illinois
Unit: Attack Carrier Air Wing 16, U.S.S. *Oriskany*
Served as: Pilot, Senior Naval Officer
Battle or Place of Action: Hoa Lo Prison, Hanoi
Date of Action: 4 September 1969
Date of Presentation: 6 March 1976
Place of Presentation: The White House, presented by Pres. Gerald R. Ford
Citation: For conspicuous gallantry and intrepidity at the risk of his life above and beyond the call of duty while senior naval officer in the prisoner-of-war camps of North Vietnam. Recognized by his captors as the leader in the prisoners' of war resistance to interrogation and in their refusal to participate in propaganda exploitation, Rear Adm. Stockdale was singled out for interrogation and attendant torture after he was detected in a covert communications attempt. Sensing the start of another purge, and aware that his earlier efforts at self-disfiguration to dissuade his captors from exploiting him for propaganda purposes had resulted in cruel and agonizing punishment, Rear Adm. Stockdale resolved to make himself a symbol of resistance regardless of personal sacrifice. He deliberately inflicted a near-mortal wound to his person in order to convince his captors of his willingness to give up his life rather than capitulate. He was subsequently discovered and revived by the North Vietnamese who, convinced of his indomitable spirit, abated in their employment of excessive harassment and torture toward all the prisoners of war. By his heroic actions, at great peril to himself, he earned the everlasting gratitude of his fellow prisoners and of his country. Rear Adm. Stockdale's valiant leadership and extraordinary courage in a hostile environment sustain and enhance the finest traditions of the U.S. Naval Service.
Notes: POW from 9 September 1965—February 1973

3366 ◆ *STONE JR., LESTER RAYMOND

Rank: Sergeant
Service: U.S. Army
Birthday: 4 June 1947

Place of Birth: Binghamton, Broome County, New York
Date of Death: 3 March 1969
Place of Death: Republic of Vietnam
Cemetery: Chenango Valley Cemetery (MH)—Binghamton, New York
Entered Service at: Syracuse, Onondaga County, New York
Unit: 1st Platoon, Company B, 1st Battalion, 20th Infantry, 11th Infantry Brigade, 23d Infantry Division (Americal)
Served as: Squad Leader
Battle or Place of Action: west of Landing Zone Liz, Republic of Vietnam
Date of Action: 3 March 1969
G.O. Number, Date: 14, 23 April 1970
Date of Presentation: 7 April 1970
Place of Presentation: The White House, presented by Pres. Richard M. Nixon to his family
Citation: For conspicuous gallantry and intrepidity in action at the risk of his life above and beyond the call of duty. Sgt. Stone distinguished himself while serving as squad leader of the 1st Platoon. The 1st Platoon was on a combat patrol mission just west of Landing Zone Liz when it came under intense automatic-weapons and grenade fire from a well-concealed company-size force of North Vietnamese regulars. Observing the platoon machine gunner fall critically wounded, Sgt. Stone remained in the exposed area to provide cover fire for the wounded soldier who was being pulled to safety by another member of the platoon. With enemy fire impacting all around him, Sgt. Stone had a malfunction in the machine gun, preventing him from firing the weapon automatically. Displaying extraordinary courage under the most adverse conditions, Sgt. Stone repaired the weapon and continued to place on the enemy positions effective suppressive fire which enabled the rescue to be completed. In a desperate attempt to overrun his position, an enemy force left its cover and charged Sgt. Stone. Disregarding the danger involved, Sgt. Stone rose to his knees and began placing intense fire on the enemy at point-blank range, killing six of the enemy before falling mortally wounded. His actions of unsurpassed valor were a source of inspiration to his entire unit, and he was responsible for saving the lives of a number of his fellow soldiers. His actions were in keeping with the highest traditions of the military profession and reflect great credit on him, his unit, and the U.S. Army.

3367 ◆ *STOUT, MITCHELL WILLIAM

Rank: Sergeant
Service: U.S. Army
Birthday: 24 February 1950
Place of Birth: Knoxville, Knox County, Tennessee
Date of Death: 12 March 1970
Place of Death: Republic of Vietnam
Cemetery: Virture Cemetery (MH)—Concord, Tennessee
Entered Service at: Raleigh, Wake County, North Carolina
Unit: Battery C, 1st Battalion, 44th Artillery
Battle or Place of Action: Khe Gio Bridge, Republic of Vietnam
Date of Action: 12 March 1970
G.O. Number, Date: 42, 12 September 1974
Date of Presentation: 17 July 1974

Place of Presentation: Blair House (Courtyard), presented by Vice Pres. Gerald R. Ford to his family
Citation: Sgt. Stout distinguished himself during an attack by a North Vietnamese Army Sapper company on his unit's firing position at Khe Gio Bridge. Sgt. Stout was in a bunker with members of a searchlight crew when the position came under heavy enemy mortar fire and ground attack. When the intensity of the mortar attack subsided, an enemy grenade was thrown into the bunker. Displaying great courage, Sgt. Stout ran to the grenade, picked it up, and started out of the bunker. As he reached the door, the grenade exploded. By holding the grenade close to his body and shielding its blast, he protected his fellow soldiers in the bunker from further injury or death. Sgt. Stout's conspicuous gallantry and intrepidity in action, at the cost of his own life, are in keeping with the highest traditions of the military service and reflect great credit upon him, his unit, and the U.S. Army.

3368 ◆ *STRYKER, ROBERT FRANCIS

Rank: Specialist Fourth Class
Service: U.S. Army
Birthday: 9 November 1944
Place of Birth: Auburn, Cayuga County, New York
Date of Death: 7 November 1967
Place of Death: Republic of Vietnam
Cemetery: Pine Hill Cemetery—Throopsville, New York
Entered Service at: Throop, Cayuga County, New York
Unit: Company C, 1st Battalion, 26th Infantry, 1st Infantry Division
Served as: Grenadier
Battle or Place of Action: near Loc Ninh, Republic of Vietnam
Date of Action: 7 November 1967
G.O. Number, Date: 72, 20 November 1969
Date of Presentation: 4 November 1969
Place of Presentation: The White House, presented by Vice Pres. Spiro T. Agnew to his family
Citation: For conspicuous gallantry and intrepidity at the risk of his life above and beyond the call of duty. Sp4c. Stryker, U.S. Army, distinguished himself while serving with Company C. Sp4c. Stryker was serving as a grenadier in a multicompany reconnaissance-in-force near Loc Ninh. As his unit moved through the dense underbrush, it was suddenly met with a hail of rocket, automatic-weapons, and small-arms fire from enemy forces concealed in fortified bunkers and in the surrounding trees. Reacting quickly, Sp4c. Stryker fired into the enemy positions with his grenade launcher. During the devastating exchange of fire, Sp4c. Stryker detected enemy elements attempting to encircle his company and isolate it from the main body of the friendly force. Undaunted by the enemy machine-gun and small-arms fire, Sp4c. Stryker repeatedly fired grenades into the trees, killing enemy snipers and enabling his comrades to sever the attempted encirclement. As the battle continued, Sp4c. Stryker observed several wounded members of his squad in the killing zone of an enemy claymore mine. With complete disregard for his safety, he threw himself upon the mine as it was detonated. He was mortally wounded as his body absorbed the blast and shielded his comrades from the explosion. His unselfish actions were

responsible for saving the lives of at least six of his fellow soldiers. Sp4c. Stryker's great personal bravery was in keeping with the highest traditions of the military service and reflects great credit upon himself, his unit, and the U.S. Army.

3369 ◆ STUMPF, KENNETH EDWARD

Rank: Sergeant (rank at time of action: Specialist Fourth Class) (highest rank: Sergeant Major)
Service: U.S. Army
Birthday: 28 September 1944
Place of Birth: Neenah, Winnebago County, Wisconsin
Entered Service at: Milwaukee, Milwaukee County, Wisconsin
Unit: 3d Platoon, Company C, 1st Battalion, 35th Infantry, 25th Infantry Division
Served as: Squad Leader
Battle or Place of Action: near Duc Pho, Republic of Vietnam
Date of Action: 25 April 1967
G.O. Number, Date: 64, 22 October 1968
Date of Presentation: 19 September 1968
Place of Presentation: The White House, presented by Pres. Lyndon B. Johnson
Citation: For conspicuous gallantry and intrepidity in action at the risk of his life above and beyond the call of duty. S/Sgt. Stumpf distinguished himself while serving as a squad leader of the 3d Platoon, Company C, on a search-and-destroy mission. As S/Sgt. Stumpf's company approached a village, it encountered a North Vietnamese rifle company occupying a well-fortified bunker complex. During the initial contact, three men from his squad fell wounded in front of a hostile machine-gun emplacement. The enemy's heavy volume of fire prevented the unit from moving to the aid of the injured men, but S/Sgt. Stumpf left his secure position in a deep trench and ran through the barrage of incoming rounds to reach his wounded comrades. He picked up one of the men and carried him back to the safety of the trench. Twice more S/Sgt. Stumpf dashed forward while the enemy turned automatic weapons and machine guns upon him, yet he managed to rescue the remaining two wounded squad members. He then organized his squad and led an assault against several enemy bunkers from which continuously heavy fire was being received. He and his squad successfully eliminated two of the bunker positions, but one to the front of the advancing platoon remained a serious threat. Arming himself with extra hand grenades, S/Sgt. Stumpf ran over open ground, through a volley of fire directed at him by a determined enemy, toward the machine-gun position. As he reached the bunker, he threw a hand grenade through the aperture. It was immediately returned by the occupants, forcing S/Sgt. Stumpf to take cover. Undaunted, he pulled the pins on two more grenades, held them for a few seconds after activation, then hurled them into the position, this time successfully destroying the emplacement. With the elimination of this key position, his unit was able to assault and overrun the enemy. S/Sgt. Stumpf's relentless spirit of aggressiveness, intrepidity, and ultimate concern for the lives of his men, are in the highest traditions of the military service and reflect great credit upon himself and the U.S. Army.

3370 ◆ TAYLOR, JAMES ALLEN

Rank: Captain (rank at time of action: First Lieutenant) (highest rank: Major)
Service: U.S. Army
Birthday: 31 December 1937
Place of Birth: Arcata, Humboldt County, California
Entered Service at: San Francisco, San Francisco County, California
Unit: Troop B, 1st Squadron, 1st Cavalry, Americal Division
Served as: Executive Officer
Battle or Place of Action: west of Que Son, Republic of Vietnam
Date of Action: 9 November 1967
G.O. Number, Date: 78, 10 December 1968
Date of Presentation: 19 November 1968
Place of Presentation: The White House, presented by Pres. Lyndon B. Johnson
Citation: Capt. Taylor, Armor, was serving as executive officer of Troop B, 1st Squadron. His troop was engaged in an attack on a fortified position west of Que Son when it came under intense enemy recoilless-rifle, mortar, and automatic-weapons fire from an enemy strong point located immediately to its front. One armored cavalry assault vehicle was hit immediately by recoilless-rifle fire and all five crewmembers were wounded. Aware that the stricken vehicle was in grave danger of exploding, Capt. Taylor rushed forward and personally extracted the wounded to safety despite the hail of enemy fire and exploding ammunition. Within minutes a second armored cavalry assault vehicle was hit by multiple recoilless-rifle rounds. Despite the continuing intense enemy fire, Capt. Taylor moved forward on foot to rescue the wounded men from the burning vehicle and personally removed all the crewmen to the safety of a nearby dike. Moments later the vehicle exploded. As he was returning to his vehicle, a bursting mortar round painfully wounded Capt. Taylor yet he valiantly returned to his vehicle to relocate the medical evacuation zone to an area closer to the front lines. As he was moving his vehicle, it came under machine-gun fire from an enemy position not 50 yards away. Capt. Taylor engaged the position with his machine gun, killing the three-man crew. Upon arrival at the new evacuation site, still another vehicle was struck. Once again Capt. Taylor rushed forward and pulled the wounded from the vehicle, loaded them aboard his vehicle, and returned them safely to the evacuation site. His actions of unsurpassed valor were a source of inspiration to his entire troop, contributed significantly to the success of the overall assault on the enemy position, and were directly responsible for saving the lives of a number of his fellow soldiers. His actions were in keeping with the highest traditions of the military profession and reflect great credit upon himself, his unit, and the U.S. Army.

3371 ◆ *TAYLOR SR., KARL GORMAN

Rank: Staff Sergeant
Service: U.S. Marine Corps
Birthday: 14 July 1939
Place of Birth: Laurel, Prince George's County, Maryland
Date of Death: 8 December 1968
Place of Death: Republic of Vietnam
Cemetery: Independence Cemetery—Independence, Pennsylvania
Entered Service at: Baltimore, Baltimore County, Maryland
Unit: Company I, 3d Battalion, 26th Marines Regiment, 3d Marine Division (Rein) FMF
Served as: Gunnery Sergeant
Battle or Place of Action: Republic of Vietnam
Date of Action: 8 December 1968
Date of Presentation: 16 February 1971
Place of Presentation: The White House, presented by Pres. Richard M. Nixon to his family
Citation: For conspicuous gallantry and intrepidity at the risk of his life above and beyond the call of duty while serving at night as a company gunnery sergeant during Operation Meade River. Informed that the commander of the lead platoon had been mortally wounded when his unit was pinned down by a heavy volume of enemy fire, S/Sgt. Taylor, along with another marine, crawled forward to the beleaguered unit through a hail of hostile fire, shouted encouragement and instructions to the men, and deployed them to covered positions. With his companion, he then repeatedly maneuvered across an open area to rescue those marines who were too seriously wounded to move by themselves. Upon learning that there were still other wounded men lying in another open area, in proximity to an enemy machine-gun position, S/Sgt. Taylor, accompanied by four comrades, led his men forward across the fire-swept terrain in an attempt to rescue the marines. When his group was halted by devastating fire, he directed his companions to return to the company command post; whereupon he took his grenade launcher and, in full view of the enemy, charged across the open rice paddy toward the machine-gun position, firing his weapon as he ran. Although wounded several times, he succeeded in reaching the machine-gun bunker and silencing the fire from that sector, moments before he was mortally wounded. Directly instrumental in saving the lives of several of his fellow marines, S/Sgt. Taylor, by his indomitable courage, inspiring leadership, and selfless dedication, upheld the highest traditions of the Marine Corps and of the U.S. Naval Service.

3372 ◆ THACKER, BRIAN MILES

Rank: First Lieutenant
Service: U.S. Army
Birthday: 25 April 1945
Place of Birth: Columbus, Franklin County, Ohio
Entered Service at: Salt Lake City, Salt Lake County, Utah
Unit: Battery A, 1st Battalion, 92d Artillery
Served as: Team Leader
Battle or Place of Action: Fire Base 6, Kontum Province, Republic of Vietnam
Date of Action: 31 March 1971
G.O. Number, Date: 42, 5 November 1973
Date of Presentation: 15 October 1973
Place of Presentation: The White House, presented by Pres. Richard M. Nixon
Citation: For conspicuous gallantry and intrepidity in action at the risk of his life above and beyond the call of duty. 1st

Lt. Thacker, Field Artillery, Battery A, distinguished himself while serving as the team leader of an Integrated Observation System collocated with elements of two Army of the Republic of Vietnam units at Fire Base 6. A numerically superior North Vietnamese Army force launched a well-planned dawn attack on the small, isolated, hilltop fire base. Employing rockets, grenades, flamethrowers, and automatic weapons, the enemy forces penetrated the perimeter defenses and engaged the defenders in hand-to-hand combat. Throughout the morning and early afternoon, 1st Lt. Thacker rallied and encouraged the U.S. and Republic of Vietnam soldiers in heroic efforts to repulse the enemy. He occupied a dangerously exposed observation position for a period of four hours while directing friendly air strikes and artillery fire against the assaulting enemy forces. His personal bravery and inspired leadership enabled the outnumbered friendly forces to inflict a maximum of casualties on the attacking enemy forces and prevented the base from being overrun. By late afternoon, the situation had become untenable. 1st Lt. Thacker organized and directed the withdrawal of the remaining friendly forces. With complete disregard for his personal safety, he remained inside the perimeter alone to provide covering fire with his M-16 rifle until all other friendly forces had escaped from the besieged fire base. Then, in an act of supreme courage, he called for friendly artillery fire on his own position to allow his comrades more time to withdraw safely from the area and, at the same time, inflict even greater casualties on the enemy forces. Although wounded and unable to escape from the area himself, he successfully eluded the enemy forces for eight days until friendly forces regained control of the fire base. The extraordinary courage and selflessness displayed by 1st Lt. Thacker were an inspiration to his comrades and are in the highest traditions of the military service.

3373 ◆ THORNTON, MICHAEL EDWIN

Rank: Engineman First Class (highest rank: Lieutenant)
Service: U.S. Navy
Birthday: 23 March 1949
Place of Birth: Greenville, Greenville County, South Carolina
Entered Service at: Spartanburg, Spartanburg County, South Carolina
Unit: Naval Advisory Group
Served as: Assistant U.S. Navy Advisor
Battle or Place of Action: Republic of Vietnam
Date of Action: 31 October 1972
Date of Presentation: 15 October 1973
Place of Presentation: The White House, presented by Pres. Richard M. Nixon
Citation: For conspicuous gallantry and intrepidity at the risk of his life above and beyond the call of duty while participating in a daring operation against enemy forces. PO Thornton, as assistant U.S. Navy adviser, along with a U.S. Navy lieutenant serving as senior adviser, accompanied a three-man Vietnamese Navy SEAL patrol on an intelligence-gathering and prisoner capture operation against an enemy-occupied naval river base. Launched from a Vietnamese Navy junk in a rubber boat, the patrol reached land and was continuing on foot toward its objective when it suddenly came

under heavy fire from a numerically superior force. The patrol called in naval gunfire support and then engaged the enemy in a fierce firefight, accounting for many enemy casualties before moving back to the waterline to prevent encirclement. Upon learning that the senior adviser had been hit by enemy fire and was believed to be dead, PO Thornton returned through a hail of fire to the lieutenant's last position, quickly disposed of two enemy soldiers about to overrun the position, and succeeded in removing the seriously wounded and unconscious Senior Naval Advisor to the water's edge. He then inflated the lieutenant's lifejacket and towed him seaward for approximately two hours until picked up by support craft. By his extraordinary courage and perseverance, PO Thornton was directly responsible for saving the life of his superior officer and enabling the safe extraction of all patrol members, thereby upholding the highest traditions of the U.S. Naval Service.

3374 ◆ THORSNESS, LEO KEITH

Rank: Lieutenant Colonel (rank at time of action: Major) (highest rank: Colonel)
Service: U.S. Air Force
Birthday: 14 February 1932
Place of Birth: Walnut Grove, Redwood County, Minnesota
Entered Service at: Walnut Grove, Redwood County, Minnesota
Unit: 357th Tactical Fighter Squadron, 355th Tactical Fighter Wing
Served as: Pilot of a F-105
Battle or Place of Action: over North Vietnam
Date of Action: 19 April 1967
G.O. Number, Date: GB-796, 6 November 1973
Date of Presentation: 15 October 1973
Place of Presentation: The White House, presented by Pres. Richard M. Nixon
Citation: For conspicuous gallantry and intrepidity in action at the risk of his life above and beyond the call of duty. As pilot of an F-105 aircraft, Lt. Col. Thorsness was on a surface-to-air missile suppression mission over North Vietnam. Lt. Col. Thorsness and his wingman attacked and silenced a surface-to-air missile site with air-to-ground missiles, and then destroyed a second surface-to-air missile site with bombs. In the attack on the second missile site, Lt. Col. Thorsness' wingman was shot down by intensive antiaircraft fire, and the two crewmembers abandoned their aircraft. Lt. Col. Thorsness circled the descending parachutes to keep the crewmembers in sight and relay their position to the Search and Rescue Center. During this maneuver, a MIG-17 was sighted in the area. Lt. Col. Thorsness immediately initiated an attack and destroyed the MIG. Because his aircraft was low on fuel, he was forced to depart the area in search of a tanker. Upon being advised that two helicopters were orbiting over the downed crew's position and that there were hostile MIGs in the area posing a serious threat to the helicopters, Lt. Col. Thorsness, despite his low fuel condition, decided to return alone through a hostile environment of surface-to-air missile and antiaircraft defenses to the downed crew's position. As he approached the area, he spotted four MIG-17 aircraft and

immediately initiated an attack on the MIGs, damaging one and driving the others away from the rescue scene. When it became apparent that an aircraft in the area was critically low on fuel and the crew would have to abandon the aircraft unless they could reach a tanker, Lt. Col. Thorsness, although critically short on fuel himself, helped to avert further possible loss of life and a friendly aircraft by recovering at a forward operating base, thus allowing the aircraft in emergency fuel condition to refuel safely. Lt. Col. Thorsness' extraordinary heroism, self-sacrifice, and personal bravery involving conspicuous risk of life were in the highest traditions of the military service, and have reflected great credit upon himself and the U.S. Air Force.

Notes: POW from April 1967—March 1973

3375 ◆ VARGAS, JAY R.

Rank: Major (rank at time of action: Captain) (highest rank: Colonel
Service: U.S. Marine Corps
Birthday: 29 July 1937
Place of Birth: Winslow, Navajo County, Arizona
Entered Service at: Winslow, Navajo County, Arizona
Unit: Company G, 2d Battalion, 4th Marines, 9th Marine Amphibious Brigade
Served as: Commanding Officer
Battle or Place of Action: Dai Do, Quang Tri Province, Republic of Vietnam
Date of Action: 30 April-2 May 1968
Date of Presentation: 14 May 1970
Place of Presentation: The White House, presented by Pres. Richard M. Nixon
Citation: For conspicuous gallantry and intrepidity at the risk of his life above and beyond the call of duty while serving as commanding officer, Company G, in action against enemy forces from 30 April to 2 May 1968. On 1 May 1968, though suffering from wounds he had incurred while relocating his unit under heavy enemy fire the preceding day, Maj. Vargas combined Company G with two other companies and led his men in an attack on the fortified village of Dai Do. Exercising expert leadership, he maneuvered his marines across 700 meters of open rice paddy while under intense enemy mortar, rocket, and artillery fire and obtained a foothold in two hedgerows on the enemy perimeter, only to have elements of his company become pinned down by the intense enemy fire. Leading his reserve platoon to the aid of his beleaguered men, Maj. Vargas inspired his men to renew their relentless advance, while destroying a number of enemy bunkers. Again wounded by grenade fragments, he refused aid as he moved about the hazardous area reorganizing his unit into a strong defensive perimeter at the edge of the village. Shortly after the objective was secured the enemy commenced a series of counterattacks and probes which lasted throughout the night but were unsuccessful as the gallant defenders of Company G stood firm in their hard-won enclave. Reinforced the following morning, the marines launched a renewed assault through Dai Do on the village of Dinh To, to which the enemy retaliated with a massive counterattack resulting in hand-to-hand combat. Maj. Vargas

remained in the open, encouraging and rendering assistance to his marines when he was hit for a third time in the three-day battle. Observing his battalion commander sustain a serious wound, he disregarded his excruciating pain, crossed the fire-swept area, and carried his commander to a covered position, then resumed supervising and encouraging his men while simultaneously assisting in organizing the battalion's perimeter defense. His gallant actions uphold the highest traditions of the Marine Corps and the U.S. Naval Service.

3376 ◆ *WARREN JR., JOHN EARL

Rank: First Lieutenant
Service: U.S. Army
Birthday: 16 November 1946
Place of Birth: Brooklyn, Kings County, New York
Date of Death: 14 January 1969
Place of Death: Republic of Vietnam
Cemetery: Long Island National Cemetery (0-33144) (MH)—Farmingdale, New York
Entered Service at: New York, New York
Unit: Company C, 2d Battalion (Mechanized), 22d Infantry, 25th Infantry Division
Served as: Platoon Leader
Battle or Place of Action: Tay Ninh Province, Republic of Vietnam
Date of Action: 14 January 1969
G.O. Number, Date: 49, 8 September 1970
Date of Presentation: 6 August 1970
Place of Presentation: The White House, presented by Pres. Richard M. Nixon to his family
Citation: For conspicuous gallantry and intrepidity in action at the risk of his life above and beyond the call of duty. 1st Lt. Warren distinguished himself at the cost of his life while serving as a platoon leader with Company C. While moving through a rubber plantation to reinforce another friendly unit, Company C came under intense fire from a well-fortified enemy force. Disregarding his safety, 1st Lt. Warren with several of his men began maneuvering through the hail of enemy fire toward the hostile positions. When he had come to within six feet of one of the enemy bunkers and was preparing to toss a hand grenade into it, an enemy grenade was suddenly thrown into the middle of his small group. Thinking only of his men, 1st Lt. Warren fell in the direction of the grenade, thus shielding those around him from the blast. His action, performed at the cost of his life, saved three men from serious or mortal injury. 1st Lt. Warren's ultimate action of sacrifice to save the lives of his men was in keeping with the highest traditions of the military service and reflects great credit on him, his unit, and the U.S. Army.

3377 ◆ *WATTERS, CHARLES JOSEPH

Rank: Major
Service: U.S. Army
Birthday: 17 January 1927
Place of Birth: Jersey City, Hudson County, New Jersey
Date of Death: 19 November 1967
Place of Death: Republic of Vietnam

Cemetery: Arlington National Cemetery (2-E-186-A) (MH)—Arlington, Virginia
Entered Service at: Fort Dix, Mercer County, New Jersey
Unit: Company A, 173d Support Battalion, 173d Airborne Brigade
Served as: Chaplain
Battle or Place of Action: Hill 875, near Dak To, Kontum Province, Republic of Vietnam
Date of Action: 19 November 1967
G.O. Number, Date: 71, 20 November 1969
Date of Presentation: 4 November 1969
Place of Presentation: The White House, presented by Vice Pres. Spiro T. Agnew to his family
Citation: For conspicuous gallantry and intrepidity in action at the risk of his life above and beyond the call of duty. Chaplain Watters distinguished himself during an assault in the vicinity of Dak To. Chaplain Watters was moving with one of the companies when it engaged a heavily armed enemy battalion. As the battle raged and the casualties mounted, Chaplain Watters, with complete disregard for his safety, rushed forward to the line of contact. Unarmed and completely exposed, he moved among, as well as in front of, the advancing troops, giving aid to the wounded, assisting in their evacuation, giving words of encouragement, and administering the last rites to the dying. When a wounded paratrooper was standing in shock in front of the assaulting forces, Chaplain Watters ran forward, picked the man up on his shoulders, and carried him to safety. As the troopers battled to the first enemy entrenchment, Chaplain Watters ran through the intense enemy fire to the front of the entrenchment to aid a fallen comrade. A short time later, the paratroopers pulled back in preparation for a second assault, Chaplain Watters exposed himself to both friendly and enemy fire between the two forces in order to recover two wounded soldiers. Later, when the battalion was forced to pull back into a perimeter, Chaplain Watters noticed that several wounded soldiers were lying outside the newly formed perimeter. Without hesitation and ignoring attempts to restrain him, Chaplain Watters left the perimeter three times in the face of small-arms, automatic-weapons, and mortar fire to carry and to assist the injured troopers to safety. Satisfied that all of the wounded were inside the perimeter, he began aiding the medics—applying field bandages to open wounds, obtaining and serving food and water, giving spiritual and mental strength and comfort. During his ministering, he moved out to the perimeter from position to position redistributing food and water and tending to the needs of his men. Chaplain Watters was giving aid to the wounded when he himself was mortally wounded. Chaplain Watters' unyielding perseverance and selfless devotion to his comrades was in keeping with the highest traditions of the U.S. Army.

3378 ◆ *WAYRYNEN, DALE EUGENE

Rank: Specialist Fourth Class
Service: U.S. Army
Birthday: 18 January 1947
Place of Birth: Moose Lake, Carlton County, Minnesota
Date of Death: 18 May 1967

Place of Death: Republic of Vietnam
Cemetery: Rice River Lutheran Cemetery (MH)—McGregor, Minnesota
Entered Service at: Minneapolis, Hennepin County, Minnesota
Unit: Company B, 2d Battalion, 502d Infantry, 1st Brigade, 101st Airborne Division
Battle or Place of Action: near Duc Pho, Quang Ngai Province, Republic of Vietnam
Date of Action: 18 May 1967
G.O. Number, Date: 66, 27 October 1969
Date of Presentation: 16 October 1969
Place of Presentation: The White House, presented by Pres. Richard M. Nixon to his family
Citation: For conspicuous gallantry and intrepidity in action at the risk of his life above and beyond the call of duty. Sp4c. Wayrynen distinguished himself with Company B, during combat operations near Duc Pho. His platoon was assisting in the night evacuation of the wounded from an early enemy contact when the leadman of the unit met face to face with a Viet Cong soldier. The American's shouted warning also alerted the enemy who immediately swept the area with automatic-weapons fire from a strongly built bunker close to the trail and threw hand grenades from another nearby fortified position. Almost immediately, the leadman was wounded and knocked from his feet. Sp4c. Wayrynen, the second man in the formation, leaped beyond his fallen comrade to kill another enemy soldier who appeared on the trail, and he dragged his injured companion back to where the point squad had taken cover. Suddenly, a live enemy grenade landed in the center of the tightly grouped men. Sp4c. Wayrynen, quickly assessing the danger to the entire squad as well as to his platoon leader who was nearby, shouted a warning, pushed one soldier out of the way, and threw himself on the grenade at the moment it exploded. He was mortally wounded. His deep and abiding concern for his fellow soldiers was significantly reflected in his supreme and courageous act that preserved the lives of his comrades. Sp4c. Wayrynen's heroic actions are in keeping with the highest traditions of the service, and they reflect great credit upon himself and the U.S. Army.

3379 ◆ *WEBER, LESTER WILLIAM

Rank: Lance Corporal
Service: U.S. Marine Corps
Birthday: 30 July 1948
Place of Birth: Aurora, Du Page County, Illinois
Date of Death: 23 February 1969
Place of Death: Republic of Vietnam
Cemetery: Clarendon Hills Cemetery (MH)—Westmont, Illinois
Entered Service at: Chicago, Cook County, Illinois
Unit: 2d Platoon, Company M, 3d Battalion, 7th Marines, 1st Marine Division (Rein) FMF
Served as: Squad Leader/Machine Gunner
Battle or Place of Action: Bo Ban area, Hieu Duc District, Quang Nam Province, Republic of Vietnam
Date of Action: 23 February 1969
Date of Presentation: 16 February 1971

Place of Presentation: The White House, presented by Pres. Richard M. Nixon to his family

Citation: For conspicuous gallantry and intrepidity at the risk of his life above and beyond the call of duty while serving as a machine-gun squad leader with Company M, in action against the enemy. The 2d Platoon of Company M was dispatched to the Bo Ban area of Hieu Duc district to assist a squad from another platoon which had become heavily engaged with a well-entrenched enemy battalion. While moving through a rice paddy covered with tall grass L/Cpl. Weber's platoon came under heavy attack from concealed hostile soldiers. He reacted by plunging into the tall grass, successfully attacking one enemy, and forcing 11 others to break contact. Upon encountering a second North Vietnamese Army soldier he overwhelmed him in fierce hand-to-hand combat. Observing two other soldiers firing upon his comrades from behind a dike, L/Cpl. Weber ignored the frenzied firing of the enemy and, racing across the hazardous area, dived into their position. He neutralized the position by wrestling weapons from the hands of the two soldiers and overcoming them. Although by now the target for concentrated fire from hostile riflemen, L/Cpl. Weber remained in a dangerously exposed position to shout words of encouragement to his emboldened companions. As he moved forward to attack a fifth enemy soldier, he was mortally wounded. L/Cpl. Weber's indomitable courage, aggressive fighting spirit, and unwavering devotion to duty upheld the highest traditions of the Marine Corps and of the U.S. Naval Service. He gallantly gave his life for his country.

3380 ◆ WETZEL, GARY GEORGE

Rank: Specialist Fourth Class [rank at time of action: Private First Class]
Service: U.S. Army
Birthday: 29 September 1947
Place of Birth: South Milwaukee, Milwaukee County, Wisconsin
Entered Service at: Milwaukee, Milwaukee County, Wisconsin
Unit: 173d Assault Helicopter Company, 11th Combat Aviation Battalion, 1st Aviation Brigade
Served as: Door Gunner
Battle or Place of Action: near Ap Dong An, Republic of Vietnam
Date of Action: 8 January 1968
G.O. Number, Date: 79, 10 December 1968
Date of Presentation: 19 November 1968
Place of Presentation: The White House, presented by Pres. Lyndon B. Johnson
Citation: Sp4c. Wetzel, 173d Assault Helicopter Company, distinguished himself by conspicuous gallantry and intrepidity at the risk of his life above and beyond the call of duty. Sp4c. Wetzel was serving as door gunner aboard a helicopter which was part of an insertion force trapped in a landing zone by intense and deadly hostile fire. Sp4c. Wetzel was going to the aid of his aircraft commander when he was blown into a rice paddy and critically wounded by two enemy rockets that exploded just inches from his location. Although bleeding profusely due to the loss of his left arm and severe wounds in his right arm, chest, and left leg, Sp4c. Wetzel staggered back to his original position in his gun-well and took the enemy forces under fire. His machine gun was the only weapon placing effective fire on the enemy at that time. Through a resolve that overcame the shock and intolerable pain of his injuries, Sp4c. Wetzel remained at his position until he had eliminated the automatic-weapons emplacement that had been inflicting heavy casualties on the American troops and preventing them from moving against this strong enemy force. Refusing to attend his own extensive wounds, he attempted to return to the aid of his aircraft commander but passed out from loss of blood. Regaining consciousness, he persisted in his efforts to drag himself to the aid of his fellow crewman. After an agonizing effort, he came to the side of the crew chief who was attempting to drag the wounded aircraft commander to the safety of a nearby dike. Unswerving in his devotion to his fellow man, Sp4c. Wetzel assisted his crew chief even though he lost consciousness once again during this action. Sp4c. Wetzel displayed extraordinary heroism in his efforts to aid his fellow crewmen. His gallant actions were in keeping with the highest traditions of the U.S. Army and reflect great credit upon himself and the Armed Forces of his country.

3381 ◆ *WHEAT, ROY MITCHELL

Rank: Lance Corporal
Service: U.S. Marine Corps
Birthday: 24 July 1947
Place of Birth: Moselle, Jones County, Mississippi
Date of Death: 11 August 1967
Place of Death: Republic of Vietnam
Cemetery: Eastabuchie Cemetery (MH)—Eastabuchie, Mississippi
Entered Service at: Jackson, Hinds County, Mississippi
Unit: Company K, 3d Battalion, 7th Marines, 1st Marine Division
Served as: Fire Team Leader
Battle or Place of Action: along Liberty Road, Dien Ban District, Quang Nam Province, Republic of Vietnam
Date of Action: 11 August 1967
Date of Presentation: 23 September 1968
Place of Presentation: Marine Barracks, Washington, D.C., presented by Sec. of the Navy Paul R. Ignatius to his family
Citation: For conspicuous gallantry and intrepidity at the risk of his life above and beyond the call of duty. L/Cpl. Wheat and two other marines were assigned the mission of providing security for a Navy construction battalion crane and crew operating along Liberty Road in the vicinity of the Dien Ban district, Quang Nam Province. After the marines had set up security positions in a treeline adjacent to the work site, L/Cpl. Wheat reconnoitered the area to the rear of their location for the possible presence of guerrillas. He then returned to within 10 feet of the friendly position and here unintentionally triggered a well-concealed, bounding type antipersonnel mine. Immediately, a hissing sound was heard which was identified by the three marines as that of a burning time fuse. Shouting a warning to his comrades, L/Cpl. Wheat in a valiant act of heroism hurled himself upon the mine, absorbing the tremendous impact of the explosion with his body. The inspirational personal heroism and extraordinary valor of his unselfish action saved his fellow marines from cer-

tain injury and possible death, reflected great credit upon himself, and upheld the highest traditions of the Marine Corps and the U.S. Naval Service. He gallantly gave his life for his country.

3382 ◆ *WICKAM, JERRY WAYNE

Rank: Corporal
Service: U.S. Army
Birthday: 19 January 1942
Place of Birth: Rockford, Winnebago County, Illinois
Date of Death: 6 January 1968
Place of Death: Republic of Vietnam
Cemetery: Lightsville Cemetery—Leaf River, Illinois
Entered Service at: Chicago, Cook County, Illinois
Unit: Troop F, 2d Squadron, 11th Armored Cavalry Regiment
Battle or Place of Action: near Loc Ninh, Republic of Vietnam
Date of Action: 6 January 1968
G.O. Number, Date: 78, 4 December 1969
Date of Presentation: 18 November 1969
Place of Presentation: The White House, presented by Vice Pres. Spiro T. Agnew to his family
Citation: For conspicuous gallantry and intrepidity in action at the risk of his life above and beyond the call of duty. Cpl. Wickam distinguished himself while serving with Troop F. Troop F was conducting a reconnaissance-in-force mission southwest of Loc Ninh when the lead element of the friendly force was subjected to a heavy barrage of rocket, automatic-weapons, and small-arms fire from a well-concealed enemy bunker complex. Disregarding the intense fire, Cpl. Wickam leaped from his armored vehicle and assaulted one of the enemy bunkers and threw a grenade into it, killing two enemy soldiers. He moved into the bunker and, with the aid of another soldier, began to remove the body of one Viet Cong when he detected the sound of an enemy grenade being charged. Cpl. Wickam warned his comrade and physically pushed him away from the grenade thus protecting him from the force of the blast. When a second Viet Cong bunker was discovered, he ran through a hail of enemy fire to deliver deadly fire into the bunker, killing one enemy soldier. He also captured one Viet Cong who later provided valuable information on enemy activity in the Loc Ninh area. After the patrol withdrew and an air strike was conducted, Cpl. Wickam led his men back to evaluate the success of the strike. They were immediately attacked again by enemy fire. Without hesitation, he charged the bunker from which the fire was being directed, enabling the remainder of his men to seek cover. He threw a grenade inside of the enemy's position killing two Viet Cong and destroying the bunker. Moments later he was mortally wounded by enemy fire. Cpl. Wickam's extraordinary heroism at the cost of his life were in keeping with the highest traditions of the military service and reflect great credit upon himself and the U.S. Army.

3383 ◆ *WILBANKS, HILLIARD ALMOND

Rank: Captain
Service: U.S. Air Force
Birthday: 26 July 1933
Place of Birth: Cornelia, Habersham County, Georgia
Date of Death: 24 February 1967
Place of Death: Republic of Vietnam
Cemetery: Fayette Methodist Cemetery—Fayette, Mississippi
Entered Service at: Atlanta, Fulton County, Georgia
Unit: 21st Tactical Air Support Squadron, Nha Trang Air Force Base, Republic of Vietnam
Served as: Pilot of a O-E1 Bird Dog
Battle or Place of Action: near Dalat, Republic of Vietnam
Date of Action: 24 February 1967
G.O. Number, Date: GB-50, 8 February 1968
Date of Presentation: 24 January 1968
Place of Presentation: The Pentagon, presented by Sec. of the Air Force Harold Brown to his family
Citation: For conspicuous gallantry and intrepidity in action at the risk of his life above and beyond the call of duty. As a forward air controller Capt. Wilbanks was pilot of an unarmed, light aircraft flying visual reconnaissance ahead of a South Vietnam Army Ranger Battalion. His intensive search revealed a well-concealed and numerically superior hostile force poised to ambush the advancing Rangers. The Viet Cong, realizing that Capt. Wilbanks' discovery had compromised their position and ability to launch a surprise attack, immediately fired on the small aircraft with all available firepower. The enemy then began advancing against the exposed forward elements of the ranger force which were pinned down by devastating fire. Capt. Wilbanks recognized that close support aircraft could not arrive in time to enable the rangers to withstand the advancing enemy onslaught. With full knowledge of the limitations of his unarmed, unarmored light reconnaissance aircraft, and the great danger imposed by the enemy's vast firepower, he unhesitatimgly assumed a covering, close support role. Flying through a hail of withering fire at treetop level, Capt. Wilbanks passed directly over the advancing enemy and inflicted many casualties by firing his rifle out of the side window of his aircraft. Despite increasingly intense antiaircraft fire, Capt. Wilbanks continued to completely disregard his own safety and made repeated low passes over the enemy to divert their fire away from the rangers. His daring tactics successfully interrupted the enemy advance, allowing the rangers to withdraw to safety from their perilous position. During his final courageous attack to protect the withdrawing forces, Capt. Wilbanks was mortally wounded and his bullet-riddled aircraft crashed between the opposing forces. Capt. Wilbanks' magnificent action saved numerous friendly personnel from certain injury or death. His unparalleled concern for his fellow man and his extraordinary heroism were in the highest traditions of the military service, and have reflected great credit upon himself and the U.S. Air Force.

3384 ◆ *WILLETT, LOUIS EDWARD

Rank: Private First Class
Service: U.S. Army
Birthday: 19 June 1945
Place of Birth: Brooklyn, Kings County, New York
Date of Death: 15 February 1967

Place of Death: Republic of Vietnam
Cemetery: Saint John's Cemetery (MH)—Middle Village, New York
Entered Service at: Brooklyn, Kings County, New York
Unit: Company C, 1st Battalion, 12th Infantry, 4th Infantry Division
Served as: Rifleman
Battle or Place of Action: Kontum Province, Republic of Vietnam
Date of Action: 15 February 1967
G.O. Number, Date: 52, 30 September 1968
Date of Presentation: 5 September 1968
Place of Presentation: The Pentagon, presented by Sec. of the Army Stanley R. Resor to his family
Citation: For conspicuous gallantry and intrepidity at the risk of his life above and beyond the call of duty. Pfc. Willett distinguished himself while serving as a rifleman in Company C, during combat operations. His squad was conducting a security sweep when it made contact with a large enemy force. The squad was immediately engaged with a heavy volume of automatic-weapons fire and pinned to the ground. Despite the deadly fusillade, Pfc. Willett rose to his feet firing rapid bursts from his weapon and moved to a position from which he placed highly effective fire on the enemy. His action allowed the remainder of his squad to begin to withdraw from the superior enemy force toward the company perimeter. Pfc. Willett covered the squad's withdrawal, but his position drew heavy enemy machine-gun fire, and he received multiple wounds enabling the enemy again to pin down the remainder of the squad. Pfc. Willett struggled to an upright position, and, disregarding his painful wounds, he again engaged the enemy with his rifle to allow his squad to continue its movement and to evacuate several of his comrades who were by now wounded. Moving from position to position, he engaged the enemy at close-range until he was mortally wounded. By his unselfish acts of bravery, Pfc. Willett insured the withdrawal of his comrades to the company position, saving their lives at the cost of his life. Pfc. Willett's valorous actions were in keeping with the highest traditions of the U.S. Army and reflect great credit upon himself and the Armed Forces of his country.

3385 ◆ WILLIAMS, CHARLES QUINCY

Rank: First Lieutenant (rank at time of action: Second Lieutenant) (highest rank: Major)
Service: U.S. Army
Birthday: 17 September 1933
Place of Birth: Charleston, Charleston County, South Carolina
Date of Death: 15 October 1982
Place of Death: Columbia, South Carolina
Cemetery: Arlington National Cemetery (65-1491) (MH)—Arlington, Virginia
Entered Service at: Fort Jackson, South Carolina
Unit: Detachment A, 5th Special Forces Group, 1st Special Forces
Served as: Executive Officer
Battle or Place of Action: Dong Xoai, Republic of Vietnam

Date of Action: 9-10 June 1965
G.O. Number, Date: 30, 5 July 1966
Date of Presentation: 23 June 1966
Place of Presentation: The White House, presented by Pres. Lyndon B. Johnson
Citation: 1st Lt. Williams distinguished himself by conspicuous gallantry and intrepidity at the risk of his life above and beyond the call of duty while defending the Special Forces camp against a violent attack by hostile forces that lasted for 14 hours. 1st Lt. Williams was serving as executive officer of a Special Forces detachment when an estimated Viet Cong reinforced regiment struck the camp and threatened to overrun it and the adjacent district headquarters. He awoke personnel, organized them, determined the source of the insurgents' main effort, and led the troops to their defensive positions on the south and west walls. Then, after running to the district headquarters to establish communications, he found that there was no radio operational with which to communicate with his commanding officer in another compound. To reach the other compound, he traveled through darkness but was halted in this effort by a combination of shrapnel in his right leg and the increase of Viet Cong gunfire. Ignoring his wound, he returned to the district headquarters and directed the defense against the first assault. As the insurgents attempted to scale the walls and as some of the Vietnamese defenders began to retreat, he dashed through a barrage of gunfire, succeeded in rallying these defenders, and led them back to their positions. Although wounded in the thigh and left leg during this gallant action, he returned to his position and, upon being told that communications were reestablished and that his commanding officer was seriously wounded, 1st Lt. Williams took charge of actions in both compounds. Then, in an attempt to reach the communications bunker, he sustained wounds in the stomach and right arm from grenade fragments. As the defensive position on the walls had been held for hours and casualties were mounting, he ordered the consolidation of the American personnel from both compounds to establish a defense in the district building. After radio contact was made with a friendly air controller, he disregarded his wounds and directed the defense from the district building, using descending flares as reference points to adjust air strikes. By his courage, he inspired his team to hold out against the insurgent force that was closing in on them and throwing grenades into the windows of the building. As daylight arrived and the Viet Cong continued to besiege the stronghold, firing a machine gun directly south of the district building, he was determined to eliminate this menace that threatened the lives of his men. Taking a 3.5 rocket launcher and a volunteer to load it, he worked his way across open terrain, reached the berm south of the district headquarters, and took aim at the Viet Cong machine gun 150 meters away. Although the sight was faulty, he succeeded in hitting the machine gun. While he and the loader were trying to return to the district headquarters, they were both wounded. With a fourth wound, this time in the right arm and leg, and realizing he was unable to carry his wounded comrade back to the district building, 1st Lt. Williams pulled him to a covered position and then made his way back to the district building where he sought the help of others who went out and evacu-

ated the injured soldier. Although seriously wounded and tired, he continued to direct the air strikes closer to the defensive position. As morning turned to afternoon and the Viet Cong pressed their effort with direct recoilless-rifle fire into the building, he ordered the evacuation of the seriously wounded to the safety of the communications bunker. When informed that helicopters would attempt to land as the hostile gunfire had abated, he led his team from the building to the artillery position, making certain of the timely evacuation of the wounded from the communications area, and then on to the pickup point. Despite resurgent Viet Cong gunfire, he directed the rapid evacuation of all personnel. Throughout the long battle, he was undaunted by the vicious Viet Cong assault and inspired the defenders in decimating the determined insurgents. 1st Lt. Williams' extraordinary heroism is in the highest traditions of the U.S. Army and reflect great credit upon himself and the Armed Forces of his country.

3386 ◆ *WILLIAMS, DEWAYNE THOMAS

Rank: Private First Class
Service: U.S. Marine Corps
Birthday: 18 September 1949
Place of Birth: Brown City, Sanilac County, Michigan
Date of Death: 18 September 1968
Place of Death: Republic of Vietnam
Cemetery: St. Mary's Cemetery (MH)—St. Clair, Michigan
Entered Service at: Saint Clair, Saint Clair County, Michigan
Unit: 1st Platoon, Company H, 2d Battalion, 1st Marines, 1st Marine Division
Served as: Rifleman
Battle or Place of Action: Quang Nam Province, Republic of Vietnam
Date of Action: 18 September 1968
Date of Presentation: 20 April 1970
Place of Presentation: The White House, presented by Vice Pres. Spiro T. Agnew to his family
Citation: For conspicuous gallantry and intrepidity at the risk of his life above and beyond the call of duty while serving as a rifleman with the 1st Platoon, Company H, in action against communist insurgent forces. Pfc. Williams was a member of a combat patrol sent out from the platoon with the mission of establishing positions in the company's area of operations from which it could intercept and destroy enemy sniper teams operating in the area. In the night as the patrol was preparing to move from its daylight position to a preselected night position, it was attacked from ambush by a squad of enemy using small arms and hand grenades. Although severely wounded in the back by the close intense fire, Pfc. Williams, recognizing the danger to the patrol, immediately began to crawl forward toward a good firing position. While he was moving under the continuing intense fire, he heard one of the members of the patrol sound the alert that an enemy grenade had landed in their position. Reacting instantly to the alert, he saw that the grenade had landed close to where he was lying and without hesitation, in a valiant act of heroism, rolled on top of the grenade as it exploded, absorbing the full and tremendous impact of the explosion with his

body. Through his extraordinary initiative and inspiring valor in the face of certain death, he saved the other members of his patrol from serious injury and possible loss of life, and enabled them to successfully defeat the attackers and hold their position until assistance arrived. His personal heroism and devotion to duty upheld the highest traditions of the Marine Corps and the U.S. Naval Service. He gallantly gave his life for his country.

3387 ◆ WILLIAMS, JAMES ELLIOTT

Rank: Boatswain's Mate First Class
Service: U.S. Navy
Birthday: 13 June 1930
Place of Birth: Rock Hill, York County, South Carolina
Entered Service at: Columbia, Richland County, South Carolina
Unit: River Patrol Boat 105, River Section 531, My Tho, Republic of Vietnam
Served as: Boat Captain/Patrol Officer
Battle or Place of Action: Mekong River, Republic of Vietnam
Date of Action: 31 October 1966
Date of Presentation: 14 May 1968
Place of Presentation: The Pentagon (Inner Courtyard), Hall of Heroes, presented by Pres. Lyndon B. Johnson
Citation: For conspicuous gallantry and intrepidity at the risk of his life above and beyond the call of duty. PO1c. Williams was serving as boat captain and patrol officer aboard River Patrol Boat (PBR) 105 accompanied by another patrol boat when the patrol was suddenly taken under fire by two enemy sampans. PO1c. Williams immediately ordered the fire returned, killing the crew of one enemy boat and causing the other sampan to take refuge in a nearby river inlet. Pursuing the fleeing sampan, the U.S. patrol encountered a heavy volume of small-arms fire from enemy forces, at close-range, occupying well-concealed positions along the river bank. Maneuvering through this fire, the patrol confronted a numerically superior enemy force aboard two enemy junks and eight sampans augmented by heavy automatic-weapons fire from ashore. In the savage battle that ensued, PO1c. Williams, with utter disregard for his safety, exposed himself to the withering hail of enemy fire to direct counterfire and inspire the actions of his patrol. Recognizing the overwhelming strength of the enemy force, PO1c. Williams deployed his patrol to await the arrival of armed helicopters. In the course of his movement he discovered an even larger concentration of enemy boats. Not waiting for the arrival of the armed helicopters, he displayed great initiative and boldly led the patrol through the intense enemy fire and damaged or destroyed 50 enemy sampans and seven junks. This phase of the action completed, and with the arrival of the armed helicopters, PO1c. Williams directed the attack on the remaining enemy force. Now virtually dark, and although PO1c. Williams was aware that his boats would become even better targets, he ordered the patrol boats' search lights turned on to better illuminate the area and moved the patrol perilously close to shore to press the attack. Despite a waning supply of ammunition, the patrol successfully engaged the enemy ashore and

completed the rout of the enemy force. Under the leadership of PO1c. Williams who demonstrated unusual professional skill and indomitable courage throughout the three-hour battle, the patrol accounted for the destruction or loss of 65 enemy boats and inflicted numerous casualties on the enemy personnel. His extraordinary heroism and exemplary fighting spirit in the face of grave risks inspired the efforts of his men to defeat a larger enemy force and are in keeping with the finest traditions of the U.S. Naval Service.

3388 ◆ *WILSON, ALFRED MAC

Rank: Private First Class
Service: U.S. Marine Corps
Birthday: 13 January 1948
Place of Birth: Olney, Richland County, Illinois
Date of Death: 3 March 1969
Place of Death: Republic of Vietnam
Cemetery: Sunset Memorial Cemetery (MH)—Odessa, Texas
Entered Service at: Abilene, Taylor County, Texas
Unit: 1st Platoon, Company M, 3d Battalion, 9th Marines, 3d Marine Division
Served as: Rifleman
Battle or Place of Action: Fire Support Base Cunningham, Quang Tri Province, Republic of Vietnam
Date of Action: 3 March 1969
Date of Presentation: 20 April 1970
Place of Presentation: The White House, presented by Vice Pres. Spiro T. Agnew to his family
Citation: For conspicuous gallantry and intrepidity at the risk of his life above and beyond the call of duty while serving as a rifleman with Company M in action against hostile forces. While returning from a reconnaissance-in-force mission in the vicinity of Fire Support Base Cunningham, the 1st Platoon of Company M came under intense automatic-weapons fire and a grenade attack from a well-concealed enemy force. As the center of the column was pinned down, the leading squad moved to outflank the enemy. Pfc. Wilson, acting as squad leader of the rear squad, skillfully maneuvered his men to form a base of fire and act as a blocking force. In the ensuing firefight, both his machine gunner and assistant machine gunner were seriously wounded and unable to operate their weapons. Realizing the urgent need to bring the weapon into operation again, Pfc. Wilson, followed by another marine and with complete disregard for his safety, fearlessly dashed across the fire-swept terrain to recover the weapon. As they reached the machine gun, an enemy soldier stepped from behind a tree and threw a grenade toward the two marines. Observing the grenade fall between himself and the other marine, Pfc. Wilson, fully realizing the inevitable result of his action, shouted to his companion and unhesitating threw himself on the grenade, absorbing the full force of the explosion with his own body. His heroic actions inspired his platoon members to maximum effort as they aggressively attacked and defeated the enemy. Pfc. Wilson's indomitable courage, inspiring valor, and selfless devotion to duty upheld the highest traditions of the Marine Corps and the U.S. Naval Service. He gallantly gave his life for his country.

3389 ◆ *WINDER, DAVID FRANCIS

Rank: Private First Class
Service: U.S. Army
Birthday: 10 August 1946
Place of Birth: Edinboro, Erie County, Pennsylvania
Date of Death: 13 May 1970
Place of Death: Republic of Vietnam
Cemetery: Mansfield Memorial Park—Mansfield, Ohio
Entered Service at: Columbus, Franklin County, Ohio
Unit: Headquarters & Headquarters Company, 3d Battalion, 1st Infantry, 11th Infantry Brigade, Americal Division
Served as: Senior Medical Aidman
Battle or Place of Action: Republic of Vietnam
Date of Action: 13 May 1970
G.O. Number, Date: 35, 6 September 1974
Date of Presentation: 17 July 1974
Place of Presentation: Blair House (Courtyard), presented by Vice Pres. Gerald R. Ford to his family
Citation: Pfc. Winder distinguished himself while serving in the Republic of Vietnam as a senior medical aidman with Company A. After moving through freshly cut rice paddies in search of a suspected company-size enemy force, the unit started a thorough search of the area. Suddenly they were engaged with intense automatic-weapons and rocket-propelled-grenade fire by a well-entrenched enemy force. Several friendly soldiers fell wounded in the initial contact and the unit was pinned down. Responding instantly to the cries of his wounded comrades, Pfc. Winder began maneuvering across approximately 100 meters of open, bullet-swept terrain toward the nearest casualty. Unarmed and crawling most of the distance, he was wounded by enemy fire before reaching his comrades. Despite his wounds and with great effort, Pfc. Winder reached the first casualty and administered medical aid. As he continued to crawl across the open terrain toward a second wounded soldier he was forced to stop when wounded a second time. Aroused by the cries of an injured comrade for aid, Pfc. Winder's great determination and sense of duty impelled him to move forward once again, despite his wounds, in a courageous attempt to reach and assist the injured man. After struggling to within 10 meters of the man, Pfc. Winder was mortally wounded. His dedication and sacrifice inspired his unit to initiate an aggressive counterassault which led to the defeat of the enemy. Pfc. Winder's conspicuous gallantry and intrepidity in action at the cost of his life were in keeping with the highest traditions of the military service and reflect great credit on him, his unit, and the U.S. Army.

3390 ◆ *WORLEY, KENNETH LEE

Rank: Lance Corporal
Service: U.S. Marine Corps
Birthday: 27 April 1948
Place of Birth: Farmington, San Juan County, New Mexico
Date of Death: 12 August 1968
Place of Death: Republic of Vietnam
Cemetery: Westminster Memorial Park—Westminster, California

Entered Service at: Fresno, Fresno County, California
Unit: Company L, 3d Battalion, 7th Marines, 1st Marine Division (Rein) FMF
Served as: Machine Gunner
Battle or Place of Action: Bo Ban, Quang Nam Province, Republic of Vietnam
Date of Action: 12 August 1968
Date of Presentation: 20 April 1970
Place of Presentation: The White House, presented by Vice Pres. Spiro T. Agnew to his family
Citation: For conspicuous gallantry and intrepidity at the risk of his life above and beyond the call of duty while serving as a machine gunner with Company L, 3d Battalion, in action against enemy forces. After establishing a night ambush position in a house in Bo Ban, a hamlet of Quang Nam Province, security was set up and the remainder of the patrol members retired until their respective watch. During the early morning hours the marines were abruptly awakened by the platoon leader's warning that "grenades" had landed in the house. Fully realizing the inevitable result of his actions, L/Cpl. Worley, in a valiant act of heroism, instantly threw himself upon the grenade nearest him and his comrades, absorbing with his body, the full and tremendous force of the explosion. Through his extraordinary initiative and inspiring valor in the face of almost certain death, he saved his comrades from serious injury and possible loss of life although five of his fellow marines incurred minor wounds as the other grenades exploded. L/Cpl. Worley's gallant actions upheld the highest traditions of the Marine Corps and the U.S. Naval Service. He gallantly gave his life for his country.

3391 ◆ WRIGHT, RAYMOND RICHARD "BUZZER"

Rank: Specialist Fourth Class
Service: U.S. Army
Birthday: 5 December 1945
Place of Birth: Moriah, Essex County, New York
Entered Service at: Moriah, Essex County, New York
Unit: Company A, 3d Battalion, 60th Infantry, 9th Infantry Division
Served as: Rifleman
Battle or Place of Action: Ap Bac Zone, Republic of Vietnam
Date of Action: 2 May 1967
G.O. Number, Date: 65, 22 October 1968
Date of Presentation: 19 September 1968
Place of Presentation: The White House, presented by Pres. Lyndon B. Johnson
Citation: For conspicuous gallantry and intrepidity at the risk of his life above and beyond the call of duty. While serving as a rifleman with Company A, Sp4c. Wright distinguished himself during a combat patrol in an area where an enemy ambush had occurred earlier. Sp4c. Wright's unit suddenly came under intense automatic-weapons and small-arms fire from an enemy bunker system protected by numerous snipers in nearby trees. Despite the heavy enemy fire, Sp4c. Wright and another soldier leaped to the top of a dike to assault the position. Armed with a rifle and several grenades,

he and his comrade exposed themselves to intense fire from the bunkers as they charged the nearest one. Sp4c. Wright raced to the bunker, threw in a grenade, killing its occupant. The two soldiers then ran through a hail of fire to a second bunker. While his comrade covered him with his machine gun, Sp4c. Wright charged the bunker and succeeded in killing its occupant with a grenade. A third bunker contained an automatic rifleman who had pinned down much of the friendly platoon. While his comrade again covered him with machine-gun fire, Sp4c. Wright charged in and killed the enemy rifleman with a grenade. The two soldiers worked their way through the remaining bunkers, knocking out four of them. Throughout their furious assault, Sp4c. Wright and his comrade had been almost continuously exposed to intense sniper fire from the treeline as the enemy desperately sought to stop their attack. Overcoming stubborn resistance from the bunker system, the men advanced into the treeline, forcing the snipers to retreat, giving immediate chase, and driving the enemy away from the friendly unit so that it advanced across the open area without further casualty. When his ammunition was exhausted, Sp4c. Wright returned to his unit to assist in the evacuation of the wounded. This two-man assault had driven an enemy platoon from a well-prepared position, accounted for numerous enemy casualties, and adverted further friendly casualties. Sp4c. Wright's extraordinary heroism, courage, and indomitable fighting spirit saved the lives of many of his comrades and inflicted serious damage on the enemy. His acts were in keeping with the highest traditions of the military service and reflect great credit upon himself and the U.S. Army.

3392 ◆ *YABES, MAXIMO

Rank: First Sergeant
Service: U.S. Army
Birthday: 29 January 1932
Place of Birth: Lodi, San Joaquin County, California
Date of Death: 26 February 1967
Place of Death: Republic of Vietnam
Cemetery: Fort Logan National Cemetery (R-369) (MH)—Denver, Colorado
Entered Service at: Eugene, Lane County, Oregon
Unit: Company A, 4th Battalion, 9th Infantry, 25th Infantry Division
Served as: Company First Sergeant
Battle or Place of Action: near Phu Hoa Dong, Republic of Vietnam
Date of Action: 26 February 1967
G.O. Number, Date: 71, 15 November 1968
Date of Presentation: 31 October 1968
Place of Presentation: The Pentagon, presented by Sec. of the Army Stanley R. Resor to his family
Citation: For conspicuous gallantry and intrepidity at the risk of his life above and beyond the call of duty. First Sgt. Yabes distinguished himself with Company A, which was providing security for a land-clearing operation. Early in the morning the company suddenly came under intense automatic-weapons and mortar fire followed by a ybattalion-battalion-sized assault from three sides. Penetrating the defensive

perimeter, the enemy advanced on the company command post bunker. The command post received increasingly heavy fire and was in danger of being overwhelmed. When several enemy grenades landed within the command post, 1st Sgt. Yabes shouted a warning and used his body as a shield to protect others in the bunker. Although painfully wounded by numerous grenade fragments, and despite the vicious enemy fire on the bunker, he remained there to provide covering fire and enable the others in the command group to relocate. When the command group had reached a new position, 1st Sgt. Yabes moved through a withering hail of enemy fire to another bunker 50 meters away. There he secured a grenade launcher from a fallen comrade and fired point-blank into the attacking Viet Cong, stopping further penetration of the perimeter. Noting two wounded men helpless in the fire-swept area, he moved them to a safer position where they could be given medical treatment. He resumed his accurate and effective fire, killing several enemy soldiers and forcing others to withdraw from the vicinity of the command post. As the battle continued, he observed an enemy machine gun within the perimeter which threatened the whole position. On his own, he dashed across the exposed area, assaulted the machine gun, killed the crew, destroyed the weapon, and fell mortally wounded. First Sgt. Yabes' valiant and selfless actions saved the lives of many of his fellow soldiers and inspired his comrades to effectively repel the enemy assault. His indomitable fighting spirit, extraordinary courage, and intrepidity at the cost of his life are in the highest military traditions and reflect great credit upon himself and the Armed Forces of his country.

3393 ◆ *YANO, RODNEY JAMES TADASHI

Rank: First Sergeant
Service: U.S. Army
Birthday: 13 December 1943
Place of Birth: Kealakekua Kona, Hawaii County, Hawaii
Date of Death: 1 January 1969
Place of Death: Republic of Vietnam
Cemetery: National Memorial Cemetery of the Pacific (W-614) (MH)—Honolulu, Hawaii
Entered Service at: Honolulu, Honolulu County, Hawaii
Unit: Air Cavalry Troop, 11th Armored Cavalry Regiment
Served as: Crew Chief
Battle or Place of Action: near Bien Hao, Republic of Vietnam
Date of Action: 1 January 1969
G.O. Number, Date: 15, 23 April 1970
Date of Presentation: 7 April 1970
Place of Presentation: The White House, presented by Pres. Richard M. Nixon to his family
Citation: Sfc. Yano distinguished himself while serving with the Air Cavalry Troop. Sfc. Yano was performing the duties of crew chief aboard the troop's command-and-control helicopter during action against enemy forces entrenched in dense jungle. From an exposed position in the face of small-arms and antiaircraft fire he delivered suppressive fire upon the enemy forces and marked their positions with smoke and white phosphorous grenades, thus enabling his troop com-

mander to direct accurate and effective artillery fire against the hostile emplacements. A grenade, exploding prematurely, covered him with burning phosphorous, and left him severely wounded. Flaming fragments within the helicopter caused supplies and ammunition to detonate. Dense white smoke filled the aircraft, obscuring the pilot's vision and causing him to lose control. Although having the use of only one arm and being partially blinded by the initial explosion, Sfc. Yano completely disregarded his welfare and began hurling blazing ammunition from the helicopter. In so doing he inflicted additional wounds upon himself, yet he persisted until the danger was past. Sfc. Yano's indomitable courage and profound concern for his comrades averted loss of life and additional injury to the rest of the crew. By his conspicuous gallantry at the cost of his life, in the highest traditions of the military service, Sfc. Yano has reflected great credit on himself, his unit, and the U.S. Army.

3394 ◆ *YNTEMA, GORDON DOUGLAS

Rank: Sergeant
Service: U.S. Army
Birthday: 26 June 1945
Place of Birth: Bethesda, Montgomery County, Maryland
Date of Death: 18 January 1968
Place of Death: Republic of Vietnam
Cemetery: Pilgrim Home Cemetery—Holland, Michigan
Entered Service at: Detroit, Wayne County, Michigan
Unit: Detachment A-431, Company D, 5th Special Forces Group (Airborne), 1st Special Forces
Served as: Advisor
Battle or Place of Action: near Thong Binh, Republic of Vietnam
Date of Action: 16-18 January 1968
G.O. Number, Date: 76, 3 December 1969
Date of Presentation: 18 November 1969
Place of Presentation: The White House, presented by Vice Pres. Spiro T. Agnew to his family
Citation: For conspicuous gallantry and intrepidity in action at the risk of his life above and beyond the call of duty. Sgt. Yntema, U.S. Army, distinguished himself while assigned to Detachment A-431, Company D. As part of a larger force of civilian irregulars from Camp Cai Cai, he accompanied two platoons to a blocking position east of the village of Thong Binh, where they became heavily engaged in a small-arms firefight with the Viet Cong. Assuming control of the force when the Vietnamese commander was seriously wounded, he advanced his troops to within 50 meters of the enemy bunkers. After a fierce 30-minute firefight, the enemy forced Sgt. Yntema to withdraw his men to a trench in order to afford them protection and still perform their assigned blocking mission. Under cover of machine-gun fire, approximately one company of Viet Cong maneuvered into a position which pinned down the friendly platoons from three sides. A dwindling ammunition supply, coupled with a Viet Cong mortar barrage which inflicted heavy losses on the exposed friendly troops, caused many of the irregulars to withdraw. Seriously wounded and ordered to withdraw himself, Sgt. Yntema refused to leave his fallen comrades. Under withering small-

arms and machine-gun fire, he carried the wounded Vietnamese commander and a mortally wounded American Special Forces adviser to a small gully 50 meters away in order to shield them from the enemy fire. Sgt. Yntema then continued to repulse the attacking Viet Cong attempting to overrun his position until, out of ammunition and surrounded, he was offered the opportunity to surrender. Refusing, Sgt. Yntema stood his ground, using his rifle as a club to fight the approximately 15 Viet Cong attempting his capture. His resistance was so fierce that the Viet Cong were forced to shoot in order to overcome him. Sgt. Yntema's personal bravery in the face of insurmountable odds and supreme self-sacrifice were in keeping with the highest traditions of the military service and reflect the utmost credit upon himself, the 1st Special Forces, and the U.S. Army.

3395 ◆ YOUNG, GERALD ORREN

Rank: Captain (highest rank: Lieutenant Colonel)
Service: U.S. Air Force
Birthday: 19 May 1930
Place of Birth: Chicago, Cook County, Illinois
Date of Death: 6 June 1990
Place of Death: Anacortes, Washington
Cemetery: Arlington National Cemetery (7-A-87) (MH)—Arlington, Virginia
Entered Service at: Colorado Springs, El Paso County, Colorado
Unit: 37th Air Rescue Service, Da Nang Air Force Base, Republic of Vietnam
Served as: Rescue Helicopter Crew Commander/Pilot—HH-3E
Battle or Place of Action: Khesanh, Republic of Vietnam
Date of Action: 9 November 1967
G.O. Number, Date: GB-208, 20 May 1968
Date of Presentation: 14 May 1968
Place of Presentation: The Pentagon (Inner Courtyard), Hall of Heroes, presented by Pres. Lyndon B. Johnson
Citation: For conspicuous gallantry and intrepidity at the risk of his life above and beyond the call of duty. Capt. Young distinguished himself while serving as a helicopter rescue crew commander. Capt. Young was flying escort for another helicopter attempting the night rescue of an Army ground reconnaissance team in imminent danger of death or capture. Previous attempts had resulted in the loss of two helicopters to hostile ground fire. The endangered team was positioned on the side of a steep slope which required unusual airmanship on the part of Capt. Young to effect pickup. Heavy automatic weapons fire from the surrounding enemy severely damaged one rescue helicopter, but it was able to extract three of the team. The commander of this aircraft recommended to Capt. Young that further rescue attempts be abandoned because it was not possible to suppress the concentrated fire from enemy automatic weapons. With full knowledge of the danger involved, and the fact that supporting helicopter gunships were low on fuel and ordnance, Capt. Young hovered under intense fire until the remaining survivors were aboard. As he maneuvered the aircraft for takeoff, the enemy appeared at point-blank range and raked the aircraft with

automatic-weapons fire. The aircraft crashed, inverted, and burst into flames. Capt. Young escaped through a window of the burning aircraft. Disregarding serious burns, Capt. Young aided one of the wounded men and attempted to lead the hostile forces away from his position. Later, despite intense pain from his burns, he declined to accept rescue because he had observed hostile forces setting up automatic-weapons positions to entrap any rescue aircraft. For more than 17 hours he evaded the enemy until rescue aircraft could be brought into the area. Through his extraordinary heroism, aggressiveness, and concern for his fellow man, Capt. Young reflected the highest credit upon himself, the U.S. Air Force, and the Armed Forces of his country.

3396 ◆ *YOUNG, MARVIN REX

Rank: Staff Sergeant
Service: U.S. Army
Birthday: 11 May 1947
Place of Birth: Alpine, Brewster County, Texas
Date of Death: 21 August 1968
Place of Death: Republic of Vietnam
Cemetery: Sunset Memorial Cemetery (MH)—Odessa, Texas
Entered Service at: Odessa, Ector County, Texas
Unit: Company C, 1st Battalion (Mechanized), 5th Infantry, 25th Infantry Division
Served as: Squad Leader
Battle or Place of Action: near Ben Cui, Republic of Vietnam
Date of Action: 21 August 1968
G.O. Number, Date: 27, 23 April 1970
Date of Presentation: 7 April 1970
Place of Presentation: The White House, presented by Pres. Richard M. Nixon to his family
Citation: For conspicuous gallantry and intrepidity in action at the risk of his life above and beyond the call of duty. S/Sgt. Young distinguished himself at the cost of his life while serving as a squad leader with Company C. While conducting a reconnaissance mission in the vicinity of Ben Cui, Company C was suddenly engaged by an estimated regimental-size force of the North Vietnamese Army. During the initial volley of fire the point element of the 1st Platoon was pinned down, sustaining several casualties, and the acting platoon leader was killed. S/Sgt. Young unhesitatingly assumed command of the platoon and immediately began to organize and deploy his men into a defensive position in order to repel the attacking force. As a human wave attack advanced on S/Sgt. Young's platoon, he moved from position to position, encouraging and directing fire on the hostile insurgents while exposing himself to the hail of enemy bullets. After receiving orders to withdraw to a better defensive position, he remained behind to provide covering fire for the withdrawal. Observing that a small element of the point squad was unable to extract itself from its position, and completely disregarding his personal safety, S/Sgt. Young began moving toward their position, firing as he maneuvered. When halfway to their position he sustained a critical head injury, yet he continued his mission and ordered the element to withdraw. Remaining

3397 ◆ ZABITOSKY, FRED WILLIAM

with the squad as it fought its way to the rear, he was twice seriously wounded in the arm and leg. Although his leg was badly shattered, S/Sgt. Young refused assistance that would have slowed the retreat of his comrades, and he ordered them to continue their withdrawal while he provided protective covering fire. With indomitable courage and heroic self-sacrifice he continued his self-assigned mission until the enemy force engulfed his position. By his gallantry at the cost of his life and in the highest traditions of the military service, S/Sgt. Young has reflected great credit upon himself, his unit and the U.S. Army.

3397 ◆ ZABITOSKY, FRED WILLIAM

Rank: Sergeant First Class (rank at time of action: Staff Sergeant) (highest rank: Master Sergeant)
Service: U.S. Army
Birthday: 27 October 1942
Place of Birth: Trenton, Mercer County, New Jersey
Entered Service at: Trenton, Mercer County, New Jersey
Unit: 5th Special Forces Group (Airborne), 1st Special Forces
Served as: Assistant Team Leader
Battle or Place of Action: Laos
Date of Action: 19 February 1968
G.O. Number, Date: 27, 17 April 1969
Date of Presentation: 7 March 1969
Place of Presentation: The White House (East Ballroom), presented by Pres. Richard M. Nixon
Citation: For conspicuous gallantry and intrepidity in action at the risk of his life above and beyond the call of duty. Sfc. Zabitosky, U.S. Army, distinguished himself while serving as an assistant team leader of a nine-man Special Forces long-range reconnaissance patrol. Sfc. Zabitosky's patrol was oper-

ating deep within enemy controlled territory when they were attacked by a numerically superior North Vietnamese Army unit. Sfc. Zabitosky rallied his team members, deployed them into defensive positions, and, exposing himself to concentrated enemy automatic weapons fire, directed their return fire. Realizing the gravity of the situation, Sfc. Zabitosky ordered his patrol to move to a landing zone for helicopter extraction while he covered their withdrawal with rifle fire and grenades. Rejoining the patrol under increasing enemy pressure, he positioned each man in a tight perimeter defense and continually moved from man to man, encouraging them and controlling their defensive fire. Mainly due to his example, the outnumbered patrol maintained its precarious position until the arrival of tactical air support and a helicopter extraction team. As the rescue helicopters arrived, the determined North Vietnamese pressed their attack. Sfc. Zabitosky repeatedly exposed himself to their fire to adjust suppressive helicopter-gunship fire around the landing zone. After boarding one of the rescue helicopters, he positioned himself in the door delivering fire on the enemy as the ship took off. The helicopter was engulfed in a hail of bullets and Sfc. Zabitosky was thrown from the craft as it spun out of control and crashed. Recovering consciousness, he ignored his extremely painful injuries and moved to the flaming wreckage. Heedless of the danger of exploding ordnance and fuel, he pulled the severely wounded pilot from the searing blaze and made repeated attempts to rescue his patrol members but was driven back by the intense heat. Despite his serious burns and crushed ribs, he carried and dragged the unconscious pilot through a curtain of enemy fire to within 10 feet of a hovering rescue helicopter before collapsing. Sfc. Zabitosky's extraordinary heroism and devotion to duty were in keeping with the highest traditons of the military serrvice and reflect great credit upon himself, his unit, and the U.S. Army.

SOMALIA
(OPERATION RESTORE HOPE)

3398 ◆ *GORDON, GARY IVAN

Rank: Master Sergeant
Service: U.S. Army
Birthday: 30 August 1960
Place of Birth: Lincoln, Penobscot County, Maine
Date of Death: 3 October 1993
Place of Death: Mogadishu, Somalia
Cemetery: Lincoln Cemetery—Lincoln, Maine
Entered Service at: Lincoln, Penobscot County, Maine
Unit: Task Force Ranger, Special Operations Command
Served as: Sniper Team Leader
Battle or Place of Action: Mogadishu, Somalia
Date of Action: 3 October 1993
Date of Presentation: 23 May 1994
Place of Presentation: The White House, presented by Pres. William J. Clinton to his Widow
Citation: M/Sgt. Gary I. Gordon, United States Army, distinguished himself by action above and beyond the call of duty on 3 October 1993, while serving as a Sniper Team Leader, United States Army Special Operations Command with Task Force Ranger in Mogadishu, Somalai. M/Sgt. Gordon's sniper team provided precision fires from the lead helicopter during an assault, and at two helicopter crash sites, while subjected to intense automatic weapons and rocket propelled grenade fires. When M/Sgt. Gordon learned that ground forces were not immediately available to secure the crash site, he and another sniper unhesitatingly volunteered to be inserted to protect the four critcally wounded personnel, despite being well aware of the growing number of enemy personnel closing in on the site. After his third request to be inserted, M/Sgt. Gordon received permission to perform his volunteer mission. When debris and enemy ground fires at the site caused him to abort the first attempt, M/Sgt. Gordon was inserted one hundred meters south of the crash site. Equipped with only his sniper rifle and pistol, M/Sgt. Gordon and his fellow sniper, while under intense small arms fire from the enemy, fought their way through a dense maze of shanties and shacks to reach the critically injured crew members. M/Sgt. Gordon immediately pulled the pilot and other crew members from the aircraft, establishing a perimeter which placed him and his fellow sniper in the most vulnerable position. M/Sgt. Gordon used his long range rifle and side arm to kill an undetermined number of attackers until he depleted his ammunition. M/Sgt. Gordon then went back to the wreckage, recovering some of the crew's weapons and ammunition. Despite the fact that he was critically low on ammunition he provided some of it to the dazed pilot and then radioed for help. M/Sgt. Gordon continued to travel the perimeter, protecting the downed crew. After his team member was fatally wounded, and his own rifle ammunition exhausted, M/Sgt. Gordon returned to the wreckage, recovering a rifle with the last five rounds of ammunition and gave it to the pilot with the words "Good Luck." Then, armed only with his pistol, M/Sgt. Gordon continued to fight until he was fatally wounded. His actions saved the pilot's life. M/Sgt. Gordon's extraordinary heroism and devotion to duty were in keeping with the highest standards of military service and reflect great credit on him, his unit, and the United States Army.

3399 ◆ *SHUGHART, RANDALL DAVID

Rank: Sergeant First Class
Service: U.S. Army
Birthday: 13 August 1958
Place of Birth: Lincoln, Lancaster County, Nebraska
Date of Death: 3 October 1993
Place of Death: Mogadishu, Somalia
Cemetery: Westminster Cemetery, Garden of Benediction (230-3-2)—North Middleton Township, Pennsylvania
Entered Service at: Newville, Cumberland County, Pennsylvania
Unit: Task Force Ranger, Special Operations Command
Served as: Sniper Team Member
Battle or Place of Action: Mogadishu, Somalia
Date of Action: 3 October 1993
Date of Presentation: 23 May 1994
Place of Presentation: The White House, presented by Pres. William J. Clinton to his Widow
Citation: Sfc. Randall D. Shughart, United States Army, distinguished himself by actions above and beyond the call of duty on 3 October 1993, while serving as a Sniper Team Member, United States Army Special Operations Command with Task Force Ranger in Mogadishu, Somalia. Sfc. Stughart provided precision sniper fires from the lead helicoper during an assault on a building and at two helicopter crash sites, while subjected to intense automatic weapons and rocket propelled grenade fires. While providing critical suppressive fires at the second crash site, Sfc. Stughart and his team leader learned that ground forces were not immediately available to secure the site. Sfc. Shughart and his team leader unhesitatingly volunteered to be inserted to protect the four critically wounded personnel, despite being well aware of the growing number of enemy personnel closing in on the site. After their third request to be inserted, Sfc. Shughart and his team leader received permission to perform this volunteer mission. When debris and enemy ground fires at the site caused them to

abort the first attempt, Sfc. Shughart and his team leader were inserted one hundred meters south of the crash site. Equipped with only his sniper rifle and a pistol, Sergeant First Class Shughart and his team leader, while under intense small arms fire from the enemy, fought their way through a dense maze of shanties and shacks to reach the critically injured crew members. Sfc. Shughart pulled the pilot and the other crew members from the aircraft, establishing a perimeter which placed him and his fellow sniper in the most vulnerable position. Sfc. Shughart used his long range rifle and side arm to kill an undetermined number of attackers while travelling the perimeter, protecting the downed crew. Sfc. Shughart continued his protective fire until he depleted his ammunition and was fatally wounded. His actions saved the pilot's life. Sfc. Shughart's extraordinary heroism and devotion to duty were in keeping with the highest standards of military service and reflect great credit on him, his unit, and the United States Army.

MEDALS OF HONOR AWARDED TO UNKNOWNS

On Armistice Day, 1921, the Medal of Honor was pinned to the flag-draped coffin of the American Unknown Soldier by President Harding during services at the Arlington National Cemetery. A special bill was passed by Congress permitting the award to an unknown as "typifying the gallantry and intrepidity, at the risk of life above and beyond the call of duty, or our beloved heroes who made the supreme sacrifice in the World War." Medals of Honor were also awarded by special legislation to the unknown soldiers of Belgium, Great Britain, France, Italy, and Rumania.

BELGIUM

* * *By virtue of the authority vested in the President of the United States, The Congressional Medal of Honor, emblem of the highest military ideals and virtues, is bestowed in the name of the Congress of the United States upon the unknown, unidentified Belgian soldier in a desire to add all that is possible to the imperishable glory won by the soldiers of Belgium who fought as comrades of the American soldiers during the World War, and to commemorate with them the deeds of the nations associated with the United States of America, by paying this tribute to their unknown dead (A.G. 220.523) (War Department General Orders, No.52, 1 December 1922, Sec. I).

GREAT BRITAIN AND FRANCE

* * * By virtue of an act of Congress approved 4 March 1921, the Medal of Honor, emblem of highest ideals and virtues, is bestowed in the name of the Congress of the United States upon the unknown, unidentified British soldier and French soldier buried, respectively, in Westminster Abbey and Arc de Triomphe.

Whereas Great Britain and France, two of the Allies of the United States in the World War, have done honor to the unknown dead of their armies by placing with fitting ceremony the body of an unidentified soldier, respectively, in Westminster Abbey and in the Arc de Triomphe; and

Whereas animated by the same spirit of comradeship in which we of the American Forces fought alongside these allies, we desire to add whatever we can to the imperishable glory won by the deeds of our Allies and commemorated in part by this tribute to their unknown dead:

Now therefore,

Be it enacted by the Senate and House of Representatives of the United States of America assembled, That the President of the United States of America be, and he hereby is, authorized to bestow with appropriate ceremonies, military and civil, the Congressional Medal of Honor upon the unknown, unidentified British soldier buried in Westminster Abbey, London, England, and upon the unknown, unidentified French soldier buried in the Arc de Triomphe, Paris, France (A.G. 220.523) (War Department General Orders, No. 52, 1 December 1922, Sec. II).

ITALY

* * * By virtue of a joint resolution of Congress, approved 12 October 1921, the Medal of Honor, emblem of highest ideals and virtues, is bestowed in the name of Congress of the United States of America upon the unknown, unidentified Italian soldier to be buried in the National Monument to Victor Emanuel II, in Rome.

Whereas the Congress has authorized the bestowal of the Congressional Medal of Honor upon the unknown, unidentified British and French soldiers buried in Westminster Abbey, London, England, and the Arc de Triomphe, Paris, France, respectfully, who fought beside our soldiers in the recent war; and

Whereas, animated by the same spirit of friendship toward the soldiers of Italy who also fought as comrades of the American soldiers during the World War, we desire to add whatever we can to the imperishable glory won by their deeds and to participate in paying tribute to their unknown dead: Now, therefore, be it

Resolved by the Senate and House of Representatives of the United States of America in Congress assembled, That the President of the United States be, and he is hereby, authorized to bestow, with appropriate ceremonies, military and civil, the Congressional Medal of Honor upon the unknown, unidentified Italian soldier to be buried in the National Monument to Victor Emanuel II, in Rome, Italy (A.G. 220.523) (War Department General Orders, No. 52, 1 December 1922, Sec. III).

RUMANIA

* * * By virtue of the authority vested by law in the President of the United States, The Congressional Medal of Honor, emblem of the highest military ideals and virtues, is bestowed in the name of the Congress of the United States upon the unknown, unidentified Rumanian soldier in a desire to add all that is possible to the imperishable glory won by the soldiers of Rumania who fought as comrades of the American soldiers during the World War, and to commemorate with them the deeds of the nations associated with the United States of America, by paying tribute to their unknown dead. The medal is on display at the National Minority Museum in Bucharest, Rumania (A.G. 220.52, 17 May 1923) (War Department General Orders, No. 22, 6 June 1923).

UNITED STATES

* * * By virtue of an Act of Congress approved 24 August 1921, the Medal of Honor, emblem of highest ideals and virtues is bestowed in the name of Congress of the United States upon the unknown American, typifying the gallantry and intrepidity, at the risk of life above and beyond the call of duty, of our beloved heroes who made the supreme sacrifice in the World War. They died in order that others might live (293.8, A.G.O.) (War Department General Orders, No. 59, 13 December 1921, Sec. I).

AN ACT To authorize the President to award the Medal of Honor to the unknown Americans who lost his life while serving overseas in the armed forces of the United States during the Second World War.

Be it enacted by the Senate and House of Representatives of the United States of America assembled, That the President is hereby authorized and directed to award, in the name of Con-

gress, a Medal of Honor to the unknown American who lost his life while serving overseas in the armed forces of the United States during the Second World War, and who will lie buried in the Memorial Amphitheater of the National Cemetery at Arlington, Virginia, as authorized by the Act of June 24, 1946, Public Law 438, Seventy-ninth Congress.

Approved March 9, 1948, Public Law 438, Eightieth Congress.

AN ACT TO authorize the President to award the Medal of Honor to the unknown American who lost his life while serving overseas in the Armed Forces of the United States during the Korean War.

Be it enacted by the Senate and the House of Representatives of the United States of America assembled, That the President is hereby authorized and directed to award, in the name of Congress, a Medal of Honor to the unknown American who lost his life while serving overseas in the Armed Forces of the United States during the Korean War, and who will lie buried in the Memorial Amphitheater of the National Cemetery at Arlington, Virginia, as authorized by the Act of August 3, 1956, Public Law 975, Eighty-fourth Congress.

Approved August 31, 1957, Public Law 85-251, Eighty-fifth Congress.

AN ACT TO authorize the President to award the Medal of Honor to the unknown American who lost his life while serving in the Armed Forces of the United States in Southeast Asia during the Vietnam Era and who has been selected to be buried in the Memorial Amphitheater at Arlington National Cemetery.

Be it enacted by the Senate and the House of Representatives of the United States of America assembled, That the President may award, and present in the name of Congress, the Medal of Honor to the unknown American who lost his life while serving in Southeast Asia during the Vietnam Era as a member of the Armed Forces of the United States of America and who has been selected to lie buried in the Memorial Amphitheater of the National Cemetery at Arlington, Virginia, as authorized by Section 9 of the National Cemeteries Act of 1973 (Pubic Law 93-43), Ninety-third Congress.

Approved May 25, 1984. Public Law 98-301, Ninety-eighth Congress.

APPENDIXES

ABBREVIATIONS

A1c.	airman first class	LCS	landing craft, support
A.A.C.	army air corp	LST	landing ship tank
A.G.	adjutant general	Lt.	lieutenant
Adm.	admiral	M/Sgt.	master sergeant
AFB	air force base	Maj.	major
AGTR	technical research ship	MH	Medal of Honor
ARNG	Army National Guard	PBR	patrol boat, river
Brig.	brigadier	Pfc.	private first class
C.B.	cabin boy	PmS.	paymaster's steward
C.G.	chief gunner	Pvt.	private
C.H.	coal heaver	Q.G.	quarter gunner
C.S.A.	Confederate States of America	Q.M.	quartermaster
C.S.S.	Confederate steamship	Recon.	reconnaissance
Capt.	captain	Rein	Reinforced (unit composed of men from other units to bring the unit up to full strength)
Col.	colonel		
Comdr.	commander	Ret.	retired
Cpl.	corporal	S/man	seaman
CWO	chief warrant officer	S/Q.M.	signal quartermaster
DE	destroyer escort	S/Sgt.	staff sergeant
Ens.	ensign	SCARNG	South Carolina Army National Guard
FAC	forward air controller	SEAL	sea, air and land
FMF	fleet marine force	Sec.	secretary
G.O.#	general order number	Sfc.	sergeant first class
G/Sgt.	gunnery sergeant	Sgt.	sergeant
Gen.	general	Sp4c.	specialist fourth class
Gp.	group	Sp5c.	specialist fifth class
HC2c.	hospital corpsman second class	Surg.	surgeon
HC3c.	hospital corpsman third class	T/Sgt.	technical sergeant
HC	hospital corpsman	Tech.	technician
j.g.	junior grade	U.S.A.	U.S. Army
L/Cpl.	lance corporal	U.S.S.	United States ship
LCI(G)	landing craft infantry gunboat	WO	warrant officer

RECIPIENTS BY STATE OF ENLISTMENT & BIRTH

ALABAMA

U.S. Army

BOLDEN, Paul Luther	ES: Madison, Madison Co., AL B: Hobbes Island, AL
BOLTON, Cecil Hamilton	ES: Huntsville, Madison Co., AL B: Crawfordville, Wakulla Co., FL
DAVIS, Charles Willis	ES: Montgomery, Montgomery Co., AL B: Gordo, Pickens Co., AL
*EVANS, Rodney John	ES: Montgomery, Montgomery Co., AL B: Chelsea, Suffolk Co., MA
HOWARD, Robert Lewis	ES: Montgomery, Montgomery Co., AL B: Opelika, Lee Co., AL
JOHNSTON, Gordon	ES: Birmingham, Jefferson Co., AL B: Charlotte, Mecklenburg Co., NC
*LEONARD, Matthew	ES: Birmingham, Jefferson Co., AL B: Eutaw, Greene Co., AL
LINDSEY Sr., Jake William	ES: Lucedale, George Co., MS B: Isney, AL
MANNING, Sidney E.	ES: Flomaton, Escambia Co., AL B: Butler Co., AL
*MICHAEL, Don Leslie	ES: Montgomery, Montgonery Co., AL B: Florence, Lauderdale Co., AL
MIZE, Ola Lee	ES: Gadsden, Etowah Co., AL B: Albertville, Marshall Co., AL
*SEAY, William Wayne	ES: Montgomery, Montgomery Co., AL B: Brewton, Escambia Co., AL
SPRAYBERRY, James Michael	ES: Montgomery, Montgomery Co., AL B: LaGrange, Troup Co., GA
TAYLOR, Richard	ES: Indianapolis, Marion Co., IN B: Madison Co., AL
TREADWELL, Jack Lemaster	ES: Snyder, Kiowa Co., OK B: Ashland, Clay Co., AL

U.S. Army Air Corps/U.S. Air Force

ERWIN, Henry Eugene "Red"	ES: Bessemer, Jefferson Co., AL B: Adamsville, Jefferson Co., AL
LAWLEY Jr., William Robert	ES: Birmingham, Jefferson Co., AL B: Leeds, Jefferson Co., AL

U.S. Navy

*GILMORE, Howard Walter	ES: LA B: Selma, Dallas Co., AL
HOBSON, Richmond Pearson	ES: NY B: Greensboro, Hale Co., AL
HOUGHTON, Edward J.	ES: AL B: Mobile, Mobile Co., AL
*INGRAM, Osmond Kelly	ES: AL B: Platt City, AL
McCAMPBELL, David	ES: West Palm Beach, Palm Beach Co., FL B: Bessemer, Jefferson Co., AL

U.S. Marine Corps

*GRAY, Ross Franklin	ES: AL B: Marvel Valley, AL
McLAUGHLIN, Alford Lee	ES: Leeds, Jefferson Co., AL B: Leeds, Jefferson Co., AL
*NEW, John Dury	ES: AL B: Mobile, Mobile Co., AL
WATSON, Wilson Douglas	ES: Earle, Crittenden Co., AR B: Tuscumbia, Colbert Co., AL
WILSON, Harold Edward "Speedy"	ES: Birmingham, Jefferson Co., AL B: Birmingham, Jefferson Co., AL

ALASKA

U.S. Marine Corps

VAN WINKLE, Archie	ES: Arlington, Snohomish Co., WA B: Juneau, Juneau Co., AK

ARIZONA

U.S. Army

ALCHESAY, William	ES: Camp Verde, Yavapai Co., Arizona Territory B: AZ
BACON, Nicky Daniel	ES: Phoenix, Maricopa Co., AZ B: Caraway, Craighead Co., AR
BLANQUET	B: AZ

CHIQUITO	ES: San Carlos, Gila Co., AZ B: AZ
DUNAGAN, Kern Wayne	ES: Los Angeles, Los Angeles Co., CA B: Superior, Pinal Co., AZ
ELSATSOOSH	B: Arizona Territory
FERGUSON, Frederick Edgar	ES: Phoenix, Maricopa Co., AZ B: Pilot Point, Denton Co., TX
HERRERA, Silvestre Santana	ES: Phoenix, Maricopa Co., AZ B: El Paso, El Paso Co., TX
JIM	ES: Camp Verde, Yavapia Co., Arizona Territory B: Arizona Territory
KELSAY	ES: Arizona Territory B: Arizona Territory
KOSOHA	B: Arizona Territory
*LAUFFER, Billy Lane	ES: Phoenix, Maricopa Co., AZ B: Murray, Calloway Co., KY
MACHOL	B: Arizona Territory
NANNASADDIE	B: Arizona Territory
NANTAJE (NANTAHE)	B: Arizona Territory
ROWDY	ES: San Carlos, Gila Co., AZ B: Arizona Territory
SMITH, Cornelius Cole	ES: Helena, Lewis & Clark Co., MT B: Tucson, Pima Co., AZ

U.S. Army Air Service

*LUKE Jr., Frank	ES: Phoenix, Maricopa Co., AZ B: Phoenix, Maricopa Co., AZ

U.S. Marine Corps

*AUSTIN, Oscar Palmer	ES: Phoenix, Maricopa Co., AZ B: Nacogdoches, Nacogdoches Co., TX
*JIMENEZ, Jose Francisco	ES: Phoenix, Maricopa Co., AZ B: Mexico City, Mexico
*PRUITT, John Henry	ES: Phoenix, Maricopa Co., AZ B: Fayetteville, Washington Co., AR
VARGAS, Jay R.	ES: Winslow, Navajo Co., AZ B: Winslow, Navajo Co., AZ

ARKANSAS

U.S. Army

BACON, Nicky Daniel	ES: Phoenix, Maricopa Co., AZ B: Caraway, Craighead Co., AR
BRITT, Maurice Lee "Footsie"	ES: Lonoke, Lonoke Co., AR B: Carlisle, Lonoke Co., AR
BURKE, Lloyd Leslie "Scooter"	ES: Stuttgart, Arkansas Co., AR B: Tichnor, Arkansas Co., AR
*CHILES, Marcellus Holmes	ES: Denver, Denver Co., CO B: Eureka Springs, Carroll Co., AR
*COLLIER, Gilbert G.	S: Tichnor, Arkansas Co., AR B: Hunter, Woodruff Co., AR
FACTOR, Pompey	ES: Fort Duncan, TX B: AR
*GILLILAND, Charles L.	ES: Yellville, Marion Co., AR B: Mountain Home, Baxter Co., AR

HENDRIX, James Richard	ES: Lepanto, Poinsett Co., AR B: Lepanto, Poinsett Co., AR
*LLOYD, Edgar Harold	ES: Blytheville, Mississippi Co., AR B: Blytheville, Mississippi Co., AR
MacARTHUR, Douglas	ES: Ashland, Ashland Co., WI B: Little Rock, Pulaski Co., AR
*MILLER, Oscar F.	ES: Los Angeles, Los Angeles Co., CA B: Franklin Co., AR
STONE, James Lamar	ES: Houston, Harris Co., TX B: Pine Bluff, Jefferson Co., AR
*TERRY, Seymour W.	ES: Little Rock, Pulaski Co., AR B: Little Rock, Pulaski Co., AR
*THOMAS, William H.	ES: Ypsilanti, Washtenaw Co., MI B: Wynne, Cross Co., AR
WARD, John	ES: Fort Duncan, TX B: AR
*WATKINS, Travis E.	ES: TX B: Waldo, Columbia Co., AR
WHEELER, Henry W.	ES: Bangor, Penobscot Co., ME B: Fort Smith, Sebastian Co., AR

U.S. Navy

FRANKS, William J.	ES: De Valls Bluff, Prairie Co., AR B: Chatham Co., NC
GORDON, Nathan Green	ES: Morrilton, Conway Co., AR B: Morrilton, Conway Co., AR
*WILLIAMS, Jack	ES: AR B: Harrison, Boone Co., AR

U.S. Marine Corps

*LITTLETON, Herbert A.	ES: Black Hawk, Meade Co., SD B: Mena, Polk Co., AR
*PRUITT, John Henry	ES: Phoenix, Maricopa Co., AZ B: Fayetteville, Washington Co., AR
WATSON, Wilson Douglas	ES: Earle, Crittenden Co., AR B: Tuscumbia, Colbert Co., AL

CALIFORNIA

U.S. Army

BACA, John Philip	ES: Fort Ord, Monterey Co., CA B: Providence, Providence Co., RI
BARNES, Will Croft	ES: Washington, D.C. B: San Francisco, San Francisco Co., CA
*BELLRICHARD, Leslie Allen	ES: Oakland, Alameda Co., CA B: Janesville, Rock Co., WI
BROPHY, James	ES: Stockton, San Joaquin Co., CA B: Kilkenny, Ireland
BURKE, Patrick J.	ES: Vallejo, Solano Co., CA B: Kilkenny, Ireland
CARR, John	ES: San Jose, Santa Clara Co., CA B: Columbus, Franklin Co., OH
CARTER, George	ES: Vallejo, Solano Co., CA B: Dublin, Ireland
CAVAIANI, Jon Robert	ES: Fresno, Fresno Co., CA B: Royston, England
CRAFT, Clarence Byrle	ES: Santa Ana, Orange Co., CA B: San Bernardino, San Bernardino Co., CA
CROCKER, Henry H.	ES: San Francisco, San Francisco Co., CA B: Colchester, New London Co., CT

DEAN Sr., William Frishe | ES: CA
B: Carlyle, Clinton Co., IL

*DESIDERIO, Reginald Benjamin | ES: Gilroy, Santa Clara Co., CA
B: Clairton, Allegheny Co., PA

*DEVORE Jr., Edward Allen | ES: Harbor City, Los Angeles Co., CA
B: Torrance, Los Angeles Co., CA

DICKENS, Charles H. | ES: San Francisco, San Francisco Co., CA
B: Dublin, Ireland

DUNAGAN, Kern Wayne | ES: Los Angeles, Los Angeles Co., CA
B: Superior, Pinal Co., AZ

ELWOOD, Edwin L. | ES: San Jose, Santa Clara Co., CA
B: St. Louis, St Louis Co., MO

*EVANS Jr., Donald Ward | ES: Covina, Los Angeles Co., CA
B: Covina, Los Angeles Co., CA

FALCOTT, Henry | ES: San Francisco, San Francisco Co., CA
B: Champagne, France

GARDNER, Charles | ES: San Francisco, San Francisco Co., CA
B: Bavaria, Germany

GOLDEN, Patrick | ES: San Francisco, San Francisco Co., CA
B: County Sligo, Ireland

*GONZALES, David M. | ES: Pacoima, Los Angeles Co., CA
B: Pacoima, Los Angeles Co., CA

GREEN, Francis C. | ES: Sacramento, Sacramento Co., CA
B: Mount Vernon, Posey Co., IN

GUMPERTZ, Sydney G. | ES: Chicago, Cook Co., IL
B: San Raphael, Marin Co., CA

HALL, John | ES: Sacramento, Sacramento Co., CA
B: Logan Co., IL

HAMILTON, Frank | ES: Sacramento, Sacramento Co., CA
B: County Tyrone, Ireland

*HARMON, Roy W. | ES: Pixley, Tulare Co., CA
B: Talala, Rogers Co., OK

HARVEY, Raymond | ES: Pasadena, Los Angeles Co., CA
B: Ford City, Armstrong Co., PA

HAWK, John Druse "Bud" | ES: Bremerton, Kitsap Co., WA
B: San Francisco, San Francisco Co., CA

HEARTERY, Richard | ES: San Francisco, San Francisco Co., CA
B: Ireland

HERNANDEZ, Rodolfo Perez | ES: Fowler, Fresno Co., CA
B: Colton, San Bernardino Co., CA

HIGGINS, Thomas P. | ES: Napa, Napa Co., CA
B: Longford, Ireland

HIGH, Frank Charles | ES: Ashland, Jackson Co., OR
B: Dunningham, Yolo Co., CA

HOLDERMAN, Nelson Miles | ES: Santa Ana, Orange Co., CA
B: Trumbull, Clay Co., NE

HOOPER, Joe Ronnie | ES: Los Angeles, Los Angeles Co., CA
B: Piedmont, Greenville Co., SC

*INGALLS, George Alan | ES: Los Angeles, Los Angeles Co., CA
B: Hanford, Kings Co., CA

JENNINGS, Delbert Owen | ES: San Francisco, San Francisco Co., CA
B: Silver City, Grant Co., NM

*KANDLE, Victor Leonard | ES: Redwood City, San Mateo Co., CA
B: Roy, Pierce Co., WA

KATZ, Phillip Carl | ES: San Francisco, San Francisco Co., CA
B: San Francisco, San Francisco Co., CA

KEENAN, John | ES: San Francisco, San Francisco Co., CA
B: Tubbercurry, County Sligo, Ireland

LAWRENCE, James | ES: Sacramento, Sacramento Co., CA
B: Aberdeen, Scotland

*LEAHY, Cornelius J. | ES: San Francisco, San Francisco Co., CA
B: Limerick, Ireland

*LEISY, Robert Ronald | ES: Seattle, King Co., WA
B: Stockton, San Joaquin Co., CA

LITTRELL, Gary Lee | ES: Los Angeles, Los Angeles Co., CA
B: Henderson, Henderson Co., KY

LYTTON, Jeptha L. | ES: San Francisco, San Francisco Co., CA
B: Lawrence Co., IN

MAHERS, Herbert | ES: Wilmington, Los Angeles Co., CA
B: Canada

McKINLEY, Daniel | ES: San Francisco, San Francisco Co., CA
B: Boston, Suffolk Co., MA

McMAHON, Martin Thomas | ES: CA
B: LaPrairie, Quebec, Canada

McVEAGH, Charles H. | ES: San Francisco, San Francisco Co., CA
B: New York, NY

*MILLER, Oscar F. | ES: Los Angeles, Los Angeles Co., CA
B: Franklin Co., AR

*MOLNAR, Frankie Zoly | ES: Fresno, Fresno Co., CA
B: Logan, Logan Co., WV

*MOON Jr., Harold Herman | ES: Gardena, Los Angeles Co., CA
B: Albuquerque, Bernalillo Co., NM

MORAN, John | ES: Marysville, Yuba Co., CA
B: Lyon, France

*MUNEMORI, Sadao S. | ES: Los Angeles, Los Angeles Co., CA
B: Los Angeles, Los Angeles Co., CA

MURPHY, Thomas | ES: San Francisco, San Francisco Co., CA
B: County Kerry, Ireland

O'CALLAGHAN, John | ES: San Francisco, San Francisco Co., CA
B: New York, NY

PENRY, Richard Allen | ES: Oakland, Alameda Co., CA
B: Petaluma, Sonoma Co., CA

*PIERCE, Larry Stanley | ES: Fresno, Fresno Co., CA
B: Wewoka, Seminole Co., OK

QUINN, Peter H. | ES: San Francisco, San Francisco Co., CA
B: San Francisco, San Francisco Co., CA

REED, James C. | ES: San Francisco, San Francisco Co., CA
B: Kilkenny, Ireland

REGAN, Patrick J. | ES: Los Angeles, Los Angeles Co., CA
B: Middleboro, Plymouth Co., MA

*ROARK, Anund Charles | ES: Los Angeles, Los Angeles Co., CA
B: Vallejo, Solano Co., CA

*ROBERTS, Harold W. | ES: San Francisco, San Francisco Co., CA
B: San Francisco, San Francisco Co., CA

ROCCO, Louis Richard | ES: Los Angeles, Los Angeles Co., CA
B: Albuquerque, Bernalillo Co., NM

RODRIGUEZ, Joseph Charles | ES: San Bernardino, San Bernardino Co., CA
B: San Bernardino, San Bernardino Co., CA

SEIBERT, Lloyd Martin | ES: Salinas, Monterey Co., CA
B: Caledonia, Kent Co., MI

SHIELS, George Franklin | ES: CA
B: CA

*SHOCKLEY, William Ralph | ES: Selma, Fresno Co., CA
B: Bokoshe, LeFlore Co., OK

SMITH, Otto | ES: Sacramento, Sacramento Co., CA
B: Baltimore, Baltimore Co., MD

SMITH, William | ES: San Francisco, San Francisco Co., CA
B: Bath, Sagadahoc Co., ME

STANLEY, Edward	ES: San Francisco, San Francisco Co., CA B: New York, NY	*JONES, Herbert Charpoit	ES: CA B: Los Angeles, Los Angeles Co., CA
STRIVSON, Benoni	ES: Sacramento, Sacramento Co., CA B: Overton, TN	*KOELSCH, John Kelvin	ES: Los Angeles, Los Angeles Co., CA B: London, EnglandU.S. Marine Corps
TAYLOR, James Allen	ES: San Francisco, San Francisco Co., CA B: Arcata, Humboldt Co., CA	LAVERTY, John	ES: CA B: County Tyrone, Ireland
TURNER, George Benton	ES: Los Angeles, Los Angeles Co., CA B: Longview, Gregg Co., TX	McALLISTER, Samuel	ES: CA B: Belfast, County Antrim, Ireland
*VIALE, Robert M.	ES: Ukiah, Mendocino Co., CA B: Bayside, Humboldt Co., CA	McGONAGLE, William Loren	ES: Thermal, Riverside Co., CA B: Wichita, Sedgwick Co., KS
*VILLEGAS, Ysmael R.	ES: Casa Blanca, CA B: Casa Blanca, CA	PHARRIS, Jackson Charles	ES: CA B: Columbus, Muscogee Co., GA
VON SCHLICK, Robert H.	ES: San Francisco, San Francisco Co., CA B: Germany	SMITH, Eugene P.	ES: CA B: Illinois
WARE, Keith Lincoln	ES: Glendale, Los Angeles Co., CA B: Denver, Denver Co., CO	STOLTENBERG, Andrew Vincent	ES: CA B: Bodo, Norway
WAYBUR, David Crowder	ES: Piedmont, Alameda Co., CA B: Oakland, Alameda Co., CA	VOLZ, Robert	ES: VA B: San Francisco, San Francisco Co., CA
WEAVER, Amos	ES: San Francisco, San Francisco Co., CA B: Niles Township, Delaware Co., IN	WESTERMARK, Axel	ES: CA B: Bergo, Finland
WEST, Chester Howard	ES: Los Banos, Merced Co., CA B: Fort Collins, Larimer Co., CO	WILLIAMS, Louis	ES: CA B: Christiana (now Oslo), Norway
WILLISTON, Edward Bancroft	ES: San Francisco, San Francisco Co., CA B: Norwich, Windsor Co., VT	WOODS, Samuel	ES: CA B: San Francisco, San Francisco Co., CA
*YABES, Maximo	ES: Eugene, Lane Co., OR B: Lodi, San Joaquin Co., CA		
*YOUNG, Robert Harley	ES: Vallejo, Solano Co., CA B: Oroville, Butte Co., CA		

U.S. Marine Corps

*ANDERSON Jr., James	ES: Los Angeles, Los Angeles Co., CA B: Los Angeles, Los Angeles Co., CA
BOYDSTON, Erwin Jay	ES: CA B: Deer Creek, CO
BURNES, James	ES: CA B: Worcester, Worcester Co., MA
COLEMAN, John	ES: CA B: County Cork, Ireland
DAHLGREN, John Olof	ES: CA B: Kahliwar, Sweden
*FOSTER, Paul Hellstrom	ES: San Francisco, San Francisco Co., CA B: San Mateo, San Mateo Co., CA
*GONSALVES, Harold	ES: CA B: Alameda, Alameda Co., CA
HEISCH, Henry William	ES: CA B: Latendorf, Germany
HULBERT, Henry Lewis	ES: CA B: Kingston upon Hull, Humberside Co., England
*JOHNSON, Ralph Henry	ES: Oakland, Alameda Co., CA B: Charleston, Charleston Co., SC
*KELSO, Jack William	ES: Caruthers, Fresno Co., CA B: Madera, Madera Co., CA
*MATTHEWS, Daniel Paul	ES: Van Nuys, Los Angeles Co., CA B: Van Nuys, Los Angeles Co., CA
*MAXAM, Larry Leonard	ES: Los Angeles, Los Angeles Co., CA B: Glendale, Los Angeles Co., CA
McNALLY, Michael Joseph	ES: CA B: New York, NY
MOORE, Albert	ES: CA B: Merced, Merced Co., CA
*OBREGON, Eugene Arnold	ES: Los Angeles, Los Angeles Co., CA B: Los Angeles, Los Angeles Co., CA
ORNDOFF, Harry Westley	ES: CA B: Sandusky, Erie Co., OH

YOUNT, John P.	ES: Sacramento, Sacramento Co., CA B: Putnam Co., IN

U.S. Army Air Corps/U.S. Air Force

*CHELI, Ralph	ES: Brooklyn, Kings Co., NY B: San Francisco, San Francisco Co., CA
DOOLITTLE, James Harold	ES: Berkeley, Alameda Co., CA B: Alameda, Alameda Co., CA

U.S. Air Force

FISHER, Bernard Francis	ES: Kuna, Ada Co., ID B: San Bernardino, San Bernardino Co., CA

U.S. Navy

BROCK, George F.	ES: CA B: Cleveland, Montgomery Co., OH
*CALLAGHAN, Daniel Judson	ES: Oakland, Alameda Co., CA B: San Francisco, San Francisco Co., CA
CLAUSEY, John Joseph	ES: CA B: San Francisco, San Francisco Co., CA
COVINGTON, Jesse Whitfield	ES: CA B: Haywood, TN
FINN, John William	ES: Belle Vernon Acres, CA B: Los Angeles, Los Angeles Co., CA
FISHER, Frederick Thomas	ES: CA B: England
HALFORD, William	ES: San Francisco, San Francisco Co., CA B: Gloucester, Gloucestershire, England
HANSEN, Hans Anton	ES: CA B: Germany
HENRECHON, George Francis	ES: CA B: Hartford, Hartford Co., CT
ITRICH, Franz Anton	ES: CA B: Gross Katz, Germany

*PERKINS Jr., William Thomas   ES: San Francisco, San Francisco Co., CA
B: Rochester, Monroe Co., NY

PHILLIPS, Reuben Jasper   ES: CA
B: Cambria, San Luis Obispo Co., CA

*PHIPPS, Jimmy Wayne   ES: Culver City, Los Angeles Co., CA
B: Santa Monica, Los Angeles Co., CA

PITTMAN, Richard Allan   ES: Stockton, San Joaquin Co., CA
B: French Camp, San Joaquin Co., CA

*POYNTER, James Irsley   ES: Downey, Los Angeles Co., CA
B: Bloomington, McLean Co., IL

SILVA, France   ES: San Francisco, San Francisco Co., CA
B: Hayward, Alameda Co., CA

SWETT, James Elms   ES: San Mateo, San Mateo Co., CA
B: Seattle, King Co., WA

*WORLEY, Kenneth Lee   ES: Fresno, Fresno Co., CA
B: Farmington, San Juan Co., NM

ZION, William F.   ES: CA
B: Knightstown, Henry Co., IN

COLORADO

U.S. Army

*CHILES, Marcellus Holmes ES: Denver, Denver Co., CO
B: Eureka Springs, Carroll Co., AR

CRAWFORD, William John   ES: Pueblo, Pueblo Co., CO
B: Pueblo, Pueblo Co., CO

DIX, Drew Dennis   ES: Denver, Denver Co., CO
B: West Point, Orange Co., NY

*FRYAR, Elmer E.   ES: Denver, Denver Co., CO
B: Denver, Denver Co., CO

FUNK, Jesse N.   ES: Calhan, El Paso Co., CO
B: New Hampton, Harrison Co., MO

GROVE, William Remsburg   ES: Denver, Denver Co., CO
B: Montezuma, Poweshiek Co., IA

KNIGHT, Joseph F.   ES: Denver, Denver Co., CO
B: Danville, Vermilion Co., IL

*LINDSTROM, Floyd K.   ES: Colorado Springs, El Paso Co., CO
B: Holdrege, Phelps Co., NE

*MARTINEZ, Joe P.   ES: Ault, Weld Co., CO
B:aos, Taos Co., NM

MAXWELL, Robert Dale   ES: Creswell, Larimer Co., CO
B: Boise, Ada Co., ID

*McWETHY Jr., Edgar Lee   ES: Denver, Denver Co., CO
B: Leadville, Lake Co., CO

WALLACE, George Weed   ES: Denver, Denver Co., CO
B: Fort Riley, Geary Co., KS

WARE, Keith Lincoln   ES: Glendale, Los Angeles Co., CA
B: Denver, Denver Co., CO

WEST, Chester Howard   ES: Los Banos, Merced Co., CA
B: Fort Collins, Larimer Co., CO

*WICKERSHAM, J. Hunter   ES: Denver, Denver Co., CO
B: New York, NY

U.S. Army Air Corps/U.S. Air Force

*PUCKET, Donald Dale   ES: Boulder, Boulder Co., CO
B: Longmont, Boulder Co., CO

*WALKER, Kenneth Newton   ES: Denver, Denver Co., CO
B: Cerrillos, Santa Fe Co., NM

YOUNG, Gerald Orren   ES: Colorado Springs, El Paso Co., CO
B: Chicago, Cook Co., IL

U.S. Navy

GRAVES, Ora   ES: NE
B: Las Animas, Bent Co., CO

McCANDLESS, Bruce   ES: CO
B: Washington, D.C.

ROSS, Donald Kirby   ES: Denver, Denver Co., CO
B: Beverly, Lincoln Co., KS

UPTON, Frank Monroe   ES: CO
B: Loveland, Larimer Co., CO

U.S. Marine Corps

BOYDSTON, Erwin Jay   ES: CA
B: Deer Creek, CO

*COKER, Ronald Leroy   ES: Denver, Denver Co., CO
B: Alliance, Box Butte Co., NE

*GUILLEN, Ambrosio   ES: El Paso, El Paso Co., TX
B: La Junta, Otero Co., CO

MURPHY, Raymond Gerald ES: Pueblo, Pueblo Co., CO
B: Pueblo, Pueblo Co., CO

SITTER, Carl Leonard   ES: Pueblo, Pueblo Co., CO
B: Syracuse, Morgan Co., MO

CONNECTICUT

U.S. Army

BABCOCK, John   ES: Stonington, New London Co., CT
B: New Orleans, Orleans Co., LA

BABOCK, William J.   ES: South Kingston, Washington Co., RI
B: Griswold, CT

*BACON, Elijah William   ES: New Britain, Hartford Co., CT
B: Burlington, Hartford Co., CT

BAIRD, George William   ES: Milford, New Haven Co., CT
B: Milford, New Haven Co., CT

BECKWITH, Wallace A.   ES: New London, New London Co., CT
B: New London, New London Co., CT

BRIGGS, Elijah A.   ES: Salisbury, Litchfield Co., CT
B: Salisbury, Litchfield Co., CT

BUCK, Frederick Clarence   ES: Windsor, Hartford Co., CT
B: Hartford, Hartford Co., CT

BURKE, Daniel Webster   ES: New Haven, New Haven Co., CT
B: New Haven, New Haven Co., CT

CANFIELD, Heth   ES: Carlisle, Cumberland Co., PA
B: New Milford, Litchfield Co., CT

CORLISS, George W.   ES: Hartford, Hartford Co., CT
B: CT

CROCKER, Henry H.   ES: San Francisco, San Francisco Co., CA
B: Colchester, New London Co., CT

CURTIS, John Calvin   ES: Bridgeport, Fairfield Co., CT
B: Bridgeport, Fairfield Co., CT

DALY, Michael Joseph   ES: Southport, Fairfield Co., CT
B: New York, NY

DOWNS, Willis H.   ES: Jamestown, Stutsman Co., ND
B: Mount Carmel, CT

ENNIS, Charles D.   ES: Charleston, Washington Co., RI
B: Stonington, New London Co., CT

FLYNN, Christopher   ES: Hartford, Hartford Co., CT
B: Ireland

FORSYTH, Thomas Hall   ES: St. Louis, St. Louis Co., MO
B: Hartford, Hartford Co., CT

*FOURNIER, William Grant   ES: Winterport, Waldo Co., ME
B: Norwich, New London Co., CT

FOX, Nicholas   ES: Greenwich, Fairfield Co., CT

*FRATELLENICO, Frank Rocco   ES: Albany, Albany Co., NY
                             B: Sharon, Litchfield Co., CT

GIBBS, Wesley   ES: Salisbury, Litchfield Co., CT
                             B: Sharon, Litchfield Co., CT

GRAY, Robert A.   ES: Groton, New London Co., CT
                             B: Philadelphia, Philadelphia Co., PA

*HARTELL, Lee Ross   ES: Danbury, Fairfield Co., CT
                             B: Philadelphia, Philadelphia Co., PA

HICKOK, Nathan E.   ES: Danbury, Fairfield Co., CT
                             B: Danbury, Fairfield Co., CT

HINCKS, William B.   ES: Bridgeport, Fairfield Co., CT
                             B: Bucksport, Hancock Co., ME

HOOPER, William B.   ES: Jersey City, Hudson Co., NJ
                             B: Willimantic, Windham Co., CT

HORNE, Samuel Belton   ES: Winsted, Litchfield Co., CT
                             B: Belleek, County Fermanagh, Ireland

HUBBELL, William Stone   ES: North Stonington, New London Co.,
                                CT
                             B: Wolcottville, New Haven Co., CT

JACKSON, Frederick
Randolph   ES: New Haven, New Haven Co., CT
                             B: New Haven, New Haven Co., CT

JOHNSTON Sr., William
James   ES: Colchester, New London Co., CT
                             B: Trenton, Mercer Co., NJ

LANFARE, Aaron Steven   ES: Branford, New Haven Co., CT
                             B: Branford, New Haven Co., CT

*LIBBY, George Dalton   ES: Waterbury, New Haven Co., CT
                             B: Bridgton, Cumberland Co., ME

*MAGRATH, John D.   ES: East Norwalk, Fairfield Co., CT
                             B: East Norwalk, Fairfield Co., CT

MARSH, Charles H.   ES: New Milford, Litchfield Co., CT
                             B: Milford, New Haven Co., CT

MURPHY, James T.   ES: New Haven, New Haven Co., CT
                             B: Canada

NETT, Robert Burton   ES: New Haven, New Haven Co., CT
                             B: New Haven, New Haven Co., CT

NEVILLE, Edwin Michael   ES: Waterbury, New Haven Co., CT
                             B: Waterbury, New Haven Co., CT

NORTON, Elliott Malloy   ES: Cooper, MI
                             B: CT

O'NEILL, William   ES: New York, NY
                             B: Tariffville, Hartford Co., CT

PALMER, John Gideon   ES: Montville, New London Co., CT
                             B: Montville, New London Co., CT

SCOFIELD, David H.   ES: Stamford, Fairfield Co., CT
                             B: Mamaroneck, Westchester Co., NY

SHALER, Alexander   ES: New York, NY
                             B: Haddam, Middlesex Co., CT

*SHEA, Daniel John   ES: New Haven, New Haven Co., CT
                             B: Norwalk, Fairfield Co., CT

SHEPPARD, Charles   ES: St. Louis, St. Louis Co., MO
                             B: Rocky Hill, Hartford Co., CT

SIMONDS, William Edgar   ES: Canton, Hartford Co., CT
                             B: Collinsville, Hartford Co., CT

SODERMAN, William
Adolph   ES: West Haven, New Haven Co., CT
                             B: West Haven, New Haven Co., CT

SWIFT, Frederic William   ES: Detroit, Wayne Co., MI
                             B: Mansfield Center, Tolland Co., CT

TINKHAM, Eugene M.   ES: Waterloo, Seneca Co., NY
                             B: Sprague, CT

TRACY, Charles H.   ES: Springfield, Hampden Co., MA
                             B: Jewett City, New London Co., CT

TUCKER, Allen   ES: Sprague, CT
                             B: Lyme, CT

WEEKS, John Henry   ES: Hartwick Seminary, Oswego Co., NY
                             B: Hampton, Windham Co., CT

WHITAKER, Edward
Washburn   ES: Hartford, Hartford Co., CT
                             B: Killingly, CT

WILLIAMS, George C.   ES: New London, New London Co., CT
                             B: England

WILSON, Christopher W.   ES: West Meriden, New Haven Co., CT
                             B: Ireland

WRIGHT, Robert   ES: Woodstock, Windham Co., CT
                             B: Ireland

U.S. Air Force

LEVITOW, John Lee   ES: New Haven, New Haven Co., CT
                             B: Hartford, Hartford Co., CT

U.S. Navy

BREAULT, Henry   ES: VT
                             B: Putnam, Windham Co., CT

CANN, Tedford Harris   ES: NY
                             B: Bridgeport, Fairfield Co., CT

CRANDALL, Orson Leon   ES: CT
                             B: St. Joseph, Buchanan Co., MO

*DENNING, Lorenzo   ES: New Britain, Hartford Co., CT
                             B: Granby, Hartford Co., CT

GARVIN, William   ES: Plymouth, Litchfield Co., CT
                             B: west Canada

HARDING, Thomas   ES: CT
                             B: Middletown, Middlesex Co., CT

HENRECHON, George
Francis   ES: CA
                             B: Hartford, Hartford Co., CT

JONES, John   ES: Acton, Middlesex Co., MA
                             B: Bridgeport, Fairfield Co., CT

MacKENZIE, John   ES: MA
                             B: Bridgeport, Fairfield Co., CT

MANNING, Henry J.   ES: CT
                             B: New Haven, New Haven Co., CT

MONTGOMERY, Robert
William   ES: Norwich, New London Co., CT
                             B: Ireland

NEIL, John   ES: Norwich, New London Co., CT
                             B: Newfoundland, Canada

PECK, Oscar E.   ES: CT
                             B: Bridgeport, Fairfield Co., CT

*REEVES, Thomas James   ES: CT
                             B: Thomaston, Litchfield Co., CT

ROBERTS, James   ES: Hartford, Hartford Co., CT
                             B: England

ROSE, George Harry   ES: CT
                             B: Stamford, Fairfield Co., CT

RYAN, Richard   ES: CT
                             B: CT

SULLIVAN, James   ES: Danbury, Fairfield Co., CT
                             B: New York, NY

U.S. Marine Corps

BARNUM Jr., Harvey
Curtiss "Barney"   ES: Cheshire, New Haven Co., CT
                             B: Cheshire, New Haven Co., CT

HILL, Frank	ES: CT B: Hartford, Hartford Co., CT
KELLOGG Jr., Allan Jay	ES: Bridgeport, Fairfield Co., CT B: Bethel, Fairfield Co., CT
*SKINNER Jr., Sherrod Emerson	ES: East Lansing, Ingham Co., MI B: Hartford, Hartford Co., CT
*TALBOT, Ralph	ES: CT B: South Weymouth, Norfolk Co., MA
*WITEK, Frank Peter	ES: Illinois B: Derby, New Haven Co., CT

DELAWARE

U.S. Army

BUCKINGHAM, David E.	ES: Wilmington, New Castle Co., DE B: Pleasant Hill, DE
CONNOR, James Phillip	ES: Wilmington, New Castle Co., DE B: Wilmington, New Castle Co., DE
Du PONT, Henry Algernon	ES: Wilmington, New Castle Co., DE B: Eleutherean Mills, New Castle Co., DE
MAYBERRY, John B.	ES: Dover, Kent Co., DE B: Smyrna, Kent Co., DE
McCARREN, Bernard	ES: Wilmimgton, New Castle Co., DE B: Ireland
*NELSON, William Lancaster	ES: Middletown, New Castle Co., DE B: Dover, Kent Co., DE
PALMER, William Jackson	ES: Philadelphia, Philadelphia Co., PA B: Leipsic, Kent Co., DE
PIERCE, Charles H.	ES: Delaware City, New Castle Co., DE B: Cecil Co., MD
POSTLES, James Parke	ES: Wilmimgton, New Castle Co., DE B: Camden, Kent Co., DE
SACRISTE, Louis Jeanottelle	ES: Philadelphia, Philadelphia Co., PA B: New Castle Co., DE
SEWARD, Griffin	ES: Philadelphia, Philadelphia Co., PA B: Dover, Kent Co., DE
SHILLING, John	ES: Felton, Kent Co., DE B: England
SMITH, Samuel Rodmond	ES: Wilmington, New Castle Co., DE B: Wilmington, New Castle Co., DE
TANNER, Charles B.	ES: Wilmimgton, New Castle Co., DE B: Philadelphia, Philadelphia Co., PA

U.S. Navy

BALDWIN, Charles H.	ES: Philadelphia, Philadelphia Co., PA B: Wilmington, New Castle Co., DE
CHADWICK, Leonard B.	ES: DE B: Middletown, New Castle Co., DE
HAND, Allexander	ES: DE B: DE

FLORIDA

U.S. Army

*BENNETT, Emory L.	ES: Cocoa, Brevard Co., FL B: New Smyrna Beach, Volusia Co., FL
BOLTON, Cecil Hamilton	ES: Huntsville, Madison Co., AL B: Crawfordville, Wakulla Co., FL
*BOWEN Jr., Hammett Lee	ES: Jacksonville, Duval Co., FL B: LaGrange, Troup Co., GA

CONDON, Clarence Milville	ES: St. Augustine, St. Johns Co., FL B: South Brooksville, Hancock Co., ME
*CUTINHA, Nicholas Joseph	ES: Coral Gables, Dade Co., FL B: Fernandina Beach, Nassau Co., FL
MILLS, James Henry	ES: Fort Meade, Polk Co., FL B: Fort Meade, Polk Co., FL
*NININGER Jr., Alexander Ramsey	ES: Fort Lauderdale, Broward Co., FL B: Gainesville, Hall Co., GA
PAINE, Adam	ES: Fort Duncan, TX B: FL
*SIMS, Clifford Chester	ES: Jacksonville, Duval Co., FL B: Port St. Joe, Gulf Co., FL
VARNUM, Charles Albert	ES: Pensacola, Escambia Co., FL B: Troy, Rensselaer Co., NY

U.S. Army Air Corps

*FEMOYER, Robert Edward	ES: Jacksonville, Duval Co., FL B: Huntington, Cabell Co., WV
*McGUIRE Jr., Thomas Buchanan	ES: Sebring, Highlands Co., FL B: Ridgewood, Bergen Co., NJ

U.S. Navy

*CORRY Jr., William Merrill	ES: FL B: Quincy, Gadsden Co., FL
LASSEN, Clyde Everett	ES: Jacksonville, Duval Co., FL B: Fort Myers, Lee Co., FL
McCAMPBELL, David	ES: West Palm Beach, Palm Beach Co., FL B: Bessemer, Jefferson Co., AL
NORRIS, Thomas Rolland	ES: Silver Spring, Montgomery Co., MD B: Jacksonville, Duval Co., FL
ORMSBEE Jr., Francis Edward	ES: FL B: Providence, Providence Co., RI

U.S. Marine Corps

*CARTER, Bruce Wayne	ES: Jacksonville, Duval Co., FL B: Schenectady, Schenectady Co., NY
*JENKINS Jr., Robert Henry	ES: Jacksonville, Duval Co., FL B: Interlachen, Putnam Co., FL
*LOPEZ, Baldomero	ES: Tampa, Hillsborough Co., FL B: Tampa, Hillsborough Co., FL
*McTUREOUS Jr., Robert Miller	ES: FL B: Altoona, Lake Co., FL
*SMEDLEY, Larry Eugene	ES: Orlando, Orange Co., FL B: Front Royal, Warren Co., VA

GEORGIA

U.S. Army

*BOWEN Jr., Hammett Lee	ES: Jacksonville, Duval Co., FL B: LaGrange, Troup Co., GA
BROWN Jr., Bobbie Evan	ES: Atlanta, Fulton Co., GA B: Dublin, Laurens Co., GA
*BRYANT, William Maud	ES: Detroit, Wayne Co., MI B: Cochran, Bleckley Co., GA
CARTER, Mason	ES: Augusta, Richmond Co., GA B: Augusta, Richmond Co., GA
*DURHAM Jr., Harold Bascom	ES: Atlanta, Fulton Co., GA B: Rocky Mount, Edgecombe Co., NC

GARLINGTON, Ernest Albert
   ES: Athens, Clarke Co., GA
    B: Newberry Hill, Newberry Co., SC

*JOHNSTON, Donald Ray
   ES: Columbus, Muscogee Co., GA
    B: Columbus, Muscogee Co., GA

LEE Sr., Daniel Warnel
   ES: Alma, Bacon Co., GA
    B: Alma, Bacon Co., GA

*McKIBBEN, Ray
   ES: Atlanta, Fulton Co., GA
    B: Felton, Haralson Co., GA

McKINNEY, John R.
   ES: Woodcliff, GA
    B: Woodcliff, GA

*NININGER Jr., Alexander Ramsey
   ES: Fort Lauderdale, Broward Co., FL
    B: Gainesville, Hall Co., GA

RAY, Ronald Eric
   ES: Atlanta, Fulton Co., GA
    B: Cordele, Crisp Co., GA

SPRAYBERRY, James Michael
   ES: Montgomery, Montgomery Co., AL
    B: LaGrange, Troup Co., GA

*STORY, Luther H.
   ES: GA
    B: Buena Vista, Marion Co., GA

U.S. Air Force

JACKSON, Joe Madison
   ES: Newnan, Coweta Co., GA
    B: Newnan, Coweta Co., GA

WILBANKS, Hilliard Almond
   ES: Atlanta, Fulton Co., GA
    B: Cornelia, Habersham Co., GA

U.S. Navy

LELAND, George W.
   ES: GA
    B: Savannah, Chatham Co., GA

PHARRIS, Jackson Charles
   ES: CA
    B: Columbus, Muscogee Co., GA

U.S. Marine Corps

*BONNYMAN Jr., Alexander "Sandy"
   ES: NM
    B: Atlanta, Fulton Co., GA

DAVIS, Raymond Gilbert
   ES: Atlanta, Fulton Co., GA
    B: Fitzgerald, Ben Hill Co., GA

*DAVIS, Rodney Maxwell
   ES: Macon, Bibb Co., GA
    B: Macon, Bibb Co., GA

*DYESS, Aquilla James
   ES: GA
    B: Augusta, Richmond Co., GA

*ELROD, Henry Talmage
   ES: Ashburn, Turner Co., GA
    B: Rebecca, Turner Co., GA

LIVINGSTON, James Evertte
   ES: McRae, Telfair Co., GA
    B: Towns, Telfair Co., GA

*PHILLIPS, Lee Hugh
   ES: Ben Hill, Fulton Co., GA
    B: Stockbridge, Henry Co., GA

PLESS, Stephen Wesley
   ES: Atlanta, Fulton Co., GA
    B: Newnan, Coweta Co., GA

*THOMASON, Clyde A.
   ES: GA
    B: Atlanta, Fulton Co., GA

HAWAII

U.S. Army

*KAWAMURA, Terry Teruo
   ES: Oahu, HI
    B: Wahiawa, Honolulu Co., Oahu, HI

*MENDONCA, Leroy A.
   ES: Honolulu, Honolulu Co., Territory of Hawaii
    B: Honolulu, Honolulu Co., Territory of Hawaii

*PILILAAU, Herbert K.
   ES: Oahu, Territory of Hawaii
    B: Waianae, Oahu, Territory of Hawaii

*SMITH, Elmelindo Rodriques
   ES: Honolulu, Honolulu Co., HI
    B: Honolulu, Honolulu Co., HI

*YANO, Rodney James Tadashi
   ES: Honolulu, Honolulu Co., HI
    B: Kealakekua Kona, Hawaii Co., HI

U.S. Navy

SMITH, James
   ES: New York
    B: Hawaiian Islands

IDAHO

U.S. Army

BLEAK, David Bruce
   ES: Shelley, Bingham Co., ID
    B: Idaho Falls, Bonneville Co., ID

*BROSTROM, Leonard C.
   ES: Preston, Franklin Co., ID
    B: Preston, Franklin Co., ID

MAXWELL, Robert Dale
   ES: Creswell, Larimer Co., CO
    B: Boise, Ada Co., ID

McCARTER, Lloyd G.
   ES: Tacoma, Pierce Co., WA
    B: St. Maries, Benewah Co., ID

NEIBAUR, Thomas Croft
   ES: Sugar City, Madison Co., ID
    B: Sharon, ID

*SCHOONOVER, Dan D.
   ES: Boise, Ada Co., ID
    B: Boise, Ada Co., ID

*VAN NOY Jr., Nathan
   ES: Preston, Franklin Co., ID
    B: Grace, Caribou Co., ID

U.S. Air Force

FISHER, Bernard Francis
   ES: Kuna, Ada Co., ID
    B: San Bernardino, San Bernardino Co., CA

U.S. Marine Corps

BOYINGTON, Gregory "Pappy"
   ES: WA
    B: Coeur D'Alene, Kootenai Co., ID

*JOHNSON, James Edmund
   ES: Washington, D.C.
    B: Pocatello, Bannock Co., ID

MYERS, Reginald Rodney
   ES: Boise, Ada Co., ID
    B: Boise, Ada Co., ID

*REASONER, Frank Stanley
   ES: Kellogg, Shoshone Co., ID
    B: Spokane, Spokane Co., WA

ILLINOIS

U.S. Army

ALLEN, Abner Peeler
   ES: Bloomington, McLean Co., IL
    B: Woodford Co., IL

ALLEX, Jake
   ES: Chicago, Cook Co., IL
    B: Streska, near Prizren, Serbia

ANDERSON, Johannes Seigfried
   ES: Chicago, Cook Co., IL
    B: Bjoroky, Finland

ARCHER, James W.
   ES: Spencer, Owen Co., IN
    B: Edgar Co., IL

AYERS, John G. K.
   ES: Pekin, Tazwell Co., IL
    B: Washtenaw Co., MI

BAKER Jr., John Franklin
   ES: Moline, Rock Island Co., IL
    B: Davenport, Scott Co., IA

BANCROFT, Neil — ES: Chicago, Cook Co., IL
B: Oswego, Oswego Co., NY

BATSON, Matthew Arlington — ES: Carbondale, Jackson Co., IL
B: Anna, Union Co., IL

BENDER, Stanley — ES: Chicago, Cook Co., IL
B: Carlisle, WV

BERG, George Francis — ES: Fort Omaha, Douglas Co., NE
B: Mount Erie, Wayne Co., IL

BERTOLDO, Vito R. — ES: Decatur, Macon Co., IL
B: Decatur, Macon Co., IL

BICKFORD, Matthew — ES: Trivolia, Peoria Co., IL
B: Peoria Co., IL

BLACK, John Charles — ES: Danville, Vermillion Co., IL
B: Lexington, Holmes Co., MS

BLACK, William Perkins — ES: Danville, Vermillion Co., IL
B: Woodford, KY

*BLANCHFIELD, Michael Reinert — ES: Chicago, Cook Co., IL
B: Minneapolis, Hennepin Co., MN

BLODGETT, Wells H. — ES: Chicago, Cook Co., IL
B: Downer's Grove, Du Page Co., IL

BOURKE, John Gregory — ES: Chicago, Cook Co., IL
B: Philadelphia, Philadelphia Co., PA

BOWEN, Emmer — ES: Hampshire, Kane Co., IL
B: Erie Co., NY

BURRITT, William Wallace — ES: Chicago, Cook Co., IL
B: Campbell, Steuben Co., NY

CALLAHAN, John H. — ES: Scottville, Macoupin Co., IL
B: Shelby Co., KY

CALVERT, James Spencer — ES: Springfield, Sangamon Co., IL
B: Athens Co., OH

*CAPRON Jr., Horace — ES: Peoria, Peoria Co., IL
B: Laurel, Prince George's Co., MD

CARROLL, Thomas — ES: Chicago, Cook Co., IL
B: Kilkenny, Ireland

CHOATE, Clyde Lee — ES: Anna, Union Co., IL
B: West Frankfort, Franklin Co., IL

CHURCH, James Robb — ES: Washington, D.C.
B: Chicago, Cook Co., IL

CHURCHILL, Samuel Joseph — ES: DeKalb, DeKalb Co., IL
B: Rutland, Rutland Co., VT

COLBY, Carlos W. — ES: Madison Co., IL
B: Merrimack, Hillsborough Co., NH

COOK, John Henry — ES: Quincy, Adams Co., IL
B: London, England

COX, Robert Mitchell — ES: Prairie City, McDonough Co., IL
B: Guernsey Co., OH

CRAIG, Samuel Henry — ES: Chicago, Cook Co., IL
B: New Market, Rockingham Co., NH

CREED, John — ES: Chicago, Cook Co., IL
B: Tipperary, County Tipperary, Ireland

CUNNINGHAM, James Smith — ES: Bloomington, McLean Co., IL
B: Washington Co., PA

DANIELS, James Thomas — ES: Fort Leavenworth, Leavenworth Co., KS
B: Richland Co., IL

DARROUGH, John S. — ES: Concord, Morgan Co., IL
B: Maysville, Mason Co., KY

DAVIS, Martin K. — ES: Stonington, Christian Co., IL
B: Marion, Williamson Co., IL

DEAN Sr., William Frishe — ES: California
B: Carlyle, Clinton Co., IL

DICKIE, David — ES: Gillespie, Macoupin Co., IL
B: Scotland

DUNHAM, Russell — ES: Brighton, Jersey Co., IL
B: East Carondelet, St. Clair Co., IL

DUNNE, James — ES: Chicago, Cook Co., IL
B: Detroit, Wayne Co., MI

ELLIS, Michael B. — ES: East St. Louis, St. Clair Co., IL
B: St. Louis, St. Louis Co., MO

FARQUHAR, John Mcgreath — ES: Chicago, Cook Co., IL
B: near Ayr, Scotland

FISHER, John H. — ES: Chicago, Cook Co., IL
B: Monmouth, PA

FLYNN, James Edward — ES: St. Louis, St. Louis Co., MO
B: Pittsfield, Pike Co., IL

FOX, Henry — ES: Lincoln, Logan Co., IL
B: Reuthingen, Wurtemberg, Germany

FRASER, William W. — ES: Alton, Madison Co., IL
B: Burn Brac, Scotland

FRITZ, Harold Arthur — ES: Milwaukee, Milwaukee Co., WI
B: Chicago, Cook Co., IL

GAGE, Richard J. — ES: Ottawa, La Salle Co., IL
B: Grafton Co., NH

GARMAN, Harold Alva — ES: Albion, Edwards Co., IL
B: Fairfield, Wayne Co., IL

GERSTUNG, Robert E. — ES: Chicago, Cook Co., IL
B: Chicago, Cook Co., IL

GESCHWIND, Nicholas — ES: Pleasant Hill, Pike Co., IL
B: France

*GIBSON, Eric Gunnar — ES: Chicago, Cook Co., IL
B: Nysund, Sweden

GOLDIN, Theodore W. B. — ES: Chicago, Cook Co., IL
B: Avon, Rock Co., WI

GOLDSBERY, Andrew E. — ES: St. Charles, Kane Co., IL
B: St. Charles, Kane Co., IL

GOULD, Newton Thomas — ES: Elk Grove, Cook Co., IL
B: Elk Grove, Cook Co., IL

GUMPERTZ, Sydney G. — ES: Chicago, Cook Co., IL
B: San Raphael, Marin Co., CA

HALL, John — ES: Sacramento, Sacramento Co., CA
B: Logan Co., IL

*HAMMOND Jr., Lester — ES: Quincy, Adams Co., IL
B: Wayland, Clark Co., MO

HANEY, Milton Lorenzi — ES: Bushnell, McDonough Co., IL
B: Savannah, Ashland Co., OH

HAPEMAN, Douglas — ES: Ottawa, La Salle Co., IL
B: Ephrata, Fulton Co., NY

*HARDENBERGH, Henry M. — ES: Bremen, IL
B: Noble Co., IN

*HARVEY Jr., Carmel Bernon — ES: Chicago, Cook Co., IL
B: Montgomery, Fayette Co., WV

HENRY, James — ES: Kankakee, Kankakee Co., IL
B: Sunfish, OH

HIGGINS, Thomas J. — ES: Barry, Pike Co., IL
B: Riverlequerre, Quebec, Canada

HIGHLAND, Patrick — ES: Chicago, Cook Co., IL
B: Tipperary, Ireland

HILL, Ralyn M. — ES: Oregon, Ogle Co., IL
B: Lindenwood, Ogle Co., IL

HOBDAY, George — ES: Memphis, Shelby Co., TN
B: Pulaski Co., IL

HOLLAND, Lemuel F.	ES: Tiskilwa, Bureau Co., IL
B: Burlington, OH

HOLMES, William T.	ES: Indanapolis, Marion Co., IN
B: Vermilion Co., IL

HOUGHTON, George L.	ES: Brookfield, Cook Co., IL
B: Yarmouth, West Canada

HOWE, Orion P.	ES: Waukegan, Lake Co., IL
B: Hiram, Portage Co., OH

HUGGINS, Eli Lundy	ES: MN
B: Schuyler Co., IL

HUGHEY, John P.	ES: Anna, Union Co., IL
B: Louisville, Jefferson Co., KY

HYATT, Theodore	ES: Gardner, Grundy Co., IL
B: PA

HYMER, Samuel	ES: Rushville, Schuyler Co., IL
B: Harrison Co., IN

JOHNS, Elisha	ES: Martinton, Iroquois Co., IL
B: Clinton, Summit Co., OH

JOHNSON, Andrew	ES: Assumption, Christian Co., IL
B: Delaware Co., OH

JOHNSTON, David H.	ES: Warsaw, Hancock Co., IL
B: Indiana Co., PA

JOHNSTON, Edward	ES: Chicago, Cook Co., IL
B: Pen Yan, Yates Co., NY

JOHNSTON, Harold Irving	ES: Chicago, Cook Co., IL
B: Kendall, Hamilton Co., KS

JOSSELYN, Simeon T.	ES: Amboy, Lee Co., IL
B: Buffalo, Erie Co., NY

KAYS, Kenneth Michael	ES: Fairfield, Wayne Co., IL
B: Mount Vernon, Jefferson Co., IL

KELLER, Leonard Bert	ES: Chicago, Cook Co., IL
B: Rockford, Winnebago Co., IL

KELLEY, Leverett Mansfield	ES: Rutland, La Salle Co., IL
B: Schenectady, Schenectady Co., NY

KELLY, John J. H.	ES: Springfield, Sangamon Co., IL
B: Schuyler Co., IL

*KENNEDY, Philip	ES: Evansville, Randolph Co., IL
B: County Galway, Ireland

KLOTH, Charles H.	ES: Chicago, Cook Co., IL
B: Europe

KNIGHT, Joseph F.	ES: Denver, Denver Co., CO
B: Danville, Vermilion Co., IL

KRETSINGER, George	ES: Chicago, Cook Co., IL
B: Fairfield, Herkimer Co., NY

*KROTIAK, Anton L.	ES: Chicago, Cook Co., IL
B: Chicago, Cook Co., IL

*KRZYZOWSKI, Edward C.	ES: Cicero, Cook Co., IL
B: Chicago, Cook Co., IL

LABILL, Joseph S.	ES: Vandalia, Fayette Co., IL
B: Belgium

LARRABEE, James W.	ES: Mendota, La Salle Co., IL
B: Rensselaer Co., NY

*LOGAN Jr., John Alexander	ES: Youngstown, Mahoning Co., OH
B: Carbondale, Jackson Co., IL

LOMAN, Berger Holton	ES: Chicago, Cook Co., IL
B: Bergen, Norway

LONGFELLOW, Richard Moses	ES: Mandan, Morton Co., ND
B: Logan Co., IL

LOWER, Robert A.	ES: Elmwood, Peoria Co., IL
B: IL

LUCAS, George Washington	ES: Mount Sterling, Brown Co., IL
B: Adams Co., IL

LUCE, Moses Augustine	ES: Adrian, Lenawee Co., MI
B: Payson, Adams Co., IL

LYNCH, Allan James	ES: Chicago, Cook Co., IL
B: Chicago, Cook Co., IL

MARSH, George	ES: Brookfield, Cook Co., IL
B: Brookfield, Cook Co., IL

McCLERNAND, Edward John	ES: Springfield, Sangamon Co., IL
B: Jacksonville, Morgan Co., IL

McCONNELL, Samuel	ES: Bushnell, McDonough Co., IL
B: Belmont Co., OH

McCORNACK, Andrew	ES: Rutland, La Salle Co., IL
B: Kane, Greene Co., IL

McDONALD, James	ES: Chicago, Cook Co., IL
B: Edinburgh, Scotland

McDONALD, John Wade	ES: Waynesville, DeWitt Co., IL
B: Lancaster, Fairfield Co., OH

McGRAW, Thomas	ES: Chicago, Cook Co., IL
B: Ireland

McGUIRE, Patrick	ES: Chicago, Cook Co., IL
B: Ireland

McKEEN, Nineveh S.	ES: Marshall, Clark Co., IL
B: Marshall, Clark Co., IL

MERRIFIELD, James K.	ES: Manlius, Bureau Co., IL
B: Hyde Park, Westmoreland Co., PA

MILLER, Archie	ES: St. Louis, St. Louis Co., MO
B: Fort Sheridan, Lake Co., IL

MILLER, Henry August	ES: Decatur, Macon Co., IL
B: Germany

MILLER, Jacob C.	ES: Elgin, Kane Co., IL
B: Bellevue, Huron Co., OH

MITCHELL, John	ES: Peoria, Peoria Co., IL
B: Dublin, Ireland

*MONROE, James Howard	ES: Chicago, Cook Co., IL
B: Aurora, Du Page Co., IL

MOORE, Wilbur F.	ES: Lebanon, St. Clair Co., IL
B: Lebanon, St. Clair Co., IL

MORELOCK, Sterling Lewis	ES: Oquawka, Henderson Co., IL
B: Silver Run, MD

MORFORD, Jerome	ES: Bridgers Co., IL
B: Mercer Co., PA

*MOSKALA, Edward J.	ES: Chicago, Cook Co., IL
B: Chicago, Cook Co., IL

MURPHY, Philip	ES: Chicago, Cook Co., IL
B: County Killkenny, Ireland

MURPHY, Robinson Barr	ES: Oswego, Kendall Co., IL
B: Oswego, Kendall Co., IL

MURPHY, Thomas C.	ES: Pekin, Tazewell Co., IL
B: Ireland

NEWMAN, Marcellus J.	ES: Richview, Washington Co., IL
B: Richview, Washington Co., IL

O'DEA, John	ES: Bloomington, McLean Co., IL
B: Limerick, County Limerick, Ireland

O'DONNELL, Menomen	ES: Sumner, Lawrence Co., IL
B: Drumbarty, Ireland

OGDEN Sr., Carlos Carnes	ES: Fairmount, Vermillion Co., IL
B: Borton, Edgar Co., IL

*OLIVE III, Milton Lee	ES: Chicago, Cook Co., IL
B: Chicago, Cook Co., IL

PALMER, George Henry	ES: Monmouth, Warren Co., IL
B: NY

PARKS, James W.   ES: Xenia, Clay Co., IL
                         B: Lawrence Co., OH

PAYNE, Thomas H. L.   ES: Mendota, La Salle Co., IL
                         B: Boston Suffolk Co., MA

PENTZER, Patrick Henry   ES: Gillespie, Macoupin Co., IL
                         B: Marion Co., MO

*PEREZ Jr., Manuel   ES: Chicago, Cook Co., IL
                         B: Oklahoma City, Oklahoma Co., OK

PIKE, Edward M.   ES: Bloomington, McLean Co., IL
                         B: Casco, Cumberland Co., ME

POND, George F.   ES: Fairwater, Fond du Lac Co., WI
                         B: Libertyville, Lake Co., IL

POPE, Thomas A.   ES: Chicago, Cook Co., IL
                         B: Chicago, Cook Co., IL

POST, Philip Sidney   ES: Galesburg, Knox Co., IL
                         B: Florida, Orange Co., NY

POWERS, Wesley James   ES: Virgil, Kane Co., IL
                         B: Orono, Ontario, Canada

PUTNAM, Winthrop D.   ES: Peoria, Peoria Co., IL
                         B: Southbridge, Worcester Co., MA

REBMANN, George F.   ES: Rushville, Schuyler Co., IL
                         B: Schuyler Co., IL

REED, William   ES: Pekin, Tazewell Co., IL
                         B: Union Co., PA

*ROBINSON Jr., James
William   ES: Chicago, Cook Co., IL
                         B: Hinsdale, Du Page Co., IL

ROSS, Frank Fulton   ES: Langdon, Cavalier Co., ND
                         B: Avon, Fulton Co., IL

RUNDLE, Charles Wesley   ES: Oakley, Macon Co., IL
                         B: Covington, Campbell Co., KY

SANFORD, Jacob   ES: Prairie City, McDonough Co., IL
                         B: Fulton Co., IL

SCHENCK, Benjamin W.   ES: Maroa, Macon Co., IL
                         B: Butler Co., OH

SCHOFIELD, John McAllister ES: Freeport, Stephenson Co., IL
                         B: Gerry, Chautauga Co., NY

SCHROEDER, Henry Frank   ES: Chicago, Cook Co., IL
                         B: Chicago, Cook Co., IL

SHAPLAND, John   ES: Ottawa, La Salle Co., IL
                         B: Barnstable, Devonshire, England

SIMMONS, William Thomas ES: Springfield, Sangamon Co., IL
                         B: Greene Co., IL

SLAGLE, Oscar   ES: Manlius, Bureau Co., IL
                         B: Fulton Co., OH

SMALLEY, Reuben S.   ES: Brookfield, Cook Co., IL
                         B: Washington Co., PA

*SMITH, Fred E.   ES: Bartlett, ND
                         B: Rockford, Winnebago Co., IL

SNOW, Elmer A.   ES: Chicago, Cook Co., IL
                         B: Hardwick, Worcester Co., MA

SPALDING, Edward Burson ES: Rockford, Winnebago Co., IL
                         B: Byron, Ogle Co., IL

SPRAGUE, Benona   ES: Cheney Grove, IL
                         B: Satina Onondaga Co., NY

STEPHENS, William G.   ES: Chicago, Cook Co., IL
                         B: New York, NY

STERLING, John T.   ES: Indianapolis, Marion Co., IN
                         B: Edgar Co., IL

STOCKMAN, George Henry   ES: Chicago, Cook Co., IL
                         B: Muenden, Germany

STOKES, George   ES: Jerseyville, Jersey Co., IL
                         B: England

SUMNER, James   ES: Chicago, Cook Co., IL
                         B: London, England

TAYLOR, Henry H.   ES: Galena, Jo Daviess Co., IL
                         B: Near Galena, Jo Daviess Co., IL

THOMPSON, John   ES: Chicago, Cook Co., IL
                         B: Glasgow, Scotland

TOOMER, William   ES: Chicago, Cook Co., IL
                         B: Dublin, Ireland

TOY, Frederick Ernest   ES: Chicago, Cook Co., IL
                         B: Buffalo, Erie Co., NY

TRACY, John   ES: Chicago, Cook Co., IL
                         B: Dublin, Ireland

VERNAY, James David   ES: Lacon, Marshall Co., IL
                         B: Lacon, Marshall Co., IL

VOKES, Leroy H.   ES: St. Louis, St. Louis Co., MO
                         B: Lake Co., IL

WARD, Thomas J.   ES: Decatur, Macon Co., IL
                         B: Romney, Hampshire Co., WV

WARDEN, John   ES: Lemont, Du Page Co., IL
                         B: Cook Co., IL

WATSON, Joseph   ES: Chicago, Cook Co., IL
                         B: Union City, Branch Co., MI

WHEATON, Loyd   ES: Peoria, Peoria Co., IL
                         B: Penfield, MI

WHITE, Patrick H.   ES: Chicago, Cook Co., IL
                         B: County Sligo, Ireland

WHITMORE, John W.   ES: Camden, Schuyler Co., IL
                         B: Brown Co., IL

*WICKAM, Jerry Wayne   ES: Chicago, Cook Co., IL
                         B: Rockford, Winnebago Co., IL

WIDICK, Andrew J.   ES: Decatur, Macon Co., IL
                         B: Macon Co., IL

WILLIAMS, Elwood N.   ES: Havana, Mason Co., IL
                         B: Philadelphia, Philadelphia Co., PA

WILSON, Arthur Harrison ES: Springfield, Sangamon Co., IL
                         B: Springfield, Sangamon Co., IL

WILSON, Charles   ES: Springfield, Sangamon Co., IL
                         B: Petersburg, Menard Co., IL

*WILSON, Richard G.   ES: Cape Girardeau, Cape Girardeau Co., MO
                         B: Marion, Williamson Co., IL

WOOD, Richard H.   ES: Woodburn, Macoupin Co., IL
                         B: Canton, NJ

U.S. Army Air Corps/U.S. Air Force

*BAKER, Addison Earl   ES: Akron, Summit Co., OH
                         B: Chicago, Cook Co., IL

*GOETTLER, Harold Ernest ES: Chicago, Cook Co., IL
                         B: Chicago, Cook Co., IL

MICHAEL, Edward Stanley ES: Chicago, Cook Co., IL
                         B: Chicago, Cook Co., IL

*SEBILLE, Louis Joseph   ES: Chicago, Cook Co., IL
                         B: Harbor Beach, Huron Co., MI

*TRUEMPER, Walter Edward ES: Aurora, Du Page Co., IL
                         B: Aurora, Du Page Co., IL

YOUNG, Gerald Orren   ES: Colorado Springs, El Paso Co., CO
                         B: Chicago, Cook Co., IL

U.S. Navy

ASTEN, Charles   ES: Chicago, Cook Co., IL
                         B: Halifax, Nova Scotia, Canada

BADDERS, William ES: Indianapolis, Marion Co., IN
 B: Harrisburg, Saline Co., IL

*BIGELOW, Elmer Charles ES: IL
 B: Hebron, McHenry Co., IL

CATHERWOOD, John Hugh ES: IL
 B: Springfield, Sangamon Co., IL

COURTNEY, Henry C. ES: IL
 B: Springfield, Sangamoh Co., IL

*CROMWELL, John Philip ES: IL
 B: Henry, Marshall Co., IL

CRONAN, William (Willie) ES: IL
 B: Chicago, Cook Co., IL

DOW, Henry ES: IL
 B: Scotland

FERRELL, John H. ES: IL
 B: Bedford Co., TN

FLUCKEY, Eugene Bennett ES: Neoga, Cumberland Co., IL
 B: Washington, D.C.

GRBITCH, Rade ES: IL
 B: Austria

HOLYOKE, William Edward ES: IL
 B: Groveton, Coos Co., NH

HULL, James Lott ES: IL
 B: Patoka, Marion Co., IL

HYLAND, John ES: IL
 B: Ireland

IZAC, Edouard Victor Michel ES: IL
 B: Cresco, Howard Co., IA

JOHNSTON, William P. ES: Chicago, Cook Co., IL
 B: Chicago, Cook Co., IL

*KILMER, John Edward ES: Houston, Harris Co., TX
 B: Highland Park, Lake Co., IL

*LESTER, Fred Faulkner ES: IL
 B: Downers Grove, Du Page Co., IL

MARTIN, William ES: Cairo, Alexander Co., IL
 B: New York, NY

McCORMICK, Michael ES: Chicago, Cook Co., IL
 B: Ireland

MEYER, William ES: IL
 B: Germany

MOLLOY, Hugh ES: Joliet, Will Co., IL
 B: County Wexford, Ireland

MULLIN, Hugh Patrick ES: Chicago, Cook Co., IL
 B: Richmond, McHenry Co., IL

NOBLE, Daniel ES: Chicago, Cook Co., IL
 B: Bath Co., KY

*OSBORNE, Weedon E. ES: IL
 B: Chicago, Cook Co., IL

ROBERTS, Charles Church ES: IL
 B: Newton, Middlesex Co., MA

SMITH, Eugene P. ES: CA
 B: IL

STOCKDALE, James Bond ES: Abingdon, Knox Co., IL
 B: Abingdon, Knox Co., IL

U.S. Marine Corps

*BAILEY, Kenneth Dillon ES: Illinois
 B: Pawnee, Pawnee Co., OK

*BRUCE, Daniel Dean ES: Chicago, Cook Co., IL
 B: Michigan City, La Porte Co., IN

*BURKE, Robert Charles ES: Chicago, Cook Co., IL
 B: Monticello, Piatt Co., IL

*De La GARZA Jr., Emilio Albert ES: Chicago, Cook Co., IL
 B: East Chicago, Lake Co., IN

DUNLAP, Robert Hugo ES: Monmouth, Warren Co., IL
 B: Abingdon, Knox Co., IL

*FARDY, John Peter ES: Illinois
 B: Chicago, Cook Co., IL

HELMS, John Henry ES: Illinois
 B: Chicago, Cook Co., IL

HORTON, William M. Charlie ES: Philadelphia, Philadelphia Co., PA
 B: Chicago, Cook Co., IL

KELLY, John Joseph ES: Chicago, Cook Co., IL
 B: Chicago, Cook Co., IL

*KRAUS, Richard Edward ES: MN
 B: Chicago, Cook Co., IL

LEIMS, John Harold ES: Chicago, Cook Co., IL
 B: Chicago, Cook Co., IL

McCARTHY, Joseph Jeremiah ES: Chicago, Cook Co., IL
 B: Chicago, Cook Co., IL

*OZBOURN, Joseph William ES: IL
 B: Herrin, Williamson Co., IL

*POYNTER, James Irsley ES: Downey, Los Angeles Co., CA
 B: Bloomington, McLean Co., IL

ROBINSON, Robert Guy ES: Chicago, Cook Co., IL
 B: New York, NY

SCHILT, Christian Franklin ES: IL
 B: Richland Co., IL

UPHAM, Oscar Jefferson ES: IL
 B: Toledo, Lucas Co., OH

*WEBER, Lester William ES: Chicago, Cook Co., IL
 B: Aurora, Du Page Co., IL

WILLIAMS, Ernest Calvin ES: IL
 B: Broadwell, Elkhart Co., IL

*WILSON, Alfred Mac ES: Abilene, Taylor Co., TX
 B: Olney, Richland Co., IL

*WILSON, Robert Lee ES: IL
 B: Centralia, Marion Co., IL

*WINDRICH, William Gordon ES: Hammond, Lake Co., IN
 B: Chicago, Cook Co., IL

*WITEK, Frank Peter ES: IL
 B: Derby, New Haven Co., CT

INDIANA

U.S. Army

ANDERSON, Marion T. ES: Kokomo, Howard Co., IN
 B: Decatur Co., IN

ARCHER, James W. ES: Spencer, Owen Co., IN
 B: Edgar Co., IL

ARMSTRONG, Clinton Lycurgus ES: Indianapolis, Marion Co., IN
 B: Franklin, Johnson Co., IN

BANKS, George Lovell ES: Lafayette, Tippecanoe Co., IN
 B: Lake Co., OH

BIDDLE, Melvin Earl ES: Anderson, Madison Co., IN
 B: Daleville, Delaware Co., IN

BIEGLER, George Wesley ES: Terre Haute, Vigo Co., IN
 B: Terre Haute, Vigo Co., IN

BLASDEL, Thomas A. ES: Guilford, Dearborn Co., IN
 B: Dearborn Co., IN

BOX, Thomas J.   ES: Bedford, Lawrence Co., IN
B: IN

BROUSE, Charles W.   ES: Indianapolis, Marion Co., IN

BROWN, Lorenzo Dow   ES: Indianapolis, Marion Co., IN
B: Davidson Co., NC

BRUNER, Louis J.   ES: Clifty Brumer, IN
B: Monroe Co., IN

BUCKLES, Abram J.   ES: Muncie, Delaware Co., IN
B: Delaware Co., IN

CHAMBERLAIN, Orville
Tyron   ES: Elkhart, Elkhart Co., IN
B: Leesburgh, Kosciusko Co., IN

CHISMAN, William W.   ES: Wilmington, IN
B: Dearborn Co., IN

CONAWAY, John Wesley   ES: Hartford, Blackford Co., IN
B: Dearborn Co., IN

CUMMINS, Andrew Johnson   ES: Alexandria, Madison Co., IN
B: Alexandria, Madison Co., IN

DAVIS, John   ES: Indanapolis, Marion Co., IN
B: Carroll, KY

DAVIS, Sammy Lee   ES: Indianapolis, Marion Co., IN
B: Dayton, Montgomery Co., OH

DOUGALL, Allan Houston   ES: New Haven, Allen Co., IN
B: Scotland

DUNLAVY, James   ES: Bloomfield, Davis Co., IA
B: Decatur Co., IN

EVANS, Coron D.   ES: Madison, Jefferson Co., IN
B: Jefferson Co., IN

*FAITH Jr., Don Carlos   ES: Washington, Daviess Co., IN
B: Washington, Daviess Co., IN

FALL, Charles S.   ES: Hamburg, Livingston Co., MI
B: Noble Co., IN

FANNING, Nicholas   ES: Independence, Buchanan Co., IA
B: Carroll Co., IN

FERRIER, Daniel Tweed   ES: Delphi, Carroll Co., IN
B: IN

FOUT, Frederick W.   ES: Indanapolis, Marion Co., IN
B: Germany

FRANTZ, Joseph   ES: Osgood, Ripley Co., IN
B: Eurapae, France

GARLAND, Harry   ES: Indianapolis, Marion Co., IN
B: Boston, Suffolk Co., MA

GRAHAM, Thomas N.   ES: Westville, La Porte Co., IN

GRANT, George   ES: Indianapolis, Marion Co., IN
B: Raleigh, Shelby Co., TN

GRAVES, Thomas J.   ES: Millville, IN
B: Milton, Wayne Co., IN

GREEN, Francis C.   ES: Sacramento, Sacramento Co., CA
B: Mount Vernon, Posey Co., IN

*HARDENBERGH,
Henry M.   ES: Bremen, IL
B: Noble Co., IN

HARRIS, David W.   ES: Cincinnati, Hamilton Co., OH
B: Indianapolis, Marion Co., IN

HELMS, David H.   ES: Farmers Retreat, IN
B: Dearborn Co., IN

HOLMES, William T.   ES: Indanapolis, Marion Co., IN
B: Vermilion Co., IL

HORNADAY, Elisha Simpson   ES: Des Moines, Polk Co., IA
B: Hendricks Co., IN

HOUGH, Ira   ES: Middletown, Henry Co., IN
B: Henry Co., IN

HUDSON, Aaron R.   ES: Indanapolis, Marion Co., IN
B: Madison Co., KY

HUNT, Louis T.   ES: Jefferson Co., MO
B: Montgomery Co., IN

HYMER, Samuel   ES: Rushville, Schuyler Co., IL
B: Harrison Co., IN

JOHNSON, Ruel M.   ES: Goshen, Elkhart Co., IN
B: Harbor Creek Township, Erie Co., PA

JORDAN, Absalom   ES: North Madison, Jefferson Co., IN
B: Brown Co., OH

KELLEY, Andrew John   ES: Ypsilanti, Washtenaw Co., MI
B: La Grange Co., IN

KENDALL, William Wesley   ES: Jeffersonville, Clark Co., IN
B: Hall Township, Dubois Co., IN

KISTERS, Gerry Herman   ES: Bloomington, Monroe Co., IN
B: Salt Lake City, Salt Lake Co., UT

KUDER, Jeremiah   ES: Warsaw, Kosciusko Co., IN
B: Tiffin, Seneca Co., OH

LAWTON, Henry Ware   ES: Fort Wayne, Allen Co., IN
B: Manhattan, Lucas Co., OH

LYTTON, Jeptha L.   ES: San Francisco, San Francisco Co., CA
B: Lawrence Co., IN

MASON, Elihu H.   ES: Pemberville, Wood Co., OH
B: Wayne Co., IN

McCALL, Thomas Edward   ES: Veedersburg, Fountain Co., IN
B: Burrton, Harvey Co., KS

*McGEE, William D.   ES: Indianapolis, Marion Co., IN
B: Indianapolis, Marion Co., IN

*MICHAEL, Harry J.   ES: Milford, Kosciusko Co., IN
B: Benton, IN

MORGAN, Richard H.   ES: Taylor, Freemont Co., IA
B: Dubois Co., IN

NOLAN, Joseph A.   ES: South Bend, St. Joseph Co., IN
B: Elkhart, Elkhart Co., IN

OPEL, John N.   ES: Rossburg, Decatur Co., IN
B: Hoflas, Bavaria, Germany

OVERTURF, Jacob H.   ES: Holton, Ripley Co., IN
B: Jefferson Co., IN

PRENTICE, Joseph Rollin   ES: Fort Wayne, Allen Co., IN
B: Lancaster, Fairfield Co., OH

ROOD, Oliver P.   ES: Terre Haute, Vigo Co., IN
B: Frankfort Co., KY

RUSSELL, Milton F.   ES: North Salem, Hendricks Co., IN
B: Hendricks Co., IN

RYAN, Peter J.   ES: Terre Haute, Vigo Co., IN
B: Tiperrary, County Tiperrary, Ireland

*SESTON, Charles H.   ES: New Albany, Floyd Co., IN
B: New Albany, Floyd Co., IN

SHEPHERD, William   ES: Washington, D.C.
B: Dillsboro, Ohio Co., IN

SMALLEY, Reuben   ES: Holton, Ripley Co., IN
B: Reading, Schuyler Co., NY

STEINMETZ, William   ES: Sunman, Ripley Co., IN
B: Newport, Campbell Co., KY

STERLING, John T.   ES: Indianapolis, Marion Co., IN
B: Edgar Co., IL

STOLZ, Frank   ES: Sunman, Ripley Co., IN
B: Dearborn Co., IN

SUTHERLAND, John
Alexander   ES: Indianapolis, Marion Co., IN
B: Harrodsburg, Monroe Co., IN

TAYLOR, Richard   ES: Indianapolis, Marion Co., IN
B: Madison Co., AL

*THOMPSON, William P.   ES: Lafayette, Tippecanoe Co., IN
B: Brooklyn, Kings Co., NY

TIBBETS, Andrew W.   ES: Centerville, Appanoose Co., IA
B: Clark Co., IN

WALKER, Allen   ES: Cincinnati, Hamilton Co., OH
B: Patriot, Switzerland Co., IN

WEAVER, Amos   ES: San Francisco, San Francisco Co., CA
B: Niles Township, Delaware Co., IN

WEISS, Enoch R.   ES: St. Louis, St. Louis Co., MO
B: Kosciusko Co., IN

*WETHERBY, John C.   ES: Martinsville, Morgan Co., IN
B: Morgan Co., IN

WHITEHEAD, John Milton   ES: Westville, La Porte Co., IN
B: Wayne Co., IN

*WIGLE, Thomas W.   ES: Detroit, Wayne Co., MI
B: Indianapolis, Marion Co., IN

WINDUS, Claron   ES: Indianapolis, Marion Co., IN
B: Janesville, Rock Co., WI

WOODFILL, Samuel   ES: Bryantsburg, IN
B: Jefferson Co., IN

WRIGHT, Samuel   ES: Mankato, Blue Earth Co., MN
B: IN

YOUNT, John P.   ES: Sacramento, Sacramento Co., CA
B: Putnam Co., IN

U.S. Navy

ANTRIM, Richard Nott   ES: IN
B: Peru, Miami Co., IN

BADDERS, William   ES: INpolis, Marion Co., IN
B: Harrisburg, Saline Co., IL

BUCHANAN, Allen   ES: IN
B: Evansville, Vanderburgh Co., IN

CAMPBELL, William   ES: IN
B: IN

DITZENBACK, John   ES: IN
B: New York, NY

HILL, Frank Ebenezer   ES: IN
B: La Grange, La Grange Co., IN

INGRAM, Jonas Howard   ES: IN
B: Jeffersonville, Clark Co., IN

*SCOTT, Norman   ES: IN
B: INpolis, Marion Co., IN

WILKES, Perry   ES: Jeffersonville, Clark Co., IN
B: IN

WILLIAMS, Jay P.   ES: OH
B: Orland, Steuben Co., IN

U.S. Marine Corps

*ABRELL, Charles Gene   ES: Terre Haute, Vigo Co., IN
B: Terre Haute, Vigo Co., IN

BEARSS, Hiram Iddings   ES: IN
B: Peru, Miami Co., IN

*BRUCE, Daniel Dean   ES: Chicago, Cook Co., IL
B: Michigan City, La Porte Co., IN

*De La GARZA Jr., Emilio Albert   ES: Chicago, Cook Co., IL
B: East Chicago, Lake Co., IN

SHOUP, David Monroe   ES: IN
B: Battle Ground, Tippecanoe Co., IN

WINANS, Roswell   ES: WA
B: Brookville, Franklin Co., IN

*WINDRICH, William Gordon   ES: Hammond, Lake Co., IN
B: Chicago, Cook Co., IL

ZION, William F.   ES: CA
B: Knightstown, Henry Co., IN

IOWA

U.S. Army

BAKER Jr., John Franklin   ES: Moline, Rock Island Co., IL
B: Davenport, Scott Co., IA

BATES, Norman Francis   ES: Grinnell, Poweshiek Co., IA
B: Derry, VT

BEBB, Edward James   ES: Mount Pleasant, Henry Co., IA
B: Butler Co., OH

BENNETT, Orson W.   ES: Dubuque, Dubuque Co., IA
B: Union City, Branch Co., MI

BEYER, Arthur O.   ES: St. Ansgar, Mitchell Co., IA
B: Rock Township, Mitchell Co., IA

BIRDSALL, Horatio L.   ES: Keokuk, Lee Co., IA
B: Monroe Co., NY

BIRKHIMER, William Edward   ES: IA
B: Somerset, Perry Co., OH

BOUQUET, Nicholas S.   ES: Burlington, Des Moines Co., IA
B: Landau, Bavaria, Germany

BRAS, Edgar A.   ES: Wapello, Louisa Co., IA
B: Jefferson Co., IA

BRILES, Herschel Floyd "Pete"   ES: Fort Des Moines, Polk Co., IA
B: Colfax, Jasper Co., IA

*CHRISTENSEN, Dale Eldon   ES: Gray, Audubon Co., IA
B: Cameron Township, Audubon Co., IA

CODY, William Frederick "Buffalo Bill"   ES: Fort McPherson, NE
B: Scott Co., IA

COSGRIFF, Richard H.   ES: Wapello, Louisa Co., IA
B: Dunkirk Co., NY

DUNLAVY, James   ES: Bloomfield, Davis Co., IA
B: Decatur Co., IN

*EDWARDS, Junior Dean   ES: Indianola, Warren Co., IA
B: Indianola, Warren Co., IA

ELSON, James M.   ES: Shellsburg, Benton Co., IA
B: Coshocton, Coshocton Co., OH

FANNING, Nicholas   ES: Independence, Buchanan Co., IA
B: Carroll Co., IN

GATES, George   ES: Dubuque, Dubuque Co., IA
B: Delaware Co., OH

GODLEY, Leonidas Mahlon   ES: Ashland, IA
B: Mason Co., WV

GROVE, William Remsburg   ES: Denver, Denver Co., CO
B: Montezuma, Poweshiek Co., IA

HAYS, John H.   ES: Oskaloosa, Mahaska Co., IA
B: Jefferson Co., OH

HEALEY, George Washington   ES: Dubuque, Dubuque Co., IA
B: Dubuque, Dubuque Co., IA

HERINGTON, Pitt B.   ES: Tipton, Cedar Co., IA
B: MI

*HIBBS, Robert John   ES: Des Moines, Polk Co., IA
B: Omaha, Douglas Co., NE

HILL, James | ES: Cascade, Dubuque Co., IA
B: Bristol, Avon Co., England

HORNADAY, Elisha Simpson | ES: Des Moines, Polk Co., IA
B: Hendricks Co., IN

HUNTSMAN, John A. | ES: Lawrence, Douglas Co., KS
B: Oskaloosa, Mahaska Co., IA

KALTENBACH, Luther | ES: Honey Creek, Pottawattamie Co., IA
B: Germany

KEPHART, James | ES: Dubuque, Dubuque Co., IA
B: Venango Co., PA

KNOX, John W. | ES: Fort Leavenworth, Leavenworth Co., KS
B: Burlington, Des Moines Co., IA

LAWTON, Louis Bowem | ES: Auburn, Cayuga Co., NY
B: Independence, Buchanan Co., IA

*LEMERT, Milo | ES: Crossville, Cumberland Co., TN
B: Marshalltown, Marshall Co., IA

MAY, William C. | ES: Maysville, Franklin Co., IA
B: PA

MAYES, William B. | ES: DeWitt, Clinton Co., IA
B: Marion Co., OH

MILLER, James P. | ES: Henry Co., IA
B: Franklin, Warren Co., OH

MORGAN, Richard H. | ES: Taylor, Freemont Co., IA
B: Dubois Co., IN

NEPPEL, Ralph George | ES: Glidden, Carroll Co., IA
B: Willey, Carroll Co., IA

*OLSON, Arlo L. | ES: Toronto, Deuel Co., SD
B: Greenville, Clay Co., IA

PHIFE, Lewis | ES: Marion, Marion Co., OR
B: Des Moines Co., IA

*PIKE, Emory Jenison | ES: Sigourney, Keokuk Co., IA
B: Columbus City, Louisa Co., IA

POWER, Albert | ES: Bloomfield, Davis Co., IA
B: Liberty, Guernsey Co., OH

*RIORDAN, Paul F. | ES: Kansas City, Clay Co., MO
B: Charles City, Floyd Co., IA

SALE, Albert | ES: Dubuque, Dubuque Co., IA
B: Broome Co., NY

SLOAN, Andrew Jackson | ES: Colesburg, Delaware Co., IA
B: Bedford Co., PA

SMITH, Henry I. | ES: Shell Rock Fall, Butler Co., IA
B: Nottingham, Nottinghamshire, England

STANLEY, Eben | ES: Santa Fe, Santa Fe Co., NM
B: Decatur Co., IA

STRAUB, Paul Frederick | ES: Mount Pleasant, Henry Co., IA
B: Baden, Germany

SWAN, Charles Alexander | ES: Mount Pleasant, Henry Co., IA
B: Greene Co., PA

*THORSON, John F. | ES: Armstrong, Emmet Co., IA
B: Armstrong, Emmet Co., IA

TIBBETS, Andrew W. | ES: Centerville, Appanoose Co., IA
B: Clark Co., IN

TITUS, Calvin Pearl | ES: IA
B: Vinton, Benton Co., IA

TWOMBLY, Voltare Paine | ES: Keosauqua, Van Buren Co., IA
B: Farmington, Van Buren Co., IA

WELCH, George W. | ES: Keokuk, Lee Co., IA
B: Brown Co., IA

WILLIAMSON, James Alexander | ES: Des Moines, Polk Co., IA
B: Columbia, Adair Co., KY

YOUNG, Calvary Morris | ES: Hopeville, Clark Co., IA
B: Washington Co., OH

U.S. Army Air Corps/U.S. Air Force

DAY, George Everette "Bud" | ES: Sioux City, Woodbury Co., IA
B: Sioux City, Woodbury Co., IA

DETHLEFSEN, Merlyn Hans | ES: Royal, Clay Co., IA
B: Greenville, Clay Co., IA

*LINDSEY, Darrell Robins | ES: Storm Lake, Buena Vista Co., IA
B: Jefferson, Greene Co., IA

U.S. Navy

DEIGNAN, Osborn Warren | ES: IA
B: Stuart, Guthrie Co., IA

FITZ, Joseph | ES: Des Moines, Polk Co., IA
B: Austria

FLETCHER, Frank Friday | ES: IA
B: Oskaloosa, Mahaska Co., IA

FLETCHER, Frank Jack | ES: IA
B: Marshalltown, Marshall Co., IA

IZAC, Edouard Victor Michel | ES: IL
B: Cresco, Howard Co., IA

PIERCE, Francis Junior | ES: IA
B: Earlville, Delaware Co., IA

U.S. Marine Corps

HOWARD, Jimmie Earl | ES: Burlington, Des Moines Co., IA
B: Burlington, Des Moines Co., IA

KANSAS

U.S. Army

ADAMS, Stanley Taylor | ES: Olathe, Johnson Co., KS
B: DeSoto, Johnson Co., KS

*COWAN, Richard Eller | ES: Wichita, Sedgwick Co., KS
B: Lincoln, Lancaster Co., NE

DANIELS, James Thomas | ES: Fort Leavenworth, Leavenworth Co., KS
B: Richland Co., IL

EHLERS, Walter David | ES: Manhattan, Riley Co., KS
B: Junction City, Geary Co., KS

FERGUSON, Arthur Medworth | ES: Burlington, Coffey Co., KS
B: Coffey Co., KS

FUNSTON Sr., Frederick | ES: Iola, Allen Co., KS
B: New Carlisle, Clark Co., OH

*HADDOO Jr., John | ES: Columbus, Cherokee Co., KS
B: Hooksett, Merrimack Co., NH

HAY, Fred Stewart | ES: Fort Leavenworth, Leavenworth Co., KS
B: Stirlingshire, Scotland

HENDERSON, Joseph | ES: Leavenworth, Leavenworth Co., KS
B: Leavenworth, Leavenworth Co., KS

HOLLAND, David | ES: Fort Leavenworth, Leavenworth Co., KS
B: Dearborn, Wayne Co., MI

HUNT, Frederick O. | ES: Fort Leavenworth, Leavenworth Co., KS
B: London, England

HUNTSMAN, John A. | ES: Lawrence, Douglas Co., KS
B: Oskaloosa, Mahaska Co., IA

IMMELL, Lorenzo Dow	ES: Fort Leavenworth, Leavenworth Co., KS
	B: Ross, Butler Co., OH
JOHNSTON, Harold Irving	ES: Chicago, Cook Co., IL
	B: Kendall, Hamilton Co., KS
KNOX, John W.	ES: Fort Leavenworth, Leavenworth Co., KS
	B: Burlington, Des Moines Co., IA
MALLON, George H.	ES: Minneapolis, Hennepin Co., MN
	B: Ogden, Riley Co., KS
McCALL, Thomas Edward	ES: Veedersburg, Fountain Co., IN
	B: Burrton, Harvey Co., KS
*PEDEN, Forrest E.	ES: Wathena, Doniphan Co., KS
	B: St. Joseph, Buchanan Co., MO
*PETERSEN, Danny John	ES: Kansas City, Clay Co., MO
	B: Horton, Brown Co., KS
*PITTS, Riley Leroy	ES: Wichita, Sedgwick Co., KS
	B: Fallis, OK
POPPE, John A.	ES: Fort Dodge, Ford Co., KS
	B: Cincinnati, Hamilton Co., OH
ROACH, Hampton Mitchell	ES: Fort Dodge, Ford Co., KS
	B: Concord, LA
ROBB, George Seanor	ES: Salina, Saline Co., KS
	B: Assaria, Saline Co., KS
RODENBURG, Henry	ES: Fort Leavenworth, Leavenworth Co., KS
	B: Germany
SCHMIDT, Conrad	ES: Fort Leavenworth, Leavenworth Co., KS
	B: Wurttemberg, Germany
TREMBLEY, William Beattie	ES: Kansas City, Wyandotte Co., KS
	B: Johnson, Stanton Co., KS
WALLACE, George Weed	ES: Denver, Denver Co., CO
	B: Fort Riley, Geary Co., KS
WHITE, Edward	ES: Kansas City, Wyandotte Co., KS
	B: Seneca, Nemaha Co., KS

U.S. Army Air Corps/U.S. Air Force

*BLECKLEY, Erwin Russell	ES: Wichita, Sedgwick Co., KS
	B: Wichita, Sedgwick Co., KS
JOHNSON, Leon William	ES: Moline, Elk Co., KS
	B: Columbia, Boone Co., MO

U.S. Navy

BALCH, John Henry	ES: Kansas City, Clay Co., MO
	B: Edgerton, Johnson Co., KS
FOSTER, Paul Frederick	ES: KS
	B: Wichita, Sedgwick Co., KS
McGONAGLE, William Loren	ES: Thermal, Riverside Co., CA
	B: Wichita, Sedgwick Co., KS
ROSS, Donald Kirby	ES: Denver, Denver Co., CO
	B: Beverly, Lincoln Co., KS
TRIPLETT, Samuel S.	ES: NY
	B: Cherokee, Crawford Co., KS

U.S. Marine Corps

*BAUER, Harold William "Indian Joe"	ES: NE
	B: Woodruff, KS
*DAVENPORT, Jack Arden	ES: Mission, Johnson Co., KS
	B: Kansas City, Clay Co., MO
*HAWKINS, William Deane	ES: El Paso, El Paso Co., TX
	B: Fort Scott, Bourbon Co., KS

| *TIMMERMAN, Grant Frederick | ES: KS |
| | B: Americus, Lyon Co., KS |

KENTUCKY

U.S. Army

BELL, James Franklin	ES: Shelbyville, Shelby Co., KY
	B: Shelbyville, Shelby Co., KY
BLACK, William Perkins	ES: Danville, Vermillion Co., IL
	B: Woodford, KY
*BRATLING, Frank	ES: Louisville, Jefferson Co., KY
	B: Bavaria, Germany
CALLAHAN, John H.	ES: Scottville, Macoupin Co., IL
	B: Shelby Co., KY
*COLLIER, John Walton	ES: Worthington, Greenup Co., KY
	B: Worthington, Greenup Co., KY
*CRAIN, Morris E.	ES: Paducah, McCracken Co., KY
	B: Bandana, Ballard Co., KY
CRUSE, Thomas	ES: Owensboro, Daviess Co., KY
	B: Owensboro, Daviess Co., KY
DARROUGH, John S.	ES: Concord, Morgan Co., IL
	B: Maysville, Mason Co., KY
DAVIS, John	ES: Indanapolis, Marion Co., IN
	B: Carroll, KY
DAY, William L.	ES: Louisville, Jefferson Co., KY
	B: Barron Co., KY
DODD, Carl Henry	ES: Kenvir, Harlan Co., KY
	B: Coats, Harlan Co., KY
*FLEEK, Charles Clinton	ES: Cincinnati, Hamilton Co., OH
	B: Petersburg, Boone Co., KY
*GIVEN, John J.	ES: Cincinnati, Hamilton Co., OH
	B: Daviess Co., KY
HARDAWAY, Benjamin Franklin	ES: Fort Totten, Benson Co., Dakota Territory
	B: Benleyville, KY
HARRIS, William M.	ES: Mount Vernon, Rockcastle Co., KY
	B: Madison Co., KY
HAWTHORNE, Harry Leroy	ES: KY
	B: MN
HORSFALL, William H.	ES: Fort Cox, Charleston, WV
	B: Campbell Co., KY
HUDSON, Aaron R.	ES: Indanapolis, Marion Co., IN
	B: Madison Co., KY
HUGHES, Oliver	ES: Albany, Clinton Co., KY
	B: Fentress Co., TN
HUGHEY, John P.	ES: Anna, Union Co., IL
	B: Louisville, Jefferson Co., KY
JENKINS, Don	ES: Nashville, Davidson Co., TN
	B: Quality, Butler Co., KY
JONES, William H.	ES: Louisville, Jefferson Co., KY
	B: Davidson Co., NC
KERR, John Brown	ES: Hutchison Station, Bourbon Co., KY
	B: Lexington, Fayette Co., KY
*KYLE, Darwin K.	ES: Racine, Boone Co., WV
	B: Jenkins, Letcher Co., KY
*LAUFFER, Billy Lane	ES: Phoenix, Maricopa Co., AZ
	B: Murray, Calloway Co., KY
LITTRELL, Gary Lee	ES: Los Angeles, Los Angeles Co., CA
	B: Henderson, Henderson Co., KY

*LONG, Donald Russell
ES: Ashland, Boyd Co., KY
B: Blackfork, OH

MATTINGLY, Henry B.
ES: Lebanon, Marion Co., KY
B: Marion Co., KY

McDONALD, Franklin M.
ES: Fort Griffin, TX
B: Bowling Green, Warren Co., KY

McDONALD, Robert
ES: Newport, Campbell Co., KY
B: Erie Co., NY

McLOUGHLIN, Michael
ES: Louisville, Jefferson Co., KY
B: County Sligo, Ireland

McMILLEN, Francis M.
ES: Piqua, Miami Co., OH
B: Bracken Co., KY

MORRIS, William W.
ES: Louisville, Jefferson Co., KY
B: Stewart Co., TN

*NASH, David Paul
ES: Louisville, Jefferson Co., KY
B: Whitesville, Daviess Co., KY

NASH, James J.
ES: Louisville, Jefferson Co., KY
B: Louisville, Jefferson Co., KY

ROOD, Oliver P.
ES: Terre Haute, Vigo Co., IN
B: Frankfort Co., KY

ROSS, Wilburn Kirby
ES: Strunk, McCreary Co., KY
B: Strunk, McCreary Co., KY

RUNDLE, Charles Wesley
ES: Oakley, Macon Co., IL
B: Covington, Campbell Co., KY

SANDLIN, Willie
ES: Hyden, Leslie Co., KY
B: Jackson, Breathitt Co., KY

SCOTT, George D.
ES: Mount Vernon, Rockcastle Co., KY
B: Lancaster, Garrard Co., KY

SHAW, Thomas
ES: Baton Rouge, Baton Rouge Co., LA
B: Covington, Kenton Co., KY

*SMITH, David Monroe
ES: Livingston, Rockcastle Co., KY
B: Livingston, Rockcastle Co., KY

SPURRIER, Junior James
ES: Riggs, KY
B: Russell Co., KY

*SQUIRES, John C.
ES: Louisville, Jefferson Co., KY
B: Louisville, Jefferson Co., KY

STEINMETZ, William
ES: Sunman, Ripley Co., IN
B: Newport, Campbell Co., KY

STEVERS, Thomas W.
ES: Mount Vernon, Rockcastle Co., KY
B: Madison Co., KY

*STEWART, Jimmy Goethel
ES: Ashland, Boyd Co., KY
B: West Columbia, Mason Co., WV

SULLIVAN, Thomas
ES: Cincinnati, Hamilton Co., OH
B: Covington, Kenton Co., KY

SWEGHEIMER, Jacob
ES: Paducah, McCracken Co., KY
B: Oldtown, Baden, Germany

THORN, Walter
ES: Camp Nelson, KY
B: Brooklyn, Kings Co., NY

VOIT, Otto Emil
ES: Louisville, Jefferson Co., KY
B: Baden, Germany

WALKER, Mary Edwards
ES: Louisville, Jefferson Co., KY
B: Oswego Co., NY

WEST, Ernest Edison
ES: Wurtland, Greenup Co., KY
B: Russell, Greenup Co., KY

WESTON, John Francis
ES: Camp Anderson, KY
B: Louisville, Jefferson Co., KY

WHITEHEAD, Patton G.
ES: Louisville, Jefferson Co., KY
B: Russell Co., VA

WILLIAMSON, James Alexander
ES: Des Moines, Polk Co., IA
B: Columbia, Adair Co., KY

WOODS, Brent
ES: Louisville, Jefferson Co., KY
B: Pulaski Co., KY

U.S. Navy

BOERS, Edward William
ES: KY
B: Cincinnati, Hamilton Co., OH

CLARY, Edward Alvin
ES: KY
B: Foxport, KY

HOLT, George
ES: KY
B: KY

NOBLE, Daniel
ES: Chicago, Cook Co., IL
B: Bath Co., KY

U.S. Marine Corps

BARBER, William Earl
ES: West Liberty, Morgan Co., KY
B: Dehart, Morgan Co., KY

*BAUGH, William Bernard
ES: Harrison, Hamilton Co., OH
B: McKinney, Lincoln Co., KY

BUSH, Richard Earl
ES: KY
B: Glasgow, Barren Co., KY

*MASON, Leonard Foster
ES: OH
B: Middlesboro, Bell Co., KY

*PAUL, Joe Calvin
ES: Dayton, Montgomery Co., OH
B: Williamsburg, Whitley Co., KY

*PHELPS, Wesley
ES: KY
B: Neafus, Grayson Co., KY

SKAGGS Jr., Luther
ES: KY
B: Henderson, Henderson Co., KY

LOUISIANA

U.S. Army

BABCOCK, John
ES: Stonington, New London Co., CT
B: New Orleans, Orleans Co., LA

BEAUFORT, Jean J.
ES: New Orleans, Orleans Co., LA
B: France

CLARKE, Powhatan Henry
ES: Baltimore, Baltimore Co., MD
B: Alexandria, Rapides Co., LA

*DIAMOND, James H.
ES: Gulfport, Harrison Co., MS
B: New Orleans, Orleans Co., LA

*FOURNET, Douglas Bernard
ES: New Orleans, Orleans Co., LA
B: Lake Charles, Calcasieu Co., LA

GREELY, Adolphus Washington
ES: LA
B: Newburyport, Essex Co., MA

*JOHNSON, Leroy
ES: Oakdale, Allen Co., LA
B: Caney Creek, LA

*LEE, Milton Arthur
ES: San Antonio, Bexar Co., TX
B: Shreveport, Caddo Co., LA

NOVOSEL, Michael Joseph
ES: Kenner, Jefferson Co., LA
B: Etna, Allegheny Co., PA

RILEY, Thomas
ES: New Orleans, Orleans Co., LA
B: Ireland

ROACH, Hampton Mitchell
ES: Fort Dodge, Ford Co., KS
B: Concord, LA

SCHOWALTER Jr., Edward Rightor
ES: Metairie, Jefferson Co., LA
B: New Orleans, Orleans Co., LA

SHAW, Thomas
ES: Baton Rouge, Baton Rouge Co., LA
B: Covington, Kenton Co., KY

STANCE, Emanuel
ES: East Carroll Parish, LA
B: Carroll Parish, LA

WHITTINGTON, Hulon
Brooke ES: Bastrop, Morehouse Co., LA
B: Bogalusa, Washington Co., LA

WILLIAMS, Moses ES: East Carroll Parish, LA
B: Carrollton, Orleans Parish, LA

WISE, Homer L. ES: Baton Rouge, East Baton Rouge Co.,
LA
B: Baton Rouge, East Baton Rouge Co.,
LA

U.S. Army Air Corps/U.S. Air Force

*BENNETT, Steven Logan ES: Lafayette, Lafayette Co., LA
B: Palestine, Anderson Co., TX

*HUGHES, Lloyd Herbert ES: San Antonio, Bexar Co., TX
B: Alexandria, Rapides Co., LA

KANE, John Riley ES: Shreveport, Caddo Co., LA
B: McGregor, McLennan Co., TX

U.S. Navy

*GILMORE, Howard Walter ES: LA
B: Selma, Dallas Co., AL

OSBORNE, John ES: LA
B: New Orleans, Orleans Co., LA

RYAN Jr., Thomas John ES: LA
B: New Orleans, Orleans Co., LA

WEISBOGEL, Albert ES: LA
B: New Orleans, Orleans Co., LA

WILKINSON Jr., Theodore
Stark ES: LA
B: Annapolis, Anne Arundel Co., MD

WILLIAMS, John ES: LA
B: New Orleans, Orleans Co., LA

U.S. Marine Corps

CLAUSEN Jr., Raymond
Michael "Red" ES: New Orleans, Orleans Co., LA
B: New Orleans, Orleans Co., LA

DeBLANC, Jefferson Joseph ES: Lockport, Lafourche Co., LA
B: Lockport, Lafourche Co., LA

MAINE

U.S. Army

AMES, Adelbert ES: Rockland, Knox Co., ME
B: Rockland, Knox Co., ME

BAILEY, James E. ES: Boston, Suffolk Co., MA
B: Dexter, Penobscot Co., ME

BELCHER, Thomas ES: Bangor, Penobscot Co., ME
B: Bangor, Penobscot Co., ME

BOODY, Robert M. ES: Amesbury, Essex Co., MA
B: Lemington, ME

BOWMAN, Alonzo ES: Boston, Suffolk Co., MA
B: Washington Township, Knox Co., ME

BRETT, Lloyd Milton ES: Malden, Middlesex Co., MA
B: Dead River, ME

*BUKER, Brian Leroy ES: Bangor, Penobscot Co., ME
B: Benton, ME

CARTER, Robert
Goldthwaite ES: Bradford, Essex Co., MA
B: Bridgton, Cumberland Co., ME

CHAMBERLAIN, Joshua
Lawrence ES: Brunswick, Cumberland Co., ME
B: Brewer, Penobscot Co., ME

CHAPMAN, John ES: Limerick, York Co., ME
B: Strasburg, France

CHASE, John F. ES: Augusta, Kennebec Co., ME
B: Chelsea, ME

CLARK, Charles Amory ES: Forcroft, ME
B: Sangerville, Piscataquis Co., ME

CONDON, Clarence Milville ES: St. Augustine, St. Johns Co., FL
B: South Brooksville, Hancock Co., ME

DAHLGREN, Edward Carl ES: Caribou, Aroostook Co., ME
B: Perham, Aroostook Co., ME

DOHERTY, Thomas M. ES: Newcastle, Lincoln Co., ME
B: Mitchelstown, County Cork, Ireland

ESTES, Lewellyn Garrish ES: Oldtown, Penobscot Co., ME
B: Oldtown, Penobscot Co., ME

FERNALD, Albert E. ES: Winterport, Waldo Co., ME
B: Winterport, Waldo Co., ME

*FOURNIER, William Grant ES: Winterport, Waldo Co., ME
B: Norwich, New London Co., CT

*GOODBLOOD, Clair ES: Burnham, Waldo Co., ME
B: Fort Kent, Aroostook Co., ME

*GORDON, Gary Ivan ES: Lincoln, Penobscot Co., ME
B: Lincoln, Penobscot Co., ME

HANNA, Marcus A. ES: Rockport, Essex Co., MA
B: Bristol, Lincoln Co., ME

HANSCOM, Moses C. ES: Bowdoinham, Sagadahoc Co., ME
B: Danville, Androscoggin Co., ME

HARRINGTON, Ephraim W. ES: Kirby, VT
B: Waterford, Oxford Co., ME

HASKELL, Frank W. ES: Waterville, Kennebec Co., ME
B: Benton, ME

HAYNES, Asbury F. ES: Passadumkeag, Penobscot Co., ME
B: Edinburgh, ME

HESSELTINE, Francis Snow ES: Waterville, Kennebec Co., ME
B: Bangor, Penobscot Co., ME

HINCKS, William B. ES: Bridgeport, Fairfield Co., CT
B: Bucksport, Hancock Co., ME

HOWARD, Oliver Otis ES: Leeds, Androscoggin Co., ME
B: Leeds, Androscoggin Co., ME

HYDE, Henry J. ES: New York, NY
B: Bangor, Penobscot Co., ME

HYDE, Thomas Worcester ES: Bath, Sagadahoc Co., ME
B: Florence, Italy

KING, Horatio Collins ES: Brooklyn, Kings Co., NY
B: Portland, Cumberland Co., ME

KNOWLES, Abiather J. ES: Willets Point, Queens Co., NY
B: La Grange, Penobscot Co., ME

*LIBBY, George Dalton ES: Waterbury, New Haven Co., CT
B: Bridgton, Cumberland Co., ME

LITTLEFIELD, George H. ES: Skowhegan, Somerset Co., ME
B: Skowhegan, Somerset Co., ME

LUNT, Alphonso M. ES: Cambridge, Middlesex Co., MA
B: Berwick, York Co., ME

MATTOCKS, Charles Porter ES: Portland, Cumberland Co., ME
B: Danville, Caledonia Co., VT

*McMAHON, Thomas Joseph ES: Portland, Cumberland Co., ME
B: Washington, D.C.

*McMASTERS, Henry A. ES: Augusta, Kennebec Co., ME
B: Augusta, Kennebec Co., ME

MERRIAM, Henry Clay ES: Houlton, Aroostook Co., ME
B: Houlton, Aroostook Co., ME

MERRILL, Augustus ES: Lyndon, ME
B: Byron, ME

MILLETT, Lewis Lee "Red" ES: Mechanic Falls, Androscoggin Co., ME
B: Mechanic Falls, Androscoggin Co., ME

MORRILL, Walter Goodale ES: Brownville, Piscataquis Co., ME
B: Williamsburg, ME

O'BRIEN, Henry D. ES: St. Anthony Falls, MN
B: Colois, ME

PIKE, Edward M. ES: Bloomington, McLean Co., IL
B: Casco, Cumberland Co., ME

REED, Axel Hayford ES: Glencoe, McLeod Co., MN
B: Hartford, Oxford Co., ME

*RICHMOND, James ES: Fremont, Sandusky Co., OH
B: ME

ROBERTS, Otis O. ES: Dexter, Penobscot Co., ME
B: Sangerville, Piscataquis Co., ME

*SKIDGEL, Donald Sidney ES: Bangor, Penobscot Co., ME
B: Caribou, Aroostook Co., ME

SMITH, Charles Henry ES: Eastport, Washington Co., ME
B: Hollis, York Co., ME

SMITH, Joseph Sewall ES: Wiscasset, Lincoln Co., ME
B: Wiscasset, Lincoln Co., ME

SMITH, William ES: San Francisco, San Francisco Co., CA
B: Bath, Sagadahoc Co., ME

SPURLING, Andrew Barclay ES: Augusta, Kennebec Co., ME
B: Cranberry Isles, Hancock Co., ME

TAYLOR, Wilbur Nelson ES: Boston, Suffolk Co., MA
B: Hampden, Penobscot Co., ME

TERRY, John Darling ES: Boston, Suffolk Co., MA
B: Montville, ME

THAXTER, Sidney Warren ES: Bangor, Penobscot Co., ME
B: Bangor, Penobscot Co., ME

TOBIE Jr., Edward Parsons ES: Lewiston, Androscoggin Co., ME
B: Lewiston, Androscoggin Co., ME

TOZIER, Andrew Jackson ES: Bangor, Penobscot Co., ME
B: Monmouth, Kennebec Co., ME

TRACY, Amasa Sawyer ES: Middlebury, Addison Co., VT
B: Dover, Piscataquis Co., ME

*WAUGH, Robert T. ES: Augusta, Kennebec Co., ME
B: Ashton, RI

WHEELER, Henry W. ES: Bangor, Penobscot Co., ME
B: Fort Smith, Sebastian Co., AR

WHITMAN, Frank M. ES: Ayersville, MA
B: Woodstock, ME

WHITTIER, Edward Newton ES: Gorham, Cumberland Co., ME
B: Portland, Cumberland Co., ME

WOOD, Henry Clay ES: Winthrop, Kennebec Co., ME
B: Winthrop, Kennebec Co., ME

U.S. Army Air Corps/U.S. Air Force

*LORING Jr., Charles Joseph ES: Portland, Cumberland Co., ME
B: Portland, Cumberland Co., ME

ZEAMER Jr., Jay ES: Machias, Washington Co., ME
B: Carlisle, Cumberland Co., PA

U.S. Navy

ANGLING, John ES: Portland, Cumberland Co., ME
B: Portland, Cumberland Co., ME

BIBBER, Charles James ES: Portland, Cumberland Co., ME
B: Portland, Cumberland Co., ME

BICKFORD, John F. ES: Boston, Suffolk Co., MA
B: Tremont, ME

BLAIR, Robert M. ES: Portland, Cumberland Co., ME
B: Peacham, Caledonia Co., VT

BOWMAN, Edward R. ES: ME
B: Eastport, Washington Co., ME

DAVIS, Samuel W. ES: ME
B: Brewer, Penobscot Co., ME

DUNCAN, Adam ES: Boston, Suffolk Co., MA
B: ME

DUNN, William ES: ME
B: Lisbon, Androscoggin Co., ME

FARLEY, William ES: ME
B: Whitefield, Lincoln Co., ME

FOSS, Herbert Louis ES: ME
B: Belfast, Waldo Co., ME

FRISBEE, John B. ES: Brookline, Norfolk Co., MA
B: Phippsburg, Sagadahoc Co., ME

GIDDING, Charles ES: ME
B: Bangor, Penobscot Co., ME

HAYDEN, Cyrus ES: ME
B: York, York Co., ME

KENDRICK, Thomas ES: ME
B: Bath, Sagadahoc Co., ME

MACK, John ES: ME
B: Brooksville, Hancock Co., ME

McCULLOCK, Adam ES: Augusta, Kennebec Co., ME
B: ME

McLEOD, James ES: ME
B: Scotland

MILLIKEN, Daniel ES: New York, NY
B: Saco, York Co., ME

POOLE, William B. ES: ME
B: Cape Elizabeth, Cumberland Co., ME

RICE, Charles ES: Portland, Cumberland Co., ME
B: Russia

ROBINSON, John ES: ME
B: Cuba

SAVAGE, Auzella ES: Boston, Suffolk Co., MA
B: Anson, Somerset Co., ME

SCHONLAND, Herbert Emery ES: Portland, Cumberland Co., ME
B: Portland, Cumberland Co., ME

SEWARD, Richard Henry ES: Kittery, York Co., ME
B: Kittery, York Co., ME

SMITH, Charles H. ES: ME
B: Standish, Cumberland Co., ME

TAYLOR, Thomas ES: ME
B: Bangor, Penobscot Co., ME

TRIPP, Othniel ES: ME
B: ME

VERNEY, James W. ES: Portland, Cumberland Co., ME
B: Bath, Sagadahoc Co., ME

WILLIAMS, Anthony ES: Portsmouth, ME
B: Plymouth, Plymouth Co., MA

YOUNG, Horatio Nelson ES: Boston, Suffolk Co., MA
B: Calais, Washington Co., ME

U.S. Marine Corps

*CHAMPAGNE, David Bernard ES: Wakefield, Washington Co., RI
B: Waterville, Kennebec Co., ME

MARYLAND

U.S. Army

ANDERSON, Charles W. ES: near Winchester, Frederick Co., VA
B: Baltimore, Baltimore Co., MD

BARNES, William Henry ES: Norfolk, Norfolk Co., VA
B: St. Marys Co., MD

BEAUFORD, Clay ES: Nashville, Davidson Co., TN
B: Washington Co., MD

BOYNE, Thomas ES: Norfolk, Norfolk Co., VA
B: Prince Georges Co., MD

BUFFINGTON, John C. ES: Westminster, Carroll Co., MD
B: Carroll Co., MD

CADWALLADER, Abel G. ES: Frederick, Frederick Co., MD
B: Baltimore, Baltimore Co., MD

*CAPRON Jr., Horace ES: Peoria, Peoria Co., IL
B: Laurel, Prince George's Co., MD

CARTER, Joseph Franklin ES: Baltimore, Baltimore Co., MD
B: Baltimore, Baltimore Co., MD

CLARKE, Powhatan Henry ES: Baltimore, Baltimore Co., MD
B: Alexandria, Rapides Co., LA

*COSTIN, Henry G. ES: Baltimore, Baltimore Co., MD
B: Baltimore, Baltimore Co., MD

CRIST, John ES: Baltimore, Baltimore Co., MD
B: Baltimore, Baltimore Co., MD

DEETLINE, Frederick ES: Baltimore, Baltimore Co., MD
B: Offenheim, Germany

DONAHUE, John L. ES: Baltimore, Baltimore Co., MD
B: Baltimore Co., MD

DORSEY, Decatur ES: Baltimore, Baltimore Co., MD
B: Howard Co., MD

FLEETWOOD, Christian A. ES: Baltimore, Baltimore Co., MD
B: Baltimore, Baltimore Co., MD

FOSTER, William ES: Bakersville, MD
B: Somerset Co., England

GALT, Sterling Archibald ES: Taneytown, Carroll Co., MD
B: Taneytown, Carroll Co., MD

GREAVES, Clinton ES: Baltimore, Baltimore Co., MD
B: Madison Co., VA

HARRIS, James H. ES: Great Mills, St. Mary's Co., MD
B: St. Mary's Co., MD

HART, John William ES: Cumberland, Allegany Co., MD
B: Germany

*HARTSOCK, Robert Willard ES: Fairmont, Marion Co., WV
B: Cumberland, Allegany Co., MD

HAUPT, Paul ES: Baltimore, Baltimore Co., MD
B: Germany (Prussia)

*HILTON, Alfred B. ES: Baltimore, Baltimore Co., MD
B: Harford Co., MD

HINEMANN, Lehmann ES: Baltimore, Baltimore Co., MD
B: Lanback, Germany

*HOOKER, George ES: Washington, D.C.
B: Frederick, Frederick Co., MD

*JACHMAN, Isadore Seigfreid ES: Baltimore, Baltimore Co., MD
B: Berlin, Germany

*JECELIN, William R. ES: Baltimore, Baltimore Co., MD
B: Baltimore, Baltimore Co., MD

KEOUGH, John ES: Annapolis, Anne Arundel Co., MD
B: County Tipperary, Ireland

KOOGLE, Jacob ES: Middletown, Frederick Co., MD
B: Frederick, Frederick Co., MD

MATHEWS, William Henry ES: Baltimore, Baltimore Co., MD
B: Devizes, Wiltshire, England

MAUS, Marion Perry ES: Tennallytown, Montgomery Co., MD
B: Burnt Mills, Montgomery Co., MD

McALWEE, Benjamin Franklin ES: Baltimore, Baltimore Co., MD
B: Washington, D.C.

McGONNIGLE, Andrew Jackson ES: Cumberland, Allegany Co., MD
B: New York, NY

McNAMARA, William ES: Baltimore, Baltimore Co., MD
B: County Cork, Ireland

MILES, Louis Wardlaw ES: Princeton, Mercer Co., NJ
B: Baltimore, Baltimore Co., MD

MORELOCK, Sterling Lewis ES: Oquawka, Henderson Co., IL
B: Silver Run, MD

MOTT, John ES: Baltimore, Baltimore Co., MD
B: Fifeshire, Scotland

MURRAY Jr., Charles Patrick "Chuck" ES: Wilmington, New Hanover Co., NC
B: Baltimore, Baltimore Co., MD

MYERS, William H. ES: Baltimore, Baltimore Co., MD
B: Philadelphia, Philadelphia Co., PA

OLIVER, Francis ES: Fort Filmore, NM
B: Baltimore, Baltimore Co., MD

PENNSYL, Josiah ES: Carlisle, Cumberland Co., PA
B: Frederick Co., MD

PHELPS, Charles Edwards ES: Baltimore, Baltimore Co., MD
B: Guilford, VT

PHILIPSEN, Wilhelm O. ES: Baltimore, Baltimore Co., MD
B: Schleswig, Germany

PIERCE, Charles H. ES: Delaware City, New Castle Co., DE
B: Cecil Co., MD

PORTER, Ambrose ES: Rockport, Atchison Co., MO
B: Allegany Co., MD

*PORTER, Donn F. ES: Baltimore, Baltimore Co., MD
B: Sewickley, Allegheny Co., PA

PORTER, Samuel ES: Washington, D.C.
B: Montgomery Co., MD

*PRUSSMAN, Ernest W. ES: Brighton, Suffolk Co., MA
B: Baltimore, Baltimore Co., MD

SCHNEIDER, George ES: Baltimore, Baltimore Co., MD
B: Baltimore, Baltimore Co., MD

SHEA, Joseph Henry ES: New Bern, Craven Co., NC
B: Baltimore, Baltimore Co., MD

SHEERIN, John ES: Baltimore, Baltimore Co., MD
B: Camden Co., NJ

*SHERIDAN, Carl Vernon ES: Baltimore, Baltimore Co., MD
B: Baltimore, Baltimore Co., MD

SKINNER, John Oscar ES: MD
B: Baltimore, Baltimore Co., MD

SMITH, Andrew J. ES: Baltimore, Baltimore Co., MD
B: Baltimore, Baltimore Co., MD

SMITH, Francis M. ES: Frederick, Frederick Co., MD
B: Baltimore, Baltimore Co., MD

SMITH, Otto ES: Sacramento, Sacramento Co., CA
B: Baltimore, Baltimore Co., MD

STEWART, Joseph ES: Baltimore, Baltimore Co., MD
B: Ireland

TAYLOR, Charles ES: St. Louis, St. Louis Co., MO
B: Baltimore, Baltimore Co., MD

TAYLOR, William	ES: Frederick, Frederick Co., MD B: Washington, D.C.	JONES, Thomas	ES: Baltimore, Baltimore Co., MD B: Baltimore, Baltimore Co., MD
THOMPSON, John J.	ES: Baltimore, Baltimore Co., MD B: Holstein, Germany	JORDAN, Thomas H.	ES: Baltimore, Baltimore Co., MD B: Portsmouth, Portsmouth Co., VA
TUCKER, Jacob R.	ES: Baltimore, Baltimore Co., MD B: Chester Co., PA	LAKIN, Daniel	ES: MD B: Baltimore, Baltimore Co., MD
VEAL, Charles	ES: Baltimore, Baltimore Co., MD B: Portsmouth, Portsmouth Co., VA	MAGEE, John W.	ES: MD B: MD
WAGNER, John W.	ES: St. Louis, St. Louis Co., MO B: Clear Spring, Washington Co., MD	McDONNELL, Edward Orrick	ES: MD B: Baltimore, Baltimore Co., MD
WALLEY, Augustus	ES: Baltimore, Baltimore Co., MD B: Reistertown, Baltimore Co., MD	McNAIR Jr., Frederick Vallette	ES: Appointed at large B: Maryland
WARFEL, Henry Clay	ES: Monocacy Junction, MD B: Mill Creek, Huntingdon Co., PA	MORTON, Charles W.	ES: MD B: Ireland
WEINERT, Paul H.	ES: Baltimore, Baltimore Co., MD B: Frankfort, Germany	MULLEN, Patrick	ES: Baltimore, Baltimore Co., MD B: Ireland
WELD, Seth Lathrop	ES: Altamont, Grundy Co., TN B: Sandy Hook, MD	NORRIS, Thomas Rolland	ES: Silver Spring, Montgomery Co., MD B: Jacksonville, Duval Co., FL
WIEDORFER, Paul Joseph	ES: Baltimore, Baltimore Co., MD B: Baltimore, Baltimore Co., MD	PRESTON, Arthur Murray	ES: MD B: Washington, D.C.
WILSON, William O.	ES: St. Paul, Ramsey Co., MN B: Hagerstown, Washington Co., MD	*RICKETTS, Milton Ernest	ES: MD B: Baltimore, Baltimore Co., MD
WOODWARD, Evan M.	ES: Sandy Hook, MD B: Philadelphia, Philadelphia Co., PA	RINGOLD, Edward	ES: MD B: Baltimore, Baltimore Co., MD
*YNTEMA, Gordon Douglas	ES: Detroit, Wayne Co., MI B: Bethesda, Montgomery Co., MD	SHUTES, Henry	ES: MD B: Baltimore, Baltimore Co., MD
ZIEGNER, Herman	ES: Baltimore, Baltimore Co., MD B: Aploda, Germany	STERLING, James E.	ES: MD B: Baltimore, Baltimore Co., MD

U.S. Air Force

*WALMSLEY Jr., John Springer	ES: Baltimore, Baltimore Co., MD B: Baltimore, Baltimore Co., MD	SWEARER, Benjamin	ES: MD B: Baltimore, Baltimore Co., MD
		*TALLENTINE, James	ES: Baltimore, Baltimore Co., MD B: England

U.S. Navy

ANDREWS, John	ES: MD B: York Co., PA	TRUETT, Alexander H.	ES: MD B: Baltimore, Baltimore Co., MD
BROWN, John	ES: MD B: Denmark	WILKINSON Jr., Theodore Stark	ES: LA B: Annapolis, Anne Arundel Co., MD
BROWN, William H.	ES: MD B: Baltimore, Baltimore Co., MD	WRIGHT, William	ES: Baltimore, Baltimore Co., MD B: London, England
BUCK, James	B: Baltimore, Baltimore Co., MD		

U.S. Marine Corps

CARR, William M.	ES: Baltimore, Baltimore Co., MD B: Baltimore, Baltimore Co., MD	*GRAHAM, James Albert	ES: Prince Georges, Prince Georges Co., MD B: Wilkinsburg, Allegheny Co., PA
CHATHAM, John Purness	ES: MD B: Warchester, MD	*SHUCK Jr., William Edward	ES: Cumberland, Allegany Co., MD B: Cumberland, Allegany Co., MD
CONNOR, Thomas	ES: Baltimore, Baltimore Co., MD B: Ireland	*TAYLOR Sr., Karl Gorman	ES: Baltimore, Baltimore Co., MD B: Laurel, Prince George's Co., MD
DIGGINS, Bartholomew	ES: MD B: Baltimore, Baltimore Co., MD		

MASSACHUSETTS

U.S. Army

DURNEY, Austin Joseph	ES: Woodland, MD B: Philadelphia, Philadelphia Co., PA	ADAMS, John Gregory Bishop	ES: West Newbury, Essex Co., MA B: Groveland, Essex Co., MA
HAMMANN, Charles Hazeltine	ES: MD B: Baltimore, Baltimore Co., MD	ALLEN, Nathaniel M.	ES: Boston, Suffolk Co., MA B: Boston, Suffolk Co., MA
HAYDEN, Joseph B.	ES: MD B: St. Mary's City, St. Mary's Co., MD	ANDERSON, Frederick Charles	ES: Dedham, Norfolk Co., MA B: Boston, Suffolk Co., MA
JARRETT, Berrie Henry	ES: MD B: Baltimore, Baltimore Co., MD	BAILEY, James E.	ES: Boston, Suffolk Co., MA B: Dexter, Penobscot Co., ME
JOHANSON, John Peter	ES: MD B: Oskarshamn, Sweden		

*BARNES III, John Andrew   ES: Boston, Suffolk Co., MA
                           B: Boston, Suffolk Co., MA

BAYBUTT, Philip   ES: Fall River, Bristol Co., MA
                           B: Manchester, Greater Manchester Co.,
                           England

*BEAUDOIN, Raymond Ovila   ES: Holyoke, Hampden Co., MA
                           B: Holyoke, Hampden Co., MA

BERGENDAHL, Frederick   ES: Boston, Suffolk Co., MA
                           B: Gothenburg, Sweden

BESSEY, Charles Albert   ES: Boston, Suffolk Co., MA
                           B: Reading, Middlesex Co., MA

BOODY, Robert M.   ES: Amesbury, Essex Co., MA
                           B: Lemington, ME

BOSS, Orlando Phidelio   ES: Fitchburg, Worcester Co., MA
                           B: Fitchburg, Worcester Co., MA

BOWDEN, Samuel   ES: Boston, Suffolk Co., MA
                           B: Salem, Essex Co., MA

BOWMAN, Alonzo   ES: Boston, Suffolk Co., MA
                           B: Washington Township, Knox Co., ME

BOYNTON, Henry Van Ness   ES: Hamilton, Butler Co., OH
                           B: West Stockbridge, Berkshire Co., MA

BRADY, James   ES: Kingston, Rockingham Co., NH
                           B: Boston, Suffolk Co., MA

BRETT, Lloyd Milton   ES: Malden, Middlesex Co., MA
                           B: Dead River, ME

BROWN, John   ES: Cincinnati, Hamilton Co., OH
                           B: Boston, Suffolk Co., MA

BROWN, John Harties   ES: Charlestown, Suffolk Co., MA
                           B: New Brunswick, Canada

BRYANT, Andrew Symmes   ES: Springfield, Hampden Co., MA
                           B: Springfield, Hampden Co., MA

BUFFUM, Robert   ES: Gilead, Wood Co., OH
                           B: Salem, Essex Co., MA

BURT, James Montross   ES: Lee, Berkshire Co., MA
                           B: Hinsdale, Berkshire Co., MA

CALLEN, Thomas Joseph   ES: Boston, Suffolk Co., MA
                           B: County Louth, Ireland

CARNEY, William Harvey   ES: New Bedford, Bristol Co., MA
                           B: Norfolk, Norfolk Co., VA

CARSON, Anthony J.   ES: Malden, Middlesex Co., MA
                           B: Boston, Suffolk Co., MA

CARTER, Robert Goldthwaite ES: Bradford, Essex Co., MA
                           B: Bridgton, Cumberland Co., ME

CASEY, David P.   ES: Northbridge, Worcester Co., MA
                           B: Ireland

CHANDLER, Henry Flint   ES: Andover, Essex Co., MA
                           B: Andover, Essex Co., MA

COSGROVE, Thomas   ES: East Stoughton, Norfolk Co., MA
                           B: County Galway, Ireland

*CRAIG, Gordon Maynard   ES: Brockton, Plymouth Co., MA
                           B: Brockton, Plymouth Co., MA

CRANDALL, Charles   ES: Philadelphia, Philadelphia Co., PA
                           B: Worcester, Worcester Co., MA

DAVIS, George Evans   ES: Burlington, Chittenden Co., VT
                           B: Dunstable, Middlesex Co., MA

DAWSON, Michael   ES: New York, NY
                           B: Boston, Suffolk Co., MA

DEANE, John Milton   ES: Freetown, Bristol Co., MA
                           B: Assonet Village, Bristol Co., MA

DeCASTRO, Joseph H.   ES: Boston, Suffolk Co., MA
                           B: Boston, Suffolk Co., MA

*DeFRANZO, Arthur
Frederick   ES: Saugus, Essex Co., MA
                           B: Saugus, Essex Co., MA

DELAND, Frederick Nelson   ES: Great Barrington, Berkshire Co., MA
                           B: Sheffield, Berkshire Co., MA

DILLON, Michael A.   ES: Wilton, Hillsborough Co., NH
                           B: Chelmsford, Middlesex Co., MA

*DOANE, Stephen Holden   ES: Albany, Albany Co., NY
                           B: Beverly, Essex Co., MA

DODGE, Francis Safford   ES: Danvers, Essex Co., MA
                           B: Danvers, Essex Co., MA

DOWNEY, William   ES: Fall River, Bristol Co., MA
                           B: Ireland

DUFFEY, John   ES: New Bedford, Bristol Co., MA
                           B: New Bedford, Bristol Co., MA

EDDY, Samuel E.   ES: Chesterfield, Hampshire Co., MA
                           B: Whitingham, Windham Co., VT

ELLIOTT, Russell C.   ES: Boston, Suffolk Co., MA
                           B: Concord, Merrimack Co., NH

ELLSWORTH, Thomas
Foulds   ES: Boston, Suffolk Co., MA
                           B: Ipswich, Essex Co., MA

*EVANS, Rodney John   ES: Montgomery, Montgomery Co., AL
                           B: Chelsea, Suffolk Co., MA

*FALLS, Benjamin Frank   ES: Lynn, Essex Co., MA
                           B: Portsmouth, Rockingham Co., NH

FERRIS, Eugene W.   ES: Lowell, Middlesex Co., MA
                           B: Springfield, Windsor Co., VT

FOLEY, John H.   ES: Boston, Suffolk Co., MA
                           B: Cork, Ireland

FOLEY, Robert Franklin   ES: Newton, Middlesex Co., MA
                           B: Newton, Middlesex Co., MA

FUNK, West   ES: Philadelphia, Philadelphia Co., PA
                           B: Boston, Suffolk Co., MA

GARDNER, Charles N.   ES: Scituate, Plymouth Co., MA
                           B: South Scituate, Plymouth Co., MA

GARDNER, Robert J.   ES: Egremont, Berkshire Co., MA
                           B: Livingston, Columbia Co., NY

GARLAND, Harry   ES: Indianapolis, Marion Co., IN
                           B: Boston, Suffolk Co., MA

GAY, Thomas H.   ES: Boston, Suffolk Co., MA
                           B: Prince Edward Island, Canada

GAYLORD, Levi B.   ES: Boston, Suffolk Co., MA
                           B: Boston, Suffolk Co., MA

GIBSON, Edward Herrick   ES: Boston, Suffolk Co., MA
                           B: Boston, Suffolk Co., MA

GIFFORD, David L.   ES: New Bedford, Bristol Co., MA
                           B: Dartmouth, Bristol Co., MA

GOODMAN, David   ES: Boston, Suffolk Co., MA
                           B: Paxton, Worcester Co., MA

GRACE, Peter   ES: Berkshire, Berkshire Co., MA
                           B: Berkshire, Berkshire Co., MA

*GRANT, Joseph Xavier   ES: Boston, Suffolk Co., MA
                           B: Cambridge, Middlesex Co., MA

GREELY, Adolphus
Washington   ES: LA
                           B: Newburyport, Essex Co., MA

GRIMES, Edward P.   ES: Boston, Suffolk Co., MA
                           B: Dover, Strafford Co., NH

HALL, George John   ES: Boston, Suffolk Co., MA
                           B: Stoneham, Middlesex Co., MA

HANLEY, Richard P.   ES: Cincinnati, Hamilton Co., OH
                          B: Boston, Suffolk Co., MA

HANNA, Marcus A.   ES: Rockport, Essex Co., MA
                          B: Bristol, Lincoln Co., ME

HARBOURNE, John H.   ES: Readville, Suffolk Co., MA
                          B: England

HARRIS, Moses   ES: Boston, Suffolk Co., MA
                          B: Andover, Merrimack Co., NH

HASKELL, Marcus M.   ES: Chelsea, Suffolk Co., MA
                          B: Chelsea, Suffolk Co., MA

HOLDEN, Henry   ES: Boston, Suffolk Co., MA
                          B: Brighton, Sussex Co., England

HOLEHOUSE, James   ES: Fall River, Bristol Co., MA
                          B: Stockport, Greater Manchester Co.,
                          England

HOMAN, Conrad   ES: Boston, Suffolk Co., MA
                          B: Roxbury, Suffolk Co., MA

HOOKER, George White   ES: Boston, Suffolk Co., MA
                          B: Salem, Washington Co., NY

HOWE, William H.   ES: Boston, Suffolk Co., MA
                          B: Haverhill, Essex Co., MA

HUNTER, Charles Adams   ES: Spencer, Worcester Co., MA
                          B: Spencer, Worcester Co., MA

INGALLS, Lewis J.   ES: Belvidere, Lamoille Co., VT
                          B: Boston, Suffolk Co., MA

JELLISON, Benjamin H.   ES: Newburyport, Essex Co., MA
                          B: Newburyport, Essex Co., MA

JOHNS, Henry T.   ES: Hinsdale, Berkshire Co., MA
                          B: Philadelphia, Philadelphia Co., PA

*JOHNSON, Elden Harvey   ES: East Weymouth, Norfolk Co., MA
                          B: Bivale, Cumberland Co., NJ

KARPELES, Leopold   ES: Springfield, Hampden Co., MA
                          B: Prague, Austria-Hungary

KEATING, Daniel   ES: Boston, Suffolk Co., MA
                          B: County Cork, Ireland

LARKIN, David   ES: Boston, Suffolk Co., MA
                          B: Cork, Ireland

LAWTON, John Sterling   ES: Boston, Suffolk Co., MA
                          B: Bristol, Bristol Co., RI

LEONARD, Edwin   ES: Agawam, Hampden Co., MA
                          B: Agawam, Hampden Co., MA

LEWIS, William B.   ES: Boston, Suffolk Co., MA
                          B: Boston, Suffolk Co., MA

LORD, William   ES: Lawrence, Essex Co., MA
                          B: Bradford, England

LOVERING, George Mason   ES: East Randolph, Norfolk Co., MA
                          B: Springfield, NH

LOWTHERS, James   ES: Boston, Suffolk Co., MA
                          B: Boston, Suffolk Co., MA

LUNT, Alphonso M.   ES: Cambridge, Middlesex Co., MA
                          B: Berwick, York Co., ME

LUTHER, James Hezikiah   ES: Taunton, Bristol Co., MA
                          B: Dighton, Bristol Co., MA

LYON, Frederick A.   ES: Burlington, Chittenden Co., VT
                          B: Williamsburg, Hampshire Co., MA

MacARTHUR Jr., Arthur   ES: Milwaukee, Milwaukee Co., WI
                          B: Springfield, Hampden Co., MA

MacGILLIVARY, Charles
Andrew   ES: Boston, Suffolk Co., MA
                          B: Charlottetown, Prince Edward Island,
                          Canada

MAHONEY, Gregory   ES: Boston, Suffolk Co., MA
                          B: Pettypool, South Wales

MAHONEY, Jeremiah   ES: Fall River, Bristol Co., MA

MANNING, Joseph S.   ES: Boston, Suffolk Co., MA
                          B: Ipswich, Essex Co., MA

MARLAND, William   ES: Andover, Essex Co., MA
                          B: Andover, Essex Co., MA

MATHEWS, George William   ES: Worcester, Worcester Co., MA
                          B: Worcester, Worcester Co., MA

MATTHEWS, David A.   ES: Boston, Suffolk Co., MA
                          B: Boston, Suffolk Co., MA

MAXHAM, Lowell Mason   ES: Taunton, Bristol Co., MA
                          B: Carver, Plymouth Co., MA

MAYNARD, George Henry   ES: Boston, Suffolk Co., MA
                          B: Waltham, Middlesex Co., MA

McGAR, Owen   ES: Providence, Providence Co., RI
                          B: North Attleboro, Bristol Co., MA

McKINLEY, Daniel   ES: San Francisco, San Francisco Co., CA
                          B: Boston, Suffolk Co., MA

McNERNEY, David Herbert   ES: Fort Bliss, El Paso Co., TX
                          B: Lowell, Middlesex Co., MA

MILES, Nelson Appleton   ES: Roxbury, Suffolk Co., MA
                          B: Westminster, Worcester Co., MA

MILLER, George   ES: Boston, Suffolk Co., MA
                          B: Brooklyn, Kings Co., NY

MORIARITY, John   ES: Boston, Suffolk Co., MA
                          B: Huddersfield, Yorkshire, England

MOSHER, Louis C.   ES: Brockton, Plymouth Co., MA
                          B: Westport, Bristol Co., MA

MOYLAN, Myles   ES: Essex, Essex Co., MA
                          B: Amesbury, Essex Co., MA

*MULLER, Joseph E.   ES: New York, NY
                          B: Holyoke, Hampden Co., MA

MURPHY, Daniel J.   ES: Lowell, Middlesex Co., MA
                          B: Philadelphia, Philadelphia Co., PA

MURPHY, Dennis J. F.   ES: Lowell, Middlesex Co., MA
                          B: County Cork, Ireland

*MURPHY, Frederick C.   ES: Weymouth, Norfolk Co., MA
                          B: Boston, Suffolk Co., MA

MURPHY, Jeremiah J.   ES: Boston, Suffolk Co., MA
                          B: County Cork, Ireland

NEAL, Solon D.   ES: Boston, Suffolk Co., MA
                          B: Hanover, Grafton Co., NH

NEE, George Henry   ES: Boston, Suffolk Co., MA
                          B: Boston, Suffolk Co., MA

NEILON, Frederick S.   ES: Watertown, Middlesex Co., MA
                          B: Boston, Suffolk Co., MA

O'REGAN, Michael   ES: Boston, Suffolk Co., MA
                          B: Fall River, Bristol Co., MA

OSBORNE, William   ES: Boston, Suffolk Co., MA
                          B: Boston, Suffolk Co., MA

OSBORNE, William Henry   ES: East Bridgewater, Plymouth Co., MA
                          B: Scituate, Plymouth Co., MA

*OUELLETTE, Joseph R.   ES: Lowell, Middlesex Co., MA
                          B: Lowell, Middlesex Co., MA

PAYNE, Thomas H. L.   ES: Mendota, La Salle Co., IL
                          B: Boston Suffolk Co., MA

*PERKINS, Michael J.   ES: Boston, Suffolk Co., MA
                          B: Boston, Suffolk Co., MA

PINKHAM, Charles H.   ES: Worcester, Worcester Co., MA
                          B: Grafton, Worcester Co., MA

PLUNKETT, Thomas   ES: West Boylston, Worcester Co., MA
                          B: Ireland

*PRUSSMAN, Ernest W.   ES: Brighton, Suffolk Co., MA
                          B: Baltimore, Baltimore Co., MD

PUTNAM, Winthrop D.   ES: Peoria, Peoria Co., IL
                          B: Southbridge, Worcester Co., MA

PYM, James   ES: Boston, Suffolk Co., MA
                          B: Oxfordshire, England

REED, Charles Wellington ES: Malden, Middlesex Co., MA
                          B: Charlestown, Suffolk Co., MA

REGAN, Patrick J.   ES: Los Angeles, Los Angeles Co., CA
                          B: Middleboro, Plymouth Co., MA

RICE, Edmund   ES: Cambridge, Middlesex Ccounty, MA
                          B: Brighton, Suffolk Co., MA

RICH, Carlos H.   ES: Northfield, Franklin Co., MA
                          B: Canada

ROBBINS, Marcus M.   ES: Boston, Suffolk Co., MA
                          B: Elba, Dodge Co., WI

ROBINSON, John H.   ES: Roxbury, Suffolk Co., MA
                          B: Ireland

ROBINSON, Joseph   ES: Boston, Suffolk Co., MA
                          B: Montreal, Canada

SAXTON Jr., Rufus   ES: Deerfield, Franklin Co., MA
                          B: Greenfield, Franklin Co., MA

SCANLAN, Patrick   ES: Spencer, Worcester Co., MA
                          B: Ireland

SCHWENK, Martin   ES: Boston, Suffolk Co., MA
                          B: Baden, Germany

SLADEN, Joseph Alton   ES: Lowell, Middlesex Co., MA
                          B: Rockdale, England

SMITH, Thomas   ES: Fort Adams, RI
                          B: Boston, Suffolk Co., MA

SNOW, Elmer A.   ES: Chicago, Cook Co., IL
                          B: Hardwick, Worcester Co., MA

STEWART, Benjamin F.   ES: Boston, Suffolk Co., MA
                          B: Norfolk, Norfolk Co., VA

STRONG, James N.   ES: Pittsfield, Berkshire Co., MA
                          B: Pittsfield, Berkshire Co., MA

SWEATT, Joseph Sewell
Gerrish   ES: Lowell, Middlesex Co., MA
                          B: Boscawen, Merrimack Co., NH

TABOR, William L. S.   ES: Concord, Merrimack Co., NH
                          B: Metheun, Essex Co., MA

TAGGART, Charles A.   ES: Otis, Berkshire Co., MA
                          B: Blandford, Hampden Co., MA

TAYLOR, Wilbur Nelson   ES: Boston, Suffolk Co., MA
                          B: Hampden, Penobscot Co., ME

TERRY, John Darling   ES: Boston, Suffolk Co., MA
                          B: Montville, ME

TOBIN, John Michael   ES: Boston, Suffolk Co., MA
                          B: Waterford, Ireland

TOLAN, Frank   ES: Boston, Suffolk Co., MA
                          B: Malone, Franklin Co., NY

TRACY, Charles H.   ES: Springfield, Hampden Co., MA
                          B: Jewett City, New London Co., CT

TRUELL, Edwin M.   ES: Mantson, WI
                          B: Lowell, Middlesex Co., MA

*TURNER, Charles William ES: MA
                          B: Boston, Suffolk Co., MA

*TURNER, William Bradford ES: Garden City, Nassau Co., NY
                          B: Dorchester, Suffolk Co., MA

TURPIN, James H.   ES: Boston, Suffolk Co., MA
                          B: Easton, Bristol Co., MA

WALKER, Frank T. O.   ES: Burlington, Middlesex Co., MA
                          B: South Boston, Suffolk Co., MA

WALSH, John   ES: Springfield, Hampden Co., MA
                          B: Tipperary, Ireland

WARD, James   ES: Boston, Suffolk Co., MA
                          B: Quincy, Norfolk Co., MA

WARREN, Francis Emroy   ES: Hinsdale, Berkshire Co., MA
                          B: Hinsdale, Berkshire Co., MA

WELCH, Richard   ES: Williamstown, Berkshire Co., MA
                          B: Ireland

WHITMAN, Frank M.   ES: Ayersville, MA
                          B: Woodstock, ME

WHITTLESEY, Charles White ES: Pittsfield, Berkshire Co., MA
                          B: Florence, Florence Co., WI

WILBUR, William Hale   ES: Palmer, Hampden Co., MA
                          B: Palmer, Hampden Co., MA

*WILKIN, Edward G.   ES: Longmeadow, Hampden Co., MA
                          B: Burlington, Chittenden Co., VT

WINTERBOTTOM, William   ES: Boston, Suffolk Co., MA
                          B: Manchester, Greater Manchester Co.,
                             England

WITHINGTON, William
Herbert   ES: Jackson, Jackson Co., MI
                          B: Dorchester, Suffolk Co., MA

WOOD, Leonard   ES: Boston, Suffolk Co., MA
                          B: Winchester, Cheshire Co., NH

WORTMAN, George G.   ES: Boston, Suffolk Co., MA
                          B: Monckton, New Brunswick, Canada

WRIGHT, Samuel Cole   ES: Plympton, Plymouth Co., MA
                          B: Plympton, Plymouth Co., MA

U.S. Army Air Corps

*PEASE Jr., Harl   ES: Boston, Suffolk Co., MA
                          B: Plymouth, Grafton Co., NH

U.S. Navy

ARTHER, Matthew   ES: Boston, Suffolk Co., MA
                          B: Scotland

ATKINSON, Thomas E.   ES: MA
                          B: Salem, Essex Co., MA

BAKER, Benjamin F.   B: Dennis Port, Barnstable Co., MA

BARNUM, James   ES: MA
                          B: MA

BAZAAR, Philip   ES: New Bedford, Bristol Co., MA
                          B: Chile

BEYER, Albert   ES: Boston, Suffolk Co., MA
                          B: Hanover, Germany

BICKFORD, John F.   ES: Boston, Suffolk Co., MA
                          B: Tremont, ME

BOIS, Frank   ES: Northampton, Hampshire Co., MA
                          B: Quebec, Canada

BOND, William S.   ES: Boston, Suffolk Co., MA
                          B: Boston, Suffolk Co., MA

BRADLEY, Alexander   ES: MA
                          B: Boston, Suffolk Co., MA

BRENNAN, Christopher   ES: Boston, Suffolk Co., MA
                          B: Ireland

BRESNAHAN, Patrick Francis ES: VT
                          B: Peabody, Essex Co., MA

*CARON, Wayne Maurice ES: Boston, Suffolk Co., MA
                      B: Middleboro, Plymouth Co., MA

CHANDLER, James B.   ES: Boston, Suffolk Co., MA
                      B: Plymouth, Plymouth Co., MA

CHARETTE, George   ES: Lowell, Middlesex Co., MA
                      B: Lowell, Middlesex Co., MA

CONNOLLY, Michael   ES: MA
                      B: Boston, Suffolk Co., MA

CRAMEN, Thomas   ES: MA
                      B: Ireland

DEMPSEY, John   ES: Boston, Suffolk Co., MA
                      B: Ireland

DENEEF, Michael   ES: MA
                      B: MA

DENNIS, Richard   ES: Boston, Suffolk Co., MA
                      B: Charlestown, Suffolk Co., MA

*DEWERT, Richard David ES: Taunton, Bristol Co., MA
                       B: Taunton, Bristol Co., MA

DORAN, John James   ES: MA
                      B: Boston, Suffolk Co., MA

DUNCAN, Adam   ES: Boston, Suffolk Co., MA
                      B: ME

ENRIGHT, John   ES: MA
                      B: Lynn, Essex Co., MA

FITZPATRICK, Thomas   ES: Taunton, Bristol Co., MA
                      B: Canada

FOY, Charles H.   ES: Springfield, Hampden Co., MA
                      B: Portsmouth, Rockingham Co., NH

FRISBEE, John B.   ES: Brookline, Norfolk Co., MA
                      B: Phippsburg, Sagadahoc Co., ME

GILE, Frank S.   ES: MA
                      B: MA

GILL, Freeman   ES: MA
                      B: Boston, Suffolk Co., MA

GISBURNE, Edward Allen ES: MA
                       B: Providence, Providence Co., RI

GRADY, John   ES: MA
                      B: New Brunswick, Canada

GRIFFITHS, John   ES: MA
                      B: Wales

GRISWOLD, Luke M.   ES: Springfield, Hampden Co., MA
                      B: MA

HAMILTON, Thomas W.   ES: Weymouth, Norfolk Co., MA
                      B: Scotland

HANDRAN, John   ES: MA
                      B: MA

HARCOURT, Thomas   ES: MA
                      B: Boston, Suffolk Co., MA

HARRINGTON, Daniel C. ES: MA
                      B: Ireland

HARRISON, George H.   ES: Somerset, Bristol Co., MA
                      B: Middleton, Essex Co., MA

HART, William   ES: MA
                      B: MA

HATHAWAY, Edward W.   ES: Plymouth, Plymouth Co., MA
                      B: Plymouth, Plymouth Co., MA

HAYES, John   ES: New Bedford, Bristol Co., MA
                      B: Brogus, Newfoundland, Canada

HORTON, James   ES: MA
                      B: England

HORTON, James   ES: MA
                      B: Boston, Suffolk Co., MA

HORTON, Lewis Augustine ES: Taunton, Bristol Co., MA
                        B: Bristol Co., MA

HOWARD, Peter   ES: Boston, Suffolk Co., MA
                      B: France

HUDNER Jr., Thomas Jerome ES: Fall River, Bristol Co., MA
                          B: Fall River, Bristol Co., MA

JAMES, John H.   ES: MA
                      B: Boston, Suffolk Co., MA

JONES, John   ES: Acton, Middlesex Co., MA
                      B: Bridgeport, Fairfield Co., CT

KELLEY, Thomas Gunning ES: Boston, Suffolk Co., MA
                       B: Boston, Suffolk Co., MA

KELLY, Francis   ES: MA
                      B: Boston, Suffolk Co., MA

KENNA, Barnett   ES: Newburyport, Essex Co., MA
                      B: Canterbury, Kent Co., England

KERSEY, Thomas Joseph ES: MA
                      B: St. Johns, Newfoundland, Canada

KRAMER, Franz   ES: MA
                      B: Nierstein, Germany

KYLE, Patrick J.   ES: MA
                      B: Ireland

LAFFEY, Bartlett   ES: Boston, Suffolk Co., MA
                      B: Galway, County Galway, Ireland

LOGAN, Hugh   ES: Boston, Suffolk Co., MA
                      B: Ireland

LYLE, Alexander Gordon ES: MA
                       B: Gloucester, Essex Co., MA

LYONS, Thomas G.   ES: MA
                      B: Salem, Essex Co., MA

MacKENZIE, John   ES: MA
                      B: Bridgeport, Fairfield Co., CT

MADDIN, Edward   ES: MA
                      B: Newfoundland, Canada

MAHONEY, George   ES: Pennsylvania
                      B: Worcester, Worcester Co., MA

McDONALD, John   ES: Boston, Suffolk Co., MA
                      B: Perth, Scotland

McFARLAND, John C.   ES: Boston, Suffolk Co., MA
                      B: Boston, Suffolk Co., MA

MIHALOWSKI, John   ES: MA
                      B: Worcester, Worcester Co., MA

MILLER, Harry Herbert ES: MA
                      B: Noel Shore, Hants Co., Nova Scotia, Canada

MILLER, James   ES: Boston, Suffolk Co., MA
                      B: Denmark

MILLER, Willard D.   ES: MA
                      B: Noel Shore, Hants Co., Nova Scotia, Canada

MOORE, George   ES: Boston, Suffolk Co., MA
                      B: Philadelphia, Philadelphia Co., PA

MOORE, William   ES: MA
                      B: Boston, Suffolk Co., MA

MULLER, Frederick   ES: MA
                      B: Copenhagen, Denmark

NEWLAND, William D.   ES: MA
                      B: Medway, Norfolk Co., MA

O'BRIEN, Oliver Albert ES: Boston, Suffolk Co., MA
                       B: Boston, Suffolk Co., MA

O'CALLAHAN, Joseph
Timothy   ES: MA
                      B: Boston, Suffolk Co., MA

OLSEN, Anton	ES: MA B: Christiana (now Oslo), Norway	THOMPSON, William	ES: Boston, Suffolk Co., MA B: Cape May Co., NJ
*OUELLET, David George	ES: Boston, Suffolk Co., MA B: Newton, Middlesex Co., MA	TROY, William	ES: MA B: Boston, Suffolk Co., MA
PARKER, William	ES: MA B: Boston, Suffolk Co., MA	WILLEY, Charles H.	ES: MA B: East Boston, Suffolk Co., MA
PILE, Richard	ES: MA B: West Indies	WILLIAMS, Anthony	ES: Portsmouth, ME B: Plymouth, Plymouth Co., MA
PRANCE, George	ES: Boston, Suffolk Co., MA B: France	WILLIAMS, Augustus	ES: MA B: Kristiansand, Norway
PRESTON, John	ES: Boston, Suffolk Co., MA B: Ireland	WILLIS, George	ES: MA B: Boston, Suffolk Co., MA
PROVINCE, George	ES: Boston, Suffolk Co., MA B: Newport, Newport Co., RI	YOUNG, Horatio Nelson	ES: Boston, Suffolk Co., MA B: Calais, Washington Co., ME

OLSEN, Anton — ES: MA / B: Christiana (now Oslo), Norway

*OUELLET, David George — ES: Boston, Suffolk Co., MA / B: Newton, Middlesex Co., MA

PARKER, William — ES: MA / B: Boston, Suffolk Co., MA

PILE, Richard — ES: MA / B: West Indies

PRANCE, George — ES: Boston, Suffolk Co., MA / B: France

PRESTON, John — ES: Boston, Suffolk Co., MA / B: Ireland

PROVINCE, George — ES: Boston, Suffolk Co., MA / B: Newport, Newport Co., RI

RAMAGE, Lawson Paterson "Red" — ES: VT / B: Monroe Bridge, Franklin Co., MA

REGAN, Jeremiah — ES: Boston, Suffolk Co., MA / B: Boston, Suffolk Co., MA

RILEY, John Phillip — ES: MA / B: Allentown, Lehigh Co., PA

ROBERTS, Charles Church — ES: IL / B: Newton, Middlesex Co., MA

ROUNTRY, John — ES: Boston, Suffolk Co., MA / B: MA

RYAN, Francis Thomas — ES: MA / B: MA

SADLER, William — ES: MA / B: Boston, Suffolk Co., MA

SAUNDERS, James — ES: Boston, Suffolk Co., MA / B: MA

SAVAGE, Auzella — ES: Boston, Suffolk Co., MA / B: Anson, Somerset Co., ME

SEACH, William — ES: MA / B: London, England

SEANOR, James — ES: New York, NY / B: Boston, Suffolk Co., MA

SMITH, Frank Elmer — ES: VA / B: Boston, Suffolk Co., MA

SMITH, John — ES: MA / B: Boston, Suffolk Co., MA

STACY, William Bradford — ES: New Bedford, Bristol Co., MA / B: Fall River, Bristol Co., MA

STANLEY, William A. — ES: MA / B: MA

STEVENS, Daniel Dickerson — ES: MA / B: La Grange, Fayette Co., TN

STICKNEY, Herman Osman — ES: MA / B: Pepperell, Middlesex Co., MA

SULLIVAN, James F. — ES: MA / B: Lowell, Middlesex Co., MA

SWANSON, John — ES: MA / B: Gothenburg, Sweden

SWATTON, Edward — ES: Boston, Suffolk Co., MA / B: New York, NY

SWEENEY, William — ES: MA / B: Boston, Suffolk Co., MA

TALBOTT, William — ES: Boston, Suffolk Co., MA / B: England

THIELBERG, Henry — ES: Dudley, Webster Co., MA / B: Germany

THOMPSON, William — ES: Boston, Suffolk Co., MA / B: Cape May Co., NJ

TROY, William — ES: MA / B: Boston, Suffolk Co., MA

WILLEY, Charles H. — ES: MA / B: East Boston, Suffolk Co., MA

WILLIAMS, Anthony — ES: Portsmouth, ME / B: Plymouth, Plymouth Co., MA

WILLIAMS, Augustus — ES: MA / B: Kristiansand, Norway

WILLIS, George — ES: MA / B: Boston, Suffolk Co., MA

YOUNG, Horatio Nelson — ES: Boston, Suffolk Co., MA / B: Calais, Washington Co., ME

U.S. Marine Corps

ADAMS, John Mapes — ES: MA / B: Haverhill, Essex Co., MA

ADRIANCE, Harry Chapman — ES: MA / B: Oswego, Oswego Co., NY

BURNES, James — ES: CA / B: Worcester, Worcester Co., MA

*CADDY, William Robert — ES: MA / B: Quincy, Norfolk Co., MA

CAMPBELL, Daniel J. — ES: Boston, Suffolk Co., MA / B: Prince Edward Island, Canada

CARR, William Louis — ES: Boston, Suffolk Co., MA / B: Peabody, Essex Co., MA

COONEY, James — ES: MA / B: Limerick, Ireland

FORSTERER, Bruno Albert — ES: MA / B: Koenigsberg, Germany

*HANSON, Robert Murray — ES: MA / B: Lucknow, India

HILL, Walter Newell — ES: MA / B: Haverhill, Essex Co., MA

HUNT, Martin — ES: Boston, Suffolk Co., MA / B: County Mayo, Ireland

*JULIAN, Joseph Rodolph — ES: MA / B: Sturbridge, Worcester Co., MA

KEARNEY, Michael — ES: MA / B: Newmarket, County Cork, Ireland

McGINTY III, John James — ES: Laurel Bay, SC / B: Boston, Suffolk Co., MA

MEREDITH, James — ES: Boston, Suffolk Co., MA / B: Omaha, Douglas Co., NE

*MONEGAN Jr., Walter Carleton — ES: Seattle, King Co., WA / B: Melrose, Middlesex Co., MA

NUGENT, Christopher — ES: MA / B: County Cavan, Ireland

POPE, Everett Parker — ES: Quincy, Norfolk Co., MA / B: Milton, Norfolk Co., MA

*POWER, John Vincent — ES: MA / B: Worcester, Worcester Co., MA

PRENDERGAST, Thomas Francis — ES: MA / B: Waterford, Ireland

SCANNELL, David John — ES: Boston, Suffolk Co., MA / B: Boston, Suffolk Co., MA

SCOTT, Joseph Francis — ES: Cambridge, Middlesex Co., MA / B: Boston, Suffolk Co., MA

SULLIVAN, Edward | ES: MA
B: Cork, Ireland

*TALBOT, Ralph | ES: CT
B: South Weymouth, Norfolk Co., MA

*VITTORI, Joseph | ES: Beverly, Essex Co., MA
B: Beverly, Essex Co., MA

*WALSH, William Gary | ES: MA
B: Roxbury, Suffolk Co., MA

MICHIGAN

U.S. Army

ALBER, Frederick | ES: Manchester, Washtenaw Co., MI
B: Germany

AYERS, John G. K. | ES: Pekin, Tazwell Co., IL
B: Washtenaw Co., MI

BALDWIN, Frank Dwight | ES: Constantine, St. Joseph Co., MI
B: Manchester, Washtenaw Co., MI

BALLEN, Frederick A. | ES: Adrian, Lenawee Co., MI
B: Germany

BARRELL, Charles L. | ES: Leighton, Allegan Co., MI
B: Conquest, NY

BENNETT, Orson W. | ES: Dubuque, Dubuque Co., IA
B: Union City, Branch Co., MI

BICKFORD, Henry H. | ES: Middleport, Niagara Co., NY
B: Ypsilanti, Washtenaw Co., MI

BONDSTEEL, James Leroy | ES: Detroit, Wayne Co., MI
B: Jackson, Jackson Co., MI

BRANDLE, Joseph E. | ES: Colon, St. Joseph Co., MI
B: Seneca Co., OH

*BRYANT, William Maud | ES: Detroit, Wayne Co., MI
B: Cochran, Bleckley Co., GA

CAWETZKA, Charles | ES: Wayne, Wayne Co., MI
B: Detroit, Wayne Co., MI

CHANDLER, Stephen Edwin | ES: Grandby, Oswego Co., NY
B: Convis, MI

CHAPMAN, Amos | ES: Fort Supply, Indian Territory
(Oklahoma)
B: Kalamazoo, Kalamazoo Co., MI

CHRISTIANCY, James Isaac | ES: Monroe Co., MI
B: Monroe Co., MI

CLUTE, George Washington | ES: Marathon, MI
B: Marathon, MI

COLE, Gabriel | ES: New Salem, Washtenaw Co., MI
B: Chenango Co., NY

CUSTER, Thomas Ward | ES: Monroe, Monroe Co., MI
B: New Rumley, Harrison Co., OH

CUTCHEON, Byron M. | ES: Ypsilanti, Washtenaw Co., MI
B: Pembroke, Suncook Co., NH

DePUY, Charles H. | ES: St. Louis, St. Louis Co., MO
B: Sherman, MI

DODD, Robert Fulton | ES: Detroit, Wayne Co., MI
B: Canada

DOUGHERTY, William | ES: Philadelphia, Philadelphia Co., PA
B: Detroit, Wayne Co., MI

DROWLEY, Jesse Ray | ES: Wayne Co., MI
B: St. Charles, Saginaw Co., MI

DUNNE, James | ES: Chicago, Cook Co., IL
B: Detroit, Wayne Co., MI

ELDRIDGE, George H. | ES: Detroit, Wayne Co., MI
B: Sackets Harbor, Jefferson Co., NY

*ESSEBAGGER Jr., John | ES: Holland, Ottawa Co., MI
B: Holland, Ottawa Co., MI

FALCONER, John A. | ES: Manchester, Washtenaw Co., MI
B: Washtenaw, MI

FALL, Charles S. | ES: Hamburg, Livingston Co., MI
B: Noble Co., IN

FORMAN, Alexander A. | ES: Jonesville, Hillsdale Co., MI
B: Scipio Township, Hillsdale Co., MI

FOX, Henry M. | ES: Coldwater, Branch Co., MI
B: Trumbull, OH

FRENCH, Samuel S. | ES: Gifford, Tuscola Co., MI
B: Erie Co., NY

FURLONG, Harold Arthur | ES: Detroit, Wayne Co., MI
B: Pontiac, Oakland Co., MI

GAUJOT, Antoine August | ES: Williamson, Mingo Co., WV
B: Keweenaw, Baraga Co., MI

GAUJOT, Julien Edmund | ES: Williamson, Mingo Co., WV
B: Keweenaw, Baraga Co., MI

HACK, John | ES: Adrian, Lenawee Co., MI
B: Germany

HADLEY, Cornelius Minor | ES: Adrian, Lenawee Co., MI
B: Sandy Creek, Oswego Co., NY

HAIGHT, Sidney | ES: Goodland, MI
B: Reading, Hillsdale Co., MI

HARRINGTON, John | ES: Cleveland, Cuyahoga Co., OH
B: Detroit, Wayne Co., MI

HARTZOG, Joshua B. | ES: Detroit, Wayne Co., MI
B: Paulding Co., OH

HASTINGS, Smith H. | ES: Coldwater, Branch Co., MI
B: Quincy, Branch Co., MI

HERINGTON, Pitt B. | ES: Tipton, Cedar Co., IA
B: MI

HILL, Edward | ES: Detroit, Wayne Co., MI
B: Liberty, Sullivan Co., NY

HILLOCK, Marvin C. | ES: Detroit, Wayne Co., MI
B: Port Huron, St. Clair Co., MI

HODGES, Addison J. | ES: Adrian, Lenawee Co., MI
B: Hillsdale, Hillsdale Co., MI

HOLLAND, David | ES: Fort Leavenworth, Leavenworth Co.,
KS
B: Dearborn, Wayne Co., MI

HOLTON, Charles Maynard | ES: Battle Creek, Calhoun Co., MI
B: Potter, Yates Co., NY

IRWIN, Patrick | ES: Ann Arbor, Washtenaw Co., MI
B: Ireland

JARVIS, Frederick | ES: Hudson, Lenawee Co., MI
B: Essex Co., NY

JOHNSON, Dwight Hal | ES: Detroit, Wayne Co., MI
B: Detroit, Wayne Co., MI

JOHNSON, Henry | ES: Detroit, Wayne Co., MI
B: Boydton, Mecklenburg Co., VA

JOHNSON Jr., Oscar Godfrey | ES: Foster City, Dickinson Co., MI
B: Foster City, Dickinson Co., MI

KEEN, Joseph S. | ES: Detroit, Wayne Co., MI
B: Vale, Guernsey, England

KELLEY, Andrew John | ES: Ypsilanti, Washtenaw Co., MI
B: La Grange Co., IN

KEMP, Joseph Bell | ES: Sault Ste. Marie, Chippewa Co., MI
B: Lima, Allen Co., OH

LAMBERS, Paul Ronald | ES: Holland, Ottawa Co., MI
B: Holland, Ottawa Co., MI

LANE, Morgan D.	ES: Allegan, Allegan Co., MI B: Monroe, Orange Co., NY	SHEPARD, Irwin	ES: Chelsea, Washtenaw Co., MI B: Skaneateles, Onondaga Co., NY
LEMON, Peter Charles	ES: Tawas City, Iosco Co., MI B: Toronto, Canada	SIDMAN, George Dallas	ES: Owosso, Shiawassee Co., MI B: Rochester, Monroe Co., NY
LEONARD, William	ES: Detroit, Wayne Co., MI B: Ypsilanti, Washtenaw Co., MI	SJOGREN, John Carleton	ES: Rockford, Kent Co., MI B: Rockford, Kent Co., MI
LEWIS, Henry	ES: Adrian, Lenawee Co., MI B: Belleville, Wayne Co., MI	SMITH, Alonzo	ES: Jonesville, Hillsdale Co., MI B: Niagara Co., NY
LUCE, Moses Augustine	ES: Adrian, Lenawee Co., MI B: Payson, Adams Co., IL	SMITH, William H.	ES: Cincinnati, Hamilton Co., OH B: Lapeer, Lapeer Co., MI
McCONNELL, James	ES: Detroit, Wayne Co., MI B: Syracuse, Onondaga Co., NY	SWIFT, Frederic William	ES: Detroit, Wayne Co., MI B: Mansfield Center, Tolland Co., CT
McFALL, Daniel Robert	ES: Ypsilanti, Washtenaw Co., MI B: Niagara Co., NY	SYPE, Peter	ES: Adrian, Lenawee Co., MI B: Monroe Co., MI
McHALE, Alexander U.	ES: Muskegon, Muskegon Co., MI B: Ireland	THATCHER, Charles M.	ES: Grand Haven, Ottawa Co., MI B: Coldwater, Branch Co., MI
MENTER, John William	ES: Detroit, Wayne Co., MI B: Palmer, NY	*THOMAS, William H.	ES: Ypsilanti, Washtenaw Co., MI B: Wynne, Cross Co., AR
MORSE, Benjamin	ES: Grand Rapids, Kent Co., MI B: Livingston, Columbia Co., NY	THOMPSON, Charles Augustus	ES: Kalamazoo, Kalamazoo Co., MI B: Perrysburg, Wood Co., OH
*MOYER, Donald Raymond	ES: Keego Harbor, Oakland Co., MI B: Pontiac, Oakland Co., MI	TOBAN, James W.	ES: Northfield, MI B: Northfield, MI
MUNDELL, Walter L.	ES: Dallas, MI B: MI	VLUG, Dirk John	ES: Grand Rapids, Kent Co., MI B: Maple Lake, Wright Co., MN
NASH, Henry H.	ES: Adrian, Lenawee Co., MI B: Lenawee Co., MI	WALKER, John	ES: Detroit, Wayne Co., MI B: Leon, France
NOLL, Conrad	ES: Ann Arbor, Washtenaw Co., MI B: Germany	WARD, William Henry	ES: Adrian, Lenawee Co., MI B: Adrian, Lenawee Co., MI
NORTON, Elliott Malloy	ES: Cooper, MI B: CT	WATSON, Joseph	ES: Chicago, Cook Co., IL B: Union City, Branch Co., MI
NORTON, John R.	ES: Grand Rapids, Kent Co., MI B: St. John's Parish, Roscommon, County Ballaugh, Ireland	*WETZEL, Walter C.	ES: Roseville, Macomb Co., MI B: Huntington, Cabell Co., WV
PETERS, Henry Carlton	ES: Adrian, Lenawee Co., MI B: Monroe Co., MI	WHEATON, Loyd	ES: Peoria, Peoria Co., IL B: Penfield, MI
PLANT, Henry E.	ES: Cockery, MI B: Oswego Co., NY	WHITNEY, William G.	ES: Quincy, Branch Co., MI B: Allen, Hillsdale Co., MI
POLOND, Alfred	ES: Lapeer, Lapeer Co., MI B: Lapeer, Lapeer Co., MI	*WIGLE, Thomas W.	ES: Detroit, Wayne Co., MI B: INpolis, Marion Co., IN
POWERS, Thomas	ES: Detroit, Wayne Co., MI B: New York, NY	WILDER, Wilber Elliott	ES: Detroit, Wayne Co., MI B: Atlas, Genesee Co., MI
*POXON, Robert Leslie	ES: Detroit, Wayne Co., MI B: Detroit, Wayne Co., MI	WILLCOX, Orlando Bolivar	ES: Detroit, Wayne Co., MI B: Detroit, Wayne Co., MI
RANNEY, George E.	ES: Grand Rapids, Kent Co., MI B: Batavia, Genesee Co., NY	WITHINGTON, William Herbert	ES: Jackson, Jackson Co., MI B: Dorchester, Suffolk Co., MA
RHODES, Julius Dexter	ES: Springville, Erie Co., NY B: Monroe Co., MI	WOODRUFF, Alonzo	ES: Ionia, Ionia Co., MI B: Ionia, Ionia Co., MI
*ROBINSON, James H.	ES: Victor, MI B: Oakland Co., MI	*YNTEMA, Gordon Douglas	ES: Detroit, Wayne Co., MI B: Bethesda, Montgomery Co., MD
ROMEYN, Henry	ES: MI B: Galen, Wayne Co., NY	YOUNG, Benjamin F.	ES: Detroit, Wayne Co., MI B: Canada
SANCRAINTE, Charles Francis	ES: Monroe, Monroe Co., MI B: Monroe, Monroe Co., MI	*ZUSSMAN, Raymond	ES: Detroit, Wayne Co., MI B: Hamtramck, Wayne Co., MI
SAVACOOL, Edwin F.	ES: Marshall, Calhoun Co., MI B: Jackson, Jackson Co., MI		

U.S. Army Air Corps/U.S. Air Force

SEIBERT, Lloyd Martin	ES: Salinas, Monterey Co., CA B: Caledonia, Kent Co., MI	*CRAW, Demas Thurlow	ES: MI B: Traverse City, Grand Traverse Co., MI
SHAFTER, William Rufus	ES: Galesburg, Kalamazoo Co., MI B: Kalamazoo, Kalamazoo Co., MI	LINDBERGH Jr., Charles Augustus	ES: Little Falls, Morrison Co., MN B: Detroit, Wayne Co., MI
SHAW, George Clymer	ES: Washington, D.C. B: Pontiac, Oakland Co., MI	*SEBILLE, Louis Joseph	ES: Chicago, Cook Co., IL B: Harbor Beach, Huron Co., MI

SMITH Sr., Maynard
Harrison ES: Cairo, MI
 B: Cairo, MI

U.S. Navy

CHARETTE, William Richard ES: Ludington, Mason Co., MI
 B: Ludington, Mason Co., MI

CRONIN, Cornelius ES: MI
 B: Ireland

*FLAHERTY, Francis Charles ES: MI
 B: Charlotte, Eaton Co., MI

*HAMMERBERG, Owen
Francis Patrick ES: MI
 B: Daggett, Menominee Co., MI

STODDARD, James ES: Detroit, Wayne Co., MI
 B: Port Robinson, Canada (West)

ZUIDERVELD, William ES: MI
 B: MI

U.S. Marine Corps

*CANNON, George Ham ES: MI
 B: Webster Groves, St. Louis Co., MO

DEWEY, Duane Edgar ES: Muskegon, Muskegon Co., MI
 B: Grand Rapids, Kent Co., MI

GLOWIN, Joseph Anthony ES: MI
 B: Detroit, Wayne Co., MI

SIMANEK, Robert Ernest ES: Detroit, Wayne Co., MI
 B: Detroit, Wayne Co., MI

*SKINNER Jr., Sherrod
Emerson ES: East Lansing, Ingham Co., MI
 B: Hartford, Hartford Co., CT

SMITH, Albert Joseph ES: MI
 B: Calumet, Houghton Co., MI

*STOCKHAM, Fred William ES: New York, NY
 B: Detroit, Wayne Co., MI

*WILLIAMS, Dewayne
Thomas ES: Saint Clair, Saint Clair Co., MI
 B: Brown City, Sanilac Co., MI

MINNESOTA

U.S. Army

ALBEE, George Emerson ES: Owatonna, Steele Co., MN
 B: Lisbon, Grafton Co., NH

BARRICK, Jesse ES: Fort Snelling, St. Paul Co., MN
 B: Columbiana Co., OH

BELL, Harry ES: Minneapolis, Hennepin Co., MN
 B: Milwaukee, Milwaukee Co., WI

*BIANCHI, Willibald Charles ES: New Ulm, Brown Co., MN
 B: New Ulm, Brown Co., MN

*BLANCHFIELD, Michael
Reinert ES: Chicago, Cook Co., IL
 B: Minneapolis, Hennepin Co., MN

BURGER, Joseph ES: Crystal Lake, Hennepin Co., MN
 B: Austria or Swiss Tyrol

BURKARD, Oscar R. ES: Fort Snelling, St. Paul Co., MN
 B: Baden Achern, Germany

CILLEY, Clinton Albert ES: Sasioja, MN
 B: Rockingham Co., NH

CLARK, William A. ES: Shelbyville, MN
 B: PA

COLALILLO, Michael "Mike" ES: Duluth, St. Louis Co., MN
 B: Hibbing, St. Louis Co., MN

DAVIS, Charles P. ES: Valley City, Barnes Co., ND
 B: Long Prairie, Todd Co., MN

FLANNIGAN, James ES: Fort Snelling, St. Paul Co., MN
 B: Canada

GERE, Thomas Parke ES: Fort Snelling, St. Paul Co., MN
 B: Wellsburg, Chemung Co., NY

HANNA, Milton ES: Henderson, Sibley Co., MN
 B: Licking Co., OH

HAWKS, Lloyd C. ES: Park Rapids, Hubbard Co., MN
 B: Becker, Sherburne Co., MN

HAWTHORNE, Harry Leroy ES: KY
 B: MN

HOLMES, Lovilo N. ES: Mankato, Blue Earth Co., MN
 B: Farmersville, Cattaraugus Co., NY

HUGGINS, Eli Lundy ES: MN
 B: Schuyler Co., IL

MALLON, George H. ES: Minneapolis, Hennepin Co., MN
 B: Ogden, Riley Co., KS

McMILLIAN, Albert Walter ES: Jefferson Barracks, MO
 B: Stillwater, Washington Co., MN

MERRITT, John G. ES: Fort Snelling, St. Paul Co., MN
 B: New York, NY

MONTROSE, Charles H. ES: New York, NY
 B: St. Paul, Ramsey Co., MN

MORGAN, George Horace ES: Minneapolis, Hennepin Co., MN
 B: St. Catherines, Canada

O'BRIEN, Henry D. ES: St. Anthony Falls, MN
 B: Colois, ME

*OLSON, Kenneth Lee ES: Minneapolis, Hennepin Co., MN
 B: Willmar, Kandiyohi Co., MN

*PAGE, John Upshur Dennis ES: St. Paul, Ramsey Co., MN
 B: Malahi Island, Luzon, Philippine Islands

PAY, Byron E. ES: Mankato, Blue Earth Co., MN
 B: LeRoy Township, Jefferson Co., NY

PICKLE, Alonzo H. ES: Dover, Olmsted Co., MN
 B: Canada

*PRUDEN, Robert Joseph ES: Minneapolis, Hennepin Co., MN
 B: St.Paul, Ramsey Co., MN

*RABEL, Laszlo ES: Minneapolis, Hennepin Co., MN
 B: Budapest, Hungary

REED, Axel Hayford ES: Glencoe, McLeod Co., MN
 B: Hartford, Oxford Co., ME

RUDOLPH, Donald Eugene ES: Minneapolis, Hennepin Co., MN
 B: South Haven, Wright Co., MN

SHERMAN, Marshall ES: St. Paul, Ramsey Co., MN
 B: Burlington, Chittenden Co., VT

VALE, John ES: Rochester, Olmsted Co., MN
 B: London, England

VLUG, Dirk John ES: Grand Rapids, Kent Co., MI
 B: Maple Lake, Wright Co., MN

*WAYRYNEN, Dale Eugene ES: Minneapolis, Hennepin Co., MN
 B: Moose Lake, Carlton Co., MN

WELCH, Charles H. ES: Fort Snelling, St. Paul Co., MN
 B: New York, NY

WILSON, William O. ES: St. Paul, Ramsey Co., MN
 B: Hagerstown, Washington Co., MD

*WOLD, Nels T. ES: Minnewaukan, Benson Co., ND
 B: Winger, Polk Co., MN

WRIGHT, Samuel ES: Mankato, Blue Earth Co., MN
 B: IN

U.S. Army Air Corps/U.S. Air Force

LINDBERGH Jr., Charles Augustus	ES: Little Falls, Morrison Co., MN B: Detroit, Wayne Co., MI
THORSNESS, Leo Keith	ES: Walnut Grove, Redwood Co., MN B: Walnut Grove, Redwood Co., MN

U.S. Navy

DAVIS, Raymond Erwin	ES: Puget Sound, WA B: Mankato, Blue Earth Co., MN
NELSON, Oscar Frederick	ES: MN B: Minneapolis, Hennepin Co., MN
*RUD, George William	ES: MN B: Minneapolis, Hennepin Co., MN
*VAN VALKENBURGH, Franklin	ES: WI B: Minneapolis, Hennepin Co., MN

U.S. Marine Corps

CATLIN, Albertus Wright	ES: MN B: Gowanda, Cattaraugus Co., NY
*COURTNEY Jr., Henry Alexius	ES: MN B: Duluth, St. Louis Co., MN
CUKELA, Louis	ES: Minneapolis, Hennepin Co., MN B: Spalato, Yugoslavia
DYER, Jesse Farley	ES: MN B: St. Paul, Ramsey Co., MN
*FLEMING, Richard Eugene	ES: MN B: St. Paul, Ramsey Co., MN
*HAUGE Jr., Louis James	ES: MN B: Ada, Norman Co., MN
*KRAUS, Richard Edward	ES: MN B: Chicago, Cook Co., IL
*La BELLE, James Dennis	ES: MN B: Columbia Heights, Hennepin Co., MN
SORENSON, Richard Keith	ES: Anoka, Anoka Co., MN B: Anoka, Anoka Co., MN

MISSISSIPPI

U.S. Army

BARFOOT, Van Thomas	ES: Carthage, Leake Co., MS B: Edinburg, Leake Co., MS
BLACK, John Charles	ES: Danville, Vermillion Co., IL B: Lexington, Holmes Co., MS
*DIAMOND, James H.	ES: Gulfport, Harrison Co., MS B: New Orleans, Orleans Co., LA
DORLEY, August	ES: Natchez, Adams Co., MS B: Germany
*HANSON, Jack G.	ES: Galveston, Galveston Co., TX B: Escatawpa, Jackson Co., MS
HEARD, John William	ES: MS B: Woodstock, MS
*HENRY, Robert T.	ES: Greenville, Washington Co., MS B: Greenville, Washington Co., MS
*JORDON, Mack A.	ES: Collins, Covington Co., MS B: Collins, Covington Co., MS
LEE, Hubert Louis	ES: Leland, Washington Co., MS B: Arburg, MO
LINDSEY Sr., Jake William	ES: Lucedale, George Co., MS B: Isney, AL

PITTMAN, John Albert	ES: Carrollton, Carroll Co., MS B: Carrollton, Carroll Co., MS
SLATON, James Daniel	ES: Gulfport, Harrison Co., MS B: Laurel, Jones Co., MS
WELBORN, Ira Clinton	ES: Mico, MS B: Mico, MS

U.S. Navy

BROWN, Wilson	ES: MS River, MS B: Natchez, Adams Co., MS
FREEMAN, Martin	ES: Ship's Island, Jackson Co., MS B: Germany
MADISON, James Jonas	ES: MS B: Jersey City, Hudson Co., NJ

U.S. Marine Corps

COMMISKEY Sr., Henry Alfred	ES: Hattiesburg, Forrest Co., MS B: Hattiesburg, Forrest Co., MS
*WHEAT, Roy Mitchell	ES: Jackson, Hinds Co., MS B: Moselle, Jones Co., MS
WILSON Jr., Louis Hugh	ES: MS B: Brandon, Rankin Co., MS

MISSOURI

U.S. Army

*ADAMS, William Edward	ES: Kansas City, Clay Co., MO B: Casper, Natrona Co., WY
ANDERSON, James	ES: St. Louis, St. Louis Co., MO B: East Canada
BARGER, Charles Denver	ES: Stotts City, Lawrence Co., MO B: Mount Vernon, Lawrence Co., MO
BARKLEY, John Lewis	ES: Blairstown, Henry Co., MO B: Blairstown, Henry Co., MO
BIEGER, Charles	ES: St. Louis, St. Louis Co., MO B: Wiesbaden, Germany
*BRANT, Abram B.	ES: St. Louis, St. Louis Co., MO B: New York, NY
BRYAN, William C.	ES: St. Louis, St. Louis Co., MO B: Zanesville, Muskingum Co., OH
BURR, Herbert Hoover	ES: Kansas City, Clay Co., MO B: St. Joseph, Buchanan Co., MO
CABLE, Joseph A.	ES: Madison, Dane Co., WI B: Cape Girardeau, Cape Girardeau Co., MO
DePUY, Charles H.	ES: St. Louis, St. Louis Co., MO B: Sherman, MI
ELLIS, Michael B.	ES: East St. Louis, St. Clair Co., IL B: St. Louis, St. Louis Co., MO
ELWOOD, Edwin L.	ES: San Jose, Santa Clara Co., CA B: St. Louis, St Louis Co., MO
EPPS, Joseph L.	ES: Oklahoma Indian Territory B: Jamestown, Moniteau Co., MO
EVANS, William	ES: St. Louis, St. Louis Co., MO B: Annagh, Ireland
FLYNN, James Edward	ES: St. Louis, St. Louis Co., MO B: Pittsfield, Pike Co., IL
FOLLETT, Joseph Leonard	ES: St. Louis, St. Louis Co., MO B: Newark, Essex Co., NJ
FORAN, Nicholas	ES: St. Louis, St. Louis Co., MO B: County Waterford, Ireland

FORREST, Arthur J.	ES: Hannibal, Marion Co., MO B: St. Louis, St. Louis Co., MO
FORSYTH, Thomas Hall	ES: St. Louis, St. Louis Co., MO B: Hartford, Hartford Co., CT
FRIZZELL, Henry F.	ES: Pilot Knob, Iron Co., MO B: Madison Co., MO
FUNK, Jesse N.	ES: Calhan, El Paso Co., CO B: New Hampton, Harrison Co., MO
GEIGER, George	ES: St. Louis, St. Louis Co., MO B: Cincinnati, Hamilton Co., OH
GREBE, M. R. William	ES: St. Louis, St. Louis Co., MO B: Hildesheim, Germany
GUERIN, Fitz W.	ES: St. Louis, St. Louis Co., MO B: New York, NY
GWYNNE, Nathaniel McClean	ES: Fairmount, MO B: Urbana, Champaign Co., OH
HALL, William Preble	ES: Huntsville, Randolph Co., MO B: Randolph Co., MO
HAMMEL, Henry A.	ES: St. Louis, St. Louis Co., MO B: Germany
*HAMMOND Jr., Lester	ES: Quincy, Adams Co., IL B: Wayland, Clark Co., MO
HARDING, Mosher A.	ES: St. Louis, St. Louis Co., MO B: West Canada
HATLER, M. Waldo	ES: Neosho, Newton Co., MO B: Bolivar, Polk Co., MO
HILL, Frank E.	ES: St. Louis, St. Louis Co., MO B: Mayfield, WI
HUNT, Louis T.	ES: Jefferson Co., MO B: Montgomery Co., IN
*KANELL, Billie Gene	ES: Poplar Bluff, Butler Co., MO B: Poplar Bluff, Butler Co., MO
*KELLEY, Ova Art	ES: Norwood, Wright Co., MO B: Norwood, Wright Co., MO
KIRBY, Dennis Thomas	ES: St. Louis, St. Louis Co., MO B: Niagara Falls, Niagara Co., NY
LEE, Hubert Louis	ES: Leland, Washington Co., MS B: Arburg, MO
*LONG, Charles Richard	ES: Kansas City, Clay Co., MO B: Kansas City, Clay Co., MO
McCAMMON, William Wallace	ES: Montgomery City, Montgomery Co., MO B: Shippensburg, Cumberland Co., PA
McGANN, Michael A.	ES: St. Louis, St. Louis Co., MO B: County Roscommon, Ireland
McMILLIAN, Albert Walter	ES: Jefferson Barracks, MO B: Stillwater, Washington Co., MN
MILLER, Archie	ES: St. Louis, St. Louis Co., MO B: Fort Sheridan, Lake Co., IL
MYERS, Fred	ES: St. Louis, St. Louis Co., MO B: Brunswick, Germany
NEDER, Adam	ES: St. Louis, St. Louis Co., MO B: Bavaria, Germany
*PEDEN, Forrest F.	ES: Wathena, Doniphan Co., KS B: St. Joseph, Buchanan Co., MO
PENTZER, Patrick Henry	ES: Gillespie, Macoupin Co., IL B: Marion Co., MO
PESCH, Joseph M.	ES: St. Louis, St. Louis Co., MO B: Grossleiton, Prussia
*PETERSEN, Danny John	ES: Kansas City, Clay Co., MO B: Horton, Brown Co., KS

PHILLIPS, Samuel D.	ES: St. Louis, St. Louis Co., MO B: Butler Co., OH
PHOENIX, Edwin	ES: St. Louis, St. Louis Co., MO B: St. Louis, St. Louis Co., MO
PORTER, Ambrose	ES: Rockport, Atchison Co., MO B: Allegany Co., MD
RAY, Charles W.	ES: St. Louis, St. Louis Co., MO B: Pensacola, Yancey Co., NC
*RIORDAN, Paul F.	ES: Kansas City, Clay Co., MO B: Charles City, Floyd Co., IA
SCHROETER, Charles	ES: St. Louis, St. Louis Co., MO B: Lindberg, Hanover, Germany
SCOTT, Robert B.	ES: St. Louis, St. Louis Co., MO B: Washington Co., NY
SHEPPARD, Charles	ES: St. Louis, St. Louis Co., MO B: Rocky Hill, Hartford Co., CT
SHINGLE, John Henry	ES: St. Louis, St. Louis Co., MO B: Philadelphia, Philadelphia Co., PA
*SISLER, George Kenton	ES: Dexter, Stoddard Co., MO B: Dexter, Stoddard Co., MO
*SKINKER, Alexander Rives	ES: St. Louis, St. Louis Co., MO B: St. Louis, St. Louis Co., MO
SMITH, Charles E.	ES: St. Louis, St. Louis Co., MO B: Auburn, Cayuga Co., NY
*SPECKER, Joe C.	ES: Odessa, Lafayette Co., MO B: Odessa, Lafayette Co., MO
STEINER, Christian	ES: St. Louis, St. Louis Co., MO B: Wurttemberg, Germany
*TAYLOR, Bernard	ES: Washington, D.C. B: St. Louis, St. Louis Co., MO
TAYLOR, Charles	ES: St. Louis, St. Louis Co., MO B: Baltimore, Baltimore Co., MD
TROGDEN, Howell G.	ES: St. Louis, St. Louis Co., MO B: Cedar Falls, Randolph Co., NC
TURNER, Harold Leo	ES: Seminole, Seminole Co., OK B: Aurora, Lawrence Co., MO
VOKES, Leroy H.	ES: St. Louis, St. Louis Co., MO B: Lake Co., IL
WAGNER, John W.	ES: St. Louis, St. Louis Co., MO B: Clear Spring, Washington Co., MD
WEISS, Enoch R.	ES: St. Louis, St. Louis Co., MO B: Kosciusko Co., IN
WHERRY, William Macky	ES: St. Louis, St. Louis Co., MO B: St. Louis, St. Louis Co., MO
WILLS, Henry	ES: St. Louis, St. Louis Co., MO B: Gracon, VA
*WILSON, Richard G.	ES: Cape Girardeau, Cape Girardeau Co., MO B: Marion, Williamson Co., IL
WORTICK, Joseph	ES: Hannibal, Marion Co., MO B: Fayette Co., PA

U.S. Army Air Corps/U.S. Air Force

FLEMING, James Phillip	ES: Pullman, Whitman Co., WA B: Sedalia, Pettis Co., MO
HOWARD, James Howell	ES: St. Louis, St. Louis Co., MO B: Canton, China
JOHNSON, Leon William	ES: Moline, Elk Co., KS B: Columbia, Boone Co., MO

U.S. Navy

BALCH, John Henry	ES: Kansas City, Clay Co., MO B: Edgerton, Johnson Co., KS

BALLARD, Donald Everett   ES: Kansas City, Clay Co., MO
                          B: Kansas City, Clay Co., MO

CARY, Robert Webster   ES:ton, Cooper Co., MO
                          B: Kansas City, Clay Co., MO

CRANDALL, Orson Leon   ES: CT
                          B: St. Joseph, Buchanan Co., MO

*DAVID, Albert Leroy   ES: MO
                          B: Maryville, Nodaway Co., MO

FUQUA, Samuel Glenn   ES: Laddonia, Audrain Co., MO
                          B: Laddonia, Audrain Co., MO

HOLTZ, August   ES: St. Louis, St. Louis Co., MO
                          B: St. Louis, St. Louis Co., MO

McGUIRE, Fred Henry   ES: Gordonville, Cape Girardeau Co., MO
                          B: Gordonville, Cape Girardeau Co., MO

O'HARE, Edward Henry
"Butch"   ES: St. Louis, St. Louis Co., MO
                          B: St. Louis, St. Louis Co., MO

TOWNSEND, Julius Curtis   ES: Athens, MO
                          B: Athens, MO

U.S. Marine Corps

BUTTON, William Robert   ES: St. Louis, St. Louis Co., MO
                          B: St. Louis, St. Louis Co., MO

*CANNON, George Ham   ES: MI
                          B: Webster Groves, St. Louis Co., MO

*COLE, Daril Samuel   ES: Esther, San Francois Co., MO
                          B: Flat River, San Francois Co., MO

*CREEK, Thomas Elbert   ES: Amarillo, Potter Co., TX
                          B: Joplin, Jasper Co., MO

*DAVENPORT, Jack Arden   ES: Mission, Johnson Co., KS
                          B: Kansas City, Clay Co., MO

GAIENNIE, Louis Rene   ES: St. Louis, St. Louis Co., MO
                          B: St. Louis, St. Louis Co., MO

HANNEKEN, Herman Henry   ES: St. Louis, St. Louis Co., MO
                          B: St. Louis, St. Louis Co., MO

*PHILLIPS, George   ES: Labadie, Franklin Co., MO
                          B: Rich Hill, Vernon Co., MO

SITTER, Carl Leonard   ES: Pueblo, Pueblo Co., CO
                          B: Syracuse, Morgan Co., MO

MONTANA

U.S. Army

*GALT, William Wylie   ES: Stanford, Judith Basin Co., MT
                          B: Geyser, Judith Basin Co., MT

McLENNON, John   ES: Fort Ellis, MT
                          B: Fort Belknap, TX

MORAN, John E.   ES: Cascade Co., MT
                          B: Vernon, Windham Co., VT

*PARRISH, Laverne   ES: Ronan, Lake Co., MT
                          B: Knox City, MT

POWERS, Leo J.   ES: Alder Gulch, Madison Co., MT
                          B: Anselmo, Custer Co., NE

SCHAUER, Henry   ES: Scobey, Daniels Co., MT
                          B: Clinton, Custer Co., OK

SMITH, Cornelius Cole   ES: Helena, Lewis & Clark Co., MT
                          B: Tucson, Pima Co., AZ

U.S. Marine Corps

*RUHL, Donald Jack   ES: MT
                          B: Columbus, Stillwater Co., MT

NEBRASKA

U.S. Army

BERG, George Francis   ES: Fort Omaha, Douglas Co., NE
                          B: Mount Erie, Wayne Co., IL

*BOOKER, Robert D.   ES: Callaway, Custer Co., NE
                          B: Callaway, Custer Co., NE

CO-RUX-TE-CHOD-ISH
(MAD BEAR)   ES: Columbus, Platte Co., NE
                          B: NE

CODY, William Frederick
"Buffalo Bill"   ES: Fort McPherson, NE
                          B: Scott Co., IA

*COWAN, Richard Eller   ES: Wichita, Sedgwick Co., KS
                          B: Lincoln, Lancaster Co., NE

*FOUS, James William   ES: Omaha, Douglas Co., NE
                          B: Omaha, Douglas Co., NE

HAGEMEISTER, Charles Cris ES: Lincoln, Lancaster Co., NE
                          B: Lincoln, Lancaster Co., NE

*HIBBS, Robert John   ES: Des Moines, Polk Co., IA
                          B: Omaha, Douglas Co., NE

HOLDERMAN, Nelson Miles   ES: Santa Ana, Orange Co., CA
                          B: Trumbull, Clay Co., NE

KIRKWOOD, John A.   ES: North Platte Barracks, Lincoln Co., NE
                          B: Allegheny City, Allegheny Co., PA

KOUMA, Ernest Richard   ES: Dwight, Butler Co., NE
                          B: Dwight, Butler Co., NE

*LINDSTROM, Floyd K.   ES: Colorado Springs, El Paso Co., CO
                          B: Holdrege, Phelps Co., NE

LOHNES, Frank W.   ES: Omaha, Douglas Co., NE
                          B: Oneida Co., NY

POWERS, Leo J.   ES: Alder Gulch, Madison Co., MT
                          B: Anselmo, Custer Co., NE

*SHUGHART, Randall David ES: Newville, Cumberland Co., PA
                          B: Lincoln, Lancaster Co., NE

VIFQUAIN, Victor   ES: Salene Co., NE
                          B: Brussels, Belgium

U.S. Navy

EHLE, John Walter   ES: NE
                          B: Kearney, Buffalo Co., NE

GRAVES, Ora   ES: NE
                          B: Las Animas, Bent Co., CO

KERREY, Joseph Robert   ES: Omaha, Douglas Co., NE
                          B: Lincoln, Lancaster Co., NE

*PARLE, John Joseph   ES: NE
                          B: Omaha, Douglas Co., NE

SCHMIDT, Otto Diller   ES: NE
                          B: Blair, Washington Co., NE

VOLZ, Jacob   ES: NE
                          B: Sutton, Clay Co., NE

U.S. Marine Corps

*BAUER, Harold William
"Indian Joe"   ES: NE
                          B: Woodruff, KS

*COKER, Ronald Leroy   ES: Denver, Denver Co., CO
                          B: Alliance, Box Butte Co., NE

*GOMEZ, Edward   ES: Omaha, Douglas Co., NE
                          B: Omaha, Douglas Co., NE

*HANSEN, Dale Merlin   ES: NE
                          B: Wisner, Cuming Co., NE

*KEITH, Miguel   ES: Omaha, Douglas Co., NE
                                     B: San Antonio, Bexar Co., TX

MEREDITH, James   ES: Boston, Suffolk Co., MA
                                     B: Omaha, Douglas Co., NE

NEVADA

U.S. Army

BLAIR, James   ES: Camp Winfield Scott, Humbolt Co., NV
                                     B: Schuyler Co., PA

U.S. Navy

*VAN VOORHIS, Bruce Avery   ES: NV
                                     B: Aberdeen, Grays Harbor Co., WA

NEW HAMPSHIRE

U.S. Army

ALBEE, George Emerson   ES: Owatonna, Steele Co., MN
                                     B: Lisbon, Grafton Co., NH

APPLETON, William H.   ES: Portsmouth, Rockingham Co., NH
                                     B: Chichester, NH

BARKER, Nathaniel C.   ES: Manchester, Hillsborough Co., NH
                                     B: Piermont, Grafton Co., NH

BATCHELDER, Richard Napoleon   ES: Manchester, Hillsborough Co., NH
                                     B: Lake Village (Now Lakeport), Belknap Co., NH

BOUTWELL, John W.   ES: West Lebanon, Grafton Co., NH
                                     B: Hanover, Grafton Co., NH

BRADY, James   ES: Kingston, Rockingham Co., NH
                                     B: Boston, Suffolk Co., MA

CAMP, Carlton N.   ES: Hanover, Grafton Co., NH
                                     B: Hanover, Grafton Co., NH

CARR, Chris   ES: Manchester, Hillsborough Co., NH
                                     B: Manchester, Hillsborough Co., NH

CILLEY, Clinton Albert   ES: Sasioja, MN
                                     B: Rockingham Co., NH

COHN, Abraham   ES: Campton, Grafton Co., NH
                                     B: Guttentag, Silesia, Prussia

COLBY, Carlos W.   ES: Madison Co., IL
                                     B: Merrimack, Hillsborough Co., NH

COPP, Charles Dearborn   ES: Nashua, Hillsborough Co., NH
                                     B: Warren Co., NH

COUGHLIN, John   ES: Manchester, Hillsborough Co., NH
                                     B: VT

CRAIG, Samuel Henry   ES: Chicago, Cook Co., IL
                                     B: New Market, Rockingham Co., NH

CUTCHEON, Byron M.   ES: Ypsilanti, Washtenaw Co., MI
                                     B: Pembroke, Suncook Co., NH

*DILBOY, George   ES: Keene, Cheshire Co., NH
                                     B: Greece

DILLON, Michael A.   ES: Wilton, Hillsborough Co., NH
                                     B: Chelmsford, Middlesex Co., MA

DOW, George P.   ES: Manchester, Hillsborough Co., NH
                                     B: Atkinson, Rockingham Co., NH

ELLIOTT, Russell C.   ES: Boston, Suffolk Co., MA
                                     B: Concord, Merrimack Co., NH

EVANS, Ira Hobart   ES: Barre, Washington Co., VT
                                     B: Piermont, Grafton Co., NH

*FALLS, Benjamin Frank   ES: Lynn, Essex Co., MA
                                     B: Portsmouth, Rockingham Co., NH

GAGE, Richard J.   ES: Ottawa, La Salle Co., IL
                                     B: Grafton Co., NH

GOODALL, Francis Henry   ES: Bath, Grafton Co., NH
                                     B: Bath, Grafton Co., NH

GRIMES, Edward P.   ES: Boston, Suffolk Co., MA
                                     B: Dover, Strafford Co., NH

*HADDOO Jr., John   ES: Columbus, Cherokee Co., KS
                                     B: Hooksett, Merrimack Co., NH

HADLEY, Osgood Towns   ES: Peterborough, Hillsborough Co., NH
                                     B: Nashua, Hillsborough Co., NH

HARRIS, Moses   ES: Boston, Suffolk Co., MA
                                     B: Andover, Merrimack Co., NH

KIMBALL, Joseph   ES: Ironton, Lawrence Co., OH
                                     B: Littleton, Grafton Co., NH

KNIGHT, Charles H.   ES: Keene, Cheshire Co., NH
                                     B: Keene, Cheshire Co., NH

LITTLE, Henry F. W.   ES: Manchester, Hillsborough Co., NH
                                     B: Manchester, Hillsborough Co., NH

LOVERING, George Mason   ES: East Randolph, Norfolk Co., MA
                                     B: Springfield, NH

NEAL, Solon D.   ES: Boston, Suffolk Co., MA
                                     B: Hanover, Grafton Co., NH

NOLAN, John J.   ES: Nashua, Hillsborough Co., NH
                                     B: Thurles, County Tipperary, Ireland

PINGREE, Samuel E.   ES: Hartford, Windsor Co., VT
                                     B: Salisbury, Merrimack Co., NH

ROBIE, George Frank   ES: Manchester, Hillsborough Co., NH
                                     B: Candia, Rockingham Co., NH

ROWE, Henry Walker   ES: Candia, Rockingham Co., NH
                                     B: Candia, Rockingham Co., NH

SIMONS, Charles Jenks   ES: Exeter, Rockingham Co., NH
                                     B: Bombay, India

SWEATT, Joseph Sewell Gerrish   ES: Lowell, Middlesex Co., MA
                                     B: Boscawen, Merrimack Co., NH

TABOR, William L. S.   ES: Concord, Merrimack Co., NH
                                     B: Metheun, Essex Co., MA

TILTON, William   ES: Hanover, Grafton Co., NH
                                     B: St. Albans, Franklin Co., VT

VEAZEY, Wheelock Graves   ES: Springfield, Windsor Co., VT
                                     B: Brentwood, Coos Co., NH

WILCOX, William H.   ES: Lempster, Sullivan Co., NH
                                     B: Lempster, Sullivan Co., NH

WILKINS, Leander A.   ES: Northumberland, NH
                                     B: Lancaster, Coos Co., NH

WOOD, Leonard   ES: Boston, Suffolk Co., MA
                                     B: Winchester, Cheshire Co., NH

WOODBURY, Eri Davidson   ES: St. Johnsbury, Caledonia Co., VT
                                     B: Francistown, Hillsborough Co., NH

U.S. Army Air Corps

*PEASE Jr., Harl   ES: Boston, Suffolk Co., MA
                                     B: Plymouth, Grafton Co., NH

U.S. Navy

ANDERSON, Robert N.   ES: NH
                                     B: Ireland

FOY, Charles H.   ES: Springfield, Hampden Co., MA
                                     B: Portsmouth, Rockingham Co., NH

FRANKLIN, Frederick H.   ES: NH
                            B: Portsmouth, Rockingham Co., NH

GEORGE, Daniel Griffin   ES: NH
                            B: Plaistow, Rockingham Co., NH

HAM, Mark G.   ES: Portsmouth, Rockingham Co., NH
                            B: Portsmouth, Rockingham Co., NH

HAWKINS, Charles   ES: Portsmouth, Rockingham Co., NH
                            B: Scotland

HOLYOKE, William Edward   ES: IL
                            B: Groveton, Coos Co., NH

MELVILLE, Charles   ES: NH
                            B: Dover, Strafford Co., NH

MERTON, James F.   ES: Portsmouth, Rockingham Co., NH
                            B: Cheshire, England

O'KANE, Richard
Hetherington   ES: Durham, Strafford Co., NH
                            B: Dover, Strafford Co., NH

SMITH, William   ES: Concord, Merrimack Co., NH
                            B: Ireland

TODD, Samuel   ES: NH
                            B: Portsmouth, Rockingham Co., NH

U.S. Marine Corps

*BARKER, Jedh Colby   ES: Park Ridge, Bergen Co., NJ
                            B: Franklin, Merrimack Co., NH

WEST, Walter Scott   ES: NH
                            B: Bradford, Merrimack Co., NH

NEW JERSEY

U.S. Army

BART, Frank J.   ES: Newark, Essex Co., NJ
                            B: New York, NY

BEECH, John P.   ES: Trenton, Mercer Co., NJ
                            B: Stratfordshire Co., England

*BENJAMIN Jr., George   ES: Carney's Point, Salem Co., NJ
                            B: Philadelphia, Philadelphia Co., PA

BRADBURY, Sanford   ES: Washington, D.C.
                            B: Newton, Sussex Co., NJ

BRANT Jr., William   ES: Trenton, Mercer Co., NJ
                            B: Elizabeth, Union Co., NJ

BREWSTER, Andre Walker   ES: Philadelphia, Philadelphia Co., PA
                            B: Hoboken, Hudson Co., NJ

*BRITTIN, Nelson Vogel   ES: Audubon, Camden Co., NJ
                            B: Audubon, Camden Co., NJ

BURKE, Francis Xavier   ES: Jersey City, Hudson Co., NJ
                            B: New York, NY

CARMIN, Isaac Harrison   ES: New Lexington, Perry Co., OH
                            B: Monmouth Co., NJ

CARPENTER, Louis Henry   ES: Philadelphia, Philadelphia Co., PA
                            B: Glassboro, Gloucester Co., NJ

CLANCY, James T.   ES: Camden, Camden Co., NJ
                            B: Albany, Albany Co., NY

CONNER, Richard   ES: Burlington, Burlington Co., NJ
                            B: Philadelphia, Philadelphia Co., PA

*COURSEN, Samuel Streit   ES: Madison, Morris Co., NJ
                            B: Madison, Morris Co., NJ

CUMMINGS, Amos Jay   ES: Irvington, Essex Co., NJ
                            B: Conklin, Broome Co., NY

DONELLY, John S.   ES: Jersey City, Hudson Co., NJ
                            B: County Kerry, Ireland

DRAKE, James Madison   ES: Elizabeth, Union Co., NJ
                            B: Washington Valley, Somerset Co., NJ

*DUTKO, John W.   ES: Riverside, Burlington Co., NJ
                            B: Dilltown, Indiana Co., PA

EGGERS, Alan Louis   ES: Summit, Union Co., NJ
                            B: Saranac Lake, Franklin Co., NY

ENGLISH, Edmund   ES: Newark, Essex Co., NJ
                            B: New York, NY

FALLON, Thomas Timothy   ES: Freehold, Monmouth Co., NJ
                            B: County Galway, Ireland

FESQ, Frank E.   ES: Newark, Essex Co., NJ
                            B: Germany

FOLLETT, Joseph Leonard   ES: St. Louis, St. Louis Co., MO
                            B: Newark, Essex Co., NJ

FOLLY, William H.   ES: New York, NY
                            B: Bergen Co., NJ

*GERTSCH, John Gerry   ES: Buffalo, Erie Co., NY
                            B: Jersey City, Hudson Co., NJ

GRANT, Gabriel   ES: Trenton, Mercer Co., NJ
                            B: Newark, Essex Co., NJ

GREGG, Stephen Raymond   ES: Bayonne, Hudson Co., NJ
                            B: New York, NY

HEYL, Charles Pettit heath ES: Camden, Camden Co., NJ
                            B: Philadelphia, Philadelphia Co., PA

HOOPER, William B.   ES: Jersey City, Hudson Co., NJ
                            B: Willimantic, Windham Co., CT

HOPKINS, Charles F.   ES: Trenton, Mercer Co., NJ
                            B: Hope, Warren Co., NJ

*HOSKING Jr., Charles Ernest ES: Fort Dix, Mercer Co., NJ
                            B: Ramsey, Bergen Co., NJ

HOWARD, James   ES: Brooklyn, Kings Co., NY
                            B: Newton, Sussex Co., NJ

JACKSON, James   ES: NJ
                            B: NJ

JACOBS, Jack Howard   ES: Trenton, Mercer Co., NJ
                            B: Brooklyn, Kings Co., NY

*JOHNSON, Elden Harvey   ES: East Weymouth, Norfolk Co., MA
                            B: Bivale, Cumberland Co., NJ

JOHNSTON Sr., William
James   ES: Colchester, New London Co., CT
                            B: Trenton, Mercer Co., NJ

LATHAM, John Cridland   ES: Rutherford, Bergen Co., NJ
                            B: Windemere, Cumbria Co., England

LOCKE, Lewis   ES: Jersey City, Hudson Co., NJ
                            B: Clintonville, Essex Co., NY

MAGEE, William   ES: Newark, Essex Co., NJ
                            B: Newark, Essex Co., NJ

*MAY, Martin O.   ES: Phillipsburg, Warren Co., NJ
                            B: Phillipsburg, Warren Co., NJ

*McGRAW, Francis Xavier   ES: Camden, Camden Co., NJ
                            B: Philadelphia, Philadelphia Co., PA

MEAGHER, John William   ES: Jersey City, Hudson Co., NJ
                            B: Jersey City, Hudson Co., NJ

MILES, Louis Wardlaw   ES: Princeton, Mercer Co., NJ
                            B: Baltimore, Baltimore Co., MD

*MINUE, Nicholas   ES: Carteret, Middlesex Co., NJ
                            B: Sedden, Poland

*O'SHEA, Thomas E.   ES: Summit, Union Co., NJ
                            B: New York, NY

ORESKO, Nicholas   ES: Bayonne, Hudson Co., NJ
                            B: Bayonne, Hudson Co., NJ

OSS, Albert | ES: Newark, Essex Co., NJ
B: Belgium

PARKER, James | ES: Newark, Essex Co., NJ
B: Newark, Essex Co., NJ

PITMAN, George J. | ES: Philadelphia, Philadelphia Co., PA
B: Recklestown, NJ

PORTER, William | ES: Trenton, Mercer Co., NJ
B: New York, NY

QUINN, Alexander M. | ES: Philadelphia, Philadelphia Co., PA
B: Passaic, Passaic Co., NJ

*SADOWSKI, Joseph John | ES: Perth Amboy, Middlesex Co., NJ
B: Perth Amboy, Middlesex Co., NJ

SAGELHURST, John Christopher | ES: Jersey City, Hudson Co., NJ
B: Buffalo, Erie Co., NY

*SAWELSON, William | ES: Harrison, Hudson Co., NJ
B: Newark, Essex Co., NJ

SEWELL, William Joyce | ES: Camden, Camden Co., NJ
B: Castlebar, County Mayo, Ireland

SHEERIN, John | ES: Baltimore, Baltimore Co., MD
B: Camden Co., NJ

SMITH, Theodore F. | ES: Harrisburg, Dauphin Co., PA
B: Rahway, Union Co., NJ

SOUTHARD, David | ES: Florence, Burlington Co., NJ
B: Ocean Co., NJ

STEWART, George W. | ES: Salem, Salem Co., NJ
B: Salem, Salem Co., NJ

STREILE, Christian | ES: Jersey City, Hudson Co., NJ
B: Germany

SULLIVAN, Thomas | ES: Newark, Essex Co., NJ
B: County Meath, Ireland

TAYLOR, Anthony | ES: Philadelphia, Philadelphia Co., PA
B: Burlington, Burlington Co., NJ

TAYLOR, Forrester L. | ES: Beverly, Burlington Co., NJ
B: Philadelphia, Philadelphia Co., PA

THOMPKINS, William H. | ES: Paterson, Passaic Co., NJ
B: Paterson, Passaic Co., NJ

*THORNE, Horace Marvin | ES: Keyport, Monmouth Co., NJ
B: Keansburg, Monmouth Co., NJ

TILTON, Henry Remsen | ES: Jersey City, Hudson Co., NJ
B: Barnegat, Ocean Co., NJ

TITUS, Charles | ES: New Brunswick, Middlesex Co., NJ
B: Millstone, NJ

TOFFEY, John James | ES: Hudson, Hudson Co., NJ
B: Quaker Hill, Dutchess Co., NY

TOMPKINS, Aaron B. | ES: Jersey City, Hudson Co., NJ
B: Orange, Essex Co., NJ

TRAYNOR, Andrew | ES: Rome, Oneida Co., NY
B: Newark, Essex Co., NJ

VAN IERSEL, Ludovicus M. M. | ES: Glen Rock, Bergen Co., NJ
B: Dussen, Holland

VEALE, Moses | ES: Philadelphia, Philadelphia Co., PA
B: Bridgeton, Cumberland Co., NJ

WANTON, George Henry | ES: Paterson, Passaic Co., NJ
B: Paterson, Passaic Co., NJ

*WATTERS, Charles Joseph | ES: Fort Dix, Mercer Co., NJ
B: Jersey City, Hudson Co., NJ

WILSON, Charles E. | ES: Hatborough, Montgomery Co., NJ
B: Bucks Co., PA

WILSON, John | ES: Jersey City, Hudson Co., NJ
B: England

WOOD, Richard H. | ES: Woodburn, Macoupin Co., IL
B: Canton, NJ

ZABITOSKY, Fred William | ES: Trenton, Mercer Co., NJ
B: Trenton, Mercer Co., NJ

U.S. Army Air Corps

*CASTLE, Frederick Walker | ES: Mountain Lakes, Morris Co., NJ
B: Manila, Philippine Island

*McGUIRE Jr., Thomas Buchanan | ES: Sebring, Highlands Co., FL
B: Ridgewood, Bergen Co., NJ

U.S. Navy

BEHNE, Frederick | ES: NJ
B: Lodi, Bergen Co., NJ

BLUME, Robert | ES: NJ
B: Pittsburgh, Allegheny Co., PA

BREEMAN, George | ES: NJ
B: Passaic, Passaic Co., NJ

*CHOLISTER, George Robert | ES: NJ
B: Camden, Camden Co., NJ

COONEY, Thomas C. | ES: NJ
B: Westport, Nova Scotia, Canada

CRILLEY, Frank William | ES: PA
B: Trenton, Mercer Co., NJ

DAVIS, John | ES: NJ
B: Cedarville, Cumberland Co., NJ

EILERS, Henry A. | ES: NJ
B: Newark, Essex Co., NJ

HAMBERGER, William Francis | ES: NJ
B: Newark, Essex Co., NJ

KANE, Thomas | ES: NJ
B: Jersey City, Hudson Co., NJ

MADISON, James Jonas | ES: MS
B: Jersey City, Hudson Co., NJ

MAGER, George Frederick | ES: NJ
B: Phillipsburg, Warren Co., NJ

PARKER, Alexander | ES: NJ
B: Kensington, NJ

PETERSEN, Carl Emil | ES: NJ
B: Hamburg, Germany

SHERIDAN, James | ES: New York, NY
B: Newark, Essex Co., NJ

SIEGEL, John Otto | ES: NJ
B: Milwaukee, Milwaukee Co., WI

STRAHAN, Robert | ES: NJ
B: NJ

SWEENEY, Robert Augustus | ES: NJ
B: Montserrat, West Indies

TEYTAND, August P. | ES: NJ
B: Santa Cruz, West Indies

THOMPSON, William | ES: Boston, Suffolk Co., MA
B: Cape May Co., NJ

*TOMICH, Peter | ES: NJ
B: Prolog, Austria

VAN ETTEN, Hudson | ES: NJ
B: Port Jervis, Orange Co., NY

WEEKS, Charles H. | ES: NJ
B: NJ

WHITFIELD, Daniel | ES: NJ
B: Newark, Essex Co., NJ

WILLIAMS II, John | ES: NY
| B: Elizabethtown, NJ

YOUNG, Edward B. | ES: NJ
| B: Bergen, Hudson Co., NJ

U.S. Marine Corps

*BARKER, Jedh Colby | ES: Park Ridge, Bergen Co., NJ
| B: Franklin, Merrimack Co., NH

BASILONE, John
"Manila Jonn" | ES: NJ
| B: Buffalo, Erie Co., NY

CAFFERATA Jr., Hector
Albert | ES: Dover, Morris Co., NJ
| B: New York, NY

*CONNOR, Peter Spencer | ES: South Orange, Essex Co., NJ
| B: Orange, Essex Co., NJ

FIELD, Oscar Wadsworth | ES: NY
| B: Jersey City, Hudson Co., NJ

FRYER, Eli Thompson | ES: NJ
| B: Hightstown, Mercer Co., NJ

HARVEY, Harry | ES: NJ
| B: New York, NY

PFEIFER, Louis Fred | ES: NJ
| B: Philadelphia, Philadelphia Co., PA

PRESTON, Herbert Irving | ES: NJ
| B: Berkeley, Union Co., NJ

ROUH, Carlton Robert | ES: NJ
| B: Lindenwold, Camden Co., NJ

SHIVERS, John | ES: NJ
| B: Canada

SIGLER, Franklin Earl | ES: Little Falls, Passaic Co., NJ
| B: Glen Ridge, Essex Co., NJ

TOMLIN, Andrew J. | ES: NJ
| B: Goshen, Cape May Co., NJ

NEW MEXICO

U.S. Army

*FERNANDEZ, Daniel | ES: Albuquerque, Bernalillo Co., NM
| B: Albuquerque, Bernalillo Co., NM

JENNINGS, Delbert Owen | ES: San Francisco, San Francisco Co., CA
| B: Silver City, Grant Co., NM

*MARTINEZ, Joe P. | ES: Ault, Weld Co., CO
| B: Taos, Taos Co., NM

MILLER, Franklin Douglas | ES: Albuquerque, Bernalillo Co., NM
| B: Elizabeth City, Pasquotank Co., NC

MIYAMURA, Hiroshi | ES: Gallup, McKinley Co., NM
| B: Gallup, McKinley Co., NM

*MOON Jr., Harold Herman | ES: Gardena, Los Angeles Co., CA
| B: Albuquerque, Bernalillo Co., NM

OLIVER, Francis | ES: Fort Filmore, NM
| B: Baltimore, Baltimore Co., MD

ROCCO, Louis Richard | ES: Los Angeles, Los Angeles Co., CA
| B: Albuquerque, Bernalillo Co., NM

RUIZ, Alejandro Renteria | ES: Carlsbad, Eddy Co., NM
| B: Loving, Eddy Co., NM

SCOTT, Robert Sheldon | ES: Santa Fe, Santa Fe Co., NM
| B: Washington, D.C.

STANLEY, Eben | ES: Santa Fe, Santa Fe Co., NM
| B: Decatur Co., IA

*VALDEZ, Jose F. | ES: Pleasant Grove, Utah Co., UT
| B: Governador, NM

U.S. Army Air Corps

*WALKER, Kenneth
Newton | ES: Denver, Denver Co., CO
| B: Cerrillos, Santa Fe Co., NM

U.S. Marine Corps

*BONNYMAN Jr., Alexander
"Sandy" | ES: NM
| B: Atlanta, Fulton Co., GA

*WORLEY, Kenneth Lee | ES: Fresno, Fresno Co., CA
| B: Farmington, San Juan Co., NM

NEW YORK

U.S. Army

ALLEN, James | ES: Potsdam, St. Lawrence Co., NY
| B: Ireland

ANDERSON, Bruce | ES: Albany, Albany Co., NY
| B: Mexico City, Mexico

*ARCHER, Lester | ES: Plattsburgh, Clinton Co., NY
| B: Fort Ann, Washington Co., NY

*ASHLEY Jr., Eugene | ES: New York, NY
| B: Wilmington, New Hanover Co., NC

AUSTIN, William Grafton | ES: New York, NY
| B: Galveston, Galveston Co., TX

BAKER, John | ES: Brooklyn, Kings Co., NY
| B: Hessen, Germany

*BAKER Jr., Thomas Alexander | ES: Troy, Rensselaer Co., NY
| B: Troy, Rensselaer Co., NY

BANCROFT, Neil | ES: Chicago, Cook Co., IL
| B: Oswego, Oswego Co., NY

BARNUM, Henry Alanson | ES: Syracuse, Onondaga Co., NY
| B: Jamesville, Onondaga Co., NY

BARRELL, Charles L. | ES: Leighton, Allegan Co., MI
| B: Conquest, NY

BARRETT, Carlton William | ES: Albany, Albany Co., NY
| B: Fulton, Oswego Co., NY

BARRETT, Richard | ES: Buffalo, Erie Co., NY
| B: County Mayo, Ireland

BARRY, Augustus | ES: New York, NY
| B: Ireland

BART, Frank J. | ES: Newark, Essex Co., NJ
| B: New York, NY

BATES, Delavan | ES: Mohawk, Herkimer Co., NY
| B: Schoharie Co., NY

BEDDOWS, Richard | ES: Flushing, Queens Co., NY
| B: Liverpool, Merseyside Co., England

BEEBE, William Sully | ES: Philadelphia, Philadelphia Co., PA
| B: Ithaca, Tompkins Co., NY

*BEGLEY, Terrence | ES: Albany, Albany Co., NY
| B: Ireland

BEIKIRCH, Gary Burnell | ES: Buffalo, Erie Co., NY
| B: Rochester, Monroe Co., NY

BELL, Bernard Pious | ES: New York, NY
| B: Grantsville, Calhoun Co., WV

BELL, James | ES: Troy, Rensselaer Co., NY
| B: County Antrim, Ireland

BENJAMIN, John Francis | ES: Newburgh, Orange Co., NY
| B: Orange Co., NY

BENJAMIN, Samuel Nicholl | ES: New York, NY
| B: New York, NY

BICKFORD, Henry H. — ES: Middleport, Niagara Co., NY; B: Ypsilanti, Washtenaw Co., MI

BIRDSALL, Horatio L. — ES: Keokuk, Lee Co., IA; B: Monroe Co., NY

BLUNT, John W. — ES: Four Corners, Chatham, Columbia Co., NY; B: Columbia Co., NY

BOEHM, Peter Martin — ES: Brooklyn, Kings Co., NY; B: Albany, Albany Co., NY

BOWEN, Chester Bennett — ES: Nunda, Livingston Co., NY; B: Nunda, Livingston Co., NY

BOWEN, Emmer — ES: Hampshire, Kane Co., IL; B: Erie Co., NY

*BOYCE Jr., George W. G. — ES: Cornwall, Orange Co., NY; B: New York, NY

BRADLEY, Thomas Wilson — ES: Walden, Orange Co., NY; B: Sheffield, Yorkshire Co., England

BRANAGAN, Edward — ES: New York, NY; B: County Louth, Ireland

*BRANT, Abram B. — ES: St. Louis, St. Louis Co., MO; B: New York, NY

BREWER, William John — ES: Newburgh, Orange Co., NY; B: Putnam Co., NY

BRINGLE, Andrew — ES: Buffalo, Erie Co., NY; B: Buffalo, Erie Co., NY

BRONNER, August Frederick — ES: New York, NY; B: Germany

BROSNAN, John — ES: New York, NY; B: Ireland

BROWN, Henri Le Fevre — ES: Ellicott, Erie Co., NY; B: Jamestown, Chautauqua Co., NY

BROWN, James — ES: New York, NY; B: Wexford, Ireland

BROWN Jr., Edward — ES: New York, NY; B: Ireland

*BROWN Jr., Morris — ES: Geneva, Ontario Co., NY; B: Hammondsport, Steuben Co., NY

BROWNELL, Francis Edwin — ES: Troy, Rensselaer Co., NY; B: Troy, Rensselaer Co., NY

BRUSH, George Washington — ES: Huntington, Suffolk Co., NY; B: West Hills, Suffolk Co., NY

BRUTON, Christopher C. — ES: Riga, Monroe Co., NY; B: Ireland

BUCHA, Paul William — ES: USMA West Point, Orange Co., NY; B: Washington, D.C.

*BUCHANAN, George A. — ES: Canaoaigua, Ontario Co., NY; B: Victor, Ontario Co., NY

*BUCKLEY, Denis — ES: Avon, Livingston Co., NY; B: Canada

BURK, E. Michael — ES: Troy, Rensselaer Co., NY; B: Ireland

BURK, Thomas — ES: Harrisburgh, Lewis Co., NY; B: Lewis Co., NY

BURKE, Francis Xavier — ES: Jersey City, Hudson Co., NJ; B: New York, NY

BURKE, Richard — ES: New York, NY; B: Tipperary, Ireland

BURKE, Thomas — ES: New York, NY; B: Ireland

BURRITT, William Wallace — ES: Chicago, Cook Co., IL; B: Campbell, Steuben Co., NY

BUTLER, Edmond Thomas — ES: Brooklyn, Kings Co., NY; B: Clonmel, County Tipperary, Ireland

BUTTERFIELD, Daniel Adams — ES: Washington, D.C.; B: Utica, Oneida Co., NY

*BUTTS, John Edward — ES: Buffalo, Erie Co., NY; B: Medina, Orleans Co., NY

BYRNE, Denis — ES: New York, NY; B: Wexford, Ireland

CADWELL, Luman Lewis — ES: Troy, Rensselaer Co., NY; B: Nanticoke Springs, Broome Co., NY

CALKIN, Ivers S. — ES: Willsboro, Essex Co., NY; B: Elizabethtown, Essex Co., NY

CALL, Donald Marshall — ES: France; B: New York, NY

CAMPBELL, James A. — ES: New York, NY; B: Brooklyn, Kings Co., NY

*CAREY, Hugh — ES: New York, NY; B: Ireland

CAREY, James Lemuel — ES: Syracuse, Onondaga Co., NY; B: Jamesville, Onondaga Co., NY

CARMAN, Warren — ES: Victor, Ontario Co., NY; B: England

CARR, Eugene Asa — ES: Hamburg, Erie Co., NY; B: Boston Corner, Erie Co., NY

CARTER, John Joice — ES: Nunda, Livingston Co., NY; B: Troy, Rensselaer Co., NY

CARTER, William Harding — ES: New York, NY; B: Nashville, Davidson Co., TN

CARUANA, Orlando Emanuel — ES: New York, NY; B: Ca Valletta, Malta

CASEY, James Seaman — ES: New York, NY; B: Philadelphia, Philadelphia Co., PA

CATLIN, Isaac Swartwood — ES: Owego, Tioga Co., NY; B: Near Owego, Tioga Co., NY

CAYER, Ovila — ES: Malone, Franklin Co., NY; B: St. Remi, Canada

CHANDLER, Stephen Edwin — ES: Grandby, Oswego Co., NY; B: Convis, MI

CHAPIN, Alaric B. — ES: Pamelia, Jefferson Co., NY; B: Ogdensburg, St. Lawrence Co., NY

*CHARLTON, Cornelius H. — ES: Bronx Co., NY; B: East Gulf, Raleigh Co., WV

CLANCY, James T. — ES: Camden, Camden Co., NJ; B: Albany, Albany Co., NY

CLANCY, John E. — ES: Vancouver Barracks, Clark Co., WA; B: New York, NY

CLAPP, Albert Adams — ES: Painesville, Lake Co., OH; B: Pompey, Onondaga Co., NY

CLARK, Francis J. — ES: Salem, NY; B: Whitehall, Washington Co., NY

CLARK, Harrison — ES: Chatham, Columbia Co., NY; B: Chatham, Columbia Co., NY

CLARKE, Dayton P. — ES: Hermon, St. Lawrence Co., NY; B: DeKalb, St. Lawrence Co., NY

CLEVELAND, Charles Franklin — ES: Elmira, Chemung Co., NY; B: Hartford, Washington Co., NY

COEY, James — ES: Oswego, Oswego Co., NY; B: New York, NY

COLE, Gabriel	ES: New Salem, Washtenaw Co., MI B: Chenango Co., NY
COLLINS Sr., Thomas D.	ES: Liberty, Sullivan Co., NY B: Neversink Flats, Sullivan Co., NY
*COLYER, Wilbur E.	ES: South Ozone, Queens Co., NY B: Brooklyn, Kings Co., NY
COMPSON, Hartwell B.	ES: Seneca Falls, Seneca Co., NY B: Seneca Falls, Seneca Co., NY
CONBOY, Martin	ES: New York, NY B: Roscommon, Ballagh Co., Ireland
CONNORS, James	ES: Canajoharie, Montgomery Co., NY B: Kildare, Ireland
CORLISS, Stephen Potter	ES: Albany, Albany Co., NY B: Albany, Albany Co., NY
COSGRIFF, Richard H.	ES: Wapello, Louisa Co., IA B: Dunkirk Co., NY
COYNE, John Nicholas	ES: New York, NY B: New York, NY
CROSIER, William Henry Harrison	ES: Skaneateles, Onondaga Co., NY B: Skaneateles, Onondaga Co., NY
CROSS, James Edwin	ES: Batavia, Genesee Co., NY B: Darien, Genesee Co., NY
CROWLEY, Michael	ES: Rochester, Monroe Co., NY B: Rochester, Monroe Co., NY
CULLEN, Thomas	ES: New York, NY B: Ireland
CUMMINGS, Amos Jay	ES: Irvington, Essex Co., NJ B: Conklin, Broome Co., NY
CUNNINGHAM, Charles	ES: New York, NY B: Hudson, Columbia Co., NY
CURRAN, Richard J.	ES: Seneca Falls, Seneca Co., NY B: Ennis, County Clare, Ireland
CURREY, Francis Sherman "Frank"	ES: Hurleyville, Sullivan Co., NY B: Loch Sheldrake, Sullivan Co., NY
CURTIS, Newton Martin	ES: De Peyster, St. Lawrence Co., NY B: De Peyster, St. Lawrence Co., NY
DALESSONDRO, Peter Joseph	ES: Watervliet, Albany Co., NY B: Watervliet, Albany Co., NY
DALY, Michael Joseph	ES: Southport, Fairfield Co., CT B: New York, NY
DAVIDSON, Andrew	ES: Middlefield, Otsego Co., NY B: Morebattle, Roxburgshire, Scotland
DAVIS, Thomas	ES: New York, NY B: Haverford, West Wales
DAWSON, Michael	ES: New York, NY B: Boston, Suffolk Co., MA
DAY, Charles	ES: Richmond, Philadelphia Co., PA B: West Laurens, Otsego Co., NY
*De ARMOND, William	ES: New York, NY B: Butler Co., OH
*DeGLOPPER, Charles N.	ES: Grand Island, Erie Co., NY B: Grand Island, Erie Co., NY
DENNY, John	ES: Elmira, Chemung Co., NY B: Big Flats, Chemung Co., NY
Di CESNOLA, Louis Palma	ES: New York, NY B: Rivarola, Piedmont, Italy
DICKEY, William Donaldson	ES: Newburgh, Orange Co., NY B: Newburgh, Orange Co., NY

*DIETZ, Robert H.	ES: Kingston, Ulster Co., NY B: Kingston, Ulster Co., NY
DILGER, Hubert	ES: New York, NY B: Germany
DIX, Drew Dennis	ES: Denver, Denver Co., CO B: West Point, Orange Co., NY
*DOANE, Stephen Holden	ES: Albany, Albany Co., NY B: Beverly, Essex Co., MA
DOCKUM, Warren C.	ES: Plattsburgh, Clinton Co., NY B: Clintonville, Clinton Co., NY
DODDS, Edward Edwin	ES: Rochester, Monroe Co., NY B: Canada
DOLLOFF, Charles W.	ES: St. Johnsbury, Caledonia Co., VT B: Parishville, St. Lawrence Co., NY
DONALDSON, Michael Aloyisius	ES: Haverstraw, Rockland Co., NY B: Haverstraw, Rockland Co., NY
DONAVAN, Cornelius	ES: New York, NY B: County Cork, Ireland
DONLON, Roger Hugh Charles	ES: Saugerties, Ulster Co., NY B: Saugerties, Ulster Co., NY
DONOGHUE, Timothy	ES: New York, NY B: Ireland
DONOVAN, William Joseph "Wild Bill"	ES: Buffalo, Erie Co., NY B: Buffalo, Erie Co., NY
DOODY, Patrick H.	ES: New York, NY B: Ireland
DORE, George H.	ES: West Bloomfield, Ontario Co., NY B: England
*DUNN, Parker F.	ES: Albany, Albany Co., NY B: Albany, Albany Co., NY
DURHAM, John S.	ES: Malone, Fond Du Lac Co., WI B: New York, NY
EDWARDS, David	ES: Sangerfield, Oneida Co., NY B: Wales
EDWARDS, William D.	ES: Brooklyn, Kings Co., NY B: Brooklyn, Kings Co., NY
EGGERS, Alan Louis	ES: Summit, Union Co., NJ B: Saranac Lake, Franklin Co., NY
ELDRIDGE, George H.	ES: Detroit, Wayne Co., MI B: Sackets Harbor, Jefferson Co., NY
EMBLER, Andrew Henry	ES: NY B: New York, NY
EMMET, Robert Temple	ES: New York, NY B: New York, NY
ENGLISH, Edmund	ES: Newark, Essex Co., NJ B: New York, NY
EVANS, James Robert	ES: New York, NY B: New York, NY
EVERSON, Adelbert	ES: Salina, Onondaga Co., NY B: Cicero, Onondaga Co., NY
FARNSWORTH, Herbert E.	ES: Gowanda, Cattaraugus Co., NY B: Perrysburg, Cattaraugus Co., NY
FEGAN, James	ES: New York, NY B: Athlone, County Westmeath, Ireland
FERRARI, George	ES: Cleveland, Cuyahoga Co., OH B: New York, NY
FICHTER, Hermann Emil	ES: New York, NY B: Baden, Germany

FISHER, Almond Edward   ES: Brooklyn, Kings Co., NY
                         B: Hume, Allegany Co., NY

FOLLY, William H.   ES: New York, NY
                         B: Bergen Co., NJ

FORD, George W.   ES: New York, NY
                         B: Ireland

FOURNIA, Frank Ottis   ES: Plattsburgh, Clinton Co., NY
                         B: Rome, Oneida Co., NY

*FRATELLENICO, Frank
Rocco   ES: Albany, Albany Co., NY
                         B: Sharon, Litchfield Co., CT

FREEMAN, Archibald   ES: Newburgh, Orange Co., NY
                         B: Newburgh, Orange Co., NY

FREEMAN, William Henry   ES: Troy, Rensselaer Co., NY
                         B: Troy, Rensselaer Co., NY

FREEMEYER, Christopher   ES: New York, NY
                         B: Bavaria, Germany

FRENCH, Samuel S.   ES: Gifford, Tuscola Co., MI
                         B: Erie Co., NY

FUGER, Frederick W.   ES: New York, NY
                         B: Wurttemberg, Germany

GAFFNEY, Frank J.   ES: Niagara Falls, Niagara Co., NY
                         B: Buffalo, Erie Co., NY

GARDINER, Peter W.   ES: New York, NY
                         B: Carlisle, Schoharie Co., NY

GARDNER, Robert J.   ES: Egremont, Berkshire Co., MA
                         B: Livingston, Columbia Co., NY

*GASSON, Richard   ES: New York, NY
                         B: Ireland

GEORGIAN, John   ES: Buffalo, Erie Co., NY
                         B: Germany

GERBER, Frederick William ES: Brooklyn, Kings Co., NY
                         B: Dresden, Germany

GERE, Thomas Parke   ES: Fort Snelling, St. Paul Co., MN
                         B: Wellsburg, Chemung Co., NY

*GERTSCH, John Gerry   ES: Buffalo, Erie Co., NY
                         B: Jersey City, Hudson Co., NJ

GIFFORD, Benjamin   ES: German Flats, Herkimer Co., NY
                         B: German Flats, Herkimer Co., NY

GILMORE, John Curtis   ES: Potsdam, St. Lawrence Co., NY
                         B: Canada

GINLEY, Patrick   ES: New York, NY
                         B: Ireland

GLOVER, Thaddeus Brown   ES: New York, NY
                         B: New York, NY

GLYNN, Michael   ES: New York, NY
                         B: Galway, Ireland

GOETTEL, Philip   ES: Syracuse, Onondaga Co., NY
                         B: Salina, Onondaga Co., NY

GOHEEN, Charles Arthur   ES: Rochester, Monroe Co., NY
                         B: Groveland, Livingston Co., NY

GOODRICH, Edwin   ES: Westfield, Chautauqua Co., NY
                         B: New York, NY

GOURAUD, George Edward   ES: New York, NY
                         B: New York, NY

*GRABIARZ, William J.   ES: Buffalo, Erie Co., NY
                         B: Buffalo, Erie Co., NY

GREENE, Oliver Duff   ES: Scott, Cortland Co., NY
                         B: Scott, Cortland Co., NY

GREGG, Stephen Raymond   ES: Bayonne, Hudson Co., NJ
                         B: New York, NY

GREIG, Theodore W.   ES: Staten Island, Richmond Co., NY
                         B: NY

GRIBBEN, James H.   ES: New York, NY
                         B: Ireland

GRINDLAY, James G.   ES: Utica, Oneida Co., NY
                         B: Odinburgh, Scotland

GRUEB, George M.   ES: Brooklyn, Kings Co., NY
                         B: Wurttemberg, Germany

*GUENETTE, Peter Mathew ES: Albany, Albany Co., NY
                         B: Troy, Rensselaer Co., NY

GUERIN, Fitz W.   ES: St. Louis, St. Louis Co., MO
                         B: New York, NY

HACK, Lester Goodel   ES: Salisbury, Addison Co., VT
                         B: Cadwell, Warren Co., NY

HADLEY, Cornelius Minor ES: Adrian, Lenawee Co., MI
                         B: Sandy Creek, Oswego Co., NY

HAGERTY, Asel   ES: New York, NY
                         B: Canada

HAIGHT, John H.   ES: Westfield, Chautauqua Co., NY
                         B: Westfield, Chautauqua Co., NY

HALL, Francis Bloodgood ES: Plattsburgh, Clinton Co., NY
                         B: New York, NY

HALL, Henry Seymour   ES: Elmira, Chemung Co., NY
                         B: Barkersville, Saratoga Co., NY

HALLOCK, Nathan Mullock ES: Middletown, Orange Co., NY
                         B: Mount Hope, Orange Co., NY

HAMILTON, Mathew H.   ES: New York, NY
                         B: Hobart, Australia

HANFORD, Edward R.   ES: Cortland, Cortland Co., NY
                         B: Allegany Co., NY

HAPEMAN, Douglas   ES: Ottawa, La Salle Co., IL
                         B: Ephrata, Fulton Co., NY

HARING, Abram Pye   ES: New York, NY
                         B: New York, NY

HARRIS, Charles D.   ES: Rochester, Monroe Co., NY
                         B: Albion, Orleans Co., NY

HART, William E.   ES: Rushville, Yates Co., NY
                         B: Rushville, Yates Co., NY

HARVEY, Harry   ES: Rochester, Monroe Co., NY
                         B: England

HATCH, John Porter   ES: Oswego, Oswego Co., NY
                         B: Oswego, Oswego Co., NY

HAWTHORNE, Harris Smith ES: Otsego Co., NY
                         B: Salem, Washington Co., NY

HEERMANCE, William Laing ES: Kinderhook, Columbia Co., NY
                         B: Kinderhook, Columbia Co., NY

HEISE, Clamor   ES: New York, NY
                         B: Germany

HIBSON, Joseph C.   ES: New York, NY
                         B: London, England

HICKEY, Dennis William   ES: Plattsburgh, Clinton Co., NY
                         B: Troy, Rensselaer Co., NY

HILL, Edward   ES: Detroit, Wayne Co., MI
                         B: Liberty, Sullivan Co., NY

HILL, James Samuel   ES: Lyons, Wayne Co., NY
                         B: Lyons, Wayne Co., NY

HILLIKER, Benjamin F.   ES: Waupaca Township, Waupaca Co., WI
                         B: Golden, Erie Co., NY

HILLS, William Giles   ES: East Randolph, Cattaraugus Co., NY
                         B: Conewango, Cattaraugus Co., NY

HOGAN, Henry   ES: New York, NY
                         B: County Clare, Ireland

HOGARTY, William P.   ES: Elmira, Chemung Co., NY
                           B: New York, NY

HOLMES, Lovilo N.   ES: Mankato, Blue Earth Co., MN
                           B: Farmersville, Cattaraugus Co., NY

HOLTON, Charles Maynard   ES: Battle Creek, Calhoun Co., MI
                           B: Potter, Yates Co., NY

HOOKER, George White   ES: Boston, Suffolk Co., MA
                           B: Salem, Washington Co., NY

HORAN, Thomas   ES: Dunkirk, Chautauqua Co., NY

HOUGHTON, Charles H.   ES: Ogdensburg, St. Lawrence Co., NY
                           B: Macomb, St. Lawrence Co., NY

HOULTON, William M.   ES: Athens, Athens Co., OH
                           B: Clymer, Chautauqua Co., NY

HOWARD, James   ES: Brooklyn, Kings Co., NY
                           B: Newton, Sussex Co., NJ

HUMPHREY, Charles
Frederic   ES: Buffalo, Erie Co., NY
                           B: Cortland, Cortland Co., NY

HYDE, Henry J.   ES: New York, NY
                           B: Bangor, Penobscot Co., ME

IRSCH, Francis   ES: New York, NY
                           B: Saarburg, Germany

IRWIN, Bernard John
Dowling   ES: New York, NY
                           B: Ireland

JACOBS, Jack Howard   ES: Trenton, Mercer Co., NJ
                           B: Brooklyn, Kings Co., NY

JACOBSON, Eugene Philip   ES: New York, NY
                           B: Prussia

JAMES, John   ES: Albany, Albany Co., NY
                           B: Manchester, Greater Manchester Co.,
                              England

JAMIESON, Walter   ES: New York, NY
                           B: Boulogne, France

JARVIS, Frederick   ES: Hudson, Lenawee Co., MI
                           B: Essex Co., NY

JETTER, Bernhard   ES: New York, NY
                           B: Wurttemberg, Germany

JOEL, Lawrence   ES: New York, NY
                           B: Winston-Salem, Forsyth Co., NC

JOHNDRO, Franklin   ES: Queensbury, Warren Co., NY
                           B: Highgate Falls, Franklin Co., VT

JOHNSON, Follett   ES: Ogdensburg, St. Lawrence Co., NY
                           B: Brasher, St. Lawrence Co., NY

JOHNSON, Wallace W.   ES: Waverly, Tioga Co., NY
                           B: Newfield, Thompkins Co., NY

JOHNSTON, Edward   ES: Chicago, Cook Co., IL
                           B: Pen Yan, Yates Co., NY

JOHNSTON, William "Willie" ES: St. Johnsbury, Caledonia Co., VT
                           B: Morristown, Morristown Co., NY

*JONES, William   ES: New York, NY
                           B: Wicklow, County Wicklow, Ireland

JOSSELYN, Simeon T.   ES: Amboy, Lee Co., IL
                           B: Buffalo, Erie Co., NY

JUDGE, Francis W.   ES: New York, NY
                           B: England

KAISER, John   ES: New York, NY
                           B: Nerzogenaurach, Germany

KANE, John   ES: Marilla, Erie Co., NY
                           B: Ireland

KAPPESSER, Peter   ES: Syracuse, Onondaga Co., NY
                           B: Germany

*KAROPCZYC, Stephen
Edward   ES: Bethpage, Nassau Co., NY
                           B: New York, NY

KAUFMAN, Benjamin   ES: Brooklyn, Kings Co., NY
                           B: Buffalo, Erie Co., NY

KAUSS, August   ES: New York, NY
                           B: Germany

*KEDENBURG, John James   ES: Brooklyn, Kings Co., NY
                           B: Brooklyn, Kings Co., NY

KEELE, Joseph   ES: Staten Island, Richmond Co., NY
                           B: Ireland

KEENAN, Bartholomew T.   ES: Cincinnati, Hamilton Co., OH
                           B: Brooklyn, Kings Co., NY

KEENE, Joseph   ES: Utica, Oneida Co., NY
                           B: England

KELLER, William G.   ES: Buffalo, Erie Co., NY
                           B: Buffalo, Erie Co., NY

KELLEY, Charles   ES: New York, NY
                           B: County Clare, Ireland

KELLEY, Leverett Mansfield ES: Rutland, La Salle Co., IL
                           B: Schenectady, Schenectady Co., NY

KELLY, Daniel   ES: Groveland, Livingston Co., NY
                           B: Groveland, Livingston Co., NY

KELLY, Thomas   ES: New York, NY
                           B: Ireland

KELLY, Thomas   ES: New York, NY
                           B: County Mayo, Ireland

KELLY, Thomas   ES: NY
                           B: Ireland

KELLY, Thomas Joseph   ES: Brooklyn, Kings Co., NY
                           B: Brooklyn, Kings Co., NY

KENNEDY, John   ES: New York, NY
                           B: Cavan, County Cavan, Ireland

KENYON, John Snyders   ES: Schenevus, Otsego Co., NY
                           B: Grosvenors Corners, Schoharie Co., NY

KENYON, Samuel P.   ES: Augusta, NY
                           B: Ira, Cayuga Co., NY

KERRIGAN, Thomas   ES: New York, NY
                           B: County Tipperary, Ireland

KIGGINS, John   ES: Syracuse, Onondaga Co., NY
                           B: Syracuse, Onondaga Co., NY

KING, Horatio Collins   ES: Brooklyn, Kings Co., NY
                           B: Portland, Cumberland Co., ME

KING Jr., Rufus   ES: NY
                           B: NY

KIRBY, Dennis Thomas   ES: St. Louis, St. Louis Co., MO
                           B: Niagara Falls, Niagara Co., NY

KLINE, Harry   ES: Syracuse, Onondaga Co., NY
                           B: Germany

KNOWLES, Abiather J.   ES: Willets Point, Queens Co., NY
                           B: La Grange, Penobscot Co., ME

KNOX, Edward M.   ES: New York, NY
                           B: New York, NY

KOELPIN, William   ES: Brooklyn, Kings Co., NY
                           B: Stetten, Prussia

KRETSINGER, George   ES: Chicago, Cook Co., IL
                           B: Fairfield, Herkimer Co., NY

KUDER, Andrew   ES: Rochester, Monroe Co., NY
                           B: Groveland, Livingston Co., NY

LADD, George   ES: Camillus, Onondaga Co., NY
                           B: Camillus, Onondaga Co., NY

*LAING, William	ES: Brooklyn, Kings Co., NY B: Hempstead, Nassau Co., NY	MARSH, Albert	ES: Randolph, Cattaraugus Co., NY B: Randolph, Cattaraugus Co., NY
LANE, Morgan D.	ES: Allegan, Allegan Co., MI B: Monroe, Orange Co., NY	MARTIN, Patrick	ES: New York, NY B: County Offaly, Ireland
LANG, George Charles	ES: Brooklyn, Kings Co., NY B: Flushing, Queens Co., NY	McBRIDE, Bernard	ES: Washington, D.C. B: Brooklyn, Kings Co., NY
LANGBEIN, Johann Christoph Julius	ES: New York, NY B: Germany	McBRYAR, William	ES: New York, NY B: Elizabethtown, Bladen Co., NC
*LANGHORN, Garfield McConnell	ES: Brooklyn, Kings Co., NY B: Cumberland, Cumberland Co., VA	McCANN, Bernard	ES: New York, NY B: County Roscommon, Ireland
LARRABEE, James W.	ES: Mendota, La Salle Co., IL B: Rensselaer Co., NY	McCARTHY, Michael	ES: New York, NY B: St. John's, Newfoundland, Canada
LAWTON, Louis Bowem	ES: Auburn, Cayuga Co., NY B: Independence, Buchanan Co., IA	McCONNELL, James	ES: Detroit, Wayne Co., MI B: Syracuse, Onondaga Co., NY
LEONARD, Patrick Thomas	ES: New York, NY B: County Clare, Ireland	McDONALD, Robert	ES: Newport, Campbell Co., KY B: Erie Co., NY
LESLIE, Frank	ES: New York, NY B: London, England	McENROE, Patrick H.	ES: Schodack, Rensselaer Co., NY B: Ireland
LEVY, Benjamin Bennett	ES: Newport News, Newport News Co., VA B: New York, NY	McFALL, Daniel Robert	ES: Ypsilanti, Washtenaw Co., MI B: Niagara Co., NY
LIBAIRE, Adolph	ES: New York, NY B: Baccarat, France	McGINN, Edward	ES: Cincinnati, Hamilton Co., OH B: New York, NY
LITEKY, Charles James (Angelo)	ES: Fort Hamilton, Kings Co., NY B: Washington, D.C.	McGONNIGLE, Andrew Jackson	ES: Cumberland, Allegany Co., MD B: New York, NY
LITTLE, Thomas	ES: New York, NY B: Barbados, West Indians	McGOUGH, Owen	ES: Cornwall, Orange Co., NY B: Monaghan, Ireland
LOCKE, Lewis	ES: Jersey City, Hudson Co., NJ B: Clintonville, Essex Co., NY	McHUGH, John	ES: New York, NY B: Syracuse, Onondaga Co., NY
LOHNES, Frank W.	ES: Omaha, Douglas Co., NE B: Oneida Co., NY	McKAY, Charles W.	ES: Allegany, Cattaraugus Co., NY B: Mansfield, Cattaraugus Co., NY
LONG, Oscar Fitzalan	ES: Utica, Oneida Co., NY B: Utica, Oneida Co., NY	McKEE, George	ES: Rochester, Monroe Co., NY B: County Tyrone, Ireland
LONSWAY, Joseph	ES: Sackets Harbor, Jefferson Co., NY B: Clayton, Jefferson Co., NY	McMURTRY, George G.	ES: New York, NY B: Pittsburgh, Allegheny Co., PA
LORISH, Andrew J.	ES: Attica, Wyoming Co., NY B: Dansville, Livingston Co., NY	McNALLY, James	ES: Albany, Albany Co., NY B: County Monaghan, Ireland
LOVE, George Maltby	ES: Elmira, Chemung Co., NY B: Buffalo, Erie Co., NY	McPHELAN, Robert	ES: New York, NY B: County Laois, Ireland
*LOZADA, Carlos James	ES: New York, NY B: Caguas, Caguas Co., Puerto Rico	McVEAGH, Charles H.	ES: San Francisco, San Francisco Co., CA B: New York, NY
*LUCAS, Andre Cavaro	ES: West Point, Orange Co., NY B: Washington, D.C.	*McVEANE, John P.	ES: Buffalo, Erie Co., NY B: Toronto, Canada
LUDGATE, William	ES: New York, NY B: London, England	MEACH, George E.	ES: New York, NY B: NY
LUDWIG, Carl	ES: Flushing, Queens Co., NY B: France	MEAGHER, Thomas	ES: Brooklyn, Kings Co., NY B: Scotland
LUTES, Franklin W.	ES: Geddes, NY B: Dundee, Yates Co., NY	MENTER, John William	ES: Detroit, Wayne Co., MI B: Palmer, NY
LYMAN, Joel H.	ES: Randolph, Cattaraugus Co., NY B: East Randolph, Cattaraugus Co., NY	*MERRELL, Joseph Frederick	ES: Staten Island, Richmond Co., NY B: Staten Island, Richmond Co., NY
MADDEN, Michael	ES: New York, NY B: County Limerick, Ireland	MERRILL, George	ES: Moreau, NY B: Queensberry, Warren Co., NY
MADISON, James	ES: Fairport, Monroe Co., NY B: Niagara, Niagara Co., NY	MERRILL, John Mitchell	ES: New York, NY B: New York, NY
MANDY, Harry J.	ES: New York, NY B: England	MERRITT, John G.	ES: Fort Snelling, St. Paul Co., MN B: New York, NY
MANGAM, Richard Christopher	ES: Auburn, Cayuga Co., NY B: Ireland	MEYER, Henry Coddington	ES: Dobbs Ferry, Westchester Co., NY B: Hamburg, Erie Co., NY
		MILLER, Frank	ES: Jamaica, Queens Co., NY B: NY

MILLER, George   ES: Boston, Suffolk Co., MA
B: Brooklyn, Kings Co., NY

MILLER, John   ES: Rochester, Monroe Co., NY
B: Kurhessen, Germany

MILLS, Albert Leopold   ES: New York, NY
B: New York City (Washington Heights), NY

MILLS, Frank W.   ES: Middletown, Orange Co., NY
B: Middletown, Orange Co., NY

MOFFITT, John Henry   ES: Plattsburgh, Clinton Co., NY
B: Chazy, Clinton Co., NY

MONTROSE, Charles H.   ES: New York, NY
B: St. Paul, Ramsey Co., MN

MOQUIN, George   ES: Brooklyn, Kings Co., NY
B: New York, NY

MORSE, Benjamin   ES: Grand Rapids, Kent Co., MI
B: Livingston, Columbia Co., NY

MORSE, Charles E.   ES: NY
B: France

*MULLER, Joseph E.   ES: New York, NY
B: Holyoke, Hampden Co., MA

MUNSELL, Harvey May   ES: Philadelphia, Philadelphia Co., PA
B: Painted Post, Steuben Co., NY

MURPHY, Charles Joseph   ES: New York, NY
B: Stockport, Greater Manchester Co.,
England

MURPHY, Edward   ES: New York, NY
B: County Cork, Ireland

MURPHY, Michael C.   ES: New York, NY
B: Limerick, County Limerick, Ireland

MURPHY, Thomas   ES: Brooklyn, Kings Co., NY
B: New York, NY

MURPHY, Thomas J.   ES: New York, NY
B: Ireland

*MURRAY, Robert Charles   ES: New York, NY
B: Bronx Co., NY

MURRAY, Thomas   ES: New York, NY
B: County Monaghan, Ireland

NEAHR, Zachariah C.   ES: Canajoharie, Montgomery Co., NY
B: Palatine, Montgomery Co., NY

NEWMAN, William Henry   ES: Port Jervis, Orange Co., NY
B: Highland Mills, Orange Co., NY

NIHILL, John   ES: Brooklyn, Kings Co., NY
B: Nenagh, County Tipperary, Ireland

NIVEN, Robert   ES: Rochester, Monroe Co., NY
B: Harlem, NY

NORTON, Llewellyn Powell   ES: Scott, Cortland Co., NY
B: Scott, Cortland Co., NY

NUTTING, Lee   ES: New York, NY
B: New York, NY

O'BEIRNE, James Rowan   ES: New York, NY
B: Roscommon, County Ballagh, Ireland

O'BRIEN, Peter   ES: New York, NY
B: Dublin, County Dublin, Ireland

O'BRIEN, William Joseph   ES: Troy, Rensselaer Co., NY
B: Troy, Rensselaer Co., NY

O'CALLAGHAN, John   ES: San Francisco, San Francisco Co., CA
B: New York, NY

O'NEILL, Richard William   ES: New York, NY
B: New York, NY

O'NEILL, Stephen   ES: New York, NY
B: St. Johns, New Brunswick, Canada

O'NEILL, William   ES: New York, NY
B: Tariffville, Hartford Co., CT

*O'SHEA, Thomas E.   ES: Summit, Union Co., NJ
B: New York, NY

O'SULLIVAN, John Francis   ES: New York, NY
B: County Kerry, Ireland

OLIVER, Paul Ambrose   ES: New York, NY
B: At sea in the English Channel aboard
American flagship Louisiana.

ORR, Charles Alvin   ES: Bennington, Wyoming Co., NY
B: Holland, Erie Co., NY

PACKARD, Loron F.   ES: Cuba, Allegany Co., NY
B: Cattaraugus Co., NY

PALMER, George Henry   ES: Monmouth, Warren Co., IL
B: NY

PARKS, Henry Jeremiah   ES: Orangeville, Wyoming Co., NY
B: Orangeville, Wyoming Co., NY

PARNELL, William Russell   ES: Brooklyn, Kings Co., NY
B: Dublin, Ireland

PATTERSON, John Henry   ES: NY
B: NY

PAY, Byron E.   ES: Mankato, Blue Earth Co., MN
B: LeRoy Township, Jefferson Co., NY

PAYNE, Irvin C.   ES: New York, NY
B: Wayne Co., PA

PECK, Archie A.   ES: Hornell, Steuben Co., NY
B: Tyrone, Schuyler Co., NY

PENGALLY, Edward   ES: Albany, Albany Co., NY
B: Devonshire, England

*PETERSON, George   ES: Brooklyn, Kings Co., NY
B: Brooklyn, Kings Co., NY

PFISTERER, Herman   ES: New York, NY
B: Brooklyn, Kings Co., NY

PHILLIPS, Josiah   ES: Ulysses, Potter Co., PA
B: Wyoming Co., NY

PLANT, Henry E.   ES: Cockery, MI
B: Oswego Co., NY

PLATTEN, Frederick   ES: New York, NY
B: Torbeck, Ireland

PLIMLEY, William   ES: Catskill, Greene Co., NY
B: Catskill, Greene Co., NY

POND, James Burton   ES: Janesville, Rock Co., WI
B: Allegany, Cattaraugus Co., NY

PORTER, William   ES: Trenton, Mercer Co., NJ
B: New York, NY

POST, Philip Sidney   ES: Galesburg, Knox Co., IL
B: Florida, Orange Co., NY

POTTER, Norman F.   ES: Pompey, Onondaga Co., NY
B: Pompey, Onondaga Co., NY

POWERS, Thomas   ES: Detroit, Wayne Co., MI
B: New York, NY

PRESTON, Noble Delance   ES: Fulton, Oswego Co., NY
B: Madison, Madison Co., NY

PUTNAM, Edgar Pierpont   ES: Stockton, Chautauqua Co., NY
B: Stockton, Chautauqua Co., NY

QUINLAN, James   ES: New York, NY
B: Clomwell, County Tipperary, Ireland

RAFFERTY, Peter F.   ES: New York, NY
B: County Tyrone, Ireland

RAGNAR, Theodore   ES: New York, NY
B: Linkoping, Sweden

RAND, Charles Franklin ES: Batavia, Genesee Co., NY
B: Batavia, Genesee Co., NY

RANNEY, George E. ES: Grand Rapids, Kent Co., MI
B: Batavia, Genesee Co., NY

RANNEY, Myron H. ES: Dansville, Livingston Co., NY
B: Franklinville, Cattaraugus Co., NY

*RAY, Bernard James ES: Baldwin, Nassau Co., NY
B: Brooklyn, Kings Co., NY

RAYMOND, William H. ES: Penfield, Monroe Co., NY
B: Penfield, Monroe Co., NY

READ, Morton A. ES: Brockport, Monroe Co., NY
B: Brockport, Monroe Co., NY

REYNOLDS, George ES: New York, NY
B: Ireland

RHODES, Julius Dexter ES: Springville, Erie Co., NY
B: Monroe Co., MI

RIDDELL, Rudolph R. ES: Hamilton, Madison Co., NY
B: Hamilton, Madison Co., NY

ROBERTSON, Robert
Stoddart ES: Argyle, Washington Co., NY
B: Argyle, Washington Co., NY

ROBINSON, John Cleveland ES: Binghamton, Broome Co., NY
B: Binghamton, Broome Co., NY

ROCHE, David ES: New York, NY
B: County Kerry, Ireland

ROCKEFELLER, Charles
Mortimer ES: New York, NY
B: Gallatin Columbia Co., NY

ROMEYN, Henry ES: MI
B: Galen, Wayne Co., NY

ROONEY, Edward ES: Poughkeepsie, Dutchess Co., NY
B: Poughkeepsie, Dutchess Co., NY

*ROOSEVELT Jr., Theodore ES: Oyster Bay, Nassau Co., NY
B: Oyster Bay, Nassau Co., NY

ROSSBACH, Valentine ES: Flushing, Queens Co., NY
B: Germany

ROTH, Peter Paul ES: Brooklyn, Kings Co., NY
B: Wurttemberg, Germany

ROUNDS, Lewis A. ES: Norwalk, Huron Co., OH
B: Cattaraugus Co., NY

RUSSELL, Charles L. ES: Malone, Franklin Co., NY
B: Malone, Franklin Co., NY

RUSSELL, James ES: New York, NY
B: New York, NY

RUTHERFORD, John T. ES: Canton, St. Lawrence Co., NY
B: Russell, St. Lawrence Co., NY

RYAN, Denis ES: New York, NY
B: Cork, Ireland

SAGE, William Hampden ES: Binghamton, Broome Co., NY
B: Centerville, Allegany Co., NY

SAGELHURST, John
Christopher ES: Jersey City, Hudson Co., NJ
B: Buffalo, Erie Co., NY

SALE, Albert ES: Dubuque, Dubuque Co., IA
B: Broome Co., NY

*SANTIAGO-COLON,
Hector ES: New York, NY
B: Salinas, Salinas Co., Puerto Rico

SARTWELL, Henry ES: Fort Ann, Washington Co., NY
B: Ticonderoga, Essex Co., NY

SCHAEFER, Joseph E. ES: Long Island, NY
B: New York, NY

SCHILLER, John ES: New York, NY
B: Hessen, Germany

SCHLACHTER, Philipp ES: New York, NY
B: Germany

SCHMAL, George William ES: Buffalo, Erie Co., NY
B: Germany

SCHNITZER, John ES: New York, NY
B: Kempten, Bavaria, Germany

SCHOFIELD, John
McAllister ES: Freeport, Stephenson Co., IL
B: Gerry, Chautauga Co., NY

SCHOU, Julius Alexis ES: Brooklyn, Kings Co., NY
B: Copenhagen, Denmark

SCHUBERT, Martin ES: Elmira, Chemung Co., NY
B: Germany

SCHWAN, Theodore ES: NY
B: Hanover, Germany

SCOFIELD, David H. ES: Stamford, Fairfield Co., CT
B: Mamaroneck, Westchester Co., NY

SCOTT, Robert B. ES: St. Louis, St. Louis Co., MO
B: Washington Co., NY

SEARS, Cyrus ES: Bucyrus, Crawford Co., OH
B: Meredith Township, Delaware Co., NY

SHALER, Alexander ES: New York, NY
B: Haddam, Middlesex Co., CT

SHEA, Charles William ES: New York, NY
B: Bronx Co., NY

SHEPARD, Irwin ES: Chelsea, Washtenaw Co., MI
B: Skaneateles, Onondaga Co., NY

SHIPLEY, Robert F. ES: Penn Yan, Yates Co., NY
B: Wayne, Schuyler Co., NY

*SHOUP, Curtis F. ES: Buffalo, Erie Co., NY
B: Napanoch, Ulster Co., NY

SHUBERT, Frank ES: Canojaharie, Montgomery Co., NY
B: Hesse, Germany

SICKLES, Daniel Edgar ES: New York, NY
B: New York, NY

SICKLES, William H. ES: Fall River, Columbia Co., WI
B: Danube, Herkimer Co., NY

SIDMAN, George Dallas ES: Owosso, Shiawassee Co., MI
B: Rochester, Monroe Co., NY

SIMMONS, John ES: Liberty, Sullivan Co., NY
B: Bethel, Sullivan Co., NY

SKELLIE, Ebenezer ES: Mina, Chautauqua Co., NY
B: Mina, Chautauqua Co., NY

SMALLEY, Reuben ES: Holton, Ripley Co., IN
B: Reading, Schuyler Co., NY

SMITH, Alonzo ES: Jonesville, Hillsdale Co., MI
B: Niagara Co., NY

SMITH, Charles E. ES: St. Louis, St. Louis Co., MO
B: Auburn, Cayuga Co., NY

SMITH, David Lafayette ES: Bath, Steuben Co., NY
B: Cameron, Steuben Co., NY

*SMITH, George W. ES: New York, NY
B: Greenfield, Saratoga Co., NY

SMITH, Richard ES: Haverstraw, Rockland Co., NY
B: Haverstraw, Rockland Co., NY

SMITH, Thomas J. ES: New York, NY
B: Liverpool, Merseyside Co., England

SMITH, Wilson ES: Madison, Madison Co., NY
B: Madison, Madison Co., NY

SOVA, Joseph E.	ES: Rochester, Monroe Co., NY B: Chili, Monroe, NY	TRACY, William Gardner	ES: Albany, Albany Co., NY B: Syracuse, Onondaga Co., NY
SPILLANE, Timothy	ES: Waterford, Saratoga Co., NY B: County Kerry, Ireland	TRAYNOR, Andrew	ES: Rome, Oneida Co., NY B: Newark, Essex Co., NJ
SPRAGUE, Benona	ES: Cheney Grove, IL B: Satina Onondaga Co., NY	TREMAIN, Henry Edwin	ES: New York, NY B: New York, NY
*SPRAGUE, John Wilson	ES: Sandusky, Erie Co., OH B: White Creek, Washington Co., NY	TRIBE, John	ES: Oswego, Oswego Co., NY B: Tioga Co., NY
STAHEL, Julius H.	ES: New York, NY B: Szegedin, Hungary	*TURNER, William Bradford	ES: Garden City, Nassau Co., NY B: Dorchester, Suffolk Co., MA
STANLEY, Edward	ES: San Francisco, San Francisco Co., CA B: New York, NY	UHRL, George	ES: New York, NY B: Baden, Germany
STARKINS, John H.	ES: Flushing, Queens Co., NY B: Great Neck, Nassau Co., NY	URBAN, Matt Louis	ES: Fort Bragg, Cumberland Co., NC B: Buffalo, Erie Co., NY
STEPHENS, William G.	ES: Chicago, Cook Co., IL B: New York, NY	URELL, Michael Emmet	ES: New York, NY B: County Cork, Ireland
STEWART, George Evans	ES: New York, NY B: New South Wales (Australia)	VALENTE, Michael	ES: Ogdensburg, St. Lawrence Co., NY B: Cassino, Italy
*STONE Jr., Lester Raymond	ES: Syracuse, Onondaga Co., NY B: Binghamton, Broome Co., NY	VAN SCHAICK, Louis Joseph	ES: Cobleskill, Schoharie Co., NY B: Cobleskill, Schoharie Co., NY
*STRYKER, Robert Francis	ES: Throop, Cayuga Co., NY B: Auburn, Cayuga Co., NY	VAN WINKLE, Edward (Edwin)	ES: Phelps, Ontario Co., NY B: Phelps, Ontario Co., NY
SWAP, Jacob E.	ES: Springs, Somerset Co., PA B: Coeymans, Albany Co., NY	VARNUM, Charles Albert	ES: Pensacola, Escambia Co., FL B: Troy, Rensselaer Co., NY
SWIFT, Harlan J.	ES: Buffalo, Erie Co., NY B: New Hudson, Columbia Co., NY	VON MEDEM, Rudolph	ES: New York, NY B: Germany (Prussia)
THACKRAH, Benjamin	ES: Johnsonville, Rensselaer Co., NY B: Scotland	VON VEGESACK, Ernest	ES: New York, NY B: Gotland, Sweden
THOMPKINS, George W.	ES: Port Jervis, Orange Co., NY B: Orange Co., NY	WAALER, Reidar	ES: New York, NY B: Christiana, now Oslo, Norway
THOMPSON, Allen	ES: Sandy Creek, Oswego Co., NY B: New York, NY	WAINWRIGHT IV, Jonathan Mayhew	ES: Skaneateles, Onondaga Co., NY B: Fort Walla Walla, Walla Walla Co., WA
THOMPSON, George Washington	ES: Syracuse, Onondaga Co., NY B: Victory, Cayuga Co., NY	WAINWRIGHT, John	ES: West Chester, Chester Co., PA B: Syracuse, Onondaga Co., NY
THOMPSON, James Granville	ES: Sandy Creek, Oswego Co., NY B: Sandy Creek, Oswego Co., NY	WALKER, Mary Edwards	ES: Louisville, Jefferson Co., KY B: Oswego Co., NY
THOMPSON, James Harry	ES: New York, NY B: England	WALL, Jerry C.	ES: Milo, NY B: Geneva Ontario Co., NY
*THOMPSON, William Henry	ES: Bronx Co., NY B: New York, NY	WALLACE, William	ES: New York, NY B: County Donegal, Ireland
*THOMPSON, William P.	ES: Lafayette, Tippecanoe Co., IN B: Brooklyn, Kings Co., NY	WALLING, William Henry	ES: Folly Island, Charleston Co., SC B: Hartford, Washington Co., NY
THOMSON, Clifford	ES: New York, NY B: Fulton, Oswego Co., NY	WAMBSGAN, Martin	ES: Clyde, Wayne Co., NY B: Nusdorof, Bavaria, Germany
THORN, Walter	ES: Camp Nelson, KY B: Brooklyn, Kings Co., NY	*WARREN Jr., John Earl	ES: New York, NY B: Brooklyn, Kings Co., NY
TINKHAM, Eugene M.	ES: Waterloo, Seneca Co., NY B: Sprague, CT	WATSON, James C.	ES: Philadelphia, Philadelphia Co., PA B: Cochecton, Sullivan Co., NY
TOFFEY, John James	ES: Hudson, Hudson Co., NJ B: Quaker Hill, Dutchess Co., NY	WEBB, Alexander Stewart	ES: New York, NY B: New York, NY
TOLAN, Frank	ES: Boston, Suffolk Co., MA B: Malone, Franklin Co., NY	WEBB, James W.	ES: New York, NY B: Brooklyn, Kings Co., NY
TOMPKINS, Charles Henry	ES: Brooklyn, Kings Co., NY B: Fort Monroe, Hampton Co., VA	WEBBER, Alason P.	ES: Chillicothe, Ross Co., OH B: Greene Co., NY
TOOHEY, Thomas	ES: Milwaukee, Milwaukee Co., WI B: New York, NY	WEEKS, John Henry	ES: Hartwick Seminary, Oswego Co., NY B: Hampton, Windham Co., CT
TOY, Frederick Ernest	ES: Chicago, Cook Co., IL B: Buffalo, Erie Co., NY	WEIR, Henry Cary	ES: Bolivar, WV B: West Point, Orange Co., NY
TRACY, Benjamin Franklin	ES: Owego, Tioga Co., NY B: Owego, Tioga Co., NY	WELCH, Charles H.	ES: Fort Snelling, St. Paul Co., MN B: New York, NY

WELCH, Michael	ES: New York, NY B: Poughkeepsie, Dutchess Co., NY		BATES, Richard	ES: NY B: Wales
WELCH, Stephen	ES: Allegany, Cattaraugus Co., NY B: Groton, Tompkins Co., NY		BELL, George	ES: New York, NY B: Sunderland, England
*WELLS, Henry S.	ES: Phelps, Ontario Co., NY		*BENFOLD, Edward Clyde "Ted"	ES: Philadelphia, Philadelphia Co., PA B: Staten Island, Richmond Co., NY
WELLS, Thomas McCoy	ES: DeKalb, St. Lawrence Co., NY B: Ather, Ireland		BENNETT, Floyd	ES: NY B: Warrensburg, Warren Co., NY
WEST, Frank	ES: Mohawk, Herkimer Co., NY B: Mohawk, Herkimer Co., NY		BENNETT, James Harvey	ES: NY B: Haverstraw, Rockland Co., NY
WESTERHOLD, William	ES: New York, NY B: Binde, Prussia		BETHAM, Asa	ES: New York, NY B: New York, NY
*WICKERSHAM, J. Hunter	ES: Denver, Denver Co., CO B: New York, NY		BJORKMAN, Ernest H.	ES: NY B: Malmo, Sweden
*WILL, Walter J.	ES: West Winfield, Herkimer Co., NY B: Pittsburgh, Allegheny Co., PA		BLAGHEEN, William	ES: New York, NY B: Devonshire Co., England
*WILLETT, Louis Edward	ES: Brooklyn, Kings Co., NY B: Brooklyn, Kings Co., NY		BOURNE, Thomas	ES: New York, NY B: England
WILLIAMS, Leroy	ES: Batavia, Genesee Co., NY B: Oswego, Oswego Co., NY		BRADLEY, Amos	ES: NY B: Dansville, Livingston Co., NY
WINDOLPH, Charles	ES: Brooklyn, Kings Co., NY B: Bergen, Germany		BRADLEY, Charles	ES: New York, NY B: Ireland
WINEGAR, William W.	ES: Mount Morris, Livingston Co., NY B: Springport, NY		BRADLEY, George	ES: Rhode Island B: New York, NY
WISNER, Lewis S.	ES: Wallkill, Ulster Co., NY B: Wallkill, Ulster Co., NY		BRADLEY Jr., Willis Winter	ES: North Dakota B: Ransomville, Niagara Co., NY
WOODRUFF, Carle Augustus	ES: Washington, D.C. B: Buffalo, Erie Co., NY		BRADY, George F.	ES: NY B: Ireland
WRIGHT, Raymond Richard "Buzzer"	ES: Moriah, Essex Co., NY B: Moriah, Essex Co., NY		BREEN, John	ES: New York, NY B: New York, NY
YOUNG, James Marvin	ES: Chautauqua Co., NY B: Ellicott, Erie Co., NY		BRINN, Andrew	ES: New York, NY B: Scotland
			BROWN, James	ES: NY B: Rochester, Monroe Co., NY

U.S. Army Air Corps

*CHELI, Ralph	ES: Brooklyn, Kings Co., NY B: San Francisco, San Francisco Co., CA		BROWN, John	ES: New York, NY B: Glasgow, Scotland
HAMILTON, Pierpont Morgan	ES: New York, NY B: Tuxedo Park, Orange Co., NY		BROWN, Robert	ES: NY B: Norway
*VANCE Jr., Leon Robert	ES: Garden City, Nassau Co., NY B: Enid, Garfield Co., OK		BROWNELL, William P.	ES: NY B: NY
VOSLER, Forrest Lee "Woody"	ES: Rochester, Monroe Co., NY B: Lyndonville, Orleans Co., NY		BURKE, Thomas	ES: NY B: Ireland
			BURNS, John M.	ES: NY B: Hudson, Columbia Co., NY

U.S. Navy

AHERN, William	ES: NY B: Ireland		BURTON, Albert	ES: NY B: England
ALLEN, Edward G.	ES: NY B: Amsterdam, Holland		BUTTS, George	ES: Cleveland, Cuyahoga Co., OH B: Rome, Oneida Co., NY
ANDERSON, William	ES: NY B: Sweden		BYRNES, James	ES: NY B: Ireland
AUER, John F.	ES: NY B: NY		CAHEY, Thomas	ES: NY B: Belfast, County Antrim, Ireland
AVERY, James	ES: NY B: Scotland		CANN, Tedford Harris	ES: NY B: Bridgeport, Fairfield Co., CT
BAKER, Charles	ES: New York, NY B: Georgetown, D.C.		*CAPODANNO, Vincent Robert	ES: Staten Island, Richmond Co., NY B: Staten Island, Richmond Co., NY
BARTER, Gurdon H.	ES: New York, NY B: Williamsburg, Kings Co., NY		CAREY, James	ES: NY B: Ireland
BASS, David L.	ES: New York, NY B: Ireland		CASSIDY, Michael	ES: New York, NY B: Ireland

CAVANAUGH, Thomas   ES: NY
B: Ireland

CHANDRON, August   ES: NY
B: France

CHAPUT, Louis G.   ES: New York, NY
B: Canada

CLANCY, Joseph   B: New York, NY

CLAUSEN, Claus Kristian
Randolph   ES: NY
B: Denmark

COLBERT, Patrick   ES: NY
B: Ireland

CONLAN, Dennis   ES: New York, NY
B: New York, NY

COOPER, John   ES: New York, NY
B: Dublin, County Dublin, Ireland

CORAHORGI, Demetri   ES: NY
B: Trieste, Austria

CORCORAN, Thomas E.   ES: New York, NY
B: Dublin, County Dublin, Ireland

COREY, William   ES: NY
B: New York, NY

COSTELLO, John   ES: NY
B: Rouses Point, Clinton Co., NY

COTTON, Peter   ES: NY
B: New York, NY

CREELMAN, William James   ES: NY
B: Brooklyn, Kings Co., NY

CREGAN, George   ES: NY
B: New York, NY

DAVIS, John   ES: New York, NY
B: Germany

DEAKIN, Charles   ES: Philadelphia, Philadelphia Co., PA
B: New York, NY

DECKER, Percy A.   ES: NY
B: New York, NY

DENHAM, Austin   ES: NY
B: England

DENSMORE, William   ES: NY
B: NY

DITZENBACK, John   ES: IN
B: New York, NY

DONNELLY, John C.   ES: New York, NY
B: England

DOUGHERTY, Patrick   ES: New York, NY
B: Ireland

DUNPHY, Richard D.   ES: New York, NY
B: Ireland

EGLIT, John   ES: NY
B: Finland

ENGLISH, Thomas   ES: New York, NY
B: New York, NY

ERICKSON, John P.   ES: Brooklyn, Kings Co., NY
B: London, England

ERICKSON, Nicholas   ES: NY
B: Finland

EVERETTS, John   ES: NY
B: Thorold, Canada

FARRELL, Edward   ES: New York, NY
B: Saratoga, Saratoga Co., NY

FLANNAGAN, John   ES: NY
B: Ireland

FLOOD, Thomas S.   ES: NY
B: Ireland

FORBECK, Andrew Peter   ES: NY
B: NY

FOWLER, Christopher   ES: NY
B: NY

GALBRAITH, Robert   ES: NY
B: Brooklyn, Kings Co., NY

GARDNER, William   ES: New York, NY
B: Ireland

GARRISON, James R.   ES: New York, NY
B: Poughkeepsie, Dutchess Co., NY

GIBBONS, Michael   ES: NY
B: Ireland

GOWAN, William Henry   ES: NY
B: Rye, Westchester Co., NY

GRAHAM, Robert   ES: NY
B: England

GREENE, John   ES: NY

HALLING, Luovi   ES: NY
B: Stockholm, Sweden

HALSTEAD, William W.   ES: NY
B: Alplaus, Schenectady Co., NY

HAMILTON, Hugh   ES: New York, NY
B: New York, NY

HARLEY, Bernard   ES: New York, NY
B: Brooklyn, Kings Co., NY

HARRIS, John   ES: New York, NY
B: Norway

HARTIGAN, Charles Conway   ES: Norwich, Chenango Co., NY
B: Middletown, Orange Co., NY

HILL, George   ES: New York, NY
B: England

HILL, William Lowell   ES: NY
B: Brooklyn, Kings Co., NY

HINNEGAN, William   ES: NY
B: Ireland

HOBAN, Thomas   ES: NY
B: New York, NY

HOBSON, Richmond Pearson   ES: NY
B: Greensboro, Hale Co., AL

HOLLAT, George   ES: NY

HOWARD, Martin   ES: New York, NY
B: Ireland

HUSE, Henry McLaren
Pinckney   ES: NY
B: USMA, West Point, Orange Co., NY

HUSKEY, Michael   ES: NY
B: Niagara Co., NY

*HUTCHINS, Carlton
Barmore   ES: NY
B: Albany, Albany Co., NY

IRLAM, Joseph   ES: New York, NY
B: Liverpool, Merseyside Co., England

IRVING, John   ES: New York, NY
B: East Brooklyn, Kings Co., NY

IRVING, Thomas   ES: New York, NY
B: England

IRWIN, Nicholas   ES: New York, NY
B: Denmark

JOHANSSON, Johan J.   ES: NY
B: Sweden

JOHNSON, Henry	ES: New York, NY B: Norway	McKNIGHT, William	ES: New York, NY B: Ulster Co., NY
JOHNSON, William	ES: NY B: St. Vincent, West Indies	MILLIKEN, Daniel	ES: New York, NY B: Saco, York Co., ME
JONES, Andrew	ES: New York, NY B: Limerick, County Limerick, Ireland	MILLMORE, John	ES: NY B: New York, NY
JONES, John E.	ES: NY B: New York, NY	MILLS, Charles	ES: Brooklyn, Kings Co., NY B: Ulster, Ulster Co., NY
JORDAN, Robert	ES: NY B: New York, NY	MITCHELL, Thomas	ES: NY B: New York, NY
KENYON, Charles W.	ES: New York, NY B: Oneida, Madison Co., NY	MOORE, Charles	ES: New York, NY B: Ireland
KING, Hugh	ES: NY B: Ireland	MOORE, Francis	ES: NY B: NY
KING, John	ES: NY B: County Mayo, Ireland	MORGAN, James H.	ES: New York, NY B: NY
KING, Robert Henry	ES: NY B: NY	MORIN, William Henry	ES: NY B: Birmingham, West Midlands Co., England
KINNAIRD, Samuel W.	ES: New York, NY B: New York, NY	MORRISON, John G.	ES: Lansingburg, Tompkins Co., NY B: Ireland
KRAUSE, Ernest	ES: NY B: Lubeck, Germany	MORSE, William	ES: NY B: Germany
LAFFERTY, John	ES: PA B: New York, NY	MURPHY, John Edward	ES: NY B: Ireland
LAKIN, Thomas	ES: NY B: NY	MURPHY, Patrick	ES: New York, NY B: Ireland
LANN, John S.	ES: New York, NY B: Rochester, Monroe Co., NY	NAYLOR, David Johnson	ES: New York, NY B: Thompsonville, Sullivan Co., NY
LEE, James H.	ES: New York, NY B: NY	NIBBE, John H.	ES: NY B: Germany
LEJEUNE, Emile	ES: NY B: France	NICHOLS, William	ES: NY B: New York, NY
LLOYD, John W.	ES: NY B: New York, NY	NOIL, Joseph B.	ES: NY B: Nova Scotia, Canada
LOW, George	ES: NY B: Canada	NORDSIEK, Charles Luers	ES: NY B: New York, NY
LUCY, John	ES: NY B: New York, NY	NORDSTROM, Isador A.	ES: NY B: Goteborg, Sweden
MACHON, James	ES: New York, NY B: Derby, Derbyshire, England	NORRIS, J. W.	ES: NY B: England
MACK, Alexander	ES: New York, NY B: Rotterdam, Holland	O'CONNELL, Thomas	ES: New York, NY B: Ireland
MADDEN, William	ES: New York, NY B: Devonshire, England	O'DONOGHUE, Timothy	ES: NY B: Rochester, Monroe Co., NY
MARTIN, William	ES: NY B: Ireland	OAKLEY, William	ES: NY B: Colchester, Essex Co., England
MARTIN, William	ES: Cairo, Alexander Co., IL B: New York, NY	OHMSEN, August	ES: NY B: Lubeck, Germany
MAXWELL, John	ES: NY B: Brooklyn, Kings Co., NY	OSEPINS, Christian	ES: NY B: Holland
McCARTON, John	ES: NY B: Brooklyn, Kings Co., NY	PARKS, George	ES: New York, NY B: Schenectady, Schenectady Co., NY
McCLELLAND, Matthew	ES: Brooklyn, Kings Co., NY B: Brooklyn, Kings Co., NY	PEASE, Joachim	ES: New York, NY B: Long Island, NY
McCLOY, John	ES: NY B: Brewster, Putnam Co., NY	PELHAM, William	ES: New York, NY B: Halifax, Nova Scotia, Canada
McGOWAN, John	ES: New York, NY B: Ireland	PERRY, Thomas	ES: NY B: NY
McINTOSH, James	ES: New York, NY B: Canada	PETERSON, Alfred	ES: New York, NY B: Sweden
McKENZIE, Alexander	ES: NY B: Glasgow, Scotland		

PHINNEY, William   ES: New York, NY
B: Norway

*POWERS, John James   ES: NY
B: New York, NY

PRICE, Edward   ES: New York, NY
B: New York, NY

PYNE, George   ES: New York, NY
B: England

QUICK, Joseph   ES: NY
B: NY

READ, Charles   ES: New York, NY
B: Cambridge, Washington Co., NY

REGAN, Patrick   ES: NY
B: Queenstown, County Cork, Ireland

REID, Patrick   ES: NY
B: Dublin, Ireland

RICHARDS, Louis   ES: New York, NY
B: New York, NY

ROBINSON, Alexander   ES: New York, NY
B: England

ROBINSON, Charles   ES: New York, NY
B: Dundee, Scotland

ROBINSON, Thomas   ES: NY
B: Norway

ROGERS, Samuel F.   ES: NY
B: Buffalo, Erie Co., NY

RUSSELL, Henry Peter   ES: NY
B: Quebec, Canada

RUSSELL, John   ES: NY
B: New York, NY

SCHEPKE, Charles Stephen   ES: NY
B: New York, NY

SCHNEPEL, Fred Jurgen   ES: NY
B: New York, NY

SCHUTT, George   ES: New York, NY
B: Ireland

SEANOR, James   ES: New York, NY
B: Boston, Suffolk Co., MA

SHANAHAN, Patrick   ES: NY
B: Shanat Castle, County Limerick, Ireland

SHARP, Hendrick   ES: New York, NY
B: Spain

SHERIDAN, James   ES: New York, NY
B: Newark, Essex Co., NJ

SHIPMAN, William   ES: New York, NY
B: New York, NY

SIMKINS, Lebbeus   ES: NY
B: Utica, Oneida Co., NY

SIMPSON, D. Henry Lakin   ES: NY
B: London, England

SMITH, Edwin   ES: NY
B: New York, NY

SMITH, James   ES: New York, NY
B: Belfast, County Antrim, Ireland

SMITH, James   ES: NY
B: Hawaiian Islands

SMITH, James A.   ES: NY
B: NY

SMITH, John   ES: New York, NY
B: Albany, Albany Co., NY

SMITH, John   ES: NY
B: Bermuda

SMITH, Oloff   ES: New York, NY
B: Sweden

SMITH, Thomas   ES: New York, NY
B: England

SMITH, Walter B.   ES: New York, NY
B: NY

SMITH, Wilhelm   ES: NY
B: Germany

SPICER, William   ES: NY
B: Liverpool, Merseyside Co., England

STANLEY, Robert Henry   ES: aboard U.S.S. *Vermont*
B: Brooklyn, Kings Co., NY

STANTON, Thomas   ES: NY
B: Ireland

STOKES, John S.   ES: NY
B: New York, NY

STOUT, Richard   ES: NY
B: Owego, Tioga Co., NY

SULLIVAN, James   ES: Danbury, Fairfield Co., CT
B: New York, NY

SULLIVAN, John   ES: NY
B: New York, NY

SULLIVAN, Timothy   ES: New York, NY
B: Ireland

SUMMERS, Robert   ES: New York, NY
B: Prussia

SUNDQUIST, Gustav Adolf   ES: NY
B: Sweden

SWATTON, Edward   ES: Boston, Suffolk Co., MA
B: New York, NY

TAYLOR, George   ES: New York, NY
B: Reddich, Hereford & Worcester Co.,
England

THOMAS, Karl   ES: NY
B: Germany

THORDSEN, William George   ES: NY
B: Fredericstadt, Germany

TRIPLETT, Samuel S.   ES: NY
B: Cherokee, Crawford Co., KS

TROY, Jeremiah   ES: NY
B: New York, NY

VADAS, Albert   ES: NY
B: Austria-Hungary

VAN ETTEN, Hudson   ES: NJ
B: Port Jervis, Orange Co., NY

WAGG, Maurice   ES: New York, NY
B: Hampshire, England

WALSH, James Aloysius   ES: New York, NY
B: New York, NY

WARD, James   ES: New York, NY
B: New York, NY

WARREN, David   ES: New York, NY
B: Glasgow, Scotland

WEBSTER, Henry S.   ES: Brooklyn, Kings Co., NY
B: Stockholm, NY

WEISSEL, Adam   ES: NY
B: Germany

WELLS, William   ES: New York, NY
B: Germany

WESTA, Karl   ES: NY
B: Norway

WILCOX, Franklin L.	ES: NY B: Paris, Oneida Co., NY
WILKE, Julius August Robert	ES: NY B: Germany
WILKES, Henry	ES: New York, NY B: New York, NY
WILLIAMS, Frank	ES: NY B: Danzig, Germany
WILLIAMS, Robert	ES: NY B: New York, NY
WILLIAMS II, John	ES: NY B: Elizabethtown, NJ
WILSON, August	ES: NY B: Danzig, Germany
WOON, John	ES: New York, NY B: England
WORAM, Charles B.	ES: New York, NY B: New York, NY
WRIGHT, Edward	ES: New York, NY B: New York, NY
YOUNG, William	ES: New York, NY B: NY

U.S. Marine Corps

ADRIANCE, Harry Chapman	ES: Massachusetts B: Oswego, Oswego Co., NY
APPLETON, Edwin Nelson	ES: NY B: Brooklyn, Kings Co., NY
BASILONE, John "Manila John"	ES: NJ B: Buffalo, Erie Co., NY
*BOBO, John Paul	ES: Buffalo, Erie Co., NY B: Niagara Falls, Niagara Co., NY
BROWN, Charles	ES: Hong Kong B: New York, NY
BUCKLEY, Howard Major	ES: NY B: Croton Falls, Westchester Co., NY
CAFFERATA Jr., Hector Albert	ES: Dover, Morris Co., NJ B: New York, NY
*CARTER, Bruce Wayne	ES: Jacksonville, Duval Co., FL B: Schenectady, Schenectady Co., NY
CASAMENTO, Anthony	ES: New York, NY B: New York, NY
CATLIN, Albertus Wright	ES: MN B: Gowanda, Cattaraugus Co., NY
*COOK, Donald Gilbert	ES: Brooklyn, Kings Co., NY B: Brooklyn, Kings Co., NY
DALY, Daniel Joseph	ES: NY B: Glen Cove, Nassau Co., NY
FIELD, Oscar Wadsworth	ES: NY B: Jersey City, Hudson Co., NJ
FITZGERALD, John	ES: NY B: Limerick, Ireland
FRANKLIN, Joseph John	ES: NY B: Buffalo, Eric Co., NY
*GRAVES, Terrence Collinson	ES: NY B: Corpus Christi, Nueces Co., TX
HARVEY, Harry	ES: NJ B: New York, NY
HOFFMAN, Charles F.	ES: Brooklyn, Kings Co., NY B: New York, NY

HUDSON, Michael	ES: NY B: County Sligo, Ireland
HUGHES, John Arthur	ES: NY B: New York, NY
JACOBSON, Douglas Thomas	ES: NY B: Rochester, Monroe Co., NY
KATES, Thomas Wilbur	ES: NY B: Shelby Center, NY
*KOCAK, Matej	ES: New York, NY B: Gbely (Slovakia), Austria
KUCHNEISTER, Hermann Wilhelm	ES: NY B: Hamburg, Germany
LEE, Howard Vincent	ES: Dumfries, Prince William Co., VA B: New York, NY
LEONARD, Joseph H.	ES: New York, NY B: Cohoes, Albany Co., NY
MACKIE, John Freeman	ES: New York, NY B: New York, NY
*MAUSERT III, Frederick William	ES: Dresher, Montgomery Co., PA B: Cambridge, Washington Co., NY
*McCARD, Robert Howard	ES: NY B: Syracuse, Onondaga Co., NY
McNALLY, Michael Joseph	ES: CA B: New York, NY
McNAMARA, Michael	ES: NY B: Clure, Ireland
MORRIS, John	ES: NY B: NY
MURPHY, John Alphonsus	ES: Washington, D.C. B: New York, NY
MURRAY, William Henry	ES: Brooklyn, Kings Co., NY B: Brooklyn, Kings Co., NY
*NOONAN Jr., Thomas Patrick	ES: Brooklyn, Kings Co., NY B: Brooklyn, Kings Co., NY
O'MALLEY, Robert Emmett	ES: New York, NY B: Woodside, Queens Co., NY
OVIATT, Miles M.	ES: NY B: Cattaraugus Co., NY
OWENS, Michael	ES: NY B: New York, NY
*PERKINS Jr., William Thomas	ES: San Francisco, San Francisco Co., CA B: Rochester, Monroe Co., NY
*PETERS, Lawrence David	ES: Binghamton, Broome Co., NY B: Johnson City, Broome Co., NY
ROANTREE, James S.	ES: NY B: Dublin, County Dublin, Ireland
ROBINSON, Robert Guy	ES: Chicago, Cook Co., IL B: New York, NY
SMITH, Willard M.	ES: NY B: Allegany, Cattaraugus Co., NY
SPROWLE, David	ES: NY B: Lisbon, St. Lawrence Co., NY
*STOCKHAM, Fred William	ES: New York, NY B: Detroit, Wayne Co., MI
WALKER, Edward Alexander	ES: Brooklyn, Kings Co., NY B: Huntley, Scotland
WALSH, Kenneth Ambrose	ES: Brooklyn, Kings Co., NY B: Brooklyn, Kings Co., NY

NORTH CAROLINA

U.S. Army

*ASHLEY Jr., Eugene
ES: New York, NY
B: Wilmington, New Hanover Co., NC

*BLACKWELL, Robert Lester
ES: Hurdle Mills, Person Co., NC
B: Person Co., NC

BROWN, Lorenzo Dow
ES: Indianapolis, Marion Co., IN
B: Davidson Co., NC

CRUMP, Jerry Kirt
ES: Forest City, Rutherford Co., NC
B: Charlotte, Mecklenburg Co., NC

*DURHAM Jr., Harold Bascom
ES: Atlanta, Fulton Co., GA
B: Rocky Mount, Edgecombe Co., NC

*EUBANKS, Ray E.
ES: LaGrange, Lenoir Co., NC
B: Snow Hill, Greene Co., NC

*GEORGE, Charles
ES: Whittier, Jackson Co., NC
B: Cherokee, Swain Co., NC

JOEL, Lawrence
ES: New York, NY
B: Winston-Salem, Forsyth Co., NC

JOHNSTON, Gordon
ES: Birmingham, Jefferson Co., AL
B: Charlotte, Mecklenburg Co., NC

JONES, William H.
ES: Louisville, Jefferson Co., KY
B: Davidson Co., NC

McBRYAR, William
ES: New York, NY
B: Elizabethtown, Bladen Co., NC

MILLER, Franklin Douglas
ES: Albuquerque, Bernalillo Co., NM
B: Elizabeth City, Pasquotank Co., NC

MURRAY Jr., Charles Patrick "Chuck"
ES: Wilmington, New Hanover Co., NC
B: Baltimore, Baltimore Co., MD

PARKER, Samuel Iredell
ES: Monroe, Union Co., NC
B: Monroe, Union Co., NC

PATTERSON, Robert Martin
ES: Raleigh, Wake Co., NC
B: Durham, Durham Co., NC

RAY, Charles W.
ES: St. Louis, St. Louis Co., MO
B: Pensacola, Yancey Co., NC

SHEA, Joseph Henry
ES: New Bern, Craven Co., NC
B: Baltimore, Baltimore Co., MD

*STOUT, Mitchell William
ES: Raleigh, Wake Co., NC
B: Knoxville, Knox Co., TN

THOMPSON, Max
ES: Canton, Haywood Co., NC
B: Bethel, Pitt Co., NC

TROGDEN, Howell G.
ES: St. Louis, St. Louis Co., MO
B: Cedar Falls, Randolph Co., NC

URBAN, Matt Louis
ES: Fort Bragg, Cumberland Co., NC
B: Buffalo, Erie Co., NY

*WARNER, Henry F.
ES: Troy, Montgomery Co., NC
B: Troy, Montgomery Co., NC

*WOMACK, Bryant Homer
ES: Mill Spring, Polk Co., NC
B: Mill Spring, Polk Co., NC

U.S. Navy

ANDERSON, Edwin Alexander
ES: Wilmington, New Hanover Co., NC
B: Wilmington, New Hanover Co., NC

BARROW, David Duffy
ES: Norfolk, Norfolk Co., VA
B: Reelsboro, NC

FRANKS, William J.
ES: De Valls Bluff, Prairie Co., AR
B: Chatham Co., NC

*HALYBURTON Jr., William David
ES: NC
B: Canton, Haywood Co., NC

HERRING, Rufus Geddie
ES: Roseboro, Sampson Co., NC
B: Roseboro, Sampson Co., NC

JOHNSTON Jr., Rufus Zenas
ES: NC
B: Lincolnton, Lincoln Co., NC

SANDERSON, Aaron
ES: Philadelphia, Philadelphia Co., PA
B: North Carolina

STATON, Adolphus
ES: NC
B: Tarboro, Edgecombe Co., NC

U.S. Marine Corps

LUCAS, Jacklyn Harold
ES: Norfolk, Norfolk Co., VA
B: Plymouth, Washington Co., NC

PARKER, Pomeroy
ES: NC
B: Gates Co., NC

NORTH DAKOTA

U.S. Army

ANDERS, Frank Lafayette
ES: Fargo, Cass Co., ND
B: Fort Lincoln, Dakota Territory

BLOCH, Orville Emil
ES: Streeter, Stutsman Co., ND
B: Big Falls, Waupaca Co., WI

BOEHLER, Otto A.
ES: Wahpeton, Richland Co., ND
B: Germany

DAVIS, Charles P.
ES: Valley City, Barnes Co., ND
B: Long Prairie, Todd Co., MN

DOWNS, Willis H.
ES: Jamestown, Stutsman Co., ND
B: Mount Carmel, CT

FITZMAURICE, Michael John
ES: Cavour, Beadle Co., SD
B: Jamestown, Stutsman Co., ND

*HAGEN, Loren Douglas
ES: Fargo, Cass Co., ND
B: Fargo, Cass Co., ND

HARDAWAY, Benjamin Franklin
ES: Fort Totten, Benson Co., Dakota Territory
B: Benleyville, KY

JENSEN, Gotfred
ES: Devils Lake, Ramsey Co., ND
B: Denmark

KINNE, John Baxter
ES: Fargo, Cass Co., ND
B: Beloit, Rock Co., WI

LONGFELLOW, Richard Moses
ES: Mandan, Morton Co., ND
B: Logan Co., IL

*PENDLETON, Jack James
ES: Yakima, Yakima Co., WA
B: Sentinel Butte, Golden Valley Co., ND

ROSS, Frank Fulton
ES: Langdon, Cavalier Co., ND
B: Avon, Fulton Co., IL

SLETTELAND, Thomas
ES: Grafton, Walsh Co., ND
B: Bergen, Norway

*SMITH, Fred E.
ES: Bartlett, ND
B: Rockford, Winnebago Co., IL

*WOLD, Nels T.
ES: Minnewaukan, Benson Co., ND
B: Winger, Polk Co., MN

U.S. Navy

BRADLEY Jr., Willis Winter
ES: ND
B: Ransomville, Niagara Co., NY

CARTER, Joseph Edward
ES: ND
B: Manchester, Greater Manchester Co., England

U.S. Marine Corps
*GURKE, Henry | ES: ND
B: Neche, Pembina Co., ND

OHIO

U.S. Army

ALBERT, Christian | ES: Cincinnati, Hamilton Co., OH
B: Cincinnati, Hamilton Co., OH

*ANTOLAK, Sylvester | ES: Clairsville, OH
B: Clairsville, OH

ARCHINAL, William J. | ES: Canaldover, OH
B: Felsburg, Hesse, Germany

ASTON, Edgar R. | ES: Cincinnati, Hamilton Co., OH
B: Clermont Co., OH

AYERS, David | ES: Upper Sandusky, Wyandot Co., OH
B: Kalida, Putnam Co., OH

*BAESEL, Albert E. | ES: Berea, Cuyahoga Co., OH
B: Berea, Cuyahoga Co., OH

BAKER Jr., Edward Lee | ES: Cincinnati, Hamilton Co., OH
B: Platte River, Laramie Co., WY

BANKS, George Lovell | ES: Lafayette, Tippecanoe Co., IN
B: Lake Co., OH

BARRICK, Jesse T. | ES: Fort Snelling, St. Paul Co., MN
B: Columbiana Co., OH

BARRINGER, William H. | ES: Mason City, Mason Co., WV
B: Long Bottom, Meigs Co., OH

BEATY, Powhatan | ES: Cincinnati, Hamilton Co., OH
B: Richmond, Richmond Co., VA

BEBB, Edward James | ES: Mount Pleasant, Henry Co., IA
B: Butler Co., OH

BELL, James Bennett | ES: Troy, Miami Co., OH
B: Branot, OH

BENNETT, Edward Andrew | ES: Middleport, Meigs Co., OH
B: Middleport, Meigs Co., OH

BENSINGER, William | ES: McComb, Hancock Co., OH
B: Waynesburg, Stark Co., OH

BERTRAM, Heinrich | ES: Cincinnati, Hamilton Co., OH
B: Brunswick, Germany

BICKHAM, Charles Goodwin | ES: Dayton, Montgomery Co., OH
B: Dayton, Montgomery Co., OH

BIRKHIMER, William Edward | ES: IA
B: Somerset, Perry Co., OH

BISHOP, Daniel | ES: Wheeling, Ohio Co., WV
B: Monroe Co., OH

BLICKENSDERGER, Milton | ES: Shanesville, OH
B: Lancaster, Lancaster Co., PA

BOURY, Richard | ES: Wirt Courthouse, WV
B: Monroe Co., OH

BOYNTON, Henry Van Ness | ES: Hamilton, Butler Co., OH
B: West Stockbridge, Berkshire Co., MA

BRANDLE, Joseph E. | ES: Colon, St. Joseph Co., MI
B: Seneca Co., OH

BRONSON, James H. | ES: Trumbell Co., OH
B: Indiana Co., PA

BROOKIN, Oscar | ES: Green Co., OH
B: Byron, Fond Du Lac Co., WI

BROWN, John | ES: Cincinnati, Hamilton Co., OH
B: Boston, Suffolk Co., MA

BROWN, Robert Burns | ES: Zanesville, Muskingum Co., OH
B: New Concord, Muskingum Co., OH

BROWN, Uriah H. | ES: Steubenville, Jefferson Co., OH
B: Covington, Miami Co., OH

BROWN, Wilson W. | ES: Findlay, Hancock Co., OH
B: Logan Co., OH

BRYAN, William C. | ES: St. Louis, St. Louis Co., MO
B: Zanesville, Muskingum Co., OH

BUFFUM, Robert | ES: Gilead, Wood Co., OH
B: Salem, Essex Co., MA

BUHRMAN, Henry G. | ES: Cincinnati, Hamilton Co., OH
B: Cincinnati, Hamilton Co., OH

BURNS, James Madison | ES: Wellsburg, Brooke Co., WV
B: Wells Township, Jefferson Co., OH

CALVERT, James Spencer | ES: Springfield, Sangamon Co., IL
B: Athens Co., OH

CAMPBELL, William | ES: New Philadelphia, Tuscarawas Co., OH
B: County Down, Ireland

CAPEHART, Henry | ES: Bridgeport, Belmont Co., OH
B: Johnstown, Cambria Co., PA

CARMIN, Isaac Harrison | ES: New Lexington, Perry Co., OH
B: Monmouth Co., NJ

CARR, Franklin | ES: Toledo, Lucas Co., OH
B: Stark Co., OH

CARR, John | ES: San Jose, Santa Clara Co., CA
B: Columbus, Franklin Co., OH

CARSON, William J. | ES: North Greenfield, Highland Co., OH
B: Washington Co., PA

CASEY, Henry | ES: Bloomingburg, Fayette Co., OH
B: New Geneva, Fayette Co., PA

*CHRISTIAN, Herbert F. | ES: Steubenville, Jefferson Co., OH
B: Byesville, Guernsey Co., OH

*CICCHETTI, Joseph J. | ES: Waynesburg, Stark Co., OH
B: Waynesburg, Stark Co., OH

CLAPP, Albert Adams | ES: Painesville, Lake Co., OH
B: Pompey, Onondaga Co., NY

COCKLEY, David L. | ES: Columbus, Franklin Co., OH
B: Lexington, Richland Co., OH

COLWELL, Oliver | ES: Columbus, Franklin Co., OH
B: Champaign Co., OH

COOK, John | ES: Cincinnati, Hamilton Co., OH
B: Cincinnati, Hamilton Co., OH

COONROD, Aquilla | ES: Bryan, Williams Co., OH
B: Williams Co., OH

COX, Robert Mitchell | ES: Prairie City, McDonough Co., IL
B: Guernsey Co., OH

*CRAIG, Robert | ES: Toledo, Lucas Co., OH
B: Scotland

CRANSTON, William Wallace | ES: Urbana, Champaign Co., OH
B: near Woodstock, Champaign Co., OH

CRISWELL, Benjamin C. | ES: Cincinnati, Hamilton Co., OH
B: Moundsville, Marshall Co., WV

CROCKER, Ulric Lyona | ES: Vergennes, OH
B: OH

CUBBERLY, William G. | ES: Cincinnati, Hamilton Co., OH
B: Butler Co., OH

CUMPSTON, James M. | ES: Portsmouth, Scioto Co., OH
B: Gallia Co., OH

CUSTER, Thomas Ward | ES: Monroe, Monroe Co., MI
B: New Rumley, Harrison Co., OH

DAVIDSON, Andrew | ES: Cincinnati, Hamilton Co., OH
B: Middlebury, Addison Co., VT

DAVIS, Freeman | ES: Newcomerstown, Tuscarawas Co., OH
B: Newcomerstown, Tuscarawas Co., OH

DAVIS, Harry Clay   ES: Columbus, Franklin Co., OH
B: Franklin Co., OH

DAVIS, Joseph   ES: East Palestine, Columbiana Co., OH
B: Monmouth Co., Wales

DAVIS, Sammy Lee   ES: Indianapolis, Marion Co., IN
B: Dayton, Montgomery Co., OH

DAY, David Frakes   ES: Cincinnati, Hamilton Co., OH
B: Dallasburg, OH

DAY, Matthias Walter   ES: Oberlin, Lorain Co., OH
B: Mansfield, Richland Co., OH

*De ARMOND, William   ES: New York, NY
B: Butler Co., OH

DeLAVIE, Hiram H.   ES: Allegheny Co., PA
B: Stark Co., OH

*DELEAU Jr., Emile   ES: Blaine, Belmont Co., OH
B: Lansing, Belmont Co., OH

DeWITT, Richard Willis   ES: Oxford, Butler Co., OH
B: Butler Co., OH

DORSEY, Daniel Allen   ES: Chillicothe, Ross Co., OH
B: Lancaster, Fairfield Co., OH

DOWLING, James   ES: Cleveland, Cuyahoga Co., OH
B: County Meath, Ireland

EDGERTON, Nathan Huntley   ES: Philadelphia, Philadelphia Co., PA
B: Barnesville, Belmont Co., OH

ELSON, James M.   ES: Shellsburg, Benton Co., IA
B: Coshocton, Coshocton Co., OH

ENDERLIN, Richard   ES: Chillicothe, Ross Co., OH
B: Germany

EVERHART Sr., Forrest Eugene   ES: Texas City, Galveston Co., TX
B: Bainbridge, Ross Co., OH

FEASTER, Mosheim   ES: Cleveland, Cuyahoga Co., OH
B: Schellsburg, Bedford Co., PA

FERRARI, George   ES: Cleveland, Cuyahoga Co., OH
B: New York, NY

FINKENBINER, Henry S.   ES: Pike Township, OH
B: North Industry, Stark Co., OH

*FLEEK, Charles Clinton   ES: Cincinnati, Hamilton Co., OH
B: Petersburg, Boone Co., KY

FORCE, Manning Ferguson   ES: Cincinnati, Hamilton Co., OH
B: Washington, D.C.

FOX, Henry M.   ES: Coldwater, Branch Co., MI
B: Trumbull, OH

FREEMAN, Henry Blanchard   ES: Mount Vernon, Knox Co., OH
B: Mount Vernon, Knox Co., OH

FREY, Franz   ES: Cleveland, Cuyahoga Co., OH
B: Switzerland

FUNSTON Sr., Frederick   ES: Iola, Allen Co., KS
B: New Carlisle, Clark Co., OH

GARRETT, William   ES: Chardon, Geauga Co., OH
B: Isle of Man, England

GATES, George   ES: Dubuque, Dubuque Co., IA
B: Delaware Co., OH

GAUNT, John C.   ES: Damascoville, OH
B: Columbiana Co., OH

GAUSE, Isaac   ES: Canfield, Mahoning Co., OH
B: Trumbull Co., OH

GEIGER, George   ES: St. Louis, St. Louis Co., MO
B: Cincinnati, Hamilton Co., OH

*GIVEN, John J.   ES: Cincinnati, Hamilton Co., OH
B: Daviess Co., KY

GODFREY, Edward Settle   ES: Ottawa, Putnam Co., OH
B: Kalida, Putnam Co., OH

GRAY, John   ES: Cincinnati, Hamilton Co., OH
B: Dundee, Scotland

GREEN, George   ES: Columbus, Franklin Co., OH
B: Elsham, Lincolnshire Co., England

GREEN, John   ES: Columbus, Franklin Co., OH
B: Wurttemberg, Germany

GREENAWALT, Abraham   ES: Salem, Columbiana Co., OH
B: Montgomery Co., PA

GREGG, Joseph Olds   ES: Columbus, Franklin Co., OH
B: Lithopolis, Fairfield Co., OH

GRIMSHAW, Samuel   ES: Smithfield, Jefferson Co., OH
B: Jefferson Co., OH

GUINN, Thomas   ES: Oxford, Butler Co., OH
B: Clinton Co., OH

GWYNNE, Nathaniel McClean   ES: Fairmount, MO
B: Urbana, Champaign Co., OH

*HALL, Lewis R.   ES: Columbus, Franklin Co., OH
B: Bloom, OH

HALL, Newton H.   ES: Brimfield, Portage Co., OH
B: Brimfield, Portage Co., OH

HANEY, Milton Lorenzi   ES: Bushnell, McDonough Co., IL
B: Savannah, Ashland Co., OH

HANKS, Joseph   ES: Chillicothe, Ross Co., OH
B: Chillicothe, Ross Co., OH

HANLEY, Richard P.   ES: Cincinnati, Hamilton Co., OH
B: Boston, Suffolk Co., MA

HANNA, Milton   ES: Henderson, Sibley Co., MN
B: Licking Co., OH

HARRINGTON, John   ES: Cleveland, Cuyahoga Co., OH
B: Detroit, Wayne Co., MI

HARRIS, David W.   ES: Cincinnati, Hamilton Co., OH
B: Indianapolis, Marion Co., IN

HARRIS, Sampson   ES: Olive, OH
B: Noble Co., OH

HARTZOG, Joshua B.   ES: Detroit, Wayne Co., MI
B: Paulding Co., OH

*HASTINGS, Joe R.   ES: Magnolia, Stark Co., OH
B: Malvern, Carroll Co., OH

HAWKINS, Martin Jones   ES: Portsmouth, Scioto Co., OH
B: Mercer Co., PA

HAWKINS, Thomas R.   ES: Philadelphia, Philadelphia Co., PA
B: Cincinnati, Hamilton Co., OH

HAYES, Webb Cook   ES: Fremont, Sandusky Co., OH
B: Cincinnati, Hamilton Co., OH

HAYS, John H.   ES: Oskaloosa, Mahaska Co., IA
B: Jefferson Co., OH

HEDGES, Joseph S.   ES: Mansfield, Richland Co., OH
B: Mansfield, Richland Co., OH

HELLER, Henry   ES: Urbana, Champaign Co., OH

HENRY, James   ES: Kankakee, Kankakee Co., IL
B: Sunfish, OH

HERDA, Frank Aloysious   ES: Cleveland, Cuyahoga Co., OH
B: Cleveland, Cuyahoga Co., OH

HILL, James Madison   ES: Cincinnati, Hamilton Co., OH
B: Washington Co., PA

HOFFMAN, Henry   ES: Cincinnati, Hamilton Co., OH
B: Wurttemberg, Germany

HOLCOMB, Daniel Irving   ES: Hartford, Trumbull Co., OH
B: Hartford, Trumbull Co., OH

HOLLAND, Lemuel F. ES: Tiskilwa, Bureau Co., IL
B: Burlington, OH

HOLLAND, Milton Murray ES: Albany, Athens Co., OH
B: Austin, Travis Co., TX

HOULTON, William M. ES: Athens, Athens Co., OH
B: Clymer, Chautauqua Co., NY

HOWARD, Hiram Reese ES: Cincinnati, Hamilton Co., OH
B: Urbana, Champaign Co., OH

HOWE, Orion P. ES: Waukegan, Lake Co., IL
B: Hiram, Portage Co., OH

HUTCHINSON, Rufus D. ES: Cincinnati, Hamilton Co., OH
B: Butlerville, OH

IMMELL, Lorenzo Dow ES: Fort Leavenworth, Leavenworth Co., KS
B: Ross, Butler Co., OH

INSCHO, Leonidas H. ES: Newark, Licking Co., OH
B: Chatham, Licking Co., OH

JAMES, Isaac ES: Mississinawa Township, OH
B: Jefferson Township, Ashtabula Co., OH

JARDINE, James ES: Hamilton Co., OH
B: Helensburgh, Dunbartonshire, Scotland

JOHN, William F. ES: Chillicothe, Ross Co., OH
B: Germany

JOHNS, Elisha ES: Martinton, Iroquois Co., IL
B: Clinton, Summit Co., OH

JOHNSON, Andrew ES: Assumption, Christian Co., IL
B: Delaware Co., OH

JONES, David ES: Washington Courthouse, Fayette Co., OH
B: Fayette Co., OH

JORDAN, Absalom ES: North Madison, Jefferson Co., IN
B: Brown Co., OH

KEENAN, Bartholomew T. ES: Cincinnati, Hamilton Co., OH
B: Brooklyn, Kings Co., NY

*KEFURT, Gus ES: Youngstown, Mahoning Co., OH
B: Greenville, Mercer Co., PA

KELLEY, George V. ES: Massillon, Stark Co., OH
B: Massillon, Stark Co., OH

KEMP, Joseph Bell ES: Sault Ste. Marie, Chippewa Co., MI
B: Lima, Allen Co., OH

*KESSLER, Patrick L. ES: Middletown, Butler Co., OH
B: Middletown, Butler Co., OH

KIMBALL, Joseph ES: Ironton, Lawrence Co., OH
B: Littleton, Grafton Co., NH

KIRK, Jonathan C. ES: Wilmington, Clinton Co., OH
B: Clinton Co., OH

KNAAK, Albert ES: Cincinnati, Hamilton Co., OH
B: Luxenburg, Switzerland

KNIGHT, William J. ES: Farmers Center, Defiance Co., OH
B: Apple Creek, Wayne Co., OH

KOUNTZ, John S. ES: Maumee, Lucas Co., OH
B: Maumee, Lucas Co., OH

KUDER, Jeremiah ES: Warsaw, Kosciusko Co., IN
B: Tiffin, Seneca Co., OH

KYLE, John ES: Nashville, Davidson Co., TN
B: Cincinnati, Hamilton Co., OH

*LAPOINTE Jr., Joseph Guy ES: Cincinnati, Hamilton Co., OH
B: Dayton, Montgomery Co., OH

LARIMER, Smith ES: Columbus, Franklin Co., OH
B: Richland Co., OH

LAWTON, Henry Ware ES: Fort Wayne, Allen Co., IN
B: Manhattan, Lucas Co., OH

LEONARD, Patrick James ES: Cincinnati, Hamilton Co., OH
B: County Meath, Ireland

*LOGAN Jr., John Alexander ES: Youngstown, Mahoning Co., OH
B: Carbondale, Jackson Co., IL

*LONG, Donald Russell ES: Ashland, Boyd Co., KY
B: Blackfork, OH

LONGSHORE, William Henry ES: Columbus, Franklin Co., OH
B: Zanesville, Muskingum Co., OH

LOYD, George A. ES: Zanesville, Muskingum Co., OH
B: Muskingum Co., OH

LYTLE, Leonidas S. ES: Cleveland, Cuyahoga Co., OH
B: Warren Co., PA

MASON, Elihu H. ES: Pemberville, Wood Co., OH
B: Wayne Co., IN

MAYES, William B. ES: DeWitt, Clinton Co., IA
B: Marion Co., OH

MAYFIELD, Melvin ES: Nashport, Muskingum Co., OH
B: Salem, Harrison Co., WV

MAYS, Isaiah ES: Columbus Barracks, Franklin Co., OH
B: Carters Bridge, VA

McCLEARY, Charles H. ES: Clyde, Sandusky Co., OH
B: Sandusky Co., OH

McCLELLAND, James M. ES: Ohio
B: Harrison Co., OH

McCONNELL, Samuel ES: Bushnell, McDonough Co., IL
B: Belmont Co., OH

McDONALD, John Wade ES: Waynesville, DeWitt Co., IL
B: Lancaster, Fairfield Co., OH

McELHINNY, Samuel O. ES: Point Pleasant, Mason Co., WV
B: Meigs Co., OH

McGINN, Edward ES: Cincinnati, Hamilton Co., OH
B: New York, NY

McGONAGLE, Wilson ES: Cadiz, Harrison Co., OH
B: Jefferson Co., OH

McMILLEN, Francis M. ES: Piqua, Miami Co., OH
B: Bracken Co., KY

MEAHER, Nicholas ES: Cincinnati, Hamilton Co., OH
B: Perry Co., OH

MILLER, Daniel H. ES: Columbus, Franklin Co., OH
B: Fairfield Co., OH

MILLER, Jacob C. ES: Elgin, Kane Co., IL
B: Bellevue, Huron Co., OH

MILLER, James P. ES: Henry Co., IA
B: Franklin, Warren Co., OH

MILLER, John G. ES: Camp Dennison, Hamilton Co., OH
B: Germany

MOREY, Delano ES: Kenton, Hardin Co., OH
B: Licking Co., OH

*MORGAN, Lewis ES: Delaware Co., OH
B: Delaware Co., OH

MURPHY, John P. ES: Cincinnati, Hamilton Co., OH
B: Killarney, County Kerry, Ireland

MYERS, George S. ES: Tiffin, Seneca Co., OH
B: Fairfield, Butler Co., OH

NEWMAN, Henry ES: Cincinnati, Hamilton Co., OH
B: Hanover, Germany

NORTH, Jasper N. ES: Amesville, Athens Co., OH
B: OH

ORBANSKY, David ES: Columbus, Franklin Co., OH
B: Lautenburg, Prussia

PARKS, James W.   ES: Xenia, Clay Co., IL
                   B: Lawrence Co., OH

PARROTT, Jacob   ES: Kenton, Hardin Co., OH
                   B: Fairfield Co., OH

PATTERSON, John T. ES: McConnelsville, Morgan Co., OH
                   B: Morgan Co., OH

PEARSALL, Platt   ES: Downington, OH
                   B: Meigs Co., OH

PEIRSOL, James Kastor ES: Waynesboro, OH
                       B: Beaver Co., PA

*PETRARCA, Frank Joseph ES: Cleveland, Cuyahoga Co., OH
                         B: Cleveland, Cuyahoga Co., OH

PHILLIPS, Samuel D. ES: St. Louis, St. Louis Co., MO
                     B: Butler Co., OH

PHISTERER, Frederick ES: Medina Co., OH
                      B: Germany

PINN, Robert A.   ES: Massillon, Stark Co., OH
                   B: Stark Co., OH

PITTINGER, William ES: Steubenville, Jefferson Co., OH
                    B: Knoxville, Jefferson Co., OH

POPPE, John A.   ES: Fort Dodge, Ford Co., KS
                   B: Cincinnati, Hamilton Co., OH

PORTER, John Reed ES: McComb, Hancock Co., OH
                   B: Delaware Co., OH

POWELL, William Henry ES: Ironton, Lawrence Co., OH
                       B: Pontypool, Monmouthshire, South Wales

POWER, Albert   ES: Bloomfield, Davis Co., IA
                   B: Liberty, Guernsey Co., OH

PRATT, James N.   ES: Bellefontaine, Logan Co., OH
                   B: Bellefontaine, Logan Co., OH

PRENTICE, Joseph Rollin ES: Fort Wayne, Allen Co., IN
                         B: Lancaster, Fairfield Co., OH

RAERICK, John   ES: Cincinnati, Hamilton Co., OH
                   B: Baden, Germany

RANSBOTTOM, Alfred ES: Nashport, Muskingum Co., OH
                    B: South Zanesville, Delaware Co., OH

REDDICK, William Henry
Harrison   ES: Portsmouth, Scioto Co., OH
                   B: Locust Grove, Adams Co., OH

RENNINGER, Louis   ES: Liverpool, OH
                   B: Liverpool, OH

RICHARDSON, William R. ES: Washington, OH
                        B: Cleveland, Cuyahoga Co., OH

RICHEY, William E. ES: New Concord, Muskingum Co., OH
                    B: Athens Co., OH

RICHMAN, Samuel   ES: Cleveland, Cuyahoga Co., OH
                   B: Cleveland, Cuyahoga Co., OH

*RICHMOND, James   ES: Fremont, Sandusky Co., OH
                   B: ME

RICKSECKER, John Henry ES: Aurora, Portage Co., OH
                        B: Mansfield, Richland Co., OH

ROBERTS, Gordon Ray ES: Cincinnati, Hamilton Co., OH
                     B: Middletown, Butler Co., OH

*ROBERTSON, Samuel ES: Boarneville, Ross Co., OH
                    B: Muskingum Co., OH

ROBINSON, Elbridge ES: McConnelsville, Morgan Co., OH
                    B: Morgan Co., OH

*ROBINSON Jr., James E. ES: Waco, McLennan Co., TX
                         B: Toledo, Lucas Co., OH

ROCK, Frederick   ES: Cleveland, Cuyahoga Co., OH
                   B: Darmstadt, Germany

*ROSS, Marion A.   ES: Christianburg, Champaign Co., OH
                   B: Christianburg, Champaign Co., OH

ROSSER, Ronald Eugene ES: Crooksville, Perry Co., OH
                       B: Columbus, Franklin Co., OH

ROUNDS, Lewis A.   ES: Norwalk, Huron Co., OH
                   B: Cattaraugus Co., NY

ROWALT, John F.   ES: Cincinnati, Hamilton Co., OH
                   B: Belleville, Richland Co., OH

ROY, Stanislaus   ES: Cincinnati, Hamilton Co., OH
                   B: France

SCHENCK, Benjamin W. ES: Maroa, Macon Co., IL
                      B: Butler Co., OH

SCHMAUCH, Andrew   ES: Portsmouth, Scioto Co., OH
                   B: Germany

SCHMIDT, William   ES: Maumee, Lucas Co., OH
                   B: Tiffin, Seneca Co., OH

SCHNELL, Christian ES: Wapakoneta, Auglaize Co., OH
                    B: VA

*SCOTT, John Morehead ES: Findley, Hancock Co., OH
                       B: Stark Co., OH

SEAMAN, Elisha B. ES: Logan Co., OH
                   B: Logan Co., OH

SEARS, Cyrus   ES: Bucyrus, Crawford Co., OH
                   B: Meredith Township, Delaware Co., NY

SHAFFER, William   ES: Cincinnati, Hamilton Co., OH
                   B: Bavaria, Germany

SHARPLESS, Edward Clay ES: Columbus, Franklin Co., OH
                        B: Marion Co., OH

SHIELDS, Bernard   ES: Ironton, Lawrence Co., OH
                   B: Ireland

SLAGLE, Oscar   ES: Manlius, Bureau Co., IL
                   B: Fulton Co., OH

*SLAVENS, Samuel   ES: Wakefield, Pike Co., OH
                   B: Pike Co., OH

SMITH, James (Ovid) ES: Circleville, Pickaway Co., OH
                     B: Fredericksburg, Fredericksburg Co., VA

SMITH, Otis W.   ES: Champaign, OH
                   B: Logan Co., OH

SMITH, William H. ES: Cincinnati, Hamilton Co., OH
                   B: Lapeer, Lapeer Co., MI

SPENCE, Orizoba   ES: Cincinnati, Hamilton Co., OH
                   B: Forest Co., PA

*SPRAGUE, John Wilson ES: Sandusky, Erie Co., OH
                       B: White Creek, Washington Co., NY

STACEY, Charles   ES: Norwalk, Huron Co., OH
                   B: England

STANLEY, David Sloane ES: Congress, Wayne Co., OH
                       B: Cedar Valley, OH

STAUFFER, Rudolph ES: Cincinnati, Hamilton Co., OH
                   B: Berne, Switzerland

STEELE, John Whedon ES: Oberlin, Lorain Co., OH
                     B: Middleburg, Logan Co., OH

STICKELS, Joseph   ES: Bethany, OH
                   B: Butler Co., OII

STICKOFFER, Julius Henry ES: Cincinnati, Hamilton Co., OH
                          B: Switzerland

STOKES, Alonzo   ES: Cincinnati, Hamilton Co., OH
                   B: Logan Co., OH

STURGEON, James K. ES: Lancaster, Fairfield Co., OH
                    B: Perry Co., OH

SULLIVAN, Thomas   ES: Cincinnati, Hamilton Co., OH
                   B: Covington, Kenton Co., KY

SURLES, William H.	ES: Steubenville, Jefferson Co., OH B: Steubenville, Jefferson Co., OH
SWAYNE, Wager	ES: Columbus, Franklin Co., OH B: Columbus, Franklin Co., OH
THACKER, Brian Miles	ES: Salt Lake City, Salt Lake Co., UT B: Columbus, Franklin Co., OH
*THOMAS, Charles L.	ES: Cincinnati, Hamilton Co., OH B: Philadelphia, Philadelphia Co., PA
THOMPSON, Charles Augustus	ES: Kalamazoo, Kalamazoo Co., MI B: Perrysburg, Wood Co., OH
THOMPSON, Freeman C.	ES: Marietta, Washington Co., OH B: Monroe Co., OH
THOMPSON, Thomas W.	ES: Urbana, Champaign Co., OH B: Champaign Co., OH
TORGLER, Ernest R.	ES: Toledo, Lucas Co., OH B: Mecklenburg, Germany
*TOWLE, John Roderick	ES: Cleveland, Cuyahoga Co., OH B: Cleveland, Cuyahoga Co., OH
TREAT, Howell B.	ES: Painesville, Lake Co., OH B: Painesville, Lake Co., OH
TYRRELL, George William	ES: Cincinnati, Hamilton Co., OH B: Ireland
VAN MATRE, Joseph	ES: Middleport, Meigs Co., OH B: Mason Co., WV
VANCE, Wilson J.	ES: Findlay, Hancock Co., OH B: Findlay, Hancock Co., OH
WAGEMAN, John H.	ES: Amelia, Clermont Co., OH B: Amelia, Clermont Co., OH
WALKER, Allen	ES: Cincinnati, Hamilton Co., OH B: Patriot, Switzerland Co., IN
WALKER, James C.	ES: Springfield, Clark Co., OH B: Harmony, Clark Co., OH
WALLER, Francis A.	ES: DeSoto, Vernon Co., WI B: Gurney, OH
WARD, Nelson W.	ES: Rutland, Meigs Co., OH B: Madison Township, Columbiana Co., OH
WEBBER, Alason P.	ES: Chillicothe, Ross Co., OH B: Greene Co., NY
WELSH, Edward	ES: Cincinnati, Hamilton Co., OH B: Ireland
WENDE, Bruno	ES: Canton, Stark Co., OH B: Germany
*WILEY, James	ES: Bellville, Richland Co., OH B: OH
WILHELM, George	ES: Lancaster, Fairfield Co., OH B: Scioto Co., OH
WILLIAMS, William Haliday	ES: Lima, Allen Co., OH B: Williamstown, Hancock Co., OH
WILSON, Benjamin	ES: Cincinnati, Hamilton Co., OH B: Pittsburgh, Allegheny Co., PA
WILSON, John Alfred	ES: Perrysburg, Wood Co., OH B: Columbus, Franklin Co., OH
WILSON, Milden H.	ES: Newark, Licking Co., OH B: Huron Co., OH
*WINDER, David Francis	ES: Columbus, Franklin Co., OH B: Edinboro, Erie Co., PA
WOLLAM, John	ES: Jackson, Jackson Co., OH B: Hamilton, Butler Co., OH
WOOD, Mark	ES: Portage, Wood Co., OH B: England

*WOODFORD, Howard E.	ES: Barberton, Summit Co., OH B: Barberton, Summit Co., OH
WOODS, Daniel A. (Wood)	ES: Wheeling, Ohio Co., WV B: OH Co., WV
YEAGER, Jacob F.	ES: Tiffin, Seneca Co., OH B: New Texas, Lehigh Co., PA
YOUNG, Calvary Morris	ES: Hopeville, Clark Co., IA B: Washington Co., OH
*YOUNG, Rodger W.	ES: Clyde, Sandusky Co., OH B: Tiffin, Seneca Co., OH
YOUNKER, John L.	ES: Lancaster, Fairfield Co., OH B: Wurttemberg, Germany

U.S. Army Air Corps

*BAKER, Addison Earl	ES: Akron, Summit Co., OH B: Chicago, Cook Co., IL
*METZGER Jr., William Edward	ES: Lima, Allen Co., OH B: Lima, Allen Co., OH
RICKENBACKER, Edward Vernon	ES: Columbus, Franklin Co., OH B: Columbus, Franklin Co., OH

U.S. Navy

BARTON, Thomas	ES: OH B: Cleveland, Cuyahoga Co., OH
BEASLEY, Harry C.	ES: OH B: OH
BOERS, Edward William	ES: KY B: Cincinnati, Hamilton Co., OH
BROCK, George F.	ES: CA B: Cleveland, Montgomery Co., OH
BUTTS, George	ES: Cleveland, Cuyahoga Co., OH B: Rome, Oneida Co., NY
DORMAN, John Henry	ES: Cincinnati, Hamilton Co., OH B: Cincinnati, Hamilton Co., OH
*ESTOCIN, Michael John	ES: Akron, Summit Co., OH B: Turtle Creek, Allegheny Co., PA
GARY, Donald Arthur	ES: OH B: Findlay, Hancock Co., OH
HALEY, James	ES: OH B: Ireland
HANFORD, Burke	ES: OH B: Toledo, Lucas Co., OH
HARNER, Joseph Gabriel	ES: OH B: Louisville, Stark Co., OH
JARDINE, Alexander	ES: OH B: Inverness, Scotland
*KIDD, Isaac Campbell	ES: OH B: Cleveland, Cuyahoga Co., OH
McGUNIGAL, Patrick	ES: OH B: Hubbard, Trumbull Co., OH
McHUGH, Martin	ES: OH B: Cincinnati, Hamilton Co., OH
PETTY, Orlando Henderson	ES: PA B: Harrison, Hamilton Co., OH
READ, Charles A.	ES: OH B: Sweden
*SCOTT, Robert Raymond	ES: OH B: Massillon, Stark Co., OH
SHEPARD, Louis Capet	ES: OH B: Ashtabula, Ashtabula Co., OH

STUPKA, Laddie	ES: OH B: Cleveland, Cuyahoga Co., OH
*WARD, James Richard	ES: Springfield, Clark Co., OH B: Springfield, Clark Co., OH
WILLIAMS, Jay P.	ES: OH B: Orland, Steuben Co., IN
WOOD, Robert B.	ES: OH B: New Garden, OH

U.S. Marine Corps

*BAUGH, William Bernard	ES: Harrison, Hamilton Co., OH B: McKinney, Lincoln Co., KY
*BERRY, Charles Joseph	ES: Ohio B: Lorain, Lorain Co., OH
*DICKEY, Douglas Eugene	ES: Cincinnati, Hamilton Co., OH B: Greenville, Darke Co., OH
*EPPERSON, Harold Glenn	ES: OH B: Akron, Summit Co., OH
*FOSTER, William Adelbert	ES: OH B: Cleveland, Cuyahoga Co., OH
JACKSON, Arthur Junior	ES: Portland, Multnomah Co., OR B: Cleveland, Cuyahoga Co., OH
*KELLY, John Doran	ES: Homestead, Allegheny Co., PA B: Youngstown, Mahoning Co., OH
*MARTIN, Harry Linn	ES: OH B: Bucyrus, Crawford Co., OH
*MASON, Leonard Foster	ES: OH B: Middlesboro, Bell Co., KY
*NEWLIN, Melvin Earl	ES: Cleveland, Cuyahoga Co., OH B: Wellsville, Columbiana Co., OH
ORNDOFF, Harry Westley	ES: CA B: Sandusky, Erie Co., OH
OSTERMANN, Edward Albert	ES: OH B: Columbus, Franklin Co., OH
*PAUL, Joe Calvin	ES: Dayton, Montgomery Co., OH B: Williamsburg, Whitley Co., KY
REID, George Croghan	ES: OH B: Lorain, Lorain Co., OH
*STEIN, Tony	ES: OH B: Dayton, Montgomery Co., OH
*THOMAS, Herbert Joseph	ES: WV B: Columbus, Franklin Co., OH
UPHAM, Oscar Jefferson	ES: IL B: Toledo, Lucas Co., OH

OKLAHOMA

U.S. Army

*BURRIS, Tony K.	ES: Blanchard, McClain Co., OK B: Blanchard, McClain Co., OK
*CAREY Jr., Charles F.	ES: Cheyenne, Laramie Co., WY B: Canadian, Pittsburg Co., OK
CHAPMAN, Amos	ES: Fort Supply, Indian Territory (Oklahoma) B: Kalamazoo, Kalamazoo Co., MI
CHILDERS, Ernest "Chief"	ES: Tulsa, Tulsa Co., OK B: Broken Arrow, Tulsa Co., OK
CREWS, John R.	ES: Bowlegs, Seminole Co., OK B: Golden, McCurtain Co., OK
EPPS, Joseph L.	ES: Indian Territory (Oklahoma) B: Jamestown, Moniteau Co., MO

*HARMON, Roy W.	ES: Pixley, Tulare Co., CA B: Talala, Rogers Co., OK
HAYS, George Price	ES: Okarche, Kingfisher Co., OK B: Chee Foo, China
*HENRY, Frederick F.	ES: Clinton, Custer Co., OK B: Vian, Sequoyah Co., OK
*KINER, Harold G.	ES: Enid, Garfield Co., OK B: Aline, Alfalfa Co., OK
*McGILL, Troy A.	ES: Ada, Pontotoc Co., OK B: Knoxville, Knox Co., TN
MONTGOMERY, Jack Cleveland	ES: Sallisaw, Sequoyah Co., OK B: Long, OK
*PEREZ Jr., Manuel	ES: Chicago, Cook Co., IL B: Oklahoma City, Oklahoma Co., OK
*PIERCE, Larry Stanley	ES: Fresno, Fresno Co., CA B: Wewoka, Seminole Co., OK
*PITTS, Riley Leroy	ES: Wichita, Sedgwick Co., KS B: Fallis, OK
*REESE Jr., John N.	ES: Pryor, Mayes Co., OK B: Muskogee, Muskogee Co., OK
SAMPLER, Samuel M.	ES: Altus, Jackson Co., OK B: Decatur, Wise Co., TX
SCHAUER, Henry	ES: Scobey, Daniels Co., MT B: Clinton, Custer Co., OK
*SHOCKLEY, William Ralph	ES: Selma, Fresno Co., CA B: Bokoshe, LeFlore Co., OK
TREADWELL, Jack Lemaster	ES: Snyder, Kiowa Co., OK B: Ashland, Clay Co., AL
TURNER, Harold Leo	ES: Seminole, Seminole Co., OK B: Aurora, Lawrence Co., MO
*WALLACE, Herman C.	ES: Lubbock, Lubbock Co., TX B: Marlow, Stephens Co., OK

U.S. Army Air Corps

| *GOTT, Donald Joseph | ES: Arnett, Ellis Co., OK
B: Arnett, Ellis Co., OK |
| *VANCE Jr., Leon Robert | ES: Garden City, Nassau Co., NY
B: Enid, Garfield Co., OK |

U.S. Navy

| *EVANS, Ernest Edwin "Chief" | ES: OK
B: Pawnee, Pawnee Co., OK |
| McCOOL Jr., Richard Miles | ES: OK
B: Tishomingo, Johnston Co., OK |

U.S. Marine Corps

*BAILEY, Kenneth Dillon	ES: IL B: Pawnee, Pawnee Co., OK
*SCHWAB, Albert Ernest	ES: Tulsa, Tulsa Co., OK B: Washington, D.C.
SMITH, John Lucian	ES: OK B: Lexington, Cleveland Co., OK

OREGON

U.S. Army

| ALLWORTH, Edward C. | ES: Corvallis, Benton Co., OR
B: Crawford, WA |
| *DAHL, Larry Gilbert | ES: Portland, Multnomah Co., OR
B: Oregon City, Clackamas Co., OR |

HIGH, Frank Charles	ES: Ashland, Jackson Co., OR B: Dunningham, Yolo Co., CA
*HOLCOMB, John Noble	ES: Corvallis, Benton Co., OR B: Baker, Baker Co., OR
*KAUFMAN, Loren R.	ES: The Dalles, Wasco Co., OR B: The Dalles, Wasco Co., OR
KILBOURNE Jr., Charles Evans	ES: Portland, Multnomah Co., OR B: Fort Myer, Arlington Co., VA
PHIFE, Lewis	ES: Marion, Marion Co., OR B: Des Moines Co., IA
ROBERTSON, Marcus William	ES: Hood River, Hood River Co., OR B: Flintville, WI
*STRYKER, Stuart S.	ES: Portland, Multnomah Co., OR B: Portland, Multnomah Co., OR
*YABES, Maximo	ES: Eugene, Lane Co., OR B: Lodi, San Joaquin Co., CA

U.S. Army Air Corps

*KINGSLEY, David Richard	ES: Portland, Multnomah Co., OR B: Portland, Multnomah Co., OR

U.S. Navy

FADDEN, Harry Delmar	ES: WA B: The Dalles, Wasco Co., OR

U.S. Marine Corps

JACKSON, Arthur Junior	ES: Portland, Multnomah Co., OR B: Cleveland, Cuyahoga Co., OH
*MARTINI, Gary Wayne	ES: Portland, Multnomah Co., OR B: Lexington, Lexington Co., VA

PENNSYLVANIA

U.S. Army

ALLEN, William	ES: Philadelphia, Philadelphia Co., PA B: Philadelphia, Philadelphia Co., PA
AMMERMAN, Robert Wesley	ES: Milesburg, Centre Co., PA B: Centre Co., PA
ANDERSON, Everett W.	ES: Philadelphia, Philadelphia Co., PA B: near Phoenixville, Chester Co., PA
ANDERSON, Thomas	ES: Wheeling, Ohio Co., WV B: Scenery Hill, Washington Co., PA
APPLE, Andrew O.	ES: New Manchester, Hancock Co., WV B: Northampton, Northampton Co., PA
ARNOLD, Abraham Kerns	ES: Bedford, Bedford Co., PA B: Bedford, Bedford Co., PA
BAIRD, Absalom	ES: Washington, Washington Co., PA B: Washington, Washington Co., PA
BEAUMONT, Eugene Beauharnais	ES: Wilks-Barre, Luzerne Co., PA B: Wilks-Barre, Luzerne Co., PA
BEEBE, William Sully	ES: Philadelphia, Philadelphia Co., PA B: Ithaca, Tompkins Co., NY
*BENJAMIN Jr., George	ES: Carney's Point, Salem Co., NJ B: Philadelphia, Philadelphia Co., PA
BENNETT, Orrin	ES: Towanda, Bradford Co., PA B: Bradford Co., PA
BENYAURD, William Henry Harrison	ES: Philadelphia, Philadelphia Co., PA B: Philadelphia, Philadelphia Co., PA

BETTS, Charles Malone	ES: Philadelphia, Philadelphia Co., PA B: Bucks Co., PA
BEYER, Hillary	ES: Philadelphia, Philadelphia Co., PA B: Montgomery Co., PA
BINGHAM, Henry Harrison	ES: Canonsburg, Washington Co., Pensylvania B: Philadelphia, Philadelphia Co., PA
BISHOP, Francis A.	ES: Harrisburg, Dauphin Co., PA B: Bradford Co., PA
BLACKMAR, Wilmon Whilldin	ES: Philadelphia, Philadelphia Co., PA B: Bristol, Bucks Co., PA
BLACKWOOD, William Robert Douglas	ES: Philadelphia, Philadelphia Co., PA B: Hollywood, County Wicklow, Ireland
BLAIR, James	ES: Camp Winfield Scott, Humbolt Co., NV B: Schuyler Co., PA
BLICKENSDERGER, Milton	ES: Shanesville, OH B: Lancaster, Lancaster Co., PA
BLUCHER, Charles	ES: Philadelphia, Philadelphia Co., PA B: Germany
BONEBRAKE, Henry G.	ES: Franklin Co., PA B: Waynesboro, Franklin Co., PA
BONNAFFON Jr., Sylvester	ES: Philadelphia, Philadelphia Co., PA B: Philadelphia, Philadelphia Co., PA
BOON, Hugh Patterson	ES: Washington, Washington Co., PA B: Washington, Washington Co., PA
BOURKE, John Gregory	ES: Chicago, Cook Co., IL B: Philadelphia, Philadelphia Co., PA
BRANNIGAN, Felix	ES: Pittsburgh, Allegheny Co., PA B: Ireland
BREST, Lewis Francis	ES: Pittsburgh, Allegheny Co., PA B: Mercer, Mercer Co., PA
BREWSTER, Andre Walker	ES: Philadelphia, Philadelphia Co., PA B: Hoboken, Hudson Co., NJ
BREYER, Charles	ES: Philadelphia, Philadelphia Co., PA B: England
BROGAN, James	ES: Harrisburg, Dauphin Co., PA B: County Donegal, Ireland
BRONSON, James H.	ES: Trumbell Co., OH B: Indiana Co., PA
BROWN, Benjamin	ES: Harrisburg, Dauphin Co., PA B: Spotsylvania Co., VA
BROWN, Charles E.	ES: Schuylkill Haven, Schuylkill Co., PA B: Schuylkill Co., PA
BROWN, Jeremiah Z.	ES: Curllsville, Clarion Co., PA B: near Rural Valley, Armstrong Co., PA
*BROWN, Melvin L.	ES: Erie, Erie Co., PA B: Mahaffey, Clearfield Co., PA
BURNETT, George Ritter	ES: Spring Mills, Centre Co., PA B: Lower Providence Township, PA
BUZZARD, Ulysses G.	ES: Pittsburgh, Allegheny Co., PA B: Armstrong, PA
CALDWELL, Daniel G.	ES: Philadelphia, Philadelphia Co., PA B: Marble Hill, Montgomery Co., PA
CANFIELD, Heth	ES: Carlisle, Cumberland Co., PA B: New Milford, Litchfield Co., CT
CAPEHART, Charles E.	ES: Washington, D.C. B: Conemaugh Township, PA
CAPEHART, Henry	ES: Bridgeport, Belmont Co., OH B: Johnstown, Cambria Co., PA

*CAREY, Alvin P.   ES: Laughlintown, Westmoreland Co., PA
                           B: Lycippus, PA

CARLISLE, Casper R.   ES: Pittsburgh, Allegheny Co., PA
                           B: Allegheny Co., PA

CARPENTER, Louis Henry   ES: Philadelphia, Philadelphia Co., PA
                           B: Glassboro, Gloucester Co., NJ

CARSON, William J.   ES: North Greenfield, Highland Co., OH
                           B: Washington Co., PA

CART, Jacob   ES: Carlisle, Cumberland Co., PA
                           B: Carlisle, Cumberland Co., PA

CASEY, Henry   ES: Bloomingburg, Fayette Co., OH
                           B: New Geneva, Fayette Co., PA

CASEY, James Seaman   ES: New York, NY
                           B: Philadelphia, Philadelphia Co., PA

CHAMBERS, Joseph B.   ES: East Brook, PA
                           B: Beaver Co., PA

CLARK, James G.   ES: Philadelphia, Philadelphia Co., PA
                           B: Germantown, Philadelphia Co., PA

CLARK, Wilfred   ES: Philadelphia, Philadelphia Co., PA
                           B: Philadelphia, Philadelphia Co., PA

CLARK, William A.   ES: Shelbyville, MN
                           B: PA

CLAUSEN, Charles H.   ES: Philadelphia, Philadelphia Co., PA
                           B: Philadelphia, Philadelphia Co., PA

CLAY, Cecil   ES: Philadelphia, Philadelphia Co., PA
                           B: Philadelphia, Philadelphia Co., PA

CLOPP, John E.   ES: Philadelphia, Philadelphia Co., PA
                           B: Philadelphia, Philadelphia Co., PA

COLLIS, Charles Henry
Tucky   ES: Philadelphia, Philadelphia Co., PA
                           B: Cork, County Cork, Ireland

COMFORT, John W.   ES: Philadelphia, Philadelphia Co., PA
                           B: Philadelphia, Philadelphia Co., PA

CONNELL, Trustrim   ES: Port Kennedy, PA
                           B: Lancaster, Lancaster Co., PA

CONNER, Richard   ES: Burlington, Burlington Co., NJ
                           B: Philadelphia, Philadelphia Co., PA

COOKE, Walter Howard   ES: Norristown, Montgomery Co., PA
                           B: Norristown, Montgomery Co., PA

CORCORAN, Michael   ES: Wheeling, Ohio Co., WV
                           B: Philadelphia, Philadelphia Co., PA

CORSON, Joseph Kirby   ES: Philadelphia, Philadelphia Co., PA
                           B: Plymouth Meeting, Montgomery Co., PA

CRANDALL, Charles   ES: Philadelphia, Philadelphia Co., PA
                           B: Worcester, Worcester Co., MA

*CRESCENZ, Michael
Joseph   ES: Philadelphia, Philadelphia Co., PA
                           B: Philadelphia, Philadelphia Co., PA

CUNNINGHAM, Francis
Marion   ES: Springfield, Delaware Co., PA
                           B: Somerset, Somerset Co., PA

CUNNINGHAM, James
Smith   ES: Bloomington, McLean Co., IL
                           B: Washington Co., PA

DAILY, Charles   ES: Philadelphia, Philadelphia Co., PA
                           B: Mallow, County Cork, Ireland

DAVIDSIZER, John A.   ES: Lewistown, Mifflin Co., PA
                           B: Milford, Pike Co., PA

DAVIS, Charles C.   ES: Harrisburg, Dauphin Co., PA
                           B: Harrisburg, Dauphin Co., PA

DAY, Charles   ES: Richmond, Philadelphia Co., PA
                           B: West Laurens, Otsego Co., NY

DEARY, George   ES: Philadelphia, Philadelphia Co., PA
                           B: Philadelphia, Philadelphia Co., PA

DeLACEY, Patrick   ES: Scranton, Lackawanna Co., PA
                           B: Carbondale, Lackawanna Co., PA

DELANEY, John Carroll   ES: Honesdale, Wayne Co., PA
                           B: Ireland

DeLAVIE, Hiram H.   ES: Allegheny Co., PA
                           B: Stark Co., OH

*DESIDERIO, Reginald
Benjamin   ES: Gilroy, Santa Clara Co., CA
                           B: Clairton, Allegheny Co., PA

DeSWAN, John Francis   ES: Philadelphia, Philadelphia Co., PA
                           B: Philadelphia, Philadelphia Co., PA

DOLBY, David Charles   ES: Philadelphia, Philadelphia Co., PA
                           B: Norristown, Montgomery Co., PA

DONALDSON, John P.   ES: Butler, Butler Co., PA
                           B: Butler Co., PA

DOUGHERTY, Michael   ES: Philadelphia, Philadelphia Co., PA
                           B: Falcarragh, County Donegal, Ireland

DOUGHERTY, William   ES: Philadelphia, Philadelphia Co., PA
                           B: Detroit, Wayne Co., MI

*DUTKO, John W.   ES: Riverside, Burlington Co., NJ
                           B: Dilltown, Indiana Co., PA

EDGERTON, Nathan
Huntley   ES: Philadelphia, Philadelphia Co., PA
                           B: Barnesville, Belmont Co., OH

ELLIOTT, Alexander   ES: North Sewickley, Allegheny Co., PA
                           B: Beaver Co., PA

ELLIS, Horace   ES: Chippewa Falls, Chippewa Co., WI
                           B: Mercer Co., PA

ENGLE, James Edgar   ES: Chester, Delaware Co., PA
                           B: Chester, Delaware Co., PA

*ENGLISH Jr., Glenn Harry ES: Philadelphia, Philadelphia Co., PA
                           B: Altoona, Blair Co., PA

EVANS, Thomas   ES: Johnstown, Cambria Co., PA
                           B: Wales

EWING, John C.   ES: Greensburg, Westmoreland Co., PA
                           B: Ligonier Valley, Westmoreland Co., PA

FARREN, Daniel   ES: Philadelphia, Philadelphia Co., PA
                           B: County Derry, Ireland

FASNACHT, Charles H.   ES: Philadelphia, Philadelphia Co., PA
                           B: Lancaster Co., PA

FASSETT, John Barclay   ES: Philadelphia, Philadelphia Co., PA
                           B: Philadelphia, Philadelphia Co., PA

FEASTER, Mosheim   ES: Cleveland, Cuyahoga Co., OH
                           B: Schellsburg, Bedford Co., PA

FISHER, John H.   ES: Chicago, Cook Co., IL
                           B: Monmouth, PA

FISHER, Joseph   ES: Philadelphia, Philadelphia Co., PA
                           B: Philadelphia, Philadelphia Co., PA

FLANAGAN, Augustin D.   ES: Chester Springs, Chester Co., PA
                           B: Loretto, Cambria Co., PA

FOX, William R.   ES: Philadelphia, Philadelphia Co., PA
                           B: Philadelphia, Philadelphia Co., PA

FRICK, Jacob G.   ES: Pottsville, Schuylkill Co., PA
                           B: Northumberland, Northumberland Co.,
                              PA

FUNK, West   ES: Philadelphia, Philadelphia Co., PA
                           B: Boston, Suffolk Co., MA

FUNK Jr., Leonard Alfred   ES: Wilkinsburg, Allegheny Co., PA
                           B: Braddock Township, Allegheny Co., PA

FURMAN, Chester S.   ES: Bloomsburg, Columbia Co., PA
                           B: Columbia, Lancaster Co., PA

FURNESS, Frank   ES: Philadelphia, Philadelphia Co., PA
                           B: Philadelphia, Philadelphia Co., PA

GALLOWAY, George Norton   ES: Philadelphia, Philadelphia Co., PA
                           B: Philadelphia, Philadelphia Co., PA

GALLOWAY, John   ES: Philadelphia, Philadelphia Co., PA
                           B: Philadelphia, Philadelphia Co., PA

GEDEON, Louis   ES: Pittsburgh, Allegheny Co., PA
                           B: Pittsburgh, Allegheny Co., PA

GILLIGAN, Edward Lyons   ES: Philadelphia, Philadelphia Co., PA
                           B: Philadelphia, Philadelphia Co., PA

GION, Joseph   ES: Allegheny Co., PA
                           B: Alsace-Lorraine area, Germany

GLAVINSKI, Albert   ES: Pittsburgh, Allegheny Co., PA
                           B: Germany (Prussia)

GOODMAN, Willaim Ernest   ES: Philadelphia, Philadelphia Co., PA
                           B: Philadelphia, Philadelphia Co., PA

GRAUL, William L.   ES: Reading, Berks Co., PA
                           B: Reading, Berks Co., PA

GRAY, Robert A.   ES: Groton, New London Co., CT
                           B: Philadelphia, Philadelphia Co., PA

GREENAWALT, Abraham   ES: Salem, Columbiana Co., OH
                           B: Montgomery Co., PA

GRESSER, Ignatz   ES: Allentown, Lehigh Co., PA
                           B: Malach, Germany

GUNTHER, Jacob   ES: Philadelphia, Philadelphia Co., PA
                           B: Schuylkill Co., PA

*HALLMAN, Sherwood H.   ES: Spring City, Chester Co., PA
                           B: Spring City, Chester Co., PA

HARMON, Amzi Davis   ES: Greensburg, Westmoreland Co., PA
                           B: Wilkinsburg, Allegheny Co., PA

*HARR, Harry R.   ES: East Freedom, Blair Co., PA
                           B: Pine Croft, PA

HARRIS, George W.   ES: Bellefonte, Centre Co., PA
                           B: Schuylkill, Philadelphia Co., PA

*HARTELL, Lee Ross   ES: Danbury, Fairfield Co., CT
                           B: Philadelphia, Philadelphia Co., PA

HARTRANFT, John Frederic   ES: Norristown, Montgomery Co., PA
                           B: New Hanover Township, Montgomery
                              Co., PA

HARVEY, Raymond   ES: Pasadena, Los Angeles Co., CA
                           B: Ford City, Armstrong Co., PA

HAWKINS, Martin Jones   ES: Portsmouth, Scioto Co., OH
                           B: Mercer Co., PA

HAWKINS, Thomas R.   ES: Philadelphia, Philadelphia Co., PA
                           B: Cincinnati, Hamilton Co., OH

HENRY, Guy Vernor   ES: Reading, Berks Co., PA
                           B: Fort Smith, Indian Territory

HERRON, Francis Jay   ES: Pittsburgh, Allegheny Co., PA
                           B: Pittsburgh, Allegheny Co., PA

HERRON, Leander   ES: Pittsburgh, Allegheny Co., PA
                           B: Bucks Co., PA

HEYL, Charles Pettit Heath ES: Camden, Camden Co., NJ
                           B: Philadelphia, Philadelphia Co., PA

HIGBY, Charles   ES: New Brighton, Beaver Co., PA
                           B: Pittsburgh, Allegheny Co., PA

HILL, Henry   ES: Harrisburg, Dauphin Co., PA
                           B: Schuylkill Co., PA

HILL, James Madison   ES: Cincinnati, Hamilton Co., OH
                           B: Washington Co., PA

HIMMELSBACK, Michael   ES: Harrisburg, Dauphin Co., PA
                           B: Allegheny Co., PA

HOFFMAN, Thomas W.   ES: Harrisburg, Dauphin Co., PA
                           B: Perrysburg, Allegheny Co., PA

HOGAN, Franklin   ES: Howard, Centre Co., PA
                           B: Centre Co., PA

HOOVER, Samuel   ES: Harrisburg, Dauphin Co., PA
                           B: Dauphin Co., PA

HORNER, Freeman Victor   ES: Shamokin, Northumberland Co., PA
                           B: Mount Carmel, Northumberland Co.,
                              PA

HOTTENSTINE, Solomon J.   ES: Philadelphia, Philadelphia Co., PA
                           B: Lehigh Co., PA

HOWARD, Henderson Calvin   ES: Indiana, Indiana Co., PA
                           B: Indiana Co., PA

HUBBARD, Thomas H.   ES: Philadelphia, Philadelphia Co., PA
                           B: Philadelphia, Philadelphia Co., PA

HUFF, James W.   ES: Vanburan, PA
                           B: Washington, Washington Co., PA

HUIDEKOPER, Henry
Shippen   ES: Philadelphia, Philadelphia Co., PA
                           B: Meadville, Crawford Co., PA

HUNTERSON, John C.   ES: Philadelphia, Philadelphia Co., PA
                           B: Philadelphia, Philadelphia Co., PA

HYATT, Theodore   ES: Gardner, Grundy Co., IL
                           B: PA

ILGENFRITZ, Charles Henry ES: Harrisburg, Dauphin Co., PA
                           B: York Co., PA

JENNINGS, James T.   ES: Luzerne, Luzerne Co., PA
                           B: Devonshire, England

JOHNS, Henry T.   ES: Hinsdale, Berkshire Co., MA
                           B: Philadelphia, Philadelphia Co., PA

JOHNSON, Joseph Esrey   ES: Philadelphia, Philadelphia Co., PA
                           B: Lower Merion, Montgomery Co., PA

JOHNSON, Ruel M.   ES: Goshen, Elkhart Co., IN
                           B: Harbor Creek Township, Erie Co., PA

JOHNSON, Samuel   ES: Connellsville, Fayette Co., PA
                           B: Springfield Township, Delaware Co., PA

JOHNSTON, David H.   ES: Warsaw, Hancock Co., IL
                           B: Indiana Co., PA

KAY, John   ES: Philadelphia, Philadelphia Co., PA
                           B: Lancashire, England

*KEFURT, Gus   ES: Youngstown, Mahoning Co., OH
                           B: Greenville, Mercer Co., PA

KELLY, Alexander   ES: Allegheny, Allegheny Co., PA
                           B: Saltsburg, Indiana Co., PA

KELLY, Charles E.   ES: Pittsburgh, Allegheny Co., PA
                           B: Pittsburgh, Allegheny Co., PA

*KELLY, John D.   ES: Cambridge Springs, Crawford Co., PA
                           B: Venango Township, Crawford Co., PA

KEPHART, James   ES: Dubuque, Dubuque Co., IA
                           B: Venango Co., PA

KERR, Thomas R.   ES: Pittsburgh, Allegheny Co., PA
                           B: near Colleraine, County Derry, Ireland

KILMARTIN, John   ES: Philadelphia, Philadelphia Co., PA
                           B: Montreal, Canada

KINDIG, John M.   ES: Wilkins, Allegheny Co., PA
                           B: East Liberty, Allegheny Co., PA

KINSEY, John   ES: Maytown, Lancaster Co., PA
                           B: Lancaster Co., PA

KIRK, John   ES: Harrisburg, Dauphin Co., PA
                           B: York, York Co., PA

KIRKWOOD, John A.   ES: North Platte Barracks, Lincoln Co., NE
                     B: Allegheny City, Allegheny Co., PA

KITCHEN, George Krause   ES: Harrisburg, Dauphin Co., PA
                         B: Lebanon Co., PA

KNAPPENBERGER, Alton W.   ES: Almount, Bucks Co., PA
                          B: Coopersburg, Lehigh Co., PA

KRAMER, Theodore L.   ES: Danville, Montour Co., PA
                      B: Luzerne Co., PA

*KREHER, Wendelin   ES: Philadelphia, Philadelphia Co., PA
                    B: Stetten, Prussia

LANDIS, James Parker   ES: Reedsville, Mifflin Co., PA
                       B: Mifflin Co., PA

LAWS, Robert Earl   ES: Altoona, Blair Co., PA
                    B: Altoona, Blair Co., PA

LEE, Fitz   ES: Philadelphia, Philadelphia Co., PA
            B: Dinwiddie Co., VA

LEONARD, William Edman   ES: Jacksonville, PA
                         B: Greene Co., PA

LEWIS, Dewitt Clinton   ES: West Chester, Chester Co., PA
                        B: West Chester, Chester Co., PA

LILLEY, John   ES: Lewistown, Mifflin Co., PA
               B: Mifflin Co., PA

*LOBAUGH, Donald Ronald   ES: Freeport, Armstrong Co., PA
                          B: Freeport, Armstrong Co., PA

LOWER, Cyrus B.   ES: New Castle, Lawrence Co., PA
                  B: Lawrence, PA

LUTY, Gotlieb   ES: West Manchester, York Co., PA
                B: Allegheny Co., PA

LYTLE, Leonidas S.   ES: Cleveland, Cuyahoga Co., OH
                     B: Warren Co., PA

MACLAY, William Palmer   ES: Altoona, Blair Co., PA
                         B: Spruce Creek, Huntingdon Co., PA

MARM Jr., Walter Joseph   ES: Pittsburgh, Allegheny Co., PA
                          B: Washington, Washington Co., PA

MARQUETTE, Charles D.   ES: Campbelltown, Lebanon Co., PA
                        B: Lebanon Co., PA

MARTIN, Sylvester Hopkins   ES: Philadelphia, Philadelphia Co., PA
                            B: Chester Co., PA

MATTHEWS, John C.   ES: Greensburg, Westmoreland Co., PA
                    B: Westmoreland Co., PA

MATTHEWS, Milton   ES: Pittsburgh, Allegheny Co., PA
                   B: Pittsburgh, Allegheny Co., PA

MAY, John   ES: Philadelphia, Philadelphia Co., PA
            B: Wurttemberg, Germany

MAY, William C.   ES: Maysville, Franklin Co., IA
                  B: PA

McADAMS, Peter   ES: Philadelphia, Philadelphia Co., PA
                 B: Armagh, County Armagh, Ireland

McANALLY, Charles   ES: Philadelphia, Philadelphia Co., PA
                    B: Ireland

McCAMMON, William
Wallace   ES: Montgomery City, Montgomery Co.,
              MO
          B: Shippensburg, Cumberland Co., PA

McCORMICK, Michael P.   ES: Harrisburg, Dauphin Co., PA
                        B: Rutland, Rutland Co., VT

*McGRAW, Francis Xavier   ES: Camden, Camden Co., NJ
                         B: Philadelphia, Philadelphia Co., PA

McKEEVER, Michael   ES: Philadelphia, Philadelphia Co., PA
                    B: Ireland

McKOWN, Nathaniel A.   ES: Philadelphia, Philadelphia Co., PA
                       B: Susquehanna Co., PA

McMURTRY, George G.   ES: New York, NY
                      B: Pittsburgh, Allegheny Co., PA

*McVEIGH, John J.   ES: Philadelphia, Philadelphia Co., PA
                    B: Philadelphia, Philadelphia Co., PA

MEARS, George W.   ES: Bloomsburg, Columbia Co., PA
                   B: Bloomsburg, Columbia Co., PA

MECHLIN, Henry W.B.   ES: Pittsburgh, Allegheny Co., PA
                      B: Mount Pleasant, Westmoreland Co., PA

MERLI, Gino Joseph   ES: Peckville, Lackawanna Co., PA
                     B: Scranton, Lackawanna Co., PA

MERRIFIELD, James K.   ES: Manlius, Bureau Co., IL
                       B: Hyde Park, Westmoreland Co., PA

*MESSERSCHMIDT,
Harold O.   ES: Chester, Delaware Co., PA
            B: Grier City, PA

*MESTROVITCH, James I.   ES: Pittsburgh, Allegheny Co., PA
                         B: Crna Cora, Yugoslavia

MILLER, George W.   ES: Philadelphia, Philadelphia Co., PA
                    B: Philadelphia, Philadelphia Co., PA

MILLER, William Edward   ES: Newville, Cumberland Co., PA
                         B: West Hill, Cumberland Co., PA

MINDIL, George Washington   ES: Philadelphia, Philadelphia Co., PA
                            B: near Frankfort, Germany

*MINICK, John W.   ES: Carlisle, Cumberland Co., PA
                   B: Wall, Allegheny Co., PA

MITCHELL, Alexander H.   ES: Hamilton, Jefferson Co., PA
                         B: Perrysville, Allegheny Co., PA

MITCHELL, John James   ES: Philadelphia, Philadelphia Co., PA
                       B: County Tyrone, Ireland

MITCHELL, Theodore   ES: Pittsburgh, Allegheny Co., PA
                     B: Tarentum, Allegheny Co., PA

MONAGHAN, Patrick H.   ES: Minersville, Schuylkill Co., PA
                       B: Ireland

MORFORD, Jerome   ES: Bridgers Co., IL
                  B: Mercer Co., PA

MORRIS, James L.   ES: Philadelphia, Philadelphia Co., PA
                   B: County Kerry, Ireland

MORRIS, William Powers   ES: Philadelphia, Philadelphia Co., PA
                        B: Philadelphia, Philadelphia Co., PA

MORRISON, Francis   ES: Drakestown, PA
                    B: Ohiopyle, Fayette Co., PA

MOSTOLLER, John William   ES: Stoystown, Somerset Co., PA
                          B: Stoystown, Somerset Co., PA

MULHOLLAND, St. Clair
Agustin   ES: Philadelphia, Philadelphia Co., PA
          B: Lisburn, County Antrim, Ireland

MUNSELL, Harvey May   ES: Philadelphia, Philadelphia Co., PA
                      B: Painted Post, Steuben Co., NY

MURPHY, Daniel J.   ES: Lowell, Middlesex Co., MA
                    B: Philadelphia, Philadelphia Co., PA

MURPHY, Edward F.   ES: Philadelphia, Philadelphia Co., PA
                    B: Wayne Co., PA

MYERS, William H.   ES: Baltimore, Baltimore Co., MD
                    B: Philadelphia, Philadelphia Co., PA

NOVOSEL, Michael Joseph   ES: Kenner, Jefferson Co., LA
                          B: Etna, Allegheny Co., PA

OLIVER, Charles   ES: Webster, Westmoreland Co., PA
                  B: Allegheny Co., PA

ORR, Moses   ES: Philadelphia, Philadelphia Co., PA
             B: County Tyrone, Ireland

ORR, Robert Levan   ES: Philadelphia, Philadelphia Co., PA
                    B: Philadelphia, Philadelphia Co., PA

ORTH, Jacob George
 ES: Philadelphia, Philadelphia Co., PA
 B: Philadelphia, Philadelphia Co., PA

PALMER, William Jackson
 ES: Philadelphia, Philadelphia Co., PA
 B: Leipsic, Kent Co., DE

PAUL, William H.
 ES: Philadelphia, Philadelphia Co., PA
 B: Philadelphia, Philadelphia Co., PA

PAYNE, Irvin C.
 ES: New York, NY
 B: Wayne Co., PA

PEARSON, Alfred L.
 ES: Pittsburgh, Allegheny Co., PA
 B: Pittsburgh, Allegheny Co., PA

PEIRSOL, James Kastor
 ES: Waynesboro, OH
 B: Beaver Co., PA

PENNSYL, Josiah
 ES: Carlisle, Cumberland Co., PA
 B: Frederick Co., MD

PENNYPACKER, Galusha
 ES: West Chester, Chester Co., PA
 B: Near Valley Forge, Chester Co., PA

PETTY, Philip
 ES: Troy, Bradford Co., PA
 B: Tingswich, Buckinghamshire, England

PHILLIPS, Josiah
 ES: Ulysses, Potter Co., PA
 B: Wyoming Co., NY

*PINDER Jr., John J.
 ES: Burgettstown, Washington Co., PA
 B: McKees Rocks, Allegheny Co., PA

PIPES, James Milton
 ES: Waynesburg, Greene Co., PA
 B: Morrisville, Bucks Co., PA

PITMAN, George J.
 ES: Philadelphia, Philadelphia Co., PA
 B: Recklestown, NJ

PLATT, George Crawford
 ES: Philadelphia, Philadelphia Co., PA
 B: Ireland

*PORT, William David
 ES: Harrisburg, Dauphin Co., PA
 B: Petersburg, Huntingdon Co., PA

*PORTER, Donn F.
 ES: Baltimore, Baltimore Co., MD
 B: Sewickley, Allegheny Co., PA

PORTER, Horace
 ES: Harrisburg, Dauphin Co., PA
 B: Huntingdon, Huntingdon Co., PA

PURCELL, Hiram W.
 ES: Doylestown, Bucks Co., PA
 B: Upper Black Eddy, Bucks Co., PA

PURMAN, James Jackson
 ES: Waynesburg, Greene Co., PA
 B: Greene Co., PA

QUAY, Matthew Stanley
 ES: Harrisburg, Dauphin Co., PA
 B: Dillsburg, York Co., PA

QUINN, Alexander M.
 ES: Philadelphia, Philadelphia Co., PA
 B: Passaic, Passaic Co., NJ

RANKIN, William
 ES: Harrisburg, Dauphin Co., PA
 B: Lewistown, Mifflin Co., PA

RAUB, Jacob F.
 ES: Weaversville, PA
 B: Raubsville, Northampton Co., PA

REED, George W.
 ES: Johnstown, Cambria Co., PA
 B: Cambria Co., PA

REED, William
 ES: Pekin, Tazewell Co., IL
 B: Union Co., PA

*REESE, James W.
 ES: Chester, Delaware Co., PA
 B: Chester, Delaware Co., PA

REID, Robert Alexander
 ES: Pottsville, Schuylkill Co., PA
 B: Raploch, Scotland

REIGLE, Daniel P.
 ES: Gettysburg, Adams Co., PA
 B: Adams Co., PA

REISINGER, James Monroe
 ES: Meadville, Crawford Co., PA
 B: Beaver Co., PA

RESSLER, Norman W.
 ES: Dalmatia, Northumberland Co., PA
 B: Dalmatia, Northumberland Co., PA

RHODES, Sylvester D.
 ES: Wilkes-Barre, Luzerne Co., PA
 B: Plains, PA

ROBINSON, Thomas
 ES: Tamaqua, Schuylkill Co., PA
 B: Ireland

RODENBOUGH, Theophilus Francis
 ES: PA
 B: Easton, Northampton Co., PA

*ROEDER, Robert E.
 ES: Summit Station, Schuylkill Co., PA
 B: Summit Station, Schuylkill Co., PA

ROGAN, Patrick
 ES: Reading, Berks Co., PA
 B: County Leitrim, Ireland

ROHM, Ferdinand Frederick
 ES: Juniata Co., PA
 B: Patterson, Juniata Co., PA

ROOSEVELT, George Washington
 ES: Chester Co., PA
 B: Chester Co., PA

ROUGHT, Stephen
 ES: Crampton, PA
 B: Bradford Co., PA

ROUSH, James Levi
 ES: Chambersburg, Franklin Co., PA
 B: Bedford Co., PA

ROWAND Jr., Archibald Hamilton
 ES: Pittsburgh, Allegheny Co., PA
 B: Philadelphia, Philadelphia Co., PA

RUTTER, James May
 ES: Wilkes-Barre, Luzerne Co., PA
 B: Wilkes-Barre, Luzerne Co., PA

RYAN, David
 ES: Philadelphia, Philadelphia Co., PA
 B: County Kilkenny, Ireland

SACRISTE, Louis Jeanottelle
 ES: Philadelphia, Philadelphia Co., PA
 B: New Castle Co., DE

SANDS, William
 ES: Reading, Berks Co., PA
 B: Reading, Berks Co., PA

*SAYERS, Foster Joseph
 ES: Howard, Centre Co., PA
 B: Marshalls Creek, Monroe Co., PA

SCHAFFNER, Dwite H.
 ES: Falls Creek, Jefferson Co., PA
 B: Arroya, PA

SCHEIBNER, Martin E.
 ES: Philadelphia, Philadelphia Co., PA
 B: Valdai, Russia

SCHOONMAKER, James Martinus
 ES: Pittsburgh, Allegheny Co., PA
 B: Pittsburgh, Allegheny Co., PA

SCOTT, John Wallace
 ES: Philadelphia, Philadelphia Co., PA
 B: Chester Co., PA

SEITZINGER, James M.
 ES: Worcester, Montgomery Co., PA
 B: Germany

SELLERS, Alfred Jacob
 ES: Philadelphia, Philadelphia Co., PA
 B: Plumsteadville, Bucks Co., PA

SEWARD, Griffin
 ES: Philadelphia, Philadelphia Co., PA
 B: Dover, Kent Co., DE

SHAMBAUGH, Charles
 ES: Indian Town, Lebanon Co., PA
 B: Prussia, Germany

SHELLENBERGER, John
 ES: Perryopolis, Fayette Co., PA
 B: Fayette Co., PA

SHEPHERD, Warren Julius
 ES: Westover, Clearfield Co., PA
 B: Cherry Tree, Indiana Co., PA

SHIEL, John
 ES: Philadelphia, Philadelphia Co., PA
 B: Scotland

SHINGLE, John Henry
 ES: St. Louis, St. Louis Co., MO
 B: Philadelphia, Philadelphia Co., PA

SHOPP, George J.
 ES: Reading, Berks Co., PA
 B: Equinunk, Wayne Co., PA

*SHUGHART, Randall David
 ES: Newville, Cumberland Co., PA
 B: Lincoln, Lancaster Co., NE

SILK, Edward A.
 ES: Johnstown, Cambria Co., PA
 B: Johnstown, Cambria Co., PA

*SITMAN, William S.	ES: Bellwood, Blair Co., PA B: Bellwood, Blair Co., PA	TWEEDALE, John	ES: Philadelphia, Philadelphia Co., PA B: Frankford, Philadelphia Co., PA
SLOAN, Andrew Jackson	ES: Colesburg, Delaware Co., IA B: Bedford Co., PA	VANDERSLICE, John Mitchell	ES: Philadelphia, Philadelphia Co., PA B: near Valley Forge, Chester Co., PA
SLUSHER, Henry C.	ES: Washington, Washington Co., PA B: Washington Co., PA	VEALE, Moses	ES: Philadelphia, Philadelphia Co., PA B: Bridgeton, Cumberland Co., NJ
SMALLEY, Reuben S.	ES: Brookfield, Cook Co., IL B: Washington Co., PA	WAINWRIGHT, John	ES: West Chester, Chester Co., PA B: Syracuse, Onondaga Co., NY
SMITH, Robert	ES: Philadelphia, Philadelphia Co., PA B: Philadelphia, Philadelphia Co., PA	WALTON, George Washington	ES: Upper Oxford Township, Chester Co., PA
SMITH, Thaddeus S.	ES: Harrisburg, Dauphin Co., PA B: Cumberland, Franklin Co., PA		B: Upper Oxford Township, Chester Co., PA
SMITH, Theodore F.	ES: Harrisburg, Dauphin Co., PA B: Rahway, Union Co., NJ	WARD, Charles H.	ES: Philadelphia, Philadelphia Co., PA B: Bradford, England
SNEDDEN, James	ES: Johnstown, Cambria Co., PA B: Edinburgh, Scotland	WARFEL, Henry Clay	ES: Monocacy Junction, MD B: Mill Creek, Huntingdon Co., PA
SOWERS, Michael	ES: Pittsburgh, Allegheny Co., PA B: Pittsburgh, Allegheny Co., PA	WATSON, James C.	ES: Philadelphia, Philadelphia Co., PA B: Cochecton, Sullivan Co., NY
*SPEICHER, Clifton T.	ES: Gray, Somerset Co., PA B: Gray, Somerset Co., PA	WEAHER, Andrew J.	ES: Philadelphia, Philadelphia Co., PA B: Philadelphia, Philadelphia Co., PA
SPENCE, Orizoba	ES: Cincinnati, Hamilton Co., OH B: Forest Co., PA	*WEICHT, Ellis R.	ES: Bedford, Bedford Co., PA B: Clearville, Bedford Co., PA
SPRINGER, George	ES: Harrisburg, Dauphin Co., PA B: York Co., PA	WHITE, John Henry	ES: Philadelphia, Philadelphia Co., PA B: Philadelphia, Philadelphia Co., PA
STOREY, John Hamilton Reid	ES: Philadelphia, Philadelphia Co., PA B: Philadelphia, Philadelphia Co., PA	WIDMER, Jacob	ES: Philadelphia, Philadelphia Co., PA B: Wurttemberg, Germany
*STRAUSBURGH, Bernard A.	ES: Warfordsburg, Fulton Co., PA B: Adams Co., PA	WILKENS, Henry	ES: Pittsburgh, Allegheny Co., PA B: Germany
STRAYER, William H.	ES: Carlisle, Cumberland Co., PA B: Maytown, Lancaster Co., PA	*WILL, Walter J.	ES: West Winfield, Herkimer Co., NY B: Pittsburgh, Allegheny Co., PA
SWAN, Charles Alexander	ES: Mount Pleasant, Henry Co., IA B: Greene Co., PA	WILLIAMS, Elwood N.	ES: Havana, Mason Co., IL B: Philadelphia, Philadelphia Co., PA
SWAP, Jacob E.	ES: Springs, Somerset Co., PA B: Coeymans, Albany Co., NY	*WILSON, Alfred Leonard	ES: Fairchance, Fayette Co., PA B: Fairchance, Fayette Co., PA
TANNER, Charles B.	ES: Wilmimgton, New Castle Co., DE B: Philadelphia, Philadelphia Co., PA	WILSON, Benjamin	ES: Cincinnati, Hamilton Co., OH B: Pittsburgh, Allegheny Co., PA
TAYLOR, Anthony	ES: Philadelphia, Philadelphia Co., PA B: Burlington, Burlington Co., NJ	WILSON, Charles E.	ES: Hatborough, Montgomery Co., NJ B: Bucks Co., PA
TAYLOR, Forrester L.	ES: Beverly, Burlington Co., NJ B: Philadelphia, Philadelphia Co., PA	WILSON, Francis A.	ES: Philadelphia, Philadelphia Co., PA B: Philadelphia, Philadelphia Co., PA
TEA, Richard Longstreet	ES: Philadelphia, Philadelphia Co., PA B: Philadelphia, Philadelphia Co., PA	WILSON, William	ES: Philadelphia, Philadelphia Co., PA B: Philadelphia, Philadelphia Co., PA
*THOMAS, Charles L.	ES: Cincinnati, Hamilton Co., OH B: Philadelphia, Philadelphia Co., PA	*WINDER, David Francis	ES: Columbus, Franklin Co., OH B: Edinboro, Erie Co., PA
THOMAS, Hampton Sidney	ES: Harrisburg, Dauphin Co., PA B: Quakertown, Bucks Co., PA	WITCOME, Joseph	ES: Carlisle, Cumberland Co., PA B: Mechanicsburg, Cumberland Co., PA
THOMPSON, James B.	ES: Perrysville, Allegheny Co., PA B: Juniata Co., PA	WOODALL, Zachariah	ES: Carlisle, Cumberland Co., PA B: Alexandria, Alexandria Co., VA
THOMPSON, Joseph Henry	ES: Beaver Falls, Beaver Co., PA B: Kilkeel, County Down, Ireland	WOODWARD, Evan M.	ES: Sandy Hook, MD B: Philadelphia Philadelphia Co., PA
THOMPSON, Peter	ES: Pittsburgh, Allegheny Co., PA B: Scotland	WORTICK, Joseph	ES: Hannibal, Marion Co., MO B: Fayette Co., PA
TOMINAC, John Joseph	ES: Conemaugh, Cambria Co., PA B: Conemaugh, Cambria Co., PA	WRAY, William J.	ES: Philadelphia, Philadelphia Co., PA B: Philadelphia, Philadelphia Co., PA
TRAUTMAN, Jacob	ES: Pittsburgh, Allegheny Co., PA B: Hamburg, Germany	WRIGHT, Albert D.	ES: Wellsboro, Tioga Co., PA B: Elkland, Tioga Co., PA
TUCKER, Jacob R.	ES: Baltimore, Baltimore Co., MD B: Chester Co., PA	YEAGER, Jacob F.	ES: Tiffin, Seneca Co., OH B: New Texas, Lehigh Co., PA
*TURNER, Day G.	ES: Nescopeck, Luzerne Co., PA B: Berwick, Columbia Co., PA	YOUNG, Andrew J.	ES: Carmichaels, Greene Co., PA B: Greene Co., PA

U.S. Army Air Corps/U.S. Air Force

*MATHIES, Archibald — ES: Pittsburgh, Allegheny Co., PA
   B: Scotland

*SARNOSKI, Joseph Raymond — ES: Simpson, Lackawanna Co., PA
   B: Simpson, Lackawanna Co., PA

SHOMO, William Arthur — ES: Westmoreland Co., PA
   B: Jeannette, Westmoreland Co., PA

ZEAMER Jr., Jay — ES: Machias, Washington Co., ME
   B: Carlisle, Cumberland Co., PA

U.S. Navy

ANDREWS, John — ES: Maryland
   B: York Co., PA

BALDWIN, Charles H. — ES: Philadelphia, Philadelphia Co., PA
   B: Wilmington, New Castle Co., DE

BARRETT, Edward — ES: PA
   B: Philadelphia, Philadelphia Co., PA

*BENFOLD, Edward Clyde "Ted" — ES: Philadelphia, Philadelphia Co., PA
   B: Staten Island, Richmond Co., NY

BISHOP, Charles Francis — ES: PA
   B: Pittsburgh, Allegheny Co., PA

BLUME, Robert — ES: NJ
   B: Pittsburgh, Allegheny Co., PA

BOONE, Joel Thompson — ES: St. Clair, Schuylkill Co., PA
   B: St. Clair, Schuylkill Co., PA

BRAZELL, John — ES: PA
   B: Philadelphia, Philadelphia Co., PA

BRUTSCHE, Henry — ES: PA
   B: Philadelphia, Philadelphia Co., PA

BUCHANAN, David M. — ES: PA
   B: Philadelphia, Philadelphia Co., PA

CLIFFORD, Robert Teleford — ES: PA
   B: PA

CONNOR, William C. — ES: PA
   B: Cork, County Coke, Ireland

CRAWFORD, Alexander — ES: Philadelphia, Philadelphia Co., PA
   B: Philadelphia, Philadelphia Co., PA

CRILLEY, Frank William — ES: PA
   B: Trenton, Mercer Co., NJ

CRIPPS, Thomas H. — ES: PA
   B: Philadelphia, Philadelphia Co., PA

CROUSE, William Adolphus — ES: PA
   B: Tannettsburg, Franklin Co., PA

CUTTER, George W. — ES: PA
   B: Philadelphia, Philadelphia Co., PA

DAVIS, Joseph H. — ES: Philadelphia, Philadelphia Co., PA
   B: Philadelphia, Philadelphia Co., PA

DEAKIN, Charles — ES: Philadelphia, Philadelphia Co., PA
   B: New York, NY

DEMPSTER, John — ES: Philadelphia, Philadelphia Co., PA
   B: Scotland

DOOLEN, William — ES: Philadelphia, Philadelphia Co., PA
   B: Ireland

*DREXLER, Henry Clay — ES: PA
   B: Braddock, Allegheny Co., PA

DRUSTRUP, Niels — ES: PA
   B: Denmark

Du MOULIN, Frank — ES: PA
   B: Philadelphia, Philadelphia Co., PA

DUNCAN, James K. L. — ES: PA
   B: Frankfort Mineral Springs, Washington Co., PA

DURNEY, Austin Joseph — ES: Woodland, MD
   B: Philadelphia, Philadelphia Co., PA

EDWARDS, Walter Atlee — ES: PA
   B: Philadelphia, Philadelphia Co., PA

*ESTOCIN, Michael John — ES: Akron, Summit Co., OH
   B: Turtle Creek, Allegheny Co., PA

GIRANDY, Alphonse — ES: PA
   B: Guadaloupe, West Indies

GRACE, Patrick Henry — ES: PA
   B: Ireland

HAFFEE, Edmund — ES: Philadelphia, Philadelphia Co., PA
   B: Philadelphia, Philadelphia Co., PA

HAMILTON, Richard — ES: PA
   B: Philadelphia, Philadelphia Co., PA

HICKMAN, John S. — ES: PA
   B: Blair Co., PA

*HILL, Edwin Joseph — ES: PA
   B: Philadelphia, Philadelphia Co., PA

HUBER, William Russell — ES: PA
   B: Harrisburg, Dauphin Co., PA

JOHNSEN, Hans — ES: PA
   B: Sandnes, Norway

JOHNSON, John — ES: PA
   B: Philadelphia, Philadelphia Co., PA

JOHNSON, Peter — ES: PA
   B: Sumerland, England

JONES, William — ES: PA
   B: Philadelphia, Philadelphia Co., PA

KILLACKEY, Joseph — ES: PA
   B: County Cork, Ireland

LAFFERTY, John — ES: PA
   B: New York, NY

LAWSON, John — ES: PA
   B: Philadelphia, Philadelphia Co., PA

LEAR, Nicholas — ES: Philadelphia, Philadelphia Co., PA
   B: Rhode Island

LEON, Pierre — ES: Philadelphia, Philadelphia Co., PA
   B: France

LEVERY, William — ES: PA
   B: Philadelphia, Philadelphia Co., PA

LLOYD, Benjamin — ES: Philadelphia, Philadelphia Co., PA
   B: Liverpool, Merseyside Co., England

LOWRY, George Maus — ES: PA
   B: Erie, Erie Co., PA

MAHONEY, George — ES: PA
   B: Worcester, Worcester Co., MA

MARTIN, Edward S. — ES: Philadelphia, Philadelphia Co., PA
   B: Ireland

MATTHEWS, Joseph — ES: PA
   B: Malta

McWILLIAMS, George Washington — ES: PA
   B: Waterford, Erie Co., PA

MILLER, Hugh — ES: PA
   B: Philadelphia, Philadelphia Co., PA

MITCHELL, Joseph Andrew — ES: PA
   B: Philadelphia, Philadelphia Co., PA

MOORE, George — ES: Boston, Suffolk Co., MA
   B: Philadelphia, Philadelphia Co., PA

O'NEAL, John ES: PA B: Ireland

ORTEGA, John ES: PA B: Spain

PETERS, Alexander ES: PA B: Russia

PETTY, Orlando Henderson ES: PA B: Harrison, Hamilton Co., OH

RILLEY, John Phillip ES: Massachusetts B: Allentown, Lehigh Co., PA

RUSH, William Rees ES: PA B: Philadelphia, Philadelphia Co., PA

SANDERSON, Aaron ES: Philadelphia, Philadelphia Co., PA B: NC

SAPP, Isaac ES: PA B: Philadelphia, Philadelphia Co., PA

SCHMIDT Jr., Oscar ES: PA B: Philadelphia, Philadelphia Co., PA

SEMPLE, Robert ES: PA B: Pittsburgh, Allegheny Co., PA

SINNETT, Lawrence Clinton ES: PA B: Burnt House, WV

SNYDER, William Ellsworth ES: PA B: South Bethlehem, Northampton Co., PA

SUNDQUIST, Axel Leohard ES: PA B: Finland

TAYLOR, William G. ES: Philadelphia, Philadelphia Co., PA B: Philadelphia, Philadelphia Co., PA

THAYER, James ES: PA B: Ireland

THORNTON, Michael ES: PA B: Ireland

TROUT, James M. ES: PA B: Philadelphia, Philadelphia Co., PA

VANTINE, Joseph E. ES: Pennslyvania B: Philadelphia, Philadelphia Co., PA

WHITE, Joseph ES: Philadelphia, Philadelphia Co., PA B: Washington, D.C.

WILLIAMS, Henry ES: PA B: Canada

WILLIAMS, John ES: PA B: Blair Co., PA

WILLIAMS, Peter ES: PA B: Norway

WILLIAMS, William ES: PA B: Ireland

WILLIS, Richard ES: Philadelphia, Philadelphia Co., PA B: England

U.S. Marine Corps

BINDER, Richard ES: PA B: Germany

BUTLER, Smedley Darlington ES: PA B: West Chester, Chester Co., PA

CAMPBELL, Albert Ralph ES: PA B: Williamsport, Lycoming Co., PA

*DAMATO, Anthony Peter ES: PA B: Shenandoah, Schuylkill Co., PA

DENIG, J. Henry ES: PA B: York, York Co., PA

*DIAS, Ralph Ellis ES: Pittsburgh, Allegheny Co., PA B: Shelocta, Armstrong Co., PA

DOUGHERTY, James ES: PA B: Langhash, Ireland

*FISHER, Harry ES: PA B: McKeesport, Allegheny Co., PA

FOLEY, Alexander Joseph ES: PA B: Heckersville, PA

FRANCIS, Charles Robert ES: Philadelphia, Philadelphia Co., PA B: Doylestown, Bucks Co., PA

FRY, Isaac N. ES: Philadelphia, Philadelphia Co., PA B: Lancaster, Lancaster Co., PA

GAUGHAN, Philip ES: PA B: Belmullet, County Mayo, Ireland

*GRAHAM, James Albert ES: Prince Georges, Prince Georges Co., MD B: Wilkinsburg, Allegheny Co., PA

GROSS, Samuel ES: PA B: Philadelphia, Philadelphia Co., PA

HORTON, William M. Charlie ES: Philadelphia, Philadelphia Co., PA B: Chicago, Cook Co., IL

IAMS, Ross Lindsey ES: PA B: Graysville, Greene Co., PA

*KELLY, John Doran ES: Homestead, Allegheny Co., PA B: Youngstown, Mahoning Co., OH

MacNEAL, Harry Lewis ES: PA B: Philadelphia, Philadelphia Co., PA

MARTIN, James ES: PA B: Derry, Ireland

MATHIAS, Clarence Edward ES: PA B: Royalton, Dauphin Co., PA

*MAUSERT III, Frederick William ES: Dresher, Montgomery Co., PA B: Cambridge, Washington Co., NY

*MORGAN, William David ES: Pittsburgh, Allegheny Co., PA B: Pittsburgh, Allegheny Co., PA

PAIGE, Mitchell ES: PA B: Charleroi, Washington Co., PA

PFEIFER, Louis Fred ES: NJ B: Philadelphia, Philadelphia Co., PA

*PROM, William Raymond ES: Pittsburgh, Allegheny Co., PA B: Pittsburgh, Allegheny Co., PA

PURVIS, Hugh ES: PA B: Philadelphia, Philadelphia Co., PA

QUICK, John Henry ES: PA B: Charleston, Kanawha Co., WV

*RAMER, George Henry ES: Lewisburg, Union Co., PA B: Meyersdale, Somerset Co., PA

RANNAHAN, John ES: PA B: County Monaghan, Ireland

*REEM, Robert Dale ES: Elizabethtown, Lancaster Co., PA B: Lancaster, Lancaster Co., PA

STEWART, James A. ES: PA B: Philadelphia, Philadelphia Co., PA

THOMPSON, Henry A. ES: PA B: England

VAUGHN, Pinkerton Ross ES: PA B: Downingtown, Chester Co., PA

RHODE ISLAND

U.S. Army

AVERY, William B. ES: Providence, Providence Co., RI B: Providence, Providence Co., RI

BABOCK, William J.   ES: South Kingston, Washington Co., RI
B: Griswold, CT

BACA, John Philip   ES: Fort Ord, Monterey Co., CA
B: Providence, Providence Co., RI

BARBER, James Albert   ES: Westerly, Washington Co., RI
B: Westerly, Washington Co., RI

BLISS, George Newman   ES: Pawtucket, Providence Co., RI
B: Tiverton, Newport Co., RI

BLISS, Zenas Randall   ES: Johnston, Providence Co., RI
B: Johnston, Providence Co., RI

BUCKLYN, John Knight   ES: Providence, Providence Co., RI
B: Foster Creek, Providence Co., RI

BURBANK, James H.   ES: Providence, Providence Co., RI
B: Stavorey, Holland

CHILD, Benjamin Ham   ES: Providence, Providence Co., RI
B: Providence, Providence Co., RI

CORCORAN, John   ES: Pawtucket, Providence Co., RI
B: Pawtucket, Providence Co., RI

CUTTS, James Madison   ES: Providence, Providence Co., RI
B: Washington, D.C.

ENNIS, Charles D.   ES: Charleston, Washington Co., RI
B: Stonington, New London Co., CT

HAVRON, John H.   ES: Providence, Providence Co., RI
B: Ireland

LAWTON, John Sterling   ES: Boston, Suffolk Co., MA
B: Bristol, Bristol Co., RI

LEWIS, Samuel E.   ES: Coventry, Kent Co., RI
B: Coventry, Kent Co., RI

McDONALD, George E.   ES: Warwick, Kent Co., RI
B: Warwick, Kent Co., RI

McGAR, Owen   ES: Providence, Providence Co., RI
B: North Attleboro, Bristol Co., MA

MOLBONE, Archibald   ES: Johnston, Providence Co., RI
B: West Greenwich, RI

PARKER, Thomas   ES: Providence, Providence Co., RI
B: England

*PETERS, George J.   ES: Cranston, Providence Co., RI
B: Cranston, Providence Co., RI

POTTER, George W.   ES: Coventry, Kent Co., RI
B: Coventry, Kent Co., RI

SMITH, Thomas   ES: Fort Adams, RI
B: Boston, Suffolk Co., MA

STEVENS, Hazard   ES: Olympia, Thurston Co., Washington
Territory
B: Newport, Newport Co., RI

TAYLOR, Joseph   ES: Burrillville, RI
B: England

WAINWRIGHT, Jonathan
Mayhew   ES: Skaneateles, Onondaga Co., NY
B: Fort Walla Walla, Walla Walla Co., WA

*WAUGH, Robert T.   ES: Augusta, Kennebec Co., ME
B: Ashton, RI

WELSH, James   ES: Slatersville, Providence Co., RI
B: Ireland

U.S. Navy

BRADLEY, George   ES: Rhode Island
B: New York, NY

EADIE, Thomas   ES: Newport, Newport Co., RI
B: Scotland

EDWARDS, John   ES: Rhode Island
B: Providence, Providence Co., RI

GILLICK, Matthew   ES: Rhode Island
B: Providence, Providence Co., RI

GISBURNE, Edward Allen   ES: Massachusetts
B: Providence, Providence Co., RI

HAYES, Thomas   ES: Rhode Island
B: Rhode Island

LEAR, Nicholas   ES: Philadelphia, Philadelphia Co., PA
B: Rhode Island

MOORE, Philip   ES: Rhode Island
B: Newfoundland, Canada

ORMSBEE Jr., Francis Edward   ES: Florida
B: Providence, Providence Co., RI

PROVINCE, George   ES: Boston, Suffolk Co., MA
B: Newport, Newport Co., RI

READ, George E.   ES: RI
B: RI

WALSH, Michael   ES: RI
B: Newport, Newport Co., RI

U.S. Marine Corps

*CHAMPAGNE, David
Bernard   ES: Wakefield, Washington Co., RI
B: Waterville, Kennebec Co., ME

SOUTH CAROLINA

U.S. Army

ANDERSON, Webster   ES: Winnsboro, Fairfield Co., SC
B: Winnsboro, Fairfield Co., SC

ATKINS, Thomas E.   ES: Campobello, Spartanburg Co., SC
B: Campobello, Spartanburg Co., SC

*BARKER, Charles H.   ES: Pickens Co., SC
B: Pickens Co., SC

DOZIER, James C.   ES: Rock Hill, York Co., SC
B: Galivants Ferry, Horry Co., SC

FOSTER, Gary Evans   ES: Inman, Spartanburg Co., SC
B: Spartanburg, Spartanburg Co., SC

GARLINGTON, Ernest Albert   ES: Athens, Clarke Co., GA
B: Newberry Hill, Newberry Co., SC

*HALL, Thomas Lee   ES: Fort Mill, York Co., SC
B: Fort Mill, York Co., SC

*HERIOT, James Davidson   ES: Providence, SC
B: Providence, SC

HILTON, Richmond Hobson   ES: Westville, Kershaw Co., SC
B: Westville, Kershaw Co., SC

HOOPER, Joe Ronnie   ES: Los Angeles, Los Angeles Co., CA
B: Piedmont, Greenville Co., SC

KENNEDY, John Thomas   ES: Orangeburg, Orangeburg Co., SC
B: Hendersonville, SC

*KNIGHT, Noah Odell   ES: Jefferson, Chesterfield Co., SC
B: Chesterfield Co., SC

MABRY Jr., George Lafayette   ES: Sumter, Sumter Co., SC
B: Sumter, Sumter Co., SC

*McWHORTER, William A.   ES: Liberty, Pickens Co., SC
B: Liberty, Pickens Co., SC

*SMITH, Furman L.   ES: Central, Pickens Co., SC
B: Six Mile, Pickens Co., SC

*STOWERS, Freddie   ES: Anderson Co., SC
B: Sandy Springs, Anderson Co., SC

VILLEPIGUE, John Cantey   ES: Camden, Kershaw Co., SC
B: Camden, Kershaw Co., SC

WALLING, William Henry   ES: Folly Island, Charleston Co., SC
B: Hartford, Washington Co., NY

WILLIAMS, Charles Quincy   ES: Fort Jackson, SC
B: Charleston, Charleston Co., SC

U.S. Navy

ELLIOTT, Middleton Stuart   ES: SC
B: Beauford, Beauford Co., SC

FLOYD, Edward   ES: SC
B: Ireland

MOFFETT, William Adger   ES: Charleston, Charleston Co., SC
B: Charleston, Charleston Co., SC

SULLIVAN, Daniel Augustus Joseph   ES: SC
B: Charleston, Charleston Co., SC

THORNTON, Michael Edwin   ES: Spartanburg, Spartanburg Co., SC
B: Greenville, Greenville Co., SC

WHEELER, George Huber   ES: Washington, D.C.
B: Charleston, Charleston Co., SC

WILLIAMS, James Elliott   ES: Columbia, Richland Co., SC
B: Rock Hill, York Co., SC

U.S. Marine Corps

*HOWE, James Donnie   ES: Fort Jackson, Richland Co., SC
B: Six Mile, Pickens Co., SC

*JOHNSON, Ralph Henry   ES: Oakland, Alameda Co., CA
B: Charleston, Charleston Co., SC

KENNEMORE, Robert Sidney   ES: Greenville, Greenville Co., SC
B: Greenville, Greenville Co., SC

McGINTY III, John James   ES: Laurel Bay, SC
B: Boston, Suffolk Co., MA

*OWENS, Robert Allen   ES: SC
B: Greenville, Greenville Co., SC

TRUESDELL, Donald Leroy   ES: SC
B: Lugoff, Kershaw Co., SC

*WATKINS, Lewis George   ES: Seneca, Oconee Co., SC
B: Seneca, Oconee Co., SC

SOUTH DAKOTA

U.S. Army

ANDERS, Frank Lafayette   ES: Fargo, Cass Co., ND
B: Fort Lincoln, Dakota Territory

BRADY, Patrick Henry   ES: Seattle, King Co., WA
B: Philip, Haakon Co., SD

FITZMAURICE, Michael John   ES: Cavour, Beadle Co., SD
B: Jamestown, Stutsman Co., ND

HARDAWAY, Benjamin Franklin   ES: Fort Totten, Benson Co., Dakota Territory
B: Benleyville, KY

*OLSON, Arlo L.   ES: Toronto, Deuel Co., SD
B: Greenville, Clay Co., IA

ROBERTS, Charles Duval   ES: Fort D.A. Russell, WY
B: Cheyenne Agency, Dakota

U.S. Marine Corps

FOSS, Joseph Jacob   ES: Sioux Falls, Minnehaha Co., SD
B: Sioux Falls, Minnehaha Co., SD

*LITTLETON, Herbert A.   ES: Black Hawk, Meade Co., SD
B: Mena, Polk Co., AR

TENNESSEE

U.S. Army

ADKINSON, Joseph B.   ES: Memphis, Shelby Co., TN
B: Egypt, TN

BEAUFORD, Clay   ES: Nashville, Davidson Co., TN
B: Washington Co., MD

CANTRELL, Charles P.   ES: Nashville, Davidson Co., TN
B: Smithville, Dekalb Co., TN

CARTER, William Harding   ES: New York, NY
B: Nashville, Davidson Co., TN

CECIL, Joseph Samuel   ES: New River, TN
B: New River, TN

COLLINS, Harrison   ES: Cumberland Gap, Claiborne Co., TN
B: Hawkins Co., TN

COOLEY, Raymond Henry   ES: Richard City, TN
B: Dunlap, Sequatchie Co., TN

COOLIDGE, Charles Henry   ES: Signal Mountain, Hamilton Co., TN
B: Signal Mountain, Hamilton Co., TN

DOZIER, James B.   ES: Fort Richardson, TX
B: Warren Co., TN

*DUKE, Ray E.   ES: Whitwell, Marion Co., TN
B: Whitwell, Marion Co., TN

*GARDNER, James Alton   ES: Memphis, Shelby Co., TN
B: Dyersburg, Dyer Co., TN

GILLESPIE Jr., George Lewis   ES: Chattanooga, Hamilton Co., TN
B: Kingston, Roane Co., TN

GRANT, George   ES: Indianapolis, Marion Co., IN
B: Raleigh, Shelby Co., TN

GREER, Allen James   ES: Memphis, Shelby Co., TN
B: Memphis, Shelby Co., TN

HOBDAY, George   ES: Memphis, Shelby Co., TN
B: Pulaski Co., IL

HUFF, Paul Bert   ES: Cleveland, Bradley Co., TN
B: Cleveland, Bradley Co., TN

HUGHES, Oliver   ES: Albany, Clinton Co., KY
B: Fentress Co., TN

JENKINS, Don   ES: Nashville, Davidson Co., TN
B: Quality, Butler Co., KY

JORDAN, George   ES: Nashville, Davidson Co., TN
B: Williamson Co., TN

KARNES, James Ernest   ES: Knoxville, Knox Co., TN
B: Arlington, Shelby Co., TN

KYLE, John   ES: Nashville, Davidson Co., TN
B: Cincinnati, Hamilton Co., OH

LAWSON, Gaines   ES: Rogersville, Hawkins Co., TN
B: Hawkins Co., TN

*LEMERT, Milo   ES: Crossville, Cumberland Co., TN
B: Marshalltown, Marshall Co., IA

*LYELL, William Franklin   ES: Old Hickory, Davidson Co., TN
B: Hickman Co., TN

McGAHA, Charles L.   ES: Crosby, TN
B: Crosby, TN

McGARITY, Vernon   ES: Model, TN
B: Right, TN

*McGILL, Troy A.   ES: Ada, Pontotoc Co., OK
B: Knoxville, Knox Co., TN

MORRIS, William W.   ES: Louisville, Jefferson Co., KY
B: Stewart Co., TN

*PENDLETON, Charles F.   ES: Fort Worth, TX
B: Camden, Benton Co., TN

*STOUT, Mitchell William	ES: Raleigh, Wake Co., NC B: Knoxville, Knox Co., TN
STRIVSON, Benoni	ES: Sacramento, Sacramento Co., CA B: Overton, TN
TALLEY, Edward R.	ES: Russellville, Hamblen Co., TN B: Russellville, Hamblen Co., TN
WARD, Calvin John	ES: Morristown, Hamblen Co., TN B: Green Co., TN
WELD, Seth Lathrop	ES: Altamont, Grundy Co., TN B: Sandy Hook, MD
YORK, Alvin Cullium	ES: Pall Mall, Fentress Co., TN B: Fentress Co., TN

U.S. Navy

BONNEY, Robert Earl	ES: Nashville, Davidson Co., TN B: Maryville, Blount Co., TN
COVINGTON, Jesse Whitfield	ES: CA B: Haywood, TN
FERRELL, John H.	ES: IL B: Bedford Co., TN
HARRISON, Bolden Reush	ES: TN B: Savannah, Hardin Co., TN
*RAY, David Robert	ES: Nashville, Davidson Co., TN B: McMinnville, Warren Co., TN
STEVENS, Daniel Dickerson	ES: MA B: La Grange, Fayette Co., TN
*WILLIS, John Harlan	ES: Tennessee B: Columbia, Maury Co., TN

U.S. Marine Corps

*KINSER, Elbert Luther	ES: Tennessee B: Greeneville, Greene Co., TN
*SINGLETON, Walter Keith	ES: Memphis, Shelby Co., TN B: Memphis, Shelby Co., TN

TEXAS

U.S. Army

ADAMS, Lucian	ES: Port Arthur, Jefferson Co., TX B: Port Arthur, Jefferson Co., TX
AUSTIN, William Grafton	ES: New York, NY B: Galveston, Galveston Co., TX
*BARKELEY, David B.	ES: San Antonio, Bexar Co., TX B: Laredo, Webb Co., TX
BENAVIDEZ, Roy Perez	ES: Houston, Harris Co., TX B: Cuero, DeWitt Co., TX
*COLE, Robert George	ES: San Antonio, Bexar Co., TX B: Fort Sam Houston, Bexar Co., TX
CONNOR, John	ES: Jefferson, Marion Co., TX B: Galway, Ireland
DOZIER, James B.	ES: Fort Richardson, TX B: Warren Co., TN
EDWARDS, Daniel Richmond	ES: Bruceville, McLennan Co., TX B: Mooreville, TX
EVERHART Sr., Forrest Eugene	ES: Texas City, Galveston Co., TX B: Bainbridge, Ross Co., OH
FACTOR, Pompey	ES: Fort Duncan, TX B: AR
FERGUSON, Frederick Edgar	ES: Phoenix, Maricopa Co., AZ B: Pilot Point, Denton Co., TX

FIELDS, James H.	ES: Houston, Harris Co., TX B: Caddo, Stephens Co., TX
*FOWLER, Thomas Weldon	ES: Wichita Falls, Wichita Co., TX B: Wichita Falls, Wichita Co., TX
GARCIA, Marcario	ES: Sugar Land, Fort Bend Co., TX B: Villa de Castano, Mexico
*HANSON, Jack G.	ES: Galveston, Galveston Co., TX B: Escatawpa, Jackson Co., MS
*HARRIS, James Lindell	ES: Hillsboro, Hill Co., TX B: Hillsboro, Hill Co., TX
HERRERA, Silvestre Santana	ES: Phoenix, Maricopa Co., AZ B: El Paso, El Paso Co., TX
HOLLAND, Milton Murray	ES: Albany, Athens Co., OH B: Austin, Travis Co., TX
HOWZE, Robert Lee	ES: Overton, Rusk Co., TX B: Overton, Rusk Co., TX
*KEATHLEY, George D.	ES: Lamesa, Dawson Co., TX B: Olney, Young Co., TX
*KIMBRO, Truman	ES: Houston, Harris Co., TX B: Madisonville, Madison Co., TX
*KNIGHT, Jack Llewellyn	ES: Weatherford, Parker Co., TX B: Garner, TX
*LAW, Robert David	ES: Dallas, Collin Co., TX B: Fort Worth, Tarrant Co., TX
*LEE, Milton Arthur	ES: San Antonio, Bexar Co., TX B: Shreveport, Caddo Co., LA
*LEONARD, Turney White	ES: Dallas, Collin Co., TX B: Dallas, Collin Co., TX
LLOYD, George	ES: Canton, Van Zandt Co., TX B: County Tyrone, Ireland
LOGAN, James Marion	ES: Luling, Caldwell Co., TX B: McNeil, Travis Co., TX
LOPEZ, Jose Mendoza	ES: Brownsville, Cameron Co., TX B: Mission, Hidalgo Co., TX
*MARTINEZ, Benito	ES: Fort Hancock, Hudspeth Co., TX B: Fort Hancock, Hudspeth Co., TX
McCABE, William	ES: Fort Duncan, TX B: Belfast, County Antrim, Ireland
McCLEERY, Finnis Dawson	ES: San Angelo, Tom Green Co., TX B: Stephenville, Erath Co., TX
McDONALD, Franklin M.	ES: Fort Griffin, TX B: Bowling Green, Warren Co., KY
McLENNON, John	ES: Fort Ellis, MT B: Fort Belknap, TX
McNERNEY, David Herbert	ES: Fort Bliss, El Paso Co., TX B: Lowell, Middlesex Co., MA
MURPHY, Audie Leon	ES: Dallas, Collin Co., TX B: near Kingston, Hunt Co., TX
PAINE, Adam	ES: Fort Duncan, TX B: FL
PAYNE, Isaac	ES: Fort Duncan, TX B: Mexico
*PENDLETON, Charles F.	ES: Fort Worth, TX B: Camden, Benton Co., TN
*ROBINSON Jr., James E.	ES: Waco, McLennan Co., TX B: Toledo, Lucas Co., OH
RODRIGUEZ, Cleto L.	ES: San Antonio, Bexar Co., TX B: San Marcos, Hays Co., TX
SAMPLER, Samuel M.	ES: Altus, Jackson Co., OK B: Decatur, Wise Co., TX
SASSER, Clarence Eugene	ES: Houston, Harris Co., TX B: Chenango, TX

SHELTON, George Mathews   ES: Bellington, TX
                                      B: Brownwood, Brown Co., TX

*STEINDAM, Russell Albert   ES: Austin, Travis Co., TX
                                      B: Austin, Travis Co., TX

STONE, James Lamar   ES: Houston, Harris Co., TX
                                      B: Pine Bluff, Jefferson Co., AR

TURNER, George Benton   ES: Los Angeles, Los Angeles Co., CA
                                      B: Longview, Gregg Co., TX

*WALLACE, Herman C.   ES: Lubbock, Lubbock Co., TX
                                      B: Marlow, Stephens Co., OK

WARD, John   ES: Fort Duncan, TX
                                      B: AR

*WATKINS, Travis E.   ES: Texas
                                      B: Waldo, Columbia Co., AR

WHITELEY, Eli Lamar   ES: Georgetown, Williamson Co., TX
                                      B: Florence, Williamson Co., TX

*YOUNG, Marvin Rex   ES: Odessa, Ector Co., TX
                                      B: Alpine, Brewster Co., TX

U.S. Army Air Corps/U.S. Air Force

*BENNETT, Steven Logan   ES: Lafayette, Lafayette Co., LA
                                      B: Palestine, Anderson Co., TX

*CARSWELL Jr., Horace
Seaver   ES: San Angelo, Tom Green Co., TX
                                      B: Fort Worth, Tarrant Co., TX

*DAVIS Jr., George Andrew   ES: Lubbock, Lubbock Co., TX
                                      B: Dublin, Erath Co., TX

*HUGHES, Lloyd Herbert   ES: San Antonio, Bexar Co., TX
                                      B: Alexandria, Rapides Co., LA

KANE, John Riley   ES: Shreveport, Caddo Co., LA
                                      B: McGregor, McLennan Co., TX

KEARBY, Neel Ernest   ES: Dallas, Collin Co., TX
                                      B: Wichita Falls, Wichita Co., TX

*KNIGHT, Raymond Larry   ES: Houston, Harris Co., TX
                                      B: Houston, Harris Co., TX

*MATHIS, Jack Warren   ES: San Angelo, Tom Green Co., TX
                                      B: San Angelo, Tom Green Co., TX

MORGAN, John Cary "Red"   ES: London, England
                                      B: Vernon, Wilbarger Co., TX

U.S. Navy

BULKELEY, John Duncan   ES: TX
                                      B: San Antonio, Bexar Co., TX

*DEALEY, Samuel David   ES: TX
                                      B: Dallas, Collin Co., TX

HARRISON, William Kelly   ES: TX
                                      B: Waco, McLennan Co., TX

HAYDEN, David Ephraim   ES: TX
                                      B: Florence, Williamson Co., TX

*HUTCHINS, Johnnie David   ES: TX
                                      B: Weimer, Colorado Co., TX

*KILMER, John Edward   ES: Houston, Harris Co., TX
                                      B: Highland Park, Lake Co., IL

PHILLIPS, George Frederick   ES: Galveston, Galveston Co., TX
                                      B: St. John, New Brunswick, Canada

U.S. Marine Corps

*ANDERSON, Richard Allen   ES: Houston, Harris Co., TX
                                      B: Washington, D.C.

*AUSTIN, Oscar Palmer   ES: Phoenix, Maricopa Co., AZ
                                      B. Nacogdoches, Nacogdoches Co., TX

*BORDELON, William James   ES: TX
                                      B: San Antonio, Bexar Co., TX

*CREEK, Thomas Elbert   ES: Amarillo, Potter Co., TX
                                      B: Joplin, Jasper Co., MO

*GONZALEZ, Alfredo
(Freddy)   ES: San Antonio, Bexar Co., TX
                                      B: Edinburg, Hidalgo Co., TX

*GRAVES, Terrence Collinson   ES: NY
                                      B: Corpus Christi, Nueces Co., TX

*GUILLEN, Ambrosio   ES: El Paso, El Paso Co., TX
                                      B: La Junta, Otero Co., CO

HARRELL, William George   ES: Mercedes, Hidalgo Co., TX
                                      B: Rio Grande City, Starr Co., TX

*HAWKINS, William Deane   ES: El Paso, El Paso Co., TX
                                      B: Fort Scott, Bourbon Co., KS

*KEITH, Miguel   ES: Omaha, Douglas Co., NE
                                      B: San Antonio, Bexar Co., TX

*LUMMUS, Jack   ES: TX
                                      B: Ennis, Ellis Co., TX

*MITCHELL, Frank Nicias   ES: Roaring Springs, Motley Co., TX
                                      B: Indian Gap, Hamilton Co., TX

*MORELAND, Whitt Lloyd   ES: Austin, Travis Co., TX
                                      B: Waco, McLennan Co., TX

O'BRIEN Jr., George Herman   ES: Big Spring, Howard Co., TX
                                      B: Fort Worth, Tarrant Co., TX

*ROAN, Charles Howard   ES: TX
                                      B: Claude, Armstrong Co., TX

*WILSON, Alfred Mac   ES: Abilene, Taylor Co., TX
                                      B: Olney, Richland Co., IL

UTAH

U.S. Army

KISTERS, Gerry Herman   ES: Bloomington, Monroe Co., IN
                                      B: Salt Lake City, Salt Lake Co., UT

THACKER, Brian Miles   ES: Salt Lake City, Salt Lake Co., UT
                                      B: Columbus, Franklin Co., OH

*VALDEZ, Jose F.   ES: Pleasant Grove, Utah Co., UT
                                      B: Governador, NM

U.S. Navy

*BENNION, Mervyn Sharp   ES: Utah
                                      B: Vernon, Tooele Co., UT

HALL, William Edward   ES: Mohrland, Emery Co., UT
                                      B: Storrs, Carbon Co., UT

WAHLEN, George Edward   ES: Ogden, Weber Co., UT
                                      B: Ogden, Weber Co., UT

VERMONT

U.S. Army

BATES, Norman Francis   ES: Grinnell, Poweshiek Co., IA
                                      B: Derry, VT

BEATTY, Alexander Mitchell   ES: Guildhall, Essex Co., VT
                                      B: Ryegate, Caledonia Co., VT

BENEDICT, George
Greenville   ES: Burlington, Chittenden Co., VT
                                      B: Burlington, Chittenden Co., VT

BUTTERFIELD, Franklin
George   ES: Rockingham, Windham Co., VT
                                      B: Rockingham, Windham Co., VT

CHURCHILL, Samuel Joseph   ES: DeKalb, DeKalb Co., IL
                                      B: Rutland, Rutland Co., VT

CLARK, John Wesley   ES: VT
                                      B: Montpelier, Washington Co., VT

COFFEY, Robert John	ES: Montpelier, Washington Co., VT B: St. John, New Brunswick, Canada
COUGHLIN, John	ES: Manchester, Hillsborough Co., NH B: VT
DAVIDSON, Andrew	ES: Cincinnati, Hamilton Co., OH B: Middlebury, Addison Co., VT
DAVIS, George Evans	ES: Burlington, Chittenden Co., VT B: Dunstable, Middlesex Co., MA
DOLLOFF, Charles W.	ES: St. Johnsbury, Caledonia Co., VT B: Parishville, St. Lawrence Co., NY
DOWNS, Henry W.	ES: Newfane, Windham Co., VT B: Jamaica, Windham Co., VT
DRURY, James	ES: Chester, Windsor Co., VT B: Limerick, County Limerick, Ireland
EDDY, Samuel E.	ES: Chesterfield, Hampshire Co., MA B: Whitingham, Windham Co., VT
EVANS, Ira Hobart	ES: Barre, Washington Co., VT B: Piermont, Grafton Co., NH
FERRIS, Eugene W.	ES: Lowell, Middlesex Co., MA B: Springfield, Windsor Co., VT
GOULD, Charles Gilbert	ES: Windham Co., VT B: Windham Co., VT
GRANT, Lewis Addison	ES: Bellows Falls, Windham Co., VT B: Winhall, VT
HACK, Lester Goodel	ES: Salisbury, Addison Co., VT B: Cadwell, Warren Co., NY
HARRINGTON, Ephraim W.	ES: Kirby, VT B: Waterford, Oxford Co., ME
HAWKINS, Gardner C.	ES: Woodstock, Windsor Co., VT B: Pomfret, VT
HENRY, William Wirt	ES: Waterbury, Washington Co., VT B: Waterbury, Washington Co., VT
HOLTON, Edward A.	ES: Williston, Chittenden Co., VT B: Westminster, Windham Co., VT
HOWARD, Squire Edward	ES: Townshend, Windham Co., VT B: Jamaica, Windham Co., VT
INGALLS, Lewis J.	ES: Belvidere, Lamoille Co., VT B: Boston, Suffolk Co., MA
JEWETT, Erastus W.	ES: St. Albans, Franklin Co., VT B: St. Albans, Franklin Co., VT
JOHNDRO, Franklin	ES: Queensbury, Warren Co., NY B: Highgate Falls, Franklin Co., VT
JOHNSTON, William (Willie)	ES: St. Johnsbury, Caledonia Co., VT B: Morristown, Morristown Co., NY
LIVINGSTON, Josiah O.	ES: Marshfield, Washington Co., VT B: Walden, VT
LONERGAN, John	ES: Burlington, Chittenden Co., VT B: Carrick, County Donegal, Ireland
LYON, Frederick A.	ES: Burlington, Chittenden Co., VT B: Williamsburg, Hampshire Co., MA
MATTOCKS, Charles Porter	ES: Portland, Cumberland Co., ME B: Danville, Caledonia Co., VT
McCORMICK, Michael P.	ES: Harrisburg, Dauphin Co., PA B: Rutland, Rutland Co., VT
MORAN, John E.	ES: Cascade Co., MT B: Vernon, Windham Co., VT
NICHOLS, Henry Clay	ES: St. Albans, Franklin Co., VT B: Brandon, Rutland Co., VT
NOYES, William W.	ES: Montpelier, Washington Co., VT B: Montpelier, Washington Co., VT

PECK, Cassius	ES: West Randolph, Orange Co., VT B: Brookfield, Orange Co., VT
PECK, Theodore Safford	ES: Burlington, Chittenden Co., VT B: Burlington, Chittenden Co., VT
PHELPS, Charles Edwards	ES: Baltimore, Baltimore Co., MD B: Guilford, VT
PINGREE, Samuel E.	ES: Hartford, Windsor Co., VT B: Salisbury, Merrimack Co., NH
RIPLEY, William Young Warren	ES: Rutland, Rutland Co., VT B: Middlebury, Addison Co., VT
ROBBINS, Augustus J.	ES: Grafton, Windham Co., VT B: Grafton, Windham Co., VT
SARGENT, Jackson	ES: Stowe, Lamoille Co., VT B: Stowe, Lamoille Co., VT
SCOTT, Alexander	ES: Winooski, Chittenden Co., VT B: Montreal, Canada
SCOTT, Julian A.	ES: Johnson, Lamoille Co., VT B: Johnson, Lamoille Co., VT
SEAVER, Thomas Orville	ES: Pomfret, VT B: Cavendish, Windsor Co., VT
SHERMAN, Marshall	ES: St. Paul, Ramsey Co., MN B: Burlington, Chittenden Co., VT
SPERRY, William Joseph	ES: Cavendish, Windsor Co., VT B: Cavendish, Windsor Co., VT
SWEENEY, James	ES: Essex, Chittenden Co., VT B: Manchester, Greater Manchester Co., England
THOMAS, Stephen	ES: West Fairlee, Orange Co., VT B: Bethel, Windsor Co., VT
TILTON, William	ES: Hanover, Grafton Co., NH B: St. Albans, Franklin Co., VT
TRACY, Amasa Sawyer	ES: Middlebury, Addison Co., VT B: Dover, Piscataquis Co., ME
VEAZEY, Wheelock Graves	ES: Springfield, Windsor Co., VT B: Brentwood, Coos Co., NH
WELLS, William	ES: Waterbury, Washington Co., VT B: Waterbury, Washington Co., VT
WHEELER, Daniel Davis	ES: Cavendish, Windsor Co., VT B: Cavendish, Windsor Co., VT
*WILKIN, Edward G.	ES: Longmeadow, Hampden Co., MA B: Burlington, Chittenden Co., VT
WILLISTON, Edward Bancroft	ES: San Francisco, San Francisco Co., CA B: Norwich, Windsor Co., VT
WOODBURY, Eri Davidson	ES: St. Johnsbury, Caledonia Co., VT B: Francistown, Hillsborough Co., NH

U.S. Navy

BLAIR, Robert M.	ES: Portland, Cumberland Co., ME B: Peacham, Caledonia Co., VT
BREAULT, Henry	ES: VT B: Putnam, Windham Co., CT
· BRESNAHAN, Patrick Francis	ES: VT B: Peabody, Essex Co., MA
RAMAGE, Lawson Paterson "Red"	ES: VT B: Monroe Bridge, Franklin Co., MA

U.S. Marine Corps

EDSON, Merritt Austin	ES: VT B: Rutland, Rutland Co., VT

VIRGINIA

U.S. Army

ANDERSON, Charles W.	ES: near Winchester, Frederick Co., VA B: Baltimore, Baltimore Co., MD
AYERS, James F.	ES: Richmond, Richmond Co., VA B: Collinstown, Henry Co., VA
BARNES, William H.	ES: Norfolk, Norfolk Co., VA B: St. Marys Co., MD
BEATY, Powhatan	ES: Cincinnati, Hamilton Co., OH B: Richmond, Richmond Co., VA
BOYNE, Thomas	ES: Norfolk, Norfolk Co., VA B: Prince Georges Co., MD
BROWN, Benjamin	ES: Harrisburg, Dauphin Co., PA B: Spotsylvania Co., VA
BYRNE, Bernard Albert	ES: Washington, D.C. B: Newport Barracks, Giles Co., VA
CARNEY, William Harvey	ES: New Bedford, Bristol Co., MA B: Norfolk, Norfolk Co., VA
DERVISHIAN, Ernest Herbert	ES: Richmond, Richmond Co., VA B: Richmond, Richmond Co., VA
DOSS, Desmond Thomas	ES: Lynchburg, Lynchburg Co., VA B: Lynchburg, Lynchburg Co., VA
DURHAM, James R.	ES: Clarksburg, Harrison Co., NV B: Richmond, Richmond Co., VA
FOLLAND, Michael F.	ES: Richmond, Richmond Co., VA B: Richmond, Richmond Co., VA
*GAMMON, Archer T.	ES: Roanoke, Roanoke Co., VA B: Chatham, Pittsylvania Co., VA
GARDINER, James	ES: Yorktown, York Co., VA B: Gloucester, Gloucester Co., VA
GILLENWATER, James Robert Lee	ES: Rye Cove, VA B: Rye Cove, VA
GREAVES, Clinton	ES: Baltimore, Baltimore Co., MD B: Madison Co., VA
GREGORY, Earl D.	ES: Chase City, Mecklenburg Co., VA B: Chase City, Mecklenburg Co., VA
GRESHAM, John Chowning	ES: Lancaster Courthouse, Lancaster Co., VA B: VA
JAMES, Miles	ES: Portsmouth, Portsmouth Co., VA B: Princess Anne Co., VA
JOHNSON, Henry	ES: Detroit, Wayne Co., MI B: Boydton, Mecklenburg Co., VA
KILBOURNE Jr., Charles Evans	ES: Portland, Multnomah Co., OR B: Fort Myer, Arlington Co., VA
*LANGHORN, Garfield McConnell	ES: Brooklyn, Kings Co., NY B: Cumberland, Cumberland Co., VA
LEE, Fitz	ES: Philadelphia, Philadelphia Co., PA B: Dinwiddie Co., VA
LEVY, Benjamin Bennett	ES: Newport News, Newport News Co., VA B: New York, NY
MAYS, Isaiah	ES: Columbus Barracks, Franklin Co., OH B: Carters Bridge, VA
*MILLER, Gary Lee	ES: Roanoke, Roanoke Co., VA B: Covington, Covington Co., VA
*MONTEITH Jr., Jimmie W.	ES: Richmond, Richmond Co., VA B: Low Moor, Alleghany Co., VA
MORRIS, Charles Bedford	ES: Roanoke, Roanoke Co., VA B: Carroll Co., VA
O'CONNOR, Timothy	ES: New Creek, VA B: Ireland
*PEREGORY, Frank D.	ES: Charlottesville, Charlottesville Co., VA B: Esmont, Albemarle Co., VA
RATCLIFF, Edward	ES: Yorktown, York Co., VA B: James Co., VA
*SARGENT, Ruppert Leon	ES: Richmond, Richmond Co., VA B: Hampton, Hampton Co., VA
SCHNELL, Christian	ES: Wapakoneta, Auglaize Co., OH B: VA
*SHEA Jr., Richard Thomas	ES: Portsmouth, Portsmouth Co., VA B: Portsmouth, Portsmouth Co., VA
SMITH, James (Ovid)	ES: Circleville, Pickaway Co., OH B: Fredericksburg, Fredericksburg Co., VA
STEWART, Benjamin F.	ES: Boston, Suffolk Co., MA B: Norfolk, Norfolk Co., VA
TOMPKINS, Charles Henry	ES: Brooklyn, Kings Co., NY B: Fort Monroe, Hampton Co., VA
VEAL, Charles	ES: Baltimore, Baltimore Co., MD B: Portsmouth, Portsmouth Co., VA
WHITEHEAD, Patton G.	ES: Louisville, Jefferson Co., KY B: Russell Co., VA
WILLS, Henry	ES: St. Louis, St. Louis Co., MO B: Gracon, VA
WOODALL, William H.	ES: Winchester, Frederic Co., VA B: Lynchburg, Lynchburg Co., VA
WOODALL, Zachariah	ES: Carlisle, Cumberland Co., PA B: Alexandria, Alexandria Co., VA

U.S. Army Air Corps/U.S. Air Force

*JONES III, William Atkinson	ES: Charlottesville, Charlottesville Co., VA B: Norfolk, Norfolk Co., VA
*WILKINS, Raymond Harrell	ES: Portsmouth, Portsmouth Co., VA B: Portsmouth, Portsmouth Co., VA

U.S. Navy

ATKINS, Daniel	ES: VA B: Brunswick, VA
BARROW, David Duffy	ES: Norfolk, Norfolk Co., VA B: Reelsboro, NC
BLAKE, Robert	ES: Port Royal, Caroline Co., VA B: VA
BRIGHT, George Washington	ES: VA B: Norfolk, Norfolk Co., VA
BYRD Jr., Richard Evelyn	ES: VA B: Winchester, Frederick Co., VA
*HAMMOND, Francis Colton	ES: Alexandria, Alexandria Co., VA B: Alexandria, Alexandria Co., VA
JORDAN, Thomas H.	ES: Baltimore, Baltimore Co., MD B: Portsmouth, Portsmouth Co., VA
LANGHORNE, Cary DeVall	ES: VA B: Lynchburg, Lynchburg Co., VA
LANNON, James Patrick	ES: VA B: Alexandria, Alexandria Co., VA
MIFFLIN, James	ES: VA B: Richmond, Richmond Co., VA
O'CONNER, James Francis	ES: VA B: Portsmouth, Portsmouth Co., VA

PENN, Robert   ES: VA
B: City Point, VA

SHACKLETTE, William
Sidney   ES: VA
B: Delaplane, Fauquier Co., VA

SMITH, Frank Elmer   ES: VA
B: Boston, Suffolk Co., MA

SMITH, Thomas   ES: VA
B: Ireland

STREET III, George Levick   ES: Richmond, Richmond Co., VA
B: Richmond, Richmond Co., VA

TAYLOR, Richard Hamilton   ES: VA
B: Staunton, Staunton Co., VA

TORGERSON, Martin
Torinus   ES: VA
B: Oleesen, Norway

VOLZ, Robert   ES: VA
B: San Francisco, San Francisco Co., CA

U.S. Marine Corps

*BAUSELL, Lewis Kenneth   ES: Washington, D.C.
B: Pulaski, Montgomery Co., VA

BERKELEY, Randolph Carter   ES: Appointed from: Washington, D.C
B: Staunton, Staunton Co., VA

FOX, Wesley Lee   ES: Leesburg, Loudoun Co., VA
B: Herndon, Fairfax Co., VA

LEE, Howard Vincent   ES: Dumfries, Prince William Co., VA
B: New York, NY

LUCAS, Jacklyn Harold   ES: Norfolk, Norfolk Co., VA
B: Plymouth, Washington Co., NC

*MARTINI, Gary Wayne   ES: Portland, Multnomah Co., OR
B: Lexington, Lexington Co., VA

NEVILLE, Wendell Cushing   ES: VA
B: Portsmouth, Portsmouth Co., VA

*SMEDLEY, Larry Eugene   ES: Orlando, Orange Co., FL
B: Front Royal, Warren Co., VA

SUTTON, Clarence Edwin   ES: Washington, D.C.
B: Urbanna, Middlesex Co., VA

UPSHUR, William Peterkin   ES: VA
B: Richmond, Richmond Co., VA

VANDEGRIFT, Alexander
Archer   ES: VA
B: Charlottesville, Charlottesville Co., VA

WASHINGTON

U.S. Army

*ALBANESE, Lewis   ES: Seattle, King Co., WA
B: Venice, Italy

ALLWORTH, Edward C.   ES: Corvallis, Benton Co., OR
B: Crawford, WA

BJORKLUND, Arnold L.   ES: Seattle, King Co., WA
B: Clinton, Island Co., WA

BRADY, Patrick Henry   ES: Seattle, King Co., WA
B: Philip, Haakon Co., SD

BRONSON, Deming   ES: Seattle, King Co., WA
B: Rhinelander, Oneida Co., WI

CLANCY, John E.   ES: Vancouver Barracks, Clark Co., WA
B: New York, NY

*GRANDSTAFF, Bruce Alan   ES: Spokane, Spokane Co., WA
B: Spokane, Spokane Co., WA

HAWK, John Druse "Bud"   ES: Bremerton, Kitsap Co., WA
B: San Francisco, San Francisco Co., CA

*KANDLE, Victor Leonard   ES: Redwood City, San Mateo Co., CA
B: Roy, Pierce Co., WA

KERSTETTER, Dexter James   ES: Centralia, Lewis Co., WA
B: Centralia, Lewis Co., WA

KINSMAN, Thomas James   ES: Seattle, King Co., WA
B: Renton, King Co., WA

*LEISY, Robert Ronald   ES: Seattle, King Co., WA
B: Stockton, San Joaquin Co., CA

LYON, Edward Eugene   ES: Amboy, Clark Co., WA
B: Hixton, Jackson Co., WI

*MANN, Joe Eugene   ES: Seattle, King Co., WA
B: Reardan, Lincoln Co., WA

McCARTER, Lloyd G.   ES: Tacoma, Pierce Co., WA
B: St. Maries, Benewah Co., ID

*PENDLETON, Jack James   ES: Yakima, Yakima Co., WA
B: Sentinel Butte, Golden Valley Co., ND

STEVENS, Hazard   ES: Olympia, Thurston Co., Washington
Territory
B: Newport, Newport Co., RI

WILSON, Benjamin F.   ES: Vashon, King Co., WA
B: Vashon, King Co., WA

WILSON, John Moulder   ES: Olympia, Thurston Co., Washington
Territory
B: Washington, D.C.

U.S. Air Force

FLEMING, James Phillip   ES: Pullman, Whitman Co., WA
B: Sedalia, Pettis Co., MO

U.S. Navy

BUSH, Robert Eugene   ES: WA
B: Tacoma, Pierce Co., WA

DAVIS, Raymond Erwin   ES: Puget Sound, WA
B: Mankato, Blue Earth Co., MN

FADDEN, Harry Delmar   ES: WA
B: The Dalles, Wasco Co., OR

*KEPPLER, Reinhardt John   ES: WA
B: Ralston, WA

*ROOKS, Albert Harold   ES: WA
B: Colton, Whitman Co., WA

*SHIELDS, Marvin Glen   ES: Seattle, King Co., WA
B: Port Townsend, Jefferson Co., WA

*VAN VOORHIS, Bruce
Avery   ES: Nevada
B: Aberdeen, Grays Harbor Co., WA

U.S. Coast Guard

*MUNRO, Douglas Albert   ES: WA
B: Vancouver, British Columbia, Canada

U.S. Marine Corps

*ANDERSON, Richard Beatty   ES: WA
B: Tacoma, Pierce Co., WA

BOYINGTON, Gregory
"Pappy"   ES: WA
B: Coeur D'Alene, Kootenai Co., ID

GALER, Robert Edward   ES: Seattle, King Co., WA
B: Seattle, King Co., WA

*MONEGAN Jr., Walter
Carleton   ES: Seattle, King Co., WA
B: Melrose, Middlesex Co., MA

*REASONER, Frank Stanley	ES: Kellogg, Shoshone Co., ID B: Spokane, Spokane Co., WA
SWETT, James Elms	ES: San Mateo, San Mateo Co., CA B: Seattle, King Co., WA
VAN WINKLE, Archie	ES: Arlington, Snohomish Co., WA B: Juneau, Juneau Co., AK
WINANS, Roswell	ES: WA B: Brookville, Franklin Co., IN

WEST VIRGINIA

U.S. Army

ADAMS, James F.	ES: Ceredo, Wayne Co., WV B: Cabell Co., WV
ANDERSON, Thomas	ES: Wheeling, Ohio Co., WV B: Scenery Hill, Washington Co., PA
APPLE, Andrew O.	ES: New Manchester, Hancock Co., WV B: Northampton, Northampton Co., PA
BARRINGER, William H.	ES: Mason City, Mason Co., WV B: Long Bottom, Meigs Co., OH
*BELCHER, Ted	ES: Huntington, Cabell Co., WV B: Accoville, Logan Co., WV
BELL, Bernard Pious	ES: New York, NY B: Grantsville, Calhoun Co., WV
BENDER, Stanley	ES: Chicago, Cook Co., IL B: Carlisle, WV
*BENNETT, Thomas William	ES: Fairmont, Marion Co., WV B: Morgantown, Monongalia Co., WV
BISHOP, Daniel	ES: Wheeling, Ohio Co., WV B: Monroe Co., OH
BOURY, Richard	ES: Wirt Courthouse, WV B: Monroe Co., OH
BUCKLEY, John C.	ES: Mount Pleasant, WV B: Fayette Co., WV
BUMGARNER, William	ES: Mason City, Mason Co., WV B: Mason Co., WV
BURNS, James Madison	ES: Wellsburg, Brooke Co., WV B: Wells Township, Jefferson Co., OH
*CHARLTON, Cornelius H.	ES: Bronx Co., NY B: East Gulf, Raleigh Co., WV
CORCORAN, Michael	ES: Wheeling, Ohio Co., WV B: Philadelphia, Philadelphia Co., PA
CRISWELL, Benjamin C.	ES: Cincinnati, Hamilton Co., OH B: Moundsville, Marshall Co., WV
CURTIS, Josiah M.	ES: West Liberty, Ohio Co., WV B: Ohio Co., WV
DIXON, William "Billy"	ES: Indian Territory B: Ohio Co., WV
DURHAM, James R.	ES: Clarksburg, Harrison Co., WV B: Richmond, Richmond Co., VA
ECKES, John N.	ES: Weston, Lewis Co., WV B: Lewis Co., WV
GAUJOT, Antoine August	ES: Williamson, Mingo Co., WV B: Keweenaw, Baraga Co., MI
GAUJOT, Julien Edmund	ES: Williamson, Mingo Co., WV B: Keweenaw, Baraga Co., MI
GODLEY, Leonidas Mahlon	ES: Ashland, IA B: Mason Co., WV
*HARTSOCK, Robert Willard	ES: Fairmont, Marion Co., WV B: Cumberland, Allegany Co., MD
*HARVEY Jr., Carmel Bernon	ES: Chicago, Cook Co., IL B: Montgomery, Fayette Co., WV

*HEDRICK, Clinton M.	ES: Riverton, Pendleton Co., WV B: Cherry Grove, WV
HORSFALL, William H.	ES: Fort Cox, Charleston, WV B: Campbell Co., KY
*KELLEY, Jonah Edward High	ES: Keyser, Mineral Co., WV B: Roda, WV
*KYLE, Darwin K.	ES: Racine, Boone Co., WV B: Jenkins, Letcher Co., KY
MAYFIELD, Melvin	ES: Nashport, Muskingum Co., OH B: Salem, Harrison Co., WV
McCAUSLIN, Joseph	ES: West Liberty, Ohio Co., WV B: Ohio Co., WV
*McDONALD, Phill Gene	ES: Beckley, Raleigh Co., WV B: Avondale, McDowell Co., WV
McELHINNY, Samuel O.	ES: Point Pleasant, Mason Co., WV B: Meigs Co., OH
McWHORTER, Walter F.	ES: Clarksburg, Harrison Co., WV B: Lewis Co., WV
*MOLNAR, Frankie Zoly	ES: Fresno, Fresno Co., CA B: Logan, Logan Co., WV
MOORE, George G.	ES: Parkersburg, Wood Co., WV B: Tyler Co., WV
PARSONS, Joel	ES: Mason City, Mason Co., WV B: Jackson Co., WV
*POMEROY, Ralph Eugene	ES: Quinwood, Greenbrier Co., WV B: Quinwood, Greenbrier Co., WV
REEDER, Charles A.	ES: Shinnston, Harrison Co., WV B: Harrison, Clay Co., WV
ROGERS, Charles Calvin	ES: Institute, Kanawha Co., WV B: Claremont, WV
SCHORN, Charles	ES: Mason City, Mason Co., WV B: Germany
SHAHAN, Emisire	ES: Clarksburg, Harrison Co., WV B: Preston Co., WV
SHANES, John	ES: Warren, WV B: Monongalia Co., WV
SHOEMAKER, Levi	ES: Clarksburg, Harrison Co., WV B: Monongalia Co., WV
*STEWART, Jimmy Goethel	ES: Ashland, Boyd Co., KY B: West Columbia, Mason Co., WV
SUMMERS, James Calvin	ES: Point Pleasant, Mason Co., WV B: on Elk River six miles above Charleston, Kanawha Co., WV
VAN MATRE, Joseph	ES: Middleport, Meigs Co., OH B: Mason Co., WV
WARD, Thomas J.	ES: Decatur, Macon Co., IL B: Romney, Hampshire Co., WV
WEIR, Henry Cary	ES: Bolivar, WV B: West Point, Orange Co., NY
*WETZEL, Walter C.	ES: Roseville, Macomb Co., MI B: Huntington, Cabell Co., WV
WHITE, Adam	ES: Parkersburg, Wood Co., WV B: Switzerland
WOODS, Daniel A. (Wood)	ES: Wheeling, Ohio Co., WV B: Ohio Co., WV

U.S. Army Air Corps

*FEMOYER, Robert Edward	ES: Jacksonville, Duval Co., FL B: Huntington, Cabell Co., WV

U.S. Navy

COX, Robert Edward	ES: WV B: St. Albans, Kanawha Co., WV

FRAZER, Hugh Carroll | ES: WV
B: Martinsburg, Berkeley Co., WV

JONES, Claud Ashton | ES: WV
B: Fire Creek, WV

NICKERSON, Henry Nehemiah | ES: WV
B: Edgewood, WV

SINNETT, Lawrence Clinton | ES: PA
B: Burnt House, WV

U.S. Marine Corps

CHAMBERS, Justice Marion | ES: Washington, D.C.
B: Huntington, Cabell Co., WV

QUICK, John Henry | ES: PA
B: Charleston, Kanawha Co., WV

*THOMAS, Herbert Joseph | ES: WV
B: Columbus, Franklin Co., OH

WILLIAMS, Hershel Woodrow "Woody" | ES: Fairmont, Marion Co., WV
B: Quiet Dell, Marion Co., WV

WISCONSIN

U.S. Army

ANDERSON, Beauford Theodore | ES: Soldiers Grove, Crawford Co., WI
B: Eagle, Waukesha Co., WI

ANDERSON, Peter T. | ES: Wiota, WI
B: Darlington, Lafayette Co., WI

BELL, Harry | ES: Minneapolis, Hennepin Co., MN
B: Milwaukee, Milwaukee Co., WI

*BELLRICHARD, Leslie Allen | ES: Oakland, Alameda Co., CA
B: Janesville, Rock Co., WI

BLOCH, Orville Emil | ES: Streeter, Stutsman Co., ND
B: Big Falls, Waupaca Co., WI

BRONSON, Deming | ES: Seattle, King Co., WA
B: Rhinelander, Oneida Co., WI

BROOKIN, Oscar | ES: Green Co., OH
B: Byron, Fond Du Lac Co., WI

*BURR, Elmer J. | ES: Menasha, Winnebago Co., WI
B: Neenah, Winnebago Co., WI

CABLE, Joseph A. | ES: Madison, Dane Co., WI
B: Cape Girardeau, Cape Girardeau Co., MO

COATES, Jefferson | ES: Boscobel, Grant Co., WI
B: Grant Co., WI

CROFT, James E. | ES: Janesville, Rock Co., WI
B: Yorkshire, England

DURHAM, John S. | ES: Malone, Fond Du Lac Co., WI
B: New York, NY

ELLIS, Horace | ES: Chippewa Falls, Chippewa Co., WI
B: Mercer Co., PA

ELLIS, William | ES: Watertown, Jefferson Co., WI
B: England

*ENDL, Gerald Leon | ES: Janesville, Rock Co., WI
B: Fort Atkinson, Jefferson Co., WI

FRITZ, Harold Arthur | ES: Milwaukee, Milwaukee Co., WI
B: Chicago, Cook Co., IL

GOLDIN, Theodore W. B. | ES: Chicago, Cook Co., IL
B: Avon, Rock Co., WI

*GRUENNERT, Kenneth E. | ES: Helenville, Jefferson Co., WI
B: Helenville, Jefferson Co., WI

*HANDRICH, Melvin O. | ES: Manawa, Waupaca Co., WI
B: Manawa, Waupaca Co., WI

HILL, Frank E. | ES: St. Louis, St. Louis Co., MO
B: Mayfield, WI

HILLIKER, Benjamin F. | ES: Waupaca Township, Waupaca Co., WI
B: Golden, Erie Co., NY

INGMAN Jr., Einar Harold | ES: West Bend, Washington Co., WI
B: Milwaukee, Milwaukee Co., WI

JOHNSON, John | ES: Janesville, Rock Co., WI
B: Toten Christiana (now Olso), Norway

KINNE, John Baxter | ES: Fargo, Cass Co., ND
B: Beloit, Rock Co., WI

LYON, Edward Eugene | ES: Amboy, Clark Co., WA
B: Hixton, Jackson Co., WI

MacARTHUR, Douglas | ES: Ashland, Ashland Co., WI
B: Little Rock, Pulaski Co., AR

MacARTHUR Jr., Arthur | ES: Milwaukee, Milwaukee Co., WI
B: Springfield, Hampden Co., MA

*McGRATH, Hugh Jocelyn | ES: Eau Claire, Eau Claire Co., WI
B: Fond Du Lac, Fond Du Lac Co., WI

*MILLER, Andrew | ES: Two Rivers, Manitowoc Co., WI
B: Manitowoc, Manitowoc Co., WI

MOORE, Daniel B. | ES: Mifflin, Iowa Co., WI
B: Mifflin, Iowa Co., WI

*MOWER, Charles E. | ES: Chippewa Falls, Chippewa Co., WI
B: Chippewa Falls, Chippewa Co., WI

NEWMAN, Beryl Richard | ES: Baraboo, Sauk Co., WI
B: Baraboo, Sauk Co., WI

NOLAN, Richard J. | ES: Milwaukee, Milwaukee Co., WI
B: Ireland

O'CONNOR, Albert | ES: Lodi, Columbia Co., WI
B: Herford, Canada

*OLSON, Truman O. | ES: Cambridge, Dane Co., WI
B: Christiana, WI

POND, George F. | ES: Fairwater, Fond du Lac Co., WI
B: Libertyville, Lake Co., IL

POND, James Burton | ES: Janesville, Rock Co., WI
B: Allegany, Cattaraugus Co., NY

*RED CLOUD Jr., Mitchell | ES: Merrillan, Jackson Co., WI
B: Hatfield, WI

ROBBINS, Marcus M. | ES: Boston, Suffolk Co., MA
B: Elba, Dodge Co., WI

ROBERTSON, Marcus William | ES: Hood River, Hood River Co., OR
B: Flintville, WI

SICKLES, William H. | ES: Fall River, Columbia Co., WI
B: Danube, Herkimer Co., NY

SLACK, Clayton Kirk | ES: Madison, Dane Co., WI
B: Plover, Portage Co., WI

STUMPF, Kenneth Edward | ES: Milwaukee, Milwaukee Co., WI
B: Neenah, Winnebago Co., WI

*SUDUT, Jerome A. | ES: WI
B: Wausau, Marathon Co., WI

TOOHEY, Thomas | ES: Milwaukee, Milwaukee Co., WI
B: New York, NY

TRUELL, Edwin M. | ES: Mantson, WI
B: Lowell, Middlesex Co., MA

WALLER, Francis A. | ES: DeSoto, Vernon Co., WI
B: Gurney, OH

WETZEL, Gary George | ES: Milwaukee, Milwaukee Co., WI
B: South Milwaukee, Milwaukee Co., WI

WHITTLESEY, Charles White   ES: Pittsfield, Berkshire Co., MA
   B: Florence, Florence Co., WI

WINDUS, Claron   ES: Indianapolis, Marion Co., IN
   B: Janesville, Rock Co., WI

U.S. Army Air Corps/U.S. Air Force

BONG, Richard Ira   ES: Poplar, Douglas Co., WI
   B: Superior, Douglas Co., WI

*JERSTAD, John Louis   ES: Racine, Racine Co., WI
   B: Racine, Racine Co., WI

*SIJAN, Lance Peter   ES: Milwaukee, Milwaukee Co., WI
   B: Milwaukee, Milwaukee Co., WI

U.S. Navy

CASTLE, Guy Wilkinson
Stuart   ES: WI

De SOMER, Abraham   ES: WI
   B: Milwaukee, Milwaukee Co., WI

*PETERSON, Oscar Verner   ES: WI
   B: Prentice, Price Co., WI

SIEGEL, John Otto   ES: NJ
   B: Milwaukee, Milwaukee Co., WI

*VAN VALKENBURGH,
Franklin   ES: WI
   B: Minneapolis, Hennepin Co., MN

YOUNG, Cassin   ES: WI
   B: Washington, D.C.

U.S. Marine Corps

*AGERHOLM, Harold
Christ   S: Wisconsin
   B: Racine, WI

*CHRISTIANSON, Stanley
Reuben   ES: Mindoro, La Crosse Co., WI
   B: Mindoro, La Crosse Co., WI

MODRZEJEWSKI, Robert
Joseph   ES: Milwaukee, Milwaukee Co., WI
   B: Milwaukee, Milwaukee Co., WI

YOUNG, Frank Albert   ES: Wisconsin
   B: Milwaukee, Milwaukee Co., WI

WYOMING

U.S. Army

*ADAMS, William Edward   ES: Kansas City, Clay Co., MO
   B: Casper, Natrona Co., WY

BAKER Jr., Edward Lee   ES: Cincinnati, Hamilton Co., OH
   B: Platte River, Laramie Co., WY

*CAREY Jr., Charles F.   ES: Cheyenne, Laramie Co., WY
   B: Canadian, Pittsburg Co., OK

ROBERTS, Charles Duval   ES: Fort D.A. Russell, WY
   B: Cheyenne Agency, Dakota

WASHINGTON, D.C.

U.S. Army

BARNES, Will Croft   ES: Washington, D.C.
   B: San Francisco, San Francisco Co., CA

BELL, Dennis   ES: Washington, D.C.
   B: Washington, D.C.

BERKELEY, Randolph Carter   ES: Washington, D.C.
   B: Stauton, Stauton Co., VA

BRADBURY, Sanford   ES: Washington, D.C.
   B: Newton, Sussex County, New Jersey

BUCHA, Paul William   ES: USMA West Point, Orange County,
New York
   B: Washington, D.C.

BUTTERFIELD, Daniel
Adams   ES: Washington, D.C.
   B: Utica, Oneida County, New York

BYRNE, Bernard Albert   ES: Washington, D.C.
   B: Newport Barracks, Giles County, Virginia

CAPEHART, Charles E.   ES: Washington, D.C.
   B: Conemaugh Township, Pennsylvania

CHEEVER Jr., Benjamin
Harrison   ES: Washington, D.C.
   B: Washington, D.C.

CHURCH, James Robb   ES: Washington, D.C.
   B: Chicago, Cook County, Illinois

CUTTS, James Madison   ES: Providence, Providence County, Rhode
Island
   B: Washington, D.C.

FORCE, Manning Ferguson   ES: Cincinnati, Hamilton County, Ohio
   B: Washington, D.C.

*HOOKER, George   ES: Washington, D.C.
   B: Frederick, Frederick County, Maryland

LENIHAN, James   ES: Washington, D.C.
   B: County Kerry, Ireland

LITEKY, Charles James
(Angelo)   ES: Fort Hamilton, Kings County, New York
   B: Washington, D.C.

*LUCAS, Andre Cavaro   ES: West Point, Orange County, New York
   B: Washington, D.C.

McALWEE, Benjamin
Franklin   ES: Baltimore, Baltimore County, Maryland
   B: Washington, D.C.

McBRIDE, Bernard   ES: Washington, D.C.
   B: Brooklyn, Kings County, New York

*McGOVERN, Robert Milton   ES: Washington, D.C.
   B: Washington, D.C.

*McMAHON, Thomas
Joseph   ES: Portland, Cumberland County, Maine
   B: Washington, D.C.

PLOWMAN, George H.   ES: Washington, D.C.
   B: Oxford, Oxfordshire, England

PORTER, Samuel   ES: Washington, D.C.
   B: Montgomery County, Maryland

SCOTT, Robert Sheldon   ES: Santa Fe, Santa Fe County, New Mexico
   B: Washington, D.C.

SHAW, George Clymer   ES: Washington, D.C.
   B: Pontiac, Oakland County, Michigan

SHEPHERD, William   ES: Washington, D.C.
   B: Dillsboro, Ohio County, Indiana

*TAYLOR, Bernard   ES: Washington, D.C.
   B: St. Louis, St. Louis County, Missouri

TAYLOR, William   ES: Frederick, Frederick County, Maryland
   B: Washington, D.C.

WARRINGTON, Lewis   ES: Washington, D.C.
   B: Washington, D.C.

WILSON, John Moulder   ES: Olympia, Thurston County,
Washington Territory
   B: Washington, D.C.

WOODRUFF, Carle Augustus   ES: Washington, D.C.
   B: Buffalo, Erie County, New York

U.S. Navy

BADGER, Oscar Charles   ES: Washington, D.C.
B: Washington, D.C.

BAKER, Charles   ES: New York, NY
B: Washington, D.C.

BEHNKE, Heinrich   ES: Washington, D.C.
B: Germany

COURTS, George McCall   ES: Washington, D.C.
B: Washington, D.C.

FLUCKEY, Eugene Bennett   ES: Neoga, Cumberland County, Illinois
B: Washington, D.C.

HARRINGTON, David   ES: Washington, D.C.
B: Washington, D.C.

HAYDEN, John   ES: Washington, D.C.
B: Washington, D.C.

KEEFER, Philip Bogan   ES: Washington, D.C.
B: Washington, D.C.

LIPSCOMB, Harry   ES: Washington, D.C.
B: Washington, D.C.

McCANDLESS, Bruce   ES: Colorado
B: Washington, D.C.

McDONALD, James Harper   ES: Washington, D.C.
B: Newmaud, Scotland

PRESTON, Arthur Murray   ES: Maryland
B: Washington, D.C.

RUSH, John   ES: Washington, D.C.
B: Washington, D.C.

WAINWRIGHT Jr., Richard   ES: Washington, D.C.
B: Washington, D.C.

WHEELER, George Huber   ES: Washington, D.C.
B: Charleston Co., S.C.

WHITE, Joseph   ES: Philadelphia, Philadelphia County,
Pennsylvania
B: Washington, D.C.

YOUNG, Cassin   ES: Wisconsin
B: Washington, D.C.

U.S. Marine Corps

*ANDERSON, Richard Allen   ES: Houston, Harris County, Texas
B: Washington, D.C.

*BAUSELL, Lewis Kenneth   ES: Washington, D.C.
B: Pulaski, Montgomery County, Virginia

CHAMBERS, Justice Marion   ES: Washington, D.C.
B: Huntington, Cabell County, West Virginia

*JOHNSON, James Edmund   ES: Washington, D.C.
B: Pocatello, Bannock County, Idaho

MILLER, Andrew   ES: Washington, D.C.
B: Germany

MURPHY, John Alphonsus   ES: Washington, D.C.
B: New York, New York

PORTER, David Dixon   ES: Washington, D.C.
B: Washington, D.C.

*SCHWAB, Albert Ernest   ES: Tulsa, Tulsa County, Oklahoma
B: Washington, D.C.

STEWART, Peter   ES: Washington, D.C.
B: Airdrie, Scotland

SUTTON, Clarence Edwin   ES: Washington, D.C.
B: Urbanna, Middlesex County, Virginia

FOREIGN-BORN RECIPIENTS

AUSTRALIA

BELPITT, William Henry, USN	B: Sydney, Australia
HAMILTON, Mathew H., USA	B: Hobert, Australia
STEWART, George Evans, USA	B: New South Wales (Australia)

AUSTRIA

BURGER, Joseph, USA	B: Swiss Tyrol, Austria
CORAHORGI, Demetri, USN	B: Triste, Austria
CUKELA, Louis, USMC	B: Sebenes, Austria
FITZ, Joseph, USN	B: Austria
GRBITCH, Rade, USN	B: Austria
KARPELES, Leopold, USA	B: Prague, Austria - Hungary
*KOCAK, Matej, USMC	B: Gbely, Austria
*TOMICH, Peter, USN	B: Prolog, Austria
VADAS, Albert (WADAS), USN	B: Austria - Hungary

BELGIUM

LABILL, Joseph S., USA	B: Belgium
OSS, Albert, USA	B: Belgium
VIFQUAIN, Victor, USA	B: Brussels, Belgium

BERMUDA

SMITH, John, USN	B: Bermuda

CANADA

ANDERSON, James (SMYTH), USA	B: Canada (east)
ASTEN, Charles (Michael), USN	B: Halifax, Nova Scotia, Canada
BOIS, Frank, USN	B: Canada
BROWN, John Harties, USA	B: New Brunswick, Canada
*BUCKLEY, Denis, USA	B: Canada
CAMPBELL, Daniel J., USMC	B: Prince Edward Island, Canada
CAYER, Ovila, USA	B: St. Remi, Canada
CHAPUT, Louis G., USN	B: Canada
COFFEY, Robert John, USA	B: St. John, New Brunswick, Canada
COONEY, Thomas C., USN	B: Westport, Nova Scotia, Canada
DODD, Robert Fulton, USA	B: Canada
DODDS, Edward Edwin, USA	B: Canada
EVERETTS, John, USN	B: Therold, Canada
FITZPATRICK, Thomas, USN	B: Canada
FLANNIGAN, James (FLANAGAN), USA	B: Canada
GARVIN, William, USN	B: Canada (west)
GAY, Thomas H., USA	B: Prince Edward Island, Canada
GILMORE, John Curtis, USA	B: Canada
GRADY, John, USN	B: New Brunswick, Canada
HAGERTY, Asel (HAGERT, Asa), USA	B: Canada
HARDING, Mosher A., USA	B: Canada (west)
HAYES, John, USN	B: Brogus, Newfoundland, Canada
HIGGINS, Thomas J., USA	B: Riverlequerre, Quebec, Canada
HOUGHTON, George L., USA	B: Yarmouth, Canada (west)
KERSEY, Thomas Joseph, USN	B: St. Johns, Newfoundland, Canada
KILMARTIN, John (GILMARTIN), USA	B: Montreal, Canada
LEMON, Peter Charles, USA	B: Toronto, Canada
LOW, George (EVATT), USN	B: Canada
MacGILLIVARY, Charles Andrew, USA	B: Prince Edward Island, Canada
MADDIN, Edward (MADDEN), USN	B: Newfoundland, Canada
McCARTHY, Michael, USA	B: St. Johns, Newfoundland, Canada
McINTOSH, James, USN	B: Canada
McMAHON, Martin Thomas, USA	B: LaPraire, Quebec, Canada
*McVEANE, John P. (McVEAN), USA	B: Toronto, Canada
MILLER, Harry Herbert, USN	B: Nova Scotia, Canada
MILLER, Willard D., USN	B: Nova Scotia, Canada
MOORE, Philip, USN	B: Newfoundland, Canada
MORGAN, George Horace, USA	B: Canada
*MUNRO, Douglas Albert, USCG	B: Vancouver, British Columbia, Canada
MURPHY, James T., USA	B: Canada
NEIL, John, USN	B: Newfoundland, Canada
NOIL, Joseph B., USN	B: Nova Scotia, Canada
O'CONNOR, Albert, USA	B: Herford, Canada
O'NEILL, Stephen, USA	B: St. John, New Brunswick, Canada
PELHAM, William, USN	B: Halifax, Nova Scotia, Canada
PHILLIPS, George Frederick, USN	B: St. John, New Brunswick, Canada
PICKLE, Alonzo H., USA	B: Canada

842

POWERS, Wesley James, USA	B: Orono, Ontario, Canada	ELMORE, Walter, USN	B: England
RICH, Carlos H., USA	B: Canada	ERICKSON, John P., USN	B: London, England
ROBINSON, Joseph, USA	B: Montreal, Canada	FISHER, Frederick Thomas, USN	B: England
RUSSELL, Henry Peter, USN	B: Quebec, Canada	FOSTER, William, USA	B: Somerset Co., England
SCOTT, Alexander, USA	B: Canada	GARRETT, William, USA	B: Isle of Man, England
SHIVERS, John, USMC	B: Canada	GRAHAM, Robert (HALL, Fred), USN	B: England
STODDARD, James, USN	B: Port Robinson, Canada (west)	GREEN, George, USA	B: Elsham, Lincolnshire
WILLIAMS, Henry, USN	B: Canada	HALFORD, William, USN	B: Gloucester, Gloucestershire
WORTMAN, George G., USA	B: Monckton, New Brunswick, Canada	HARBOURNE, John H., USA	B: England
		HARVEY, Harry (HUCKMAN), USA	B: England
YOUNG, Benjamin F., USA	B: Canada	HIBSON, Joseph C., USA	B: London, England
		HILL, George, USN	B: England

CHILE

BAZAAR, Philip, USN	B: Chile	HILL, James, USA	B: Bristol, Avon Co., England
		HOLDEN, Henry, USA	B: Brighton, Sussex Co.,

CHINA

HAYS, George Price, USA	B: China	HOLEHOUSE, James, USA	B: Stockport, Greater Manchester Co.
HOWARD, James Howell, USAAC/USAF	B: Canton, China		
		HORTON, James (Joseph), USN	B: England

CUBA

ROBINSON, John, USN	B: Cuba	HULBERT, Henry Lewis, USMC	B: Kingston-upon-Hull, Humberside Co.

DENMARK

BENSON, James, USN	B: Denmark	HUNT, Frederick O., USA	B: London, England
BROWN, John, USN	B: Denmark	IRLAM, Joseph, USN	B: Liverpool, Merseyside Co.
CLAUSEN, Claus Kristian Randolph, USN	B: Denmark	IRVING, Thomas, USN	B: England
DRUSTRUP, Niels, USN	B: Denmark	JAMES, John, USA	B: Manchester, Greater Manchester Co.
IRWIN, Nicholas, USN	B: Denmark		
JENSEN, Gotfred, USA	B: Denamrk	JENNINGS, James T., USA	B: Devonshire, England
MILLER, James, USN	B: Denmark	JOHNSON, Peter, USN	B: Sumerland, England
MULLER, Frederick, USN	B: Copenhagen, Denmark	JUDGE, Francis W., USA	B: England
SCHOU, Julius Alexis, USA	B: Copenhagen, Denamrk	KAY, John, USA	B: Lancashire Co., England
		KEEN, Joseph S., USA	B: Vale, Guernsey, England
		KEENE, Joseph, USA	B: England

ENGLAND

BAYBUTT, Philip, USA	B: Manchester, Greater Manchester Co.	KENNA, Barnett, USN	B: Canterbury, Kent Co., England
		*KOELSCH, John Kelvin, USN	B: London, England
BEDDOWS, Richard, USA	B: Liverpool, Merseyside Co.	LATHAM, John Cridland, USA	B: Windemere, Cumbria Co., England
BEECH, John P., USA	B: Stratfordshire, England	LESLIE, Frank, USA	B: London, England
BELL, George H., USN	B: Sunderland, England	LLOYD, Benjamin, USN	B: Liverpool, Merseyside Co.
BLAGHEEN, William (BLAGDEN), USN	B: Devonshire, England	LORD, William, USA	B: Bradford, England
BOURNE, Thomas, USN	B: England	LUDGATE, William, USA	B: London, England
BRADLEY, Thomas Wilson, USA	B: Sheffield, Yorkshire, England	MACHON, James, USN	B: Derby, Derbyshire, England
BREYER, Charles, USA	B: England	MADDEN, William, USN	B: Devonshire, England
BURTON, Albert, USN	B: England	MANDY, Harry J., USA	B: England
CARMAN, Warren, USA	B: England	MATHEWS, William Henry	B: Devizes, Wiltshire, England
CARTER, Joseph Edward, USN	B: Manchester, Greater Manchester Co.	MERTON, James F., USN	B: Cheshire, England
		MORIARITY, John, USA	B: Huddersfield, Yorkshire
CAVAIANI, Jon Robert, USA	B: Royston, England	MORIN, William Henry, USN	B: Birmingham, West Midlands Co.
COOK, John Henry, USA	B: London, England		
CROFT, James E., USA	B: Yorkshire, England	MURPHY, Charles Joseph, USA	B: Stockport, Greater Manchester Co.
DENHAM, Austin, USN	B: England		
DONNELLY, John C., USN	B: England	NORRIS, J. W., USN	B: England
DORE, George H., USA	B: England	OAKLEY, William, USN	B: Colchester, Essex Co., England
ELLIS, William, USA	B: England	PARKER, Thomas, USA	B: England
		PENGALLY, Edward, USA	B: Devonshire, England
		PETTY, Philip, USA	B: Tingswich, Buckinghamshire
		PLOWMAN, George H., USA	B: Oxford, Oxfordshire
		PYM, James, USA	B: Oxfordshire, England
		PYNE, George, USN	B: England

ROBERTS, James, USN	B: England
ROBINSON, Alexander, USN	B: England
SEACH, William, USN	B: London, England
SHAPLAND, John, USA	B: Barnstable, Devonshire
SHILLING, John, USA	B: England
SIMPSON, D. Henry Lakin, USN	B: London, England
SLADEN, Joseph Alton, USA	B: Rockdale, England
SMITH, Henry I., USA	B: Nottingham, Nottinghamshire
SMITH, Thomas, USN	B: England
SMITH, Thomas J., USA	B: Liverpool, Merseyside Co.
SPICER, William, USN	B: Liverpool, Merseyside Co.
STACEY, Charles, USA	B: England
STOKES, George, USA	B: England
SUMNER, James, USA	B: London, England
SWEENEY, James (2nd), USA	B: Manchester, Greater Manchester Co.
TALBOTT, William, USN	B: England
*TALLENTINE, James, USN	B: England
TAYLOR, George (JOHNSON), USN	B: Reddich, Hereford & Worcester Co.
TAYLOR, Joseph, USA	B: England
THOMPSON, Henry A. (CONNELLY, Roderick P.), USMC	B: England
THOMPSON, James Harry, USA	B: England
VALE, John, USA	B: London, England
WAGG, Maurice, USN	B: Hampshire Co. England
WARD, Charles H., USA	B: Bradford, England
WILLIAMS, George C., USA	B: England
WILLIS, Richard, USN	B: England
WILSON, John, USA	B: England
WINTERBOTTOM, William, USA	B: Manchester, Greater Manchester Co.
WOOD, Mark, USA	B: England
WOON, John, USN	B: England
WRIGHT, William, USN	B: London, England

FINLAND

ANDERSON, Johannes Seigfried, USA	B: Bjoroky, Finland
EGLIT, John, USN	B: Finland
ERICKSON, Nicholas, USN	B: Finland
WESTERMARK, Axel, USN	B: Bergo, Finland

FRANCE

BEAUFORT, Jean J., USA	B: France
CHANDRON, August, USN	B: France
CHAPMAN, John (KAUFMAN, Charles F.), USA	B:Strasburg, France
FALCOTT, Henry, USA	B: Champagne, France
FRANTZ, Joseph, USA	B: Eurapae, France
GESCHWIND, Nicholas, USA	B: France
HOWARD, Peter, USN	B: France
JAMIESON, Walter, USA	B: Boulogne, France
LEJEUNE, Emile, USN	B. France
LEON, Pierre, USN	B: France
LIBAIRE, Adolph, USA	B: Bacarrt, France

LUDWIG, Carl, USA	B: France
MORAN, John, USA	B: Lyon, France
MORSE, Charles F., USA	B: France
PRANCE, George, USN	B: France
ROY, Stanislaus (Stanilas), USA	B: France
TOBIN, Paul, USN	B: Plybin, France
WALKER, John, USA	B: Leon, France

GERMANY & PRUSSIA

ALBER, Frederick, USA	B: Germany
ARCHINAL, William J., USA	B: Felsburg, Hesse, Germany
BAKER, John, USA	B: Hesse, Germany
BALLEN, Frederick A., USA	B: Germany
BEHNKE, Heinrich, USN	B: Germany
BERTRAM, Heinrich, USA	B: Brunswick, Germany
BEYER, Albert, USN	B: Hanover, Germany
BIEGER, Charles, USA	B: Wiesbaden, Germany
BINDER, Richard, USMC	B: Germany
BLUCHER, Charles, USA	B: Germany
BOEHLER, Otto A., USA	B: Germany
BOUQUET, Nicholas S., USA	B: Landau, Bavaria, Germany
*BRATLING, Frank, USA	B: Bavaria, Germany
BRONNER, August Frederick, USA	B: Germany
BURKARD, Oscar R., USA	B: Achern, Baden, Germany
COHN, Abraham, USA	B: Guttentag, Silesia, Prussia
DAVIS, John, USN	B: Germany
DEETLINE, Frederick, USA	B: Offenheim, Germany
DILGER, Hubert, USA	B: Germany
DORLEY, August (DOERLE), USA	B: Germany
ENDERLIN, Richard, USA	B: Germany
FESQ, Frank E., USA	B: Germany (Purssia)
FICHTER, Hermann Emil, USA	B: Baden, Germany
FORSTERER, Bruno Albert, USMC	B: Koenigsberg, Germany
FOUT, Frederick W., USA	B: Germany
FOX, Henry, USA	B: Reuthingen, Wurttemberg, Germany
FREEMAN, Martin, USN	B: Germany
FREEMEYER, Christopher, USA	B: Bavaria, Germany
FUGER, Frederick W., USA	B: Wurttemberg, Germany
GARDNER, Charles (SCHLER, Simon), USA	B: Bavaria, Germany
GEORGIAN, John, USA	B: Germany
GERBER, Frederick William, USA	B: Dresden, Germany
GION, Joseph, USA	B: Alsace-Lorraine area, Germany
GLAVINSKI, Albert (GLAWINSKI), USA	B: Hildesheim, Germany
GREBE, M. R. William, USA	B: Hildesheim, Germany
GREEN, John, USA	B: Wurttemberg, Germany
GRESSER, Ignatz, USA	B: Malach, Germany
GRUEB, George M., USA	B: Wurttemberg, Germany
HACK, John, USA	B: Germany
HAMMEL, Henry A., USA	B: Germany
HANSEN, Hans Anton, USN	B: Germany
HART, John William, USA	B: Germany
HAUPT, Paul, USA	B: Prussia (Germany)
HEISCH, Henry William, USMC	B: Latendorf, Germany

HEISE, Clamor, USA | B: Germany
HENDRICKSON, Henry, USN | B: Germany
HINEMANN, Lehmann, USA | B: Lanback, Germany
HOFFMAN, Henry, USA | B: Wurttemberg, Germany
IRSCH, Francis, USA | B: Saarburg, Germany
ITRICH, Franz Anton, USN | B: Gross Katz, Germany
*JACHMAN, Isadore Seigfried, USA | B: Berlin, Germany
JACOBSON, Eugene Philip, USA | B: Prussia
JETTER, Bernard, USA | B: Wurttemberg, Germany
JOHN, William F., USA | B: Germany
KAISER, John, USA | B: Nerzogenaurach, Germany
KALTENBACH, Luther, USA | B: Germany
KAPPESSER, Peter, USA | B: Germany
KAUSS, August, USA | B: Germany
KLEIN, Robert, USN | B: Gerdonen, Germany
KLINE, Harry (KLIEN, Henry), USA | B: Germany
KOELPIN, William, USA | B: Stetten, Prussia
KRAMER, Franz, USN | B: Nierstein, Germany
KRAUSE, Ernest, USN | B: Lubeck, Germany
*KREHER, Wendelin, | B: Stetten, Prussia
KUCHMEISTER, Hermann W., USMC | B: Hamburg, Germany
LANGBEIN, Johann Christian Julius, USA | B: Germany
LUKES, William F., USN | B: Niderbergdorf, Bohemia
MAY, John, USA | B: Wurttemberg, Germany
MEYER, William, USN | B: Germany
MILLER, Andrew, USMC | B: Germany
MILLER, Henry August, USA | B: Germany
MILLER, John (FEY, Henry), USA | B: Kurhessen, Germany
MILLER, John G., USA | B: Germany
MINDIL, George Washington, USA | B: near Frankfort, Germany
MORSE, William, USN | B: Germany
MYERS, Fred, USA | B: Brunswick, Germany
NEDER, Adam, USA | B: Bavaria, Germany
NEWMAN, Henry, USA | B: Hanover, Germany
NIBBE, John H., USN | B: Germany
NOIL, Joseph B., USA | B: Germany
OHMSEN, August, USN | B: Lubeck, Germany
OPEL, John N., USA | B: Hoflas, Bavaria, Germany
ORBANSKY, David (URBANSKY), USA | B: Lautenburg, Prussia
PESCH, Joseph M., USA | B: Grossleiton, Prussia
PETERSEN, Carl Emil, USN | B: Hamburg, Germany
PHILIPSEN, Wilhelm O., USA | B: Schleswig, Germany
PHISTERER, Frederick, USA | B: Germany
RAERICK, John, USA | B: Baden, Germany
ROCK, Frederick, USA | B: Darmstadt, Germany
RODENBURG, Henry, USA | B: Germany
ROSSBACH, Valentine, USA | B: Germany
ROTH, Peter Paul, USA | B: Wurttemberg, Germany
SCHILLER, John (SCHILLING), USA | B: Hesse, Germany
SCHLACHTER, Philipp, USA | B: Germany
SCHMAL, George William, USA | B: Germany

SCHMAUCH, Andrew, USA | B: Germany
SCHMIDT, Conrad, USA | B: Wurttemberg, Germany
SCHNITZER, John, USA | B: Kempten, Bavaria, Germany
SCHORN, Charles, USA | B: Germany
SCHROETER, Charles, USA | B: Lindberg, Hanover, Germany
SCHUBERT, Martin, USA | B: Germany
SCHWAN, Theodore, USA | B: Hanover, Germany
SCHWENK, Martin (MARTIN, George), USA | B: Baden, Germany
SEITZINGER, James M., USA | B: Germany
SHAFFER, William (SCHAFFER), USA | B: Bavaria, Germany
SHAMBAUGH, Charles, USA | B: Prussia, Germany
SHUBERT, Frank, USA | B: Hesse, Germany
SMITH, Wilhelm, USN | B: Germany
STEINER, Christian, USA | B: Wurttemberg, Germany
STOCKMAN, George Henry, USA | B: Muenden, Germany
STRAUB, Paul Frederick, USA | B: Baden, Germany
STREILE, Christian, USA | B: Germany
SUMMERS, Robert (SOMMERS), USN | B: Prussia
SWEGHEIMER, Jacob (John Jacob), USA | B: Oldtown, Baden, Germany
THIELBERG, Henry, USN | B: Germany
THOMAS, Karl, USN | B: Germany
THOMPSON, John J., USA | B: Holstein, Germany
THORDSEN, William George, USN | B: Fredericstadt, Germany
TORGLER, Ernest R., USA | B: Mecklenburg, Germany
TRAUTMAN, Jacob, USA | B: Hamburg, Germany
UHRL, George (Uhri), USA | B: Baden, Germany
VOIT, Otto Emil, USA | B: Baden, Germany
VON MEDEM, Rudolph, USA | B: Germany (Prussia)
VON SCHLICK, Robert H., USA | B: Germany
WAMBSGAN, Martin, USA | B: Nusdorof, Bavaria, Germany
WEINERT, Paul H., USA | B: Frankfort, Germany
WEISSEL, Adam, USN | B: Germany
WELLS, William, USN | B: Germany
WENDE, Bruno, USA | B: Germany
WESTERHOLD, William, USA | B: Binde, Prussia
WIDMER, Jacob, USA | B: Wurttemberg, Germany
WILKE, Julius August Robert, USN | B: Germany
WILKENS, Henry, USA | B: Germany
WILLIAMS, Frank, USN | B: Danzig, Germany
WILSON, August, USN | B: Danzig, Germany
WINDOLPH, Charles, USA | B: Bergen, Germany
YOUNKER, John L., USA | B: Wurttemberg, Germany
ZIEGNER, Herman, USA | B: Aploda, Germany

GREECE

*DILBOY, George, USA | B: Greece

HOLLAND

ALLEN, Edward G., USN | B: Amsterdam, Holland
BURBANK, James H., USA | B: Stavorey, Holland
FASSEUR, Isaac L., USN | B: Fushing, Holland
MACK, Alexander, USN | B: Rotterdam, Holland

MOORE, Charles, USN	B: Holland
OSEPINS, Christian, USN	B: Holland
VAN IERSEL, Ludovicus M. M., USA	B: Dussen, Holland

HUNGARY

*RABEL, Laszlo, USA	B: Budapest, Hungary
STAHEL, Julius H., USA	B: Szegedin, Hungary

INDIA

*HANSON, Robert Murray, USMC	B: Lucknow, India
SIMONS, Charles Jenks, USA	B: India

IRELAND

AHERN, William, USN	B: Ireland
ALLEN, James, USA	B: Ireland
ANDERSON, Robert N., USN	B: Ireland
BARRETT, Richard, USA	B: County Mayo, Ireland
BARRY, Augustus, USA	B: Ireland
BASS, David L., USN	B: Ireland
*BEGLEY, Terrence, USA	B: Ireland
BELL, James, USA	B: County Antrim, Ireland
BLACKWOOD, William Robert Douglas, USA	B: Hollywood, County Wicklow, Ireland
BRADLEY, Charles, USN	B: Ireland
BRADY, George F., USN	B: Ireland
BRANAGAN, Edward, USA	B: County Louth, Ireland
BRANNIGAN, Felix, USA	B: Ireland
BRENNAN, Christopher, USN	B: Ireland
BROGAN, James (Edward James), USA	B: County Donegal, Ireland
BROPHY, James, USA	B: Kilkenny, Ireland
BROSNAN, John, USA	B: Ireland
BROWN, Edward Jr. (BROWNE), USA	B: Ireland
BROWN, James, USA	B: Wexford, Ireland
BRUTON, Christopher C.	B: Ireland
BURK, E. Michael (BURKE, Michael),USA	B: Ireland
BURKE, Patrick J., USA	B: Kilkenny, Ireland
BURKE, Richard, USA	B: Tipperary, Ireland
BURKE, Thomas, USN	B: Ireland
BURKE, Thomas, USN	B: Ireland
BUTLER, Edmond Thomas, USA	B: Clonmel, County Tipperary, Ireland
BYRNE, Denis, USA	B: Wexford, Ireland
BYRNES, James, USN	B: Ireland
CAHEY, Thomas, USN	B: Belfast, County Antrim, Ireland
CALLEN, Thomas Joseph (CALLAN), USA	B: County Louth, Ireland
CAMPBELL, William, USA	B: County Down, Ireland
CAREY, Hugh, USA	B: Ireland
CAREY, James, USN	B: Ireland
CARROLL, Thomas, USA	B: Kilkenny, Ireland
CARTER, George, USA	B: Dublin, Ireland

CASEY, David P., USA	B: Ireland
CASSIDY, Michael, USN	B: Ireland
CAVANAUGH, Thomas, USN	B: Ireland
COLBERT, Patrick, USN	B: Ireland
COLEMAN, John, USMC	B: County Cork, Ireland
COLLIS, Charles Henry Tucky, USA	B: County Cork, Ireland
CONBOY, Martin, USA	B: Roscommon, County Ballagh, Ireland
CONNOR, John, USA	B: Galway, Ireland
CONNOR, Thomas, USN	B: Ireland
CONNOR, William C., USN	B: County Cork, Ireland
CONNORS, James, USA	B: Kildare, Ireland
COONEY, James, USMC	B: Limerick, Ireland
COOPER, John (MATHER, John Laver), USN	B: County Dublin, Ireland
CORCORAN, Thomas E., USN	B: Dublin, County Dublin, Ireland
COSGROVE, Thomas, USA	B: County Galway, Ireland
CRAMEN, Thomas, USN	B: Ireland
CREED, John, USA	B: Tipperary, County Tipperary, Ireland
CRONIN, Cornelius, USN	B: Ireland
CULLEN, Thomas, USA	B: Ireland
CURRAN, Richard J., USA	B: Ennis, County Clare, Ireland
DAILY, Charles, USA	B: Mallow, County Cork, Ireland
DELANEY, John Carroll, USA	B: Ireland
DEMPSEY, John, USN	B: Ireland
DICKENS, Charles H., USA	B: Dublin, Ireland
DOHERTY, Thomas M., USA	B: Mitchelstown, County Cork, Ireland
DONAVAN, Cornelius (DONOVAN), USA	B: County Cork, Ireland
DONELLY, John S. (DONNELLY), USA	B: County Kerry, Ireland
DONOGHUE, Timothy (DONAHUE), USA	B: Ireland
DOODY, Patrick H., USA	B: Ireland
DOOLEN, William, USN	B: Ireland
DOUGHERTY, James, USMC	B: Langhash, Ireland
DOUGHERTY, Michael, USA	B: Falcarragh, County Donegal, Ireland
DOUGHERTY, Patrick, USN	B: Ireland
DOWLING, James, USA	B: County Meath, Ireland
DOWNEY, William, USA	B: Ireland
DRURY, James, USA	B: Limerick, County Limerick, Ireland
DUNPHY, Richard D., USN	B: Ireland
EVANS, William, USA	B: Annagh, Ireland
FALLON, Thomas Timothy, USA	B: County Galway, Ireland
FARREN, Daniel, USA	B: County Derry, Ireland
FEGAN, James, USA	B: Athlone, County Westmeath, Ireland
FITZGERALD, John, USMC	B: Limerick, Ireland
FLANNAGAN, John, USN	B: Ireland
FLOOD, Thomas S., USN	B: Ireland
FLOYD, Edward, USN	B: Ireland
FLYNN, Christopher, USA	B: Ireland
FOLEY, John H., USA	B: Cork, Ireland

FORAN, Nicholas, USA | B: County Waterford, Ireland
FORD, George W., USA | B: Ireland
GARDNER, William, USN | B: Ireland
*GASSON, Richard, USA | B: Ireland
GAUGHAN, Philip, USMC | B: Belmullet, County Mayo, Ireland

GIBBONS, Michael, USN | B: Ireland
GINLEY, Patrick, USA | B: Ireland
GLYNN, Michael, USA | B: Galway, Ireland
GOLDEN, Patrick, USA | B: County Sligo, Ireland
GRACE, Patrick Henry (Henry Patrick), USN | B: Ireland
GRIBBEN, James H., USA | B: Ireland
HALEY, James, USN | B: Ireland
HAMILTON, Frank, USA | B: County Tyrone, Ireland
HARRINGTON, Daniel C., USN | B: Ireland
HAVRON, John H., USA | B: Ireland
HEARTERY, Richard, USA | B: Ireland
HIGGINS, Thomas P., USA | B: Longford, Ireland
HIGHLAND, Patrick, USA | B: Tipperary, Ireland
HINNEGAN, William, USN | B: Ireland
HOGAN, Henry, USA | B: County Clare, Ireland
HORNE, Samuel Belton, USA | B: Belleek, County Fermanagh, Ireland

HOWARD, Martin (HORGAN, Michael C.), USN | B: Ireland
HUDSON, Michael, USMC | B: County Sligo, Ireland
HUNT, Martin, USMC | B: County Mayo, Ireland
HYLAND, John, USN | B: Ireland
IRWIN, Bernard John Dowling, USA | B: Ireland
IRWIN, Patrick, USA | B: Ireland
JONES, Andrew, USN | B: Limerick, County Limerick, Ireland

JONES, William, USA | B: Wicklow, County Wicklow, Ireland

KANE, John, USA | B: Ireland
KEARNEY, Michael, USMC | B: Newmarket, County Cork, Ireland

KEATING, Daniel, USA | B: County Cork, Ireland
KEELE, Joseph, USA | B: Ireland
KEENAN, John, USA | B: Tubbercurry, County Sligo, Ireland

KELLEY, Charles, USA | B: County Clare, Ireland
KELLEY, John, USN | B: Ireland
KELLY, Thomas, USA | B: County Mayo, Ireland
KELLY, Thomas Gunning, USA | B: Ireland
KENNEDY, John, USA | B: Cavan, County Cavan, Ireland
KENNEDY, Philip, USA | B: County Galway, Ireland
KEOUGH, John, USA | B: County Tipperary, Ireland
KERR, Thomas R., USA | B: Near Colleraine, County Derry, Ireland

KERRIGAN, Thomas, USA | B: County Tipperary, Ireland
KILLACKEY, Joseph, USN | B: County Cork, Ireland
KING, Hugh, USN | B: Ireland
KING, John, USN | B: County Mayo, Ireland
KYLE, Patrick J., USN | B: Ireland

LAFFEY, Bartlett, USN | B: Galway, County Galway, Ireland
LARKIN, David, USA | B: Cork, Ireland
LAVERTY, John, USN | B: County Tyrone, Ireland
*LEAHY, Cornelius J., USA | B: Limerick, Ireland
LENIHAN, James, USA | B: County Kerry, Ireland
LEONARD, Patrick James, USA | B: County Meath, Ireland
LEONARD, Patrick Thomas, USA | B: County Clare, Ireland
LLOYD, George (LOYD), USA | B: County Tyrone, Ireland
LOGAN, Hugh, USN | B: Ireland
LONERGAN, John, USA | B: Carrick, County Donegal, Ireland
MADDEN, Michael, USA | B: County Limerick, Ireland
MANGAM, Richard Christopher, USA | B: Ireland
MARTIN, Edward S., USN | B: Ireland
MARTIN, James, USMC | B: Derry, Ireland
MARTIN, Patrick, USA | B: County Offaly, Ireland
MARTIN, William, USN | B: Ireland
McADAMS, Peter, USA | B: Armagh, County Armagh, Ireland
McALLISTER, Samuel, USN | B: Belfast, County Antrim, Ireland
McANALLY, Charles, USA | B: Ireland
McCABE, William, USA | B: Belfast, County Antrim, Ireland
McCANN, Bernard, USA | B: County Roscommon, Ireland
McCARREN, Bernard, USA | B: Ireland
McCORMICK, Michael, USN | B: Ireland
McENROE, Patrick H., USA | B: Ireland
McGANN, Michael A., USA | B: County Roscommon, Ireland
McGOUGH, Owen, USA | B: Monaghan, Ireland
McGOWAN, John, USN | B: Ireland
McGRAW, Thomas, USA | B: Ireland
McGUIRE, Patrick, USA | B: Ireland
McHALE, Alexander U., USA | B: Ireland
McKEE, George, USA | B: County Tyrone, Ireland
McKEEVER, Michael, USA | B: Ireland
McLOUGHLIN, Michael, USA | B: County Sligo, Ireland
McNALLY, James, USA | B: County Monaghan, Ireland
McNAMARA, Michael, USMC | B: Clure, Ireland
McNAMARA, William, USA | B: County Cork, Ireland
McPHELAN, Robert, USA | B: County Laois, Ireland
MITCHELL, John, USA | B: Dublin, Ireland
MITCHELL, John James, USA | B: County Tyrone, Ireland
MOLLOY, Hugh, USN | B: County Wexford, Ireland
MONAGHAN, Patrick H., USA | B: Ireland
MONTAGUE, Daniel, USN | B: Wicklow, Ireland
MONTGOMERY, Robert William, USN | B: Ireland
MOORE, Charles, USN | B: Ireland
MORRIS, James L., USA | B: County Kerry, Ireland
MORRISON, John G., USN | B: Ireland
MORTON, Charles W., USN | B: Ireland
MULHOLLAND, St. Clair Agustin, USA | B: Lisburn, County Antrim, Ireland

MULLEN, Patrick, USN | B: Ireland
MURPHY, Dennis J. F., USA | B: County Cork, Ireland
MURPHY, Edward, USA | B: County Cork, Ireland

MURPHY, Jeremiah J., USA	B: County Cork, Ireland
MURPHY, John Edward, USN	B: Ireland
MURPHY, John P., USA	B: Killarney, County Kerry, Ireland
MURPHY, Michael C,, USA	B: Limerick, County Limerick, Ireland
MURPHY, Patrick, USN	B: Ireland
MURPHY, Philip, USA	B: County Killkenny, Ireland
MURPHY, Thomas, USA	B: County Kerry, Ireland
MURPHY, Thomas C., USA	B: Ireland
MURPHY, Thomas J., USA	B: Ireland
MURRAY, Thomas, USA	B: County Monaghan, Ireland
NIHILL, John, USA	B: Nenagh, County Tipperary, Ireland
NOLAN, John J., USA	B: Thurles, County Tipperary, Ireland
NOLAN, Richard J., USA	B: Ireland
NORTON, John R., USA	B: St. John's Parish, County Roscommon, Ireland
NUGENT, Christopher, USMC	B: County Cavan, Ireland
O'BEIRNE, James Rowan, USA	B: Roscommon, County Ballagh, Ireland
O'BRIEN, Peter, USA	B: Dublin, County Dublin, Ireland
O'CONNELL, Thomas, USN	B: Ireland
O'CONNOR, Timothy, USA	B: Ireland
O'DEA, John, USA	B: Limerick, County Limerick, Ireland
O'DONNELL, Menomen, USA	B: Drumbarty, Ireland
O'NEAL, John, USN	B: Ireland
O'SULLIVAN, John Francis, USA	B: County Kerry, Ireland
ORR, Moses, USA	B: County Tyrone, Ireland
PARNELL, William Russell, USA	B: Dublin, Ireland
PLATT, George Crawford, USA	B: Ireland
PLATTEN, Frederick, USA	B: Torbeck, Ireland
PLUNKETT, Thomas, USA	B: Ireland
PRENDERGAST, Thomas Francis, USMC	B: Waterford, Ireland
PRESTON, John, USN	B: Ireland
QUINLAN, James, USA	B: Clomwell, County Tipperary, Ireland
RAFFERTY, Peter F., USA	B: County Tyrone, Ireland
RANNAHAN, John, USMC	B: County Monaghan, Ireland
REED, James C., USA	B: Kilkenny, Ireland
REGAN, Patrick, USN	B: Queenstown, County Cork, Ireland
REID, Patrick, USN	B: Dublin, Ireland
REYNOLDS, George, USA	B: Ireland
RILEY, Thomas, USA	B: Ireland
ROANTREE, James S., USMC	B: Dublin, County Dublin, Ireland
ROBINSON, John H., USA	B: Ireland
ROBINSON, Thomas, USA	B: Ireland
ROCHE, David, USA	B: County Kerry, Ireland
ROGAN, Patrick, USA	B: County Lietrim, Ireland
RYAN, David, USA	B: County Kilkenny, Ireland
RYAN, Denis, USA	B: Cork, Ireland
RYAN, Peter J., USA	B: Tipperary, Ireland

SCANLAN, Patrick (SCANLON), USA	B: Ireland
SCHUTT, George, USN	B: Ireland
SEWELL, William Joyce, USA	B: Castlebar, County Mayo, Ireland
SHANAHAN, Patrick, USN	B: Shanat Castle, County Limerick, Ireland
SHIELDS, Bernard, USA	B: Ireland
SMITH, James, USN	B: Belfast, County Antrim, Ireland
SMITH, Thomas, USN	B: Ireland
SMITH, William, USN	B: Ireland
SPILLANE, Timothy, USA	B: County Kerry, Ireland
STANTON, Thomas, USN	B: Ireland
STEWART, Joseph, USA	B: Ireland
SULLIVAN, Edward, USMC	B: Cork, Ireland
SULLIVAN, Thomas, USA	B: County Meath, Ireland
SULLIVAN, Timothy, USN	B: Ireland
THAYER, James, USN	B: Ireland
THOMPSON, Joseph Henry, USA	B: Kilkeel, County Down, Ireland
THORNTON, Michael, USN	B: Ireland
TOBIN, John Michael, USA	B: Waterford, Ireland
TOOMER, William, USA	B: Dublin, Ireland
TRACY, John (NABERS, Henry G.), USA	B: Dublin, Ireland
TYRRELL, George William, USA	B: Ireland
URELL, Michael Emmet, USA	B: County Cork, Ireland
WALLACE, William, USA	B: County Donegal, Ireland
WALSH, John, USA	B: Tipperary, Ireland
WELCH, Richard, USA	B: Ireland
WELLS, Thomas McCoy, USA	B: Ather, Ireland
WELSH, Edward, USA	B: Ireland
WELSH, James, USA	B: Ireland
WHITE, Patrick H., USA	B: County Sligo, Ireland
WILLIAMS, William, USN	B: Ireland
WILSON, Christopher W., USA	B: Ireland
WRIGHT, Robert, USA	B: Ireland

ITALY

*ALBANESE, Lewis, USA	B: Venice, Italy
Di CESNOLA, Louis Palma, USA	B: Rivarola, Piedmont, Italy
HYDE, Thomas Worcester, USA	B: Florence, Italy
VALENTE, Michael, USA	B: Cassino, Italy

MALTA

CARUANA, Orlando Emanuel, USA	B: Ca Valletta, Malta
MATTHEWS, Joseph, USN	B: Malta
WILLIAMS, Antonio, USN	B: Malta

MEXICO

ANDERSON, Bruce, USA	B: Mexico City, Mexico
GARCIA, Marcario, USA	B: Villa de Castano, Mexico
*JIMENEZ, Jose Francisco, USMC	B: Mexico City, Mexico
PAYNE, Isaac, USA	B: Mexico

NORWAY

BROWN, Robert, USN	B: Norway
HARRIS, John, USN	B: Norway

JOHANNESSEN, Johannes J., USN	B: Bodo, Norway
JOHNSEN, Hans, USN	B: Sandnes, Norway
JOHNSON, Henry, USN	B: Norway
JOHNSON, John, USA	B: Toten Christiania, (now Oslo), Norway
LOMAN, Berger Holton, USA	B: Bergen, Norway
MONSSEN, Mons, USN	B: Bergen, Norway
NELSON, Lauritz, USN	B: Norway
OLSEN, Anton, USN	B: Christiana, (now Oslo), Norway
PHINNEY, William, USN	B: Norway
ROBINSON, Thomas, USN	B: Norway
SLETTELAND, Thomas, USA	B: Bergen, Norway
STOLTENBERG, Andrew Vincent, USN	B: Boto, Norway
TORGERSON, Martin Torinus, USN	B: Oleesen, Norway
WAALER, Reidar, USA	B: Christiana, (now Oslo), Norway
WESTA, Karl, USN	B: Norway
WILLIAMS, Augustus, USN	B: Kristiansand, Norway
WILLIAMS, Louis, USN	B: Christiana, (now Oslo), Norway
WILLIAMS, Peter, USN	B: Norway

PHILIPPINE ISLANDS

CALUGAS, Jose, USA	B: Iliolo, Leon, Barrio Tagsing, PI
*CASTLE, Frederick Walker, USAAC	B: Manila, PI
*DAVIS, George Fleming, USN	B: Manila, PI
NISPEROS, Jose B., USA	B: San Fernandos Union, PI
*PAGE, John Upshur Dennis, USA	B: Luzon, Malahi Island, PI
TRINIDAD, Telesforo Delacruz, USN	B: New Washington Capig, PI

POLAND

MINUE, Nicholas, USA	B: Sedden, Poland

PUERTO RICO

*GARCIA, Fernando Luis, USMC	B: Utuado, Utusdo Co. PR
*LOZADA, Carlos James, USA	B: Caguas, Caguas Co. PR
*RUBIO, Euripides, USA	B: Ponce, Ponce Co. PR
*SANTIAGO-COLON, Hector, USA	B: Salinas, Salinas Co. PR

RUSSIA

PETERS, Alexander, USN	B: Russia
RICE, Charles, USN	B: Russia
SCHEIBNER, Martin E., USA	B: Valdia, Russia
SUNDQUIST, Axel Leohard, USN	B: Finland, Russia
TURVELIN, Alexander Haure, USN	B: Russia

SCOTLAND

ARTHER, Matthew, USN	B: Scotland
AVERY, James, USN	B: Scotland
BRINN, Andrew, USN	B: Scotland
BROWN, John (HAYES, Thomas), USN	B: Glasgow, Scotland
*CRAIG, Robert, USA	B: Scotland
DAVIDSON, Andrew, USA	B: Morebattle, Scotland
DEMPSTER, John, USN	B: Scotland
DICKIE, David, USA	B: Scotland
DOUGALL, Allan Houston, USA	B: Scotland
DOW, Henry, USN	B: Scotland
EADIE, Thomas, USN	B: Scotland
FARQUHAR, John McGreath, USA	B: Near Ayr, Scotland
FRASER, William W., USA	B: Burn Brac, Scotland
GRAY, John, USA	B: Dunde, Scotland
GRINDLAY, James G., USA	B: Odinburgh, Scotland
HAMILTON, Thomas W., USN	B: Scotland
HAWKINS, Charles, USN	B: Scotland
HAY, Fred Stewart (SCHWABE, Frederick H.), USA	B: Stirlingshire, Scotland
JARDINE, Alexander, USN	B: Inverness, Scotland
JARDINE, James, USA	B: Helensburg, Dumbartonshire, Scotland
LAWRENCE, James, USA	B: Aberdeen, Scotland
*MATHIES, Archibald, USAAC	B: Scotland
McDONALD, James, USA	B: Edinburgh, Scotland
McDONALD, James Harper, USN	B: Newmaud, Scotland
McDONALD, John, USN	B: Perth, Scotland
McKENZIE, Alexander, USN	B: Glasgow, Scotland
McLEOD, James, USN	B: Scotland
MEAGHER, Thomas (MARR, Thomas W.), USA	B: Scotland
MOTT, John (McMAHAN, John Mott), USA	B: Fifeshire County, Scotland
REID, Robert Alexander, USA	B: Raplock, Scotland
ROBINSON, Charles, USN	B: Dundee, Scotland
SHIEL, John, USA	B: Scotland
SNEDDEN, James, USA	B: Edinburgh, Scotland
STEWART, Peter, USMC	B: Airdrie, Scotland
THACKRAH, Benjamin, USA	B: Scotland
THOMPSON, John, USA	B: Glasgow, Scotland
THOMPSON, Peter, USA	B: Scotland
WALKER, Edward Alexander, USMC	B: Huntley, Scotland
WARREN, David, USN	B: Glasgow, Scotland

SPAIN

ORTEGA, John, USN	B: Spain
SHARP, Hendrick, USN	B: Spain

SWEDEN

ANDERSON, William, USN	B: Sweden
BERGENDAHL, Frederick, USA	B: Gothenburg, Sweden
BJORKMAN, Ernest H., USN	B: Malmo, Sweden
DAHLGREN, John Olof, USMC	B: Kahliwar, Sewden
*GIBSON, Eric Gunnar, USA	B: Nysund, Sweden
HALLING, Luovi, USN	B: Stockholm, Sweden
JOHANSON, John Peter, USN	B: Oskarshamn, Sweden
JOHANSSON, Johan J., USN	B: Sweden
NORDSTROM, Isador A., USN	B: Gotegorg, Sweden
PETERSON, Alfred, USN	B: Sweden
RAGNAR, Theodore, USA	B: Linkoping, Sweden
READ, Charles A., USN	B: Sweden
SMITH, Oloff, USN	B: Sweden

SUNDQUIST, Gustav Adolf, USN B: Sweden
SWANSON, John, USN B: Gothenburg, Sweden
VON VEGESACK, Ernest, USA B: Gotland, Sweden

SWITZERLAND

FREY, Franz (Frank Xaiver), USA B: Switzerland
KNAAK, Albert, USA B: Luxenburg, Switzerland
STAUFFER, Rudolph, USA B: Berne, Switzerland
STICKOFFER, Julius Henry, USA B: Switzerland
VEUVE, Ernest, USA B: New Castle, Switzerland
WHITE, Adam, USA B: Switzerland

WALES

BATES, Richard, USN B: Wales
DAVIS, Joseph, USA B: Monmouth County, Wales
DAVIS, Thomas, USA B: Haverford, West Wales
EDWARDS, David, USA B: Wales
EVANS, Thomas, USA B: Wales

GRIFFITHS, John, USN B: Wales
MAHONEY, Gregory, USA B: Pettypool, South Wales
POWELL, William Henry, USA B: Pontypool, Monmouthshire, South Wales

WEST INDIES

DAVIS, John, USN B: Kingslow, Jamaica, West Indies
GIRANDY, Alphonse, USN B: Guadaloupe, West Indies
JOHNSON, William, USN B: St. Vincent, West Indies
LITTLE, Thomas, USA B: Barbados, West Indies
PILE, Richard, USN B: West Indies
SWEENEY, Robert Augustus, USN B: Montserrat, West Indies
TEYTAND, August P. (TEYTARD), USN B: Santa Cruz, West Indies

YUGOSLAVIA

ALLEX, Jake (MANDUSHICH, Jake Allex), USA B: near Prizren, Streska, Serbia
*MESTROVITCH, James I., USA B: Crna Cora, Yugoslavia

TABLE OF MEDAL RECIPIENTS
1863–1994

ACTION	ARMY	NAVY	MARINE CORPS	AIR FORCE	COAST GUARD	TOTAL
CIVIL WAR	1195	308	17	0	0	1520
INTERIM 1865-1870	0	13	0	0	0	13
INDIAN CAMPAIGNS	424	0	0	0	0	424
KOREAN CAMPAIGN 1871	0	8	7	0	0	15
INTERIM 1871-1898	0	98	2	0	0	100
SPANISH-AMERICAN WAR	30	64	15	0	0	109
SAMOA CAMPAIGN	0	1	3	0	0	4
PHILILIPPINE INSURRECT.	69	5	6	0	0	80
CHINA RELIEF EXPEDITION	4	22	33	0	0	59
INTERIM 1899-1910	0	48	2	0	0	50
PHILIPPINES 1911	1	5	0	0	0	6
MEXICAN CAMPAIGN	1	46	9	0	0	56
HAITIAN CAMPAIGN 1915	0	0	6	0	0	6
INTERIM 1915-1916	0	8	0	0	0	8
DOMINICAN CAMPAIGN	0	0	3	0	0	3
WORLD WAR I	90	21	8	0	0	119
HAITIAN CAMPAIGN 1919-1920	0	0	2	0	0	2
2ND NICARAGUAN CAMPAIGN	0	0	2	0	0	2
INTERIM 1919-1940	2	15	1	0	0	18
WORLD WAR II	294	57	81	0	1	433
KOREAN WAR	78	7	42	4	0	131
VIETNAM WAR & ERA	155	15	57	12	0	239
SOMALIA	2	0	0	0	0	2
UNKNOWNS	9	0	0	0	0	9
TOTALS	2354	741	296	16	1	3408*

*Seven double awardees won medals in two different actions

A SELECT MEDAL OF HONOR BIBLIOGRAPHY

This Medal of Honor bibliography is somewhat selective. To include all sources would involve an endless compilation of materials, the good with the bad, the scholarly with the unscholarly. The exclusion and/or inclusion of entries was solely my decision. So, too, was the method of presentation and the division of titles.

I've attempted to shorten the list in various ways. For example, hundreds of military units have written their own histories, detailed accounts of their combat action in the campaigns of the various wars. Many contain accounts where Medals were won; to include all of these would mean nearly 600 more entries.

There is much information about actions where Medals were awarded in the excellent official histories published by the services. Here I've listed the series name rather than individual titles, in order to call the reader's attention to them.

Not all Medal of Honor biographies are listed. Some Medal winners have had many volumes written about them, for instance Douglas MacArthur, O. O. Howard and Leonard Wood, all of whom were controversial figures. Nearly 20 books cover the various aspects of Howard's career, much of this material being redundant, poorly written or just boring. Those works included here are well written and very much to the point. This basis for selection has been applied to other material throughout.

Similarly the section "Books with Anecdotes about the Medals and Their Recipients" has been edited to present only the relevant material. For example, Edward Beach's *The Wreck of the Memphis* focuses on the *Memphis* disaster, but within the main story lies the story of how three of her crew won Medals of Honor. And then again, just two brief paragraphs in Ross Carter's *Those Devils in Baggy Pants* relate how Pvt. John R. Towle announced to his comrades that he was going to win a Medal of Honor, as he took on two German tanks and their infantry, stopping them cold, winning a Medal posthumously.

GENERAL BIBLIOGRAPHY

Anders, Curt. *Fighting Generals.* New York: Putnam, 1965.

Army Times (eds.). *American Heroes of Asian Wars.* New York: Dodd, Mead, 1968.

Barrows, N. *Blow All Ballast: The Story of the Squalus.* New York: Dodd, Mead, 1940.

Belden, Bauman. *United States War Medals.* Greenwich, Conn.: F. Flayderman, 1962.

Benavidez, Roy B. *The Last Medal of Honor Winner.* McLean, Va.: Brasseys U.S., 1995.

Beyer, W. F., and O.F. Keyel (eds.). *Deeds of Valor from Records in the Archives of the United States Government: How American Heroes Won the Medal of Honor.* 2 vols. Detroit: Perrien-Keydel, 1906-07.

Bigler, Philip. *In Honored Glory: the Story of Arlington Cemetery.* New York: Vandamere, 1966.

Blakeney, Jane. *Heroes, U.S. Marine Corps, 1861-1955.* Washington, D.C.: Blakeney Pub., 1957.

Blassingame, Wyatt. *Medical Corps Heroes of World War II.* New York: Garrard, 1969.

Boswell, Rolfe. *Medals for Marines.* New York: Thomas Y. Crowell, 1945.

Bozich, Stanley J. *Detroit's Own.* Frankenmuth, Mich.: Polar Bear Pub., 1985.

Braun, Saul M. *Seven Heroes . . . Medal of Honor Stories of the War in the Pacific.* New York: Putnam, 1965.

Chase, Joseph C. *Soldiers All: Portraits and Sketches of the Men of the A.E.F.* New York: George H. Doran, 1920.

Cook, John L. *Dust Off.* Toronto: Bantam Books, 1988.

Cooke, Donald E. *For Conspicuous Gallantry: Winners of the Medal of Honor.* Maplewood, N.J.: Hammond, 1966.

Curtis, Arthur S. *The Congressional Medal of Honor.* Annapolis, Md.: The American Serviceman's Library, 1945.

Dell Publishing (ed.). *The Congressional Medal of Honor Library: the Names, the Deeds, Korea.* New York: Dell Publishing, 1987.

———. *Congressional Medal of Honor Library: The Names, the Deeds, World War II.* New York: Dell Publishing, 1986.

Delong, Kent. *War Heroes: True Stories of Congressional Medal of Honor Recipients.* Westport, Conn.: Praeger, 1993.

Donovan, Frank. *The Medal: The Story of the Medal of Honor.* New York: Dodd, Mead, 1962.

Dorling, H. Taprell. *Ribbons and Medals.* London: Philip, 1963.

DuPre, Flint O. *U.S. Air Force Biographical Dictionary.* New York: Watts, 1965.

Engle, Eloise K. *Medic: America's Medical Soldiers, Sailors and Airmen from the Revolutionary War to Vietnam.* New York: Day, 1967.

Faber, Harold and Doris. *American Heroes of the 20th Century.* New York: Random House, 1967.

Feeny, William D. *In Their Honor.* New York: Duell, 1963.

Ferrel, P. V. *The Heroes of the War for the Union and Their Achievements.* Cincinatti, 1865.

Floherty, John J. *The Courage and the Glory.* New York: J. B. Lippincott, 1942.

Fredman, J. George, and Louis A. Falk. *Jews in American Wars.* New York: Jewish War Veterans of the United States, 1943.

Friederich, Rudolf J. *Medal of Honor Citation Supplements.* Chicago: Orders & Medals Society of America, 1968.

Gallery, Daniel V. *Twenty Million Tons Under the Sea (U-505).* Chicago: H. Regnery, 1956.

Garland, Albert N. (ed.). *Infantry in Vietnam.* New York: Jove Pubns., 1985.

Gibbons, Cromwell. *Military Decorations and Campaign Service Bars of the United States.* New York: U.S. Insignia, 1943.

Greene, J. I. (ed.). *The Infantry Journal Reader.* Garden City, N.Y.: Doubleday, Doran, 1943.

Gurney, Gene. *Arlington National Cemetery: a Picture Story.* New York: Crown Publishers, 1965.

———. *Five Down and Glory.* New York: Putnam, 1958.

Harr, B. *Combat Boots.* New York: Exposition Press, 1952.

Heaps, Willard A. *The Bravest Teenage Yanks.* New York: Duell, 1963.

Hero Tales of the American Soldier and Sailor as Told by the Heroes Themselves and Their Comrades. Philadelphia: merchants Library Association, 1899.

Hicken, Victor. *The American Fighting Man.* New York: Macmillan, 1969.

Hinkel, John V. *Arlington: Monument to Heroes.* Englewood Cliffs, N.J.: Prentice Hall, 1965.

Hirsch, Phil (ed.). *Great Combat Stories of the Korean War.* New York: Pyramid, 1968.

Holbrook, Stewart. *None More Courageous: American War Heroes of Today.* New York: Macmillan, 1942.

Howell, Glenn. *Medals of Honor.* New York: L. MacVeagh, Dial Press, 1931.

Hume, Edgar E. *The Medical Book of Merit.* Washington, D.C.: The Association of Medical Surgeons, 1925.

Jacobs, Bruce. *Heroes of the Army: The Medal of Honor and Its Winners.* New York: Norton, 1956.

———. *Korea's Heroes: The Medal of Honor Story.* New York, Berkley Pub., 1961.

Kayser, Hugh F. *The Spirit of America.* Palm Springs, Calif: ETC Publs., 1982.

Kerrigan, Evans E. *American War Medals and Decorations.* New York: Macmillan, 1964.

———. *American Medals and Decorations.* Westport, Conn.: Medallic Pub., 1990.

———. *Current American War Medals and Decorations, 1963-1969.* Noroton Heights, Conn.: Medallic Pub., 1969.

Lavender, David. *Mike Maroney, Raider.* Philadelphia: Westminster Press, 1945.

———. *Medal of Honor in Vietnam.* Westport, Conn.: Medallic Pub., 1976.

Lee, Irvin H. *Negro Medal of Honor Men.* New York: Dodd, Mead, 1967.

———. *Medal of Honor.* New York: Dodd, Mead, 1967.

Lockwood, C., and H. C. Adamson. *Hellcats of the Sea.* New York: Greenberg, 1955.

Lockwood, Charles. *Sink 'Em All.* New York: Dutton, 1951.

Look Magazine (eds.). *Our American Heroes.* New York: Look, 1943.

Loubat, Joseph F. *The Medallic History of the United States of America, 1776-1876.* New York: the author, 1880.

Merrill, James M. (ed.). *Uncommon Valor: The Exciting Story of the Army.* New York, 1964.

Meyer, N. S. *Military Insignia and Equipment.* New York: N. S. Meyer, 1930.

Millbook, Minnie. *A Study in Valor: Michigan Medal of Honor Winners in the Civil War.* Lansing, Mich., 1966.

Miller, Warren H. *Boys of 1917: Famous American Heroes of the World War.* Boston: L. C. Page, 1939.

Mingos, Howard. *American Heroes of the War in the Air.* 2 vols. New York: Lanciar Publishers, 1943.

Mitchell, Joseph B. *The Badge of Gallantry: Recollections of the Civil War Congressional Medal of Honor Winners.* New York: Macmillan, 1968

Morgan, Joseph M. *Military Medals and Insignia of the United States.* Glendale, Calif.: Griffin-Patterson Publishing, 1941.

Mulholland, St. Clair A. *Medal of Honor Legion of the United States.* Philadelphia: Town Printing, 1905.

Murphy, Edward F. *World War II Heroes.* Novato, Calif., Presidio Press, 1990.

————. *Korean War Heroes.* Novato, Calif.: Presidio Press, 1992.

————. *Vietnam Medal of Honor Heroes.* New York: Ballantine Books, 1987.

Musciano, Walter A. *Corsair Aces: The Bent-Wing Birds over the Pacific.* New York: Prentice Hall, 1979.

Nagle, John T. *The Status of Acting Assistant Surgeons of the United States Army.* New York: M. B. Brown, printer, 1893.

National Geographic Society. *Insignias and Decorations of the U.S. Armed Forces.* Washington, D.C.: National Geographic Society, 1944.

Navy Times (eds.). *They Fought Under the Sea.* Washington, D.C.: Navy Times Books, 1968.

Official Records of the Union and Confederate Navies in the War of Rebellion. 31 vols. Washington, D.C.: U.S. Naval War Records Office, 1894-1927.

O'Neill, Charles K. *Wild Train: The Story of the Andrews Raiders.* New York: Random House, 1956.

Parker, William R. (ed.). *Above and Beyond the Call of Duty; Commemorating the One Hundredth Anniversary of the Medal of Honor.* New York: McFadden Books, 1963.

Petersen, Gordon A. *A Guide to U.S. Army Insignia and Decorations.* Racine, Wis.: Whitman, 1942.

Pullen, John J. *A Shower of Stars: The Medal of Honor and the 27th Maine.* Philadelphia: Lippincott, 1966.

Reck, Franklin M. *Beyond the Call of Duty.* New York: Thomas Y. Crowell, 1944.

Reeder, Russell P. (Red). *Medal of Honor Heroes.* New York: Random House, 1965.

Reynolds, Quentin J. *Known But to God.* New York: John Day, 1962.

Roberts, MacLennan. *The Great Locomotive Chase.* New York: Dell Publishing, 1956.

Rodenbough, Theo. F.(ed. and comp.). *The Bravest Five Hundred of '61.* New York: G. W. Dillingham, 1891.

Rovere, Richard H., and Athur A. Schlesinger. *The MacArthur Controversy and American Foreign Policy.* New York: Farrar, Straus, & Giroux, 1965.

Schott, Joseph L. *Above and Beyond: The Story of the Congressional Medal of Honor.* New York: Putnam, 1963.

Schuon, Karl. *U.S. Marine Corps Biographical Dictionary.* New York: Franklin Watts, 1963.

Scott, J. (pseudo.). *Marine War Heroes: Daring Exploits of Marine Winners of the . . . Medal of Honor.* Derby, Conn.: Monarch Books, 1963.

Scott, Jay. *America's War Heroes: Dramatic True Tales of . . . Men Whose Exploits Won Them the . . . Medal of Honor.* Derby, CT, 1963.

Shane, Ted. *Heroes of the Pacific.* New York: J. Messner, 1944.

Sims, Edward H. *Greatest Fighter Missions of the Top Navy and Marine Air Aces of World War II.* New York: Harper, 1962.

————. *The Greatest Aces.* New York: Harper, 1968.

Snowden, James R. *A Description of the Medals of Washington.* Philadelphia: J. B. Lippincott, 1861.

South Carolina Adjutant-General's Office. *The Medal of Honor, Army and Navy.* Columbia, S.C.: South Carolina State Adjutant General's Office, 1956.

Stillman, Richard J. *The U.S. Infantry: Queen of Battle.* New York: Franklin Watts, 1965.

Stringer, Harry. *Heroes All!* Washington, D.C.: Fassett, 1919.

Studley, George W. *Regulation War Medals.* Avon, N.Y.: Studley, G.W., 1939.

Talley, Naomi. *Medals for Brave Men.* New York: Dial Press, 1963.

Tassin, R. *Double Winners of the Medal of Honor.* Canton, Ohio: Daring Books, 1987.

Tibbets, Albert B. *American Heroes All.* Boston: Little, Brown, 1966.

Thomas, Lowell J. *These Men Shall Never Die.* Philadelphia: The John C. Winston, 1943.

Tolliver, Raymond F. *Fighter Aces.* New York: Macmillan, 1965.

Townsend, Edward D. *Anecdotes of the Civil War in the United States.* New York: D. Appleton, 1884.

U.S. Army Artillery and Missile School. *The Medal of Honor Among Artillerymen.* Ft. Sill, Okla.: 1961.

U.S. Army Corps of Engineers. *Medal of Honor Winners.* Washington, D.C.: 1964.

U.S. Infantry Association. *Army Regulations Applicable to Individual Soldiers and the Administration of Units of the Army.* Washington, D.C.: 1923.

U.S. Military Academy. *Memorial Booklet West Point Graduate . . . Medal of Honor.* West Point, N.Y.: U.S. Military Academy, 1963.

U.S. National Historic Publishers Association. *The World War and Historic Deeds of Valor from Official Records and Illustrations of the Untied States and Allied Governments. Vol. VI.* Chicago: U.S. Hist. Publ. Assn., 1919.

Wells, Linton. *Salute to Valor.* New York: Random House, 1942.

Werlich, Robert. *Orders and Decorations of All Nations.* Washington, D.C.: Quaker Press, 1966.

Whitehouse, Arthur G. J. *Epics and Legends of the First War.* London: F. Muller, 1964.

Wyllie, Robert E. *Orders, Decorations and Insignia: Military and Civil.* New York: G. P. Putnam's Sons, 1921.

Yolen, Will, and Kenneth Seeman. *Heroes for Our Times.* Harrisburg, Pa.: Stackpole Books, 1968.

AUTOBIOGRAPHIES AND BIOGRAPHIES OF MEDAL OF HONOR WINNERS

Army Times (eds.). *The Banner and the Glory: The Story of Gen. Douglas MacArthur.* New York: Dodd, Mead, 1966.

Baldwin, Alice B. *Memoirs of the Late Major-General Frank D. Baldwin.* Los Angeles: Wetzel Publishing, 1929.

Beamish, Richard J. *The Boy's Story of Lindbergh, The Lone Eagle.* Chicago: John C. Winston, 1928.

Benavidez, Roy, and Oscar Griffin. *The Three Wars of Roy Benavidez.* San Antonio, Tex., 1988.

Billac, Pete (ed.). *The Last Medal of Honor.* New York: Swan Publications, 1990.

Bourke, John G. *Apache Campaign.* New York: Scribner, 1958.

———. *On the Border with Crook.* Lincoln, Neb.: University of Nebraska Press, 1971.

Boyington, Gregory. *Baa Baa Black Sheep.* New York: Putnam, 1958.

Boynton, Henry V. (ed.). *U.S. Congress, Joint Committee on Dedication of Chickamauga and Chattanooga National Military Park Sept. 18-20, 1895.* Washington, D.C.: U.S. Government Printing Office, 1896.

Bradley, James H. *The March of the Montana Column: Godfrey's Diary.* Norman, Okla.: University of Oklahoma Press, 1963.

Brent, Rafer (pseud.). *Great War Stories.* New York: Bartholemew House, 1957.

Breuer, William B. *Sea Wolf.* Novato, Calif.: Presidio Press, 1987.

Butler, Smedley D. *War Is a Racket.* New York: Round Table Press, 1935.

Butterfield, Julia L. (ed.). *A Biographical Memorial of General Daniel Butterfield.* New York: Grafton Press, 1904.

Byrd, Richard E. *Alone.* New York: G. P. Putnam's Sons, 1938.

———. *Little America.* New York: Putnam, 1930.

Carpenter, John A. *Sword and Olive Branch: Oliver Otis Howard.* Pittsburgh: University of Pittsburgh Press, 1964.

Carr, William H. A. *The DuPonts of Delaware.* Toronto: Dodd, 1964.

Carter, R. G. *The Old Sergeant's Story.* New York: Hitchcock, 1926.

Cavanagh, Michael. *Memoirs of Gen. Thomas Francis Meagher.* Worcester, Mass.: Messenger Press, 1892.

Chamberlain, Joshua L. *The Passing of the Armies.* New York: G. P. Putnam's Sons, 1915.

Cleveland, E. J. *The Genealogy of the Cleveland and Cleaveland Families.* Hartford, Conn.: Case, Lockwood & Brainard, 1899.

Cody, William F. *The Adventures of Buffalo Bill.* New York: Harper & Row, 1904.

Considine, Robert B. *General Douglas MacArthur.* New York, 1964.

Cowan, Sam K. *Sergeant York and His People.* New York: Funk & Wagnalls, 1922.

Cruse, Thomas. *Apache Days and After.* Caldwell, Idaho: Caxton Printers, 1941.

Cummings, Damon E. *Admiral Richard Wainwright and the United States Fleet.* Washington, D.C.: U.S. Government Printing Office, 1962.

Cutler, Thomas J. *Brown Water, Black Berets.* Annapolis, Md.: Naval Institute Press, 1988.

Davis, Kenneth S. *Hero: Charles A. Lindbergh and the American Dream.* New York: Doubleday, 1959.

Day, George E. *Return with Honor.* Mesa, AZ: 1989

Dean, William F. *General Dean's Story.* New York: Viking Press, 1954.

Donlon, Roger. *Outpost of Freedom.* New York: McGraw-Hill, 1965.

Dougherty, Michael. *Prison Diary of Michael Dougherty.* Bristol, Pa.: C. A. Dougherty, 1908.

DuPont, Henry A. *Campaign of 1864 in the Valley of Virginia.* New York: National Americana Society, 1925.

Eadie, Tom. *I Like Diving: A Professional's Story.* Boston: Houghton Mifflin, 1929.

Edwards, D. K. *This Side of Hell.* New York: Doubleday, 1932.

Ellsberg, Edward. *Men Under the Sea.* New York: Dodd, Mead, 1940.

———. *On the Bottom.* Rahway, N.J.: 1939.

Fluckey, Eugene B. *Thunder Below!* Chicago: University of Illinois Press, 1992.

Force, Manning F. . . . *General Sherman*. New York: D. Appleton and Company, 1899.

Foss, Joe. *Joe Foss, Flying Marine*. New York: Books, Inc., 1943; distributed by E. P. Dutton.

Foss, Joe, and Donna W. Foss. *Proud American*. New York: Pocket Books, 1992.

Foster, C. *Rear Admiral Byrd and the Polar Expeditions*. New York: Burt, 1930.

Foster, John. *Guadalcanal General: The Story of A. A. Vandergrift, USMC*. New York: Morrow, 1966.

Fredericks, Edgar J. *MacArthur: His Mission and Meaning*. Philadelphia: J. Whitmore, 1969.

Funston, Frederick. *Memories of Two Wars*. New York: Scribner, 1914.

Ganoe, William A. *MacArthur Close-Up: Much Then and Some Now*. New York: Vantage, 1962.

Gladych, Michael. *Admiral Byrd of Antarctica*. New York: Messner, 1960.

Glines, Carroll V. *Doolittle's Tokyo Raiders*. New York: Van Nostrand, 1964.

Godfrey, Edward S. *Some Reminiscences, Including the Washita Battle November 27, 1868*. Reprinted from the Cavalry Journal 37 No. 153; (1928).

Graham, Don. *No Name on the Bullet*. New York: Viking Press, 1989.

Greely, Maj. Gen. A. W. *Reminiscences of Adventure and Service*. New York: C. Scribner's Sons, 1927.

Greely, Lt. A. W. *Three Years of Arctic Service*. New York: C. Scribner's Sons, 1886.

Gumpertz, Sydney G. *The Jewish Legion of Valor*. New York: S. G. Gumpertz, 1946.

Hagedorn, Hermann. *Leonard Wood: A Biography*. 2 vols. New York: Harper & Brothers, 1931.

Hall, Norman S. *The Balloon Buster*. New York: Bantam Books, 1928, 1966.

Herndon, B. *The Unlikeliest Hero: The Story of PFC Desmond Doss, Conscientious Objector Who Won His Nation's Highest Military Honor*. Mountain View, Calif.: Pacific, 1967.

Hobson, Richmond P. *The Sinking of the Merrimac: A Personal Narrative*. New York: Century, 1899.

Howard, James H., Paul McCarthy (ed.). *Roar of the Tiger*. New York: Crown Publishing Group, 1991.

Howard, Oliver O. *Autobiography of Oliver Otis Howard*. 2 vols. New York: Baker & Taylor, 1907.

Hoyt, Edwin P. *The Last Explorer: The Adventures of Admiral Byrd*. New York: John Day, 1968.

Huff, Sidney. *My Fifteen Years with General MacArthur*. New York: Paperback Library, 1964.

Huie, William B. *The Hero of Iwo Jima*. New York: New American Library, 1962.

Hunt, Frazier. *MacArthur and the War Against Japan*. New York: C. Scribner's Sons, 1944.

———. *Untold Story of Douglas MacArthur*. New York: Devin-Adair, 1954.

Izac, Edouard. *Prisoner of the U-90*. Boston: Houghton, Mifflin, 1919.

Jablonski, Edward. *Flying Fortress: Illustrated Biography of the B-17s and the Men Who Flew Them*. New York: Doubleday, 1965.

Johnson, Virginia W. *The Unregimented General; a Biography of Nelson A. Miles*. Cambridge, Mass.: Houghton Mifflin, 1962.

Kelly, Charles. *One Man's War*. New York: A. A. Knopf, 1944.

Kenney, George C. *Dick Bong; Ace of Aces*. New York: Duell, 1960.

Keyhoe, Donald E. *Flying with Lindbergh*. New York: Putnam, 1928.

King, James T. *War Eagle: A Life of General Eugene A. Carr*. Lincoln, Neb.: University of Nebraska Press, 1963.

Klemme, Otto. *General Lawton's Day*. Leipzig: Verlag fur Literatur, Kunst und Musik, 1907.

Langford, Laura C. Holloway. *Howard: The Christian Hero*. New York: Funk & Wagnalls, 1885.

Lawrence, J. S. *The Descendants of Moses and Sarah Kilham Porter*. Grand Rapids, Mich.: F. A. Onderdonk, printer, 1910.

Lawson, Ted. *Thirty Seconds Over Tokyo*. New York: Random House, 1953.

Lindbergh, Charles A. *Of Flight and Life*. New York: Scribner's Sons, 1948.

———. *The Spirit of St. Louis*. New York: Scribner, 1953.

———. *We*. New York: Putnam, 1927.

Lockwood, Charles A., and Hans C. Adamson. *Through Hell and Deep Water: The Story of the Submarine U.S.S. Harder*. New York: Greenberg, 1956.

Lowry, Timothy S. *And Brave Men, Too*. New York: Crown Pub., 1985.

MacArthur, Douglas. *Reminiscences*. New York: McGraw-Hill, 1964.

Mende, Elsie P. *An American Soldier and Diplomat: Horace Porter*. New York: Frederick A. Stokes, 1927.

Merrill, James M. *Target Tokyo: The Halsey-Doolittle Raid*. New York: Rand-McNally, 1964.

Miles, Nelson A. *Personal Recollections and Observations of General Nelson A. Miles.* New York: Werner, 1896.

———. *Serving the Republic.* New York: Harper, 1911.

Miley, John D. *In Cuba with Shafter.* New York: C. Scribner's Sons, 1899.

Miller, Franklin D. with Elwood J. C. Kureth. *Reflections of a Warrior.* Novato, Calif.: Presidio Press, 1991.

Miller, Francis T. *General Douglas MacArthur.* Philadelphia: John C. Winston, 1944.

Mullholland, St. Clair A. *The Story of the 116th Regiment, Pennsylvania Infantry.* Philadelphia: F. McManus, Jr., printer, 1899.

Murphy, Audie. *To Hell and Back.* New York: H. Holt, 1949.

Murphy, Francis X. *Fight Admiral.* New York: Vantage Press, 1952.

New York Monuments Commission. *In Memoriam, Alexander Steward Webb.* Albany, N.Y.: New York Monuments Commission, 1916.

Nicolay, Helen. *MacArthur of Bataan.* New York: D. Appleton-Century, 1942.

O'Callahan, Joseph, S. J. *I Was a Chaplain on the Franklin.* New York: Macmillan, 1956.

O'Kane, Richard H. *Clear the Bridge.* Chicago: Rand McNally, 1977.

———. *Wahoo.* Novato, Calif: Presidio Press, 1987.

Parker, James. *The Mounted Rifleman.* Menasha, Wis.: Banta, 1916.

Pearl, Jack. *General Douglas MacArthur.* Derby, Conn.: Monarch Books, 1961.

Pinchon, Edgcumb. *Dan Sickles: Hero of Gettysburg and "Yankee King of Spain."* Garden City, N.Y.: Doubleday, Doran, 1945.

Pittenger, William. *Daring and Suffering: a History of the Great Railroad Adventure.* Philadelphia: J. W. Daughaday, 1863.

———. *In Pursuit of the General.* reprint, San Marino, Calif.: Golden West Books, 1966.

Place, Marion. *The Frontiersman:.* New York: Holt, 1967.

Pond, George. *The Shenandoah Valley in 1864.* New York: C. Scribner's Sons, 1883.

Porter, Horace. *Campaigning with Grant.* New York: Century, 1897.

Reynolds, Quentin. *The Amazing Mr. Doolittle.* New York: Appleton-Century Crofts, 1953.

Rickenbacker, Edward V. *Fighting the Flying Circus.* Garden City, N.Y.: Doubleday, 1965.

———. *Rickenbacker.* Englewood Cliffs, N.J.: Prentice Hall, 1967.

———. *Seven Came Through.* New York: Doubleday, 1943.

Roosevelt, E. B. A. *Day Before Yesterday; Reminiscences.* New York: Doubleday, 1959.

Roske, Ralph, and C. Van Doren. *Lincoln's Commando.* New York: Harper, 1957.

Ross, Helen L. *Touch of Smile.* Burley, Wash.: Coffee Break Press, 1978.

Ross, Walter S. *The Last Hero: Charles A. Lindbergh.* New York: Harper, 1968.

Rovere, Richard H., and Arthur M. Schlesinger, Jr. *The General and the President.* New York: Farrar, Straus and Young, 1951.

Schofield, John M. *Forty-six Years in the Army.* New York: Century, 1897.

Stanley, David S. *Personal Memoirs of Major-General D. S. Stanley.* Cambridge, Mass.: Harvard University Press, 1917.

Strandberg, John E., and Roger James Bender. *Call of Duty: Military Awards & Decorations of the United States of America.* San Jose, Calif.: Bender, 1994.

Swanberg, W. A. *Sickles the Incredible.* New York: Scribner, 1956.

Thomas, Lowell J. *Old Gimlet Eye.* New York: Farrar & Rinehart, 1933.

Todd, Alden L. *Abandoned: The Story of the Greely Arctic Expedition, 1881-1884.* New York: McGraw-Hill, 1961.

Tolman, Newton F. *The Search for General Miles.* New York: Putnam, 1968.

Tremain, Henry E. *Sailor's Creek to Appomattox Court House.* New York: C. H. Ludwig, printer, 1885.

———. *Two Days of War: A Gettysburg Narrative.* New York: Bonnell, 1905.

Urban, Matt, and Charles F. Conrad. *Matt Urban Story: Life and World War Two Experiences.* Holland, Mich.: Matt Urban Story, 1989.

Vandegrift, Alexander A. *Once a Marine: The Memoirs of General A. A. Vandegrift, U.S.M.C.* New York: Norton, 1964.

Vanderslice, John M. *Gettysburg.* Philadelphia: J. B. Lippincott, 1897.

Wainwright, Jonathan, Robert Considine (ed.). *General Wainwright's Story.* Garden City, N.Y.: Doubleday & Co., 1946.

Wallace, Willard M. *Soul of the Lion: A Biography of General Joshua L. Chamberlain.* New York: Nelson, 1960.

Webb, Alexander S. *The Peninsula: McClellan's Campaign of 1862.* New York: C. Scribner's Sons, 1881.

Wetzel, Gary G. *Jake: The Forgotten Warrior.* Oak Creek, WI: 1984.

Wheeler, Richard. *The Bloody Battle for Suribachi.* New York: Crowell, 1965.

White, W. L. *They Were Expendable.* New York: Harcourt, 1942.

Whiting, Charles. *Hero: The Life and Death of Audie Murphy.* Chelsea, Mich.: Madison Books, 1990.

Whitney, Courtney. *MacArthur, His Rendezvous with History.* New York: Knopf, 1956.

Whorf, Mike. *Old Soldiers Never Die.* Birmingham, Mich.: Mike Whorf, 1970, 1964.

Wilhelm, Maria. *The Fighting Irishman: The Story of "Wild Bill" Donovan.* New York: Hawthorn Books, 1964.

Willcox, Orlando B. (Majro March, Pseud.). *Faca, An Army Memoir.* Boston, E. O. Libby, 1858.

Wilson, D Ray. *Episode on Hill 616.* Alton, IL., 1981.

Wilson, John A. *Adventures of Alf Wilson.* Toledo, Ohio: Blade Printing & Paper, 1880.

Windolph, Charles A. *I Fought with Custer.* New York: C. Scribner's Sons, 1947.

Woodfill, Samuel. *Woodfill of the Regulars.* New York: Doubleday, Doran, 1929.

York, Alvin, and Tom Skeyhill (ed.). *Sergeant York: His Own Life Story and War Diary.* Garden City, N.Y.: Doubleday, Doran, 1931.

GOVERNMENT DOCUMENTS
(Washington, D.C., U.S. Government Printing Office, unless otherwise noted.)

Annual Report of the Chief of the Record and Pension Office, 1901-1906

Annual Report of the Secretary of Defense, 1948-1969.

Annual Report of the Secretary of the Navy, 1863-1947.

Annual Report of the Secretary of War, 1863-1865, 1890-1947.

Congressional Document. *Medal of Honor, 1863-1968. (Revision of 1964 ed.)* 90th Cong., 2nd Sess., Washington, D.C., 1968.

———. *General Staff Corps and Medals of Honor.* S. Doc. 58, 66th Cong., 1st Sess., 1919.

U.S. Army and Navy Regulations, 1895-1969; Air Force Regulations, 1948-1969. (Pertinent to wearing the Medals, display and Medal design.)

U.S. Army War College. *Rewards and Commendations.* Fort Carlysle, 1928.

U.S. Congress. House Committee on Military Affairs. *Presenting A Medal of Honor to General (A.L.) Greely, Feb. 22, 1935.* House Rpt. No. 210, 74th Cong., 1st Sess., 1935.

U.S. Commission of Fine Arts. *Critical Appraisal of the Present Medal of Honor.* 1920.

U.S. Department of the Army. *The Medal of Honor of the United States Army. 1948.*

U.S. Department of Defense. *The Unknowns of World War II and Korea. 1960.*

U.S. Department of the Navy. *Roll of Honor: a Record of the Medals of Honor Issued to the Enlisted Men and Marines of the Navy. 1888.*

U.S. Department of the Navy. Bureau of Naval Personnel. *Records of Medals of Honor Issued to Bluejackets and marines of the United States Navy, 1862-1910. 1910.*

U.S. Department of the Navy. Bureau of Naval Personnel. *Record of Medals of Honor Issued to the Bluejackets and Marines of the United States Navy, 1862-1920. 1921.*

U.S. Department of the Navy. *Medal of Honor, 1861-1949. 1950.*

U.S. Navy. Division of Naval Intelligence. *Decorations, Medals and Campaign Ribbons of the U.S. Armed Forces. 1943.*

U.S. Senate, Committee on Pensions. *Petition of Wilson W. Brown and Other Members of the "Mitchell Raiders".* Rpt. No. 361, 48th Cong., 1st Sess., 1884.

U.S. Senate, Committee on Rules and Administration. *Representative Speeches of General of the Army Douglas MacArthur.* S. Doc. 95, 88th Cong., 2nd Sess., 1964.

U.S. Senate, Subcommittee on Veterans' Affairs of the Committee on Labor and Public Welfare. *Medal of Honor, 1863-1964.* 88th Cong., 2nd Sess., Washington, 1964.

U.S. War Department. *Regulations for the Army of the United States.* Washington, D.C., 1889.

———. *Medals of Honor and Certificates of Merit. 1904.*

———. *Medals of Honor Issued by the War Department from January 1, 1907 to December 31, 1909. 1910.*

———. *Medals of Honor Issued by the War Department from September 1, 1904 to June 30, 1915, together with the List of Corrections Made in the Medal of Honor Circular of September 1, 1904.*

War Department Document. *Medals of Honor Issued by the War Department Up to and Including October 31, 1897.* Washington, D.C., 1897.

———. Adjutant-General's Office. *Congressional Medal of Honor, the Distinguished Service Cross and the Distinguished Service Medal Issued by the War Department Since April 6, 1917, Up To and Including General Orders, No. 126, War Department, November 11, 1919.*

———. *American Decorations: A List of the Awards of the Congressional Medal of Honor. . . 1862-1926. 1927.*

———. *Decorations, United States Army, Supplements to 1927 Report, Nos. I, II, III, IV and V. 1937-1940.*

MEDAL OF HONOR FICTION

Condon, Richard. *The Manchurian Candidate*. New York: McGraw, 1959.

Hoffenberg, John. *A Hero for Regis*. New York: Dutton, 1963.

Huie, William B. *The Klansman*. New York: Dial Press, 1968.

King, Charles. *The Medal of Honor*. New York: H. B. Claflin, 1905.

Little, Charles. *The Bold and the Lonely*. New York: McKay, 1966.

Myrer, Anton. *Once an Eagle*. New York: Holt, 1968.

Swarthout, Glendon. *They Came to Cordura*. New York: Random House, 1958.

Taggart, Donald G. *Reunion of the 108th*. New York: Doubleday, 1968.

BOOKS BY MEDAL WINNERS

Birkhimer, William E. *Historical Sketch of the Organization, Administration, Material, and Tactics of the Artillery, United States Army*. Washington, D.C.: J. J. Chapman, agent, 1884.

Carter, Robert G. *The Art and Science of War Versus the Art of Fighting*. Washington, D.C.: National Publishing, 1922.

Wood, Leonard. *America's Duty as Shown by Our Military History: Its Facts and Fallacies*. Chicago: Reilly & Lee, 1921.

BOOKS WITH ANECDOTES ABOUT THE MEDALS AND THEIR RECIPIENTS

American Council of Learned Societies. Schuyler, R. L. (ed.). *Dictionary of American Biography*. *22 vols*. New York: Schribner, 1958.

Anders, Curtis. *Fighting Airmen*. New York: Putnam, 1966.

Anderson, Bern. *By Sea and By River: The Naval History of the Civil War*. New York: A. Knopf, 1962.

Appleman, Roy E. *The U.S. Army in Korea*. vol. 1: *South to the Naktong, North to the Yalu*. Rutland, Vt.: C. E. Tuttle, 1961.

Army Times (eds.). *The Daring Regiments: Adventures of the A.E.F. in World War I*. New York: Dodd, Mead, 1967.

———. *The Yanks Are Coming, Story of General John J. Pershing*. New York: Putnam, 1960.

Asprey, Robert B. *At Belleau Wood*. New York: Putnam, 1965.

Bailey, Tom. *Tarawa*. Derby, CT, 1962.

Bartley, Whitman S. *Iwo Jima: Amphibious Epic*. Nashville, Tenn.: Battery Press, 1954.

Bayler, Walter Louis John as told to Cecil Carnes. *Last Man Off Wake Island*. New York: Bobbs Merrill, 1943.

Beach, Edward I. *The Wreck of the Memphis*. New York: Holt Rinehart, 1966.

Belote, James H., and William M. *Corregidor: the Saga of a Fortress*. New York: Harper, 1968.

Boatner, Mark M. *The Civil War Dictionary*. New York: David McKay 1959.

Boswell, Rolfe. *Leathernecks: Our Marines in Fact & Picture*. New York: Thomas Y. Crowell, 1943.

Bourke, John G. *An Apache Campaign*. New York, 1958.

Brininstool, E. A. *Troopers with Custer: historic incidents of the battle of the Little Big Horn*. Harrisburg: Pa.: Stackpole, 1952.

Brown, Ashley. *U.S. Marines in Action*. New York: Villard Books, 1986.

Brown, Ashley, and Jonathan Reed. *Marines*. Harrisburg, Penna.: Nat'l Hist. Soc., 1983.

Bryan, J. *Aircraft Carrier*. New York: Ballantine Books, 1954.

Bulkley, Robert J. *At Close Quarters: PT Boats in the United States Navy*. Washington, D.C.: The Naval History Division, 1962.

Burchard, Peter. *One Gallant Rush: Robert Gould Shaw and His Brave Black Regiment*. New York: St. Martin's Press, 1965.

Cagle, Malcolm W., and F. A. Manson. *The Sea War in Korea*. Annapolis, Md.: U.S. Naval Institute, 1957.

Caldin, Martin. *Air Force: A Pictorial History of American Airpower*. New York: Bramhall House, 1957.

———. *Black Thursday*. New York: Dutton, 1960.

———. *The Ragged, Rugged Warriors: The Heroic Story of American Pilots in the Early Air War Against Japan*. New York: Dutton, 1966.

Carter, Ross S. *Those Devils in Baggy Pants*. New York: Appleton-Century Crofts, 1951.

Cass, Bevan G. (ed.). *History of the Sixth Marine Division, Melanesia, Micronesia, Orient*. Washington, D.C.: Infantry Journal Press, 1948.

Catlin, Albertus Wright. *With the Help of God and a Few Marines*. Garden City, N.Y.: Doubleday, Page, 1919.

Chadwick, Joseph. *The Apache Wars*. Derby, Conn.: Monarch Books, 1961.

———. *The Sioux Indian Wars*. Derby, Conn.: Monarch Books, 1962.

Chambliss, Wiliam. *The Silent Service*. New York: New American Library, 1959.

Cohlmia, Robert A., Arthur and Kenneth. *The Third Marine Division*. Washington, D.C.: Infantry Press Journal, 1948.

Congdon, Don (ed.). *Combat: the Civil War*. New York: Dial Press, 1968.

Conner, Howard. *The Spearhead: The World War II History of the Fifth Marine Division*. Washington, D.C.: Infantry Journal Press, 1950.

Crane, Stephen. *Red Badge of Courage and Other Stories.* New York: Collier, 1962.

Cunningham, W. Scott. *Wake Island Command.* New York: Little, 1962.

Custer, Elizabeth. *Boots and Saddles.* New York: Harper & Brothers, 1885.

———. *Following the Guidon.* New York: Harper, 1890.

Devereux, James. *The Story of Wake Island.* New York: J. B. Lippincott, 1947.

Dornbusch, Charles E. (comp.). *Histories of American Army Units, World Wars I and II and Korean Conflict.* Washington, D.C.: Adjutant General's Office, 1956.

Downey, Fairfax D. *General Crook, Indian Fighter.* Philadelphia: Westminster Press, 1957.

Dugan, James, and Stewart Carroll. *Ploesti: the Great Ground-Air Battle of 1 August 1943.* New York: Random House, 1963.

Dupuy, Richard E. *Brave Men and Great Captains.* New York: Harper, 1959.

———. *The Compact History of the United States Army.* Englewood Cliffs, N.J.: Hawthorn Books, 1961.

———. *Men of West Point.* New York: McLeod, 1952.

Dupuy, R. Ernest. *Where They Have Trod.* New York: Stokes, 1940.

Dupuy, R. Ernest, and William H. Baumer. *The Little Wars of the United States.* New York: Hawthorn Books, 1968.

Dupuy, R. Ernest, and N. Trevon. *Military Heritage of America.* New York: McGraw, 1956.

Edmonds, James E. *Fighting Fools.* New York: D. Appleton-Century, 1938.

Elsinger, Larry (ed.). *Sky Fighters of World War I.* Greenwich, Conn.: Fawcett, 1961.

Faulk, Odie B. *The Geronimo Campaign.* New York: Oxford, 1969.

Fehrenbach, T. R. *This Kind of War: A Study in Unpreparedness.* New York: Macmillan, 1963.

Field, James A. Jr. *History of U.S. Naval Operations: Korea.* Washington, D.C., 1962.

Forsberg, Franklin (ed.). *Highlights from "Yank," The Army Weekly.* New York: Royal Books, 1953.

Foster, John. *Hell in the Heavens.* New York: Putnam, 1961.

Freidel, Frank. *Over There: The Story of America's First Great Overseas Crusade.* New York: McGraw Hill, 1990.

Futrell, Robert F. *The United States Air Force in Korea, 1950-1953.* New York: Duell, 1961.

Gallant, Thomas G. *On Valor's Side.* New York: Doubleday, 1963.

———. *The Friendly Dead.* New York: Doubleday, 1964.

Garroe, William A. *The History of the United States Army.* New York, 1924.

Gibbons, Floyd. *And They Thought We Wouldn't Fight.* New York: George H. Doran, 1918.

Glass, E. L. N. *The History of the Tenth Cavalry.* Tucson, Ariz.: Acme Printing, 1921.

Glazier, Willard. *The Capture, Prison Pen and the Escape.* New York, United States Publishing, 1868.

Greer, Andrew C. *The New Breed: The Story of the U. S. Marines in Korea.* New York: Harper, 1952.

Grider, George W. *War Fish.* Boston: Little, Brown & Co., 1958.

Grolier's History of the First World War. 4 vols. New York: Grolier, 1966.

Gugeler, Russell A. *Combat Actions in Korea.* Washington, D.C.: Combat Forces Press, 1954.

Gurney, Gene. *Flying Aces of World War I.* New York: Random House, 1965.

———. *Journey of the Giants (Story of the B-29).* New York: Cowar-McCann, 1961.

———. *The War in the Air: A Pictorial History of World War II Air Forces in Combat.* New York: Crown, 1962.

Hammer, Kenneth. *Little Big Horn Biographies.* Brookings, S. Dak.: Custer Battlefield Historical & Museum Association, 1965.

Handleman, Howard. *Bridge to Victory.* New York: Random House, 1943.

Harbord, James G. *The American Army in France, 1917-19.* Boston: Little, Brown, 1936.

Harper, Robert S. *Ohio Handbook of the Civil War.* Columbus, Ohio: LBS Archival Products, 1961.

Heavey, William F. *Down Ramp!.* Washington, D.C.: Infantry Journal Press, 1947.

Heinl, Robert D. Jr. *Victory at High Tide: The Inchon-Seoul Campaign.* New York: Lippincott, 1968.

Heitman, Francis B. *Historical Register and Dictionary of the United States Army.* Washington, D.C.: U.S. Government Printing Office, 1903. Revised, 1965.

Hilliard, Jack B. *An Annotated Reading List of United States marine Corps History.* Washington, D.C.: U.S. Marine Corp, Historical Branch, G3 Div., 1966.

Hirsh, Phil. *Fighting Eagles.* New York: Pyramid Books, 1961.

Hoehling, Adolph A. *The Fierce Lambs.* Boston: Little, Brown, 1960.

Honeywell, Roy J. *Chaplains of the United States Army.* Washington, D.C.: Office of Chief of Chaplains, 1958.

Hough, Frank O. *The Island War: The United States Marine Corps in the Pacific.* Philadelphia: J. B. Lippincott, 1947.

Hoyt, Edwin P. *The Battle of Leyte Gulf.* New York: Jove Publications, 1988.

Hubler, Richard G., and John A. DeChant. *Flying Leathernecks.* Garden City, N.Y.: Doubleday, Doran, 1944.

Hunt, George P. *Coral Comes High.* New York: Harper & Brothers, 1946.

———. *The Story of the United States Marines.* New York: Random House, 1951.

Jablonski, Edward. *Pictorial History of World War I Years.* New York: Doubleday, 1985.

Jacobs, Bruce. *Soldiers: The Fighting Divisions of the Regular Army.* New York: Norton, 1958.

Johnston, R. W. *Follow Me!* New York: Random House, 1948.

Karig, Walter. *Battle Report. vol. 6.* New York: Farrar & Rinehart, 1944-52.

Kenney, George C. *General Kenney Reports: A Personal History of the Pacific War.* New York: Duell, Sloan & Pearce, 1949.

King, Charles. *Campaigning with Crook.* Norman, Okla: University of Oklahoma Press, 1964.

Knox, Dudley W. *A History of the United States Navy.* New York, 1963.

Leckie, Robert. *Challenge for the Pacific.* New York: Doubleday, 1965.

———. *Conflict: The History of the Korean War.* New York: Putnam, 1962.

———. *March to Glory.* New York: Bantam, 1990.

———. *Strong Men Armed: The United States Marines Against Japan.* New York: Random House, 1962.

Leckie, William H. *The Buffalo Soldiers: A Narrative of the Negro Cavalry in the West.* Norman, Okla.: University of Oklahoma Press, 1967.

———. *The Military Conquest of the Southern Plains.* Norman, Okla.: University of Oklahoma Press, 1963.

Lejeune, John A. *Reminiscences of a Marine.* Philadelphia: Dorrance, 1930.

Lewis, Winston B. *The Battle of Savo Island.* Washington, D.C.: Naval Historical Center, 1993.

Life Magazine (eds.). *The First World War.* New York: Life, 1965.

Livesay, Anthony. *Great Battles of World War I.* New York: Macmillan, 1989.

Lockwood, Charles. *Sink 'Em All.* New York: Dutton, 1951.

Lockwood, Charles A., and H. C. Adamson. *Hell at 50 Fathoms.* Philadelphia: Chilton, 1962.

Loomis, Robert. *Great American Fighter Pilots of World War II.* New York: Random House, 1961.

Lord, Walter. *Day of Infamy.* New York: Holt, 1957.

———. *Incredible Victory.* New York: Harper & Row, 1967.

Love, Edmund G. *War Is a Private Affair.* New York: Harcourt, 1959.

Mandel, Paul, and Life Magazine (eds.). *Great Battles of the Civil War.* New York: Life, 1961.

Mann, Carl. *Air Heraldry.* New York: R. M. McBride, 1944.

Marshall, S. L. A. *The American Heritage History of World War I.* New York: Dell, 1966.

———. *Battle at Best.* New York: Morrow, 1963.

———. *Battles in the Monsoon: Campaigning in the Central Vietnam, Summer 1966.* New York: Morrow, 1967.

———. *Men Against Fire.* New York: Morrow, 1947.

———. *Night Drop.* New York: Macmillan, 1963.

———. *The Officer as a Leader.* Harrisburg, Pa.: Stackpole Co., 1966.

———. *Pork Chop Hill: the American Fighting Man in Action, Korea, Spring, 1952.* Nashville, Battery Press, 1986.

———. *West to Cambodia.* New York: Cowles, 1968.

Macaulay, Neill W. *The Sandino Affair.* Chicago: Quadrangle Books, 1967.

MacDonald, Charles B. *The Battle of the Huertgen Forest.* New York: Lippincott, 1963.

McCahill, William. *First to Fight.* Philadelphia: David McKay, 1943.

McCollum, Lee Charles. *History and Rhymes of the Lost Battalion.* Chicago: Foley, printers, 1922.

McMillan, George. *The Old Breed.* Washington, D.C.: Infantry Journal Press, 1949.

———. *Uncommon Valor: Marine Divisions in Action.* Washington, D.C.: Infantry Journal Press, 1946.

Mercey, A. A. *Sea, Surf and Hell.* New York: Prentice Hall, 1945.

Merrill, James M. (ed.). *Uncommon Valor: The Exciting Story of the Army.* New York: Rand-McNally, 1964.

Metcalfe, Clyde H. *A History of the United States Marine Corps.* New York: G. Putnam's Sons, 1939.

———. *Marine Corps Reader.* New York: Putnam, 1944.

Miller, F. T. *World in the Air: The Story of Flying in Pictures.* 2 vols. New York: Putnam, 1930.

Miller, Harold B. *Navy Wings*. New York: Dodd, Mead, 1937, 1942.

Monks, John, Jr. *Ribbon and Star: The Third Marines at Bougainville*. Washington, D.C.: Zenger, 1979.

Montross, Lynn. *The United States Marines: A Pictorial History*. New York: Holt, Rinehart & Winston, 1959.

Moore, Robin. *The Green Berets*. New York: Crown, 1965.

Morison, Samuel Eliot. *History of United States Naval Operations in World War II*. 15 vols. Boston: Little, Brown, 1947-1962.

Mulvey, Timothy J. *These Are Your Sons*. New York: McGraw-Hill, 1952.

Muphy, Jack. *History of United States Marine Corps Operations in World War II*. 3 vols. Washington, D.C.:, 1961-1968.

———. *A History of the United States*. Stamford, Conn.: Longmeadow Press,1993.

Murphy, Robert. *Diplomat Among Warriors* New York: Doubleday, 1964.

Murphy, Thomas D. *Ambassadors in Arms*. Honolulu: University of Hawaii Press, 1954.

Nason, Elias. *The Life and Public Services of Henry Wilson*. Boston: D. Lothrup, c. 1881.

Navy Times (eds.). *They Fought Under the Sea*. Springfield, Va: Navy Times Publishing, 1963.

Newcomb, Richard F. *Battle of Iwo Jima*. New York: Crowell, 1966.

———. *Savo: the Incredible Naval Debacle Off Guadalcanal*. New York: Holt, Rinehart & Winston, 1961.

Nolan, Alan T. *The Iron Brigade*. New York: Macmillan, 1961.

Office of the Chief of Military History. *The United States Army in World War II*. 84 vols. Washington, D.C.: U.S. Government Printing Office, 1947-1968.

Official Records of the Union and Confederate Navies in the War of Rebellion. 31 vols. Washington, D.C.: U.S. Naval War Records Office, 1894-1927.

Parrott, Marc. *Hazard: Marines on Mission*. Garden City, N.Y.: Doubleday, 1962.

Pearl, Jack. *Aerial Dogfights of World War II*. Derby, Conn.: Monarch Books, 1962.

Pershing, John J. *My Experiences in the World War*. New York: Frederick A. Stokes, 1931.

Phisterer, Frederick (comp.). *New York in the War of the Rebellion, 1861 to 1865, vol. 5*, Albany, N.Y.: J. B. Lyon, State Printers, 1912.

Pierce, Philip N., and Frank D. Hough. *The Compact History of the United States Marine Corps*. New York: Hawthorn Books, 1960.

Plank, Will. *Banners and Bugles*. Marlborough, N.Y.: Centennial Press, 1963.

Platt, Frank C. (ed.). *Great Battles of World War I: In the Air*. New York: New American Library, 1966.

———. *Great Battles of World War I; On the Land*. New York, 1966.

Powell, William H. *Officers of the Army and Navy: Volunteers Who Served in the Civil War*. Philadelphia: L. R. Hamersly, 1893.

Pratt, Fletcher. *The Compact History of the U.S. Navy*. New York: Hawthorn Books, 1962.

Proehl, Carl W. (ed.). *The Fourth Marine Division in World War II*. Nashville: Battery Press, 1988.

Public Papers of the Presidents of the United States. Harry S. Truman, 1945-1953. 8 vols. *Dwight D. Eisenhower, 1953-1961. John F. Kennedy, 1961-1963*. 3 vols.*Lyndon B. Johnson, 1963-1967*. 5 vols. Millwood, N.Y.: KTO Press, 1978.

Pullen, John. *The 20th Maine: a Volunteer Regiment in the Civil War*. Philadelphia: Lippincott, 1962.

Quarles, Benjamin. *The Negro in the Civil War*. Boston: Little, Brown, 1953.

Randall, Ruth. *Colonel Elmer Ellsworth*. Boston: Little, Brown, 1960.

Reeder, Russell P. (Red), and N. R. Campion. *The West Point Story*. New York: Random House, 1956.

Reynolds, Quentin J. *They Fought for the Sky [The Dramatic Story of the First War in the Air]*. New York: Rinehart, 1957.

Rickey, Don Jr. *Forty Miles a Day on Beans and Hay*. Norman, Okla.: University of Oklahoma Press, 1963.

Ridgway, Matthew B. *The Korean War*. New York: Doubleday, 1967.

Riesnberg, Felix. *The Story of the Naval Academy*. New York: Random House, 1958.

Robinson, D. B. (ed.). *The Dirty Wars*. New York, Dial Press,1967.

Robinson, Donald (ed.). *The Day I Was Proudest To Be An American*. Garden City, N.Y.: Doubleday, 1958.

Roosevelt, Theodore. *The Rough Riders*. New York: New American Library, 1961.

Roscoe, Theodore. *Pig Boats: The True Story of the Fighting Submarines of World War II*. New York: Bantam Books, 1958.

Ryan, Cornelius. *The Longest Day: June 6, 1944*. New York: Simon & Schuster, 1959.

Saturday Evening Post (eds.). *Battle: Great True Stories of Combat in World War II*. New York: Saturday Evening Post, 1968.

Schott, Joseph L. *The Ordeal of Samar.* Indianapolis: Bobbs-Merrill, 1965.

Schuon, Karl (ed.). *The Leathernecks: an Informal History of the U.S. Marine Corps.* New York: Franklin Watts, 1963.

Shaw, Henry T. Jr. *Tarawa: A Legend Is Born.* New York: Ballantine Books, 1968.

Shelford, W. *Subsunk.* Garden City, N.Y.: Doubleday, 1960.

Sherrod, Robert. *History of Marine Corps Aviation in World War II.* Washington, D.C.: Combat Forces Press, 1952.

———. *On To Westward.* New York: Duell, 1945.

Sims, William S., and Burton Jesse Hendrick. *Victory at Sea.* New York: Doubleday, 1920.

Smith, Holland. *Coral and Brass.* New York: C. Scribner's Sons, 1949.

Smith, Stanley E. *The U.S. in Navy World War II.* New York: Morrow, 1966.

Smith, William W. *Midway, Turning Point of the Pacific.* New York: Crowell, 1966.

Stackpole Co. (eds.). *The Army Almanac.* Harrisburg, Pa.: Stackpole Co., 1959.

Stallings, Laurence. *The Doughboys: The Story of the AEF, 1917-1918.* New York: Harper & Row, 1963.

Sterling, Forest J. *Wake of the Wahoo.* Philadelphia: Chilton Co., 1960.

Stewart, Edgar I. *Custer's Luck.* Norman, Okla.: University of Oklahoma Press, 1955.

Sweetman, Jack. *The Landing at Veracruz: 1914.* Annapolis, Md.: U.S. Naval Institute, 1968.

Thomason, John W. *And a Few Marines.* New York: Scribner, 1943.

———. *Fix Bayonets.* New York: Scribner, 1926.

Todd, Frederick P., and Fritz Kredel. *Soldiers of the American Army, 1775-1954.* Chicago: H. Regnery, 1954.

Toand, John. *Battle: The Story of the Bulge.* New York: Random House, 1959.

———. *But Not in Shame: The Six Months After Pearl Harbor.* New York: Random House, 1961.

———. *The Last 100 Days.* New York: Random House, 1966.

Townsend, Thomas S. *The Honors of the Empire State in the War of the Rebellion.* New York: A. Lovell, 1889.

Tregaskis, Richard. *Guadalcanal Diary.* New York: Random House, 1955.

True, The Man's Magazine. *True Civil War Stories.* *Edited by Joseph Millard.* Greenwich, Conn., Fawcett, 1961.

Ulanoff, Stanley. *Fighter Pilot.* Garden City, N.Y.: Doubleday, 1962.

U.S. Marine Corps and Nicholas Canzona. *United States Marine Operations in Korea, 1950-1953.* 4 vols. Grosse Point, Mich.: Scholarly Press, 1969.

U.S. Naval History Division. *Aviation in the United States Navy.* Washington, D.C.: U.S. Government Printing Office, 1961.

———. *The Submarine in the United States Navy.* Washington, D.C.: U.S. Government Printing Office, 1969.

Warner, Ezra J. *Generals in Blue.* Baton Rouge, La.: Louisiana State University Press, 1964.

Weigley, Russell F. *History of the United States Army.* New York: Macmillan, 1967.

Wellman, Paul I. *The Indian Wars of the West.* New York: Doubleday, 1954.

Westermier, Clifford P. *Who Rush to Glory: the Cowboy Volunteers of 1898.* Caldwell, Idaho: Caxton Printers, 1958.

White, W. L. *They Were Expendable.* New York: 1942.

Whitehouse, A. G. L. (Arch). *The Years of the War Birds.* Garden City, N.Y.: Doubleday, 1960.

———. *The Years of the Sky Kings.* Garden City, N.Y.: Doubleday, 1959.

Whitman, Sidney E. *The Troopers: An Informal History of the Plains Cavalry, 1865-1890.* New York: Hastings House Publishers, 1962.

Wiley, Bell I. *The Common Soldier of the Union.* Indianapolis: Bobbs-Merrill, 1952.

Willson, Arobella M. *Disaster, Struggle, Triumph.* Albany, N.Y.: Argus, 1870.

Wise, Frederick M. *A Marine Tells It to You.* New York: J. H. Sears Co., 1929.

Wise, Wm. H. and Company Inc.(ed.). *The 100 Best True Stories of World War II.* New York: W. H. Wise, 1945.

Wolff, Leon. *Little Brown Brother.* New York: Doubleday, 1961.

———. *Low Level Mission.* New York: Doubleday, 1957.

Wormser, Richard. *The Yellowlegs: the Story of the United States Cavalry.* Garden City, N.Y.: Doubleday, 1966.

Wright, Elsie N. (Grayson, J. J. Pseud.). *Famous Flyers.* Cleveland, Ohio: World Syndicate Pub., 1932.

— Eugene V. McAndrews

INDEX

BAKER, Addison Earl, *U.S. Army Air Corps*	2603	BEAUMONT, Eugene Beauharnais, *U.S. Army*	62
BAKER, Benjamin F., *U.S. Navy*	2073	BEBB, Edward James, *U.S. Army*	63
BAKER, Charles, *U.S. Navy*	37	BECKWITH, Wallace A., *U.S. Army*	64
BAKER Jr., Edward Lee, *U.S. Army*	2074	BEDDOWS, Richard, *U.S. Army*	65
BAKER, John, *U.S. Army*	1544	BEEBE, William Sully, *U.S. Army*	66
BAKER Jr., John Franklin, *U.S. Army*	3168	BEECH, John P., *U.S. Army*	67
BAKER Jr., Thomas Alexander, *U.S. Army*	2604	BEGLEY, Terrence, *U.S. Army*	68
BALCH, John Henry, *U.S. Navy*	2459	BEHNE, Frederick, *U.S. Navy*	2325
BALDWIN, Charles H., *U.S. Navy*	38	BEHNKE, Heinrich, *U.S. Navy*	2326
BALDWIN, Frank Dwight, *U.S. Army*	39, 1545	BEIKIRCH, Gary Burnell, *U.S. Army*	3173
BALLARD, Donald Everett, *U.S. Navy*	3169	BELCHER, Ted, *U.S. Army*	3174
BALLEN, Frederick A., *U.S. Army*	40	BELCHER, Thomas, *U.S. Army*	69
BANCROFT, Neil, *U.S. Army*	1546	BELL, Bernard Pious, *U.S. Army*	2611
BANKS, George Lovell, *U.S. Army*	41	BELL, Dennis, *U.S. Army*	2076
BARBER, James Albert, *U.S. Army*	42	BELL, George, *U.S. Navy*	70
BARBER, William Earl, *U.S. Marine Corps*	3030	BELL, Harry, *U.S. Army*	2189
BARFOOT, Van Thomas, *U.S. Army*	2605	BELL, James, *U.S. Army*	1550
BARGER, Charles Denver, *U.S. Army*	2460	BELL, James Bennett, *U.S. Army*	71
BARKELEY, David B., *U.S. Army*	2461	BELL, James Franklin, *U.S. Army*	2190
BARKER, Chalres H., *U.S. Army*	3031	BELLRICHARD, Leslie Allen, *U.S. Army*	3175
BARKER, Jedh Colby, *U.S. Marine Corps*	3170	BELPITT, William Henry, *U.S. Navy*	1978
BARKER, Nathaniel C., *U.S. Army*	43	BENAVIDEZ, Roy Perez, *U.S. Army*	3176
BARKLEY, John Lewis, *U.S. Army*	2462	BENDER, Stanley, *U.S. Army*	2612
BARNES, Will Croft, *U.S. Army*	1547	BENEDICT, George Greenville, *U.S. Army*	72
BARNES, William H., *U.S. Army*	44	BENFOLD, Edward Clyde "Ted", *U.S. Navy*	3033
BARNES III, John Andrew, *U.S. Army*	3171	BENJAMIN Jr., George, *U.S. Army*	2613
BARNUM Jr., Harvey Curtiss "Barney", *U.S. Marine Corps*	3172	BENJAMIN, John Francis, *U.S. Army*	73
BARNUM, Henry Alanson, *U.S. Army*	45	BENJAMIN, Samuel Nicholl, *U.S. Army*	74
BARNUM, James, *U.S. Navy*	46	BENNETT, Edward Andrew, *U.S. Army*	2614
BARRELL, Charles L., *U.S. Army*	47	BENNETT, Emory L., *U.S. Army*	3034
BARRETT, Carlton William, *U.S. Army*	2606	BENNETT, Floyd, *U.S. Navy*	2578
BARRETT, Edward, *U.S. Navy*	1977	BENNETT, James Harvey, *U.S. Navy*	2077
BARRETT, Richard, *U.S. Army*	1548	BENNETT, Orrin, *U.S. Army*	75
BARRICK, Jesse, *U.S. Army*	48	BENNETT, Orson W., *U.S. Army*	76
BARRINGER, William H., *U.S. Army*	49	BENNETT, Steven Logan, *U.S. Air Force*	3177
BARROW, David Duffy, *U.S. Navy*	2075	BENNETT, Thomas William, *U.S. Army*	3178
BARRY, Augustus, *U.S. Army*	50	BENNION, Mervyn Sharp, *U.S. Navy*	2615
BART, Frank J., *U.S. Army*	2463	BENSINGER, William, *U.S. Army*	77
BARTER, Gurdon H., *U.S. Navy*	51	BENSON, James, *U.S. Navy*	1979
BARTON, Thomas, *U.S. Navy*	52	BENYAURD, William Henry Harrison, *U.S. Army*	78
BASILONE, John "Manila Jonn", *U.S. Marine Corps*	2607	BERG, George Francis, *U.S. Army*	2078
BASS, David L., *U.S. Navy*	53	BERGENDAHL, Frederick, *U.S. Army*	1551
BATCHELDER, Richard Napoleon, *U.S. Army*	54	BERKELEY, Randolph Carter, *U.S. Marine Corps*	2384
BATES, Delavan, *U.S. Army*	55	BERRY, Charles Joseph, *U.S. Marine Corps*	2616
BATES, Norman Francis, *U.S. Army*	56	BERTOLDO, Vito R., *U.S. Army*	2617
BATES, Richard, *U.S. Navy*	1521	BERTRAM, Heinrich, *U.S. Army*	1552
BATSON, Matthew Arlington, *U.S. Army*	2187	BESSEY, Charles Albert, *U.S. Army*	1553
BAUER, Harold William "Indian Joe", *U.S. Marine Corps*	2608	BETHAM, Asa, *U.S. Navy*	79
BAUGH, William Bernard, *U.S. Marine Corps*	3032	BETTS, Charles Malone, *U.S. Army*	80
BAUSELL, Lewis Kenneth, *U.S. Marine Corps*	2609	BEYER, Albert, *U.S. Navy*	2079
BAYBUTT, Philip, *U.S. Army*	57	BEYER, Arthur O., *U.S. Army*	2618
BAZAAR, Philip, *U.S. Navy*	58	BEYER, Hillary, *U.S. Army*	81
BEARSS, Hiram Iddings, *U.S. Marine Corps*	2188	BIANCHI, Willibald Charles, *U.S. Army*	2619
BEASLEY, Harry C., *U.S. Navy*	2383	BIBBER, Charles James, *U.S. Navy*	82
BEATTY, Alexander Mitchell, *U.S. Army*	59	BICKFORD, Henry H., *U.S. Army*	83
BEATY, Powhatan, *U.S. Army*	60	BICKFORD, John F., *U.S. Navy*	84
BEAUDOIN, Raymond Ovila, *U.S. Army*	2610	BICKFORD, Matthew, *U.S. Army*	85
BEAUFORD, Clay, *U.S. Army*	1549	BICKHAM, Charles Goodwin, *U.S. Army*	2191
BEAUFORT, Jean J., *U.S. Army*	61	BIDDLE, Melvin Earl, *U.S. Army*	2620

BIEGER, Charles, *U.S. Army*	86	BOWDEN, Samuel, *U.S. Army*	1557
BIEGLER, George Wesley, *U.S. Army*	2192	BOWEN, Chester Bennett, *U.S. Army*	118
BIGELOW, Elmer Charles, *U.S. Naval Reserve*	2621	BOWEN, Emmer, *U.S. Army*	119
BINDER, Richard, *U.S. Marine Corps*	87	BOWEN Jr., Hammett Lee, *U.S. Army*	3182
BINGHAM, Henry Harrison, *U.S. Army*	88	BOWMAN, Alonzo, *U.S. Army*	1558
BIRDSALL, Horatio L., *U.S. Army*	89	BOWMAN, Edward R., *U.S. Navy*	120
BIRKHIMER, William Edward, *U.S. Army*	2193	BOX, Thomas J., *U.S. Army*	121
BISHOP, Charles Francis, *U.S. Navy*	2385	BOYCE Jr., George W. G., *U.S. Army*	2630
BISHOP, Daniel, *U.S. Army*	1554	BOYDSTON, Erwin Jay, *U.S. Marine Corps*	2270
BISHOP, Francis A., *U.S. Army*	90	BOYINGTON, Gregory "Pappy", *U.S. Marine Corps Reserve*	2631
BJORKLUND, Arnold L., *U.S. Army*	2622	BOYNE, Thomas, *U.S. Army*	1559
BJORKMAN, Ernest H., *U.S. Navy*	2327	BOYNTON, Henry Van Ness, *U.S. Army*	122
BLACK, John Charles, *U.S. Army*	91	BRADBURY, Sanford, *U.S. Army*	1560
BLACK, William Perkins, *U.S. Army*	92	BRADLEY, Alexander, *U.S. Navy*	1980
BLACKMAR, Wilmon Whilldin, *U.S. Army*	93	BRADLEY, Amos, *U.S. Navy*	123
BLACKWELL, Robert Lester, *U.S. Army*	2464	BRADLEY, Charles, *U.S. Navy*	124
BLACKWOOD, William Robert Douglas, *U.S. Army*	94	BRADLEY, George, *U.S. Navy*	2386
BLAGHEEN, William, *U.S. Navy*	95	BRADLEY, Thomas Wilson, *U.S. Army*	125
BLAIR, James, *U.S. Army*	1555	BRADLEY Jr., Willis Winter, *U.S. Navy*	2467
BLAIR, Robert M., *U.S. Navy*	96	BRADY, George F., *U.S. Navy*	2081
BLAKE, Robert, *U.S. Navy*	97	BRADY, James, *U.S. Army*	126
BLANCHFIELD, Michael Reinert, *U.S. Army*	3179	BRADY, Patrick Henry, *U.S. Army*	3183
BLANQUET, *U.S. Army*	1556	BRANAGAN, Edward, *U.S. Army*	1561
BLASDEL, Thomas A., *U.S. Army*	98	BRANDLE, Joseph E., *U.S. Army*	127
BLEAK, David Bruce, *U.S. Army*	3035	BRANNIGAN, Felix, *U.S. Army*	128
BLECKLEY, Erwin Russell, *U.S. Army Air Service*	2465	BRANT, Abram B., *U.S. Army*	1562
BLICKENSDERGER, Milton, *U.S. Army*	99	BRANT Jr., William, *U.S. Army*	129
BLISS, George Newman, *U.S. Army*	100	BRAS, Edgar A., *U.S. Army*	130
BLISS, Zenas Randall, *U.S. Army*	101	BRATLING, Frank, *U.S. Army*	1563
BLOCH, Orville Emil, *U.S. Army*	2623	BRAZELL, John, *U.S. Navy*	131
BLODGETT, Wells H., *U.S. Army*	102	BREAULT, Henry, *U.S. Navy*	2579
BLUCHER, Charles, *U.S. Army*	103	BREEMAN, George, *U.S. Navy*	2330
BLUME, Robert, *U.S. Navy*	2080	BREEN, John, *U.S. Navy*	132
BLUNT, John W., *U.S. Army*	104	BRENNAN, Christopher, *U.S. Navy*	133
BOBO, John Paul, *U.S. Marine Corps Reserve*	3180	BRESNAHAN, Patrick Francis, *U.S. Navy*	2331
BOEHLER, Otto A., *U.S. Army*	2194	BREST, Lewis Francis, *U.S. Army*	134
BOEHM, Peter Martin, *U.S. Army*	105	BRETT, Lloyd Milton, *U.S. Army*	1564
BOERS, Edward William, *U.S. Navy*	2328	BREWER, William John, *U.S. Army*	135
BOIS, Frank, *U.S. Navy*	106	BREWSTER, Andre Walker, *U.S. Army*	2271
BOLDEN, Paul Luther, *U.S. Army*	2624	BREYER, Charles, *U.S. Army*	136
BOLTON, Cecil Hamilton, *U.S. Army*	2625	BRIGGS, Elijah A., *U.S. Army*	137
BOND, William S., *U.S. Navy*	107	BRIGHT, George Washington, *U.S. Navy*	2082
BONDSTEEL, James Leroy, *U.S. Army*	3181	BRILES, Herschel Floyd "Pete", *U.S. Army*	2632
BONEBRAKE, Henry G., *U.S. Army*	108	BRINGLE, Andrew, *U.S. Army*	138
BONG, Richard Ira, *U.S. Army Air Corps*	2626	BRINN, Andrew, *U.S. Navy*	139
BONNAFFON Jr., Sylvester, *U.S. Army*	109	BRITT, Maurice Lee (Footsie), *U.S. Army*	2633
BONNEY, Robert Earl, *U.S. Navy*	2329	BRITTIN, Nelson Vogel, *U.S. Army*	3036
BONNYMAN Jr., Alexander "Sandy", *U.S. Marine Corps Reserve*	2627	BROCK, George F., *U.S. Navy*	2332
BOODY, Robert M., *U.S. Army*	110	BROGAN, James, *U.S. Army*	1565
BOOKER, Robert D., *U.S. Army*	2628	BRONNER, August Frederick, *U.S. Army*	140
BOON, Hugh Patterson, *U.S. Army*	111	BRONSON, Deming, *U.S. Army*	2468
BOONE, Joel Thompson, *U.S. Navy*	2466	BRONSON, James H., *U.S. Army*	141
BORDELON, William James, *U.S. Marine Corps*	2629	BROOKIN, Oscar, *U.S. Army*	2083
BOSS, Orlando Phidelio, *U.S. Army*	112	BROPHY, James, *U.S. Army*	1566
BOUQUET, Nicholas S., *U.S. Army*	113	BROSNAN, John, *U.S. Army*	142
BOURKE, John Gregory, *U.S. Army*	114	BROSTROM, Leonard C., *U.S. Army*	2634
BOURNE, Thomas, *U.S. Navy*	115	BROUSE, Charles W., *U.S. Army*	143
BOURY, Richard, *U.S. Army*	116	BROWN, Benjamin, *U.S. Army*	1567
BOUTWELL, John W., *U.S. Army*	117	BROWN Jr., Bobbie Evan, *U.S. Army*	2635

BROWN, Charles, *U.S. Marine Corps*	1959	BURKE, Thomas, *U.S. Army*	183
BROWN, Charles E., *U.S. Army*	144	BURKE, Thomas, *U.S. Navy*	1523
BROWN Jr., Edward, *U.S. Army*	145	BURNES, James, *U.S. Marine Corps*	2272
BROWN, Henri Le Fevre, *U.S. Army*	146	BURNETT, George Ritter, *U.S. Army*	1574
BROWN, James, *U.S. Army*	1568	BURNS, James Madison, *U.S. Army*	184
BROWN, James, *U.S. Navy*	147	BURNS, John M., *U.S. Navy*	185
BROWN, Jeremiah Z., *U.S. Army*	148	BURR, Elmer J., *U.S. Army*	2638
BROWN, John, *U.S. Army*	150	BURR, Herbert Hoover, *U.S. Army*	2639
BROWN, John, *U.S. Navy*	149	BURRIS, Tony K., *U.S. Army*	3039
BROWN, John, *U.S. Navy*	1522	BURRITT, William Wallace, *U.S. Army*	186
BROWN, John Harties, *U.S. Army*	151	BURT, James Montross, *U.S. Army*	2640
BROWN, Lorenzo Dow, *U.S. Army*	1569	BURTON, Albert, *U.S. Navy*	187
BROWN, Melvin L., *U.S. Army*	3037	BUSH, Richard Earl, *U.S. Marine Corps Reserve*	2641
BROWN Jr., Morris, *U.S. Army*	152	BUSH, Robert Eugene, *U.S. Navy Reserve*	2642
BROWN, Robert, *U.S. Navy*	153	BUTLER, Edmond Thomas, *U.S. Army*	1575
BROWN, Robert Burns, *U.S. Army*	154	BUTLER, Smedley Darlington, *U.S. Marine Corps*	2388, 2437
BROWN, Uriah H., *U.S. Army*	155	BUTTERFIELD, Daniel Adams, *U.S. Army*	188
BROWN, William H., *U.S. Navy*	156	BUTTERFIELD, Franklin George, *U.S. Army*	189
BROWN, Wilson, *U.S. Navy*	157	BUTTON, William Robert, *U.S. Marine Corps*	2573
BROWN, Wilson W., *U.S. Army*	158	BUTTS, George, *U.S. Navy*	190
BROWNELL, Francis Edwin, *U.S. Army*	159	BUTTS, John Edward, *U.S. Army*	2643
BROWNELL, William P., *U.S. Navy*	160	BUZZARD, Ulysses G., *U.S. Army*	2084
BRUCE, Daniel Dean, *U.S. Marine Corps*	3184	BYRD Jr., Richard Evelyn, *U.S. Navy*	2580
BRUNER, Louis J., *U.S. Army*	161	BYRNE, Bernard Albert, *U.S. Army*	2196
BRUSH, George Washington, *U.S. Army*	162	BYRNE, Denis, *U.S. Army*	1576
BRUTON, Christopher C., *U.S. Army*	163	BYRNES, James, *U.S. Navy*	191
BRUTSCHE, Henry, *U.S. Navy*	164	CABLE, Joseph A., *U.S. Army*	1577
BRYAN, William C., *U.S. Army*	1570	CADDY, William Robert, *U.S. Marine Corps Reserve*	2644
BRYANT, Andrew Symmes, *U.S. Army*	165	CADWALLADER, Abel G., *U.S. Army*	192
BRYANT, William Maud, *U.S. Army*	3185	CADWELL, Luman Lewis, *U.S. Army*	193
BUCHA, Paul William, *U.S. Army*	3186	CAFFERATA Jr., Hector Albert, *U.S. Marine Corps Reserve*	3040
BUCHANAN, Allen, *U.S. Navy*	2387	CAHEY, Thomas, *U.S. Navy*	2333
BUCHANAN, David M., *U.S. Navy*	1981	CALDWELL, Daniel G., *U.S. Army*	194
BUCHANAN, George A., *U.S. Army*	166	CALKIN, Ivers S., *U.S. Army*	195
BUCK, Frederick Clarence, *U.S. Army*	167	CALL, Donald Marshall, *U.S. Army*	2469
BUCK, James, *U.S. Navy*	168	CALLAGHAN, Daniel Judson, *U.S. Navy*	2645
BUCKINGHAM, David E., *U.S. Army*	169	CALLAHAN, John H., *U.S. Army*	196
BUCKLES, Abram J., *U.S. Army*	170	CALLEN, Thomas Joseph, *U.S. Army*	1578
BUCKLEY, Denis, *U.S. Army*	171	CALUGAS, Jose, *U.S. Army*	2646
BUCKLEY, Howard Major, *U.S. Marine Corps*	2195	CALVERT, James Spencer, *U.S. Army*	1579
BUCKLEY, John C., *U.S. Army*	172	CAMP, Carlton N., *U.S. Army*	197
BUCKLYN, John Knight, *U.S. Army*	173	CAMPBELL, Albert Ralph, *U.S. Marine Corps*	2273
BUFFINGTON, John C., *U.S. Army*	174	CAMPBELL, Daniel J., *U.S. Marine Corps*	2085
BUFFUM, Robert, *U.S. Army*	175	CAMPBELL, James A., *U.S. Army*	198
BUHRMAN, Henry G., *U.S. Army*	176	CAMPBELL, William, *U.S. Army*	199
BUKER, Brian Leroy, *U.S. Army*	3187	CAMPBELL, William, *U.S. Navy*	200
BULKELEY, John Duncan, *U.S. Navy*	2636	CANFIELD, Heth, *U.S. Army*	1580
BUMGARNER, William, *U.S. Army*	177	CANN, Tedford Harris, *U.S. Navy*	2470
BURBANK, James H., *U.S. Army*	178	CANNON, George Ham, *U.S. Marine Corps*	2647
BURGER, Joseph, *U.S. Army*	179	CANTRELL, Charles P., *U.S. Army*	2086
BURK, E. Michael, *U.S. Army*	180	CAPEHART, Charles E., *U.S. Army*	201
BURK, Thomas, *U.S. Army*	181	CAPEHART, Henry, *U.S. Army*	202
BURKARD, Oscar R., *U.S. Army*	1571	CAPODANNO, Vincent Robert, *U.S. Navy*	3189
BURKE, Daniel Webster, *U.S. Army*	182	CAPRON Jr., Horace, *U.S. Army*	203
BURKE, Francis Xavier, *U.S. Army*	2637	CAREY, Alvin P., *U.S. Army*	2648
BURKE, Lloyd Leslie "Scooter", *U.S. Army*	3038	CAREY Jr., Charles F., *U.S. Army*	2649
BURKE, Patrick J., *U.S. Army*	1572	CAREY, Hugh, *U.S. Army*	204
BURKE, Richard, *U.S. Army*	1573	CAREY, James, *U.S. Navy*	1524
BURKE, Robert Charles, *U.S. Marine Corps*	3188	CAREY, James Lemuel, *U.S. Army*	205

COLLINS, Harrison, *U.S. Army*	260	CRAIG, Samuel Henry, *U.S. Army*	1601
COLLINS Sr., Thomas D., *U.S. Army*	261	CRAIN, Morris E., *U.S. Army*	2672
COLLIS, Charles Henry Tucky, *U.S. Army*	262	CRAMEN, Thomas, *U.S. Navy*	1988
COLWELL, Oliver, *U.S. Army*	263	CRANDALL, Charles, *U.S. Army*	1602
COLYER, Wilbur E., *U.S. Army*	2472	CRANDALL, Orson Leon, *U.S. Navy*	2583
COMFORT, John W., *U.S. Army*	1596	CRANSTON, William Wallace, *U.S. Army*	289
COMMISKEY SR., Henry Alfred, *U.S. Marine Corps*	3047	CRAW, Demas Thurlow, *U.S. Army Air Corps*	2673
COMPSON, Hartwell B., *U.S. Army*	264	CRAWFORD, Alexander, *U.S. Navy*	290
CONAWAY, John Wesley, *U.S. Army*	265	CRAWFORD, William John, *U.S. Army*	2674
CONBOY, Martin, *U.S. Army*	266	CREED, John, *U.S. Army*	291
CONDON, Clarence Milville, *U.S. Army*	2200	CREEK, Thomas Elbert, *U.S. Marine Corps*	3197
CONLAN, Dennis, *U.S. Navy*	267	CREELMAN, William James, *U.S. Navy*	1989
CONNELL, Trustrim, *U.S. Army*	268	CREGAN, George, *U.S. Navy*	2392
CONNER, Richard, *U.S. Army*	269	CRESCENZ, Michael Joseph, *U.S. Army*	3198
CONNOLLY, Michael, *U.S. Navy*	1984	CREWS, John R., *U.S. Army*	2675
CONNOR, James Phillip, *U.S. Army*	2665	CRILLEY, Frank William, *U.S. Navy*	2444
CONNOR, John, *U.S. Army*	1597	CRIPPS, Thomas H., *U.S. Navy*	292
CONNOR, Peter Spencer, *U.S. Marine Corps*	3195	CRIST, John, *U.S. Army*	1603
CONNOR, Thomas, *U.S. Navy*	270	CRISWELL, Benjamin C., *U.S. Army*	1604
CONNOR, William C., *U.S. Navy*	271	CROCKER, Henry H., *U.S. Army*	293
CONNORS, James, *U.S. Army*	272	CROCKER, Ulric Lyona, *U.S. Army*	294
COOK, Donald Gilbert, *U.S. Marine Corps*	3196	CROFT, James E., *U.S. Army*	295
COOK, John, *U.S. Army*	273	CROMWELL, John Philip, *U.S. Navy*	2676
COOK, John Henry, *U.S. Army*	274	CRONAN, William (Willie), *U.S. Navy*	2338
COOKE, Walter Howard, *U.S. Army*	275	CRONIN, Cornelius, *U.S. Navy*	296
COOLEY, Raymond Henry, *U.S. Army*	2666	CROSIER, William Henry Harrison, *U.S. Army*	297
COOLIDGE, Charles Henry, *U.S. Army*	2667	CROSS, James Edwin, *U.S. Army*	298
COONEY, James, *U.S. Marine Corps*	2277	CROUSE, William Adolphus, *U.S. Navy*	2093
COONEY, Thomas C., *U.S. Navy*	2092	CROWLEY, Michael, *U.S. Army*	299
COONROD, Aquilla, *U.S. Army*	1598	CRUMP, Jerry Kirt, *U.S. Army*	3050
COOPER, John, *U.S. Navy*	276, 1525	CRUSE, Thomas, *U.S. Army*	1605
COPP, Charles Dearborn, *U.S. Army*	277	CUBBERLY, William G., *U.S. Army*	1606
CORAHORGI, Demetri, *U.S. Navy*	2336	CUKELA, Louis, *U.S. Marine Corps*	2475
CORCORAN, John, *U.S. Army*	278	CULLEN, Thomas, *U.S. Army*	300
CORCORAN, Michael, *U.S. Army*	1599	CUMMINGS, Amos Jay, *U.S. Army*	301
CORCORAN, Thomas E., *U.S. Navy*	279	CUMMINS, Andrew Johnson, *U.S. Army*	2094
COREY, William, *U.S. Navy*	1985	CUMPSTON, James M., *U.S. Army*	302
CORLISS, George W., *U.S. Army*	280	CUNNINGHAM, Charles, *U.S. Army*	1607
CORLISS, Stephen Potter, *U.S. Army*	281	CUNNINGHAM, Francis Marion, *U.S. Army*	303
CORRY Jr., William Merrill, *U.S. Navy*	2582	CUNNINGHAM, James Smith, *U.S. Army*	304
CORSON, Joseph Kirby, *U.S. Army*	282	CURRAN, Richard J., *U.S. Army*	305
COSGRIFF, Richard H., *U.S. Army*	283	CURREY, Francis Sherman "Frank", *U.S. Army*	2677
COSGROVE, Thomas, *U.S. Army*	284	CURTIS, John Calvin, *U.S. Army*	306
COSTELLO, John, *U.S. Navy*	1986	CURTIS, Josiah M., *U.S. Army*	307
COSTIN, Henry G., *U.S. Army*	2473	CURTIS, Newton Martin, *U.S. Army*	308
COTTON, Peter, *U.S. Navy*	285	CUSTER, Thomas Ward, *U.S. Army*	309
COUGHLIN, John, *U.S. Army*	286	CUTCHEON, Byron M., *U.S. Army*	310
COURSEN, Samuel Streit, *U.S. Army*	3048	CUTINHA, Nicholas Joseph, *U.S. Army*	3199
COURTNEY Jr., Henry Alexius, *U.S. Marine Corps Reserve*	2668	CUTTER, George W., *U.S. Navy*	1990
COURTNEY, Henry C., *U.S. Navy*	1987	CUTTS, James Madison, *U.S. Army*	311
COURTS, George McCall, *U.S. Navy*	2391	DAHL, Larry Gilbert, *U.S. Army*	3200
COVINGTON, Jesse Whitfield, *U.S. Navy*	2474	DAHLGREN, Edward Carl, *U.S. Army*	2678
COWAN, Richard Eller, *U.S. Army*	2669	DAHLGREN, John Olof, *U.S. Marine Corps*	2278
COX, Robert Edward, *U.S. Navy*	2337	DAILY, Charles, *U.S. Army*	1608
COX, Robert Mitchell, *U.S. Army*	287	DALESSONDRO, Peter Joseph, *U.S. Army*	2679
COYNE, John Nicholas, *U.S. Army*	288	DALY, Daniel Joseph, *U.S. Marine Corps*	2279, 2438
CRAFT, Clarence Byrle, *U.S. Army*	2670	DALY, Michael Joseph, *U.S. Army*	2680
CRAIG, Gordon Maynard, *U.S. Army*	3049	DAMATO, Anthony Peter, *U.S. Marine Corps*	2681
CRAIG, Robert, *U.S. Army*	2671	DANIELS, James Thomas, *U.S. Army*	1609

DOUGHERTY, William, *U.S. Army*	1623	ELMORE, Walter, *U.S. Navy*	1997
DOW, George P., *U.S. Army*	366	ELROD, Henry Talmage, *U.S. Marine Corps*	2702
DOW, Henry, *U.S. Navy*	367	ELSATSOOSH, *U.S. Army*	1628
DOWLING, James, *U.S. Army*	1624	ELSON, James M., *U.S. Army*	392
DOWNEY, William, *U.S. Army*	368	ELWOOD, Edwin L., *U.S. Army*	1629
DOWNS, Henry W., *U.S. Army*	369	EMBLER, Andrew Henry, *U.S. Army*	393
DOWNS, Willis H., *U.S. Army*	2202	EMMET, Robert Temple, *U.S. Army*	1630
DOZIER, James B., *U.S. Army*	1625	ENDERLIN, Richard, *U.S. Army*	394
DOZIER, James C., *U.S. Army*	2479	ENDL, Gerald Leon, *U.S. Army*	2703
DRAKE, James Madison, *U.S. Army*	370	ENGLE, James Edgar, *U.S. Army*	395
DREXLER, Henry Clay, *U.S. Navy*	2584	ENGLISH, Edmund, *U.S. Army*	396
DROWLEY, Jesse Ray, *U.S. Army*	2695	ENGLISH Jr., Glenn Harry, *U.S. Army*	3215
DRURY, James, *U.S. Army*	371	ENGLISH, Thomas, *U.S. Navy*	397
DRUSTRUP, Niels, *U.S. Navy*	2395	ENNIS, Charles D., *U.S. Army*	398
Du MOULIN, Frank, *U.S. Navy*	1526	ENRIGHT, John, *U.S. Navy*	1998
Du PONT, Henry Algernon, *U.S. Army*	379	EPPERSON, Harold Glenn, *U.S. Marine Corps Reserve*	2704
DUFFEY, John, *U.S. Army*	372	EPPS, Joseph L., *U.S. Army*	2203
DUKE, Ray E., *U.S. Army*	3059	ERICKSON, John P., *U.S. Navy*	399
DUNAGAN, Kern Wayne, *U.S. Army*	3213	ERICKSON, Nicholas, *U.S. Navy*	2103
DUNCAN, Adam, *U.S. Navy*	373	ERWIN, Henry Eugene "Red", *U.S. Army Air Corps*	2705
DUNCAN, James K. L., *U.S. Navy*	374	ESSEBAGGER Jr., John, *U.S. Army*	3061
DUNHAM, Russell, *U.S. Army*	2696	ESTES, Lewellyn Garrish, *U.S. Army*	400
DUNLAP, Robert Hugo, *U.S. Marine Corps Reserve*	2697	ESTOCIN, Michael John, *U.S. Navy*	3216
DUNLAVY, James, *U.S. Army*	375	EUBANKS, Ray E., *U.S. Army*	2706
DUNN, Parker F., *U.S. Army*	2480	EVANS, Coron D., *U.S. Army*	401
DUNN, William, *U.S. Navy*	376	EVANS Jr., Donald Ward, *U.S. Army*	3217
DUNNE, James, *U.S. Army*	377	EVANS, Ernest Edwin "Chief", *U.S. Navy*	2707
DUNPHY, Richard D., *U.S. Navy*	378	EVANS, Ira Hobart, *U.S. Army*	402
DURHAM Jr., Harold Bascom, *U.S. Army*	3214	EVANS, James Robert, *U.S. Army*	403
DURHAM, James R., *U.S. Army*	380	EVANS, Rodney John, *U.S. Army*	3218
DURHAM, John S., *U.S. Army*	381	EVANS, Thomas, *U.S. Army*	404
DURNEY, Austin Joseph, *U.S. Navy*	2100	EVANS, William, *U.S. Army*	1631
DUTKO, John W., *U.S. Army*	2698	EVERETTS, John, *U.S. Navy*	1999
DYER, Jesse Farley, *U.S. Marine Corps*	2396	EVERHART Sr., Forrest Eugene, *U.S. Army*	2708
DYESS, Aquilla James, *U.S. Marine Corps Reserve*	2699	EVERSON, Adelbert, *U.S. Army*	405
EADIE, Thomas, *U.S. Navy*	2585	EWING, John C., *U.S. Army*	406
ECKES, John N., *U.S. Army*	382	FACTOR, Pompey, *U.S. Army*	1632
EDDY, Samuel E., *U.S. Army*	383	FADDEN, Harry Delmar, *U.S. Navy*	2340
EDGERTON, Nathan Huntley, *U.s. Army*	384	FAITH Jr., Don Carlos, *U.S. Army*	3062
EDSON, Merritt Austin, *U.S. Marine Corps*	2700	FALCONER, John A., *U.S. Army*	407
EDWARDS, Daniel Richmond, *U.S. Army*	2481	FALCOTT, Henry, *U.S. Army*	1633
EDWARDS, David, *U.S. Army*	385	FALL, Charles S., *U.S. Army*	408
EDWARDS, John, *U.S. Navy*	386	FALLON, Thomas Timothy, *U.S. Army*	409
EDWARDS, Junior Dean, *U.S. Army*	3060	FALLS, Benjamin Frank, *U.S. Army*	410
EDWARDS, Walter Atlee, *U.S. Navy*	2586	FANNING, Nicholas, *U.S. Army*	411
EDWARDS, William D., *U.S. Army*	1626	FARDY, John Peter, *U.S. Marine Corps*	2709
EGGERS, Alan Louis, *U.S. Army*	2482	FARLEY, William, *U.S. Navy*	412
EGLIT, John, *U.S. Navy*	2101	FARNSWORTH, Herbert E., *U.S. Army*	413
EHLE, John Walter, *U.S. Navy*	2102	FARQUHAR, John Mcgreath, *U.S. Army*	414
EHLERS, Walter David, *U.S. Army*	2701	FARRELL, Edward, *U.S. Navy*	415
EILERS, Henry A., *U.S. Navy*	1996	FARREN, Daniel, *U.S. Army*	1634
ELDRIDGE, George H., *U.S. Army*	1627	FASNACHT, Charles H., *U.S. Army*	416
ELLIOTT, Alexander, *U.S. Army*	387	FASSETT, John Barclay, *U.S. Army*	417
ELLIOTT, Middleton Stuart, *U.S. Navy*	2397	FASSEUR, Isaac L., *U.S. Navy*	2000
ELLIOTT, Russell C., *U.S. Army*	388	FEASTER, Mosheim, *U.S. Army*	1635
ELLIS, Horace, *U.S. Army*	389	FEGAN, James, *U.S. Army*	1636
ELLIS, Michael B., *U.S. Army*	2483	FEMOYER, Robert Edward, *U.S. Army Air Corps*	2710
ELLIS, William, *U.S. Army*	390	FERGUSON, Arthur Medworth, *U.S. Army*	2204
ELLSWORTH, Thomas Foulds, *U.S. Army*	391	FERGUSON, Frederick Edgar, *U.S. Army*	3219

GARDNER, Charles N., *U.S. Army*	464	GOHEEN, Charles Arthur, *U.S. Army*	488
GARDNER, James Alton, *U.S. Army*	3233	GOLDEN, Patrick, *U.S. Army*	1658
GARDNER, Robert J., *U.S. Army*	465	GOLDIN, Theodore W. B., *U.S. Army*	1659
GARDNER, William, *U.S. Navy*	466	GOLDSBERY, Andrew E., *U.S. Army*	489
GARLAND, Harry, *U.S. Army*	1647	GOMEZ, Edward, *U.S. Marine Corps*	3066
GARLINGTON, Ernest Albert, *U.S. Army*	1648	GONSALVES, Harold, *U.S. Marine Corps Reserve*	2733
GARMAN, Harold Alva, *U.S. Army*	2728	GONZALES, David M., *U.S. Army*	2734
GARRETT, William, *U.S. Army*	467	GONZALEZ, Alfredo (Freddy), *U.S. Marine Corps*	3235
GARRISON, James R., *U.S. Navy*	468	GOODALL, Francis Henry, *U.S. Army*	490
GARVIN, William, *U.S. Navy*	469	GOODBLOOD, Clair, *U.S. Army*	3067
GARY, Donald Arthur, *U.S. Navy*	2729	GOODMAN, David, *U.S. Army*	1660
GASSON, Richard, *U.S. Army*	470	GOODMAN, Willaim Ernest, *U.S. Army*	491
GATES, George, *U.S. Army*	1649	GOODRICH, Edwin, *U.S. Army*	492
GAUGHAN, Philip, *U.S. Marine Corps*	2109	GORDON, Gary Ivan, *U.S. Army*	3398
GAUJOT, Antoine August, *U.S. Army*	2210	GORDON, Nathan Green, *U.S. Navy*	2735
GAUJOT, Julien Edmund, *U.S. Army*	2403	GOTT, Donald Joseph, *U.S. Army Air Corps*	2736
GAUNT, John C., *U.S. Army*	471	GOULD, Charles Gilbert, *U.S. Army*	493
GAUSE, Isaac, *U.S. Army*	472	GOULD, Newton Thomas, *U.S. Army*	494
GAY, Thomas H., *U.S. Army*	1650	GOURAUD, George Edward, *U.S. Army*	495
GAYLORD, Levi B., *U.S. Army*	473	GOWAN, William Henry, *U.S. Navy*	2344
GEDEON, Louis, *U.S. Army*	2211	GRABIARZ, William J., *U.S. Army*	2737
GEIGER, George, *U.S. Army*	1651	GRACE, Patrick Henry, *U.S. Navy*	1963
GEORGE, Charles, *U.S. Army*	3064	GRACE, Peter, *U.S. Army*	496
GEORGE, Daniel Griffin, *U.S. Navy*	474	GRADY, John, *U.S. Navy*	2405
GEORGIAN, John, *U.S. Army*	1652	GRAHAM, James Albert, *U.S. Marine Corps*	3236
GERBER, Frederick William, *U.S. Army*	1527	GRAHAM, Robert, *U.S. Navy*	497
GERE, Thomas Parke, *U.S. Army*	475	GRAHAM, Thomas N., *U.S. Army*	498
GERSTUNG, Robert E., *U.S. Army*	2730	GRANDSTAFF, Bruce Alan, *U.S. Army*	3237
GERTSCH, John Gerry, *U.S. Army*	3234	GRANT, Gabriel, *U.S. Army*	499
GESCHWIND, Nicholas, *U.S. Army*	476	GRANT, George, *U.S. Army*	1661
GIBBONS, Michael, *U.S. Navy*	2110	GRANT, Joseph Xavier, *U.S. Army*	3238
GIBBS, Wesley, *U.S. Army*	477	GRANT, Lewis Addison, *U.S. Army*	500
GIBSON, Edward Herrick, *U.S. Army*	2212	GRAUL, William L., *U.S. Army*	501
GIBSON, Eric Gunnar, *U.S. Army*	2731	GRAVES, Ora, *U.S. Navy*	2490
GIDDING, Charles, *U.S. Navy*	2003	GRAVES, Terrence Collinson, *U.S. Marine Corps*	3239
GIFFORD, Benjamin, *U.S. Army*	478	GRAVES, Thomas J., *U.S. Army*	2112
GIFFORD, David L., *U.S. Army*	479	GRAY, John, *U.S. Army*	502
GILE, Frank S., *U.S. Navy*	480	GRAY, Robert A., *U.S. Army*	503
GILL, Freeman, *U.S. Navy*	2111	GRAY, Ross Franklin, *U.S. Marine Corps Reserve*	2738
GILLENWATER, James Robert Lee, *U.S. Army*	2213	GRBITCH, Rade, *U.S. Navy*	2345
GILLESPIE Jr., George Lewis, *U.S. Army*	481	GREAVES, Clinton, *U.S. Army*	1662
GILLICK, Matthew, *U.S. Navy*	2004	GREBE, M. R. William, *U.S. Army*	504
GILLIGAN, Edward Lyons, *U.S. Army*	482	GREELY, Adolphus Washington, *U.S. Army Ret.*	2587
GILLILAND, Charles L., *U.S. Army*	3065	GREEN, Francis C., *U.S. Army*	1663
GILMORE, Howard Walter, *U.S. Navy*	2732	GREEN, George, *U.S. Army*	505
GILMORE, John Curtis, *U.S. Army*	483	GREEN, John, *U.S. Army*	1664
GINLEY, Patrick, *U.S. Army*	484	GREENAWALT, Abraham, *U.S. Army*	506
GION, Joseph, *U.S. Army*	485	GREENE, John, *U.S. Navy*	507
GIRANDY, Alphonse, *U.S. Navy*	2343	GREENE, Oliver Duff, *U.S. Army*	508
GISBURNE, Edward Allen, *U.S. Navy*	2404	GREER, Allen James, *U.S. Army*	2214
GIVEN, John J., *U.S. Army*	1653	GREGG, Joseph Olds, *U.S. Army*	509
GLAVINSKI, Albert, *U.S. Army*	1654	GREGG, Stephen Raymond, *U.S. Army*	2739
GLOVER, Thaddeus Brown, *U.S. Army*	1655	GREGORY, Earl D., *U.S. Army*	2491
GLOWIN, Joseph Anthony, *U.S. Marine Corps*	2451	GREIG, Theodore W., *U.S. Army*	510
GLYNN, Michael, *U.S. Army*	1656	GRESHAM, John Chowning, *U.S. Army*	1665
GODFREY, Edward Settle, *U.S. Army*	1657	GRESSER, Ignatz, *U.S. Army*	511
GODLEY, Leonidas Mahlon, *U.S. Army*	486	GRIBBEN, James H., *U.S. Army*	512
GOETTEL, Philip, *U.S. Army*	487	GRIFFITHS, John, *U.S. Navy*	513
GOETTLER, Harold Ernest, *U.S. Army Air Service*	2489	GRIMES, Edward P., *U.S. Army*	1666

HATHAWAY, Edward W., *U.S. Navy*	571	HICKOK, Nathan E., *U.S. Army*	597
HATLER, M. Waldo, *U.S. Army*	2495	HIGBY, Charles, *U.S. Army*	598
HAUGE Jr., Louis James, *U.S. Marine Corps Reserve*	2756	HIGGINS, Thomas J., *U.S. Army*	599
HAUPT, Paul, *U.S. Army*	1680	HIGGINS, Thomas P., *U.S. Army*	1687
HAVRON, John H., *U.S. Army*	572	HIGH, Frank Charles, *U.S. Army*	2219
HAWK, John Druse "Bud", *U.S. Army*	2757	HIGHLAND, Patrick, *U.S. Army*	600
HAWKINS, Charles, *U.S. Navy*	573	HILL, Edward, *U.S. Army*	601
HAWKINS, Gardner C., *U.S. Army*	574	HILL, Edwin Joseph, *U.S. Navy*	2765
HAWKINS, Martin Jones, *U.S. Army*	575	HILL, Frank, *U.S. Marine Corps*	2117
HAWKINS, Thomas R., *U.S. Army*	576	HILL, Frank E., *U.S. Army*	1688
HAWKINS, William Deane, *U.S. Marine Corps*	2758	HILL, Frank Ebenezer, *U.S. Navy*	2348
HAWKS, Lloyd C., *U.S. Army*	2759	HILL, George, *U.S. Navy*	2008
HAWTHORNE, Harris Smith, *U.S. Army*	577	HILL, Henry, *U.S. Army*	602
HAWTHORNE, Harry Leroy, *U.S. Army*	1681	HILL, James, *U.S. Army*	603
HAY, Fred Stewart, *U.S. Army*	1682	HILL, James Madison, *U.S. Army*	1689
HAYDEN, Cyrus, *U.S. Navy*	1964	HILL, James Samuel, *U.S. Army*	604
HAYDEN, David Ephraim, *U.S. Navy*	2496	HILL, Ralyn M., *U.S. Army*	2499
HAYDEN, John, *U.S. Navy*	2007	HILL, Walter Newell, *U.S. Marine Corps*	2409
HAYDEN, Joseph B., *U.S. Navy*	578	HILL, William Lowell, *U.S. Navy*	2009
HAYES, John, *U.S. Navy*	579	HILLIKER, Benjamin F., *U.S. Army*	605
HAYES, Thomas, *U.S. Navy*	580	HILLOCK, Marvin C., *U.S. Army*	1690
HAYES, Webb Cook, *U.S. Army*	2217	HILLS, William Giles, *U.S. Army*	606
HAYNES, Asbury F., *U.S. Army*	581	HILTON, Alfred B., *U.S. Army*	607
HAYS, George Price, *U.S. Army*	2497	HILTON, Richmond Hobson, *U.S. Army*	2500
HAYS, John H., *U.S. Army*	582	HIMMELSBACK, Michael, *U.S. Army*	1691
HEALEY, George Washington, *U.S. Army*	583	HINCKS, William B., *U.S. Army*	608
HEARD, John William, *U.S. Army*	2115	HINEMANN, Lehmann, *U.S. Army*	1692
HEARTERY, Richard, *U.S. Army*	1683	HINNEGAN, William, *U.S. Navy*	609
HEDGES, Joseph S., *U.S. Army*	584	HOBAN, Thomas, *U.S. Navy*	2118
HEDRICK, Clinton M., *U.S. Army*	2760	HOBDAY, George, *U.S. Army*	1693
HEERMANCE, William Laing, *U.S. Army*	585	HOBSON, Richmond Pearson, *U.S. Navy*	2119
HEISCH, Henry William, *U.S. Marine Corps*	2287	HODGES, Addison J., *U.S. Army*	610
HEISE, Clamor, *U.S. Army*	1684	HOFFMAN, Charles F., *U.S. Marine Corps*	2501
HELLER, Henry, *U.S. Army*	586	HOFFMAN, Henry, *U.S. Army*	611
HELMS, David H., *U.S. Army*	587	HOFFMAN, Thomas W., *U.S. Army*	612
HELMS, John Henry, *U.S. Marine Corps*	2347	HOGAN, Franklin, *U.S. Army*	613
HENDERSON, Joseph, *U.S. Army*	2218	HOGAN, Henry, *U.S. Army*	1694
HENDRICKSON, Henry, *U.S. Navy*	2116	HOGARTY, William P., *U.S. Army*	614
HENDRIX, James Richard, *U.S. Army*	2761	HOLCOMB, Daniel Irving, *U.S. Army*	615
HENRECHON, George Francis, *U.S. Navy*	2377	HOLCOMB, John Noble, *U.S. Army*	3247
HENRY, Frederick F., *U.S. Army*	3075	HOLDEN, Henry, *U.S. Army*	1695
HENRY, Guy Vernor, *U.S. Army*	588	HOLDERMAN, Nelson Miles, *U.S. Army*	2502
HENRY, James, *U.S. Army*	589	HOLEHOUSE, James, *U.S. Army*	616
HENRY, Robert T., *U.S. Army*	2762	HOLLAND, David, *U.S. Army*	1696
HENRY, William Wirt, *U.S. Army*	590	HOLLAND, Lemuel F., *U.S. Army*	617
HERDA, Frank Aloysious, *U.S. Army*	3245	HOLLAND, Milton Murray, *U.S. Army*	618
HERINGTON, Pitt B., *U.S. Army*	591	HOLLAT, George, *U.S. Navy*	619
HERIOT, James Davidson, *U.S. Army*	2498	HOLMES, Lovilo N., *U.S. Army*	620
HERNANDEZ, Rodolfo Perez, *U.S. Army*	3076	HOLMES, William T., *U.S. Army*	621
HERRERA, Silvestre Santana, *U.S. Army*	2763	HOLT, George, *U.S. Navy*	2010
HERRING, Rufus Geddie, *U.S. Navy*	2764	HOLTON, Charles Maynard, *U.S. Army*	622
HERRON, Francis Jay, *U.S. Army*	592	HOLTON, Edward A., *U.S. Army*	623
HERRON, Leander, *U.S. Army*	1685	HOLTZ, August, *U.S. Navy*	2349
HESSELTINE, Francis Snow, *U.S. Army*	593	HOLYOKE, William Edward, *U.S. Navy*	2288
HEYL, Charles Pettit heath, *U.S. Army*	1686	HOMAN, Conrad, *U.S. Army*	624
HIBBS, Robert John, *U.S. Army*	3246	HOOKER, George, *U.S. Army*	1697
HIBSON, Joseph C., *U.S. Army*	594	HOOKER, George White, *U.S. Army*	625
HICKEY, Dennis William, *U.S. Army*	595	HOOPER, Joe Ronnie, *U.S. Army*	3248
HICKMAN, John S., *U.S. Navy*	596	HOOPER, William B., *U.S. Army*	626

JOHNDRO, Franklin, *U.S. Army*	684	KARNES, James Ernest, *U.S. Army*	2506
JOHNS, Elisha, *U.S. Army*	685	KAROPCZYC, Stephen Edward, *U.S. Army*	3265
JOHNS, Henry T., *U.S. Army*	686	KARPELES, Leopold, *U.S. Army*	715
JOHNSEN, Hans, *U.S. Navy*	2124	KATES, Thomas Wilbur, *U.S. Marine Corps*	2291
JOHNSON, Andrew, *U.S. Army*	687	KATZ, Phillip Carl, *U.S. Army*	2507
JOHNSON, Dwight Hal, *U.S. Army*	3261	KAUFMAN, Benjamin, *U.S. Army*	2508
JOHNSON, Elden Harvey, *U.S. Army*	2775	KAUFMAN, Loren R., *U.S. Army*	3083
JOHNSON, Follett, *U.S. Army*	688	KAUSS, August, *U.S. Army*	716
JOHNSON, Henry, *U.S. Army*	1714	KAWAMURA, Terry Teruo, *U.S. Army*	3266
JOHNSON, Henry, *U.S. Navy*	689	KAY, John, *U.S. Army*	1718
JOHNSON, James Edmund, *U.S. Marine Corps*	3080	KAYS, Kenneth Michael, *U.S. Army*	3267
JOHNSON, John, *U.S. Army*	690	KEARBY, Neel Ernest, *U.S. Army Air Corps*	2784
JOHNSON, John, *U.S. Navy*	2013	KEARNEY, Michael, *U.S. Marine Corps*	2126
JOHNSON, Joseph Esrey, *U.S. Army*	691	KEATHLEY, George D., *U.S. Army*	2785
JOHNSON, Leon William, *U.S. Army Air Corps/U.S. Air Force*	2776	KEATING, Daniel, *U.S. Army*	1719
JOHNSON, Leroy, *U.S. Army*	2777	KEDENBURG, John James, *U.S. Army*	3268
JOHNSON Jr., Oscar Godfrey, *U.S. Army*	2778	KEEFER, Philip Bogan, *U.S. Navy*	2127
JOHNSON, Peter, *U.S. Navy*	2125	KEELE, Joseph, *U.S. Army*	717
JOHNSON, Ralph Henry, *U.S. Marine Corps*	3262	KEEN, Joseph S., *U.S. Army*	718
JOHNSON, Ruel M., *U.S. Army*	692	KEENAN, Bartholomew T., *U.S. Army*	1720
JOHNSON, Samuel, *U.S. Army*	693	KEENAN, John, *U.S. Army*	1721
JOHNSON, Wallace W., *U.S. Army*	694	KEENE, Joseph, *U.S. Army*	719
JOHNSON, William, *U.S. Navy*	2014	KEFURT, Gus, *U.S. Army*	2786
JOHNSTON, David H., *U.S. Army*	695	KEITH, Miguel, *U.S. Marine Corps*	3269
JOHNSTON, Donald Ray, *U.S. Army*	3263	KELLER, Leonard Bert, *U.S. Army*	3270
JOHNSTON, Edward, *U.S. Army*	1715	KELLER, William G., *U.S. Army*	2128
JOHNSTON, Gordon, *U.S. Army*	2222	KELLEY, Andrew John, *U.S. Army*	720
JOHNSTON, Harold Irving, *U.S. Army*	2505	KELLEY, Charles, *U.S. Army*	1722
JOHNSTON Jr., Rufus Zenas, *U.S. Navy*	2414	KELLEY, George V., *U.S. Army*	721
JOHNSTON, William (Willie), *U.S. Army*	697	KELLEY, John, *U.S. Navy*	722
JOHNSTON, William P., *U.S. Navy*	696	KELLEY, Jonah Edward High, *U.S. Army*	2787
JOHNSTON Sr., William James, *U.S. Army*	2779	KELLEY, Leverett Mansfield, *U.S. Army*	723
JONES, Andrew, *U.S. Navy*	698	KELLEY, Ova Art, *U.S. Army*	2788
JONES, Claud Ashton, *U.S. Navy*	2445	KELLEY, Thomas Gunning, *U.S. Navy*	3271
JONES, David, *U.S. Army*	699	KELLOGG Jr., Allan Jay, *U.S. Marine Corps*	3272
JONES, Herbert Charpoit, *U.S. Naval Reserve*	2780	KELLY, Alexander, *U.S. Army*	724
JONES, John, *U.S. Navy*	700	KELLY, Charles E., *U.S. Army*	2789
JONES, John E., *U.S. Navy*	701	KELLY, Daniel, *U.S. Army*	725
JONES, Thomas, *U.S. Navy*	702	KELLY, Francis, *U.S. Navy*	2129
JONES, William, *U.S. Army*	704	KELLY, John D., *U.S. Army*	2790
JONES, William, *U.S. Navy*	703	KELLY, John Doran, *U.S. Marine Corps*	3084
JONES, William H., *U.S. Army*	1716	KELLY, John J. H., *U.S. Army*	1723
JONES III, William Atkinson, *U.S. Air Force*	3264	KELLY, John Joseph, *U.S. Marine Corps*	2509
JORDAN, Absalom, *U.S. Army*	705	KELLY, Thomas, *U.S. Army (Civil War)*	726
JORDAN, George, *U.S. Army*	1717	KELLY, Thomas, *U.S. Army (Indian Campaigns)*	1724
JORDAN, Robert, *U.S. Navy*	706	KELLY, Thomas, *U.S. Army (Sp.-Am. War)*	2130
JORDAN, Thomas H., *U.S. Navy*	707	KELLY, Thomas Joseph, *U.S. Army*	2791
JORDON, Mack A., *U.S. Army*	3081	KELSAY, *U.S. Army*	1725
JOSSELYN, Simeon T., *U.S. Army*	708	KELSO, Jack William, *U.S. Marine Corps*	3085
JUDGE, Francis W., *U.S. Army*	709	KEMP, Joseph Bell, *U.S. Army*	727
JULIAN, Joseph Rodolph, *U.S. Marine Corps Reserve*	2781	KENDALL, William Wesley, *U.S. Army*	728
KAISER, John, *U.S. Army*	710	KENDRICK, Thomas, *U.S. Navy*	729
KALTENBACH, Luther, *U.S. Army*	711	KENNA, Barnett, *U.S. Navy*	730
KANDLE, Victor Leonard, *U.S. Army*	2782	KENNEDY, John, *U.S. Army*	731
KANE, John, *U.S. Army*	712	KENNEDY, John Thomas, *U.S. Army*	2223
KANE, John Riley, *U.S. Army Air Corps/U.S. Air Force*	2783	KENNEDY, Philip, *U.S. Army*	1726
KANE, Thomas, *U.S. Navy*	713	KENNEMORE, Robert Sidney, *U.S. Marine Corps*	3086
KANELL, Billie Gene, *U.S. Army*	3082	KENYON, Charles W., *U.S. Navy*	732
KAPPESSER, Peter, *U.S. Army*	714	KENYON, John Snyders, *U.S. Army*	733

LEJEUNE, Emile, *U.S. Navy*	2020	LORD, William, *U.S. Army*	799
LELAND, George W., *U.S. Navy*	778	LORING Jr., Charles Joseph, *U.S. Air Force*	3098
LEMERT, Milo, *U.S. Army*	2512	LORISH, Andrew J., *U.S. Army*	800
LEMON, Peter Charles, *U.S. Army*	3285	LOVE, George Maltby, *U.S. Army*	801
LENIHAN, James, *U.S. Army*	1743	LOVERING, George Mason, *U.S. Army*	802
LEON, Pierre, *U.S. Navy*	779	LOW, George, *U.S. Navy*	2021
LEONARD, Edwin, *U.S. Army*	780	LOWER, Cyrus B., *U.S. Army*	803
LEONARD, Joseph H., *U.S. Marine Corps*	2227	LOWER, Robert A., *U.S. Army*	804
LEONARD, Matthew, *U.S. Army*	3286	LOWRY, George Maus, *U.S. Navy*	2417
LEONARD, Patrick James, *U.S. Army*	1744	LOWTHERS, James, *U.S. Army*	1752
LEONARD, Patrick Thomas, *U.S. Army*	1745	LOYD, George A., *U.S. Army*	805
LEONARD, Turney White, *U.S. Army*	2811	LOZADA, Carlos James, *U.S. Army*	3292
LEONARD, William, *U.S. Army*	1746	LUCAS, Andre Cavaro, *U.S. Army*	3293
LEONARD, William Edman, *U.S. Army*	781	LUCAS, George Washington, *U.S. Army*	806
LESLIE, Frank, *U.S. Army*	782	LUCAS, Jacklyn Harold, *U.S. Marine Corps Reserve*	2820
LESTER, Fred Faulkner, *U.S. Navy*	2812	LUCE, Moses Augustine, *U.S. Army*	807
LEVERY, William, *U.S. Navy*	2135	LUCY, John, *U.S. Navy*	2022
LEVITOW, John Lee, *U.S. Air Force*	3287	LUDGATE, William, *U.S. Army*	808
LEVY, Benjamin Bennett, *U.S. Army*	783	LUDWIG, Carl, *U.S. Army*	809
LEWIS, Dewitt Clinton, *U.S. Army*	784	LUKE Jr., Frank, *U.S. Army Air Service*	2514
LEWIS, Henry, *U.S. Army*	785	LUKES, William F., *U.S. Navy*	1965
LEWIS, Samuel E., *U.S. Army*	786	LUMMUS, Jack, *U.S. Marine Corps Reserve*	2821
LEWIS, William B., *U.S. Army*	1747	LUNT, Alphonso M., *U.S. Army*	810
LIBAIRE, Adolph, *U.S. Army*	787	LUTES, Franklin W., *U.S. Army*	811
LIBBY, George Dalton, *U.S. Army*	3094	LUTHER, James Hezikiah, *U.S. Army*	812
LILLEY, John, *U.S. Army*	788	LUTY, Gotlieb, *U.S. Army*	813
LINDBERGH Jr., Charles Augustus, *U.S. Army Air Corp Reserve*	2590	LYELL, William Franklin, *U.S. Army*	3099
LINDSEY, Darrell Robins, *U.S. Army Air Corps*	2813	LYLE, Alexander Gordon, *U.S. Navy*	2515
LINDSEY Sr., Jake William, *U.S. Army*	2814	LYMAN, Joel H., *U.S. Army*	814
LINDSTROM, Floyd K., *U.S. Army*	2815	LYNCH, Allan James, *U.S. Army*	3294
LIPSCOMB, Harry, *U.S. Navy*	2353	LYON, Edward Eugene, *U.S. Army*	2230
LITEKY, Charles James (Angelo), *U.S. Army*	3288	LYON, Frederick A., *U.S. Army*	815
LITTLE, Henry F. W., *U.S. Army*	789	LYONS, Thomas G., *U.S. Navy*	816
LITTLE, Thomas, *U.S. Army*	1748	LYTLE, Leonidas S., *U.S. Army*	1753
LITTLEFIELD, George H., *U.S. Army*	790	LYTTON, Jeptha L., *U.S. Army*	1754
LITTLETON, Herbert A., *U.S. Marine Corps Reserve*	3095	MABRY Jr., George Lafayette, *U.S. Army*	2822
LITTRELL, Gary Lee, *U.S. Army*	3289	MacARTHUR Jr., Arthur, *U.S. Army*	817
LIVINGSTON, James Evertte, *U.S. Marine Corps*	3290	MacARTHUR, Douglas, *U.S. Army*	2823
LIVINGSTON, Josiah O., *U.S. Army*	791	MacGILLIVARY, Charles Andrew, *U.S. Army*	2824
LLOYD, Benjamin, *U.S. Navy*	792	MACHOL, *U.S. Army*	1755
LLOYD, Edgar Harold, *U.S. Army*	2816	MACHON, James, *U.S. Navy*	818
LLOYD, George, *U.S. Army*	1749	MACK, Alexander, *U.S. Navy*	819
LLOYD, John W., *U.S. Navy*	793	MACK, John, *U.S. Navy*	820
LOBAUGH, Donald Ronald, *U.S. Army*	2817	MacKENZIE, John, *U.S. Navy*	2516
LOCKE, Lewis, *U.S. Army*	794	MACKIE, John Freeman, *U.S. Marine Corps*	821
LOGAN, Hugh, *U.S. Navy*	795	MACLAY, William Palmer, *U.S. Army*	2231
LOGAN, James Marion, *U.S. Army*	2818	MacNEAL, Harry Lewis, *U.S. Marine Corps*	2136
LOGAN Jr., John Alexander, *U.S. Army*	2228	MADDEN, Michael, *U.S. Army*	822
LOHNES, Frank W., *U.S. Army*	1750	MADDEN, William, *U.S. Navy*	823
LOMAN, Berger Holton, *U.S. Army*	2513	MADDIN, Edward, *U.S. Navy*	2023
LONERGAN, John, *U.S. Army*	796	MADISON, James, *U.S. Army*	824
LONG, Charles Richard, *U.S. Army*	3096	MADISON, James Jonas, *U.S. Naval Reserve Force*	2517
LONG, Donald Russell, *U.S. Army*	3291	MAGEE, John W., *U.S. Navy*	2024
LONG, Oscar Fitzalan, *U.S. Army*	1751	MAGEE, William, *U.S. Army*	825
LONGFELLOW, Richard Moses, *U.S. Army*	2229	MAGER, George Frederick, *U.S. Navy*	2137
LONGSHORE, William H., *U.S. Army*	797	MAGRATH, John D., *U.S. Army*	2825
LONSWAY, Joseph, *U.S. Army*	798	MAHERS, Herbert, *U.S. Army*	1756
LOPEZ, Baldomero, *U.S. Marine Corps*	3097	MAHONEY, George, *U.S. Navy*	2138
LOPEZ, Jose Mendoza, *U.S. Army*	2819	MAHONEY, Gregory, *U.S. Army*	1757

McHALE, Alexander U., *U.S. Army*	878	MESTROVITCH, James I., *U.S. Army*	2522
McHUGH, John, *U.S. Army*	1775	METZGER Jr., William Edward, *U.S. Army Air Corps*	2856
McHUGH, Martin, *U.S. Navy*	879	MEYER, Henry Coddington, *U.S. Army*	903
McINTOSH, James, *U.S. Navy*	880	MEYER, William, *U.S. Navy*	2141
McKAY, Charles W., *U.S. Army*	881	MICHAEL, Don Leslie, *U.S. Army*	3306
McKEE, George, *U.S. Army*	882	MICHAEL, Edward Stanley, *U.S. Army Air Corps/U.S. Air Force*	2857
McKEEN, Nineveh S., *U.S. Army*	883	MICHAEL, Harry J., *U.S. Army*	2858
McKEEVER, Michael, *U.S. Army*	884	MIFFLIN, James, *U.S. Navy*	904
McKENZIE, Alexander, *U.S. Navy*	1966	MIHALOWSKI, John, *U.S. Navy*	2592
McKIBBEN, Ray, *U.S. Army*	3302	MILES, Louis Wardlaw, *U.S. Army*	2523
McKINLEY, Daniel, *U.S. Army*	1776	MILES, Nelson Appleton, *U.S. Army*	905
McKINNEY, John R., *U.S. Army*	2848	MILLER, Andrew, *U.S. Army*	2859
McKNIGHT, William, *U.S. Navy*	885	MILLER, Andrew, *U.S. Marine Corps*	906
McKOWN, Nathaniel A., *U.S. Army*	886	MILLER, Archie, *U.S. Army*	2235
McLAUGHLIN, Alford Lee, *U.S. Marine Corps*	3104	MILLER, Daniel H., *U.S. Army*	1788
McLENNON, John, *U.S. Army*	1777	MILLER, Frank, *U.S. Army*	907
McLEOD, James, *U.S. Navy*	887	MILLER, Franklin Douglas, *U.S. Army*	3307
McLOUGHLIN, Michael, *U.S. Army*	1778	MILLER, Gary Lee, *U.S. Army*	3308
McMAHON, Martin Thomas, *U.S. Army*	888	MILLER, George, *U.S. Army*	1789
McMAHON, Thomas Joseph, *U.S. Army*	3303	MILLER, George W., *U.S. Army*	1790
McMASTERS, Henry A., *U.S. Army*	1779	MILLER, Harry Herbert, *U.S. Navy*	2142
McMILLEN, Francis M., *U.S. Army*	889	MILLER, Henry August, *U.S. Army*	908
McMILLIAN, Albert Walter, *U.S. Army*	1780	MILLER, Hugh, *U.S. Navy*	2028
McMURTRY, George G., *U.S. Army*	2521	MILLER, Jacob C., *U.S. Army*	909
McNAIR Jr., Frederick Vallette, *U.S. Navy*	2420	MILLER, James, *U.S. Navy*	910
McNALLY, James, *U.S. Army*	1781	MILLER, James P., *U.S. Army*	911
McNALLY, Michael Joseph, *U.S. Marine Corps*	2185	MILLER, John, *U.S. Army*	912
McNAMARA, Michael, *U.S. Marine Corps*	1967	MILLER, John G., *U.S. Army*	913
McNAMARA, William, *U.S. Army*	1782	MILLER, Oscar F., *U.S. Army*	2524
McNERNEY, David Herbert, *U.S. Army*	3304	MILLER, Willard D., *U.S. Navy*	2143
McPHELAN, Robert, *U.S. Army*	1783	MILLER, William Edward, *U.S. Army*	914
McTUREOUS Jr., Robert Miller, *U.S. Marine Corps*	2849	MILLETT, Lewis Lee "Red", *U.S. Army*	3106
McVEAGH, Charles H., *U.S. Army*	1784	MILLIKEN, Daniel, *U.S. Navy*	915
McVEANE, John P., *U.S. Army*	890	MILLMORE, John, *U.S. Navy*	2029
McVEIGH, John J., *U.S. Army*	2850	MILLS, Albert Leopold, *U.S. Army*	2144
McWETHY Jr., Edgar Lee, *U.S. Army*	3305	MILLS, Charles, *U.S. Navy*	916
McWHORTER, Walter F., *U.S. Army*	891	MILLS, Frank W., *U.S. Army*	917
McWHORTER, William A., *U.S. Army*	2851	MILLS, James Henry, *U.S. Army*	2860
McWILLIAMS, George Washington, *U.S. Navy*	892	MINDIL, George Washington, *U.S. Army*	918
MEACH, George E., *U.S. Army*	893	MINICK, John W., *U.S. Army*	2861
MEAGHER, John William, *U.S. Army*	2852	MINUE, Nicholas, *U.S. Army*	2862
MEAGHER, Thomas, *U.S. Army*	894	MITCHELL, Alexander H., *U.S. Army*	919
MEAHER, Nicholas, *U.S. Army*	1785	MITCHELL, Frank Nicias, *U.S. Marine Corps*	3107
MEARS, George W., *U.S. Army*	895	MITCHELL, John, *U.S. Army*	1791
MECHLIN, Henry W.B., *U.S. Army*	1786	MITCHELL, John James, *U.S. Army*	1792
MELVILLE, Charles, *U.S. Navy*	896	MITCHELL, Joseph Andrew, *U.S. Navy*	2297
MENDONCA, Leroy A., *U.S. Army*	3105	MITCHELL, Theodore, *U.S. Army*	920
MENTER, John William, *U.S. Army*	897	MITCHELL, Thomas, *U.S. Navy*	2030
MEREDITH, James, *U.S. Marine Corps*	2140	MIYAMURA, Hiroshi, *U.S. Army*	3108
MERLI, Gino Joseph, *U.S. Army*	2853	MIZE, Ola Lee, *U.S. Army*	3109
MERRELL, Joseph Frederick, *U.S. Army*	2854	MODRZEJEWSKI, Robert Joseph, *U.S. Marine Corps*	3309
MERRIAM, Henry Clay, *U.S. Army*	898	MOFFETT, William Adger, *U.S. Navy*	2421
MERRIFIELD, James K., *U.S. Army*	899	MOFFITT, John Henry, *U.S. Army*	921
MERRILL, Augustus, *U.S. Army*	900	MOLBONE, Archibald, *U.S. Army*	922
MERRILL, George, *U.S. Army*	901	MOLLOY, Hugh, *U.S. Navy*	923
MERRILL, John Mitchell, *U.S. Army*	1787	MOLNAR, Frankie Zoly, *U.S. Army*	3310
MERRITT, John G., *U.S. Army*	902	MONAGHAN, Patrick H., *U.S. Army*	924
MERTON, James F., *U.S. Navy*	1968	MONEGAN Jr., Walter Carleton, *U.S. Marine Corps*	3110
MESSERSCHMIDT, Harold O., *U.S. Army*	2855	MONROE, James Howard, *U.S. Army*	3311

NICHOLS, William, *U.S. Navy*	973	OLSON, Arlo L., *U.S. Army*	2886
NICKERSON, Henry Nehemiah, *U.S. Navy*	2423	OLSON, Kenneth Lee, *U.S. Army*	3321
NIHILL, John, *U.S. Army*	1815	OLSON, Truman O., *U.S. Army*	2887
NININGER Jr., Alexander Ramsey, *U.S. Army*	2880	OPEL, John N., *U.S. Army*	998
NISPEROS, Jose B., *U.S. Army*	2379	ORBANSKY, David, *U.S. Army*	999
NIVEN, Robert, *U.S. Army*	974	ORESKO, Nicholas, *U.S. Army*	2888
NOBLE, Daniel, *U.S. Navy*	975	ORMSBEE Jr., Francis Edward, *U.S. Navy*	2528
NOIL, Joseph B., *U.S. Navy*	2035	ORNDOFF, Harry Westley, *U.S. Marine Corps*	2301
NOLAN, John J., *U.S. Army*	976	ORR, Charles Alvin, *U.S. Army*	1000
NOLAN, Joseph A., *U.S. Army*	2238	ORR, Moses, *U.S. Army*	1821
NOLAN, Richard J., *U.S. Army*	1816	ORR, Robert Levan, *U.S. Army*	1001
NOLL, Conrad, *U.S. Army*	977	ORTEGA, John, *U.S. Navy*	1002
NOONAN Jr., Thomas Patrick, *U.S. Marine Corps*	3317	ORTH, Jacob George, *U.S. Army*	1003
NORDSIEK, Charles Luers, *U.S. Navy*	2424	OSBORNE, John, *U.S. Navy*	2040
NORDSTROM, Isador A., *U.S. Navy*	2357	OSBORNE, Weedon E., *U.S. Navy*	2529
NORRIS, J. W., *U.S. Navy*	2036	OSBORNE, William, *U.S. Army*	1822
NORRIS, Thomas Rolland, *U.S. Navy*	3318	OSBORNE, William Henry, *U.S. Army*	1004
NORTH, Jasper N., *U.S. Army*	978	OSEPINS, Christian, *U.S. Navy*	2041
NORTON, Elliott Malloy, *U.S. Army*	979	OSS, Albert, *U.S. Army*	1005
NORTON, John R., *U.S. Army*	980	OSTERMANN, Edward Albert, *U.S. Marine Corps*	2441
NORTON, Llewellyn Powell, *U.S. Army*	981	OUELLET, David George, *U.S. Navy*	3323
NOVOSEL, Michael Joseph, *U.S. Army*	3319	OUELLETTE, Joseph R., *U.S. Army*	3117
NOYES, William W., *U.S. Army*	982	OVERTURF, Jacob H., *U.S. Army*	1006
NUGENT, Christopher, *U.S. Marine Corps*	983	OVIATT, Miles M., *U.S. Marine Corps*	1007
NUTTING, Lee, *U.S. Army*	984	OWENS, Michael, *U.S. Marine Corps*	1969
O'BEIRNE, James Rowan, *U.S. Army*	985	OWENS, Robert Allen, *U.S. Marine Corps*	2889
O'BRIEN Jr., George Herman, *U.S. Marine Corps Reserve*	3116	OZBOURN, Joseph William, *U.S. Marine Corps*	2890
O'BRIEN, Henry D., *U.S. Army*	986	PACKARD, Loron F., *U.S. Army*	1008
O'BRIEN, Oliver Albert, *U.S. Navy*	987	PAGE, John Upshur Dennis, *U.S. Army*	3118
O'BRIEN, Peter, *U.S. Army*	988	PAIGE, Mitchell, *U.S. Marine Corps*	2891
O'BRIEN, William Joseph, *U.S. Army*	2881	PAINE, Adam, *U.S. Army*	1824
O'CALLAGHAN, John, *U.S. Army*	1817	PALMER, George Henry, *U.S. Army*	1009
O'CALLAHAN, Joseph Timothy, *U.S. Naval Reserve*	2882	PALMER, John Gideon, *U.S. Army*	1010
O'CONNELL, Thomas, *U.S. Navy*	989	PALMER, William Jackson, *U.S. Army*	1011
O'CONNER, James Francis, *U.S. Navy*	2037	PARKER, Alexander, *U.S. Navy*	2042
O'CONNOR, Albert, *U.S. Army*	990	PARKER, James, *U.S. Army*	2239
O'CONNOR, Timothy, *U.S. Army*	991	PARKER, Pomeroy, *U.S. Marine Corps*	2154
O'DEA, John, *U.S. Army*	992	PARKER, Samuel Iredell, *U.S. Army*	2531
O'DONNELL, Menomen, *U.S. Army*	993	PARKER, Thomas, *U.S. Army*	1012
O'DONOGHUE, Timothy, *U.S. Navy*	994	PARKER, William, *U.S. Navy*	1013
O'HARE, Edward Henry "Butch", *U.S. Navy*	2884	PARKS, George, *U.S. Navy*	1014
O'KANE, Richard Hetherington, *U.S. Navy*	2885	PARKS, Henry Jeremiah, *U.S. Army*	1015
O'MALLEY, Robert Emmett, *U.S. Marine Corps*	3322	PARKS, James W., *U.S. Army*	1016
O'NEAL, John, *U.S. Navy*	2039	PARLE, John Joseph, *U.S. Naval Reserve*	2892
O'NEILL, Richard William, *U.S. Army*	2527	PARNELL, William Russell, *U.S. Army*	1825
O'NEILL, Stephen, *U.S. Army*	997	PARRISH, Laverne, *U.S. Army*	2893
O'NEILL, William, *U.S. Army*	1819	PARROTT, Jacob, *U.S. Army*	1017
O'REGAN, Michael, *U.S. Army*	1820	PARSONS, Joel, *U.S. Army*	1018
O'SHEA, Thomas E., *U.S. Army*	2530	PATTERSON, John Henry, *U.S. Army*	1019
O'SULLIVAN, John Francis, *U.S. Army*	1823	PATTERSON, John T., *U.S. Army*	1020
OAKLEY, William, *U.S. Navy*	2152	PATTERSON, Robert Martin, *U.S. Army*	3324
OBREGON, Eugene Arnold, *U.S. Marine Corps*	3115	PAUL, Joe Calvin, *U.S. Marine Corps*	3325
OGDEN Sr., Carlos Carnes, *U.S. Army*	2883	PAUL, William H., *U.S. Army*	1021
OHMSEN, August, *U.S. Navy*	2038	PAY, Byron E., *U.S. Army*	1022
OLIVE III, Milton Lee, *U.S. Army*	3320	PAYNE, Irvin C., *U.S. Army*	1023
OLIVER, Charles, *U.S. Army*	995	PAYNE, Isaac, *U.S. Army*	1826
OLIVER, Francis, *U.S. Army*	1818	PAYNE, Thomas H. L., *U.S. Army*	1024
OLIVER, Paul Ambrose, *U.S. Army*	996	PEARSALL, Platt, *U.S. Army*	1025
OLSEN, Anton, *U.S. Navy*	2153	PEARSON, Alfred L., *U.S. Army*	1026

PRUITT, John Henry, *U.S. Marine Corps*	2537	REIGLE, Daniel P., *U.S. Army*	1106
PRUSSMAN, Ernest W., *U.S. Army*	2913	REISINGER, James Monroe, *U.S. Army*	1107
PUCKET, Donald Dale, *U.S. Army Air Corps*	2914	RENNINGER, Louis, *U.S. Army*	1108
PURCELL, Hiram W., *U.S. Army*	1077	RESSLER, Norman W., *U.S. Army*	2161
PURMAN, James Jackson, *U.S. Army*	1078	REYNOLDS, George, *U.S. Army*	1109
PURVIS, Hugh, *U.S. Marine Corps*	1970	RHODES, Julius Dexter, *U.S. Army*	1110
PUTNAM, Edgar Pierpont, *U.S. Army*	1079	RHODES, Sylvester D., *U.S. Army*	1111
PUTNAM, Winthrop D., *U.S. Army*	1080	RICE, Charles, *U.S. Navy*	1112
PYM, James, *U.S. Army*	1838	RICE, Edmund, *U.S. Army*	1113
PYNE, George, *U.S. Navy*	1081	RICH, Carlos H., *U.S. Army*	1114
QUAY, Matthew Stanley, *U.S. Army*	1082	RICHARDS, Louis, *U.S. Navy*	1115
QUICK, John Henry, *U.S. Marine Corps*	2159	RICHARDSON, William R., *U.S. Army*	1116
QUICK, Joseph, *U.S. Navy*	2360	RICHEY, William E., *U.S. Army*	1117
QUINLAN, James, *U.S. Army*	1083	RICHMAN, Samuel, *U.S. Army*	1843
QUINN, Alexander M., *U.S. Army*	2160	RICHMOND, James, *U.S. Army*	1118
QUINN, Peter H., *U.S. Army*	2243	RICKENBACKER, Edward Vernon, *U.S. Army Air Service*	2539
RABEL, Laszlo, *U.S. Army*	3339	RICKETTS, Milton Ernest, *U.S. Navy*	2920
RAERICK, John, *U.S. Army*	1839	RICKSECKER, John Henry, *U.S. Army*	1119
RAFFERTY, Peter F., *U.S. Army*	1084	RIDDELL, Rudolph R., *U.S. Army*	1120
RAGNAR, Theodore, *U.S. Army*	1840	RILEY, Thomas, *U.S. Army*	1121
RAMAGE, Lawson Paterson "Red", *U.S. Navy*	2915	RILLEY, John Phillip, *U.S. Navy*	2162
RAMER, George Henry, *U.S. Marine Corps Reserve*	3126	RINGOLD, Edward, *U.S. Navy*	1122
RAND, Charles Franklin, *U.S. Army*	1085	RIORDAN, Paul F., *U.S. Army*	2921
RANKIN, William, *U.S. Army*	1841	RIPLEY, William Young Warren, *U.S. Army*	1123
RANNAHAN, John, *U.S. Marine Corps*	1086	ROACH, Hampton Mitchell, *U.S. Army*	1844
RANNEY, George E., *U.S. Army*	1087	ROAN, Charles Howard, *U.S. Marine Corps Reserve*	2922
RANNEY, Myron H., *U.S. Army*	1088	ROANTREE, James S., *U.S. Marine Corps*	1124
RANSBOTTOM, Alfred, *U.S. Army*	1089	ROARK, Anund Charles, *U.S. Army*	3343
RATCLIFF, Edward, *U.S. Army*	1090	ROBB, George Seanor, *U.S. Army*	2540
RAUB, Jacob F., *U.S. Army*	1091	ROBBINS, Augustus J., *U.S. Army*	1125
RAY, Bernard James, *U.S. Army*	2916	ROBBINS, Marcus M., *U.S. Army*	1845
RAY, Charles W., *U.S. Army*	2244	ROBERTS, Charles Church, *U.S. Navy*	2362
RAY, David Robert, *U.S. Navy*	3340	ROBERTS, Charles Duval, *U.S. Army*	2163
RAY, Ronald Eric, *U.S. Army*	3341	ROBERTS, Gordon Ray, *U.S. Army*	3344
RAYMOND, William H., *U.S. Army*	1092	ROBERTS, Harold W., *U.S. Army*	2541
READ, Charles, *U.S. Navy*	1093	ROBERTS, James, *U.S. Navy*	1126
READ, Charles A., *U.S. Navy*	1094	ROBERTS, Otis O., *U.S. Army*	1127
READ, George E., *U.S. Navy*	1095	ROBERTSON, Marcus William, *U.S. Army*	2245
READ, Morton A., *U.S. Army*	1096	ROBERTSON, Robert Stoddart, *U.S. Army*	1128
REASONER, Frank Stanley, *U.S. Marine Corps*	3342	ROBERTSON, Samuel, *U.S. Army*	1129
REBMANN, George F., *U.S. Army*	1097	ROBIE, George Frank, *U.S. Army*	1130
RED CLOUD Jr., Mitchell, *U.S. Army*	3127	ROBINSON, Alexander, *U.S. Navy*	1131
REDDICK, William Henry Harrison, *U.S. Army*	1098	ROBINSON, Charles, *U.S. Navy*	1132
REED, Axel Hayford, *U.S. Army*	1099	ROBINSON, Elbridge, *U.S. Army*	1133
REED, Charles Wellington, *U.S. Army*	1100	ROBINSON Jr., James E., *U.S. Army*	2923
REED, George W., *U.S. Army*	1101	ROBINSON, James H., *U.S. Army*	1134
REED, James C., *U.S. Army*	1842	ROBINSON Jr., James William, *U.S. Army*	3345
REED, William, *U.S. Army*	1102	ROBINSON, John, *U.S. Navy*	1530
REEDER, Charles A., *U.S. Army*	1103	ROBINSON, John Cleveland, *U.S. Army*	1135
REEM, Robert Dale, *U.S. Marine Corps*	3128	ROBINSON, John H., *U.S. Army*	1136
REESE, James W., *U.S. Army*	2917	ROBINSON, Joseph, *U.S. Army*	1846
REESE Jr., John N., *U.S. Army*	2918	ROBINSON, Robert Guy, *U.S. Marine Corps*	2542
REEVES, Thomas James, *U.S. Navy*	2919	ROBINSON, Thomas, *U.S. Army*	1137
REGAN, Jeremiah, *U.S. Navy*	1104	ROBINSON, Thomas, *U.S. Navy*	1531
REGAN, Patrick, *U.S. Navy*	2044	ROCCO, Louis Richard, *U.S. Army*	3346
REGAN, Patrick J., *U.S. Army*	2538	ROCHE, David, *U.S. Army*	1847
REID, George Croghan, *U.S. Marine Corps*	2425	ROCK, Frederick, *U.S. Army*	1138
REID, Patrick, *U.S. Navy*	2361	ROCKEFELLER, Charles Mortimer, *U.S. Army*	1139
REID, Robert Alexander, *U.S. Army*	1105	RODENBOUGH, Theophilus Francis, *U.S. Army*	1140

SCOTT, John Wallace, *U.S. Army*	1192	SHOCKLEY, William Ralph, *U.S. Army*	2946
SCOTT, Joseph Francis, *U.S. Marine Corps*	2165	SHOEMAKER, Levi, *U.S. Army*	1223
SCOTT, Julian A., *U.S. Army*	1193	SHOMO, William Arthur, *U.S. Army Air Corps/U.S. Air Force*	2947
SCOTT, Norman, *U.S. Navy*	2941	SHOPP, George J., *U.S. Army*	1224
SCOTT, Robert B., *U.S. Army*	1864	SHOUP, Curtis F., *U.S. Army*	2948
SCOTT, Robert Raymond, *U.S. Navy*	2942	SHOUP, David Monroe, *U.S. Marine Corps*	2949
SCOTT, Robert Sheldon, *U.S. Army*	2943	SHUBERT, Frank, *U.S. Army*	1225
SEACH, William, *U.S. Navy*	2308	SHUCK Jr., William Edward, *U.S. Marine Corps*	3135
SEAMAN, Elisha B., *U.S. Army*	1194	SHUGHART, Randall David, *U.S. Army*	3399
SEANOR, James, *U.S. Navy*	1195	SHUTES, Henry, *U.S. Navy*	1226
SEARS, Cyrus, *U.S. Army*	1196	SICKLES, Daniel Edgar, *U.S. Army*	1227
SEAVER, Thomas Orville, *U.S. Army*	1197	SICKLES, William H., *U.S. Army*	1228
SEAY, William Wayne, *U.S. Army*	3352	SIDMAN, George Dallas, *U.S. Army*	1229
SEBILLE, Louis Joseph, *U.S. Air Force*	3133	SIEGEL, John Otto, *U.S. Navy*	2549
SEIBERT, Lloyd Martin, *U.S. Army*	2548	SIGLER, Franklin Earl, *U.S. Marine Corps Reserve*	2950
SEITZINGER, James M., *U.S. Army*	1198	SIJAN, Lance Peter, *U.S. Air Force*	3355
SELLERS, Alfred Jacob, *U.S. Army*	1199	SILK, Edward A., *U.S. Army*	2951
SEMPLE, Robert, *U.S. Navy*	2428	SILVA, France, *U.S. Marine Corps*	2309
SESTON, Charles H., *U.S. Army*	1200	SIMANEK, Robert Ernest, *U.S. Marine Corps*	3136
SEWARD, Griffin, *U.S. Army*	1865	SIMKINS, Lebbeus, *U.S. Navy*	1230
SEWARD, Richard Henry, *U.S. Navy*	1201	SIMMONS, John, *U.S. Army*	1231
SEWELL, William Joyce, *U.S. Army*	1202	SIMMONS, William Thomas, *U.S. Army*	1232
SHACKLETTE, William Sidney, *U.S. Navy*	2365	SIMONDS, William Edgar, *U.S. Army*	1233
SHAFFER, William, *U.S. Army*	1866	SIMONS, Charles Jenks, *U.S. Army*	1234
SHAFTER, William Rufus, *U.S. Army*	1203	SIMPSON, D. Henry Lakin, *U.S. Navy*	2050
SHAHAN, Emisire, *U.S. Army*	1204	SIMS, Clifford Chester, *U.S. Army*	3356
SHALER, Alexander, *U.S. Army*	1205	SINGLETON, Walter Keith, *U.S. Marine Corps*	3357
SHAMBAUGH, Charles, *U.S. Army*	1206	SINNETT, Lawrence Clinton, *U.S. Navy*	2429
SHANAHAN, Patrick, *U.S. Navy*	2366	SISLER, George Kenton, *U.S. Army*	3358
SHANES, John, *U.S. Army*	1207	SITMAN, William S., *U.S. Army*	3137
SHAPLAND, John, *U.S. Army*	1208	SITTER, Carl Leonard, *U.S. Marine Corps*	3138
SHARP, Hendrick, *U.S. Navy*	1209	SJOGREN, John Carleton, *U.S. Army*	2952
SHARPLESS, Edward Clay, *U.S. Army*	1867	SKAGGS Jr., Luther, *U.S. Marine Corps Reserve*	2953
SHAW, George Clymer, *U.S. Army*	2249	SKELLIE, Ebenezer, *U.S. Army*	1235
SHAW, Thomas, *U.S. Army*	1868	SKIDGEL, Donald Sidney, *U.S. Army*	3359
SHEA, Charles William, *U.S. Army*	2944	SKINKER, Alexander Rives, *U.S. Army*	2550
SHEA, Daniel John, *U.S. Army*	3353	SKINNER, John Oscar, *U.S. Army*	1872
SHEA, Joseph Henry, *U.S. Army*	1210	SKINNER Jr., Sherrod Emerson, *U.S. Marine Corps Reserve*	3139
SHEA Jr., Richard Thomas, *U.S. Army*	3134	SLACK, Clayton Kirk, *U.S. Army*	2551
SHEERIN, John, *U.S. Army*	1869	SLADEN, Joseph Alton, *U.S. Army*	1236
SHELLENBERGER, John, *U.S. Army*	1211	SLAGLE, Oscar, *U.S. Army*	1237
SHELTON, George Mathews, *U.S. Army*	2250	SLATON, James Daniel, *U.S. Army*	2954
SHEPARD, Irwin, *U.S. Army*	1212	SLAVENS, Samuel, *U.S. Army*	1238
SHEPARD, Louis Capet, *U.S. Navy*	1213	SLETTELAND, Thomas, *U.S. Army*	2252
SHEPHERD, Warren Julius, *U.S. Army*	2166	SLOAN, Andrew Jackson, *U.S. Army*	1239
SHEPHERD, William, *U.S. Army*	1214	SLUSHER, Henry C., *U.S. Army*	1240
SHEPPARD, Charles, *U.S. Army*	1870	SMALLEY, Reuben, *U.S. Army*	1241
SHERIDAN, Carl Vernon, *U.S. Army*	2945	SMALLEY, Reuben S., *U.S. Army*	1242
SHERIDAN, James, *U.S. Navy*	1215	SMEDLEY, Larry Eugene, *U.S. Marine Corps*	3360
SHERMAN, Marshall, *U.S. Army*	1216	SMITH, Albert Joseph, *U.S. Marine Corps*	2594
SHIEL, John, *U.S. Army*	1218	SMITH, Alonzo, *U.S. Army*	1243
SHIELDS, Bernard, *U.S. Army*	1217	SMITH, Andrew J., *U.S. Army*	1873
SHIELDS, Marvin Glen, *U.S. Navy*	3354	SMITH, Charles E., *U.S. Army*	1874
SHIELS, George Franklin, *U.S. Army*	2251	SMITH, Charles H., *U.S. Navy*	1244
SHILLING, John, *U.S. Army*	1219	SMITH, Charles Henry, *U.S. Army*	1245
SHINGLE, John Henry, *U.S. Army*	1871	SMITH, Cornelius Cole, *U.S. Army*	1875
SHIPLEY, Robert F., *U.S. Army*	1220	SMITH, David Lafayette, *U.S. Army*	1246
SHIPMAN, William, *U.S. Navy*	1221	SMITH, David Monroe, *U.S. Army*	3140
SHIVERS, John, *U.S. Marine Corps*	1222	SMITH, Edwin, *U.S. Navy*	1247

STRYKER, Robert Francis, *U.S. Army*	3368	TAYLOR Sr., Karl Gorman, *U.S. Marine Corps*	3371
STRYKER, Stuart S., *U.S. Army*	2965	TEA, Richard Longstreet, *U.S. Army*	1905
STUMPF, Kenneth Edward, *U.S. Army*	3369	TERRY, John Darling, *U.S. Army*	1334
STUPKA, Laddie, *U.S. Navy*	2370	TERRY, Seymour W., *U.S. Army*	2967
STURGEON, James K., *U.S. Army*	1301	TEYTAND, August P., *U.S. Navy*	2371
SUDUT, Jerome A., *U.S. Army*	3144	THACKER, Brian Miles, *U.S. Army*	3372
SULLIVAN, Daniel Augustus Joseph, *U.S. Naval Reserve Force*	2555	THACKRAH, Benjamin, *U.S. Army*	1335
SULLIVAN, Edward, *U.S. Marine Corps*	2168	THATCHER, Charles M., *U.S. Army*	1336
SULLIVAN, James, *U.S. Navy*	1302	THAXTER, Sidney Warren, *U.S. Army*	1337
SULLIVAN, James F., *U.S. Navy*	2055	THAYER, James, *U.S. Navy*	2059
SULLIVAN, John, *U.S. Navy*	1303	THIELBERG, Henry, *U.S. Navy*	1338
SULLIVAN, Thomas, *U.S. Army*	1898	THOMAS, Charles L., *U.S. Army*	1906
SULLIVAN, Thomas, *U.S. Army*	1899	THOMAS, Hampton Sidney, *U.S. Army*	1339
SULLIVAN, Timothy, *U.S. Navy*	1304	THOMAS, Herbert Joseph, *U.S. Marine Corps Reserve*	2968
SUMMERS, James Calvin, *U.S. Army*	1305	THOMAS, Karl, *U.S. Navy*	2315
SUMMERS, Robert, *U.S. Navy*	1306	THOMAS, Stephen, *U.S. Army*	1340
SUMNER, James, *U.S. Army*	1900	THOMAS, William H., *U.S. Army*	2969
SUNDQUIST, Axel Leohard, *U.S. Navy*	2169	THOMASON, Clyde A., *U.S. Marine Corps Reserve*	2970
SUNDQUIST, Gustav Adolf, *U.S. Navy*	2170	THOMPKINS, George W., *U.S. Army*	1341
SURLES, William H., *U.S. Army*	1307	THOMPKINS, William H., *U.S. Army*	2171
SUTHERLAND, John Alexander, *U.S. Army*	1901	THOMPSON, Allen, *U.S. Army*	1342
SUTTON, Clarence Edwin, *U.S. Marine Corps*	2314	THOMPSON, Charles Augustus, *U.S. Army*	1343
SWAN, Charles Alexander, *U.S. Army*	1308	THOMPSON, Freeman C., *U.S. Army*	1344
SWANSON, John, *U.S. Navy*	1309	THOMPSON, George Washington, *U.S. Army*	1907
SWAP, Jacob E., *U.S. Army*	1310	THOMPSON, Henry, *U.S. Navy*	2060
SWATTON, Edward, *U.S. Navy*	1311	THOMPSON, Henry A., *U.S. Marine Corps*	1345
SWAYNE, Wager, *U.S. Army*	1312	THOMPSON, James B., *U.S. Army*	1346
SWEARER, Benjamin, *U.S. Navy*	1313	THOMPSON, James Granville, *U.S. Army*	1347
SWEATT, Joseph Sewell Gerrish, *U.S. Army*	1314	THOMPSON, James Harry, *U.S. Army*	1348
SWEENEY, James, *U.S. Army*	1315	THOMPSON, John, *U.S. Army*	1908
SWEENEY, Robert Augustus, *U.S. Navy*	2056	THOMPSON, John J., *U.S. Army*	1349
SWEENEY, William, *U.S. Navy*	2057	THOMPSON, Joseph Henry, *U.S. Army*	2558
SWEGHEIMER, Jacob, *U.S. Army*	1316	THOMPSON, Max, *U.S. Army*	2971
SWETT, James Elms, *U.S. Marine Corps Reserve*	2966	THOMPSON, Peter, *U.S. Army*	1909
SWIFT, Frederic William, *U.S. Army*	1317	THOMPSON, Thomas W., *U.S. Army*	1350
SWIFT, Harlan J., *U.S. Army*	1318	THOMPSON, William, *U.S. Navy*	1351
SYPE, Peter, *U.S. Army*	1319	THOMPSON, William Henry, *U.S. Army*	3145
TABOR, William L. S., *U.S. Army*	1320	THOMPSON, William P., *U.S. Army*	1352
TAGGART, Charles A., *U.S. Army*	1321	THOMSON, Clifford, *U.S. Army*	1353
TALBOT, Ralph, *U.S. Marine Corps*	2556	THORDSEN, William George, *U.S. Navy*	2256
TALBOTT, William, *U.S. Navy*	1322	THORN, Walter, *U.S. Army*	1354
TALLENTINE, James, *U.S. Navy*	1323	THORNE, Horace Marvin, *U.S. Army*	2972
TALLEY, Edward R., *U.S. Army*	2557	THORNTON, Michael, *U.S. Navy*	2061
TANNER, Charles B., *U.S. Army*	1324	THORNTON, Michael Edwin, *U.S. Navy*	3373
TAYLOR, Anthony, *U.S. Army*	1325	THORSNESS, Leo Keith, *U.S. Air Force*	3374
TAYLOR, Bernard, *U.S. Army*	1902	THORSON, John F., *U.S. Army*	2973
TAYLOR, Charles, *U.S. Army*	1903	TIBBETS, Andrew W., *U.S. Army*	1355
TAYLOR, Forrester L., *U.S. Army*	1326	TILTON, Henry Remsen, *U.S. Army*	1910
TAYLOR, George, *U.S. Navy*	1327	TILTON, William, *U.S. Army*	1356
TAYLOR, Henry H., *U.S. Army*	1328	TIMMERMAN, Grant Frederick, *U.S. Marine Corps*	2974
TAYLOR, James Allen, *U.S. Army*	3370	TINKHAM, Eugene M., *U.S. Army*	1357
TAYLOR, John, *U.S. Navy*	1533	TITUS, Calvin Pearl, *U.S. Army*	2316
TAYLOR, Joseph, *U.S. Army*	1329	TITUS, Charles, *U.S. Army*	1358
TAYLOR, Richard, *U.S. Army*	1330	TOBAN, James W., *U.S. Army*	1359
TAYLOR, Richard Hamilton, *U.S. Navy*	2058	TOBIE Jr., Edward Parsons, *U.S. Army*	1360
TAYLOR, Thomas, *U.S. Navy*	1331	TOBIN, John Michael, *U.S. Army*	1361
TAYLOR, Wilbur Nelson, *U.S. Army*	1904	TOBIN, Paul, *U.S. Navy*	2062
TAYLOR, William, *U.S. Army*	1332	TODD, Samuel, *U.S. Navy*	1362
TAYLOR, William G., *U.S. Navy*	1333	TOFFEY, John James, *U.S. Army*	1363

WALMSLEY Jr., John Springer, *U.S. Air Force*	3149	WELLS, William, *U.S. Army*	1437
WALSH, James Aloysius, *U.S. Navy*	2434	WELLS, William, *U.S. Navy*	1436
WALSH, John, *U.S. Army*	1413	WELSH, Edward, *U.S. Army*	1438
WALSH, Kenneth Ambrose, *U.S. Marine Corps*	2997	WELSH, James, *U.S. Army*	1439
WALSH, Michael, *U.S. Navy*	2372	WENDE, Bruno, *U.S. Army*	2178
WALSH, William Gary, *U.S. Marine Corps Reserve*	2998	WEST, Chester Howard, *U.S. Army*	2567
WALTON, George Washington, *U.S. Army*	1414	WEST, Ernest Edison, *U.S. Army*	3152
WAMBSGAN, Martin, *U.S. Army*	1415	WEST, Frank, *U.S. Army*	1936
WANTON, George Henry, *U.S. Army*	2176	WEST, Walter Scott, *U.S. Marine Corps*	2179
WARD, Calvin John, *U.S. Army*	2566	WESTA, Karl, *U.S. Navy*	2373
WARD, Charles H., *U.S. Army*	1925	WESTERHOLD, William, *U.S. Army*	1440
WARD, James, *U.S. Army*	1926	WESTERMARK, Axel, *U.S. Navy*	2321
WARD, James, *U.S. Navy*	1416	WESTON, John Francis, *U.S. Army*	1441
WARD, James Richard, *U.S. Navy*	2999	WETHERBY, John C., *U.S. Army*	2263
WARD, John, *U.S. Army*	1927	WETZEL, Gary George, *U.S. Army*	3380
WARD, Nelson W., *U.S. Army*	1417	WETZEL, Walter C., *U.S. Army*	3006
WARD, Thomas J., *U.S. Army*	1418	WHEAT, Roy Mitchell, *U.S. Marine Corps*	3381
WARD, William Henry, *U.S. Army*	1419	WHEATON, Loyd, *U.S. Army*	1442
WARDEN, John, *U.S. Army*	1420	WHEELER, Daniel Davis, *U.S. Army*	1443
WARE, Keith Lincoln, *U.S. Army*	3000	WHEELER, George Huber, *U.S. Navy*	2374
WARFEL, Henry Clay, *U.S. Army*	1421	WHEELER, Henry W., *U.S. Army*	1444
WARNER, Henry F., *U.S. Army*	3001	WHERRY, William Macky, *U.S. Army*	1445
WARREN, David, *U.S. Navy*	1422	WHITAKER, Edward Washburn, *U.S. Army*	1446
WARREN, Francis Emroy, *U.S. Army*	1423	WHITE, Adam, *U.S. Army*	1447
WARREN Jr., John Earl, *U.S. Army*	3376	WHITE, Edward, *U.S. Army*	2264
WARRINGTON, Lewis, *U.S. Army*	1928	WHITE, John Henry, *U.S. Army*	1448
WATKINS, Lewis George, *U.S. Marine Corps*	3150	WHITE, Joseph, *U.S. Navy*	1449
WATKINS, Travis E., *U.S. Army*	3151	WHITE, Patrick H., *U.S. Army*	1450
WATSON, James C., *U.S. Army*	1929	WHITEHEAD, John Milton, *U.S. Army*	1451
WATSON, Joseph, *U.S. Army*	1930	WHITEHEAD, Patton G., *U.S. Army*	1937
WATSON, Wilson Douglas, *U.S. Marine Corps Reserve*	3002	WHITELEY, Eli Lamar, *U.S. Army*	3007
WATTERS, Charles Joseph, *U.S. Army*	3377	WHITFIELD, Daniel, *U.S. Navy*	1452
WAUGH, Robert T., *U.S. Army*	3003	WHITMAN, Frank M., *U.S. Army*	1453
WAYBUR, David Crowder, *U.S. Army*	3004	WHITMORE, John W., *U.S. Army*	1454
WAYRYNEN, Dale Eugene, *U.S. Army*	3378	WHITNEY, William G., *U.S. Army*	1455
WEAHER, Andrew J., *U.S. Army*	1931	WHITTIER, Edward Newton, *U.S. Army*	1456
WEAVER, Amos, *U.S. Army*	2261	WHITTINGTON, Hulon Brooke, *U.S. Army*	3008
WEBB, Alexander Stewart, *U.S. Army*	1424	WHITTLESEY, Charles White, *U.S. Army*	2568
WEBB, James W., *U.S. Army*	1425	WICKAM, Jerry Wayne, *U.S. Army*	3382
WEBBER, Alason P., *U.S. Army*	1426	WICKERSHAM, J. Hunter, *U.S. Army*	2569
WEBER, Lester William, *U.S. Marine Corps*	3379	WIDICK, Andrew J., *U.S. Army*	1457
WEBSTER, Henry S., *U.S. Navy*	1427	WIDMER, Jacob, *U.S. Army*	1938
WEEKS, Charles H., *U.S. Navy*	1428	WIEDORFER, Paul Joseph, *U.S. Army*	3009
WEEKS, John Henry, *U.S. Army*	1429	WIGLE, Thomas W., *U.S. Army*	3010
WEICHT, Ellis R., *U.S. Army*	3005	WILBANKS, Hilliard Almond, *U.S. Air Force*	3383
WEINERT, Paul H., *U.S. Army*	1932	WILBUR, William Hale, *U.S. Army*	3011
WEIR, Henry Cary, *U.S. Army*	1430	WILCOX, Franklin L., *U.S. Navy*	1458
WEISBOGEL, Albert, *U.S. Navy*	2066	WILCOX, William H., *U.S. Army*	1459
WEISS, Enoch R., *U.S. Army*	1933	WILDER, Wilber Elliott, *U.S. Army*	1939
WEISSEL, Adam, *U.S. Navy*	2067	WILEY, James, *U.S. Army*	1460
WELBORN, Ira Clinton, *U.S. Army*	2177	WILHELM, George, *U.S. Army*	1461
WELCH, Charles H., *U.S. Army*	1934	WILKE, Julius August Robert, *U.S. Navy*	2180
WELCH, George W., *U.S. Army*	1431	WILKENS, Henry, *U.S. Army*	1940
WELCH, Michael, *U.S. Army*	1935	WILKES, Henry, *U.S. Navy*	1462
WELCH, Richard, *U.S. Army*	1432	WILKES, Perry, *U.S. Navy*	1463
WELCH, Stephen, *U.S. Army*	1433	WILKIN, Edward G., *U.S. Army*	3012
WELD, Seth Lathrop, *U.S. Army*	2262	WILKINS, Leander A., *U.S. Army*	1464
WELLS, Henry S., *U.S. Army*	1434	WILKINS, Raymond Harrell, *U.S. Army Air Corps*	3013
WELLS, Thomas McCoy, *U.S. Army*	1435	WILKINSON Jr., Theodore Stark, *U.S. Navy*	2435

ZABITOSKY, Fred William, *U.S. Army*   3397   ZION, William F., *U.S. Marine Corps*   2324
ZEAMER Jr., Jay, *U.S. Army Air Corps*   3026   ZUIDERVELD, William, *U.S. Navy*   2436
ZIEGNER, Herman, *U.S. Army*   1957   ZUSSMAN, Raymond, *U.S. Army*   3027